The Encyclopedia of Crafts

F to P
VOLUME 2

The Encyclopedia of Crafts

LAURA TORBET, Editor

Gary Tong, Illustrator

CHARLES SCRIBNER'S SONS • NEW YORK

Library of Congress Cataloging in Publication Data
Main entry under title:

The encyclopedia of crafts.

    1. Handicraft—Dictionaries. I. Torbet, Laura.
TT9.S37   745'.03'21   80-13431
ISBN 0-684-16409-4   Set
ISBN 0-684-16661-5   Volume 1
ISBN 0-684-16662-3   Volume 2
ISBN 0-684-16663-1   Volume 3

1 3 5 7 9 11 13 15 17 19 C/V 20 18 16 14 12 10 8 6 4 2

Printed in the United States of America

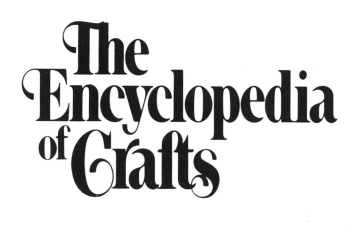

The Encyclopedia of Crafts

f

Fabdec. Batik and Tie-dye. See **fiber-reactive dye** and **Batik and Tie-dye: Dyes.**

Fabergé, Peter Carl. Enameling. See **Enameling.**

fabric. Batik and Tie-dye. Puppets. Quilts. Stitchery. (Also called cloth.) A material, usually woven, in which the interlacing of **lengthwise (warp)** and **crosswise (weft)** threads produces any of a great variety of textures and patterns. While the terms fabric and **textile** are often used interchangeably, fabric usually includes the woven materials, and textiles is a broader term including many other **fiber** methods. Also see **Stitchery: Materials.**

fabric. Block Printing. Fabric Printing. Cloth woven or knit from fibers, usually measured in length by the yard. Standard widths vary from 36″ to 54″.

The kinds of material generally used for fabric printing are those with a smooth surface, such as cotton or linen, although various other types of fabric can also be used. It is advisable first to experiment on scraps of the fabric to determine the suitability of the fabric for printing. Heavy, rough fabrics may yield interesting effects, although it is difficult to obtain a clear print. Fabrics with woven textures, such as twill, will take a block print only on the raised diagonal ribs, with no color reaching the grooves in between. Extremely thin fabrics such as chiffon should be printed with very little paint, to avoid a heavy, stiff layer. Knit fabrics do not print well.

Materials for **dye printing** should first be tested for their absorption of dye. Some fiber blends, such as polyester and cotton, do not dye well. Usually, fabrics with anticrease finishes repel dye. All new fabrics should be washed before printing to remove any **size.** Also see **Fabric Printing: Preparing Fabric.**

fabric. Stenciling. Almost any fabric can be used for stenciling, although medium-weight fabrics with a smooth surface are best. A smooth fabric such as cotton will produce a smooth design with crisp edges. A fabric with texture or nap will produce an uneven print with blurry edges. New fabric should first be washed to remove any sizing. Also see **stenciling fabric.**

fabric. Weaving. The finished **web** or **cloth.** The word refers to something that has been constructed, built, fabricated, or put together.

fabric adhesive. Quilts. Stitchery. Toys. **Adhesive** material used to adhere one piece of **fabric** to another. Fabric adhesive may be applied by means of a spray can, as a viscous liquid, or as a weblike material that is permeated or coated with a heat-setting adhesive. Some adhesive sprays are intended for temporary use, such as those specifically designed to hold pattern pieces in place while fabrics are cut. These spray adhesives work well in holding fabric or **felt** in place for **appliqué** since they replace the need for either pins or basting. They supposedly do not affect the surface of the fabric though when the sprayed parts are separated some particles and dust do stick. Various fabric spray adhesives work with varying degrees of success on different materials, so they should be experimented with for particular needs. New sprays are continuously being developed and made available.

Various liquid fabric glues which look similar to household glue or **white glue** are also available. Care must be taken with appliqué fabrics to avoid any **glue** that soaks into the material which will discolor it or change its texture.

Those adhesives which come in sheet form, such as **iron-on interfacing**s, are of a weblike **synthetic** material. They are placed between two layers of fabric and ironed to permanently bond or weld the materials together. Instructions must be carefully followed, as too low a heat or too short a time period will not set the materials. A few one-way adhesives allow the webbing to be ironed onto a fabric so that shapes cut from the fabric are slightly stiff, or have more **body,** which is a help especially when the fabrics are used for **machine appliqué.** It is important to check temperatures required to set the adhesives to make sure the heat required does not exceed the maximum ironing temperature for the fabrics. Some synthetics, for example, would melt before they were adhered. Read labels carefully in using any adhesive, as various fibers require different treatment.

fabric analysis. Weaving. The breaking down of a swatch of fabric so that all information necessary for reproducing it can be obtained. Besides the **weave analysis,** this includes determining the fabric or **thread count,** which is the number of **ends** and **picks per inch;** the type of **finishing** as it affects the **shrinkage** or **felting** of the fabric, and the type of yarn used in regard to **fiber** content, **twist,** and count. Although the weave analysis is simple for any weaver to do, complete fabric analysis is best done in a laboratory or textile office because it requires the use of a grain scale to accurately determine **yarn count** and often the use of chemicals to establish fiber content. Also see **sett.**

fabrication. Jewelry. Any method of putting pieces of metal together to form jewelry, including **soldering, sweat soldering, riveting,** and hinging.

fabric book. Batik and Tie-dye. Quilts. Stitchery. Toys. (Also called rag book.) A book, either for children or adults, made up from sheets of **fabric** instead of paper. The contents can be **stitch**ed, painted, **batik**ed, **appliqué**d, or ink-ed. Usually pages are sewn back to back and may be finished with **binding.** Children's books made this way are usually washable. Cloth books or stitched books for adults are usually one-of-a-kind, containing collage, poems, epigrams, etc. Some stitchers have made sampler books of fabric for collections of embroidery stitches, appliqué designs, or **quilt block**s; any series of tests, experiments, or finished pieces can be **join**ed at one edge, booklike, for easy access and filing.

fabric collage. Stitchery. The layering of soft materials or **fabric**s in a collagelike arrangement on a large piece of **background** material. **Appliqué** is often employed in fabric collage, though sometimes gluing, stapling, and nailing may be used. The technique utilized in the collage depends upon the intended use of the work. A collage dress would be sewn, for example, whereas a collage wall might be stapled.

fabric construction. Knitting. A term for the basic finished knit fabric (e.g., garment or wall hanging) upon which embroidery, **Swiss darning, cross stitch** (or any other decorative trim) is applied. Also see **Knitting: Basic Procedures.**

fabric crayon. Stitchery. A special crayon made for use on fabric. The crayons are first applied to drawing or **tracing paper** as designs or drawings. Then the crayon drawing is placed facedown over a piece of white or light-colored **synthetic fabric.** The **synthetic** material should be laid over a padding of newspapers with clean white paper as the top sheet.

A hot iron is used to transfer the design; the heat sets the color onto the fabric. Most synthetic fabrics work well, especially Dacron and polyester **blend**s. **Cotton**s can be used, although the fabric crayon colors are not as permanent on them as on the synthetics. Crayola fabric crayons are a commonly available brand. This technique can be used on **quilt**s, **pillow**s, clothing, and toys. It is especially adaptable for using children's drawings.

fabric cutter. Rugmaking. See **strip cutter.**

fabric doll. Stitchery. Toys. Any **doll** made from woven or knitted material. It is usually a doll with a **fabric** head, as fabric bodies were not uncommon for dolls with heads of **bisque, composition,** or porcelain. **Art fabric dolls, felt** dolls, cloth dolls, stocking dolls, and **rag doll**s are all fabric dolls. Also see **nylon stocking doll, sock doll.**

fabric finish. Batik and Tie-dye. Stitchery. See **finish.**

fabric for batik. Batik and Tie-dye. See **Batik and Tie-dye: Fabrics for Dyeing.**

fabric for tie-dye. Batik and Tie-dye. See **Batik and Tie-dye: Fabrics for Dyeing.**

fabric head. Puppets. See **soft head.**

fabric ink. Fabric Printing. See **textile color.**

fabric joint. Toys. A connection between two parts, usually wood, made by attaching a single piece of fabric between them. The fabric can be **glue**d or stapled to the wood. A **hinge joint** or a series of hinged joints can be made with fabric. Also see **stitched joint.**

fabric paint. Batik and Tie-dye. Stitchery. See **textile paint.**

fabric painting. Batik and Tie-dye. Stitchery. Toys. See **direct-dye painting.**

fabric print. Fabric Printing. Any design or pattern printed on **fabric** using almost any printing process with fabric ink or **textile color** as the medium. Fabrics are generally printed with repeated design motifs. Also see **Fabric Printing: Printing Techniques.**

FABRIC PRINTING

From earliest times people have decorated the fabric surfaces of their clothing and environment. The first printed patterns were probably made by dipping leaves and sticks in some colored substance and pressing them on cloth.

Gradually the processes became more intricate. Designs were printed with incised clay and rollers, and bamboo stamps. The sculptures and murals of the Babylonians, Assyrians, and Egyptians depicted figures with patterned clothing suggestive of stamped patterns as well as of hand painting, although no such fabrics have survived. Some Egyptian mummy cloths from the fifth century A.D. have been found with **mordant dye printing** in clay or wax **resist patterns.**

India probably has the longest history of fabric decoration. Printing blocks have been found dating from 3000 B.C. **Mordant** dyeing may have been known in India 5,000 years ago. Although no early fabrics have survived, records of travelers to India always mentioned cloth decorated with flowers. These printed silks and cottons influenced many other cultures. Indian fabrics discovered in Egypt, with block-printed resist patterns dyed either blue with **indigo** or red with **madder,** indicate that there was extensive trading between the two countries.

Fabrics from Asia and Africa were known to medieval Europe through travel and trade; but it was not until the eleventh century that fabric printing was tried in Europe. The techniques of **wood-block printing,** developed in Germany for book illustration, were applied to fabric decoration. Patterns imitating brocades and damasks were printed in black on a natural or colored fabric. Although the techniques were limited, a feeling of luxury was attained with very complicated linear patterning. Silver or gold leaf was occasionally adhered to the decorated fabric with gum.

Fabric-printing processes continued to improve; by 1676 in England, cottons were being printed with blocks. The dye processes were limited, however, and the decorated fabrics were a poor imitation of those from India. As the popularity of Indian cottons grew, English silk and wool merchants felt threatened. By 1700, the importation of printed fabrics from India was prohibited. In spite of the ban, the use of both Indian calicoes and English copies increased. The conflict led to riots in which the weavers and their supporters attacked women wearing printed cotton garments.

The production of printed fabrics in England increased considerably after the introduction of the roller in the 1770s. The small size of the roller limited the size of the **repeat,** however, and therefore also limited the scale of the design. Roller-printed fabrics were used for clothing, but **block printing** continued to be used for the large designs of furnishings fabrics. Increasing industrialization brought about further technical developments in dye chemistry and cloth production. Fabric printing declined as a craft and became part of the new textile industry.

By the middle of the nineteenth century there was strong opposition to the Industrial Revolution, on both political and philosophical grounds. **William Morris,** one of the leading figures of the arts-and-crafts movement, was largely responsible for the revival of many crafts, including fabric printing. He reintroduced hand printing methods and, in design, stressed motifs based on natural forms. Art Nouveau, which followed, fully developed this approach to decoration.

The modern craftsperson has an unlimited choice of printing tools, from simple cork and potato stamping to more sophisticated techniques. The **wood block** probably remains the most popular method in the history of fabric printing. The **linoleum block** is a fairly recent innovation and has proved to be an efficient printing tool that has soft, easily cut surfaces. The knowledge of historical methods, coupled with the improved **textile color** available today, provides valuable tools for exciting fabric decoration.

TOOLS AND MATERIALS For designing and printing, the following materials will be needed: drawing board, paper, tracing paper, scissors, brushes, felt-tip marking pens, watercolor or tempera paint, palette or piece of glass, masking tape, staple gun, thumbtacks, ruler, newspaper, cloths, a padded printing table on properly prepared **fabric, textile color, extender,** and **thinner.** For **linoleum**—or **wood-block printing,** a carpenter's **bench hook** for cutting, a rubber **brayer,** a sheet of glass or an **inking pad,** cutting tools, and a sharpening stone will be needed. **Flocking powder** may be needed to prepare the blocks for printing.

Other tools may be needed for specific techniques, such as a stencil knife and stencil paper for **stenciling,** or a knife and vegetables for **potato-block printing.** A heavy T-square is necessary for the **registration** of **repeat** designs. The equipment needed for techniques that apply only to limited areas of fabric printing—such as **steaming,** which is used only for fabrics printed with **dye paste** colors—are listed under the specific entries.

For drying printed fabrics, a clothesline and plastic clothespins are efficient, although the fabrics can be laid on newspaper on a table. For cleaning up, kitchen cleanser, household bleach, and turpentine or mineral spirits are essential. Also see **Fabric Printing: Setting Up a Workshop, Preparing Fabric.**

SETTING UP A WORKSHOP The work area should be well lighted and near a source of water, to make cleaning up easier. It is advisable to have the **textile color,** palette, **brayer,** and **mallet** (or whatever tools are needed for the specific technique) placed on a small table near the printing table.

The most important requirement for fabric printing is the padded printing table. It is much more satisfactory to print the entire piece of cloth rather than work on small sections of fabric and then move it. The size of the printing table depends on the type of printing to be done. Because most fabrics are decorated in lengths of about 3 yds., the table should be more than 3 yds. long, and 6″ wider than the width of the **fabric** to be used. The table height should be about 30″. The top should be of ½″–1″ thick plywood reinforced with 1″ × 2″ pine stock. The table top can be mounted on wood or metal legs or set on sawhorses. For perfect color application, the table top (**a.**) must have a resilient padding. First, tack a ⅜″ layer of felt or rug underpadding (**b.**) to the plywood. Then staple a muslin cover cloth (**c.**) over the underpadding. Next, pin a muslin backing cloth (**d.**) down tightly with T-pins (**e.**), making sure it is straight with the table. This backing cloth is the base for the printing fabric and can be removed and washed after use. Attach the fabric to be printed (**f.**) with T-pins, stretching the fabric as it is pinned. Begin stretching, aligning the fabric along one side and one end. Place pins about every inch, then stretch and pin the second side and end, pulling from opposite sides. Place masking tape (**g.**) along the edges for making **registration** marks. See ill.

Printing table

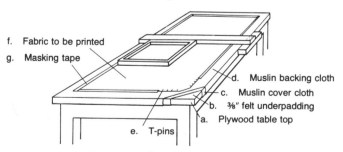

f. Fabric to be printed
g. Masking tape
d. Muslin backing cloth
c. Muslin cover cloth
b. ⅜″ felt underpadding
a. Plywood table top
e. T-pins

DESIGNING In designing for fabric printing, the characteristics of the technique are an important consideration because they determine the general appearance of the design. **Linoleum-block printing** gives crisp, opaque areas; **wood-block printing** gives a more textured, bolder surface;

stenciling has a sharp, patterned look; and **potato-block-printing** patterns give a stamped effect. The complexity of the design should be appropriate to the technique used.

Another element of fabric printing is the placement of the design on the fabric. Since fabrics are decorated as a continuous length of cloth rather than as an individual picture, the arrangement—the way in which the designs are repeated to fill out the cloth—is as important as the design itself and can add to the richness and complexity of the pattern. The designs can be randomly scattered over the fabric; they can be repeated in vertical, horizontal, or diagonal stripes or in closely patterned rows. Remember that fabric is generally used in three-dimensional ways, for interior decoration and for garments, so the design may not always be viewed on a flat plane. Allow extra fabric if needed for seams, hems, and so on.

In designing the basic unit, or **repeat,** the size of the repeat is an important aspect of the pattern. This size may be determined by the width of the fabric (how many repeats will be placed across it). Planning should be done on tracing paper to determine the proper size and placement of the repeat across the width and along the length of the fabric. The repeat motifs can be cut out of paper and placed on another piece of paper the same size as fabric to be printed, and moved around until the placement is determined. Corner joinings should also be worked out on paper. When the design is completed, it can be glued down and used as a pattern. Careful **registration** marks must be planned in advance for all printing procedures. In planning the repeat pattern, the way in which each repeat unit will join or meet the next one should be considered. Units in straight rows can meet with a butt joint, one next to the other, or they can overlap. However, overlapping produces a darker color, so this must be worked into the design. For units with irregular edges (as contrasted to rectangular or square units), a part of one unit can fit into a hollow or negative area of the next one, without touching it, in a dovetail joint.

As a final note on designing, it must be remembered that in all **block-printing** techniques the image will be reversed, left to right, when printed. Unless the design is symmetrical, it must be reversed before it is traced onto the block.

PREPARING FABRIC New material usually contains a stiffening substance called **size.** This must be removed by washing the fabric, rinsing it, and ironing it smooth before printing. However, if fabric that will never be washed (such as satin or velvet) is used, this is not necessary.

PRINTING TECHNIQUES Printing should be done with the fabric pinned taut to a padded table. Before color is applied, the printing method should be planned. For the general placement of motifs, guiding folds can be pressed into the fabric with an iron; the outline of the design can be stitched with basting thread (do not print over thread); or a paper pattern can be placed over the fabric and dots or guidelines marked through the paper onto the fabric with a sharp pencil. For accurate planning of a **repeat, registration** marks can be made on the masking tape along the edges of the table, on the T-square, and on the block,

screen, or stencil. Since each type of fabric and color behaves differently when printed, samples should first be made on scraps of the fabric. Additional cutting corrections can be made to blocks after these test prints.

In order to obtain smooth, opaque colors from a **linoleum block** or **wood block** it may be necessary to sand the block or to apply **flocking** to it before printing. If white paint has been applied to the linoleum block to facilitate cutting, it should be removed by sanding before printing. Before **dye printing,** blocks must receive either sanding or flocking. Linoleum contains a large amount of oil and, because dye-printing colors are rather watery, the oily surface of the linoleum has a tendency to reject the color, resulting in a mottled print. This tendency can be corrected by moderately sanding the block with medium-grade sandpaper held against a hard, flat surface to roughen the slick linoleum surface or by applying **flocking powder** to the adhesive (**flocking-mordant**) coated linoleum for a surface resembling the nap of velvet. Either of these methods will produce a linoleum surface that will accept the paint, producing an even, opaque print. Wood blocks to be used for dye printing must be coated with two coats of shellac as a protection from **dye** and moisture. Because shellac causes the color to "take" unevenly, an absorbent surface must be given to the printing surface with flocking. Even when oil-base textile ink is used, a wood block will print more efficiently when sanded lightly with fine sandpaper and rubbed with even pressure in all directions to give the printing surface "tooth."

Textile color can be applied in various ways—through a stencil, by brushing, by spraying, by rolling, or by sponging. In **block printing** with textile ink, the color is spread on a palette or piece of glass, then rolled out evenly with a **brayer.** The brayer picks up an even coat of ink, which is then rolled onto the block. The block should be inked with several light coats of color rather than one heavy coat.

In block printing with **dye paste,** color the consistency of honey is brushed evenly on an **inking pad.** The block is then stamped on the pad several times until the printing surface is evenly coated with color.

When two or more colors are to be printed, print all of one color first and allow it to dry before printing the second color. The additional color can be applied as **overprinting** or **partial overprinting,** or it can be coordinated to produce a final **fitted print** of several colors.

The first print from a clean block is usually uneven, so first make a few tests on a scrap of the fabric. Hold the inked block face down over the fabric and press straight down, pressing your little fingers against the fabric to steady your hands. Never move the block once it is down. Print it by pressing it with your hands or pounding it with a **mallet;** then pick the block straight up. When using a mallet, move the left hand to different parts of the block to steady the block as the mallet strikes it firmly. Hit the block with several sharp, firm blows at regular intervals.

The block must be carefully inked before each print is made. Care must be taken to keep fingers clean. There will be minor imperfections in hand printing; however, if the color is blotchy or uneven, the block may have been moved, pressure may not have been evenly applied, or the ink may have been unevenly or too heavily applied. Similar care must be taken with **silkscreen printing, stenciling,** and other techniques. Also see **Fabric Printing: Setting Up a Workshop.**

FINISHING   All printed colors must be dried thoroughly, for from two to four days depending on the thickness of the fabric and color layer. Pieces should be placed on newspaper or hung to dry over a taut line. Fabric colors usually require a **fixation** treatment to make them washable. However, if the trial prints on scrap fabrics come through a wash successfully, then this step is not needed. The fixation process is achieved by exposure to the heat of an iron or a **steamer.** Most **textile color** can be set with ironing. **Dye paste** colors require **steaming.** Manufacturers of dye or pigment will generally specify the finishing treatment required.

To set the color by ironing, place a press cloth or paper between the dry, printed fabric and the iron (preferably a steam iron). Use the setting for cotton. Take care when ironing to expose every part of the cloth to the heat.

For a more efficient ironing process, use a press cloth wrung out in white vinegar. Place it over the printed fabric and press with a hot iron until the press cloth is dry. Wet it again with vinegar, and continue the process until all of the fabric is treated. This is an unpleasant operation, but the dual effect of the acetic acid in the vinegar and the steam acts to make the colors fast.

CARE AND MAINTENANCE OF TOOLS   Scrape remaining ink from the **brayer,** glass plate, and other equipment after printing. When **dye paste** or water-based inks are used, all blocks and equipment should be cleaned with water, a sponge, and a stiff brush. For oil-base **textile colors,** clean the equipment with mineral spirits or turpentine. Blocks and brayers can be soaked in a deep metal pan of solvent. The depressions in the printing surfaces of blocks must be thoroughly scrubbed with a stiff brush. Before storing clean, dry equipment, cover the printing blocks with cardboard to protect the printing surfaces from scratches. The brayer may be dusted with talcum powder.

CARE AND MAINTENANCE OF FABRICS   Hand-printed fabrics should be hand laundered or machine-washed for a short time in mild soap or detergent and lukewarm water. Rinse them in warm water and hang them up to dry. Never leave damp printed fabrics rolled up for ironing later. Let the piece line-dry until it is almost dry; then iron it on the wrong side. Finish by ironing lightly on the right side. Dry cleaning is not advisable.

fabric printing. Block Printing. Fabric Printing. The decoration of fabric by means of the application of insoluble color such as **textile color** or **dye paste** in repeated patterns over the surface of the fabric. Various methods are used to apply the color, such as **linoleum block printing, potato block printing, stenciling,** and **wood block printing.** The unit of design, the **repeat,** is usually printed in a regular pattern across the width and down the length of the fabric by means of **registration.**

Fabric printing differs from fabric dyeing techniques (batik, tie-dyeing, etc.) in that the printed textile color adheres to the surface of the fiber whereas **dye** combines chemically with the fiber. Textile color is thicker than dye, so printed fabric has opaque, flat color rather than the transparent color characteristic of dyed fabrics. Printed designs, generally produced with a **printing block,** have crisp, definite edges, not the soft, fluid shapes and lines of dyed designs.

Fabric printing has traditionally been a hand process. However, with the invention of roller printing in the 1770s, it became successful commercially. The patterns were printed with engraved copper rollers, enabling thousands of yards of fabric to be produced per day. Recently, silkscreen printing, a form of stencil printing through a fabric mesh in which areas of pattern have been stopped out, has become widely used to mass produce printed fabrics.

face. Stitchery. See **right side of fabric.**

face grain. Woodworking. See **wood.**

faceplate turning. Woodworking. See **wood turning.**

face shield. Metalworking. See **arc-welding equipment, eye protector.**

facet. Gemcutting. A small **flat** face ground and polished on the surface of a gem for the purpose of reflecting light.

The large flat-top facet is called the table. The upper portion of a faceted gem is called the crown; the band separating the crown and pavillion is called the girdle; this is the part held by the bezel in a jewelry mounting. The lower part is called the pavillion; the large facets on the sides are called mains. The base of a faceted gem is called the culet (**a.**), see next page.

The table cut is the simplest of the faceted forms. It consists of a flat top and a flat bottom with single or double-beveled edges; the stone may have any geometric outline. The angle of a single-beveled, table-cut stone on the edge from the girdle to the back is 80° or less; on a double-beveled stone the included angle of the girdle is 160° or less. The table may vary in size from one-quarter to one-half the height of the stone; generally the pavillion is twice as deep as the crown. Opaque stones, such as onyx and bloodstone, are table cut and set in rings. This form developed from the octahedron, a natural crystal shape.

The buff top is a single or double-beveled table cut with a convex crown.

The step cut (also called trapeze cut) is similar to the double-beveled table cut with straight edges and a series of rectangular facets parallel to the girdle arranged in steps. The facets may be of uniform width or the girdle facets may be wider (**b.**).

The emerald cut is a step cut in elongated octagon form (**c.**).

Diamonds faceted in rectangular step cuts are called baguettes. The majority of step-cut gems are light-hued and transparent.

Another variety of the step cut is the cross-cut, distinguished by facets at an angle between the step facets. The octagon form develops a maltese cross.

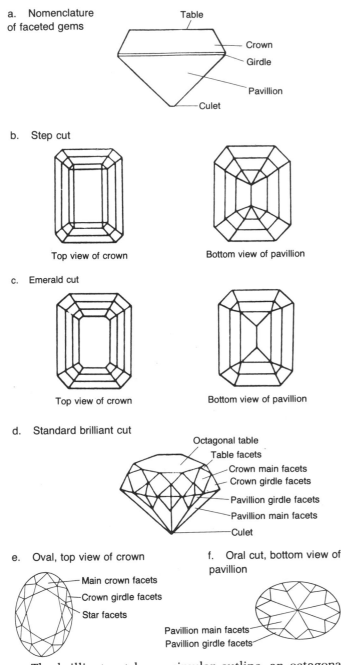

a. Nomenclature of faceted gems

Table
Crown
Girdle
Pavillion
Culet

b. Step cut

Top view of crown

Bottom view of pavillion

c. Emerald cut

Top view of crown

Bottom view of pavillion

d. Standard brilliant cut

Octagonal table
Table facets
Crown main facets
Crown girdle facets
Pavillion girdle facets
Pavillion main facets
Culet

e. Oval, top view of crown

Main crown facets
Crown girdle facets
Star facets

f. Oral cut, bottom view of pavillion

Pavillion main facets
Pavillion girdle facets

The brilliant cut has a circular outline, an octagonal table, and 58 facets, consisting of the table, 8 main crown facets, 8 crown table facets (also called star facets), 16 crown girdle facets, 8 main pavillion facets, 16 pavillion girdle facets, and the culet. (The culet is absent on small stones.) A series of 8 star facets is sometimes arranged around the culet. The majority of colorless transparent stones are brilliant-cut (**d.**).

The mixed cut is a combination, with a brilliant-cut crown and a step-cut pavillion.

The marquise cut is a standard brilliant cut with a pointed elliptical outline.

The oval cut is a brilliant cut with an elliptical shape. The brilliance and fire is not equal to the round brilliant, as two of the pavillion mains must be cut at too flat an angle (**e., f.**).

The double mirror brilliant is an improvement designed for gems with low refractive indices. It consists of a series of facets on the pavillion directly below the crown main facets and the crown girdle facets, both in the same arrangement.

The rose cut is an old style, today used mainly on **garnet**s and iron **pyrite**s (called marcasite). It consists of a flat base and a rounded top covered with triangular facets, often arranged in three rows terminating in six facets meeting at a point. The double rose cut is developed from two rose cuts sharing the girdle; this form is used for pendants.

A pendeloque is a pear-shaped double rose cut.

Briolettes are drop forms with triangular facets arranged over the surface of the stone. The cross-section of a briolette may be either round or oval.

Cap cut refers to freeform, irregular, nonstandard faceted shapes. See ill. Also see **faceting, lap, preforming.**

faceted beads. Beadwork. See **crystal beads.**

faceting. Gemcutting. A process of grinding small **flat** faces on the surface of a transparent or semitransparent gem in a regular order to improve its **reflection** of light. Faceting is done on a horizontal **abrasive** surface called a **lap.** A **faceting unit** is used to accurately hold the stone in the desired orientation to the lap for grinding and **polishing.**

After the gem rough has been **preform**ed and **dop**ped, and the girdle trued and centered, the pavillion **facet**s are ground. The pavillion facets are polished and the stone is turned and transferred to another dop to expose the crown in true alignment with the facets already cut. The crown facets are ground and polished, then the finished gem is cleaned of dop.

Faceting angles are determined by the refractive index

Steps in faceting a standard brilliant cut

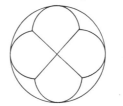

a. Main facets of the pavillion

b. Completion of the mains

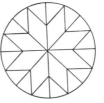

c. Addition of pavillion girdle facets

d. Main crown facets

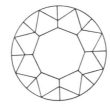

e. Crown girdle facets

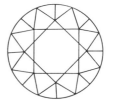

f. Addition of star (or table) facets

Facets of the double-mirror brilliant cut

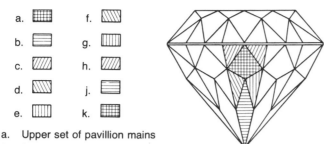

a.
b.
c.
d.
e.

f.
g.
h.
j.
k.

a. Upper set of pavilion mains
b. Lower set of pavilion mains
c. Girdle facets
d., e. Additional facets cut between the two sets of mains
f.-k. Polishing order

of the gem. These angles are designed to produce the best play of light for each type of stone. Many recipes for cutting faceted gems are found in two volumes called *The Book of Gem Cuts* by M.D.R. Company of Los Angeles, California. These formulas are given for **quartz** but can be converted for use with any material. Until experience is gained, it is best to follow the tested procedures for faceting and to keep a record of the cutting angles and positions on the **faceting unit** for each particular piece. See ill. Also see **preforming, refraction.**

faceting. Stained Glass. (Also called knapping.) A process used to create a sparkling effect on pieces of **dalle-de-verre.** It is achieved by creating an irregular surface on the edges of the glass with random light hammer blows.

faceting head. Gemcutting. See **faceting unit.**

faceting unit. Gemcutting. (Also called faceting head.) A device for holding a stone in the proper position to the **lap** for cutting and **polishing facet**s.

The jamb peg is an old technique that uses an inverted cone that stands perpendicular to the lap. It has holes in it for supporting the **dop stick** at different angles (**a.**).

The back rest is an adjustable plate attached to a perpendicular mast with perforations; it is used similarly to the jamb peg (**b.**).

The Williams facet head uses an aluminum inverted cone girdled with steplike gradations to support a Y-shaped attachment on the end of the dop stick.

The modern faceting head is a more complicated and efficient unit. Its components are a base, parallel to the plane of the rotating abrasive lap surface, that supports a mast to which the sleeve and yoke are attached by a clamp. It has a fine elevation adjustment for determining the faceting angle, a handpiece for holding the dopped stone in its chuck or collet, a pointer and scale that shows the exact faceting angle, and a stop that allows the angle to be set and repeated. The index gear rotates the handpiece and the gem material for cutting facets at proper intervals around the stone. A release lever locks the position of the index gear and a cheater adjustment allows sideplay of the handpiece for the fine adjustment of facet position (**c., d.**). See ill. Also see **faceting, machinery** and **Gemcutting: Tools and Materials.**

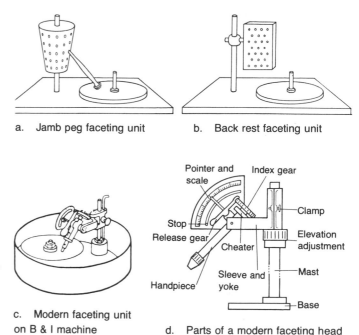

a. Jamb peg faceting unit

b. Back rest faceting unit

c. Modern faceting unit on B & I machine

d. Parts of a modern faceting head

facing. Stitchery. A material used on the reverse side of another **fabric,** to face or line it. In a **wall hanging,** the facing may also be the **backing.** Sometimes a facing is added to give extra **body** during sewing, then an additional backing or **lining** is added. If the facing is covered on each side, it then becomes an **interfacing.**

facing sand. Metalworking. See **molding sand.**

fadeless paper. Toys. The trademark name of an all-purpose paper for schoolroom or studio use. It is resistant to fading and water and is available in a wide range of sizes, from **construction paper** size to rolls 48″ wide. It is made in a great variety of colors for paper sculpture, crayon resist, painting, cutouts, murals, and display work.

faggoted seam. Stitchery. A **seam** used to join two pieces of material in which **faggoting** is employed as the connecting element.

faggot filling stitch. Crewel. Embroidery. See **sheaf stitch filling.**

faggoting. Quilts. Stitchery. An insertion **stitch,** used to **join** two pieces of **fabric** in such a way that an open space shows between the fabrics with threads making a decorative pattern in the opening.

faggot stitch. Knitting. This is a basic light, open lace stitch. There are two basic units to the stitch: a **yarn over** and a right-angle or left-angle decrease. The yarn-over stitch can be made before or after the decrease and the second row of the pattern may be purled, depending upon the particular faggot stitch variation. Faggot-stitch knit fabric has a tendency to angle slightly on the bias unless the decreases are made alternately between the left and right sides of the yarn overs. Also see **bébé buttonhole, lace faggot stitch** and **Knitting: Decreasing.**

faience. Beadwork. An ancient type of **bead,** generally blue or green, the body of which is made of powdered sandy quartz colored with a vitreous glaze plus copper for blue, or manganese for purple and black. The faience technique was a predecessor of that for making **glass beads.** Faience beads, the first to be mass-produced, were made in Egypt, Crete, Greece, Syria, and possibly India. By 1400 B.C. they had been spread throughout the world by expedition voyages. Also see **Beadmaking.**

faience. Ceramics. A **lead-tin glaze** on earthenware. The word derives from a French term for earthenware produced by Italian potters in Faenza during the Renaissance as an imitation of Spanish **majolica.** Also see **Delft ware.**

Fair Charlotte. Toys. See **Frozen Charlotte.**

Fair Isle knitting. Knitting. The style of **color knitting** from Fair Island, Scotland. Fair Isle designs are linked with Catholic tradition. There is evidence that Fair Isle sweaters are patterned after the sweaters worn by sailors washed ashore from their wrecked ships during the Spanish Armada in 1588. Genuine Fair Isle knitting is practiced only on Fair Island. The designs are based on two factors—the method in which the color designs are worked and the sequence of patterning, which varies all the way up the garment. A broad pattern is knitted in a number of colors, usually followed by a narrow pattern carried out in only two or three colors. The patterning is done in bold, clear colors on a more neutral background of white, fawn, gray, or brown.

fairy cross. Gemcutting. See **staurolite.**

fake fur. Stitchery. Toys. A woven or knitted **fabric,** usually **synthetic,** that has an extra-long **nap** to resemble fur. It is made in a variety of colors, patterns, and naps to imitate everything from leopard to zebra. It is often used in making children's **stuffed toys.**

Falling Star. Quilts. (Also called Circling Swallows, Flying Star, Flying Swallows.) An eight-pointed star **block pieced** of diamonds and triangles in which the "birds" all fly in a circle. The pattern is dated at about 1800. Also see **star patterns.**

Falling Timbers. Quilts. A variation of **Drunkard's Path** that uses the **Robbing Peter to Pay Paul** motif. See ill.

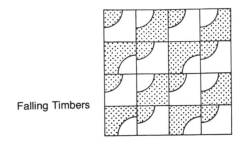

Falling Timbers

false damask. Weaving. See **damask.**

false French seam. Stitchery. A **seam finish** which has an appearance similar to the **French seam.** A **plain seam** is first sewn (**a.**), then the **raw edges** of the **seam allowance**s are turned in toward each other so that the **fold**ed edges match. The two are then **join**ed with a line of machine **straight stitch**es sewn near the folded edge (**b.**). See ill.

False French seam

false heddle. Weaving. A term sometimes used for **string heddles** made to correct an error in **threading.**

false plaid. Weaving. See **plaid.**

false saffron. Dyeing. See **saffron.**

family-record quilt. Quilts. A family record, in **appliqué,** set into a quilt. The center **block** usually shows the family home. Around it are the trees, lawn, flowers, children, ponies, and pets. Each block records some memory, and aunts, cousins, and daughters-in-law all make and sign blocks. Familiar sights are often included, as well as famous people and historical events. This quilt is a variation of the **album quilt.**

Fan. Quilts. See **Quilts: Quilting.**

fancy crossed throw. Knitting. A method of making an elongated cross stitch. See ill.

Fancy crossed throw

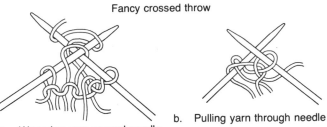

a. Wrapping yarn around needle

b. Pulling yarn through needle

fancy quilting. Quilts. Quilting patterns more elaborate than those of **plain quilting.** They employ curved and sometimes complex shapes in running designs and **block** designs. Also see **Quilts: Quilting.**

fancy quilting patterns. Quilts. The best known of the "fancy" or ornate **quilting pattern** names are:

Acanthus	Feather Wreath	Slave Chain
American eagle	Oak Leaf	Spider Web
Arabesque	Ocean Wave	Star and Crown
Bell flower	Peacock Fan	Starfish
Bouquet	Pineapple	Swirl
Clamshell	Princess Feather	Teacup
Daisy	Rope	Weeping Willow
Day Lily	Running Vine	Wheel of Fortune
Dove of Peace	Sausage	Widening Circles
Fan	Serpentine	Wineglass
Feathered Plumes		

fancy running quilting design. Quilts. See **Quilts: Quilting.**

fancy twill. Weaving. See **twill weave.**

fancy weave. Weaving. A catch-all term for **weaves** that have no definite category. These could be **combination weaves** or simple or **basic weaves** that have been embellished by changes in the **drawing-in draft** and **chain draft** so that they no longer belong strictly in the category where they originated.

fanfare. Bookbinding. (Also called à la fanfare.) A decorative style in which a book cover is divided into geometric compartments bounded by **fillets** and profusely decorated with small **tools** and branching foliage.

fan fold. Papercrafts. A fan-shaped fold achieved by **accordion pleating** a paper circle or rectangle. Cut out a circle and mark the center point. Mark regular intervals around the circumference for the fold lines. Cut a slit from one of these marks to the center. Begin accordion pleating at one cut side and continue to the other. The fan folds will vary in depth depending on how far they are opened. A rectangle folded in accordion pleating will form a fan shape when crimped at the bottom. A full medallion can be made by creasing an accordion-folded rectangular strip at the center, bringing the sides toward each other, and **fastening** the folds where they meet at the center. See ill.

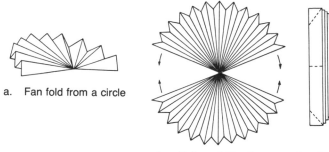

a. Fan fold from a circle

b. Full medallion from a rectangle

fanning out. Bookbinding. (Also called fanning over.) Manipulating a pile of paper sheets, **boards**, or book **sections** so that each unit is slightly exposed along one edge. It is usually achieved by rapidly flexing or flipping through the materials.

fanning over. Bookbinding. See **fanning out.**

fanny frame. Crewel. Embroidery. Needlepoint. See **embroidery frame.**

fan quilt. Quilts. Any of a great variety of quilts based on **pieced** or **appliquéd blocks** that depict fans. It is most often a quarter-circle fan shape filling more than half the block. The fan blocks can be set to make rainbows or full circles, although they are most commonly used so that the fan appears in the same corner of each block. Among the most common fan quilts are Grandmother's Fan, Japanese Fan, and Rebecca's Fan. **Harvest Sun** is a fan block set in

such a way as to form radiating circular designs. Many **Victorian crazy quilts** are based on fan designs.

Fans. Quilts. A variation of **Drunkard's Path** that uses the **Robbing Peter to Pay Paul** motif. See ill.

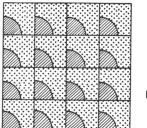

Fans

fan stitch. Lacemaking. See **leaf stitch.**

fantasy toy. Toys. Any toy that allows for and encourages fantasy on the part of the child. Masks are among the best for this, allowing a child to assume the role or identity suggested by the mask. Simple paper masks are as effective as any.

Costumes allow for much of the same fantasizing. Almost all children fantasize to some extent and the most insignificant prop may be all that is needed. Cardboard structures that let children crawl inside to "drive" or "fly" the objects are also excellent fantasy toys.

Farbigem process for laminated glass. Stained Glass. A technique for laminating glass that is carried out by the Willet Studios in Philadelphia, Pennsylvania. They imported the technique from Holland in 1965. It uses a secret gluing process that is stronger than epoxy-type glues and is patented under the name Farbigem. The process uses layers of ¼" plate glass fixed vertically to the surface of colored glass. Materials such as **glass rods**, marbles, faceted glass, and so on, can be incorporated in the **lamination** process. Also see **faceting.**

farm set. Toys. See **farm toy.**

farm toy. Toys. (Also called farm set.) A collection of small playthings that relate to farm activities. Animals are always included, along with any of the following: barns or other buildings, fences, **wagons**, and the farmer family. Most farm sets now are made of plastic, but they have been made in numerous materials including wood, paper, cardboard, and metal.

A farm toy is also any single toy of farm activity, such as a hay wagon, a barn, or a tractor.

Faroe Island knitting. Knitting. (Also called Faroe Island.) The style of knitting that originated in the Faroes, a group of Danish islands located in the North Atlantic Ocean between the Shetlands and Iceland. Faroe Island knitting follows the same two knitting principles as **Fair Isle knitting;** however, the background color is always off-white, in about 4-ply weight, and the designs are based on simple geometric patterns that are much bolder in color than those found in Fair Isle knitting. Each section of a Faroe Island design is knit in a different color. Also see **color knitting**.

farrier's nail. Stained Glass. A horseshoe nail. They are used to hold the **lead came** and glass pieces in place while **glazing**. They are nailed at an angle into the workboard just far enough to keep the piece from sliding around. See ill. Also see **grazing strips** and **Stained Glass: Glazing, Tools and Materials**.

Farrier's nails holding lead and glass in place

fashion doll. Toys. (Also called French fashion doll.) A small wood **mannequin** first made in France in the early 1700s. It was made to model the latest in fashionable clothes for women. The Parisian costumes were thus introduced to England and later to America. They were not really toys, but many found their way into children's hands after serving their purposes of displaying the latest in hairstyles and fashions. By the end of the eighteenth century the dolls were replaced by colored, engraved fashion plates.

fashioning. Knitting. The use of **increases** and **decreases** to give shape to a garment. For example, stitches are decreased beginning under the arms in a sweater to narrow the garment sufficiently to fit snugly across the chest; a knit skirt must be fashioned similarly to fit properly, i.e., to be full at the bottom and tapered in toward the waist. Fashioning is an intrinsic part of almost any knitting.

fast. Batik and Tie-dye. Stitchery. Permanent, or lasting, as colors or dyes which are fast. Dyes are usually fast to certain conditions, for example, fast to sunlight. The term "colorfast" is not very reliable since it does not describe the conditions under which the dye or color is permanent. Some dyes may be fast to water but not to **dry cleaning**, or vice versa. Dyes may be fast on some **fabric**s and not others. Also see **boilfast color**.

fast color. Batik and Tie-dye. Dyeing. Quilts. Stitchery. See **colorfast**.

fast-color salts. Batik and Tie-dye. (Also called colorfast salts.) The **dyestuff** used in **naphthol dye** mixes. Also see **Batik and Tie-dye: Dyes**.

fastening. Papercrafts. Various methods are used to secure or attach pieces of paper in making **paper sculpture**. The overlapped edges of paper may be secured with transparent tape, masking tape, double-coated masking tape, or **glue**. A stapler, metal brads, pins, needle and thread, and paper clips are useful for some projects. To pierce holes for joining or hanging with thread, an awl, bodkin, or darning needle inserted in a cork may be needed. A system of tabs and slits can be used to fasten paper.

fastening device. Plastics. A mechanical fastener, such as a **screw**, pin, hinge, **dowel**, rod, bead chain, **rivet**, spiral book binding, staple, and tack, used according to the thickness and weight of the plastic. Thin sheeting can be fastened with ordinary staples or snap fittings used for cloth. Heavier, solid pieces can be fastened and jointed in ways common to wood and metal. Use screws and **bolts** for joining parts that will be disassembled for transportation, or for joints that move when they expand and contract under extreme changes of temperature. Spray painting **acrylic** causes it to stress. Do not drill a hole for a mechanical fastener in a spray-painted area or near corners if pressure is to be put on them because the joint will break. Also see **heat bonding**.

fastening off. Batik and Tie-dye. Tying the ends of the **binding material**s together in the final step of **binding** for **tie-dye**. A ¾" length of the string or cord is left free when the binding is started. When binding has been completed, this free end is tied in a tight double knot to the finishing end so that both are secured. Fastening off, or tying off, must be carefully done, especially in the **tritik** method.

When only one string or cord end is available for fastening off, a loop can be made (**a.**) and the end brought around (**b.**) and knotted to the loop (**c.**). When another knot is visible (**d.**), an end thread can be wrapped diagonally to meet the knot and tied to the double strands (**e.**). See ill.

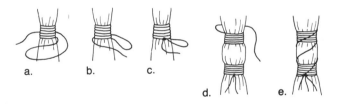

a.   b.   c.

d.   e.

fastening on. Batik and Tie-dye. Attaching the threads or **binding material**s to the fabric in the **tie-dye** process. The thread must first be fastened on securely so that it can be pulled and wound tightly. If the fastening on is carelessly done, the threads may loosen and the pattern will be lost in the subsequent dyeing process. A simple way of fastening on is to place the string on a diagonal and hold it in place with one finger, usually the left thumb. Wrap the thread over the diagonal five or six times (**a.**) and pull tight until there is no give and the thread does not slide loose (**b.**). If the tail end of this diagonal is left exposed, it can later be tied to the other end of the string in **fastening off**.

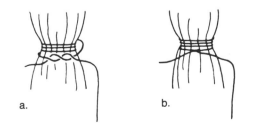

a.   b.

A slip knot is also commonly used in fastening on; any knot that holds securely will be adequate. See ill.

fastness. Fabric Printing. A term used to describe the ability of color printed on a **fabric** to withstand washing and exposure to sunlight.

fat clay. Ceramics. See **Ceramics: Clay.**

fat liquoring. Leatherwork. The wet chemical operation during the **tanning** process of lubricating hides in a solution of oils and fatty substances to ensure pliability and add **tensile strength.** The fat liquoring process can be regulated to produce soft or strong leathers. Also see **Leatherwork: Tanning and Manufacture.**

fat oil. Ceramics. A thick varnish that results from exposing turpentine to air for a period of time. It is used as a vehicle for **underglaze** and **overglaze** pigments.

fat oil of turpentine. China and Glass Painting. (Also called thick oil.) A **medium** for mixing powdered **on glaze color** that aids in blending colors without leaving brush marks. It is also used with **enamel** and **raised paste.** Make the fat oil by pouring a few drops of pure turpentine into a saucer and leaving it in a dust-free place, exposed to air, until the turpentine spirits evaporate, leaving the thick oil. Add a few more drops of turpentine to the saucer and let it stand for another three or four days, repeating this process until enough oil has been collected.

favrile glass. Stained Glass. The trademark for Louis **Tiffany**'s blown glass, which was described as "a composition of various colored glasses worked together while hot." In an 1896 brochure, the choice of the name Favrile was explained as a derivative of the Renaissance English word "fabrile," which meant "belonging to a craftsman or his craft." It was advertised as "a material produced by what is believed to be a new formula, the outcome of a number of experiments instituted by and carried on by Mr. Louis C. Tiffany." (From *Louis C. Tiffany: Rebel in Glass* by Robert Koch.) Also see **Tiffany, Louis Comfort** and **Stained Glass.**

feather. Metalworking. See **flame.**

Feather Crown. Quilts. An **appliqué wreath** that uses the feather pattern in a continuous circle. The wreath fits into a **square block,** and the blocks are **set** to form an **all-over pattern** or are alternated with solid blocks. It is sometimes described as being a variation of **Princess Feather,** but the arrangements are completely different. The similarity is only in the feathered edge.

The Feather Crown is almost always used to surround a **Ragged Robin** center. See ill.

feather cutting. Découpage. A technique of cutting **print**s for découpage in which scissors are held steady while the print is fed into the scissors with a back-and-forth motion producing deep, fine zigzags along the cut edge. These cuts, which resemble feathers, tufts of grass, or dry-brush paint strokes, are usually made along the outer edges of the **cutout.** Also see **Découpage: Cutting.**

feathered plumes. Quilts. See **border.**

feather fastening. Weaving. Attaching feathers to weaving, either in the **fringe** or in the body of the woven piece. The use of feathers as decoration on textiles was developed to a fine degree by the Peruvians. In the sixteenth century their Spanish conquerors wrote of their astonishment at the beauty of Peruvian feather work. The North American Indians also used feathers for embellishment, but they were used in headdresses, baskets, and hide clothing, not incorporated into a woven textile.

Feathers to be incorporated into weaving are made into a strand to be used as the **filling.** To prepare this strand, two horizontally parallel cords or yarns are used; the top one is securely anchored and the bottom one is considered the working cord. The quill of the feather is bent down and over the top holding cord, thus hooking the feather onto it. The second and lower cord is wrapped around the folded quill in a simple or looped knot, securing the hooked quill to the top cord. Working from left to right, a strand of attached feathers is created. Attention should be given to the direction in which the feathers are falling, where the knot appears, how conspicuous it is, and the color of the cord or yarn used. If necessary, another working cord can be introduced and used to stabilize the feather positions. This third strand is tied around the base of the neck of the feather. This is often done with very large feathers. Large feathers also, because of their long, rigid quills, often have loops tied around the quills for stringing onto an anchored cord.

In a fringe, the feathers can be attached singly or in groups by **whipping** around the tip of the fringe strands and the unbent quill of the feather or feathers. Trim off the whipping end and any of the tip if it shows. See ill. Also see **taaniko twining.**

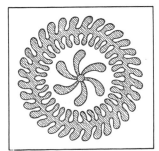

Feather Crown

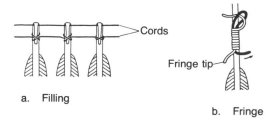

a. Filling

b. Fringe

feathering. Jewelry. Small grooves or tapered lines caused by improper **buffing.** If while buffing the work is held in the same direction and at the same angle for too long a time—and this can be a very short period—the **buffing compound,** which acts as a fine abrasive, will begin to cut grooves into the metal. Similarly, if there is a pit or scratch in the metal that was not removed prior to buffing, the buffing compound will build up in these areas and cause feathering. Also see **bobbing compounds, breaking in a buffing wheel, buffing, buffing compounds.**

feathers. Featherwork. Usually the feathers from the wings and tails of birds are used for featherwork. The central shaft of the feather is called the **quill.** The soft, fluffy feathers growing at the base of the large feathers are called **down.** Feathers can be obtained without killing birds. Zoo aviaries or pet shops can be contacted to collect feathers that drop during molting season. Feathers may be purchased from hobby shops. Feathers from game and food birds, such as turkeys, pheasants, and guinea hens, are available in their natural coloring or dyed. When purchasing dyed feathers, buy enough for the whole project. Because dye lots vary, the next time you purchase feathers the color may be slightly different.

Feather Star. Quilts. (Also called Twinkling Star.) A **block** pattern that uses numerous small triangles **pieced** together to form a square. The small triangles at the edges of the star make an active **sawtooth** pattern.

When this block is pieced with a **hexagon** as the central block the name changes to **Radiant Star.** If a **nine-patch** is used, it becomes a **California Star.** Because of the zigzag pattern, it is sometimes also called the Chestnut Burr.

feather stitch. Crewel. Embroidery. See **cretan stitch.**

FEATHERWORK

The craft of applying bird **feathers** by gluing or stitching to decorate surfaces or objects has an ancient history. Certain cultures come to mind as outstanding in their creative uses of feathers. The Hawaiians made elaborate feathered capes and headdresses for their royalty. The North American plains Indians used feathers to decorate clothing and ceremonial objects. Perhaps the best-known example is the war bonnet, the feathered headdress that was worn as a symbol of bravery. Feathers from the Golden Eagle (a symbol of courage) were collected by braves, but could not be worn until they were awarded as a token of valor for brave deeds, each feather being rewarded for a specific feat of bravery. When a brave had won enough feathers to make a war bonnet, he and his friends would ceremoniously recount the stories of his prowess as each feather was prepared and fastened to the war bonnet. Occasionally a warrior would earn enough feathers to make a double-tailed war bonnet, which had a double row of feathers hanging down the back. The feathers were attached to the bonnet by softening the end of the **quill** in hot water, notching it with a knife, and then tucking the slender quill end up into the hollow center of the quill to form a loop;

this loop was then laced to the leather backing. The base of each feather was covered with a **fluff** and bound with yarn. The front of the bonnet was finished with a strip of beadwork and beadwork rosettes at each side.

Featherwork as a decorative craft has fluctuated in popularity, reaching a peak during the nineteenth century in Europe and the U.S.A. The most common use of feathers was to adhere them to pictures as added embellishment. And the most popular picture subject was, of course, birds. One or two birds would be sketched on the paper with some suggestion of a naturalistic background. The feathers were then carefully **glued** to the paper, accurately following the coloring of the bird depicted, working from the tail to the neck so that the quill end was never seen. Then the head and neck were filled with tiny feathers, beginning at the beak and proceeding down to join and cover the neck feathers. These pictures were then framed under glass.

In the late eighteenth century feathers were often used in interior decoration. Cornice designs and murals were executed with feathers adhered to the walls, sometimes in combination with sea shells. Since it was popular to raise exotic birds (many homes had aviaries) feathers could easily be collected. Another source of feathers was the kitchen, where game birds were plucked in preparation for cooking.

Perhaps the most charming form of traditional featherwork was the feather nosegay, in which tiny pieces of feathers, usually cut into petal shapes, were assembled into realistic looking floral bouquets. The nosegays were generally mounted in a shadow box under glass. Another popular eighteenth-century featherwork item was the feather tippet, a neck scarf that hung down in front, upon which were stitched varicolored feathers.

The tradition of stitching feathers to cloth again became popular in the late 1800s. Feathers were stitched to buckram or other stiff fabric, arranged in patterns to completely cover the backing material. This featherwork was used for muffs and dress trimmings and for such household decorations as fire screens and valances. For small pieces, pheasant, peacock, ostrich, parrot, marabou, guinea fowl, pigeon, and blackcock feathers were used. For large pieces Aylesbury duck or white poultry feathers were used, dyed in various colors.

PREPARING FEATHERS Traditionally the feathers from domestic poultry were prepared by first washing the bird in lukewarm water with soapsuds and a bit of whiskey and then leaving it in a clean, warm place to dry. The bird was then killed and its feathers plucked. The feathers were placed loosely in a cloth bag and set in a warm oven for a few minutes to make them fluffy. Each feather was trimmed with scissors, the little hard piece at the top of the **quill** was removed, and the **fluff** clipped away.

To prepare purchased feathers, first wash them gently in soap and water if feathers need to be cleaned. When they are dry, fluff them up by holding them in the steam from the spout of a teapot or by placing them in the sunshine (but not long enough to make them fade). Shake each one to fluff it further. Clip away the fluff from the base of each feather. This can be a messy job if there is a draft in the room (you will need a vacuum cleaner to clean up). If the feathers are to cover a rounded form, the stiff quill can be broken by pulling the feather over a scissors blade, making the feather more pliable. Some feathers may need to be shaped with the fingers to straighten them.

Store feathers loosely in tightly closed plastic bags with a mothball in each bag.

DYEING FEATHERS   Prepare a pan of liquid household dye on top of the stove. The proportion of dye to water will depend on the color intensity desired. Experiments should be made with a few feathers before dyeing is begun. Steep the feathers in the pan of hot dye until the desired shade is obtained, then remove them one by one with tongs and place them on newspaper to dry.

WORKING WITH FEATHERS   Featherwork techniques are in general based on adhering the feathers to the background material. They are glued, or sometimes stitched, to the backing. The particular method is dictated by the backing material used, but in most cases, **glue,** scissors, and tweezers will be the only tools required. Occasionally feathers are cut or trimmed to desired shapes. The one method that seems universal in featherwork is that of applying the feathers, usually one at a time, in overlapping rows so that the unsightly quill end and exposed background are covered by the tip of the feather overlapping it. The backing can be almost any material. Feathers have been combined with leather, fabric, wood, and even ceramics. The glue is brushed on the surface to be decorated with feathers. Experimentation may be necessary to determine the correct amount of glue to apply. Too much glue will show through the feather, making it translucent; too little glue may not give proper adhesion. Pins may be inserted to hold feathers in position while drying, but should be removed before the glue completely dries.

Stitching feathers to fabric is also done in overlapping rows. Beginning at one end of the fabric, sew feathers one by one in a line across the fabric, stitching each feather close to the end of the quill with **waxed thread.** Stitch on both sides of the quill. Subsequent rows of feathers should overlap the previous row to conceal the securing stitches and completely cover the backing.

CARE AND MAINTENANCE OF FEATHERWORK   Feather designs should be stored with moth balls in tightly closed containers or plastic bags. Feather arrangements are best protected when mounted or framed under glass as a permanent protection from dust, insects, and general wear and tear. If it is necessary to clean feathers, remove them from the piece and wash them in soap and water as described in **Featherwork: Preparing Feathers.** Since birds oil their feathers from ducts at the tips of their tails by preening, feathers may be given a light coating of oil with any unsalted animal grease, applied lightly with the fingertips.

feather wreath. Quilts. See **Quilts: Quilting.**

feed. Metalworking. Plastics. Woodworking. The process of pushing material into a cutting or drilling tool, or the tool into the material. Use a slow, even rate of feed when

machining plastics to prevent overheating them. Also see **Plastics: Cutting, Drilling, Filing.**

feldspar. Ceramics. A major ingredient of porcelain and white ware bodies. Feldspar is an insoluble, inexpensive, high fire **flux.** Also see **nepheline syenite.**

feldspar. Gemcutting. A mineral composed of aluminum silicates, soda, lime, and potash. It has a **hardness** of 6, a **specific gravity** of 2.5–2.7, refractive indices of 1.525 and 1.536, and a vitreous luster. It occurs in colorless, white, yellow, brown, green, and red varieties in varying degrees of opacity and translucency. Feldspar is polished with cerium oxide on a felt or leather buff. Crushed feldspar is mixed with **quartz** and clay to make porcelain.

Potash feldspars **crystal**lize in the monoclinic system and are called orthoclase because the crystal faces meet at right angles. Other types crystallize in the triclinic system and are called oligioclase because the faces meet at angles slightly greater than 90°. Both types have good **cleavage** parallel to the faces and the basal plane.

Amazonite (also called amazon stone) is a deep-green orthoclase.

Sunstone exhibits a red metallic glitter against a pale white or yellow background due to inclusions of mica and **hematite** arranged along the **C axis.** It is similar in appearance to avanturine **quartz.**

Moonstone (also called adularia) is a translucent orthoclase and occurs in pale white, green, yellow, or reddish-brown varieties. It exhibits a blue-white milky chatoyance when viewed in the proper direction. To best display its **luster,** moonstone is cut in very high **cabochon** with the table parallel to the chatoyant face. Sometimes the back of the stone is hollowed to increase translucence.

Albite is a semitransparent white oligioclase. Like moonstone it exhibits a blue-white milky chatoyance when viewed in the proper direction.

Labradorite, an opaque feldspar, exhibits a colored sheen when viewed from the proper direction. Its body color is dark gray and reflects a bright metallic luster with a display of blue, violet, red, and green colors similar to the wings of a tropical butterfly. To produce this effect gems are cut either into **flat**s or slightly convex. Also see **polishing, refraction.**

feldspar glaze. Ceramics. **Glaze**s containing **feldspar** are normally applied to **stoneware** and **porcelain.** Feldspar glazes are very hard and resistant to most acids. The fired surface may be either matte or smooth, but never glossy like unfired glazes.

fell. Stitchery. To sew in such a way that the material is held flat. Sometimes **appliqué** is referred to as "felled work." More commonly, fell refers to a **seam finish.** When two pieces of **fabric** have been sewn at the **seam allowance,** one **raw edge** is cut back, then the other is folded over it, turned under, and **hem**med in place. It is referred to as a **flat fell seam.**

fell. Weaving. The last **pick** of **filling** beaten down by the weaver. This is the pick that is already in position as part of the cloth, not the pick waiting in the **shed** for the **beater** to push it down. An older name for fell is beat-up point. Also see **bubbling.**

felled work. Stitchery. See **fell.**

felling. Stitchery. See **hemming.**

felt. Crewel. Embroidery. Needlepoint. A nonwoven fabric made of compressed wool fibers. It is used as a **background fabric** and as a backing on a completed piece to hide the rough backside. Most dyes used on felt are not colorfast.

felt. Puppets. Quilts. Stitchery. Toys. A resilient, smooth, **nonwoven material,** usually made of all **wool** or wool/**rayon** combination, though sometimes of wool, hair and/or fur. It is a non**fray**ing material and the edges require no **finishing.** Felt is made by a process called **felting.** One of the oldest methods of **fabric** construction known, it depends on the property of wool **fibers** to coil and mat so that they tangle themselves, becoming permanently interlocked. Heat, moisture, agitation, and pressure are all necessary to produce the compressed layers of fibers.

Felts are commonly available in 72″ widths from fabric shops or department stores which also carry an assortment of precut rectangles of felt in a wide range of colors. Fiber contents and gauges vary, as do prices. The commonly available felts of 50% wool are used in most **felt appliqué.**

Special felts, suitable for large stitchery **wall hangings** and **mural**s are made from 100% wool which has been treated to make it **moth repellent, fire retardant,** and resistant to mildew, soil, and water. These special **preshrunk** felts, 60″ wide, are not usually stocked though they can be ordered through interior design shops or from interior decorators.

The primary limitation of felt in **quilting** is that it is nonwashable, so soil must be removed by **dry cleaning.** The brilliant flat colors of felt are well suited to decorative **appliqué,** however, and it is easy to sew, comes in a bright array of colors, has a smooth texture and is visually warm. Because of the thickness of felt, it develops a **relief** pattern when sewn, as in **stacked felt,** or when it is appliquéd. The soft surface of the felt shows the patterns of **stitch**es to advantage especially when stitches are drawn tight.

Felt is used in a variety of ways in stitchery. Suitable for **banner**s, wall hangings, or rugs, it is especially adaptable for those projects incorporating lettering. Felt is excellent for **cut-through appliqué** and **French knot appliqué. Shadow work** and **transparent appliqué** both utilize felt.

All wool or part wool felts are sometimes used in the **tie-dye** process. While the felt is somewhat **bulky** to handle, it dyes well and has been successfully used in this way.

For **doll**making and **stuff**ed **toys,** felt is a material especially well suited since it can be stitched from the top side. Because it is heavy, the surface remains smooth even if the toys or animals are stuffed with nylon stockings or crumbled **foam rubber.** The primary disadvantage of using felt

in stuffed animals or figures is that it is not washable and must be dry cleaned. Also see **arm puppet.**

felt. Weaving. See **felting.**

felt appliqué. Stitchery. An **appliqué** technique in which cut pieces of **felt** are sewn to a felt or a woven **fabric background.** Because the felt is nonwoven and will not **ravel,** there are no limitations to the kinds of shapes that can be cut and sewn. The most common **stitch**es for appliquéing felt are **running stitch,** French knots, and **overcast stitch.**

Felt appliqués are usually very bright and cheerful since the felt is a smooth, flat **nonwoven material** and the colors are intense.

Because the felt offers so little resistance to the **needle,** felt appliqué is appropriate for the beginner. This technique also allows the stitcher to concentrate on the problems of color and design without becoming overly involved in sewing techniques, since no edges are turned under or **hem**med.

felt buff. Jewelry. A pressed felt polishing attachment used with fine **abrasive** grit on a **buffing machine** to **buff** work that must retain a flat surface. Felt buffs are available in several shapes and densities. They can be shaped somewhat by allowing them to run over a metal edge. Similar smaller felt buffs are available for use on the **flexible-shaft machine.** Also see **buffing compound, felt polishing stick, ring buff.**

felted rug. Rugmaking. See **felting.**

felting. Knitting. After the knit fabric has been soaked to ensure against shrinkage, the fabric is **blocked,** dried, and brushed with a **teasel brush** to give it a feltlike texture. Also see **Knitting.**

felting. Rugmaking. Spinning. Weaving. In spinning, the undesirable matting or pressing together of animal **fibers** in the presence of moisture and heat. It occurs during the scouring by too high a temperature of the wash water, too much agitation, or too sudden a change in the temperature of the next water into which the **fleece** is put.

In rugmaking or weaving, felting is the process of making a fabric by pressing and rubbing together natural or man-made fibers in the presence of moisture and heat. The fibers tangle and interlock to form a compact cloth called felt. In most felt there is no weaving involved. However, fibers can be spun and woven, then felted to cover up the spaces in the weaving. The texture of some blankets is obtained in this way.

Rugs also can be made by felting. Usually the felt is the base fabric, which is either appliquéd or embroidered over. The felt can also be cut into shapes and appliquéd over a base of felt or some other cloth.

Felted fabrics are excellent insulators against cold and noise. They can be cut and shaped easily and there is no raveling of fiber or threads. The most important fiber for felt is short **staple** wool **noil.** Also see **finishing, fulling.**

felting. Stitchery. A process of shrinking and matting a woven **wool fabric**. When moisture and heat are applied, the woolen material can be made to **shrink** excessively so that the weave tends to disappear, leaving a smooth **napped** surface, similar to that of **felt**. Felting is usually used to refer to the treatment of woven wool fabric, though it is sometimes used to refer to the process of making felt from **fiber**s.

felt polishing stick. Jewelry. A flat wooden stick with thick felt glued to one side that can be impregnated with **tripoli** or rouge for **hand polishing**. See ill. Also see **crocus composition**.

Felt polishing stick

felt-tip pen. Batik and Tie-dye. Stitchery. See **marking pen**.

female mold. Plastics. See **mold**.

fence. Woodworking. An adjustable guide attached to a **table saw**, portable **router**, or other power tool. Its purpose is to align and fix the material being cut at a set distance from the blade so as to control the amount, depth, shape, or dimension of the cut.

Fence Rail. Quilts. A quilt name that refers to a particular **set** of **Roman Stripe block**. In this, the rectangles are joined to form squares, and the top rectangle in each block is a dark color. Set at right angles in an **all-over block pattern**, the stripes join to make a zigzag pattern of the black lines.

fermentation. Dyeing. See **indigo, lichen dye**.

fern. Quilts. See **Princess feather**.

fern stitch. Crewel. Embroidery. A simple technique consisting of three **straight stitch**es of equal size radiating from the same hole at the base of the stitch. The center stitch can move straight upward or diagonally to define a direction, as in a plant vein or a spray of flowers.

fern stitch. Needlepoint. This stitch resembles a neat braid when completed. It should be worked from top to bottom in vertical or diagonal rows using every or every other mesh. Begin with a small **cross stitch**. The larger stitches are worked one mesh apart and are two meshes long. See ill.

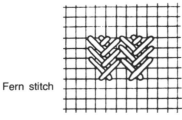

Fern stitch

ferric chloride. Enameling. See **etching**.

ferrous metals. Jewelry. Metalworking. Iron and **alloys** containing iron.

festoons and bowknots. Quilts. See **border**.

fettling. Ceramics. A process by which **mold** marks and rough edges are removed from leather hard or dry ware with a **fettling knife**.

fettling knife. Ceramics. (Also called a potter's knife.) A fine-bladed knife that comes to a sharp point and is used in **fettling**. Also see **Ceramics: Tools and Materials**.

Fezan. Batik and Tie-dye. See **acid dye, direct dye**.

fiber. Spinning. Weaving. Any thin single hair or threadlike strand of animal, vegetable, mineral, or synthetic origin. Several fibers are combined or spun to make a single continuous element called a **thread** or **yarn** that can be used for weaving, knitting, crochet, etc. Fibers are short in length and are measured in inches averaging from ¾ to 15″. This can be a natural length, or the cutting of **filaments** of silk and man-made substances. Fibers have characteristics according to their source and are classified as either natural or man-made. Natural fibers are those derived from living and growing things and are usually designated as animal, vegetable, or mineral fibers.

Animal fibers are obtained from animals or filaments from the abdomen of an insect. The continuous filament comes from the silkworm and is called **silk.** Short fibers are the hair, fur, and wool that serve as protective skin coverings of certain mammals. Fibers of this type are not continuous and must be spun into thread or yarn in order to be used, or they can be **felted**. The chief hair fiber is **wool**. It differs in structure from other hair in that a wool fiber is composed of overlapping scales (as seen under a microscope), whereas hairs are smooth. Wool comes from sheep, but there are many animals whose hair or fur can be used. Among these are **alpaca, Angora** and **cashmere** goats, **camel, llama, vicuña, horse**, chinchilla, angora rabbit, and beaver. Fur from animals such as fox, mink, or even dog and cat is sometimes added to wool for softness and textural interest.

Vegetable or plant fibers have their origin in some part of a plant. They can be the soft hairs that surround the seeds of certain plants; **cotton** is the best example of a seed-hair fiber. Bast fibers are found in the stem or stalk just under the outer covering or bark of a number of plants. They are used for a wide variety of purposes, ranging from the weaving of fine **linen**, which derives from the **flax** plant, to the manufacture of coarser textiles and **cordage** from **hemp, ramie,** or **jute**. The North American Indians used bast fibers derived from willow, cedar, basswood, nettle, milkweed, and mulberry. Leaf fibers are found in the leaves or leaf stems and are tough and stiff. They are used almost entirely for **cordage** making. They include **sisal**, pineapple, and palm. Certain other vegetable fibers have limited uses. These would include fibers from a fruit casing (such as coconut fibers), entire stems of grasses, and the bark and roots of some trees. The term "fiber" is sometimes extended to include basket-weaving materials such as rattan.

Asbestos is perhaps the one true natural mineral fiber because it is the only one **carded** into **roving** and spun much as cotton and wool are spun. It can be woven or felted into coarse fabrics that are valuable as insulation or fire protection. Fiberglass is derived from a mineral source, but because of its manner of production—drawing molten glass into thin flexible filaments—it is considered man-made. There are some metallic yarns that have been drawn from sheets of gold, silver, copper, and aluminum and slit into fine strips or ribbons. Coating with plastic renders them tarnishproof and in some cases color is added to the plastic. However, most so-called metallic yarns consist of a **core** thread wound with a thin metal strip, or a core thread that has been painted or sprayed with metal powder or dipped into it. An adhesive applied beforehand attaches the powder to the core.

Man-made fibers are the products of laboratory research that has taken raw materials, changed them to a liquid, and then forced or pumped this liquid through a **spinneret.** This nozzle-shaped piece can have holes in it that are smaller than the diameter of a human hair. After the liquid passes through the spinneret it is solidified into fiber. The synthetic cellulose fibers first came into commercial use at the end of the nineteenth century and are still very important.

Man-made fibers are most conveniently classified according to the raw materials from which they are made. They can be regenerated fibers with a cellulose base; these are the rayons produced by several processes. Other regenerated fibers have a natural protein base from either a vegetable (seaweed, soybean, cornmeal, peanuts) or an animal (casein, skim milk) source. Then there are the true synthetics, which have chemically engineered resin bases. Nylon was the first successful one on the market. Also see **camel's hair, horsehair, mohair, raffia, staple fiber.**

fiber. Stitchery. A thread or threadlike filament which can be spun or woven. It may be either a **natural fiber** or a **man-made fiber.** The natural ones are vegetable or **cellulosic fiber**s; the man-made ones include all **synthetics** such as **nylon** and **polyester.**

fiber dyeing. Dyeing. See **dyed-in-the-wool, stock dyeing.**

fiber fabricated. Weaving. A recently coined term referring to any art object constructed by a technique out of **fiber.**

fiberglass. Plastics. See **glass fiber.**

fiberglass. Stained Glass. See **polyester resin technique.**

fiber mallet. Metalworking. See **hammer.**

fiber-reactive dye. Batik and Tie-dye. Dyeing. A **colorfast dye** of fairly recent origin, also known by such trade names as Dylon, Fabdec, Fibrec, **Putman,** and **Procion dye.** This class of dyes is used for **cold water dye**ing cotton, linen,

viscose rayon, and, to a lesser degree, silk and wool in both the **tie-dye** and **batik** processes. With these dyes, the color is impregnated into the fiber by direct chemical linkage. They are called fiber-reactive dyes because of the reaction that causes the dye molecule to form a bond with the fiber.

Fiber-reactive dyes are sold through various distributors, so many different names may all refer to the same product. They use **salt** as the **assistant** and **washing soda** (sal soda) as the **fix**er, except when used to dye wool. The action of the washing soda creates an alkaline solution that is essential to making the dye and fiber molecules react. If any dye, regardless of brand name, requires salt for the assistant and washing soda (sal soda) as the fixer, it is fiber-reactive. The temperature of the **dyebath** should be 90–100° F. To react to this dye, the fiber must be well washed and absorbent.

Fiber-reactive dyes can be used for **direct-dye painting** when a **thickener** is added to the dye solution. To thicken, use **chemical water** and sodium alginate or a commercially packaged **alginate thickener,** usually sold by the distributor of the dye. After painting, the fabric may be **heat-set** by **steaming.** To thin the dyes, use chemical water. The very thin dyes can then be sprayed or airbrushed onto fabric. Because of the **colorfast**ness of these dyes they are not suitable for **discharge dyeing.**

For tie-dye, the fabric should be wet out before dyeing. After fabric is removed from the dyebath, it should be immediately and thoroughly rinsed to remove all excess dye particles. It should not be untied until it is dry. Hot soapy water is sometimes needed to remove final residue of **dyestuff** from the fabric.

In **dyeing** with fiber-reactive dyes allow the following amounts of dyestuff for each pound of fabric to be dyed:

¼ tsp. dyestuff to 3 tbs. salt for light intensity
½ tsp. dyestuff to 6 tbs. salt for medium intensity
1 tsp. dyestuff to 9 tbs. salt for strong intensity
3 tsp. dyestuff to 15 tbs. salt for very strong intensity

The dyestuff is **pasted** in cold water, then dissolved in 1 cup hot water (140° F) and mixed with sufficient water to make the dyebath. It should be heated to 90–100° F for best results. The salt is added to the dyebath, then the fabric is added for 10 minutes, stirring the material constantly. The **dye liquor** can be scooped out with a cup and poured over the **wax**ed fabric to avoid excess **fractures** or **crackles** in batik.

Two tablespoons of washing soda (sal soda), or some other fixer as designated in the directions, are dissolved into 2 tablespoons warm water. The fabric is removed from the dyebath, the soda is added and stirred, and the fabric is replaced. It is stirred in the dyebath for 15 minutes. When dyeing is finished, remove the fabric and rinse it. Let it dry slowly, as fiber-reactive dyes continue to **set** as they dry.

The soda sometimes eats into the wax when batik fabric is dyed, so rewaxing may be necessary between dyeings.

To dye silk with fiber-reactive dyes, use 2 tablespoons **Glauber's salt** in place of table salt and only 1 teaspoon soda. Dye for 1 hour at 120° F, then rinse and dry.

Dyeing wool with fiber-reactive dye requires heat, so it cannot be used for batik. The wool is heated to simmering in the salt solution and kept at that level for 10 minutes. Then 1 cup of white vinegar is added to the dyebath, or about ¼ cup vinegar for every gallon of water. Simmer an additional 10 minutes. Do not add soda or other fixer. Remove it from the heat and rinse it in hot water to avoid a change in temperature, which can shrink or damage wool. Finally wash it by hand in hot soapy water, rerinse, and let dry. Also see **Batik and Tie-dye: Dyes.**

fiber sculpture. Weaving. The use of **weaving** and related fiber techniques to make three-dimensional constructions. Just about all fiber sculpture is made **off-loom** and employs such techniques as **knotting, netting, coiling, braiding, plaiting, finger weaving,** knitting, **wrapping,** and crochet. Some fiber sculpture depends on armatures or some means of keeping the shape up and intact; other fiber sculpture becomes three-dimensional by virtue of the material and the technique used. Also see **three-dimensional weaving.**

Fibrec. Batik and Tie-dye. See **fiber-reactive dye** and **Batik and Tie-dye: Dyes.**

fibrolite. Gemcutting. A light-blue mineral with a **hardness** of 7½, a **specific gravity** of 3.25, and refractive indices of 1.658 and 1.677. It is used for **facet**ed gems. Fibrolite is cut with 400-grit silicon carbide **abrasive** on a lead **lap** and polished with Linde A on a tin lap. Also see **cabochon, faceting, polishing, refraction.**

fid. Leatherwork. (Also called lacing fid.) A square-pointed tool similar to an awl used to tighten laces and enlarge existing holes for **lacing.** See ill. Also see **awl and haft.**

Fid

field of diamonds. Quilts. A **hexagon quilt** that uses a Grandmother's Flower Garden arrangement with additional hexagons at top and bottom to form **diamond** shapes. The diamond **blocks** are then **set** with a row of plain hexagons between, forming an **all-over** crisscross lattice pattern.

50/50 weaves. Weaving. See **balanced weave.**

figure. Woodworking. See **wood.**

figure and ground. In visual compositions, the subject and its background. An ink blot is often taken to be a figure against a ground of white paper (as in a Rorschach test). That the eye tends to see images in terms of figure and ground leads to some interesting anomalies or so-called optical illusions. The accompanying illustration shows an instance where the eye is somewhat confused as to figure and ground. At first glance, it may seem to be a drawing of a bird bath or goblet, but on further inspection, the figure and ground reverse, and we see two faces. See ill.

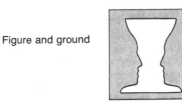
Figure and ground

figure eight stitch. Basketry. See **Basketry: Coil Basket Construction.**

figure eight warp. Weaving. See **continuous warp.**

filament. Lacemaking. Tatting. A single, very fine thread or threadlike structure.

filament. Spinning. Weaving. A very long continuous strand of **fiber** that is usually measured in yards, but conceivably could be miles long. The only natural filament is **silk,** which is extruded by a silkworm in the making of a cocoon. All man-made fibers start out as filaments. They are drawn out of a spinneret as a liquid solution and are immediately coagulated into a solid. This filament is then either left as a continuous filament, or cut up into **staple fiber** lengths and spun up in this form. Filaments can be texturized, a method of deforming its smooth surface for bulkiness, improved absorbency, softer **hand,** and a pleasant surface texture. Yarns made from filaments are of two types, monofilament and multifilament. Monofilament yarns are made of a single solid strand of great strength and smoothness. These yarns are used where sheerness with strength is desired, such as for hosiery. A multifilament yarn is composed of two or more filaments twisted together, usually with only a slight twist. The size and number of filaments are variable. Silk, rayon, acetate, and nylon, among others, are often found as multifilament yarns. Also see **spun yarn, textured yarns.**

file. Enameling. See **firescale** and **Enameling: Tools and Materials.**

file. Glasswork. Files are often used in glasswork to cut a notch or ring in rod or tubular glass to start a break. A sharp, fine file like a Nicholson-brand Warding Bastard is best. The 6″ size is adequate for notching a rod or tube; the 12″ size is best for starting a crack to separate free-blown work from the **blowing iron.** Files can be resharpened on an abrasive wheel by grinding the edge to expose still-sharp file cuts on the flat. Also see **freeblowing.**

file. Jewelry. Metalworking. Plastics. Woodworking. A steel bar with a rough ribbed surface used for shaping or smoothing plastic, metal, or wood. Files used on metals are also used on plastics. Files used in jewelrymaking, metalworking, and plastics are of two main types of cut or arrangements of the file's teeth: single-cut, with one set of parallel rows of ribs cut diagonally across the face, and double-cut, with two sets of cuts crossing on the face to form diamond-shaped points (**a.**, **b.**). The single-cut face gives a smoother finish but cuts more slowly.

Files come in various lengths of from 6 to 12″ and in three grades of coarseness: bastard cut (rough), second cut (medium), and smooth (for finishing). The longer a file is, the coarser it is; a 12″ smooth file is coarser than a 10″ smooth file.

Files are named according to the shape of their cross section—triangular, round, half-round, or oval. A file is classified by length, shape, and cut. All files are designed to remove metal on the forward stroke.

Files are classified into three groups: machinist's files, jeweler's files (or Swiss pattern), and special-purpose files.

Machinist's files are commonly used for general metalworking where quick removal of the metal is desired. Examples of machinist's files are:

MILL FILE   Used for sharpening **saws** and edged tools, for **drawfiling**, lathe filing, and finishing. The single-cut is used mostly in the smooth and second-cut grades to give a fine finish. It got its name because it was first used for filing saws used in lumber mills (**c.**).

HAND FILE   This file does not decrease in width at the end. One edge is uncut, and the file is used to finish flat surfaces and corners of rectangular openings (**d.**).

SQUARE FILE   Used for filing slots, rectangular openings, and for some general surface filing. It is often double-cut (**e.**).

ROUND FILE   Use this file to smooth round openings and concave surfaces. Round files over 6″ long are usually double-cut; others are single-cut (**f.**).

HALF-ROUND FILE   Use this file for concave, convex, and flat surfaces. The flat side is single-cut; the curved side can be of a different cut and coarseness (**g.**).

THREE-SQUARE FILE   Use this for filing acute angles and cleaning square corners. It is generally double cut (**h.**).

RASP   (Also called rasp-cut file.) The rasp has pointed separate teeth instead of the ridges of a file, and is used only on soft or hot metal or wood. The other files may all be used on cold metal or plastic (**j.**). See **rasp.**

Needle files and **riffler**s are used in jewelrymaking. American files are graded as follows: 00 (2/0), rough file; 0 (zero), bastard file; 1 (one), second cut; 2, smooth cut. Files finer than 2 are supersmooth. Files manufactured in foreign countries use different systems to indicate cut or coarseness. "Swiss files" refers to foreign files which are available in grades of 00 (2/0) as the coarsest and 8 as the finest.

Files used in woodworking are only slightly different from those used in metalworking. Since wood is relatively soft, wood files need not be made of high-tempered steel, and the spaces between the teeth are larger to prevent clogging with wood chips. Since rasps tend to clog less easily and cut more quickly, they are used for coarser wood shaping.

Wood files should be cared for in the same way as metal files are; to prevent damage to the teeth, they should never come in contact with metal. See ill.

CARE OF FILES   Attach a tight-fitting handle by tapping the handle with the file in it on a workbench until the file slides into the handle. Do not hit the file with a hammer to force it into the handle. Clean the file after every few strokes by tapping the handle on the workbench to remove chips. If it becomes clogged with material, brush the file with a **file card.** Do not strike the file face or edge against a hard surface to clean it because the teeth may break. Keep the files separated in storage so that they don't touch each other and dull or break the teeth. Also keep them dry so they don't rust. Also see **filing** and **Metalworking: Filing, Plastics: Filing.**

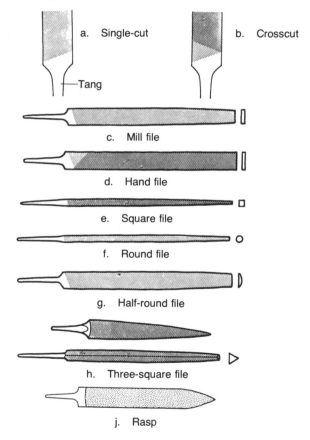

c.   Mill file

d.   Hand file

e.   Square file

f.   Round file

g.   Half-round file

h.   Three-square file

j.   Rasp

file card. Jewelry. Metalworking. Plastics. A brush with many closely placed short steel bristles used to clean **files.** Some file cards come with a detachable steel pick.

Place the file on a flat surface for support. Brush the file card in the direction of the cut of the file as many times as necessary to remove the metal which has been caught in its grooves. A delicate pressure is applied to **needle files** so as not to break them. Harder pressure may be needed for larger files. Use the pick to remove metal which the file card cannot reach. See ill.

File card

file cleaner. Metalworking. See **file card.**

filet. Lacemaking. A French word meaning net. The structure of this lace is similar to that of fishing nets. The name "filet" is also given to certain **bobbin lace** and **crochet,** done with the same square meshed look as a filet net. Also see **bobbin lace filet, crochet filet, knotted lace filet.**

filet. Stitchery. Hand-knotted mesh, as in fish nets or hand-made lace. The weave is imitated in machine production. While similar to **net,** it is always made with threads which cross at right angles, making a **grid pattern.**

filet crochet. Crochet. (Also called filet mesh.) A series of small squares created by **double crochet** and chain stitch. The double-crochet stitches are worked in blocks and form the design, and the chain stitches form the netlike background (**a., b.**). The pattern is charted on graph paper and it is possible to do very detailed work (**c.**). This technique is particularly suited to monograms. See ill. Also see **edging.**

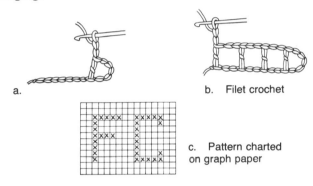

a.

b. Filet crochet

c. Pattern charted on graph paper

filet mesh. Crochet. See **filet crochet.**

filet mesh. Rugmaking. A crocheted open mesh that can be used alone or with ribbons or cloth strips threaded through the open spaces. There are many variations on filet mesh that produce larger or smaller openings, or simpler or fancier bars (called trebles) between openings. One version is made by first chaining for the desired length, then double crocheting in the sixth chain from the hook. Chain 2 and skip two chains in the original length before double crocheting again. This is repeated to the end of the row where 5 chains are made and the work is turned to begin the second row. For each succeeding row, the double crochet can go either right above the previous double crochet bar or in a staggered pattern between them. See ill.

Filet mesh

filet work. Weaving. See **netting.**

file wax. Jewelry. A **wax** containing plastic that can be filed and altered with heat. It is used in making the model in preparation for **lost-wax casting.** Also see **filing, sawing.**

filigree. Jewelry. A fine, delicate tracery of metal wires soldered together to produce a lacelike effect.

filigree. Stained Glass. A decorative lacelike pattern applied over glass and tinned with **solder.** Also see **brass, copper sheeting, tinning.**

filigree blade. Leather. See **swivel knife.**

filing. Jewelry. The process of removing metal with a **file** to create and refine form. Work can be supported against the **bench pin** or **bench** and held with the hand, a **ring clamp,** or any clamp that will hold the work stationary during filing.

Files are designed to cut on the forward stroke. It is often advisable to lift the file and inspect the work with each stroke. If it seems more practical or expedient to use a back-and-forth motion, use more pressure on the forward stroke and less on the return stroke. Attach wooden handles to the **tang** of larger, standard files. Grasp the file handle and extend the forefinger along its length to increase your control of larger files. Long, smooth strokes cut better than short, choppy ones. The larger files are used to remove metal quickly and can be used on heavy gauge metal. **Needle file**s are used to refine the form after large areas of metal are removed.

Needle files are used for all kinds of filing for which a small file is required. Needle files can handle very sensitive forms, curves, and angles. Two of their major uses are to refine designs that have been sawed out of sheet metal and to create form. They cut at any angle on the forward stroke.

Hold a file parallel to the surface of the metal, to remove metal efficiently; when held at a slight angle, filing is somewhat slower but this can be useful when perfecting forms and edges. Also see **beveling, file card.**

fill. Weaving. See **filling.**

filler. Découpage. Various compounds are available for filling cracks, holes, or open grain in wood surfaces to be used for découpage. Plastic wood is used for cracks and holes, and spackling compound for smaller blemishes. When dry, the filler should be sanded until the surface is smooth. The filler is applied before the wood is sealed or **finish**ed.

filler. Plastics. Materials added to **resin**s to change one or more of their basic properties; for example, to reduce **exotherm,** to extend resin, or to add strength or flexibility. Examples of fillers are cotton, jute, hemp, sisal, whiting, **glass fiber, cabosil,** talc, nylon, Dacron, mica, china clay, asbestos fibers, calcium carbonate, and chalk.

filler. Quilts. Any material used as the middle layer in a quilt is called the filler. Originally, pieces of old clothes or blankets were used, as they added weight and warmth, and the **quilting stitch**es held all these pieces of filler in place. Later, **cotton** and **wool wadding** or **batting** were used.

Muslin, batting, blankets of cotton, wool, **synthetic,**

flannel, or any other material will work satisfactorily as filler. But to achieve the sculptured relief surface so highly prized on a **quilt top,** batting is preferred. Also see **Quilts: Definition.**

filler. Stitchery. Toys. Any **stuffing** material used in **appliqué** stitchery, **doll**making, or **toy**making is called the filler. Usually, filler designates a loose **batt:** that is, one not packaged in blanket form, as for quilting. A loose batt contains either **cotton** or **kapok,** Dacron polyester, or other filler in bulk state, from which smaller pieces can be pulled off.

The filler for toys may also come in other forms. Shredded **foam rubber** or **Styrofoam** pellets are often used though they will sometimes disintegrate with use. Cotton wadding or kapok may eventually mat down, getting more compact. The **Dacron polyester batting** is best for resilience and washability.

Nylon stockings make a good filler for stuffed toys if the toy is made from a **fabric** that is heavy enough to maintain a smooth surface. **Sawdust** has traditionally been used as a filler, but it is not washable and should be used only with a closely woven fabric.

filler. Weaving. See **filling.**

filler. Woodworking. See **grain filler, wood filler.**

filler metal. Metalworking. Metal that is added to the **base** or **parent metal** when **welding, soldering,** or filling holes and cracks in a metal object. It does not necessarily have to be in the form of a filler rod or **welding rod** but may be a piece of wire, a piece cut off a bar or ingot, or a piece of the same type of metal taken from another object. When patching holes or cracks in a cast bronze, it is preferable to use a piece of the same metal, often from the **gate** system surrounding the original casting, so that the metal will be the same color and strength and take a uniform **patina.**

filler rod. Metalworking. See **welding rod.**

fillet. Bookbinding. A cylindrical revolving metal disk or barrel attached to a wooden handle. The barrel is engraved with one or more lines or decorative motifs. A fillet is used to run continuous lines or designs in **tooling** the casings of bindings. See ill. Also see **roll.**

a. One-line fillet

b. The notch enables corners to be neatly joined

fillet weld. Metalworking. See **weld.**

filling. Lacemaking. A broad term used in lacemaking that refers to the stitches in **needle lace** and **bobbin lace** that "fill in" certain areas of the design. Also see **filling stitches, leaf stitch.**

filling. Stitchery. (Also called pick, shot, woof.) The yarn or threads that run **crosswise** in a woven **fabric.** Each filling thread, or **weft** thread, is carried alternately over and under the **warp** threads.

filling. Weaving. (Also called fill, filler, **weft,** woof.) The crosswise or horizontal threads that interlace at right angles with the **warp** to form **cloth.** The filling is inserted between the warp **ends** by way of the **shed** with a **shuttle** or some other yarn carrier. Filling is often inserted **selvage** to selvage, but in **finger-manipulated** techniques the filling can be put in only for short sections and not always at right angles to the warp, in which case it then becomes known as **eccentric weft.** Filling can be loosely put in for **lace** or **gauze** effects or, as in **tapestry weave,** can be beaten down to cover the warp entirely so that all the interest is in the filling alone. Filling yarn can be softer, with less **twist,** and more **textured** than warp yarns because there is no stress or tension put on it during weaving. It should, however, be strong enough to hold up for the use for which it was intended. Individual filling yarns are known as **picks** or **shots,** and the number of **picks per inch** helps determine the thickness and the weight of a fabric.

filling arrangement. Weaving. One repeat of the pattern of the filling in terms of yarn. This repeat shows the order of placing the filling during weaving in terms of color, type of yarn (weight and texture), and fiber content.

filling brocade. Weaving. See **brocade.**

filling calculation. Weaving. See **yarn calculation.**

filling-face. Rugmaking. Weaving. A term denoting that the **filling** predominates on the face or the top side of a cloth. In some cases, such as **tapestry** and **flatweave rug**s, it may completely cover the **warp.** There are some weaves that have so few **raiser**s that a filling-face look results. However, a filling-face structure usually comes about not due to the **weave** but through an open **sett** and a heavy **beat.** The weight of the warp yarn in relation to the filling yarn also plays an important part. For example, a lightweight warp yarn set loosely could be very easily covered by a thick, soft filling yarn. Filling-face constructions are usually not as durable as **warp-face** ones. Most patterns are horizontal stripes, although with a **pick-and-pick** arrangement it is possible to achieve a vertical stripe. Also see **boundweave, satin weave.**

filling in. Bookbinding. Raising the height of **cloth** or **paper** siding with manila paper so that it lays flush with leather corners to give a neater appearance.

filling pattern. Quilts. The **quilting** that is used to fill in the areas between the larger, more important parts of the quilting designs. These usually are **geometric,** and may be straight lines, diagonals, plaids, **scallops,** circles, etc. They are always small repetitive units of **all-over** design. Also see **teacup quilting** and **Quilts: Quilting.**

filling stitch. Crewel. Embroidery. Needlepoint. A **stitch** used for filling in an area of the background fabric.

Crewel and embroidery stitches effective as filling stitches are **block shading, couching, cross stitch, detached chain stitch, ermine stitch, french knot, line stitch,** raised stem stitch, Roumanian stitch, seed stitch, sheaf stitch filling, stem stitch, and squared filling.

Needlepoint stitches used to fill in areas or background are brick stitch, cross stitch, French cut, French stitch, Gobelin stitch, notted stitch, Montenegrin cross stitch, old Florentine stitch, Parisian embroidery stitch, plaited Gobelin stitch, rice stitch, and stem stitch. Also see open filling stitch.

filling stitch. Lacemaking. In **bobbin lace** there can be a **filling** of a **ground** stitch, **bars**, or **leaf stitch**.

In **needle lace** the area in which these stitches go is outlined by a raised or flat **cordonnet** that serves as a foundation for **buttonhole stitch**es worked in a dense or open manner.

Fillings may also be made with a grouping of **wheel**s, or, as in **knotted lace filet** and **bobbin lace filet**, the design can have a filling of **darning stitch**es. Also see **basketry, bobbin lace filet, knotted lace filet, leaf stitch**.

filling thread. Quilts. Stitchery. See **weft**.

Filo floss. Embroidery. Needlepoint. A trade name for a fine silk floss. Also see **silk yarn**.

Filoselle. Embroidery. Needlepoint. A trade name for a fine twisted silk thread. Also see **silk yarn**.

filter press. Ceramics. A machine which is used to extract water from **slip**. The clay is forced under pressure into chambers lined with material. The water is squeezed out and the remaining clay is thicker. Also see **bat, canvas bag**.

fin. Jewelry. Thin extensions of metal caused by cracks in the **investment** during **lost wax casting**. Cracks are produced in the investment by incorrect mixing, incorrect firing during **burnout**, and sometimes, although rarely, caused by the thrust of molten metal from the **centrifugal casting machine**. Small fins are not uncommon and often can be easily chiseled, filed, or peeled away. Also see **flash**.

fin. Metalworking. Plastics. See **flash**.

finding. Jewelry. A commercially manufactured unit, such as a **joint** (**a.**), catch (**b.**), pinstem (**c.**), **rivet wire** (**d.**), earring backing, or cuff link back (**e.**). Rivet wire is used to hold the pinstem and joint together for soldering. See ill. Also see **jump ring, spring ring**.

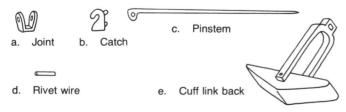

a. Joint b. Catch c. Pinstem d. Rivet wire e. Cuff link back

finding. Leatherwork. Various commercially available accessories, usually metal, added to leather designs for decorative and functional purposes, such as **belt finding**s,

eyelets, grommets, rivets, snaps, etc. Also see **Leatherwork: Setting up a Workshop, Tools and Materials**.

fine gold. Jewelry. **Pure gold**. Also see **karat**.

fine silver. Jewelry. **Silver** that is 999.0 parts silver per 1000 parts.

fine stitch. Quilts. Stitchery. Any small, delicate, carefully sewn **appliqué stitch** in which little or no thread shows on the surface of the **fabric**.

fine weave linen. Crewel. Embroidery. A **background fabric** excellent for crewel worked with crewel yarn, single-strand **Persian yarn**, 6-ply **cotton embroidery floss**, silk floss. Also see **linen fabric**.

finger bobbin. Weaving. See **butterfly**.

fingered hand. Puppets. See **glove-type hand**.

finger hank. Weaving. See **butterfly**.

finger hole. Puppets. The opening at the **base** of any **puppet head** through which the finger is inserted. It may accommodate one or two fingers. Also see **Puppets: Making the Puppet Head**.

finger joint. Woodworking. See **joint**.

finger-manipulated. Weaving. A term referring to woven techniques that are done by the fingers working in and around the **warp** threads and not by raising or lowering the **harnesses**. This includes **lace weave**s, **laid-in weave**s, **knotted pile, tapestry, wrapping**, and **soumak**. Finger-manipulated techniques can be done on any type of **loom**. A **butterfly** is used extensively with them and, in some cases, weaving aids such as a **gauge** or a **pick-up stick**. "Finger-manipulated" can also refer to opening the **shed** on a **frame** or **backstrap loom** with the fingers rather than with a **shed stick** or **heddles**. The shed openings can be for any weave or technique desired and not necessarily for one of those listed above. Finger-manipulated is often called hand-manipulated and, sometimes, **free weaving**. However, it is not synonymous with **finger weaving**, which is a type of **plaiting**.

finger puppet. Puppets. Any of a great variety of small puppets that fit over the ends of the fingers. They may be made in any of a variety of ways.

A piece of **felt** can be rolled around the finger to determine size, the overlapping end sewn down to make a small tube, and features added with embroidery.

In another method, two arch-shaped pieces can be cut and joined, inserting arms into the seams if desired (**a.**). A face can be added on a small circle of felt appliquéd to the arch shape, or the features can be sewn directly onto the arch.

The head, body, and arms of the figure can be cut as a single shape. A duplicate is used for the reverse side, and the two pieces are stitched together.

Profile finger puppets work very well for specific faces or animals. For example, a horse finger puppet is easily made by cutting a profile of the horse's head with a long neck that slips over the finger. The horse shape is duplicated and the two pieces are sewn together to make the puppet. Yarn can be added for a mane.

Another type of finger puppet consists of features painted or drawn directly on the pad of the finger with a **marking pen** or watercolor pen or watercolor paint. A tiny bit of cloth tied onto the finger or held in place by a rubber band completes the costume. See ill.

Finger puppets

a.   b.

finger-puppet stage. Puppets. See **Puppets: The Puppet Stage.**

finger top. Toys. (Also called spool top, whirly top.) A simple **spin top** made from the cylinder left over from a spool of sewing thread. A **dowel**, cut so that it is longer than the spool, is inserted through the hole in the center of the spool. The dowel is **glue**d in place so that it is tight and firm. Then the spool is **lathe turned** so that a V-shape is cut from each end of the spool edge to the center (**a.**). In this way two tops are made from one spool. The dowel extending from the end of each top makes a peg or handle and the top is spun on the point (**b.**). See ill.

Finger top

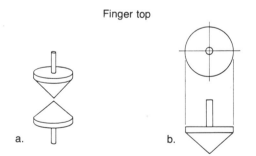

a.   b.

finger treadle. Weaving. See **lever, table loom.**

finger weaving. Weaving. A technique in which fingers are the only tool used to interlace strands of yarn. The most common use of the term is in relationship to **plaiting,** for which it is a synonym. However, when speaking of North American Indian methods of fiber construction, the term is also used in regard to other techniques that employ mainly the fingers. For example, **Salish weaving,** whether **twill weaving** on a **frame** (two-bar) **loom,** or **twining** on a **warp-weighted** (single-bar) **loom,** is referred to as finger weaving. In the case of the twill weaving, the pattern is picked up by the fingers for each **shed.** The Salish called twining on the warp-weighted loom "loose warp weaving" due to the warp being secured only at one end.

Other types of twining, such as that used in **Chilkat**

blankets, **Taaniko twining,** and twining done by the **Ojibwa** Indians, is also referred to as finger weaving. The twining of the Ojibwas was also known as the "old Indian weave."

As can be seen in many instances, finger weaving does not even imply the over and under interlacing of weaving. Sometimes **looping** and **netting** are also included under finger weaving constructions, whereas they should properly be designated as finger techniques. Finger weaving has also grown away from the idea that just the fingers are to be used, as sometimes a frame, needles, or a **shed stick** are used as aids. Also see **Indian weaving, Swedish braid.**

finial. Puppets. Stitchery. Toys. A decorative piece added to the end of a **rod** or a **staff.** The ornamental finial usually ends in a point or round ball and adds a flourish to the blunt end of a rod. The most common finials for **banner**s or wall hangings are made of wood. Some have **dowel** ends by which they can be attached to a rod. Wood finials are often added to give decorative detail to toy trains, cars, or building blocks.

fining. Glasswork. (Also called planing.) The process whereby small bubbles of air trapped in a molten batch of glass are allowed to float to the surface. This requires holding the **melt** at a very high temperature for some time, typically for 24 hours at 1500° C. The process can be speeded up somewhat by pushing wet wood to the bottom of the melt. The large bubbles produced this way rise quickly and carry the smaller natural bubbles, or **seed**s, to the surface, and the wood leaves little residue.

finish. Batik and Tie-dye. Quilts. Stitchery. Any of a variety of processes or treatments added to **fabric**s after they are constructed. The fabric finish may be chemical (permanent) or additive (permanent or nonpermanent). Finishing is added for a number of reasons and may be applied for the specific purpose of adding sheen or weight. The finish may add features that make the fabric **crease resistant, moth repellant, fireproof,** or **fire retardant.** It may give a shiny coating, as in **chintz** or glazed cotton, or impart a property such as **permanent press, wash-and-wear,** or stain-resistance. The finish of a fabric is of great importance if the fabric is to be dyed. A permanent-press finish treats the fabric to make it resistant to dye, which would affect its performance for **batik** or **tie-dye.** Also see **removing fabric finish.**

finish. Découpage. Any of the clear-drying **varnish**es that protect the surface and enhance it with a glossy sheen. Varnish is commonly used for découpage finish, applied in many layers over a painted and sealed surface, then sanded until smooth, and **wax**ed. Also see **Découpage: Varnishing and Sanding.**

finish. Leatherwork. After **tanning,** leather is given various finishes, according to its function. It may be hammered and machine-rolled for shoe soles, glass-rollered for a glossy finish, or machine-buffed for soft leathers. Also see **embossing, suede.**

finish. Toys. The final surface or coating applied over a stain or paint to protect it or to add texture.

Tempera or **watercolor paint,** when applied to cardboard, wood, **dough art,** or paper, often requires a finish that serves as a **sealer.** It prevents smearing or rubbing of the paint and, if adequately fixed, makes the surface waterproof. Shellac, varnish, or urethane liquid plastic can be brushed on, or acrylic plastic spray or other clear aerosol spray finishes can be used.

Enamel paints offer a finish that is part of the paint itself, usually **glossy** or matte. The process of **antiquing** requires a finish coat of various stains and colors. When a natural wood finish is desired a shellac is sometimes used as a sealer, followed by sanding and waxing. A complete natural finish can be obtained, especially on **hardwood**s, by sanding and rubbing with steel wool to a glossy surface.

finish. Woodworking. The result of **sanding,** filling, **painting, staining, bleaching, sealing, rubbing,** or **wax**ing a wood surface. It is employed to bring out the natural beauty, **grain,** and color of a wood; to facilitate cleaning; to prevent it from absorbing moisture and thus splitting, staining, or **warp**ing; and in some cases to produce a uniformity of color or surface if it lacks one. A variety of **stain**s, **abrasive**s, **wood filler**s, **rubbing compound**s, and **sealer**s are employed. The most common final finishes are **linseed oil, paint, shellac, lacquer,** and **varnish,** which are usually rubbed and polished to produce a gloss finish. Study each type of finish and finishing process for its specific usage and methods of application. Also see **Woodworking: Finishing.**

finished length. Weaving. The length of the fabric after weaving and **finishing.** Also see **yarn calculations.**

finished picks. Weaving. See **picks per inch.**

finished size. Quilts. The size of a piece, **block,** or unit after seams or hems are taken. The finished size is usually ¼" smaller in all around than the cut size.

finishing. Bookbinding. The impressing or **tooling** of design or letters for the **title,** applying gilt or **edge coloring,** or any other decorative procedure done after the construction of the book is complete.

finishing. Candlemaking. See **Candlemaking: Finishing the Candle.**

finishing. Macramé. The process of securing cords and knots at the end of a piece of macramé. There are various finishing techniques, including the **overhand knot;** the **gathering knot,** which forms a border of tasseled fringe; and the **accumulating bar,** which ends the piece with a smooth, solid row of knots. If the accumulating bar is used, the loose ends of **cord** are woven into the fabric with either a **tapestry needle** or a **crochet hook** on the back of the work. A piece of macramé can also be finished in the **compact half hitch,** the **chain stitch,** and the chain stitch with crossed loops.

finishing. Metalworking. The use of a process, in making a metal object, that improves the final appearance, prevents corrosion, improves the wearing qualities of the surface, or covers an inexpensive or soft metal with a more expensive or more durable one. Traditional craft procedures usually include **chasing, polishing, buffing,** and **coloring.** Today, however, many sculptors working on large outdoor constructions employ methods usually associated with industrial products, such as spray coating with paints or plastics, **sandblasting, aluminum anodizing,** etc. (The work is usually done by commercial fabricators because home studio space and equipment are inadequate.) The finishing methods listed in **Metalworking** require only supplies and equipment of moderate cost for the home shop. Also see **Metalworking: Finishing.**

finishing. Plastics. See **Plastics: Finishing.**

finishing. Quilts. The trimming, basing, **binding,** and hemming of a quilt when it is removed or **taken out** of the **quilting frame.** Also see **Quilts: Definition, Binding.**

finishing. Rugmaking. Weaving. In rugmaking, steps taken at the end of making a rug to secure the edges to make sure that the rug retains its shape and attractiveness and to add to the durability of the rug. These steps can involve **blocking** or **steam pressing** in order to control or correct the shape; **joining** sections if the rug has been made in small pieces; **hemming, binding,** making a **fringe,** or otherwise finishing raw edges on a rug; adding a fringe or **tassels** for decoration; lining the rug; or latexing the back. Which of these steps is used depends on the technique employed, whether or not a **rug backing** was used, and what kind it was. For example, an **embroidered rug** might need to be blocked and backed with a lining, but a woven rug might need only a fringe knotted out of its **warp end**s. Likewise, a rug made on a **burlap** backing would have to have the hem taken care of differently from one made on a **Swedish rug backing.**

In weaving, steps that a **fabric** undergoes after weaving and prior to putting it to use or on display. In some cases the various steps are optional; in other cases, necessary. This depends on the fiber content, the type of yarn, the weave or technique employed, and what the end use is to be. For example, a **wall hanging** might only have a fringe made and be lightly pressed, whereas a coating fabric may be washed and shrunk and steam pressed.

The following are the finishing steps in the order they are considered after cutting the fabric off the **loom:** 1) mending, which is the darning in of **broken end**s and the beginning and ending tails of **filling** yarn that have not been taken care of during weaving; some weaving mistakes can be corrected through darning; 2) securing the first and last pick so that the fabric does not unravel; this can be a machine stitching, **overcasting,** or making some sort of **finishing edge** or a **fringe;** 3) washing the piece in lukewarm or hot water with a mild detergent so that the surface dirt that accumulated in the yarn during weaving is taken out, so that the yarn blooms and the weave shrinks or compresses; the amount of dirt and the fiber content determine the water temperature; 4) **piece dyeing;** 5) blocking; 6) **tentering**; 7) **fulling**; 8) **felting**; 9) **napping**; 10) **steam pressing**; 11) **hemming**; and 12) adding trim or fringe.

Natural finishing is when the least possible finishing has been done in order to allow the fibers and yarn to keep their natural texture. Also see **backing the rug, blooming, finishing edges, shrinkage, sponging.**

finishing. Stitchery. The final steps in making a **banner, wall hanging,** or other **fabric** article. It includes **binding** or **hemming** as well as supplying the means by which the piece may be hung. Finishing involves covering **raw edges** with bias strips, **bias tape,** or **band**s of fabric. Raw edges are turned back and covered with a **backing** or they are **fold**ed and hemmed. The finishing edge may also make provision for a supporting **rod** at top and bottom. This can be a stitched **channel** or added loops through which a dowel or **rod** can be inserted.

Finishing may also refer to the way in which any raw edge is treated. **Appliqué**ing, hemming or **fell**ing is a means of finishing a single raw edge. When there are two raw edges, as in a **plain seam,** various **seam finish**es may be used, including **French seam, flat fell seam,** and **topstitched seam.** Some materials, such as **felt, bonded fabric,** or leather do not require any edge finishing. Also see **Stitchery: Finishing.**

finishing. Tatting. See **tie off ends** and **Tatting: Finishing.**

finishing. Woodworking. See **Woodworking: Finishing.**

finishing edge. Quilts. Any of a variety of edges added to the finished quilt. It might be a **bias binding** used to make a narrow **border,** or it may be a wide border sewn on and backed or faced. On some quilts the top layer is turned to the back and **slipstitch**ed in place, or the **backing** may be brought over to the face of the quilt and slipstitched in place to make a border, **miter**ing the corner. The addition of the finishing edge is the final step of a quilt. Also see **Quilts: Binding.**

finishing edge. Rugmaking. Weaving. A technique applied to the edges of a woven rug or other weaving to secure the first and last **pick**s and to complete the work. A finishing edge can often work in conjunction with **hemming.** At other times it takes the place of a hem. If this involves a self-fringe or an added **fringe,** then a technique must be used that will keep the **warp end**s from fraying and tangling, and that looks attractive. If the function of the finishing edge is to secure the picks, it is called a weft protector and could involve, besides hems, machine or hand stitching, knotting, twining, or looping. If the finishing edge serves mainly to protect the warp, it is called a warp protector and could include such methods as braiding, knotting, plying, or **whipping** the fringe. There are also finishing edges that are both warp and weft protectors. Under this category is the **Swedish braid** and various **twined** and **wrapped edge**s.

Darning the warp ends back into the edge is probably the simplest way to both protect them and give a neat, crisp edge to the piece. Another simple way is through the use of **overhand knot**s that can serve as a weft protector or be extended into a warp protector as well. Any of the warp protecting methods can be used with fringes added on to rugs made on **rug backing**s or by any technique other than weaving. See ill. Also see **Damascus Edge, looped edge, Philippine Edge.**

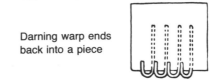

Darning warp ends back into a piece

finishing leather. Leatherwork. See **Leatherwork: Finishing.**

finishing nail. Woodworking. See **nail.**

finishing press. Bookbinding. A wooden clamp used to hold a book while the title and decorations are applied to the **spine.**

finishing stove. Bookbinding. The heater used to heat **tool**s employed in **titling** and cover decoration. It can be fueled by gas, electricity, or oil. Its shape is usually circular to allow the brass ends of the tools to be heated in the center of the stove; an outside rim supports the handles and keeps them cool. It is also possible to use the heater for keeping glue warm. See ill.

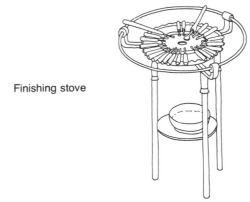

Finishing stove

finish removal. Batik and Tie-dye. The process of removing a **fabric finish** to make the fibers more receptive to dye. New material should always be washed in hot water with soap or detergent to extract **sizing.** Other formulas can be used to remove other fabric finishes. Also see **removing fabric finish, removing size,** and **Batik and Tie-dye: Fabrics for Dyeing.**

Finnweave. Weaving. A type of **double cloth pick-up weave** that can be used for designs of great detail and intricacy as well as for simple designs. A **pick-up stick,** along with a **shed stick** and a round rod, are used for obtaining the **shed**s. The **warp** is made of two colors—those of the face and back layers. The colors reverse positions from front to back; the pattern color on the face will become the background color on the back side, and the face background color will become the pattern color on the back. Finnweave is worked out as a design on **graph paper**

and then, following the graph paper, the pattern sheds are picked up. **Plain weave** is used for both top and bottom layers. Finnweave is used for towels, blankets, pillow covers, and wall hangings. It is a very slow technique in which strict adherence to the graph paper design is essential or the pattern and background will not be in solid colors but peppered by "raindrops," mistakes showing the opposite color. This is one of the most popular weaves in Finland, with its history going back to the sixteenth century. It is known there as *takana* and *lastakudos*—the last term meaning stick weaving.

To do Finnweave, set up the warp so that dark threads are on harnesses 1 and 2 and light on 3 and 4. Raise harnesses 1 and 2 and pick up the first line of the pattern with the pick-up stick. No **filling** is inserted, but the stick is pushed back against the **reed** and the **treadling** is changed to 3 and 4, so that a cross is produced behind the reed and between the parts of the warp. The round rod is placed in this cross and the pick-up stick removed. Treadling is changed to 1-2-4 and the shed stick is inserted through the shed that develops above the round rod. The shed stick is turned to make a shed and a **pick** of light filling is woven. The shed stick is removed, the treadling is changed to 1-2-3, the shed stick is reinserted into the new shed, and the second pick of light filling is woven. Both shed stick and round rod are now removed.

The steps for the background on harnesses 3 and 4 are the same as for the pattern with the background being picked up when 3-4 are raised. The treadling, after 3-4, is 1-2, 2-3-4, 1-3-4. Two picks of dark filling are woven. This completes one line on graph paper. The same procedure is carried through for each line.

Mexican double weave (sometimes called Peruvian double weave) is similar but easier and faster. Using the same threading and color order, treadle 1-2, pick up the background, and leave the pick-up stick flat in the warp and pushed back to the reed. Treadle harness 3 and weave a light pick. Treadle harness 4, beat down and then push the stick up against the reed. Insert the second light pick, remove the stick, and beat.

For the pattern treadle 3-4, pick up the pattern and repeat the above actions with the pick-up stick, treadling 1 and then 2 and weaving with the dark filling.

fir. Woodworking. A **softwood** grown in the western and northwestern United States. It is related and is similar in appearance to **spruce.** Although it bruises and dents easily, it is recommended as practice or starter wood for beginning woodcarvers because it is soft and therefore easy to carve. Commercially, it is used for **plywood**, packing cases, and boxes. Douglas fir may be used for high-finish surfaces in grades C and better.

fire. Ceramics. See **Ceramics: Firing.**

fire. Gemcutting. See **refraction.**

fire agate. Gemcutting. See **quartz.**

fire brick. Ceramics. See **insulation.**

firebrick plug. Stained Glass. Cone-shaped pieces of firebrick used as plugs and protective coverings for the spyhole of a **kiln.** They can easily be carved from a piece of firebrick. Also see **firing, inspection plug.**

fire clay. Ceramics. See **Ceramics: Clay.**

firecord. Ceramics. A straw rope soaked in salt water and wrapped around a **pot.** When fired the rope burns away, leaving a semiglazed line. This technique originated in Japan. Also see **salt glaze.**

firecrack. Stained Glass. (Also called crack.) These are glass breakages that occur during **firing** in the **kiln.** They occur either when the glass has not been annealed properly during manufacturing or when the glass is heated up too quickly in the kiln. There are two kinds of firecracks. Star cracks are breakages in which the glass explodes over the other glass in the kiln. Cooling cracks occur when the glass separates, usually in the shape of a curve. Also see **annealing, Norman slab glass.**

fire gilding. Jewelry. A simple but highly toxic plating technique in which gold is dropped into mercury and instantly dissolved into an **amalgam.** A completed piece of copper jewelry is rubbed with the amalgam, taking on the appearance of the mercury. When the work is heated in a flame the mercury volatizes, leaving a deposit of gold. One of the earliest forms of gold plating, it is a somewhat heavier plating than is done today. Pieces that have been fire gilded retain their finish for centuries. This technique should not be attempted without instruction. Also see **percel-gilt, water gilding.**

Fire Lily. Quilts. See **Lily.**

fire polishing. Glasswork. A method of reducing the sharpness of broken glass. When a rod or tube is nicked and cracked off, the edges are sharp and often ragged. Simply holding the sharp end in a **glass fire** will cause the end to soften, and surface tension effects will neatly round over the edges.

fireproofing. Papercrafts. A chemical treatment used to make papier mâché designs fire resistant. Add 1 teaspoon of sodium phosphate, available from the drugstore, for every 1 cup of **flour paste** or other liquid **papier mâché** paste to be used.

fire resistant. Stitchery. A treatment or **finish** given to **fabrics** so that they will prevent the spread of flame.

A **fabric** can be chemically treated to make the materials fire retardant. Fire retardant fabrics are neither fireproof nor flameproof; the treatment slows the burning process. Chemicals used to make materials retardant include ammonium phosphate, ammonium sulfate, borax, boric acid, and zinc chloride.

A fabric not affected by fire may be said to be fireproof. It is able to withstand exposure to flame or high temperature and still remain intact and usable. Fabrics used in public buildings are required to be fire-resistant or flameproof although rarely fireproof.

firescale. Enameling. The oxidation of some **metals,** such as sterling silver and copper, when they are heated for cleaning, annealing, and **firing.** This tarnishing is avoided when fine silver or high-karat gold are used.

Firescale forms a black incrustation on copper; small bits loosen when cooling and may stick in the **enamel.** It is sometimes used to create designs in and around enamels.

Firescale peels off when cool and must be dry when fired. Metal surfaces may be protected from firescale by a coating of scale inhibitor such as Amacote or Scale. Avoid contamination of unfired materials. Do not use the brush for scale treatment for applying enamel or **binder.**

Firescale is removed by **cleaning metal** surfaces. Metal edges are cleaned with a file. Also see **camel's hair brush, color testing, liver of sulfur** and **Enameling: Basic Operations, Tools and Materials.**

firescale. Jewelry. (Also called scale.) An **oxide** that forms on and below the surface of copper-bearing **alloys,** such as sterling **silver,** when exposed to heat. Firescale is reduced by coating the metal with **flux** before **soldering** or **annealing.** Areas that are not fluxed will develop heavy coats of firescale. The exception to this rule is seams, which are covered with **yellow ochre casein** to prevent the solder from flowing out of them. Remove firescale by **pickling** or by rubbing with **carborundum paper, emery paper, Scotch stone,** or **pumice.** Small amounts can even be removed by **buffing,** although too much metal may be removed, causing the form to lose definition. It is impossible to completely prevent firescale, but most of it can be avoided if fluxing and soldering are done properly. It should also be noted that where there is firescale, solder will not flow; this is true of all copper bearing metals such as sterling silver, **karat** golds, **bronze, brass,** and **copper** itself. Firescale on copper comes off easily and completely when it is pickled. On sterling silver firescale usually appears after buffing, in the form of bluish-gray splotches mixed with the more yellowish tone of the unaffected areas. Also see **Prip's flux.**

firescale. Metalworking. See **scale.**

firing. Ceramics. The heat treatment of ceramic materials to the **sintering** stage of a **kiln.** The standard firing procedure consists of a slow **bisque fire** to burn out any organic matter and chemically combined water. The resultant **bisque** is strong enough to be handled, but still porous enough to absorb **glaze.** The **glaze fire,** which follows **glazing,** is hotter and faster than the bisque fire. Also see **once fired ware** and **Ceramics: Firing.**

firing. China and Glass Painting. The final process in china and glass decoration, in which the colors are exposed to the high heat of the **kiln** to fuse the colors into the background **glaze.**

Onglaze color fires, or fuses, at around 750–800° C, or between pyrometric cone 017 (1328° F) and 019 (1166° F).

Colors vary in their firing properties, reds usually requiring greater heat.

Increase the heat slowly so the china expands slowly, with the peephole of the kiln left open for about half an hour to allow the fumes from oils used in mixing the colors to escape. Then close the muffle and increase the heat as required. The cooling-off period should be gradual. Leave the china in the kiln until it is quite cool to avoid quick contraction resulting in breakage. Repeat the firing for each additional coat of china paint. These additional firings enhance the glaze.

Glass is fired at lower temperatures than china. Use a separating powder such as whiting to coat the kiln shelves to prevent glass from sticking. For best results, sift a high-fire kiln wash over the whiting before firing to give a good surface to the underside of the fired piece. When firing glass, take care to open the kiln door about 1" the moment the firing is completed to release hot air, thereby halting the effects of the heat to keep the glass firm and to avoid melting it. During firing glassware appears black when the red glow begins, then slowly lightens and becomes hazy and finally transparent. Stop the heat when the glass appears transparent. Overfiring, firing too fast, or too close to the elements will distort glass.

firing. Enameling. Heating the **enamel** to melt it and fuse it to the **metal.** Firing is done either in a **kiln** or with a **torch.** The piece of enameling must be supported on a **trivet,** screen, or brick during firing as the high temperature causes the metal to "relax." A long-handled **firing fork** or **spatula** is used to handle the trivet.

Preheat the kiln to at least 1700° F. Opening the kiln door causes a drop of about 150° F in kiln temperature. A **pyrometer** is used to measure kiln temperature, but the most practical guide is visual appraisal of color. A reddish glow is visible at about 1100° F, dull red at 1400° F, cherry red at 1500° F, orange at 1700° F, and yellow at 1850° F.

Be sure enamel is dry before firing. Place the piece in the center of the kiln. The time varies, but after 1½ to 2 minutes, open the kiln and look in. The enamel becomes dark, then craterous, then pebbly, and finally shiny and smooth.

Remove the piece to a stone slab or asbestos board in a draft-free place to cool. After the red glow has faded, weights may be applied to flatten the piece or to prevent warping. It's advisable to wear an asbestos glove to avoid burns.

Some metals, such as copper and sterling silver, form **firescale** when they are fired. Trivets and screens are often made of monel, stainless steel, or nichrome because these metals do not form firescale, which can contaminate the enamel. Nonflammable fireboard, pieces of refractory brick, and sheets of mica are used to support flat pieces. Also see **binder, cloison, color testing, overfiring, overglaze, underglaze.**

firing. Stained Glass. The heat treatment used to adhere pigment and stain to glass, to fuse glass pieces together, and to slump glass into molds. Firing involves heating and cooling in a **kiln.**

If using a closed kiln, arrange the glass pieces on the **kiln** trays and load the trays into the firing chamber. Close the door and seal it with a piece of asbestos rope. Raise the heat slowly to 450−480° C and maintain this temperature for about four hours. Most glass in a closed kiln will be overfired at 600° C (about 1120° F). If the temperature rises too quickly, the glass in trays in the bottom of the kiln will be fired hard and appear bubbly and that in trays at the top will be unfired. After the glass is fired, shut off the kiln and allow it to cool for 12 hours. Then remove the glass.

If using an open kiln, while the kiln is heating up, place one tray on the bottom shelf of the firing chamber and the other tray in the **annealing chamber.** When, at about 650° C, the paint pigment is fired, remove the annealed tray to the first shelf of the preheating rack underneath the kiln. Then take out the tray in the firing chamber and place it in the annealing chamber. Place the annealed tray on the preheating rack. Place the **baffle** into the top position. Place the fired tray in the annealing chamber, and the preheated tray into the firing chamber under the baffle. After waiting a few minutes, withdraw the baffle and place the annealed tray on the preheating rack to avoid cracking.

In cooling the glass the first 100° C are most important to avoid cracking. The trays should be moved quickly from the firing chamber to the annealing chamber.

Firing is often done by eye. Following is how glass looks at certain temperatures:

Temperature (in degrees Celsius)	Appearance
400°	The glass begins to glow red at the edges but has no color otherwise.
500°	The glass is a dull red; glass paint at this point looks gray and flat.
600°	The surface of glass paint looks glossy; temperature should be held for 15 minutes or more on thick glass to get a good-quality firing.
650°	The glass is bright red; if glass remains longer than 5 minutes in firing chamber it will begin to change shape.
700°	The glass is very red and puttylike.
800°	The glass will be fused together.

Also see **blistered paint, firing out, metaling, overfiring.**

firing chamber. Stained Glass. See **firing.**

firing cone. See **pyrometric cone.**

firing fork. Enameling. A tool used for moving **trivet**s and enameled pieces in and out of the **kiln** when **firing.** Firing forks may be two-tined with a heat guard or constructed of a heavy-gauge steel. They come in a range of sizes. See ill. Also see **Enameling: Tools and Materials.**

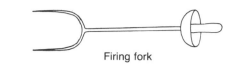
Firing fork

firing out. Stained Glass. A form of overfiring in which the glass paint disappears. The solution is to reapply the paint and fire again. Also see **firing stain, painting on glass.**

firing stain. Stained Glass. Stain or glaze should be fired at a low temperature. The best time to fire stain is after a day of **firing** paint, when the **kiln** has been turned off. At that point there is a declining but long-lasting heat known as a soaking fire that reduces the chance of **overfiring** the stain.

Glass varies in its response to stain. Yellow glasses stain well; very deep ambers can be obtained. English **reamy glass** at a very low temperature, whites, and French and some German whites are very susceptible to stain, with results from a light yellow to deep amber. French greens are somewhat susceptible. French and English blues generally stain well, producing a wide range of lovely greens. The English make a staining blue just for this purpose. Reds take stain well on the white side of the glass; otherwise the stain replaces the red with a yellow. Also see **firing out, staining.**

firmer chisel. Woodworking. See **chisel.**

firmer gouge. Woodworking. See **gouge.**

first aid. Candlemaking. See **Candlemaking: Safety Precautions.**

first clip. Spinning. See **lamb's wool.**

fishbone stitch. Crewel. Embroidery. Needlepoint. (Also called attached flystitch, long and short oblique stitch, short oblique stitch.) A combination of straight and **tacking stitch**es worked on cloth or canvas. It can be worked closely to form a leaf shape or widely for a border pattern. See ill. Also see **Cretan stitch, fly stitch.**

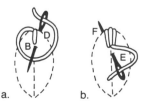

a.   b.   c.

d. Fishbone stitch worked on fabric

e. Fishbone stitch worked on canvas

fisherman's knot. Weaving. See **netting.**

fisherman's sweater patterns. Knitting. The pattern of sweater traditionally knit by the fishermen of the Channel Islands, located off the coast of Normandy in the English Channel. Fishermen's sweaters may be made from a composite of stitches, such as the cable, ribbing, **double moss stitch,** and a combination of garter and stocking stitches. Blue and off-white are two of the most commonly used colors. Also see **Aran knitting, Guernsey, Jersey sweater.**

fishline. Stained Glass. A strong, thin filament of clear plastic sold in different strengths on reels in sporting goods stores. It is practically invisible when hanging and is used to hold pieces of glass in **mobile**s, and to hang finished **panel**s or **freeform** pieces in front of a window.

fish net. Stitchery. A **cotton net fabric** with a wide, coarse mesh.

fishnet knot. Weaving. See **netting.**

fishtail chisel. Woodworking. See **chisel.**

fitching. Basketry. A form of **twined weaving** used to hold the stakes securely. It is commonly used after a space or opening in the **siding.** Also see **Basketry: Woven Basket Construction.**

fitch pairing. Basketry. The action or motion of twisting the **weaver**s in order to secure the **stake**s while **fitching.** Here, the furthest left weaver is always taken and twisted under the right-hand weaver. Also see **Basketry: Woven Basket Construction.**

fitted print. Block Printing. Fabric Printing. A multicolored block print that is printed in stages, one block being cut for each color, with color areas finally fitting together according to the original design.

First, a multicolored layout is done in poster or tempera paint, with paint colors that match the printing inks to be used. Large, clearly defined color areas are most suitable to fabric printing. Then the color separations are traced onto tracing paper placed over the painted design. One tracing is made for each color, with all lines and shapes of one color carefully isolated and traced on the corresponding sheet. These shapes are then transferred with carbon paper to blocks the same size as the layout, one for each color. The blocks are cut and then printed, one after another. Care must be taken to line up each block correctly, so that the final print will be identical to the design. Also see **registration.**

fitting. Stained Glass. (Also called installation.) The process in which a finished work is fitted to a window space. The stained-glass work may be a **panel** left unframed and hung in front of a strong light or window. Heavy copper wire loops can be soldered to the top of the panel and thin wire or **fishline** threaded through them. If H-section **lead came** is used for the border lead, copper wire, fishline, or a small decorative chain can be fitted into the opening of the

outer channel of the lead and soldered or tied together, leaving slack at the top of the panel for hanging.

Glass panels made to size for an existing window can be fitted into the window by nailing a **stop** or wooden molding the length and width of all four sides of the window frame to the inside window trim.

This spacer can be as narrow as ⅛″ thick. Place the panel against this stop and carefully nail another four pieces of molding in place. This holds the panel against the window while leaving an air space between them.

Fitting the stained-glass panel permanently into a window opening is called fixing. Often, reinforcing rods such as division bars and saddle bars are needed to support the window. Also see **banding, needle-nose pliers, pointing, rebate, reglet, solder.**

Five-minute Epoxy. Plastics. See **epoxy.**

Five-point Star. Quilts. See **star patterns.**

fix. Batik and Tie-dye. To **set** color in the **dyeing** process through the use of various methods, usually involving the application of heat. In fixing color the heat may be applied by **ironing** or **steaming**, or by simmering or boiling the **dyebath**, depending upon the particular type of **dye** used. Some dyes can be set through exposure to the sun. Also see **heat set, sodium bicarbonate, washing soda.**

fixation. Fabric Printing. The process—generally exposure to heat—by which colors are permanently fixed to the fiber. **Steaming** is the common method of fixation. Any fabric decorated with **dye paste** will require fixation for **fastness** of color because most of the **dye** remains in the dried film of the **thickener** on the surface of the fabric. Little or none will penetrate the fiber until exposure to heat. Then, with the absorption of moisture, each printed area becomes a highly concentrated **dyebath** and the dye penetrates the fiber. Fixation can also be done by ironing the fabric. Also see **Fabric Printing: Finishing.**

fixative. Puppets. Toys. A protective coating for paper or painted surfaces to prevent smearing. It is transparent and **lacquer**like. When water-soluble paints or inks are used, fixative will check the likelihood of smears. It is available in aerosol spray cans.

fixing. Stained Glass. See **fitting.**

flake yarn. Spinning. Weaving. See **novelty yarn.**

flambé. Ceramics. (Also called rouge flambé.) A **porcelain glaze** of Chinese origin. It has a flamelike appearance because it is streaked with **reduction** copper red or purples. Flambé literally means ''flaming.'' Also see **copper carbonate.**

flame. Jewelry. The burning gas coming from the tip of a **torch.** The size and type of flame used depends on the operation performed. Most torches, save the propane variety, have interchangeable torch tips that adjust the size of the flame. Propane torches, such as the Bernz-O-Matic, produce one type of flame, although the size of the flame can be adjusted by a valve on the side of the nozzle. A propane torch is suitable for soldering and fluxing work up to 3". Acetylene torches (Prest-O-Lite) contain acetylene gas and produce a clean, quick-heating flame; a slightly reducing or brushing flame contains the best proportion of acetylene to air. **Gas-air torch**es have separate hoses for gas and air; regulating the quantity of gas and air produces the different types of flames.

A neutral flame is recommended for **soldering,** although some metals require a brushing flame. A neutral flame burns an equal amount of air and gas (**a.**). A brushing flame (also called slight reducing flame) has a pale blue inner cone, a deep blue outer cone with a yellow tip (**b.**). This flame is suitable for **fluxing** and **annealing** because it heats the metal evenly and prohibits the formation of **firescale.** A fluxing flame produces a slight hissing sound, whereas a soldering flame produces a whooshing sound.

Use a needle flame to **solder** small pieces (not **filigree**) or whenever a concentrated heat source is necessary. The needle flame is a very pointed, extremely blue flame caused by an excess of air and a deficiency of gas (**c.**). It is an extremely hot flame that heats the metal unevenly and promotes firescale which inhibits the flow of solder.

Use a torch in a dimly lit room to facilitate seeing the color changes in the metal as it reaches the correct temperature for annealing, fluxing, and soldering. Different metals melt at different temperatures; however, all metals vary in coloration from normal through the red, orange, yellow spectra to white. It is advisable to **flux** a test piece and make note of the color changes to avoid overheating the metal when working a piece.

During all operations keep the flame moving in a circular to figure-eight motion to keep the metal evenly heated. The hottest part of the flame is the point before the inner cone. When soldering, concentrate the flame on the metal adjacent to the **seam;** the solder will flow when the solder-flowing temperature is reached. Solder will not flow until the metal adjacent to it is hot enough. As the metal approaches soldering temperature, bring the torch in closer and concentrate the hottest part of the flame along the seam. Continue the movement of the torch tip, even though, at this point, it is covering a much smaller area. Pull the flame away should the metal get too hot; move in closer if it cools too rapidly. If the flame is uncontrollable produce a reducing atmosphere by fluxing the entire piece. The flux can be removed with a toothbrush. Use a large flame to heat a large surface; it will heat the surface more evenly, thus preventing the formation of firescale and warpage.

The reducing flame and the oxidizing flame are not used in jewelrymaking because both promote firescale. A soft yellow flame with a small blue inner cone (reducing flame) indicates a deficiency of air and an excess of gas (**d.**). The reducing flame is not hot enough for soldering; the metal never reaches the solder-flowing temperature. The oxidizing flame is an intense blue-pointed flame resembling a needle flame (**e.**). The oxidizing flame is used for metalworking. See ill. Also see **encrustation, flux, inlay, pick soldering, sweat soldering.**

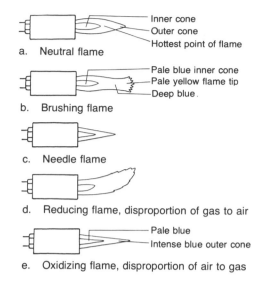

a. Neutral flame — Inner cone / Outer cone / Hottest point of flame

b. Brushing flame — Pale blue inner cone / Pale yellow flame tip / Deep blue

c. Needle flame

d. Reducing flame, disproportion of gas to air

e. Oxidizing flame, disproportion of air to gas — Pale blue / Intense blue outer cone

flame. Metalworking. The burning gas coming from the tip of a welding or cutting torch. The parts of the **oxyacetylene** flame are the feather, the inner cone, and the envelope or outer cone. It is by recognizing the appearance of the parts that one may regulate the specific types of flame for welding.

The three basic welding flames are: the oxidizing flame, carburizing flame (or reducing flame), and the neutral flame. A fourth is acetylene burning in air, but this is not used for welding.

OXIDIZING FLAME This flame, which contains an excess of oxygen, has only two well-defined parts: an inner cone, which is shorter and more sharply pointed than in a neutral flame, and an outer envelope, which is ragged at the end and purple in color. The torch emits a hissing sound when there is an oxidizing flame. Although it is the hottest of the flames, having a temperature range from 6300° F at the inner cone to 2300° F at the tip of the envelope, it is used only for specific kinds of metals. This is because it produces **oxide**s, which make ordinary **steel** welds very brittle. A slightly oxidizing flame is used only on the **braze welding** of **copper** and copper **alloys** such as **bronze** and **brass,** and also on **cast iron.**

CARBURIZING FLAME This flame has oxygen in it but also contains an excess of **acetylene.** If used for ordinary welding it will produce a weld that is brittle because the carbon is absorbed by the steel from the flame. A strongly carburizing flame will boil steel, but a slightly carburizing one is used for **silver soldering,** and a more carburizing one is sometimes used to weld **nickel** or nickel alloys. The temperature is approximately 5700° F at the inner cone tip.

NEUTRAL FLAME This flame may be recognized by an inner round-tipped cone and a blue outer envelope. It is recommended for most **oxyacetylene welding,** and occurs when there is an equal mixture of both oxygen and acetylene coming from the torch. Its temperature ranges from 5900° F at the inner cone to 2300° F at the tip of the envelope.

ACETYLENE BURNING IN AIR This is a long yellow flame without a cone or feather and is the first one you see when igniting the torch before you turn the oxygen torch valve on. Its temperature is approximately 1500° F, which is too low for welding. It also covers the metal with carbon soot.

The oxyacetylene cutting torch employs these same flames for different functions. The acetylene burning in air is again not suitable for any working. The carburizing flame may be used for **preheating** when cutting cast iron because the excess acetylene aids heat penetration to the bottom of the material. The oxidizing flame is not commonly used with an ordinary hand cutting torch, but may be used with an industrial torch for cutting heavy steel pieces. The neutral flame is the normal one used for both preheating and cutting. See ill.

Oxyacetylene welding flame

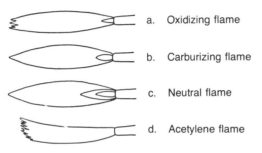

a. Oxidizing flame

b. Carburizing flame

c. Neutral flame

d. Acetylene flame

flame cutting. Metalworking. The process of cutting **ferrous** metal with the flame from an oxyacetylene cutting torch. First the metal is preheated to molten hot, then the oxygen lever or trigger on the cutting torch is depressed to release a stream of oxygen. The resulting intense flame oxidizes the metal and cuts a **kerf** through it. Also see **oxyacetylene welding equipment** and **Metalworking: Cutting.**

flameproof. Stitchery. A fabric treated to make it resistant to after-flaming. This means that when the source of flame is removed, the fabric does not continue to glow or burn. A difficulty in flameproofing is that the chemicals affect the feel of the fabric. There are flameproofing sprays available on the market which may be applied to yardage or to finished sewn or stitched **panel**s. Flameproofing companies will also treat finished panels when that is required for public installation. A charge is usually made according to the number of yards being treated, with a minimum handling charge. A certificate is supplied by the flameproofing company so that the finished work will be accepted when the craftsman delivers it for installation and approval by fire inspectors. Be sure to obtain the necessary certifying papers with commercial sprays, and supply the necessary information with the work. If large **stitchery panel**s or **mural**s must be flameproofed for public installation, it is better to have this treatment given to the fabric before **appliqué** or embroidery or other embellishments. Flameproofing involves dipping the material into a liquid, so thorough pressing is essential afterward. The surface of **felt**, for example, is changed by this process. It is preferable to press felt before applying appliqué; it is difficult to **press** the pieces completely afterward.

Fabrics may be treated at home to make them **fire-retardant**, but the treatment is not acceptable under state laws for fire protection.

Textiles made of synthetic fibers are inherently flame retardant. They do not support combustion when flame or heat is applied. Some **nylon**s are high temperature resistant. **Cotton** and **rayon** burn rapidly, but most fabrics can be treated with chemicals. Cellulosic **natural fiber**s are easily flammable, burn quickly, carry flame, and glow red—all dangerous points. **Animal fiber**s burn less readily but are not considered dangerous. **Wool** ignites slowly and goes out by itself. Flame resistant techniques impregnate fabric with borax or boric acid.

flame stitch. Needlepoint. See **Bargello.**

flame stitch. Rugmaking. See **Hungarian stitch.**

flamework. Glasswork. One of the **glasswork** crafts, often called **lampwork.** Flamework entails heating a glass tube or rod, customarily in an air-gas or oxygen-air-gas flame (which is hotter) and then deforming the tube or rod through tool manipulation or by moving the ends of the tube or rod by hand. One of the more important uses of these techniques is the fabrication of chemical laboratory equipment. Novelties and some sculpture are made with flameworking techniques also.

Flamework is the least expensive of glass crafts to equip for. Most important is the **glass fire.** Often two or more glass fires are set up in a cross-fire so that both sides of the stock tube or rod can be heated at once. When tubing is heated to a soft state, it can be drawn or pulled apart to form pipettes; the end can be closed off, and small bubbles can be formed at the end by blowing; or the rod can be drawn very thin for **spun-glass work.**

flaming. Plastics. A finishing process of heating only the edge of a sheet of plastic with an open flame from a **propane torch** to smooth the surface. Also see **Plastics: Finishing.**

flamskvavnad. Weaving. See **tapestry.**

Flanders baby. Toys. See **penny wooden doll.**

flange. Ceramics. See **Ceramics: Form.**

flange. Jewelry. Any rim of metal that extends beyond the boundaries of the basic form in a piece of jewelry. It can be left in position as a reinforcing or decorative element, or it can be removed, as with the extensions or flanges of metal in **box construction.** A flange is also an extension of metal that can be bent over or around another piece of metal to hold it in position.

flange. Puppets. A raised edge or rim at the **base** of the **puppet head** on the neck. The flange flares out from the neck so that fabric can be fastened or tied above it without slipping off. Also see **Puppets: Making the Puppet Head.**

flannel. Quilts. Stitchery. A **napped fabric** of firm weave. It may be **wool, cotton,** or **synthetic.** Flannel made only of cotton fibers is usually called **cotton flannel.** Also see **baby flannel.**

flannel board. Toys. A panel, often **Celotex,** covered with **felt** or flannel and used as a storytelling board. Cutouts of flannel or felt placed on the board are kept in place by the naps of the materials. Shapes can be stuck on and removed repeatedly. Cutouts are often made so that the animals or figures fit a specific story.

flannelette. Quilts. See **baby flannel.**

flap jack. Toys. See **jumping jack.**

flash. Jewelry. Metalworking. Plastics. (Also called fin.) A thin protruding film or sheet of metal or plastic formed in a casting at the point where the edges of a mold join together.

flashback. Metalworking. Flame burning inside the welding **torch** but not extending out of the torch tip. The external welding flame goes out, accompanied by a squealing or hissing sound at the tip. Black smoke may pour out of the tip. This is dangerous because the flame could progress back through the hoses to the **cylinder**s and cause an explosion. If a flashback occurs while welding, shut off the torch valves (oxygen first), and then the tank valves. Common causes of flashback are: welding with incorrect gas pressures, touching the metal with the torch tip, using a match instead of a **flint lighter** to ignite the torch, or a blockage in the torch tip. Check your equipment before relighting the torch. A safety device called a flashback arrestor may be installed if additional safety protection is desired when fuel source pressures are low. Flashback is not to be confused with **backfire.**

flashed glass. Stained Glass. A variant of **antique glass** made by **gather**ing a molten blob of glass (generally of a light color), quickly dipping the blob into a molten pot of a darker color, then blowing the glass into a cylindrical shape. The second pot of color is kept at a hotter temperature to give the glass more fluidity in blowing. The two colors do not mix but are layered in a sheet with a thicker light color and a thin skin of darker color over it. Red glass, when it is not colored with selenium, is usually flashed. Greens are often flashed, and blues sometimes are. Some common examples of flashed glass are red on white, red on yellow, and red on blue. The combination of tones adds depth. The sheet often contains beautiful gradations from light to dark that result from an uneven second coating of the glass blob when it is dipped. To test for flashed glass, chip off a piece of a sheet and hold it on end against the light to see the layers of color.

In France, flashed glass is called plaquée; in Germany, it is called überfang. Also see **aciding, antique glass colorants, English antique glass, French antique glass, German antique glass, sandblasting.**

flashing. Ceramics. Smoke stained **bisque** or **glaze** surfaces caused by partial **reduction** conditions or **overfiring.**

flashing. Glasswork. See **casing.**

flask. Jewelry. A tubular piece of stainless steel used as a container and support collar for the wax model and **investment** during the pouring of the investment, **burnout,** and **centrifugal casting.** The flask size needed is determined by the size of the wax mold used and the capacity of the **centrifugal casting machine.** Flasks are commonly available in sizes of $1-1\frac{1}{4}'' \times \frac{1}{2}-1''$ to $4'' \times 6''$, although larger ones may be obtained. Stainless steel flasks should be used with **nonferrous** metals, and high-temperature nickel alloy flasks with platinum and other metals and alloys with high melting points. Flasks are numbered, according to size, corresponding with the numbers on the flask cradle that holds and centers the **crucible** in the rotating arm of the centrifugal casting machine. See ill.

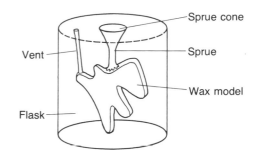

flask. Metalworking. (Also called sand-casting flask.) A two-piece wooden or metal box in which sand is packed around a **pattern** in sandcasting. Also see **sandcasting molding equipment.**

flask tongs. Jewelry. A pair of metal tongs used for turning and changing the position of **investment flask**s during **burnout,** for removing the hot flasks from the burnout **kiln,** and for placing them in the cradle of the **centrifugal casting machine.** See ill. Also see **asbestos gloves.**

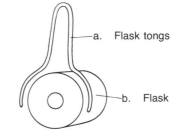

a. Flask tongs
b. Flask

flask tongs. Metalworking. See **tongs.**

flat. Gemcutting. A smooth, polished section or slab of stone used for display. A flat surface may be made with the **slabbing saw** and requires only **sanding** and **polishing** to finish.

A flat may be ground on the edge of a vertical **grinding wheel** and finished on the side of the wheel. Keep the stone moving straight up and down against the middle of the wheel and use plenty of water.

Horizontal **laps** are a desirable surface on which to grind flats. Keep the stone moving across the entire surface of the running lap to avoid excess wear on any part.

Small flats may be ground by hand on a piece of plate glass using loose **abrasive** progressively from 100 to 1000 grit. Be sure to clean the glass, the work, and yourself carefully between each grit. Larger flats are worked by hand with the same technique on a steel plate.

Overarm slab machines are manufactured with attachments to grind, sand, and polish flats up to 2 × 3'.

The easiest way to grind flats is with a reciprocating or orbital flat lapping machine. Several rough pieces are put on the work surface with a slurry of abrasive and water (if possible, weights are stuck onto the top of the pieces) and the machine is put into motion. The same formula of grinding, sanding, and polishing is followed but the machine does all the work.

Flats must be sanded carefully on drum sanders to avoid making grooves or waves caused by stationary contact with the curved surface. If a disk sander is used it should be slightly domed with felt of rubber to avoid overcutting the edges and corners of the flat.

If polishing disks are used they also should be slightly domed for the same reason. A polishing buff is useful for stubborn spots but will not produce a truly flat surface.

Sanding on a horizontal lap is done with sanding disks or with loose grits and followed by polishing on leather, wood, felt, canvas, or carpet laps with compounds of tripoli or tin oxide.

Grinding and polishing flat surfaces is the starting point for **cabochon** cutting and **faceting** gems and the last step of **intarsia**.

Petrified wood makes interesting flats showing grain patterns of the original tree. Agates are slabbed in a style called *libro aperto* (meaning open book) in which facing sections are chosen for their bilateral symmetry to each other and are used for construction of stone butterfly shapes. Also see **facet, machinery.**

flat. Puppets. Any scenery painted or depicted on a flat and usually rigid piece of material. Sometimes a flat is dropped in front of the **back curtain** to suggest the interior of a room. The **backdrop** is sometimes a flat, and **wings** may be referred to as "flats." Also see **set** and **Puppets: The Puppet Stage.**

flat-backed book. Bookbinding. A book with a flat **back** finished without **rounding** and **backing.**

flat block. Toys. A building **block** or **alphabet block** made flat instead of as a cube. Some flat blocks are halved cubes. Any flat pieces of wood make flat blocks. Originally they were embossed with letters and numerals.

flat braiding. Weaving. See **plaiting.**

flat doll. Stitchery. Toys. An unstuffed doll or figure made of **fabric.** Either **jointed** or as a **single-shape doll,** the clothes are usually suggested by the fabrics from which

the doll parts are cut. Flat dolls may be used as toys or applied decoratively to **banners** or **panels.**

flat double fold. Batik and Tie-dye. A pair of folds or **pleats** in fabric or other flexible material in which the folds face one another; one pleat is laid flat to face the center and a second pleat, next to it, faces the first. A series of such flat double folds can then be **tied** or bound in the **tie-and-dye** process.

flat double knot. Macramé. See **square knot.**

flat fell seam. Stitchery. (Also called flat felled seam.) An extension of the **plain seam** in which both **seam allowances** are **press**ed flat to one side. The seam allowance which is underneath is trimmed so that the remaining allowance can be **hem**med down flat over the first. It gives a finished look to both sides and is a good **seam** to use when the appearance of the back side is of concern. See ill. Also see **finishing, seam finish.**

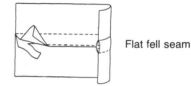
Flat fell seam

flat figure. Puppets. Stitchery. See **flat doll, flat puppet.**

flat-head screw. Woodworking. See **screw.**

flat kite. Kites. See **diamond kite.**

flat knot. Macramé. See **half knot.**

flat knot with picot. Macramé. See **square knot with picots.**

flat modeling. Leatherwork. A **tooling** method in which designs are outlined and cut with the **swivel knife,** then the background is pressed down with modeling tools, leaving raised designs.

flat-nose pliers. Jewelry. See **pliers.**

flat power bit. Woodworking. See **drill bit.**

flat puppet. Puppets. (Also called flat figure.) Either of two types of two-dimensional puppets. One is the **shadow puppet,** with "flat puppet" simply being another name for it. It is sometimes called a **silhouette puppet.**

A second kind of flat puppet is one that uses figures simply drawn on cardboard. It usually has a base to make it freestanding, and the **puppeteer** slides it on or off the stage by means of a wire. Flat puppets are descendants of the old English flat puppets, which were sold "**penny plain and tuppence colored.**"

Sometimes figures are cut out from magazines or children's books, glued to cardboard, and used as flat puppets.

If an old book is used, it sometimes offers a single character in several different poses.

The flat puppet, while very simple to construct and use, offers great possibilities in performance. Flat-puppet performances are given on a simply constructed stage called the **toy theater.** Also see **cut-out figure, paper cut-out puppet, rod puppet.**

flat-puppet stage. Puppets. See **Puppets: The Puppet Stage.**

flat quilting. Quilts. Stitchery. **Quilting Stitch**es taken through two layers of **fabric,** but having no **filler** or **padding** between them, produce a nonrelief, or flat, surface. This is known as flat quilting, having almost no dimension. Its primary value is decorative, although it sometimes functions to strengthen a flimsy fabric. It may be used to join two layers of fabric in clothing or in articles of household use.

flat reed. Basketry. See **cane.**

flat rug. Rugmaking. A smooth-faced rug without **pile.** It can be an embroidered, crocheted, knit, **braided,** or **flatweave rug.**

flats. Toys. (Also called flat tin figure.) Old pressed or cut figures, such as **toy soldiers** and mounted horsemen, that stood on a base but were essentially two-dimensional. Some were made of **cardboard,** others of tin or lead. Flat figure **model**s were made of various famous people, including Frederick the Great.

flat shuttle. Weaving. See **stick shuttle.**

flat stitch. Needlepoint. A group of long and short **satin stitch**es that produce a smooth flat effect. The stitches slant diagonally over one, two, three, four, three, two, and finally one mesh forming a perfect square (**a.**). It is often done with the squares slanting in alternating directions for a textured effect. Another variation is to alternate the flat stitch squares with squares of **tent stitch.** Scottish stitch is done by outlining each block of the flat stitch with a row of tent stitch (**b.**). Any of these variations can be worked as a border stitch. See ill. Also see **border stitch.**

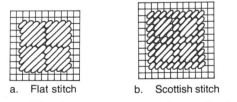

a.   Flat stitch   b.   Scottish stitch

flat tapestry. Weaving. A **tapestry** without **pile,** loop, or surface texture of any sort. In its strictest application, the same type and weight of yarn is used throughout the entire work and the weave is all **plain weave.** A **cartoon** is strictly followed and any texture is obtained by color mixing through **hatching** and **stippling.** Most Aubusson tapestries are of this type and are so flat that from a few feet away it is difficult to tell whether the work is woven or painted.

flattening. Metalworking. See **blacksmithing techniques.**

flattening. Tincrafting. **Tinplate,** the basic material for tincrafting, is a highly malleable material that can be fairly easily hammered into the desired shape. To flatten tinplate, hit the plate on both sides an equal number of times, first one side, then the other, alternating sides, or the tin will curve upward with each blow. Also see **Tincrafting: Preparing the Tincan.**

flatter. Metalworking. See **blacksmithing tools.**

flat tin figure. Toys. See **flats.**

flat twill. Weaving. See **twill weave.**

flat varnish. Woodworking. See **varnish.**

flatware. Ceramics. Tablewear that is generally flat in shape and is cast in a single **mold,** such as dishes and saucers. Also see **hollowware.**

flatweave rugs. Rugmaking. Weaving. (Also called flatwoven rugs.) Woven rugs without a **pile.** The method used to obtain a flat weave rug can be chosen from many techniques. They are roughly divided into being either **filling-face** or **warp-face.** In filling-face, the easiest to accomplish are stripes completely covering the **warp,** and woven **selvage** to selvage. **Rolakan** is a popular Scandinavian technique that is good for stylized geometric patterns. More time-consuming, but offering unlimited design or pictorial possibilities are **tapestry rugs, kilims** and **soumak,** or any mixture of these techniques. Contemporary **Navajo weaving** is a good example of flatweave tapestry rugs.

Warp-face rugs are generally warp **stripe** rugs or a variation on this produced by a crammed warp for a **log cabin pattern** or the Scandinavian **mattor** weaves. There are also rugs that show both warp and **filling,** such as **rag rug**s, **double cloth,** or **ingrain rug**s, or those woven in any **loom-controlled** weave using heavy enough warp and filling yarn. Rugs in a laid-in technique usually show the warp, but in some cases are beaten down enough so that only the filling shows. In addition, flatwoven rugs can be first finger or card-woven and then the strips sewn together, or they can be made using **weft twining,** as are the blankets of the **Chilkat** and Salish Indians. Also see **card weaving, finger weaving, joining, Salish weaving, sett, weft twining.**

flatwoven rug. Rugmaking. Weaving. See **flatweave rug.**

flax. Batik and Tie-dye. Quilts. Stitchery. The **natural fiber**s of the flax plant that are used to make linen.

flax. Spinning. The plant that produces the **bast fibers** from which **linen** yarn is spun. It is the oldest known **vegetable fiber** plant and was used during the Stone Age almost 10,000 years ago. Remnants of linen fishing nets, clothing, and unworked flax have been in the lake dwellings in Switzerland dating back to that era. Fragments of linen cloth from 2000 B.C. and pictures of flax culture on the walls of Egyptian tombs have been found. Flax is now grown in many areas of the world. In the United States it is cultivated mainly for its seed, which is used in the production of linseed oil.

The fiber is found in the stalk and extends down to the roots. In planting flax, seeds are sown evenly and close together so that the plants grow long stalks (up to 40") that branch only at the top.

Extracting the fibers from the flax plant is a long and somewhat complicated procedure, with good results depending on how well the procedure is called out. There are several steps in obtaining and preparing the fibers of the flax plant. The plant is pulled up by the roots, rather than cut off, to obtain the longest possible fiber. It is tied into bundles and left to dry. The stalks undergo deseeding by pulling the flax heads through a coarse steel rippling comb (**a.**). Once again, the stalks are tied into bundles, this time for retting. In retting, the stalks are soaked in pure, clear water, which rots away the woody outer core, leaving the fibers inside intact. At the same time, the bacterial action of the water dissolves the adhesive gums that bind the fibers together. There are choices in the matter of retting. The flax can be dew-retted, which is exposure to the action of dew moisture and sunlight in a field. This requires a period of 4 to 6 weeks, gives uneven results, and darkens the color of the fiber. However, the best-wearing fiber is pro-

duced this way. There are also pool retting and steam retting. Both are quicker than dew retting with pool retting being the fastest, because excess bacteria to speed up the rotting is present in stagnant water. The lightest color in flax would come from stream retting, which flows away the decomposing vegetable matter. The flax is then dried and pounded on a flax brake to break up the rotted stalk clinging to the fiber inside (**b.**). At the same time, the process of separating the line from the tow is started. A large bundle of flax is laid across the brake at the hinged end. The upper portion of the brake, which resembles a mallet with teeth, is brought down with force upon the flax. The flax moves away from the hinged section with each blow. The stalks are separated from the fiber by a scutcher or swingle, which is a rack with a heavy wooden blade. The flax is held across the rack and beaten down against the side of the rack with the wooden blade. This **scutching** further breaks up the plant and beats away the other parts (**c.**). Hackling (or heckling) is a combing action that is the last process in the dressing, or preparation, of flax. The flax is held by the root end and thrown on and pulled through the hackle (or heckle, hatchel, hetchle), a heavy iron comb (**d.**). The flax is drawn across a coarse comb first, then across a fine one. The fibers are now cleaned, smoothed, and straightened. They have been separated into short lengths called tow, or long lengths called line. They are in a tidy bundle called a strick that has all the long, loose strands removed. See ill.

The last step is spinning. This converts the flax fibers into linen yarn. The process differs from ordinary wool spinning in that great care must be exercised in preparing the flax around the **distaff**. This is necessary to insure a steady, even flow of fibers from the distaff to the **spindle** or **spinning wheel**. Flax can be spun either wet or dry. Also see **dressing the distaff**.

flax brake. Spinning. See **flax**.

flax top. Spinning. **Flax** that has been prepared into a long coil prior to spinning. It is held in the spinner's lap as it is drafted and spun. Also see **linen**.

flax wheel. Spinning. See **treadle wheel**.

fleece. Spinning. The coat of wool shorn from a sheep's back. Also see **sorting, wool**.

fleece dyeing. Dyeing. See **dyed-in-the-wool, stock dyeing**.

Flemish glass. Stained Glass. A **rolled glass** with uniform indentations made by the roller. It is a cheap glass that is not particularly unusual or attractive in large quantity. Also see **machine-made glass**.

Flemish weave. Weaving. See **high-warp, tapestry**.

flesher. Leatherwork. A term for the layer taken from the underside, or flesh side, of the pelt. It is generally used to make **chamois**. Also see **Leatherwork**.

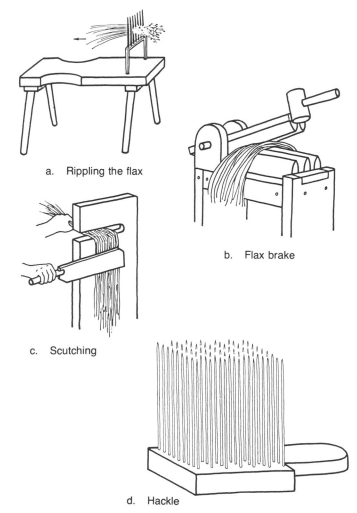

a. Rippling the flax

b. Flax brake

c. Scutching

d. Hackle

fleshing. Leatherwork. The machine operation in which the under layer of fat and flesh is scraped from the skin by revolving knives in preparation for **tanning.** Also see **bating** and **Leatherwork: Tanning and Manufacture.**

fleur-de-lis. Crewel. Embroidery. Needlepoint. A heraldic emblem symbolizing a lily or an iris, the coat of arms of a former French royal family; it is frequently represented in needlework. See ill.

Fleur-de-lis

flexibilizer. Plastics. See **plasticizer.**

flexible cover. Bookbinding. A thin cover constructed of a lightweight material, such as cardboard, laminated sheets of **paper,** or a heavy **leather** without **boards.** It may be covered with **cloth** or a thin leather. A very narrow turn-up is left when **backing** and the boards are fitted for a **tight-backed case.** If using leather without boards, **board paper** is pasted to the flesh side of the leather. Thick leather is pared and turned in, or the edge can simply be cut and dyed. The book is pressed as usual. Also see **pairing.**

flexible mold. Plastics. See **mold.**

flexible sewing. Bookbinding. Sewing through the fold of each **signature,** looping the thread around an outside **cord,** as opposed to burying the threads in the **back** of the book. First the **all-along stitching** and then the **off-and-on stitching** method is used, so that the bulk the threads create is evenly distributed. Books sewn in this manner require heavy-duty **endpapers.** They are easy to open and the binding lasts a long time. Large or heavy books should be sewn on double cords. Also see **sewing on cords.**

flexible shaft machine. Gemcutting. Jewelery. Metalworking. Plastics. A multiuse motor-driven tool run by a foot-operated **rheostat.** The motor is usually AC and DC current, small and varies from $^1/_{10}$th to $^1/_{15}$th horsepower Extending from the motor, which is hung on a hook, is a hard rubber hose containing a flexible steel shaft 30–36″ long. This is connected to a handpiece. The motor turns the shaft at speeds of 1500–14,000 rpm.

There are numerous handpieces of different constructions available, some stationary and others with flexible sections. At the end and on the inside of the handpiece is a **collet,** which holds the **mandrel** (the shaft of an accessory to the handpiece). The standard collet usually can hold shafts from zero to $^1/_8$″ in diameter; there are other size collets that can take larger-diameter mandrels. The collets are interchangeable within the handpiece, depending on the model. This type of handpiece is usually hand tightened. In other handpieces, the mandrel of the accessory is

tightened into place with a chuck key. This type of handpiece has a greater range in the size of the opening of the collet, but each time an accessory is inserted or removed the handpiece must be tightened and loosened with the chuck key. Most handpieces of this type tend to be of a bulkier size.

The handpieces themselves are often interchangeable. The accessories available that fit into the handpiece are capable of grinding, **drilling, buffing,** and brushing and are available in thousands of shapes, sizes, and materials. It is a versatile and valuable machine for working small gem carvings such as **cameos** and **intaglios.** See ill. Also see **bristle brush, bur, carving point, drills, hand drill, point carver, separating disk** and **Gemcutting: Tools and Materials.**

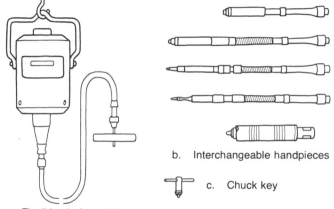

a.   Flexible shaft machine

b.   Interchangeable handpieces

c.   Chuck key

Flex-Span. Plastics. See **dipping resin.**

flicker book. Tools. See **animated booklet.**

flint. Gemcutting. See **quartz.**

flint. Metalworking. See **abrasive.**

flint clay. Ceramics. See **Ceramics: Clay.**

flint lighter. Metalworking. See **oxacetylene welding equipment.**

flint sandpaper. Woodworking. See **abrasive.**

flip ball. Toys. See **cup-and-ball.**

flipperdinger. Toys. An **American folk toy** that consists of a **blowpipe,** a ring, and a **ball** with a hook through it. When air is blown through the blowpipe it comes out a hole or outlet on the top at the opposite end and raises the small lightweight ball. A **pith ball** was used in the original versions. The challenge of the toy is to hook the ball onto the ring, which is mounted on a vertical wire at the end of the blowpipe.

A similar toy, and probably the original on which the flipperdinger is based, is the hangman's noose. It was popular in France and was inspired by the French Revolution; it was then called *le pendu.* See ill., next page. Also see **action toy.**

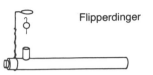

Flipperdinger

flip toy. Toys. See **acrobat.**

float. Basketry. A term used in **plaited basketry** when the structure departs from the normal over-one, under-one **stroke.** When the elements are floated over two or over three, many pattern variations result as seen in **twilled plaiting.**

float. Weaving. A **warp** or **filling** thread that skips over or under other threads without interlacing. The length of a float is measured by the number of skipped threads. The shortest float would be a thread skipping over two warp threads or two filling threads. Whether or not a float is desirable depends on the **sett,** or **picks per inch,** or the effect that is to be obtained. It is assumed that floats are put there for the purpose of forming designs or textural effects. Indeed, some patterns, such as **overshot,** exist only because of the floats. However, undesirable floats occur when **harness**es are not functioning properly and **end**s are not being woven into the fabric. Incorrect **drawing-in** or **treadling** is another cause of floats. Also see **cut-float.**

floated solder seams. Stained Glass. In **copper foiling,** flat soldered seams are built up to rounded ones by holding the **soldering iron** about ⅛″ above the seam and adding **solder** until a nicely rounded seam develops. Also see **lampshade construction.**

floating selvage. Weaving. See **selvage.**

floating toy. Toys. See **bath toy, boat, camphor toy, soap carving.**

flocculant. Ceramics. An **electrolyte** that speeds up the drying time of clay, or acts as a thickening agent in **slip** or **glaze,** so that it needs more water to render it fluid. This will make it adhere more easily to a **pot.** Flocculants include aluminum sulfate and epsom salts. Also see **alumina.**

flocculant condition. Ceramics. Clay particles mixed in water, as in a **slip,** are attracted to each other by electrical impulse forming "flocks." Also see **deflocculant.**

flock. Fabric Printing. See **flocking powder.**

flock. Stitchery. See **flocked fabric.**

flocked fabric. Stitchery. A **fabric** with a pattern of raised particles (called flock) on the surface. Flock is tiny particles of cotton or fiber that are mixed with a binder and printed on the woven material. **Dotted swiss** is a flocked material sometimes used in **transparent appliqué.**

flocking. Fabric Printing. The process of coating a **linoleum block** or **wood block** with **flocking powder** over an adhesive called **flocking mordant** to make the inking surface more absorbent, enabling it to pick up more color. Flocking is applied after the pattern has been cut.

With a **brayer,** roll the **mordant** on a flat, nonabsorbent surface such as glass. Then roll it onto the surface of the printing block, making sure it is evenly spread on the printing surface. Using a kitchen strainer, sift the flocking powder over the mordanted surface until the mordant cannot be seen. Press a piece of cardboard or wood over the flocked area to achieve better adhesion. Let dry 24 hours, then blow or shake off the excess. The flocking must be renewed when it wears off or when the block is to be used for another color. Also see **Fabric Printing: Printing Techniques.**

flocking. Stitchery. The process used in making **flocked fabric** either commercially or at home. Some **wall hangings, banners,** and **soft sculptures** are made using a flocking process. Designs are painted using **white glue** and before it dries the glue is sprinkled with tiny particles of various materials. Fabrics flocked this way will not withstand cleaning or washing.

flocking mordant. Fabric Printing. A term for the adhesive, usually an oil paint with an excess of varnish, used as the glue size for adhering **flocking powder** to printing blocks to make the surface more absorbent to dye or paint. Flocking mordant is available as a white adhesive in a tube. Adequate substitutes are the waterproof varnish called spar varnish, just as it is, or pure copal varnish, after it has been left to thicken in an open dish for a day. Also see **Fabric Printing: Printing Techniques.**

flocking powder. Fabric Printing. (Also called flock.) Finely pulverized particles of wool or rayon fluff, available in loose powder form, that is applied over **flocking mordant** to a **linoleum block** or **wood block** to provide a more absorbent inking surface. Also see **Fabric Printing: Printing Techniques.**

flock of geese. Quilts. See **Birds in Flight.**

flogging chisel. Metalworking. See **blacksmithing tools.**

floor loom. Weaving. A **harness loom** built to stand on the floor with the **harness**es controlled by the feet pressing on **treadles.** Also see **foot-power loom, jack-type loom, loom, table loom.**

floor swift. Spinning. Weaving. See **swift.**

floor tile. Mosaics. An unglazed commerical **tile,** used in flooring, available in a limited color range. Floor tile tends to be thicker than **ceramic tile,** and the coloring, unlike that of ceramic tile, is mixed with the clay and runs throughout the tile. Because of the relative difficulty of cutting floor tile, it is often shattered with a hammer to produce smaller fragments for mosaic work. Also see **Mosaics: Tools and Materials, Cutting the Material.**

floor toy. Toys. Any **pull toy, wheeled toy,** or **fraction toy** that rests on the floor or is pulled over the floor.

floral tape. Beadmaking. A tape used in **bead flowermaking,** available in rolls ½″ wide in many colors. Each side is slightly adhesive, with no right or wrong side. The tape should be stretched while working to make it tacky and to reduce bulk. Floral tape is used for assembling beaded flowers, for adding flowers and leaves to stems, and for finishing off stem ends. To wrap a stem, begin at the base of the flower and wrap downward at a diagonal, pressing down with the fingers against the **stem wire.** Join leaves to the stem with more tape.

Florentine embroidery. Needlework. See **Bargello.**

Florentine finish. Jewelry. A finish produced by using **liner**s (specialized engraving tools) to create a series of parallel lines to partially or completely cover a metal surface. After the basic pattern of parallel lines is engraved, the liner goes over the area again from a different angle.

Florentine knitting. Knitting. (Also called jacquard knitting.) The elaborate color knitting that flourished during the Renaissance in Florence, Italy. It comprises animal, floral, and insect motifs. Because this type of knitting is so intricate, the use of bobbins is generally recommended.

Florentine lace. Leatherwork. (Also called Venetian lace.) A soft, pliable kidskin lace, available commercially in ¼″ and ⅜″ widths. Strips for **Florentine lacing** can also be cut from very light leather in any desired width.

Florentine lacing. Leatherwork. The **whipstitch** done with **Florentine lace.** In this form of whipstitching, holes are prepunched, as usual, at a distance apart the width of the lace, but the holes are much smaller than the width of the lace. The lace is pointed at one end, and the end inserted into a hook and eye needle or a life eye needle and whipstitched in the normal way. Florentine lacing is distinctive because of the soft luxurious "gathered" look of the wide lace going through the small holes, and because the wide lace completely covers the edge of the leather. Care must be taken to keep the lace from twisting as it is worked. See ill. Also see **edge stitch, lacing.**

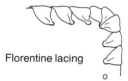

Florentine lacing

Florentine Stitch. Needlepoint. See **mosaic stitch diagonally.**

Florentine stitch. Rugmaking. See **Hungarian stitch.**

florists' wire. Puppets. A thin, malleable wire used for attaching or joining where flexibility is more important than strength.

floss. Spinning. Weaving. A yarn that has several plies that lie separately or have a very loose **twist.** The yarn is soft and traditionally of **silk,** in a size suitable for embroidery. Floss can also be of **linen;** both silk and linen floss are used as **filling** in weaving. The sheen of the long, loose fibers in floss make it a popular yarn for ornamentation in weaving. Heavy floss is used in **wall hanging**s and some **fiber sculpture.** Also see **ply.**

floss. Stitchery. See **embroidery floss.**

flossa. Rugmaking. Weaving. A Scandinavian term for cut, short, **knotted pile** made over a pile **gauge.** Traditionally it is knotted during weaving, using a Ghiordes or Turkish knot. Today flossa encompasses also those rugs needleworked on a prepared backing, and in some woven flossa rugs. Sehna and Spanish knots are also used. Flossa rugs are of pile 1″ or under in height and knotted very close together so that the pile is dense and stands up straight. Also see **flossa rod, pile height, rug backing.**

flossa rod. Rugmaking. Weaving. A metal bar or stick used in making short **pile** on a **horizontal loom.** Usually it is a long piece of iron with a groove on the upper side for a flossa knife to travel along to cut the pile. The pile yarn goes around the rod in making every row of pile. The width of the rod determines the height of the pile. The usual width is ½ – ⅝″. If the pile is to be higher, the rod should then be made of wood because the metal would be too heavy to work with. Also see **flossa, gauge.**

flour-and-water paste. Puppets. Toys. See **wheat paste.**

flour paste. Batik and Tie-dye. Toys. Any of several flour and water mixtures used as a paper **adhesive.**

In the **tie-dye**ing process, flour paste is used to **resist dye.** The mixture is painted over the **binding**s and dried before the fabric is dipped in the dye.

In **batik,** a **paste batik** method may be used in which flour paste mixture may be substituted for the **wax.** It does not prevent **dye penetration** as well as wax, but it has the advantage of not needing to be hot. The paste is applied to fabric that has been treated with skim milk. It is an excellent way for children to explore the batik method.

Mix 3 level tablespoons of flour with a little warm water to make a smooth paste. Pour over ½ cup boiling water. If it does not thicken it can be boiled.

In gluing paper, flour and water paste should be used only on rough work because the water base may warp paper or light cardboard. It is safe for children, dries hard, and is inexpensive to make. Also see **paste-resist batik.**

flour paste. Papercrafts. The traditional paste for **papier mâché** is made from common flour thinned with water to the consistency of heavy cream, about 1 part flour to 2 parts water. A tablespoon of **white glue** may be added for extra strength. This paste should be used right away.

A cooked flour paste, called flour sauce glue, is made by heating flour and water in about the same proportions in a saucepan over low heat. Stir and add more water if necessary until the mixture is a creamy liquid. The flour paste is then cooled, and may be kept in the refrigerator. If not refrigerated, a few drops of oil of wintergreen from the drugstore may be added as a preservative.

flour sauce glue. Papercrafts. See **flour paste.**

flow. Basketry. The difference in size between the top and bottom of a **basket.** This outward slope is referred to as the flow of the basket. Also see **spring.**

flower designs. Quilts. Any of a seemingly infinite variety of **appliqué block** designs that incorporate flowers. Seldom do any two quiltmakers use the same **set** for the same patterns and prints. Flowers change in shape and color, so that a new name is born with almost every new quilt. Lilies, peonies, tulips, dahlias, daisies, and sunflowers predominate in a profusion of reds, greens, and golds, but no flower has been given so much inspiration for the artistic bent as the rose. Sometimes a variety of flowers is collected in one block because the limitations of **piecing** do not carry over into appliqué. **Rose of Sharon,** Radical Rose, **Whig Rose, Combination Rose** (or California Rose), **Tulip,** and Sunflower are among the best known. No two Rose of Sharons will be found exactly alike. Other patterns are Indiana Rose, Lotus Flower, North Carolina Rose, Ohio Rose, Original Rose, Rose and Buds, Rose in Bud, Rose of Tennessee, Coxcomb, and Spice Pink. Also see **appliqué patterns.**

flower doll. Toys. A doll made by joining various parts of flowers with toothpicks. Camelias and hollyhocks are often used, with a flower in full bloom inverted to suggest a skirted figure. Partially open buds suggest faces, and hats or bonnets are made of smaller flowers. Flower dolls are **ephemeral toy**s.

flowers. Beadwork. See **bead flowermaking.**

flowers. Papercrafts. See **paper flowers.**

Flowers in a Pot. Quilts. See **vase and urn patterns.**

fluff. Featherwork. Any small, fluffy feather, such as **down,** or a tuft of small feathers.

fluff rug. Rugmaking. Weaving. See **corduroy.**

fluidity. Jewelry. The capacity of a metal to flow readily when heated to a certain temperature.

fluorite. Gemcutting. A fluoride of calcium **crystal**lized in the isometric system with perfect **cleavage** in four directions. It has a **hardness** of 4, a **specific gravity** of 3.1–3.2, and a refractive index of 1.434. Fluorite is translucent to transparent with a moist vitreous **luster.** It occurs in colorless, white, yellow, red, green, blue, and violet varieties. It has a white **streak** and is decomposed by sulfuric acid. Main crown **facet**s are cut at an angle of 41° and main pavillion facets at 43°. It is polished with tin oxide on a wax wooden lap, or with cerium oxide on a plastic lap.

Because fluorite has the same cleavage characteristics as **diamond,** it is sometimes used to make models for practicing diamond cutting.

Also see **faceting, polishing, refraction,** and **Gemcutting: Rough Shaping.**

flush cover. Bookbinding. A cover with the same measurements as the leaves; a cover with no **square.**

flute. Weaving. (Also called Aubusson bobbin.) A **bobbin** used in the weaving of tapestries in Aubusson, France. It is a thin, wooden spool about 5″ long. There are bulges at each end to prevent the yarn from sliding off. Sometimes one side is flattened out to prevent the bobbin from rolling off the **loom.** It is associated with weaving tapestries on a **low-warp** loom. Because these tapestries are often quite intricate, with many color changes within small areas, the flute holds small amounts of yarn and many of them can be worked simultaneously without crowding the working surface. See ill.

Aubusson flute with yarn

fluting. Ceramics. A decorative motif consisting of a series of long, rounded, parallel grooves cut into the surface of a soft or **leather-hard** pot.

flux. Ceramics. China and Glass Painting. Enameling. A body or **glaze** ingredient that melts during **firing** to bond the other ingredients together. Flux is added to the body to lower the **maturity** temperature. Common alkaline fluxes are **borax, boric acid,** colemanite, and **soda ash. Bone ash** and **white lead** are low fire fluxes. High fire fluxes are **feldspar, whiting,** and **zinc oxide.** Also see **barium, volcanic ash.**

In china and glass painting flux refers to a powdered, colorless glass composed of lead oxide. It is mixed with **mineral color** pigments to make them fuse to the china or glass, giving the surface a higher gloss or **glaze.** Some **onglaze color** may contain enough flux when purchased (called well-fluxed or **fluxed color**), but most will need to have flux added. Make firing tests of all colors to see if they glaze properly. In firing, the flux blends with the glaze of the china and thus adheres the color to the surface. As a general guide for mixing flux, add 1 part flux to 3 parts powdered color for painting, or 1 part flux to 2 parts color for **tinting.** Too much flux will cause colors to fade. The colorless flux can also be applied as a shiny glaze by **dusting** over the painted but still tacky surface. To add flux to tube colors, first mix the powdered flux with a **medium** until it is the same consistency as the tube colors, then blend it with the color in the same proportions as above.

In enameling flux refers to a transparent **enamel** in liquid or powder form that contains no **metal oxide** coloring, used either as the first base coat over the **metal** or as a final finish coat. Flux does not require **counterenamel**ing, as it is elastic. It is fired at high temperatures. Flux is used over **underglaze,** fire with **cloison** wires on it, or as an undercoat for **metal foil.** On copper, flux retains a more golden color than the red hue of the metal would reflect through transparent enamels. Silver requires flux under warm colors; different products are used for sterling than for fine silver. Gold requires flux only if it is neither fine nor 18K nontarnishing; i.e., alloys of 18K or 14K zinc-free gold should be fluxed. Also see **barium, camel's-hair brush, frit** and **Enameling: Tools and Materials.**

flux. Glasswork. Any one of a number of materials, usually metallic oxides such as potassium oxide (KO), soda ash (Na_2CO_3), red lead (Pb_3O_4), or boric oxide (B_2O_3), that are mixed with silica sand (SiO_2) to lower the fusion point of the resultant glass. See **borosilicate glass, lead-crystal glass, soda-lime glass.**

flux. Jewelry. Metalworking. A chemical used to prevent **firescale** and to allow **solder** to flow.

There are many types of flux available in many forms. The two basic fluxes are a paste and a liquid. They are basically borax fluxes, and are suitable for fluxing in preparation for **soldering** or **annealing** gold, silver, copper, brass, bronze, and some steels.

WELDING FLUX Although flux is not needed for welding most **ferrous** metals, it is used for welding aluminum or stainless steel with gas. The flux is usually contained in the electrode coating when **arc-welding** or **heliarc-welding** those metals.

Flux is also used on **welding rod**s to weld dissimilar metals together. For example, copper, brass, nickel, and nickel alloys can be welded to low-carbon steel or cast iron, or to each other, with the aid of flux. (Aluminum can be welded only to itself.) When gas-welding, ask your metals distributor to recommend a commercial brand of flux for your particular alloy.

BRAZE-WELDING FLUX Use this flux by dipping a heated brazing rod into the powdered flux to coat the rod, or use a rod that has been precoated with flux. The most common brazing flux is **borax** (sodium tetraborate). It may be purchased in a ready-made powder, paste, or in sticks or rods from which you can make a paste.

CASTING FLUX This flux is usually added to the molten metal in the **crucible** to purify the metal and to eliminate gas, which could ruin the casting. It is added just before pouring the metal into the **mold.** Powdered charcoal is used for **lead,** but commercially manufactured fluxes are added to **aluminum, brass,** and other alloys.

SOFT-SOLDERING FLUX There are two basic classifications of fluxes for soft or common solder: corrosive flux and noncorrosive flux.

Corrosive fluxes are acid or chloride fluxes made principally of zinc chloride and ammonium, and must be washed off after the soldering is finished. An example is sal ammoniac (ammonium chloride), which is used on **copper, iron, steel, stainless steel, zinc, aluminum bronze,** and **galvanized iron.** Another common flux is **cut acid** (zinc chloride) which may be used on iron, galvanized iron, **tin plate,** copper, brass, lead, stainless steel, and nickel.

Noncorrosive fluxes need not be removed after soldering. They are not as efficient in removing oxides from metal, but prevent additional formation of oxides during soldering. Some noncorrosive fluxes are rosin, tallow, and stearin (for lead and lead alloys). Commercially made mixes are also available. These fluxes are recommended for tin, pewter, copper, brass, and other copper alloys, and when soldering connections on electrical equipment or on other objects where corrosion must be avoided. Also see **flux brushing, glycerine.**

flux. Stained Glass. A substance that must be applied to **lead came** or **copper foil** before soldering. It removes oxides formed by exposure of the metal's surface to the atmosphere and increases the fusion of the **solder** to the metal. Also, the process of applying flux to lead or copper foil.

Liquid flux is most commonly used. There are two kinds: Oleic acid is an organic, noncaustic acid applied with a brush to the solder joints on lead came. It is the most popular all-round flux. Although it can also be used on copper foil, zinc chloride (ruby fluid) is preferred because oleic acid does not react as well with copper. Paste flux is used for general soldering work in both lead and copper. It comes in a can and is applied with a stiff brush. Also see **copper foiling** and **Stained Glass: Glazing, Tools and Materials.**

flux. Tincrafting. A chemical agent used in **soldering** tin to prevent the formation of an oxide film at the heated joint during the application of the **solder.** Zinc chloride and ammonium chloride are common flux materials. Flux can be purchased as either a paste, a liquid, or a powder. It is applied to the metal surfaces to be joined after they have been scraped clean with a steel brush or metal file. Also see **Tincrafting: Joining the Tin.**

flux brush. Jewelry. A **brush** used for **fluxing** metal in preparation for **soldering.** It should be a tapered, round, sable brush; sable is the only material that will spring back to its original shape when wet, which is most important for fluxing and picking up and placing **solder pallion**s. A good size to use is #8.

A flux brush must be new. It should never be used for anything but **flux** and should be kept meticulously clean. If it is accidentally dropped on the floor, it should be rinsed in running water. When it is in use, it should be put down on the bench with the bristles extending over the edge of the **bench.** Contamination of the flux brush, flux, or metal is the major cause of soldering failures.

fluxed color. Color and Glass Painting. Color containing enough **flux** to fuse the color onto the surface of the china during **firing.**

fluxed gold. China and Glass Painting. See **Roman gold.**

fluxing. Jewelry. Coating metals with **flux** in preparation for **soldering.** Flux promotes the flow of **solder** and prevents the formation of **firescale.** Flux is available as a liquid or as a paste. To flux metal **pickle** the metal. Remove it from the pickle with **pickling tongs** and rinse it. From this point on hold the metal by the edges or with **tweezers.** The metal must remain completely free of any grease or contamination, including oil from the hands.

Place the work on a **heating frame** resting on an **asbestos pad** or a **carborundum pan.** Apply a thin coat of liquid flux with a **flux brush** to all surfaces of the metal. Remove excess flux from the brush before applying the flux to the metal. Excess flux appears as thick white clumps when dried with the torch. Using the **torch** heat the metal with a soft brushing **flame** until the coat of liquid flux turns white. The idea is to get the metal hot enough to dry the flux, but not hot enough to cause even the slightest discoloration to form on any area of the metal. Apply flux with very quick strokes to any area that is not white. Heat the metal to dry out this new application of flux. Repeat until the entire surface of the metal has a white coat. The flux is applied with quick strokes to prevent the brush from sticking to the hot metal and burning. Also be careful not to ignite the bristles with the torch. Remove excess flux with tweezers held parallel to the surface of the metal. Excess flux must be removed to prevent solder pallions from slipping when the flux melts during soldering.

Cut solder into **pallion**s using **snips.** Clip the pallions on clean white paper and coat with a brush full of liquid flux. Smear the flux around on the paper so that all surfaces of the solder are covered. Do not use lined paper because the ink may contaminate the flux. Paper towels are equally unsuitable because they are absorbent. White typing paper is the best. Position the pallions on the work for soldering while the flux is still wet. Slowly heat the work until the liquid flux on the pallions dries and turns white. The wet flux on the pallions will spread to the immediate surrounding areas. Move the torch slowly to avoid blowing the pallions out of position. Brush the flame directly on the piece, taking it across the full surface. Pause for a second and repeat. As the flux dries, it will bubble and the solder will begin to move. Pause longer and brush with flame, repeating until everything is dry, then solder.

Fluxing is one of the most important steps in the making of jewelry which is to be soldered or **anneal**ed. Most failures are caused during **soldering** by incorrect fluxing and lack of cleanliness.

fly cutter. Metalworking. Plastics. See **circle cutter.**

flyer. Spinning. A U-shaped wooden device with a set of **guide hooks** found on **treadle wheels.** This device twists the yarn and then guides it for winding on the **bobbin.** Also see **flyer assembly.**

flyer assembly. Spinning. A yarn **bobbin** with a rotating attachment called a **flyer** that is added to a **spinning wheel** so that the spinning and winding can be done in one operation. This assembly replaces the regular **spindle head.** The flyer assembly includes a **flyer,** which is located at the outside end of the **spindle shaft** with its open end facing the bobbin and the two shaft pulleys. A **driving band** on one of the pulleys, called the **spindle pulley,** rotates the flyer. As it does so the spun yarn passes through the **orifice,** or small opening at the tip of the spindle shaft, and emerges from another opening at the side of the shaft and in back of the flyer. The yarn is twisted and runs along the top arm of the flyer, then passes through a hook that holds

it in position to be wound on the bobbin. The bobbin, with its **bobbin pulley,** is located between the flyer and the pulley flyer. The pulley of the bobbin turns at a different speed than that of the flyer because the pulleys are of different sizes. The action of the flyer is simultaneous with the action of the bobbin, that is, the flyer twists the yarn at the same time that the bobbin winds it up. The yarn is moved from one hook to another as each section of the bobbin is filled so that the winding is even along the length of the bobbin.

The flyer assembly was an immense step forward in spinning because it eliminated winding up each length of spun yarn before drawing out the next length. Leonardo da Vinci was credited with this invention, but it wasn't until some years after his death that, in 1530, Johann Jürgen, a German wood carver, made it practical for the spinning wheel. See ill. Also see **treadle wheel.**

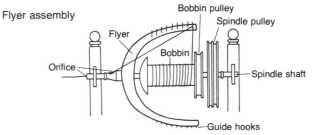

Flyer assembly

flyer pulley. Spinning. See **flyer assembly, spindle pulley.**

flyer wheel. Spinning. See **treadle wheel.**

Fly Foot. Quilts. See **Swastika.**

Flying Darts. Quilts. See **David and Goliath.**

Flying Dutchman. Quilts. See **Kansas Troubles.**

Flying Geese. Quilts. See **Birds in Flight.**

flying jenny. Toys. See **merry-go-round.**

flying machine. Toys. (Also called flying propeller.) A simply made **propeller toy** that operates in somewhat the same way as the **alouette.** It is an old **toy,** predating propeller aircraft, although children now often call it a **helicopter.** The toy consists of a carved wood propeller that is fastened at the top of a wood **dowel.** The shaft of the dowel is usually about the diameter of a pencil and the propellers measure about 8″ from tip to tip. The toy is operated by rapidly rotating the stick in the palms. The propeller will rise into the air. As it slows, the propeller will gradually sink to the ground.

flying propeller. Toys. See **alouette, flying machine.**

Flying Star. Quilts. See **Falling Star.**

Flying Swallows. Quilts. See **Falling Star.**

flyleaves. Bookbinding. Denotes all the free leaves of an **endpaper** section. The flyleaf is the uppermost free leaf of the section next to the cover board.

fly shuttle. Weaving. A shuttle resembling a **boat shuttle,** but larger and much heavier. It is made for use on a **flying shuttle loom** and has lead weights at each end and points of solid metal. The yarn feeds or slips off the end of a tapered nonrotating spool called a pira. The yarn tension is controlled by passing it through holes in the side of the shuttle. Also see shuttle loom, **shuttle.**

fly-shuttle loom. Weaving. A floor loom with a simple mechanism for propelling the **shuttle** at great speed across the width of the entire **beater.** This mechanism is attached to the shuttle boxes built onto the sides of the beater, one on each side. In the center of each box is a movable metal rod called a picker. The shuttle is pushed out of the box by the picker and "flies" along a shuttle race on the lower edge of the beater to the other box. The weaver's hand never touches the shuttle or picker. Instead, a handle hanging in the center of the loom, directly above the beater, is pulled. This handle, called a picking stick, is attached to a cord which in turn is attached to the outer point of each of the two pickers. Pulling the handle to the right tugs at the left-hand picker, which throws the shuttle across to the right. A left-handed pulling throws the shuttle to the left from the right-hand box. One hand works the handle while the other hand beats back and forth with the beater. The feet change the **shed.** Because this loom is used for rapid production of wide fabrics there is usually not much complex patterning; only two or four **harness**es are used, with minimal changes in the **treadling.**

Before the advent of mechanized equipment, it required two persons to work very wide looms—the weaver and a helper who caught and threw back the shuttle from the other side of the loom. With the invention of the fly-shuttle loom in England in 1733 by John Kay, a weaver could work alone. This was the first important step on the road to power looms. It was the cause of riots and strikes in the early days of the Industrial Revolution because many people were thrown out of work by this invention. The unrest was such that Kay's home was sacked and burned by an angry mob. Today fly-shuttle looms are used by few handweavers. Mainly they are found in studios or companies specializing in handwoven **yardage** for sale. These looms also have let-off and take-up motions so that the unwoven **warp** and the woven cloth move forward a fraction of an inch automatically with each beat. The tension is controlled at both the back and front of the loom so that it remains constant. The weaver never spends the time to do this by hand. Fabrics woven on a fly-shuttle loom are labeled "hand-loomed," rather than handwoven. Also see **fly shuttle.**

fly stitch. Crewel. Embroidery. (Also called detached fly stitch.) A **detached** stitch resembling a fly that can be used to fill in large areas for an open scattered effect, or to tie down **laidwork.** When scattered over any ground stitch it can be used for various textural effects (as in a feathered animal design). See ill.

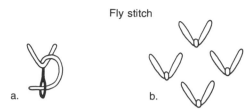

Fly stitch

a.   b.

foam. Metalworking. Plastics. (Also called cellular plastic, expanded plastic, expanded polystyrene, urethane, vinyl.) Lightweight cellular plastics are manufactured in rigid and flexible forms. Rigid varieties are more often used in crafts.

In metalworking, rigid expanded **polystyrene** and urethane (e.g., Art Foam) forms are used for **pattern**s in **foam-vaporization casting.** The foam is burned by the molten metal being poured into the **mold.**

In plastics, rigid foam is used for direct **carving** of objects or for carving and constructing shapes to be covered with reinforced **resin.** Expanded **polystyrene** (e.g., Styrofoam, Dylite, Dyplast) and expanded polyurethane (or urethane) are available in sheets, slabs, and blocks and are easily shaped and sanded with common hand and power tools. Join expanded polystyrene with **rubber cement** and expanded polyurethane with either rubber cement or epoxy. High-density urethane foam ranges from 6 to 25 pounds per cubic foot in weight, with the 6-pound variety the most common for precision model and art carving. It has a tight, smooth surface suitable for fine detail and may be directly covered with **polyester** resin or painted with a wide range of products. Expanded polystyrene comes only in one grade, which is rather coarse and is less expansive, but it is attacked by polyester resin and many spray paints. The surface should be sealed with a **polymer-emulsion gesso,** synthetic rubber, or other sealant before being coated with resin.

Some craftspersons purchase reactant chemicals to produce each specific foam and form objects by spraying or foaming the **plastic** in place. Also see **Plastics: Carving.**

foam rubber. Stitchery. Toys. (Also called latex foam.) A spongy but firm mass of a foamy latex material prepared in premolded shapes, in sheets, or as **shredded foam rubber.** It is available in various thicknesses and can be cut with a saber saw or an electric knife. It is used for **stuffing pillows,** and for mats, **bath toys, stuffed animal**s, **doll**s, or **soft sculpture.** Bags of the shredded foam rubber are packaged for use as a loose stuffing material.

In the manufacture of foam rubber, the latex is mixed with various ingredients and whipped into a foam that is about 85% air. It is a nonabsorbent, flexible, soft material.

foam-vaporization casting. Metalworking. A casting process using plastic foam (Styrofoam, for example) for a pattern in **investment** or **sandcasting.** The foam is burned out or vaporized when the molten metal is poured into the **mold.**

foil. Bookbinding. Foil is used to apply lettering or decoration to a binding with the aid of heated **tools**. It is composed of gold or other metal or pigment sandwiched between a plastic film and a heat sensitive adhesive. The adhesive side is placed next to the work, and **titling** or decoration is accomplished by impressing a heated metal tool onto the upper side of the foil.

foil. Jewelry. Very thin **sheet metal**, generally not more than 0.005″ thick. Also see **gold leaf.**

foil. Papercrafts. See **aluminum foil.**

foil. Stained Glass. See **copper foil, copper foiling.**

foil embossing. Papercrafts. A technique of incising designs with a blunt tool on padded layers of **aluminum foil.** The foil surface is made of several sheets of foil mounted over blotting paper or several layers of paper toweling on a cardboard backing. All layers are glued down with rubber cement. Any blunt, pointed tool, such as a comb tail or a dull pencil, may be used for drawing, pressing down gently to avoid tearing the foil. Often the finished design is coated with a stain of artist's oil paint thinned with turpentine, then wiped away with a cloth, leaving color mostly in the indented lines.

folder. Leatherwork. (Also called bone folder.) A tool, usually made of plastic or bone, used for defining or creasing lines in leather before folding. The line is creased on the fold line on the flesh side. Some have a **circle edge slicker** at one end for heavy leathers. See ill.

folding. Batik and Tie-dye. A simple means of manipulating **fabric** to produce bands, **stripes**, **chevrons**, **zigzag patterns**, and other designs in **tie-dye**ing. One method is called **spiral folding** because the folding process leaves a spiral line on the material.

In the simplest spiral method the length of material is folded in half and **crease**d on the center line. It may, for a wider piece of material, be folded or **accordion pleat**ed a number of times to make a long, narrow strip. Then the end of the strip is placed at a diagonal on top of a ruler (or a strip of cardboard), folded over the edge, and held in place until the rest of the strip has been wrapped diagonally around the ruler, forming a spiral line. The base of the ruler can then be slid out so that the entire flat, spiral tube can be folded in half and tied into lines, bands, or crisscross (trellis) patterns. After it is dyed and rinsed, more binding may be added before a second **dye** process.

Another folding method, which does not use a ruler as the base, is more precise and better suited for long pieces of fabric. The fabric is folded lengthwise into one double panel (for a very large pattern) or accordion pleated (for a smaller repeat pattern). Folding can begin at either end. The open end is folded at a right angle to the long strip so that the end is lined up exactly on top of a folded edge.

This makes a right triangle on the end, with a 45° corner pointing out from the length of the strip. The length of the material is now folded over itself, parallel to and touching the first fold to make a 45° angle and another right triangle. The folding process is continued until all the fabric is used, with folds held in place with pins or **bulldog clip**s. After **binding** and **dyeing**, the binding process can be repeated for an additional dyeing.

A folding method to produce a chevron pattern starts with a long, folded strip of material. A fold is made at the end to form a right triangle (**a.**). The strip of material is folded again, so that the second fold meets the first (**b., c.**). The folds continue in a spiral pattern to the end of the strip (**d.**). Band tying is added to produce the chevron pattern when it is dyed (**e.**). Line binding may also be used, either on the first dyeing or after the first and before the second dyeing (**f.**). See ill.

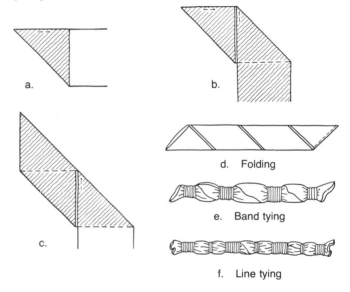

a.

b.

d.   Folding

e.   Band tying

c.

f.   Line tying

folding. Bookbinding. Folding is simple if done properly. Paper that is folded incorrectly can be refolded, but the mark of the wrong fold will always show. Use the **bone folder** to produce a smooth surface and a tight clean fold. When folding a sheet that is cut crookedly, be certain to line up the top edges even if this means that the outer ones don't line up. The general practice is to fold the long side of the rectangle each time and to slit the fold to a point just beyond the center of the next intended fold. Slitting prevents creasing on the inside of the fold; the thicker the folds get, the more likely they are to crease and should therefore be slit before making the next fold. If you are folding printed pages, raise up the corner so that you can align the printing on facing pages. Hold down the sheet you are folding firmly with one hand where the two outside corners meet. With your other hand run the bone folder from the cut edges back toward the fold (to prevent wrinkling), then run the folder along the fold to make the crease. Also see **section.**

folding. Tincrafting. See **Tincrafting: Folding the Tin.**

folding leather. Leatherwork. See **Leatherwork: Creasing, Scoring, and Folding Leather.**

folding loom. Weaving. A **harness loom** so constructed that it can be folded when not in use. Although it is assumed that a folding loom is a **floor loom,** there are **table loom**s also that fold up. Some looms fold up completely, which, if the loom is of narrow width, makes for easy storage and portability. Other floor models only fold partway in that the **back** and **warp beam**s are on hinged wooden supports that fold forward for a more compact structure that is easier to move about.

folding rule. Woodworking. See **measuring tool.**

folio. Bookbinding. A sheet folded only once, or a book made up of such sheets. Folio books are usually **saddle-stitch**ed. Also see **section.**

folk art. Stitchery. A traditional or ethnic expression which combines decorative and utilitarian functions and styles. Most folk arts are produced to be consumed or used by the people who make them since they relate to the ordinary needs of day to day living. Their appeal is a very human one because they are so personal in nature. Folk arts may be referred to as naive, primitive, pioneer, natural, home art, provincial, amateur, or self-taught. None of these gives an accurate idea of the whole range, but each helps to define it. Folk artists are usually untrained academically, since folk arts grow out of the needs, tools, and uses of everyday life. While American folk art is often used to refer only to the traditional folk arts of early America, these arts are not just a part of the past; they never completely died out or disappeared. Though the Industrial Revolution replaced many handmade articles with machine-made ones, there is still a flourishing of the hand arts today. Some folk art forms such as **quilt**making, dollmaking and the decoration of clothes may have diminished in importance but maintained a hold in many areas and households. The whole **making do** approach and the craft renaissance of the 1960s and 1970s has reestablished the importance of many folk art and handcraft forms.

folk toy. Toys. A toy of unknown origin, the design of which is passed from one generation to another. A folk toy is usually used by the people who produce it, in contrast to a manufactured toy. A toy must be fairly popular in order to survive over many generations, which means that it has been appreciated by numerous people at different times. Many folk toys are based on principles of physics, which make them intriguing to adults as well as children. **Jumping jacks, peashooter**s, **slingshot**s, and **balance toy**s are among these. Also see **Toys: Folk Toys.**

follow-the-leader. Quilts. A variation of the **pieced block** pattern called **windmill.**

follow-up. Basketry. Any variety of **border** that is put on top or beside a previous border and going in the same direction. It is used to thicken the border for strength, or for decoration. It may also be used as an edge for a **cover** or as a **foot.**

food coloring. Toys. A nontoxic dye used in foods, particularly to color frostings or icings in **cookie art.** It is available in liquid form at any grocery store. Some more intense colors are available as **food coloring paste**s from shops that specialize in kitchenware.

Food coloring is a safe, easy-to-use material. It is frequently used in **baker's art** and **dough sculpture.** Also see **baker's clay glazes, egg-yolk painting.**

food coloring paste. Toys. An intense coloring material used in frostings and doughs. Like the liquid **food coloring,** it is edible. The pastes are thick and dissolve readily when mixed into batters or with fluids. They may be used in **egg-yolk painting** and all types of **baker's art.** The colors remain bright after baking.

Fool's Puzzle. Quilts. See **Drunkard's Path.**

foot. Basketry. An extra piece of work, usually a **border,** added to the bottom of a **basket** for stability. It may sometimes be one or two **round**s of **waling** woven in during the **upsetting** of the basket.

foot. Ceramics. The base of a piece of pottery as in a vase. Also see **foot ring** and **Ceramics: Form.**

foot border. Basketry. See **border.**

footman. Spinning. (Also called pitman.) A flat piece of wood or a straight rod or wire that connects the treadle with the **axle** crank on a **treadle wheel.**

foot-operated rheostat. Jewelry. An enclosed foot-operated unit used to control the speed of the **flexible shaft machine** and some **drill press**es. The advantage of this device is that it frees both hands for working. See ill.

Foot-operated rheostats

foot-operated shears. Jewelry. A large, expensive piece of floor-standing equipment with a broad surface plate. **Sheet metal** is placed on this plate to keep it level and then is pushed under the cutting edges of the **shears.** A foot pedal operates the shears, which cut off the metal at a perfect right angle, eliminating the twisting and bevel on each side of the sheet metal that occur when it is cut by hand shears. Don't attempt to use this piece of machinery without instruction. Also see **bench shears.**

foot-power loom. Weaving. A **loom** in which the **harness**es are moved by the feet pressing on the **treadle**s. The loom can be **counterbalanced, jack-type,** or **countermarch.** It is a freestanding floor structure with a central upright frame or **castle** from which hang 2 to 16 harnesses. Attached to the harnesses are **lam**s and to the lams, treadles. In counterbalanced, or **sinking shed** looms, pressing on the treadles pulls the harnesses down. In jack-type, or **rising shed loom**s, the harnesses are pushed up when the treadles are depressed. In a countermarch loom there are two sets of lams for double **tie-up** so that stepping on the treadles moves the harnesses both up and down. Foot-power looms may be rigid or folding, narrow or wide, with an overhead **beater** or one set into the floor supports, or with one or two **warp beam**s or a **sectional warp beam.**

Foot-power looms are thought to have originated in Asia, probably in China, where early drawings show a jack-type loom being used in silk weaving. The earliest counterbalanced loom may have been invented in India in the form of a pit loom with the weaver sitting on the edge of a small pit with the feet placed down in it. Two harnesses were raised and lowered by cords running from them to big loops slipped around the toes. The early European foot-power loom was built like a cage with four sides and top and bottom supports, which contained the weaver, the bench, and the working parts of the loom. Drawings show this loom in use in the early fifteenth century in France. As time went on it was simplified, first by removing the outside cage structure. Some later models appeared in which the bench was unattached and there was no structure over the harnesses so that the loom had a low, streamlined appearance. The changes are only in appearance, not in function. Colonial looms with top structures and overhead beaters are still used today, and in some countries the cagelike structure is still an accepted part of the loom. Foot-power looms are the most popular looms in general use because they free the weaver's hands for the **shuttle** throwing and **beating.** This provides for a rhythm in weaving unavailable in any other type of loom. Also see **counterbalanced loom, countermarch loom, jack-type loom, loom.**

foot rim. Ceramics. See **foot ring.**

foot ring. Ceramics. (Also called foot rim.) A low pedestal or foot on a bowl, plate, or other ceramic form. It can be thrown on the piece, but is usually trimmed out of the thick base once the piece is **leather hard.** The foot rim assures a firm base for the form, and gives it a light, floating feeling. See ill. Also see **Ceramics: Form.**

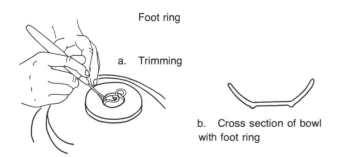

Foot ring

a.   Trimming

b.   Cross section of bowl with foot ring

footwheel. Spinning. See **treadle wheel.**

Forbidden Fruit. Quilts. See **Pine Tree.**

force fracture. Plastics. A fracture resembling a feathery branch caused by plunging a knife or other sharp object into **gel**led **resin.** It does not greatly weaken the plastic. It

can be a blunder, or a desired effect, depending upon your objective. Also see **curing.**

foredge. Bookbinding. The outside edges of the leaves and **board**s of a book directly opposite the **back edge.**

fore plane. Woodworking. See **plane.**

foreshortening. An aspect of **perspective** that involves shortening the length of an object in a drawing or painting proportionately as that length runs in a line away from the **picture plane** toward the vanishing point. Note how, in the illustration of a tumbling cylinder, the height of the cylinder is drawn shorter and shorter as the base moves toward the viewer. See ill.

Foreshortening

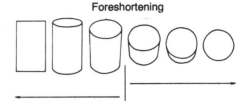

Forest Path. Quilts. See **Kansas Troubles.**

forge. Metalworking. (Also called hearth.) The furnace used to heat metal for the process of **forging.** (In that process, forge is also used as a verb.) The traditional blacksmith's forge was a fireplace or rectangular brick or stone enclosure about 30" high and 24–40" across. One day of **blacksmithing** might cost the smith several hundred pounds of coal to heat it. Ready-made manufactured forges of cast iron have been sold since the mid-nineteenth century, and today they are commonly heated by gas. Instead of the traditional **bellow**s, an automatic blower now fans traditiona **bellow**s, an automatic blower now fans the fire.

To use a gas-fueled forge, light the gas and allow the forge to preheat. Adjust the fuel mixture until the flame is blue or **neutral.** An excess of air will cause too much **scale** to form on your metal.

To use a coal-fueled forge, remove the clinkers and ashes from the remains of the old fire. Clinkers are heavy metallic particles. Save the coke, which is the lightweight crumbly material left after the gas has been removed from the green coal. Position wood shavings over the air holes and light the fire. Pump air on the fire to start it, using either bellows or a **blower.** Add the coke. Pack dampened coal around the sides, but not at the front, of the forge. Add more coal to the outside as the fire burns. Avoid applying too much air. Poke a hole into the center of the pile if the flames smoke too much at first. Place the metal to be forged in the center, lying horizontally (never standing vertically) to ensure even heating. Check the temperature of the metal by examining its color frequently, so as not to overheat and burn the metal.

forge tools. Metalworking. See **blacksmithing tools.**

forge welding. Metalworking. See **blacksmithing techniques, welding** and **Metalworking: Blacksmithing, Welding.**

forging. Jewelry. Metalworking. (Also called smithing.) The process of shaping and **forming** metals by compression, using hammers and support devices such as **anvils, mandrel**s, **steel block**s, and **stakes**. Sheet metal can be forged, but generally forging is done with wire from fine to very thick **gauge**s. Forging can produce sensitive, articulate forms. Some simple procedures can be learned quickly, but forging as a whole takes time to master. Some general rules are:

Metal will require **annealing** if it is worked for any length of time.

Wire becomes compressed, flatter, thinner, and longer depending on the **forging hammers** used. Bend wire before forging to help in achieving the desired contours. Extend the forefinger along the handle of the hammer to maintain more control of the blow of the hammer. The hammer should always strike the metal perpendicularly. It is this sensitive control of the hammer that takes time and feel to achieve. If the hammer does not strike the wire in a direct perpendicular fashion, but is slightly tipped, for example, the metal will begin to swing to the right. This can be used to advantage if you want the metal to move in that direction. If the hammer used is tipped such that an edge on the face of the hammer strikes the metal, a gash will result. This could be used as a deliberate textural surface treatment.

It is necessary to be aggressive with the metal when forging, unless it is very fine. Strike the metal fairly hard to make it move. This takes some getting used to. The striking ends of forging hammers should be cared for, as any marks in the face of the hammer will be transferred to the metal being forged. Also see **bending, cold forging, drawing out, edge thickening, planishing, planishing hammer, quench.**

forging anvil. Metalworking. See **anvil.**

forging brass. Metalworking. See **brass.**

forging down. Jewelry. (Also called drawing out.) Thinning or decreasing the thickness of metal, thereby increasing its length.

forging down. Metalworking. See **blacksmithing techniques.**

forging hammer. Jewelry. Steel-faced hammers available in a variety of shapes and contours. They are primarily silversmithing hammers. Also see **cold forming, forging.**

forging hammer. Metalworking. See **hammer.**

forging tong. Metalworking. See **tong.**

format. Bookbinding. A term used to indicate the number of times the original sheets have been folded to form the sections of a book. Also see **section.**

former. Ceramics. A natural or informal **mold** for shaping clay. In Japan, bowls were made for centuries over the elbow, knee, or hand from **slab**s of clay. **Balloon**s, bags of sand, and paper can also be used as formers.

Formica. Woodworking. A **laminated plastic** used for surfacing cabinets, countertops, desks, etc., where durability and resistance to stain and heat are required. It is not recommended for application to plaster walls, **gypsum board,** concrete walls, exteriors, or to areas exposed to temperatures exceeding 275° F. Formica is composed of bonded layers of phenolic resin-impregnated paper filler and a layer of melamine resin impregnated with colored pigment. It comes in a wide range of colors, patterns, and woodgrains in sizes from 24″ × 72″ to 60″ × 144″.

To cut Formica, use **carbide-tip**ped blades and high-speed **router**s.

Install Formica by bonding it with a **contact cement** to rigid, relatively nonporous materials such as **particle board** or **plywood.** Ideal installation conditions call for a temperature of not less than 65° F and a humidity of 35–80%.

Clean Formica with a damp cloth or ordinary bar soap and water, but do not use **abrasive** cleaners. Remove grease or glue with **solvents** such as lacquer thinner, **methyl ethyl ketone** (MEK), or contact cement solvent. Long exposure to high temperatures will dull the surface.

forming. Jewelry. A generic term that includes many techniques used in shaping metals, some of which are rolling, **bending, forging, box construction, chasing, répoussé, drawing wire,** and **doming.** Also see **bench anvil, rolling mill.**

forming block. Glasswork. See **blocking.**

forming leather. Leatherwork. See **Leatherwork: Forming Leather.**

forstner bit. Woodworking. See **drill bit.**

fortification agate. Gemcutting. See **Quartz.**

forwarding. Bookbinding. A general term for all operations in the making or binding of a book up to the stage of lettering and decorating the cover. Also see **Bookbinding.**

Forward Together. Quilts. See **presidents' quilt.**

fossil ivory. Ivory and Bone Carving. Fossil ivory is a true ivory and not silicified as are most other fossils. Although there are occasional samples with occurrences of spiral twists, the material is like green, or freshly removed, tusk. The largest deposits of fossil ivory were found in Russia, although it has been found in numerous locations in England. Vast quantities of the fossil remains of mastodon and mammoth tusks were exported to China from Russia. Tusks are sometimes stained bright blue from the minerals they were buried in, producing a material called odontolite, which is sometimes used to imitate turquoise. In the main, the tusks are well preserved; live ivory accounts for less than half the ivory on the market.

foulard. Batik and Tie-dye. A thin, soft **fabric** woven from **silk** or from silk and cotton. It has a smooth satin **finish** and is used in dyeing **batik** or **tie-dye** fabrics.

foundation. Basketry. The structural **element** or material that is bound into each **coil** in coiled basketry. It may be a single **reed rod** or a series of sticks or twigs.

foundation chain. Crochet. The chain of crochet into which the first row of actual crochet stitches is worked. Also see **chain, chain stitch** and **Crochet: Basic Procedures.**

foundation coil. Basketry. The basic structure of **coiled basketry.** It is composed of a **binder** and a **foundation** element. The foundation element is coiled around the basket while the binding element joins it to the previous coils in any number of different **stitches**. See ill. Also see **Basketry: Coiled, Coil Basket Construction.**

Beginning of a crude
foundation coil

foundation fabric. Rugmaking. See **backing, ground cloth.**

foundation loop. Lacemaking. (Also called stirrup.) A large **loop** pinned to a firm cushion. The **netting needle** thread is tied to this loop. The first row of meshes in knotted lace filet is started on the foundation loop. Also see **knotted lace filet.**

foundation selvage. Knitting. The **edge** created by the **stitches cast on** prior to the first **row** of knitting. Usually, these cast-on stitches will be the bottom edge of a piece of knitting, i.e., the bottom of a sweater or dress body. Also see **Knitting: Casting On.**

foundation yarn. Spinning. Weaving. See **novelty yarn.**

founder's sand. Metalworking. See **molding sand.**

founding. Metalworking. See **casting.**

found material. Puppets. Stitchery. Those stock or staple items commonly available anywhere that may be had for the asking or taking. Found materials such as cork, paper cups, or socks may be used in **puppetry.** A temporary head might be made of a potato, a turnip, or whatever is available. An apple corer will cut the hole in the bottom. A wad of **cotton** or a Styrofoam ball will also work as the head. Two disks of cardboard, **glue**d together at the edges but with an opening at the bottom, make a simple head. Stitchery may incorporate shells, buttons, or pieces of wood in compositions with **fibers** and **fabrics. Toys** offer endless possibilities for the use of found objects, and imaginative children readily turn discarded boxes into houses or vehicles. The use of found objects is related to **making do.** Also see **puppet head, scrap puppet.**

found object. Mosaics. Any material not originally intended for, but suitable for, mounting within a mosaic. Found objects include such natural items as rocks, **pebbles,** and shells and manufactured items such as bits of broken bottles, cracked china, wood turnings, and so on. There is almost no restriction on the kind of object that can be found and used in mosaic work. The only caution is a creative one; found objects should be selected and arranged with a sense of design, not randomly, if they are to be effective. Also see **Mosaics: Tools and Materials.**

found object. Papercrafts. Many of the basic materials for papercrafts are gathered from daily life: all kinds of paper, toothpicks, paper doilies, string, containers, and various other odds and ends. Drinking straws offer many possibilities for constructing geometric forms by stapling them together or by stringing them on a needle and thread. To make straw structures sturdier, make joint pieces by flattening several straws, then cutting them into short lengths. Bend each joint piece in half lengthwise, dip the ends in **white glue,** and then insert the ends onto the rounded straw ends of the sculpture.

Various types of cardboard containers are useful as basic shapes, or as a support on which to build or attach lightweight forms. **Papier mâché** applied by the **paper-strip method** is often worked over supports that combine containers, cans, paper-towel tubes, paper cups, and so on, secured in position with masking tape. Sculptural details may be modeled from **aluminum foil,** then taped in place on the design. Care should be taken that the design constructed from found objects is securely taped together and balanced, if it is to be free-standing, before the papier mâché process is begun.

Egg cartons provide interesting shapes when cut apart and combined in **paper sculpture** or covered with papier mâché. Cardboard egg cartons or other heavy cardboard containers may be soaked in **papier mâché paste** and modeled into desired forms, or crushed to make **paper mash.** See ill.

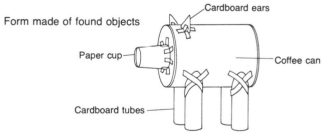

Form made of found objects

Cardboard ears

Paper cup

Coffee can

Cardboard tubes

found object beads. Beadwork. Many objects on hand can be used for or made into **beads.** Natural materials such as bamboo, beans, bone, **quill, seeds, shell,** and **wood** provide varied shapes and textures for beadwork. Household items may also provide an interesting source for beads, such as bottle caps, plastic lids, straws, **paper,** and pasta. Some found objects already have openings for stringing; others, particularly bone and wood, must be drilled. Also see **Beadmaking: Basic Operations.**

found object mold. Candlemaking. Containers or receptacles made of any material that will hold up under the relatively high heat of melted wax can be used as candle **mold**s. The container cannot be narrower than its opening at any point unless it is made of a material that can be cut, torn, or broken away. Also see **cardboard container candle, container candle, eggshell candle, gelatin mold, glass bottle candle, paper mold, sand candle, shell candle.**

found object printing. Block Printing. Many objects found in daily life can be used for printing simply by inking them. Various materials such as curtain lace, coarse fabric, wire mesh, leaves, and so on can be glued down on flat cardboard or wood backing, then inked and printed. Cord or string can be laid out in the desired design and glued to a backing, then inked and printed for intricate linear patterns. These are only a few of the variations of **relief printing** that are possible.

Many hard fruits and vegetables can be cut in half, inked, and printed. Hard vegetables such as turnips, beets, carrots, and potatoes can be cut as a **printing block,** as described under **potato block printing. Stamping** can be done with many household materials, from rubber erasers to corks. Shapes can be cut from household sponges, then inked and printed. Although these methods are simple, interesting patterns can be printed by the repetition of basic shapes. Also see **rubbing** and **Block Printing: Printing Techniques.**

found objects. Puppets. Stitchery. See **found material.**

foundry. Metalworking. A shop in which objects are made by **casting** or founding molten metal into molds.

foundry metal. Metalworking. See **metal.**

foundry sand. Metalworking. See **molding sand.**

foundry tongs. Metalworking. See **tongs.**

foundation shell. Shell carving. See **queen conch.**

four-coil weave. Basketry. See **waling.**

Four Darts. Quilts. See **David and Goliath.**

four-harness loom. Weaving. A table or **floor loom** having four **harness**es, the most popular number of harnesses that weavers choose to use. Two-harness loom models are few in number and are considered too limiting for pattern weaving. **Multiharness loom**s are more expensive and their possibilities as to pattern and complex cloth structure are not fully realized by many weavers. Four-harness looms are the happy medium; because of this popularity, most weaving books concentrate on weaving possible only with four harnesses. Some very complex patterns were developed during colonial times, or shortly thereafter, when four-harness looms were the most common available. Early four-harness looms were all **counterbalanced loom**s, but today they are available also in jack-type models. Also see **jack-type loom, table loom.**

Four Little Fans. Quilts. See **Circular Saw.**

four-patch. Quilts. A basic and simple **block** arrangement that consists of four **patch**es, or pieces, of equal size. Each patch may be divided and subdivided into triangles, smaller squares, etc. A four-patch could be formed, for example, by two **nine-patch**es in diagonally opposed corners with solid blocks in the remaining two corners. The **split four-patch** is considered to be a four-patch design.

The four-patch tends to resolve itself into flock, star, or **wreath** designs, although there are many exceptions. More than half of all quilt patterns are based on this and the nine-patch design. Also see **Birds in Flight, Dutchman's Puzzle, Swastika, Windmill, Yankee Puzzle.**

four-rod wale. Basketry. See **waling.**

four-row crossover. Beadwork. See **continuous crossover loop.**

four-selvages weaving. Weaving. See **selvage.**

four-sided fringe. Weaving. See **weft fringe.**

Four Star. Quilts. See **World Without End.**

Four Stars. Quilts. See **star patterns.**

Four-X Star. Quilts. (Also called Sister's Choice.) A pieced block that is made up of a basic **nine-patch** surrounded by another row of squares, some of which are split for the X's. See ill.

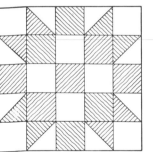

Four-X Star

fowlerite. Gemcutting. See **rhodonite.**

Fox and Geese. Quilts. See **Crosses and Losses.**

fracture. Batik and Tie-dye. The lines or cracks that occur in **wax**ed areas of **batik** fabric. When dyed, there is some **dye penetration** of these lines, which forms a pattern known as **crackle,** or veining.

fracture. Gemcutting. The uneven, irregular surface of a stone which does not have **cleavage** when it is broken.

A conchoidal fracture is so named for its resemblance to a mollusk shell. It exhibits deep circular ridges and grooves, concentric around the point where the specimen received the blow that caused the fracture.

A splintery fracture (also called hackly) is descriptive of

a break that has loosely attached splinters lighter in color than the rest of the material.

An uneven fracture (also called subconchoidal, granular) is characteristic of compact aggregates, such as agate.

An even fracture approximates a plane surface.

Also see **abrasive, beryl, chrysoberyl.**

fracture. Jewelry. A crack in metal that can be caused in a number of ways, including **forging**, continuous **bending** or **forming** without **annealing**, improper quenching, or during **casting**. Also see **air quench, quench, soldering point.**

fragrance. Candlemaking. See **scent.**

fraille. Stained Glass. A light wooden frame constructed to support stained-glass **panel**s while they are being transported to their destination. It is constructed to lie back at a slight angle so that the panels can be leaned against it, and can then be temporarily secured into a truck or van for transporting.

frame. Lacemaking. The filling stitches done on **knotted lace filet** are more easily worked if the **net** is secured to a frame. Stretcher bars put together in the size and shape needed would work very well and are obtainable in any art supply store. A frame at least 3–4″ larger than the knotted net (when it is stretched) is advisable.

Thread a strong cord or twine through a **mesh** on the edge of the net, out over the frame, and back to the next mesh. Continue in this manner until all the outer-edge meshes are secured and the netting is reasonably taut. Allow about 2–3″ between the netting edge and the frame. The knotted lace is now ready to have the design done in the filling stitches.

frame. Quilts. See **quilting frame.**

frame. Rugmaking. See **hooking frame.**

frame. Weaving. See **harness.**

frame knitting. Knitting. An early method of producing knitlike fabrics that were too large or too heavy to be worked on knitting needles. The frames were either circular or rectangular. Also see **rake knitting, spool knitting, straight frame knitting** and **Knitting.**

frame loom. Beadwork. A simple **loom** for bead weaving used by the American Indians to make wide strips of beadwork. A rectangle is made of thin wood strips with the warp threads running all the way around in one continuous piece (belt warp). The side pieces should be straight-grained, flexible wood so that when the beadwork is ready to be shifted, the sides can be pressed in to loosen the warp threads enough to shift the finished work to the back of the loom. The warp should be of strong **thread**, waxed after the loom is strung. It is not necessary to cut notches in the frame because the beads themselves regulate the spacing regardless of how far apart the warp threads are. See ill.

Frame loom

frame loom. Weaving. A simple **loom** made out of a wooden frame. The frame should be strong and rigid so that it cannot shift or give way under **warp tension.** The frame loom can have endless variations in shape, method of putting on a **warp, shedding device**s, and tensioning means.

The shape is normally square or rectangular, and the looms are usually constructed at home out of a picture frame, canvas stretchers (available at an art supply store) or spare lumber. Rug **hooking frame**s can be converted to serve as a loom (**a.**). It is also possible to buy frame looms that come with specific patented shedding and tensioning devices. A common size for a frame loom is 18×20″, although it can be much smaller or larger. A **Navajo loom** is a large frame loom placed and held vertically. The smaller frame looms are usually placed against a table or other support in a diagonal position. Mounted on legs a large frame loom is often called either an **upright loom** or a **tapestry loom.**

A variation on the above four-sided frame is an I-frame. It operates in exactly the same manner as a frame loom made with four sides but the two short sides are supported from underneath by a long wooden piece. Finishing nails (headless nails or brads) are used to hold the warp on I-frame looms. Related to the frame loom is the **box loom,** also square or rectangular. More distant relations are the **hoop loom** or the **cardboard loom,** which give other shape possibilities.

For attaching the warp to the frame loom some models have notches filed or sawed into the two short sides. Others have straight rows of finishing nails driven into the two short sides, although the nails can be put into the long sides as well. Frame looms with nails have the warp running back and forth between the nails. The looms with notches can have the warp running between the notches in the same manner as between the nails if the notches are deep enough to hold the warp, or the warp can go around the outside of the frame sides with the **end**s falling into and being spaced by the notches. All frame looms have a **continuous warp** of one sort or another put on them (**b.**). The length of this warp is dictated by whether it simply goes around the nails or notches or whether some provision such as a **warp end bar** is made to extend its length to almost twice the length of the loom. The length of the warp in turn dictates the length of the weaving to be done. The width is controlled by the number of notches or nails used within the width of the frame.

The most common shedding devices are a **shed stick** for one **shed** and a **heddle bar** with **string heddle**s for the other. The second shed can also be picked up by the fingers. Some weavers prefer pulling the **filling** through the warp with a long needle rather than using any sort of shedding device.

More sophisticated two-shed or two-**harness** frame looms can be constructed by making two supports on each long side of the frame loom. These wooden supports should have a notch or shallow groove in each support to hold each harness as it is lifted in the up position. These harnesses are still merely heddle bars with string heddles, but have an aid to keep the shed open that facilitates **selvage** to selvage weaving on a frame loom. The same idea can be extended so that there are four harnesses on a frame loom. This type of frame loom is often found in weaving supply stores.

Warp tension controls on frame looms come in many varieties. The simplest are the **tension stick**s, but for better control many weavers prefer to have a **tensioner**. Beating on a frame loom is done with a **hand beater** or a simple kitchen fork. Butterflies are usually used to carry the filling but a flat or **stick shuttle** or one of the **tapestry tools** can often be used as well. Wooden **needle**s are often used to carry the filling through at the top of a weaving when the shed will no longer open.

Although with patience anything can be woven on a frame loom it is commonly used for tapestry or **free weaving**. In the weaving process a row of **chaining** or **twining** is first put in before any weaving takes place. This is done at the bottom starting edge to space the warp evenly and give a firm beginning edge. Some weavers like to put it in also at the top of the warp. Beyond this, the weaving is dictated by the type of work being done and the variety of frame loom being used. See ill. Also see **butterfly, Salish weaving, tapestry weaving**.

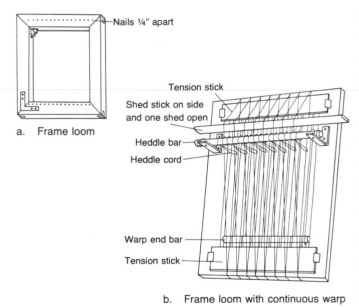

a. Frame loom

b. Frame loom with continuous warp

frame plaiting. Weaving. **Plaiting** with **warp** yarns fixed at both extremities as opposed to the usual type of plaiting in which the warp threads hang free at one end. **Sprang** is an example of the openwork fabric possible with this type of plaiting; **Hopi Indian wedding sash** is an example of a compact, firm fabric that can also be achieved with this method of plaiting.

framework. Kites. (Also called framing.) The basic structure of a kite. The purpose of the framework is to maintain the shape of the kite **covering** in the face of all the elements or forces that act upon it. The framework must be light enough to fly, but strong enough to endure. Most kite frameworks are constructed with a **wood** such as **bamboo, spruce,** or **balsa** (for very lightweight, light-wind kites). Some modern structures, however, require aluminum struts to withstand the stress. Also see **Kites: Construction**.

framework. Puppets. The **skeleton** or body of a **marionette**. Because the body is often a **jointed** figure of square sticks or round **dowels**, it appears to be less a body than a skeleton. In order to **dress the figure** more naturally, the framework is sometimes padded with strips of cloth. Also see **Puppets: Making the Marionette Skeleton**.

framing. Kites. See **framework**.

framing materials. Kites. See **Kites: Tools and Materials**.

framing square. Woodworking. See **squaring tools**.

Franklin, Benjamin. Kites. An American entrepreneur of the eighteenth century who flew a kite on a wire line in a storm to prove that lightning is electricity. To our generation of kite-fliers, his experiment serves as a reminder that a wire is nothing to send to the heavens with a kite attached. Also see **Kites**.

Fraternity of Leatherworkers. Leatherwork. During the middle ages, the Fraternity of Leatherworkers was one of the earliest (1397) of a number of crafts guilds established in a variety of crafts in Spain. The guilds were powerful associations, protecting their members and imposing upon them strict regulations to ensure high-quality workmanship. Soon similar guilds were established in England. Royal charters or licenses were issued to permit people to practice **tanning**. Also see **Leatherwork**.

fray. Puppets. Stitchery. The raveling or loosening of threads at a **raw edge** of **fabric**. To **ravel** a fabric suggests achieving a deliberate effect, whereas fray connotes a condition which occurs from wear. Also see **fringe**.

freeblowing. Glasswork. The process by which glass vessels are formed by hand, without the use of molds, on a **blowing iron**. Freeblown work, also called **off hand**, entails gathering molten glass, called "metal," from a **tank furnace** onto a blowing iron or **punty**. The softened glass is then blown into a bubble or shaped with the use of tools or gravity.

freedom quilt. Quilts. A quilt made for a young man and presented on his twenty-first birthday. A man's labor belonged to his parents until he reached this age. The father then "gave him his time," and he was free to work for himself. The freedom quilt was often made by the girls of his acquaintance. Few of these quilts were made after 1825, when the custom fell from fashion.

Freedom quilts were revived briefly in the 1870s, but with a new meaning. They were **patriotic quilt**s celebrating the centennial, and usually incorporated flags and stars in their designs.

freeform. Stained Glass. Not conforming to a predetermined border. Freeform stained glass pieces include window hangings, window-shade pulls, **mobiles**, and standing sculptures. Also see **fishline, lamination.**

freeform rug. Rugmaking. See **shaped rug.**

free-form shaping. Metalworking. See **raising technique.**

freehand batik. Batik and Tie-dye. A hand-painted **batik** in which no diagram or pattern is used. Either a paint-**brush** or **tjanting** is used to apply the **batiking wax** to fabric in the same approach as in freehand drawing. This method is preferred by many artists who use batik as a painting medium, working spontaneously and directly with the **wax** on fabric.

freehanging warp. Weaving. A **warp** not under tension, i.e., not attached to warp and **cloth beam**s or to the supports of a **frame loom**. One end of a freehanging warp is attached to a bar or cord and the other hangs loose. This type of warp is associated with **Ojibwa weaving** and the **loom** used is called an Ojibwa loom, or a freewarp loom. This loom consists of two wooden side supports between which a cord is strung, from which the warp is suspended. A **warpweighted loom** also has a freehanging warp, but in this case a wooden bar holds the warp on top and it hangs down with weights added to the warp **end**s. This gives some tension but still leaves the ends free for manipulation. Frechanging warps are used in weaving, **twining**, and **chaining** with the work proceeding from the top down. Also see **warp beam.**

free joint. Puppets. A **joint** that allows for movement in any direction. It may be back and forth, up and down, or swivel. Most joints in **marionette**s must be more controlled, for example, by a **hinge joint**. Two **screw eye**s joined together would form a fairly free joint limited only by their set. Also see **swivel joint.**

freestanding stumpwork with wire. Embroidery. A decorative embellishment used in **stumpwork** for freestanding figures, flowers, and ornaments.

Embroider a shape on a fabric (**a.**). Join it to the backing with right sides facing. Leave one section open. Snip

Freestanding stumpwork with wire

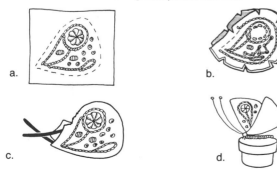

a.

b.

c.

d.

notches in the turnbacks for smooth seams and rounded finished edges (**b.**). Turn it to the right side and insert a loop of wire through the open end. Leave the ends of the wire long enough to use for attaching to the main design (**c.**). Attach by taking the wire through to the wrong side. Blind-stitch the last opening. Add final embroidery details (**d.**). See ill.

freewarp loom. Weaving. See **freehanging warp.**

free weaving. Weaving. Weaving in which the **filling** does not weave **selvage** to selvage, but only in areas desired by the weaver, and in which the **warp end**s are picked up by hand in order to obtain the correct color or pattern placement. Some examples of free weaving are **tapestry, laid-in soumak,** and **knotted pile.** Free weaving can be easily done on a frame, backstrap, or **warpweighted loom,** but can sometimes also be adapted to **harness loom treadling.** Also see **frame loom, backstrap loom.**

freeze. Jewelry. In regard to **solder,** to suddenly cool from a liquid to solid state. For example, when solder is flowing in a **joint** and needs to be pulled along the seam with a **soldering point** or **machinist's scribe,** if the tool has not been heated as well as the metal and the solder, the cold tool will pull the heat from the solder and cause it to "freeze" or stop flowing.

When solder flows into a section where it is not wanted, such as into the mechanism of a catch or a hinge, it is said to lock or freeze the mechanism into position. Also see **capillarity, yellow ochre.**

French antique glass. Stained Glass. This glass is very receptive to stain. The French are best regarded for their blues, browns, and yellowish greens. Their **flashed glass** is often produced in unusual combinations such as red on rose-pink, red on light green, and red on deep blue. Their panels measure 34×36″. Also see **antique glass, striations** and **Stained Glass: Tools and Materials.**

French chalk. Bookbinding. A variety of very soft chalk used by binders to remove grease spots.

French chalk. China and Glass Painting. An inert, white, powdered pigment with a smooth texture, commonly called talc.

French chalk. Crewel. Embroidery. Needlepoint. A white talc useful for cleaning any needlework. Also see **Crewel: Care and Maintenance, Needlepoint: Care and Maintenance.**

French chalk. Quilts. See **tailor's chalk.**

French clay. Découpage. A light-gray powdered clay that is mixed with water or **white glue** to make a claylike mixture for filling **repoussé** areas.

French dot. Crewel. Embroidery. See **French knot.**

French fashion doll. Toys. See **fashion doll.**

French groove. Bookbinding. The French groove is the indentation that runs the length of the cover near the **back edge**. The added space between the **backing** and the **board**s provides more flexibility than a **tight-backed** joint. The gap is usually equal to twice the thickness of the board (about ⅛″). French grooves are used on books that are sewn on tapes to accommodate the extra bulk. If **leather** is used for the backing material, as in **library style binding**, a ¼″ space is allowed for the added thickness. A French groove is formed with **grooving boards** in a press or by drawing a **bone folder** back and forth in the groove and then tying a piece of cord tightly around the book so that it falls in the groove until the binding is dry. Also see **sewing on tapes**.

French knot. Crewel. Embroidery. Needlepoint. Stitchery. (Also called French dot, knotted stitch, twisted knot.) A knot formed by wrapping the thread around the needle and inserting it back into the original needlehole. It can be used as a **filling stitch** over a large area and, depending on the density, can create various textural effects. It is often used as a highlight, especially for animal eyes or the center of a flower. This stitch must be worked on an **embroidery frame**. The thread is wrapped around the needle once only; the size of the knot is determined by the number of threads and the size of the needle used. See ill.

a.   b.   c.   Finished knot

French knot. Rugmaking. Weaving. An embroidery stitch used by rugmakers and weavers to create a texture on top of the work. When making an embroidered rug, French knots are used to simulate a knotted pile effect in scattered areas over or next to a flatter stitch. It creates high and low-relief areas in tapestries as well as rugs and has become popular with weavers involved with **wall hangings** or **needle weaving**.

French knot appliqué. Stitchery. The **appliqué** of one material, usually **felt** (though vinyl, suede cloth, or other nonwoven fabric can be used), to another material through the use of French knots as the attaching **stitch**. The knots add a bright, decorative pattern to the appliqué. When felt is used, the French knots are easily sewn with two to six strands of **embroidery floss**. This method can be worked on pieces of large scale, though French knots are more time-consuming than other **appliqué stitches,** so often a combination of stitches is used.

   French knot appliqué can also be accomplished using yarn for the knots.

French knot on stalks. Crewel. Embroidery. (Also called long stitch.) This stitch is worked in the same manner as the **French knot** except that the needle returns through a second hole about ¼″ from the first instead of being reinserted in the first. This stitch can be done **detached,** over-

lapping, or radiating from a point. It must be worked on an **embroidery frame.** See ill.

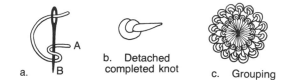

a.   B   b. Detached completed knot   c. Grouping

French laid-in. Weaving. See **laid-in**.

French paring knife. Bookbinding. A tool employed to shave or pare the leather used for book covers. **Paring** facilitates folding, reduces bulk, and allows for easy opening and closing. See ill.

French paring knife

French rand. Basketry. A type of **randing** that is most suitable for **willow** or **hedgerow baskets**. The **stroke** is used for putting on the **siding** and requires one **weaver** per **stake**. A weaver is inserted between each stake after the **upsetting** and worked consecutively in front of one stake and behind the next.

French sand. Metalworking. See **molding sand**.

French seam. Stitchery. A **seam finish** made by first sewing a **plain seam** with wrong sides of the **fabric**s together, so that the **stitch** is taken on the right sides. The **raw edge** of the **seam allowance** is then trimmed to ⅛″, and the material is turned, now with right sides together, and stitched again. This conceals all raw edges, and is a good seam where the back side of the material is exposed to view. See ill. Also see **finishing**.

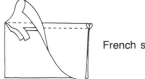

French seam

French skiver. Leatherwork. A tool used for **skiving** even bands of leather to reduce their thickness.

French slew. Basketry. Exactly like **French rand** but using double **weavers**.

French Star. Quilts. A **pieced block** design of an eight-pointed star with a complex pattern of arcs and a diagonally divided circle in the center. Also see **star patterns**.

french stitch. Needlepoint. A group of two long stitches worked over 4 mesh and tacked down in the middle of each with a small slanting stitch. The stitches are arranged in a brick wall fashion. It is excellent as a **filling stitch,** although it tends to work up slowly. See ill. (next page).

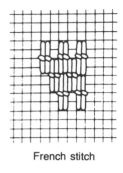

French stitch

French tapestry yarn. Crewel. Embroidery. Needlepoint. See **Broder Medici wool.**

French wool. Crewel. Embroidery. Needlepoint. See **Broder Medici wool.**

fresco. An architectural decoration in which water color is applied to damp plaster walls or ceilings. The water color soaks into the freshly applied plaster and becomes incorporated into the surface. Lime in the plaster mixture can cause bleaching of some pigments, so the **palette** is limited to colors that are not affected, mostly to **earth colors.** Alterations to fresco work are difficult because the plaster has already dried. This dry fresco painting has a tendency to peel off with age.

fretwork. Shell Carving. Carved or pierced patterns of openwork, or work in relief.

Cover the shell with Chinese white and outline the design in India ink. Color the sections to be removed. Fill the shell with melted **beeswax**; after it has solidified, dop it to a board or work surface with additional melted beeswax. With a twist drill, drill all holes necessary to your pattern and all necessary holes to permit the entry of a jeweler's sawblade. Saw out the portions that are to be removed, lubricating the blade with water. Always work from the interior portion of the shell to the outer edges when sawing. Clean the edges of the cuts with a needle file. Polish.

Panels for fretwork should be cut from the edges of the shell, which are thinner and flatter. Also see **needle drill, scratch carving** and **Shell Carving: Shell, Tools and Preparation, Sawing.**

fretwork. Woodworking. See **woodcarving.**

friction brake. Weaving. A brake found on some **floor looms** for releasing unwoven warp. By stepping on a foot pedal at the right side of the loom, the warp is released gradually and in small amounts. The type of friction brake most often found on looms is composed of a steel wire or very narrow band going around the right end of the **warp beam.** One end of the wire is attached to the **back beam** support and the other to a spring. Stepping on the pedal pulls a cord that stretches the spring and releases the brake so the warp can be pulled forward. Because the control over the amount of warp released is very fine, the action is sometimes called "automatic let-off." However, it is not truly automatic because it still depends on the

weaver to activate the release of the warp. Also see **fly shuttle loom, jack-type loom, pawl, ratchet.**

friction spark lighter. Metalworking. See **oxyacetylene welding equipment.**

friction toy. Toys. A **wheeled toy** pulled by a **string** so that the wheels are forced to turn as they are drawn over the floor. This sets a **friction wheel** or type of flywheel in motion to animate some other part of the toy.

In some toys the flywheel was set in motion by **tug-start**ing it with a string, or by ratchet.

friction wheel. Toys. A wheel that is turned when it is in contact with another turning wheel. In **wheeled toy**s, the wheels attached to the **axle** and on which the toy moves would in turn set another wheel in motion. This would then animate or activate some part of the toy.

Friendship Medley. Quilts. The name of a quilt made for a girl upon the announcement of her engagement. Each of her friends made and signed a **block.** The blocks were later **set** and the **assemble**d quilt was **put in.** The group of friends customarily met to do the **quilting.** The **bride's quilt** was also started upon the engagement announcement in addition to the friendship medley. Also see **autograph quilt, friendship quilt.**

friendship quilt. Quilts. A quilt made from a collection of **block**s that were exchanged among friends. Each woman sewed a series of blocks, signed them, and exchanged them with friends. According to custom, when she had enough blocks she **set** and quilted them.

Occasionally each member of a group contributed a block for a quilt that was given to an individual. This also is called a friendship quilt. Someone moving away might receive such a quilt with a name embroidered on each block. This gift quilt was sometimes called a **presentation quilt.** Also see **album quilt, autograph quilt, Friendship Medley, remembrance quilt.**

Friendship Ring. Quilts. See **Dresden Plate.**

friendship tablecloth. Stitchery. A table cover made from a collection of needlework and lace. Like the friendship quilt, the friendship tablecloth is composed of lace parts made and presented by a group of friends. Each piece is contributed by one of the group. Remnants and scraps of special pieces of either artistic or sentimental value are included, along with pieces of needle lace, **edg-ing**s, and doilies. The whole is worked on a large piece of **net,** with the laces added in such a way that a finished edge always overlaps **raw edges.** Sometimes a special medallion or doily is used as the center.

friendship wheel. Spinning. See **double spinning wheel.**

frilled border. Knitting. See **border.**

frilling. Knitting. A frilled or ruffled surface created by welt patterns or by systematic increasing within a group of stitches. The frill is completed when the increased stitches are cast off. Also see **Knitting: Casting Off.**

fringe. Leatherwork. A border or decorative edging in which the leather is cut into narrow strips, leaving an uncut band at the top. The fringe strips may be measured and drawn with a ruler in regular widths, then cut with a knife drawn along a metal edge ruler. Fringe may also be cut with a **scissors** in random widths.

fringe. Macramé. Rugmaking. Weaving. The word "macramé" derives from the Arabic *migramh*, which means "ornamental fringe or braid." Fringe can be knotted by various means—the **gathering knot, overhand knot, accumulating bar,** and **chain stitch.**

In rugmaking a fringe can be composed of unwoven ends of **warp** or **filling** or the frayed-out strands of a **rug backing.** It is then an extension of the yarns making up some portion of the finished article and is called a "self-fringe." This can also occur in **braided rugs** when the braids are joined to form a rectangular rug and the rag strips are left free to form the fringe. A self-fringe occurs in **braiding** and **plaiting** in general.

An applied fringe is an attached group of short pieces of yarn. They are inserted into the hem or other **finished edge** of a piece, usually with the help of a crochet hook, and are held in place with a **lark's head knot. Thrum**s are often used for this purpose. An applied fringe can be woven in strips and then attached. It is woven lengthwise on the **loom,** two strips at a time. At both outside edges the **warp ends** are closely spaced to form the heading by which the fringe will be attached to the piece for which it is meant. Between these edges there are no warp ends so that as the **filling** is put in it remains unwoven in the center. When it is taken off the loom, this unwoven part is cut down the center and becomes the fringe.

In allowing for a fringe, whether self or applied, there should be enough length to easily knot, braid, or otherwise manipulate the fringe if this is desired. A fringe can be left loose, and then **overcasting, hemstitching,** or machine stitching put in to keep the cloth from unraveling. An **overhand knot** is the simplest manner of knotting a fringe and also acts to hold the **filling** in place without additional stitching. Overhand knots can be repeated and worked into an elaborate fringe. Alternate methods are other forms of knotting such as macramé, a twisted or **plied fringe,** a **braided fringe,** or **whipping** (which is especially good for short fringes). A short fringe is about 2″ in length. Fringe can be very long, and in some wall hangings is longer than the worked piece itself.

Fringe can also be made as part of the construction in a **Damascus edge, Philippine edge,** or **Swedish braid** edge. Beads, feathers, bells, or other ornaments can be added to a fringe by slipping the object onto the strand(s), tying on, or **wrapping.** Also see **feather fastening, finishing, pompoms, tassels, weft fringe** and **macramé.**

fringe. Stitchery. The **frayed** edge of a **fabric** where the threads parallel to the cut edge have been pulled away. Also, a decorative trimming or **edging** which consists of a series of **yarns** or cords which extend, like fraying, from the edge of a fabric. Sometimes the yarns of a fringe are tied or knotted to the fabric. Other fringes are sewn on and are twisted, plaited, or worked in macramé.

fringe. Tatting. A decorative border. In tatting, because it is a single-**filament lace,** there are ends from the **thread**s when they are tied off. With planning, they might be used to advantage as fringe in the **design.** Also, many regular **picots** can be made sufficiently long and close together, as to make a fringelike decorative element in the design. A **gauge** is useful in making fringe with picots.

fringe and tassel. Knitting. To form a tassel, wrap yarn around a piece of cardboard the desired length of the tassel until as thick as you like. Thread a strand of yarn through the looped yarn at one end of the cardboard and tie tightly (**a.**). Cut through the looped yarn at the other (bottom) end of the cardboard. Wrap a strand of yarn a few times a little below the top of the tassel, and trim the tassel ends (**b.**).

To make fringe, wind yarn around a flat object slightly more than twice the desired length of the fringe. Cut at one end, leaving yarn doubled over (**c.**). With a crochet hook at the fold (**d.**), pull it through the edge of the work (**e.**). Pull the ends back through the loop (**f.**) and tighten (**g.**). See ill.

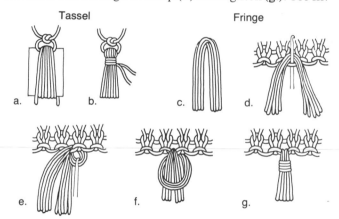

Tassel   Fringe

a.   b.   c.   d.

e.   f.   g.

fringe stitch. Crochet. See **loop stitch.**

fringing. Tincrafting. The cutting of fine strips into the outer edge of **tinplate** to provide a decorative effect. Tin curls naturally as it is cut—the finer the cut, the tighter the curl. Unless tight curls are desired, the thin strips must be handpressed, hammered, or worked with round-nosed **pliers** to flatten them to the desired tightness of curl. Also see **Tincrafting: Cutting the Tin.**

frisket paper. Stenciling. An adhesive-backed paper with a protective backing, used as a **stencil paper,** available from art supply stores in sheets or rolls. After cutting the stencil design the protective backing film is peeled away and the frisket is adhered to the surface to be decorated. Frisket paper is also available as a paper only, without the adhesive backing, and this must be coated with rubber cement before applying it to the surface to be decorated. Also see **Stenciling: Tools and Materials.**

frit. Ceramics. A partial or complete **glaze** that is melted and reground to eliminate the toxicity of lead or the solubility of **borax** and **soda ash.** Fritting improves glaze suspension, color dispersion, and eliminates the lump quality of borax in crystalline, copper red, and similar glazes. Also see **copper carbonate, lead silicate, raw glaze, white lead.**

frit. China and Glass Painting. A colorless powdered glass, similar to **flux** but different in formula, used in preparing color for decorating glass.

frit. Enameling. (Also called **flux.**) The glassy constituents of **enamel;** also, chunks of unground enamels.

Frit consists of silica (sand), borax, lead, and soda or potash. Lead, potash, and soda contribute brilliance. The amount of lead in the fruit determines its hardness. Higher temperatures are required for fusing hard enamels. Borax aids the union of the frit with the **metal oxide** coloring of the enamel, makes the enamel softer, and reduces its elasticity. Potash and soda are alkalis added to make the frit elastic so that it will adhere to the **metal** when fired and cooled.

Frobel, Ernest. Toys. See **Toys.**

frog. Stitchery. A fastener which consists of a loop made of braid or cord which is used in place of a buttonhole and a twisted or knotted piece which is used in place of a button.

front. Basketry. The side of the **basket** facing the worker.

front apron bar. Weaving. See **apron, apron bar.**

front beam. Weaving. See **breast beam.**

front bridge. Puppets. A **bridge** at the front of the **marionette stage.** The top of the front bridge provides a bar from which the **proscenium curtain**s are hung. Also see **Puppets: The Puppet Stage.**

front of knitting. Knitting. See **right side.**

frosting. Glasswork. See **etching.**

frost marks. Candlemaking. Cloudy, frostlike marks that appear on the sides of molded candles if the wax was poured at too low a **temperature** or if the mold was not heated prior to pouring. Usually frost marks can be polished away with a nylon stocking. If polishing fails to correct the problem a **wax bath** can be used. Also see **Candlemaking: Possible Flaws in Candles.**

Frozen Charlotte. Toys. (Also called all-in-one doll, pillar doll.) A doll manufactured shortly after the middle 1800s that had no movable limbs. The head, arms, and legs were all permanently positioned, and it usually had molded hair or a bonnet. The term is now used to refer to any single-piece doll of no movable parts; the original Frozen Charlottes were made of **Parian.**

There are varying theories regarding the origin of the Frozen Charlotte doll. One is that she was derived from a folk ballad of the 1830s. Another places her origin in 1840, based on a newspaper account in that year of a young woman who froze during a sleigh ride to a New Year's Eve ball. Vanity apparently prevented her from wrapping a blanket around her silken ball gown. The ballad of Fair Charlotte or Frozen Charlotte was sung in at least thirty variations, and the doll was made—or at least named—for the ill-fated and thinly clad maiden. Also see **all-bisque, bisque doll.**

fruit designs. Quilts. Any of numerous **blocks** with **appliqué** designs based on fruits. They range from the exotic pomegranate and pineapple to the love apple, or tomato. Cherries, grapes, and melons spill profusely on **quilt tops.** Variations from one **appliqué quilt** to the next are so frequent that seldom are any two appliqué quilts identical in shapes, **set,** or use of color. They do not fall neatly into categories but remain clearly individual.

frying. Stained Glass. Tiny pinholes that develop in glass paint during firing. It is usually caused by an excess of **gum arabic** in the paint formula. Also see **painting on glass.**

fugitive color. Batik and Tie-dye. Transient or fading **dye** color. A fugitive color will fade on exposure to light or sun.

fugitive dye. Dyeing. A color that is uncertain as to fastness and liable to fade in sunlight or bleed during washing. Indigo, used for denim, is a prime example; it is valued for this very quality. Also see **colorfast.**

fulgurite. Glasswork. A naturally occurring black glass that is formed when sand or any rocky substance has been fused or vitrified by a stroke of lightning.

full. Stained Glass. See **full and slack.**

full and slack. Stained Glass. These terms are used to denote inaccuracy in **cutting glass** which results in failure of the **panel** to match the working drawing after **glazing.** Full refers to cutting the pieces of glass so that the **panel** is too large for the working drawing. Slack is the opposite situation, in which the panel is too small for the working drawing.

full binding. Bookbinding. (Also called whole binding.) A binding entirely of leather.

full cloth. Bookbinding. An entirely cloth cover.

fuller. Metalworking. See **blacksmithing tools.**

fullering. Metalworking. See **blacksmithing techniques.**

Fuller's earth. Weaving. See **fulling.**

full gilt. Bookbinding. A book with all edges gilded.

full grain. Leatherwork. See **top grain.**

fulling. Weaving. A **finishing** process of shrinking and thickening woven wool fabrics through moisture, heat, and agitation. The fabric is placed in warm, soapy water and is beaten or twisted to make the fabric "felt." When the desired thickness has been achieved, it is rinsed in cold water. Fulling or milling, which increases the weight of a cloth and can obscure its weave, is not true **felting.** Felting can be a spontaneous liability, whereas fulling is planned and has a desirable effect. The original agitation was produced by wooded mallets or paddles. Now, commercially, the cloth to be fulled is pressed between hot cylinders. Home fulling is still done by foot in the outlying areas of some countries. The cloth is stomped or kicked about in a soapy bath. Fulling was known and practiced by the ancient Romans who in the eleventh century had fulling mills. By the thirteenth century fulling mills were common throughout Europe, and in the United States fulling was the first process in the making of wool fabrics to be mechanized. Fuller's earth, a claylike mineral, was mined and exported from England to the United States in the nineteenth century. It helped to absorb the last grease in the wool and then itself had to be rinsed out. Certain fabrics need more fulling than others, so the amount of water used and the length of time needed for felting and shrinking has to be controlled. A weaver has to anticipate fulling and must weave his fabric wider and longer if fulling is to take place. The fabric should be woven so it will not be stiff and boardlike after fulling, but will retain its softness and pliancy.

full pass. Weaving. See **tapestry.**

full-size. Stained Glass. A term in referring to the full dimensions of the cartoon, including the two sides, the top, and the bottom of the drawing. The daylight measurement is the visible part of the cartoon inside the edge formed by the **lead came.**

full turn. Rugmaking. Weaving. A term applied to a technique of **weft twining** in which a full twist or turn is made by the two wefts between each **warp end** or groups of warp ends. This results in one weft always going over the warp end and the other always going under. If two colors are used a solid line of one color will result. Full turn twining also makes for a very firm fabric and gives a sturdy means by which a warp can be spaced evenly on a **frame loom.** See ill.

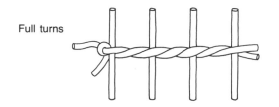

Full turns

fuming. Enameling. A technique of treating an enamel surface with chemicals while it is still hot from firing to produce an iridescent effect.

Stannic chloride and silver nitrate crystals are dissolved in water and sprayed onto the piece just as the heat glow is fading. The chemicals react with the **metal oxide** (the coloring agent in the enamel), releasing fumes that are dangerous to breathe. Also see **raku** and **Enameling: Basic Operations.**

fuming muffle. Glasswork. A kind of metal cabinet used to contain **glasswork** pieces while they are exposed to an atmosphere of stannous chloride fumes. Fumes from stannous chloride attack the surface of glass and allow it to absorb some parts of the spectrum, making the glass iridescent.

funk. A style of work which tends to use, borrow, or appropriate objects and designs from what is popular and available. "Pop" art may draw upon these themes, but funk art often incorporates them. Anything considered to be poor design or bad taste can appropriately be used in funk art. Thus a satin "Sweetheart" **pillow** emblazoned with the name of an army base might be sewn onto a piece of clothing to give it a funky quality. Old transfer patterns of stereotyped subjects are favorites of stitchers who work in this area. Funk takes the familiar out of context, and much of its humor lies in this change, since it deprives the original object of its function or sense. The funk object pokes fun at what our society may regard in an almost reverent fashion. In **soft sculpture**, everyday objects are constructed in three-dimensional **stuff**ed forms, with refrigerators, automobiles, canned foods and commercially packaged boxes among the most often represented. Even settings, such as a cottage in the woods, or rain clouds and rainbows are favorite subjects of soft sculptors.

funk pottery. Ceramics. A term for the numerous, colorful, and nonfunctional ceramic objects produced in America. Funk pottery began in the 1960s as a commentary on the society and the objects in it.

funny-paper toy. Toys. See **comic-strip toy.**

fur rug. Rugmaking. Rugs using fur in cut, woven strips, crocheted into or appliquéd on a background or done as patchwork. It is assumed that the fur is scrap pieces or a cut-up old coat. The fur should be clean and not dried out. The fur is cut on the reverse side (fur side down) using a sharp razor blade to cut the skin only and not the fur. The cut pieces or strips can be sewn together using a fine needle and nylon or silk thread, working in small **lacing stitch**es. They should not be overlapping when joining, but sewn side by side or end to end. A paper pattern should be used for the pieces; the strips can be measured out with a ruler and marked with chalk.

In weaving, a strong and compatible (in color and texture) **warp** should be used. The fur must be brushed so that it stands out between and over the warp ends, otherwise its texture and beauty will be closed into the **shed.** In crochet, a **filet mesh** is made first and then the fur strips are woven into it. As in weaving, care must be taken that the fur hairs are not held down by the mesh, but brought to the surface above the mesh. In both weaving and crochet, it is wiser to use long-haired furs because flat furs would not stand out against the warp or the filet mesh. Also, long-haired furs roll over on themselves so that the cut edges are concealed. The ends of the fur strips at the selvage should be tapered and tucked back in unobtrusively.

In appliquéing the fur pieces, the background material should be firm, such as heavy felt. Instead of sewing the pieces to the background, there are certain fabric glues available that work just as well. Any kind of fur can be used and often it is quite attractive to mix various furs; fake fur can also be used instead of the real thing. Also see **appliquéd rug, rug weaving.**

fused glass. Stained Glass. See **fused glass technique.**

fused glass technique. Stained Glass. One of the methods for bringing about a change in the color of stained glass. It should not be confused with the **polyester resin technique** of cementing bits and pieces of glass together in a composition.

In this method of changing the color of the glass, pieces of glass are fused together at a temperature several hundred degrees higher than the normal firing temperature for stained glass. Tests should be made to determine the exact glass bending temperature. In general, **antique glass** fuses at 1300° F and **machine-made glass** fuses at 1400° F.

Glass can be fused at random or small pieces can be fused onto a ¼" piece of **plate glass** that has already been cut to a desired shape. Both methods are plagued by cracking and splits because of the varying rates of expansion.

fusible thermoplastic. Plastics. Plastics formed by being heated in an oven at about 350° F until it softens, fuses, and sometimes expands. Fusible thermoplastic decomposes at temperatures above 400° F. After cooling, it is easily machined and sanded. Two common craft forms are cooking pellets (used in molds) and mosaic tiles.

fusing. Jewelry. The joining of two or more pieces of metal by heating without the use of solder. **Karat** gold and sterling **silver** fuse beautifully, but copper crystallizes. Tests should be made with other metals. The metal may or may not be **flux**ed. The two ways cause fusing at different speeds and produce different effects when the surface of the metal melts. All surfaces of the metals to be fused are heated with a **gas-air torch** until they melt and interpenetrate, and then the heat is withdrawn. Any number of pieces may be added on in this manner. Care must be taken not to overheat the metal or it will collapse completely and withdraw upon itself into a blob. **Pickle. File** to add form and textural contrast if desired. **Solder** on **findings** if required. Add **liver of sulfur** to oxidize if desired. Buff or give **Swedish finish.**

Wire may be fused, but the heat should be applied carefully as wire will melt and collapse quickly. However, since wire does melt quickly, it can be utilized as an embellishment technique for a raised linear, almost drawing like effect. By melting wire—fluxing the wire will help control its melting—on a **baseplate** of metal, the surface of the baseplate will melt and the wire will fuse to the surface.

When fusing sterling silver, the copper content is burned out, producing a gray-black surface. Pickle to expose an extremely thin deposit of fine silver. The surface will be a very dull white.

fustic. Batik and Tie-dye. Dyeing. A yellow dye obtained from the wood of a tree known as "dyer's mulberry" because the tree is a member of the mulberry family. Fustic was native to Brazil and some West Indian islands and was introduced into Europe after the mid-seventeenth century. The knotty parts of the wood are especially good as a source of the **dyestuff.** Because the yellow obtained from this wood was liable to turn brown with exposure to light, the dyestuff was used primarily as bottoming in **top-dyeing** to get various greens. While no **mordant** is necessary for fustic, mordants do make the color more fast. The addition of **alum** gives a dull yellow; **chrome,** a golden yellow; and **tin,** a bright yellow, with lesser **colorfastness** properties. Fustic is available in chip form or as extract.

fuzz. Weaving. See **pilling.**

g

gadget tie-dye. Batik and Tie-dye. The use of various devices in the **tie-dye** process. Any available gadget that is suitable for holding or blocking the fabric can be used. Some gadgets commonly used are clothespins, safety pins, plastic bags, nets, nylon stockings, **bulldog clip**s, pipe cleaners, and **plastic clip peg**s. Also see **bundle tie-dye.**

gaffer. Glasswork. The head of a commercial glassblowing team or **shop.** The team of five people consists of the gaffer, or master glassblower, who sits in the **glassworker's chair** and directs the operations of the servitor, who makes the **gather** in the furnace; the blower, who starts the **parison;** the bit gatherer, who gathers small gobs of glass for the application of handles, legs, feet, knobs, etc.; and the taker-in, who carries the finished piece to the **lehr** for controlled cooling.

Galla Placidia. Mosaics. The sister of Honorius, who, following his death, for a time lavishly governed the Roman Empire from its relatively new capital in **Ravenna.** The mid-fifth-century mausoleum built in her honor is believed to be the oldest structure in Ravenna. The **mosaics** in the mausoleum are considered to be among the finest examples of Byzantine art. Also see **Mosaics.**

gallery wire. Jewelry. Flat, square, or round wire that has had a pattern stamped on it with special punches or **repoussé tools.** Gallery wire can be used as a decorative element in combination with **fabrication** techniques such as **appliqué.** In making gallery wire, a fairly heavy **gauge** is used, generally not less than 16-gauge. To create a uniform pattern, round wire should be slightly flattened so that it will not roll, causing the pattern to twist as it is worked. This can be done by **forging** or by running the wire through a **rolling mill.** For deep impressions in the metal, small punches should be used to give a design or pattern of ⅛″ or less. It is important to use a heavy hammer; a **ball-peen hammer** would work well and ensure a good impression. Positioning of the punch before each strike is important if you are to maintain a constant pattern. If the punch is wider than the wire, it can change the outer contour of the wire to look like small balls or ovals soldered together, or many other configurations, depending on the spacing and groupings between punch marks and on changes in the rotation of the punch.

gallows. Puppets. Any device over the acting area to which the **puppet control** can be attached, leaving the **puppeteer's** hands free. There is a hook at the top of the **control bar** that can be attached to a hook on the gallows.

galvanized. Metalworking. Sheet **mild steel** covered with a coating of **zinc** to protect it from rusting. This protective coating melts if the pieces of metal are welded or soldered after the metal is galvanized. Provide adequate ventilation when **welding** galvanized metal because the zinc oxide fumes are toxic. To make galvannealed metal, the galvanized sheet is kept hot longer so that the zinc mixes more thoroughly with the steel to give it additional surface protection.

galvanized steel. Stained Glass. A metal used in modern stained-glass windows for bracing. Steel cannot be soldered unless it is coated with zinc. Pieces of galvanized steel can also be cut for use as crossbars in stained-glass lanterns. They support the socket from below and the hanging ring from above. Also see **banding, saddle bar.**

galvanized wire. Puppets. A zinc-coated nonrusting wire used on the **control bar** for **marionette**s. Also see **arm bar.**

galvannealed. Metalworking. See **galvanized.**

gamboge. Stained Glass. A resin derived from an Asiatic tree that yields a yellow pigment. Also see **staining.**

game. Toys. An amusement or play, usually competitive, in which set rules are followed and for which there may or may not be special equipment. The games that are related to toys are often **board game**s, in contrast to activity games such as softball or fox-and-geese. Most craftspeople who produce handmade games are as concerned with the design of both tactile and visual qualities as with the activity itself. Toss games, board games, chessmen, and checkerboards are games that appeal particularly to craftspeople. Also see **Toys: Games and Other Toys.**

game board. Toys. A flat sheet of rigid material on which **game**s are played. Wood and **cardboard** are the most commonly used materials. Some games require particular patterns on the board, as do backgammon and Monopoly. The checkerboard, used for both chess and checkers, has probably been made in greater variety than any other board. Inlaid wood, ceramic, needlepoint, appliqué, leather, collage, and painted boards are among those handmade by craftspeople.

gamps. Weaving. A colloquial term for a wide **sampler blanket.** It comes from the multicolored umbrella of Charles Dickens's character Sairey Gamp.

ganging. Jewelry. Placing two or more wax models in the same **flask** for simultaneous **burnout** and subsequent **casting.** Also see **centrifugal casting.**

garbo. Shell Carving. See **Shell Carving: Cameo Carving.**

Garden Island. Quilts. See **Hawaiian quilt.**

garden wreath. Quilts. See **wreath patterns.**

Garfield monument. Quilts. A **block** design that depicts Garfield's tomb, using **appliqué** as the decorative method. It was designed to honor President Garfield after his assassination. Also see **presidents' quilt.**

garnet. Gemcutting. A group of several silicate minerals **crystal**lized in the isometric system that have single **refraction** and granular to uneven **fracture.** Garnets that are transparent to cloudy are cut into **facet**ed gems.

Andradite (also called demantoid) is a green-colored garnet composed of calcium, iron, and aluminum silicates. It has a **hardness** of 6½, a **specific gravity** of 3.83–3.85, a refractive index of 1.888, and a vitreous to greasy **luster.** Its color varies from yellow-green to deep green. Andradite is easily decomposed by acids.

Spessartite is a warm yellow-red garnet composed of magnesium aluminum silicates. It has a hardness of 7, a specific gravity of 4–4.3, and a refractive index of 1.8.

Grossularite (also called Transvaal jade) is composed of calcium and aluminum silicates with a brown-green color, a hardness of 7–7¼, a specific gravity of 3.6–3.67, and a refractive index of 1.744. Grossularite is **cabochon** cut. Avoid overheating during **sanding** and **polishing** operations.

Pyrope is a manganese, iron, calcium, chrome, and aluminum silicate with rich blood-red color tinged with yellow. It has hardness of 7¼, specific gravity of 3.7–3.8, and a refractive index of 1.747.

Almandine (also called carbuncle) is a deep violet-red garnet composed of magnesium, manganese, iron, calcium, chromium, and aluminum silicates, with a hardness of 7¼, a specific gravity of 3.84, a refractive index of 1.8, and vitreous luster. Almandine is cut into cabochons and sometimes exhibits a chatoyant four-rayed star. Both types are brittle and should not be overheated when sanding and polishing.

Hessonite (also called essonite) is a yellow-red garnet composed of iron, magnesium, and aluminum silicates, with hardness of 7½, specific gravity of 3.67, refractive index of 1.74 and vitreous to resinous luster.

Uvarovite is green, with a hardness of 7½, a specific gravity of 3.77, and a refractive index of 1.87.

Rhodolite is rose-red garnet with specific gravity of 3.8 and refractive index of 1.75. It combines qualities of pyrope and almandine garnets.

Melanite is a black garnet used for mourning jewelry.

Yttrium aluminum garnet (also called Yag) is a synthetic gem faceting material with hardness of 8½, specific gravity of 4.6, and a refractive index of 1.83. It is available transparent and colored yellow, pink, lavender, blue, and green.

Transparent garnets with pale color are faceted with main crown facets at an angle of 37° and pavillion facets at 42°. Dark-colored stones are cut with crown mains at 43° and pavillion mains at 40°.

Impure garnet is crushed for use as an **abrasive** on coated papers. Gemmy masses are available for **tumbling.** Also see **Gemcutting: Application of Gems.**

garnet. Metalworking. See **abrasive.**

garnet paper. Metalworking. See **abrasive.**

garnet sandpaper. Woodworking. See **abrasive.**

Garrick's bend. Macramé. See **Josephine knot.**

garter stitch. Knitting. The easiest of all knitting stitches, the garter stitch consists of **plain knitting** every row of your pattern. For the circular knitting version of this, **knit** one row and then **purl** the next. The garter stitch is used most often on children's clothing, babies' bonnets, collars, and socks. See ill. Also see **Knitting: Stitches and Patterns.**

Garter stitch

gas-air torch. Jewelry. (Also called air-gas torch.) A heat source for **soldering** and **annealing** that consists of a head with two adjustable valves attached to a natural or manufactured gas source and an air source. The torch head is designed specifically for either natural or manufactured gas and a variety of tips may be used to control the size of the **flame.** The adjustable valves are used to control the proportion of gas to air. Oxygen also is used with gas instead of compressed air, and also requires a specific head. Gas-air torches are easily lit with a pilot flame from an alcohol lamp or with a friction flint spark lighter; these sources of ignition require the use of only one hand. Have the igniter in your hand before opening the gas valve. Allow a small amount of gas to escape before lighting the torch. A soft yellow flame indicates too much gas and not enough air. This will leave soot deposits on the metal. An intense, blue, pointy flame indicates too much air or oxygen and not enough gas. When extinguishing a gas-air torch, turn the air off first and the gas second.

gas kiln. Ceramics. A type of **kiln** fired by fuel and air at the point of the burner. It is a very practical kiln if gas is readily available, though secondary air control is essential and large flues are needed. Because both **reduction** and oxidation firing can be performed with this type of kiln, it is the favorite of most potters. See ill.

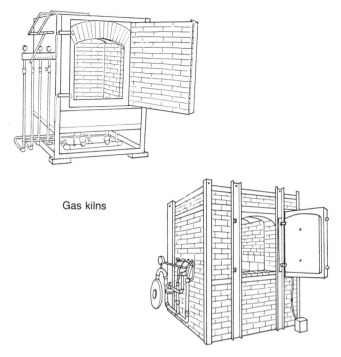

Gas kilns

gas kiln. Stained Glass. See **kiln.**

gas metal-arc welding. Metalworking. See **welding.**

gas tungsten-arc welding. Metalworking. See **welding.**

gas welding. Metalworking. See **welding.**

gate. Metalworking. See **gating system.**

gate. Plastics. The opening in a **mold** through which the **casting** material is poured or forced into the mold.

gate cutter. Metalworking. See **sandcasting molding equipment.**

gate pin. Metalworking. See **sandcasting molding equipment.**

gather. Batik and Tie-dye. To draw together a fabric by taking short stitches or folds and compressing or pulling them tight. Gathers are used in **tie-dye** to create patterns that follow the line of the gathering stitch or that run parallel to the **binding** used over the fabric.

gather. Bookbinding. See **collate.**

gather. Glasswork. (Also called gob.) The mass of molten glass, or **metal,** that is twisted onto the end of the **blowing iron,** or **punty,** and taken from the furnace. A gather on the blowing iron is best taken "off the end," pulling and rotating the iron in the metal so that the opening in the end of the iron does not become clogged with glass.

gather. Stitchery. To draw fullness into a **fabric,** usually by taking small **stitches** which are then pulled tight. Various

effects can be achieved according to the size, direction, and number of rows of the stitches. Gathers are frequently used in developing three-dimensional shapes in **stuffed fabric** forms and to add rich texture in **wall hangings** or in clothing.

gathered quilting. Quilts. Stitchery. A method of adding a richly textured area to the surface of a panel, quilt, or clothing. It is not actually **quilting,** but because it looks filled or padded it is referred to as such.

In this process an area to be textured is marked. It may be, for example, a circle, and its outline drawn on the **backing** material. Then another circle, almost twice that size, is drawn onto a different piece of fabric and cut out. The edge is turned under or hemmed, and the large circle is sewn, or **appliqué**d, to the small circular outline. The edge has to be **gather**ed to make the large circle fit, and it will then be **slip-stitch**ed into place. The gathered circle, shaped like an inverted bowl, is attached to the backing fabric. The bowl shape is pressed flat with the hand, and a small **tack**ing stitch or **catch stitch** is used to hold it in place. Small folds, gathers, and puckers will texture the entire area of the circle, and as the material puckers the catch stitches will be hidden from view.

Any simple shape can be used for gathered quilting. The shapes may have folds or tucks of more uniform pattern or may be completely random. The areas of gathered quilting are often used on **blocks** of equal size. For example, circles of the gathered material may be sewn to hexagons, which are then joined to make an **all-over pattern.**

gathering. Knitting. Gathering creates a bloused or softly puckered effect. It is done by increasing or decreasing the **stitch**es in even number, across the **row.** Gathering is often done at the waist or at the sleeve cuffs of a garment. The number of stitches increased or decreased is usually half or a third of the initial number of stitches, and is specified by the pattern. Also see **Knitting: Increasing, Decreasing.**

gathering knot. Macramé. (Also called collecting knot.) A knot frequently used in **finishing** a piece of macramé. The end result is a **fringe**d tassel.

To make this knot, the **cord**s are separated into equal groups (four if **square knot**s were worked most recently) and then the groups are separated into three. Either the left or right cord group is brought around the others horizontally and then looped through itself, pulling all three cord groups together securely to form a knot. See ill.

Gathering knot

gating. Metalworking. See **gating system.**

gating. Weaving. Adjusting a loom after it has been threaded and the **warp** tied onto the front **apron bar.** Gating includes checking the **heddles** to see that they are properly spaced and in a vertical position; that the warp in the **reed** is in the center of the **beater** and the reed set firmly in the beater so that it cannot slide back and forth; that the **tie-up** ties are of equal length so that the lower part of the **shed** is perfectly flat; and that the shed opening is perfectly clear and that there are no quickly apparent **sleying** errors. In addition, on a **counterbalanced loom** the **harness**es must be balanced so that they will all hang at the same level, and straightened so that they hang horizontally at the correct height (which is having the **heddle eye** in a straight line with a point midway between the top and bottom of the reed). This gating is done by adjusting the cords around the harness **rollers** and **pulleys** from which the harnesses are suspended. Some weavers include weaving the **heading** as part of gating because some **threading** and sleying mistakes can be seen in the heading and corrected before beginning to weave on the cloth proper.

gating system. Metalworking. (Also called gating.) The system of cavities in a **mold,** including the **pouring basin, vents, sprues,** and **runners,** through which the molten metal runs into the mold, and into which gases and steam escape during casting. See ill.

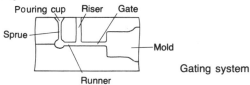

Gating system

Gaudí, Antonio (1852–1926). Mosaics. A Catalan architect, craftsperson, early exponent of **Art Nouveau,** and restorer of faith in the grandeur and brilliant potential of the **mosaic** craft. He utilized **mosaics** as an integral part of his structures and brought to the form a baroque excitement and inventive originality that raised the craft from the setback it had suffered during the Italian Renaissance. The **Sagrada Familia** church in Barcelona, begun by Gaudí in 1883, has been praised as one of the most important buildings of our time, and it certainly is one of the finest examples of mosaic ingenuity since the time of the Byzantine Empire.

gauffered edge. Bookbinding. A book edge decoration with a design, frequently in color, tooled over a gilded edge.

gauge. Crochet. Gauge refers to the number of stitches (horizontally) and the number of rows (vertically) to be made in a square inch of crochet. It is essential that your gauge for a particular piece of crochet match that specified by the pattern. Gauge varies widely depending upon the type of **yarn,** the size of the **crochet hook,** and your own particular style of crocheting (some crocheters produce much tighter crochet than others). Any deviation from the stated gauge will directly affect the size and proportions of the finished object. To determine gauge, use the suggested size of hook and yarn to be used to make the particular object; crochet a sample of single crochet approximately 4″ × 4″. Dampen this sample and press it into shape, or

follow the actual **blocking** procedure, and then count the number of stitches and the number of rows worked in one square inch. If you have more stitches and rows than the pattern calls for, use a hook one size larger; if you have less, try a smaller hook.

gauge. Jewelry. The thickness of metals. There are many gauge systems used throughout the world. In the United States the B & S (Brown & Sharpe) gauge is the standard for **nonferrous** sheet metal and wire. It is also called the American Standard Gauge, or American Wire Gauge (AWG). The United States Standard Gauge (USSG) is used for measuring steel plate and wire. Also see **gauge wheel.**

gauge. Knitting. The number of stitches per inch specified by a pattern. To gauge knitting, knit a sample of at least two pattern repeats wide and two pattern repeats long, or a sample approximately four inches square. Dampen and block the knitting sample, and then use a ruler to measure the number of stitches per inch horizontally, and the number of rows per inch vertically. Check these two figures against the gauge specified at the beginning of the knitting pattern. If the gauge figures do not match exactly, adjustments must be made. Use knitting needles one size larger if the gauge of knitting sample is larger than the number specified in the pattern gauge. Use needles one size smaller if the knitting sample is less than the pattern gauge. Knit a sample with these new needles, block, and check gauge before beginning. See ill. Also see **blocking.**

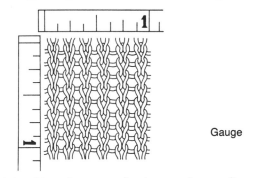

Gauge

gauge. Metalworking. A term referring to the grading of sheet metals less than ⅛″ thick. The higher the gauge number, the thinner the metal. Metal ⅛″ thick is 11 gauge, metal 1/16″ thick is 16 gauge, 1/32″ thick is 21 gauge, etc.

Gauge is also a name for a part of the gas **regulator** in **oxyacetylene welding equipment.** Also see **sheet metal gauge.**

gauge. Rugmaking. Weaving. A wooden or cardboard device used to measure the **pile** height of a **Ghiordes knot** for latch-hooked, needleworked, or woven rugs. The gauges, usually homemade, are of two types. One is for **rya,** or long pile, in which the yarn is precut and later knotted to a backing or the **warp.** Precutting enables the worker to mix a variety of yarns (changing with every knot if desired), to use small scraps or leftover yarns, and to obtain an uneven, shaggy look. There is available in stores a yarn cutter with a rotating handle that slices the yarn into uniform 2½″ lengths. This length gives a pile of ¾–1″, with the rest of the yarn taken up in the knot; this is the height usually seen in latch-hooked rugs. For a higher pile the gauge must be made at home out of wood or cardboard. If wood is used it should be ¼″ thick with grooves cut into the two widthwise sides so that a mat knife or scissors can cut through the yarn. The cardboard gauge is made of two pieces of sturdy cardboard with cardboard filler between to keep the two pieces approximately ¼″ apart. The cardboard is taped together on the lengthwise sides with the two widthwise sides left open for the cutting action. The width of a rya gauge is up to the individual. The length is twice the desired pile height plus 1″ take-up for the knot. The yarn is wound around the gauge in either a uniform manner (which makes every cut piece exactly the same size) or in a random way with the yarn falling where it will (rendering cut pieces of varying lengths for a more shaggy texture to the rug). When enough yarn is wound, a rubber band is placed around the middle section of the wound yarn and cut at the top and bottom widthwise sides (**a.**). There is another homemade gauge, in which the length is once the pile height plus 1″ for the knot. The wound yarn is cut on only one side of this gauge, giving half the amount that is wound and cut on a longer gauge.

The second type of gauge is for short pile made directly on the backing or warp and either cut or left as **loop pile.** Short pile is difficult to knot with precut lengths, so the yarn for the pile is in long, continuous lengths carried either by a needle for needleworked rugs or in **butterfly** form for woven rugs. The yarn knots around the backing or warp, goes over the gauge and then back to make the next knot and pile loop, going on in this manner until the length of yarn is finished. These pile gauges or guides can be homemade of wood or cardboard. They are usually of short lengths (about 12″) so that as one area is knotted, the gauge is pushed on to the next area in line. The height of the gauge is exactly that of the desired pile, which can be as short as ½″. There is a slit on the top side so that a mat knife or scissors can cut through the yarn. If wood is used, the wood should be cut in a V- or U-shape instead of square-cornered because the latter lengthens the pile height (**b.**). For short spaces, the hand or fingers can be used as a gauge. For long rows a **flossa rod** can be bought (**c.**). See ill. Also see **knotted rugs, pile, rug backing.**

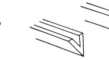

a. Gauge for precutting yarn for rya or long pile

b. V- or U-shaped wooden pile gauges

c. Homemade pile gauge (flossa rod) here used in making Ghiordes knots on a woven background

gauge. Stained Glass. The form in which wire or metal is graded. The higher the gauge number, the thinner the metal or wire.

gauge. Tatting. A tool over which the thread is placed to check the uniformity of size. It is especially useful in making **fringe** and **picot**s.

A gauge may be any suitable tool, such as firm cardboard or a ruler.

To measure a large picot, place a gauge of the desired width between the **loop thread** and the **knot bearer** before the **double stitch** is made to close the picot.

gauge. Woodworking. A tool used to measure or control the depth and angle of a mark, hole, or cut.

A bit gauge (also called bit stop, depth gauge, drill stop) is a round stop screwed or clamped over a **drill bit** to control the depth of the hole drilled. To use a bit gauge, measure and mark the desired depth of cut on your drill bit. Slip the bit gauge over the drill bit to the desired mark and secure. Proceed to drill, stopping when the gauge hits the surface of the wood. See ill. Also see **marking tools.**

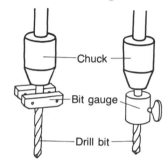

Chuck

Bit gauge

Drill bit

gauge bar. Rugmaking. Weaving. See **flossa rod.**

gauge wheel. Jewelry. A wheel-shaped or rectangular metal plate used for measuring the thickness of sheet metal and the diameter of wire. The perimeter of the wheel is notched with a series of graduated slots that are in thousandths of an inch. At the end of each notch, which is numbered to indicate its **gauge,** is a cut-out circular form; the circle is a manufacturing device and has nothing to do with measuring gauge.

To check the gauge of a piece of metal, insert the edge of the metal into the smallest slot into which it fits tightly. If it seems too tight to fit into the slot, do not force it but rather go to the next larger slot. Metals are not always milled precisely and can be slightly curved along the edge or have a small **burr** from cutting. Try the gauge at more than one point on the edge of the sheet. One side of the B & S gauge wheel is marked in the gauge number, the opposite side is marked in its equivalent in decimals. See ill.

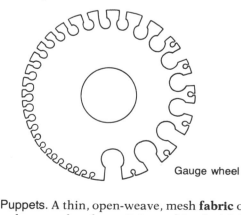

Gauge wheel

gauze. Puppets. A thin, open-weave, mesh **fabric** of **cotton** used to make gauze bandages. It is combined with layers of paper in **papier-mâché** projects to add thickness and strength without weight. Also see **Puppets: Making the Puppet Head.**

gauze. Stitchery. See **cheesecloth.**

gauze weave. Weaving. A technique that takes the **warp** yarns away from their normal parallel position to each other and crosses or half-twists them. These twists are secured by the **filling** yarn and the crossed elements recross each other to go back to their original positions. Because the twist performed is only a half-twist, there is no **twining** in a gauze weave and it is still basically an interlacing action between warp and filling, with the half-twist worked between every **pick** of filling and giving the fabric an open, airy look. The warp **end**s are crossed either in pairs or groups, with the crossing and twist being manipulated by the fingers or with the help of a crochet hook, **batten,** or **pick-up stick,** or through the use of **doup**s or beads.

Although the term **leno** tends to be used interchangeably with "gauze weave," there is a difference in that leno is combined with **plain weave,** but a gauze weave is entirely open and twisted, with no areas of plain weave. There is also a tendency to catalogue all **openwork technique** as gauze weaves, but in many openwork weaves there is no crossing or twisting of warp threads at all. The word "gauze" by itself has become a general term that denotes any light, thin, airy, transparent fabric.

The simplest gauze weave is with the warp yarns all crossed in pairs—that is, alternate warp threads are drawn sidewise and under their neighboring warp threads, thus forming the pair, and then the **shed** is opened for the filling to go through. A variation can be done so that two warp ends twist with another two, as well as variations on the direction, position, and extent of the twist. More complex gauze structures change the twisting pattern even more in that larger groups are used in the twisting and, within the group, the twisting and the way one group twists with another group vary. The groups divide and combine with other groups, and a larger **repeat** structure, in which the position of the warp ends keeps alternating, is composed.

Twists can also be omitted so that larger open spaces occur. By arranging the open spaces, elaborate open patterns can be constructed. All this was known and perfected by the ancient Peruvian weavers who also used embroidery in conjunction with some gauze weaves. Their work in gauze weaves was so lovely and extensive that the name Peruvian lace is given to some examples of it—notably to one in which the principle of the twist is applied to a 2-color, closely spaced warp in which the openings are not readily evident in the finished fabric, but the twist is there to manipulate the two colors into a design. See ill. Also see **bead leno.**

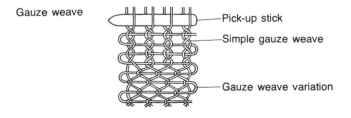

Gauze weave

- Pick-up stick
- Simple gauze weave
- Gauze weave variation

gazinta. Toys. See **spear-the-fish.**

gee-haw whimmydiddle. Toys. See **whimmydiddle.**

gel. Plastics. (Also called gellation.) The stage in curing **catalyzed resin** when the material looks like gelatin. In the soft gel stage, when it is partially set, it can be **gel molded.** In the hard gel, or completely set stage, the edges fracture rather than cut smoothly. Also see **gel point.**

gelatin. A colorless to white colloidal organic material obtained from the cartilages of animals and fish air bladders; used as an ingredient in cements and glues. It absorbs water and becomes jellylike. Also see **isinglass.**

gelatin mold. Candlemaking. The commercially available metal gelatin molds can greatly add to the candlemaker's repertoire by the variety of their shapes and sizes. Because they cannot be pierced at the bottom for **wick**ing like paper or cardboard **found object mold**s, candles made with gelatin molds must be wicked after they have hardened. This may be done in the standard way or by sandwiching a wick between two masses of hardened wax molded from the same mold. With the latter technique, one of the molded masses should be notched down the center to provide a groove for the wick before the two pieces are heated on a hot surface and pressed together to form one candle. To better bond the two halves and smooth the joined surfaces, a **wax bath** for the hardened finished candle is suggested. Also see **Candlemaking: Molding.**

gel coat. Plastics. The layer of **resin** applied for **lamination** or **lay-up.** The gel coat often contains **additive**s, such as **antioxidant**s, pigments, dyes, or other **filler**s to **light-stabilize** the resin.

gellation. Plastics. See **gel.**

gellation time. Plastics. See **gel time.**

gel medium. Plastics. See **polymer emulsion.**

gel molding. Plastics. The process of hand forming **polyester** or **epoxy resin** in the soft stages of **curing.** Pieces can be cut, bent, twisted, and rolled, or objects can be embedded in the resin. Also see **embedment.**

gel point. Plastics. The stage in **resin curing** when the liquid has the consistency of sugar syrup and the molecules start to hang together in chains.

gel time. Plastics. (Also called gellation time.) The amount of time a **catalyzed resin** takes to change from a liquid to a **gel.** Each resin has its own gel time, which varies depending on the room temperature, the percentage of catalyst added, and the addition of an **accelerator** to the mixture. Colorants may slow the gel time.

gem. Gemcutting. A mineral or rock valuable for aesthetic reasons, the surface of which has been worked (typically by grinding, **faceting,** and **polishing**) to increase its value.

GEMCUTTING

Since the Stone Age, man has used certain minerals and rocks for work and adornment. As early as 25,000 B.C., amber was mined in the Baltic Sea area. Archaeologists have unearthed Egyptian burial bracelets made of gold, **turquoise,** amethyst, and **lapis lazuli** beads dated 4500 B.C. Ancient Chinese lapidaries carved **jade,** amber, coral, emerald, ruby, and sapphire. Greek and Roman records describe vessels carved from **quartz** and engraved figures of onyx commemorating persons and events. When the Spanish arrived in America, the natives made gifts of various green gems called "chalchihuitl."

The first gems were cut with quartz sand and pointed wooden tools. Harder stones required harder abrasive, iron tools, and arduous technique. So valuable an article of trade were gems that their possession was restricted to the wealthy, and lapidaries closely guarded their "secret" methods. Gems have been attributed with supernatural powers and treasured as amulets.

The desire of European governments for gems played a part in the exploration and exploitation of colonial states around the world. Although commercial gem production has shifted from Europe to Africa, then to Asia, South America, and back to Africa, production is almost completely controlled by private individuals.

Gemcutting is a process of shaping and **polishing** a stone by wearing away its surface with **abrasives** of greater **hardness** than the stone, proceeding from coarse to progressively finer grits. It is a means of removing the best portion of a stone from the less attractive surrounding material (the matrix) to display its aesthetic properties to best advantage. Gemcutting produces ornaments of beauty and durability.

Stones for gemcutting are available in several forms—rough, removed from their natural state by shovel, pick, and hammer; slabbed, sliced into sections usually ¼″ thick; crushed, for sorting and **tumbling;** and **preform**ed, for **cabochon, facet**ed, and novelty cuts. Stones are available from rock shops and dealers, many by mail order.

Opaque materials are usually cut and polished into flat sections, tumbled to smooth, irregular shapes called baroques, and made into gemstone novelties such as **sphere**s, **intarsia,** and **cameo**s. These forms maximize the color and **luster** of opaque materials. Translucent, asteriated, and chatoyant stones are cut in cabochon form—a smooth domed surface atop a flat shape, such as an ellipse, circle, triangle, heart, etc. Transparent gem material is faceted to optimize the play of light—small flat surfaces are ground and arranged symmetrically around the stone for the enrichment of its color and brilliant reflection of light. Each stone has an optimum **faceting** procedure based on its refractive index.

Identification of gem material is made by analysis of the **hardness, specific gravity,** color, **streak, refraction,** and **crystal** structure of a specimen.

Information on gem material and gemcutting equipment may be found in magazines such as *Gems and Minerals,* Box 687, Mentone, California 92359; and *Lapidary Journal,* Box 80837, San Diego, California 92138.

APPLICATIONS OF GEMS   Gemstones are used for **abrasive**s, the fabrication of durable tools, and precious ornaments.

Emery is an abrasive variety of **corundum;** Linde A is a polishing compound made from synthetic corundum; ruby and sapphire are gem varieties of corundum. Diamonds that are unsuitable for jewelry are used in well drilling, and in grinding, **polishing,** and carving gems. Other examples of natural stone abrasives are flint and **garnet** sandpaper and pumice.

Some applications of stone for tools are agate dies for drawing wire, agate burnishers for leather and metal leaf work, agate knife edges and flat bearings in balance scales, and agate mortar-and-pestle sets. **Chrysoberyl, topaz,** and **spinel** are used as pivot bearings in watches and chronometers. **Quartz** is fashioned into lenses and used in radio transmitters and dental fillings.

Gems are also made into works of art and art objects.

TOOLS AND MATERIALS   Scales, **specific gravity** indicators, a **streak plate,** and a **dichroscope** are tools used to identify gems.

An **aluminum pencil** and a **template** are used for transferring a pattern to a gem rough.

A sharp pair of dividers is useful for measuring the work accurately.

Slabbing saws are used for sectioning large pieces of gem rough. The gem material is held in a vise or a slab grabber. A slabbing saw is not a crucial piece of equipment because cut slabs are available from a lapidary. Trim saws are smaller units used for slitting hand-held work.

An alcohol lamp, **dop** wax, a dopping plate, a dopping jig, a knock-off stick, **dop stick**s, and tweezers are necessary for **dopping.**

Machines with **grinding wheel**s, **sanding** drums and disks, and polishing buffs are used for grinding, **sanding,** and **polishing.**

A lapping machine is a horizontal rotating iron plate; loose abrasives or prepared **lap**s are placed on the master lap for grinding and polishing gem material.

A drill press is used with a **drilling jig** or **tube drill**s to bore holes in gem material.

Point carvers and **flexible-shaft machine**s fitted with small **carving points** are used to engrave and sculpture gem material. The points are interchangeable and available in many shapes.

Tumbling machines rotate several pounds of gem rough in **abrasive**s for weeks or months to produce polished, irregular-shaped gems called "**baroque**s."

Faceting units are attached perpendicular to the lap for positioning the arrangement of **facet**s on a gem.

SETTING UP A WORKSHOP   Setting up a workshop for gemcutting requires enough space for the operation of the machines and the storage of materials. A craftsperson will require from 10 to 100 square feet, depending on the amount of equipment. Direct incandescent lighting is necessary for proper viewing of the work; machines are powered by one-quarter to one-half horsepower electric motors that use 120 volt, 60-cycle AC (normal household) current, or 220 volt if available.

A separate, clean, lighted space is needed for the **dopping** operation. A separate area for **polishing** is desirable, if possible, to avoid contamination in the final operations.

Water is necessary as a coolant for **abrasive** operations; it is usually supplied from sump tanks or a can above the machine.

Water is also useful in reducing the dust from grinding and **sanding.** Running water is necessary for washing the stone, the dop stick, and the hands of the gemcutter between operations to avoid contamination of finer grits by coarser ones. Water is also used as a vehicle in **polishing.** Do not discard silicon carbide grits down the drain to avoid clogging and expensive plumbing repairs. They quickly precipitate out, leaving the water to be poured off and the sludge disposed of properly.

Goggles should be worn to protect your eyes when breaking stones and during grinding operations. A rubber apron protects clothing from water damage.

ORIENTATION Carefully plan the cutting of a gem to ensure the quality of the finished piece. Unusual properties, such as **color,** markings, clarity, **cleavage,** and **luster,** are considered before beginning. The final shape is planned and the stone is oriented and examined in the desired direction. Unless the material has been slabbed, a flat surface should be ground that will be the bottom of a **cabochon** or the top of a faceted gem.

The pattern or outline is marked on the flat surface with an **aluminum pencil;** use a **template** if you wish the finished gem to fit a commercially available jewelry mounting. Incline the pencil away from the template so that the point will mark as close to the edge as possible.

ROUGH SHAPING The stone is reduced to its rough shape by removing the material outside the drawn line. A hacksaw can be used to cut materials with a hardness of 3 or less. Score obsidian with a glass cutter before breaking. Use pliers to nibble small shallow bites down to within a millimeter of the marked outline.

Grinding wheels of 60–100 grit are used to shape stones to rough form quickly. Attach stones that are too small to hold to a **dop stick.** Further shaping is done with **abrasives** of finer grit, such as 180, 220, and 320. The stone is sanded to remove all scratches and surface irregularities caused by grinding; sanding cloths of 400–1200 grit are used to give the gem its final shape. **Sanding** is a most important operation because no imperfections are removed by **polishing.**

Gem materials having a **hardness** of 6 or less are soft enough to be worked without machinery. These include soapstone, **gypsum,** ivory, bone, amber, **serpentine,** meerschaum, tortoise shell, jet, **calcite, lepidolite,** obsidian, **azurite, cuprite, fluorite, malachite, lapis lazuli, rhodochrosite, hematite, opal, turquoise,** moonstone, and **jade.** Also see **Moh's scale of hardness.**

HAND GRINDING AND POLISHING To grind stones by hand, several **abrasive** cloths of different grits tacked to blocks of wood are necessary. Begin with a coarse grindstone or 80–100 grit abrasive for rough shaping. Smooth the stone using 220, 400, and 600 grit cloths on felt, leather, or rubber-padded wood blocks. Break in sanding cloths before using; to do so, scrape the surface with a flat rock to dislodge loose and oversize grits.

After the stone has been examined in detail and the design planned and transferred to the stone, the stone is ground to its rough shape. The bottom edge is smoothed and a back bevel is ground to prevent chipping. Then the top is rounded and smoothed until it assumes a well-proportioned symmetrical shape when viewed from all angles. Wash the stone and your hands carefully between each abrasive application; proceed to coarse sanding. Work against the cloth, rolling and rocking the stone to avoid flat spots and distortion of the smooth curve being developed. Continue sanding with finer grit cloths; check the work with dividers or against the **template** to avoid overcutting. Begin polishing when the stone shows no scratches when examined with a magnifier.

Prepolishing is an aid to achieving an easier final polish. Prepolish a well-cleaned stone until a dull gloss appears; use tripoli, rottenstone, or 1000-grit silicon carbide on a block padded with six layers of cotton fabric. Mix polishing compounds with water to a thick creamy consistency. Final polishing is done on felt or leather with tin, chrome, or cerium oxide or Linde A. The best test of a perfect polish is the inability to focus a ten-power magnifier on the surface.

SAFETY PRECAUTIONS Gemcutting saws are not dangerous, as they have no teeth, but the wheel can cause abrasions. Diamond saw blades are not dangerous if tightened and the work is held firmly when sawing. Avoid loose clothing around running machinery. Wear goggles during machining. Keep electrical connections dry and secure.

gemmaux. Stained Glass. (Also called crushed glass.) A technique of sticking tiny particles of stained glass to **plate glass** to reproduce the works of great painters such as Van Gogh, Monet, and Picasso. The technique is sometimes used commercially in France, as in the Paris Métro. Also see **lamination.**

geometric. Quilts. Stitchery. Figures or shapes founded on geometry that provide the basis of all **pieced quilt**s and are used in **piecing** fabric designs. Those figures most frequently used in quilt design include the circle, diamond, equilateral triangle, hexagon, isosceles triangle, octagon, parallelogram, rectangle, right triangle, square, and trapezoid.

geometric forms. Papercrafts. Three-dimensional papercraft constructions of the five regular geometric solids, in which all the faces are regular polygons. Each of these basic shapes can be made from one piece of paper, leaving tabs for gluing or taping together. See ill.

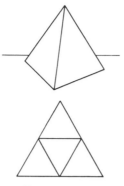

a. Tetrahedron (4 triangles)

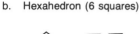

b. Hexahedron (6 squares)

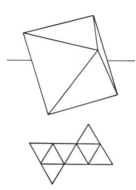

c. Octahedron (8 triangles)

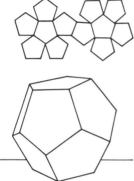

d. Dodecahedron
    (12 pentagons)

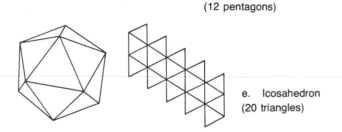

e. Icosahedron
    (20 triangles)

geometric knitting. Knitting. Geometric knitting is **colored knitting** patterned with geometric shapes. The yarns are carried on balls or **bobbin**s, and when changing from one color to another the first color is looped around the second to prevent holes from being made in the fabric. Geometric patterns are charted on **graph paper**. See ill. Also see **Argyle knitting.**

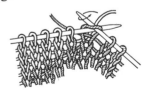

Geometric knitting

geometric puzzle. Toys. A popular **game** that originated in the Orient. It consists of a square cut into 7 pieces. The object of the game is to start with scrambled pieces and reassemble them into a square. The name is also used to refer to some three-dimensional puzzles of a similar nature.

geometric star. Quilts. Any of several **pieced quilt** designs based on **geometric** shapes that form stars. One geometric

star pattern from Pennsylvania uses small **one-patch** squares in a **checkerboard** arrangement. The colors are so arranged that some of the **blocks** outline an eight-pointed star shape in the manner of the **Texas lone star.**

The geometric star may also be a simple pieced block pattern. Also see **star patterns.**

Georgetown circle. Quilts. See **Crown of Thorns.**

German antique glass. Stained Glass. (Also called West German glass.) Germany specializes in ochre, gray, white, dull bottle-green, green-blue, deep-blue, and deep-red glass. Their panels measure 34″ × 36″. They also specialize in opalescent antique glass, a **flashed glass** with a stronger base color than regular flashed glass and with a translucent whitish-gray flash added. Also see **antique glass, striations** and **Stained Glass: Tools and Materials.**

German knitting. Knitting. The style of knitting that originated in Germany, with patterns and stitches interrelated with those of **Austrian Knitting.** Also see **Knitting: How to Knit.**

German knot stitch. Crewel. Embroidery. See **coral knot.**

German silver. Jewelry. Metalworking. See **brass, nickel silver.**

Germantown. Weaving. See **Navajo weaving.**

German wheel. Spinning. (Also called cottage wheel, parlor wheel, visiting wheel.) A **treadle wheel** with the **flyer** above the **drive wheel.** The drive wheel is supported by

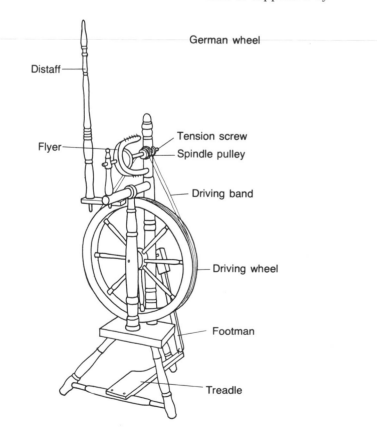

German wheel

Distaff

Flyer

Tension screw

Spindle pulley

Driving band

Driving wheel

Footman

Treadle

posts set into a base with three or four legs. The German wheel is smaller than the Saxony wheel or Brunswick wheel so it takes up less room and is easy to transport. See ill. on previous page.

gesso. Découpage. A thick mixture of inert white pigment, such as chalk or whiting, with an aqueous binder, such as a solution of **hide glue** or casein. It is available in most art supply stores as dry, cold-water gesso.

Gesso is traditionally used for sizing canvas and new wooden surfaces in preparation for painting, **gilding,** or découpage. After coatings of gesso have been applied and dried, sand the surface until smooth with wet-or-dry **sandpaper** and then with fine **steel wool** until ivory smooth.

Acrylic gesso is often substituted for gesso but does not sand to as smooth a surface.

gesso. Plastics. Traditional gesso was chalk, or whiting bound with a gelatin or casein glue. It was brushed on canvas or wood as a ground on which to paint. Now, synthetic, ready-to-use **polymer emulsion** or acrylic gesso can be used on flexible or rigid plastic supports. It is fast drying and nonyellowing, and may be used under oil or synthetic media paints. It is often used to seal expanded **foams** before they are covered with **resin.** Dilute with water and apply more than one coat by brushing, rolling, or spraying. For toned grounds, gesso may be tinted with polymer emulsion paints; for relief sculpture or for textural effects add polymer emulsion modeling paste or inert **additives.**

gesso. Toys. A thick white opaque material that dries rock-hard. It is applied by brush to wood, **papier mâché,** and other materials to smooth them, add a relief pattern, or prepare them for painting. It can be sandpapered when dry. Also see **antiquing.**

gesso beads. Beadwork. A traditional **bead** made from a combination of **whiting** and glue, strengthened by the addition of cotton fibers. Gesso beads are lightweight, practically unbreakable, and easy to make. Place ½ lb. of fine gilder's whiting in a bowl and cover it with cold water. Stir to dissolve, then let it stand overnight or longer. Strain this paste through a mesh cloth, letting it stand until the excess liquid has drained off. Dissolve 2 tablespoons of French carpenter's glue and place it on a dish or marble slab. Gradually add whiting to the glue, mixing with a palette knife, until a brownish, thick gesso is formed. During this mixing step, fine shreds of cotton or wool can be added to strengthen the mixture. Dust the hands with dry whiting, knead well, and add more whiting if necessary to make the paste as malleable as modeling clay. If possible, let the paste stand, covered with a damp cloth, for a few days. When forming beads, dust the fingers with dry whiting. Beads can be modeled into the desired shape, then pierced with a needle or wire, or they can be molded in greased molds for identical beads. Powdered color may be added to the whiting mixture to color the beads.

Ghiordes knot. Rugmaking. Weaving. See **knotted pile.**

Ghiordes knot stitch. Crewel. Embroidery. Needlepoint. See **Turkey work.**

ghost. Jewelry. (Also called skull.) A slight pale impression left by **solder** after it has flowed.

gift pillow. Stitchery. A **pincushion** made as a gift for a special occasion, especially during Victorian times. Names or initials and dates were included, as well as **ribbon**s of **satin** or **velvet.** Gift cushions were also made in the shape of hearts, sometimes a series stacked one on another, and were usually scented.

gigged. Stitchery. See **napped fabric.**

gild. Alternate spelling of **guild.**

gilding. Bookbinding. The process of burnishing **gold leaf** on a book.

gilding. Ceramics. A process that involves applying metallic decoration to ceramic ware. Liquid **gold** is applied to glazed ware and refired. Gold leaf is glued to the ware. Also see **burnishing.**

gilding. China and Glass Painting. See **gold.**

gilding. Découpage. (Also called gold leafing.) An ancient technique of adhering thin sheets of precious metals as embellishment on decorations and paintings. In general, gilding refers to coating surfaces with any kind of metal. Gold leafing implies coating with leaves of real **gold leaf,** not imitation. Other metallic leaf is available: silver, which tarnishes; palladium, which doesn't tarnish; and various types of imitation gold, such as bronze leaf, Dutch metal, and metal leaf, all of which tarnish unless protected by **varnish.**

The surface to be gilded should be smooth, preferably coated with **gesso,** and usually colored red, yellow, or green to add tone to the gold. Paint and hobby stores carry gold leaf and various **gold size** or mordant mixtures to apply as the **glue** to the surface to be gilded, gold leafing kits, and other types of gold paint and **bronze powder.**

There are two techniques of gilding: water gilding and oil, or mordant, gilding. Water gilding requires more preparation of the surface and more skill in its application, but with burnishing can supply a mirrorlike gold surface. Water gilding is generally used over gesso surfaces and is particularly good for three-dimensional carvings, furniture, and frames. Since it is too tedious and too expensive for general use in découpage, only the basics will be given. The background surface should not be coated with a **sealer** before water gilding. The gold leaf is carefully floated onto a surface wet with a solution of glue-water and grain alcohol. When dry, the surface is burnished with an agate burnisher, gently at first, then gone over again with firmer strokes. Reburnishing after a few days brings up the gloss to a high sheen.

Oil, or mordant gilding, easier to apply and generally used on flat surfaces, is more appropriate for découpage.

The resulting surface, called mat-leafed, is a dull, rich gold. Oil gilding can be done on any nonabsorbent surface. If the surface is absorbent, like gesso, it should first have several coats of a sealer, such as one part **shellac** to one part denatured alcohol.

The drying time of the gold size should be determined by the speed of the work you plan to do. The size is brushed over the surface thinly and smoothly, and allowed to dry until **tacky.** Pick up a sheet of gold leaf, holding it with the tissue paper sheet, and apply it to edge of sized area. Then slip away the tissue paper, keeping the gold leaf flat. Press the gold down with a bit of absorbent cotton. Don't rub, or you will mar the surface. Continue laying gold squares, being careful to overlap each edge until the area is covered. Patch gaps immediately with scrap leaf. Allow gilded piece to dry overnight. Then apply a sealer before varnishing.

gilding metal. Jewelry. Metalworking. A **brass alloy** of 95 parts copper and 5 parts zinc. It can be used for making jewelry that is to be gold-plated because it has good working qualities and is itself a golden color.

gimlet. Woodworking. See **drilling tools.**

gimp. Lacemaking. In **bobbin lace,** an outlining thread around a **motif, pattern,** or unit of **design.** It is usually a larger, heavier thread of a softer twist than the thread in the lacework. The gimp is worked with a single **bobbin** through the threads as the bobbins hang on the **pillow** in the making of the lace, and works independent of the stitches in the lacework. The gimp is usually the same color as the main lacework, but can be a contrasting color or a metallic thread. It is distinguished from the main body of the lacework by its shinier finish. See ill.

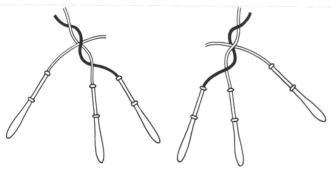

a.   Gimp passing right to left   b.   Gimp passing left to right

gimp yarn. Spinning. See **novelty yarn.**

gingham. Quilts. Stitchery. A closely woven, **cotton fabric** of **plain weave.** It is usually **yarn-dyed** to create stripes, checks, or plaids. It is sized, making it easy to handle in sewing and a popular fabric in quiltmaking.

gingham. Weaving. See **plain weave.**

Gingham Dog. Toys. A **stuffed animal** made famous in Eugene Field's poem "The Duel" about "the Gingham Dog and the Calico Cat."

ginning. Spinning. Weaving. See **cotton.**

gird. Toys. See **cleek.**

girdle. Gemcutting. See **cabochon, facet.**

girdle-back loom. Weaving. See **backstrap loom.**

girth hitch. Weaving. See **tie-on knot.**

glacial acetic acid. Batik and Tie-dye. A chemical compound (100% **acetic acid**) that may be used as the **assistant** in dyeing silks and woolens, though it must be diluted with water by 30%. It is available at photo suppliers. Use care in handling this acid and keep it out of reach of children. Observe precautions given on the label. White vinegar, a dilute acetic acid, may be substituted.

glaire. Bookbinding. An albuminous mordant made from egg white and vinegar. Glaire is used when **tooling** with **gold leaf** to help the leaf adhere to the cover. Beat 1 teaspoon vinegar into the white of an egg; allow the mixture to stand overnight and then strain it through a fine piece of muslin. Apply the mixture to the areas you plan to leaf and allow to dry. Apply a thin coat of vaseline over the glaire. The leaf will adhere to the vaseline temporarily. The pressure of the finishing tools will make the glaire congeal and fix the gold impression.

glass. Ceramics. Stained Glass. Glass is a supercooled liquid of inorganic materials—cooled rapidly enough to prevent crystallization. One of the main ingredients in glass is **silica,** which melts at a temperature of 1700° C. When combined with lower oxides and a **flux,** however, it becomes fluid material as low as 650° C.

The glass used in stained glass comes in sheet or slab form. It may be handmade or **machine-made glass,** and it may be textured in a variety of ways. Also see **ballast, antique glass, cathedral glass, crackle glass, crossed slab glass, crown glass, curious glass, flashed glass, Flemish glass, granite-backed glass, hammered glass, Kelp, Norman slab glass, opalescent glass, opaque glass, plate glass, pot-metal glass, reamy glass, rolled glass, slab glass, streaky glass.**

glass. Découpage. See **découpage under glass** and **Découpage: Preparing the Surface, Care and Maintenance.**

glass. Mosaics. A hard, breakable substance, very often transparent or translucent, that is made by melting a silicate such as sand with potash, **lime,** or soda. By the fourth century A.D., glassmaking skills in the West had improved to such an extent that glass tiles or **tesserae,** with their far greater brilliance and color variation, had replaced **marble** and stone as the basic mosaic ingredient. All the grandeur that was Byzantine **mosaics** was glass, and, to this day, so-called Byzantine glass, or **smalti,** is still considered the finest mosaic material available. It is exquisite, exhilirating, and awfully expensive. **Pressed glass,** although inferior to smalti, is far more reasonable in price and is readily available in most hobby shops in enough of a color range to satisfy the beginning mosaicist. Sheet or plate glass, cut with a **glass cutter,** or a **found object** of glass can also readily be worked into the creative mosaic, as in the work of **Rodia** and his Watts Towers. Whatever the type—smalti, pressed, cut, or found—glass still reigns supreme as the basic mosaic material. Also see **glass tiles.**

glass assemblage. Stained Glass. A method developed by Fredrica H. Fields in which layers of glass are compressed between two sheets of glass in a box frame. Light traveling through these many layers of glass produces a very interesting effect.

glass beads. Beadwork. Imported most commonly from Czechoslovakia, France, Italy, and Japan, glass beads are commercially available in a variety of colors and shapes. The transparent variety are clear and usually brilliant in color. Opaque glass beads, solid in color, and usually bright, are sometimes called chalk beads. Iridescent glass beads are permanent in color with a glossy outside finish. Glass beads are either faceted, with small plane surfaces cut to produce sparkle, or round and smooth, with uniformity of size, color, and surface. Also see **bugle beads, lined beads, millefiori** and **Beadmaking.**

glass-bending temperature. Stained Glass. See **fused glass techniques, lampshade mold.**

glassblowing. Glasswork. See **Glasswork: Glassblowing.**

glass bottle candle. Candlemaking. Glass bottles make excellent **found object mold**s because of their various shapes, and the soft sheen they give to the finished candle. General **molding** techniques should be followed. However, since most ordinary bottle glass is not heat resistant, candles should be poured at a lower temperature. To be safe, the bottle should be oven-warmed and the wax should be poured at 150–165° F. To release any air bubbles trapped by the narrow bottle neck, probe the melted wax at the top with a thin wire or **ice pick.** To remove the bottle from the hardened candle, submerge it in cold water to contract the wax, then gently tap the bottle with a hammer to break it. After all the glass has been removed the candle can be finished by **buffing** it with a nylon stocking. Also see **Krystalline.**

glass brush. China and Glass Painting. A brush composed of hundreds of strands of spun glass tightly packed together and bound with cord, used in **burnishing** gold on china or glass for a lustrous finish. The use of a glass brush is highly hazardous. Take care not to inhale the tiny glass particles that result from burnishing. Protect the skin and hold your breath during use.

glass brush. Enameling. A bundle of glass fibers used for **cleaning metal,** especially silver, with running water. Also see **Enameling: Tools and Materials.**

glass bubbles. Stained Glass. See **bubbles.**

glass cement. Stained Glass. See **cementing, grout, kwik solder.**

glass color. China and Glass Painting. See **ice.**

glass curtain. Stitchery. See **transparent fabric.**

glasscutter. Glasswork. Mosaics. There are two main types of glass cutter, the steel-wheel cutter and the diamond-point (or silicon carbide point) cutter. The diamond-point cutter lasts longer and is somewhat easier to learn to use. Steel-wheel cutters must be used carefully to avoid dulling the wheel, which happens quickly if a line is scribed a second time. The steel-wheel cutter is more convenient if accuracy of the scribed line is important, since the cutting edge is in view while scribing. See ill. Also see **glass cutting** and **Mosaics: Cutting the Material.**

glass cutter. Stained Glass. A tool used to **score** glass so that it can be broken. The score is made with a steel wheel inserted at the end of a tiny spindle resembling a unicycle and having the same kind of maneuverability. The cutter has a cast iron or wooden handle.

There are often metal serrations on one side of the tool that can be used for **grozing** off small pieces of glass. The **carbide glass cutter** and **diamond glass cutter** are specialized cutters, both having longer cutting lives than the standard **steel-wheel glass cutter.** See ill. Also see **circle cutter, running pliers, scribe, tungsten wheel** and **Stained Glass: Tools and Materials.**

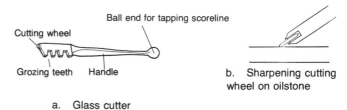

Ball end for tapping scoreline

Cutting wheel

Grozing teeth   Handle

a.   Glass cutter

b.   Sharpening cutting wheel on oilstone

glass cutting. Glasswork. Any of the methods by which glass is fractured along lines or curves, predetermined by scoring the glass with a steel or diamond or silicon carbide edge. Glass should be broken at the score immediately after the score is made; glass has a tendency to "heal," so if cutting is delayed, the cut will not run true. Glass has very little resistance to tensile forces if even minute surface scratches exist in the piece, and it is this property that makes glass cutting possible.

To cut sheet glass, first place the glass on a surface that will support it evenly. A blanket on a flat table or floor works quite well. For straight cuts a wooden straightedge is laid along the desired line and a **glass cutter** is drawn along the straightedge while a pressure of about eight pounds is exerted through the cutter. The cutter, if it is sharp and the pressure is correct, will "sing" as it cuts. After the score is made, the ball at the end of the cutter is tapped gently on the opposite side from the score to begin a crack. The crack can be led all the way through the cut this way just by tapping the opposite side of the cut about ⅛" behind the tip of the crack. A faster way is to move the sheet of glass so that the score is at the edge of the table and to exert force down on the overhanging piece while steadying the remainder on the table.

Alternatively, lay the sheet, scratch upward, on a pencil so that the line of the pencil lies along the line of the score at the end you have started to tap. Press gently down on both sides; the fracture should run true the length of the cut.

For very thin cuts, the slots in the working end of the wheel cutter can be used like pliers to engage the edge of the glass near the cut, producing the necessary tensile force by bending the glass down. It may be necessary to break off the cut in sections and then grind or polish any irregularities.

For circular, curved, or concave cuts in sheet glass, first inscribe the desired shape on the glass. It will usually be necessary to "relieve" the cut by running auxiliary break lines to the edge of the sheet intermittently along the curve and then breaking out sections. For such complex shapes, tapping the cut from the reverse side is recommended.

To cut tube or rod, score one-third of the way around the diameter to a depth of about one-third the way through the wall of tubing with one of the sharp corners of a fine **file.** A rocking motion of the file will accomplish this most easily. Exerting the necessary tension force for tubing is more complex than for sheet glass. One good way is to hold the scored tube in both hands at the stomach with the score facing away from you and then pull apart on the ends. The combination of tension and imperceptible bending should sever the glass evenly. This may take some practice. See ill. Also see **bottle cutting.**

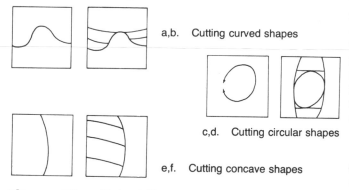

a,b.   Cutting curved shapes

c,d.   Cutting circular shapes

e,f.   Cutting concave shapes

glass cutting. Stained Glass. See **Stained Glass: Cutting Glass.**

glass drill. Stained Glass. Special abrasive drill bits made of silicon carbide can be fitted to a standard hand drill and are generally used wet against the **glass** to drill holes in it.

The special bits, which are from ⅛ to ¼", can be used in an electric drill if a **rheostat** unit is attached to slow down the revolutions of the drill. Too much heat causes the glass to crack.

Use a fine machine oil or water to wet the glass during drilling.

glass dust. Stained Glass. Finely ground glass dust is used in combination with metal oxides and **flux** in **painting on glass.** It is obtainable in bulk form from stained-glass suppliers.

glass fiber. Plastics. (Also called Fiberglas, fiberglass.) A **reinforcing material** made of supple spun-glass fibers that has high tensile strength and will take hard blows without breaking when impregnated with cured **resin.** Glass fiber will not rot, mildew, oxidize, or shrink, and isn't affected by most acids and weak alkalis. It was shown in women's gowns and lamp shades in 1893 at Chicago's Columbian Exposition but was not commercially practical until the 1930s.

Glass fiber comes in several stock forms. Unwoven roving (also called milled fibers or spun roving) is made of parallel glass filaments and is used to reinforce long, narrow objects, especially when one-directional strength is needed. Woven roving is a coarse fabric of loose strands of glass.

Mat (also called chopped strand mat or reinforcing mat) is a sheet of unwoven random lengths of chopped glass fiber that is used as a low-cost reinforcing material. Bonded mat is sprayed with a binder to hold the fibers together. Surfacing mat texture disappears when soaked with **polyester resin,** giving a smooth surface finish.

Glass fiber tape and cloth is a woven fabric made of glass fibers. It is the strongest of the stock glass fiber forms and is used as a reinforcing material with **epoxy, silicone,** and polyester.

glass fiber tape. Plastics. See **glass fiber.**

glass fire. Glasswork. In **flamework,** the gas burner that produces the intense, directed flame that is the most controllable and simple to use. An example of the metal casting nozzle that produces an acceptable glass fire is the No. 3151JC New Style Glass Fire, available from the American Gas Furnace Co., Elizabeth, N.J. Glass fires require compressed air and home gas or bottled propane to reach a high enough temperature. Many available glass fire burners permit the addition of oxygen to the air-gas mixture, which makes the flame hotter and suitable for working **borosilicate glass.** See ill.

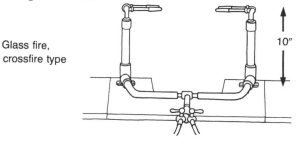

Glass fire, crossfire type

10"

glassforming. Glasswork. See **Glasswork.**

glass glob. Stained Glass. Marblelike transparent pieces of solid **glass** varying in shape and color produced in a freeform manner in a **kiln.** They can be up to 1" in size and can be foiled, leaded, or glued. Special glue that will not shrink and that dries to a transparent rapid finish is needed. These globs can be adapted to windows, lamps, and many other uses. Also see **copper foiling** and **Stained Glass: Glazing.**

glass jewel. Stained Glass. Small glass forms originally made of solid **glass rod**s heated in a beehive furnace until molten and then pressed into a mold, removed, and allowed to cool slowly. They were originally produced by the **Heidt Co.**, Brooklyn, New York, and were known as Heidt jewels. Some of these jewels are still produced today. They and other forms of glass jewels are used for decorative purposes in stained glass panels and lampshades, and in jewelry. Also see **lampshade construction.**

glass mold. Candlemaking. Professional glass molds for candlemaking can be found in certain hobby supply shops. They are used the same way as any other **found object mold**s of glass, such as drinking glasses or glass containers. Also see **glass bottle candle.**

glass muller. Ceramics. A flat-ended pestle used for mixing enamels and color on a glass slab.

glass painting. China and Glass Painting. See **China and Glass Painting: Glass Painting.**

glass pliers. Stained Glass. See **plate pliers.**

glass rack. Stained Glass. See **sample rack.**

glass reflector. Stitchery. See **reflector.**

glass rod. Stained Glass. Solid **glass** cores produced in a variety of sizes and thicknesses. They are used in **mobiles** and **wind chimes** and melted in the **kiln** to form interesting shapes. Use a glass saw blade to make a groove around the rod. Wrap **fishline** around the groove so the rod can be hung. The cut edges should be sanded with **abrasive paper.** Also see **glass glob, Farbigem process for laminated glass, glass jewels.**

glass saw blade. Stained Glass. A hacksaw fitted with a special carborundum blade can be used to cut **glass** in special situations. Also see **glass rod.**

glass storage. Stained Glass. See **sample rack** and **Stained Glass: Setting Up a Workshop.**

glass stress. Stained Glass. The addition of **metallic oxide**s to **antique glass** and the different rates of molecular expansion that occur in making the glass cause internal stress and strain not present in **plate glass.** Glass is a homogeneous liquid and is therefore subject to the same laws of physics as liquids; it expands when heated, contracts when cooled. The pressure placed on one part of a glass sheet may cause a fracture in another area of the sheet as part of a strain pattern. Sometimes, especially if a sheet is badly annealed, it may fly apart with very little pressure. Also see **annealing, antique glass colorants.**

glass tile. Mosaics. One of the oldest types of mosaic tile. Commercially produced glass tiles are available in several types: Italian glass tiles in a variety of colors, transparent or opaque; Mexican glass tiles, less dense than Italian, with some colors having a frosty appearance and a grainy sur-

face; and **Smalti,** or Byzantine glass, considered the finest of glass tiles, irregular in shape and opaque. Also see **glass.**

GLASSWORK

Any of several glass crafts including, in ascending order of difficulty or skill required, **flamework,** glassforming, and glassblowing. The term "glassblowing" is applied to both flamework and **freeblowing.** In this book, work with stock glass tube and rod is referred to as "flamework."

Glasswork was practiced as early as 1500 B.C. in Egypt, and there is evidence that glassblowing, much as we know it, was practiced there in 50 B.C. Glasswork has always been something of a mystery to the uninitiated, and its apparent dangerousness, the sharpness of broken glass, and the high temperatures necessary to melt or fuse it have kept the studio craftsperson from becoming deeply involved. However, many operations require fairly simple equipment and fairly easily learned skills. The amateur is encouraged to begin with flamework, which requires not much more than a simple **glass fire** and a supply of stock rod and tube glass of various dimensions. Fairly quickly, the beginner can learn to bend, shape, and assemble heated glass parts and to form small bubbles and pleasing shapes.

Glassforming requires an oven of some sort. For some kinds of fusion, **lamination,** and **sagging,** a pottery kiln develops enough heat; for **cast**ing a simple oven can be made from refractory bricks and a gas burner or electric heating element, the details of which the local power company can advise you about.

Freeblowing is the most demanding of the glass arts and requires a **tank furnace,** a **lehr,** blowing **iron**s, punties, and a few simple tools. Drawing molten glass from the furnace and blowing or shaping the hot **metal** is a dramatic and fascinating employ and one that is sure to draw onlookers. The kinds of work and the variety of natural shapes that can be made in freeblowing are almost endless. The action of gravity alone can stretch and pull a gob of molten glass into a pleasant waisted shape; a vessel blown in such a way that the bottom rests on a metal plate develops a natural flat-to-round transition that is difficult to achieve, for example, on a pottery wheel.

PRECAUTIONS   The obvious dangers of working with molten glass, the temperature of which may reach 1500° C, and the sharpness of broken glass make for fewer injuries among experienced glassworkers than might be imagined; glassworkers have a respect for their tools and materials. A less obvious danger is that fragments of unannealed glass have a tendency to explode. A **cullet bin,** made of metal and fitted with some sort of cover, is a necessity for containing cooling glass. **Blowing iron**s and punties are sometimes left in the cullet bin while they cool. The sound of the glass breaking away from the irons as they cool is sometimes explosive. An ordinary 30-gallon garbage can with a lid can serve as a cullet bin.

The eyes should be protected from the glare from the **tank furnace** with dark-tinted glasses. When using a **glory hole,** dark-tinted glasses are a necessity, not only so that the worker can see where the piece is being heated but also to protect the eyes from what could be damaging light. In **flameworking**, the bright yellow flare that comes off the glass where the glass fire impinges upon it is so bright that it is often difficult to see what the work is doing. To reduce this problem, **didymium goggles** are worn. These lenses tend to reduce the brightness of the glare and make working easier while they protect the eyes from possible glass fragments.

The use of acids for acid polishing and **etching** requires special care because the acids not only eat through unprotected skin but also do it slowly enough so that the damage is often not noticed until sometime later. Rubber gloves that have been carefully checked for pinholes and a rubber apron are advisable when using acids, as well as some sort of goggles to protect the eyes. When working with acids, it is a good idea to regard anything wet as acid and not just water.

Most industrial tank furnaces are allowed to stay hot 24 hours a day, 7 days a week. The studio craftsperson may wish to use the furnace only on weekends, for example, starting a batch of glass heating on a Friday night and beginning work on Saturday morning after the glass has finished **fining.** It is necessary, before allowing the tank furnace to cool, to remove as much of the **melt** as possible with blowing irons or punties, or the glass will adhere to the sides of the refractory brick inside the furnace and, in the course of contraction, dislodge brick or even destroy the furnace.

SETTING UP A WORKSHOP Flameworking. The bench can be set up nearly anywhere in a home or apartment, the glass fire being not substantially more dangerous than a stove. The top of the bench should be covered in some material that will not burn. Flameworking tools include the basic glass fire; auxiliary heating fires that have handles so that the flame can be played on portions of large pieces without having to lift the whole work into the cross-fired burners; an **annealing** oven, or **lehr,** for controlled heating and cooling of finished pieces; tweezers and pliers for pulling and twisting molten parts of glass being heated; corks for plugging ends of tubing to be blown; and such other jigs and holding devices as the glassworker may deem necessary. See ill.

GLASSFORMING Glassforming, since the principal pieces of equipment and forming methods require a fair amount of space, and since the oven produces quite a bit of heat, is best consigned to a basement or separate outbuilding. Forming glass in plaster molds requires a linoleum (or equivalent material) **dam,** putty knives, a pan for mixing the **refractory** plaster, and possibly grinding equipment for finishing molded pieces.

GLASSBLOWING Glassblowing requires the furnace and lehr mentioned above, pieces of equipment entailing the outlay of substantial time and money, or both. The workshop for glassblowing needs to be well ventilated to carry away the products of combustion as well as the great heat that spills into the surrounding area. Some workers in relatively mild climates set up the glassblowing studio out of doors with a simple canopy to keep off the rain. The floor

must be of nonflammable material such as iron sheet, concrete, or earth. **Blowing irons**, punties, **jacks**, **shears**, **files**, **blocking molds**, **paddles**, and a **glassworker's chair** are essential pieces of equipment, and after a certain level of proficiency is acquired, a **glory hole** becomes a great convenience for quickly reheating work on the irons. Reheating work in the furnace mouth will serve for a while, but the selective area heating of a glory hole and its speed are almost essential to fine work. Also see **punty.**

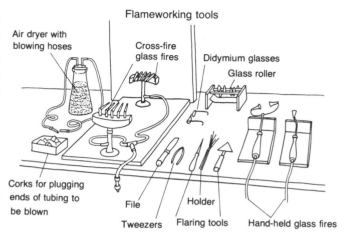

Flameworking tools

Air dryer with blowing hoses — Cross-fire glass fires — Didymium glasses — Glass roller — Corks for plugging ends of tubing to be blown — File — Holder — Tweezers — Flaring tools — Hand-held glass fires

glassworker's chair. Glasswork. The chairlike workbench in which the glassblower, or **gaffer,** sits while forming freeblown work. It is customarily made of wood, with a metal rail covering the arm of the chair where the hot end of the **blowing iron** rests while being worked. The chair has an extended seat at the working side that serves as a shelf for tools. A pail of water in which blocking molds and a file are kept wet is kept near this shelf. See ill. Also see **blocking, jack, paddle.**

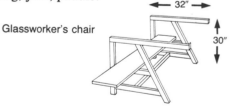

Glassworker's chair — 32″ — 30″

Glauber's salt. Batik and Tie-dye. Sodium sulfate. An **assistant** used in dyeing silk with **fiber-reactive dyes.** Also see **Batik and Tie-dye: Dyes.**

glaze. Ceramics. A thin glasslike coating fused to the surface of **bisque** by **firing** in a **kiln.** Glaze can be applied to **leather-hard** clay as in **once-fired ware.** A glaze consists of three necessary ingredients: **silica,** a **flux,** which lowers the **melting point** of the silica; and **alumina,** which gives added strength to the glazed surface, prevents **devitrification,** and increases the maturing temperature and **viscosity.** Also see **binder, blistering, bloating, chemistry of pottery, crackle, crater glaze, crawling, crazing, dunting, earthenware glaze, glaze fire, glazing, Harkort test, lead glaze, lime blowing, luster, majolica, moisture crazing, opaque glaze, overglaze, pigment oxide, pinhole, porcelain glaze, raku, raw glaze, salt glaze, slip glaze, shivering, soft glaze, stain, stemware glaze, underglaze pigment.**

glaze. China and Glass Painting. A glass (flux) applied to decorated china or glass by **dusting** over the surface for a lustrous, glassy surface after firing. It is available as a colorless, ivory-colored, or tinted liquid or powder. The glaze eliminates brushstrokes and produces a smooth surface over the painted design. A glaze may be dusted over the half-dry or dry design each time it is fired. Glazes affect iron colors such as reds and flesh tones, so they should be used sparingly over them.

glaze. Stained Glass. See **firing stain.**

glaze. Toys. See **baker's clay glazes.**

glazed greenware. Ceramics. See **once-fired ware.**

glazed polyester filler. Quilts. (Also called bonded polyester filler.) A **filler** or **batt** that has a polished surface. The batt unrolls readily into a thick sheet; the glazed or polished surface keeps bits from pulling off. It is best suited for **tied quilts** or **comforters** because the glazing holds the batt in place and prevents any bunching or slipping of the batting when the quilt is washed.

glaze fire. Ceramics. (Also called glost fire.) **Firing** glazed ware to the maturing temperature to produce a **vitreous** body. The glaze fire is to the body **maturity** temperature which is much higher than the **bisque fire** temperature.

glazier's pie. Stained Glass. The lifting up of a central portion of a leaded stained-glass **panel** before it is soldered. It is caused by too much pressure being placed on the outer edge of the panel during **glazing.** It is most likely to happen when there are many horizontal or vertical parallel pieces exerting pressure from the sides, forcing the center up. Placing a weight in the center during glazing can help prevent this. Also see **Stained Glass: Glazing.**

glazing. Batik and Tie-dye. A **fabric finish** applied commercially in textile mills to impart a smooth glazed surface. Various materials can be used for glazing, including starch, glue, mucilage, shellac, and resin. The resins offer **permanent finish** glazes, and some are stain or oil resistant. Glazed material must be thoroughly washed in hot water with soap or detergent to remove all surface treatment before the fabric can be **tie-dye**d or **batik**ed. Permanent finish glazes cannot always be removed, so test any fabrics before dyeing. Also see **removing fabric finish.**

glazing. Ceramics. The application of **glaze** to **bisque** or **leather-hard** clay. Also see **glaze fire** and **Ceramics: Glazing.**

glazing. Leatherwork. A commercial process in finishing leather in which the surface is polished to a high gloss under pressure by glass or steel rollers.

glazing. Stained Glass. (Also called leading, leading up.) The process of putting precut pieces of stained glass together with **lead cames.** Also see **joints** and **Stained Glass: Glazing.**

glazing bench. Stained Glass. See **Stained Glass: Setting Up a Workshop.**

glazing hammer. Stained Glass. Special hammers for **glazing** available through supply house catalogues. A small to medium tacking hammer will do very well. It should not have too heavy a head and should be double-ended rather than clawed. Also see **Stained Glass: Glazing.**

glazing knife. Stained Glass. (Also called lead knife.) A tool used in cutting **lead came,** available from stained-glass equipment houses. See ill. Also see **lead shears** and **Stained Glass: Glazing, Tools and Materials.**

Glazing knife

glazing strip. Stained Glass. Usually made from wooden lath strips, which are ¼″ × 1½″, or from furring strips, which are ¾″ × 1½″ wide. They are used in **glazing** a stained-glass **panel** to hold the panel stationary and to act as a support to work against. Two pieces are nailed at right angles in one corner of the workboard. Also see **farrier's nails, handrest** and **Stained Glass: Glazing, Tools and Materials.**

Glenshea linen. Crewel. Embroidery. A trade for evenly woven linen fabric manufactured in Scotland. It is excellent for **counted-thread embroidery.**

glory hole. Glasswork. A reheating furnace used in glassblowing. It is typically a metal cylinder lined with **refractory** material and fitted with gas burners that keep the interior at a steady heat of about 1400° C, which is considerably hotter than the customary temperature of the **tank furnace.**

As a blown vessel cools to a point where the thicker parts begin to lose the orange-yellow glow, the vessel requires reheating to the working temperature. This can be done in the furnace mouth, but it is difficult to control the area being heated and the piece frequently drops back into the soup. The glory hole solves this problem.

The glory hole is so named because the glare from the working hole, as a piece is heated, is so bright it can damage the eyes. Protective dark goggles must be worn if the work is to be viewed while heating.

The glory hole is very hot to work near and consumes a lot of fuel to maintain its heat, even if the chamber is surrounded with insulation brick to prevent heat loss. It is, however, a necessary convenience when work of a delicate nature has to be reheated.

gloss. Glasswork. Woodworking. A shiny or lustrous surface finish. Glass can be said to have a gloss finish. If the same glass is abraded with sandpaper or by means of acid etching, the surface can be made **matte.** Varnishes applied to wood usually leave a gloss surface, although matte-finish varnishes are available. Also see **finish.**

gloss finish enamel. Toys. See **enamel paint.**

glossy. Stitchery. Shiny, reflective, or lustrous **fabrics** with a shiny surface, such as **satin** or **silk**, may be referred to as glossy. **Plastic-coated fabrics** often have a very shiny, glossy surface.

glossy cane. Basketry. See **cane.**

glossy wrapping cane. Basketry. See **cane.**

glost fire. Ceramics. See **glaze fire.**

glove leather. Leatherwork. A term denoting any fine lightweight leather commonly used for making gloves, such as **kidskin, goatskin, calfskin,** or **cabretta.**

glove puppet. Puppets. See **hand puppet.**

glover's needle. Leatherwork. See **needle.**

gloves. Knitting. Knit gloves play a special role in the history of knitting. Over the centuries the traditional designs, patterns, and colors of gloves have been refined and perfected to such a degree that it is possible to know approximately where and when a glove or mitten was knit. Also see **Knitting.**

glove-type hand. Puppets. A fingered hand made for the end of an open sleeve of the **hand puppet** or **marionette.** It may be made in any of several ways, each of which shows a thumb and fingers.

Lines of stitching on a **hand** shape that is cut from one or two layers of **felt** will serve to depict the fingers, with the thumb cut out. Chamois may be cut into finger shapes after 2 layers have been glued together. Or the fingers can be sewn of fabric, turned, and **stuff**ed, although this is difficult to do on such small shapes. Finally, an **armature** can be built using **florist's wire.** The hand is outlined in wire and the fingers are added, and then all these extensions are wrapped with strips of cloth or **gauze** and coated with **wheat paste** or **papier mâché.** Some marionettes are made with hands of **sheet lead.** In adding the glove-type hands to the garment of the hand puppet, the hands must face the front with thumbs up. Also see **mitten-type hand.**

glow candle. Candlemaking. An attractive molded candle with a hard-wax outer shell and soft-wax inner core. Clear high-**melting point** wax is heated to 200° F, combined with a teaspoon of **stearic acid** to further harden it, and poured into a tall metal **mold.** If a professional mold is used, the wick hole in the bottom should be sealed with clay or **caulking compound.** The wax is allowed to cool until it builds up to roughly ¼–½" thick around the sides. Any remaining wax is then poured out. The candle may then be wicked with a **wire wick,** or with a stiffened **braided wick.** Pierce a hole in the bottom wax. Set the wick with a small amount of soft wax heated to 190° F, with no stearic acid, but poured at 160° F. Allow to harden. Pull the wick taut, center it up through the mold, secure it with a rod across the top of the mold, and pour in the remainder of the soft wax. A similar candle can be made by the reverse process in which a soft core candle is molded, then dipped in hard wax heated to 200–210° F. Also see **Candlemaking: Dipping.**

glue. Bookbinding. Glue is used to adhere endpapers to the boards and to laminate sheets of paper together. Flexible glue is used in back gluing processes such as **back lining, backing,** and **rounding.** Electric and Sterno-heated **glue pots** are commonly used in the bindery. Glue spoils when heated above 150° F; it is adequately heated at 120–130° F. Occasional heating of stored glue will prevent the formation of mold.

glue. Découpage. Papercrafts. For general use in découpage, **white glue** is adequate. Thin it with water for gluing thin paper or **gold braid.** White glue is difficult to wipe completely off the surface after it begins to harden, so it is better to use for applying simple shapes rather than intricately cut ones. A few drops of glycerin from the drugstore can be added to make white glue dry more slowly.

Découpage studios and hobby shops carry specially prepared découpage glue, which may be better for work with very intricate **cutouts** when the surface itself receives the glue.

For glass, use white glue thinned with water, or Adhesium glue from paint stores. Also see **flour paste, papier-mâché paste.**

glue. Featherwork. Various adhesives are available for gluing feathers. Rubber cement and white glue are most commonly used. Barge Cement is a popular brand that comes with a brush applicator. The cement container should be tightly closed when not in use as it will thicken and the fumes are strong. Brush the glue or cement on the backing surface, then place the feathers as desired.

glue. Leatherwork. See **rubber cement.**

glue. Mosaics. See **adhesive.**

glue. Puppets. Stitchery. Toys. An **adhesive** made from gelatin, obtained by boiling animal hoofs, bones, skins, and often referred to as **animal glue.** The gelatinous material is mixed with water or other substances to make various glue products. This glue is often light brown in color. Any viscous or adhesive substance may be referred to as a glue even if it has a vegetable base (such as **mucilage**) or a synthetic base (such as **white glue**). Also see **acetate glue, sawdust** and **Stitchery: Gluing.**

glue. Tincrafting. See **Tincrafting: Joining the Tin.**

glue. Woodworking. See **adhesive.**

glue gun. Toys. See **hot melt glue gun.**

gluepot. Bookbinding. A cast-iron double boiler in a water jacket with a built-in heating unit designed to melt dry glue and keep it fluid while binding.

gluing. Amber Carving. See **Amber Carving: Finishing.**

glycerin. Metalworking. (Also called glycerol, glycol alcohol.) A colorless, odorless, syrupy liquid made from fats and oils, used for preparing a **flux** for **soldering pewter.** To prepare the flux, mix 10 drops of **hydrochloric acid** with 1 ounce of glycerin.

glycerin. Toys. See **alcohol.**

glycerol. Metalworking. See **glycerin.**

glycerol. Toys. See **alcohol.**

glycol alcohol. Metalworking. See **glycerin.**

GMA welding. Metalworking. See **welding.**

goatskin. Leatherwork. The skin from mature goats. It is durable and pliable and is used for gloves, linings, and lacing. Also see **glove leather.**

Gob. Glasswork. See **gather.**

gobbler box. Toys. See **turkey call.**

Gobelin bobbin. Weaving. A long **bobbin** with a pointed end used in the weaving of Gobelin tapestries. The pointed end serves to beat down the **filling.** The bobbins are about 8″ long and have an indentation at about the middle, where the yarn is wound. When not in use but still attached to the tapestry a half-hitch is made with the yarn around the neck of the bobbin. This allows it to hang down without unwinding. See ill. Also see **high-warp.**

Gobelin bobbin with yarn

Gobelin droit. Needlepoint. See **Gobelin stitch.**

Gobelin loom. Weaving. See **high-warp, tapestry loom.**

Gobelin stitch. Needlepoint. (Also called Gobelin droit, Renaissance stitch, straight Gobelin, tapestry stitch, upright Gobelin.) An upright stitch worked over any number of mesh that is excellent for backgrounds and as a **filling stitch** because it is fast, easy to work up, and gives a firm backing to a piece. It can also be used as a **border stitch.**

In appearance it resembles a woven tapestry. It should be worked with an even tension, as stitches pulled too tightly will expose the **canvas** threads. If the stitches are pulled too tightly, a **back stitch** can be worked over the exposed canvas threads. In working this stitch, it is important to remember to always come up in an empty hole and down into an occupied one.

The Gobelin stitch is the basis for the **encroaching Gobelin** and **slanting Gobelin.** See ill.

a.   b.   Gobelin stitch

Gobelin stitch. Rugmaking. See **tapestry stitch.**

Gobelin tapestry. Weaving. A **tapestry** originating from the Gobelins Factory in Paris, which was sponsored as the royal tapestry factory under Louis XIV. The French tapestry weavers were brought together as a group at Gobelins, which is on the site of a dyeworks founded by Jehan Gobelin in the fifteenth century. It is now a national museum and factory. Also see **high-warp, interlocking, slit tapestry.**

Godey, Louis Antoine. Découpage. Godey, with a partner, founded the first successful women's magazine, "The Lady's Book," in 1830. Later, after the partner withdrew, the name was changed to "Godey's Lady's Book."

Most prized today are the full-color illustrations of ladies' fashions, with figures shown in atmospheric settings of the opera, taking tea, in the park, and so on. These plates were originally hand-colored lithographs. Today, copies of these prints are available for use in découpage.

goggles. Jewelry. Protective, shatterproof glasses that encompass the eyes should always be worn when using a motor-driven **grinding wheel** to recondition tools. They should be worn even if the **grinding** machine has a glass protective device mounted on the motor.

goggles. Metalworking. See **eye protector, oxyacetylene welding equipment.**

goggles. Stained Glass. See **dalle-de-verre** and **Stained Glass: Safety Precautions.**

gold. Ceramics. An element that is used in pottery. Usually twenty-four-karat gold is used in the form of an **overglaze** or enamel is fired onto ceramic **ware** in the process called **gilding.** The gold liquid is brushed on to the piece and then must be fired precisely at 1085° F. The applied gold decoration will fire **matte** or glossy depending on the glaze.

gold. China and Glass Painting. Available in powdered or liquid form, it has a metallic gloss after **firing,** and is used for decorating china and glass. It is all right to add the gold after a design has been painted on china but not yet fired if the paint is carefully removed from the areas to be gold. Clear these areas with a cloth dampened in turpentine; remove the paint from small areas with a cloth over the end of a brush handle. The china must be absolutely clean where gold is to be painted. Gold may be applied over colors that have been fired, then refired. When gold is applied over another color, it will have a matte surface after firing. A **banding wheel** may be used to apply gold bands and circles. A rich ground can be achieved by **dusting** powdered gold. Neither the brushes for adding gold nor the small palette knife for mixing it should be used for anything else. Manufacturers of gold usually give directions on the package for the correct **medium** to be used for mixing.

Gold pigment available in powder form, called matte gold, needs grinding and mixing with **lavender oil** and has a dull finish after firing. If a high luster is wanted, polish by **burnishing** after firing. However, unburnished gold will wear brighter with use. There are two types of matte gold:

Roman gold, also called fluxed gold, which contains **flux,** and hard, or unfluxed, gold. Since unfluxed gold does not contain the flux necessary to bind the color to the glaze, it must be used in combination with **fluxed color,** i.e., over **tinting,** or over **raised paste** designs. Unfluxed gold is not used on white china, as there would not be enough flux present to fuse it to the china. After firing, unfluxed gold is much brighter than fluxed gold. To apply matte gold, dip a brush into the paint, making sure to keep the paint mixed while working, and cover the surface with smooth, even strokes.

Liquid bright gold is a brown, oily liquid available in jars or small bottles. Stir the liquid, then paint it on the china with a camel's-hair brush. It is generally used just as it is in the bottle, but it can be thinned with lavender oil or a commercially available essence for thinning gold. Use the thinner supplied by the manufacturer of the gold. Thin sparingly; too much oil makes gold bubble and peel in firing. Never use turpentine with it; it will become discolored. After firing, the gold has a bright luster and does not require burnishing. Liquid gold is used over raised paste applied with a fine sable liner brush.

Liquid bright gold can be used to cover large surfaces for the first firing, then covered by dusting with matte gold for a second firing for a lustrous matte finish. Or the two golds can be mixed about half and half, using a bit more than half of matte gold and thinning with lavender oil if necessary.

A metallic green-gold paint can be mixed from 1 part **silver** and 3 parts matte gold.

Gold for glass, which is mixed with anise oil, must be fixed at lower temperatures than china. Gold especially prepared for use on glass is available. After firing, it has a brilliant finish, and is also gold when seen on the reverse side of the transparent glass. It may be polished by burnishing with sand. Also see **white gold.**

gold. Enameling. See **metal, metal foil, metallic luster.**

gold. Mosaics. See **smalti.**

gold beads. Beadwork. Gold, treasured since ancient times, has a long history of use in jewelry and beadwork. Various techniques have been used for making gold beads. It has been hammered into thin sheets, then bent into desired shapes, and it has been melted and poured into bead molds. Gold beads can be finished with smooth or textured surfaces, or with fine, raised gold wire designs. The technique of designing with raised gold wires and tiny gold dots, called granulation, was perfected by the Etruscans.

Since its discovery, gold has been venerated as a source of life-giving heat. On the African Gold Coast it has been considered the embodiment of the spirit of the sun. It is not hard to understand why this glowing metal, which never changes color or tarnishes and which has been venerated for its mystical powers, has inspired intricate and rich design work in nearly every civilization.

gold braid. Découpage. See **gold-paper trim.**

gold cord. Embroidery. Plyed strands and braids made of metal or metal combined with silk, rayon, or other fibers used in **metallic thread embroidery.** They are applied to the **background fabric** by **couching** with a strong waxed cotton or silk thread to form the design entirely or be used as an outline. Also see **Lurex thread.**

gold cushion. Bookbinding. A block of wood, padded on the top and covered with rough calf or other nongreasy leather. It is used for laying **gold leaf** out or for **titling** or **tooling.**

Golden Glow. Quilts. See **Star Flower.**

Golden section. The mathematical **proportion** 1.0:.618. This proportion, known to the ancient Greeks, is one of the most pleasing ways to relate two lengths of line, two volumes, or two areas. A line divided into two parts at the golden section point has a kind of balance that is clearer to see than to try to explain. In the illustration, the line AC has been divided at the point B. The ratio of the distance AB to the distance BC is the same as the ratio between the distance BC to the distance AC. Applications of this proportion to designs include the proportion of the height to the width of the Parthenon, and the placement of lines in compositions by Mondrian. See ill.

Golden section

gold filled. Jewelry. A term used to indicate that a base metal has been mechanically coated with a thin layer of gold by brazing, **soldering,** or welding. The gold can be applied only to the top surface or to both top and bottom; in the case of wire, all surfaces may be coated. Usually jewelry is marked "GF" (gold filled) or gold rolled. They are really commercial terms, and although correct are misleading because gold filled implies "filled with gold." The label "$^1/_{10}$ 12K gold filled" means that the base metal has been covered with 12K gold, and that the gold **alloy** makes up $^1/_{10}$ the total weight of the piece. Also see **gold leaf. leaf.**

golding rims. China and Glass Painting. See **banding.**

gold knife. Bookbinding. An 8″ × 1″ blade with one slightly rough edge (not sharp enough to cut the **gold cushion**) that is used to cut **gold leaf.** The blade must be kept grease-free.

gold leaf. Bookbinding. Gold leaf is used for **gilding** the edges of the leaves of a book and for titles and decorations. It is about 23 carats, beaten to a thickness generally of .000004″, and sold in books of 25 leaves, or sheets, of 3¼ inch square.

gold leaf. Découpage. Extremely thin sheets of pure or synthetic gold used for **gilding.** Gold leaf, available at craft and paint stores, comes in tissue-paper books, usually 3½″ square with 25 sheets to the book. Various shades are available, from deep, rich gold to lemon gold to white.

A patent gold for "gilding in the wind" is also available. It is easier to handle but not really suitable for work to be closely observed, such as découpage. It is used on outdoor objects, such as balls on flag poles.

To apply, cut the gold-leaf book along the binding to free the sheets. The gold leaf is always picked up by the tissue paper sheet.

gold leaf. Jewelry. Gold that has been beaten or rolled into tissue-thin sheets. It is always **fine gold,** or nearly so. It is often used for decoration and is extremely fragile. It is glued into place with a glue referred to as a "size." It can also be placed within a bezel or between a transparent or translucent gemstone, such as a Mexican opal, and the base metal to enhance the stone's color and to reflect light. This works especially well if the work is of silver, as the silver will eventually tarnish under the stone and turn black, but the gold **foil** will remain bright and shiny. Silver and platinum leaf are also available.

gold leaf. Toys. See **gold metal leaf.**

gold leafing. Découpage. See **gilding.**

gold metal leaf. Toys. (Also called gold leaf.) A **metallic paper,** thinner than tissue paper, used in gold leafing to add a lustrous surface, often for **antiquing.** It can be applied to small areas of most surfaces with **white glue.** If large areas are to be gold-leafed, a **gold sizing** should be painted on first.

gold oxide. Stained Glass. See **antique glass colorants.**

gold-paper trim. Découpage. A variety of gold-foil paper, gold-braid borders, and ornamental designs manufactured in West Germany and available in craft shops. The trims are embossed with raised parts and die-cut in intricate patterns. The borders range from a fine line to several inches wide. These decorations are glued to the surface and combined with **cutout**s to give added luster to the découpage design. They are frequently combined with Victorian cutouts.

The gold trims come in a bright gold. They may be antiqued by spraying or wiping sparingly with an oil paint color, such as raw umber, burnt umber, or Venetian red.

Before applying to the surface, the trim should be sprayed with clear **acrylic** to protect the gold color from running when the **sealer** is applied. It is helpful to coat the back of the trim with sealer to keep it stiff. When the sealer is dry, **white glue** thinned with water is applied to the back of the trim. In working with bulky trims, use thinned sealer and **glue** to prevent adding more thickness. Allow glued trim to set until **tacky** before applying; then press in place. Roll down trim with a brayer to ensure a tight bond and to flatten as much as possible so that the **varnish** does not form puddles around the edges. When the trim has dried, the sealer and then the découpage **finish** may be applied.

gold purl. Embroidery. Twisted metallic thread used in **metallic thread embroidery.** Also see **bullion thread.**

gold ringer cowrie. Shell Carving. (*Cypraea annula.*) A shell with a gray exterior layer, a thin layer of gray **middle color,** and a black to violet **ground color** used in **cameo carving.** It is small and can be used for a ring-sized cameo without trimming. Also see **cowrie, helmet,** and **Shell Carving: Shell Preparation and Tools.**

gold rolled. Jewelry. See **gold filled.**

gold size. Découpage. The adhesive used to glue **gold leaf** to surfaces in **gilding.** Two types of size are available. Burnish size is used for water gilding, which requires burnishing. It combines rabbit-skin glue, grain alcohol, and water in a solution applied over a base of finely ground, tinted clay, called "bole," mixed with water. Oil-base size is used for oil, or mordant gilding for surface called mat-leafed, the technique generally used in découpage. Oil-base size comes as a slow- or quick-drying varnishlike liquid, so it should be selected according to the speed at which you plan to work. The time it takes for the glue to dry to the **tacky** stage, when gilding can be applied, varies from 30 minutes to 48 hours, depending on the weather.

Regular gilder's oil size, tinted with yellow, is slow-drying and remains tacky for 48 hours, so should be applied the night before gilding.

Japan gold size, or quick-drying size, is an amber-tinted varnish that usually becomes tacky within an hour.

gold sizing. Toys. A slow-drying amber-colored liquid used under **gold metal leaf** to simulate the appearance of gold. Several hours should elapse after painting the gold sizing onto a surface before the gold leaf is added so that it becomes tacky enough for the leaf to adhere. Also see **antiquing.**

goldsmith. Jewelry. An artisan who works with gold.

Goldsmith's Hall. Jewelry. See **Worshipful Company of Goldsmiths.**

goldstone. Gemcutting. A man-made material composed of glass with copper filings. It resembles sunstone or avanturine **quartz** in **luster** and **color.**

gold tooling. Bookbinding. The application of **gold leaf** with heated decorative tools to the cover of a book. Also see **glaire, tooling.**

Golgotha. Quilts. See **Three Crosses.**

Golliwog. Toys. A popular **stuffed toy** based on a nursery character in a book by Florence Upton, "The Adventure of Two Dutch Dolls and a Golliwog." The character is usually a gangling **rag doll** with fuzzy hair, black face, and wide eyes. The Golliwog was as popular in England as the **teddy bear** was in America. Golliwogs were often homemade rag dolls as variable as **Raggedy Ann.**

goose-eye pattern. Weaving. A variety of **diamond twill** in which the **threading** and **treadling** are identical, i.e., it is **treadled as-drawn-in.** This produces a **filling-face**d diamond effect. Also see **twill weave.**

Goose-in-the-Pond. Quilts. (Also called Young Man's Fancy.) A **pieced quilt block** design of 25 squares. The squares may be made up of triangles, bands, prints, and solids, or some of the squares may be **nine-patch** designs. A slight variation in the arrangement gives a block design called Missouri Puzzle. See ill.

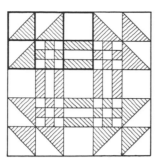

Goose-in-the-Pond

Goose Tracks. Quilts. See **Bear's Paw.**

goshenite. Gemcutting. See **beryl.**

gossip wheel. Spinning. See **double spinning wheel.**

gouache. A kind of watercolor prepared with gum that produces opaque paints. Also, a painting done with these kinds of paints. They are sometimes called designer's colors.

gouge. Bookbinding. A finishing tool used to apply curved lines; when applied end to end they form a circle.

gouge. Leatherwork. A tool used for cutting grooves in leather as a preparation for recessed stitching or for folding and creasing leather. To use the gouge, adjust the blade for the groove depth desired, mark a line where you want the groove to be, and, holding the gouge firmly at about a 45° angle to the leather, push it along the line at an even pressure, making one continuous cut. Also see **adjustable gouge, adjustable V-gouge** and **Leatherwork: Tools and Materials.**

gouge. Metalworking. See **blacksmithing tools.**

gouge. Woodworking. A cutting tool differing from a **chisel** in that the cutting blade is U-shaped or V-shaped, rather than flat, in cross-section. Gouges are used for **roughing out** large areas of wood in **carpentry, wood turning,** and **woodcarving.**

There are two types of tips. Firmer gouges are most common; the tip is beveled on the outside of the tool for easy-to-reach cuts (**a.**). Pairing gouges are beveled on the inside of the cutting tip and are used for deep straight or curved cuts (**b.**).

Carpenter's gouges have straight blades with parallel sides. Blade widths range from ⅛ to 2″. Wood-turning gouges are like carpenter's gouges except that the handles are longer and the blades shorter; they are used only on the wood-turning lathe.

Woodcarving gouges are made in a great variety of shapes and sizes for different operations. Straight gouges are most common; the cross-section can be anything from a broad to a deep U, for cuts ranging from broad and shallow to deep and narrow (**c.**). Spoon or bent gouge blades are

slightly bent or spoon-shaped to permit carving in deep holes (**d.**). Parting or V gouges are used for cutting a V-shaped groove between two forms (**e.**).

Carpenter's and woodcarving gouges are used by striking the handle with the palm of the hand or a **mallet;** wood-turning gouges are fed into the wood spinning on a lathe. All are sharpened similarly to chisels, except that they are rolled on the grinding wheel or sharpening stone to conform to the shape of the blade. See ill. Also see **sharpening, woodcarving tools, wood-turning tools** and **Woodworking: Grinding and Sharpening, Whittling and Woodcarving, Wood Turning.**

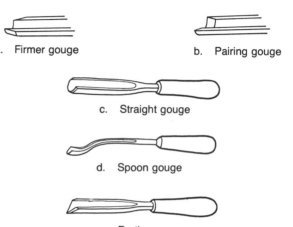

a. Firmer gouge   b. Pairing gouge

c. Straight gouge

d. Spoon gouge

e. Parting gouge

gouge stone. Woodworking. See **sharpening stone.**

grade. Gemcutting. See **grinding wheel.**

grading. Basketry. See **Basketry: Preparing the Materials.**

grading. Leatherwork. See **Leatherwork: Weight Designations and Grading.**

grading. Woodworking. See **wood.**

Grafting. Knitting. Grafting is done to unite two knitted fabrics in an invisible way. It is usually used to replace the toes of socks or fingers of gloves. A tapestry needle is threaded with very thin yarn and threaded in and out, following the pattern of the stitches. The grafting must be done according to pattern. See ill.

Grafting

grain. Bookbinding. Papercrafts. (Also called machine direction.) The cellulose fibers that compose **paper** and **board**s tend to run in one general direction (especially true of machine-made paper) called "grain." The term also refers to the lengthwise fibers of **cloth** (fibers that run parallel to the selvage).

With the exception of oblong format books, the grain of all the materials used in **bookbinding** always runs **head** to

tail, parallel to the binding. In the case of paper, it will bend more easily along the grain than against it; leaves that are used crosswise, or against the grain, will **cockle** with the application of moist adhesives, while those used with the grain is sometimes referred to as just the **grain,** while the along the lengthwise grain, pages will turn more easily and endpapers are less likely to crease. Boards cut grain-wise will tend not to warp, and are more rigid and stable.

The stability and quality of a finished binding is heavily dependent on the direction of the grain. If the grain is not readily apparent, there are some simple tests to determine its direction. Cut two strips of paper from the sheet in question, at right angles to each other, and moisten them with a sponge; the strip that tunnels lengthwise is cut along the grain. Crease a sheet of paper and wet it along the fold line; if the fold cockles, it has been folded against the grain. Paper will tear in a straighter line with the grain than against it. Sheets of paper will roll up more easily with the grain.

grain. Leatherwork. The outer layer or hair side of a skin, which retains the characteristics of the skin or hide of the animal. Grain leather is the strongest leather. **Top grain** leather is the leather split from the outside of the animal. Also see **casing, embossing, grain side, snuffed, splitting** and **Leatherwork: Gluing and Bonding Leather.**

grain. Metalworking. See **metal.**

grain. Quilts. Stitchery. The direction of the **fibers** or the direction of the weave of a **fabric.** There is always a **lengthwise grain** and a **crosswise** grain. The lengthwise grain is sometimes referred to as just the **grain,** while the **weft** or crosswise grain is sometimes called across the grain. Fabric will tear **"on the grain"** but tears best across the grain. Cutting on the grain is done by cutting a line exactly parallel to the threads of the material, either the **warp (lengthwise threads)** or weft (woof, filler, or **crosswise threads**). In **quilting** and **stitchery** it is important that fabrics be cut according to the grain or in line with the grain.

In cutting fabric for **garments,** the length of a pattern (top of skirt to hem) is aligned with the lengthwise grain. In some cutting, as in **quilt blocks,** cutting **"on the grain"** may simply mean to align a pattern with either the warp or weft thread. A **bias** cut is always **"off the grain,"** or at an angle to the grain.

grain. Woodworking. See **wood.**

grain filler. Woodworking. A colored material used to fill in the pores of **wood** grain to produce a smooth wood finish. The two basic types of grain fillers are: liquid fillers, used to fill the pores of close-grain wood such as **birch** and **maple;** and paste fillers, used on open grain wood such as **oak, mahogany,** and **walnut.** Woods such as **pine, poplar,** and **cherry** do not require a grain filler because their pores are very small. Fillers tend to stain the wood darker when applied, so it is advisable to first seal the surface with a coat of **shellac** to preserve the original wood color or **stain.**

To apply a paste grain filler, thin the paste to a creamy consistency with the appropriate **solvent** or thinner. On a small section at a time, brush on the filler across the grain, allowing it to dry to a dull finish. With a coarse rag, such as a piece of burlap, remove all the excess by wiping across the grain. With a soft cloth, lightly wipe the surface in the direction of the grain. Use a cloth wrapped around a **dowel** to remove extra filler from crevices and grooves. Let dry and seal it with a **sealant.**

To apply a liquid grain filler, use the same application procedures as you would for a paste filler. The liquid is absorbed more readily than paste, so there will be little excess. Also see **wood filler** and **Woodworking: Finishing.**

grains. Jewelry. See **casting grains.**

grain side. Leatherwork. See **grain.**

grain size. Gemcutting. See **grinding wheel.**

graissage. Stained Glass. The French term for **cementing lead came.**

grandfather candle. Candlemaking. An unusual type of candle, still found in rural Balkan areas, made to burn throughout the entire period of Lent for the souls of deceased grandparents. It is made by feeding a long **wick** through a hot **wax bath,** allowing the wax to accumulate in thin **taper** fashion. Once the wax has hardened sufficiently it is coiled or wrapped like thread around a specially designed candle holder. The taper is reeled out like a rope as it is consumed by the flame. See ill.

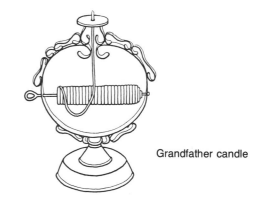

Grandfather candle

Grandma's Dream. Quilts. See **Trip Around the World.**

Grandmother's Fan. Quilts. Any of a variety of **fan quilt** patterns, most of which use a series of radiating bands of color. It can be **pieced** or **appliqué**d, or the **block** can be

Grandmother's Fan

made using a combination of the two techniques. The arrangement suggests a fan placed in one corner of the block. When **set** with fans together, the block is similar to **Harvest Sun.** See ill.

Grandmother's Flower Garden. Quilts. See **hexagon quilt.**

grandrelle yarn. Spinning. Weaving. See **novelty yarn.**

granite-backed glass. Stained Glass. A **machine-made** glass designed with a rough back that helps disperse light. It is easy to work with if no attempt is made to cut on the granite side.

granny square. Crochet. One of the best known of all **double crochet** patterns. The granny square is seen most often sewn together in afghans.

granular fracture. Gemcutting. See **fracture.**

granulation. Beadwork. See **gold beads.**

granulation. Jewelry. A technique in which minute spheres, or grains, of metal are attached to a base without the use of **solder.** This technique is usually done with **fine gold** or **fine silver,** but it is also possible with some **karat** golds and sterling if a fine gold or fine silver surface is first developed on them. The granules are attached through a molecular exchange. The Greeks, Romans, and other ancient cultures, especially the Etruscans, were accomplished in this art. As gemstones gained favor, the technique lost popularity.

Making the grains is somewhat time consuming, but it is the simplest part of granulation. A layer of crushed charcoal is placed in a small steel box or small **graphite crucible.** The most direct method is to cut small lengths of fine silver, gold **cloison** or other wire, or sheet metal pallions. Very fine balls can be made by drawing a coarse file across a bar or sheet of gold or silver. Place the metal pieces on a bed of charcoal; keep them separate or they will join and form shot instead of granules. Add another ½" layer of charcoal, then more metal, alternating until the container is full and ending with charcoal. Place the crucible in a preheated kiln and allow it to heat up to the point that the metal becomes molten. (Fine silver becomes molten at 1761° F and fine gold becomes molten at 1945° F.) As the metal becomes molten it pulls in on itself and begins to roll within the layers of charcoal, forming spheres. After formations allow the crucible to cool at a natural rate, dump the contents into sudsy water to separate the charcoal, which will float, from the granules, which will sink.

The granules themselves are separated according to size by hand or by sifting them through different-mesh screens. A solution is prepared of copper filings soaked in ammonia for a few days to dissolve them. As the liquid evaporates, water is added. The dilute solution is mixed with **Klyr Fyre,** which acts as a temporary binder when placing the grains on the work to which they will be granulated.

To affix granules of pure gold, a copper salt, such as cupric hydroxide, $CU(OH)_2$ is mixed with an organic glue, such as gum tragacanth, acacia, or fish, in equal amounts. This provides copper to form an alloy at the point of contact between the **base metal** and the granule when the surface is melted. The base metal must be free of grease and oxides before being coated with the solution. The base metal should be of the same metal as the grains. The small grains, which can be minuscule if desired, are picked up and placed in position with a fine sable brush. After the work is thoroughly dry it is placed in a trinket kiln, a small kiln 4–6" across, with a removable cover, usually of aluminum. The coils of the kiln should be completely embedded in a **refractory material.**

The trinket kiln is preheated and the work, with the grains in position, is placed inside. When the metal becomes bright red—this procedure should be done in a dimmed light—a **torch** is used to further and uniformly heat the work. The evenness of the heat from the kiln and the added temperature of the **oxidizing flame** of the torch cause the upper surfaces, or skins, of the base metal and the granules to become molten. The molecules interchange between the two, securing the granules in position. There is great danger at this point of the entire work becoming molten and collapsing. As soon as the granules have adhered (this is instantaneous), the torch must instantly be pulled away and the work blown on to cool it, however slightly, and removed from the kiln at once.

After the work has cooled it is **pickle**d and then polished with a brass **brush** and a solution of detergent and water. A final **bright dip** can also be used. Shapes other than round also may be adhered with this technique.

Grapevine. Quilts. See **Hawaiian quilt.**

grapevine and grapes. Quilts. See **border.**

graphite. Jewelry. A soft native carbon with a black metallic luster, a hardness of 1–2, and a specific gravity of 2.09–2.23. In powder form combined with clay it is called **plumbago** and used to make metal-melting **crucible**s. In the form of **graphite rod**s it is used for stirring molten metal.

graphite rod. Jewelry. An eight-inch rod of **graphite** used in special circumstances for stirring molten precious metals. Graphite rods are enduring, unaffected by extreme temperature changes, may be handled with bare hands, and metals do not stick to them. They are also used in **niello.**

graphoscope. Toys. An **optical toy** that is a simplified variation of the **stereoscope,** having only a single large lens.

graph paper. Beadwork. Knitting. Graph paper available from art supply stores, printed with a grid of about ⅛" squares, can be used in planning patterns for bead weaving. However, because beads are not perfectly square, as the grid is, this should be used only as a general guide. Special bead graph papers are available for more accurate designing.

In knitting it refers to the paper marked off in an even, over-all grid used to chart knitting designs or patterns. The size of the grid varies, but the sizes include 4, 5, 6, 8, 10, and

12 squares to the inch; each square represents one stitch. The pattern is charted on this paper and is then followed stitch by stitch and row by row as the knitting progresses. Also see **charting** and **Knitting: Knitting Terms and Abbreviations.**

graph paper. Crewel. Embroidery. Needlepoint. Paper with a grid of evenly spaced horizontal and vertical lines. It is available in art supply and stationery stores in many sizes that correspond to the sizes of **canvas,** for example, 10 squares to the inch. For this reason it is very useful in plotting out your own designs and **enlarging and reducing designs.** It also is available as tracing paper, which can be laid over an existing design and transferred to a canvas. Also see **clear plastic grid overlay** and **Needlepoint: Transferring Designs.**

graph paper. Rugmaking. Weaving. Paper used by weavers to draft out the **drawing-in draft, chain draft, tie-up, treadling sequence,** and any other drafts associated with weaving. The paper is in small squares—4, 8, or 10 to an inch being the sizes preferred by most weavers. Often the paper has a heavier line at every inch, horizontally and vertically, to make the drafting and counting easier. Rugmakers use graph paper to plot out their designs in small sizes. Then when they **latch hook,** embroider, or weave them, every square represents a space, or threads, in a **canvas** or **warp end**s on a **loom.** Also see **drafting.**

grass bleaching. Quilts. Stitchery. A **bleaching** method which is accomplished by placing **fabric**s on the grass, exposed to sun and air. In Ireland this process is called "crofting."

grass fiber. Spanning. Weaving. A broad term pertaining to coarse vegetable **fiber**s and reeds and including **ramie, jute, hemp,** yucca, palm, ordinary grasses, and young bamboo. Grass fibers can be combined with yarn or other natural elements such as bark. Grass cloth woven totally of grass fiber, usually ramie, is found in native bazaars and shops all over the world. Before the advent of **loom**s, ancient peoples twined grass fibers into **cordage,** baskets, mats, and other household items. Also see **twining.**

grassing. Spinning. See **Spinning.**

graver. Jewelry. (Also called burin, scorper.) A small sharpened steel chisel used to engrave designs into metal. Gravers are available in many widths and shapes, but the sharpened ends fall into four basic categories, round, flat, point, and square.

Although engraving is a relatively simple process, it takes a great deal of time to become technically proficient.

Position the work securely in the **engraver's block, pitch, sealing wax,** or **shellac stick.** Support oversized pieces against a **sandbag.** Lubricate the cutting tip of the graver with wintergreen oil; the graver can also be used without lubrication.

Hold the graver with the wooden handle against the outer side of the palm, near the wrist. Use thumb and first two fingers to hold the shank of the tool near the cutting end. The thumb can be used as a guide or pivot point when engraving a curve.

Cut the point of the graver slightly into the metal and move it with a smooth motion just below the surface of the metal. Keep the same angle and pressure while cutting, otherwise the graver will burrow into the metal and stop.

To disengage the graver, stop the forward motion and pressure of the graver, dig in slightly, and lift up with a slight backing up movement. This may possibly produce a **burr,** which can be easily removed by using a scraper.

If a slip occurs and metal is cut which was not intended to be, all that can be done is to try to incorporate the mistake into the design, or remove it by **filing** with a **needle file, riffler,** or fine **emery paper.** If it is not too deep, a **Scotch stone** can be used. However, the metal must be thick enough to allow for the removal of errors with all of the above possibilities.

Gravers are almost always sharp when purchased and must be sharpened often to maintain the best cutting tip. Fine points break easily. Reshape a broken point on a **grinding wheel.** Keep dipping the tool in water to keep it cool; if it gets too hot the metal will lose its temper. If a grinding wheel is not available, a file can be used, although this is much more difficult.

The best cutting angle for the edge is a 45° angle to the shank. A lesser angle produces a deeper cut, preventing the tip from breaking as easily, but the tip is harder to control. A greater angle produces a shallow cut and increases the chances of the tip breaking.

Sharpen the point on an **Arkansas oilstone** or an **India oilstone** and then on very fine **emery paper.** Place the emery paper rough side up on a very flat surface such as a piece of glass. During grinding and sharpening of a graver, a constant angle must be maintained to produce a uniform and sufficient cutting edge. This is the most difficult procedure in sharpening. A tool called an **engraver's sharpener** can be used to combat this problem.

To test the sharpness of a graver, push it with a slight pressure lengthwise against the fingernail. If it produces a cut in the nail it is sharp and ready to use. See ill. Also see **electric engraving tool, liner, transferring designs to metal.**

Graver

gravity toy. Toys. See **balance toy.**

gray compound. Jewelry. See **buffing compound.**

gray glass. Stained Glass. A term denoting the color of glass that is dulled by the addition of nickel or other metallic oxides while making the glass. Also see **antique glass colorants.**

Gray Goose. Quilts. A **pieced** quilt **block** that shows a **geometric** hourglass superimposed on a large X. It is an **overall** pattern, although sometimes it is **set** so that the blocks are separated with contrasting **band**s of color. Because it is not difficult to sew, it is a much-used pattern.

Long before the Civil War, babies were sung to sleep to the lullaby, "Go tell Aunt Rhoda . . . the old gray goose is dead." This was probably the derivation for its original name. Since then it has been known as Brown, Brown Goose, **Devil's Claws,** and Double Z.

gray scale. The ten or so readily distinguishable shades of gray arrayed in even steps between pure white and pure black.

greaseless compound. Jewelry. Metalworking. **Cutting compound**s made of glue combined with a sharp abrasive used to produce a **matte** finish on **copper** and **brass.** They come in stick form, usually protected by a metal covering to prevent them from drying out. The compounds are applied to a **buff** while it is in rotation and allowed to dry before use. Also see **bobbing compound, buffing compound, Lea's compound.**

greaseless steel wool. Metalworking. See **abrasive.**

greasy luster. Gemcutting. See **luster.**

great. Basketry. The largest available size of **willow rod,** 8'6" to 10' long.

Great Divide, the. Quilts. See **Rocky Mountain.**

great wheel. Spinning. See **wool wheel.**

Greek Cross. Quilts. A simple **pieced nine-patch** that consists of a cross in a plain field. Triangles fill each of the four corners of the **block.**

Greek laid-in. Weaving. See **laid-in.**

Greek Soumak. Rugmaking. Weaving. See **Soumak.**

Greek stitch. Needlepoint. See **long-armed cross stitch.**

green. Basketry. Woodworking. The term used to describe freshly cut reed, willow, or other basketry material, or any wood, before it is dried.

green. Woodworking. See **wood.**

Greenaway, Kate. Découpage. Kate Greenaway was an illustrator of children's books whose drawings of charming children in fashionable clothing have become collector's items. Reproductions of these are popular for use in découpage.

Greenaway was born in England in 1846, the daughter of an engraver and illustrator for *Punch* Magazine. She began doing pen-and-ink drawings of gnomes, sprites, and fairies, many of which were reproduced in *The People's Magazine.* She then did illustrations for sheet music, greeting cards, and various publications. She also wrote poetry; the best-known volume, "Under the Window," published in 1878, sold 70,000 copies.

green colorants. Ceramics. See **pigment oxide.**

green compound. Metalworking. See **polishing compound.**

green glaze. Ceramics. The basic **pigment oxide**s for green color are 1 to 3% **copper carbonate** or nickel oxide used with magnesia flux. Iron oxide produces gray-green in **reduction.**

green glazing. Ceramics. Glazing unfired pots to produce **once-fired ware.**

green ivory. Ivory and Bone Carving. See **elephant ivory.**

green rouge. Jewelry. See **buffing compound.**

green sand. Metalworking. See **molding sand.**

green soap. Puppets. See **liquid soap.**

green turtle. Shell Carving. See **Shell Carving: Tortoiseshell.**

greenware. Ceramics. Ceramic **ware** that has not yet been fired.

grid. Needlepoint. Straight lines intersecting at even intervals. Also see **clear plastic grid overlay, graph paper** and **Needlepoint: Transferring Designs.**

grid overlay. Crewel. Embroidery. Needlepoint. See **clear plastic grid overlay.**

grid pattern. Quilts. An arrangement of parallel lines that cross other parallel lines at right angles. All lines are equally spaced and intersect to make a kind of linear **checkerboard.**

grille. Stained Glass. A metal network into which **glass** can be leaded or puttied. Sculptural in form and often cast in aluminum, the metalwork can be as important as the glass. There are also regular grilles used for protecting the stained-glass window in outdoor installations. Also see **Stained Glass: Glazing.**

grin. Basketry. A space or opening that sometimes occurs in a loosely wrapped **handle.** See ill.

grinder. Metalworking. See **grinding tools.**

grinding. Gemcutting. See **grinding wheel.**

grinding. Jewelry. Removing metal with a motor-driven wheel, bandsander, or other device on which **abrasive** wheels, belts, bands, or disks can be used. Grinding is usually done in preparation for further finishing or for reconditioning tools. Also see **buffing machine, eye shields, polishing.**

grinding. Metalworking. Woodworking. Abrasive machining that removes large amounts of material and is accomplished by holding the material against a hard revolving abrasive surface to smooth or shape it. Also see **Metalworking: Finishing, Woodworking: Grinding and Sharpening.**

grinding stone. Woodworking. See **grinding wheel, sharpening stone.**

grinding tool. Metalworking. Woodworking. (Also called grinder.) Abrasive wheels or disks turned by an electric motor. There are many different wheels and disks for different metals, other materials, and different purposes (e.g., rapid stock removal or finishing work). A variety of grades of grinding abrasives from fine to coarse are available.

BENCH GRINDER   The main function of this tool in a wood or metalshop is to renew or maintain the sharp edges of cutting blades or carving tools (a.). It consists of two **grinding wheels,** usually of different grades, one mounted on each end of a shaft connected to an electric motor, and equipped with wheel covers, eye shield, and adjustable tool rests. Its size is determined by the diameter of grinding wheel it will accept—a 7″ bench grinder, for instance, will accept a 7″ grinding wheel. Common home shop sizes are from 5 to 7″ with ¼–½ horsepower motors and speeds from 1750 to 3500 rpm.

The bench grinder is a common source of injuries. Before operating it, check the stone or wheel for cracks. Make sure the eye guard is in place and the tool rest is properly adjusted and secure before turning on the power. If there is no eye guard mounted to the unit, wear protective eye goggles or face shield. When grinding, hold the object to be ground firmly on the tool rest with both hands. Do not touch the turning grinding wheel with your fingers to stop it, even after the power has been turned off.

ANGLE GRINDER   A portable power grinder used especially in metalworking for smoothing welds or removing excess rough metal on large pieces of stock or finished products (b.). A variety of grinding disks, from fine to coarse, are available.

A **flexible-shaft machine** may be used for grinding also. See ill. Also see **Woodworking: Grinding and Sharpening.**

a. Bench grinder   b. Angle grinder

grinding wheel. Ceramics. A bonded, silicon carbide disk turned on an axis. The old ones were operated by a treadle, the new ones by electric motor; they are used for grinding **glaze** off fired pots.

grinding wheel. Gemcutting. A disk with a silicon carbide **abrasive** molded in a porous bond. Grinding wheels range in size from 6 to 12″ in diameter and 1 to 2½″ in thickness. The diameter of the arbor of the machinery must be large enough to support the size of the grinding wheel used; for example, an 8″ × 1½″ wheel should not be run on an arbor of less than ¾″ diameter. The diameter of the metal washers or flanges on the arbor should be at least one-third the diameter of the grinding wheel. The constitution of grinding wheels is given in a number-letter code on the paper flange on the side of the wheel. The last numbers in the first group refer to grain size, the next letter gives the grade of the bond, the next number indicates the pore spacing between grains, and the next letter indicates the type of bonding material.

Grain size (also called sieve or mesh size) is graded by the size of the holes in an imaginary screen that would allow the grains of abrasive to pass through. Silicon carbide wheels are used in grain sizes from 80 to 400.

The grade of a grinding wheel is the strength of the bonding agent. A soft bond cuts quicker because the wheel is worn down faster, exposing fresh abrasive; a hard bond lasts longer but cuts more slowly and can become dull and glazed, causing overheating and possible damage to the gem material. For gemcutting, grades H, I, and J are soft; grades K and L are medium; and grades M and N are hard. Soft material is cut on hard grades; materials over 8 in **hardness** are best cut with **diamond** powder.

Pore spacing is designated by number from 1 (dense) to 10 (wide).

Bonding material is classified by letter. V stands for vitrified bond, S for silicate bond, R for rubber, B for resinoid, and E for shellac.

For best results the grinding wheel should be operated at proper speeds. These speeds are expressed in surface feet per minute and are determined by the speed of the arbor (expressed in revolutions per minute) and the diameter of the wheel. For example, a 6″ wheel operating at 2865 rpm provides a peripheral speed of 4500 fpm, whereas a 12″ wheel turning at 1432 rpm produces the same surface speed. Operation at too low a speed can cause irregularities and bumps in the wheel, requiring resurfacing with a **wheel dresser.**

Water, dripping from a can above the tool, serves as a coolant. If there is no such can, a sponge may be placed in the drain pan so that it comes in contact with the bottom of the wheel. The wheel should not stand in water because it will absorb the water and unbalance its weight, possibly breaking when it is restarted.

A hand rest is helpful for grinding and necessary for dressing the wheel and handling stones the weight of which approaches the weight of the wheel.

The metal shield over the grinding wheel prevents the splashing of water and, in the event of accidental breakage, fragments from striking the operator. As a safety precaution, when the wheel is started, it is best to stand to the side until it reaches speed.

The side of the wheel is rarely used for grinding because it is brittle. The running periphery is used to grind **flats, cabochons,** and **preforms.**

When working small pieces on the grinding wheel keep

the stone moving from side to side to avoid deforming the wheel's surface; the center of the wheel tends to wear more than the edges. When grinding away a sharp point round it gradually, with light pressure. Grind smoothly and steadily; do not bump the work against the wheel. See ill. Also see **machinery** and **Gemcutting: Rough Shaping, Tools and Materials.**

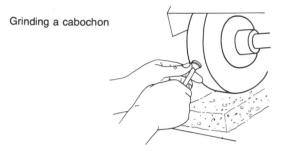

Grinding a cabochon

grinding wheel. Jewelry. Metalworking. Woodworking. A wheel composed of an abrasive bonded with ceramic material, waterglass, **resin,** or **shellac,** and used on a bench grinder, or a **flexible-shaft machine.** The wheel is classified by the type of abrasive, grain size, grade of hardness, and type of bond used.

Common grinding-wheel **abrasives** include **aluminum oxide** or **emery** for grinding metals of high tensile strength (such as carbon steel and wrought iron) and silicon carbide for hard, brittle metals (such as **brass, aluminum,** or **gray iron**).

The grain or grit number refers to the size of the abrasive particle used. The ranges are: coarse (numbers 6–24); medium (30 medium-coarse to 60 medium-fine); and fine (numbers 70–600). Number 36 is considered to be a standard wheel.

The grade of the wheel is determined by both its degree of hardness and its porosity, and is indicated by letters. Very soft grades are letters C to G, soft are H to K, medium are L to O, hard are P to S, and very hard are T to Z. The porosity is how closely packed the particles are. Hard, brittle metals are best ground on closely packed wheels of number 60–80 grit; soft metals require more widely spaced particles, so as not to clog the wheel, or a grit of number 36–46.

Choice of bonding material is determined by the type of material you will be grinding. Baked silicate of soda (or waterglass) is used to keep grinding heat to a minimum, and is designated by the symbol S on the wheel. Vitrified baked clay is used for precision work and is not corroded by acid, oil, or water. It is noted by the letter V. Shellac (letter E) and rubber (letter R) are used for thin wheels. Resin (letter B) wheels are used for making cool cuts at high speeds.

It is important never to run a grinding wheel faster than its recommended speed or it may fly apart, causing injury. Always wear goggles or a face shield when using a grinding wheel.

Grinding wheel

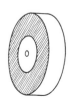

grindstone. Stained Glass. A small, hand-turned instrument that can be attached to an end of the **cutting bench** to grind off sharp points or edges left after cutting glass that are difficult to get with the **grozer** or **plate pliers.** Also see **Stained Glass: Cutting Glass.**

grisaille. Découpage. A term, from the French word for "gray," for a color scheme using only tones of gray; grisaille often simulates marble bas-relief sculpture. Black-and-white **print**s for découpage are often tinted en grisaille, using black, white, and gray **color pencils** to mix several shades of gray.

grisaille. Enameling. A style of enameling using no colored **enamel**s. This term is derived from the French word *gris,* meaning gray. Finely ground opaque white enamel is applied over a fired black enamel base in successive coats to form a structure of tones of varying shades of gray. Occasionally an **overglaze** of gold, silver, or thin coats of transparent enamel is used to accentuate details. Grisaille is similar to the Limoges technique, but uses an oil medium and **binder.** Grisaille white #497, 150–250 mesh, is available from Schauer of Vienna, Austria.

grisaille. Stained Glass. The French word for glass paint. Also the name of a type of window using mostly clear or pale glass with designs painted in black. Also see **painting on glass.**

grist. Spinning. Weaving. See **yarn count.**

grit. Gemcutting. See **abrasive.**

grit. Woodworking. See **abrasive.**

grog. Ceramics. Clay particles that have been fired and ground into various sizes. Grog is used to reduce **shrinkage,** promote drying, and to give structure to large ceramic sculptures.

grommet. Kites. A metal ring that can be punched into the cloth kite **covering** to serve as an **eyelet** to accept a **bridle string** or tying line. Grommets and grommet punchers can be found at most hardware and dime stores.

grommet. Leatherwork. A metal **finding** in various sizes shaped like an **eyelet** with a washerlike piece for the reverse side of the leather. It is used for reinforcing prepunched holes in heavy leather. The process for setting is similar to setting an eyelet, but a grommet setter is used. The correct setting tool and die is required for each size grommet. To set, first punch a hole in the leather just large enough for the eyelet part to go through; put this eyelet section face-down on the die; place leather over eyelet right-side down (**a.**); place the punch vertically in the hole of the **grommet die** (**b.**); and strike the punch with **mallet** (**c.**). See ill. next page.

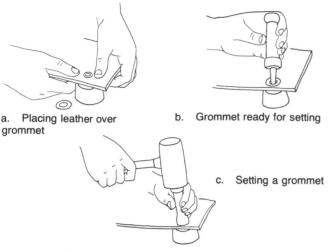

a. Placing leather over grommet

b. Grommet ready for setting

c. Setting a grommet

grommet. Stitchery. A metal eyelet set into **fabric,** leather, or **twill tape** to provide a means of fastening. Grommets may be set into fabrics or **bindings** to facilitate hanging **banner**s, flags, pennants, or panels. They are sometimes used decoratively on body coverings or to provide tiny peep holes in freehanging stitchery panels. Grommets are sometimes combined with **reflector**s and **rivet**s in decorative patterns of fabric.

grommet die. Leatherwork. (Also called grommet setter.) A two-part tool with a tube and a base with a hole used with a **mallet** for inserting **grommet**s. Grommet dies are available in various sizes. See ill.

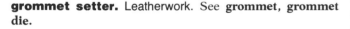

a. Grommet die

b. Grommets

grommet setter. Leatherwork. See **grommet, grommet die.**

groove. Woodworking. A slot with a rectangular cross-section cut on the surface of a board in the direction of the **grain,** as distinct from a **dado,** which is cut across the grain. Grooves are commonly used to inset or secure sliding doors, partitions, or the bottoms of cabinet drawers. Grooves are most efficiently made with a **power saw** using a **dado-head** assemble.

grooving. Plastics. Any of the following power tools are recommended for cutting grooves in plastics: **router,** metal **lathe,** abrasive wheel on a **circular saw,** or grinding head on a **flexible shaft machine.** Also see **inlaying, lathe turning, routing.**

grooving board. Bookbinding. A board with a metal projection on one edge used in a pair in the **book press** or the **lying press** to produce the **French groove.** It is usually made of plywood ⅜–½″ thick with a strip of brass, aluminum, or iron projecting ¹/₁₆″ past the edges of the board.

gros point. Needlepoint. This term refers to the number of **tent stitch**es worked on a large-gauge mono **canvas** (size 5,

7, or 8), or on penelope canvas as a **half cross stitch** (which uses less wool). Its heavy texture and speed in working up make this technique very useful for large projects.

gros point. Rugmaking. See **tent stitch.**

gros point canvas. Needlepoint. A **penelope** or mono **canvas** of sizes 5, 7, or 8.

grossularite. Gemcutting. See **garnet.**

grotesque doll. Toys. Any **doll** made with exaggerated or deliberately ugly features. These grotesques may originally have served some magical purpose unrelated to children's playthings, although children are often delighted in the half-frightening aspects of grotesque masks and figures. Some early **jack-in-the-box**es had grotesque faces, **Punch**-like in appearance. Trolls are an example of a more recent doll that, although ugly, were favorites of many children.

ground. Lacemaking. That area of **lace** serving as a background to the bolder, usually floral **motif**s of the **pattern.** There are two kinds of grounds—réseau, a netlike texture, and bride, a texture made of **bar**s.

The netlike réseau grounds are the most delicate and the most difficult to make, whether made with needle or bobbin, and therefore the most costly. When **machine lace** was created early in the nineteenth century, lace with réseau or net ground became less costly.

The bride grounds, in **needle lace,** are usually **buttonhole bar**s; in **bobbin lace,** the bars can be a **braid** or can be constructed with a **cloth stitch.**

ground cloth. Rugmaking. Weaving. In rugmaking, the foundation or body of the rug. Usually this is a woven fabric on which the pattern or **pile** is superimposed, as in **embroidered** or **hooked** rugs. In weaving, the body of the fabric, on which are interwoven the figures, fancy effects, and motifs desired. Also see **ground weave, rug backing.**

ground color. Shell Carving. In cameo carving, the background or bottom layer of shell. The carved design in the **middle color** stands in the ground color. Also see **black helmet, bull-mouth helmet, gold ringer cowrie, horned helmet, king helmet, money cowrie, panther cowrie, poached egg, queen cowrie, snakeshead cowrie, tiger cowrie** and **Shell Carving: Cameo Carving.**

grounder. Jewelry. A tool with a deeply engraved pattern on one end used to create an all-over pattern or background texture on a metal surface. Also see **chasing, matting tool, punch, repoussé tool.**

grounding. China and Glass Painting. A **ground laying** method in which **grounding oil** is applied with a large, soft brush to the area to be colored. The oiled area is then patted with a **silk pad** until the oil seems tacky. Additional patting results in a smoother surface. For any areas not to be colored, remove the oil with a cloth. Then pour powdered color that has been strained through lint-free cloth or a copper-wire sieve onto a plate. Drop some of the powdered color on the oiled surface and use cotton to push it over the surface, keeping the powder well ahead of the cotton. Continue pushing until the color is even and the surface is dry, the color having been absorbed by the oil. Dust again over the surface until no more color is absorbed. Brush away excess color. The piece is then ready for **firing;** a strong, glossy surface will result.

grounding oil. China and Glass Painting. Various oils for adhering color in **grounding,** such as copaiba balsam oil, pure balsam, or English grounding oil.

ground laying. China and Glass Painting. (Also called background laying.) Any of various techniques used to tint or color part or all of a piece of china. After coloring is applied, the piece is fired. **Grounding** is a method of applying powdered color to a tacky, oiled surface. **Tinting** is a ground-laying method of painting colors on the surface to be colored, then patting them with a **silk pad** to blend. **Dusting** with powdered color may be done after tinting to add depth to the color. Stippling is a technique of applying thickly mixed color to the background in an evenly speckled texture, using a stippling brush, sponge, or steel wool, and dabbing the color in vertical strokes, without dragging from side to side.

Mix **onglaze color** for ground laying in the same way as for painting, using a specially prepared **grounding oil.** Add a few drops of oil of cloves to prevent the color from drying too quickly. After the color is prepared, strain it through 2 thicknesses of organdy muslin stretched over a cup. Hold the muslin in place with a rubber band. A test firing on broken china scraps should be made first, as some colors are more suited to ground laying than others.

ground loom. Weaving. A **horizontal loom** fixed by pegs parallel and low to the ground for tension. It is one of the earliest known looms and is portrayed in a drawing inside a dish belonging to an early Egyptian civilization of about 4400 B.C. It is not necessarily the earliest loom in use, as some believe that the **warp-weighted loom** preceded the ground loom. It is, however, the earliest loom still in use; the warp-weighted loom is rarely seen these days but the ground loom is still common among the Egyptian peasants for weaving the black goat's hair cloth for tents, and among the Arabs in Palestine, the bedouins of the Arabian peninsula and the Libyan desert, and the Kashkai tribes of Iran. All are nomads to whom this loom has appeal because, like the **backstrap loom,** it is extremely portable, simple, and cheap. At any time, the pegs can be uprooted and the work rolled up on the beams attached to the pegs to be unrolled and repegged at some future time and place. It has perhaps some advantages over the backstrap loom in that the weaver is physically free of the loom.

Besides the four corner pegs the loom is composed of two horizontal poles or beams lashed to the pegs. These serve as the breast and **warp beam**s. A **continuous warp** is wound in a figure-eight between the two beams. **Warp tension** is adjusted by the lashings between the beams and pegs. An added refinement is a metal rod that is laced to the wooden beams. It aids in controlling the tension and is an easier device for the warp to go around while being wound. It

could compare to an **apron bar** on a **harness loom.** The distance between the beams is determined by the length of the article to be woven. A **shed stick** and **heddle bar** are used as **shedding device**s. In using the heddle bar, the weaver sometimes rests it on short wooden posts, a large stone, or a pile of stones on either side of the **warp** in order to keep the **shed** open while freeing the hands for weaving. No **reed** is used, but often a **sword** is used to beat down and then is followed by some sort of **hand beater.** A long stick with yarn wound around it is used as the **shuttle** and resembles the ancient type of **spindle bobbin.** Usually the weaver sits or squats in front of or on a completed part of the weaving. If the piece being woven is wide, two or three weavers work on the fabric simultaneously. Because the weaving position is rather uncomfortable, it is not surprising that through the centuries and in various places attempts have been made to put the weaver in a better position. In Ecuador and a few other places the pegs are stakes off the ground sufficiently high so that the weaver can sit on a stool. There is also the **pit loom,** in which the pegged loom is put over a pit dug in the ground under the loom and enabling the weaver to sit on the ground at a level with the loom with his or her feet in the pit. In this version the shedding device has evolved into a **harness** arrangement so that **treadles** for the harnesses are in the pit. This type of ground loom also has a reed and is said to have developed in India for use with cotton yarn. It is the forerunner of the **counterbalanced loom.**

In ancient days the loom was used in Egypt for **linen** weaving and in India for **cotton** weaving. Today it is used mainly with **wool** and sometimes camel's or goat's hair. Items woven on the ground loom include **flatweave, soumak,** and **knotted pile** rugs, storage bags, sling cradles, saddle bags, and tent material. See ill. Also see **breast beam.**

Ground loom without shedding devices and with a figure-8 continuous warp

ground weave. Weaving. The **weave** used to hold the background together in **pattern weaving.** It is usually **plain weave (tabby)** but can be any one of the simple standard weaves. Ground weaves are uniform and sunk, whereas the pattern weave is raised. **Overshot** and **laid-in** are examples of fabrics with a ground weave. **Pile weave**s also have a ground weave, which is in most cases invisible.

ground yarn. Weaving. The **warp** and **weft** threads used to make the **ground weave.** They are usually of the same size, type, and color, and finer than the pattern yarns that stand out against the background. Often the warp is the same for both ground and pattern but the weft is composed of two elements—the yarn similar to the warp that makes up the ground, and the heavy yarn for the pattern. Certain ground warps are put on separate **warp beam**s. An extra warp then forms the raised pattern or **pile.**

grouped thread. Weaving. Several **warp end**s or **filling pick**s that act together as a single thread to form **texture** or color effects. Grouped warp threads can be handled in two ways. The ends can be threaded side by side in a group of **heddle**s on the same **harness,** or they can be threaded according to a pattern and then treadled so that they are raised as one. The grouped ends can also be threaded in one heddle if they can fit comfortably into the **heddle eye.** Weak but lovely threads can be used in the warp if they are grouped in and thereby reinforced with other, stronger yarns.

In the filling, grouped threads are achieved by throwing two or more filling picks in the same **shed** or by winding two or more yarns on one **bobbin.**

The placement of grouped warp, or filling threads, may be regular or completely random. If texture is the desired result, the more random the groupings are the greater the texture effect will be. For example, a single thread may be followed by a group of three, then a single thread, then a group of four, then a group of two, etc., changing all the way across the warp or while weaving in the filling. The smallest number of grouped threads is two, as in a standard 2–2 **basket weave.** Several warp threads grouped together might be classified as rib weaves because warp ribs can be produced with grouped threads. Likewise, filling ribs can be made by groupings of filling yarn alternating with single threads. **Undulating twill**s can also be achieved through the planned grouping of warp threads. Grouped yarns can also create specific pattern blocks as in **M's and O's** and **canvas weave**s. Also see **drawing-in draft, treadling order.**

grout. Mosaics. (Also called grouting.) A mixture of a fine grade of **cement** plus **hydrated lime** and fine sand used to fill in the crevices between the individual bits of material in a completed **mosaic.** The question of whether or not to use grout is usually a matter of aesthetics rather than necessity, except in cases in which the finished work is to be exposed to the elements. Outdoor pieces do need some filler to prevent water damage. Ready-made grout in a wide range of colors can be bought at most building supply outlets. Grout can also be prepared from scratch by mixing approximately 6 parts cement, 6 parts fine sand, and 1 part hydrated lime with enough water to give the mixture the consistency of pancake batter. The grout may be applied to the crevices with either a **palette knife** or the fingers. Any excess may be wiped away with a clean rag once the mixture has been allowed to set for a full 24 hours. To ensure proper curing, the grout should be moistened with damp rags rather frequently during the drying process. Also see **Mosaics: Tools and Materials, Setting the Material.**

grout. Stained Glass. (Also called tile grout.) A mixture of refractory clay and cement. It is powder that when mixed with water forms a paste that can be used as a glass cement. Also see **kwik solder, lamination, lampblack.**

grouting. Mosaics. See **grout.**

grozer. Stained Glass. See **grozing pliers.**

grozing. Stained Glass. (Also called nibbling.) The removal of unwanted glass from a shaped piece of cut glass either with **grozing pliers** or with grozing teeth on a **glass cutter.** There are different-width teeth in the handle of the glass cutter for grozing thick and thin pieces of glass. Grozing is a delicate nibbling process. The pliers are held loosely and rolled over the edge of the glass. Pliers give better leverage and less chance of breakage. See ill. Also see **Stained Glass: Tools and Materials.**

a. Using the grozing pliers
b. Rolling pliers over edge of glass
c. Using the grozing teeth of the glass cutter

grozing pliers. Stained Glass. (Also called grozer, nippers.) These are small- to medium-sized pliers with flush, smooth, narrow jaws. There should be no lateral play and a fairly short bite that meets firmly and smoothly. It is possible to make pliers that will do by grinding down a small pair of pliers to get smooth jaws. They are used for **grozing** glass after it has been cut. See ill. Also see **grozing** and **Stained Glass: Tools and Materials.**

Grozing pliers

grubby. Shell Carving. The pitted, blistered, flaky condition of the surface of a shell that has been attacked by parasites and disease. A severely affected shell can be undesirable to work because of its weakened structure and dull appearance. A moderately grubby shell can be used in **fretwork,** as the pitted sections can be removed to create the design. Pieces around the pitted areas can be utilized in smaller work such as jewelry, inlay, and mosaic. Also see **blind.**

GTA. Metalworking. See **welding.**

guarding. Bookbinding. A method employed to attach single sheets or plates by adding a strip of paper along the **back edge** and inserting it in its proper place so that it may be bound with the **section**s. Guarding is done in exactly the same way as **strip repair**ing except that the strip is attached to the back of the plate or sheet.

An alternative is **tipping** the single, but it will not open to the back of the book as the guarded one will.

Exercise discretion when guarding sheets, as too many will create unsightly **swell.** Also see **Bookbinding: Repair and Restoration.**

Guernsey. Knitting. A style of sweater knit on the Isle of Guernsey in the Channel Islands, off the coast of Normandy. Guernsey sweaters have a square-shaped body and are knit in thick, dark blue wool. The design is a simple, decorative rib, with side vents and **gusset**s at the underarms and neck. The sleeves are set into an armhole with either a knit or a cut edge. The gussets add years to the life of the garment because there is no seam strain under the arms. Also see **Aran knitting.**

Guernsey casting on. Knitting. See **Knitting: Casting On.**

guide hook. Spinning. The metal hook on the arms of the U-shaped **flyer** on the **treadle wheel.** The spinner moves the spun yarn from hook to hook so that it will be guided down for an even winding of the **bobbin.** A former name for a guide hook was a "hetch." Also see **flyer assembly.**

guide string. Weaving. See **measuring cord.**

guideline. Kites. The line or **string** that is fitted around the outside ends of the kite **framework** to serve as an outer edge for the kite **covering. Notching** the stick ends helps hold the guideline in place. To prevent splitting, all sticks should be lashed near the ends with fine thread. Also see **Kites: Construction.**

guild. (Also spelled gild.) An association or society of merchants or craftsmen organized for purposes of self-protection and to further the economic and social gain of its members. The merchant guilds were the forerunners of modern trade associations as the craft guilds were forerunners of modern labor unions. Guilds flourished in western Europe from the eleventh to the sixteenth centuries.

MERCHANT GUILDS After the fall of the Roman Empire, trade between distant areas diminished, both because of the difficulty of travel over roads increasingly in disrepair, and the problem of brigands. The earliest guilds were associations of traders who traveled together for self-protection, and who often hired armed escorts to ensure their safe arrival, and the safe arrival of the goods they carried.

During the tenth and eleventh centuries, as towns began to spring up at points where there was heavy travel, local lords or kings, who profited from tolls and taxes levied on commercial enterprises, began to offer certain advantages and freedoms to traders willing to settle in towns within the lords' domains. Guild members balked at being considered serfs. The guilds negotiated with local lords to provide articles in the charter for towns that stipulated that many of the governmental functions of the lord be entrusted to the guilds. Thus the guilds came to manage the market in such a way as to exclude outside competition. They did this by levying tolls on traveling merchants, fixing prices at which goods could be sold, and establishing standards of quality.

These operations, in restraint of free trade, ensured a market for the local craftsmen and shopkeepers and provided the stability necessary for growth. Almost every sizable town in England had one or more guilds by the thirteenth century.

Not all of the merchant guild's activities were solely economic and monopolistic. Some of the more successful guilds became the equivalent of modern powerful corporations—they dealt in a variety of goods, purchased raw materials wholesale, provided insurance against losses, paved streets, policed highways, and regulated wages, hours, conditions of labor, terms of apprenticeship, methods of production and sale, and prices of materials and products. Guilds weighed, tested, or counted all products bought or sold in their area, and did their best to keep inferior goods and dishonest practices out of the market. Guilds provided their members with insurance against fire, flood, theft, imprisonment, disability, and old age; they built hospitals, orphanages, and schools; they shared the financing of churches and public facilities with the town government; and they paid for funerals and masses for deceased members.

CRAFT GUILDS Around the twelfth century, craftsmen, who were normally excluded from the merchant guilds, began to form their own guilds. At the middle of the thirteenth century, Paris had 101 different craft guilds, many of them highly specialized. There was a chest-makers' guild, a cabinet-makers' guild, a coffin-makers' guild, a boat-builders' guild, etc.—all in the field of woodworking.

Like the merchant guilds, the craft guilds worked to ensure quality, fix prices, and to establish a monopoly for its members in the trade. Guild rules limited the number of masters in an area, decided how many apprentices a master could employ, established working hours and wages for journeymen, fined members for charging unjustly, and attempted to prevent dishonest dealing and shoddy goods from appearing in the marketplace. Each guild had a guildhall, sometimes of an elaborate architectural design, that functioned as meeting place, trading hall, and courtroom for trying members accused of infractions of rules. Guilds also often had a distinctive trademark or hallmark that was stamped or printed on members' products as an assurance of quality to the buyer.

Members of the craft guilds considered themselves "brothers," and the guild rules that reduced competition did allow a sharing of trade secrets among members.

The **apprentice,** a boy of ten or so, was bound over to a **master** by the boy's parents for a period up to age twelve, during which time he lived with the master and served the master both in the shop and home. A runaway apprentice was to be returned to his master and punished. At the end of the apprenticeship, the boy became a **journeyman** and could continue to work for the same master, or choose another master for whom to work at a daily wage. In two to seven years, if a journeyman had saved enough money to provide himself with sufficient tools and a shop, and could pass an examination by the guild governors, he was made a master. The master customarily owned his own tools and worked directly for the consumer. In the case of important trade goods, like woven materials, the customer was often enough a merchant guild that had the capital necessary to start large enterprises such as weaving mills.

In time, the same aristocratic leanings of the system that made the merchant guilds oligarchies made the craft guilds elite organizations that denied master status to any but masters' sons, underpaid their journeymen, and discouraged the sense of freedom and dignity of craftsmen they were originally formed to foster.

guilloche. Enameling. A wavy-grained pattern produced by machine-turning a **metal** surface to achieve a high polish. Guilloche adds subtle reflections under a field of transparent **enamel.** Also see **Enameling.**

guilloche stitch. Crewel. Embroidery. A **border stitch** formed by combining several stitches, usually worked on an evenly woven fabric.

Begin by working two lines of **stem stitch** the desired distance apart, using a pointed needle. Next, work small blocks of three horizontal **satin stitch**es in the middle of the rows of stem stitch, making the space between them the same as the space between the rows of stem stitch. Then, using a **blunt needle**, slip it under the horizontal satin stitches, leaving the thread loose so that it curves. The needle passes up under one block of horizontal stitches, down under the next block, and then reverses the pattern on the return stroke to complete the interlacing. Finally, work a **French knot** in the center of each circle. See ill.

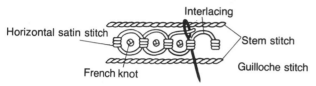

guillotine. Papercrafts. See **paper cutter.**

guillotine cutter. Bookbinding. A heavy-duty paper cutter, so named because the blade is capable of cutting through an inch or more of paper depending on the size of the cutter. Guillotines can be purchased in hand or power models. They consist essentially of a table on which the work rests, an adjustment gauge that determines the depth of the cut, a clamp that keeps the work correctly positioned, and a blade suspended from a carriage. The blade descends, strikes its cut, and returns to its raised position. This tool is dangerous to use without instruction. Also see **plow, trimming.**

guimpe yarn. Spinning. Weaving. See **novelty yarn.**

guipure. Lacemaking. A type of cord covered with thread used to raise into relief the chief parts of a design. The term "guipure" gradually came to be applied to all laces of large patterns that were connected with the **bride ground** or required no roundings, but lately the word has also been applied to large, flowing pattern laces worked with coarse net grounds. It is impossible to lay down any hard-and-fast rules about it, but no fine-patterned laces or delicately grounded laces are called guipures. Usually it refers to a coarser lace put together with brides or **bars.**

gum acacia. China and Glass Painting. See **gum arabic.**

gum arabic. Ceramics. Gum arabic and gum tragacanth are natural gums used in glazes as **binder**s to promote better glaze adhesion to the body. Soak the gum in water overnight; shake vigorously before applying. Pots should be fired within a few days of applying the glazes, since the gums will decay in time and can spoil the glaze. Binders are necessary for **fritt**ed glazes containing little or no raw clay. Binders are used when a **bisque fire** accidentally goes too high or in reglazing. The gum burns out completely during **firing.**

gum arabic. China and Glass Painting. Stained Glass. (Also called gum acacia.) An adhesive made from the hardened sap of various trees of tropical Asia, Australia, and Africa. Gum arabic, either powdered or crushed, is available from the druggist. To dissolve, pour boiling water on the gum and allow it to stand for several hours.

In stained glass gum arabic (or gum tragacanth) is mixed with paint pigments and helps adhere the paint to the glass surface. Also see **acetic acid, blistered paint, painting on glass, staining.**

gum arabic. Enameling. See **binder.**

gum arabic. Toys. A rubbery resinous substance obtained from acacia trees. It was used in molding small, simple toys and had the advantage of being edible. Combined with sweetening and flavoring, it could be used for **edible toy**s. When used alone, the toys (while not inedible) actually lasted longer. Some materials were coated with gum arabic to give them a more natural feel.

gum arabic and gum tragacanth. Jewelry. Water-soluble organic gums used as a temporary glue to hold work in position for techniques such as **niello** and **granulation,** and sometimes in **soldering.** Their advantage is that they completely volatize under heat, leaving no ash residue. Also see **Klyr Fyre.**

gum arabic glue. Mosaics. With the **indirect method** a water soluble **glue** is used to fix the **tesserae** to the **mounting paper.** For the purist, this glue has traditionally consisted of a mixture of gum arabic, blackstrap molasses, and flour. Although the proportions may vary, one known working recipe calls for 1 part gum arabic solution, 1 part blackstrap molasses, and 2 parts flour. The gum arabic solution is prepared by dissolving 1 ounce of gum arabic crystals in 1–1½ cups of boiling water, with repeated strainings through a fine sieve or cheesecloth to remove all lumps. Also see **Mosaics: Setting the Material.**

gumbo clay. Ceramics. See **Ceramics: Clay**

gum mastic. A semihard resin obtained from the mastic tree *Pistacia lentiscus* of southern Europe and Asia that is used as a waterproofing ingredient in varnish, caulking compound, and cement. Gum mastic melts at 221–248° F and dissolves in amyl alcohol, benzene, and ether.

gum tragacanth. A nearly colorless, water-soluble adhesive commonly used with paper; it is obtained from the gum of the plant *Astragalus gummifer.* It is available in plate and stick form.

gum tragacanth. Ceramics. See **gum arabic.**

gum tragacanth. Enameling. See **binder.**

gum tragacanth. Stained Glass. See **gum arabic.**

gum tragacanth. Toys. A resinous substance obtained from certain shrubs. Both colorless and odorless, it was used in the 1600s for **dollmaking** and toymaking. It was similar to **gum arabic** and **gutta percha.**

gumwood. Woodworking. (Also called red gumwood, sweet gumwood.) A reddish-brown wood with a straight, close **grain** common to the southeastern United States. It is not recommended for woodcarving because it warps badly, gives a slight odor and taste to food when used for food containers, and decays in contact with the earth. It is used to imitate **walnut** in inexpensive furniture, cabinet work, and interior trim work.

gun. Toys. See **peashooter, popgun, rubber-band gun.**

gunmetal. Metalworking. Metal used for the barrels of guns. **Nickel steel** and chromium steel **alloys** are commonly used although a **carbon steel** (called black-powder steel, ordnance steel) is also employed. Nickel steel is often favored because of its high tensile strength, good wearability, good corrosion resistance, good impact and fatigue strength, easy machinability, and ease of **heat treatment.** **Stainless steel** is a **nickel-chromium steel** (10% chromium) that is corrosion-resistant also. However, it is not absolutely rustproof and will corrode if exposed long enough to moisture. It is also more difficult to blue than other alloys. A nickel-manganese alloy steel with a low carbon content is also highly recommended.

gunny sack. Stitchery. See **burlap.**

gunny sack swing. Toys. A **bag swing** or sack swing in which gunny sack or burlap is used for the bag. Because burlap is loosely woven, the gunny sack must be lined with another fabric, such as a flour sack, if sand is used as the filler.

gusset. Knitting. The shaped knit space created to absorb continued strain either under the arm in a **Guernsey** sweater or in the heel of a sock. Specific gusset directions vary depending on pattern and use. Generally, in the knitting of a sock, stitches are first picked up on the left of the heel (after the heel has been knit) with a separate needle, then knitting is continued around to the heel flap, where additional stitches are picked up. The stitches are then redistributed on three needles, and decreasing is done until the original number of stitches (found in the leg of the sock) is obtained.

gutta percha. A semisolid bonding resin used in many formulations where some flexibility and elasticity is desirable. It is similar to rubber and is obtained from the latex of certain tropical trees. When pure it is odorless, tasteless, and colorless. Crude gutta percha is white to brown. It softens at 99° F, becomes moldable at 195° F, and melts into a colorless oil at 265° F. It dissolves in toluene, chloroform, and carbon disulfide.

gutta percha. Toys. A resinous substance once used in modeling **toys.** Its plasticity made it easy to shape, but it was not permanent. Some **doll head**s were made of gutta percha, as were assorted molded animals and figures. It was somewhat similar to **gum arabic.** With the advent of **rubber toy**s, gutta percha was no longer used.

guttering. Candlemaking. The production of more wax than the flame can handle during burning, resulting in excessive **dripping** or drowning of the flame. Also see **Candlemaking: Possible Flaws in Candles.**

gypsum. Gemcutting. A mineral composed of calcium sulphate and water. It has a **hardness** of 2 and a **specific gravity** of 2.2 to 2.24. Gypsum cut into **cabochon**s is polished with cerium oxide on a felt buff, with Linde A on leather, or with rouge on muslin.

Alabaster is white gypsum. Satin spar is gypsum that has a fibrous structure. Selenite is colorless, semitransparent gypsum. Also see **polishing** and **Gemcutting: Hand Grinding and Polishing.**

gypsum board. Woodworking. (Also called plasterboard, sheetrock, wallboard.) A board of plaster covered on both sides with strong paper. It is used for interior walls and ceilings, and may commonly be purchased in 4′ × 8′ panels in ⅜″, ½″, or ⅝″ thicknesses. It is the contemporary replacement for the lath-and-plaster wall.

gypsy setting. Jewelry. A setting in which the gemstone is set nearly flush with the surface of the metal. The metal surrounding the stone is then chased into position over the edges of the stone to hold it in place. A small groove can be engraved in the metal close to and around the stone to facilitate **chasing.** Because chasing requires some force, using a stone of less than 6 on the Mohs scale is inadvisable, as it could crack or chip.

h

hackle. Spinning. See **flax.**

hackling. Spinning. See **flax.**

hackly fracture. Gemcutting. See **fracture.**

hacksaw. Metalworking. A handsaw for cutting metal. Hacksaw frames are usually adjustable to receive 8–12″ blades that come in hard, semiflexible, or flexible types in a variety of different **steel alloys**. The type of blade is chosen according to its intended use. For example, flexible blades are useful for sawing where pressure may be put on the blade in awkward sawing positions. The number of teeth per inch on the blade should vary with the type of metal being cut. Use a blade with 14 teeth per inch on soft **steel, bronze,** and **cast iron;** 18 per inch on **mild steel, high-carbon steel,** and for general work; 24 per inch for iron pipe, **brass,** and **copper;** and 32 per inch for thin tubing and thin sheet metal.

To use a hacksaw, insert the correct blade for the metal being sawed into the frame, with the teeth pointing away from the handle. The blade should always have at least three teeth in contact with the metal; therefore, use fine blades when cutting thin pieces. Tighten the nut or handle until the blade is secure. Then make a few cuts and re-tighten it. Clamp or secure the object to be cut and protect it from being marked by the vise by covering the vise jaws with a covering material such as thin scrap wood strips or soft metal. Start cutting with one or two light strokes, and then progress to uniform full-length strokes, applying pressure on the forward motion only. Do not twist the blade or the cut will be uneven. See ill.

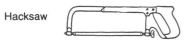

Hacksaw

haft. Leatherwork. See **awl and haft.**

hair. Toys. Hair can be added to dolls by a great variety of methods, depending largely upon the intended use of the doll. A **portrait doll,** or a stuffed **nylon stocking doll,** might be coiffed in real hair or with sections cut from a wig. **Felt** dolls may have hair of felt, **ball fringe,** etc. Very generally, the material from which the doll is fabricated suggests the material for its hair.

Most washable **rag dolls** or **fabric dolls** have hair of yarn. Cotton roving, unspun wool, and **Dacron polyester batting** can all be used, although yarns are most popular. Synthetic yarns are washable, making them especially suitable for cloth dolls.

Yarn hair can be added to dolls in a variety of ways. Stitch lengths of yarn at the top of the stuffed head (**a.**). Then add a ribbon to cover the seam (**b.**). Hair can be stitched on the line of the forehead and drawn back so that it covers the stitches where side locks are joined to the head (**c.**). Curls may be added with individual stitches, or yarn can be looped on top of the head and be tacked in place with a lighter weight thread (**d., e.**). Other hairstyles are suggested by attaching short or long lengths of yarn (**f., g.**). Long pieces of yarn can be stitched in place on a part line so that hair can be tied or braided, then tacked at the point the hair is gathered (**h., j.**). See ill.

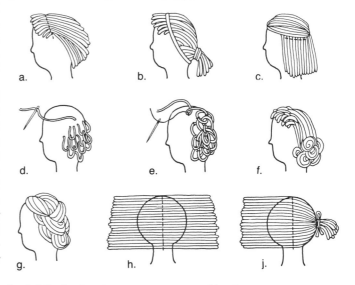

hair blade. Leatherwork. See **swivel knife.**

hair calf. Leatherwork. Calf or cowhide which has been tanned with the hair intact, often with the hair sheared to an even length. Hair calf is often printed to imitate zebra or tiger skin.

hairpin lace. Crochet. Hairpin lace is the intricate lace made on a hairpin lace fork with a crochet hook. This delicate, centuries-old lace was originally made on real hairpins.

hairpin lace. Lacemaking. A **crochet** lace made on a hairpin frame. Work this lace in bands and join together later by crocheting, or use in combination with other lacework. The widths of the lace bands vary according to the size of the hairpin frame. A very fine lace **insertion** can be made on an ordinary hairpin, if one uses a sturdy pin with straight sides. Hairpin lace has a very lacy appearance if done in an artful manner.

hairpin lace fork. Crochet. See **hairpin lace** and **Crochet: Tools and Materials.**

hair stone. Gemcutting. See **quartz.**

hakame. Ceramics. A decoration in white **slip,** applied thickly with a stiff-bristle brush made of ends of rice straw. Hakame is a base for **iron brushwork.**

halation. Stained Glass. A shimmering, halo effect occurring when the light of one piece of **glass** expands beyond the dimensions of the piece onto other pieces in a **panel.** It can change the tone of the color of neighboring pieces of glass.

half-and-half solder. Metalworking. See **solder.**

half binding. Bookbinding. A book cover that has added **cloth,** or **leather corners** and **back.**

half calf. Leatherwork. See **slink.**

half cross stitch. Needlepoint. A **tent stitch** worked on a penelope **canvas.** This technique uses less wool than the other tent stitches, but it does not give a very firm backing to the finished piece. The half cross stitch should always be worked on a penelope canvas. The upright stitches formed on the reverse side cannot slip between the mesh, as they might on single or mono canvas.

Come up at A, count one doubled thread up and one double thread over to the right, and go in at B. Come up at C, one thread immediately below B. The needle is always vertical (**a.**). Work to the end of the line, then turn the canvas completely upside down, and make another identical row below, fitting the new stitches into the holes made by the previous ones. Continue, turning the canvas at the end of each row. This shows the small upright stitches formed on the reverse side (**b.**). See ill.

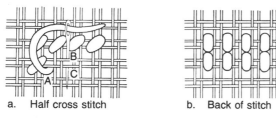

a.   Half cross stitch   b.   Back of stitch

half cross stitch. Rugmaking. See **tent stitch.**

half Damascus edge. Rugmaking. Weaving. See **Damascus edge.**

half double crochet. Crochet. (Abbr. hdc.) See **Crochet: Basic Stitches.**

half-drop principle. Knitting. A principle used to balance pattern designs or to convert a panel-type pattern into an isolated pattern. This allows great flexibility for elaborating a pattern, which may be geometric or floral.

The half-drop principle uses an extra half repeat of a pattern to balance the work. Example: *K 2, P 2 * repeat * to *, end K 2. In a geometric pattern (such as a diamond shape), one complete pattern, along with the adjoining half of the next diamond, may be charted and then knit. The half-drop principle may also be used to chart a **ribbed pattern.** Also see **charting.**

half flossa. Rugmaking. Weaving. The use of **flossa pile** areas in combination with a flat background. The flossa design areas stand out from this background, which can be either woven or embroidered. In traditional Scandinavian rugs, the background is woven in **plain weave.**

half-Gobelin. Weaving. See **HV technique.**

half-heddle. Weaving. See **doup.**

half hitch. Lacemaking. The loop used in making **bobbin lace** to tighten and hold the thread after it has been wound on the **bobbin**s. Place a half hitch around the head of the bobbin to secure the thread of the already wound bobbin. If properly done, the bobbin will not unwind too easily. Reverse the direction of the half hitch on the bobbin head, and continue to do the lacework. As the lace progresses, it will be necessary to let the thread out from the bobbin from time to time. To do this, put a thumb under the thread that goes between the thread wound on the bobbin shaft and the head, holding this thread up, or in a released tension, and without removing the half hitch from the bobbin head, unwind the bobbin slowly in the direction indicated. When the thread is adjusted, remove the thumb, tighten the half hitch, and continue the lacework. See ill.

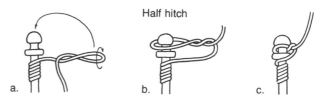

Half hitch

a.   b.   c.

half hitch. Macramé. (Also called simple knot, tatting knot.) The half hitch is one of two basic knots in macramé. It is used to produce the **double half hitch** and many other variations.

Hold one of the extreme outside cords taut (usually either horizontally or diagonally) across the work. With the free hand, pick up the cord immediately next to the taut one, loop it away from the taut cord, up over the top of the taut

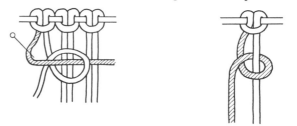

a.   Horizontal half hitch   b.   Vertical half hitch

cord, and finally behind the knotting cord inside the loop it has made. Tighten firmly.

The double half hitch is completed by repeating this loop once again with the same piece of cord. See ill. Also see **reverse double half hitch.**

half hitch. Tatting. One-half of the **double stitch** in tatting. A hitch is a loop that secures a **thread** to another thread, the hitch being made with the active thread, the **loop thread,** while the **knot bearer** remains inactive. Also see **making the double stitch.**

half knot. Macramé. The half knot is an integral part of the **square knot,** which is one of the two basic knots in macramé.

Cord #1 is placed over cords #2 and #3; cord #4 is placed over #1, brought behind #3 and #2, and pulled to the front over #1. If continued, a **sennit** with a left-to-right twist is formed (**a.**).

For a right-to-left twist, cord #4 is placed over cords #3 and #2; cord #1 is placed over #4, brought behind #2 and #3, and pulled to the front over #4 (**b.**). The square knot is made by completing each direction one below the other. See ill.

Half knot a.   b.   1 2 3 4

half-lap joint. Woodworking. See **joint.**

half-pass. Weaving. See **tapestry.**

half-pattern. Stitchery. A pattern for **symmetrical** design, in which the pattern is flipped over to make the second half. Sometimes this is accomplished by cutting the half-pattern on folded paper.

half-round. Woodworking. See **molding.**

half-round file. Metalworking. See **file.**

half rya. Rugmaking. Weaving. The use of **rya pile** areas in combination with a flat background. The rya design areas fall over and lie flat against the background which could be either woven or embroidered. In traditional Scandinavian rugs, the background is woven in **plain weave.**

half stitch. Lacemaking. A basic movement in making **bobbin lace,** in which you **cross** and **twist** two pairs of **bobbin**s. This constitutes the half stitch. It is commonly called the **net stitch.**

half stitch plait. Lacemaking. See **bar, braid, half stitch.**

half-tapestry. Weaving. See **HV technique.**

half title page. Bookbinding. The first printed page of a book, usually with only the book's title.

half turn. Rugmaking. Weaving. A term often used when speaking of an elementary weft **twining** technique in which the 2 **weft**s alternately go over and under the **warp end**s. The wefts cross each other as they go over and under, and this gives a half twist or turn between the warp ends or groups of warp ends. A horizontal twisted line occurs that can be a solid color or alternating colors depending on the colors of the 2 wefts. See ill.

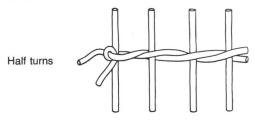

Half turns

hallmark. Jewelry. A name, symbol, or design which is stamped into the metal to identify the maker of the piece. Also see **United States Stamping Law, Worshipful Company of Goldsmiths.**

Halltex. Batik and Tie-dye. A trade name for an **alginate thickener.**

Haman knocker. Toys. A **folk toy** from Israel that is basically a **sound toy** or **noisemaker.** It consists of a handle above which is a small platform. A wooden hammer at the top moves back and forth when the toy is shaken, causing the hammer to knock against the platform. The toy can be simply made from wood and is used in the Jewish festival of Purim. The noise from the toy is so deafening that it is supposed to blot out any mention of the name of Haman, who was minister to a Persian king and persecutor of the Jews.

The original toy was made with a one-piece handle notched to fit the knocker arm. Making the handle with three pieces of lattice stock simplifies the construction. Lattice stock is available at lumberyards. See ill.

Haman knocker

hambergite. Gemcutting. A white or yellow, transparent gem **faceting** material with a **hardness** of 7½, a **specific gravity** of 2.35, and refractive indices of 1.556 and 1.628. It is polished with tin oxide on a tin **lap.** Also see **abrasive, polishing, refraction.**

hammer. Jewelry. See **ball-peen hammer, forging hammer, mallet, planishing hammer, repoussé hammer, rivet hammer.**

hammer. Leatherwork. See **mallet.**

hammer. Metalworking. Woodworking. A hand tool with a heavy head, usually steel, on a handle made of wood, steel, or **glass fiber** used to exert a force by striking, especially for the purpose of driving nails.

Hammers are used in **metalworking** for **bench work, raising,** and **forging** or **blacksmithing.** Most of the **raising hammers** can also be used for bench work, and for forging small objects. Raising hammers include:

RAISING HAMMER   This hammer has a wide edge-rounded face and is used for early raising stages when working the outside surfaces of an object (**a.**).

PLANISHING HAMMER   This has either two flat faces or one rounded end and one flat-faced end (**b.**). It is used for finishing and smoothing a formed or raised object.

PEEN HAMMER   This has one flat face and one rounded face. The ball-peen (or machinist's) hammer may be used for striking a **center punch** or **cold chisel,** for flattening **rivet** heads, or for embossing. Use the cross-peen hammer for **crimping** and **angle raising** (**c.**).

COLLET HAMMER   A small 9-ounce hammer used for edge thickening, forming deep curves, and other operations where a narrow hammer face is needed.

EMBOSSING HAMMER (ALSO CALLED DOMING HAMMER)   This hammer is used to hammer inner surfaces of objects while raising contours when **free forming** with a **sandbag** (**d.**).

MALLET   Hammerlike tools with heads made of wood, rubber, fiber, leather, or rawhide, used for **bouging** and raising **pewter, lead,** and other soft metals, or where a minimum of surface marking is required (**e.**).

Forging hammers (also called blacksmithing hammers) are similar to raising hammers such as the peen hammers; the only difference is that these are heavier and larger, and are designed specifically for working **iron** and **steel.**

Forging hammers include:

PEEN HAMMER   The ball-peen and cross-peen are used for general hammering.

SLEDGEHAMMER   Any hammer over 5 pounds. It is used where great force is necessary (**f.**).

SET HAMMER (ALSO CALLED SMITH'S FORGING HAMMER)   This is used to strike the back of **set tools** (**g.**) See ill.

In **woodworking,** a **mallet** is used for hitting wood or other tools such as **chisels;** the only hammer commonly used is the claw hammer, for driving nails. There are two types of claw: the curved claw, which gives more leverage for pulling nails; and the straight (or ripping) claw, which is better for pulling boards apart (**h., j.**). There is also a choice of two types of faces: the flat face is better for rough hammering, because it has a larger flat area with which to hit the nail head; the slightly convex face of the other type permits hammering nails flush without denting the wood surface. The steel head may weigh anywhere from 5 to 20 ounces; 14–16 ounces is a good weight for finishing work, and 16–20 ounces for rough construction. Long-handled hammers give more swing leverage and are generally used for framing work; short-handled hammers are used for finishing. See ill. Also see **nailing** and **Woodworking: Nailing.**

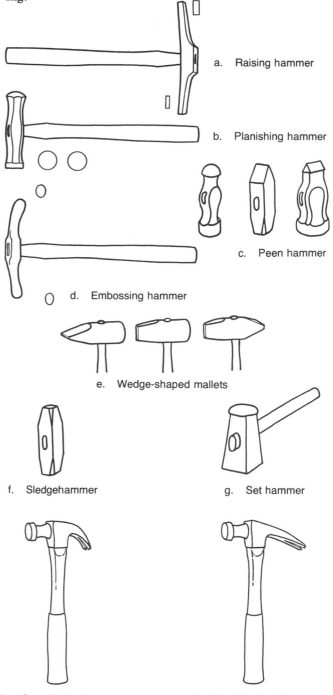

a.   Raising hammer

b.   Planishing hammer

c.   Peen hammer

d.   Embossing hammer

e.   Wedge-shaped mallets

f.   Sledgehammer

g.   Set hammer

h.   Curved claw hammer

j.   Straight claw hammer

hammer. Mosaics. (Also called mosaic hammer.) A slightly curved tungsten carbide-tipped tool used to strike a blow against a **tessera** held against a **hardie** or metal **chisel** for the purpose of fragmenting the tessera into a workable object. See ill., page 402. Also see **Mosaics: Tools and Materials, Cutting the Material.**

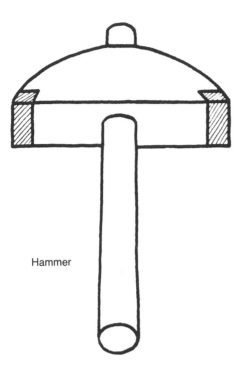

Hammer

hammer. Tincrafting. See **ball-peen hammer.**

hammered glass. Stained Glass. A type of **cathedral glass** with a uniform texture that looks hammered on one side while the other has a smooth texture. Also see **machine-made glass.**

hammering. Metalworking. See **Metalworking: Raising.**

hammering. Tincrafting. Hammering is one of the joys of tincrafting. Hammering not only flattens, curves, raises, or depresses the metal, but also makes it softer and easier to work with. Both ends of a **ball-peen hammer** are used in **beating** the metal, the flat end for **flattening,** the ball end for rounding (in conjunction with a **dapping block**). When hammering raised or depressed areas with the hammer and dapping block, the blows should begin at the outer rim and work around as the metal works with you. Hammer smoothly, slowly, and at length. It can only improve the quality of the surface and the work. Also see **Tincrafting: Preparing the Tincan.**

hammering. Woodworking. See **nailing** and **Woodworking: Nailing.**

hammering board. Tincrafting. Any hardwood board that will absorb the punches of the **awl** and the banging of the **hammering** action. Also see **Tincrafting: Cutting the Tin.**

hammer toy. Toys. A **folk toy** made in many countries but probably of Russian origin. Two movable figures, each holding a hammer, are mounted on square sticks. When the sticks are slid back and forth the figures move, one flopping forward as the other moves back. They appear to hammer in an alternating pattern. Another traditional version of the **toy** has figures of a peasant and a bear. A similar toy made in France is called a cock-and-hen or the blacksmiths. A Czech folk toy that operates on the same principle shows a ploughman struggling with a reluctant horse. Also see **carpenters.**

Hancock's paste. China and Glass Painting. A heavy, yellow-brown powder that is mixed with **fat oil of turpentine** to make a thick paste used for **raised paste** designs. Mix the powder with a palette knife on a glass slab, using just enough oil to dampen the powder, then thin with **lavender oil** or pure turpentine until the paste is as thick as cream but will not spread. To stiffen the mixture, breathe on it while turning it with a horn or bone knife. Apply the paste with a pointed **brush,** preferably a sable watercolor brush, in the desired design. Allow the paste to dry. **Roman gold** or any good matte **gold** may be painted over the raised paste lines when the paste has thoroughly dried, or the dry paste may be fired first, then the gold applied. If mixed to the proper consistency, the paste will become dull about half an hour after application. After firing, the paste is light yellow.

hand. Puppets. The **glove-type hand** or **mitten-type hand** used on the **puppet** or **marionette.** The **hand-puppet** hand may be made of **felt, fabric,** chamois, or **papier mâché.** If the **puppeteer**'s fingers fit into the hand of the hand puppet, it will aid in picking up and moving objects during the performance.

The marionette hand is made of **carved wood,** papier mâché, or **sheet lead,** or a wire hand may be formed of **florist's wire.** The **hand string** is attached between the hand and the **arm bar.** Also see **lead.**

hand. Weaving. A term used to describe how a fabric feels to handle and to touch and thereby determining some of the fabric's characteristics. A fabric's hand can tell something about its fiber content and its working properties.

hand appliqué. Quilts. Stitchery. A method of applying one piece of material to another using any of several **appliqué stitch**es to produce a decorative design or pattern. It is commonly used on **appliqué quilt**s, banners, **coverlet**s, toys, and **wall hanging**s.

There are various methods used for hand appliqué, all of which will work. Only through experience does any stitcher determine which is preferable and most easily controlled. All cutting for **appliqué** must allow an extra ¼" of material at each **raw edge.** This allowance is to be turned under and stitched. The stitches most often used are **running stitch, whip stitch,** and **blind stitch.** Occasionally **buttonhole stitch** or other similar decorative stitches are used though the patterns they make are so active that they sometimes detract from the appliqué. When the running stitch is used the stitches are taken so that only a tiny part of each stitch shows on the top. The length of the stitch occurs under the fabric. A pointed shape is the most difficult to appliqué. Working from right to left, sew the appliqué stitches at one edge first (**a.**). When a corner or point is reached, use the needle to turn under the second edge, taking a whip stitch at the tip to keep it from fraying (**b.**, **c.**). If a thread that contrasts slightly with the appliqué fabric color is used, the stitches will show up better. A red thread, for example, used on bright pink makes a decorative edge pattern. The running stitch must be taken very near the **hem** or **fold**ed edge of the appliqué. When whip stitches or blind stitches are used the thread should be of matching color to help conceal the stitches. Most appliqué stitching is sewn with mercerized thread used in a single strand. **Embroidery floss,** also used singly, is somewhat thicker and adds a more attractive pattern of stitches.

In one method of hand appliqué the pieces of the appliqué fabric are cut and pinned in place. Raw edges are turned under as they are sewn, using any of the stitches listed above. The point of the **needle** may be used to assist in turning the edges under. The sewing thread should be pulled tight every three or four stitches to be sure there is no slack in it. If pieces of appliqué overlap it is not necessary to sew any areas that are covered by another piece. In sewing curves, only the inside curves are clipped. The **clip**s should be very short, using as many as necessary but none should be as deep as the hem allowance. Outside curves need not be clipped.

In another method the appliqué fabrics are again cut with **seam allowance** added, then edges are **basted** under and **press**ed before they are pinned to the **backing** material. Many quilters prefer this method since quilt designs often use predetermined shapes to be repeated. Stitchers often prefer the first approach, which allows for the shaping of the appliqué beneath the fingers as it is sewn. The disadvantage to pressing and basting is that the pressing may stretch **bias** edges of the material. A disadvantage of the nonbasting method is that some beginners find it difficult to control placement. Either method requires practice to develop skill and control.

A beginner in hand appliqué should try various ways of working to see which works best. Any other hand stitching method may be used for appliqué. If edges are not turned under, stitches may crisscross over the raw edges. In wall hangings, and **soft sculpture** forms, the cut edges often take advantage of **fray**ed or **ravel**ed areas for textural change. See ill. Also see **Stitchery: Cutting, Hand Appliqué.**

Hand appliqué

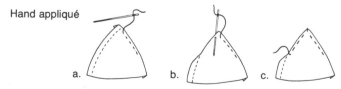

a.   b.   c.

hand beater. Rugmaking. Weaving. (Also called tapestry beater.) A tool used in the hand in **tapestry** and **rug weaving, Navajo weaving,** and **frame loom weaving** to beat the **filling** down. In the case of Navajo weaving, it is used to force down the filling between **warp** threads before beating down with the **batten.** Hand beaters come in a variety of shapes and sizes, but almost all are of a hard, smooth wood. They resemble a fork or comb and, in some cases, the tines are of steel or brass instead of wood. They are made to fit well into the hand with the exception of rug combs that are larger and heavier than other weaving combs and have a handle by which they can be grasped while beating. In many cases, weavers use a common table fork instead of a true hand beater. Also see **tapestry tools.**

hand bobbin. Macramé. Long, loose ends of macramé **cord** can be wound around the hand to prevent tangling while working.

To make a hand bobbin, each cord is held about 18″ beyond the work and wound in circles around the fingers of one hand until all the cord is wound. The bobbin is then removed from the hand and secured around the middle with a knot or small elastic band. If the cord is wound in figure-8's between the thumb and little finger of the hand, the **bobbin** is called a **butterfly.** See ill.

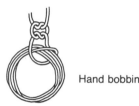

Hand bobbin

hand brace. Bookbinding. A tool used in conjunction with the **stabbing clamp** to make holes through the back **section**s of books so they may be sewn. A ¹/₁₆″ drill bit is commonly used.

hand card. Spinning. See **carder.**

hand coloring. Découpage. Uncolored **prints** to be used for découpage may be tinted by hand with oil-base **color pencils,** watercolor, or **acrylic** paints thinned with water. Also see **Découpage: Hand Coloring.**

hand drill. Jewelry. A hand-operated device used to bore holes into metal. The hand drill is fitted with twist drill bits up to ¼″ diameter. There are two basic types of hand drills. One is equipped with gears which mesh into one another to turn the **collet** holding the drill. This hand drill is held in position with one hand and turned with the other. Hold the tool so that it is perpendicular to the metal during drilling. Do not use too much pressure as the drill is sharp. Allow it to cut easily at its own rate. The metal must be held stationary while it is being drilled. Since both hands are used to operate this hand drill, it is necessary to clamp the metal down. Place a piece of flat wood beneath the metal to protect the drill point as it comes through the metal and to protect the surface of the workbench. Place heavy cardboard or a piece of leather between the clamp and the metal while drilling; otherwise the metal will be badly scratched.

The other type of hand drill, of which there are several models, basically entails a system of pumping a drill up and down by hand, which is translated into a drilling motion. This type of hand drill frees one hand to hold the metal. See ill., page 404. Also see **automatic center punch, center punch, drill press, drilling, flexible-shaft machine.**

Twist drill bit

hand drill. Woodworking. See **drilling tools.**

hand file. Jewelry. A flat file with parallel **filing** surfaces available in numerous cuts from fine to coarse. It is ¾″ wide and approximately 8½″ long including the **tang.** It has a wide variety of uses. Also see **needle file, riffler.**

hand file. Metalworking. See **file.**

hand hook. Rugmaking. A metal shank fitted into a wooden handle and traditionally used with fabric strips to make **hooked rug**s. The shank has a hook at its tip and is fitted into the handle either straight or at an angle. In olden days it was a hand-wrought bent nail or one tine of a two-pronged fork bent to form a hook and the other tine filed off. These, too, were inserted in wooden handles to make for a more comfortable tool. Some hookers still prefer to make their own hooks in this manner, or they buy either the hook mentioned above, or use a steel **crochet hook** in either a #1 or #2 size. Whatever the tool, it must go easily through the **rug backing** without tearing or pulling it. This is considered the "true" way of hooking, as opposed to using either a **punch needle** or a **speed hook,** and is done from the front of the rug. The hand hook is held in one hand with the handle usually in the palm and the index finger on its shank. The other hand holds the fabric strip under the backing and feeds it to the hook. The hook is pushed through the backing as far as it will go, catches the strip, and pulls it up through. The height of the loops formed is determined by the eye. A **frame** can be used to steady the backing, and yarn can be used as well as fabric strips. See ill. Also see **strip cutter.**

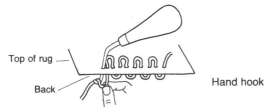

Top of rug —

Back —

Hand hook

handkerchief print. Batik and Tie-dye. See **bandana work.**

handkerchief puppet. Puppets. A simple **hand puppet** that uses a handkerchief over the index, middle, and fourth fingers. The cover may be a real handkerchief or any similar-size piece of fabric. Three holes, just big enough for the ends of the fingers to slip into, are cut into the fabric in a straight line, about 2″ to 3″ apart. The middle finger goes through the center hole, the other fingers in remaining holes. A face can then be added to the middle finger in any of several ways. The simplest way is to draw a face directly onto the finger with **marking pens.** Or an oval of cardboard or paper can be cut to suggest a face. After drawing features on it, a strip of fabric tape or ribbon may be cut for the back of the oval. It is glued at the ends, allowing just enough slack for the middle finger to slip into it to hold the head in place. Another way of making the face for this simple puppet is to use sticky-backed paper features stuck directly on the finger. Or a small cloth hood on which a marking-pen face is drawn can be slid over the finger.

hand-knotted pile. Rugmaking. Weaving. See **knotted pile.**

handle. Basketry. Something by which to hold or grasp a **basket.** It may be made of one stout rod or **bow,** or made up of a number of thinner rods wrapped or woven together. See ill. Also see **Basketry: Woven Basket Construction.**

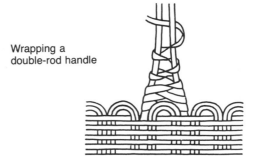

Wrapping a double-rod handle

handle. Ceramics. See **pulling a handle.**

handle bow. Basketry. See **bow.**

handle letters. Bookbinding. (Also called hand letters.) Individual letters engraved on the end of a short brass rod and attached to a handle, usually of wood. This tool and a **type clamp** are used when it is inconvenient to use a **type holder** (which holds lines of type) for **titling** a book. The letters are heated on a stove, cooled on a cotton pad, then impressed through gold or colored foil onto the **cloth** or **leather** of the binding.

handle liner. Basketry. (Also called liner, representative). A stout **rod** the thickness of the **handle bow** inserted into the weaving where the handle is expected to go. It is used to keep a space or **bow mark** open for the eventual handle. The **handle liner** permits weaving without having to negotiate around an entire handle; it should extend only slightly higher than the expected **border.** See ill.

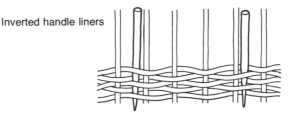

Inverted handle liners

hand letters. Bookbinding. See **handle letters.**

hand levers. Weaving. See **lever, table loom.**

hand loom. Weaving. A term referring to any **harness loom** that is not power-driven, or a semiautomatic foot-power loom. Usually a hand loom is taken to be a horizontal loom with harnesses controlled by foot-power, or its smaller table equivalent, where the harnesses are operated by hand. The former is called a **foot-power loom** or **floor loom**, while the latter is known as a **table loom.** Also see **jack-type loom.**

handmade glass. Stained Glass. See **antique glass.**

hand-manipulated. Weaving. See **finger-manipulated.**

Hand of Friendship. Quilts. See **Bear's Paw.**

hand-painted batik. Batik and Tie-dye. The traditional Javanese art of hand-drawn or hand-painted batik is called **tulis** work, or tulis batik, in contrast to **tjap printing.** Most contemporary **batik** work is accomplished by the hand-painted method. The **wax** can be applied either with a **brush** or a **tjanting.**

hand polishing. Jewelry. Generally used for delicate pieces or to reach areas inaccessible to a **buffing machine.** Burnishing and **thrumming** are two methods of hand polishing. Many of the same **buffing compound**s used in machine polishing are used for hand polishing. Also see **abrasive, buffing, chamois, chamois polishing stick, emery stick, felt polishing stick, polishing, polishing cloth, red rouge cloth, steel wool.**

hand punch. Leatherwork. See **drive punch.**

hand puppet. Puppets. (Also called fist puppet.) Any **puppet** that fits over and is **manipulate**d by the **puppeteer's** hand. It is sometimes, though less commonly, referred to as a **glove puppet.**

The **puppet head,** with arms and skirt attached, should be just large enough for the puppeteer's hand to be slipped into it. His fingers are spread to fit into the puppet's head and arms. It is the puppeteer's fingers that control the arm movements of the hand puppet. For the hand puppet that uses finger control, the coat or shirt is cut and sewn in such a way that the arms are short and wide enough for one or two fingers, since the fingers must slip into the arms if they are to be moved.

Sometimes the arm movement is ignored and only the grosser whole body movements are made, which means that fingers need not fit into the puppet arms. The hand can be used only to hold the puppet head upright and to move it. The use of the whole hand, rather than the fingers, is more easily managed by small children.

The simplest version of the hand puppet consists of the decorative front side of the puppet with an extra piece of fabric or **felt,** into which the flat of the hand can be slipped. This is easily controlled by a small child. Another very simple puppet is the **handkerchief puppet.**

The clothing for a hand puppet usually consists of just the shirt or dress, since the garment must extend down to conceal the hand. When legs are essential (as for a cowboy or a sailor), the pants can be cut, sewn, and **stuff**ed (if

desired) before being added at the waistline. They will then hang down in front, at least partially concealing the hand. See ill. Also see **apple-head puppet, arm puppet, base, batik puppet, felt puppet, hand, nylon-stocking puppet, playboard, "playing the puppet," prop shelf, Punch and Judy show, puppet play, rod puppet, scrap puppet, Sesame Street puppet, sock puppet, two-faced puppet** and **Puppets: Making the Puppet Head.**

a.   Position of fingers inside a puppet with a hollow head

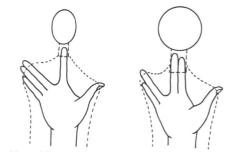

b.   Position of fingers inside a puppet with a hollow neck

hand-puppet stage. Puppets. See **boxed in** and **Puppets: The Puppet Stage.**

hand quilting. Quilts. See **Quilts: Quilting, Hand Quilting.**

hand reel. Spinning. See **reel.**

hand rest. Stained Glass. A useful piece of equipment to steady the hand while **painting on glass** and to prevent smearing areas already painted. It is made by taking a lath strip about 12″ long and nailing a small block at either end to lift the strip of wood off the table. Also see **maulstick.**

Hands All Around. Quilts. A **pieced block** pattern very similar to **Bear's Paw** with the exception of the central **patch.** Here a curved line replaces the straight one.

handsaw. Woodworking. A hand tool consisting of a handle and a thin metal blade with a series of sharpened teeth used to cut wood.

CROSSCUT SAW   The most common handsaw, used to cut the wood across **grain (a.).** It may be used to cut fabricated woods and panels without a specific grain, such as **plywood, hardboard,** and **particle board.** It is 12–28″ long and has 4–12 teeth per inch. The teeth are knifelike and **bevel**ed, and **set** alternately to right and left, making two pointed grooves in a **kerf.** A good general-purpose crosscut saw is 22″ long and has 10 **point**s (i.e., 9 teeth per inch).

RIPSAW Although the general shape is identical to that of the crosscut saw, the ripsaw is designed to cut with the grain—literally to "rip" the board (**b.**). The teeth are raked more forward, are unbeveled, and are set at less of an angle than those in a crosscut saw. A 26″, 6-point ripsaw is good for general use.

BACKSAW This is a crosscut saw with a reinforced back on a rectangular blade with fine teeth (11–14 points) (**c.**). The fine teeth and thin blade are required for finishing work where precise, straight cutting is important; it is often used in a **miter box** for cutting **joint**s. Very fine-toothed backsaws (up to 20 points) are known also as tenon saws.

COMPASS SAW A 12″ blade with a pointed tip used to cut curves; it may be used to cut a circular hole by inserting the blade into a 1″ hole bored into the board (**d.**). The teeth are like those on a crosscut saw.

KEYHOLE SAW A smaller version of the compass saw. The handle is usually metal, and the detachable blade may be replaced with a **hacksaw** blade (**e.**). It is used for cutting out small curves, such as, obviously, keyholes.

COPING SAW (ALSO CALLED FRETSAW, JIGSAW) This has a very thin blade held under tension by a U-shaped frame; it is used for cutting intricate patterns in thin wood (**f.**). See ill.

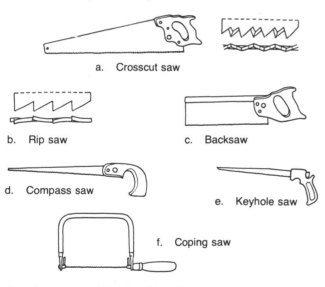

a. Crosscut saw

b. Rip saw

c. Backsaw

d. Compass saw

e. Keyhole saw

f. Coping saw

hand scraper. Woodworking. See **scraper.**

hand-screw clamp. Woodworking. See **clamping tools.**

hand snips. Metalworking. See **snips.**

hand spindle. Spinning. See **spindle.**

handspun. Spinning. A yarn spun by hand on a **spindle** or **spinning wheel.** It can be a very fine and perfect yarn, although most spinners seem to prefer an irregular, more interesting and unusual yarn than can be made by a machine.

hand stitching. Stitchery. See **hand appliqué.**

hand string. Puppets. The cord or **string** attached to the **hand** of a **puppet** by which the hand is made to move and to gesture. If there are no **elbow string**s, the arm movements are made by raising or lowering the hand strings. Simpler **marionette**s have only a hand string, eliminating the elbow string of the more complex figures. The placement of the hand strings is important and will affect the kinds of gestures made by the figure. A string attached to the forefingers makes the hand point, whereas attached behind the wrist, so the hand dangles, it gives a limp-wristed effect. Proper placement requires trial and error as well as consideration of the role or character played by the marionette. The hand strings are connected to the **arm bar.** If a continuous string is used from one hand to the other, going through **screw eyes** on the **horizontal control**, the arms can be moved either individually or together. On the **vertical control**, the hand strings may be attached to wires that replace the arm bar. The wires are lifted up or down, either individually or simultaneously, to **manipulate** the arms. Also see **arm string** and **Puppets: Stringing the Marionette.**

hand tool work. Metalworking. See **bench work.**

hand vise. Jewelry. A **vise** that can be held in one hand used for holding work that is too small or too difficult to hold in the hand. It can be used to hold wire while forming one head of a **rivet** or twisting it. The hand vise is tightened by means of a wing nut. Also see **clamp.**

handweaving. Weaving. A term that originally came into being to differentiate between that work produced by weavers at power looms in commercial mills, and that made by handweavers using a hand **shuttle** on either a **hand loom** or a **foot-power loom.** It has been expanded to include all work woven **off-loom** as well as that done on frame, backstrap, and other **primitive loom**s. Also see **backstrap loom, frame loom.**

Handy Andy. Quilts. A variation of the **geometric pieced-block** design commonly known as **Shoo-fly.** See ill.

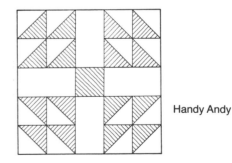

Handy Andy

hanger. Lacemaking. See **passive.**

hanging rod. Stitchery. The **rod** or dowel from which a **panel** is suspended. The **stitchery panel** or batik or other **fabric** is **fold**ed and **hem**med at the top to make a channel through which the rod is inserted. The rod can be solid brass or brass-coated, a standard drapery or curtain rod, or a wood dowel.

hanging two pairs from a pin. Lacemaking. See **bobbin.**

hangman's noose. Toys. See **flipperdinger.**

hank. Basketry. The commercial amount or standardized length in which **cane, raffia,** or other basketry material may be bought. The length of each hank depends on the material being sold, e.g., **winding** reed is commonly sold in 500' hanks, raffia in 50' hanks.

hank. Knitting. (Also called skein.) A length of yarn (usually weighing several ounces) wound into a coil. The yarn is wound either before or after the dyeing process (before if the yarn has been handspun). The yarn is wound into **balls** from these hanks or skeins.

hank. Spinning. Weaving. See **skein.**

hardanger fabric. Embroidery. A heavy fabric of evenly woven double thread linen. Also see **background fabric.**

hardboard. Woodworking. (Also called Masonite, pressboard.) A manufactured panel consisting of wood fibers bonded together at high temperatures with a natural binder called lignin. (In contrast, **particle board** is made from wood chips.) Hardboard is used for interior paneling, drawer bottoms, hidden parts of cabinets, and work surfaces; it does not split or warp because it has no **grain,** but it will sag or break under stress. There are two types. Standard hardboard is the softer of the two; it usually has one smooth and one rough side, and is less resistant to moisture and abrasion than tempered hardboard, which is usually smooth on both sides, feels harder, and is recognizable by its very dark brown color. Both types come in ⅛" and ¼" thicknesses in standard 4' × 8' or 4' × 12' panels.

hard enamel. Enameling. See **enamel, frit.**

hardener. Plastics. See **catalyst.**

hardening. Metalworking. A **heat treatment** process consisting of heating **steel** to a specific temperature to increase its hardness and **tensile strength.** The steel must have a carbon content of 1–3% for the treatment to be effective. This process also gives the metal a finer grain and reduces its **ductility,** thus making it more brittle. It is often followed by another heat treatment process called **tempering** to reduce the brittleness. Gradual natural hardening occurs in some metals. This may take only a few days or as with some alloys of **aluminum,** several years. Also see **Metalworking: Heat Treatment.**

hard ground. Enameling. See **resist.**

hardie. Metalworking. (Also called hardy.) See **blacksmithing tools.**

hardie. Mosaics. An object like a chisel with a slightly curved tungsten carbide edge upon which a **tessera** is set to receive a blow to break it into smaller pieces. The hardie is most often secured in a wooden block or table so that it can handle the **hammer** rap. **Clippers** are surer for the amateur, but for accurate cutting of fine-quality tesserae nothing can compare with the hammer-and-hardie technique. Experienced mosaicists usually embed the hardie in an upended wooden log of substantial girth, cut to a working height they find comfortable when standing. See ill. Also see **Mosaics: Tools and Materials, Cutting the Material.**

Hardie

hardie hole. Metalworking. See **anvil.**

hard jet. Jet Carving. Hard jet is mined from the lower beds of lias rock and has a hardness of 3–4 on the Mohs scale. It is the preferred material for carving. Also see **jet, soft jet.**

hardness. Amber Carving. Gemcutting. The resistance of a material to being scratched or marked by another material. A material of greater hardness will abrade materials of inferior hardness. Harder stones take and retain a superior polish.

Hardness is not a measure of resistance to shock and is not to be confused with toughness. The hardest gems are brittle, yet **jade's** fibrous structure lends it toughness—greater than steel though it is of moderate hardness. Hardness is useful information for identification and cutting of gems. The **Mohs scale of hardness** is used to rate relative hardness by gem cutters.

The following is a list of some stones arranged in order of hardness: amber 2½, jet 3½, **malachite** 3½, **fluorite** 4, **dioptase** 5, **kyanite** 5–7, **hauynite** 5½, **lapis lazuli** 5½, sphene 5½, **hematite** 5½, **obsidian** 5½, **moldavite** 5½, **opal** 5½–6½, nephrite 5¾, diopside 6, **turquoise** 6, adularia 6, amazon stone 6, labradorite 6, **pyrites** 6, **prehnite** 6½, **epidote** 6½, demantoid 6½, idocrase 6½, **olivine** 6½, chalcedony 6½, **axinite** 6¾, jadeite 6¾, **quartz** 7, **tourmaline** 7, cordierite 7¼, **garnet** 7¼, **andalusite** 7½, **staurolite** 7½, euclase 7½, **zircon** 7½, **beryl** 7¾, phenakite 7¾, **spinel** 8, topaz 8, **chrysoberyl** 8½, **corundum** 9, **diamond** 10.

Stones vary slightly in hardness, depending on the part of the world they derive from. In some cases the hardness of the same stone varies in different directions; **kyanite,** for example, has hardness of 5 across the **crystal** and 7 parallel to its **C** axis. Also see **abrasive** and **Gemcutting: Identifications of Gems.**

hardness. Glasswork. A characteristic of glass determined by the temperature to which it must be heated to become workable. The terms "hardness" and "softness" as used in the industry do not actually refer to a material's ability to withstand abrasion or cutting. Thus, **soda-lime glass** or **lead-crystal glass** are both considered soft glasses even though lead-crystal glass is considerably softer in terms of abrasion resistance than soda-lime glass. Borosilicate glass has both high resistance to abrasion and a high melting point.

hard porcelain. Ceramics. A type of **porcelain** developed in the 1600s. It is composed of three main ingredients: **kaolin, flint,** and **feldspar.**

hard solder. Jewelry. **Solder** that melts at temperatures above 1000° F. Soft, or lead, solder has undesirable qualities for jewelrymaking. Also see **silver solder.**

hard solder. Metalworking. See **solder.**

hard soldering. Metalworking. See **soldering.**

hard temper. Jewelry. Metal that has been worked cold, i.e., at room temperature, and becomes harder due to being worked. Also see **temper.**

hard twist yarn. Spinning. Weaving. See **twist.**

hardware. Woodworking. Metal parts used in building cabinets, furniture, or other wood products. Builder's or cabinet hardware includes hinges, pulls, latches, doorknobs, locks, **nails, screws, bolts,** etc.

hardware cloth. Stitchery. (Also called screen.) A wire screening material which has a crisscross or **grid pattern** of lines. It is available in various widths and can be purchased by the foot at many hardware or builders' supply stores. It is especially well suited for use in children's **yarn stitchery** projects, since the hardware cloth itself remains rigid, avoiding the usual problems children encounter in puckering the **fabric**s they are sewing. Another advantage in the use of this material by children is that it is unnecessary to use a **needle.** The ends of large yarns, or several yarns held together, may be wrapped with masking tape to form a cone-shaped end which serves as needle for the sewing through of the open spaces of the wire.

When cut (with wire cutters) the edges of the hardware cloth are sharp and should be covered with adhesive tape or masking tape to avoid cuts. Screens are often constructed with a wire mesh or hardware cloth as a base over which yarns may easily be sewn.

hardwood. Puppets. Toys. Fine, even-grained heavy woods that, if seasoned, are excellent for wood carving. They are more difficult to cut than **softwood**s but they are not apt to split. The designation "hardwood" does not necessarily mean that the wood is more durable than softwood; oak, for example, is a hardwood which is less durable than red cedar, a softwood.

All the fruitwoods are hard, as are beech, birch, boxwood, holly, mahogany, maple, oak, olive, and walnut. Because they are dense, the hardwoods can be sanded to a hard, smooth **finish.** They take on a good polish and luster and can be painted to a glossy surface. Exotic and imported hardwoods and **dark wood**s are available, such as ebony, lignum vitae, rosewood, and zebrawood, but they are not easily obtained and are often expensive. Hardwood scraps from a cabinet shop are excellent for small toys.

hardwood. Woodworking. One of the two main classifications of wood. Hardwoods come from deciduous trees (those with broad, flat leaves that fall annually); the woods are generally hard, heavy, and close-grained, although there is great variation in their quality. Because they are durable and able to take a high polish, they are commonly used for fine cabinet work, furniture, handles, interior paneling, and woodcarving. Some examples of hardwoods are **ash, beech, birch, cherry, mahogany, maple, oak,** and **walnut.** Also see **wood.**

hardwood lap. Gemcutting. See **lap.**

hardwood plywood. Woodworking. See **plywood.**

hardwood wheel. Leatherwork. A tool which is used for burnishing the edges of leather to give it a fine finish. Also see **circle edge slicker.**

hardy. Metalworking. See **blacksmithing tools, hardie.**

Hargrave, Lawrence. Kites. See **box kite.**

Harkort test. Ceramics. A test of the craze potential of a **glaze.** The test involves heating and plunging glazed ware into cold water repeatedly, while increasing the kiln temperature. It is important to make note of the temperature at which a given **glazed ware** will craze. Also see **crazing, kiln log.**

harlequin opal. Gemcutting. See **opal.**

harness. Weaving. Also called frame, shaft. A wooden or metal movable frame hung in the center of the **loom** and containing the **heddle**s through which the **warp end**s are threaded. Through the up and down movement of the harnesses, the warp ends are raised and lowered, and **shed**s come into being so that the warp can be interlaced with the **filling** to form **cloth.** The harnesses are found in, and supported by, the **castle** of a **counterbalanced loom, countermarch loom,** or **jack-type loom.** It is the distinguishing feature of a **harness loom,** be it a floor or table model, and is what differentiates the harness loom from **primitive loom**s. With the addition of harnesses, the sheds no longer need be picked up by hand or depend on a **shed stick** or a **heddle bar** (1). The harnesses are attached to and controlled by the **lams** which in turn are operated by **treadle**s or **lever**s as in the case of a **table loom.** This hand or foot mechanism allows for easy and quick shed openings. The order in which the harnesses are threaded and treadled controls the type of pattern or design the cloth will have.

The simplest harness is composed of just the frame, the top of which passes through the top loop of a **string heddle,** and the bottom through the bottom loop. Most present-day harnesses have extra flat, thin, metal bars attached to the inner edge of the top and bottom of the frame. On these are strung the heddles which can be easily shifted and added to or decreased at will. The **heddle bars** (2) are held in place at each vertical edge of the frame by a locking or hooking device. If the harness is wide, there is also a hook in the center between the bar and the horizontal frame.

The least number of harnesses a loom can have is two while the maximum is usually 16. Most handweavers start off with looms having 4 harnesses. The number of harnesses usually increases by groups of 4 so that the next step from a **four-harness loom** would be an eight-harness and anyone wishing more than 16 would jump to 20 or 24 harnesses, although this high a number is quite unusual, and the loom would have to be specially built. A loom with more than 4 harnesses is known as a **multi-harness** loom. When a loom has more than 4 harnesses, many handweavers mark the harness with a number to facilitate **threading** and to quickly spot treadling mistakes. Harnesses number from front to back, so that the harness facing the weaver at the front of the loom is always harness #1. On the number of harnesses depends the possibility of being able to weave complex or elaborate weave structures. Also see **foot-power loom, treadling order.**

harness draft. Weaving. See **drawing-in draft.**

harness leather. Leatherwork. Leather, usually vegetable-tanned cattle hide, used in saddlery.

harness loom. Weaving. A **loom** having **harness**es or frames suspended in the central structure, or **castle,** which open the **shed**s and control the pattern and structural development of the cloth. Without the castle and harnesses, the loom depends on either a **rigid heddle** arrangement, a heddle bar, or **finger-manipulated** techniques to open the sheds and achieve a fabric. A harness loom can be either floor or **table** model, have either a **rising** or **sinking shed** or both, and have the harnesses operated either by hand or foot through the use of **treadle**s, pedals, levers, wheels, or ropes. Most harness looms easily available to handweavers have from 2 to 16 harnesses. **Foot-powered** floor **loom**s have up to 16 harnesses and **table loom**s up to either 8 or 12. It is also possible to obtain looms with as many as 24 harnesses and some **dobby loom**s have even more. Although a harness loom is considered a mechanical loom by some weavers, it is very much a **hand loom** that allows the weaver greater speed in the weaving process and frees him from the monotony of picking up by hand weave **pattern**s that can be easily translated into the **threading** patterns used on a harness loom. Also see **counterbalanced loom, countermarch loom, jack-type loom.**

harness-manipulated. Weaving. Fabrics in which the weave pattern or structure has been achieved through the use of a **harness loom.** How the **harness**es are threaded, and how they are raised or lowered, is part of the harness manipulated process. The direct opposite are **finger-manipulated** weaves that depend only on the action of the fingers for the interlacing necessary to weaving, or the ornamentation that is an accessory to a woven background.

harness needle. Leatherwork. A sturdy needle with an egg-shaped eye and a dull point. It is the best stitching needle for leather. Use with waxed thread through pre-punched holes on medium and heavyweight leather. Harness needles are often used in pairs, and come in various sizes. See ill. Also see **double needle stitch.**

Harness needles

harp. Ceramics. (Also called bow.) A clay cutter used for trimming and cutting **slab**s and edges of **pot**s. It consists of steel piano wire stretched on a somewhat flexible bamboo or metal hoop. See ill.

Harp

Harriet Powers Quilt. Quilts. Among the most unusual of all **storytelling quilt**s or one-of-a-kind quilts. Harriet Powers, a black woman, made the **appliqué quilt** in Athens, Georgia, in the 1890s. It is composed of **block**s, each of which tells a biblical story or describes an exciting event. It is a beautiful quilt using simplified forms and symbols in a masterful way. Mrs. Powers wrote information about each of the blocks. Among the events depicted are Jonah being swallowed by the whale; the "dark day of May 19, 1780"; Adam and Eve with the serpent, rib, sun, moon, and "God's all-seeing eye and the merciful hand"; the "cold Thursday 10 of February, 1855: a woman frozen while at prayer . . ."; the creation of the animals; and the Crucifixion. This quilt is in the Boston Museum of Fine Arts.

Harrison Rose. Quilts. Any of several variations of an **appliqué block** design, also known as **Whig Rose.** One depicts a large rose located in the center of a block, with stem and leaves to one corner. Another is a geometric arrangement of four roses with leaves that point from the center out to the corners. These were named for President Harrison and were designed after the spirited campaign of 1840. See ill. Also see **presidents' quilt.**

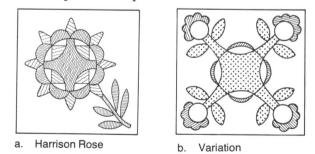
a. Harrison Rose   b. Variation

Harry's Star. Quilts. See **Star of the West.**

Harvest Sun. Quilts. (Also called Prairie Star, Ship's Wheel, Wheel of Chance.) The name given to either of two completely different **pieced block** designs. In one, the block contains a **fan** shape and is **set** so that the fans form a circle. The other is a pieced diamond block pattern that forms an eight-pointed star. It is almost identical to **Star of Bethlehem,** which is usually an **overall** pattern. See ill., page 410. Also see **fan quilt.**

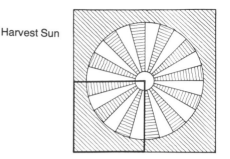

Harvest Sun

hasp. Basketry. A wrapped loop that is attached to the **cover** of a basket to keep it closed. It is located to fit over a **noose** on the body of the basket and made to accept a **peg** to secure it.

To make a hasp, **slype** both ends of a piece of cane so that when joined they form a continuous loop. With the loop well soaked, shape it into a figure-eight shape and clamp it with a **clothespin.** When it has dried, glue the ends together. Then, wrap the center section of the hasp with very fine **wrapping cane** and tie or glue the ends secure. See ill.

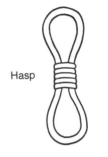

Hasp

hatchel. Spinning. See **flax.**

hatching. Weaving. A **tapestry** shading technique which allows for a gradual change from one color to its neighboring color. The term is French, *hachure*, and its traditional meaning is "a blending of colors." Hatching came in with Gothic tapestries and was used extensively in classic tapestries to delineate facial features and contours, and give depth and perspective to objects. Also, with a limited number of colors, a true tapestry artist could greatly increase his "palette" through clever hatching. The line between two colors becomes "feathery" with hatching and appears to "bleed" from one solid color to the next, while a third color appears where the two mix. Aside from being a half-tone device, hatching is used also as a textural effect to give interest to one-color flat areas.

There are many possibilities and variations that can come under the heading of hatching, but the main classifications are two: simple hatching, which is merely alternating straight lines of two colors of **filling,** and triangular hatching, which builds up the two colors into elongated spire or spikelike lines. In simple hatching, each color goes forward and back to meet the other, but there is no **slit tapestry** developed, since the meeting points are never in the same place.

Triangular hatching starts as simple hatching, but after the initial passing of the first color yarn forward and back, other passes of the first color are made that are each short-

er. The second color comes in always longer with each passage back and forth until it reaches the area of solid first color or penetrates it. The tip of each color always remains a fine line, but on either side of this line the color broadens as it radiates out from its solid area. This is the type of hatching commonly found in Gothic and Renaissance tapestries when the vogue was for more lifelike renderings. Another type of triangular hatching is more like a triangle, with the triangles of both colors merging or fitting into each other. This type does not have as subtle color qualities as the extended line. There are many more irregular triangular hatchings that are invented by the weaver as the need arises when weaving.

Besides being a Gothic tapestry trademark, hatching can also be seen in **Navajo weaving.** See ill. Also see **color blending.**

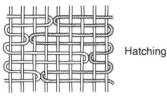

Hatching

haute-lisse. Weaving. See **high-warp, tapestry loom.**

hauyne. Gemcutting. See **hauynite.**

hauynite. Gemcutting. (Also called hauyne.) An aluminum silicon sulfate **crystal**lized in the orthorhombic system with some **cleavage.** It is a transparent, blue gem with **hardness** of 5½ and **specific gravity** of 2.4. Hauynite is a constituent of **lapis lazuli.**

Hawaiian quilt. Quilts. **Quilt**s made in Hawaii that combine the techniques of traditional Early American quilting with the island style of living and design. Since Hawaiians never had woven fabrics at all until the material arrived by the bolt, they were not limited by a necessarily frugal use of scraps, as were colonial quiltmakers. These quilts use a large piece of material for the **quilt top,** to which a second large piece is ordinarily applied. From the second piece, one strong, intricate design is cut and applied to the quilt top, usually in a **medallion quilt** design. This method makes lavish use of new fabric. The quilters of Hawaii have adapted this approach to quilting and blended it with their own ideas, materials, and skill.

While Hawaiian quilts were individually designed, some have been repeated and are typical of the vigorous and intricate style. Among those that typify the patterns are Breadfruit, Garden Island, Grapevine, Koomi Malie (or Press Gently), and Ke Kahi O Kaiulani (or Comb of Princess Kaiulani).

hawk-billed snips. Metalworking. See **snips.**

hawksbill tortoise. Shellcarving. See **Shellcarving: Tortoiseshell.**

hawk's eye. Gemcutting. See **quartz.**

H-came. Stained Glass. See **lead came.**

H-channel lead. Stained Glass. See **lead came.**

head. Bookbinding. The top edge of the leaves and **board**s of a book.

headband. Bookbinding. The turn-in at the **head** and **tail** (tail band) of some books designed to protect the ends. A thick piece of twine may be sewn in at the head and tail before turning in the overlap from the **back**, or it may simply be placed in position and the overlap turned in. Also see **pasting leather.**

head bar. Puppets. The **cross bar** attached to the **control bar** to which **string**s run from the head of a **marionette.** The **head string**s are usually attached at the sides of the head, though locations vary. Also see **Puppets: Stringing the Marionette, Manipulating the Marionette.**

headcap. Bookbinding. The shaped, folded piece of leather that covers the **headband.**

heading. Jewelry. Forming a **rivet** head with a technique called **upsetting, edge thickening.**

heading. Weaving. The piece of fabric woven at the beginning of a new **warp** and usually also at the end. It serves a variety of purposes: it spreads the open spaces between **bout**s, it gives a firm beginning foundation to beat against, and it enables the weaver to check the **threading** and **sleying** for mistakes and to see that **warp tension** is uniform. When the piece is finished, it prevents unraveling until some **finishing edge** is made. The heading is woven in **plain weave** and is usually about 1–2″ wide. The smaller the bout, the narrower the heading made. Since most headings are meant to be removed when weaving is finished, they are woven of heavy scrap yarn, soft string, or twine or rags, preferably in a contrasting color to the warp, so that mistakes show up quickly. Heading **filling** is wound either in butterflies or on **stick shuttle**s and beaten down very heavily.

Headings are woven on most types of looms. If the heading is woven in a better quality yarn with some color relationship to the piece itself, it can become a hem. This is true in weaving a **tapestry** and also at the beginning and end of some **rugs** and **wall hangings.** They are more loosely spaced than the weaving itself, so that there will be a minimum of bulk when the hem is turned. Sometimes the tapestry **cartoon** is pinned to this heading during the weaving. Also see **hemming.**

head knife. Leatherwork. A knife used for cutting heavy leather. To use the model shown, hold the leather in one hand and pull the knife toward you through the leather. A deft worker can skive heavy leather with the head knife. See ill. Also see **skiving** and **Leatherwork: Cutting and Edging Leather, Tools and Materials.**

Head knife

head string. Puppets. The connecting **string** or line between the **head bar** and the side of the **marionette head.** The two head strings are most often attached at the temples, just in front of the ears. They must be of exactly the same length if the puppet is to appear to stand straight. For special movements of the marionette's head, the string may have to be attached in different spots, but the most common attachment is at each side. Also see **control point** and **Puppets: Stringing the Marionette.**

heart. Stained Glass. The central section of a piece of **lead came.**

hearth. Metalworking. See **forge.**

Hearts and Gizzards. Quilts. (Also called Lazy Daisy, Petal Quilt, Pierrot's Pompom, Springtime Blossom, **Wheel of Fortune.**) A quilt **block** design that is a variation of **Drunkard's Path.** In this one, a triangle has a portion of a circle sewn into each of two corners. When **set,** the blocks join to form circles of alternating colors. When solid blocks are alternated with the **pieced** blocks of Hearts and Gizzards, the quilt is called Borrow and Return.

Heart's Desire. Quilts. See **Little Giant, The.**

heartwood. Woodworking. The inner core or structure of a tree. The heartwood is that portion of the **sapwood** that has died and no longer carries sap. It is generally harder, stronger, and darker in color than the surrounding sapwood. Because of these qualities, heartwood is the finest and choicest wood of a tree. Also see **wood.**

heat. Metalworking. The process of heating a metal to red-hot. Blacksmiths try to shape **iron** with as few heats as possible to avoid damaging the metal quality and to avoid accumulation of **scale.**

heat bonding. Plastics. (Also called thermal bonding, thermal fastening.) The process of fastening rigid **thermoplastic**s to themselves by using heat to soften the surfaces and weld them together. Some plastics may be heat bonded with an electric soldering pen or hot iron. For example, this is how many food supermarkets seal **cellophane** produce packages. This process is more common to industry now but may become more widespread in crafts soon.

The surfaces to be joined are heated with a soldering iron or commercial hot plate unit until the plastic softens enough to bond. Then the hot surfaces are held or clamped together to set the joint. Although the joint is strong and can be done quickly, stress may occur in the joined area and **crazing** may occur later. Commercial industry also uses tools emitting ultrasonic vibrations with high frequency voltage and specially designed hot gas welding guns to weld plastics. This equipment is very expensive and unavailable to the general public.

heat forming. Plastics. See **thermoforming** and **Plastics: Thermoforming and Molding.**

heat fracture. Plastics. Fracturing caused by unequal expansion due to high **exotherm** temperatures while **curing resin.** Fracturing greatly weakens the plastic.

heating frame. Jewelry. A flat iron or stainless steel wire screen available in various gauges used on top of an **asbestos pad, tripod,** or **carborundum pan** in **fluxing** and **soldering.** Also see **mop.**

heat lamp. Plastics. (Also called infrared heat lamp.) A lamp with a heat throwing bulb used to hasten the **curing** of **thermosetting resins.** A recommended lamp is an industrial type 250 watt infrared reflector heat lamp. Red glass bulbs are not more efficient but are more expensive. Place the heat lamp about 2″ away from the **gel**led surface of the plastic to speed hardening. This method is particularly useful where room temperatures are low. The longer a resin surface remains tacky, the greater the chance of floating dust particles becoming embedded in the surface unless protected by an **air shield.**

heat loss. Ceramics. The escaping of heat through the chimney and walls. Proper insulation deters heat loss. **Chamber kiln**s utilize heat loss to heat the next chamber during firing. Industrial, **continuous-firing kiln**s waste the least amount of heat.

heat oxidizing. Jewelry. **Coloring** and toning metals with the use of heat. This works best with low karat golds such as 10K and 14K; it also works fairly well with **bronze** and **copper.**

Thoroughly wash the completed, buffed work in a dilute solution of sudsy household ammonia to degrease it, using an old toothbrush. Rinse it well, and dry completely. Play a soft reducing **flame** across the surface of the metal, heating it slowly. The metal will gradually change color. If heated slowly this color on gold is quite permanent. It changes from a soft brown to a deeper brown, then to a soft black on 10K gold, especially if the work has been cast (in which case the area to be oxidized should not be polished, as there is already a fine layer of **cupric oxide** on the surface that becomes coal black when treated with **liver of sulfur**). On 14K gold a deep brown can be obtained through heat oxidation. As copper is oxidized it passes through light yellow and red violet hues. During the red violet stage, copper oxide is being formed, which can easily be flaked off. Unfortunately, the colors on copper are not permanent although they can be made slightly more lasting by stopping the application of heat at the desired color, allowing the metal to cool somewhat, and then, while it is still hot, plunging it into oil. A light household oil can be used for this purpose. Good ventilation is important, as this procedure can produce clouds of thick white smoke. Bronze, when heat oxidized, retains the color more lastingly than copper. Bronze, heat oxidized on a stove flame that is low, but high enough so the work is surrounded by an extremely soft brushing flame, will turn some beautiful tones of soft brown. Placing the bronze on a sheet of **mica** resting on a **heating frame** on top of a **tripod** and heating it from underneath with a torch using a soft brushing flame produces the same result. Do not allow the bronze to become too

dark, as it will begin forming an oxide that will flake off. Also see **antiquing, patina.**

heat set. Batik and Tie-dye. To **fix** or **set** a **dye** by applying heat. **Ironing, steaming,** simmering, heating in the oven, or exposing to the sun are all methods used. The best heat set method is usually specified for any given dye. Also see **autodave.**

heat soaking. Ceramics. The process of maintaining the maturing temperature of a **glaze** or **clay body** in a **kiln.** This allows for a glaze to release gases and smooth out in a fluid state. A controlling **pyrometer** is used in an **electric kiln** to maintain the soak temperature, or it can be done by switching the kiln on and off at intervals. Also see **maturity.**

heat storage. Ceramics. The amount of heat retained by **kiln furniture,** fire bricks, **muffles,** and **sagger**s. Also, the amount of heat required to heat a kiln to the point where the amount of heat radiations and absorption is equal. Dense materials retain more heat than porous materials. Kiln bricks should be as low in **heat storage** as possible. Also see **insulation, thermal conductivity.**

heat treatment. Metalworking. The process of heating metal to specific high temperatures to toughen, harden, or soften it or to increase its **tensile strength.** Basic heat treatments include **hardening, tempering,** and **annealing.** Also see **Metalworking: Heat Treatment.**

heat work. Ceramics. Heat work is the actual effect of heat on **ware**s at a given temperature over a given period of time. **Pyrometer**s measure temperature only; pyrometric **cones** measure heat work. Heat soaking alters **glaze** results even though the temperature remains the same or constant.

Heavenly Steps. Quilts. See **Box Quilt.**

heavy-duty thread. Stitchery. A **mercerized sewing thread** made in a thicker or heavier gauge. It is used for **machine appliqué** since the thicker thread gives a better coverage at **raw edge**s of material. This thread is also used for any heavy-duty sewing. It is available in most fabric shops and department stores, though not in as full a range of colors as regular sewing thread.

heckle. Spinning. See **flax.**

heckling. Spinning. See **flax.**

heddle. Weaving. The part of a **harness loom** that holds the **warp end** in position. Heddles are made of flat steel strips, twisted wire, or string. There is a loop or **heddle eye** in the center through which the warp end is threaded. Heddles are suspended between the **harness** frames on a steel bar attachment called a **heddle bar** or rod. The heddles have loops at the top and bottom through which the heddle bars are threaded. Simpler looms using **string heddle**s sometimes have the heddles attached directly to the harness frames. The length of a heddle varies with the loom used, with the shortest length being 6″ and the longest 12″. The eyes are approximately ½″ long. They can be threaded with the fingers or with the aid of a **reed hook.** Synonyms for this type of heddle are headle, heald, and sometimes needle. There are other types of heddles found on backstrap, frame, Navajo, inkle, and **tapestry loom**s. These are simple string loops that go underneath all the even-numbered ends or all the odd-numbered ends. They are attached to a heddle bar or stick. Also see **backstrap loom, counterbalanced loom, frame loom, heddle cord, inkle loom, Navajo loom.**

heddle bar. Weaving. (Also called heddle rod, heddle stick.) The wooden bar found in **primitive loom**s that acts as a **shedding device.** Around it the **heddle cord** is passed, looped or half-hitched. By lifting or pulling up on the bar the cord raises the **warp end**s and one **shed** of **plain weave** is formed. The alternate or **countershed** is obtained with a **shed stick.** In some frame and **tapestry loom**s, the bar is permanently attached. The shed is then opened in sections by pulling down on groups of **string heddles.**

Heddle bar also refers to the removable metal, inner bar found in each **harness** frame of contemporary **harness loom**s. These bars are the means of attaching the **heddle**s to the harnesses. There is one bar at the top of the frame and one at the bottom. Both are threaded through the top and bottom of the heddles. Also see **backstrap loom, counterbalanced loom, frame loom, Navajo loom.**

heddle block. Weaving. See **heddle jig.**

heddle board. Weaving. See **heddle jig.**

heddle cord. Weaving. A piece of strong string or cord that, in conjunction with the **heddle bar,** works as a **shedding device** on **primitive loom**s. This continuous cord is attached to the heddle bar and goes under every other **warp end** and acts as the **heddles.** When the heddle bar is lifted or pulled up, it raises those warp ends. The weaver can either hold the heddle bar and insert the **filling,** or temporarily put in a **shed stick** to maintain the shed while the filling goes through. There are many ways to attach the cord around the bar. A very simple method is to go under the warp end and then merely around the bar, repeating this sequence across the width of the loom. A slight variation is to make a simple loop around the heddle bar so that the cord will not shift about. A half-hitch is more stable than the loop, and two or more half-hitches can be made between every heddle to space them evenly. The cord initially is tied at the right side of the bar. The under and around procedure moves to the left, and at the left side of the bar, the cord is tied once again. A new cord has to be put on with each new warp. An alternate method is to attach a permanent cord to the heddle bar and suspend reusable loop **string heddles** from the permanent cord. The permanent cord is half-hitched to the bar loosely, so that a slight loop is left at the bottom of the bar. The half-hitches are about ¼″ apart. After this cord is in place, the individual string heddle cords are threaded through the loops and tied under every other warp end. See ill. Also see **backstrap loom, frame loom, Navajo loom, tapestry loom.**

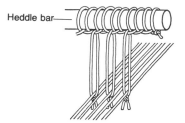

String heddles attached to a permanent half-hitched heddle cord

heddle eye. Weaving. The loop or opening in the center of a metal, wire, or string **heddle** on a **harness loom.** The **warp end** is pulled through or threaded through this opening. The eyes are usually just large enough to let the **reed** or threading **hook** through. Also see **string heddle.**

heddle gauge. Weaving. See **heddle jig.**

heddle hook. Weaving. See **reed hook.**

heddle jig. Weaving. (Also called heddle block, heddle board, heddle gauge.) A wooden block with four dowel posts sunk into it. It is used to make individual **string heddles.** The string or cord is tied in square knots on one side of the two center posts. The open area between the knots forms the **heddle eye.** The cord is square-knotted twice to close the heddle. Ten or twelve heddles are made in this manner before transferring them to the **harness.** See ill.

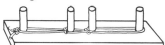

Heddle jig for making string heddles

heddle-reed. Weaving. See **rigid heddle.**

heddle rod. Weaving. See **backstrap loom, frame loom, heddle bar, Navajo loom, tapestry loom.**

heddle stick. Weaving. See **backstrap loom, frame loom, heddle bar, Navajo loom, tapestry loom.**

hedebo. Embroidery. See **whitework.**

hedgehog. Stained Glass. See **striations.**

heel. Bookbinding. The lower portion of the engraved figure or design of a finishing tool.

heel bar. Puppets. The **cross bar,** attached to the **rod** of the **control,** which is connected by **strings** to the back of the **marionette**'s foot. By manipulating the strings of the heel bar the marionette is made to step backward or to dance.

Walking is accomplished by manipulating the strings attached to the knees, and only the most complex movements require a heel bar. Most marionettes are without them. Also see **heel string** and **Puppets: Stringing the Marionette.**

heel string. Puppets. The connecting line or **string** between the **marionette's** heel and the **heel bar.** Also see **Puppets: Stringing the Marionette.**

Heidt jewels. Stained Glass. See **glass jewel.**

Heidt, Louis. Stained Glass. Owner and operator of the Heidt Glass Factory, Brooklyn, New York, during the early 1900s. He was one of the early suppliers of **cathedral glass** and **drapery glass** to **Tiffany** before Tiffany started making his own. Also see **glass jewel.**

heishi. Beadwork. See **shell.**

heliarc welding. Metalworking. See **welding.**

helicopter. Toys. A floating or flying toy similar to the **paper airplane,** but that tends to float down, twirling on the way. In one, a strip of paper is folded twice to make a Z shape. In another, a more elaborate fold makes a **propeller** of the projecting ends. Also see **flying machine.**

heliotrope. Gemcutting. See **quartz.**

heliweld. Metalworking. See **welding.**

helmet. Shell Carving. The traditional material of the **cameo** carver. Often it is possible to obtain only one good cameo blank from an entire shell. Also see **black helmet, bull-mouth helmet, cowrie, horned helmet, king helmet, queen conch** and **Shell Carving: Shell.**

hem. Knitting. The straight bottom (or top) **edge** of a knitted garment or any piece of knitting. There are several methods of forming a hem.

A picot edge creates a scalloped edge. When work is the desired size, follow these directions.

Row 1: K 1, * yo, K 2 tog * repeat * to *, end K 1.
Row 2: P across row.
Continue in stockinette stitch to the desired width of hem, and cast off. Fold the work on the rows where the overs were made, and hem.

For a hand-sewn hem, the last row of knitting is cast off, and the knitting is folded under to the desired length and sewn as for any other hem.

An alternate method is to sew each loop of the last row to the back-of-knitting side.

hem. Stitchery. An allowance at the edge of a **fabric** to be turned under and finished. It is usually preferable that a hem be inconspicuous, unless it serves some decorative purpose. The process involves measuring, pinning, and basting the edge to be hemmed. For example, on a **wall hanging,** an edge is measured and the **hemline** is marked for the finished edge of the **panel.** The edge is turned under on that line and **basted,** after which the **raw edge** of the material must also be turned under and stitched. It is then hemmed and sewn to the **background** fabric, **press**ed, and the basting stitches removed. In hemming a heavy fabric, a **seam binding** can be sewn onto the raw edge, extending it, so that an additional **fold** is not needed.

If a hem must make allowance for a **rod,** as in a **banner** or wall hanging, the hem must be carefully measured or folded over the rod to determine the amount of fabric needed. A **slip stitch** or **blind stitch** is most often used to **tack** the hem in place.

hematite. Gemcutting. Ferrous oxide occurring in colors ranging from dark gray to black or red varieties. It has **hardness** of 6, **specific gravity** of 4.7, red **streak,** and metallic luster. Hematite is often chatoyant. It is polished with cerium oxide on muslin, leather, or wood. Also see **abrasive, cabochon, chatoyance, feldspar, pyrite** and **Gemcutting: Hand Grinding and Polishing, Rough Shaping.**

hemimorphite. Gemcutting. A hydrous silicate of zinc with **hardness** of 4½, and **specific gravity** of 3.25 to 3.5. It is **color**ed green or blue.

hemline. Stitchery. The **fold** line on which material is turned under to make a **hem.**

hemming. Rugmaking. Weaving. The **finishing** of the rug or woven piece by folding back the raw edges and sewing to the back of the piece. Hemming can be done by using **rug binding** or softer binding to cover the raw edge of the hem that has been folded back, by folding once more to hide these raw edges, or by **overcasting** them before sewing down as double protection against unraveling. Which method is used is determined by the softness and pliancy of the backing or woven piece. A **canvas mesh rug backing,** for example, would not lend itself to double fold hemming, but would have to be bound. Woven pieces lend themselves to either, depending on how stiffly or tightly the hems are woven. They should not be beaten down as much as the body of the weaving. A hem allowance should be left at the beginning of a project so that about 2″ can be folded back, the raw edges taken care of, and then sewn to the back with **carpet thread,** heavy duty cotton thread, or yarn matching in color to the item. The corners of a square or rectangular rug that has been hooked, latch-hooked, or embroidered have to be mitered so that the rug will lie flat on the ground. This is not necessary with woven rugs or other objects, since only two edges can be hemmed for the other two are **sel-vage**s. Round rugs need their hem slit or made with small tucks or gathers in order to take out the fullness of the hem so that it will be flat against the rug. See ill. Also see **heading.**

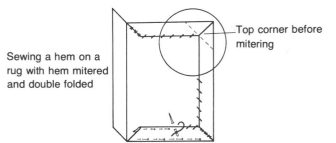

Sewing a hem on a rug with hem mitered and double folded

Top corner before mitering

hemming. Stitchery. (Also called felling.) A **finishing** process which uses a twice-turned edge which maintains a uniform width for its entire distance. Also see **hem.**

hemming bird. Stitchery. See **sewing bird.**

hemming press. Stitchery. See **sewing bird.**

hemp. Batik and Tie-dye. Stitchery. A **natural fiber** from the hemp plant used to make a heavy string or cord. It is sometimes woven into coarse, heavy **fabrics** such as sacking or burlap, although **jute** is more commonly used. Hemp is also used to make rope.

hemp. Plastics. See **filler, reinforcing material.**

hemp. Spinning. Weaving. Hemp is the common name of an Asiatic annual herb which produces strong, pliable fibers in the inner bark of its hollow stem. The plant is also cultivated in Europe and the United States. Unrelated plants, like **sisal,** are sometimes called hemp. Hemp is stronger than **jute** and withstands water better than any other natural fiber. It is used for heavy fabrics and rugs, but more likely for **cordage.** The fibers are removed and processed by methods similar to those used in processing **flax.**

hemstitch. Stitchery. A decorative **stitch,** often used on lightweight or **transparent fabrics,** where a delicate, fine pattern is needed. Several threads of the **fabric** are drawn out in the direction the stitch is to be sewn, leaving an open area with threads running in one direction only. Starting at the right, the needle is used to pick up 3 or 4 of these threads. The **needle** is brought up and then a short stitch is taken back down through the fabric edge. This gives the effect of gathering the loose threads into bundles and secures them at the edge. In double hemstitching, the stitch is repeated at each side.

This stitch was a popular one for **linens** and for fine edgings on handkerchiefs, baby clothes, and blouses. It is seldom used in clothing today.

hemstitching. Crewel. Embroidery. A technique best worked on a woven material whose threads can be drawn out easily. After the horizontal threads have been drawn out, a hemstitch secures the vertical thread groupings. See ill. Also see **drawn thread border, whitework.**

Drawn threads—
Hemstitching—

hemstitching. Rugmaking. Weaving. A manner of stitching the first and last **picks** in weaving or on a **rug backing** so that they will not fray out and a **warp fringe** is left. This can also be done on the **selvage** sides so that a **weft fringe** is possible. In weaving, hemstitching can be done either when the article is on the loom or taken off. Yarn of the same color as the warp or **filling** is threaded through a **needle.** A holding stitch or two is taken in the selvage and the needle is passed under, between, over, and behind a desired number of threads (this number depends on the **sett** and weight of the warp yarns), going from right to left and brought to the surface to the left of the group of yarns, two or three picks in from the **fell.** The yarn is pulled snugly and the procedure is repeated with the next group of warp yarns to the left. In some forms of hemstitching, an additional holding stitch is taken in the fell between each group of warp yarns encircled. The direction of stitching can also be from left to right. Also see **finishing edge.**

Hen and Chickens. Quilts. See **Shoo-fly.**

henna. Batik and Tie-dye. A **natural dye** of reddish-orange hue extracted from the henna shrub.

Henry of the West. Quilts. See **Star of the West.**

heraldry. Stained Glass. The designing of armorial bearings (originally shields for battle), using simple decorative shapes that could be easily read. The designers used attractive, simple colors and well-designed arrangements of shapes to fit the area of the shield. Heraldry can be studied as an introduction to designing simple stained-glass panels.

Hero of Alexandria (ca. 150 B.C.). Toys. A genius and inventor whose early hydraulic toys were marvels of scientific experiment. While many of his works were **water toys,** he also devised **automatic toys** that were set in motion by forced hot air or by pneumatic and mechanical action.

herringbone. Basketry. A decorative twilled weaving pattern used in **plaited basketry.** Also see **twilled plaiting** and **Basketry: Plaited Basket Construction.**

Herringbone. Quilts. See **Tree Everlasting.**

herringbone. Weaving. A term that refers to a **threading** pattern as well as a weave effect based on the **twill weave.** It is commonly used in apparel fabrics. The fabric has a small weave pattern resembling the spine of a fish with diagonal rows coming to a center. This center can have either a point to it or have a **break** to it. Contemporary herringbones have a break and so belong to the broken twill category. All broken twills are not herringbones. A true herringbone, whether with a break or a point, has long enough "spines" for the diagonal to be seen, and is evenly proportioned on both sides of the break or the point. A herringbone with a break is sometimes called a dornik twill. Herringbones usually reverse directions in the warp so that a special threading draft is necessary to make this reversal possible. The herringbone threading draft is either pointed or broken to fit the final weave effect desired. See ill. Also see **twill.**

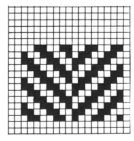

Herringbone weave draft

herringbone stitch. Crewel. Embroidery. (Also called mossoul stitch, Russian cross stitch, witch stitch.) This stitch is a variation of the **cross stitch**—the two stitches cross near either end, not in the middle. The stitch must always be worked evenly. This stitch can be used to mount needlework to a board. The raw edges are folded around the edges of the board and sewn together with a herringbone stitch that spans the distance between the edges.

This simple, versatile stitch has been used for hundreds of years. It can be identified in the fourteenth-century paintings of Giotto and Fra Angelico. See ill. Also see **closed herringbone stitch, rice stitch, shadow stitch.**

a.   b.   Herringbone stitch

heshe. Beadwork. See **shell.**

Hessian fabric. Crewel. Embroidery. A strong coarse cloth made of a mixture of hemp and jute used as a **background fabric** for embroidery with heavy yarns to achieve a rough effect. Also see **rug wool.**

hessonite. Gemcutting. See **garnet.**

hetch. Spinning. See **guide hook.**

hetchle. Spinning. See **flax.**

Hewson Quilt, The. Quilts. A **medallion quilt** sewn in 1800 by Zibiah Hewson, wife of John Hewson, who printed the fabrics from which it is made. He was the first American to print on **cotton.**

hexagonal kite. Kites. See **Kites: Design.**

hexagonal plaiting. Basketry. A form of **lattice plaiting** in which three sets of parallel elements are woven together. See ill.

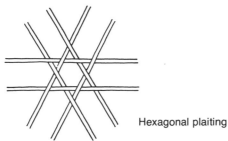

Hexagonal plaiting

hexagonal quilt. Quilts. Any of several **pieced** quilt designs requiring great perseverance to produce, because the **fabric** pieces are cut into numerous small hexagons of identical size. These shapes are often backed with paper that is cut smaller than the fabric so that the **seam allowance** of the fabric is folded back over the paper. The edges of the hexagons are then stitched together. When the hexagons are arranged with one in the center, surrounded by six others, they produce a small flowerlike shape. There are endless variations of the design, depending on the use of color and the number of circles used in each flower. When flowerlike forms of two or three circles are used the quilt is known as Grandmother's Flower Garden. When joined in a random pattern it is called Honeycomb.

Hexagonal Star. Quilts. See **star patterns.**

hexagonal system. Gemcutting. See **crystal.**

hickory. Woodworking. A tough elastic **hardwood** grown best in the eastern United States. Its most common use is in tool handles. Hickory heartwood is brown and its **sapwood** is almost white. It can be carved but **checks** extensively if not seasoned. Also see **wood.**

hiddenite. Gemcutting. See **spodumene.**

hidden whip stitch. Stitchery. Basically the same as a **whip stitch,** but in which the **needle** comes out exactly on the **fold** of the piece being **appliquéd.** The needle is then slipped under the fold before it bites into the material and comes out exactly on the fold again. Carefully done, this stitch leaves no thread showing on the top. Also see **blind stitch.**

hide. Leatherwork. The whole skin or pelt of a large animal, such as steer, cow, bull, horse, or buffalo. For convenience in handling, hides are split into two halves, or **sides.** Also see **belly, kip, skin, splitting** and **Leatherwork.**

hide glue. Découpage. Skin or hide glue, made from the skins of animals, is used to prepare **gesso.** Rabbit-skin glue, the most commonly used hide glue, is available in dry sheets or pieces. It is soaked in water overnight until it has swollen to about three times its dry volume. The glue is then hcatcd, but never boiled, in a double boiler until the glue has dissolved into a hot liquid.

hide glue. Woodworking. See **adhesive.**

Hi-Dye. Batik and Tie-dye. See **fiber-reactive dye** and **Batik and Tie-dye: Dyes.**

high-carbon steel. Metalworking. See **steel.**

high-density foam. Plastics. See **foam.**

high fine silver. Jewelry. See **silver.**

high firing enamel. Enameling. See **enamel.**

high-gloss lacquer. Toys. A fast-drying brilliant colored **lacquer** available in aerosol spray cans. It is flammable and must be used with adequate ventilation. Also see **lacquer enamel.**

high-heart came. Stained Glass. See **lead came.**

high-speed drill. Jewelry. A drill made of special high-speed steel that is resistant to burning out. Small high-speed drills, however, burn out quickly at excessively high speeds. Also see **beeswax.**

high-speed steel. Metalworking. See **steel.**

high-warp. Weaving. (Also called *haute-lisse.*) Refers to a **warp** that is running vertically on an upright or **vertical**

loom. This is the method used at the Gobelin tapestry factory in France. The looms there are quite huge with several people working at them simultaneously. **Shed stick** and **heddle rod** make the **shed**s. Since the weavers work on the back of the tapestry, there are mirrors in back of the warp so that the weaver can see the right side. Weavers working at home make high-warp tapestries on many different models of upright or **tapestry loom**s. Some of these use shed sticks while others have foot pedals or other means of opening up the shed. Also see **Gobelin bobbin, tapestry, upright loom.**

high wheel. Spinning. See **wool wheel.**

Hills and Valleys Quilt. Quilts. A **contemporary quilt** made of **velvet, velveteen,** or other heavy, soft-textured materials cut into strips and rolled to enclose the **bat**ting or **stuffing.** Technically it is not a quilt, but a **coverlet,** as no actual **quilting** is involved. The finished quilt looks like a series of small velvet logs, laid side by side, sewn to a **backing** material. It makes a luxurious, heavy, bulky bedcover.

hinge. Basketry. The simplest hinge to hold a **cover** to its basket is a closed loop of **cane** or **reed** that loosely connects the **border**s of both. It may be wrapped like a **hasp** or woven to hold it secure.

hinge. Bookbinding. The material used to fasten the text of a book to its cover **board**s.

hinge. Jewelry. A device that permits a section of a piece of jewelry to move or swing on an axis, which is fastened to another section. One of the basic types of jewelry hinge is made with a minimum of three tubular sections of equal length and **gauge.** Two of the tubular sections are soldered onto one piece of metal, and the third soldered onto another. It is imperative that the sections line up exactly, as they must interlock. A round wire exactly the same diameter as the hole of the tubing can then be put through them to act as the pivot point. A smoother-working and stronger hinge consists of five units of tubing, three on one piece of metal and two on the other. Also see **chenier, fabrication, tube-holding jig.**

hinged board. Bookbinding. See **binding single sheets with cloth-hinged boards.**

hinge joint. Puppets. A one-way joint, as at the knee or elbow of a **marionette.** It functions in the same way as any ordinary hinge, allowing movement in one direction only. The hinges can be made of various materials, with **leather hinge**s being one of the most favored. Beveling the area under the leather strips allows for even more control. See ill.

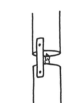

Hinge joint

hippopotamus tooth. Ivory and Bone Carving. The curved canine teeth of the hippo are harder than elephant ivory but used in much the same way. Before working them, the outer layer of porcelaneous enamel must be removed. This may be accomplished with a grindstone. Hippopotamus tooth was the preferred substance for dentures during the eighteenth century, as it was the most durable. Also see **Ivory and Bone Carving: Preparation, Carving, Finishing.**

hip string. Puppets. The cord or string that connects points on the **marionette**'s hips to the **control bar.** Hip strings are ordinarily used only with the **horizontal control.** The **back string** replaces the hip strings if the **vertical control** is used. Also see **Puppets: Stringing the Marionette.**

historical doll. Toys. See **Toys: Doll**s.

historical toy. Toys. See **Toys.**

historiscope. Toys. A **panorama toy** that consisted of a box with one side cut out to suggest a stage. It was first manufactured in 1868. A series of panoramic pictures was shown by unrolling a long strip of paper from one cylinder, or roller, to another. The earliest gave a "Panorama and History of America from Columbus to the Civil War." Children's **homemade movie screen**s or homemade television sets are based on the same principle of using drawings on a rolling cylinder. Also see **Toys: Optical Toys.**

Hitchcock, Lambert. Stenciling. See **Stenciling.**

hit-or-miss. Quilts. A method of combining **block**s in an **all-over pattern** in which no specific color arrangement is followed. The "hit-or-miss" arrangement was sometimes used on **medallion quilts** to make the rows of blocks that outlined the central block.

"Hit-or-miss" is not a haphazard arrangement, but rather an approach that allows for variations within one set dimension. For example, in the **strip quilt**s, the fabrics for any one strip are all the same width—only the color, pattern, and length are hit-or-miss. In a **checkerboard** pattern, a hit-or-miss arrangement is used on multicolored blocks of the same size.

hit-or-miss rug. Rugmaking. Weaving. See **rag rug.**

H-lead. Stained Glass. See **lead came.**

hobbyhorse. Toys. (Also called stick horse.) A horsehead, usually made of wood or fabric, mounted on a stick on which children pretend to ride. Some have small wheels at the end of the stick so that they can be rolled easily across the floor. The child straddles the stick and holds the reins or the part of the stick just under the head.

The hobby horse may be called a broom-handle horse, a riding horse, or a riding-stick horse. The **rocking horse** is also sometimes referred to as a hobbyhorse.

hobnail pattern. Macramé. See **berry knot.**

hog-hair brush. Stained Glass. See **brush.**

Holbein stitch. Embroidery. See **blackwork, double running stitch.**

holding cord. Macramé. (Also called knot-bearing cord.) Any cord on which knots, such as the **half hitch,** are made. It is held taut in place by a **pin** and by retaining the loose end in the free hand while the knotting cords are worked around it. Also see **mounting cord.**

hole-and-slot heddle. Weaving. See **rigid heddle.**

Hole-in-the-Barn-Door. Quilts. See **Shoo-fly.**

hole saw. Metalworking. Plastics. Woodworking. See **drill bits.**

hollie point. Embroidery. A needle lace made entirely of closely worked **buttonhole stitch**es. Possibly its name was derived from "holy" point because church vestments were frequently done in this technique, and because it originally was brought from the Holy Land. It was also used a great deal for household items. When closely worked in silk, it becomes an ideal close covering for the raised portions of **stumpwork.**

hollow back. Bookbinding. The hollow back lining is a stronger form of paper lining that produces a slightly elevated **back.** It is usually associated with leather bindings, although it is sometimes used with cloth. The elevation is created by folding a stiff paper into a tube and gluing it in place over the **back lining** on the **back** of the book.

hollow-bit tongs. Metalworking. See **tongs.**

hollow construction. Jewelry. Type of construction in which walls completely enclose an empty space such as a cube or sphere. Also see **air hole, blowhole, box construction, scorer.**

hollow dish-mold. Ceramics. The easiest type of **mold** to make, consisting of a concave mold of **plaster** or **bisque** in which a **slab** of clay is placed to form a plate or bowl. As the clay dries, it shrinks away from the sides, and removal is easy.

hollow egg. Toys. An **egg** with perforations at each end through which the egg yolk and egg white have been forced out. A sturdy T-pin or pointed nut pick can be used to poke holes at the ends of the egg. One hole should be slightly larger than the other and about the size of a pea. The mouth is placed over the smaller hole and, by blowing, the contents are forced out the other hole. The empty eggshell, or blown egg, is rinsed and can then be used for making a **peep-egg** or for painting and decorating. Also see **Toys: Ephemeral Toys.**

hollow ground. Woodworking. A blade with a hollow or concave surface instead of a bevel behind the cutting edge. It makes for easier cutting and carving by reducing the amount of friction on the blade. This hollow is a characteristic of better **whittling** and **woodcarving tool**s and knives. A blade can be hollow-ground on a **grinding wheel** using the convex shape of the wheel to produce a concavity on the blade. See ill. Also see **Woodworking: Grinding and Sharpening.**

Hollow ground

hollowing. Tincrafting. Creating a concave depression in **tinplate** with a **dapping block** as the hammering surface and a **ball-peen hammer** as the tool. Hollowing can produce either concave or convex bowls depending on which side the tin is hammered. The **hammering** itself should begin at the outer edge or outer rim of the area to be lowered and then gradually worked around toward the center as the metal works inward.

hollowing. Woodworking. A term in **woodcarving** to describe the removing of the interior back of a carved form, to remove a rotten core, or to accelerate seasoning, by exposing the interior to the air.

hollow ware. Ceramics. Dishes that have volume, such as cups, bowls, and tureens. Also see **flatware.**

hollow ware. Metalworking. Hollow metal forms, usually made by **raising techniques.** These may be jewelry, sculpture, or dishes and bowls, and are generally rounded in shape.

holly. Woodworking. A white or cream-colored wood that is very hard and has little visible grain. Because holly trees do not grow large, the wood comes in small pieces and is mainly used for **inlaying** and **marquetry.**

homemade movie screen. Toys. A simple device made from a cardboard box in which drawings made in series are unrolled from a cylinder held vertically at one side of the screen onto a cylinder at the other side of the screen. It is made in much the same way as the nineteenth-century **historiscope.**

homemade paste. Toys. See **flour paste.**

homero. Ivory and Bone Carving. See **vegetable ivory.**

Homespun. Quilts. See **Burgoyne Surrounded.**

homespun. Quilts. Stitchery. Originally, **fabrics** woven from homespun yarns, now machine-made of uneven yarns with slight irregularities to imitate the original. Spun **rayon** and **wool blend**s are now used. Homespun also refers to natural colored **plain weave**s of **cotton.** It is woven in varying widths, some wide enough to be used as bed covers without piecing.

In **quilting** and stitchery homespun is often used because of its uneven texture.

homespun. Spinning. Weaving. A term that has come to mean yarn that has been commercially produced but has the qualities of a handmade product. It is a coarse and rugged yarn with an uneven surface. Spinners use home-spun interchangeably with **handspun** to denote a yarn spun at home by hand.

In weaving, the term originally stood for a rough but very serviceable fabric handwoven by peasants in their homes out of handspun yarn. Today it means a cloth of coarse texture woven in **plain weave** on either a hand or power loom.

Honeycomb. Quilts. A **pieced quilt** pattern using the hexagon shape. It is similar to the **hexagon quilt,** but it uses no specific arrangement of the colors. See ill.

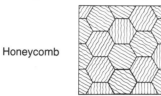

Honeycomb

honeycomb filling. Crewel. Embroidery. This technique begins with a block of squares as in **squared filling.** Using a blunt tapestry and contrasting thread, weave over and under the laid threads diagonally across the square. The needle pierces the background fabric at the outline of the pattern only. See ill. Also see **raised honeycomb filling.**

Honeycomb filling 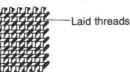 Laid threads

honeycombing. Knitting. A method of decorating ribbed, knit fabrics with a smocklike embroidering technique. Either the same color yarn or contrasting color(s) is used to catch the first and second ribs together, the third and fourth, etc., all with single embroidery back stitches. Do this the width of the ribbed fabric. Move down the fabric slightly to make the second row of honeycombing, this time catching the second and third ribs, the fourth and fifth, the sixth to the seventh, etc. At the end of this second row, begin the two-row pattern again and repeat as many times as desired. The honeycombing should pull the ribs into small evenly spaced diamonds. Also see **smocking.**

honeycomb sheet. Candlemaking. See **Candlemaking: Rolling.**

honeycomb weave. Weaving. Weaves that pit the fabric surface with cell-like shapes so that it resembles a honeycomb. A definite three-dimensional effect is achieved through the construction which is made up of **warp** and **filling float**s held together with **plain weave** and which uses more than four **harness**es. The most common and most popular honeycomb is one with floats on the four sides of a square and an indented center of plain weave. It looks like a waffle and so has taken on the name of waffle weave. There are other honeycombs in which circles, ovals, diamonds, and other shapes are made with the filling or warp floating against the plain weave. The three-dimensional effect can be heightened by heavy yarn in an open **sett,** but this makes for a very loose structure in what

is already a sparse interlacing. Honeycomb is a soft, spongy fabric which is most often used for towels, dress goods, bedspreads, and baby blankets. However, some weavers, notably Sherri Smith, have taken advantage of its three-dimensional qualities to create new effects in **wall hanging**s and **fiber sculpture.**

Honduras mahogany. Woodworking. See **mahogany.**

Hong Kong grass. Basketry. A commercial name for a coarse grass or **sedge** that is twisted to form a continuous length or rope. It is used for stool and chair seating.

honing. Woodworking. See **sharpening, whetting.**

hooey stick. Toys. See **whimmydiddle.**

hook. Rugmaking. Weaving. See **hand hook, latch hook, reed hook.**

hook-and-eye needle. Leatherwork. See **lacing needle** and **Leatherwork: Tools and Materials.**

hooked knitting. Knitting. An early form of knitting done with knitting needles that had a hook at one end.

hooked rug. Rugmaking. **Pile rug**s constructed by pulling or pushing loops of yarn into a woven **rug backing.** There is evidence that prehistoric man hooked materials for use as clothing, as the Copts, Chinese, Moors, and Arabs did with yarn in the early Christian era. Later, hooked fabrics appeared in parts of Europe, Scandinavia, and England. The colonists brought the craft to America, substituted strips of old cloth in place of yarn, and used it primarily for floor and bedcoverings. Thrift was the motive to hook a rug and, in this, it shares a similarity with **rag rug**s. The colonists cut their worn woven cloth into strips, dyed them and pushed them through coffee, grain, and sugar bags which were split open for use as rug backing. The craft flourished in America and became an expressive outlet for the hookers; the rugs became scenes of home, garden, forest, seasonal or family life. Daily activities were pictured, as were portraits of animals and momentous occasions. Edward S. Frost, a Yankee Civil War veteran, was the first to make hooked rug patterns for sale. However, not too many years after the Civil War, hooking lapsed and it was not until World War I that it was revived again, when it was very popular during the Depression and especially so during World War II. It seems that in troubled times, the popularity of hooking rugs grows.

As the yarn or fabric goes through the backing, it forms continuous loops on the right side of the backing. These loops form the **pile** which can be left as loops, or later sheared, or cut through. The loops can be put in at different **pile height**s. Purists claim that true hooking is done with a **hand hook,** or crochet hook, which pulls the material up from the back to the front or right side. However, today, there are many innovations on the hand hook that go by names like **speed hook** or **punch needle.** What these new hooks have in common is that the yarn or fabric is threaded through a needle and is pushed through the backing from back to front. The next step in speediness is electric hooking, but most of the guns or needles are too large to be practical for home-hooking. Commercially made hooked rugs are called tufted rugs. Tufting is the prime method of manufacturing most of our floor coverings, and is based on the same principle as hooking; that of pushing yarn through a pre-made backing.

The only other piece of equipment necessary for hooking is a **frame** to hold the backing taut as the yarn is pushed through it. It is also possible with the hand hook to simply hold the fabric in the hand as the hook goes in and out. Also see **bent-handled scissors, pegged rug, shearing rug, shirred rug, strip cutter, thrummed rug, yarn sewn rug.**

hooking frame. Rugmaking. A rectangular, oval, or round structure over which a **rug backing** is stretched and held taut for ease in hooking. It is essential when hooking is done with a **speed hook,** and less so when hooking is done with a **hand hook** or a **punch needle.** A frame can be used when working with soft backings in **embroidered rug**s. Simple frames that are homemade can also serve as a loom for **frame loom** weaving.

In hooking, the backing is attached to the frame with thumb tacks, staples, or by **lacing.** For the last, a lacing set can be bought with special lacing cord and metal clips that attach the cord to the backing. On oval or hoop frames, an adjustable tension screw holds the backing firmly between the two concentric circles. Frames are either of the small or lap variety, or the large or standing variety. A lap frame can be homemade and is an excellent learning tool, but generally impractical for making large rugs. It can be easily put together out of canvas stretchers (available at art supply stores) or out of an old picture frame. Its size should preferably be smaller than 20″ × 26″ for ease in handling. This lap frame can be mounted on four long, flat-topped bolts in each corner, and thus be raised and used on a tabletop, making it excellent for speed hooking. A further improvement on the lap frame is to make it bigger so that it can accommodate up to 3′ × 5′ rugs. This is possible by using 2″ × 4″ boards and extending the lengthwise sides so that the frame now has legs to support it as it leans against a wall. It will be more comfortable to work on if the legs are long enough to give foot room underneath the frame. The frame without the lengthwise extension can also be supported across chair backs or sawhorses, or it can have legs screwed into each corner.

Frames that are purchased are on trestle stands that tilt for ease in working, and many can be adjusted to comfortable working heights. All fold for storage and are easy to move about. In all cases, as the hooking proceeds and one area is finished, the work is removed from the frame and shifted to an unworked area. Some of the rectangular frames have rollers at the top and bottom so that the finished area can be rolled out of the way, exposing an unworked one. A spiral wool holder can be attached across the top of the frame with the various yarn colors needed inserted into the coils of the spring. See ill. Also see **hooked rug, rug hook.**

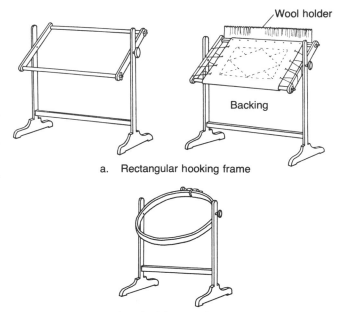

a. Rectangular hooking frame

b. Oval hooking frame

hoop. Basketry. A **rod** tied together at the ends to form a circle. This hoop is used to keep the ends of the **stake**s upright while **upsetting** or weaving in the **siding** of a basket. See ill.

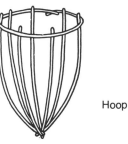

Hoop

hoop. Crewel. Embroidery. Needlepoint. See **embroidery frame.**

hoop. Lacemaking. A hand-held hoop is useful in doing **needle lace.** A hoop, smaller than a **tambour frame,** either oval or round, will hold the **net ground** taut while doing the lacework. A hoop is actually two circles of polished wood; they fit one inside the other. Hoops are available that have an adjusting clamp to tighten them together when the net is in place, or the inside hoop may be wrapped with ribbon or a tape to make the fit tighter as needed.

hoop. Toys. A ring or circle of any rigid nonbreakable material. Hoops have been popular for centuries with both adults and children. They were used in various **toss game**s, **hoop roll,** and for exercising. The Greeks had bronze hoops and the Romans used hoops made of iron. Hoops made of wood have been around for centuries, and were only recently replaced by plastic hoops such as the **hula hoop.** Also see **cleek.**

hoop-and-pole. Toys. See **spear-the-fish.**

hoop loom. Rugmaking. Weaving. A circular **loom** made out of a metal or a wooden hoop. This hoop can be constructed out of heavy gauge wire that is bent into a round shape and the ends can be attached firmly together by tying, taping, or soldering. It can also be a round form such as a bicycle tire rim, an old wooden wheel, or an embroidery hoop. For the most part, **wall hanging**s are the items constructed on a hoop loom; the hoops usually remain in place after the weaving is finished and form the support by which the piece is hung. This means that, in most cases, it is desirable to cover the metal or wood with yarn prior to weaving by using some embroidery **edging stitch,** such as a **blanket stitch.** The threads that will serve as **warp** are then attached through the edging stitch. In cases where no edging stitch is used, the warp threads are tied around the rim or wire and held in place with tape or a little dab of fabric glue. Holes can be bored in wooden hoops through which a **continuous warp** can be threaded.

The warp threads are attached in a straight line from one side to the opposite one by always going through the imaginary center of the hoop. When all the warp pieces are in place, a taut knot is made in the center with an extra length of yarn. This holds the warp firmly in place. The yarn used for the knot can also become the **filling,** in which case, after the knot is made, the yarn would continue to interlace with the warp threads with the weaving progressing from the center out. The weaving is done with a needle and it can also proceed in the opposite direction from the rim down to the center. The weaving can go around and around, or back and forth in sections, as in **tapestry** weaving. The concentration of warp yarns in the center can be used as part of the design and calls for a lesser amount of filling. Warp **end**s can be put in after the weaving starts in the center. They are then attached to the hoop edge and to some point in the already woven section. They go from the hoop to the woven area and then return to the side from which they came.

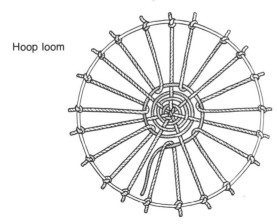

Hoop loom

RUGMAKING   If a hoop loom (see above) is of sufficient size, a small round rug can be made of either yarn or rag strips. In this case, the hoop must be removed and the warp is only temporarily attached to it by sewing, tying, or pinning the individual yarn strands, or rag strips. **Bodkins** can be used with the heavier yarn, but the rag strips can be interlaced by hand. Weaving would proceed as a continu-

ous round-and-round movement. See ill. Also see **needle-weaving.**

hoop roll. Toys. A **game** played with a **hoop** and a T-shaped stick, sometimes called a **skimmer.** The crosspiece is added at the very end of the stick and is used to push the hoop. The object is to keep the hoop upright and steer it around obstacles and corners.

In a variation of the hoop roll, a device similar to the skimmer was attached to the hoop. Made of metal, the **cleek** or stick had a ring formed at each end. One was linked to the hoop and the other was held in the hand to control the hoop. Also see **action toy.**

hop hornbeam. Woodworking. See **birch.**

Hopi Indian wedding sash. Weaving. A sash of white cotton constructed by **plaiting** in a 3/3 **twill** pattern on a frame that holds the **warp** strands rigid. It is both a wedding sash and a rain sash which is woven by the Hopi man for the Hopi bride and is carried in her reed bundle on the day of her wedding when she gives it to her husband who will wear it in ceremonial rain dances. The technique is also called **frame plaiting** or braiding in that the warp **end**s are fixed and held firmly at both ends while plaiting. It is worked on the principle of **sprang,** in that what is plaited at one end repeats itself at the other. The weaver works from both directions to the center where a few rows of 3/3 twill weave are woven in with the help of a tapestry **needle** to finish the fabric. Sprang is an open fabric, but the wedding sash is done as a very compact cloth that has a faint chevron pattern due to the twill plaiting. The warp is wound around a frame as a **continuous warp** would be. Each taut end is taken in turn and pulled under three and over three neighboring ends, and held in place with a **shed stick** until subsequent twists secure it. After the finished belt is cut off the frame, the ends are finished off as a **fringe** and often decorated with wood or cornhusk rings.

hopsacking. Puppets. Quilts. Stitchery. An open **basket weave fabric** made of medium to heavy yarns. It is textured, and is usually a **cotton** or **cotton blend.** Its texture makes it a popular choice for stitchery, especially with **machine appliqué.** Hopsacking is occasionally used in contemporary **quilt**s.

horizontal. Quilts. See **Quilts: Quilting.**

horizontal bar. Puppets. See **horizontal rod.**

horizontal clove hitch. Macramé. See **horizontal double half hitch.**

horizontal control. Puppets. (Also called aeroplane control.) A special arrangement of **control bar** and **cross bar**s to which a **marionette** is strung and which are held horizontally to **manipulate** the marionette. This type of control is necessary to suggest the movement of a four-legged animal. Also see **arm bar, arm string, back string, hand string, hip string, horizontal rod, rod, simplified horizon-**

tal control, **suspended head bar** and **Puppets: Manipulating the Marionette, Stringing the Marionette.**

horizontal double half hitch. Macramé. (Also called horizontal clove hitch.) A **double half hitch** worked on a horizontal **holding cord.** Also see **angling, Cavandoli work.**

horizontal half hitch. Macramé. See **half hitch.**

horizontal loom. Weaving. A loom in which the **warp** is in a horizontal position when weaving. This would include all **harness looms,** horizontal frame and **tapestry looms,** and **ground looms.** Also see **floor loom, frame loom, low-warp, table loom.**

horizontal rod. Puppets. (Also called horizontal bar.) The **control bar** of the **horizontal control** for a **marionette.** The **rod** is grasped in one hand when the figure is performing. Also see **Puppets: Stringing the Marionette.**

horizontal roll. Batik and Tie-dye. In **tie-dye, rolling** the fabric horizontally so that the roll runs from one **selvage** to the other. After it is rolled it can be **bound, tied,** or held in place with various tools, such as **bulldog clip**s and clothespins. Both **gadget tie-dye** and **knotted tie-dye** sometimes use this roll. Tying on the horizontal roll produces a vertical pattern, since the **bindings** go across the roll.

horizontal stitch. Knitting. The horizontal stitch in knitting is a variation on the **one-over-one principle.** *K 1, over 1, transfer the stitch from right needle to left needle, *rep * to * across the **row.** Be sure the transferred stitch is on the needle in the same direction as the stitches on the left-handle needle. Purled stitches or rows are done in the same manner. (This gives a truly horizontal stitch.) See ill.

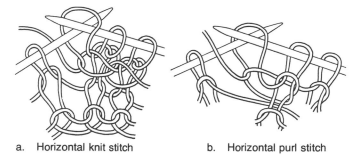

a. Horizontal knit stitch   b. Horizontal purl stitch

horizontal Tunisian stitch. Knitting. See **Tunisian horizontal stitch.**

horn. (Ivory and Bone Carving.) The hard bony growth on the head borne permanently by cattle, goats, oxen, sheep, etc., or the solid bonelike antler of the deer family that is shed annually.

Horn objects have been utilized since prehistoric times; the natural shape of the horn made it useful as a vessel for liquids and powders and as a funnel. It was used by the Vikings to cover the stocks of their broadswords and on their fierce-looking helmets. In biblical times the shofar, a ram's horn, was blown to call men to arms and to announce ceremonies. Horns were tooted through the ages to

glorify, inspire, strike fear, alert, and summon. These uses of animal horn inspired the Bronze Age Danish metal lur horn.

Horn may be obtained from slaughterhouses or from hobby supply houses, which sell cleaned, imported horns. The horn purchased from a slaughterhouse should be boiled until the membrane that attached it to the animal's skull can be removed; this should be done immediately or it will decompose. Allow the horn to dry before working it, as it can warp if you don't. Deer antlers and bull, cow, buffalo, and steer horn are the most commonly used; the cow horn is more solid than the steer horn, which is shell-thin.

Scrutinize the horn before buying it as this was once the animal's tool and weapon and may bear the scars of its service. A scar can become more prominent as a piece is worked. Horn is tough and durable and is worked with the same tools as tortoiseshell. It can also be formed with heat.

The rough cutting of antler and horn is accomplished with a hacksaw, and the finer cuts with a coping saw or jeweler's saw. Horn may be boiled until it is malleable (about an hour), and then hand-shaped, shaped in a mold, clamped into the shape you wish with a holding jig, or flattened (after sawing it in half) between two boards clamped at the four corners with C-clamps. It can also be softened with a propane torch or bunsen burner, but must first be coated with waterglass (fireproofing sodium silicate dissolved in water) to keep it from igniting. Overheating the horn will cause it to become brittle and alter its color. Allow the waterglass to dry before subjecting it to the flame. When heating it, rotate and keep the piece moving to ensure even heating. When cool, it will retain the shape you have made.

Refining the shape after sawing is accomplished with fine and coarse crosscut files of different profiles, rasps, and gouges. These may be hand- or power-operated. Use a hand drill with metal-working bits for drilling. To prepare it for polishing, use a scraper that has been filed smooth or sandpaper to remove grooves left by sawing and filing or natural ridges in the horn. Use #1 sandpaper first, then #1/0 and 2/0. Begin polishing with a rag dipped in water and pulverized **pumice** powder. After rinsing the pumice off, powdered **clear coal** and water is used. For the final polish, use a paste of soap and powdered **whiting.** Chamois is used to maintain the polish of horn, and soap and water to clean it.

horn. Metalworking. See **anvil.**

Hornbill ivory. Ivory and Bone Carving. Ivory derived from the casque or epithema of the helmeted hornbill, a bird native to the East Indies. The ivory is a close-textured and hard material. A cross-section reveals a scarlet-rimmed yellow interior. It has been mainly employed by the Chinese for small carved objects such as brooches and buckles.

Hornby. Toys. A name associated with the manufacture of fine **clockwork** and electric trains in the early 1900s. They were designed by Frank Hornby, who originally made them for his sons. He also developed the **Meccano** system.

horned helmet. Shell Carving. (*Cassis cornuta.*) A shell used in cameo carving that provides a white exterior color, a white **middle color,** and an orange **ground color.** Fished from Japan, the Philippines, and the West Indies, it is of doubtful value for cameos as it has a tendency to separate. Also see **cowrie, helmet** and **Shell Carving: Shell, Tools and Preparation.**

horn hammer. Jewelry. A hammer on which the striking face is made of horn; this hammer is used for small areas. The horn hammer provides more power to bend metal than a **rawhide mallet,** but is less forceful than a steel hammer. Also see **piqué work.**

hornstone. Gemcutting. See **quartz.**

horse. Weaving. A horizontal wooden piece found on a **counterbalanced loom** as one means of supporting the **harness**es. Horses are hung in pairs on cords from the top of the loom, and from them are hung two harnesses, or two smaller horses, that have the harnesses hung from them. They are practically noiseless in operation. Alternate ways of hanging harnesses are through the use of either **pulleys** or **rollers.** See ill.

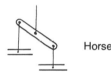

Horse

horse. Woodworking. See **sawhorse.**

horse fiddle. Toys. See **rattletrap.**

horsehair. Rugmaking. Spinning. Weaving. The lustrous body hair of a horse that is usually spun into a heavy, thick yarn. It is a tough fiber suitable for rugs that need solidity and that will receive a great deal of wear. It does not give to compressing much under **beating** on the loom. The hair length ranges from 1 cm to 2 cm when taken from the body, and from a few inches to several feet when removed from the mane or tail.

horsehide. Leatherwork. Leather made from the skin of a horse or colt. Also see **cordovan.**

horse reins. Toys. See **weaving spool.**

horsetail. Embroidery. See **Maltese silk.**

Hosanna. Quilts. See **Palm, The.**

hot dyeing. Batik and Tie-dye. A process used to add color to **fabric** in which the **dyebath** is 140° F or higher. Also see **direct dye.**

hot forming. Jewelry. Working on metals that have been heated and are still hot. Hot forming can facilitate the

twisting of some metals. It works beautifully on heavy-**gauge** square sterling silver wire. Hold one end of the work in a vise and do the twisting by using two pairs of wrenches as turning devices. This procedure requires two people, one holding the Prest-o-lite **torch** and the other doing the twisting. The metal must be red-hot at the area being twisted and the twisting must be done with an even, smooth turning. See ill.

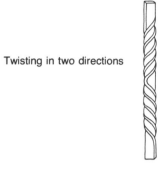

Twisting in two directions

hot melt glue gun. Toys. (Also called glue gun.) An electric hand tool in which pellets of plastic **glue** are inserted to be heated and melted. A trigger device releases the hot liquid glue through a nozzle. The glue works best in adhering wood to wood, although it is recommended for use on an assortment of materials. It is available at hardware stores and some hobby shops. Also see **adhesive.**

hot rolled. Metalworking. See **metal.**

hot set. Metalworking. See **blacksmithing tools.**

hot-short. Jewelry. The tendency in metals to become brittle at high temperatures. It can result in the cracking of the metal and the formation of minute flaws.

hound's-tooth check. Weaving. A popular **check** pattern appearing like a four-pointed star and achieved by alternating 4 dark threads with 4 light ones in the **warp** and **filling.** A 2/2 **twill** is most often used as the **weave.** The size of the pattern is determined by the yarn size and **sett.**

Hourglass. Quilts. The name given to two different **pieced block** designs. One is a **nine-patch** in which two of the pieces are split to suggest an hourglass shape.

In the second, a **split two-patch** makes a simple X or hourglass, as in the **Octagons** quilt. It is sometimes called

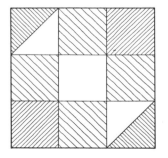

Hourglass

Windmill, although the old traditional Windmill was a **split four-patch.** See ill.

household cement. Toys. A fast-drying, clear, and commonly available all-purpose **glue** that dries transparent. Common brand names are **Duco cement** and Testor's. Warnings and cautions given on the **adhesive** containers must be observed. Also see **acetate glue.**

household dye. Batik and Tie-dye. The all-purpose dye most commonly available for all **fabrics**, including **natural fibers**, **man-made fibers**, and **blends**. The **assistant** used is determined by the fiber being dyed. A package of such dye usually contains a mixture of direct, acid, and other dye particles so that the fibers being dyed absorb the molecules of the appropriate dye, and the rest remain in the **dyebath.** This dye colors best in hot or simmering water, but it must be used cool for **batik.**

With **hot dyeing** the colors can be strong, but they are not fast. They tend to run when laundered and fade in light or sun. **Cold dyeing** produces colors of lower intensity than the hot process. Any of the fabrics dyed with household dyes can be dry cleaned.

Salt is the assistant in most of these dyes, and some have salt already added. Vinegar may be required by some to dye wool. The all-purpose Dick Blick dye uses wood alcohol to **paste** the **dyestuff** and for the assistant, but salt should still be added. The colors are **set** by **ironing** while the fabric is still damp.

Household dye is sometimes called "all-purpose" or union dye. Among the brand names of the most common household dyes are Cushing's Perfection, Drummer, Keystone, Dylon Liquid, Dylon Multicolor or Multipurpose, Putnam All-purpose, Rit (liquid and powder) and Tintex. Also see **Batik and Tie-dye: Dyes.**

household dye. Dyeing. Dyes easily available in most dime stores or supermarkets. They are also known as all-purpose dyes and come in a few familiar brand names. They are packaged to contain enough dye for 1 pound of yarn or fabric. Follow directions on the package for the best results.

household glue. Stitchery. Toys. See **white glue.**

House of Cards. Toys. A visually elegant **constructional toy** that consists of a stack of slotted cards. The cards can be fitted together to make buildings, towers, etc. The designs of the cards are varied, colorful, and sophisticated and appeal to adults as well as children. The toy was created by designer Charles Eames.

howler. Toys. A type of **bull-roarer** that sometimes has a notched edge.

H-section lead. Stained Glass. See **lead came.**

huckabuck weave. Weaving. See **huck weave.**

huck weave. Weaving. (Also called huckabuck weave.) A type of weave associated with a soft, absorbent, cotton fabric. It is composed of a **plain weave ground** with small **warp float** spots or areas that give it a pebbly pattern effect. The floats and their spacing give the fabric good absorbency so it is often used for toweling. Friction is also produced by the irregular and slightly rough surface caused by the floats. The plain weave background of the fabric gives it strength, providing that at least 50% of the surface is in plain weave. Although the tendency is to use cotton when weaving it, the texture of the pattern looks equally well in linen, wool, or synthetics. Besides toweling, it has found wide use in table linens, scarves, stoles, upholstery, drapery, and apparel fabrics. There are many **threading** and **treadling** variations that alter the placement of the spots, and the design is achieved by the grouping of spots. The term originated with the linen toweling and other cloth carried by the textile merchants on their backs from town to town in the British Isles. See ill.

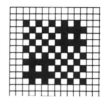
Huckabuck weave draft

Hudson River quilt. Quilts. A unique **one-of-a-kind quilt** made up of thirty **appliqué block**s, each sewn by a skilled needleworker. Irene Preston Miller of Croton-on-Hudson, New York, invited 29 people equally concerned about the beauty of the Hudson River to join her in producing the blocks, which depict scenes ranging from the source of the Hudson down to New York Harbor. Funds raised by the quilt will be used to aid in the preservation of the unique beauty of this river valley.

hue. One of the three properties of a color, sometimes **color** itself. Hue refers to a color's position in the **spectrum** or **hue circle.** Examples of hues are green, turquoise, and red. Hue is independent of **value** and **saturation.** A pink made by the addition of white **pigment** to red pigment is still of the same hue as the unmixed red. **Monochromatic** color schemes are selections of colors using one hue mixed with various proportions of black and white. Also see **color clash, color harmony, discord.**

hue circle. A circular arrangement of samples of colors such that **complementary color**s fall opposite each other across the center, and the change in **hue** between adjacent colors is gradual.

Many color theorists have approached the problem of showing all perceptibly different hues in an orderly way. Wilhelm Ostwald (1853–1932) constructed what is perhaps the most familiar system, using 24 different hues arranged with the intention that opposite or complementary colors, when mixed as pigments, would produce a neutral gray. Additional colors can be added, ad infinitum, between the named colors in the circle, as in any hue circle scheme.

Ostwald felt there were four primary colors—namely, red, blue, yellow, and green—even though he knew that some yellow and blue pigments can be mixed to produce quite brilliant greens. In the interest of placing complementary colors opposite each other in a more or less symmetrical way, he included green as a **primary color.** Colors that can be made by mixtures of primary color pigments are called secondary colors, and these are arranged between the primaries that make them.

A somewhat simpler arrangement of colors in a hue circle is suggested by fairly recent research in physics and psychology. It is most convenient to consider three primary colors: red, green, and blue. Projected spots of these colors, in varying intensities, on a white screen, are sufficient to produce pretty much any desired color at the overlapping of the three spots. The complement of red, which can be shown on the same screen by turning off the red projected spot, is a blue-green color called cyan after the pigment that closely approximates that color, phthalocyanine blue GB 4804. The complement of green, produced on the screen by turning off the green light (while blue and red continue to illuminate the spot) is a magenta color, approximated by the pigment lithol rubine or linear quinacridone red. The complement of blue, produced in like manner, is yellow, approximated by the pigment benzidene yellow YB-5704, or by hansa yellow 10G.

The complements of the primary light colors are the pigment primaries used for full-color printing and are the colors of dyes used in color photographic film. The arrangement of the color primaries of light—red, blue, and green—together with the color primaries of pigments produces an array in which complementary colors fall opposite each other and pigments of those colors do tend to produce neutral grays. See ill.

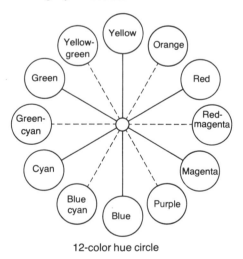

12-color hue circle

hula hoop. Toys. A large plastic ring or circle, semirigid and usually bright in color. The hula hoop, like all **hoop**s, had various uses, but was popularly slipped over the body and then kept going in a circular motion by rotating the body. It was tremendously popular with children as a **game** and with adults as an exercise. The hoop, as with other **universal toy**s, appears periodically, slips into oblivion for a while, and then later emerges again as a new toy.

hulling. Basketry. Four-foot rod of green **willow.**

hummer. Toys. See **bull roarer.**

hummer button. Toys. See **buzz button.**

humming top. Toys. Any **top** that makes a low humming sound while spinning. It may also be called a singing top.

hump mold. Ceramics. (Also called mushroom mold, drape mold.) A **mold** with a convex surface over which a slab of clay is draped or placed; the excess is trimmed away with a **fettling** knife. Forms must be removed from the mold when **leather hard** or the drying clay may crack as it shrinks.

Humpty Dumpty Circus. Toys. A series of toys produced in America in the early twentieth century, consisting of figures and animals. They were made of wood and the segmented parts were held together with **elastic** cord. The **joint**ed figures could thus be set in various positions.

Hungarian embroidery stitch. Needlepoint. A very old and simple technique which forms small diamond shapes, each consisting of three vertical stitches worked over two, four, and two mesh. The next diamond is started either diagonally with the first short stitch coming below the last short stitch of the previous diamond, or horizontally after skipping two meshes. In the finished effect, all short stitches are underneath one another. It is very effective when worked in two colors. See ill.

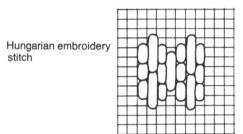

Hungarian embroidery stitch

Hungarian point. Needlepoint. A type of **Bargello** which was widely used by Italian embroiderers for church vestments, altar fronts, and wall and bed hangings. Some very beautiful pieces exist today in the Bargello Museum in

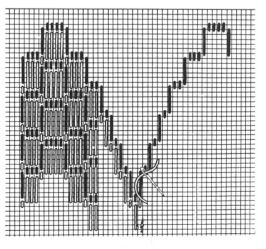

Hungarian point

Florence, Italy, and the Victoria and Albert Museum in London, England. Although its origin is unknown, perhaps the pattern originated in Hungary. It became very popular in eighteenth-century America. Hungarian point is more difficult to work than Bargello because the patterns are so intricate.

The patterns are worked in rows of a long vertical stitch over 6 mesh and one short stitch over 2 mesh. Each row varies slightly in placement of these stitches, but the overall pattern is maintained throughout. The color scheme adds greatly to the interest of this pattern. See ill.

Hungarian stitch. Rugmaking. A vertical stitch forming a brick formation. It is a stitch with many versions, variations, and names. Some of the versions place the brickwork effect so that it forms diamonds. A variation would be with long stitches in one vertical row and smaller ones in the next row, and then alternating in this manner. In names, it is also known as the Florentine stitch, the flame stitch, bargello stitch, brick stitch, and the Irish stitch. When it is known as the flame or bargello brick, the color placement is very critical in order to get the correctly shaded effect. In its simplest version, with all stitches being of equal length, the Hungarian stitch is started with the needle being brought back to front, and then inserted a certain number of holes directly above. Using **canvas mesh,** four holes up would give a good length. Emerge now to the right of the beginning of the first stitch. Insert two holes up and emerge at the lower right again. By starting every other row in a shorter stitch, the alternate stitches will be centered. Insert four holes up and continue across the bottom of the rug in a 4–2–4–2 arrangement. The next row starts in the same hole as the top of the stitches in the preceding hole. Hungarian stitch can be worked in a zig-zag manner across the **rug backing** rather than in more or less horizontal rows. See ill.

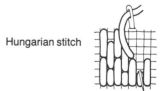

Hungarian stitch

hunter's star. Quilts. A **pieced-block** pattern of an eight-pointed star in which the points and background alternate in color. When the **quilt** is **set,** diamonds set into the corners of the blocks join to make additional stars. Also see **star patterns.**

hurricane candle. Candlemaking. A candle similar in construction to the glow candle, with the exception that the soft inner core is not melted in. A small soft-wax candle is inserted in the outer hard-wax shell. To maximize the amount of light given off, this small candle should be no thicker than ¼". To remove excess wax formed during the initial cooling (beyond what is needed to create a shell), hot wax may be poured into the mold to melt part of the previous layer.

HV technique. Weaving. A term coined from the Swedish "halvgobeläng" or half-tapestry (half-Gobelin). It is actually not a tapestry technique, but a form of **laid-in** that gives a transparent effect. The pattern thread is put in every **shed** to make an opaque pattern against a background of quite sheer **warp** and **filling.** Traditionally, the background threads are fine linen, and the pattern thread, fine wool, with often two colors on one **shuttle,** or a heavier wool used one color to a shuttle. The pattern part usually covers the greater section of the surface and the sheer areas are narrow areas between pattern portions. Also see **transparent tapestry.**

hyalite. Gemcutting. See **opal.**

hydrated lime. Mosaics. Commercial **lime** that has been mixed with water to the consistency of table cream, allowed to settle (with any excess water poured off the top), and then set aside to age several days until it becomes pliable, like bread dough. Dried aged lime can be crumbled for use without the addition of any extra water. The **mortar** used as an **adhesive** in the construction of mosaics is a mixture of sand, cement, and hydrated lime. The addition of the hydrated lime produces a more plastic mixture. It also tends to slow down the hardening of the cement and to reduce shrinkage during the process.

Hydrocal. Plastics. See **casting plaster.**

hydrocarbon. Plastics. Compounds of carbon, hydrogen, and oxygen commonly found together in coal, petroleum, and natural gas. These elements are then recombined to form benzene, toluene, ethylene, **ethylene dichloride** (EDC), **methylene dichloride** (MDC) and other base chemicals for making plastics. Some are **solvent**s that cause **crazing** of plastics. They are also used in printing inks, contact adhesives, and synthetic varnishes. They are highly flammable and give off toxic vapors.

hydrochloric acid. Metalworking. (Also called muriatic acid.) A colorless acid used for coloring, etching, cleaning, and preparing **flux** for metals. It is made by chemically combining hydrogen and chlorine (or salt) with **sulfuric acid.**

hydrochloric acid. Mosaics. (Also called muriatic acid.) A strong acid solution used at full strength in the final cleaning of the completed mosaic. Considerable care should be taken in handling the solution. Heavy gloves, preferably rubber, and protective clothing must be worn. The hydrochloric acid application, best carried out with a small stiff brush, should be followed immediately by a soda-and-water rinse, and finally by a clear-water wash-down. Also see **Mosaics: Cleaning the Mosaic.**

hydrofluoric acid. China and Glass Painting. A colorless fuming liquid, available from the drugstore, necessary for **acid etching** in china or glass. Be extremely careful when handling this strong acid. Wash all exposed skin immediately in ammonia and water, using ½ teaspoon of ammonia per cup of water. Never add water to acid.

hydrofluoric acid. Enameling. See **etching, matte finish.**

hydrofluoric acid. Stained Glass. An acid produced by the reaction of concentrated sulfuric acid with solid fluorides. It is a colorless, fuming, and corrosive liquid that reacts with silicates and is used in **aciding** glass.

Hydrofluoric acid is extremely dangerous. Instead of using plastic gloves, or protective clothing, dip your hands in a bucket of cold water after each contact with the acid. Wash your hands with soap and water after working.

If a burn should occur, it will look like a reddish irritation with a red bloodspot in the middle. It quickly becomes painful and ulcerous. Hydrofluoric acid works subcutaneously, beginning slowly, so that when the burn is detected, it is usually too late to stop. Pack **bicarbonate of soda** around the wound and consult a doctor as soon as possible.

hydrogen peroxide. Stitchery. See **bleach, bleaching.**

hydrometer. Ceramics. An instrument for measuring the specific gravity of a liquid/solid mixture. The hydrometer is a glass or wooden rod that is weighted at one end and which floats horizontally in water. The more solid matter present in a mixture, the greater the length of the hydrometer showing above the surface.

hydrophane. Gemcutting. See **opal.**

hypersthene. Gemcutting. A mineral of the **pyroxene** group with **hardness** of 6 and **specific gravity** of 3.4; hypersthene is often found with **feldspar.** The mineral has a brown-black opaque body with a coppery-red metallic sheen due to **inclusion**s of brookite arranged parallel to the orthorhombic **crystal** structure. If the stone is oriented, cut, and polished properly as a **flat,** the entire surface reflects light uniformly; when cut **cabochon,** the **luster** is intensified into a thin bright chatoyancy.

Bronzite is a variety of hypersthene that is lighter in **color** and density, with specific gravity of 3.2, and exhibits a bronze-yellow sheen. Bronzite may exhibit a fibrous structure similar to cat's eye.

Bastite is mineralogically similar to bronzite but it has a gray-green body color and metallic to pearly luster. Bastite is often found embedded in **serpentine.** Also see **Gemcutting: Hand Grinding and Polishing.**

i

ice. China and Glass Painting. An **enamel** formulated especially for use on glass. Clear ice, a **flux,** is sifted as a **glaze** over opaque enamel powders to prevent them from chipping.

ice cream stick. Toys. See **craft stick.**

ice-cube candle. Candlemaking. (Also called Swiss-cheese candle.) A candle with a lacelike surface made by pouring hot wax over ice packed in a candle **mold.** A store-bought candle or dipped **taper** of the same height as the planned pouring level serves as **wick.** Pack ice cubes or ice chips in the mold around the taper; melt the wax to a relatively low **temperature** (about 160° F) and pour it into the mold; allow the candle to cool for roughly two hours and remove it from the mold over a sink; dip the candle in a hot **wax bath** to soften the edges left by the melted ice cubes. When completely dry, the candle may be placed in the mold again to be filled with a different color of wax. Shake the mold gently to assure that the second color penetrates the cavities left by the ice. See ill.

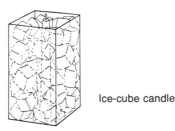

Ice-cube candle

ice pick. Candlemaking. An ice pick, a skewer, or a knitting needle can be used to pierce a hole in the hardened wax in order to **wick** the candle.

Idaho white pine. Woodworking. See **pine.**

identifying fibers. Batik and Tie-dye. It is important in **tie-dye** and **batik** to identify the fibers in any given **fabric** because dyes are selected in terms of the fabric content. The best source of information for fiber identification comes from the bolt when fabric is purchased. An indelible **marking pen** can be used to label the material at one end or at the **selvage,** or a number can be written on the fabric with the information about it kept on paper under a corresponding number.

If fabrics of an undetermined origin are being used, the **burn test** will offer the easiest home method of analysis.

Many people can, of course, recognize by appearance and feel the contents of numerous fabrics. **Blends,** however, make this difficult. A sample dye test is advised when there is any uncertainty. Also see **alkali test, oil test** and **Batik and Tie-dye: Identifying Fibers.**

idiochromatic. Gemcutting. See **color.**

idocrase. Gemcutting. A mineral composed of calcium aluminum silicate **crystal**lized in the tetragonal system with a **hardness** of 6½, a **specific gravity** of 3.42, and granular **fracture.** Idocrase occurs in transparent brown and green crystals with refractive indices of 1.708 and 1.716 and has a vitreous to greasy **luster.** It also may be colorless or yellow, red or blue with weak dichroism.

It is **fac**eted in the step or **emerald cut** and polished with tin oxide on a tin **lap** or cerium oxide on a plastic lap. Also see **abrasive, faceting, polishing, refraction.**

I-frame. Weaving. See **frame loom.**

igniter. Metalworking. See **oxyacetylene welding equipment.**

ikat. Batik and Tie-dye. Dyeing. Weaving. The process of covering portions of the **warp** or **filling** before weaving, so that it can be dyed with the covered portions resisting the dye. The covered areas are put in according to a pattern which can be small, precise and complex, or a large, random mottling. When both the warp and filling are covered, it is called double ikat. In this case, the design of both either coincides to form one pattern, or the warp and filling designs are independent of each other. The most common way to ikat is to tie off the areas which are not meant to take the dye; hence it has become known as a variation of **tie dye**ing. However, other methods of coating the design areas to make them waterproof are acceptable under the category of ikat.

For warp ikat, after the warp is taken from the **warping board** or **reel,** it is spread out to its full length and width and stretched on a frame or table. The pattern areas are wrapped very tightly with waxed cord, rags, or plastic so that the dye will not penetrate. After the tying, the warp is chained loosely and put into the **dye bath** where it is stirred constantly to make sure that the loose areas are fully penetrated. Then follows thorough drying, and the wrappings are removed. The process is repeated for every color. After the complete pattern with all its colors is finished, the warp is chained and very carefully put on the **loom.** If it is to be weft or filling ikat, the filling yarns are measured out according to the width of the warp in the **reed** and then stretched with the same procedure following as for the warp ikat. The dye used depends on the fiber content of the yarns used. The most often used are the **acid** and **direct dye**s.

Ikat was known to the ancient Peruvians, who practiced it in simple designs and in limited quantities prior to the Spanish conquest. It is practically unknown in Peru today. The peoples of southeast Asia developed ikat into a complex, exacting art, and today are practicing masters of it. It is also known and used in Japan, Guatemala, and Mexico.

illusion. Stitchery. See **tulle.**

illusion circle. Toys. See **buzz button.**

imitation gauze. Weaving. See **mock leno weaves.**

imitation tapestry. Weaving. See **clasped weft laid-in.**

impervious. Ceramics. See **permeability.**

impregnation. Plastics. Painting, dipping, or soaking of semiporous objects or materials in **catalyzed resin** to preserve or to prepare them for lamination. Also see **gel coat.**

impress. Ceramics. A method of decoration that involves pressing a decoration into **leather-hard** clay usually with a **roulette** or **stamp.** Impressing is a very popular technique. Almost anything is usable for impressed decoration. **Overglaze** buildup in the impressed areas will yield interesting effects. See ill.

Impressing

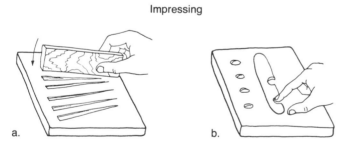

a.   b.

incidental. Weaving. The extra thread or **heddle** inserted into the **drawing-in draft**s of certain **block weave**s in order to join blocks or make a smooth transition from one block to the other. Also see **crackle.**

incised batik. Batik and Tie-dye. (Also called scratch batik.) A **batik** process in which **wax**ed areas of the fabric are cut into or drawn on with various tools. These incised lines must cut deeply enough to expose the fabric. **Dye** is then applied by **direct dye painting** or by **dip dyeing** so that color can penetrate into these lines. This method produces a fine line pattern where the wax is incised. Among the most common incising tools are awls, mimeograph stencil tools, and dental tools.

incised carving. Woodworking. See **woodcarving.**

incised cutting. Découpage. See **Découpage: Cutting.**

inclusion. Amber Carving. Inclusions are foreign bodies enclosed in the mass of a mineral. They can be liquid, gas, or solid. Inclusions have either been forced into a material as a result of pressure or are formed simultaneously with, and enveloped by, minerals in a hot liquid state that eventually solidified, incorporating the alien substances. They may also have formed later, from liquids and gases that were trapped in the hardened host mineral. Inclusions are sometimes perfectly formed crystals of another mineral, insects, small particles of plant life. Generally an inclusion will increase the value of a gem, although it is possible for it to detract from the beauty of a stone. Some gems that occur with inclusions are amber, ruby, sapphire, zircon, and emerald.

Inclusions can provide proof of the origin of a mineral and aid in determining the authenticity of a gemstone. Perfectly round bubbles are a good indication that the specimen is a fake, as gas and water inclusions would have to conform to the structure of crystals that form the gem; however, it is possible to squeeze round bubbles into irregular shapes to make a fake look authentic. Occasionally both liquid and gas are trapped within a specimen, and movement of the liquid may be observed. Also see **jet, spar.**

inclusion. Gemcutting. See **cabochon, C-axis.**

inclusion. Plastics. An object or material **laminate**d or embedded in **plastic** which remains visible in the finished form. Also see **dip coating, embedment, lamination.**

increase. Crochet. (Abbr. inc.) To increase, or add, a stitch by making two stitches in one loop or by adding a chain stitch. Also see **Crochet: Increasing.**

increasing. Knitting. See **Knitting: Increasing.**

index of refraction. Glasswork. One of the properties of transparent materials. The angle of refraction changes as light passes from a medium of one density to another. The denser the material, the greater the angle of refraction. In undergoing such change, light entering obliquely will be bent toward an imaginary line perpendicular to the interface, the blue end of the spectrum being bent more than the red end of the spectrum by virtue of its higher frequency. In passing into a less dense medium, light will be refracted in a direction closer to the line of the interface. Light passing between two media exactly perpendicular is not refracted.

The ratio of change of angle that light undergoes in passing from air to other materials is a constant for those materials; transparent materials are given a numerical index of refraction relative to air. The higher the index of refraction, the more the light is bent in passing from air into the material. Diamond, because of its high density, has a high index of refraction. Colors are refracted selectively, giving diamond the property of reflecting light in spectral array. The refraction that occurs normally in a pane of window glass becomes "corrected" as light leaves the glass, and no color spectrum is visible. A prism bends light in the same direction twice so that the spectrum can easily be seen. Certain types of glass, notably **lead-crystal glass** and **silica glass,** have high indices of refraction and tend to sparkle.

The inquisitive mind can find food for thought in the consideration of a pencil standing obliquely in a tumbler of water. The apparent bending of the pencil is an illustration of the index of the refraction of water.

Indiana Puzzle. Quilts. An old **four-patch** and **two-patch pieced block** pattern from pioneer days in Indiana. The **patch**es are combined in an **all-over pattern** to suggest a reel, as though the four corners of the block had spun out in a spiraling pattern. A variation is the Virginia Reel.

Indiana Rose. Quilts. See **Original Rose.**

Indian filling stitch. Crewel. Embroidery. See **Roumanian stitch.**

Indian Meadow. Quilts. See **Queen Charlotte's Crown, Rocky Glen.**

Indian River. Quilts. See **Queen Charlotte's Crown.**

Indian Trail. Quilts. A **quilt block** of **pieced** triangular shapes. It is one of many variations of the popular **Kansas Troubles.** See ill.

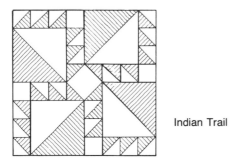

Indian Trail

Indian weaving. Weaving. A term referring to the weaving done by the Indians of North America. It can also rightfully include the weaving done by the Indians of Central and South America, but usually this work is referred to by the name of the country such as **Peruvian weaving,** Guatemalan weaving, and so on. Currently in North America, most of the Indian weaving being done is by the Navajos of the Southwest who have been carrying on a long weaving tradition learned from the Pueblo Indians. However, at one time weaving was carried on in areas as far apart as the northwest coast (**Salish** and **Chilkat weaving**), the Great Lakes (**Ojibwa weaving**), the Mississippi Basin, and the Eastern woodlands. Other than **Navajo weaving** little, if any, is being done in the other areas although scattered attempts to revive it are being made.

Although Indian textiles are generally alluded to as being woven, in reality, many techniques other than weaving were employed depending on the area and the availability of materials there and the type of **loom** used. **Finger weaving** without a loom was carried on quite extensively.

Usually just the fingers were used, but at times needles and later weaving frames also were employed. There is also much evidence of **twining, plaiting, netting, looping,** knitting, and crochet.

In terms of the equipment used, weaving on what is known as a true loom, i.e., a loom with a **shedding device,** was done only by the Indians of the Southwest. This would include the **backstrap belt loom** as well as the vertical **Navajo loom.** The backstrap, thought to have come from middle America, is older than the Navajo loom but operates on the same basis with a **shed stick** and a **heddle rod.** Loom development among the Indians most likely followed the same path as it did in other corners of the world. From a simple support for the **warp,** such as one horizontal bar or the **warp-weighted loom,** undoubtedly grew the idea to build a total frame or two-bar loom so that the warp could be rigid and more easily manipulated. The introduction of the backstrap perhaps was the stimulus for adding a shedding device to the frame. A **rigid heddle** loom was introduced from Europe. On this type of loom beadwork, using European trade beads, was woven as well as belts by some tribes, while others used a **bow loom** for belts and beadwork.

The history of Indian weaving in North America can be traced to about 2,000 years ago through the discovery of woven sashes and pack straps in caves in the Southwest. These had been woven by the predecessors of the Anasazi or Basketmakers (or perhaps the Anasazi themselves) who were, in turn, the predecessors of the Pueblos, the most sophisticated weavers in North America. There is also some evidence that the weaving of mats, sandals, and other objects of reeds and rushes could have existed as early as 9,000 years ago during the time of Archaic Indian cultures in the Southwest, while in other parts of the country it is thought that weaving was in existence as early as 1500 B.C. The Anasazi spun the fibers of yucca, milkweed, Indian hemp, and cedar bark, along with some animal fibers, into yarn. They used a single bar loom. The true loom (i.e., two-bar loom) did not make its appearance until after the first century A.D. The upright, vertical loom eventually associated with the Navajos was in use during the Great Pueblo Period of 1050–1300 A.D., but its exact date of appearance is unknown. It was during this time that the Pueblos began the growing and weaving of cotton which it is supposed had been introduced earlier also from Middle America. The spinning of all fibers was done by hand twisting or on a **spindle** since the spinning wheel was unknown.

By 1600, sheep raising was practiced by the Pueblos and they had switched from using cotton to wool. The Navajos took on this practice along with the art of weaving. They migrated northward with their knowledge between 1300 and 1600, giving rise to the speculation that the true weaving found along the northwest coast was due to some Navajos settling here.

India oilstone. Jewelry. A synthetic stone made of an **aluminum oxide abrasive,** used for sharpening steel cutting tools. Although the stone is impregnated with oil, additional light oil should be used during sharpening to prevent the metal particles from filling the pores of the stone.

Use a rotating motion when sharpening. The stone should be washed from time to time with plain soap and water to remove old oil. Also see **Arkansas oilstone, graver, engraver's sharpener.**

India rubber. Toys. Pure **rubber.** The term may refer to the substance or any object made from it. The India rubber balls were first made after the 1840s, when rubber was imported to England. Undoubtedly children elsewhere had played with the naturally resilient and bouncy substance earlier. India **rubber toy**s were popular from 1880 through the early 1900s. Also see **balls.**

India stone. Woodworking. See **sharpening stone.**

indicolite. Gemcutting. See **tourmaline.**

indigo. Batik and Tie-dye. A blue **vat dye.** Originally this dye was derived primarily from the indigo plant *Indigofera.* The plant is native to the West Indies; the name means "Indian blue." Today the indigo blue dye has been replaced with synthetically produced **aniline dye.**

Indigo can be vatted for home dyeing, although it is complex and great caution must be used to handle the materials or ingredients.

To make indigo dye mix 1 teaspoon 60% indigo grains with a little warm water. Dissolve in the **dye vessel** ½ teaspoon **caustic soda** flakes and ½ teaspoon sodium hydroxide in a little cold water. Add 2 pints hot water. Gently add 1½ teaspoons **salt** and the warm indigo solution to the dye vessel. Avoid stirring air bubbles into this mixture. Stir gently with a glass rod. Vat 10 minutes or until the solution turns yellow-green. Keep the vat at body temperature during the dyeing process. Immerse the fabric into the **dyebath** gently, taking care not to add air bubbles. Dye for 10 minutes.

Remove fabric and **oxidize** or expose to air for about 10 minutes or until the material turns blue. Repeated dyeings will make the color stronger.

The dyed fabric should be rinsed in cold water to which 1 teaspoon **acetic acid** (or a little white vinegar) has been added. Wash, rinse, and iron while damp.

Indigo can be used on either **batik** or **tie-dye** fabrics. Also see **leuco.**

indigo. Crewel. Embroidery. Needlepoint. A **colorfast** dye made from a blue flax flower growing wild in Massachusetts in colonial times. The name Massachusetts itself is said to come from the Indian word meaning blue hills. Also see **aniline dye.**

indigo. Dyeing. An ancient blue **dyestuff** made from the leaves of a plant in the pea family. Various species of this genus grow all over the world and indigo was used in China, India, Egypt, Italy, and Peru. Its use in Europe began at the end of the sixteenth century when it was imported from India. Both **woad** and indigo are chemically similar; however, indigo is a much stronger dye than woad. Woad growers strongly opposed this importation since it was a threat to their livelihood. In England, Queen Elizabeth I prohibited the importation of indigo in order to protect the growers. The dyestuff is obtained through fermentation of the leaves, but most home dyers purchase indigo powder ready to use.

Indigo is not water soluble, so the first step in using this dyestuff is to make it water soluble through a process of reduction (removing the oxygen) with sodium hydrosulfite. This process can also be done naturally through fermentation of indigo with bran and madder. In the old world the reducing agent was fermented urine. Whichever way reduction is accomplished, the resulting material, known as indigo white, is then dissolved in an alkaline solution such as **caustic soda** (a dangerous chemical). After the dyestuff is in the yarn or fabric and exposed to air, the oxygen reverses the reduction process and the indigo slowly turns blue. The **colorfast** quality of this dye is heightened by its not being water soluble and further increased by repeated dippings in the dyebath and exposing to air between dips. The Persians used as many as forty dips at times. Another method of increasing fastness is double dyeing, first with woad in the bottom dyeing and then with indigo as the **top dyeing.** The process of fewer and longer repeated dips in the dyebath also has the effect of making the blue more vivid. In the mid-nineteenth century, **aniline dye**s were developed and the first produced was a synthetic indigo. The word "aniline" is derived from anil, the name for the indigo plant, which in turn is derived from the Sanskrit *nila,* meaning blue or indigo. Also see **vat dye.**

indigo. Fabric Printing. A dark-blue dye obtained from plants of the genus *Indigofera.*

indigo white. Dyeing. See **indigo.**

indirect dye. Dyeing. See **adjective dye.**

indirect method. Mosaics. (Also called reverse method.) The approach to setting a **mosaic** in which the **tesserae** or mosaic materials are first fixed reverse-side out with a **gum arabic glue** to a heavy **mounting paper** upon which a mirror image of the final mosaic design has been sketched. (Since the work is laid out on the mounting paper in reverse, the pattern should also be drawn in reverse unless the design is symmetrical.) The completed mosaic, glued in reverse upon the mounting paper, is then transported from the artist's studio to the installation site, where it is permanently set in **mortar** or **adhesive** right-side out. For large-scale mosaics, the paper pattern can be subdivided into smaller segments to facilitate the transporting of the work from the studio to the site. When the mosaic has been installed and allowed to set for several hours, the mounting paper can be removed by dissolving the glue in water and peeling the paper away.

The indirect method was developed during the Italian Renaissance in response to a demand for mosaics that far surpassed the productive capacities of craftsmen using the traditional **direct method.** The advantage of the indirect approach for handling the work and easy accessibility to materials is apparent; by completing the project in the studio the artist eliminates the need to transport large quantities of tesserae to the installation site. The disadvantages of the technique are far more subjective and relate primarily to the artist's lack of control over the angle and height of the individual pieces as they will be viewed once the mosaic is installed. Creatively, the direct method would seem to be the more satisfactory approach, but any working mosaicist will no doubt explore both approaches before making any judgment. Also see **sandcasting** and **Mosaics: Tools and Materials, Setting the Material.**

indirect tie-up. Weaving. See **tie-up.**

inedible dough. Toys. A **clay**like mixture that can be made at home for use in dough art. Among the most common and popular of these doughs are **baker's clay, salt clay,** and **cornstarch dough.** Because of the high salt content, most are considered inedible. Also see **edible dough.**

infrared. See **color.**

infrared heat lamp. Plastics. See **heat lamp.**

infrared quartz lamp kiln. Enameling. See **kiln.**

inglaze color. China and Glass Painting. See **underglaze color.**

ingot. Metalworking. A quantity of metal cast into a rectangular shape; originally the word designated the mold for so casting the metal. Ingots are cast to recover scrap metal, to make **alloys,** and as a first step in the manufacturing of stock metal shapes. An ingot may also be made when a shape of substantial thickness is required, instead of fabricating it by building up thin layers of metal.

Molds for ingots are available in assorted lengths, widths, and thicknesses, and in upright or horizontal models. They are generally 3–16″ long, up to 2¾″ wide and ⅛–¹⁄₁₆″ thick; the interior of the ingot mold is coated with machine oil, fat, soot, or carbon to prevent the hot metal from sticking to it. Then it is heated to receive the molten metal. After the metal is heated to slightly above its boiling point, it is poured into the heated mold in one continuous stream, allowed to cool, and removed from the mold.

ingot. Stained Glass. A mass of metal that has been cast into a convenient shape, such as a bar. Also see **lead came.**

ingrain rug. Rugmaking. Weaving. A reversible pattern **flat rug** made in a **double cloth** or triple cloth construction. Ingrain rugs were eighteenth and nineteenth century products made in England and Scotland on either hand or power looms. They were woven of either wool or cotton **warp** with a wool **filling.** They were exported to the States where they were known also as Scotch rugs, Kilmarnock rugs, Kidderminster rugs, and English rugs. The hand-loomed ones were only a yard wide and had to be pieced together to form larger rugs. This might account for the poor reputation they had for durability, although there always seemed to be a steady demand for them. In 1790, Tobias Lear went to New York City to purchase floor covering for President Washington and complained, "We get no carpet in New York to suit the room, nor carpeting of

the best kind. Scotch carpeting is almost the only kind to be found here." Also see **Peruvian ingrain.**

inhibitor. Plastics. (Also called stabilizer, retarding agent.) Substances which slow **curing** and increase **self life.** Sometimes an **accelerator** is added to **catalyzed resin** to overcome the action of an inhibitor which was premixed into the uncatalyzed **resin** by the manufacturer.

ink. Block Printing. See **block printing ink.**

inking pad. Fabric Printing. A padded surface on which **textile color** is applied, and on which the printing block is stamped to coat it with color for printing. This technique is commonly used for **dye printing** on **fabric.**

To make an inking pad, use a piece of ¾″ plywood of about twice the dimensions of the printing block. Cover the wooden base with resilient padding such as ironing-board padding or rug underpadding, cut slightly smaller than the plywood. Cover this padding with a piece of heavy-duty plastic or oilcloth, pulled around and tacked or stapled on the reverse side. Then tack or pin on a piece of absorbent fabric such as felt; this is the inking surface. Replace this layer of cloth for each color.

To print, press the printing block onto the color-coated pad several times at various angles until the color is evenly distributed. Take care not to fill up small depressions in the block. See ill.

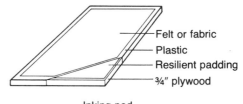

Felt or fabric
Plastic
Resilient padding
¾″ plywood

Inking pad

inking roller. Block Printing. Découpage. Fabric Printing. See **brayer.**

inkle loom. Weaving. A very simple two-**shed** loom used for weaving narrow bands or belts of limited length. It is a wooden frame with a number of pegs for the **warp** to go around. One of these pegs is movable in its socket and works as the tension regulator. There is one set of **string**

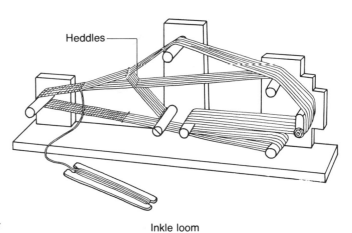

Heddles

Inkle loom

heddles used to make the shed. They are a series of single loops attached to a central peg. The loom can be either a table or floor model. The **warping** and **threading** are done at one and the same time. As the **warp end** goes around the pegs it also is put through a heddle. The warp is circular with the warp ends tied to themselves and not to the pegs since the warp must be free to slide around the pegs during the weaving. See ill. Also see **continuous warp, inkle weaving.**

inkle weaving. Weaving. The weaving of narrow tapes, bands, or belts on a specially designed loom. The **sheds** are opened by lifting up or pushing down on the **warp** by hand. Usually a **flat shuttle** is used with a sharp edge that beats down the **weft.** The belts are **warp-face**d on both sides with a thick weft hidden inside the warp and visible at the **selvage**s. Only **plain weave** is possible. Patterns are usually lengthwise color **stripe**s of two or more **end**s of each color. If colors are put in so that they alternate with each other then horizontal stripes are possible. Combining the two kinds of stripes can give patterns with more variety. If even more complex designs are desired then two-harness **rep weave**s or **pick-up pattern**s can be used. The narrow tapes or bands can be sewn together to make wider pieces of fabric. Also see **inkle loom** and **Weaving: Definitions.**

Inkodye. Batik and Tie-dye. The trade name of a particular **vat dye** used for **dip dyeing** or **direct dye painting.** Also see **leuco.**

inkrastacja. Jewelry. A technique in which wood is carved and inlaid with flat **brass** wire. Also see **inlay, tarkashi work.**

inlay. Bookbinding. (Also called onlay.) A thin piece of colored leather or some other material that is pasted into an outlined tool form, border, or panel on the cover of a book.

inlay. Ceramics. A decorative technique used on medieval floor **tile**s, in which clay is inlaid with a clay of a contrasting color. Wooden stamps were used to impress a pattern, which was then filled with **slip** or soft clay and fired.

inlay. Découpage. Various materials, from paper to eggshell, can be glued in tiny pieces as an embellishment in découpage designs. These mosaiclike patterns are then buried, along with the cut-out **prints,** under the découpage **finish** until they resemble inlaid work. Also see **eggshell inlay, intarsia, mother-of-pearl** and **Découpage: Varnishing and Sanding.**

inlay. Jewelry. To fit material into grooves cut into another material. It can be one metal into another, wood into wood, shell into metal, **ivory** into metal, or even silk thread into **ebony** or feathers into metal. The inlaid material is usually at the same level as the material into which it has been placed. This is usually accomplished by **cement**ing, **filing** or sandpapering. Also see **abalone, bidri, damascene, inkrastacja.**

inlay. Weaving. The action of placing various colors of **filling** in certain areas of the **warp** as opposed to traveling **selvage** to selvage with one filling. This can be done with any **weave** and does not require having **ground yarn**s weaving a background. However, a means of joining the various fillings must be arrived at which usually involves the **tapestry** joinings. Inlay is also another name for the **laid-in** techniques.

inlay. Woodworking. A decorative woodworking process in which a pattern is cut into the surface of a wood panel to a depth of ⅛ – ¼″. The depression is then filled with pieces of wood (or other materials, such as metal, ivory, or horn) until the surface is flush and smooth again.

The origin of inlaying and **marquetry** dates back to Egypt in the fourteenth century B.C. Furniture from the tombs of Tutankhamen and Rameses was constructed from layers of veneer with inlays of ivory, gold, and precious stones. Some wealthy Romans and Greeks inlaid ivory and pearls into feasting tables.

The craft of inlaying was called intarsia or intarsiatura in fourteenth- and fifteenth-century Italy, where at first only dark and light woods were inlaid into the surfaces of furniture. Later, woods stained and colored with acid solutions, gilding, and paints were used for inlay.

inlaying. Plastics. The process of setting different-colored plastics or other materials into the surface of a plastic. There are several methods: Cut out grooves or areas in the plastic surface, or drill holes, and replace with pieces of different colors, **cement**ing the inlays in place (**a.**). Cut two sheets of plastic with a coping saw to make a full depth inlay (**b.**). Match the pieces together and use the capillary cementing method to cement the bicolored inlay together (**c., d.**). Carve a design with the **intaglio process,** then fill

Inlaying

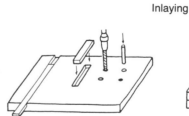

a. Drilling holes and grooving

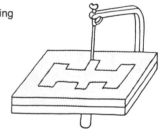

b. Cutting plastic with coping saw

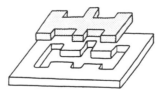

c. Matching two pieces of different colors

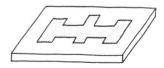

d. Finished bicolored inlay

e. Carving using intaglio process

the grooves with **lacquer, paint,** or **resin** of the desired colors (**e.**). See ill. Also see **grooving.**

inlaying ivory. Ivory and Bone Carving. See **Ivory and Bone Carving: Carving.**

inlay puzzle. Toys. A very simple **jigsaw puzzle** in which background areas are permanently **glued** into place. Only smaller shapes must be fitted into openings provided for them.

insertion. Lacemaking. Tatting. A narrow strip of tatting with both edges worked the same placed between two pieces of fabric or two pieces of **lace.** The tatting insertion shown has two bands of **attached rings,** decorated with **picots.** This insertion was made using one **shuttle,** indicated by the **single thread** joining the rings; it also shows the **reverse work** method. An insertion is also known by its French term *entre-deux.* See ill.

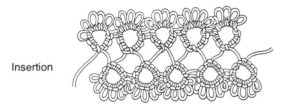

Insertion

inserts. Bookbinding. Material not printed and collated in the same manner as the rest of the text that must be inserted by hand. It is material that must for some reason be printed separately, such as maps and overlays.

inside caliper. Woodworking. See **measuring tools.**

insoluble. Ceramics. A material that will not dissolve in water. Clay will mix with water but will not dissolve. **Borax** can be rendered insoluble only by **fritting** with **silica.** Ninety percent of all ceramic minerals are insoluble.

inspection plug. Stained Glass. A piece of firebrick carved into a cone shape. It is inserted into a hole in the **kiln** called the spyhole. It can be removed during firing to check temperature, melting rate, color, etc. Also see **firebrick plug.**

installation. Stained Glass. See **fitting.**

instant dye. Batik and Tie-dye. A liquid household **dye.**

instant papier mâché. Papercrafts. Commercial mixtures of ground-up paper pulp are available from art supply stores. These mixtures are combined with water to make a **paper mash** that is easy to work with, as malleable as clay, and dries hard when left in the open air. When thoroughly dry, it can be smoothed with sandpaper, if desired, and painted.

instant papier mâché. Toys. A clean, odorless, nontoxic commercial product available in hobby stores and craft shops. It is used in place of newspapers and **glue** as a modeling material. Water is added and the mixture kneaded to make it uniformly wet. It is a versatile medium that is heavy when wet but dries light. It does not adhere to plastic. It should dry thoroughly before sanding; this takes several days. When dry it can be coated with **gesso,** then painted with **tempera, casein,** or **acrylic paint.** It can be sprayed with metallic sprays or gold-leafed or antiqued. Also see **celluclay.**

instant puppet. Puppets. See **scrap puppet.**

insulation. Ceramics. Prevention of **heat loss** or **thermal conductivity** through the walls of the **kiln.** Efficient insulators do not store heat, and will cool rapidly when the **firing** process is complete. Common insulators used in kilns are **firebrick, kaolwool blanket,** and **asbestos.** Also see **heat storage, kiln wash.**

intaglio. Bookbinding. A **tool** is said to be cut intaglio when the design is cut in such a way that, when stamped on a surface, it appears raised against a sunken background.

intaglio. Gemcutting. Gem material with a figure or design engraved into the surface; varieties of chalcedony **quartz** are often used for intaglios. The engraving is made with a **point carver** or **flexible-shaft machine** with **carving point**s. The intaglio can be embellished with burnished gold or encrusted with gems. Black-and-white onyx, called nicolo, is carved into intaglios; the design is cut through the white upper layer into the black layer. See ill. Also see **cameo.**

Intaglio surface

intaglio. Jewelry. A method in which an **acid** solution is used to etch designs into metal. All surfaces not to be etched, including the edges, are covered with a **resist.** The design is then scratched through the resist with a sharp instrument such as an **etching needle.** The areas in which the metal surface is exposed are then etched with acid; the etched area is the intaglio. Also see **asphaltum, etching, niello.**

intaglio cutting. Glasswork. See **engraving.**

intaglio process. Plastics. (Also called dry point, engraving.) Carving a design into the plastic surface using sharp hand tools such as a **burin** or etching needle. The process is used for direct display of the engraved plastic—often combined with **light piping** or **inlaying.** The engraved plastic may be used as a print-making plate. Printing plates may be made with the dry-point process, which imitates the effects of traditional dry-point engraving, using shallow scratches on the plastic's surface, or by engraving, which calls for deeper cuts and therefore produces more reproductions before the plate wears out. (Engraving is sometimes called etching—inaccurately, since no acid is used to etch the design.) See ill. Also see **Plastics: Carving.**

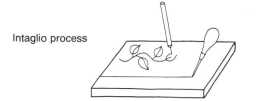

Intaglio process

intarsia. Découpage. A term from the Italian word for **inlay** for a style of wood inlay popular in Italy during the fourteenth and fifteenth centuries. Mosaiclike pieces of wood were fitted and glued into a wooden support. The style later spread to Germany, Holland, and Spain. As the craft spread, the designs became more varied, with scrolls, arabesques, scenes, and geometric patterns. In the eighteenth century, marble and semiprecious stones were added, inlaid in rectangular pieces.

This inlay style is imitated in découpage with a **trompe l'oeil** usage of marbelized **decorative paper,** which is glued to the surface as a paper mosaic, and then coated with découpage **finish.**

intarsia. Gemcutting. (Also called pietra dura.) A picture made by fitting and cementing gem material together that is cut to exact shape and ground to the same thickness. Parquetry is similar to intarsia but the stones are cut into geometric composition.

Draw two copies of the pattern; one of these should be a mirror image; the finished pieces are set upside down on this copy. Carefully cut the other copy into separate parts and glue onto slabs of the gem materials. The face of the pieces is the side with the paper. Use a trim saw to cut out the shapes; thin-pointed shapes will shatter on the **grinding wheel.** The curvature of the saw blade will over-cut the pieces on the back. Place all the pieces together face down on a sheet of glass or other flat surface for the final fitting. Remove the paper from the face of the stones. Bend a strip of one-inch-wide metal around the outside of the picture as tightly as possible as a mold for casting; the bottom edge of the metal strip should be flush with the glass. Cut a piece of ¼″ mesh wire screen to fit the base, and mix equal parts of portland cement and sand with water. Moisten the stones, and fill the mold with enough cement to cover the stones. Add screening. Add the remaining cement to fill the mold. A wire loop can be attached to the wire edge for hanging. Let the cement set overnight, and water it each day for three or four days to cure. Remove the glass and the metal strip. The picture is then lapped flat and polished. It is helpful if the pieces at the corners are made of harder material to resist wear during **lapping.**

Small intarsias are sometimes finished in **cabochon** form. A variation of intarsia is carving a depression in a blank and inlaying it with pieces to make a design.

intarsia. Woodworking. See **inlay.**

intarsiatura. Woodworking. See **inlay.**

intensity. See **saturation.**

interbraiding. Rugmaking. Weaving. The process of making individual braids and at the same time joining them by **braiding** into a solid surface so that no stitching or lacing of individual braids is necessary. It is often used in rugmaking for square or rectangular **braided rug**s, but also has made its appearance in **off-loom wall hanging**s. Interbraiding is best started on a narrow strip of wood slightly longer than the width of the piece being made. All strips for the braid should be tied individually to the wood, which can be then anchored with clamps. The number of strips used must be based on the number of braids used for making the rug. For example, if a 5-strand braid is used and the piece will have 30 braids across in the width, then 150 strips must be fastened to the wooden support. To start the piece, the first group of 5 strips at the left are braided the usual way for between 12–18″. The braid is pinned so that it will not unbraid and the next 5 ends to the right are braided. However, as they are being braided, each strip, as it comes next to the finished braid, is taken through the right loop of the first braid. If there is difficulty in going through the loop, a crochet hook is used to pull through or a large safety pin is attached to the end of the strip being pushed through. The piece is made by working across the width and down the length at the same time. When the desired length is reached, the ends can be knotted into a **fringe** or finished by **overcasting** or machine-sewing. This secures the ends from unbraiding so that the strips can then be trimmed or tapered down and slipped back through the edge loops and finally sewn down securely on the back side. Yarn can be used as well as rag strips.

interfacing. Stitchery. A woven or **nonwoven material** placed between the surface or top fabric and the **facing** to give added **body,** firmness, or shape.

interior spar varnish. Woodworking. See **varnish.**

interlaced backstitch. Crewel. Embroidery. See **back stitch threaded.**

interlaced cable chain stitch. Crewel. Embroidery. A variation of the **chain stitch** that is effective worked in single line or in rows and interlaced for a border or **open filling stitch.** When used as the latter it is more effective to use double thread for the cable and single for the interlacing; use a blunt needle for the interlacing.

To make the cable chain stitch, work a chain stitch, except instead of tacking down the loop with another loop, twist the yarn once around the needle (**a.**). Draw the twist

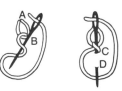

a.   b.   c. Cable chain stitch   d. Interlaced cable chain stitch

tight and put the needle in at C, slightly outside the loop. Come up at D forming another loop (**b.**). Repeat (**c.**).

For interlacing, thread a blunt needle with a contrasting colored thread and lace through the cables (**d.**). Be careful not to pull the thread too tightly. See ill.

interlaced running stitch. Crewel. Embroidery. See **running stitch threaded.**

interlacing. Weaving. The interaction between the **warp** and the **filling** in weaving. In some patterns known as the **weave,** the filling either goes over or under the warp so that the warp and filling form a unit called **cloth.** The order of interlacing comprises the weave pattern and there are endless variations. The places where warp goes over filling, or filling over warp, are called interlacing points. There may be many or few of them. If there are few in each row of warp or filling, the noninterlaced yarn between the interlacing points is known as a **float.** In most cases, the filling interlaces at right angles to the warp. Interlacing is also used when speaking of **braiding** or **plaiting,** but then the over and under process goes on at an oblique angle.

interlining. Quilts. Stitchery. The **filler** or **padding** of a **quilt** or **wall hanging** is known as interlining. The selection of the interlining is determined by the need for warmth, available materials, the thickness desired, and the method of stitching. The most common filler has been **cotton batting;** now, **Dacron polyester batting** is most popular. Sometimes a **wool** blanket, **cotton flannel,** a sheet of **muslin,** or overlapped portions of cotton blanket are used.

Also, material placed between the top fabric and the **lining** of a garment to add warmth or **body.** Also see **batt.**

interlocked canvas. Needlepoint. See **canvas.**

interlocking. Weaving. A **tapestry** technique of joining two **filling** colors without creating a slit. A vertical joining is made by looping the filling threads coming from different directions around each other. This simple step, known as single interlocking, is done between **warp ends** whenever the threads meet. They are both in the same **shed** of **plain weave.** After the looping, the shed is changed and they return to their starting points. Care must be taken that both filling threads are weaving in a straight line with each other and that a loose loop is not left at the point of interlocking. The interlocking must be kept carefully centered between the two warp ends or the resulting line will have a fuzzy appearance. Interlocking is one of the slower tapestry techniques, but it gives a firm joining with only a slight feathering, or indistinctness, where the two colors meet. It is completely reversible and can be used in **diagonals.** There are variations as to direction from which each of the fillings comes, position of the joining, and whether or not to stay in the same shed when returning from the joining.

Double interlocking is the joining twice of the two colors at the meeting point. This produces a distinct ridge on the working side and a clean, straight line on the reverse side; but as traditional tapestries are all done with the wrong side facing the weaver, this presents no problems. It is a very strong joining that came about as a variation of simple interlocking in the eighteenth century at the Gobelin factory. It was quickly adopted since the finished effect was considered to give a more painterly look. Both adjacent fillings move in the same direction in the same shed and interlock twice between the warp ends. The left thread moves left to right and is dropped at the joining point. The right thread is inserted at the joining point and is then carried to the right and then back in the next shed to the joining point and dropped. The left thread, which has been dangling at this joining point, is carried under and over the right thread and then woven to the left in the next shed. The shed is changed again and the left thread comes back to the right again to the joining point. The right thread is picked up, goes under and over the left thread, and then moves right and then back left again. This same sequence is repeated for the length of the joining. It can also be used for diagonals. It is closely associated with Swedish weaving. Both interlockings are also found in Norwegian, Coptic, Gothic, Aubusson, **Navajo,** and **Peruvian weaving.** Interlocking is a controversial term which some weavers use in reference to **dovetailing,** others use it only in reference to double interlocking, and still others have dropped it from their vocabularies, preferring to coin new terms that they feel are more descriptive of the technique. Also see **rölakan.**

interlocking Gobelin. Needlepoint. See **encroaching Gobelin stitch.**

interlocking parts. Toys. Pieces that **join** or fit together in such a way that they lock. Many children's toys have simple interlocking parts. Most **jigsaw puzzles** are cut so that pieces are interlocking. Children's trains and cars are sometimes made with interlocking wood parts.

interlocking stitch. Rugmaking. Weaving. See **lacing stitch.**

internal-release agent. Plastics. See **mold-release agent.**

interpenetrating dovetailing. Weaving. See **dovetailing.**

interweaving. Weaving. Often used interchangeably with **interlacing** when speaking of the action of the **warp** and **filling,** but the term is more apt when talking about the over and under movement of other elements in imitation of weaving. For example, if one were to take an already woven band and work this over and under another band or some long ropes of **wrapping,** this would then be properly called interweaving. Interweaving of elements often takes place **off-loom** because of the size or dimension of the elements and their rigidity.

in the grease. Spinning. See **wool.**

intrinsic mold. Plastics. A material used as a **mold** which becomes either a visible **inclusion** or a structural part of the finished form.

inversion point. Ceramics. The **firing** temperature at which a change in crystalline structure takes place. The **clay body** expands and hardens during the heating cycle of firing and contracts during cooling. Fast or uneven heating and cooling results in **cracking** which is why firing and cooling are done very slowly.

inverted border. Basketry. See **border** and **Basketry: Plaited Basket Construction.**

inverted stitch. Knitting. Another term for the **purl** stitch. Also see **Knitting: Knitting Movements.**

investing. Jewelry. Covering and surrounding a **wax model** with **investment** in preparation for **burnout** and casting. Select the appropriate size **flask** for the wax model. The **sprue**s, **sprue cone**s, and **vent**s are attached to the wax model so it will fit into the flask properly when invested. Use additional wax to attach the sprues, sprue cones, etc., to the wax model and to attach the sprued wax model to a flat surface such as masonite or glass. Coat the wax model with **debubblizer**; dry. Mix a small amount of investment in a rubber bowl, just enough to coat the entire surface of the wax model including the sprues and the sprue cones. Coating the sprues and sprue cones helps support the weight of the investment covering the model. Apply the investment with a small round brush; the investment should evenly cover the wax model. If the wax model is very detailed, use a thinner investment in two coats to insure transference of the design. Allow each coat of investment to dry before applying the next. Place the flask over the coated model in preparation for the investment. Space must be left between the model and the flask on all sides to compensate for the expansion of the investment during **centrifugal casting.** Leave a minimum of ¼″ all around the wax model in a small flask (ring size) and a minimum of ½″ in a medium flask (pin size). A large or very irregular shaped wax model requires more space between it and the flask. It may be necessary to place the model at an angle. Consequently, it is preferable to position the flask over the wax model before attaching the sprues and sprue cones, to make sure the flask is the proper size. **Asbestos coil** can be dipped in water and smoothed around the edges of the flask, leaving ¼″ at the top and bottom of the flask. Asbestos coil is used by many craftspeople to compensate for the expansion and contraction of the investment.

Seal the bottom outer edge with Plasticene when the flask is in position.

Mix investment to fill the entire flask; it is better to mix too much than too little. Tip the flask at a slight angle when pouring the investment to prevent air bubbles being trapped on the underside of the wax model.

If the investment does not fill the entire flask, do not mix more investment in order to entirely fill the flask; two different mixtures of investment will separate and crack during burnout, causing a casting failure. If the amount of investment is insufficient to fill the flask, immediately empty the flask, remove the Plasticene, rinse the flask, and gently rinse the wax model. The model will retain the first coat of the investment. Handle the wax model carefully to avoid damaging it. Mix another batch of investment and fill the flask to the top.

Slowly rotate the filled flask while tapping lightly with a metal handle of a kitchen knife for a few minutes before the investment sets; this will release trapped air bubbles. It is crucial that the investment be bubble-free before it hardens; continue tapping lightly until no more bubbles rise to the surface. The flask can rest on a flat surface or worktable; hold the flask securely to cushion the knife handle blows. The blows must not be too hard—the model could be dislodged and float to the surface of the investment; this can be detected by a swelling of the investment surface. Should this occur, remove the wax model, sprues, sprue cones, etc., from the investment; discard investment, rinse wax model, repair any damage to the model, and begin again.

A thin film of water may accumulate on the surface of the investment as it begins to harden. Remove the water with a flat edge, a piece of metal, or cardboard, used in a back and forth sawing motion across the top of the flask. This will also remove any extra investment, producing a flat surface level with the edges of the flask. The investment must be level with the edges of the flask to insure proper fit within the centrifugal casting machine to prevent cracking the investment when the molten metal is forced into the cavity.

Allow the investment to harden. This will take anywhere from 5 to 20 minutes depending on weather conditions. Before the investment is completely hard, label the flask for content, if more than one flask is used. Each piece requires a different amount of metal to cast, so it is imperative to know what is in the flask.

After the investment has hardened, remove the Plasticene or clay from the bottom and twist the flask to separate it from the glass or masonite. The sprue cones may remain attached to the glass; it can be used for subsequent castings. It is unnecessary to remove the sprue cone; it will disintegrate during burnout. Keep the flask in a horizontal position to prevent loose particles of investment from falling into the cavity. This is especially important after burnout; any particle that falls into the cavity will cause a pit in the casting. See ill. Also see **vibrator.**

Position of flask during investing

investment. Jewelry. A finely powdered plasterlike material that is mixed with water and used to invest the **wax model** used in **lost-wax casting.** There are a number of investments available on the market, either from jewelry or dental supply houses—the same type of investment is used for casting crowns for teeth. The most available investment contains cristobalite, silica (SiO_4) and flour.

These materials allow for extreme heating and rapid cooling without cracking. Investment also contains gypsum (a form of plaster of Paris), which is the actual binder of all the materials. This type of investment, which is usually called Cristobalite Investment, is made by Kerr and is excellent. It is white in color.

There is another type of investment, gray in color, called Model Casting Investment that is made by Modern Materials Manufacturing Company, St. Louis, Missouri. It is difficult to find. Although it feels coarse, it is quite fine and picks up every detail of the wax, as does the Cristobalite Investment. Follow directions on labels for mixing investments.

Mix the investment in a **rubber bowl,** roughly 1 part water to 3 parts investment. Put the water in the rubber bowl first. Do not get any water into the can or package of investment; it will cause small portions to become hard and possibly ruin future castings. When the investment is not being used it should be kept tightly sealed and in a dry place. Slowly add investment to the water by taking a loose handful of investment and sprinkling it on the surface of the water. As it becomes wet it will sink to the bottom. Continue this process slowly until the investment stops sinking and forms a thin layer of dry investment on the top. Stick your fingers in the bowl and gently, but as quickly as possible, mix in the crust of dry investment and at the same time feel for lumps, if any, and break them. Stir as little as possible as the contents of the investment mixture produce their own heat in a chemical reaction to set the investment. Stirring the mixture speeds this chemical reaction and the investment will set before the flask is filled. The investment should be the consistency of sour cream. The mixture is too thin if it runs off your fingers. Add more powdered investment until the desired consistency is reached. If it is too thick, do not add more water. Throw the mixture out and begin again. The casting will fail if water is added to thin the mixture. Do not discard unused mixed investment down the drain because it will harden and clog the drain. Pour the mixed investment in newspaper or in a box and toss it in the trash. Also see **burnout.**

investment. Metalworking. The covering material of which a mold that surrounds a wax model in the **lost-wax casting** is made. It is usually a combination of casting plaster, refractory materials, and other additives mixed with water. At one time it was made of clay and ashes or ground charcoal. Organic matter such as manure, cloth, or straw was also often added to the basic clay mixture to reduce oxidation of the **bronze** when it was poured into the mold, and to strengthen the mold. Ready-made mixtures for metal casting may be purchased today and mixed with water as you would ordinary **casting plaster.**

The layer of investment that touches the wax model is called the facing. This mixture is often made very thin so it can penetrate small creases and details. An early recipe recommended by sixteenth-century goldsmith-sculptors was: 4 parts tripoli powder, 2 parts burnt oxhorn cores, and 1 part iron filings, all ground together and mixed with liquid manure.

Although investment formulas are numerous and subject to the preferences of individual craftspersons (Leonardo da Vinci recommended a mixture of 2 parts plaster to 1 part burnt oxhorns), the method of application is standard. Apply the investment with a spatula to the surface, making sure you get it into all the crevices and undercuts. Set this covered model into a casting flask or container, then fill the enclosure with liquid investment until the mixture reaches the top of the pouring basin. For sculpture, this enclosure is often merely a roll of heavy plastic wrapped into a tube set upright on the floor and sealed at the seams with clay. After the investment material has hardened, the plastic is removed and the mold taken to the **burn-out** kiln for drying.

investment casting. Jewelry. Metalworking. See **lost-wax casting.**

investment mold. Metalworking. See **mold.**

invisible casting on. Knitting. See **Knitting: Casting On.**

iolite. Gemcutting. (Also called cordierite, dichroite.) A mineral consisting of hydrous aluminum and magnesium silicates with a **hardness** of 7½ and a **specific gravity** of 2.6−2.66. Iolite occurs in brittle, transparent **crystal**s of the orthorhombic system having conchoidal **fracture** and a vitreous to greasy **luster.** Its refractive indices are 1.53 and 1.54 and it has a sky-blue **color** with strong dichroism. When it is viewed perpendicular to the crystal faces in three directions it appears light-blue, dark-blue, and yellow-gray alternately. As **cabochon,** it is cut shallow to prevent the deep blue from masking the pleochromism. Iolite is sometimes cut in cubes for display. **Faceting** is best done on an iron **lap** with 1000 grit silicon carbide **abrasive; polishing** is done on a tin lap with tin oxide. Also see **refraction.**

Iowa Star. Quilts. A four-pointed **star pattern.** See ill.

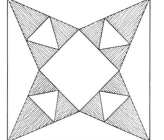

Iowa Star

iridescence. Gemcutting. See **luster.**

iris. Gemcutting. See **luster.**

Irish chain. Quilts. The **piecing** of small squares so that colored **block**s are placed with corners touching. It is a variation of a **nine-patch** block that makes a diagonal pattern. This arrangement makes an active zigzag or **saw-tooth** pattern. The chains are made in **band**s to be used between quilt blocks and are frequently used in **border**s.

All Irish chains are composed using just one piecing pattern—a square.

In each of the nine-patch blocks, a pattern print or solid color is alternated with a plain fabric of contrasting color. This makes, in effect, a checkerboard of nine squares. One nine-patch square is then used as the single square in a larger nine-patch block, creating a single Irish chain.

The double Irish chain has bands using two blocks with the corners end-to-end. When the plain blocks that alternate with the nine-patch blocks have a single small square **appliqué**d to each corner, the result is a double Irish chain. It is also called chained five-patch.

The triple Irish chain uses three blocks touching corners and makes a complex pattern.

The Irish chain has been a favorite since colonial times. Because it joins squares identical in size, it is more easily sewn than the finished quilt would suggest. See ill.

a. Nine-patch

b. Nine-patch blocks alternate with plain blocks for the single Irish chain

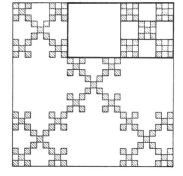

Irish crochet. Lacemaking. In the mid-nineteenth century, at about the time of the Great Famine in Ireland, an effort was made to imitate **point de Venise** in crochet. The dense, rich texture and **pattern**s achieved are today recognized as Irish crochet. Elegant floral **motif**s, flat or in relief, connected by a **ground** of netlike **mesh**es (embellished with many **picot**s on the meshes), and edges finished with scallops are characteristics of Irish crochet. The main rose floral motif is particularly distinctive, being attached to the ground only at the base of the petals.

Irish crochet lace. Crochet. A crocheted lace of rich floral motifs begun on a foundation cord instead of the usual chain. The motifs are then connected by sewing them to a background of crochet net and the work finished with a scalloped outer edge or plain edge. Irish crocheted lace is an imitation of Venetian point lace, and was introduced as a cottage industry during the Great Famine in the nineteenth century. It is still a flourishing cottage craft in Ireland.

Irish knitting. Knitting. The style of knitting that flourishes in Ireland. Irish knitting is characterized by natural colors, **cable** patterns, **crossed stitch**es, and **bobble**s. Historically, the finest examples of knitting were knit by men—in this case the Irish fishermen and sailors. Also see **Aran knitting.**

Irish linen. Crewel. Embroidery. A fine quality linen woven in Ireland and suitable as a **background fabric** for delicate embroidery.

Irish Puzzle. Quilts. See **Kansas Troubles.**

Irish stitch. Needlepoint. See **brick stitch.**

Irish stitch. Rugmaking. See **Hungarian stitch.**

Irish tambour lace. Lacemaking. See **tambour lace.**

Irish wheel. Spinning. See **treadle wheel.**

Iris leaf. Quilts. The **wandering foot** pattern, sewn in green and white, assumes this new name.

Iroba doll. Toys. A contemporary wooden **doll** made in central Africa.

iron. Metalworking. The mineral iron is combined with other substances in its natural state. Even in its simplest smelted form, it looks like a useless spongy mass, without obvious metallic properties. Iron must be forged and hammered to squeeze out the **slag** to make it usable. Iron working followed the use of copper, at about 1400 B.C.; before that time, only iron from meteorites was used. Meteoric iron was prized not only because it was associated with the heavens, but also for its hardness. Eskimos used only meteoric iron until the eighteenth century. Up to medieval times all metals were associated with astrology, and iron was thought to be connected with Mars even after iron no longer was derived only from meteorites. Iron implements were buried with their ancient owners in Europe for celestial protection. The Egyptians learned to harden iron with carbon in it, and the Greeks were familiar with **tempering.**

Today, iron ore, coke, and limestone are heated in a blast furnace and heated air is blown into the mixture. The intense heat separates the iron from the impurities; these are absorbed by the limestone and float to the top of the liquid, where they are skimmed off. There are several different types of iron, not all suitable for craft work.

Pig iron, iron directly from the blast furnace, is the base for all other **ferrous** metals. It usually contains about 5% carbon and is useless for craft work. The name comes from the early method of pouring iron into bar molds around a main channel like a litter of small pigs around a sow.

Cast iron contains 2−4% carbon and up to 3.5% silicon. It is relatively brittle and therefore not useful for forging, although it may be **braze weld**ed. There are three basic types: gray cast iron, white cast iron, and malleable cast iron (also called malleable iron). Gray cast iron is dark gray, porous, very brittle, and has a sooty surface when broken because much of its carbon is distributed throughout it in flake form. It is primarily used for machine-part castings. White cast iron has a low silicon content, and its carbon is united with the iron by rapidly cooling the metal in manufacture. Its surface has a white crystalline appearance when the metal is fractured. White cast iron is very hard and is used for castings that must resist much wear, and in the manufacturing of malleable iron. Malleable iron is really a white cast iron that has been annealed to remove the brittleness. All cast iron conducts heat so rapidly that one may have to preheat an entire surface before welding only one part. If malleable iron is heated to fusion-welding temperatures it will return to a brittle white cast iron, and must be reheated and **anneal**ed afterward to restore its malleability.

Wrought iron contains only tiny amounts of carbon and is commonly used for **blacksmithing**. When heated, it can be bent, twisted, and hammered without breaking. It melts at 2800° F and conducts heat more slowly than cast iron; it is also more expensive than the other irons.

All iron is vulnerable to corrosion, so either the surface must be given a protective coating when exposed to the elements or the material must be **alloy**ed with less corrodible metals to make it durable.

iron binding wire. Jewelry. (Also called binding wire.) Any **gauge** of iron wire used in **binding** and **soldering** operations. Also see **jig**.

iron brushwork. Ceramics. Decoration done with **iron oxide** mixed with water. Iron brushwork can be applied either under or over a **glaze** before **firing** to achieve a dark brown to green decoration, depending on the glaze with which it is used. Also see **hakame**.

iron chromate. Ceramics. Iron chromate is used in combination with manganese and **zinc oxide** to produce **underglaze** browns or with **cobalt oxide** to form a black **stain**. Also see **iron oxide**.

ironing. Batik and Tie-dye. A process used either to remove **wax** from **batik fabric** or to **set dyes**. When wax is to be removed a worktable should be padded with newspapers so that it will serve as an ironing board. The newspapers are covered first with a layer of paper towels, then the wax-coated batik, then another layer of paper towels. When pressed over with a medium-hot iron the wax is melted out into the paper towels. If the wax is thick the towels will have to be changed several times.

Ironing is also a **heat set**ting method for **fix**ing dye colors. Also see **calendering** and **Batik and Tie-dye: Fabrics for Dyeing**.

iron-on adhesive. Stitchery. A **nonwoven material**, available in sheet form or by the yard, which can be used to adhere two pieces of **fabric** together. The iron-on adhesive is placed between the two fabrics, and then a medium-hot iron is used to **set** and adhere the layers. Stitch-Witchery is one iron-on adhesive commonly available in department stores or fabric shops. Also see **fabric adhesive**.

iron-on appliqué. Stitchery. A method of applying decorative design by using **iron-on tape**s on a **background** of contrasting color, or by using **adhesive** materials between **fabric** layers. The **iron-on fabric** tapes, available in assorted colors, are cut into shapes and placed with the adhesive side facing the background fabric. They are then ironed to permanently **set** them. They will easily withstand one or two washings and sometimes more. If the iron-on fabric shapes loosen, they can sometimes be reset with ironing. The adhesive materials are applied as described in iron-on adhesives.

In dollmaking, iron-on appliqué is often used on fabric or **felt** puppets, animals, and dolls to suggest details and features. It provides a quick and easy way of adding pattern.

When used on clothing or on **quilts** where there will be wear and repeated washings, a machine-sewn **straight stitch** may be sewn at the **raw edge** of the cut **appliqué** shapes to make them more permanent. In wall **hanging**s or **banner**s where wear is not a problem or a concern, iron-on appliqué gives a speedy effect and the texture of fabric with a minimum of time and sewing.

iron-on fabric. Puppets. Stitchery. Similar to **iron-on tape**, these **fabric**s or patches are larger pieces or strips of the **adhesive**-coated cloth. Most are **permanent press, Sanforized**, washable and dry-cleanable. The iron-on fabric is used for **appliqué** or for mending.

iron-on interfacing. Puppets. Stitchery. Weblike or **bonded fabric** which can be semipermanently adhered to another **fabric** by ironing over it with a medium-hot iron. These **lining**s usually have a shiny **adhesive** side which is placed against the fabric to which it is to be applied. In **appliqué**, they may be ironed to the wrong side of lightweight fabrics to give them more **body** and make them easier to handle and sew. In making **stuffed animal**s, **hand puppet**s, **three-dimensional stitchery**, or **stuff**ed work, the **interfacing** will stiffen material enough to make some parts rigid or to help them retain a shape. Also see **batik puppet, fabric adhesive**.

iron-on patch. Stitchery. Any **iron-on fabric**, usually of twill, **denim**, or other sturdy **fabric**, meant for patching. They are preshaped, with rounded corners.

iron-on seam binding. Stitchery. See **seam binding**.

iron-on tape. Puppets. Stitchery. (Also called mending tape, press-on tape.) Strips or tapes of **fabric** which have an **adhesive** backing so that they can be applied to another fabric. They are **set** or made permanent with the heat of an iron. The tape is available in strips or patches of **iron-on fabric** in a limited range of colors, usually in packages of assorted related colors (pastels and dark colors). They are reasonably permanent, though in repeated washings the tape may loosen or **fray**. Also see **bonded tape, fabric adhesive, iron-on appliqué**.

iron-on transfer pattern. Crewel. Embroidery. A design printed on a special paper and transferable to the **background fabric** with a hot iron. Also see **Crewel: Transferring a Design**.

iron oxide. Ceramics. There are three forms of iron oxide: ferrous oxide, ferric oxide (hematite), and ferrous-ferric oxide (magnetite). Iron is the oxide that produces brown or tan bodies and glazes. It is responsible for the red color and low **firing** characteristics of **earthenware** clays. Also see **burnt sienna, iron chromate, ochre, pigment oxide, specking**.

iron pyrite. Gemcutting. See **pyrite.**

iron toy. Toys. See **cast-iron toy.**

ironwood. Woodworking. See **birch.**

ironworking. Metalworking. See **blacksmithing.**

irregular dovetailing. Weaving. See **dovetailing.**

Isaac, Susan. Toys. See **Toys.**

isinglass. A semitransparent white, pure **gelatin** that is used in glue and cement formulas. The term "isinglass" also applies to muscovite mica. Also see **diamond cement.**

isolated stitches. Crewel. Embroidery. See **detached.**

isometric system. Gemcutting. See **crystal.**

isotropic. Gemcutting. See **refraction.**

Italian laid-in. Weaving. See **laid-in.**

Italian quilting. Quilts. See **Italian trapunto.**

Italian shading. Embroidery. Italian shading is the most sophisticated method of **couching** in **metallic thread embroidery.** It is accomplished by laying down gold threads that conform to the contour of a shape. The couching stitches act as shading by varying their density and spacing over the laid gold threads. A variation on this technique is to lay the gold threads alongside each other in parallel lines (**a.**). A design is then created using the couching stitches. The gold threads have been completely covered with close couching stitches inside the lily to give a dark shadow effect. The couching stitches are then spaced gradually wider apart and the colors lightened toward the outer edge of the shape. This couching is done line by line (**b.**). See ill.

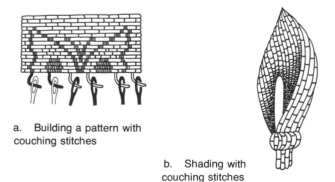

a. Building a pattern with
couching stitches

b. Shading with
couching stitches

Italian trapunto. Quilts. (Also called Italian quilting.) A decorative fabric technique often used on **quilts.** This method was favored in the southern United States, probably because there was little need for padded or heavier quilts. In this method, the two layers of fabric (the plain **quilt top** and the **backing**) are placed together, and the quilt design is outlined with two parallel lines of stitching about ¼" apart. When the sewing of the design is completed, the fabric is snipped in one spot on the back between the two lines of stitching to make a small opening. Then a cord is pulled through the opening and between the parallel lines. A soft **cotton** cord, such as **candlewicking,** or a cotton yarn is used. The cord makes the raised design between the parallel lines, giving a soft padded look. The cord is always pulled through from the back using a large blunt needle. It is also called **cord quilting,** which is a variation. Italian trapunto is always linear in design, in contrast to **English trapunto,** in which larger areas are **stuff**ed.

IT Solder. Jewelry. (Pronounced "eye-tee.") A very hard solder with a flow point of 1460° F. Also see **silver solder, soldering.**

ivory. Ivory and Bone Carving. The creamy-white, hard, opaque dentine of tooth or tusk of large land and sea mammals, or the beak of the helmeted hornbill. It has a **hardness** of 3; the **specific gravity** of dentine ivory is 1.70−1.93, and of vegetable ivory is 1.38−1.42.

The color, quality, size, hardness, and, if it is a tusk, the depth of the internal hollow all determine the value of a piece. A matched pair of tusks is extremely desirable, and of considerable value (although most matched pairs do not really match, as most animals have a tendency to use and wear down one tusk more than the other).

Ivory is a living substance that continues to grow as long as the animal lives, and hardens and yellows with age. It is susceptible to cracking and warping. It is elastic, fine-grained, and absorbs and reflects light. It carves more slowly than wood or stone.

Dentine ivory is obtained from elephants in Africa, India, Ceylon, and Thailand, and from hippopotamuses, walruses, **narwhal,** mammoths, whales, boar, crocodiles, and a species of hornbill.

One of the largest suppliers of ivory is the Soviet Union, which uncovered huge beds of fossilized mammoth and mastodon tusks well-preserved enough to be sold in huge quantities to China. Also see **elephant ivory, hippopotamus tooth, hornbill ivory, walrus ivory.**

ivory. Jewelry. The hard creamy white modified dentine composing the tusk of a tusked mammal. Probably elephant ivory is the most commonly used. It is a marvelous material to work with and polishes beautifully. It can be used as a material unto itself by **sawing,** forming, and shaping it with **files;** as a base for **inlay** and **pique work,** which is a form of inlay; or as an inlay material. Shallow designs with a sharp tool such as a **scriber** can be scratched in ivory and the cuts filled with blackberry juice for a black color, red raspberry juice for red, or with aniline dyes. Ivory has a visible grain, as opposed to bone, which shows signs of porosity and does not have grain. As ivory ages it becomes browner until it is very rich, especially if it is in a bracelet and the natural oils from the skin are slowly absorbed while it is worn. Fresh ivory is almost snow white and the grain is difficult to discern. It is difficult to work, as it is somewhat sticky and the odor is very unpleasant. Older ivory is dry, odorless, and wonderful to work. A face mask should be worn while working it as the powder from sawing or filing is very fine.

IVORY AND BONE CARVING

Although bone and ivory have been, and are, used in similar ways and are similarly worked, there are many differences in the materials themselves, and certainly in their values. Ivory is considered much superior to bone, and is indeed much rarer. Its mellowing and light-reflecting qualities make it an attractive material for carving and ornamentation. However, bone has traditionally been used in the same capacities because it was more available and manageable.

There are many well-preserved items of bone and ivory from the Stone Age, including engraved tusks, bone and antler axheads, fishhooks, and ornaments. Finely carved ivory articles such as combs, tablets, and small statues have been unearthed in Egyptian tombs that are more than 5,000 years old. From 3000 B.C., Sudanese elephants and hippopotamuses from the Nile provided the Egyptians with their ivory. Phoenicia, Babylonia, Byzantium, and Rome all excelled in carving ivory. Ivory, symbolic of virginity and purity, achieved a high development in the early Christian era, when it was used lavishly in church decoration, in shrines, altars, crucifixes, and door panels.

Ivory and carving and ornamentation reached their peak in the Middle Ages; they were carved and used to bind the illuminated manuscripts and made into caskets, combs, hunting horns, and other items too numerous to mention. Most of the ivory for these articles came from West African elephant tusks.

Bone was enjoying such popularity by the fourteenth century that, in northern Italy, Baldassare degli Embriachi founded a bone-carving school. In the French town of **Dieppe**, in Normandy, an ivory-carving industry arose about 1364; the town produced works of art that became famous the world over. Dieppe is thought to have been directly connected with trends and techniques used in the indigenous American art of **scrimshaw**, the carving of whale teeth, **panbone**, and **baleen. Les laboureurs**, ivory carvers from Dieppe who worked at their craft while imprisoned in England during the Napoleonic Wars, were later joined in detention by American prisoners of the War of 1812, where, under the tutelage of the French, they soon learned a trade to augment their finances, often prospering as they could not in civilian life. The British blockade had stopped the flow of frivolous articles from France, and the wealthy British paid handsomely for the carved objects of the prisoners. Often they would supply the carver with the best materials to work with, including gold, although the principal material was bone. Later the Americans returned to their whaling and carried with them the techniques of the Dieppe carvers.

Bone and ivory were used in furniture decoration in Europe in the sixteenth century; the Italians initiated its use. Marquetry reached its peak in the early 1700s. The most famous exponent of this veneering art was André

Charles Boulle, a French cabinetmaker, who used tortoiseshell, ebony, and brass more than bone; **Boulle work** was named after him. Often the bone or ivory was stained green to resemble foliage, or engraved and filled with black to make them conspicuous.

The Chinese have used ivory for centuries in delicate fretwork, intricate carvings on fans and of landscapes, floral motifs, and of animals. Japan had little access to ivory, and yet produced skilled carvings in the material, as in their **netsukes**; often these were of **vegetable ivory**, or other similar imitation ivory. The Eskimo has always employed bone and ivory for weapons, tools, and works of art. The Yankee whalers came in contact with other ivory carvers here and in the South Sea Islands.

TOOLS AND MATERIALS The tools used to work bone and ivory are basically those used to work wood. They include crosscut files with assorted profiles, saws, jeweler's files and rasps, a file card, gouges for hollowing, a hand drill, brace and bit, flexible shaft drill, and a **needle drill.**

Although the work is often held in the hand, it can be secured by various means. It may be dopped to a surface with **beeswax** or held steady with a **carpet underlay, wood vise wedge,** or **leather-lined vise.** Beads may be held for many operations with a **bead-holding jig, lapstick, bow-drill,** or **bead-polishing board.**

Sundries used in cleaning, bleaching, and polishing are steel wool, **whiting, tin oxide,** lime, bicarbonate of soda, **almond oil,** Q-tips, alum, and sandpaper. An X-acto knife, hammer, glue, and pliers are useful in various operations.

A favorite tool for engraving is the **Eskimo style,** and the artist's skew chisel is used for inlay.

The nature of bone varies with the type, how it has been chemically treated, and its age. **Bone** is a hard, compact, dense material on the outside, with a porous cancelled interior. The larger the bone, the deeper the compact layer. The interior section is not usually used. Store-bought slabs are usually from industrial sources and have had the fat boiled out with gasoline, making it more brittle than those you treat yourself. The degree of fat affects its yellowness. Old bone is liable to have a bad odor.

Cattle bone is the most widely used bone for working; it is whiter and smaller than horse bone. Sheep bone can be used as well, and is the hardest of the three. The color varies from chalky white through off-white to yellow.

Bone is obtained through a craft supply source or from a meathouse. If you decide to buy it and prepare it yourself for working, purchase marrow bones. Store-bought bone is dried and sliced in slabs. Available in five sizes, the smallest is suitable for very small objects such as cocktail sticks, spoons, and forks and measures about 4¾" long. The largest and thickest is approximately 6½" long and is of a size to yield salad and cake servers.

PREPARATION OF THE MATERIAL When working **whale teeth,** generally the first operation is to remove the ribs. Use a sanding disk on an electric drill unless the material is particularly hard, in which case use an abrasive stone. With **hippopotamus tooth,** the porcelaneous enamel on the outside curve of the tooth is removed with a grindstone. Large carving surfaces are obtained from elephant tusks by cutting spiral sheets around the tusk. Soft ivory, if boiled, can sometimes be twisted into shapes while still warm.

To clean a fresh bone, with a hacksaw remove the joint and then clean out the marrow. In soda water or lime water to which 1 tsp. of alum has been added for each quart, boil the bone for 1 to 3 hours, depending on its size and fat content. Rinse the bone and change the water as often as is required to achieve a thoroughly clean bone. Place it outdoors in a sunny location for several days for bleaching and airing.

After boiling the bone and cutting it to size and shape, it can be bleached in a 40% solution of hydrogen peroxide for 24 to 48 hours. It is possible to shorten the bleaching time by using only a 20% hydrogen peroxide solution and boiling it. This chemical is capable of burning your skin, so handle it with care and keep it out of the reach of children.

Cut along the length of the bone with a hacksaw to obtain the largest flat slabs possible.

Cutting bone slabs

Saw cuts

SAWING BONE   Remove unwanted bone with a coping saw with metal-cutting blades. Coarse blades may be used for the rough cut and basic shapes.

Drill a hole for the blade of the coping saw to saw a piece from the inside of the slab. Use fine-toothed metalworking blades for the more intricate or delicate sawcuts.

Hold the saw in a perpendicular position and saw up and down the whole length of the blade. Saw your line steadily and continuously, whether curved or straight, and it will be smoother than if you falter or stop. Do not push the saw to make faster progress, but let it work its way forward. Do not saw too fast or push too hard, as the blade may overheat and clog the teeth or snap.

After cutting away as much material with the saw as you can, file it to further shape it. Place bone in the vise for rough filing; a **wood vise wedge** is helpful with irregularly shaped pieces to help hold them. A fine steel brush or file card is necessary to clean the file as you work, as the fat content of the bone causes the file teeth to clog. The finer the file, the more quickly it clogs. If the file is difficult to unclog, carefully burn the bone meal out of the teeth over a flame. Too much heat will ruin the temper of your file.

Sand before or after bleaching, but always before polishing. Sand with the grain to achieve the smoothest finish. Use #1, 1/0, and 2/0 sandpaper, or 300 or 400 wet-or-dry for rough sanding. Numbers 0 and 00 steel wool are used for the final sanding before polishing. See ill.

TRANSFERRING THE DESIGN   Trace the design onto the material with a grease pencil. With intricate designs, transfer them to thin paper; it is convenient to then cement the paper tracing to the bone with a flour paste and work directly through the tracing into the bone. Apply a second layer of paste over the paper. The paper can later be removed with a damp sponge. This is the best way to transfer dotted outlines.

If you intend to make a matched set of articles, such as handles for tableware, it is time saving to make a reusable template of cardboard, plastic, or thin wood. Use a hard pencil with a sharp point and trace directly to the bone.

CARVING   Carving is best done slowly, as tools easily slip on the surface. Tools are pushed with a gentle rocking motion. They must be kept sharp to make any appreciable impression. If you are carving through a pasted paper design, the style will produce a squeaking noise when in contact with ivory.

A favorite tool for engraving is the **Eskimo style.** In all engraving, do not attempt to make deep cuts, but repeat a cut over if the depth does not suit you. Cut all vertical lines at one time and then all horizontal ones. The diamond, wedge-shaped, and V-shaped chisel are often used for carving. If the tool sticks, lift it and start again. Brace one thumb against the other to control the speed and direction in which you move the tool. See ill.

Brace thumbs while carving ivory

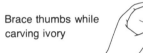

The artist's skew chisel is used to cut inlay recesses. Cut a template to use for the shape of the recess and the inlay material. Outline the design and remove the first layer inside the lines with the skew chisel. Start at the center and work out toward the outline. The inside enamel of **whale teeth** is harder than the outside, and the careful use of power tools to remove the harder material will speed up this operation.

Put a strong all-purpose glue in the recess and place the inlay into place. Lay a thin piece of wood over the inlay and tap firmly with a small wooden mallet. Ebony and other brittle materials that might split or shatter should be pressed in with your finger and burnished with the wood handle of a tool.

FINISHING   Tableware parts of stainless steel are joined to handles by embedding or **riveting** them, depending on the type of shank the part has. Some shanks may have to be sawed off to fit your handle.

Drill the hole the same size as the shank. The shank should be roughened with a file or scratched so that it will grip the glue better. The glue should be resistant to oil and water and fast-setting, such as pulverized resin glue. Fill the hole with glue or dip the shank into the glue, and embed. Remove the excess glue after one hour, and position the handle correctly.

RIVETING   To rivet handles to tableware, mark the position of the rivet holes on the material by holding the shank of the hardware against the handle. The handle works best when it is the same width as the shank you are riveting in. Drill the holes and countersink them. Drill the holes the depth of the slot and clean them out with a saw or needle file. The slot should fit the shank perfectly so that the handle won't wobble. Forcing the shank into a hole that is too small can cause the handle to split. For the rivet, use aluminum wire of the proper thickness cut to the correct depth of the hole it will fill. Carefully hammer the rivet on both sides when it is in the hole or, to avoid marring the bone surface, squeeze the rivet with pliers, protecting the bone with cardboard.

Incised lines made with an X-acto knife, style, or **needle drill** will not appear until they receive color. The colors may be inks or various-colored sealing waxes. India ink is commonly used by drawing the point of a pen along the incised lines to emphasize them. It is brushed across stippled designs and then wiped off, leaving only the dots filled.

To fill areas with sealing wax, a moderately warm soldering iron, or a blade warmed over a flame (wipe off any carbon deposit before picking up the wax) will melt the wax and can be used to apply it to the grooves. Remove the excess wax by sanding. After sanding, polish the bone carefully. Polishing with too much pressure will melt the wax.

To attach metal findings use a cellulose cement to hold the metal in place and carefully drill holes for rivets. Do not hammer the rivets in, but squeeze them with pliers while protecting the face of the piece with a piece of cardboard. Findings may be glued with a concentrated resin glue and screws may be inserted into predrilled holes.

Commercially prepared polish for bone may be obtained from craft-supply outlets. **Whiting,** paris white, and water-ground whiting are used to polish bone; the latter is preferred. Polish bone with a circular motion.

For ivory, use **pumice powder** with a soft damp rag, rubbing the tooth or piece all over. If the ivory is whale tooth you will find that the tooth will take a greater polish at the tip than near the base. Continue to rub the tooth until all traces of sandpaper marks are removed. After rinsing the pumice from the material, with a clean rag proceed to polish it with whiting. Alternative abrasives are **putty powder, tin oxide, chalk,** and **rottenstone.** The final abrasive traditionally used on **scrimshaw** is ash and then just the palm of the hand.

Often the final step is to apply a light oil and then to wipe it dry; **almond oil** is recommended. It is not certain whether or not this hastens the yellowing of ivory.

Polishing agents applied to the end of wet Q-tips help in the polishing of carved pieces.

CARE AND MAINTENANCE   The care of ivory and bone is very similar. A dry climate is best for both materials, as excessive dampness can cause separation of their layers. A piece should never be immersed in water. Bone is of a firmer texture and can withstand the effects of moisture better than the fragile ivory. The results of water can be swelling, warping, and cracking.

It is not generally advised to wash old ivory. If you choose to risk it, ivory may be cleaned with a damp sponge with a mild soap, rinsed with clean tepid water, and quickly dried with a soft nonabrasive cloth. A thin application of **almond oil** can then be applied.

Strong sunlight and heat can cause the layers to **part.**

Although it is possible to bleach ivory, it is a material whose beauty increases with age due to the gradual deepening of its color. The patina or bloom increases not only the beauty but the value of an ivory piece. Bone also can be bleached; its yellowing process is slower and not as attractive as that of ivory.

Painted ivory pieces should be cleaned dry with a soft bristle brush, as water could destroy the picture. It is best not to attempt any restoring of this type of ivory art. A soft brush is used to dust carvings as well.

Often, in spite of good care, ivory will develop cracks. The further separation of the fibers may be checked by binding them together with a liquid furniture wax. Mask off the edges of the crack to keep the wax off the surface and fill the crack with the wax, using a pointed paint brush. Let it dry two days and remove the tape. This small attention may be effective for from six months to a year. Repeat when required.

ivory black. Ivory and Bone Carving. One of the finest black pigments, made by calcining ivory.

j

jack. Glasswork. (Also called pucella.) The tongs used to handle molten glass in glassblowing (**a.**). Jacks are also used to open the necks of vessels by inserting the two points and allowing the jack to open while turning the work on the **punty.**

To open a neck with a jack, reheat the work on a punty in the mouth of the **tank furnace** or in a **glory hole** (**b.**). Insert the points of the jack into the open mouth and allow them to spread while the **blowing iron** is rolled with the other hand on the arms of the **glassworker's chair** (**c.**). After the mouth is opened sufficiently with the points of the jack, use both points together to force the soft glass outward while turning the work on the iron (**d.**).

Jacks may be of any size, depending on the size of work being done, and most glassblowers have several sizes at hand when working at the glassworker's chair. See ill.

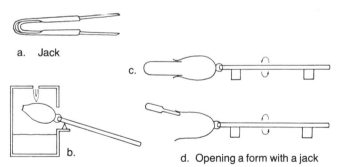

a. Jack

c.

b.

d. Opening a form with a jack

jack-in-the-box. Toys. (Also called Johnny jump-up.) A wood box that contains a clownlike head mounted on a cloth-covered spring. When the lid of the box is lifted the spring sends the head popping upward. The toy is of unknown origin, but it was formerly called a punch box, which suggests that it may have developed from the puppet character **Punch.** The faces of the jacks often have exaggerated features or masks similar to the face of Punch. The toy is also made as a musical jack-in-the-box. Also see **animated toy.**

Jack-in-the-Pulpit. Quilts. See **Toad-in-the-Puddle.**

jack knife. Woodworking. See **whittling tools.**

jack loom. Weaving. A **floor** or **table loom** in which the **harness**es are raised when a **treadle** or **lever** is pushed. All table looms are jack-type and may have a wheel, knob, or rope instead of a lever to raise each harness. There are two types of floor jack looms—those in which the harnesses are pushed up from below, and those having the harnesses lifted from the top. Directly below each harness of the first type are wooden pieces acting as levers that push the harnesses up when the treadle is pressed down. On the second type, there is an overhead or side structure to which the jack levers are connected and which pull up the harnesses when the treadle is pressed. The jack levers are attached to the lams and the lams to the treadles. Each harness can be raised by itself without disturbing the others. The rising harnesses lift the **warp** threads from a closed **shed** position, while the other threads remain stationary at the bottom of the **reed.** This independent action of each harness is different from both the **countermarch** and **counterbalanced loom**s. As opposed to the latter, a jack-type loom has greater flexibility in working with unbalanced weaves such as double weaves, **honeycomb weave**s, and many others that require either more or less harnesses raised than remain lowered. (An example would be 1 harness raised against 3 remaining stationary in a 4-harness weave.) Because of the raising of the harnesses, a jack-type loom is known as a **rising shed** loom. Commonly available weaving widths in table models are from 8″ to 26″ and for the floor jack looms from 20″ to 60″. Harnesses can range from 2 to 16 in number. See ill. Also see **balanced weave, double cloth, foot-power loom.**

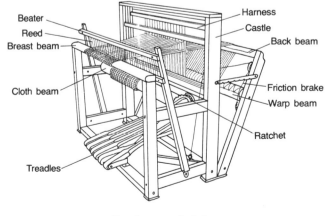

Four-harness jack loom

jack plane. Woodworking. See **plane.**

jacks. Toys. (Also called jackstones.) A **game** played with five or more small stones or specially shaped pieces of metal. A **ball** is bounced and the jacks are retrieved in a certain order while the ball is in the air.

Jackson Star. Quilts. See **star patterns.**

jackstones. Toys. See **jacks, knucklebones.**

jackstraws. Toys. A **game** similar to **pick-up-sticks** in which small carved wooden sticks, dropped in a pile, are to be picked up, or removed, one at a time. The old handmade jackstraws were carved in the shapes of hoes, rakes, shovels, etc. The sticks were a thin, lightweight, soft white wood.

Jacobean. Crewel. Embroidery. Needlepoint. The term "Jacobean" from the seventeenth-century Jacobean period includes three different pattern arrangements. The first is the Tree-of-Life design taken from the East Indian **palampores.** The second is Elizabethan scroll design which developed into a bolder design worked in wool during the seventeenth century. The third is a wavy border enclosed within straight lines. The term "Jacobean" generally refers to a very bold design.

Jacob's Ladder. Quilts. A **pieced-block** design consisting of 36 small squares, some of which are split into 2 triangles. It is pieced to give a diagonal line of **sawtooth** or ladder pattern. The Jacob's Ladder is always pieced in two colors only, those being of strong dark and light contrast. When the dark and light patterns within the block are reversed, and a third color is added, a new pattern is developed, which was called **Stepping Stones** in New England and Virginia and the Tail of Benjamin's Kite in Pennsylvania. It then became The Underground Railroad, and on the prairie was known as the Trail of the Covered Wagon or Wagon Tracks. See ill.

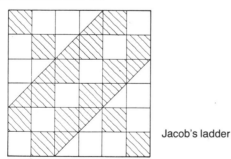

Jacob's ladder

Jacob's ladder. Toys. (Also called clatter blocks, klacker, ladder toy.) A traditional **action toy** made up of a series of flat wooden blocks linked together with cloth tapes in such

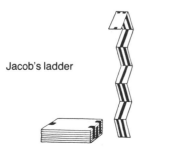

Jacob's ladder

a way that when one of the end blocks is held at the edges and tilted, it triggers a series of movements that gives the illusion of continuous tumbling actions. The action may be repeated indefinitely. Double-acting hinges allow the toy to "flip while in action." See ill.

Jacquard knitting. Knitting. See **Florentine knitting.**

Jacquard loom. Weaving. A mechanically operated loom that was based on a **draw loom** principle, but which removed the necessity of having a weaver's helper lift the extra **harness**es or **heddle**s. It was invented by Joseph Marie Jacquard in France in about 1804. The Jacquard loom has a head motion, situated on top of the loom, that controls the raising of the **warp ends.** Every heddle is governed individually so that very intricate patterns are possible. The head motion operates on the basis of a chain of cardboard or metal cards. Each card is a **pick** or **shed** in the weaving. Every card is made up of punched holes indicating a **raiser** in the pattern. As the cards mechanically are moved around, the head motion needles attached to the warp ends are activated if there is a hole in the card, and the pattern is woven. Also see **damask, dobby loom, draw loom.**

Jacquard stitch. Needlepoint. A variation of the **Byzantine stitch** which places a single row of **tent stitch** between the diagonal rows of Byzantine stitches.

jade. Beadwork. Gemcutting. An opaque to translucent gem of either nephrite or jadeite used for carving in jewelry and **beadmaking.** Jade is polished with 1,200 grit **diamond** powder, chrome, or tin oxide, and Linde A on leather over a padded wooden disk. It is sanded wet with 200−600 grit **abrasive** cloths and allowed to run dry.

Nephrite is an amphibole composed of silicates and carbonates of aluminum and magnesium with a crypto-**crystal**line structure, **hardness** of 6½, and **specific gravity** of 2.9−3.1. It occurs in shades of green, gray, yellow, and brown with variegated or uniform **color** and has refractive indices of 1.60 and 1.63. It is usually carved or cut in **cabochon** form. Nephrite is very tough and fibrous; violent temperature changes cause it to crack.

Jadeite belongs to the **pyroxene** group. It is composed of sodium and aluminum silicates in compact aggregates. It is translucent, occurring in white, green, gray, blue, or rose with a greasy **luster.** It has hardness of 6¾, specific gravity of 3.3−3.4, and refractive indices of 1.66 and 1.68. Also see **actinolite, polishing, refraction, sanding** and **Gemcutting: Hand Grinding and Polishing, Rough Shaping.**

jadeite. Beadwork. Gemcutting. See **jade.**

jamb peg. Gemcutting. See **faceting unit.**

Jansenist binding. Bookbinding. A French style of binding in which the covers are decorated only with **blind tooling.** It was named after the Roman Catholic Jansenists for the severity of its style.

Japan dryer. Woodworking. A petroleum distillate used to speed the drying of **paints** and **linseed oil.** It is especially useful to mix with paint when adverse weather conditions may delay the drying. Japan dryer is combustible and toxic, with more than 1% **lead** in it. Do not apply it to anything that might come in contact with children. Always mix it thoroughly with the paint or linseed oil and apply it where there is adequate ventilation. Protect the skin and avoid breathing its vapors.

Japanese Fan. Quilts. See **fan quilt.**

Japanese gold and silver. Embroidery. (Also called Jap gold.) To make Japanese thread, gold or silver leaf (real metal with a thin paper backing) is lightly twisted and gummed around a silk core that completely conceals the silk. The resulting thread has a beautiful luster. As it would naturally be too fragile to sew right through the **background fabric,** two threads of Jap gold are always couched down on the surface of the fabric side by side, using a fine waxed silk thread. When many rows are couched side by side, and as they curve in different directions, the effect and sheen of gold cloth is achieved.

Because of the high price of gold and silver artificial Jap golds are available. However, most of them do tarnish. Also see **couching, metallic thread embroidery.**

Japanese paper folding. Papercrafts. See **origami.**

Japanese weave. Basketry. See **rib-rand.**

japanned tin. Toys. The decorative painted metal surface of many nineteenth-century toys. The metal was covered with a **finish** coat of hard **lacquer** or varnish, giving it a glossy surface over brilliant colors. The method originally came from Japan and was adopted by toy manufacturers in the United States and Europe.

japanning. Découpage. A term used in England for the technique of imitating the **lacquer ware** that was imported to Europe from China and Japan at the end of the seventeenth and beginning of the eighteenth centuries.

European cabinetmakers could not exactly duplicate the **lacquer** process because of the long drying time required and the difference in climate. The Europeans wanted to produce the ware quickly to meet the growing demand for it, so in order to harden the lacquer quickly it was baked instead of air-dried. As a result the wood underneath the lacquer warped or cracked. The process was finally perfected by using **papier mâché** as a base.

Soon this craft of making objects of papier mâché pulp and lacquering them was pursued by many amateurs. As added decoration, hand-tinted prints were cut out and adhered to the surface—the beginning of découpage.

Later, the term "japanning" became associated more with découpage techniques as we know them, of embellishing a surface with cut-outs and burying them under layers of varnish. In 1760 the book *Ladies' Amusement* gave instructions for japanning, with prints to be cut out and techniques for applying varnish or "seedlac" coats and a final rubbing with **rottenstone.**

japanning. Tincraft. A term originating in England used to describe the effect created by the application of a glossy **varnish** or **lacquer** finish to tinware. The result was felt to resemble the Oriental lacquerware imported to Europe during the seventeenth and eighteenth centuries. Also see **Tincrafting: Finishing the Tin.**

Jap gold. Embroidery. See **Japanese gold and silver.**

jasper. Gemcutting. See **quartz.**

jaspering. Bookbinding. (Also called speckling.) Speckling the edges of the leaves of a book with color by brushing it with a stiff brush through a screen. Also see **edge coloring.**

Java cotton. Stitchery. See **kapok.**

Javanese batik. Batik and Tie-dye. The traditional **batik** produced in Java and having the characteristic stylizations of natural forms. The Javanese developed the art of batik to its most intricate and complex level; it has been an art form there since the twelfth century. The Javanese work consists of two major types: the **tulis,** or hand-drawn method, and the **tjap,** or printed method. Also see **Batik and Tie-dye.**

jaw crusher. Ceramics. An industrial machine used to crush rocks when **mixing glaze** materials.

jean. Stitchery. A **cotton** twill-weave fabric similar to **denim.** It is firm and has a smooth, durable surface. Jean is commonly used in sportswear where the term is interchangeable with denim, which it resembles. Jeans, **blue jeans,** or blue denims all use variations of this twill-weave cotton.

jeans. Stitchery. See **blue jeans.**

jersey sweater. Knitting. Fishermen's sweaters knitted in the Channel Islands (specifically, the Isle of Jersey). Jerseys are similar in design to the plain, square-shaped **Guernsey** sweaters, but the yarn is thinner and need not be blue, the traditional color of Guernseys. Also see **Aran knitting.**

Jersey wheel. Spinning. See **wool wheel.**

jet. Beadwork. Jet beads were originally made from a hard, black mineral similar to coal. Jet, considered a protection against witchcraft, was used for **rosary** beads. It wasn't until the nineteenth century that jet beads became popular for use in **bead embroidery.** The Victorians used jet almost exclusively in making tassels. Today, jet is a term loosely applied to any black, shiny bead with a faceted surface.

jet. Jet Carving. Jet is a variety of lignite coal formed chiefly of wood of the araucarian pine tree (similar to the monkey puzzle tree) that has been subjected to great heat and pressure without oxygen, thereby producing a carbonaceous substance—the same conditions that produce diamonds. It has a hardness of 2½−4, a specific gravity of 1.35, and a refractive index of 1.66. It occurs in beds and veins, and from its principal source in Whitby, England, it is mined from shale beds in the coastal waters and from the beaches and inland veins. It is found also in Colorado and Utah, and in Germany and Spain.

Jet is perfectly opaque, has a deep black color, accepts a high, lustrous polish, is tough, brittle, has an oily deposit on it, and is easily carved. Sometimes jet is called black amber; but jet is fossilized wood, often with visible growth rings, and amber is a resin, and jet is millions of years older than amber. They both become electrically charged when rubbed, and each is flammable, warm to the touch, and aromatic when sawn. Jet burns with a green flame when ignited. If scratched with an emery board a brown line should appear.

Rough **pebble jet** is dull gray except for fractures that reveal the black within. Rough **soft jet** and **hard jet** are usually covered with a hard yellow or blue skin of lias rock, the substance of the beds from which they are mined. The lias rock sometimes penetrates into the cracks of the jet, becoming an **inclusion;** the other inclusions found in jet are alum and quartz (**spar**).

jet bead. Jet Carving. See **bead-holding jig, bowdrill, lapstick** and **Jet Carving: Cutting.**

JET CARVING

Jet has been used since prehistoric times. Rings of jet were fashionable among the Romans and the Celts. During the Bronze Age, jet was used for talismans and as a trade material. Beautiful rings, beads, and other objects were produced with tools of bronze on the Yorkshire coast and were traded for gold and bronze to distant points of Europe.

The most famous jet is from Whitby, England, where for centuries the material has been mined and crafted. In the 1800s jet was machine-carved for the first time, speeding up production. Jet thus became an item of interest to wholesalers; soon the carvers could no longer take the time to obtain only the quality jet that good carving required, and the increased production forced the standards of craftsmanship down. Before long, inferior imitations and workmanship quenched the public's desire for jet. In the 1860s it celebrated a new popularity when the death of the Prince Consort required the women of upper classes to dress in mourning and black beads and tiaras were considered appropriate. The association of jet with mourning has remained, while other of its customary uses— banishing serpents, quieting barking dogs, and testing for virginity—seem to have passed out of vogue.

Jet was also used for cigar and cigarette holders, handles for various implements, boxes, and inlay, and because of the ease with which it is carved, it was a favorite material for portrait cameos.

TOOLS AND MATERIALS Exquisite carvings of jet have been executed with no more than a pen knife, but the addition of a few simple tools speeds the work.

Chinese white and colored china markers are used to outline designs. A twist drill or a **needle drill** with steel bits are sufficiently hard to drill jet. It is sawn with a jeweler's saw with a blade coarse enough to allow the jet dust to pass out of the kerf, instead of clogging it. Fine blades are too easily bent.

Files of various sizes and profiles, rifflers, a wood-carving knife, and **pumice pencils,** and the **bowdrill** are used for shaping. Fine detail can be added with gravers, wood chisels, an X-acto knife, and rolled abrasive paper.

A **lapstick, beeswax,** a **bead-holding jig,** a **bead-polishing board,** and **carpet underlay** are ways to hold the work stationary for different operations. Because of the brittleness of jet it cannot be held in a vise.

Polishing jet requires emery powder, **rottenstone,** jeweler's rouge or **crocus** powder, **tin oxide,** olive oil, **charcoal,** and chamois or flannel rags.

CUTTING Power tools should not be used with jet because the material does not respond to them, and because the flammable black dust that results could be ignited by electrical sparks.

Rough cutting of jet is done with a jeweler's saw with a fairly coarse blade, which is lubricated with water while working to reduce friction. When drilling jet with the twist drill, remove the bit from the hole and shake the powdered jet from the hole every so often; jet is an oily material and the heat caused by drilling can make this dust sticky, clogging the bit. It is therefore best to drill slowly. Always drill a piece before carving or polishing, as sometimes the kerf flakes near the edges, and this will save you the trouble of having to repeat either of these operations.

To make a jet bead, drill a hole halfway through from one side, then complete the hole by drilling from the opposite side.

If the piece has an **inclusion** in it, it will need special consideration. The mineral inclusions are harder than jet and demand different tools.

Jet may be faceted on a stationary lap.

POLISHING The traditional polish for jet is a paste of soft soap, water, and charcoal powder. Jet thrives on oil and grease; any sweet oil can be used as the medium for the polish compounds.

Although it may be unnecessarily coarse (in which case skip it), emery is used first, with olive or some other oil; next is rottenstone, jeweler's rouge, or tin oxide. The piece is then polished with only oil and finally with a clean piece of soft cloth or chamois.

Apply abrasives to a dampened bead-polishing board, using a clean piece of leather for each different abrasive. Use wide, sweeping motions to prevent the jet from overheating. Hold the piece carefully so as not to soften edges that are meant to stay sharp.

jeweler's anvil. Jewelry. See **bench anvil.**

jeweler's bench. Jewelry. See **bench.**

jeweler's coral. Coral Carving. See **coral.**

jeweler's file. Metalworking. See **file.**

jeweler's loupe. Jewelry. See **eye loupe.**

jeweler's rouge. Jewelry. Metalworking. Plastics. See **abrasive, polishing compound.**

jeweler's saw. Enameling. (Also called sawframe.) A C-shaped steel frame attached to a handle with a thin fine-toothed blade attached across it like the string on a bow. The saw is used to cut accurate shapes out of metal. If a cut is to be made inside a piece of work without touching an edge, a hole can be punched or drilled and the blade, unstrung, inserted, and then restrung. Beeswax is used to lubricate the blade.

jeweler's saw. Jewelry. See **sawframe.**

JEWELRY

The first article of clothing was probably not clothing at all but an adornment, the first form of jewelry. A feather in the hair or a white shell on a piece of vine was more than mere adornment to early man. It was a charm with mystical powers to ward off illness, promote fertility, or show wealth.

By the time of the Egyptian civilization, skills in the arts were highly developed; the Egyptians made superb jewelry, as did the Greeks and Romans. Certainly some of the greatest works of jewelry came out of these periods. Consider that they did not have saws with which to saw metal (metal was cut with chisels) or compressed gas in tanks with which to solder. On inspection we find that pure gold does things that no alloy can ever do, and that **soldering** with heat from charcoal and an oil lamp using a **blowpipe** produced incredible artifacts. Today we solder with a slightly oxidizing **flame,** but charcoal produced it automatically. We alloy solders to control the temperature at which they will flow; ancient craftspeople discovered natural alloys that melted at lower temperatures. We are constantly amazed that no solder seams show, but know they were soldered because through time the alloys in the gold solders disintegrated, leaving a film of pure gold. Their seams were superbly fitted and their skill almost unbelievable.

TOOLS AND MATERIALS For the beginning jeweler a basic tool kit can consist of the following.

   sawframe: 4″
   sawblades: one package each of sizes 2/0, 3/0, and 4/0
   ring clamp
   needle-point scriber
   tweezers: one pair
   hand file: bastard cut
   V-bar and clamp
   needle files: round, half-round, flat, square, and cross
   plastic emery stick
   steel rule: 6″ long marked in millimeters and inches
   ring sizer
   ring mandrel
   hand drill
   drills: several small ones ¹⁄₁₆″ or less in diameter

   carborundum paper: at least two sheets each of 280 and 400
   rawhide mallet: 1½″ face

For **soldering** the following equipment is needed:

   asbestos pad: two 12″ × 12″ × ½″
   charcoal block
   heating frame: 4″ × 4″
   carborundum pan with carborundum grains
   flux brush: round sable watercolor brush #8
   hard solder **flux:** green, one small bottle
   solder: one sheet or stick each of easy, medium, and hard
   soldering point
   iron binding wire: one spool each of 20-gauge and 18-gauge
   torch: propane soldering torch, canister type
   solder shears (**plate shears**)

For **pickling:**

   hotplate: electric, with one heating unit
   Sparex #2
   pyrex containers: one with lid to hold Sparex #2, and one to hold water, no lid necessary
   copper **pickling tong**s

For **buffing:**

   A **buffing machine** and two 4″ stitched muslin **buff**s

For **hand polishing:**

   felt polishing stick: two, ½″ or ¾″ wide
   Super Tripoli
   red rouge
   one bottle of sudsy household **ammonia**
   one toothbrush

It is also recommended to purchase round-nose **plier**s, flat-nose pliers, a **gauge wheel,** a **bezel pusher,** and a curved **burnisher.** A major purchase for the serious jewelry maker is a **flexible-shaft machine.**

The preceding list covers all the basic tools and materials necessary to create almost any jewelry form. As you work you can slowly acquire other tools, such as a **bracelet mandrel, circle cutter,** and a **dapping block** with **punch**es—tools that are specialized and expensive but wonderful to have. On the other hand, it is possible to make simple pieces of jewelry with no more than a design, the metal, a sawframe, sawblades, and carborundum paper or **emery paper** to create an emery paper finish.

The care and maintenance of tools is relatively simple. As the majority of tools are made of steel and can rust it is important to keep them dry, not only in storing them, but also by making sure that the metal you are working on is dry. When the metal comes out of the **pickle,** for example, it should first be rinsed and then dried before tools are used on it.

A light household oil can be applied to some tools that are not in constant use. A dapping block or a stake can be lightly wiped with oil, wrapped in an oil-impregnated rag, and then in a plastic food wrap and stored without danger of rust for a long time. Most **buffing machine**s have sealed bearings and need never be oiled, but other machines, such as the flexible shaft machine, need periodic oilings both of the motor and down the length of the flexible shaft. These tools come with directions for their care and maintenance. Most tools, however, should not be oiled because oil is undesirable on any tool that comes in contact with metal that will be soldered or colored, as cleanliness is of the utmost importance. Pickling will remove any oil or grease from metal that becomes contaminated. Files cannot be oiled, and they are particularly susceptible to rust. If you have a problem with them rusting in air, keep them in a small metal container just long enough to hold them and place a packet of silica gel in the container. Silica gel can be purchased in camera stores in small packets. It is used to protect camera equipment from rusting by pulling moisture out of the air in the container into itself, and it will work in the same manner for files. If rust does appear, remove it immediately with a **file card cleaner;** on other tools such as pliers, sawframes, steel rules, and ring sizers, use 0000 **steel wool** or very fine emery paper. Do not use the emery paper on the cutting edge of tools as it can destroy their sharpness. Repolish the tools with **tripoli,** except for the files, if you wish. They have to be washed with ammonia to remove the tripoli and then dried very thoroughly, or they will rust again. A hand-held hair dryer can be used on tools quickly and efficiently. A small amount of oil can be dabbed on the pivot points of tools such as pliers or **shears** to permit them to operate more smoothly.

SETTING UP A WORKSHOP   How you set up your workshop or studio depends on how much time you want to spend working, how much space is available, and how much money you want to spend. One of the advantages of making jewelry is that a tremendous amount can be accomplished in a small area. Good ventilation is of utmost importance to pull away fumes from **flux, pickle,** and **coloring** solutions. You need a good sturdy **bench.** Jeweler's benches can be purchased in a number of models but they are not inexpensive. It is not too difficult to construct one. Use two-by-fours for legs and supports, bolt and screw them together with white glue between the joints, and use either ½" plywood or ¾" particle board for the top surface. The most important factor is that it must not wiggle. If the bench can be attached to a wall, all the better.

Another important factor is light. The best light for the eyes is a combination of incandescent and fluorescent light, one of which can come from a freestanding lamp on the bench, the other from a general room light. The area at the back or side of the bench can be used to hang equipment so that it is within easy reach and yet off the surface of the bench. A sheet of plywood or 2½" × ¾" strips of #1 white pine, which has no knots, with finishing nails hammered in on which to hang hand tools can be attached to the wall; pegboard could also be used. **Hand polishing** causes little dust problem, but if you use a **buffing machine** the minimum protection you will need from dust is a **polishing hood.** It is best if the buffing machine is placed on a worktable away from the bench.

BASIC PROCEDURES   The basic techniques in jewelrymaking are **sawing, filing, soldering,** and **polishing.** A secondary list would include **piercing,** creating a **patina, coloring,** and many other techniques. The two most important technical things in the making of jewelry are support and cleanliness. These two items follow through all of the techniques. Make a sketch and plan the sequence of processes before beginning to make a piece. Work one step at a time. To facilitate explaining jewelrymaking procedures, a pin in silver with a sawn-out design that will be affixed to a **baseplate** by **sweat soldering** will be used as an example.

First decide which **gauge** metal is appropriate for the design. After deciding on the gauge, say 20-gauge, purchase enough metal for the top piece and the baseplate. The pin is going to be a flat disk, drawn freehand, and about 1¾" in diameter. Because the baseplate must be somewhat larger for sweat soldering, the piece of **sheet metal** should be 2" × 4". Transfer the design to the metal. Take a 3/0 **sawblade** which is the appropriate size for this work, and insert it in the **sawframe.** Saw the metal in half across; support the metal on the **bench pin** or the **v-bar and lamp** and then follow the curve. In this manner some extra metal will be saved.

Mark with the **automatic center punch** each area to be cut out, while supporting the metal on a **steel block.** Select a **hand drill** to make a hole large enough to insert the sawblade. Drill in all the marked areas; lubricate the drill with **beeswax** after each hole. A **flexible shaft machine** may also be used. After all of the areas are drilled out, support the metal on the bench pin once again and saw the areas out, sawing directly on the lines of the design. Clean up all of the sawn-out areas to perfect their contours, using the **needle file** that best fits each section of the contour. Now saw out the rest of the outside edge of the circular design. It has been left on until now to provide something more to hold on to while sawing. Remove the remains of the transferred design, depending on which method was used, and place the work in the heated **pickle** with **copper pickling tongs** to remove any grease from it in preparation for sweat soldering. After the piece is pickled, rinsed, and dried off, **flux** both sides of the metal, using the **flux brush** and resting the metal on a **heating frame** placed on a **carborundum pan.** The whole work should be resting on an **asbestos pad** to protect the **bench** from the flame while **fluxing** and later during soldering. After the piece is fluxed on both sides, apply medium **solder** that has just been cleaned with **carborundum paper** and cut into **pallions** with the **solder shears.** The pallions, too, are fluxed but left wet and placed in position on the back of the sawn-out design using the point of the flux brush to pick the solder pallions up. Use medium solder for this **joint** because the **findings** have to be soldered on later.

Using the **torch** and the correct **flame,** slowly heat the piece to dry out the flux on the solder pallions so they do not blow off, then heat the work quickly until the solder just flows. Turn off the torch and place the piece in the pickle with the pickling tongs. The baseplate, which should previously have been sawn out and is 1 mm larger all around than the piece just heated, is also placed in the pickle. The first disk is pickled to remove the flux and any **firescale** that has formed during heating and melting the solder, and the second to remove the grease. After both pieces are pickled clean, rinse them in water, dry them, and flux both sides of both pieces.

Place the baseplate on the heating frame. Place the top piece, with the sawn-out design, on top of it with the solder side down. Quickly heat both pieces and solder them together with the **soldering point** ready in case it is needed. Pickle, rinse, and dry. Saw off the extra millimeter of the baseplate as close as possible to the upper plate. Place the piece in the **ring clamp**, support it against the bench pin, and file off the rest of the metal with a flat **handfile** so that the edges of the top plate and the baseplate are level with each other. This causes the solder seam to completely disappear. Remove the piece from the ring clamp and smooth it with carborundum paper. This will remove any deeper scratches and any firescale that may still remain, although it is almost impossible to see at this point. Rinse the pin to remove any debris and dry it.

Now the **findings** must be soldered to the back of the pin. Because this is the second soldering, use easy solder, which flows at a lower temperature than the medium solder used previously. All the surfaces of the metal must again be completely fluxed. Solder the findings in position and then pickle. This time place the work on a **charcoal block** or directly on the asbestos pad for soldering, as the work might move if done on carborundum pan. After the work is again thoroughly pickled, rinsed, and dried, use carborundum paper on both surfaces to completely remove any firescale. Then use fine carborundum paper, rinse, and dry.

The baseplate can now be oxidized (oxidization) with **liver of sulfur** to turn the recessed areas black. The work can then be polished or left with an **emery paper finish.** If you are going to polish it with a **buff** on the **buffing machine,** use a **felt ring buff.** Because the surface of the ring buff and the pin are both flat, the ring buff cannot reach into the recesses and remove the liver of sulfur. In using either the buffing machine or **hand polishing** method, first use **Super Tripoli** to remove any scratches left by the finer carborundum paper, then wash it off using sudsy household **ammonia.** Rinse and dry. For the final polish, use a **red rouge cloth** or red rouge. The pinstem can then be inserted, with a **rivet** used to hold it in place, if that is the type of pinstem used, and finally the blackened areas can be coated with oil to deepen the color. The pin is then ready to be worn.

Making a pin such as the above utilizes all of the basic jewelry techniques except **bending,** which would be necessary in the **fabrication** of a piece such as a ring. In the case of a ring, the correct length of metal would be bent around a **ring mandrel** held in a **vise** and hammered over the mandrel using a **rawhide mallet.** The two ends of the metal come together when hammered with the rawhide mallet to make them flush, as the ring's roundness is unimportant at this point. The **seam** would be squeezed together with the fingers and sawn directly through, which would remove a little metal from each side. This is done while supporting the ring on a bench pin. When the joint is perfect, no light will show through it when it is squeezed

together. It is then bound with **iron binding wire** to hold the seam together for soldering. The ring is fluxed and soldered, the iron binding wire is removed, and the work pickled, rinsed, dried, and then slipped back on the ring mandrel and hammered round with the rawhide mallet. This procedure produces a plain band ring. At this point needle files could be used to create different forms in the metal. Also see **buffing compounds, drilling, polishing, transferring designs to metal.**

CLEANING AND MAINTENANCE It's a good idea to keep all finished work wrapped in a soft material such as flannel, tissue paper, or paper towels to prevent scratching. There is no tarnish produced on the surface of **fine gold,** or **karat** golds, except in 10K, which may slightly change color if left untouched for six months to a year; any color change that appears can be wiped off with the lightest of pressure. Silver forms a sulfide tarnish rather quickly unless it is worn continually. If it is wrapped, the tarnishing process slows down considerably. Some of the new liquid cleaners available commercially are quite good, but they will remove all oxidization, including **liver of sulfur,** which is really just a developed form of tarnish. Silver cleaners that come in paste form are not too good; they remove tarnish but some of them are slightly abrasive. Silver can also be cleaned by mixing a solution of baking soda and table salt with a little soap diluted in water in an old aluminum pan. Place the silver jewelry in the solution and bring it to a boil. Allow the work to stand for a few minutes and then rinse in water and dry. If the jewelry contains pearls, plastic, or soft gem stones such as opals or turquoise, this procedure is not possible as the material cannot withstand boiling. Re**polishing** is of course always possible. **Copper, brass,** and **bronze** can be lightly polished with a **red rouge cloth** to remove the discoloration that occurs rather quickly on the polished metal. However, in most instances the more copper, brass, and especially bronze oxidize, the more handsome they become.

SAFETY PRECAUTIONS Always pour acid slowly into water, never the reverse, as it can cause splattering, heavy fuming, and even an explosion. Running water and bicarbonate of soda should always be immediately available when using acids.

Pyrex containers are excellent for acid **pickle** because when acid is poured into water it generates heat. Because pickle works more efficiently when heated, pyrex is excellent from more than one point of view. **Sparex #2,** which works very efficiently as a pickle, lessens tremendously the dangers involved with liquid acids.

When preparing acid solutions for **pickling, etching,** or other techniques wear plastic goggles with plastic side panels to protect the eyes from splashing. This type of goggles is nearly always available at places that sell acids or liquid chemicals.

Acid fumes are harmful. Mixing pickle or etching solutions should be done in a well-ventilated room, preferably one with an exhaust fan. Containers in which acids are stored should be clearly marked and kept in a cool, dry place.

When disposing of acid solutions wear the protective plastic goggles. Slowly pour the solution down the drain while running the water. By pouring slowly and allowing the water to run during and for a while after disposal you will avoid damage to the drains.

Breathing fine dusts from **buffing** and **grinding** is unhealthy. If a buffing machine that has an exhaust fan and filters to trap the dust is used there is no problem. If not, a **polishing hood** that has a pan with water in the bottom of it is the next best thing. A face mask can be worn for additional protection when buffing. The respirator-type face mask should be marked "Approved by the United States Bureau of Mines." When grinding, always wear protective eyeglasses. When using a **flexible shaft machine** for grinding wear protective eyeglasses and a respirator, or at least a cotton scarf, folded double and worn like a bandit's mask with the ends tucked in at the neck of a buttoned shirt. Some people, although this is rare, are affected by buffing compounds and may develop a skin dermatitis, in which case a protective ointment may be necessary. See a doctor for advice. Keep clothing buttoned at the neck and at the sleeves to keep dust and metal fragments away from the skin.

Have a first-aid kit in the studio area that includes antiseptic, bandages, gauze, tape, and a burn ointment.

Squeeze cuts received while sawing until they bleed to remove any fine metal particles that may have entered the cut. Wash with soap and water, use antiseptic, and bandage. The same procedure is followed if injury is caused by a snapping **sawblade, needle file,** or other tools. If the puncture is deep, a tetanus shot or even stitches may be necessary.

Never use butter or grease on burns. Use an ointment that has been formulated for burns, or run cold water over or apply ice to the area. A recently discovered technique for burns referred to as a "pressure bandage" works extremely well for minor burns. Place a piece of tissue, paper towel, or any form of paper on the burn and wrap it as tightly as possible with tape. The pressure bandage must be applied right away. This bandage must be as tight as possible without cutting off circulation and left in place until the burning sensation stops, which may be anywhere from a few minutes to several hours. The tightness of the wrapping prevents the forming of liquids at the burned areas, consequently preventing blistering. When the wrapping is removed the skin may be quite red, depending on the severity of the burn, and will be sensitive. If the burn is severe, cover it with layers of gauze to keep the air from it and see a doctor.

To treat an acid burn, flush the area under running water immediately and use a neutral soap and water to alkalize the acid. If the burn is serious, apply a thick paste of bicarbonate of soda, wrap with gauze to keep air from the burn, and see a doctor.

If you get acid or any chemical in the eye, flush the eye immediately under tepid running water for at least 15 minutes. Do not apply anything other than water; substances that neutralize the acid, such as bicarbonate of soda, also produce chemical heat, which can be harmful to the eye. The eye will be red from the acid irritant and the water. If the eyeball aches see a doctor at once. If there is a delay apply 1 or 2 drops of castor oil to the eye.

jig. Jewelry. A device used to hold pieces of metal together in a tight joint in preparation for soldering. Some items that can be used as jigs are **iron binding wire, cotter pins, steel T-pins,** and **cross-locking tweezers.**

Also a guide or support for bending wire, usually made in a pattern. To make a jig, draw a design in a block of white pine. Drive finishing nails into the block of wood, along the edge of the design. Clip off the tops of the nails, leaving enough to accept the **gauge** of wire to be bent. The wire is bent along and around the pattern of the nails. Also see **soldering.**

jig. Metalworking. Plastics. Woodworking. Any of a variety of improvised or constructed holding devices to aid in the gluing or cutting of a number of similar pieces. Jigs are used to speed the process by indicating by a mark, block, or groove where a specific operation is to take place.

jigger. Ceramics. A machine used to mold **hollow ware.** The jigger squeezes clay between a profiled metal tool **template** and a revolving plaster mold. The **ware** is formed by throwing a **slab** of clay onto a revolving **mold** while a template is brought down by means of a pivoted arm onto the spinning clay, squeezing the clay up into the mold. The final step is cutting away the surplus clay. A mechanical technique used in large scale production. See ill.

Jigger

jiggering. Bookbinding. This term refers to the rocking movement used when **tooling** a line with a **pallet.**

jigsaw. Plastics. See **power saw.**

jigsaw. Woodworking. See **handsaw, power saw.**

jigsaw puzzle. Toys. A traditional **game** or toy that consists of a picture attached to a rigid backing that is then cut up into small parts to be reassembled. To make a homemade picture **puzzle** a drawing, photograph, print, or picture can be **glue**d to a backing of Masonite or wood. A magazine picture may be used, but sometimes the **adhesive** lets a color on the reverse side of the picture show through. **White glue** is painted to the backing wood which has been cut to the exact size of the picture being used, and the picture is placed on top, smoothed, and dried. It may need to be weighted if it tends to bubble or wrinkle.

After the glue is dry the puzzle is cut into **interlocking parts** with a jigsaw. It can then be reassembled. A **puzzle bag** of fabric, a large Manila envelope, or a box should be provided in which to store the puzzle parts.

Traditional puzzles, originally called **dissected puzzles**, included color pictures of historical events, scenic views, and well-known paintings. Some now have a picture on each side, making the assembly even more challenging. **Double-layer puzzles** or **inlay puzzles** are made especially for very small children. Puzzles range in complexity from thick wood ones of few shapes and simple colors for small children to large ones containing hundreds of small pieces, all similarly patterned. The appeal of puzzles is not limited to any age range.

jiki. Ceramics. The Japanese name for **porcelain.**

Job's Tears. Quilts. A **pieced** design of the four-pointed star sewn into a square **block.** It is a pattern that has been a favorite for almost two centuries. It was known by this name until 1825, when it became Slave Chain. When Texas was the issue of greatest political concern, the pattern name changed to Texas Tears. After the Civil War, Rocky Road to Kansas was used. It finally became Endless Chain.

The stars of the blocks are **set** together in rows so that diamond shapes emerge between the stars, giving a rich **all-over** design to the **quilt top.** See ill. Also see **Kansas Troubles, star patterns.**

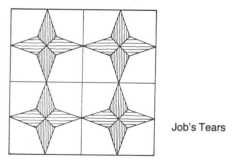

Job's Tears

jog. Bookbinding. (Also called knock up.) To align papers into compact piles from uneven bundles by gently tapping them on a level surface, **backs** first and then at the **head.**

Johnny jump-up. Toys. See **jack-in-the-box.**

Johnny-Round-the-Corner. Quilts. See **Rolling Stone.**

join. Batik and Tie-dye. A connection made between two threads in the **tritik** method of **tie-dye.** A join is needed if especially long lines of stitching are used or if a thread breaks and a new thread must be introduced. The new thread is knotted and inserted into the fabric three or four stitches back of the last stitch taken by the first thread. Several stitches are taken adjacent and parallel to the first stitches. The first thread must then be drawn tight and knotted before the stitching is continued with the new thread. If a thread is broken, several of the last stitches may have to be removed so that there is a thread end long enough to pull tight and knot.

join. Quilts. See **assemble, set.**

join. Stitchery. Toys. To fasten, combine, or connect two or more parts so that they remain connected. Papers can be joined through the use of **adhesives** or **pressure sensitive tapes. Fabrics** are joined with **iron-on adhesives, fabric glues,** or **seams.** Wood parts may be temporarily joined with **interlocking parts** as in jigsaw puzzles or **acrobats,** or they may be permanently set with wood glues, nails, screws, or epoxy resins.

join. Tatting. See **attach.**

joiner. Woodworking. Joinery is a subtrade in the larger occupation of cabinetmaking. The joiner makes or puts together **joint**s in the building of cabinets, furniture, or other **millwork.** The job requires a thorough familiarity with the basic woodworking joints and their combinations in order to select the best joint in terms of strength, the desired appearance, and the tools available. Also see **cabinetmaker.**

joinery. Woodworking. See **joiner.**

joining. Crochet. The joining together of separate pieces of a crocheted object with the **slip stitch (a, b.).** It is also the adding of a new strand of **yarn** or the changing of yarn colors, which is done as the last **yarn-over** when completing a **stitch (c, d.).** See ill.

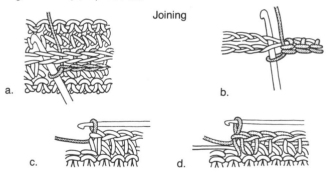

Joining

a. b. c. d.

joining. Kites. See **Kites: Construction.**

joining. Knitting. The process of adding on a new end of yarn to another. Yarn should be joined only at the beginning or cut the end of a row, to make the knotting and weaving-in of the two loose ends as unnoticeable as possible.

Joining is done by tying a fairly loose knot with the old and the new ends of yarn (leaving 3″ tails to be worked into the back of the fabric later) and continuing to knit according to the pattern. When the work is completed, the knot is

Joining

untied and woven into the edge, or the back of the work. See ill. Also see **splicing.**

joining. Lacemaking. In **bobbin lace,** when two areas of lacework need to be joined, a **sewing** is made. It is not done with needle and thread, but with the **bobbins.** In **needle lace, bars** are used to join the areas or sections together.

joining. Macramé. See **splicing.**

joining. Plastics. See **bonding, cementing** and **Plastics: Cementing.**

joining. Rugmaking. Weaving. The piecing together of premade or prewoven small sections to make a much larger item. It is done because the final item would have been too large, too cumbersome, or too heavy to make all in one, or because the craftsman is working on a narrow **rug backing** or a narrow **loom.** Joining is also done to shape garments or sculptural pieces. The point of joining can be invisible or inconspicuous, or a decorative, very visible, addition to the final piece, but the main point is that it must be strong enough to hold the joined pieces together.

If working on a rug backing, the joining can be done before the work begins on the bare backing, during the work in progress, or after individual sections are completed. All other techniques have to be joined after the sections are completed. Some edges to be joined are raw and must be either hemmed, overcast, or given some other machine or hand stitching finishing before joining.

Joining can be accomplished by overlapping and sewing through the joined pieces, piecing edge to edge with a variety of **lacing stitch**es or decorative stitches, or having an openwork joining as with a fagotting stitch. Another technique, such as crochet, can be inserted between the sections as a joining method. Decorative stitches range from very bold and rough textured ones to fine, delicate work, and can be as imaginative as the embroiderer's art allows.

Pieces to be joined usually are meant to be matched accurately. However, they can also be joined in a patchwork arrangement, or the design can be such that each piece is a different design unit, and while exact matching is not necessary, the design does not become a whole until attached to the other units. General directions for joining include the use of a large-eyed tapestry **needle,** or curved **rug needle,** to make stitching easier with thick yarn and heavy items. The joining yarn or thread should be strong, and when the stitch is invisible, **carpet warp, carpet thread,** or heavy-duty cotton thread should be used. **Braided rug**s can be joined with a rug lacer and lacing cord. The pieces should be anchored securely with heavy books or clamps during joining so that they do not shift and disturb the alignment. They can be pinned or basted together, which is particularly good for overlapping. Those backings that overlap should be matched precisely according to holes and threads. In joining edge-to-edge, it is wise to baste the edges that just meet to keep them from shifting as the final lacing stitch is put in. Also see **edging stitch, finishing, hemming, overcasting, piecing.**

joining canvas. Needlepoint. To join two pieces of **canvas,** trim a completed work with 1″ of unworked canvas showing. Turn back the raw edge on the sides to be joined and match up the canvas mesh. Using a strong button thread of the same color as the canvas, oversew the edge so that the **overcasting stitch**es are visible and the needle slants at an angle through the canvas mesh. By pulling the stitches tight in forming the next stitch, the vertical threads of canvas will merge together. It is important to remember to hold the folds together on the reverse side in order not to sew through them.

For a decorative joining stitch, use the **binding stitch.**

joining in. Basketry. (Also called piece-in.) To extend or splice together the used-up **reed, weaver,** or other material with a new length. Also see **Basketry: Woven Basket Construction, Plaited Basket Construction, Coiled Basket Construction.**

joint. Bookbinding. The hinging point, noticeable as a groove, between the **spine** and **board**s of a book and the body of a book.

joint. Jewelry. Any area where two or more pieces of metal come together, as in preparation for **soldering.** A joint is also referred to as a **seam,** solder seam, and solder joint. Good solder joints must fit perfectly. No light should show through any joint as solder will not fill gaps unless they are within thousandths of an inch tolerance. Sometimes gaps can be filled with excess applications of solder, but because solder will tarnish differently from the metal, these spots will eventually show.

Solder flows from being heated but it is capillary action that carries it along a joint. The best way to test for a joint is to hold it up to the light; if no light comes through it is perfect. To obtain perfect joints and to hold joints together for soldering, numerous methods and devices are used.

A joint is also a **finding** and is used as a flexible connecting unit or closure such as a **hinge** or a clasp. Also see **jig, machinist's scriber, soldering point, steel block, sweat soldering.**

joint. Puppets. Toys. A connection or link between parts of a figure where movement occurs. A **puppet** is usually **articulated** by the use of joints which are added in such a way that natural or human gestures can be suggested. In **puppetry, screw eye joint**s and **hinge joint**s are common.

In making **stuff**ed **toys** or **dolls,** lines of stitching may be sewn into the stuffed shapes. These **stitched joint**s are really simple hinge joints. Other dolls of wood, **composition,** or **bisque** commonly use **peg joint**s, **ball joint**s, **mortise-and-tenon joint**s, or **cord joint**s.

When parts of a figure are made separately and then connected, these points of connection are also called joints. Also see **animated figure, card marionette, elbow string, free joint.**

joint. Stained Glass. The places at which **lead came** with glass meets another piece of came with glass when a stained-glass project is put together. These joints can be made either at an angle or where the two pieces of came cross. There are two kinds of joints: lap joint and butt joint.

The lap joint is used for flat came only. The lead leaf that overlaps the lead that is to be joined must be opened wide at the joint. The joining came, which has been flattened with a hammer, is then slipped under the top and bottom leaf of the overlapping came (**a.**).

The butt joint, which is used for both flat and half-round lead, occurs where the two edges of the joining cames meet side by side. Horizontals should always join into verticals, so that the vertical remains one long piece. Care should be taken to allow for the overlap of the glass by the leaf of the vertical came (**b.**). See ill.

In mitering a butt joint, the cames are cut so that they meet at a diagonal. When lead panels are to be fixed into stonework the border leads should be mitered. Also see **copper foiling, copper tie, cutting lead, fitting, glazing** and **Stained Glass: Glazing.**

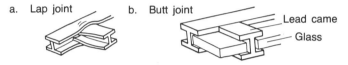

a. Lap joint   b. Butt joint   Lead came
                                      Glass

joint. Woodworking. The place where two or more pieces of wood are joined; also the type of fastening construction used. The basic types of joint are:

BUTT JOINT The simplest joint, in which the end of one board is butted against the face of another and fastened with **corrugated fastener**s, **nails**, **screws**, **dowel**s, or glue (**a.**). Because the strength of the joint comes only from the **fastener** used, the joint is relatively weak and is used where there is no sideways pressure.

LAP JOINT Two pieces of wood are crossed over each other and secured (**b.**). This can be an end-lap (the end of both boards), a cross-lap (the middles of both), or a middle-lap (the end of one and the middle of the other). The half-lap joint is a stronger variation; corresponding notches are cut halfway through each piece to accept and help hold the other.

MITER JOINT A type of butt joint in which the ends being joined are **bevel**ed or cut to corresponding angles before being fitted together and fastened like an ordinary butt joint (**c.**). Since there is more contact between the two boards, the miter is slightly stronger than the butt joint. It is usually used where it is undesirable to expose **end grain** (for aesthetic reasons, or, as in screen doors, for weather resistance) or where it is necessary to match molding patterns (as in picture frames).

BLOCKED JOINT An ordinary butt or miter joint strengthened with a small block of wood, often glued in place (**d.**).

RABBET JOINT A rectangular cut is made at the end of one board to receive the end of the other (**e.**). This provides a larger gluing surface for a stronger joint than the

butt joint; it is commonly used at the corners of drawers and boxes.

DADO JOINT Similar to the rabbet, except that the notch is cut at least an inch away from the end of the receiving board. Under pressure, the dado will prevent the sideways twisting or shifting of the joined pieces; it is a good joint for permanent shelves (**f.**).

MORTISE-AND-TENON JOINT One of the strongest joints. A **mortise** (a rectangular hole) is made in one board to ac-

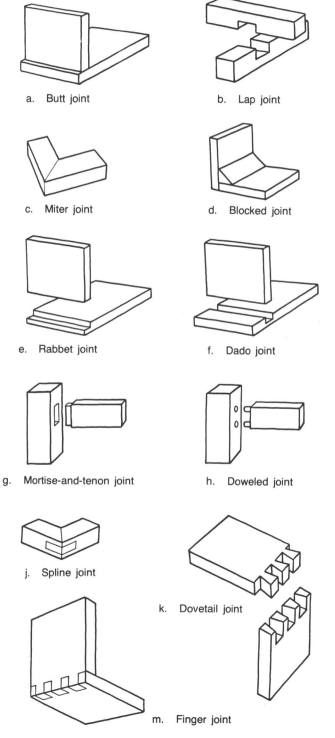

a. Butt joint   b. Lap joint

c. Miter joint   d. Blocked joint

e. Rabbet joint   f. Dado joint

g. Mortise-and-tenon joint   h. Doweled joint

j. Spline joint

k. Dovetail joint

m. Finger joint

cept the tenon (a corresponding tongue) on the end of the other. The two members are simply glued, sometimes pegged, together. When the tenon goes only partway through the other member and does not show, the result is a blind mortise-and-tenon joint. Both types are widely used in furniture (**g.**).

TONGUE-AND-GROOVE JOINT This is essentially an elongated mortise-and-tenon joint running the full length of parallel boards, each specially milled with a tongue on one edge and a groove on the other. It is used for flooring, paneling, and some furniture tops.

DOWELED JOINT This joint uses wooden pegs or **dowels** between the joined members for added strength (**h.**). Dowels may be used to reinforce almost any joint but are most commonly used with butt and miter joints, and for joining narrow parallel boards to make a wider panel. The dowels are usually pieces of **birch** or **maple** ¼–½″ in diameter and 2–36″ long. A **doweling jig** aids in placing and **drilling** the holes, and **centering pins** help to position the holes in the second piece after the first holes are drilled.

SPLINE JOINT Similar to the doweled joint in that both use an added piece of wood for reinforcement (**j.**). In this joint, both boards are grooved or mortised to accept a common tongue or spline of the same or stronger wood. The spline may be used with any number of joints, but it is used most commonly where a doweled joint would be used.

DOVETAIL JOINT A very strong joint used in building furniture and drawers (**k.**). The joint has interlocking teeth, often cut with a router. It consists of a series of grooves cut into the end of one board and a series of expanded teeth (shaped more or less like doves' tails) in the other; fitted together, they form an exceptionally strong joint, even without glue. The Shakers utilized this joint beautifully in their furniture.

FINGER JOINT Similar in appearance and function to the dovetail joint, except that the fingers are cut square, without taper, and therefore do not interlock as the dovetail does (**m.**). Consequently the joint is somewhat less strong. See ill. Also see **Woodworking: Jointing.**

jointed doll. Toys. A **doll** which has movable parts, allowing for changing positions of the arms and legs and sometimes of the head. An animated figure is a simple jointed doll. Either a **ball joint** or a **rivet joint** is commonly used on a **doll body**, although **pin joint**s and **mortise-and-tenon joint**s were used on very early dolls. For the cloth doll a joint may be made with lines of stitching called a **stitched joint**. The artist's **mannequin** is a jointed doll or an articulated figure.

jointed figure. Puppets. See **articulated puppet, card marionette.**

jointer. Woodworking. See **plane.**

jointing. Woodworking. The process of making a **joint**; a **joiner**'s work. Also see **Woodworking: Jointing.**

jolly. Ceramics. A machine used to mold **flatware**. It operates similar to a **jigger**.

Josephine knot. Macramé. (Also called Carrick bend) A graceful, pretzel-shaped knot.

Form a loop with the right-hand cord, overlapping on top and toward the left-hand cord (**a.**). Hold the loop in the left hand, resting the back of the hand firmly on top of the left-hand cord to hold it in place. The left-hand cord does all the tying.

Bring the end of the left-hand cord and put it over the right-hand cord below the loop (**b.**). Bring the left-hand cord under the right-hand cord above the loop (**c.**).

To finish, put the tying cord down through the loop, over the right-hand cord and under the left-hand cord from right to left, and out over the right-hand cord on the side of the loop (**d.**). Tighten the knot by carefully pulling out and down on both sides. The knot can also be tied in reverse (**e.**). When working a row of Josephine knots, alternate the tying directions to keep it from twisting. See ill.

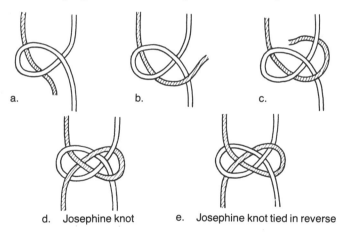

a.   b.   c.

d. Josephine knot   e. Josephine knot tied in reverse

Josephine knot. Tatting. A decorative element in tatting. This **knot** may be made on a single cord for a textured look, or on the **single thread** that joins **rings** and **chains** in a row of rings or chains.

The Josephine knot is composed of a number of **half hitch**es all done in the same direction. To work this knot, with one **shuttle** make a series of **left half hitch**es only, or a series of **right half hitch**es only.

To make a small Josephine knot, make three or four half hitches on the **knot bearer** and **close** the **loop** tightly to form the completed knot.

To make this knot another way, after the half hitches are done put the shuttle through the last loop formed by the **loop thread**, just before closing. This will make a lump or thick knot. See ill. Also see **Josephine picot.**

Josephine knots on thread separating rings, using one shuttle

Josephine picot. Tatting. A decorative **picot** in tatting, not used for joining purposes.

To make this picot, construct several **double stitch**es on the **knot bearer** with two shuttles to the place where the Josephine picot will be, and drop the knot-bearing shuttle. With the shuttle of the **loop thread,** make a series of either **left half hitch**es or **right half hitch**es, six to twelve depending on the size of the thread or picot, and **close.** Pick up the knot-bearing shuttle and continue tatting. See ill. Also see **Josephine knot.**

a.   Josephine picot knot closed   b.   Josephine picots on rings

Joseph's Coat. Quilts. (Also called Rainbow.) An **all-over** quilt design that uses bright-colored strips the length of the quilt. It is then sometimes bound in a pattern of diagonal strips of those same colors.

Another Joseph's Coat pattern is a **pieced** design of about 50 squares and triangles known as **Scrap Bag.** The name is derived from the **scrap-bag quilt,** which utilizes numerous scraps for the quilt design. See ill.

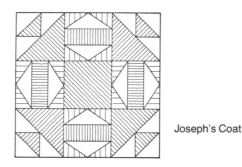

Joseph's Coat

journeyman. Under the medieval **guild** system, a practitioner of a trade or craft who, having served his time as an **apprentice** with a **master,** was entitled to work at his trade for a wage. The term comes from the Latin *diurnus* for "daily," referring to the fact that journeymen were paid on a daily basis. After two to seven years as a journeyman, a man could set up his own shop as a master, provided he had enough capital and could meet the requirements established by his guild. Such requirements sometimes included, especially in the later Middle Ages, the submitting of a completed **masterpiece** to the governors of the guild for their approval.

Judy. Puppets. A well-known character of the **Punch and Judy Show.** She is **Punch**'s wife. She was called Joan until the early 1800s and then became Judy. She has always nagged, squabbled, and behaved shrewishly. In most versions of the Punch and Judy **puppet theater,** she leaves Punch with the baby and later is the victim of his beating. Also see **Punch and Judy cast, stock character.**

Jumeau. Toys. A French family famous for **dollmaking** in the 1800s. Their best-known dolls, which are favored collectors' pieces, had beautifully made heads of **bisque** or porcelain.

jumper needles. Knitting. Special single-pointed, 18″ needles made of a flexible plastic with a disk end. They are used instead of **circular knitting needles** when extra length is needed. Also see **Knitting: Materials.**

jumping jack. Puppets. Toys. (Also called flap jack, Merry Jack, tumbler.) Either of two traditional **toys,** both of which are animated figures. One is the acrobat, or flap jack, which is manipulated by applying pressure and then relaxing it on two vertical sticks. The figure is suspended from **strings** between the two sticks and performs acrobatic stunts when operated (**a.**).

The other toy, also a traditional **folk toy** of uncertain origin, is sometimes also called the **pantin** or "jumping Tom." It is an **articulated toy** and consists of a **joint**ed, symmetrical figure. The arms and legs are attached to the body and also to strings. To manipulate the toy it is held or hung from above by a string; another string, attached to the arms and legs at a point behind the body, drops down below the figure. When it is pulled down it makes the arms and legs of the figure fly out and perform jerky erratic movements (**b.**). Animals, birds, people, or any other form can be assembled and set into action by this very simple procedure.

Elaborate versions are sometimes made of this toy, decorated and painted in intricate patterns of bright color. For these, thin wood is used and parts are jointed by using small brass screws with nuts to fit. The jumping jack is often a harlequin, or jester. See ill. Also see **athlete.**

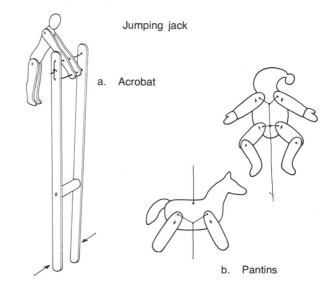

Jumping jack

a.   Acrobat

b.   Pantins

jump ring. Jewelry. A wire ring with the **joint** left unsoldered, used as a connecting device to hold units together or as part of a chain. Also see **finding.**

jump rope. Toys. (Also called skipping rope.) A length of rope about 2½ yards long held with one end in each hand and jumped over as it is swung over the head and then under the feet. Clothesline half-inch **manila rope** and synthetic rope all work well. A soft cotton rope will not do because it does not have enough weight to be swung.

Craftspeople have delighted in devising various kinds of handles for this ever-popular traditional **toy.** One involves sliding the rope through a hollow wood cylinder and knotting it at the outside edge. The wood handles are usually sanded smooth and painted. Padded hands and stuffed **doll** figures can also be used.

jute. Batik and Tie-dye. Stitchery. A glossy fiber from either of two East Indian plants. The jute fiber is used primarily for burlap, sacking, and twine. It is similar to **hemp,** and because of the textural appeal is sometimes used on large-scale stitchery or three-dimensional forms. The fibers can be dyed and may be used in **dyed-thread batik.**

jute. Knitting. Jute is made from **bast fiber** and is used in knitting; it works best in articles that call for strength and durability rather than softness or flexibility (for example, placemats or rugs).

jute. Macramé. A natural-fiber **cord** available in many weights and twists and a number of colors, it is an inexpensive material for macramé. Also see **Macramé: Tools and Materials.**

jute. Plastics. See **filler, reinforcing material.**

jute. Spinning. Weaving. A **bast fiber** of a woody plant cultivated in tropical countries of Asia and Africa. Bengal is the world market center. The plant can grow as high as 15 feet and the stalk produces 2 to 5 times as much fiber as the **flax** plant. At harvest time, the roots and foliage are removed from the stalks which are then treated like flax by rippling, retting, scutching, and **hackling.** The dry fibers are yellowish-brown, but can be bleached and dyed. They are glossy and tenacious, but brittle and easily disintegrated by water and moisture. Jute spins well, is inexpensive and used primarily in the manufacture of low-grade **twine** and **burlap.**

jute backing. Rugmaking. A **rug backing** imported in several different qualities from Germany and Scandinavia. It is made of very high quality **jute,** or of jute in combination with linen or some other fiber. In some cases, the jute fiber may not be present at all. The name "jute" seems to have been coined in reference more to a jute look or coloring (brownish-ochre) that the backing has, rather than to its actual fiber content. It comes in a variety of weaves and weights, with guidelines for **latch hook** or embroidered **rya** knots. It is available in a maximum width of 144″. It is porous, so that the threads can be shifted to allow the embroidery stitches or latch hook to be worked in any area. However, its weave structure is such that it prevents it from being a sleazy fabric.

Juvenile Drama. Puppets. (Also called Juvenile Theater.) The **toy theater** so popular in nineteenth-century England which used the printed **toy sheets** of flat figures or **"penny plain and tuppence colored"** figures. The sheets showed the characters of a particular play in full costume, and a copy of the drama usually accompanied the sheets. The most dramatic poses were used to characterize the actors who performed in the melodramas of abducted maidens and wicked uncles. Also see **Pollack's Toy Museum.**

Juvenile Theater. Puppets. See **Juvenile Drama.**

k

kachina doll. Toys. A figure used in ritual ceremony by the Hopi Indians. The kachinas are **mask**ed and painted Indians who impersonate any of hundreds of the spirits of earth and sky. The kachina dolls are replicas of these kachinas. Each **doll** is carved of cottonwood and decorated with brilliant paints and feathers.

kaleidorama. Toys. See **phenakistoscope.**

kaleidoscope. Toys. An early **optical toy** invented in 1815. An arrangement of reflective surfaces and loose colored glass pieces combine to form ever-changing symmetrical patterns as the cylinder of the **toy** is rotated. The **chromotrope,** which was developed later, is similar in design. The kaleidoscope was originally a toy for adults, but has since, because of its popularity, become a toy for children.

The kaleidoscope was probably based on the late eighteenth-century **debusscope.** Also see **teleidoscope** and **Toys: Optical Toys.**

Kaleidoscope. Quilts. An **all-over pieced quilt** pattern made up of **Maltese Cross block**s. When joined, the illusion is of a Maltese cross within a four-pointed star in a circle. If a quilt made of **Arkansas Traveler** blocks is compared with one of Kaleidoscope blocks, they will appear identical. They are simply different divisions of the larger pattern. Another variation of this design is **Spider Web.** See ill.

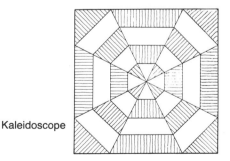

Kaleidoscope

kaleidoscope bargello. Needlepoint. See **Bargello: Patterns.**

kalem stitch. Needlepoint. (Also called reverse tent stitch.) A variation of the **knitting stitch** worked vertically rather than horizontally. It is often used for working rugs because it gives a tight backing. See ill.

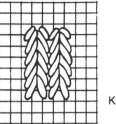

Kalem stitch

kangaroo skin. Leatherwork. **Hide** from the Australian kangaroo or wallaby.

Kansas Dugout. Quilts. An **all-over pattern** of octagonal and square shapes that interlock. Its name grew out of the hardships of pioneer life in the late 1800s.

Kansas Troubles. Quilts. A **block** of **pieced** triangular shapes. It is the same **sawtooth** pattern as the **Delectable Mountains** but does not follow that particular **set** of the blocks.

Set in another way, the block becomes an **Irish Puzzle.** When set in rows it may be call **Sawtooth,** although ordinarily "sawtooth" refers simply to a zigzag edge.

Among the other names attributed to variations of this pattern are Climbing Rose, Flying Dutchman, Forest Path, Indian Trail, North Wind, Old Maid's Ramble, Prickly Pear, Rambling Road, Rambling Rose, **Storm at Sea,** Tangled Tares, Weathervane, and Winding Walk.

Kansas Troubles is a name sometimes given to a completely different design identified also as **Job's Tears.** See ill.

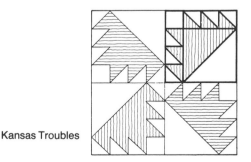

Kansas Troubles

kaolin. Ceramics. (Also called china clay.) Pure, white clay consisting largely of kaolinite. Kaolin can be either a sedimentary or residual clay. It has a low iron content and is used in making **porcelain** and white ware. It is a primary clay formed by the **weathering** of **feldspar** and tends to be coarse-grained and, therefore, low in **plasticity**. Ball clay is mixed with kaolin to increase its handling qualities. It is very **refractory** and must be combined with fluxes to lower its firing temperature. Deposits are found in the southeastern United States. Also see **Ceramics: Throwing.**

kaolinite. Ceramics. A mineral that is the principal ingredient in kaolin.

kaolwool blanket. Ceramics. A fibrous, lightweight silica blanket used for insulation in **kilns** that is now available commercially. One inch of blanket is equal to three layers of fire brick.

kapok. Stitchery. (Also called Java cotton.) A soft whitish **vegetable fiber**, silkier and finer than **cotton**, which comes from around the seeds of the tropical kapok (or silk-cotton) tree. It is available in **batts**, or by the pound, and is used to **stuff pillows** or mattresses. It is an inexpensive **filler**, although difficult to use, as the particles float so freely into the air when it is handled. At one time it was a common filler for stuffed animals, dolls, **quilts**, or **padding** of any kind. Because of its tendency to fly or spread when used, many dollmakers as well as stitchers prefer to use **Dacron polyester batting** or **cotton batting**.

karat. Jewelry. The unit of measure that indicates the amount of gold in an **alloy**. **Fine gold**, or pure gold, is 24 karat. Hence, one karat is $1/24$ part of the alloy. The jewelry term "karat" should not be confused with the gemcutting term "carat." Also see **buffing compound.**

Karvex. Jewelry. The trade name of a brittle blue **wax** that does not soften at body temperature because it has a plastic additive. It can be carved, sawed, and filed and is used to make **wax models** for **lost-wax casting.**

kawang. Batik and Tie-dye. A name given to a specific traditional Javanese **batik** design. It consists of ovals that represent the fruit and leaf of the kapok tree. The **motifs** appear in arrangements of four. This is one of the motifs that has carried over to the present from centuries ago. Also see **Batik and Tie-dye.**

kazoo. Toys. A simple musical instrument that children can make and play. It consists of a cardboard tube such as those found in paper towels or toilet tissue. One open end is covered with waxed paper or aluminum foil held in place by a **rubber band**. A hole is punched about 1″ from the paper-covered end and the would-be musician hums or sings into the opposite end. The paper vibrates to produce a buzzing sound.

Keco-Aid (Keystone). Batik and Tie-dye. See **acid dye.**

Keco-Direct. Batik and Tie-dye. See **direct dye.**

keel. Kites. A finlike surface attached at right angles to the main kite surface used to distribute the wind evenly onto both sides of the lifting surface. The keel acts as both a stabilizer and a rudder to direct the kite into the wind. Also see **delta-wing kite, dihedral angle, keel kite, spine.**

keel kite. Kites. For modern converts to the **delta-wing kite**, **keel** construction would appear to be an innovation, but the design has been used in the Far East for many centuries. The keel kite is basically a flat flying surface with a keel attached at right angles to the underside, along the center **spine**. Its function is to split the wind so that the wind works on both sides of the kite surface to stabilize the **lift** and direct the kite into the wind.

keeper. Leatherwork. See **belt finding.**

Ke Kahi O Kaiulani (Comb of Princess Kaiulani). Quilts. See **Hawaiian quilt.**

kelly. Toys. See **balance toy.**

kelp. Stained Glass. A specially prepared white **glass** made for **staining**. It is relatively expensive, but the results make it worthwhile.

kemp. Spinning. A very coarse, brittle **wool** found mostly in poorly bred cross-breeds. It is usually of inferior quality, discolored, and absorbs dye poorly.

Kensington outline stitch. Crewel. Embroidery. See **split stitch.**

Kensington stitch. Crewel. Embroidery. See **long and short stitch.**

Kentucky Coffin Quilt. Quilts. A unique and extraordinary **patchwork** and **appliqué quilt** made in 1825. The center of the quilt shows a large burial plot, surrounded by a picket fence and complete with gate and symbolic weeping willow trees. The plot is surrounded by **pieced blocks** of **LeMoyne Stars** alternated with prints. At the outside edge a picket-fence **border** outlines the quilt. Coffin shapes are appliquéd at three edges of the quilt, some embroidered with the name of a family member. As each member died his casket was removed from the edge and resewn onto the cemetery plot! Only four caskets are thus sewn and the rest remain at the edge. Apparently this memorial gesture was not carried on past the death of the quilter. This one-of-a-kind quilt is in the possession of the Kentucky Historical Society. Also see **memory quilt.**

Kentucky Flowerpot. Quilts. See **vase and urn pattern.**

kerf. Metalworking. Woodworking. The narrow section of wood or metal lost when cutting with a **saw** or **cutting torch**. Also the groove made by cutting. Be sure to allow for the kerf when planning precise cuts. Also see **kerfing.**

kerfing. Woodworking. The process of making a series of deep parallel cuts or **kerfs** on the back surface of a piece of wood. It is used to bend wood when **steaming** is impractical. The sharper the bend desired, the closer together the kerfs should be. After dry-bending wood by kerfing, the shape or curve must be held in position by a tension member or piece of wood, much as a bow needs a string.

To kerf, mark a series of evenly distributed parallel lines across the **grain** on the back of the board to be bent. With a **backsaw** or other saw, **cross-cut** most of the way through the board at each line. The closer the kerfs, the easier it will be to bend the wood. Slowly bend the wood; glue and assemble. See ill.

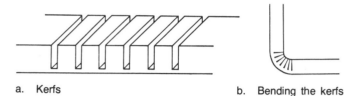

a. Kerfs   b. Bending the kerfs

kermes. Dyeing. See **cochineal.**

kern maidens. Toys. See **corn dollies.**

kettle cloth. Puppets. Stitchery. (Also called skillet cloth.) A part **cotton,** part **synthetic plain-weave** material which is commonly available in fabric shops. It has good **body,** a slightly uneven texture, and is often used in **banner**s, **panel**s, and **quilt**s. It is **piece-dye**d, and because the different **fiber**s accept the dye in different ways, there is a characteristic crisscross pattern of whitish threads mixed with the colored.

kettle stitch. Bookbinding. (Also called catch stitch.) The term "kettle stitch" is derived from the German word *kettenstitch*, meaning chain stitch. It is used to link the **section**s together when **sewing on tapes** or cords. It is executed at the **head** and **tail** of each section after the third section is sewn. See ill. Also see **sewing on cords.**

Kettle stitch

a.   b.

key. Jewelry. The bottom of the channel or lowered surface into which material will be **inlaid.** To key a surface use either a **scriber** or **graver** to make a group of channels.

key. Metalworking. Plastics. A protuberance and matching cavity on the interlocking edges of mold sections. Keys are used to assist proper alignment of pieces when the whole **piece mold** is assembled for **casting.**

key chisel. Metalworking. See **blacksmithing tools.**

keyhole saw. Woodworking. See **handsaw.**

Keystone. Batik and Tie-dye. See **household dye.**

key windup toy. Toys. See **clockwork toy, windup toy.**

kick. Glasswork. An indentation in the bottom of a glass bottle or glass vessel that reduces its capacity. Champagne bottles have a kick that makes the bottle strong enough to contain the gas pressure inside.

kick wheel. Ceramics. A foot-operated **potter's wheel** where the potter sits over the flywheel, which is operated or rotated with the sole of the foot. The main attributes of a good wheel are sturdy construction, good bearings, quietness, and comfort. A kick wheel is especially good for turning and many potters prefer it to a power wheel. See ill.

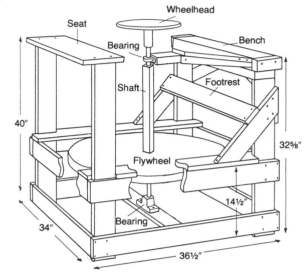

kid. Toys. The leather made from the skin of a young goat, or any imitation of it. Kid was once a popular material for making the bodies of **doll**s and **stuffed animal**s. Also see **leather doll** and **Toys: Dolls.**

kidderminster rug. Weaving. See **ingrain rug.**

kidskin. Leatherwork. Leather made from the whole skins of small animals, such as kid or young goat, generally used for shoe uppers, belts, and garments. Kidskin is thin, so during processing it is not pared or split into layers but processed as **suede.** Also see **glove leather, lining leather.**

kilim. Rugmaking. Weaving. A **flatweave rug** using **slit tapestry** techniques to affect color changes in its closely packed **filling.** Most traditional kilims are noted for being highly patterned with many changes of color going on simultaneously as each filling yarn weaves in its own area. Slits in a kilim are seldom sewn together since they are not very long, for the pattern changes so often, and the motif moves diagonally, or straight to the left or right. The earliest known kilim goes back to the days of ancient Troy. It was also familiar to the Egyptians and Persians, and is still much practiced around the world with the best examples coming from the nomad tribes of the Middle East, and the peasant weavers of Poland. Both are known for their beautiful colors and unique stylized designs, with the Middle Eastern ones being more ornate. The yarn used by the nomad weavers is much finer than that used in Poland, where a heavy **homespun** type of wool is preferred to give an irregularly textured surface. There are many spellings of kilim, with khilim being the next most common.

killed acid. Metalworking. See **cut acid.**

killed spirits. Metalworking. See **cut acid.**

Kilmarnock rug. Rugmaking. Weaving. See **ingrain rug.**

kiln. Ceramics. China and Glass Painting. A box of refractory bricks into which heath is introduced and controlled to fire clay bodies and **glaze**s. It is called an oven in the industry. The temperature is brought up slowly in firing to the required temperature and is then cooled slowly; usually the same amount of time is involved in heating as in cooling.

In china and glass painting various types of kilns may be used for **firing** china or glass to fuse the painted design into the background glaze. A muffle kiln, which has a special internal chamber for baking by slow firing, is often used. For firing glass a top-loading or front-loading kiln with an element in the door is used. Also see **bag wall, heat loss, heat storage, insulation, kiln furniture, muffle, thermal conductivity.**

kiln. Enameling. A small furnace that can maintain temperatures of 1500°–1800° F. It is used to fire enamels for which **torch firing** is inadequate. The kiln should reach a temperature of 1500° F in 45–90 minutes. Most are electric, operating on either one or two 110-volt lines, and should be connected to a separate fuse. The kiln is often made of refractory brick and has nichrome heating elements top and bottom. Keep debris away from these elements to avoid breakage. The kiln door may open in one of several directions and should be well insulated to prevent heat loss.

The infrared quartz lamp kiln heats up instantly when the door is shut. It has a tinted glass window for observation. Intense heat is generated so rapidly by the bulbs in the top of the kiln that the heat distribution suffers and an enameled piece may have to be rotated occasionally to insure even **firing**. Also see **binder, cleaning metal, firing fork, kiln wash, washing enamel** and **Enameling: Tools and Materials.**

kiln. Jewelry. A sophisticated heating oven capable of reaching very high temperatures. Kilns are used in jewelry techniques such as **niello, burnout** in preparation for **centrifugal casting, annealing** (in some instances), and enameling. Enameling and burnout for **casting** require separate kilns as the contamination from burnout can seriously contaminate enamels. Also see **lost-wax casting.**

kiln. Stained Glass. A refractory-lined furnace for **firing** stained glass. The heat source can be gas or electric. All glass must be preheated before firing and cooled down after firing.

The gas kiln employs a gas and air mixture run by an electrically driven motor. Its advantage is the saving of time and money. It is cheaper to build than an electric kiln and heats up faster, but it is not accurate in temperature control. Firing is done by eye, using an **inspection plug.**

The electric kiln most commonly used is an open kiln. It has three parts: the rack for trays that are to be fired; the firing chamber; and the **annealing chamber.** Like the gas kilns, it is designed to be fed trays of glass continually. The firing time is short and one tray follows another. The firing chamber has positions for more than one tray so that each can be moved independently. The kiln is made of firebrick threaded with electric elements to distribute heat as evenly as possible. The annealing chamber is a small, insulated, flat chamber above the firing chamber. It draws heat from the chamber below.

The other form of electric kiln is a closed kiln, similar to a ceramic kiln. It has one large firing chamber with a heavy firebrick door. Steel racks are built in to hold several trays. The kiln is set and fires in one even progression. Once the controls are set it theoretically does not have to be watched. The hardest glass should be placed in the hotter areas of the kiln and softer glass in the cooler areas. Also see **baffle, kiln tray.**

kiln drying. Woodworking. See **wood.**

kiln fuel. Ceramics. A **kiln** must be heated with a fuel or with electricity for firing ceramics; the kiln must be designed for the specific heating method to be used. In choosing the heating method, the potter must consider the economy and availability of various fuels, the flexibility and ease of control, and the relative cleanliness of the fuel.

Heat is produced when oxygen (O) combines with the carbon (C) and hydrogen (H) in the fuel, forming carbon dioxide (CO_2) and water vapor (H_2O). Other elements in the fuel produce other compounds that may not be as desirable.

The first ceramics were fired with twigs, leaves, and grass in pit firings, a method that is used to this day. The heat is not sufficient for high-fired ware, and the excess carbon blackens the pottery.

Wood gives a more controllable and hotter fire, and is still used, especially in Oriental **chambered kiln**s. The wood ash, in some cases, provides a glazelike finish (due to the **silica** it contains), but free ash in the kiln can damage glazes, making it necessary to use **muffle**s or **sagger**s to protect the glazes.

Coal, a relatively cheap fuel, was often used in early bottle kilns. Most coal contains impurities, especially **sulfur,** which injures **lead glaze**s.

Coke is a by-product of coal gas extracted from coal; its glowing, radiant heat makes it an excellent kiln fuel. Though scarce in recent years, it may become more available as coal-gas production is increased to meet the energy crisis.

Oil is relatively cheap and safe to store, but impurities such as sulfur, and the noxious fumes produced, must be accounted for in the kiln design and placement.

Manufactured gases (butane, coal gas, liquid petroleum gas, propane) are efficient fuels, but sulfur is a problem. In general, though, gas fuels burn more cleanly than oil. Bottled gas should always be stored outdoors, since the heavier-than-air gas can collect in explosive quantities indoors. In freezing temperatures, the pressure tends to fall in the tanks.

Natural gas, low in sulfur, burns cleaner than manufactured gas, and is a nearly ideal fuel.

kiln furniture. Ceramics. Pieces of refractory material placed in the **kiln** chamber to support ware while firing.

Kiln shelves are made of silicon carbide or a compacted high **alumina** clay. Silicon carbide is a refractory material that is **thermal shock** resistant, thermal conductive, and has minimal thermal expansion. Silicon carbide conducts electricity and is not a recommended shelf material for use in **electric kilns**. Shelves should be turned every few firings to correct bending due to repeated heating and cooling. A center post is necessary to prevent sagging and breaking of shelves 24″ and more. Kiln shelves are supported by props made of pieces of insulating brick.

A crank is a grooved stand used to space **tiles** and hold plates vertical during firing. Cranks are made of a coarse **grog**ged clay called crank mixture. Tiles can also be supported on saddles which are I-shaped bars. Setters are supports that follow the contours of irregular shaped ware.

A stilt has three arms, each about 2″ long, radiating from the center with a pin coming out of the top of each arm. Glazed ware is carefully placed on the pinpoints of the stilts. A stilt protects the glazed bottom of a pot from sticking to the kiln shelf during firing. Stilts can be used only a few times.

The spur is smaller than a stilt and has one point up and three points down on which pots are fired. Use several spurs for each pot and only when firing **earthenware.** Also see **heat storage, placing sand, thermal conductivity.**

kiln log. Ceramics. A record kept by the potter of firing conditions that registers length of **firing,** maturing temperature, oil or gas pressure, firing time, atmosphere, and damper positions. This log is useful in determining the optimum firing conditions of various clay bodies and **glazes.** Also see **pigment oxide.**

kiln shelves. Ceramics. See **kiln furniture.**

kiln trays. Stained Glass. All stained-glass **kilns** have removable trays made of a metal **angle-iron** holding an **asbestos** or steel sheet covered with a fine level layer of **whitening** that is dried out in the kiln. The glass rests directly on the trays, which slide in and out of the kiln. Glass pieces should be placed gently on the trays and pressed down slightly. The layer of whitening helps prevent the glass from sliding around and protects the tray from direct heat, lengthening its life. Glass of similar thickness should be kept on the same tray. Also see **Stained Glass: Setting Up a Workshop.**

kiln wash. Ceramics. A thin layer of **air-setting mortar** or heat retentive **refractory** material that is applied to the shelves to prevent glazed **ware** from sticking to the shelves. Also see **bat wash.**

kiln wash. Enameling. A chemical used to protect the floor and sides of the **kiln** from spilled molten **enamel.** Mix the dry powder with water to a thick consistency and brush onto the floor, walls, and shelves of the kiln. Apply three coats to new surfaces; one day per coat for drying. Enamel spills should be cleaned up with a metal scraper and the wash renewed. Also see **Enameling: Tools and Materials.**

kind. Basketry. Describes **stuff** that is pliable and easy to use, as opposed to **unkind,** stuff that is hard to use.

King David's Crown. Quilts. Either of two popular and well-known quilt designs. The first is a simple **pieced** four-pointed star. It is easy to construct and therefore often used. The other is a pieced **block** using over 40 squares and triangles of various sizes in a lively patterned design. See ill. Also see **star patterns.**

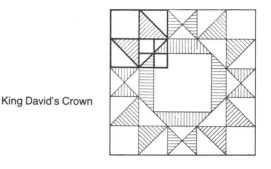

King David's Crown

king helmet. Shell Carving. (*Cassis tuberosa* Linn. Also called Sardonyx helmet.) A shell for cameo carving with a white exterior layer, a porcelaneous white **middle color,** and a light brown or buff **ground color.** Occasionally the ground color is a burnt orange. The king helmet is sometimes substituted for the black helmet, but has a tendency to separate. Also see **cowrie, helmet** and **Shell Carving: Shell, Tools and Preparations.**

king's coral. Coral Carving. See **coral.**

King's Crown. Quilts. The name given to several different designs for **pieced quilts.** All are made in squares. Also see **Coronation.**

king's water. Jewelry. See **aqua regia.**

kinora. Toys. An early form of the animated **peep show** into which three people could look at the same time. Made for home use with replacement reels, it was a small and more compact version of the mutascope, which was designed for public use. Also see **Toys: Optical Toys.**

kip. Leatherwork. (Also called kipskin.) The skin from intermediate sized cattle, such as a large calf or an undersized steer or horse. Kip is softer than **hide** leather. Also see **cattle hide** and **Leatherwork.**

kipskin. Leatherwork. See **kip.**

kistka. Batik and Tie-dye. Egg Decorating. A hand tool used in making **Pysanky** eggs. The tool, a special stylus that holds a small amount of hot **wax**, is drawn over the surface of the egg to make a line. A **tjanting** or a **brush** is often used in place of the kistka, the traditional Ukrainian tool.

kite. Kites. A kite is a structure with a relatively light-weight **framework** and a **covering** of material such as cloth or paper. It is designed to take advantage of the principles of **aerodynamics** to **lift** in the wind and remain aloft at the proper flying angle, tethered by a ground-controlled flying line.

KITES

Kites were flown in China more than two thousand years ago. For the people of the Orient, the kite has always been thought to possess certain spiritual and mystical powers. It served as a direct link to the heavens and as an expression of man's ability to exercise a kinship with the gods and nature. Very few holidays, births, seasons, or coming-of-age celebrations have ever passed in the Orient without the flying of kites. Even the practical use of kites has relied on a ritual base. Ancient stories tell of Oriental warlords sending up kites with noisemakers to frighten the enemy, or with lanterns to enlighten their own rebellious troops as to the divine importance of their cause.

Kite-flying eventually spread throughout the world. In Europe, the fervor surrounding the kite was every bit as intense as it was in the Orient, but the motivation was different. Western man began finding practical, rather than spiritual, uses for this new device.

During the eighteenth century, the West enjoyed something of a kite craze; kites became tools of meaningful inquiry. In June 1752, Benjamin Franklin raised a kite in a storm to prove his theory that lightning was electricity; his experiment also demonstrated the danger of launching a kite with a wire flying-line in a thunderstorm.

While Franklin's work may be the most noteworthy, it was by no means an isolated example of the use of kites for scientific inquiry. In the early 1800s, an Englishman named Pocock constructed a kite-drawn vehicle that he called the charlovant. With two kites and a carriage, he achieved a speed of 25 miles per hour.

Kites have been used for aerial photography, meteorological study, and atmospheric analysis. In 1901, the first transatlantic Marconi signal was received by an aerial attached to a kite.

The most important work done with kites had to do with learning about **aerodynamics** and its application to the construction, launching, and flying of the airplane. Alexander Graham Bell built his best kites with the hope of developing a powered aircraft. Lawrence Hargrave invented the **box kite** in his effort to create a kite that could carry a man. It was Hargrave's addition of vertical planes to the horizontal surface that led to the box kite, and cellular kite construction, and laid the basis of the early twentieth-century flight experiments of Alexander Graham Bell and his group. The Wright Brothers were kitesmen before they ever flew an airplane.

Aerial reconnaissance was another historical use of kites. Kite legends of the Orient tell of the warlords using kites to lift observers above battlegrounds for reconnaissance. Captain B. F. S. Baden-Powell, maker of the Marconi aerial kite, constructed several multiple-kite systems to carry observers above fighting lines during the Boer War.

As airplanes developed, kites became less frequently used as scientific tools. Western man has, in recent years, seen in kites what the people of the Far East have always seen—that the kite is a beautiful object, mystical and exciting.

TOOLS AND MATERIALS   A kite is very simple to build, and the materials are easy to come by; they are **wood**, either strips or doweling, for the framing; a material such as paper, cloth, or plastic for the **covering;** a simple **adhesive** or glue to hold everything together; and some **string** for the **guideline**, lashing, **bridling**, and flying.

A kite must have **lift** to remain in flight and must have stability to be controlled. Choose the lightest materials that will accommodate the degree of stress placed on your kite by the wind.

FRAMING MATERIALS   Most kites are built with wood framing, although some large, modern kites use aluminum struts.

Bamboo, used by Oriental kitemakers, is light, straight-grained, flexible, and very strong. Kite stores, such as Go Fly A Kite in New York City, have presplit bamboo for sale, or old bamboo rods or shades may be used. Use a sharp knife to split and scrape down the bamboo joints and the inside surface, and finish with fine sandpaper. Bamboo can be easily shaped or curved by soaking the strips overnight in water containing a small amount of ammonia and then bending and drying the strips around a form. Another shaping method is to heat the bamboo very carefully over a candle flame, moving it continuously to avoid overheating and burning it.

Most commercial kites use **spruce** strips for framing. Spruce is easy to work with, relatively strong, and sufficiently flexible for most kite designs. **Balsa,** softer than spruce, is generally too light and fragile for all but the smallest of kites.

Perhaps the best framing material for a medium-size kite of simple design is the doweling rod. Most lumber yards stock doweling in a range of diameters in standard lengths. Doweling is smooth, very strong, and easy to work with, although it is not as flexible as bamboo.

COVERING MATERIALS   Silk is about the oldest covering material for kites. Stronger than paper, tight enough in weave to provide adequate air resistance, and glorious to view, its only drawback is its cost.

Paper, the other traditional material, is much cheaper than silk and easily obtainable. The paper chosen should be strong enough to withstand normal kite-flying pressures. **Rice paper**, particularly the heavier grades, makes great kites, but even newspapers can be used.

More and more kites use plastic as a covering. Polyethelene and DuPont Mylar offer all kinds of imaginative opportunities for exciting kite construction. Plastics are light in weight, tough, easy to work with and repair, and have almost zero porosity (wind does not flow through plastic).

Perhaps the best kite covering material, certainly about the most popular for avid American kitemakers, is cloth. The preferred material is either cotton sailcloth or one of the new synthetics such as Zephyrlite, manufactured originally for the large spinnaker sails of America's racing yachts. These cloths handle easily, can be shaped to hold spars by seaming, are more durable than paper, and are fairly resistant to air.

White glue, available in most hardware stores, is an excellent bonding agent. If a plastic is to be used as a covering, any simple adhesive tape can be used to bond the edges or surfaces.

The only other material to consider is the **string**. A kite, hobby, or hardware store can supply fine cotton or linen thread suitable for the **guideline** on your kite covering. For **bridling** and flying, care should be taken to select a string strong enough to keep your kite in tow, but not heavy enough to create **drag**. Most good-quality string comes with a test strength to indicate its breaking point. As a general rule, your kite string should have a test strength equal to three times the square footage of the frontal area of the kite. Each kite will pull differently because of the way it is made, bridled, and flown, so no perfect guide to string strength can be given.

Very light thread, such as button thread, may be used for lashing the spar ends prior to **notching**. If a **tail** is needed to stabilize the kite, use a light line with crepe paper or small rags attached.

Tools for making kites include a good pair of scissors, a very sharp utility knife, a paper punch, cloth reinforcing rings to prevent tearing (or for cloth coverings, a grommeting machine with **grommet**s, or an eyeletter with **eyelet**s), pliers, sandpaper, and drawing equipment (pencil, ruler, and sometimes a compass). If the kite covering is to be decorated, you'll need paints and brushes. For a cloth covering, use either needle and thread or a sewing machine for seaming and hemming.

The kite workshop can be simply organized. All that is really needed is a worktable that is clean and large enough to spread out plans, and a cutting table. The only other requirement is adequate storage for your relatively fragile materials.

CONSTRUCTION **Balancing, joining,** the **guideline, covering, decorating, bridling, bowing,** and the **tail** are the elements of kite construction.

Balance. A kite must have balance if it is to remain aloft. Measure everything with extreme accuracy (mid-points must be exact); check the symmetry of each lateral **spar** by balancing it at mid-point on something like a knife blade to determine if extra trimming is in order. Check the final completed **framework** by resting the center **spine** lightly on your fingers to see if it balances or continually tips in one direction. It is easier to correct balancing errors in the workshop than in the field.

Joining. The function of the kite framework is to maintain kite surface rigidity in flight, and, for this to happen, the joints must be firmly secured. Because of the fragility of most framing material, however, normal joining techniques such as notching or grooving should be avoided. Joints must be overlapped rather than fitted. Overlapped joints can be greatly strengthened by wrapping or lashing them with strong but lightweight button thread. The best procedure is to carefully and accurately set the joint at the desired angle with white glue, and then, while the glue is still wet, secure the thread with a slip knot across the diagonal of the joint, and wrap it in crisscross fashion several times. The glue, which should seep up and around the thread, should be allowed to set undisturbed. Check the angle once again to be sure the wrapping has not shifted the sticks.

Guideline. Kites often need a guideline around the outer ends of the framework to provide a perimeter for the covering. Notched V-cuts in the sticks help hold the guideline in place. To avoid splitting the sticks during the notching operation, the stick ends should be lashed (prior to cutting) with fine thread about ¼" from the end.

Covering. Place the completed framework on top of the covering material. Using the framework as a pattern, cut the covering material, leaving about a 1" margin of material all around. Turn the margins over the guideline to check position. If desired, the covering is then decorated. When the decoration dries, the covering can be folded and creased around the guideline and glued or stitched in place.

Decorating. The great kites of the Orient were so elaborately decorated that decoration often dictated the design. Decoration is becoming more and more important to modern kitemakers. Coverings of paper and cloth can be painted with poster paints, watercolors, or felt tip pens, printed, stenciled, tie-dyed, batiked, etc.

Bridling. The bridle—the line that connects the kite to the flying **string**—may be attached when the covering is in place. Kites such as the diamond kite may be single- or double-leg bridled. The single bridle is attached to the center joint, holes are punched in the covering and the thread fed through (kites fly with the surface toward the flyer). Linen reinforcing rings should be glued around the holes to prevent tearing. The two-legged bridle is tied to the top and bottom of the vertical mast; the two strings should connect at a point just above the stress joint.

Bowing. Kites such as the diamond kite may be flown flat or bowed. Bowing provides a **dihedral angle,** which increases stability. To bow the kite, the two ends of the horizontal spar must be pulled toward each other to form a slightly convex outer kite surface. The depth of the bow should vary according to wind conditions—the heavier the wind, the more pronounced the bow. Bowed kites should be debowed when not in use.

Tail. A tail is mandatory for all flat kites, and may be required for some bowed versions. The tail provides stability for an otherwise fitful flying object. There are no real rules for kite tail construction, but it must be light. The tail should provide **drag**, not pounds. Crepe paper tails or string with crepe paper strips tied on will often do as well as the more traditional rag strip type. Good tail construction is the result of trial and error.

DESIGN   A quick look around the skies above a good kite-flying field on any fine windy day will tell you that the number of kite designs is practically unlimited. It would be almost impossible to cover all the variations.

The basic flat kite has many variations, both in shape (diamond, square, hexagon, etc.) and number of sticks used in the framing. The framework itself can be very elaborate, as long as it is flat.

The **diamond kite** (or "two-sticker," as it is sometimes called) seems to be the most popular. To construct one you need a vertical stick, or **mast,** and a slightly shorter horizontal stick, or **spar.** There are no set rules regarding the dimensions of spar and mast or their relative proportions, but you might try making the mast 3' long, and the spar 2½' wide. Flat **spruce** sticks (⅛" × ⅜") can be purchased in suitable lengths from some lumber yards, many hobby shops, and all kite-supply stores. Fairly stiff **bamboo** sticks or ⅜" doweling can also be used.

Notch the stick ends, then overlap the two sticks at a right angle about a quarter of the way down from the mast tip. Glue and lash the joint. Run a kite-string guideline through the notches at the stick ends. The **guideline** should be taut when secured, but not so tight as to warp the sticks.

Measure and cut the covering, decorate, fold around the guideline and glue or stitch it together. The horizontal spar should be placed closest to the paper with the vertical mast on top.

The **Eddy kite,** patented by an American, William Eddy, in the late nineteenth century, is as wide as it is tall; the horizontal **spar** is as long as the vertical **mast.** The spar crosses the mast about ⅕ of the way down. It uses **bowing** as an alternative to the tail for stabilizing flight.

The Eddy kite is easy to make. The crucial element is to cut the covering material (preferably cloth) to allow some pocketing around the sticks. The material, when wrapped around the **guideline**s, must have some slack. Keep in mind that bowing can place considerable stress on the horizontal spar, and that some reinforcing is advisable. A slightly shorter length of spruce framing material can be lashed to the midsection of the spar. The **bridle** is attached to the joint where the two sticks cross and to the vertical mast about a fifth of the way from the bottom. The Eddy kite should require no **tail.**

Another simple variation of the flat kite is the flat **hexagonal kite.** Three sticks (one horizontal and two diagonal) cross with the guideline at a point slightly above the center to form a six-sided framework. The horizontal can also be laid across the two verticals slightly above their point of intersection. This kite is bridled by attaching strings to the four ends of the diagonal sticks. The strings should meet at a point just above the crossing point. A long tail tied in the middle of a string attached to the lower ends of the diagonal sticks will stabilize the kite in flight.

In recent years the **delta-wing kite** has become extremely popular. As the name implies, it is triangular in shape, like the Greek letter delta (Δ). Fine delta-wing kites can be purchased from most hobby shops and kite stores, but you can build your own.

Plastics are often used as a covering for the delta wing, but the preferred material among experienced kitemakers is cloth; the lightweight, synthetic sailcloths are about the best of all. Doweling is about the best material for the spars.

Observe the indicated measurements as closely as possible. Once you have a feeling for the way the kite is made, there are practically no limitations to the sizes possible. To assure that both sides of the kite are equal in size, take a piece of cloth 36" high and fold the material in half vertically. Measure 39" from the center fold along the baseline and cut a diagonal line from that point to the top center. Unfold, and check your progress. You should have a triangle measuring 36" high and 78" wide. Refold the cloth exactly along the original fold line and sew a seam along the folded edge from tip to base, 1" from the outer edge of the fold. This forms a sleeve to hold the **spine,** or keel stick. The keel can be cut from a remnant of the cloth. The exact dimensions (after turning and hemming) and the precise angles of the cut are given in the diagram. To prevent raveling, hemming is recommended. If you have no protractor, remember, a 45° angle is a right angle folded in half, and a 30° angle is a right angle folded in thirds. Measure these two angles along the hemmed 28¾" baseline, leaving the remaining angle. Sew the hemmed keel to the keel sleeve, positioning the tip of the 45° angle 7½" from the very tip of the triangle.

Sleeves should now be sewn into the two leading edges of the wings to hold the side **spar**s (sometimes referred to as stiffeners, or battens). To construct a sleeve, fold over 1" of the entire leading edge on both sides of the tip, and seam the length. To keep the side spars from slipping too far forward, sew shut the sleeves 12" from the kite tip. The very tips of the outer kite edges may be trimmed back about 2" along the baseline if desired.

The lower end of both the spars and the keel stick may be drilled with a small hole to allow a small piece of string to be drawn through the cloth, the spars, and the spine to secure them in place. Should a spar break, you only have to cut the string, pull out the old stick, and slide in the new. Once drilled, the spars and spine may be slipped into their sleeves. For this particular kite, the recommended spine and spars are 36" long with 3/16" diameter doweling. Secure in place by threading a string through the cloth and hole.

Next, attach the cross spar. This stick keeps the kite wings outspread, and its placement is crucial. For this kite, the cross brace should connect with the outer spars at points 21" from the tip of the kite. Measure the distance along both edges, reinforce the spots with cloth reinforcing tape, and sink a metal **eyelet** through the sleeves at both points, about ½" from the outer edge.

The cross spar itself, 34" of 5/16" doweling, can be held in place with a variety of techniques (the connecting points are actually 32" apart, but the extra inch is needed at both ends to secure the rod). Small holes should be drilled 1" from each end of the rod. Stiff wire hooks may be bent through the holes and hooked through the eyelets to the outer spars. An alternative method is to thread small pieces of string through both the spar holes and the eyelets, and tie them in place. The best technique may be to tie one end with string and hook the other end with a wire hook. In this way you do not lose the rod because it is tied fast at one end, and you do not have to untie both pieces to roll up the kite, i.e., the hook is easier to undo than the string.

The last step is to insert the eyelets in the keel to take the flying line or bridle. Tape the lower corner of the keel with cloth reinforcing tape, and sink in two eyelets, one at the very corner of the keel and another about 2″ up along the leading edge. The two holes will give you the option of changing bridle positions if the wind requires it. When completed, the tip of the kite may be folded back about 1½″ along the keel line and sewn down.

Because the delta-wing kite is somewhat sensitive in terms of balance, it is important that the wings be of equal size and weight. If the kite fails to float on an even keel, small pieces of tape can be added to either wing tip to correct minor imbalances.

A single string through the eyelet hole in the keel will bridle and tether the kite. See ill.

FLIGHT Kites seem to fly best on slightly humid, breezy, warm summer days when warm-air thermals can come into play. You should select an open area like a park or a beach, or at least one as free of hazards as possible. Kites must never be flown near power lines, or close enough to roads or airfields to disturb or distract traffic.

To launch your kite you will need a kite line and some kind of stick, spool, or **reel** to let it out and take it in. All kinds of cord, twine, fishing line, synthetic string, etc., will do nicely, as will the kite string sold in most hobby shops. Never use any kind of metal wire or line for kite flying. To determine how strong the line must be, one simple rule of thumb is that the listed test strength in pounds should be equal to three times the total square footage of the frontal area of the kite. **Bridling,** wind force, etc., can make this rule invalid, but generally it works.

To let your string out, or take it in, anything from the crude stick to the most elaborate fishing reel rig can be used. The thing to keep in mind is that the larger the spool, the easier it is to take in the line. You can buy a kite reel or adapt something to a design of your own. The fishing reel mounted on a sturdy rod is ideal for it makes rewinding simple, and it gives you the extra reach of the pole's length for manipulating your kite in flight.

Kite launching can be very easy or very rough, depending on the winds, the flying area, and the size and design of your kite. Ideally, you should be able to get your kite airborne by standing with your back to the wind and tossing your kite upward and into the breeze. As it takes, let out the line, keeping slack to a minimum, and nudge it skyward with short, gentle tugs on the line. Do not run with

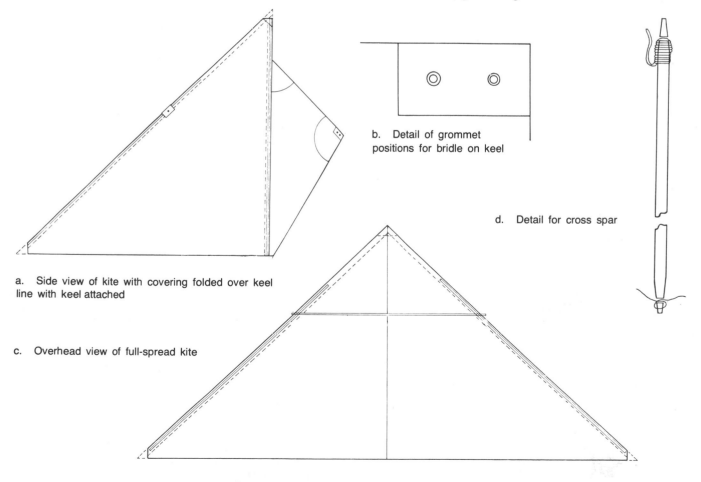

a. Side view of kite with covering folded over keel line with keel attached

b. Detail of grommet positions for bridle on keel

c. Overhead view of full-spread kite

d. Detail for cross spar

the kite. This could damage it, and it is bad form. In too light winds, it may be necessary to either prop the kite up on its tail or have someone hold it about 100' downwind and then let it go as you tug at the line with the first hint of a breeze.

Assuming your kite has the proper bridling, it should, once launched, remain aloft. Little tugs on the line, while the kite is at low levels, should further force it upward. If the flight seems jagged, it may be that your bridling system or the general balance of your kite is off. A flat flight can be caused by a bridle set too high; a top-heavy kite can be caused by a bridle set too low.

To bring the kite back home, you simply reel it in. The heavier the wind, the more you will have to play it in, like a game fish on a line, reeling in as it dives, and giving it some rope as it tries to climb. Looping must stop as the kite nears the ground or the kite will crash. If looping continues all the way down, it's best to have someone walk along the line and slowly draw it down with a gloved hand as you reel it in.

kittiscope. Toys. An early twentieth-century **optical toy** that was advertised as a "moving picture machine." It was made on the same principle as the **zoetrope**, although it was an extended version. Also see **Toys: Optical Toys.**

Kitty Corner. Quilts. See **Shoo-fly.**

klacker. Toys. See **Jacob's Ladder.**

Klyr Fyre. Enameling. See **binder.**

Klyr Fyre. Jewelry. A glue that when exposed to high heat completely volatizes, leaving no residue. It is used to hold objects temporarily in place while **soldering** and in **granulation.**

knapping. Stained Glass. See **faceting.**

kneading. Ceramics. A method of rolling and pressing clay that removes all air pockets and produces a dense, consistent **clay body** and increases **plasticity.** The clay is either rolled out with a **rolling pin** or pressed down by hand on a flat surface, such as a plaster slab. Also see **de-airing, wedging.**

knee string. Puppets. (Also called leg string.) The cord tied above the knee of a **marionette** by which the leg is **manipulate**d. The knee strings are attached to the **leg bar.** Also see **Puppets: Stringing the Marionette.**

knickknack. Toys. A small toy or trifle, usually more ornamental than useful. The term is sometimes used to refer to any **miniature** or tiny toy, especially of an animal or figure.

knife. Basketry. (Also called picking knife.) A sharp tool used to slice a reed or **willow rod** to a point or to **pick off** long ends of basketry material. Any sharp knife will do; however, blades that do not fold up are preferable. See ill.

Knife

knife. Papercrafts. Various types of knives are used in papercrafts, from a dull kitchen knife for **scoring** to sharp knives, such as a stencil, mat, and utility knives, for cutting.

To cut a straight line with a knife, a metal rule should be held firmly on the pencil line as a guide for the blade. The other hand, holding the knife lightly, pulls the blade on the pencil line, along the rule edge. If the knife is sharp, the paper will be cut with one stroke. For heavy cardboard, several strokes will have to be made along the same pencil line until the cardboard is cut. To cut a curved line, the knife is held in one place by one hand while the other hand moves the paper.

knife. Woodworking. See **whittling tool**s.

knife-edge pillow. Crewel. Embroidery. Needlepoint. A rectangular, square, or round pillow with back and front meeting at the edge with or without welting. Welting is recommended in needlepoint because it will conceal raw **canvas** edges. Also see **Crewel: Finishing, Needlepoint: Finishing.**

knit. Knitting. A single element interlooping vertically to form a knit fabric. **Plain knitting** is worked in the **garter stitch.** Also see **purl** and **knitting: Basic Procedures, Knit Movements.**

knit into stitch below. Knitting. (abbr. ksb) This is a stitch that creates a strong vertical line in knitting. One or more **throws** can be made by **purl**ing a stitch on either side of the stitch that is used when **knit**ting into the stitch below for an even more definite vertical line. Variation: k 2 tog, yo, ksb, yo, s 1, k 1, psso. Purl across this **row.** See ill.

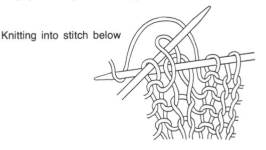

Knitting into stitch below

knitted. Rugmaking. Weaving. See **soumak.**

knitted lace. Knitting. Knitted lace has been called the perfection of the art of knitting. The repetitive use of the **yarn over** principle in lace patterns, coupled with small needles and very fine yarn, produces a very beautiful delicate lace fabric that often looks more complicated to knit than it is. Today there are dozens of lace stitch patterns to choose from, many of them quite old traditional designs, often with historical significance. Knitted sections or panels of lace can be successfully incorporated into other knitting stitches in wall hangings, sweaters, dresses, blouses, scarves, and more extensively, in shawls, curtains, bedspreads, and table coverings. Also see **faggot stitch, lace faggot stitch, Viennese lace.**

knitted lace. Lacemaking. Although knitting is usually thought of as a solid, tightly woven fabric, it can also have a lacy, open appearance. The designs of early knitted laces were imitations of the patterns for **bobbin lace** and **needle lace.**

During the nineteenth century, knitted edgings, doilies, and lacelike knitted shawls were done with what were called "fancy stitches"; they were a combination of small, dense areas with open areas created in the various stitches.

knitted rug. Rugmaking. Rugs made using two knitting needles and a ball of yarn. The rug can be a finished piece, strips or areas sewn together into a large rug, or a foundation onto which is sewn **knotted pile** or embroidery. The yarn used for a rug should be fairly heavy, both for speed in making and for a firm rug. This can be wool, cotton, synthetics, jute, twine, or even fabric strips. The needles should be a large size like a #7, #8, #9 (American size). A smaller size would make the stitch too fine and the knitting too tight. Needles made of wood come in large sizes and extra-large sizes. They are strong and well-suited to the job of holding the weight of a rug. Plastic needles can be used as long as they do not bend under the weight of the work. Designs can be knitted into a rug in the same way they are knitted into a sweater or socks. With heavy yarns, the patterns that work out best are geometric ones. The texture of a knitted rug is fairly even unless some interesting yarn enlivens it or various stitches are combined. The best shape for a knitted rug is a rectangle, square, or circle, since odd shapes may not hold their shape due to the tendency of knit fabrics to stretch. Hemming, binding, or lining a knitted rug are optional so that when the last stitch is finished nothing more is necessary and the rug is complete. Also see **shirred rug.**

KNITTING

The word "knit" is derived from the old English (Anglo-Saxon) word *Cnyttan*, meaning to form a fabric by the interlooping of successive series of loops of yarn or thread. (*Oxford Historic Principles*, 1973.) Knitting is a single-element technique and is defined by the process of pulling a loop through a loop, hence the classification of interlooping.

The origin of knitting is unknown; it is possible that it evolved in several areas. Many early fragments that appear to be knitted are not knitting but a single-element technique classified as crossed-looping. In this working process, the end of the yarn is passed through a loop of a previous row, generally with the aid of a single needle. The result resembles knitting.

The earliest extant piece of so-called knitting was found at Dura-Europos (an ancient city in Syria) and dates approximately A.D. 256; the crossed eastern stitch is used. Early sandal socks discovered in the tombs of the Copts

resemble knitting; they are probably done in the crossed-looping manner.

The discovery of a superb example of color knitting in Fostat, an ancient city on the site of Cairo, Egypt, provides a link in the evolution of color knitting. The fragment of deep-red silk on a ground of gold silk with its elaborate pattern was knit 36 stitches to the inch. Work of this caliber inspired the knitters of Spain and Italy during the twelfth through sixteenth centuries when **color knitting** reached perfection.

Before the introduction of silk in Europe, much knitting was done with wool, and in many cases felted for greater warmth and durability. With the advent of silk, cloths were knitted in elaborate designs that resembled brocade and embossed fabrics; gold and metal threads were often used to outline patterns.

The Tudor Period in England (1485–1603) was the Golden Age of knitting. Guilds were formed, and rigid standards set; only those who passed demanding examinations were admitted to these guilds. The apprenticeship was six years. The apprentice was given 13 weeks to complete a 5 × 6′ rug of intricate design, a woolen shirt, a beret, and a pair of woolen socks; the rug was probably worked on a knitting frame. Upon the approval of the guild, the apprentice was admitted as a master knitter.

Wherever knitting was introduced, it flourished. Colored knitting continued to be popular, and in the East, the colors used were particularly brilliant; an example of this is an eighteenth-century Persian sock which shows intricate bird patterns on the front, outlined in a gold metal thread and worked in chain embroidery. A nineteenth-century multicolored stocking from Asia Minor illustrates the use of color knitting in the entire sock including the heel. Such knitting is similar to the color knitting of mid-Europe and Scandinavia.

Shipwrecked sailors, according to tradition, brought color knitting to the people of Fair Isle during the time of the Spanish Armada. Meanwhile, in the Shetland Islands, lace knitting was developed into an art. Use of cobweb-thin, handspun wool produced the most intricate and delicate lace shawls imaginable. The Aran Islands, as well as the fishing ports and villages of Cornwall and Devon, made a tremendous contribution to the development of knitting. Each port produced a distinctly individual fisherman's sweater.

The careful study of the patterns used in shawls and sweaters will provide innumerable knitting stitches and motifs.

South America made essential contributions to the tradition of knitting. The work done during the Paracas and Nazca Periods (third century B.C.–third century A.D.) used the crossed loop construction. After the Spanish Conquest in the sixteenth century, knit clothing and bags became commodities which had great market value.

Knitting in colonial America was a craft of necessity; as needs changed, so did the style of knitting. Thus, the use of more color and more complex patterns came into being.

Bags and beaded knitting were a highly developed art during the nineteenth century. While lace knitting, used as trim for bedding, napery, towels, and clothing, reached a high artistic level.

Knitting in the twentieth century, aside from being a means of producing clothing and items for the home, is taking on a new dimension. It is now a recognized art form. It is being included in a well-rounded textile course as one of the many techniques for producing museum-quality textiles.

MATERIALS Knitting yarns are available in an extremely wide variety of colors, textures, and fibers, suitable for every kind of knit object. Yarns include **alpaca, angora,** camel hair, cotton yarns, **jute, linen, llama, metallic fiber, mohair, ramie,** rabbit hair, seine twine, silk, wool, **vicuña,** and **worsted.**

The choice of knitting needles is of the utmost importance. The shaft and the points must be smooth and the needles properly weighted. Knitting needles are made in a variety of materials, but the most readily obtainable are those of aluminum alloy and plastic. It is important to buy a leading brand that adheres to the standard gauge for all knitting needles. The size and length of straight or circular needles is a matter of personal choice. Knitting needles are made in steel, wood, bone, plastic, aluminum, and are single-pointed, double-pointed, circular, and jumper.

AMERICAN NEEDLE SIZES AND LENGTHS

Aluminum, single point, straight, 10 and 14″, #0−#15. double point, 7 and 10″, #0−#8.

Plastic, single or double point, straight, 10 and 14″, #1−#15.

Plastic, circular, 16″, #0−#10½.

Plastic **jumper needle**s, 18″, #5−#15; 24″, #0−#10½; 29″, #0−#15; 36″, #5−#15.

Wood, single point, 14″, #7, #9, #11, #13, #14, #15.

Needle sizes are based on English, American, Continental mm. (metric).

American	English	Continental
0000	16	1¼
000	15	1½
00	14	2
0	13	2¼
1	12	2½
2	11	3 or 2¾
3	10	3¼
4	9	3½
5	8	4
6	7	4½
7	6	5
8	5	5½
9	4	6
10	3	6½
10½	2	7
11	1	7½
12	0	8
13	00	8½
15	000	9
16	0000	9½

A cable stitch needle is used to hold **stitches in waiting** when turning a cable.

Use a crochet hook to pick up **dropped stitch**es.

Smooth rough spots on knitting needles with an emery board.

A needle **gauge** is necessary for circular or double pointed needles because these needles do not have the size imprinted upon them.

Measure the number of stitches in the width and the number of rows in the length to the inch with a measuring tape.

Protect the points of needles when not in use with rubber or cork needle guards.

Graph paper. A grid paper used for charting designs.

Notebook. For recording patterns, helpful hints, yarn sources.

Ring markers. Plastic rings which are used to separate areas in a pattern or to separate pattern repeats.

Stitch holder. A large safety-pinlike device for holding stitches waiting to be worked.

Yarn bobbins. Made of plastic to hold the different colors of yarn used in **Argyle, Florentine,** and **brocade knitting.**

Tapestry needles. Blunt pointed needles used for **Swiss darning, grafting,** and sewing finished pieces together.

KNITTING TERMS AND ABBREVIATIONS Although there are many terms and variations, knitting abbreviations are actually quite easy to understand—based either on **knit**ting (K) or **purl**ing (P). Necessary abbreviations are also usually listed at the beginning of most knitting patterns. Abbreviations are as follows:

For the knit stitch

knit	K
knit one	K 1
knit one behind (this movement will cross the stitch)	K 1 b
knit one (two throws)—to lengthen the stitch	K 1 (2 throws)
knit two together	K 2 tog
knit two together behind	K 2 tog b
slip one knit-wise	s 1 k-w
knit into stitch below	ksb
knit round	kr

For purl stitch

purl	P
purl one	P 1
purl one behind	P 1 b
purl one (two throws) to lengthen stitch	P 1 (2 throws)
purl two together	P 2 tog
purl two together behind	P 2 tog b
slip one purl-wise	s 1 p-w
purl into stitch below	psb
purl round	pr
casting off in pattern	COP
decrease (knit)	dec
left to right	K 2 tog
right to left	s 1 K 1 psso
decrease (purl)	dec

left to right	P 2 tog
right to left (purl reversed)	P rev.
increase (solid)	inc
left increase	l inc
make one increase (raised increase)	m 1 R
right increase	r inc
solid increase on knit side (bar increase)	m 1 bK
solid increase on purl side (bar increase)	m 1 bP
make **bobble**	m b
open increase (yarn over)	yo, O
pattern	pat
pass slip stitch over	psso
repeat * to * as many times as indicated	rep * to *
repeat directions within brackets as indicated	( ) × times
round knitting	rK
slip one (stitch)	s 1 (st)
slip stitch	sl st
stitch(es)	st(s)
stocking stitch (stockinette stitch)	ss
together	tog
yarn back	y b
yarn front	y f
yarn over (over) before or after a stitch	yo, O
yarn over reversed	yor, Or
yarn over two times	yo 2, O2

BASIC PROCEDURES Knitting begins with the act of **casting on** which creates the beginning **selvage.** There are many ways of casting on and each way produces a slightly different look to the selvage. Knitting is based on two movements, **knit**ting and **purl**ing. All other stitches are combinations and variations of these movements. A complete understanding of stitch movement will help to clear up a great deal of the misunderstanding concerning knitting. To learn how to look at a stitch, how to insert the needle, and take the stitch off the needle without twisting it (unless a **twisted stitch** is called for) is one of the most important points in knitting, and in many cases a subject not understood by knitters.

Knitting also involves the increasing and decreasing procedures to add stitches, or reduce stitches, as needed to create the myriad of knitting stitches and patterns. Increasing and decreasing are the determining factors in the shaping of garments and in controlling the width of a piece of knitting. There are a number of ways of increasing and decreasing and each method is important to understand. It is recommended that increasing and decreasing be given special attention by the knitter.

Casting off (binding off) is the final movement used to complete a piece of knitting. There are several methods and each method produces a smooth selvage, the appearance depending on the method used.

There are many ways to hold knitting needles, and each way is correct. The end result of knitting is the same, since the finished knitting does not depend on how the needles are held, but how the yarn is taken (or thrown) over the needle. A one-handed person can obtain the same result as the person who holds the needles in two hands. Two of the most familiar ways of holding the needles are the Continental (German) method with the yarn held in the left hand (an excellent way for the left-handed person) and the English (American) method, with the yarn in the right hand. The knowledgeable knitter will be proficient in both methods; the advantage is that in **color knitting,** one color can be held in the left hand, and the other color in the right hand for faster knitting.

Knitting in all of its ramifications is a most rewarding activity whether one is knitting a simple scarf, placemat, pillow cover, clothing, or a complicated wall hanging.

HOW TO KNIT Knit stitch uncrossed, English method. The needle with the cast-on stitches is in the left hand. Yarn is over the index finger and held by the little finger for **tension.** Insert the needle in the front of the stitch (**a.**). Take the yarn under and then over the right needle (**b.**). Pull the yarn through the loop to complete the stitch (**c.**). Slip the completed stitch off the needle (**d.**).

Purl stitch uncrossed, English method. The needle with cast on stitches is held in the left hand (**e.**). Yarn is over the index finger and held by the little finger for tension. Insert the needle in the front of the stitch (**f.**). Take the yarn behind the right needle and bring it to the front (**g.**). Pull the loop through to complete the stitch (**h., j.**). Slip the completed stitch off the needle (**k.**).

Knit stitch uncrossed, Continental (German) method. Insert the needle from front to back and with the point of

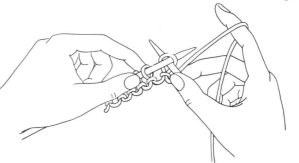

a. Correct positions of needles for knit stitch uncrossed (English method)

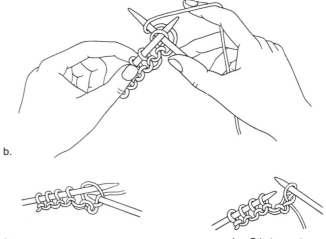

b.

c. d. Stitch made

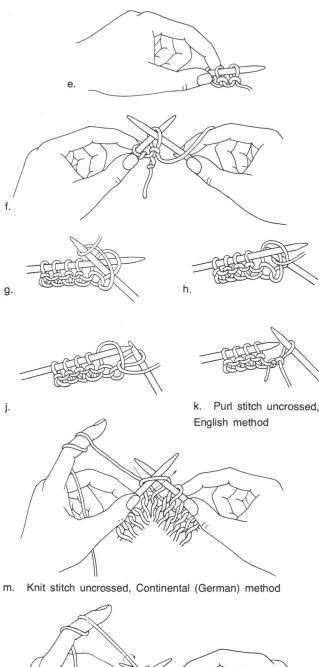

e.

f.

g.

h.

j.

k. Purl stitch uncrossed,
English method

m. Knit stitch uncrossed, Continental (German) method

n. Purl stitch uncrossed, Continental (German) method

the needle pull the yarn through the loop to make the stitch (**m.**).

Purl stitch uncrossed, Continental (German) method. Insert the right needle from the back to the front and with the point of the right needle catch the yarn over the needle and pull it through the needle to make the stitch (**n.**). See ill., pages 471–72.

KNIT MOVEMENTS All of the following stitch movements can be done holding the needles in either the English or Continental (German) manner. The knit stitch and the purl stitch uncrossed are the most common methods of knitting.

The knit stitch and purl stitch crossed are used for special effects. To make the knit stitch crossed insert the needle into the back of the stitch, right over left crossing (**a.**); the purl row is made in plain purl stitches. To make the purl stitch crossed insert the needle into the back of the stitch (**b.**); the knit row is worked in plain knitting.

Knit and purl stitch uncrossed eastern stitches are square in shape and used when a close firm fabric is needed. To make the knit stitch uncrossed eastern insert the needle into the back of the loop and take the yarn over the top of the needle (**c.**). The purl stitch uncrossed eastern is worked similarly except the yarn is pulled under the needle (**d.**).

The knit stitch and purl stitch crossed eastern is a very old method of knitting usually worked on hooked knitting needles. Work each knit and purl stitch from the front, left over right crossing (**e., f.**).

The knit stitch and purl stitch uncrossed (combined method) is a combination of western and eastern movements that produces a very even fabric. This is the best method to use when knitting with silk, cotton, linen, and wire. To work the knit stitch uncrossed eastern (combined method) insert the needle into the back of the stitch and throw the yarn under the needle (**g.**). To make the purl stitch uncrossed eastern insert the needle into the front of the stitch and throw the yarn over the needle (**h.**).

To make the knit stitch plaited (combined method) the needle is inserted into the front of the stitch, right over left cross (**j.**). Insert the needle into the back of the purl stitch to make the purl stitch plaited (combined method, left over right crossing) (**k.**). See ill. Also see **charting.**

a. Knit stitch crossed

b. Purl stitch crossed

c. Knit stitch uncrossed eastern

d. Purl stitch uncrossed eastern

e. Knit stitch crossed eastern

f. Purl stitch crossed eastern

g. Knit stitch uncrossed (combined method)

h. Purl stitch uncrossed (combined method)

j. Knit stitch plaited (combined method)

k. Purl stitch plaited (combined method)

CASTING ON This is the method by which stitches are formed on a knitting needle to begin a piece of work. There are several ways of casting on, each creating a different **tension.** The careful selection of method is important with regard to the use of the knitted item.

Cable casting on. A method of casting on similar to knitting on whereby the needle is inserted between, rather than through, the loops. If the first **row** is knit through the front, a decorative ropelike edge will be created (**a.**).

Continental casting on. Allow about ¾" of yarn per stitch when estimating how long the free end of yarn must be.

To cast on, make a slip knot and insert the needle (**b.**). Hold the needle in the right hand, the two ends of yarn between the third and fourth fingers (**c.**). With the thumb, pull the free end forward (**d.**). The ball end of yarn goes over the index finger. Pull the thumb forward (**e.**). Insert the needle through the loop and pull the yarn that is over the index finger through the loop (**f., g.**). Insert the thumb behind the free end and pull both fingers to complete the stitch (**h.**). Continue the seven-step procedure to the desired number of stiches.

Guernsey casting on. A special method of casting on that produces a knotted edge. Using the single casting on method, cast on two stitches (**j.**). Slip the first stitch over the second stitch (**k.**). *Cast on two more stitches, slip the second stitch over the first stitch* and repeat * to * for the desired number of stitches (**m.**). This method is used when knitting a traditional **Guernsey** design.

Invisible casting on. In this method of casting on, the object is to NOT create a definite **selvage.** This is achieved by laying the yarn around the needle and a foundation yarn cut slightly longer than the length of the needle (**n.**). When the knitting is finished, the foundation yarn can be withdrawn from the cast-on row, leaving a series of loops that can be used for **grafting** the knitting to a second piece of knit fabric.

Knitting on. A method of casting on using two needles. To cast on, place a slip knot on the left needle (**p.**), insert the right needle into the stitch, and knit one stitch (**q.**). Do not pull the loop off the left-hand needle, insert the right-hand needle into the new stitch front-to-back and remove right needle (**r.**), continue casting on until desired number of stitches are on the needle. For an edge with lots of stretch, insert the needle into the front of the stitch (**s.**). For a tight edge, insert the needle into the back of the stitch (**t.**).

Picot casting on. A method of forming an elaborate, scalloped selvage. Put a slip knot on the needle and **knit** on one stitch yarn forward (**u.**), S 1 p-w, K 1, psso, and turn (**v.**). Continue to work this stitch series until the number of loops on your needle is equal to the number of stitches required. Pick up and knit these loops, according to the pattern.

Round casting on. Casting on using three or more **double-pointed needle**s, one **circular needle,** as opposed to casting on using two single-pointed needles. This is the type of casting on that is done prior to beginning a piece of **circular knitting** (**w., x., y.**). Any method of casting on may be used.

Single casting on. The English method of casting on, using one needle and one end of yarn (**z.**). For a loose selvage, cast stitches on two needles using one end of yarn. See ill., pages 474–75.

INCREASING This knitting movement (abbr. inc) is made to add an extra stitch, or increase, to the row of knitting you are working. It is an important stitch movement for two reasons: first, it is used to widen a piece of knitting; and secondly, it serves as a pattern principle, especially in **faggot stitch** and **lace faggot stitch** designs. The methods of increasing are:

Bar increase. Knit into the front of the stitch (**a., b.**), then into the back of the same stitch (**c.**). In a row or section of purling, purl into the front of the stitch, then into the back of the same stitch.

Raised increase. Using the running thread between two stitches either on the front or the back of the knit fabric (**d.**). For an open stitch (visible increase) knit into the front of the stitch (**e.**); for a closed stitch (invisible increase) knit into the back of the stitch (**f.**)

Central increase. Either a double, bar, or raise increase made in the center of the knitting.

Double increase. This increase makes three stitches out of one existing stitch. K 1, P 1, K 1 into one stitch, or make a raised increase before and after the middle stitch.

Visible increase. This increase employs the **over principle,** bringing the yarn over either before or after working the stitch. This can be done in either the knit row or the purl row (**g., h.**).

Openwork increase. This increase uses the over principle as well. On the **row** following the first increase, do not twist the stitch when knitting or purling the over.

Lifted increase. To lift the loop of the stitch below into the process of increasing. In the **knit** row, knit the lifted loop, and then knit the original stitch (**j.**). In the **purl** row, follow the same procedure as for knit, but purl the stitches (**k.**). See ill., page 475.

DECREASING This is one of the most important stitch movements (abbr. dec) in knitting and serves two purposes; it is used to narrow the width of a piece of knitting, the old term for decreasing being narrowing. It also plays a vital part in the creation of patterns and is used extensively in the **faggot stitch** and **lace faggot stitch** designs. The methods of decreasing are:

Chain decrease. Work center stitch on top; s 2 kw, K 1, psso.

Double decrease-left. Knit—S 1, K 2 tog, psso. Purl—P 2 tog, return stitch to left needle, insert right needle into next stitch on left needle and bring over transferred stitch.

Double decrease-right. Knit—S 1, K 1, psso, return stitch to left needle, draw the next stitch over transferred stitch. Purl—S 1, P 1. Slip the stitch on the left needle purlwise and return it to the left needle (this will put the stitch in the correct direction for the decrease). Transfer the purled stitch to the left needle and pull the next stitch over the transferred stitch. Return the completed decrease to the right needle.

Mitre (A 45° angle). Decrease one side only after casting on two together at the beginning or end of row. Decrease at beginning and end of every other row.

Single decrease. Knit. left to right, S 1, K 1, psso (**a.**). right to left, K 2 tog (**b., c.**). K 2 tog b (**d., e.**).

Single decrease. Purl. P 2, S 1, psso. Purl 2, return stitch to left-hand needle (**f.**), insert right needle into next stitch and slip over transferred stitch (**g.**). See ill. (page 476) left to right, P 2 tog. P 2 tog b.

CASTING ON

a.   Cable casting on

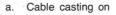

b.

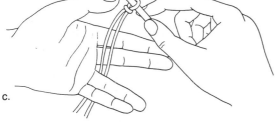

c.

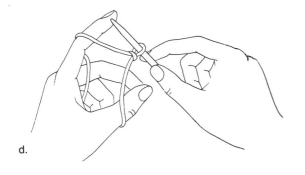

d.

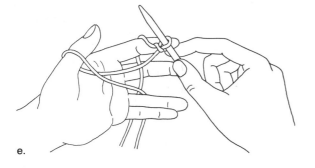

e.

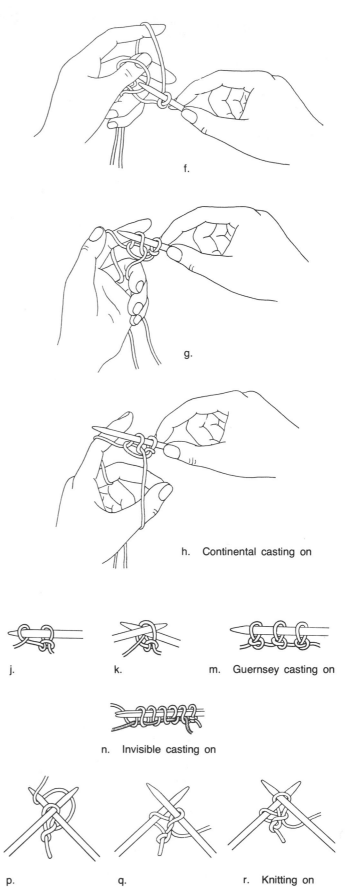

f.

g.

h.   Continental casting on

j.   k.   m.   Guernsey casting on

n.   Invisible casting on

p.   q.   r.   Knitting on

s. Knitting into the front of the stitch

t. Knitting into the back of the stitch

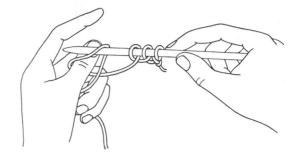

z. Single casting on, English method

u.

v. Picot casting on

INCREASING

a.

b. Bar increase, knit

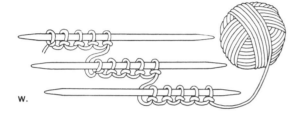

w.

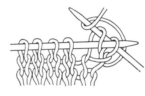

c. Bar increase, purl

d. Raised increase working method

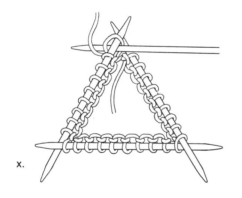

x.

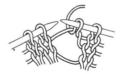

e. Visible raised increase

f. Invisible raised increase

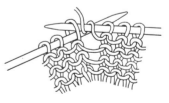

g. Visible increase, knit

h. Visible increase, purl

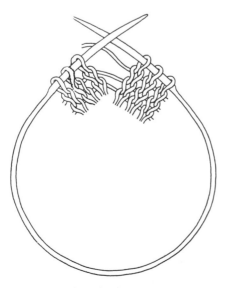

j. Lifted increase, knit

k. Lifted increase, purl

y. Round casting on

Single decrease, knit DECREASING (a–e)

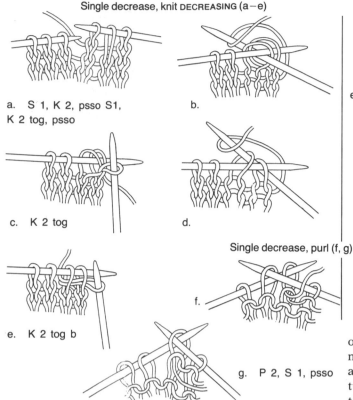

a. S 1, K 2, psso S1,
K 2 tog, psso

b.

c. K 2 tog

d.

e. K 2 tog b

Single decrease, purl (f, g)

f.

g.   P 2, S 1, psso

Single decrease cast off

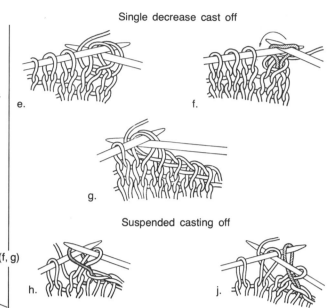

e.

f.

g.

Suspended casting off

h.

j.

Suspended casting off. Begin decreasing by casting off—do not slip the loop off the left-hand needle (**h.**). The next stitch is knit and the completed stitch is removed at the same time as the suspended stitch (**j.**). This leaves two stitches on the needle. Because of the suspended action, this method of casting off renders a loose selvage. See ill.

STITCHES AND PATTERNS

Garter stitch. Knitting every row on straight needles. Knit one round, purl round on circular needles.

Purl stitch. Inverted stocking stitch. Knit one row, purl one row.

Stocking stitch. Knit one row, purl one row on straight needles. Knit all rounds on circular needles.

Checked stitch. An arrangement of knit and purl stitches.

Even check. Cast on an even number of stitches.

Row 1–6: *K 6, P 6*, rep * to* across row.

Row 7–12: *P 6, K 6 *, rep * to * across row.

Repeat six row pattern until work is the desired length.

Broken check. Multiple of 5 stitches.

Row 1: *P 4, K 1*, rep * to *.

Row 2: *P 2, K 3*, rep * to *.

Row 3: *P 2, K 3*, rep * to *.

Row 4: *P 4, K 1*, rep * to *.

Row 5: K 5.

Moss stitch. Cast on an uneven number of stitches, *K 1, P 1*, rep * to * every row. If row ends K 1 the next will begin K 1 or vice versa.

Double moss stitch. Multiple of 4 stitches.

Row 1 and 2: *K 2, P 2*, rep * to * across row.

Row 3 and 4: *P 2, K 2*, rep * to * across row.

Plaited basket stitch. Cast on an even number of stitches, make stitch following the **one over one principle.**

Row 1: *Pass right hand needle behind first stitch, K second stitch, K first stitch * in usual manner. Repeat * to * across row, end K 1.

CASTING OFF The term used for the finishing row of a piece of knitting. As in casting on, care must be taken to maintain **tension** and to follow the **pattern.** To cast off, *K 2 tog (**a.**), pull the second stitch on the right-hand needle over the first (**b., c.**) *. Rep * to * across the row (**d.**), cut the yarn to about 4″ or more as needed, and pull the end through the final loop. Weave the end into the back side of the knit fabric along the edge. The same method is used on the purl row, with the stitches being purled.

Casting off in pattern. Casting off following the particular stitch pattern (i.e., **knit** the knit stitches, **purl** the purl stitches, and so on).

Single decrease cast off. A method of casting off where each stitch is worked twice. *K 2 tog (**e.**), transfer stitch to the left needle (**f.**) * being sure that the stitch is on the needle in the same direction as the other stitches, repeat * to * (**g.**).

Casting off

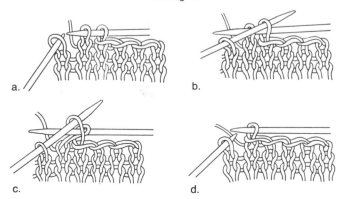

a.

b.

c.

d.

Row 2: *P second stitch, P first stitch *, rep * to * across row, end P 1.

Bias knitting. An increase and a decrease separated by several stitches. The increases and decreases are placed vertically each above its own kind. Several methods of increasing or decreasing may be used.

Right bias fabric:

Row 1: K 2 tog, K to last stitch, M 1 bK.

Row 2: K or P across row.

Left bias fabric:

Row 1: M 1 bK, knit to last 3 stitches, K 2 tog, work edge stitch.

Row 2: K or P across row. Repeat these two rows.

Spiral rib with bias areas. Multiple of 14 stitches, cast on three needles.

Row 1: *S 1, K 1, psso, K 7, m 1 bK, K 4*, rep * to *.

Row 2: K one round.

Double knitting. A double fabric knitted with two needles but with the cast-on edge closed. To make: * S 1, K 1* across row. The knit stitch is slipped in the next row.

Diamond pattern. Using the **half drop principle** two diagonal lines of stitches cross in opposite directions to produce a diamond pattern.

Dropped stitch pattern. Multiple of 10 sts plus 4.

Beginning row, do not repeat: K 2, * yo, K 10*, rep * to *, end yo, K 2.

Row 1, 3, and 5: P all stitches.

Row 2 and 4: K all stitches.

Row 6: K 2 * drop 1, K 5, yo, K 5 *, rep * to * end drop 1, K 2.

Row 7, 9, and 11: P.

Row 8 and 10: K.

Row 12: K 2 * yo, K 5, drop 1, K 5*, rep * to *, end yo, K 2.

Repeat rows 1 through 12 for pattern.

Eyelet patterns. The eyelet is the most ornamental and varied motif in knitting. The slant of the decreasing is very important in making the eyelet motif.

To make eyelet pattern: multiple of 4 sts plus 3.

Row 1: P.

Row 2: K 2, * yo, K 2 tog, K 2*, rep * to *, end yo, K 2 tog, K 3.

Row 3: P.

Row 4: K 4, * yo, K 2 tog, K 2*, rep * to *, end yo, K 2 tog, K 1, Repeat 4 rows for pattern.

The purse stitch is worked with an even number of stitches; *yo, P 2 tog*, rep * to * every row.

Lace patterns. The basis for knitted lace is the **over** and carefully planned decreasing.

Minileaf pattern. Multiple of 6 stitches plus 2 sts. over.

Row 1: K 1, *K 3, yo, K 3 tog, yo*, repeat * to *, ending with K 1.

Row 2 and 4: Purl.

Row 3: K 1, *yo, K 3 tog, you, K 3*, repeat * to *, ending with K 1.

Old shale and Shetland lace patterns. Multiple of 11 sts.

Row 1: *k 2 tog, you, K 1, yo, K 1, yo, K 1, you, K 2 tog, K 2 tog*, repeat * to *.

Row 2: Purl.

Row 3 and 4: Knit.

Brioche stitch. Multiple of 2 sts.

Row 1: This is the back of the fabric and the first row only. *yo, S 1 p-w, K 1*, repeat * to *.

Row 2: *yo, S 1 p-w, K 2 tog*, repeat * to *. Repeat row 2 to desired length. Knit one row and cast off.

Ribbed patterns. A combination of knitting and purling. Cast on an even number of stitches. To make a one and one rib, *K 1, P 1*, rep * to * every row. To make a four and four rib, * K 4, P 4*, rep * to * every row.

Uneven ribbing. Cast on uneven number of stitches.

Row 1: *K 3, P 2*, rep * to * across row.

Row 2: *K 2, P 3*, rep * to * across row.

Ribbed pleating. Multiple of 15 stitches.

Row 1: *K 4, P 1, K 1, P 1, K 1, P 1, K 1, P 5* rep * to *.

Row 2: *K 5, P 1, K 1, P 1, K 1, P 1, K 1, P 4* rep * to *.

Broken ribbing. Multiple of 6 stitches.

Row (odd): *K 6, P 6*, rep * to *.

Row (even): *P 6, K 6*, rep * to *.

Welt patterns. Patterns of horizontal ridges made by combinations of knit and purl rows worked on any number of stitches.

Three and two welt. Multiple of 5 stitches.

Row 1, 4, 7, 8, 10: K.

Row 2, 3, 5, 6, 9: P.

Two and two welt. Multiple of 4 stitches.

Row 1 and 4: P.

Row 2 and 3: K.

Ribbed welt. Any number of stitches.

Row 1, 7, 9: *K 4, P 4 *, rep * to *, end K 2.

Row 2, 8: *P 4, K 4 *, rep * to *, end K 2.

Rows 4, 6, 11: K.

Row 5, 10, 12: P.

Repeat 12 rows for pattern, bind off on either Row 3 or Row 9.

Irregular welt. Multiple of 10 plus 2.

Row 1: K.

Row 2: *K 2, P 2, K 6, P 2*, rep * to *.

Row 3: *K 2, P 6, K 2, P 2*, rep * to *.

Row 4: *K 2, P 8, K 2*, rep * to *.

Row 5: *P 2, K 8, P 2*, rep * to *.

Repeat 5 rows for pattern.

The **bobble** is an embossed motif based on increasing stitches within one stitch and working them back and forth to the desired size before knitting all increased stitches together to make the original stitch. There is no set number of stitches in a bobble but three stitches are the usual number.

Detached oval cluster. A motif that is based on one stitch and completed within that stitch. Based on five stitches.

Row 1: Use one stitch as base (K 1, yo, K 1, yo, K 1)

Row 2: P 5.

Row 3: S 1, K 4.

Row 4: S 1, P 4.

Row 5: S 1, K 4.

Row 6: P 2 tog, P 1, P rev.

Row 7: S 1, K 2 tog, psso.

Bell motif. 8 stitches plus 2.

Row 1: P 1, *turn work and cast on by knitting 8 stitches, turn work* P 1.

Row 2: K 1, * purl into the back of the next 8 stitches *, K 1.

Row 3: P 1, * S 1, K 1, psso, K 4, K 2 tog,* P 1.

Row 4: K 1, * P 6 * K 1.

Row 5: P 1, *S 1, K 1, psso, K 2, K 2 tog,* P 1.

Row 6: K 1, *P 4* K 1.

Row 7: P 1, *S 1, K 1, psso, K 2 tog,* P 1.

Row 8: K 1, *P 2* K 1.

Row 9: P 1, *S 1, K 1, psso* P 1.

Row 10: K 2 tog, K 1. This includes one stitch in the bell pattern and one of the background stitches so that the stitch count will be back to the original number before **casting-on.**

Clustering. Three or more stitches are knitted onto a separate needle. Either the working yarn or a separate color is wrapped around the stitches several times before transferring them to the right needle before continuing the pattern.

Looped knitting. A series of loops created by wrapping the yarn once or more around a measuring device. The loops formed are then worked into the fabric by including them into the actual stitch when knitted.

Medallions. Medallion knitting can be worked on two, four, five, or six needles.

Square medallion on four needles. Cast on two stitches on each of four needles (8 stitches).

Round 1: Knit into the back of each stitch.

  2: M 1 R, K into every stitch.

  3: Knit a round. (All odd number rows knit.)

  4: M 1 R, K at the beginning and end of each needle for one round. Continue rows 3 and 4 to desired size. Cast off. Variations may be made by embossed knitting, detached knots, and clustering.

Circular on two needles. Cast 12 stitches on two needles using the **invisible cast-on.** Work medallion in **stocking stitch.**

Row 1: Knit all odd number rows.

Row 2: Purl. Turn leave 2 stitches.

Row 4: Purl. Turn leave 4 sts.

Row 6: Purl. Turn leave 6 sts.

Row 8: Purl. Turn leave 8 sts.

Row 10 thru 12: Purl. Repeat from Row 1, until medallion is completed.

Also see **brocade knitting, chevron knitting, lace faggot stitch, picot eyelet, picot knot, Tunisian knitting, horizontal, Tunisian knitting, oblique, turning.**

knitting on. Knitting. See **Knitting: Casting On.**

knitting sheath. Knitting. An implement similar in shape to a miniature sword sheath that can be tucked into a belt or rested on the hip to hold a knitting needle steady. By using the knitting sheath to support the needle, the fingers of that hand are left free to manipulate the yarn. This method is rather old, and not generally in use today. Traditi—ally, knitting sheaths were elaborate in design and were often given as special presents.

knitting stitch. Needlepoint. (Also called reverse tent stitch.) This stitch looks very much like knitting and can be worked in horizontal rows. It makes an attractive, tight background, but takes a long time to work up. See ill. Also see **kalem stitch.**

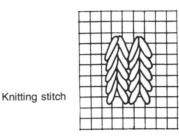

Knitting stitch

knitting stitch. Rugmaking. A closely compacted stitch that covers the **rug backing** extremely well. It is also known as a knit or soumak stitch, in that it has the herringbone rib of a knitted fabric and, to a lesser extent, that of a traditional Near Eastern woven **soumak** rug. It is a diagonal stitch that can be worked either horizontally or vertically. On a **canvas mesh** backing the stitch is worked as follows: bring needle from back to front and insert front to back in the first hole above and to the right; emerge through the hole directly below; to get the herringbone effect, move from right to left in the next row. The stitch can be made much larger by working over more threads. See ill.

Knitting stitch

knitting up. Knitting. (Also called picking up stitches.) The knitting-up process can be used to change the angle of the knitting in making **gussets** in socks or sweaters. Hold the work facing you, and pick up as many stitches as are necessary. See ill.

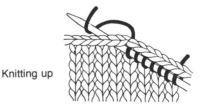

Knitting up

knitting with beads. Beadwork. The technique of combining beads with knitting in which beads are threaded onto yarn, pushed against the back of the needle, and stitched in place with a stitch of knitting. Also see **threading beads.**

knitting yarn. Crewel. Needlepoint. A multi-ply, softly twisted **yarn** generally used in knitting. In needlework it can be used for a soft, raised texture.

knit together double. Knitting. A method of decreasing used to create decorative effects, to end **mitred** knitting, or whenever there are three stitches to be cast off. Also see **Knitting: Decreasing.**

knit together simple. Knitting. (abbr. K tog) This procedure is used for decreasing, with **overs** for **faggot stitch** and **lace faggot** knitting. Also see **Knitting: Decreasing.**

knob. Ceramics. See **Ceramics: Form.**

knocking down. Bookbinding. Flattening the threads and embedding them in the paper of the **back** of a book by hammering in order to reduce **swell.** Place the book in the **lying press** with 1–2″ of the back projecting above the press. Place the **knocking-down block** behind the book and tap the book gently along the back with a mallet or hammer. Place the block on other side and repeat. Work gently and keep alternating sides until swell is no more than one-fourth greater than the width of the book at the **foredge.** Be careful not to break the threads.

knocking-down block. Bookbinding. A block of wood with a grip on the back that is placed behind the book to provide a smooth, hard brace when **knocking down** the **swell.** A knocking-down iron serves the same purpose, but is made from iron instead of wood. An antique flat iron may be substituted.

knock-off stick. Gemcutting. See **dopping.**

knock up. Bookbinding. See **jog.**

knop. Glasswork. A small rounded protuberance or knob affixed to glass vessels as ornamentation. Also see **prunt.**

knop yarn. Spinning. Weaving. See **novelty yarn.**

Knoop scale of hardness. Gemcutting. See **Mohs scale of hardness.**

knot. Macramé. A fastening made by intertwining or tying together two or more cords. Also see **accumulating bar, adding beads, alternating half hitch, alternating reverse double half hitch, angling, bobble, compact half hitch, diagonal double half hitch with center closing, diagonal double half hitch with color, double half hitch** (clove hitch), **half knot, square knot, square knot with picots, vertical double half hitch.**

knot. Spinning. See **skein.**

knot. Tatting. (abbr. k) Because tatting is a knotted **lace,** that is, lace formed by knots, very often the stitches are referred to as knots. The tatting stitch, two **half hitches** that make the double stitch, is therefore also known as the tatting knot; in this usage stitch and knot are synonymous. Also see **making the double stitch.**

knot. Woodworking. See **wood.**

knot bearer. Tatting. The **thread** from the **shuttle** held in the hand during tatting. Also the inactive thread, which carries the **double stitches,** or the thread that pulls up to close a **ring.**

knot-bearing cord. Macramé. See **holding cord.**

knotless netting. Lacemaking. See **looping.**

knotless netting. Weaving. See **netting.**

knots. Lacemaking. See **half hitch, knotted lace filet, reef knot, weaver's knot.**

knot stitch. Crewel. See **coral knot.**

knot stitch. Crochet. See **lovers' knot stitch.**

knotted fringe. Rugmaking. Weaving. See **fringe, overhand knot.**

knotted ground and drawn-thread border. Embroidery. A technique of creating a knot around drawn threads to give a highly textured effect. The same knot can be used to hold several drawn threads together to create a drawn-thread border. Both variations must be worked on an **evenweave fabric.** First lay parallel threads across the area to be covered. Using a blunt tapestry needle, slide under the first bar from right to left. Take the working thread over, then under the needle, and draw through, pulling gently upward to form a knot (**a.**). Repeat on the next bar (**b., c.**). The same knot can be used to hold a bundle of threads together on a drawn thread border. Secure the thread in the center of the buttonholing at either side of the border (**d.**). See ill. Also see **drawn thread embroidery.**

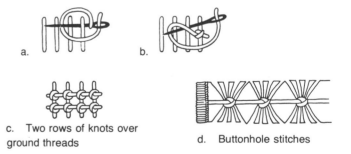

a.   b.

c. Two rows of knots over ground threads

d. Buttonhole stitches

knotted lace filet. Lacemaking. Perhaps **filet** lace is one of the earlier forms of lacemaking. Its square mesh is very similar to fisherman's net, and it is actually made in the same manner. A **netting needle** and a **mesh stick** are used. The size of each tool is determined by the size of the mesh desired, and by the fineness or coarseness of the thread, yarn, or cord used.

   Start the knotted filet from a stirrup or **foundation loop.** Tie the end of the thread from the netting needle to the foundation loop and proceed to knot as shown in the illustration (**a., b., c.**). Different shapes may be made by increasing or decreasing the number of meshes on the outer edge of the lace. Stretch the netted work on a **frame** and fill in the design with a **darning stitch.** A long blunt needle is best for filling in the **design.** Finish edge with a **buttonhole stitch.** See ill. next page. Also see **Lacemaking: Knotted Laces.**

Knotted lace filet

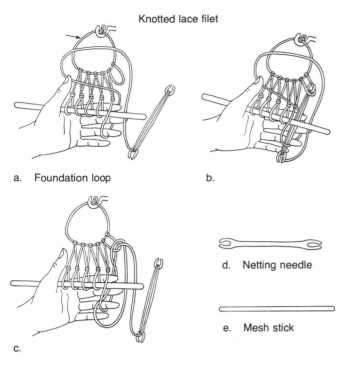

a.   Foundation loop

b.

d.   Netting needle

e.   Mesh stick

c.

knotted pearl stitch. Crewel. Embroidery. A stitch made up of a series of raised knots that form a narrow band. The **buttonhole stitch**es should not be pulled too tightly, and should always be drawn up into the center of the band. Do not attempt to work too wide a band with this stitch.

Using a blunt needle, come up at A, go down at B, and up again at C. A-B-C are all on a straight line. Slide the needle under the top of the first stitch from right to left without going through material. Holding the loop under the needle, pull flat. This forms one buttonhole stitch on the first bar (**a.**). Insert needle in background fabric, parallel to AB to begin a second buttonhole stitch (**b.**). Slip needle under top of second stitch (**c.**). Anchor row with buttonhole stitch outside last buttonhole loop (**d.**). See ill. Also see **line stitch.**

a.   One knotted pearl stitch completed

b.   Insert needle in background fabric parallel to AB beginning second stitch

c.   Slip needle under top of second stitch

d.   Knotted pearl stitch band

knotted pile. Rugmaking. Weaving. The cut or loop **pile** attached to a foundation by way of a knot. The knot is tied by hand in **woven rug**s and formed by a latch hook in **latch-hooked rug**s and a needl½ in needleworked, or **embroidered rug**s. Knotted pile can be attached with a needle

to **netting**, crochet, knitting and just about anything else that allows it to form the knot structure. The three classical knots used are the Ghiordes knot or Turkish knot, the Sehna knot or Persian knot, and the Spanish knot or single warp knot. In weaving, all three are used, but the one most commonly seen is the Ghiordes knot. In **latch hooking**, it is possible to form only the Ghiordes knot, while in working with a needle, all three knots can be made but usually only the Ghiordes knot is seen. In latch hooking or needleworking, the knot has a **rug backing** or some foundation to work into. In weaving, the foundation is woven and the knots inserted one row at a time during the weaving. After every row of knots the **filling** is put in and then the next row of knots inserted. Knotted pile is not only used for rugs but can be found in pillows, hats, purses and bags, wall hangings, towels, garments, and drapery.

The earliest examples of knotted pile come from Egypt dating back to about 1500 B.C. The knot used was the Spanish knot attached to a single **warp end.** The Egyptians freely used pile, knotted or merely looped into the background, in different materials for all sorts of articles. The earliest rug was found in a frozen tomb in Pazyryk in the mountains of southern Siberia and goes back to 500 B.C. The intricacy of the design and the subtle use of many colors in this rug indicate a long tradition of rug design and knotting. The knot used was the Ghiordes knot. By the fourteenth century, rugs using the Ghiordes and Sehna knots were being woven in Turkey and Persia and the export of Oriental rugs to Europe was under way. The height of Oriental rug knotting came in the sixteenth century with very intricate and elaborate designs that were accomplished through very fine knots; in one case there were 790 of these knots in a square inch. The more knots per square inch a rug might have, the more its value increased. The number of knots per square inch for most Oriental rugs ranges from 80 to 320. Contemporary craftsmen, using heavier yarn and long pile, put in only from four to ten knots per square inch.

The density of the pile, determined by the number of knots per square inch and the amount of backing or filling between each row of knots, depends on the desired texture, the spacing of the knots, the length of the pile, and how many strands are used in each knot. In most techniques, it is desirable to have a thick, rather than a thin or stringy, texture, since the backing in either needleworked or latch-hooked rugs is not intended to show, and in woven pieces the pile is usually also meant to cover the **plain weave** areas in between each row of knots. Knotted pile can be as short as ¼", in which case the knots must be close together. The longer the pile, the further apart the knots can be placed. They need not be aligned in rows right above each other, but can be spaced in a staggered or alternate manner, provided they cover the backing. This is true of woven or latch-hooked items. However, in needleworked pieces, the backing normally used has spaced, open-row areas for the knots, so that unless another type of **rug backing** is used, the needleworker is limited to following the open row. From two to six strands of yarn in a knot are used by modern craftsmen, whereas the traditional Middle Eastern weaver uses only one strand in a knot.

The Ghiordes or Turkish knot is made on two or more adjacent warp threads. It can be made of individual pre-cut yarn pieces, or in a continuous manner, one knot after another. The pre-cut version offers more scope for color and design variations since, with every knot, the color or color combinations can be changed. The length of pile is determined by a **gauge** or the fingers. In needleworked rugs, the choice is the same, although using pre-cut yarns involves many threadings of the needle. With latch-hooked rugs, it is all pre-cut yarn that is used since the hook can not accommodate continuous yarn. To make the knot using pre-cut yarn, lay the length of yarn over two warp ends in a closed **shed.** Pass the yarn tips behind the warp ends and up between the two ends pulling tightly forward (**a.**). With a continuous strand, working from left to right, the yarn goes down between the two ends, under the left end, up and over the left and right ends, under the right end and up between the two ends. The two yarn ends of the first knot meet in the center and are pulled tightly forward and up. The pile gauge is laid over the yarn of the first knot and the yarn goes over it and to the next set of warp ends for the next knot. As each knot is made, the yarn is pulled tightly over the **gauge.** The same path is followed by a needle in doing needleworked pile (**b.**). The pile may be cut or the gauge pulled out and the yarn left in loops (**c.**). The knots tend to fall frontward, especially the long pile. To compensate for the directional fall they can be put in backward or even sideways. The Ghiordes knot has become known as the rya knot due to its exclusive use in the popular Scandinavian rya rugs. Of the three knots mentioned, the Ghiordes knot is the most secure and so lends itself to use in long pile. It is also the knot used in **flossa** rugs. Another name for the knot is Smyrna knot after a town in the Middle East that specialized in rugs using the knot. During colonial times in America, the Ghiordes knot was called a Turkey knot after the place of origin of the Turkish Oriental rugs. Turkey knots were part of woven or needleworked rugs that made an attempt to imitate the Turkish designs and density.

A Sehna or Persian knot is made over two adjacent warp ends. One end of a cut piece of yarn is left outside the two warp threads and the other end is passed under the first thread and over and under the second, ending up between the two threads. The knots can be made so that the pile falls either to the right or left and is known as a right-hand Sehna or a left-hand Sehna (**d.**). As with the Ghiordes knot, the Sehna can also be made with a continuous yarn over a gauge. Sehna knots are seldom used by today's craftsmen even though they distribute the pile more evenly than the Ghiordes knot and more of them can be put into a square inch. It is a simpler knot than the Ghiordes, quicker to tie and only a little less secure. Sehna can also be spelled Senna.

A Spanish or single warp knot is formed over a single warp end or two warp ends used as one. Lay a pre-cut piece of yarn on top of the warp end, and then bring the two tips of the yarn under the end, cross them and bring them back to the surface (**e.**). This knot is usually made on alternate warp ends; that is, one row would have all knots on the even-numbered warp ends and the next row would have them all on odd-numbered warp ends. The knot is not really a knot,

but merely a loop around the warp end, and as such, tends to slip off the warp before the next **pick** of filling is put in to hold the knots in place. It became known as the Spanish knot since the Spaniards used it consistently for centuries in the majority of their knitted rugs. Its use dates back to the twelfth century when the Moors set up a rug-weaving industry in Spain. Because of its single warp construction it is possible to do very fine designs with the Spanish knot but by and large most Spanish rugs have bolder motifs than the Oriental rugs. See ill.

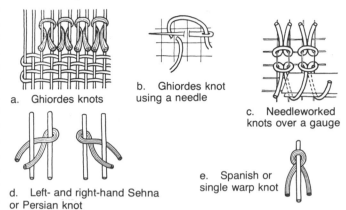

a. Ghiordes knots

b. Ghiordes knot using a needle

c. Needleworked knots over a gauge

d. Left- and right-hand Sehna or Persian knot

e. Spanish or single warp knot

knotted rug. Rugmaking. Weaving. Those rugs made by knotting **pile** onto a **rug backing,** as in latch-hooked or **needleworked rug**s, or a **warp,** as in **woven rug**s. Also see **knotted pile.**

knotted stitch. Crewel. Embroidery. See **French knot.**

knotted stitch. Needlepoint. A long diagonal stitch over 4 mesh, tacked down with a small stitch slanting in the opposite direction. Successive rows encroach on one another by one mesh. It forms a tight, firm surface, is used as a **filling stitch,** and works up quickly. See ill.

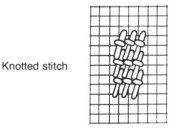

Knotted stitch

knotted tie-dye. Batik and Tie-dye. A **tie-dye** method in which lengths of material are tightly knotted to make them **resist dye penetration** when they are immersed in the **dyebath.** Also, any **batik**ed fabric treated by **knotting** and dyeing. Fine fabrics such as muslin, linen, voile, and silk chiffon work best. When the knotting process is used, two or three dyeings produce the most varied effects. The knotting may also be done over a rope that is rolled into the cloth. This is referred to as "knotted-rope tie-dye."

To do knotted tie-dye the length of fabric is measured or marked for positioning of knots (**a.**). It is then folded lengthwise and the material itself is tied into a knot (**b.**). See ill., page 482.

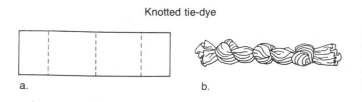

Knotted tie-dye

a.   b.

knotting surface. Macramé. See **celotex** and **Macramé: Tools and Materials.**

knotty pine. Woodworking. See **pine.**

knot yarn. Spinning. Weaving. See **novelty yarn.**

knucklebones. Toys. (Also called dibstones, jackstones.) An early form of **dice** in which the knucklebones were tossed in a **game** of chance and skill. The ankle bones of sheep were used in the original ancient Greek version; the bones were tossed and caught on the back of the hand. The game is well known through a frieze painting in Pompeii. Astrogalus is another name by which the game pieces were known.

koleidorama. Toys. See **phenakistoscope.**

Kooboo. Basketry. See **cane.**

Koomi Malie (Press Gently). Quilts. See **Hawaiian quilt.**

kraft paper. Bookbinding. A heavy paper used for the **back lining** and **endpaper**s of books. True kraft paper leaves a small quantity of very soft ash if it is burned, indicating a very pure form of cellulose fiber. It is available in a variety of colors besides natural brown and bleached.

kraft paper. Stained Glass. See **Stained Glass: Tools and Materials.**

krahen. Toys. See **paper folding.**

Kriegrocene. Batik and Tie-dye. See **acid dye.**

krokbragd. Rugmaking. Weaving. A three and **four-harness weave** producing, with the correct **sett,** a **filling-faced** fabric often used for rugs. Color placement in the filling and the **treadling order** produce steplike angular designs.

The **threading** is based on a **point draw** with either even points in each repeat or double points in each repeat. The harnesses are treadled each alone or in combinations of two. Four-harness krokbragd is quite similar to **bound-weave.** Threading is a four-harness even point and each harness is treadled alone.

Krokbragd is Norwegian for "crooked path." If lightweight **warp** is used in combination with fine filling yarns the weave is suitable for items such as pillows, bags and purses, bands and seat covers.

Krystalline. Candlemaking. A commercial plastic **additive** that hardens the candle without increasing its opacity. This substance is particularly useful when a clear wax is desirable.

kuftgari. Jewelry. A form of **damascene** that originated in India involving the **inlay**ing of gold or silver wire into steel.

Kundun work. Jewelry. An Indian technique in which gemstones are **cement**ed into another material with a small space left around the stone. Strips of **fine gold** are then forced into this space. More than one application of gold may be required. After the gold has been inserted, it is burnished down, partially over the adjoining material and partially over the stone, to hold it in place.

kunzite. Gemcutting. See **spodumene.**

kwik solder. Stained Glass. A liquid or cold **solder** that can be used as grout; available in hardware stores. Also see **lampshade construction, liquid solder, slab glass lampshade.**

kyanite. Gemcutting. A mineral composed of aluminum silicate **crystal**lized in the triclinic system with **hardness** of 5−7 and **specific gravity** of 3.56−3.6. Kyanite has two perfect **cleavage** planes parallel to the **C-axis.** It occurs in transparent or translucent blue **color** with some dichroism and a vitreous to pearly **luster.** Kyanite has refractive indices of 1.712 and 1.728; sometimes it exhibits a chatoyant band. Main crown and pavillion **facet**s are cut at 40° and polished with tin oxide on a tin **lap.** Also see **cabochon, faceting, polishing, refraction.**

L

labradorescence. Gemcutting. See **luster.**

labradorite. Gemcutting. See **feldspar.**

la cardère. Spinning. See **carder.**

lacche povero. Découpage. See **arte povero.**

lace. Lacemaking. Lace is a delicate openwork fabric worked with needles, **bobbins, shuttles,** and threads. Examples are **bobbin lace, crochet** lace, **knitted lace, knotted lace filet, needle lace,** and **tatting.** Macramé and **sprang** are laces worked with the hands and thread only. Some traditional, decorative, small lace items are the **doily, insertion,** and **lace edging;** larger pieces of lace fabric are made for wearing apparel and household accessories like curtains and tablecloths.

Generally speaking, bobbin laces are the most delicate and sheer; needle and knotted laces, because of their knotted stitch structure, are the sturdiest; and crochet and knitted laces, with the **loop** stitch structure, have a stretchy quality.

The word "lace" was not used to distinguish this fabric until the end of the seventeenth century in Europe. The Italians used the general term of *puntos;* the more universal terms were *passement au fuseau* for pillow lace or bobbin lace and *passement a l'aiguille* for needle lace; lacemakers were called *passementiers.* By the end of the sixteenth century the French used the word *dentelle* for lace.

lace. Leather. See **lacing.**

lace. Tatting. Tatted lace, a knotted lace, has a firmness of texture and structure that **bobbin lace** lacks because it is made using only the **cross** and **twist** movements of the thread. Tatted lace shares this firmness of texture with other knotted laces, e.g., **knotted lace filet** and **reticella.** Perhaps tatting has the same origin as the knotted filets, because they both are made with a shuttle and a single filament. It is possible that tatting derived from the ancient methods of making fishermen's nets. The first advance in tatting came during the fifteenth century, when a single knotted cord was made with a shuttle; this cord was then applied to fabric by embroidery stitches.

Tatting as it is today, composed of **rings** and **chains** decorated with **picots** and creating a geometric or floral appearance, enjoyed a great popularity during the nineteenth century. The threads were very fine, creating a very delicate lace.

lace appliqué. Stitchery. (Also called lace cut-through.) The use of laces, old or new, with **fabric** in appliqué **panels.** The lace may be incorporated into **appliqué** in either of two basic ways.

In **cut-through appliqué,** or **reverse appliqué,** the laces can be used as a middle layer. That is, a fabric is placed on top, another underneath with lace between them. The top layer of fabric is then cut out to reveal the laces that are beneath it. Both are sewn to the third backing layer to hold the laces secure. The third or underneath layer helps to fill any open spaces in the lace and provides some firmness to which **appliqué stitch**es may be attached.

Laces can also be used compositionally. In this approach, prefinished lace forms (doilies, **edgings,** and **medallions)** are used so as to preserve the initial character of each. Knitted, tatted, or crochet laces of all kinds, both hand and machine made, may be used as the appliqué. The lace pieces are **tack**ed in place with tiny **catch stitch**es, then elaborated with embroidery. These may be combined with areas of **transparent fabrics,** such as **net** or **organdy,** which are sewn either by hand or machine stitching.

lace beading. Beadwork. Various patterns of open **beadwork** made by the North American Indians, using stringing techniques with a needle and thread rather than a **loom.** Also see **bead mosaic work, bead weaving with needle and thread.**

lace Bronson. Weaving. See **Bronson weave.**

lace coil. Basketry. A type of **coil basket** that uses a **lace stitch** to produce openings or perforations in the **siding.** These perforations in the basket may be decorative, practical (to lighten the weight of the basket), or functional (to make the basket into a strainer). See ill. Also see **lace stitch** and **Basketry: Coiled Basket Construction.**

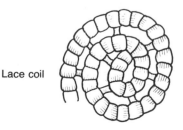

Lace coil

lace cut-through. Stitchery. See **lace appliqué.**

lace edging. Lacemaking. Tatting. A narrow strip of **lace** used to decorate the edge of clothing or household articles. It usually has one straight edge for sewing the **edging** to the fabric; the other edge is ornamented with **picot**s, **scallop**s, or the like.

lace faggot stitch. Knitting. Lace faggoting is lace knitting reduced to the bare essentials. Knitting this stitch produces an open, chainlike mesh. The design units—an **over** and a decrease—are used for every row on both sides of the fabric. For the basic lace faggot stitches, the over can be single or double, and the decrease can be knit or purled. As the over and the decrease are done every row, the fabric has little or no bias. Lace faggot stitches can be used, therefore, to create lace backgrounds and to carry solid motif patterns. Also see **Knitting: Decreasing.**

lace knot. Embroidery. An almost invisible firm knot used to join two threads, making it possible to work with one continuous thread. It is used predominantly in **whitework** and openwork filling stitches where it is important to have a continuous thread and no knots showing.

Begin working an ordinary knot in the thread; instead of pulling the end through, pull through a loop (**a.**). Push the end of the new thread to be joined through the top of this loop (**b.**). Hold the new thread firmly and pull the loop of the first thread tight (**c.**). Pull sharply on both ends of the first thread—the new thread will pop through the knot (**d.**). Pull both the first and the new thread tightly against one another to tighten the knot. The knot is so firm, if done correctly, that the ends may be trimmed quite short and the knot will be almost invisible (**e.**). See ill.

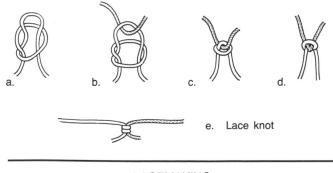

a.   b.   c.   d.

e.   Lace knot

LACEMAKING

The art or process of producing **lace.** Because lace is made of fiber, which decomposes with age, it has been difficult to find pre-Christian remnants from which to trace its history. Historians, however, have little doubt that lace, as we think of it, evolved from early techniques of the Near East and Mediterranean. These techniques can be classified into three types: **cutwork,** using needle and thread; manipulation of threads with hands or shuttles; and **sprang,** a twisting and crossing of warp threads.

Although there are different opinions as to where traditional lace fabric was first developed, Belgium and Italy each claim that distinction. The term *passement* was first used to indicate lace fabric, and late in the sixteenth cen-

tury the French term *dentelle* came into use. This would seem to indicate that lace fabric was first commonly made in Europe. The art of lacemaking was probably spread to the Mediterranean countries through trade and war. It was carried by the sea routes from Venice up into the seaports of central and northern Europe. In some Roman digs near Bologna, Italy, bones were found of the size and shape of **bobbin**s, lying in position as they would on a **bobbin lace pillow.** All fiber was gone from these bones, but a priest's robe in the Vatican dating from the fourteenth century, with a 3″ border of bobbin lace, indicates that it was known and developed before that time.

Laces made in the nunneries for use in the church vestments and as shrouds were referred to as nun's work. Lace was considered too valuable for anything but church purposes or as trimmings for the grave clothes of the saints; the patterns were either scriptural subjects or church emblems. Lacemaking was a closely guarded technique, but as the nuns taught the ladies of high birth in the church schools and the missionary nuns traveled to areas foreign to their home country, lacemaking was gradually taken up by the lay public. It was not until the Renaissance period in Europe that lace became part of the dress of the laity, and for some years was even too costly for anyone but kings. Gradually lace was used by all the nobility and, during the flowering of lacemaking in Europe from the fifteenth to the eighteenth centuries, by ladies and gentlemen in great profusion and extravagance.

Political troubles in France and Holland during the eighteenth century, the invention of the bobbin net machine by John Heathcoat and a friend named Lacy in England in 1808, the creation of a bobbin lace machine by John Leavers, also in England in 1813, all contributed to the decline in laces made by hand. The bobbin lace machine would reproduce any kind of bobbin lace so well that it was difficult to tell the difference between handmade and **machine lace;** today, although many improvements have been made, it is still called the Leavers machine. Contemporary laces express more a greatness and boldness of design than the delicate refinement of sixteenth through eighteenth century laces; even those persons who are preserving the traditional patterns of lace are not using the very, very fine threads of centuries past. Particularly in bobbin lace there is great opportunity for contemporary expression. The bobbins and yarns in this lace technique are highly maneuverable, allowing ease and freedom of design.

BOBBIN LACE   From the ancient technique of **sprang** it was a natural step to **bobbin lace.**

To begin bobbin lace, have a **dressed pillow** and other accessories, such as scissors, extra thread, and a **crochet hook** for **sewings.** Use a new pattern or take a **pricking** from another pattern. Make the lace according to the pattern instructions, **tying out** the bobbins when the lace is completed. Remove all the pins and gently lift the lace from the pillow. Press it lightly on the wrong side, using a pressing cloth and a warm, not hot, iron.

There are only two basic movements of the bobbins in bobbin lace, namely, **cross** (abbr. C.), and **twist** (abbr. T.). It is from the multiple combinations of only these two movements of the bobbins that all the beautiful laces of the past and present have been created. Bobbin lace is the most versatile in design, the lacer being completely free to execute the bobbins in any direction.

NEEDLE LACE Quite a few needle laces had their beginnings in **cutwork.** Two examples are **reticella** and **point de Venise,** sometimes called Venetian point, which attained their fullest development in Italy from the end of the fifteenth century through the beginning of the seventeenth century. The two laces are similarly worked, but reticella is geometric in design and point de Venise is flowing and floral and has the addition of **cordonnet.**

Lay a pattern drawn on paper over a double layer of cloth. With needle and thread make a structure of foundation threads, three to five together, using a thread of fine, smooth quality over the pattern lines. Secure the threads with stitches at widely spaced intervals, making these holding stitches through the paper pattern and the two layers of cloth. Upon this structure of foundation threads work the **buttonhole stitch**es, **picot**s, and, in the point de Venise, the cordonnet. When the lace is finished, cut the securing stitches holding the foundation in place by sliding the scissors between the two layers of cloth, which will release the lace from the pattern.

The **sol lace**s are **needle lace**s made in circles, squares, or rectangles that are stitched together into a large lace piece. The sol laces are made worldwide and have names indicative of their home country. They are worked in various stitches, depending on the country of origin, in knotted, darned, and buttonhole stitches. Some are made much like reticella and point de Venise. The Teneriffe lace **medallions** are worked over a frame or mold, rather than upon a base of cloth. As in all the needle laces, a fine-quality smooth thread, needles, scissors, pattern, and mold or cloth are all that are necessary.

The **appliqué** laces, some of the most delicate and beautiful of the laces, are classified as needle laces. The materials needed are lace motifs, **blue paper, net,** needles, very fine sewing thread, scissors, and a **frame** to hold the work while in progress.

On a pattern drawn on blue paper, lay lace motifs that have been previously made of either bobbin or needle lace, right-side down in the positions required by the design. Tack them in place with a **running stitch.** Pin the net over this. With an **overcast stitch,** sew around all the edges of the motifs. Cut the tacking stitches under the blue paper and remove the lace. Press with a pressing cloth on the wrong side.

Carrickmacross is an appliqué lace, worked as all the other appliqués are except that the design uses a very fine lawn or muslin instead of bobbin or needle motifs for the design areas. Once identified, one will always be able to pick out Carrickmacross in museums, collections, and illustrations in books. The materials needed are a very fine lawnlike cotton cloth, net, a fine cord, needles, fine thread, scissors, and a frame or **hoop** to hold the work firmly.

Stretch the lawn or muslin in a hoop, sketch a pattern on the wrong side of the fabric and, also on the wrong side, secure a layer of net to the lawn with running stitches, outlining the design. On the right side, edge the design with a fine cord, securing it with a moderately tight overcast stitch through the lawn and net. Use cord also to make a picot on the edge of the lace in a distinctive **loop,** rather than a worked picot. Then very carefully cut away certain areas of the lawn to give the net the appearance of the background against the figures of the design made with the lawn.

Tambour lace, another needle lace, is also called Limerick lace because it was principally made in Limerick, Ireland. The tambour stitch is made with a stitch very like a **chain stitch** in crochet lace. Using a very fine **tambour hook,** this stitch is made with thread a little heavier than the net so the stitches will show strongly. The materials needed are net, a paper pattern to be traced onto the net, a hoop or **tambour frame,** a tambour hook, smooth fine-quality thread a little heavier than the net, and scissors.

Stretch the net in the tambour frame. Place the end of the thread underneath the net and pull a **loop** on the hook up onto the top, the side toward the worker, retaining the loop on the hook. Insert the hook into the net a short space ahead, pull up the thread in another loop, and pull this loop through the previous one, which is now dropped. Retain the new loop on the hook and repeat. Follow the pattern drawn onto the net, making solid areas of stitches and outlining rows of stitches.

KNOTTED LACE **Knotted lace filet** is net, very similar in construction to fishermen's netting, embellished with **darning stitch**es to form patterns. It is a classic example of a functional material, in this case fishermen's netting, used for an art form. It is a single-**filament** lace using a **netting** to hold the thread and a **mesh stick** over which the **mesh**es are made. The size of the mesh stick determines the size of the mesh. The materials needed are a **netting needle,** mesh stick, thread, scissors, and a firm cushion to hold the starting **foundation loop** from which the net meshes are constructed.

Macramé is a knotted lace done only with the hands and thread or yarn. When it was done in the sixteenth century in Italy and Spain it was known as macramé lace. It was primarily done on the end threads of towels instead of making a hem. Because threads from the weaving were very fine, the macramé lace was very fine also. The designs were geometric, sometimes with small human figures worked in. Today macramé work is generally coarser, although still geometric in design. Tools and materials are simple: a firm board or pad to which the work can be pinned, pins, scissors, and threads, cords, or yarns.

Tatting is another single-filament knotted lace. This lace, which developed into such an art form during the nineteenth century, actually started as a knotted cord, made by a large knotting shuttle and small cord. This type of knotting was done in fifteenth-century Europe, especially in England, France, and Germany. The knotted cords were applied to fabric with embroidery stitches.

Tatting soon developed into a lace form because of the desire for fancy laces. The first tatting was done with one shuttle, and can be recognized by the single thread joining the rings and arches. By the middle of the nineteenth century, **picot**s and two shuttles were used. Some of the tatting of that century was extremely delicate, done with very fine thread. At first tatting took the form of **lace edgings** and **insertion**s, but it soon developed into very sheer, fabric-like lace for wearing apparel and table pieces. Tatting is a technique that, once mastered, does not require the concentration on design that the other laces demand during their creation. An experienced tatter can tell by the feel of the knotted lace between the fingers just how it is being done. The materials for tatting are one or two tatting shuttles, a crochet hook to pick up the picots, scissors, and very smooth, strong but fine thread. A small tatting bag is useful to keep the articles in when the work is laid aside, and it may also serve as a bag to hold the ball or other shuttle while tatting, the bag being hung from the left wrist. There is much interest in tatting, and it is perhaps one of the most popular of the laces because of its simplicity of materials and technique, and its beauty.

CROCHET AND KNITTED LACES   **Crochet** lace and **knitted lace** are similar in appearance and their softness of stitch construction and stretchability not found in bobbin lace and needle lace, which tend to be more like woven fabric.

Crochet lace is a single-filament fabric made by using a crochet hook to pull a series of loops through each succeeding one. Motifs of birds, flowers, and, particularly in **Irish crochet,** the shamrock, are first made separately, and then joined with a mesh ground embellished with many picots. The heavier, raised areas in Irish crochet are worked with stitches over a soft cotton cording. Irish crochet is the best known of the crochet laces: it has a design in imitation of **point de Venise. Crochet filet** has been popular since the eighteenth century; it copies the design of needle laces like darned, knotted filet. **Lace edging**s and **insertion**s are a frequent expression of crochet.

Another crochet lace is **hairpin lace.** This was started by some enterprising person using the tools at hand, namely, a hairpin. The early hairpin laces were very fine, but now hairpin frames are available on which lace several inches wide can be made. This lace is used as a tape, and is joined with other hairpin lace directly or by crocheting stitches between the hairpin tapes. The materials required are crochet hooks of various sizes, hairpin frames selected for the width of lace desired, yarn or thread, and scissors.

Knitted lace is a single-filament fabric worked with thread of yarn and a pair of knitting needles. It closely followed crochet lace in its development and use for insertions, lace edgings, and doilies. These were made with "fancy stitches," as the stitches were called during the nineteenth and early twentieth centuries, although knitted laces go back before that time. Lace scarves and similar articles of wearing apparel, and curtains and other household articles that require an open, lacy look may be artfully done in knitted lace.

CLEANING AND CARE OF LACE   Clean lace before it becomes too soiled. Cleaning is time-consuming and must be done with great care. The method will depend on the kind of lace and the size of the piece.

If the lace has a **pattern** that may become distorted in the washing, lay the lace on paper and sketch the design, for use when ironing. If the lace may be put into water, wash it in a solution of mild soap, well dissolved in lukewarm, soft water. Never wring or twist the lace while washing; only gently squeeze the lace if necessary, and never rub soap onto the lace. Soap is very difficult to remove from the lace without undue agitation and friction.

Supported by the hands, lift the lace piece up out of the water all at once, rather than by one section or one end only. Rinse it thoroughly in clear warm water several times, and roll it in a cloth to absorb the moisture. Lay it on a thick cushion of cloths, right-side down, cover the lace with a cloth to protect it and press it with a warm iron. If a paper pattern was made, the lace will retain the proper proportions by pinning it onto the pattern right-side down before ironing.

To clean a small piece of very fragile lace, place it in a bottle with a soap solution and shake it or soak it awhile to remove the soil.

To wash a fragile **insertion** or **lace edging,** wrap a bottle with cheesecloth and wind the lace around and around it; pin the points of the lace to the cheesecloth to retain shape if necessary, secure the end of the lace, and dip it into a soap solution. Rinse it well in warm, soft water. Dry the lace on the bottle, if necessary, to hold the shape.

Should it not be possible to wash the lace in water, clean it with powdered magnesia or French chalk. Lay the lace on a paper and cover it generously with the powder. Fold the piece in half and cover it again with powder. Continue folding and covering with powder until all surfaces are well covered. Fold the paper over and roll all together. Leave it for several days for the powder to absorb the soil and grease in the lace. Remove all the powder by shaking it out of the lace.

To store laces, lay small pieces flat between clean tissue paper and roll large pieces in tissue paper. The crease that would develop from folding would weaken the fiber in time, and it is difficult to remove with just pressing. It is also advisable to air the lace occasionally.

To mend lace, determine what kind of lace it is, and whether it is all made by hand or whether some parts are made by hand and some by machine, as in the **appliqué** laces. When mending lace, attach the thread or wound bobbins into the undamaged lace, beyond the worn or damaged area, and proceed with the lacework.

In **knotted lace filet,** cut out the broken **meshes** and work new mesh stitches into their place; take out the darned **design** beyond the line of new and old mesh, and darn the pattern back in according to the rest of the design.

In **needle lace** with machine net grounds, remove the **net** that is damaged and mend the pattern with needle and thread, putting in the **filling.** Tack the needle lace pieces onto **blue paper** right-side down, lay a new piece of net that matches the old over the **sprays,** and tack the net to the edge of the blue paper. With a fine needle and thread, sew through the net around the edge of each spray with a running stitch. Cut the tacking stitches, and remove from the blue paper.

Use the same or similar thread as in the lace to be repaired. If **reticella** or **point de Venise,** remove the damaged area by trimming out. Work a structure of foundation threads, and upon these do the **buttonhole stitches** to follow the lace pattern to fill the damaged part.

Bobbin lace is repaired on the **pillow.** Pairs of bobbins are placed into the meshes beyond the worn areas as in a **sewing.** With similar thread, work the lace in the same pattern as the original lace; sewings join the sides of the new and old lace. Tie off the bobbins, as in **tying out,** in an irregular line to avoid showing the repair. Remember that in bobbin lace the side of the lace facing the lacemaker is the wrong side.

lace patterns. Crochet. Most openwork crochet **patterns** are referred to as lace patterns. Among the best known are **filet crochet, hairpin lace, lover's knot stitch,** and **Irish crochet lace.** Also see **Crochet: Basic Stitches.**

lacer. Rugmaking. A type of broad, flat, blunt needle used in **lacing** a **braided rug.** The narrower variety are suitable for working narrower braids.

lace stitch. Basketry. (Also called Mariposa weave.) A type of knotted stitch used in **coiled basketry** that holds the **foundation** rows apart and produces spaces or openings in the **siding.** It also serves to lighten the weight of the basket by using less material. Also see **lace coil** and **Basketry: Coiled Basket Construction.**

lace stitch. Knitting. This is the stitch used to produce **knitted lace.** Lace stitches are based on two units: the **over** principle, which creates the holes, and the decrease, which controls the width of the pattern and provides the decorative aspect of the lace. Many of these stitches are traditional designs, and all but the most complex are fairly easy to knit. Also see **faggot stitch, lace faggot stitch, Viennese lace** and **Knitting: Decreasing, Stitches and Patterns.**

lace weave. Weaving. Openwork weaves produced on a **loom** that imitate lace. Lace weaves fall into two categories: **loom-controlled,** woven on a **harness loom; finger-manipulated,** woven on any kind of a loom no matter how primitive. One variety of the latter is called **gauze weave,** while the loom-controlled equivalent is sometimes referred to as imitation gauze. The chief difference between the two is the twisting or crossing of **warp** threads that occurs in finger-manipulated lace weaves which produces wider and more varied openings than is possible in loom-controlled lace weaves. Loom-controlled lace weaves often depend on the **sleying** and **beat** to get the open effect. They may be all-over open weaves or have the lace look in sections set off by blocks or areas of **plain weave.** Also see **Bronson weave, canvas weave, mock leno weave, openwork technique, Swedish lace.**

lacing. Beadwork. A technique used in **bead flowermaking** to reinforce large petals and leaves and to join petals in a continuous row.

To reinforce a large petal with wire lacing, begin in the center, using 30 or 32 gauge wire about three times the width of the petal. With the right side of the work facing up, place the wire across the middle of the **basic row** on the wrong side, then backstitch from the center row to the outside row on the right as follows: bring the wire from under the row of beads to the right of the basic row, up, back over the top, and then under again to the next row on the right. Continue working to the right until the outer row is reached, then clip off excess wire (**a.**). Turn the petal over to the wrong side and lace the other half in the same way using the remaining piece of wire.

To join petals in a row with wire lacing, start in the center of the first petal, as for lacing a large petal, and backstitch in the same way to the outer row on the right (**b.**). Place the second petal adjacent to the first one and continue lacing across it. Add the desired number of petals in this way, making sure that the tops of the petals are even. Then turn the work over and lace the other half of the first petal. Lacing should be in a straight line.

To join loop units with skip-lacing, cut a piece of wire about four times the width of the piece to be laced. Beginning at the first loop, use the backstitch wire lacing method, except lace two rows at each step to draw the loops together (**c.**). See ill.

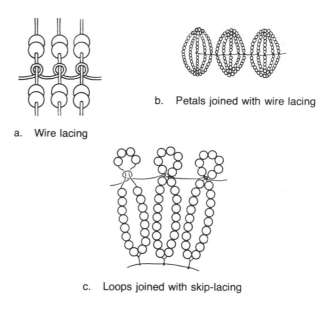

b.   Petals joined with wire lacing

a.   Wire lacing

c.   Loops joined with skip-lacing

lacing. Leather. Long, narrow lengths of leather, either flat or round, of varying thicknesses used for hand stitching, and binding pieces of leather together to give a decorative finish to edges. Lacing is inserted through holes or slits which have been punched in the leather. Lacing, usually made from **latigo,** calf, goat, or **rawhide,** can be cut from skins or brought in various widths and colors. It is available in $^3/_{32}''$, $^1/_8''$, and $^3/_{16}''$ widths, in spools of 25–50 feet. Calf and goat lace usually has one rounded side which is kept facing out as you work. Latigo lacing is wider and rougher. Vinyl imitation leather lacing is also available. Lacing is usually done with the **cross stitch,** the **single buttonhole stitch,** or the **whipstitch.** Also see **awl and haft, fid, Florentine lacing, lacing needles, lacing pliers, punch, splice** and **Leatherwork: Setting Up a Workshop, Sewing Leather.**

lacing. Rugmaking. A method of attaching the rows of braids to make a **braided rug**. This is done using a blunt needle or **lacer** threaded with lacing cord or doubled **carpet thread**. The cord or thread is drawn alternately between the loops of two adjacent braids, going from one braid to the other. The needle or lacer does not pierce the material. By drawing the cord tightly, the loops lock into each other and the cord disappears between them. Lacing should always be done on a flat surface and worked on the underside of the rug, away from the worker. In an oval or round rug, lace alternate loops in the curve to ease the fullness so that the rug will lie flat on the floor instead of rippling. The skipped loops always should be on the braid about to be attached. Lacing can be preceded by sewing to assure correct alignment of the braids. For an extra strong joining double lacing is recommended. This is done with two lengths of cord or thread and two needles or lacers. Both work from side to side but in opposition to each other so that the cords cross each other between the braids. See ill.

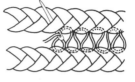

Lacing braids together

Showing position of cord before pulling closed

lacing cord. Rugmaking. See **braided rug, lacing**.

lacing fid. Leather. See **fid**.

lacing hole nippers. Leatherwork. See **lasting pincers**.

lacing needle. Leatherwork. Lacing needles enable the **lacing** to be threaded without doubling the lace over to facilitate the entry through slits or holes in the leather. To thread a hook-and-eye needle (**a.**), thread the lace through the eye and then hold fast by a prong or hook which pierces the lace. A two-prong lacing needle (**b.**) has a pronged top in which lacing can be slipped without doubling it. The curved and/or straight life-eye needle (**c., d.**) is threaded by cutting one end of the lace to a point for sewing. The other lace end is blunt and is screwed into the hollow end of the needle. Lacing needles are available in various sizes for different thicknesses of leather. See ill. Also see **needle**.

Lacing needles

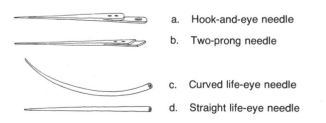

a. Hook-and-eye needle

b. Two-prong needle

c. Curved life-eye needle

d. Straight life-eye needle

lacing on. Weaving. A method of attaching the **warp ends** to the front **apron bar** as the last step in **dressing the loom**. The warp is divided into small equal groups called **bouts** which are tied at the tips so that a loop is formed. A strong cord goes around the apron bar and through these loops.

The tension is adjusted by manipulating and pulling on the cord which should be long enough so that at least 1" is left between the loop and the apron bar. It is an alternate method to **tying-on**.

lacing pliers. Leatherwork. A tool used to facilitate **lacing** and pulling straps through holes in leather. See ill.

Lacing pliers

lacing pony. Leatherwork. A viselike tool mounted on a base used to hold leather steady while punching, stitching, or **lacing**. The leather is clamped between two pieces of wood that tighten with a wing nut. The pony is mounted on a base that is set on a chair or bench and straddled so that one thigh rests on each side of the base to hold it firm. See ill. Also see **cross stitch, double needle stitch, stitching horse** and **Leatherwork: Sewing Leather**.

Lacing pony in use

lacing stitch. Rugmaking. Weaving. Any one of a variety of stitches that moves from one piece to another drawing these pieces together so that their edges meet. Lacing stitches are used in **joining** sections of rug or wall hangings, garments, or in assembling utilitarian fiber pieces. For a lacing stitch, the yarn or thread used should be about twice the length of one side of a section, if this is practical. Most craftspeople prefer to lace in a direction away from themselves; attach the yarn to the lower edge of the right or left section by looping it around the edge thread a few times. Knot the yarn if it is not too bulky and it will not show. In one of the simplest versions, the lacing stitch is worked from side to side at a diagonal pulling the sides together. It can also move horizontally so that it provides a close compact cover over the seam; this is sometimes called an overhand stitch (**a.**). At the completion of the joining, the yarn should be looped around the top threads two or three times so that it is secure and will not tend to open. The needle is run back under the last lacing stitches and clipped off. A large-eyed **needle** or **rug needle** is used with either matching yarn, **carpet warp, carpet thread,** or heavy-duty cotton thread. The stitches are spaced about ¼" apart when using heavy yarn, closer with thread. They are not pulled so tight as to cause puckering or overlapping, but just so the sections meet closely and lie smoothly next to each other. In joining crocheted or knitted items, the stitches should be aligned so as to fit in with the crochet or knit stitch.

Lacing stitches can be hidden completely, or almost so, in the cloth. The fabric that is being joined must itself be quite compact, and the stitch is made within the cloth by moving side to side as above. It is sewn close to the selvage or within a hem or turned edge (**b.**). The interlocking stitch is worked over and under the cloth and is partially hidden (**c.**). See ill.

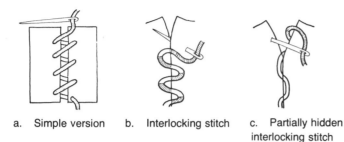

a.   Simple version   b.   Interlocking stitch   c.   Partially hidden interlocking stitch

Lacqroid. Bookbinding. See **cloth.**

lacquer. Découpage. Puppets. Toys. A resinous, natural **varnish** obtained from Asiatic sumac trees and used to finish wood with a hard, glossy surface. The trees, grown on plantations and tapped at ten years of age, yield a thick, gray syrup. When exposed to air the raw lacquer turns yellow brown and then black. The syrup is then cleaned, dehydrated, and purified.

Oriental lacquer has certain unusual characteristics. Contact with moisture hardens and strengthens it. It has high resistance to heat and acids so it is an excellent protective coating. Its only weakness is that it fades and dries out when exposed to bright light. Because Oriental lacquer is not exported and conditions of weather and materials vary greatly, lacquer has been replaced by varnish for use in découpage in this country.

lacquer. Metalworking. Woodworking. A transparent solution of lac diluted in **alcohol** used as a protective coating for wood, metal, and other surfaces. Natural lac is a resin formed on sumac trees in southern Asia by a type of scale insect. Today synthetic lacquers are produced from plastic **resin**s and **acrylic**s and occasionally combined with **celluloid**s and **alkyd**s. Contemporary lacquers dry rapidly, are relatively heatproof, waterproof, and, in some cases, alcoholproof. Lacquers, unlike some finishes, will not oxidize or powder with age.

The use of lacquer is often frowned upon by art metalworkers for aesthetic reasons. However, many metal objects placed outdoors require constant maintenance to preserve their surface qualities, and so a special metal lacquer is often applied as a sealant to reduce their upkeep.

Apply metal lacquer in a single coating only. Clean the metal thoroughly with an **abrasive** and then a chemical **solvent** such as **turpentine.** Use a soft, long-bristled brush to paint it on, avoiding brushing over the same place twice while the lacquer is wet because the previous brush strokes will show. The lacquer may turn white if applied in cold temperatures.

Clear gloss furniture lacquer is most commonly used in woodworking to bring out the natural beauty and color of a wood surface. It will take a high polish and is used extensively on table tops and drawer fronts.

Use a flat furniture lacquer when a hand-rubbed polish is not necessary, as on the sides of cabinets or drawers. Lacquer enamels are used on furniture that requires a painted finish. These come in a large variety of colors.

In woodworking, lacquers cannot be used directly over a varnished, painted, or stained surface unless it is first properly sealed with **shellac.** It should not be applied over surfaces that have not been thoroughly cleaned of paint remover or wax. All lacquers, because they are fast-drying, are best applied with an aerosol can or sprayer, although they may be brushed on for smaller jobs.

To brush on lacquer pour out only enough for the job into a clean container. Be sure the surface is free from dirt, grease, or oil. Fill the brush to capacity and, holding it at a 45° angle, begin to flow it on. Start in the center of the work and work toward the edges. Always use a fully loaded brush. Avoid overlaps and do not brush the lacquer into the surface, but let it flow on, a section at a time. Do not brush over the same area twice. Allow to dry at least two hours before applying a second coat.

To spray on lacquer, hold the gun or spray can 8–12″ from and at right angles to the surface. Begin spraying outside the edge of the piece. Spray across the **grain,** keeping the nozzle at a set distance above the surface and continue the stroke well past the edge. Continue with back-and-forth passes and overlap each pass by 50%. Let dry for at least two hours, then cover with a second coat, spraying with the direction of the **grain.** Avoid excessive buildup to prevent sags and runs.

If sanding is necessary between coats, use a 5/0 **garnet** or a 280–400 grade **wet-or-dry sandpaper.** Clean and apply additional coats as necessary.

In order to remove surface imperfections or too high a luster, the lacquered surface must be rubbed down with a rubbing compound. Also see **rubbing** and **Woodworking: Finishing.**

lacquer. Tincrafting. See **Tincrafting: Finishing the Tin.**

lacquer enamel. Toys. A **lacquer** to which pigment has been added. It gives a fast-drying glossy surface.

lacquering leather. Leather. See **Leatherwork: Finishing Leather.**

lacquer thinner. Plastics. See **solvent.**

lacquer thinner. Woodworking. See **solvent.**

lacquer ware. Découpage. During the eighteenth century, lacquered boxes, fans, writing tables, and other decorative objects imported to Europe from the Orient were so widely in demand that a popular craft, **japanning,** was developed to produce imitations.

Oriental lacquer ware was exquisitely designed and characterized by a hard, lustrous surface. This was achieved by applying **lacquer** in as many as 30 layers, with fine grinding between coats. The coats of lacquer were thinner and thinner with each application. The grinding was varied in the same way, beginning with coarse and then graduating to fine abrasives to achieve a satin polish. The piece was then kept in a dark house or cave with a damp atmosphere to ensure proper hardening.

Lacquer ware was decorated with carved, painted, or inlaid designs. Innumerable processes were used for textured lacquer grounds. Gold and silver dust were sprinkled on a black ground, or lacquer was mixed with pinewood soot for a rich black, then polished with charcoal. Some grounds were sprinkled with **mother-of-pearl** dust, then covered with transparent lacquer. Pieces of eggshell were pressed into lacquer ware which was painted with a design and then carefully polished to reveal the tiny fragments of shell. This technique was also used with the skin of ray or shark which showed through the lacquer as small white patches; sometimes the fish skin was first dyed indigo. Similarly, grains or seeds were sprinkled on a ground of wet yellow lacquer which was covered with black and then polished to reveal the seeds. The sophistication of these lacquer grounds stimulated the admiration of the Europeans and must account for the variety of materials incorporated in japanning, and now in découpage, including **eggshell inlay, mother-of-pearl,** and other **inlay** materials.

lacquer ware. Tincrafting. See **Tincrafting: Finishing the Tin.**

lacy square medallion. Crochet. An open, lacelike crocheted **medallion.**

ladder. Découpage. (Also called stay.) A simple supporting device, such as the narrow, folded strips of cardboard used to prop up separate elements in a **shadow box.** The cardboard strip, of width determined by the size of what it is to support, is glued behind the cutout and then to the background. Also see **bridge** and **Découpage: Cutting.**

ladder stitch. Knitting. This stitch creates an open, ladderlike, vertical pattern and follows the same principle as **lace faggot stitch**es. The ladder stitch is based on a **double over,** double increase into a double over, double decrease. The basic six-stitch pattern is:
   Row 1: K 1, K 2 tog, you 2, K 2 tog, K 1.
   Row 2: K 2, (K 1, P 1 into over), K 2.
Also see **Knitting: Increasing, Decreasing.**

ladder toy. Toys. See **Jacob's ladder.**

ladder walker. Toys. A toy, probably developed during the eighteenth century, that consists of a figure that moves down a ladder in a flip-flopping motion. The top and bottom of each figure is identically cut with a keyhole type of opening. The slotted portion slides over a step, then the round opening allows the figure to swing or flop down so that the slot on the opposite end slides over the next step. It is a somewhat common and ever-popular toy, and it is animated by its own weight. It requires planning and careful cutting, but it can easily be made at home with simple tools.

Ladies' Amusement. Découpage. *Ladies' Amusement, or The Whole Art of Japanning Made Easy,* published in England in 1760 by Robert Sayer at the Golden Buck, London, was the first publication of **prints** suitable for **japanning** or découpage. In 1959 a facsimile of the book was published by the Ceramic Book Co., Monmouth, Wales. About 1500 prints, by such artists as **Pillement,** Englebrecht, Fenn, Hancock, Hemerich, and June, of flowers, shells, insects, animals, landscapes, and borders were included. Also included were instructions for sizing wood, cutting out the prints, **varnishing,** and making various gums, **glue**s, and **lacquer**s which were not commercially available.

Lady-of-the-Lake. Quilts. A **block** for a **pieced quilt** that is really an elaborate **Odd Fellow's Patch.** It consists of a large cross made up of **split four-patch**es and is most effectively used as an **all-over pattern.**

La Farge, John. Stained Glass. See **Stained Glass.**

Lafayette Orange Peel. Quilts. (Also called Orange Peel.) An old **pieced** pattern of curved lines requiring great skill to sew. Each **block** consists of a **square** in which four concave lines reach from corner to corner. When the blocks are **set,** the **scallops** join to suggest overlapping circles. The quilt is often made of orange or yellow and white.

According to legend the Marquis de Lafayette brought oranges to a Philadelphia dinner party given in his honor. The exotic fruits from Barcelona were rare and highly prized, and one of the guests pared her orange in such a way that it inspired the quilt design.

It is sometimes called a **robbing Peter to pay Paul** quilt because of the set of the blocks. See ill.

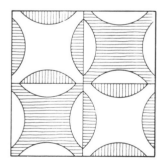

Lafayette Orange Peel

lag bolt. Woodworking. See **screw.**

lag screw. Woodworking. See **screw.**

laid-in. Weaving. (Also called onlay.) A type of **free weaving** in which the **pattern filling yarn** is "laid-in" with the fingers rather than being carried through the **shed** by a **shuttle, selvage** to selvage in the same manner as the **ground yarn.** The pattern thread is a **supplementary yarn** that moves back and forth only in the area indicated by the pattern or design. There are numerous types of laid-in weaves; the background is usually a **plain** or **twill weave,** while the pattern yarn is laid-in in the same shed or other sheds. If the pattern and background yarns are the same thickness, the design will appear faintly; if the pattern yarn is thicker, the design will be more pronounced. Should the pattern yarn **float** more on the surface than it goes under the **warp end**s, the pattern will appear even stronger. The laid-in yarn can go in every shed following every **pick** of the ground weave, every other shed, on **opposite**s or in a specific **pattern weave.** Draw the design full-size on plain paper and place it as a guide in back of the weaving, or on **graph paper** with each square equal to the number of warp and filling threads determined by the type of yarns and the laid-in technique used.

Since the pattern yarn goes back and forth only in a prescribed area, when it turns to reverse its direction, the turn may be apparent on the surface. To avoid this, work the weaving on the wrong side so that the turnings will all be on the wrong side and not seen on the surface. If the work is being done right side up, care must be taken to perform the turns on the back side, so that the face is neat and uniform. However, the turns can be left visible on the face as an added textural feature. In some varieties of laid-in, the emphasis is on the turns rather than the thread within the pattern.

Laid-in is also called **inlay, pick-up weave,** and **discontinuous brocade.** Other names not so frequently used are overlay, which indicates that most of the supplementary filling is floating on the face; and underlay, indicating that most of the supplementary filling is on the back, with the pattern appearing faintly or as dots on the face. When the pattern thread is in the same plain-weave shed as the ground thread, this is called simple, straight, regular, or plain laid-in. Turns can be made on either the top or underside. Following are some common variations on simple laid-in.

Italian laid-in utilizes two pattern-filling threads in each shed of plain weave used for the pattern. Usually there is an uneven number of plain-weave ground threads between each pair of pattern threads. The pattern fillings, normally in a heavy yarn, each come from the opposite direction and cross the pattern. Face turns leaving loops of yarn are made (**a.**).

Calabrian laid-in is related to Italian laid-in, but the pattern-filling threads are woven in a pattern shed rather than plain weave. Some patterns used for the laid-in are twill, **Summer and Winter weave,** and **rosepath.** In the twill and rosepath, the tendency is to use the 1/3 versions, so that the Calabrian laid-in has become associated with patterns that look solid because so much of the pattern thread is on the surface. The pattern yarns are put in exactly as in the Italian, but in some cases two threads from each direction are used, and the thread is soft and thick. One or more rows of plain weave ground are woven between each pattern filling (**b.**). The thickness of the pattern filling usually determines how much ground is woven.

Reverse Calabrian laid-in is in the 3/1 weave, so that the floats are below the surface and the design is mainly in outline form with the turns on the surface giving the outline. There are a number of rows of plain weave between each pattern filling.

Greek and French laid-in are woven over two ends and under two; the French alternates the pattern with a **pick** of plain weave, and connects isolated design units with a line

of the pattern filling. Without the connecting thread, this laid-in is sometimes called Mexican laid-in. Greek laid-in is woven 1–2, 3–4 for the pattern, and then a pick of plain weave ground.

Entwined laid-in takes the pattern thread into the shed and there twists it around the ground thread already in the shed. The twisting or entwining is done only around that part of the ground thread that is involved in the pattern. Both pattern and ground threads are in the usual plain-weave sheds.

Brickwork inlay gives the effect of brickwork in the pattern threads by using the 1/3 arrangement; only use the two opposite sheds in this arrangement so that each shed going-under of the pattern thread is in the middle of the three-over float. For example, if #1 thread is raised for the first pattern pick and #3 for the second, this sequence is followed throughout wherever the pattern falls.

This list for laid-in techniques could go on and on, each new name indicating a slight change usually particular to a specific region or country. Laid-in weaving has been very popular among the peasant weavers in all countries and used to be done so perfectly that it was difficult to distinguish it from embroidery. Because of this close resemblance, it is sometimes called **embroidery weave. Dukagång, HV technique,** and **transparent tapestry** are popular laid-in weaves that originated in Scandinavia.

Pile can likewise be laid-in. Cut pieces of yarn are laid-in between rows of plain weave. The length of the cut pieces varies according to the **pile height** desired. They are usually laid under and secured by three ends with the cut yarn tips protruding on the surface to give the pile effect. The density of the pile will vary according to the thickness of the yarn used, the number of yarns used in each laid-in insertion, and the spacing of the laid-in insertions. Pile done this way has a resemblance to **corduroy** pile. See ill.

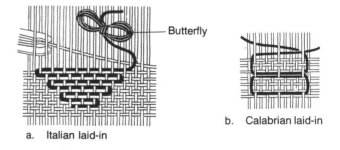

a. Italian laid-in —Butterfly b. Calabrian laid-in

laid on. Quilts. Stitchery. A term used to describe the transferring of a **quilting pattern** to the **quilt top.** This is sometimes completed before the quilt top is put into the **quilting frame,** although at other times the design is "laid on" as the **quilting** progresses. Also see **Quilts: Quilting.**

laidwork. Crewel. The technique of laying down long threads placed parallel on the **background fabric.** The laid threads are secured either by crossbars, small **tacking stitch**es, **detached** stitches such as the **fly stitch,** or any of the **line stitch**es such as **chain stitch** or **stem stitch.** Generally the edges of laidwork are uneven and require a strong outline such as stem stitch. Laidwork can be used for large areas because, unlike the satin stitch, no yarn is wasted on the reverse side. Begin laidwork at the widest point of the shape to establish desired direction. All subsequent stitches are parallel to this line (**a.**). Work stitches from the center to the edges of the shape (**b.**). To secure laidwork with crossbars, make a long stitch diagonally across the shape. The crossbars cross the laidwork at a 45° angle (**c.**). All subsequent crossbars are worked at ¼″ intervals. The crossbars can be secured with small tacking stitches at each intersection (**d.**). See ill. Also see **couching, laidwork tied diagonally.**

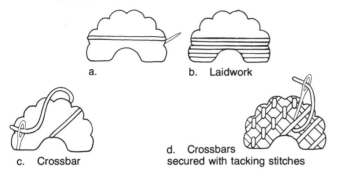

a.

b.   Laidwork

c.   Crossbar

d.   Crossbars
secured with tacking stitches

laidwork tied diagonally. Crewel. A variation of **laidwork** in which the laid threads are tied with diagonal bars. Work the diagonal stitches across the widest part of the stitch to establish the direction. Small tacking stitches hold the diagonal in place. See ill.

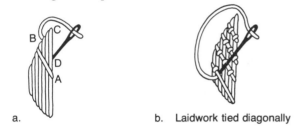

a.

b.   Laidwork tied diagonally

laitance. Stained Glass. A French word meaning "soft herring roe." The term refers to a shiny residue of cement that remains on the top of the mold after **concrete** has been vibrated during casting. Also see **dalle-de-verre, vibrator.**

lam. Weaving. (Also called lamm, marche.) A horizontal bar found in **floor loom**s directly below each **harness** and parallel to it. It serves as an intermediary connecting device between the harnesses and **treadle**s and in so doing acts as a balance between the two parts and makes possible multiple **tie-up**s of harnesses to treadle. On the top side of the lam are hooks to attach each lam to its corresponding harness. Once connected, they are rarely disconnected or changed. **Lam cord**s are used if they are attached by tying. However, many new looms have metal hingelike attachments. Eyelets or openings are found on the bottom edge of the lam, through which a cord or hook will go to attach treadles to the lam. Although only one harness is attached to one lam, many lams can be attached to one treadle, depending on the type of tie-up used and the pattern of weave involved. Most lams are of wood and hinged to one side of the loom, but they can also be of metal and suspended from the harness. In looms with a double tie-up, such as the **counter march loom**, there are two sets of lams for each harness. The shorter lams are called marches and the longer, countermarches. Also see **counterbalanced loom, jack-type loom.**

lamb's wool. Knitting. Spinning. The first **fleece** shorn from a lamb when it is about six to eight months old. It is soft and has superior spinning qualities. The **fiber** also has a natural tip which is lost after the first shearing; the ends of wool from mature sheep are very blunt. This first shearing is also known as the first of virgin clip. Also see **wool.**

lam cord. Weaving. A name given to both the cord that attaches the **harness** to the **lam** and the cord coming from the lam and attaching with a cord from the **treadle** to form the **snitch knot** used in a **tie-up.**

laminate. Metalworking. Plastics. Woodworking. A product made from bonding together layers of material. Also see **lamination.**

laminated fabric. Stitchery. Materials treated in such a way that layers of material are joined together by adhering them with **glue** or resin so that they form one **fabric.** In some cases two fabrics are laminated and in others a sheet of foam or plastic is bonded to the cloth. This **bonded fabric** is also referred to as laminated. The process gives a firmer base to some fabrics and gives them a ready-made **lining.**

laminated glass. Stained Glass. See **lamination.**

laminated papier mâché. Puppets. See **strip papier mâché.**

laminating. Leather. A process of gluing one layer of leather to another to make thick leather which is used for heavy-duty wear such as soles of shoes. The leather is first roughened with sandpaper, then each layer is brushed with contact cement, left to dry, and then pressed together. Also see **Leatherwork: Gluing and Bonding Leather.**

laminating. Papercrafts. A **papier mâché** technique in which several layers of newspaper or other **paper** are glued together with **papier-mâché paste.** This laminated sheet is then shaped or molded as desired, or cut or torn and then shaped into smaller forms. When dry, the laminated forms are stronger than a normal papier-mâché form would be. The use of laminated sheets would be helpful for applying papier mâché to large-scale sculptures, especially over **chicken-wire** forms, for added strength and smoothness. See ill.

Laminated paper cylinder

laminating. Plastics. Woodworking. See **lamination** and **Plastics: Laminating.**

laminating resin. Plastics. **Epoxy** or **polyester resin** formulated for use in thin **lamination** layers. It is used with **reinforcing material**s and usually has good surface **curing** characteristics. Also see **distortion.**

lamination. Glasswork. One of the simpler processes of glassforming. Bits of metal, including screening and wire, or bits and rods of colored glass are sandwiched between two sheets of clear or colored glass, and the whole assembly is heated in an oven to the fusing temperature. The resultant decorative piece can be used as a window or sculpture.

lamination. Jewelry. Joining one or more metals into layers. Also see **mokumé, sweat soldering.**

lamination. Plastics. Woodworking. (Also called lay-up.) Laminating is the process of sandwiching together layers of materials for thickness or strength, often used for curved forms. Lamination may refer to the process or the end product; delamination is the process of separation.

In plastics, laminating is the process of building up a form by laminating layers of a **reinforcing material** such as **glass fiber** with **catalyzed polyester** or **epoxy resin** over a form or in a **mold.**

In woodworking, laminating is the gluing together of layers of wood; **plywood** is the most familiar laminated product, and a **veneer** glued to a thick piece is considered a lamination. Lamination may provide additional thickness to a block of wood that is to be carved, or it may be used to build up a slender curved form by bending and gluing individual layers over a curved mold.

To laminate wood, check to see that the boards or veneers to be joined are **plane**d accurately so the layers will fit well. Check for **warps** or other **wood** defects that would leave space between the layers or twist the lamination out of shape. For greater structural strength, arrange the layers so that the **grain**s cross each other. Preset the boards in a trial run to check the fit and grain. Glue, align, and clamp the laminations securely. Also see **Plastics: Laminating.**

lamination. Stained Glass. A bonding process in which **gemmaux,** or crushed glass, set in **epoxy resin** is bonded to a sheet of **plate glass** producing laminated glass. Also, a process in which layers of clear epoxy resin and fiberglass are built up around pieces of glass.

Plate glass is the best surface for laminating. The bonding agent is clear, slow-drying epoxy resin. One gallon covers 200–500 sq. ft. Other equipment includes epoxy cleaner, a small **spatula** for spreading epoxy, rubber gloves, a **vitrified silicone stone, grout** or epoxy mixed with **lampblack,** and stained-glass scraps left over from other projects.

Pattern-making is the same as in traditional stained-glass paneling; cut the **template**s with regular scissors. If the piece is to be framed into a window, leave a ½" border on the plate glass free of lamination.

Tape the **cartoon** to the worktable. Cut and dull pieces of glass that need it. Nail two lath strips in the bottom corner of the cartoon as in **glazing.** Place the plate glass on top of the drawing. Mask off any area where no lamination is desired. Work must be done on a flat surface. Mix the epoxy according to the manufacturer's instructions. Using a spatula, put a thin, even layer of clear epoxy over the surface to be laminated. Starting in a corner and working outward, press the glass firmly into the epoxy until the piece is covered. When the epoxy has dried to a rubbery consistency, uncover the masked areas and use a razor and epoxy cleaner to remove unwanted epoxy.

Other applications of the technique are multiple-layer lamination, random thickness lamination, on-edge lamination (glass laminated on edge instead of being laid flat), and **free-form** sculpture. Also see **dulling, Farbigem process for laminated glass, polyester resin technique, shuttering** and **Stained Glass: Cutting Glass, Safety Precautions.**

lamm. Weaving. See **lam.**

lampascope. Toys. An **optical toy** of about 1870; it was the French variation of the **magic lantern.** It was made for use with a paraffin lamp, common in most homes of the time. Also see **Toys: Optical Toys.**

lampblack. Metalworking. A nonabrasive cleaning and burnishing agent that is used as a final finishing procedure on **pewter** to increase the luster of the metal. Oil-soluble Germantown lampblack powder is mixed with kerosene to a consistency of thick cream for use. Also see **pewterworking, polishing compound.**

lampblack. Stained Glass. An organic colorant used in paint, **epoxy resin,** and **grout** and to darken the cement for leaded glass **panels.** Also see **cementing, lamination.**

lampshade construction. Stained Glass. (Also called Tiffany lamp construction method.) Stained glass lampshades can be built either of molded glass and/or flat glass pieces arranged and soldered on a form.

The materials for the form can be inverted wooden or plastic bowls; lathe-turned wooden cone or bell shapes; papier mâché or Styrofoam molds. Laminate pieces of Styrofoam using Styrofoam glue and carve. Prefabricated Styrofoam forms are available from some stained-glass supply houses.

Wood is the traditional material, but it is also the most expensive. For beginners any of the substitutes will do. Whatever mold material is used, it should be able to hold nails; in the case of **plexiglass,** use small blobs of **Plasticene** to affix the glass to the form. The Plasticene should not touch the foil or lead because it will prevent the solder from adhering; it is a lengthy process to remove the Plasticene. Protect the surface of papier mâché and Styrofoam molds with rectangles of aluminum foil while using the **soldering iron;** use spray adhesive to adhere the foil to the mold.

Wrap drawing paper tightly around the mold or cut it in segments and tape it in place on the mold; make the drawing, number the shapes, and remove the paper. Use tracing paper to duplicate an existing lamp design. To make the **template,** use carbon paper to transfer the drawing onto heavy kraft paper or stencil paper; number the template to correspond to the **cartoon**.

Cut the template for patterns, one section at a time, using standard scissors. Use a glass cutter and cut glass in the same manner as for leading or foiling a glass **panel**.

The next step after cutting is copper foiling. Secure the foiled pieces to the form with nails, pushpins, or Plasticene, and solder them together working in sections around the mold. Use zinc chloride **flux** to coat each piece where the edges meet, and **solder** to join with the soldering iron, just enough to hold the section together. Tip the mold up to obtain a horizontal working surface. Build full rows around the form until it is completely covered. Flux and solder completely around the pieces; **floated solder seam**s make the piece look more professional. Remove the form and solder the inside of the lampshade.

A top and bottom finishing rim can be added. It can be made out of decorative **brass banding**, or the bottom can be made out of 12-gauge copper electrical wire. The top should be steel wire. Use stainless steel flux for the tops as well as for soldering the rim to the fixture. (Stainless steel flux is highly corrosive and should be kept away from tools.) Clean the flux and grease from the finished lampshade with borax soap powders and a soft brush.

Lampshades can also be made with **lead came** instead of **copper foil** and leaded as in **glazing**. Narrow came is used so that the shade doesn't become unreasonably heavy. Lead came affords fewer design possibilities than foil, but it works well for flat-sided lamps, box lights, and bent glass formed in **lampshade mold**s. Often, a lamp form is not necessary since the lead came holds the lamp together. Also see **copper foiling, slab-glass lampshade, swagging, vase cap** and **Stained Glass: Cutting Glass, Glazing.**

lampshade mold. Stained Glass. They can be of two types, either **drape mold**s or **sagging mold**s; both are used in a **kiln** to shape glass either over or inside them. Both types of mold are made of terra cotta—a low-fired, unglazed, red modeling clay—and then fired in the kiln. After the mold has cooled, a mold release, such as silica powder, is coated on the outside or inside of the mold, according to the type, to prevent the glass from sticking.

If a drape mold is used, balance the cut piece of glass on top of the mold so that it will drape around the form. Sagging molds are used for more acute bends. The flat glass pieces cut for sagging molds are called **blank**s. Place the piece so that it will sag correctly into the mold.

Place the molds and glass in a kiln and gradually heat it to 1250−1300° F (the glass-bending temperature), depending on the color and thickness of the glass. Firing is done by eye because of the varying firing times. Once all the pieces are bent, assemble them. Use small blocks or **Plasticene** to hold the bent pieces vertical while **glazing**. Also see **lampshade construction.**

lampwork. Glasswork. **Glasswork**ing using rods or tubes of preformed glass that are softened and shaped in a flame. Historically, flame hot enough for this kind of work was achieved by directing a stream of air through the flame of a wick lamp. Also see **flamework.**

lanolin. Metalworking. See **wax.**

lanolin. Spinning. The natural wool grease or fat, composed largely of cholesterol, that is extracted from raw wool during **scouring**. Also see **wool, yolk.**

lantern. Papercrafts. An **expanding** form made from a piece of paper that has been folded and slit at the fold, then rolled into a **cylinder**. The overlapping edges are then secured with **glue** or tape. By varying the proportions of this basic shape, many interesting forms can be made. See ill.

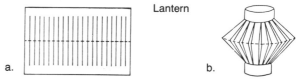

Lantern

a.   b.

lap. Gemcutting. A disk-shaped **abrasive** surface used horizontally to cut and polish **facets** on gems. Laps are recharged by spreading diamond powder in olive oil over the lap surface and pressing it into the lap with a steel roller or a rounded piece of agate with a rocking motion. Laps are operated at low speeds for cutting and **polishing**. Lapping with loose abrasive is recommended at a peripheral surface speed of under 700 feet per minute (220 rpm for a 12″ lap) to prevent the abrasive from flying off. Facet cutting on a diamond lap is done at approximately 100 rpm for a 12″ lap; harder gems require higher speeds. Lower surface speeds are obtained near the center of a rotating lap rather than at the edges.

Polishing laps are available in many materials and are used in conjunction with various polishing compounds. Polishing compounds are mixed with water to a thick creamy consistency and applied sparingly on the lap; a continuous water drip is necessary while polishing.

Soft metal and plastic polishing laps are scarified to aid retention of polishing agents. This scarification is done with a knife point or a scoring wheel in crisscrossing lines radiating from the center of the lap. See ill.

Store laps separately to avoid contamination; old record jackets are sufficient containers.

The master lap is a lathe-trued, inch-thick, cast-iron plate. Loose silicon carbide abrasive, or cloths in disk shape were previously used on the master lap, but modern gem faceters use copper disks impregnated with 400 grit diamond powder on one side and 800 grit on the other (the 600/1200 grit disk is also popular). Protect the master lap from dents and deformations. Remove accumulated cutting sludge from the master lap by sweeping it with a carborundum pocket hone while flushing it with water.

A tin lap used with tin oxide and/or Linde A is the most versatile polishing combination.

A tin-type metal lap used with tin oxide or one micron diamond powder is recommended for polishing harder stones. It has a harder surface than the tin lap.

A hardwood lap with the surface protected with paraffin or beeswax used with tin oxide is recommended for polishing soft materials.

A wax lap made on a metal base and a wax-impregnated muslin surface used with tin, chrome, or cerium oxide is recommended for polishing very soft, fragile gem material.

A linoleum lap used with tripoli or tin oxide is recommended for polishing curved tops and the girdles of gems, because linoleum is resilient.

A lucite lap used with cerium oxide is recommended for polishing **quartz** and **beryl**. Also see **faceting, faceting unit, machinery** and **Gemcutting: Tools and Materials.**

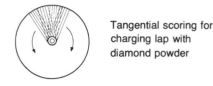

Tangential scoring for charging lap with diamond powder

lapboard. Basketry. (Also called plank.) A workboard that is held in the lap, to which the **basket** is attached to permit ease of working. See ill. Also see **Basketry: Tools and Materials.**

Lapboard

lapboard. Shell Carving. A board with a chamois overlay charged with abrasive. This device is used to hand polish fragile materials by moving them over the abrasive surface, rather than vice versa.

lapboard. Stitchery. A flat surface of wood or cardboard that is placed on the lap to facilitate sewing while sitting in a chair. It is usually a rigid surface, such as a drawing board or breadboard, which can be placed across the arms of a chair or on the lap to provide a level area. Originally, lap boards were flexible and **muslin**-covered so that they could be rolled up and easily moved.

The lapboard offers a flat surface for thread, scissors, and tools as well as an area to cut and sew against. Sometimes a piece of illustration board, cardboard, or a tray will work well. An advantage to using a lapboard is that it helps avoid the possibility of attaching the sewing to the clothes covering the lap.

lap frame. Crewel. Embroidery. Needlepoint. See **embroidery frame.**

lap frame. Rugmaking. See **hooking frame.**

lapidary. Gemcutting. A person who works at cutting, **polishing,** or engraving gems; or one who deals in precious stones. The term also applies to the workshop of a gemcutter. The word derives from the Latin *lapis*, meaning stone.

lapis lazuli. Gemcutting. A composition of **calcite, pyrite, lazulite,** some **hauynite,** and ultramarine. It has **hardness** of 5½, **specific gravity** of 2.4–2.9, a blue **streak,** and granu-

lar **fracture.** Lapis lazuli is opaque and has a deep blue **color** with yellow or reddish-brown specks of pyrite and white specks of calcite. It is decomposed by hydrochloric acid. Polish lapis lazuli with chrome oxide on a leather buff or 8,000 grit diamond powder on a wood **lap.** Also see **abrasive, cabochon, polishing** and **Gemcutting: Hand Grinding and Polishing, Rough Shaping.**

lap joint. Jewelry. A soldered joint in which the two edges overlap. Also see **soldering.**

lap joint. Stained Glass. Woodworking. See **joint.**

lap loom. Weaving. See **bandloom.**

lapping. Basketry. See **wrapping.**

lapping. Jewelry. A polishing technique used to polish metal to a mirror finish and generally reserved for polishing large, flat surfaces. It is done on a **buffing machine** with either a wheel made of a nonyielding surface such as a hard **felt buff** or a wheel that is made of a tightly grained wood. Most lapping is done against the side of the wheel, which generally, but not always, has a slightly convex surface. The wheel can be used as is or charged with **tripoli** for **polishing** or rouge for **buffing.** Also see **abrasive, super Tripoli.**

lap quilting. Quilts. **Quilting** without the use of a **quilting frame** or **quilting hoop.** Quilts may be made by quilting portions of the whole and assembling those portions when all are completed. This is especially helpful to anyone with limited work space, where it may be difficult to set up a frame. Also see **quilt-as-you-go.**

lapstick. Amber Carving. Coral Carving. Ivory and Bone Carving. Jet Carving. A piece of wood or plywood cut to the shape required to hold the material being worked. They may be shaped to hold rough or partially formed pieces (which are dopped into place) and can be used with the **bowdrill** for the final shaping and polishing of domes, spheres, or beads with rounded ends. They can also be placed in the vise to facilitate working on small pieces. See ill. Also see **beeswax.**

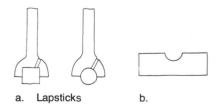

a. Lapsticks   b.

lapstick. Gemcutting. See **dop stick.**

lap weld. Metalworking. See **weld.**

large anvil. Metalworking. See **anvil.**

large saber saw. Woodworking. See **power saw.**

lark's head. Macramé. See **double half hitch.**

lark's head. Weaving. Used to attach string **heddle**s to the **heddle bar** of an **inkle loom** and for multiple other functions in weaving such as attaching the cords to the screw eyes in order to make a **snitch knot.** In spite of its many uses, it is seldom called or known by its name. See ill.

Lark's head

lary sticks. Weaving. Two long, thin sticks used as temporary supports for the **reed** while **sleying** it. They should be tied to the **breast beam** and **back beam** of the **loom,** although some weavers prefer to have them rest unattached on the beams. Lary sticks are used in just one method of sleying; use when the reed is removed from the **beater** and in a horizontal position in front of the **harness**es. This position is kept by tying the reed to the lary sticks. Since not all weavers prefer this method of sleying, lary sticks are not standard pieces of equipment that come with a loom. Instead, **lease sticks** or other rods longer than the loom are used. However, at one time, lary sticks were considered necessary and many old looms come with their own set made of the same wood as the loom. If lary sticks are used, the **raddle** can also be attached to them if desired. Also see **dressing the loom.**

lastakudos. Weaving. See **Finnweave.**

lasting pincers. Leatherwork. (Also called lacing hole nippers.) Basically a cobbler's tool, lasting pincers are used in leatherwork to pull lace or thread through small holes or to stretch shoe leather around a last. Common needlenose pliers or lasting pliers can be substituted. See ill. Also see **lacing.**

Lasting pincers

latchet hook. Rugmaking. See **latch hook.**

latch hook. Rugmaking. (Also called latchet hook.) A tool employed in making **latch-hooked rug**s. It is composed of a wooden handle with a hooked metal shank fitted into it. Attached to the hook is a small hinge; this is the "latch" that opens and closes in use. The hook pulls the yarn through the **canvas mesh,** and with the aid of the latch, forms a knot to hold the **pile** in place. The concept of the latch is based on the latch needle used in the commercial knitting industry. A crochet hook could be used in place of a latch hook, but quite a bit more skill is needed to make the knot, since no latch is present to guide and hold the yarn while making the knot. See ill.

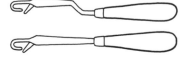

Two models of a latch hook

latch-hooked rug. Rugmaking. **Pile** rugs made with pre-cut pieces of yarn and a tool called a **latch hook.** The latch hook pulls the yarn through a stiffened **canvas mesh rug backing** and forms a Ghiordes knot to hold the pile in place. The technique has no long tradition behind it as other rugmaking methods do. It goes back to the 1920s when the latch hook was invented in England. It first became popular in America in the mid-1930s and is one of the easiest ways to make a pile rug. Yarn can be bought pre-cut in packages or cut at home with the aid of a yarn cutter or a homemade **gauge.** To use the latch hook, double a strand or strands of yarn around the shaft after inserting the shaft through the holes of the canvas mesh. The cut ends are held in the hook at the tip of the tool. Pull down with the hook so that the open latch goes through the loop of yarn, is closed, and pulls the yarn through the loop to form the knot. The **pile height** is determined by the cut lengths of yarn. The knots will stand up to give a tight pile and one that will not fall in any specific direction. The pile can be trimmed if any long or irregular ends appear after the rug is finished. See ill. Also see **knotted pile.**

Steps in using a latch hook

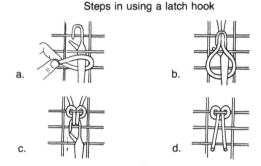

a.   b.   c.   d.

latex. Rugmaking. See **backing the rug.**

latex-coated material. Stitchery. See **backed material.**

latex foam. Toys. See **foam rubber.**

latex mold. Candlemaking. See **rubber mold.**

latex paint. Toys. A water-soluble paint that has a synthetic base. It is opaque, fast-drying, and easy to use. Once dry, it is waterproof. Latex can be brushed on for a fine, smooth **finish.**

latex paint. Woodworking. See **paint.**

latex resist. Ceramics. See **resist method.**

lathe. Metalworking. Plastics. Woodworking. A motorized shop tool used to turn a material while cutting tools shape the rotating form. It is used mainly for rounded or cylindrical forms in **metal, wood,** and **plastic.** In general, all lathes are composed of the same elements. The main parts are a headstock, which is a fixed center connected directly to the turning source, or through a belt drive; the tailstock, a movable center that is adjusted to hold the work to the headstock; and the tool rest, used to secure a carving tool while turning. Lathe sizes are determined by the maximum spindle length and diameter the machine can accept.

A lathe designed specifically for **metal spinning** and other metalworking is usually more powerful than a **wood-turning lathe.** However, some lathes may be used for both wood and plastic turning, as well as metal spinning. If you are planning to do a great deal of either plastic or metal turning, a metal-turning lathe is preferable to a wood-turning one.

lathe. Toys. (Also called wood lathe.) A machine for turning or cutting **wood.** There are some toys that cannot readily be made without a lathe. **Skittles, tops, nested eggs,** and other similar shapes are **lathe-turned.**

lathe forming. Plastics. See **lathe turning.**

lathe forming. Woodworking. See **wood turning.**

lathe tools. Woodworking. See **wood-turning tools.**

lathe-turned. Toys. **Wood** that has been shaped or cut by the use of a **lathe.** The **turned-wood animal** is produced through a combination of lathe-turning and sawing.

lathe turning. Plastics. (Also called lathe forming, turning.) The process of shaping forms on a **lathe.**

Use a lathe for plastic turning but sharpen the lathe tools as if for use on soft metal. Keep the tools very sharp.

When cutting, rest the lathe tools on a steady support. Use a high speed but make light cuts. The turning speed depends on the type of plastic and its size; check the manufacturer's recommended speeds.

Do not overheat the plastic when cutting. When turning **thermoplastics,** use a **coolant** such as a soap-and-water mixture.

Avoid stopping the **feed** in the middle of a cut or you may mark the surface. A semi-matte surface and ribbon-like shavings should result if done correctly.

lathe turning. Woodworking. See **wood turning.**

lathkin. Stained Glass. A tool used for opening the **channels** in **lead came.** Although available commercially a lathkin is generally made by the craftsman from a piece of hardwood. For example, a ⅜″ piece of round dowel 4 or 5″ long with a blunt point works well. Ivory, bone, or boxwood, or any smooth, hard substance can be used. See ill. Also see **needle-nose pliers, stopping knife, tracery** and **Stained Glass: Tools and Materials, Glazing.**

lath strips. Stained Glass. See **glazing strips.**

latigo. Leather. A term for cattle hide which has been tanned with alum and gambier. Latigo is sturdy and durable, but soft and pliable, and somewhat oily; it comes in bright yellow or dark brown. **Sides** (9–11 oz) are good for belts and bags. Latigo is used for **lacing,** saddles, and bridles. Also see **Leatherwork: Tanning and Manufacture.**

lattice. Woodworking. See **wood.**

lattice binding. Batik and Tie-dye. See **crisscross binding.**

lattice plaiting. Basketry. One of the three main types of **plaiting,** in which three or more series of flat parallel elements are woven together. It is a variation of **checked plaiting. Hexagonal plaiting** is an example of lattice plaiting.

lattice stitch. Lacemaking. See **net stitch.**

lattice-wrapped weave. Basketry. A **woven basketry weave** that uses an **active element** or **weft** to bind a parallel series of vertical **stakes** to a horizontal stake.

To make the lattice-wrapped weave, with the vertical stakes to the front, lay the waste end of your wrapping material along the horizontal stake so it points in the direction you will be weaving and will be held in place for the successive wrappings. Coming from behind, wrap it diagonally up to the right across the first stake. Next, bring it down behind the horizontal and out to the front. Then take it up to the left across the first stake and then diagonally down to the right in the back, and out to the front between the first and second stakes.

Simplified: Bottom left to top right, out the back and down. Bottom right across to top left and out the back. In the back, upper left to lower right and out the front. You are now ready to wrap the second and successive stakes. See ill.

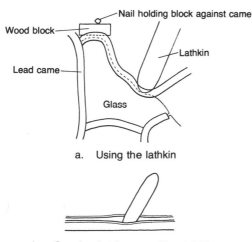

a. Using the lathkin

b. Opening lead came with a lathkin

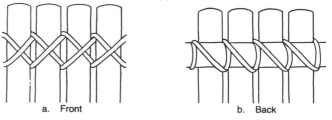

Lattice-wrapped weave

a. Front   b. Back

latticinio. Glasswork. A decorative type of glasswork highly developed by Venetian glassmakers in the eighteenth century. **Canes** of colored glass were arranged longitudinally inside a cylindrical form, picked up on a **punty gather,** and heated so that the canes fused together.

This mass, when heated again, was drawn and twisted, and sections of it were used for the stems of fancy vessels and the like. Alternatively, a ring of colored canes set in a form could be picked up around the outside of a **parison**, fused to a bubble, and then marvered. The resultant, often multicolored, parison was then blown in the usual fashion into vessels of great value. Also see **drawing, marvering**.

lauan. Woodworking. See **mahogany**.

laundry marker. Batik and Tie-dye. Stitchery. See **marking pens**.

Laurel Leaves. Quilts. An **appliqué quilt block** design showing leaves, gradually diminishing in size, pointing out to the four corners of the block.

lavender oil. China and Glass Painting. (Also called oil of lavender.) Oil extracted from garden lavender flowers, used as a **medium** for mixing **onglaze color** and for spreading **gold** over large areas.

lawn. Ceramics. A fine meshed **sieve** of silk, linen, or bronze wire mounted on a wood, metal, or plastic rim that is graded according to wires per inch. It is used to screen **glaze** in **mixing** before use.

lay cords. Bookbinding. The cord loops on the bar of the **sewing frame** to which are fastened the sewing cords used to join the **section**s of a book.

layering. Candlemaking. A decorative **molding** technique in which the candle is formed in layers of wax of different colors, each poured separately. Wait till each layer is sufficiently hard before pouring the next one. The harder the wax, the clearer the color separation; if the wax is too hard, however, the layers will not adhere. The **depressions** formed at each level should be refilled before the next layer is poured. To create various planes and levels of the colored layers, tip the mold at an angle as you are pouring. Also see **Candlemaking: Molding**.

layering. Weaving. See **padding**.

laying gold. Bookbinding. Applying **gold leaf** to a surface.

lay-up. Plastics. See **lamination**.

lazulite. Gemcutting. A mineral composed of hydrous aluminum phosphate with **hardness** of 5½ and **specific gravity** of 3.1 **crystal**lized in the monoclinic system. Lazulite is transparent blue with vitreous **luster** and granular **fracture**. Polish **facet**ed lazulite with tin oxide on a pewter or wooden **lap**. Lazulite is a constituent of **lapis lazuli**.

lazy daisy. Crewel. Embroidery. See **detached chain stitch**.

Lazy Daisy. Quilts. See **Hearts and Gizzards**.

lazy line. Weaving. A slight, often nearly invisible, oblique line sometimes found in the solid color areas in Navajo blankets. The line occurs when the color is not woven the full width of the **warp** but in sections due to the large size of the piece. In order to avoid a **slit tapestry**, the edges of the section were woven on a diagonal so that the joining would occur without any apparent breaks in the cloth. There appeared only faint open lazy lines to tell where the sections had been joined. Sometimes they could be seen only by holding up to the light. The lazy lines saved the Indian woman time and effort for otherwise she would have to move with each **filling pick** as it traveled from one **selvage** to the other. In addition, lazy lines are said to give flexibility to the blanket and thereby make it stronger.

lazy squaw stitch. Basketry. A basic **stitch** in **coiled basketry**. It consists of a long stitch interspersed with a short stitch or a series of short stitches and is used for speed in building up the fabric. Also see **Basketry: Coil Basket Construction**.

lazy squaw stitch. Beadwork. See **lazy stitch**.

lazy stitch. Beadwork. (Also called lazy squaw stitch.) A technique of stitching rows of **bead**s to skin or fabric widely used by the North American Indians. A needle with heavy, waxed, knotted thread, such as carpet thread, is pushed through to the right side of the skin. The required number of beads are threaded and pushed into place. The needle is pushed into the leather, the thread pulled tight and brought out again to begin the next row of beads, right above the last stitch. This method enables large areas to be rapidly covered with all-over patterns. For heavy skins, the stitches are not sewn through the entire thickness, but only through half of the skin so that no stitches show on the wrong side.

To stitch around a curve, rows of beads are stitched radiating from the center point of the circle, with the rows spread apart at the circumference, much the same as the rays of a setting sun. See ill.

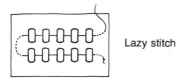
Lazy stitch

L-bar iron. Stained Glass. An L-shaped piece of iron that is screwed to the side of a **dalle-de-verre** worktable for use in making straight cuts in the **slab glass**. After the glass has been scored, hold the **cut-line** along the L-bar and bring it down sharply on the edge of the bar to make the glass break in a clean line. Also see **score** and **Stained Glass: Cutting Glass**.

lea. Spinning. Weaving. The yardage standard for **linen** yarn. One lea is equal to three hundred yards of linen spun from one pound of raw **flax**. The number of leas in one pound indicate the **yarn count**. For example, linen yarn marked "10 lea" has 3,000 yds. per pound, "10 lea, 2-ply" has 1500 yds. per pound.

lead. Metalworking. A very soft, heavy metal with a low melting point (around 600° F). It is used with tin in soft solder, or alloyed with 6–14½ antimony for casting and called type metal. It is easily cast since it does not usually adhere to cast iron, wrought iron, or steel molds or ladles. When casting, sprinkle ammonium chloride (**sal ammoniac**) on the surface. Lead fumes are poisonous and an exhaust fan and hood are necessary to draw them out of the studio. Also, never use lead for food containers or children's toys.

Lead is also sold in sheet form and has been used for **repoussé** work. It does not become **work-harden**ed, so does not require **annealing** after prolonged hammering. Lead is easily welded and soldered. Although it is low in strength, it is highly resistant to atmospheric corrosion and most acids.

lead. Puppets. A heavy, soft metallic element. Because of its weight and the ease with which it can be melted, it is excellent for weighting **puppets** and **marionettes**. **Sheet lead** is most often used for puppet **hands.**

lead. Stained Glass. See **lead came.**

lead bin. Stained Glass. (Also called lead coffin, lead rack, trough.) The best way to store **lead came** is in troughs or bins 6′ long (the commercial length of lead came) made of wood and hanging on the wall on **angle-irons** or shelf brackets. Lead can also be stored in bins 6′ long under the glazing bench, or hung from clamps nailed to the wall. See ill. Also see **Stained Glass: Setting Up a Workshop.**

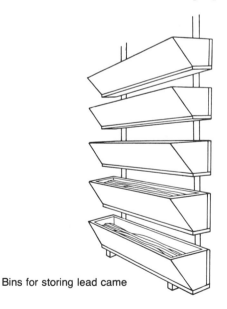

Bins for storing lead came

lead block. Jewelry. A flat lead block sometimes used in **forming. Dapping punch**es can be used with a lead block if a **dapping block** is unavailable, or a lead block can be used to form simple units of **repoussé.** Care must be taken not to contaminate precious metals because when the metal is heated for **annealing** or **soldering,** the smallest trace of the lead can attack the metal, causing pitting and holes. The lead can be removed from the metal with **files, carborundum paper,** or **steel wool.** Also see **niello.**

lead burning. Metalworking. See **lead welding.**

lead came. Stained Glass. (Also called calme, came, lead.) Strips of lead, usually 6′ long, milled in an extrusion process that channels and shapes them in a variety of ways. Lead came is the main support for the glass in a stained-glass **panel.** The top surface of came can be either round or flat, the round being tougher to cut because of the extra lead on top. The channel width measures about ¼″.

There are several basic types of lead came. H-came (also called H-channel lead, H-lead, or H-section lead) has a channel on either side of the center wall or **heart;** it is used for holding the pieces of stained glass in the panel. U-came (also called high-heart came), with one channel, is used for finishing the outer edge of a piece. H-came can be used in finishing when the window is to go in a wooden frame. The extra lead of the H provides room for error in the final measurements of the panel.

Specialized lead cames include steel-core or reinforced lead came, made by encircling a steel rod in the heart of the lead came and used for reinforcing large panels. The heart is larger than in other forms of came and should be planned for. It is cut with a hacksaw rather than a **glazing knife** and can be used in places in which **saddle bars** are inappropriate. Colonial lead came and high-heart came are very ornate leads with a heavier rounded top **leaf,** used mainly in leaded windows with clear glass. Off-center came has a heart placed to one side, with one large channel for thick glass and one small channel for a thin piece. It eliminates the need to use a larger lead (which would make the piece visually heavy) to accommodate the thicker glass. **Extra wide came** may be purchased in the same sizes as regular lead came, but with a channel almost double in width. It is used with very thick **antique glass** or in **double glazing.** See ill. Also see **casting lead came, copper foil, flux, glazing, lathkin, lead shears, needle nose pliers, side cutting pliers, stopping knife, stretching rod, template, tracery, zinc came** and **Stained Glass: Tools and Materials, Glazing.**

a. Various sections of lead came

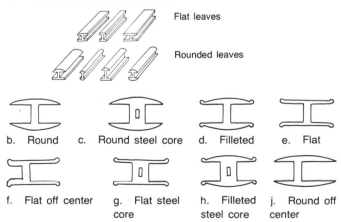

Flat leaves

Rounded leaves

b. Round   c. Round steel core   d. Filleted   e. Flat

f. Flat off center   g. Flat steel core   h. Filleted steel core   j. Round off center

lead coffin. Stained Glass. See **lead bin.**

lead-crystal glass. Glasswork. A kind of glass composed of silica (SiO_2), lead oxide (Ph_3O_4), and potash (K_2O). It is easy to work because it has a wide range of temperatures at which it is soft enough to form. Lead-crystal glass is brilliant, especially when potash is part of the formulation, because of its high index of refraction and it is fairly soft at room temperature. This softness leads to easy scratching, but also allows the glass to be cut or engraved easily. Lead crystal is used for the highest-quality tableware for its brilliance, in neon-sign work for its workability, and in television picture tubes for its ability to absorb ultraviolet light and X-rays. Also see **Worshipful Company of Glass Sellers.**

leaded brass. Metalworking. See **brass.**

leader. Basketry. A **rod** or **skein** that is run across a **handle** and **wrapped** with flat **winding reed.** It is most commonly used to give additional strength and thickness to the handle. Depending on how it is wrapped, decorative **listing** patterns may be obtained. See ill.

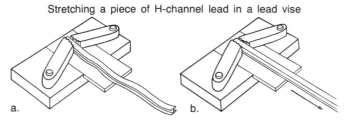
Leader

leader. Lacemaking. In **bobbin lace,** a single **bobbin** working horizontally. Also see **worker.**

leader. Spinning. (Also called starting yarn.) A short length of **spun yarn** left on an empty **bobbin** or **spindle** to facilitate beginning the new spinning. This length provides a firm strand to which the newly spun yarn can be attached, and by which it is pulled and wound around the spindle. Also see **dressing the distaff.**

lead glaze. Ceramics. Any **glaze** that contains more than 1% lead. Lead is used as a low-fire **flux. Pigment oxides** dissolved in lead are used for **underglaze** decoration; lead combined with a **tin glaze** is used in **majolica.** Lead is toxic and can be dangerous even after **firing.** Do not use on ware that will come in contact with acidic materials such as vinegar and wine. Lead should be avoided for use in any tableware, especially ovenware, where cooking temperatures can cause **metal release.** Also see **lead silicate, white lead.**

leading. Stained Glass. See **glazing** and **Stained Glass: Glazing.**

leading-up. Stained Glass. See **glazing** and **Stained Glass: Glazing.**

lead knife. Stained Glass. See **glazing knife.**

lead ladle. Stained Glass. See **casting lead came.**

lead leaf. Stained Glass. See **leaf.**

lead-lining. Stained Glass. See **cut-lining.**

lead mill. Stained Glass. See **casting lead came.**

lead poisoning. Stained Glass. See **Stained Glass: Safety Precautions.**

lead rack. Stained Glass. See **lead bin.**

lead shears. Stained Glass. A form of metal clipper used to cut **lead came.** Also see **glazing knife.**

lead silicate. Ceramics. A **frit** made of lead oxide and silica that eliminates the toxicity of lead compounds. Also see **lead glaze, white lead.**

lead soldier. Toys. See **toy soldier.**

lead substitutes. Stained Glass. See **copper foil, lead came, zinc came.**

lead-tin glaze. Ceramics. A mixture of lead and tin used in decorating pottery. Also see **majolica, tin glaze.**

lead vise. Stained Glass. A special vise available through stained-glass supply houses for stretching and straightening **lead came** before **glazing.** It is not expensive. Any vise except those for wood or pipe could be substituted. See ill. Also see **stretching lead** and **Stained Glass: Tools and Materials, Glazing.**

Stretching a piece of H-channel lead in a lead vise

a.   b.

lead welding. Metalworking. (Also called lead burning.) The process of **fusion welding lead** by heat with a **lead welding rod** and no **flux.** Clean the surfaces thoroughly and heat the metal with a small torch tip on a **propane torch** or an air-acetylene or oxyacetylene gas-fueled **flame.** Also see **oxyacetylene welding equipment.**

lead wiping. Metalworking. The process of joining lead pieces by repeatedly pouring molten **solder** containing 37−40% tin over the lead seam. Shape the solder into the seam by molding it with gloves and a cloth pad.

lead work. Lacemaking. See **leaf stitch.**

leaf. Bookbinding. A single sheet of paper that is hinged at the binding edge. A page is one side of a leaf.

leaf. Stained Glass. (Also called lead leaf.) The lip of the **lead came** or metallic foil which overlaps the **glass.** It is the section of the lead opened with the **lathkin** before **glazing.** Also see **copper foil, needle-nose pliers.**

leaf stitch. Lacemaking. A stitch that has a shaped, solid appearance. It is a very interesting bobbin-made **motif** and is found in almost all **bobbin lace**s. Honiton lacemakers call it **cutwork,** cutwork with a hole, leadwork, or "toad-in-the-hole." Other lacers may refer to the leaf stitch as blossom filling, brick filling, cushion filling, diamond filling, **filling, no-pin filling,** paddles, **pin filling,** plait, tally, and woven plait. The most common names are fan stitch, leaves, spot stitch, and wheat ears. The name varies according to the lace in which it is made, but all are constructed in the same manner.

Use two pairs of **bobbin**s; one **bobbin** becomes the **worker,** going over and under the three **passive** bobbins, back and forth; tighten or loosen the worker bobbin to shape the leaf or other **motif** as desired. Push up the thread from the worker bobbin to cover completely the threads from the passive bobbins. See ill. Also see **filling stitch.**

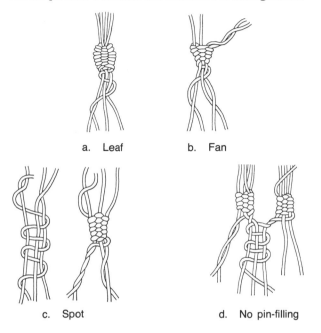

a. Leaf   b. Fan

c. Spot   d. No pin-filling

league. Basketry. A bottom **stick** that extends long enough to become a side **stake.**

leaking mold. Candlemaking. After the **wick** has been threaded through the hole pierced in the bottom of the **mold** it is necessary to seal the hole with **clay** or a **caulking compound** such as Mortite. Even with metal molds equipped with a retainer screw for plugging the hole, it is best to seal it using a caulking compound. If the candle begins to leak during pouring, reinforce the sealing or dip the candle rapidly into cold water. Also see **Candlemaking: Molding.**

lean clay. Ceramics. See **Ceramics: Clay.**

leaning bar. Puppets. See **bridge bar.**

learning toy. Toys. A toy or device designed to encourage study and exploration. All involve the use of basic skills. Most **game**s are learning toys in that they involve spelling or mathematics. Almost all toys are learning toys to some extent, although when they are designed for that specific purpose they are identified as **scientific toy**s or **educational toy**s. Also see **Toys: Constructional Toys.**

Lea's compound. Jewelry. A **greaseless compound,** generally used on a muslin **buff.** It is fast-cutting and produces a handsome **satin finish** on **copper** or **silver.** It can also be used to resurface steel tools, such as **stakes** or **steel block**s that get damaged; remove scratches or nicks using a file and then medium-grade **carborundum cloth. Buff** the tool with an **abrasive** compound such as Lea's for refining, and then with **super Tripoli** for a final smooth finish. When using Lea's compound, it is advisable to wear a face mask because of the dust. Lea's compound comes sealed in a soft metal tube. Peel off the top and part of the sides to use the compound. It dries out on exposed surfaces quite rapidly and should be stored upside-down with the exposed section underwater or wrapped tightly with a heavy-duty plastic food wrap. If it dries out, the dried portion can be cut away with a knife to expose a fresh surface. Also see **buffing compound.**

lease. Weaving. See **cross.**

lease cord. Weaving. The cord used to tie the **cross** in a **warp** in place after the warp is made, and before it is taken to the **harness loom.** On **primitive loom**s, a long lease cord is inserted the full width of the warp and stays on the loom during the weaving process. On the harness loom, **lease sticks** are substituted for the lease cord. Also see **backstrap loom.**

lease pegs. Weaving. The two pegs or rods around which the **cross** is formed on a **warping board** or **warping reel.** The yarn goes over one peg and under the other, alternately; when returning in the opposite direction the yarns are crisscrossed for the proper order of the warp.

lease rods. Weaving. See **lease sticks.**

lease sticks. Weaving. (Also called lease rods, cross sticks, rods.) A pair of thin, flat, and smooth wooden sticks that are inserted into the **warp** on either side of the **cross** to keep the cross in order while **dressing the loom.** The sticks are indispensable during **beaming,** keeping the warp organized and untangled, and during **threading** and **sleying,** insuring that the yarns are picked up in the correct order for going through the **heddle**s and **reed.** Lease rods usually have rounded edges to facilitate unencumbered movement through the yarn while beaming the warp. There are holes in each end of each rod; tie the pair together about an inch apart so that the cross is clearly visible and moved easily. Lease rods are included with the purchase of most **harness loom**s; if they have been lost, any stick meeting the above requirements can be used. On some narrow-width **table loom**s, the lease sticks are made of fiberboard.

Lease sticks are inserted into the warp after **warping** is completed and the warp is transferred to the loom. They take the place of the **lease cord** used to tie the cross. They are usually tied to the loom during beaming. However, in some methods of beaming, lease rods are left loose to be constantly pushed toward the **warp chain.** Depending on how the loom is dressed, the lease sticks can be either in the back or front of the loom; if in the front, they can be transferred to the back; this is advisable should the lease rods remain in the warp during weaving. The advantage of leaving them in is that they help to maintain the order of the yarns and mistakes and **broken end**s can be more easily spotted. Lease sticks can be removed when the loom is dressed; if retained, attach them to the **back beam** in order to prevent them from moving up with the warp and diminishing the **shed** opening.

leash. Weaving. See **cross, string heddle.**

leather. Bookbinding. Leather is a versatile and enduring material for covering books. It can be used alone to cover the entire surface of the **board**s or used only on **corner**s and **back**s in combination with cloth. It makes strong yet supple bindings, pleasing to the eye and to the touch. Because of its thickness it is not as easy to work with as cloth. Often it must be pared or shaved to facilitate its working ability and to permit or ease opening and closing of the book. Avoid leathers that imitate other skins and use only acid-free leathers to ensure durability.

Morocco is made from goat skin; it is the most useful, general purpose leather.

Niger morocco is sumac-tanned, aniline-dyed, and resistant to atmospheric pollution. Niger morocco is a popular, useful leather available only in a limited range of colors.

Levant morocco comes mostly from South Africa; it is tough, has a bold grain, and is available in many colors. It is best employed on large books.

Oasis morocco comes from Algeria; it is the cheapest and softest of the morocco leathers.

Sheepskin is not highly recommended; it is used for cheaper bindings.

Sealskin is considered to be the finest of all skins for casings. As concerned as a binder may feel about the endurance of his book, a serious consideration must be given to the rapidly diminishing number of seals and to the endurance of the species. Sealskin is recommended, therefore, as an excellent covering for seals and not for bindings.

Information on the care of leather bindings may be obtained from the Superintendent of Documents, Washington, D.C., leaflet #69: Preservation of Leather Bindings. Also see **paring, pasting leather** and **Bookbinding: Care and Maintenance.**

leather appliqué. Stitchery. Any **appliqué** work in which leather pieces are sewn to a **background** of leather or other material. Leather, being nonwoven, does not need to be **hem**med or turned under but can be **topstitch**ed. If very heavy leather is used, the edges may have to be perforated with a leather punch, an awl, or other sharp tool before sewing.

leather doll. Toys. A doll with a leather body. **Kid** was preferred, as was split leather which, because it is thinner, is even more pliable. In the 1800s leather was sometimes used for the **doll head** as well as the **doll body,** although more often the head was of wax, **composition,** or wood. Leather is seldom used in **dollmaking** now, but is occasionally used for special **stuffed animals.**

leather dye. Batik and Tie-dye. **Aniline dyes** designed for use on leather may be adapted for use in **tie-dye** and **batik.** It may be painted on directly in liquid form or diluted for **dip dyeing.** Experimentation is necessary to determine its fastness and the strength of **dye** needed. Two common

brands of leather dye are Fiebing's and Tandy's. Also see **direct dye painting.**

leather hard. Ceramics. (Also called cheese hard.) A condition of dryness that occurs in the raw ware. Also see **applied decoration** and **Ceramics: Form.**

leather hinge. Puppets. (Also called leather joint.) A **hinge joint** made from a strip of leather. It is sometimes used at the knee or elbow of a **marionette.** For example, if the upper and lower parts of a leg are made from sticks of wood, they can be hinged by placing the pieces end to end and then gluing a narrow **leather strip** on the back side. This allows the leg to move backward at the knee and prevents it from moving forward. Also see **screw-eye joint** and **Puppets: Making the Marionette Skeleton.**

leather joint. Puppets. See **leather hinge.**

leather lacing. Macramé. Long narrow strips of leather (sometimes called "thongs") that can be used in macramé in place of macramé **cord.**

leather-lined vise. Coral Carving. Ivory and Bone Carving. The modification of any vise by attaching Moroccan leather to the vise jaws to prevent marring the surface of soft materials. Also see **bead-holding jig, beeswax, carpet underlay, wood vise wedge** and **Shell Carving: Tools and Materials.**

leather needle. Stitchery. See **needle, sewing machine needle.**

leather strip. Puppets. A narrow thin piece of leather used in making a **leather hinge** for an **articulated figure.** Also see **Puppets: Making the Marionette Skeleton.**

LEATHERWORK

Leather is animal skin that has been tanned, usually with the hair removed in the process. It is a strong, flexible, durable material to work with and can readily be stitched, glued, dyed, and formed. A **hide** is a full pelt of a large animal, usually a cow or horse. The hides are usually split for easy handling into two halves, each one referred to as a **side.** A smaller skin is classified as a **kip** for an immature cow or horse or as a **skin** for a smaller animal.

Top-grain leather is the smooth hair side. A **split** is a layer that is split from the flesh side or the middle layers of the hide. A **flesher** is taken from the underside of the pelt.

Various types and grades of leather are available, such as English tooling kip and **cabretta. Suede** is any hide with a brushed surface or a nap. Certain leathers are better for certain projects, such as top-grain vegetable-tanned leather for **tooling** and **stamping,** top-grain leather (5–8 oz) for belts, or lightweight leather (2–3 oz) for garments.

The thickness of leather is measured in terms of weight, designated by the number of ounces in one square foot of leather. One **ounce** of leather is $1/64''$ thick, and so on.

Leather is marked according to the number of square

feet: 9^1 means 9¼', 9^2 means 9½', 9^3 means 9¾', and so on.

Leather is graded according to the quality of the hide surface by the letters A, B, C, and D. Grade A leather is the best, with the least amount of imperfections, scars, or marks and with the most uniform thickness.

Leather-crafted garments and decorative items have been an essential part of daily life since ancient times. Egyptian leather shoes and writing tablets have survived. Leather was used during Greek and Roman times for shoes, clothing, and decorative accessories. The Romans even used leather for money. Leather items were used early in many other civilizations, from Africa to North America. During the Middle Ages leatherworkers were organized into guilds such as the **Fraternity of Leatherworkers** in Spain. Leatherwork designing reached a period of rich ornamentation in fourteenth-century Italy with **cuirboulli work** in which softened, damp leather was shaped or molded over relief forms with intricate patterns. It was often combined with **carton-cuir work,** a process of modeling a leather and paper pulp into designs, much the same as clay. Decorative bookbindings, containers, and other household ornaments were produced with a sculptured pattern, usually finished by staining them black.

Most of the processing of leather was probably based on the "tannin" derivatives of various barks and plants. The Hebrews are credited for the development of oak bark tanning, which was the principal method used until **chrome tanning** was developed in the nineteenth century by the chemist Sir Humphry Davy. With this method the hides are soaked in chromium-salt baths for a few hours instead of months, as was necessary for vegetable-tanned leather. At about the same time, machines were developed to remove the hair and flesh from the hides and to split and shave the pelts into various uniform thicknesses. By the twentieth century, leather tanning had become so highly developed that the tanneries were producing leather in unlimited colors, textures, grains, and finishes.

TANNING AND MANUFACTURE   The **tanning** process involves three basic stages: **curing** (or pickling), tanning, and finishing. The untreated pelts are refrigerated until they reach the tannery to prevent decomposition. The curing is done with a wet salting process in which pelts are washed and then sprinkled with salt or brine cured in vats of salt crystals. The pelts are then sorted and trimmed to facilitate handling. The large **hide**s are usually **split** down the backbone into two **sides.** The hides are further processed by soaking them in water and chemicals for 10–20 hours, then rinsing in fresh water to restore moisture that is lost during the curing process. The hair and excess flesh are removed by soaking in a lime solution and then **fleshing,** or scraping with rotary blades. From this time on the hair side is called the "grain side"; the underside is referred to as the "flesh side." The skins are further purified in a **bating** treatment. The pelt is then washed and preserved in sulfuric acid until ready for tanning.

Vegetable tanning, or bark tanning (the preparation necessary for tooling leather), is soaking the skins in vegetable and oak bark derivatives for up to six months. In **chrome tanning,** more commonly used and much faster, the pelts are soaked in a solution of chromium salts for only a few hours. There are several other tanning methods, such as combinations of chrome and vegetable tanning, designed to produce various types of leathers. In oil tanning the leather is processed with fish oils for softness and pliability. This process is used for **chamois** and **latigo.** After tanning, the excess water is wrung from the hide which is then fed into a machine to be split into various thicknesses. At this time the leather is dyed by various processes.

Fat liquoring is the next process, involving soaking in vats of oils, chemicals, and fats to strengthen the leather and restore its pliability. Then the hides are stretched onto frames and dried in the open air or in ovens.

The finishing of leather consists of restoring moisture lost during dyeing by spraying the hides with water, softening the hides by machine rolling, and removing blemishes by buffing. The **finish** coatings (to protect the leather and bring out the color) are applied in thin layers that are let to dry between applications. In staking, one of the final finishing processes, the skins are drawn over metal stakes to remove any residue or encrustations and to make them more flexible. Plating, in which glass rollers are rolled over the leather under great pressure, gives a smooth surface and is also used to emboss **artificial grain. Suede** is finished by burnishing to give a soft nap.

After the processing is finished, the tanned skins are trimmed, measured, graded, and shipped to wholesalers and craft shops.

SETTING UP A WORKSHOP   Ideally, a large, well-lighted worktable and space for storage of hides, dyes, and tools should be available for leatherwork. A 4' × 8' plywood or pine tabletop provides a good cutting board for spreading out and cutting hides. The plywood board may be covered with artists' mat board for cutting. At one end of the worktable, a pounding board, such as a thick piece of Neolite from a shoemaker, should be glued for punching holes and riveting. For **stamping** and **tooling,** a marble slab around 12" square is needed.

For general storage it is helpful to have shelves close to the workbench with separate boxes or bottles for small items such as **finding**s, sewing and lacing tools, etc.

The leatherwork shop may be started on a very small scale with just a few tools and hides and then enlarged as your interest in the craft grows.

TOOLS AND MATERIALS   There are very few leatherwork tools that are considered basic to all leather techniques. Each type of operation or technique calls for different tools, so they should be purchased as you go along in accordance with your needs. It is, however, important to pay a little extra for quality in the tools that will be used with frequency and to give them the proper care. Basically, a workbench, a hardwood or rawhide **mallet, rubber cement** or leather glue, a good pair of **scissors,** a compass, **dividers,** a **square,** and a whetstone are needed.

For cutting light leathers, the scissors will suffice. For cutting heavier leather, a **bevel point knife** is the most versatile. For cutting straps for belts, bags, or sandals, buy a **Stript-Ease,** an inexpensive **draw gauge** that can be adjusted to easily cut even strips of leather. A **skiving knife** or **safety beveler** will be useful to pare away even thicknesses in heavy leather to facilitate folding or sewing together two layers without unnecessary bulk. Eventually a **head knife** or **moon knife** will be a desirable purchase.

An edge beveler, available in several sizes, is used to round the edges of heavy pieces, and a **circle edge slicker** is used to polish and smooth the beveled edge. An **edge creaser** is used to incise lines an even distance from the edges of leather in preparation for recessed stitching or for a decorative, more finished effect. A **gouge** (a **rampart gouge** is easiest to use) will take a sliver out of the dry leather (for recessed stitching) or it can be used to carve decorative motifs that can be filled in with dyes or permanent markers.

The amount and type of sewing and lacing done will determine what kinds of punches and **thonging chisel**s are needed. A good **revolving punch** is an absolute necessity. Round **drive punch**es in various sizes are also quite basic and can be bought as needed. A four-prong round hole drive punch is a great time saver for punching long rows of evenly spaced holes. Thonging chisels punch slits through the leather for sewing and lacing; they are available in a wide range of numbers of prongs and sizes of slit. **Lacing** and **thread** should also be bought as needed. A life-eye needle or a hook-and-eye needle works best for lacing. A pair of needlenose pliers or cobbler's lasting pliers is useful for pulling lace through narrow slits or holes.

The basic equipment for **tooling** and **stamping** is a piece of marble or "Marblite," the best base for absorbing the blows of the stamping hammer, and a **swivel knife,** the basic tool for incising the outline designs that are the mainstay of tooled leatherwork. **Modeler**s and **stamp**s come in a rather dazzling variety and should be bought as needed.

For coloring and finishing, it is advisable to buy **dyes**, **edge dyes**, stains, antique finishes, and **wax**es as needed. A supply of rags, daubers, sheep's wool, and small artists' paint brushes should be kept on hand.

Conditioning of leather calls for carnauba wax, **neat's-foot oil, lexol, castor oil,** Vaseline, or any number of preparations expressly sold for various types of leather. The variety of cleaning agents is also varied, but **saddle soap** is the most widely used.

Rivets, **snap**s, **eyelet**s, buckles, **finding**s, etc., should of course be bought as needed.

Keep all tools well sharpened and in good condition. A whetstone or oil stone is used for sharpening, with a few drops of oil on the stone. When sharpening knives, both sides of the blade are pulled back and forth against the stone at the angle at which the blade is ground. A leather strap may also be used for a final sharpening.

To sharpen a **swivel knife** with its two-angled sides, whet both sides and maintain the correct angle while sharpening.

A **thonging chisel** is sharpened on a stone by stroking it on the flat angle of the prongs with pressure on the motion toward the cutting points.

The **awl** is revolved on the whetstone by turning between the fingers to grind evenly all around the point. For the wedge-pointed saddler's awl, each flat surface of the point is sharpened separately. A **drive punch** is sharpened by turning it in the fingers while holding it at an oblique angle. The tubes of a **revolving punch** are sharpened with a strip of emery cloth; and the anvil, with a fine file. Stamping tools can be conditioned by rubbing them on a leather strap with some jeweler's rouge rubbed into it.

CUTTING AND EDGING   Cutting must always be done on a soft wood surface with very sharp tools. To cut straight lines, hold the knife perpendicular to the leather and pull it firmly along the edge of a metal ruler. For heavy leather, several light cuts will be needed to cut all the way through. When using a **template,** trace the lines in pencil on the leather and cut them freehand or cut along the edge of the cardboard pattern as you would use a ruler. A **head knife** or **moon knife** may be needed to cut heavy leather. For general work with lightweight and medium-weight leathers, a good pair of leather **scissors** should be adequate. Garments and curved shapes are best cut with scissors; cutting lightweight leather with a knife will pull and stretch it.

The **draw gauge** is used for quickly cutting even strap widths. The **Strip-Ease,** an inexpensive version of the draw gauge, is also adjustable for various width straps. Both of these tools take some practice to operate.

Skiving—reducing the thickness of leather by shaving off thin layers, usually from the flesh side—can be done with most knives, or with a skife, **safety beveler,** or **skiving knife.** Skiving should be done on a hard surface; a marble slab is perfect. Skiving is done with gouges along the line to be creased in preparation for folding. When joining equal thicknesses of leather or lace, skiving is done to both pieces so that, when cemented together, they will equal a single thickness, thus reducing bulk. The knife is placed almost flat on the edge of the leather and pushed with even tension along the edge, paring away a shallow wedge of even thickness.

Another cutting technique, edging (or dressing) is done to put a bevel on the edges of heavy leather belts, bags, and straps. An **edge cutter** or **common edge beveler** is used to slice off various-size bevels. To make the edge smoother, sand lightly with emery paper or fine sandpaper; the edge may be burnished even more with a **circle edge slicker,** a **modeler,** or a **burnisher.**

Regular sewing patterns may be used for sewing leather garments and accessories. If there are any alterations to be made in the pattern or if the pieces are too large for the hides and should be cut, mark the pattern before cutting. Cut out all of the paper patterns, trimming away seam allowance in any place where raw edges will be left instead of hemming or if raw edges are going to be butted together and laced in lieu of stitching seams.

Leather is not cut on the fold as fabric is. Make a paper tracing of any piece designated in the sewing pattern for cutting on the fold, marking the fold line. Flip the pattern piece over, line it up along the fold line, and trace the other half. Cut out and use the complete pattern piece. The pattern, when taped to the hide and ready to cut, should be exactly what you want.

Place the patterns to best utilize the hide, placing the large pieces along the grain or nap of the hide, which is along the animal's backbone. Tape pieces down with masking tape and trace around each one with a felt-tip pen. A ruler should be used for straight edges. Mark all darts, buttons, etc., with the pen. Remove the pattern and mark the pattern identification names on the back side of leather pieces.

GLUING AND BONDING Gluing is used for adhering folds and to hold seams in place for sewing and **lacing.** Some items can be constructed entirely by cementing. Gluing is done on dry leather, except for temporarily spot gluing while still wet. **Rubber cement** is commonly used for gluing leather. Various leathercraft cements are also available from craft shops. Leather can also be joined with **rivet**s.

To glue a seam allowance, brush on glue along the seam and press in place. For turning back an edge or hem, apply glue to the edge double the width of the hem desired. Masking tape may be used as a guide for accurate gluing and to prevent glue from adhering to unwanted areas. Remove the tape after applying the glue. When dry, fold back the hem to the glue line.

Bonding is done to join two pieces of leather to add thickness or to have two finished **grain** sides showing. Usually both pieces of leather are evenly coated with glue and allowed to dry. To spread an even coating over large areas use a piece of cardboard to spread the glue, working quickly so that it will dry in an even, thin layer. Press the pieces together; they will bond on contact. To ensure a firm bond, tap the bonded pieces lightly with a **mallet.**

Care must be taken when bonding leather to place the pieces correctly because the bond is permanent. To avoid mistakes in placement, place a sheet of tracing paper between the two layers of glued, dry leather while positioning them; the dried glue won't stick to the paper. Pull the paper down, matching up a small part of the top, then continue pulling the paper down and joining the pieces for a permanent, perfect bond.

When gluing appliqué shapes care must be taken not to leave extra glue around the edges, especially on **suede.** A paper stencil may be cut the same as the appliqué shape and placed on the background leather. Brush the glue sparingly on the leather appliqué shape so it won't smudge when pressed down. After the glue has dried press it carefully to the glued background area.

Glue may be cleaned from most smooth leathers by rubbing off the excess with fingers. Also see **laminating.**

CREASING, SCORING, AND FOLDING **Creasing,** which is done with an **edge creaser,** is used for decoration or for recessed stitching. It is done on leather dampened with a sponge, pulling the creaser back and forth until the crease is of desired depth. The edge creaser may also be used to run a decorative line along the edge of leather that has been folded under and glued to add a finished look and help the glue to bond more firmly.

Scoring leather, much the same process as that used to score heavy paper or cardboard, is done to facilitate folding lightweight leather. The folding line is marked on the flesh side. The leather may be dampened for ease in folding. Place a ruler along the line and run along the line with a modeling tool, ball-point pen, **bone folder,** or scratch **awl.** Bear down with moderate pressure.

To fold heavy leather, dampen it and score to fold or pare away layers of leather from the flesh side by **skiving** with a **skiving knife** or a **safety beveler.** For very heavy leather, a deeper gouge may need to be removed from the fold line with a **rampart gouge** or an **adjustable V-gouge.** The gouging tool used should be placed so that the cutting blade hits the line drawn for the fold. Set the tool for the desired depth and push it firmly along the fold line, using a ruler as a guide.

To make the fold, dampen the leather along the groove line on the flesh side. Press the fold in place and tap it lightly with a **mallet** to set it. Let the leather dry in position. Gluing is done after the leather has dried.

FORMING Leather, when dampened, has some flexibility and can be molded over a form with pressure applied to it. Even hats can be made by forming the leather over a hat block. Two fitting molds are needed, such as two pie tins or two bowls, one fitting snugly inside the other. Cowhide or tooling leather should be used for forming, prepared by soaking or **casing.** Stretch the leather over the top of the smaller mold; place the larger mold over it and weight it until the leather is dry; remove the leather from the mold and trim the edges with a knife.

SEWING Leather may be sewn together with **needle** and **thread** or joined by **lacing.** For sewing most leathers the holes will have to be prepunched. **Skiving** may be necessary to reduce bulk in joining pieces of heavyweight leather.

The thickness of the leather determines the length of the stitches. The lighter the leather, the closer the stitches. To mark the spaces on medium or lightweight leather, use a pounce wheel or **space marker.** For large stitches, use a **thonging chisel** or mark the intervals with a pencil and ruler or with **dividers** set at the desired stitch width.

The **saddler's haft and awl** is generally used to pierce the holes for stitching. In heavy leather the stitching may be sewn in a recessed groove to save wear and tear on the thread. Use the **stitching groover,** V-gouge, or **edge creaser** to make the groove. Then punch holes in the recessed groove. It may be helpful to hold heavy leather in a **lacing pony** or vise when enlarging the holes.

The thread is knotted at one end before sewing. When stitching is finished, pound the knot lightly with a **mallet** to flatten it. Then secure it with a bit of glue. To finish off a line of stitching, run the thread back under several stitches on the back side, then cut the thread and tap the stitching lightly with a mallet. Various stitches may be used for leatherwork; the **running stitch** is the most commonly used for seams.

To make curved seams flexible and to make a seam allowance lie flat, cut V notches along the seam allowance on the wrong side. For straight seams, stitch, flatten, cement, and pound the seam.

Various methods may be used for stitching seams. **Topstitching** and **double topstitching** add a decorative look to a plain seam and also stitch down the seam allowance. An **overlapped seam** joins two pieces of leather with topstitching from the right side.

Holes for lacing are prepunched with a thonging chisel or with round **drive punch**es. The chisel makes short slits through which flat lace passes. Round holes are easier to work with and more decorative in appearance. The thonging chisel is used with a mallet. To pierce holes around a corner, use a single-prong lacing chisel or a single-hole drive or **revolving punch,** punching them as evenly as possible to fit around the corner.

Various stitches are used for lacing. The **cross stitch, whipstitch,** and **single buttonhole stitch** are most commonly used.

Most sewing machines, with the right adjustments, will stitch leather beautifully. Nylon thread or cotton-covered polyester thread is used, with double-duty weight for heavyweight leathers. Use the same thread for the bobbin. Also, most machines accept special wedge-shaped leather needles. Set the stitch length regulator for a low number of stitches per inch, generally around six. The pressure foot regulator is adjusted to lighten the pressure, as leather is usually thicker than fabric. Stitch slowly, helping the leather along, and do not backstitch. For garments, stitch from the top toward the hemline; if there is stretching, the hem can be trimmed. To finish off seams, cut the thread and tie the ends by hand, then trim them.

V notches along a curved seam

DYEING AND COLORING   Various dyes and finishes can be used to color leather. The leather must be clean and dry. The **dye** may be applied before or after the project is assembled, depending on the coloring desired.

To dye large areas use a soft cloth or a piece of woolskin saturated with mineral oil to keep the woolskin from absorbing too much dye. Apply the dye (poured into a shallow pan for easy dabbing) with quick, broad strokes for even coverage. Work with back-and-forth strokes or with a circular motion.

For small areas, apply dye with a dauber, a small piece of woolskin attached to a wire handle rather like a liquid shoe polish applicator. For intricate or tooled areas, use a small brush to paint the dye on. After the dye has dried, rub the area with a soft cloth to remove the excess before applying a finish coating.

Special edge dyes and enamels are available for coloring leather edges. These dyes give greater penetration and the enamels give a water-resistant finish. A brush or a dauber may be used for application.

Various textures and combinations of dye can be achieved with interesting results. Texturing can be done with woolskin dipped in dye and brushed across the leather or with a toothbrush dipped in dye and spattered over dyed background. Dye can be successfully applied in layers, building up layers of translucent color.

Antiquing paste, available in jars in many colors, is rubbed in with a soft cloth to give a soft, lustrous finish. Antique finish is lovely over stamped and tooled designs.

Leather can also be painted with acrylics, which give a very smooth, glossy look. Permanent felt-tip markers are a versatile medium for decorating leather and suede.

FINISHING   For finishing leather, leather lacquer and a can of **neat's foot oil** or **Lexol** should be kept on hand. Many other finishes (**wax**es, polish, soaps, and oils) are available as a final protective coating.

Carnauba cream is applied with a cloth and polished to a soft finish to clean and soften leather. Saddle soap is applied with a sponge or brush, working it into a lather. The excess is removed with a cloth and the leather buffed to clean, soften, and polish the surface. Vaseline petroleum jelly is rubbed into the leather and then the excess is removed with a cloth to condition leather. Omega Finish Coat and Fiebing Tan-Kote are leather lacquers. Apply lacquer with a cloth and, when dry, polish to a high gloss. Lacquered leather is clear and water resistant. Neat's foot oil, the commonly used finish for making leather water resistant, also softens and lubricates and can be used periodically for reconditioning leather. Also see **buffing, plate finish.**

CARE, CLEANING, AND STORAGE   Although leather is extremely durable, dye, heat, and soaking tend to make it stiff. **Neat's foot oil** or **Lexol** should be applied to condition leather about every six months. Apply several light coats with a soft cloth, with extra oil on areas to receive extra stress.

If smooth leather becomes soiled it should first be cleaned with saddle soap, then conditioned with oil. If **suede** is soiled, try using a wire brush to clean it. Commercial suede cleaning is available for more soiled items. Leather articles should be stored flat or hung on wooden hangers, but not in sealed bags—they need air.

leaves. Lacemaking. See **leaf stitch.**

lebkuchen. Toys. An **edible dough** used in making **cookie art.** It is a **dark dough** that is rolled and cut with **cookie cutter**s to make a traditional cookie of Bavaria, Germany, and Switzerland. It is usually decorated with a linear pattern of white frosting.

Lee's Surrender. Weaving. See **overshot.**

left half hitch. Tatting. The first part of the **double stitch** in tatting. Also see **half hitch, making the double stitch.**

left-hand twill. Weaving. See **twill weave.**

left-hand weaver. Basketry. The name given to the **weaver** that is the furthest to the left of all other weavers in weaving a given stitch. The term is used primarily when giving directions on how to make a specific **weave.**

leg. Lacemaking. See **bar.**

legacy quilt. Quilts. See **sampler quilt.**

leg bar. Puppets. (Also called leg control.) The **cross bar** that controls the leg movement of the **marionette.** It is usually hung on the **control** in such a way that it can be removed easily. **String**s are run from the knees of a marionette to the leg bar and, when these strings are **manipulate**d, a walking movement is suggested in the **puppet.** Also see **knee string, rocking** and **Puppets: Manipulating the Marionette.**

leg control. Puppets. See **leg bar.**

Lego building brick. Toys. The trademark name for a variety of plastic **constructional toy**s that have fitted parts consisting of pegs and sockets. The **bricks** are made in various sizes and styles and all fit snugly. Also see **Toys: Construction Toys.**

leg string. Puppets. See **knee string.**

lehr. Glasswork. A furnace or oven, the temperature of which is lowered slowly under close control so that glass objects inside cool slowly enough to prevent cracking. Also see **annealing.**

lemel. Jewelry. Filings produced when **filing precious metals.** They should be saved and sold to the refiner. Also see **sweeps.**

lemon juice. Stitchery. A safe and effective **bleach** for lightening or whitening **fabric.** It is often used for delicate or antique materials, laces, doilies, or **antimacassars.** The lemon juice can be squeezed directly onto a stain or spot, or the juice can be diluted in water to soak the fabric. It is one of the safest of all **bleaching** agents.

Lemon Star. Quilts. A favorite **pieced-block** pattern of an eight-pointed star. It is one of the many variations of the **LeMoyne Star.** See ill.

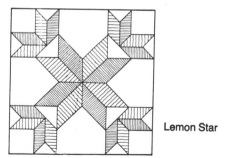

Lemon Star

LeMoyne Star. Quilts. (Also Lemoyne Star.) A popular **pieced** pattern consisting of any of a variety of eight-pointed stars set into squares. The pattern takes its name from the LeMoyne brothers, one of whom captured ports in Canada from the English in the late 1600s. The other brother founded New Orleans in the early 1700s. Yankee homemakers, unfamiliar with French, translated this to **Lemon Star,** by which the quilt pattern and others that are similar are often known.

A variation of the LeMoyne Star is **Lucinda's Star.** See ill.

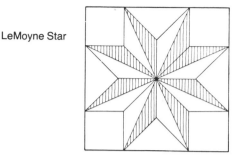

LeMoyne Star

Lend and Borrow. Quilts. See **Rocky Glen.**

lengthwise. Quilts. Stitchery. With the length of the woven fabric parallel to the **selvage** edge. The **warp** threads are those that run lengthwise.

lengthwise grain. Batik and Tie-dye. Quilts. Stitchery. The direction of the **warp** threads in a woven fabric. The lengthwise grain is the length of the **fabric,** running parallel to the **selvage** edges, and cuts made on it are parallel to both the warp threads and the selvages. The lengthwise grain is often referred to as the straight of the fabric or **"on the grain."**

The warp threads run the length of the woven material. Fabrics for **panel**s, **wall hanging**s, **quilt block**s, and dolls are placed so that the lengthwise threads or the warp threads run through the cut shapes in a straight line from top to bottom. If materials are not cut with the lengthwise grain they will sometimes stretch and eventually will become uneven.

lengthwise thread. Quilts. Stitchery. See **warp.**

leno. Weaving. An **openwork technique** created by twisting **warp ends** around each other and having the **filling** yarn hold the twist in place. It is structurally the simplest of the **cross weave**s, and also the most commonly used. Leno is basically a combination of the **gauze weave** and the **plain weave** with the leno worked **selvage** to selvage and followed by an odd number of plain weave **pick**s, or with the leno just in certain design areas surrounded by plain weave.

In commercial weaving the term "leno" refers to any **crossed warp** technique beyond a gauze weave. In hand-weaving circles, the term is used much more loosely to mean just about any cross weave, even though it has the above precise meaning. In addition, because it has a very tight twist, it is used in the making of chenille yarn (a **novelty yarn**) to hold in place the cut thread that gives the yarn its character. Leno is used in all types of fabrics as well as **wall hanging**s for ornamentation, or to form a design of open spaces versus solid areas.

Leno is done with a **pick-up stick** by most handweavers, but can be woven using **doup**s or as **bead leno.** Using a pick-up stick, leno can be done on either a closed or open **shed**; the tendency is to use the latter, because the twists are easier to control and result in a more precise and firmer look. With an open shed the warp ends from the lower layer of the shed are pulled up and to the right twisting over an equal number of warp ends in the top layer. One, two, three, or even four ends can be twisted together using the same number on both layers of the shed. Leno is worked from right to left for the first part of the twist. The remaining, or second part, of the twist is caused by the twisted lower thread returning to its original position in the pick of plain weave that follows the twist pick.

To do leno, end the plain weave on a left to right filling **shot** and open the next shed. In this shed, the edge right thread in the leno area should be in the upper layer of the shed. Insert the pick-up stick into the shed from the right. Pick up the first thread in the lower shed, lift it and move with it on the tip of the stick to the right of the first upper end. Slide the stick with the end on it over the first upper end and down to pick up the second lower end. The second lower end is also brought up by the pick-up stick to the right, up and over the second upper end. The third lower end is then picked up and worked in the same manner as the two previous ends. When the row in the design area is finished, all the ends from the lower shed should be on the stick. Close the shed and turn the pick-up stick on its edge, thereby forming a new shed. Insert the filling yarn right to left and return the stick to a level position so the shed is closed. Use the stick to push down the filling just inserted. Remove the stick and beat down with the **beater.** Open the plain weave shed and insert the filling left to right. In selvage-to-selvage leno, the twists tend to draw the edges in; therefore, the tension of the filling should be more relaxed. When weaving leno just in areas, the surrounding plain weave has extra rows of filling so that the weaving is kept at the same level across the entire cloth. Design areas of leno are often planned first on **graph paper.** See ill. Also see **Mexican lace, pick-up weave.**

Leno

leno heddle. Weaving. See **doup.**

le pendu. Toys. See **flipperdinger.**

lepidiolite. Gemcutting. A lithium mica with **hardness** of 3½, **specific gravity** of 2.8, granular **fracture,** and lilac color. Lepidiolite is often cut by hand with steel tools. Also see **Gemcutting: Hand Grinding and Polishing, Rough Shaping.**

les laboureurs. Ivory and Bone Carving. This was the term applied to the French prisoners of war held captive in England after the Napoleonic Wars who spent their time carving objects from **bone** and **ivory** and other materials available to them. It is believed that many were ivory carvers from **Dieppe** in Normandy, a town famous for its ivory carving industry. Many of these men were impressed into Napoleon's navy and were captured by the British Royal Navy; others were privateers who had left their trade because of lagging business due to the war. They were imprisoned in The Hulks and prison camps in Dartmoor, Norman's Cross, and various other locations. Their highly skilled carvings were in great demand by the wealthy Britons who were cut off from the products of France by the British blockade. Often the British became patrons to the most skilled prison artisans and would supply them with precious materials with which to execute their craft. Although through these prisoners bone came into prominence in England, it was not uncommon for them to be given ivory and even gold to work with. They were paid well for their labors and often received more money than they had ever earned as free men. Their most successful products were games, miniature guillotines, and ship models built to scale and often rigged with human hair.

With the War of 1812, into the camps began straggling the first American POWs. After a period of adjustment, the Americans sought to improve their lives in prison and paid (with whatever they had of value) the laboureurs to instruct them in carving. It is believed that this instruction later turned up in the whaling art of **scrimshaw** when the American prisoners were released and returned to the peacetime marine life of whaling. The French prisoners left the Americans their crafts, tools, and materials when they were released following the first defeat of Napoleon.

les metamorphoses. Toys. An **optical toy** of the middle nineteenth century that consisted of a highly polished cylinder and a distorted drawing. The polyoptic pictures were distorted in such a way that when the polished metal cylinder was set in a certain place the reflection of the drawing would appear normal and without distortion. Figures and faces were most often used for these pictures. Also see **Toys: Optical Toys.**

let-off motion. Weaving. See **fly shuttle loom, friction brake.**

lettering. Bookbinding. A basic **tool**ing technique that requires warmed tools and carbon paper. The ink from the carbon paper is picked up on the heated tool and transferred to the desired surface. Also see **blind tooling.**

lettering on glass. Stained Glass. Letters are painted on glass with glass paint. If light is not meant to show through the paint, the paint strokes should be applied thickly. To allow the colored glass to show inside the outline, only a strong outline of the letter should be painted. A thinly painted matt background is also used to increase the legibility of lettering. Also see **matting, painting on glass.**

lettering quill. China and Glass Painting. See **brush.**

letterpress. A printing process in which ink is transferred from a raised image to the surface to be printed by applying pressure. Linoleum block prints and **woodcuts** are simple examples of letterpress printing.

letter tools. Bookbinding. **Tool**s with letter faces used in **titling** a cover.

Letter X. Quilts. A **pieced patch** in which a square is cut on both diagonals, then rejoined in alternating colors. This makes an X, or bow-shaped, patch. The X patch can then be combined with solid patches to produce **block**s of various patterns. The **Double X** combines Xs of different sizes, and in a slight variation is called Old Maid's Puzzle. Other variations are similar to **Crosses and Losses.** See ill.

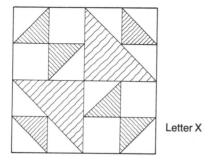

Letter X

leuco. Batik and Tie-dye. A colorless substance formed in the reduction of a **dye.** Insoluble colors to be used as dyes must be reduced chemically to make them soluble, usually with **caustic soda** or **lye.** This process is called **vatting. Vat dye**s in a leuco base allow pigments to coat **fiber**s, but until they **oxidize** the colors do not develop.

Inkodye is available already in a leuco base so that it can be used immediately; the color is developed by oxidizing it. Caledon dyes are not in a leuco state and must be vatted by the dyer. **Indigo** must also be put into a leuco state or vatted for use.

levant morocco. Bookbinding. See **leather.**

level. Woodworking. See **squaring tools.**

level dyeing. Batik and Tie-dye. An even **dye penetration,** or consistent level of color throughout the dyed fabric. To maintain level dyeing a teaspoon of detergent or soap may be added to the **dyebath,** although this quantity varies from dye to dye and from fiber to fiber. Also see **uneven dyeing.**

leveling. Candlemaking. See **Candlemaking: Finishing the Candle.**

lever. Weaving. The movable mechanism located on the front or side of a **table loom** that raises the **harness** attached to it. When it is pushed down, the harness usually rises. There are always as many levers as there are harnesses since each harness is attached to its own lever. Levers are sometimes called finger treadles.

levigated alumina. Gemcutting. See **abrasive.**

levigation. Ceramics. A process by which clay is refined through floating clay particles in water. Also see **Ceramics: Clay.**

levigation trough. Ceramics. A trough used in the process of separating fine clay particles from coarser ones by feeding them into a stream of flowing water. China clay is levigated to remove coarse micas. See ill. Also see **levigation, sedimentation.**

Levigation trough

lexol. Leatherwork. A liquid conditioner and finish for leather which softens and penetrates. Brush on and allow to soak into the leather, then polish with a soft cloth. Also see **Leatherwork: Care, Cleaning and Storage of Leather, Finishing Leather.**

library corner. Bookbinding. An attached piece of **leather** or **cloth** folded over the corner of a book cover. Because it is folded rather than cut, it affords a more enduring protection. Libraries utilize this corner in their binding because it withstands hard usage. Also see **mitered corner.**

library style binding. Bookbinding. A type of binding used for both strength and endurance. It is **cloth**-sides with **leather corners** and **back** and uses **split boards.** It is also **tight-backed.**

libro aperto. Gemcutting. See **flat.**

lichen dye. Dyeing. Dyes derived from the acids in lichens. Lichens are a combination of two organisms, algae and fungus, living together and forming a third, new and completely different organism called a thallus. Lichens grow all over the world from the top of Mt. Everest to the seashore and from Lapland to the tropics. They are classified into four groups according to their ability to yield **dyestuff**s: those that yield a dyestuff with only boiling water; those that give up the dyestuff after fermentation with ammonia (orchil lichens); those that give different colors by boiling and by fermentation; and those which yield no **dye** by any known method.

Since lichens are known all over the world, it is difficult to say where their use as a source of dyestuff originated. The Phoenicians used orchil-producing lichens (the Rocella lichens) as the bottoming in **top-dyeing** to help create Tyrian purple. In the fourteenth century this use of lichens was brought to Italy by a Florentine merchant, perfected, and from there exported all over Europe. In North America, the Navajos were also using lichen dyes. The boiling-water lichens are still used today as a source of dyes in northern Scotland, Ireland, and Wales.

The dye acids are found in the core of the thallus; the plant is bruised or crushed to get at this core. Originally, the thallus of orchil-producing lichens was decomposed by soaking it in the only ammonia available, putrid urine.

This process is called fermentation; the bacteria in the urine act to release the dye acids. Today, this process is accomplished, less odoriforously, by soaking the thallus in an ammonia solution and is called maceration. While soaking in the ammonia, the lichens undergo a somewhat similar process as in fermentation, and it is through this chemical change that the lichen acids or dyestuff are released into the solution. This process can take as long as several weeks. Then, by adjusting the solution's alkalinity, either a blue or a red dyestuff called orchil is produced. It can be dried into a powder and stored for future use. Orchil extract is commercially available from dye suppliers.

The boiling-water lichens are bruised, cracked, or crumbled and then placed in the **dyebath** with **acetic acid** to draw out the color. They are brought to a boil slowly, simmered for three or more hours and then left overnight. Immerse the material to be dyed the next day and bring the dyebath to a boil; reduce heat and simmer again. Boiling-water lichens yield yellow and oranges to browns. Since lichens contain many acids, ammonia maceration may extract one acid color while boiling water yet another acid color from the same plant. While no **mordant** is necessary for lichen dyes, mordants will increase the possibility of extending the color range. Mordants are usually necessary for dyeing cotton or linen, but on wool and silk the dyestuff works very well without a mordant.

Litmus paper is made from lichen dyes and is used as an indicator for alkalinity (the paper turns blue) or acidity (the paper turns red).

licker-in roller. Spinning. See **carding machine.**

lid. Basketry. See **cover.**

lid. Ceramics. See **Ceramics: Form.**

life-eye needle. Leatherwork. See **lacing needle** and **Leatherwork: Tools and Materials.**

lift. Kites. The force working on a kite perpendicular to the upper surface, resulting in flight. According to the principles of **aerodynamics,** as air passes over the angled edge of the kite it creates a low-pressure vacuum on the upper surface and a high-pressure area on the underside, causing the kite to rise or lift.

lifted increase. Knitting. See **Knitting: Increasing.**

lift ground. Stained Glass. A technique used in **painting on glass** in which a rubber latex glue which resists paint is brushed on the glass thickly, and then painted over, on and around it, to create a design. The glue is then removed with a razor, pin, or needle. If the glue is too thin it becomes a rubber film that is hard to see and remove. It should be removed before **firing.** Also see **staining.**

lifting plan. Weaving. See **chain draft, treadling sequence.**

light box. Crewel. Embroidery. Needlepoint. A box with a translucent glass or plastic top illuminated by an internal light, used in tracing a design. Also see **Crewel: Transferring a Design.**

light box. Stained Glass. See **cutting bench, portable light box.**

lightfast. Batik and Tie-dye. Color that is fast or permanent when exposed to light. The term is used to describe a degree and type of colorfastness in **dyes.** Some dyes are fast to one condition and not necessarily to another, so a **colorfast** dye may fade on exposure to light but still be **washfast.**

lightfastness. A quality of **dyes** and **pigments** that prevents light, especially sunlight, from bleaching or changing the color with age. Paintings or objects colored with materials that are not lightfast should not be allowed to remain in direct sunlight for long periods of time.

lighting. Puppets. See **Puppets: The Marionette Stage, The Puppet Stage.**

light piping. Plastics. (Also called edge-lighting, edge-glow.) The glowing of edges or roughened surface areas on optical glass or **acrylic** plastic is caused by light being reflected from a source outside the plastic. Light is "piped" or reflected (even around corners) by the inside of the polished surfaces to the edges and where the surface is roughened or cut, while the rest of the sheet does not light up. This characteristic is effectively used with **carving** and **intaglio** processes. See ill.

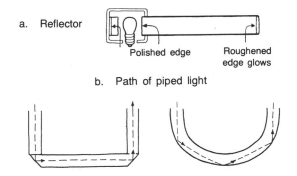

a. Reflector

Polished edge   Roughened edge glows

b. Path of piped light

light rand. Basketry. Loosely woven **randing.**

light-stabilized. Plastics. A plastic to which **antioxidants** have been added to prevent deterioration from the ultraviolet rays in sunlight.

light stabilizer. Plastics. See **antioxidant.**

light wood. Puppets. Toys. A term used to refer only to the color of wood. It has no relationship to the density or degree of hardness or softness of the wood. When wood is to be stained with color, the lighter woods will retain the colors better. Some light woods are ash, basswood, boxwood, beech, butternut, chestnut, cottonwood, holly, lime, sycamore, white oak, and white pine.

lignum vitae. Woodworking. An extremely, heavy, hard, dense, oily, fine-grained wood. It comes from Central and South America and is black to greenish-brown in color. It can be cut easily when **green** but gets harder as it **seasons.** It can take a high polish, and is difficult to glue because of its oiliness. Lignum vitae is primarily used for **mallet** heads and for fine **woodcarvings.**

Lily. Quilts. A stylized **block** design depicting an upright lily with drooping lilies on either side. It is made up using both **appliqué** and **piecing,** and was among the most favored of all geometric **flower designs.** It is an old quilt pattern dating from the early 1800s. There are numerous variations of the lily design, including: Fire Lily, Mariposa Lily, Meadow Lily, Mountain Lily, Noonday Lily, North Carolina Lily, Prairie Lily, Tiger Lily, Virginia Lily, and Wood Lily.

The **Peony** and **Tulip** quilts are similarly styled, but the peony designs usually have full-face flowers.

limber jack. Toys. See **dancing man.**

lime. Mosaics. Calcium oxide, a white substance produced by the action of heat on materials that contain calcium carbonate, such as shells or limestone. **Hydrated lime,** or lime mixed with water and allowed to set up for several days, is used to make the **mortar** that is used to **bond** mosaic material to a **backing.**

limeblowing. Ceramics. The reaction of clay in a **kiln** when pellets of **lime** in the clay turn to quicklime when fired. This causes the **pots** in the **kiln** to break.

lime glass. Glasswork. See **soda-lime glass.**

Limerick lace. Lacemaking. See **tambour lace.**

limning. Weaving. See **outlining.**

Limoges. Enameling. See **wet inlay.**

limp binding. Bookbinding. A binding with **flexible covers.**

Lincoln logs. Toys. A **constructional toy** that consists of log-shaped pieces of wood of various lengths. They are notched at the ends so that one log can fit over another to build three-dimensional structures. Also see **Toys: Constructional Toys.**

Lincoln Quilt. Quilts. A one-of-a-kind quilt made up by a group of women in 1865. The 49 **block**s of the quilt are signed on the homespun **linen** or **cotton backing**s. **Appliqué**s of cotton and **wool** are in some cases traditional blocks, but many are "current news," describing in charming pictorial detail personal feelings about the political climate, the Lincoln-Douglas debates, and the issues of the day. This quilt is in the Shelburne Museum, Shelburne, Vermont.

Lincoln's Platform. Quilts. A **block** design that consists of **pieced** triangles, squares, and strips. It suggests crossing lines and squares set over squares. The design was named for President Lincoln. See ill. Also see **presidents' quilts, Shoo-fly.**

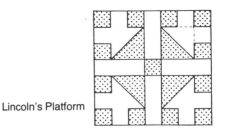

Lincoln's Platform

Linde A. Gemcutting. See **abrasive.**

Linde A. Shell Carving. A chemically prepared polishing agent of minute waferlike crystals of alumina that readily break down into smaller particles. Also see **Shell Carving: Polishing.**

line. Kites. See **string.**

line. Spinning. Weaving. See **flax, linen.**

linear foot. Metalworking. Woodworking. The measure by which materials are sold, regardless of width or weight. **Dowels,** molding, piping, and angle irons are sold by the linear foot. Planks are priced by the board foot. Also see **wood.**

line binding. Batik and Tie-dye. A **binding** method that gives a linear **resist** in the **tie-dye** process. Strong, fine cotton or linen threads work best. The **binding material** is concentrated in some areas, usually with spaces between these bound areas. The resultant effect is one of bands containing fine lines of resist.

lined beads. Beadwork. Clear **glass beads** that are painted or "lined" inside the hole during manufacture to provide special color effects. Lined beads tend to fade in intensity after prolonged exposure to sunlight.

lined-down endpaper. Bookbinding. The first leaf of an **endpaper** to which a piece of material has been affixed.

linen. Knitting. Macramé. Linen is made from flax, a bast fiber, and is spun into a high quality yarn. Linen yarn is available in many weights, plys, and colors and has a great variety of uses in knitting.

Linen produces a very handsome knot in macramé work.

linen. Quilts. Stitchery. A **natural fiber,** possibly the oldest one known, from the stem of the flax plant. The term also refers to the **fabric** woven from the linen **fibers.** Linen is very durable; it is more expensive than **cotton** and it wrinkles easily if not treated to be **wrinkle resistant.**

The texture of linen makes it an inviting surface for embroidery or for use in **wall hanging**s. It is more difficult to **hand appliqué** than is cotton, and is seldom used in **quilt**making today, although traditionally it was very common.

Because linen is a natural **vegetable fiber**, it is favored for use in tie-dye and batik since only such fiber will take certain **colorfast** dyes.

Those articles made from linen for household use, such as tablecloths and pillow cases, were referred to as "linens" when they were made up from linen fabric. While they are almost never made of linen now, these articles are still sometimes referred to in this way.

linen. Spinning. Weaving. Anything made of **flax,** such as the yarn spun from the **bast fiber** of the flax plant, or the fabric woven from this yarn. The natural color of the fiber can be silver gray, bluish gray, brown, honey beige, or creamy white, depending on the place and method of retting. It bleaches easily, either artificially or naturally, by wetting and exposing to frost or dew. The fibers are fine, smooth and soft, with a silky luster. The yarn is not elastic, which accounts for its wrinkling easily. It is not resistant to friction, but has a remarkable tensile strength. The fabric is washable and even improves in appearance with repeated washing and ironing. The fiber is coarse-pored, which makes it highly absorbent. This property, plus its ability to give off moisture rapidly by evaporation, makes linen a cool fabric to wear.

Linen yarn comes made of either tow or line. Tow are the shorter lengths of fiber taken from the flax during scutching or hackling. Fibers less than 10″ long are called tow and are used to make **twine** and low grade yarn that is not suitable for **warp.** However, tow can serve quite well as **weft.** The most desirable fibers that are left in the flax processing are the longest ones called line. They go upward from 10″ in length and are combed and spun into a strong smooth yarn best suited for warp. Linen can be spun either dry or wet; the tow is spun dry and the line wet. The **wet-spun** gives a better, finer, and more flexible yarn.

linen canvas. Needlepoint. Linen **canvas** is no longer readily available except as **petit point** canvas. It has been replaced by **cotton canvas** in all sizes because cotton is less expensive, equally strong, and a very adequate substitute.

linen count. Spinning. Weaving. See **lea, yarn count.**

linen fabric. Crewel. Embroidery. A fabric woven from flax fibers, and an excellent **background fabric** because of its strength and durability. Available in **twill,** even **weave, coarse weave,** or **fine weave.**

linen stitch. Lacemaking. See **cloth stitch.**

linen tester. Weaving. See **pick glass.**

linen thread. Embroidery. Needlepoint. A tightly twisted thread made from flax fibers and generally available in warm tones with a matte finish. This thread is often used in combination with another type of **yarn,** such as wool, for textural contrast.

linen thread. Puppets. A strong, smooth **string** or cord used in **stringing** the **marionette** to the **control bar.** A number 18 linen thread is a good weight for an average-size **puppet.** Also see **Puppets: Stringing the Marionette.**

liner. Basketry. See **handle liner.**

liner. China and Glass Painting. Stained Glass. See **brush.**

liner. Jewelry. A form of **graver** that has numerous lines on its cutting edge of different sizes and thicknesses, from coarse to fine, used to create patterns of engraved parallel lines. By using the liner at right angles, a cross-hatched surface is created. The shanks of liners are made in four shapes—straight, curved, bent, and double bent. Liners are numbered, for example, as follows: a straight liner, 10/6, is a liner with a straight shank, a coarseness of grade 10, and 6 lines.

Liners can also be used to cut grooves into the surface of metal to make a more effective gripping surface when doing **niello** or enameling, and can produce striking patterns when transparent enamels are used over the engraved metals. Liners can be used to create an all-over surface texture called **Florentine finish,** produced by cross-hatching. Other patterns created with lines are rigato, all lines cut in the same direction; ornato, a lacelike pattern; telsto, a linenlike texture, lines cut in perpendicular directions; and segrinato, a velvety texture. Also see **electric engraving tool.**

line stitch. Crewel. Embroidery. Any stitch that is worked in a narrow band that can curve around a shape as an **outline stitch,** in rows as a **filling stitch,** or can be worked as a line for the stem of a flower. Some examples are **backstitch, chain stitch, knotted pearl stitch, split stitch,** and **stem stitch.**

lining. Découpage. A decorative treatment for the interiors of boxes, drawers, secretaries, and so on. These interior spaces, which already have been sealed and painted during the découpage process, are completed with the application of fabric or **decorative paper.** The interior spaces can also be decorated with **cutouts** and a découpage **finish** at the same time the exterior is being decorated.

To make a paper lining, coat decorative paper with a **sealer** on the front and back to prevent shrinking and warping when wet with **glue.** Allow the sealer to dry thoroughly. Cut paper sections to fit inside the top and bottom of the box. A long strip for sides may be cut in one piece a little longer and wider than the area. Glue in the bottom section first by smoothing **white glue** evenly on the bottom of the box. Press the lining paper down, smoothing gently, with a finger dampened with water and glue. Then carefully apply paste to the sides. Crease the lining paper at the corners and press it into place, making sure that the corners fit tightly. Remove excess paste with the fingers. Trim off the top edges of the paper flush with the top edges of the box. Clean off any remaining paste with a damp sponge. Repeat the process to line the top of a box. Allow to dry 24 hours, then apply a sealer.

To line a box with fabric, a backing for the fabric is cut from lightweight white cardboard, such as a tablet backing. Cut cardboard pieces to fit all interior sides, top and bottom, minus ⅛″ all around the edges to allow for the thickness of the fabric. Make identifying pencil marks on the backs of the pieces so they can be replaced exactly.

On the unmarked side of the cardboard apply a coat of sealer and allow it to dry. Place the fabric on a table right-side down and lay the cardboard backing pieces on the wrong side. Allow a ½″ border of fabric all around the backing pieces, to be turned over to the wrong side. Mark cutting lines with a pencil. Cut out the fabric pieces, cutting diagonally across the ends (**a.**). Fold the fabric over and glue it down on the back of the cardboard (**b.**). For ease of handling, cut one side and one end together. Cut V's at the crease and diagonals at the end corners. Turn the fabric over and glue it to the back of the cardboard (**c.**). Repeat for the other side and end. Check for fit by placing all the pieces in the box (**d.**). If the lining fits correctly, glue it inside the box. Line the top of the box in the same way. See ill.

Lining a box

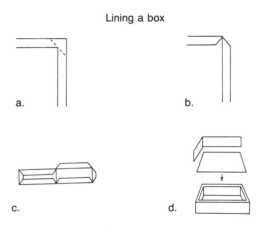

a.

b.

c.

d.

lining. Stitchery. Toys. A covering for the inner surface of a sewn article. The lining is similar in size and shape to the article being lined and is fastened or attached to it.

On a **garment** the lining may be used to ease or facilitate getting into it, since a satin or taffeta can be slid more easily over other fabrics than can wool or cotton. Lining may be used to offer opacity to a **transparent fabric,** to help it hang smoothly, to give it a finished look or to add warmth.

On a **banner** or **wall hanging,** the lining is sometimes called the **backing.** If there is an **interfacing** or **interlining,** it goes between the article and the lining. The lining conceals the wrong side of **stitch**es and may be used to cover **raw edges** of **hem**s.

Sometimes a lining is added for extra weight and strength or to provide a solid background. Batik on an organdy or batiste, for example, may require an **opaque** material behind the thin one so that the full color of the dyes can be seen.

lining leather. Leather. Generally, any very lightweight **top grain** leather (usually **calfskin, kidskin, cabreta**), 2−3

oz, used for lining such items as leather bags, wallets, etc. Also see **embossing.**

lining paper. Bookbinding. An **endpaper** that is pasted down on a cover **board,** or paper used for lining purposes.

lining paper. Découpage. See **decorative paper.**

Linmaster. Bookbinding. See **cloth.**

linocut. Block Printing. See **linoleum block.**

linoleum block. Block Printing. Fabric Printing. A readily available and versatile material for a **printing block.** Linoleum is mounted on a wood block, cut in **relief,** inked or painted, and printed on fabric or paper. Because it is easy to cut in any direction, it is perhaps the most adaptable material for both intricate patterns and clear, large designs. Linoleum is made from linseed oil and powdered cork on a base of woven jute or other fiber. It is available from art supply stores, mounted on wood blocks about ¾″ thick. Linoleum has a waxy, oily surface that rejects watery colors such as **dye-printing** colors (called **dye paste**). This tendency can be corrected by lightly sanding the block with fine sandpaper or by **flocking** the printing surface. The linoleum is sometimes coated with white poster paint so the drawing is clearly visible. Before printing, this white paint is removed by sanding.

Linoleum can be purchased for home mounting on wooden blocks. It should be at least ⅜″ thick, preferably thicker. The familiar, plain brown linoleum is available in rolls at furniture, carpet, or floor covering stores. It should be unrolled and flattened immediately after purchasing. Thicker, gray "battleship" linoleum, about ¼″ thick, is also available. The linoleum should be cemented to a piece of plywood ⅜″ thick, or thicker, with glue or linoleum mastic. Press down carefully so the surface is flat. When making blocks larger than 12″ square, heavy cardboard, instead of wood, may be used as the backing. The backing of all linoleum blocks should be shellacked as a protection from moisture. See ill. Also see **linoleum block printing.**

Linoleum block

linoleum block print. Block Printing. A print made from a **linoleum block.** Also see **Block Printing: Cutting, Printing Techniques.**

linoleum block printing. Block Printing. Fabric Printing. A basic block printing technique using a **linoleum block.** This technique is also applicable to printing on **fabric,** in which case **textile color** is used and the fabric is washed and dried before printing. Printing is done on a padded worktable. A system of **registration** should be devised before printing **repeat**ed patterns. Also see **Block Printing: Tools and Materials, Designing and Transferring, Cutting, Printing Techniques, Fabric Printing: Designing, Printing Techniques.**

linoleum lap. Gemcutting. See **lap.**

linseed oil. Woodworking. An oil made from flax seed used in wood finishing to increase the toughness and elasticity of paint, aid drying, and help preserve the wood. It creates a **gloss** finish when added to paints. Boiled linseed oil is less elastic than the raw linseed oil and not as satisfactory for exterior use, although it dries more quickly. Heated linseed oil will penetrate the wood more deeply than unheated oil. Heat it in a double boiler, but do not boil it or you will destroy its preservative properties.

Linseed oil has been used as a basic wood finish for centuries. Since early American colonial times it has been used on furniture and housewares. Its only disadvantage is that each coat takes a long time to dry and to build up a deep finish. **Japan dryer** is sometimes used to speed the process.

To use linseed oil, lightly sand the wood to expose and open the wood fibers. Mix 1 cup of linseed oil with ½ cup of **mineral spirits** and 1 heaping tablespoon of **Japan dryer.** Brush the mixture into the wood until it is saturated. After 1 hour, wipe off the excess and let the wood stand in a warm dry place for a week.

For added penetration and surface protection, apply 1 cup of linseed with 1 tablespoon of mineral spirits and 1 teaspoon of Japan dryer once a week for two or three months. Rub it in and wipe off the excess after about an hour.

linsey-wool. Quilts. Weaving. (Also called shoddy.) A coarse, fairly loose fabric handwoven of **handspun** yarns. It has a **linen warp** with a **wool filling.** It originated in England and was a common material of traditional **quilt**making.

lintless cloth. Découpage. See **tack cloth.**

lip. Ceramics. See **Ceramics: Form.**

liquid bright gold. China and Glass Painting. See **gold.**

liquid bright silver. China and Glass Painting. See **silver.**

liquid grain filler. Woodworking. See **grain filler.**

liquid petroleum gas. Ceramics. See **kiln fuel.**

liquid soap. Puppets. (Also called green soap.) A thin fluid soap used in various craft projects as a release agent. In making a strip **papier mâché** puppet head, the clay or **Plasticene** model is coated with liquid soap to facilitate separating it from the partially dried papier mâché. A liquid detergent may be used in place of liquid soap. Also see **Puppets: Making the Puppet Head.**

liquid solder. Stained Glass. A cement in which a metallic powder is suspended used mainly in repairing stained glass when the work cannot be removed and re**solder**ed. Liquid solder adheres to vertical surfaces and will not run as will conventional solder. Also see **kwik solder, slab-glass lampshade.**

Liquitex. Plastics. See **acrylic paint.**

Liquitex. Toys. The trade name of a synthetic medium for finishing. It appears white in liquid form but dries clear and hard. It may be used as a **finish** to coat wood that has a decorative surface of paint, ink, or paper. It protects the surface and, when dry, may be cleaned with a damp cloth.

lisse. Weaving. See **string heddle.**

listing. Basketry. Any of a number of ornamental patterns obtained by **wrapping** the **leader**s on a handle **bow.** See ill.

Listing patterns

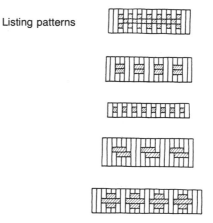

lithographic pencil. China and Glass Painting. See **china pencil.**

lithography. An art printing process wherein the image is created on a finely polished flat piece of stone, usually limestone, by drawing with a greasy crayon or ink. The image area becomes ink-receptive, while the balance of the surface is kept free of ink by treating it with a solution of acid and gum arabic in water. The principle that water and oil do not mix is responsible for keeping the printing image area separate from the nonprinting area. A rubber roller bearing a greasy ink is rolled over the whole surface of the stone, the ink transferring to the surface only in the areas that have been made ink-receptive. The water solution is also applied to the stone to prevent the image area from spreading. The water solution tends to roll off the greasy printing areas of the stone and adhere only to the untreated parts of the surface.

Finally, paper is pressed against the stone surface after it has been charged with ink and dampening solution, and the image is transferred. The design drawn or painted on the stone is reversed in the printing, so that letterforms must be drawn on the stone in mirror image. Also see **offset lithography.**

lithography. Ceramics. A process in which transfers are printed in oil on ceramics and color is dusted onto the oil. This technique has largely been replaced by commercially available glaze decals.

Little Giant, The. Quilts. (Also called Heart's Desire.) A **block** design for a **pieced quilt** that has as its central motif an eight-pointed star. The skillful use of small triangles around the star suggests a circular form. The block was named for Stephen A. Douglas in the mid-1800s.

Little Red Schoolhouse. Quilts. See **Log Cabin.**

Little Sawtooth. Quilts. See **Rocky Glen.**

Live Oak. Quilts. See **Pine Tree.**

live oak. Woodworking. See **oak.**

liver of sulfur. Enameling. A solution used for darkening metal surfaces by oxidation. Add a few crystals of potassium sulfide to boiled water and allow it to stand for fifteen minutes.

Pieces may then be dipped, or the solution brushed on. Rinse with water when the shade is dark enough. Experiment for proper concentration of solution. Also see **firescale.**

liver of sulfur. Jewelry. Potassium sulfide purchased in lump form used to oxidize and to create a **patina** on metal surfaces. It works on a number of metals but is especially effective with sterling **silver.**

Put some lukewarm water in a small jar with a lid; add some lumps of liver of sulfur; put the lid on the jar, and swirl the liquid around until the lumps are dissolved. Different strengths of the solution may be used, but for a good black the color of the liquid should be the color of tea. **Pickle** and rinse off the work to remove all dirt and grease. Apply the solution with a brush to areas where oxidation is required. The brush should be washed out with soap and water immediately afterward as the liver of sulfur will destroy the bristles quite rapidly. Warm the area covered with a **torch,** using a brushing **flame,** to hasten the action of the liver of sulfur. The solution is oxidizing only while it is wet. More of the solution must be added as soon as the previous application becomes dry. Do not overheat the work because the oxidation will become grainy and flake off in areas. It is advisable to apply several coats of liver of sulfur allowing for oxidation to occur slowly. Such is the case for any patina, both for color and permanence. Low heat and slow oxidation will produce excellent results. After oxidizing is completed, the yellow, green, and blue surface film must be rinsed off in water to reveal the true color underneath.

Work may also be dipped into the solution, and heat then applied to the piece. In this case, the entire piece will turn black. Rinse and dry the work. Removal of oxidization where not desired can be done on a **buffing wheel** charged with powdered **pumice** or by **hand polishing.** If the work has a flat upper surface and the oxidization in lower areas is to remain, the unwanted oxidization on the upper areas can be removed with a felt ring buff, as this will not reach into the recessed areas.

Liver of sulfur in lump or liquid form should be stored in a dark place or in a tinted glass container with a lid at room temperature; light, heat, and air cause rapid deterioration. If the solution begins to form a yellow scum on its surface, deterioration has begun. It should be thrown out, and a new solution mixed, just prior to using. The vapors of liver of sulfur are not good to breathe. Also see **coloring** and **Jewelry: Safety Precautions.**

liver of sulfur. Metalworking. See **patina.**

lizard skin. Leatherwork. The hide from any member of the lizard family. Lizard has a characteristic patterned grain which is often imitated by **embossing** on other leathers, such as **calfskin.**

llama. Spinning. Weaving. The largest member of the camel family native to South America whose wool is used to make durable and extremely warm fabrics. The long hair is used in the weaving of textiles; the outer coat of the **fleece** is thick and coarse, while the hair next to the body is very fine and resembles that of **alpaca.** The **staple** length is from 6 to 12″ and the color is either white blotched with black and brown, or pure shades of black, dark brown, light brown, gray, and white.

Lobster. Quilts. An **appliqué quilt block** pattern named for its resemblance to the lobster. It is a complex appliqué that repeats in such a way as to suggest a square was folded in half twice and then cut in the manner of a paper snowflake.

local dyeing. Fabric Printing. See **dye printing.**

locked double needle stitch. Leatherwork. See **double needle stitch.**

locked weft. Weaving. See **clasped weft.**

lock stitch awl. Leather. See **automatic awl.**

loft. Spinning. Weaving. The resiliency a yarn has that enables it to bounce or spring back to its original thickness after being compressed. In the fiber, loft is due to **crimp** and is found in a high quality wool. Also, the surface of a cloth woven of such a fiber.

Log Cabin. Quilts. Either of two well-known and long-favorite quilt designs. The Log Cabin design is often left unquilted and treated as a **tied quilt.** The first pattern, a popular quilt design in use since colonial times, is simple enough for a beginning quilter to make. There are inexhaustible numbers of possible variations, depending upon color and value arrangements. It consists of a central square with **band**s or strips surrounding it. A slight variation in arrangement makes a similar pattern called **Courthouse Steps.** A particular arrangement or **set** of the dark and light **pieced** Log Cabin **block**s makes a quilt called **Barn Raising.**

If the central piece of the Log Cabin block is changed from a square to a hexagon or octagon, new patterns emerge. The **Pineapple Log Cabin** and **Windmill Blades** are two of these. Among the other possible arrangements of the Log Cabin block are **Straight Furrow, Streak of Lightning**, and a **checkerboard** pattern.

The Log Cabin design is the popular block that depicts a

log cabin with chimney, door, and window (or windows). The design is usually pieced, although sometimes a combination of piecing and **appliqué** is used. It was probably named for President Lincoln's birthplace. The same pattern is also called Little Red Schoolhouse, Old Homestead, and Schoolhouse. See ill. Also see **presidents' quilt.**

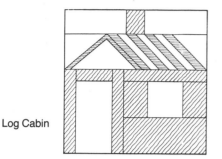

Log Cabin

log cabin pattern. Weaving. A **plain weave** that forms vertical and horizontal stripes through the color placement in the **threading** and **treadling.** Two colors, usually light and dark, are used alternately in both the **warp** and **filling.** The alternate colors are put in block groups to give a stripe in one direction. The color order changes at the edge of the block; two threads of the same color come next to each other, then the colors begin to alternate again for the next block. The change at the edge of the block causes the colors to change **harness**es and the blocks change or reverse directions. Also, the size of the yarn can be alternated to produce a difference in the stripe. The stripes, or logs, form a simple geometric pattern suitable for placemats, bags, table scarves, pillow covers, and upholstery. It can be woven on a two-**harness loom** making it an especially good pattern for beginning weavers. Also see **end-and-end.**

log-cut. Woodworking. See **wood.**

log drum. Toys. See **drum box.**

loggerhead tortoise. Shell Carving. See **Shell Carving: Tortoiseshell.**

logwood. Batik and Tie-dye. Dyeing. A natural bluish or purple **dyestuff** used primarily as an ingredient in black **dye.** The dyestuff is obtained from the heart of the logwood tree native to Mexico and Central America. The colors produced with the logwood chips are not **colorfast** unless **mordant**ed. Logwood with **alum** produces a violet to gray color; with **tin,** purple; with **chrome,** gray to black. Also see **dyewood** and **Dyeing: Natural Dyes.**

London shrinkage. Weaving. A two-hundred-year-old method of **shrinkage** associated with fine **worsted fabric.** It is a cold water method of **finishing** that prepares the fabric for cutting and insures that it will not shrink after sewing. Originally, worsted was laid out in the fields surrounding London so that the dew would improve the **hand** of the fabric and shrink it. Today, weavers tend to send their fabric to a finishing plant for London shrinkage rather than do it at home. At the plant, a wet wool

or cotton blanket is placed on a long platform and a layer of cloth is spread on top. Alternating the layers of blankets and cloth, a sufficient weight is placed on top to force the moisture from the blankets into the wool cloth. The cloth is left sandwiched between the wet blankets for twelve hours, then dried at room temperature and pressed. An equivalent home method is to roll the cloth in a wet sheet, let it stand for six hours; dry the cloth flat on a table or the floor. If the cloth is straightened out while wet, pressing may be entirely unnecessary.

Lone Ring. Quilts. A variation of **Drunkard's Path** that uses the **Robbing Peter to Pay Paul** motif. See ill.

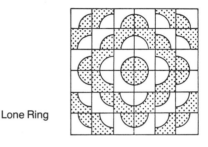

Lone Ring

Lone Star. Quilts. See **Texas Lone Star.**

long-and-short oblique stitch. Needlepoint. See **fishbone stitch.**

long-and-short stitch. Crewel. Embroidery. (Also called Kensington stitch.) Long and short stitches worked over the **split stitch.** The short stitch is ¼ shorter than the long one. The length of the stitches must be maintained, if the stitch is worked correctly. The stitches fit against each other in bricklike fashion; use a double thread for a distinctive pattern. Tapestry shading and soft shading are the two varieties of the long and short stitch; tapestry shading is the easier of the two.

Tapestry shading is worked with vertical long and short stitches over a horizontal line of split stitches (**a.**). In the second and all subsequent rows, the stitches cover ¼ of the stitch of the previous row (**b., c.**).

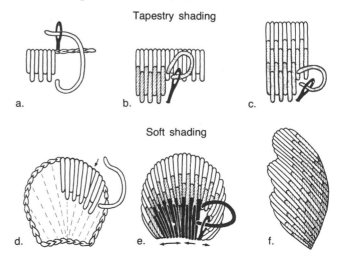

Tapestry shading

a.   b.   c.

Soft shading

d.   e.   f.

Soft shading resembles tapestry shading except that the stitches follow the direction of the shape being filled in. When working around a curve it may be necessary to add a small wedge stitch to fill in the outline (**d.**). Irregular shapes leave much to the imagination and skill (**e., f.**). It is advisable to lightly pencil in directional lines before beginning to stitch the shape. Soft shading is a difficult stitch, but when executed properly it imparts a very natural shading to the design. See ill. Also see **shading stitch.**

long-armed cross stitch. Needlepoint. (Also called Greek stitch, long-legged cross stitch, plaited Slav stitch, Tristom-and-twist stitch.) A variation of the **cross stitch** in which a long stitch crosses a short one; it is a tight stitch and is used frequently for rugmaking. Also, an old **canvas** stitch used traditionally in Swedish canvas embroidery, **Tristom.** Work horizontally in either direction; the short stitch is half the length of the long one. In this rendition the short stitch covers four mesh and the long stitch covers eight. This stitch is extremely useful for joining sections of a rug, framing a design; and finishing a canvas; work as a binding stitch on the fold. See ill. Also see **Montenegrin cross stitch** and **Needlepoint: Finishing.**

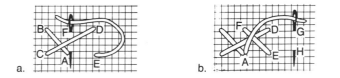

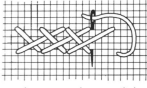

c. Long-armed cross stitch

long-armed feather stitch. Crewel. Embroidery. See **Cretan stitch.**

long double crochet. Crochet. (Abbr. ldc.) The long double crochet is a **double crochet** started on the 6th chain from the **crochet hook**, and is crocheted so that all loops are extended to the length of 3 **chain stitch**es.

longeron. Kites. The primary structural sticks used in the construction of a **box kite.** The term also applies to the main structural member that runs the length of an aircraft fuselage.

long-eye needle. Stitchery. Any **needle** which has a long opening or eye for the thread to pass through. Embroidery needles, crewel needles, and darning needles all have long eyes which make it easier to thread **yarn**s and flosses.

long-legged cross stitch. Needlepoint. See **long-armed cross stitch.**

long-oil varnish. Woodworking. See **varnish.**

long pile. Rugmaking. Weaving. See **pile, rya.**

long-small. Basketry. A 5′ length of **willow** rod.

long staple. Spinning. See **staple.**

long stitch. Crewel. Embroidery. See **French knot on stalks.**

loom. Beadwork. Various looms are available for **bead weaving.** The loom should be about 6″ longer than the item to be woven, and as wide as desired. For the warp use strong **thread**, such as buttonhole thread waxed with **beeswax.**

A simple loom can be made from a wooden box with saw grooves in the ends for spacing the warp threads. A nail or peg is driven into the outside ends for fastening the warp. The **box loom** is a variation of the **frame loom (a.).**

A roller-type loom is good for weaving long pieces because several feet of warp can be rolled up at one end. The warp threads are spaced by beads (**b.**). See ill.

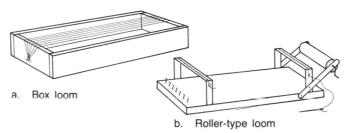

a. Box loom

b. Roller-type loom

loom. Weaving. A device used to facilitate the weaving of two sets of threads into **cloth.** A loom consists of parts necessary to hold one set, the **warp,** while the other set, the **filling,** interlaces with the warp. As such, little is necessary to make a loom; the early loom was simple, but the weaving process was tedious and time-consuming. Improvements on the first looms were made with the impetus being to save time and make weaving easier. Essentially, the same pattern is possible on a **frame loom** as on a **Jacquard loom;** however, time and patience are required for working it out on a frame loom, whereas on the power Jacquard loom it is an effortless, mechanical gesture.

The earliest known looms had one set of threads; the vertical warp hung from a bar and the filling threads interlaced crosswise through it. **Warp tension** was the first loom improvement and facilitates inserting the filling faster and easier. The warp tension was achieved by adding weights to the bottom of the **free-hanging warp,** resulting in the **warp-weighted loom,** or, by using a **continuous warp** which is attached to a support or stick. These warp supports enable the weaver to stretch out the entire warp uniformly. The warp tension can be arranged horizontally, as in the **ground loom;** the sticks are tied to pegs in the earth to hold the warp taut. The warp can remain in a vertical position, as in the **Navajo loom,** or it can run on the diagonal as in a **backstrap loom.**

The **heddle** evolved to facilitate separating the warp threads so that the filling could be carried through; previously the warp threads were picked up by the fingers. A **string heddle** is a cord that is passed under every other warp end and is attached to the **heddle bar** which lifts the warp threads caught by the cord simultaneously. The **shed stick** provided an alternate method of opening the shed; this was achieved by placing it under alternate warp threads. This heddle construction advanced to the **rigid heddle** used on **primitive loom**s. The string heddle is an example of the flexible heddle construction; a partial opening, rather than **selvage** to selvage, is possible.

The filling was carried through the warp ends by the fingers. The **spindle** was used as the first **stick shuttle**; this device made possible longer fillings and a wider cloth. Combs used as **hand beater**s replaced the fingers to beat the filling down or up. The **batten** evolved and is used in conjunction with the **heddle bar** and the **shed stick**; the batten can be used as a shed stick. The beater on the contemporary **harness loom** is a multipurpose device used to separate the warp, push down the filling, and to flatten everything evenly. It is customary to work from the bottom up or away from the weaver.

Weaving was limited in length to the amount of warp that could be stretched within the bars until the addition of two revolving beams. These beams are set at both ends of the taut warp ends. The warp is made longer than the length possible within the loom; the unwoven warp ends are wound around one beam (the **warp beam**) and the woven cloth is wound around the other beam (**cloth beam**).

Another bar was added to the heddle bar; this bar is attached to the bottom of the string heddles, permitting downward movement controlled by the feet placed in stirrups. Thus came about the first **harness** and **treadle** construction and the first **foot-powered loom**s.

Looms are classified according to type, size, position of the warp, horizontal or vertical, **shedding motion (rising shed, sinking shed)**, and number of harnesses available.

The most complex looking loom is the harness loom; it is available in a table and floor model. Basically, the harness loom is a frame loom with a wooden or metal outside frame and a sturdy inner structure, called the **castle,** that houses the harnesses. These harnesses, with their attendant heddles, treadles, **lam**s, or **lever**s, are the major difference between the harness loom and the primitive loom. The harnesses make weaving a speedy affair, but do not necessarily produce a more beautiful fabric. To add to the speed and efficiency of a harness loom, there is a warp beam in the rear that has an attached **apron bar** and **ratchet;** a cloth beam in the front also with attached apron bar and ratchet. The warp ends, in coming from the warp beam, glide over the **back beam,** run over and under a pair of flat wooden **lease stick**s, pass through the heddles and **reed,** over the **breast beam** and are attached to the cloth beam apron bar. When the process of **dressing the loom** is completed, the weaver is ready to weave.

The origin of the **counterbalanced loom, jack-type,** and **draw loom** can be traced to China where they were used for weaving silk. The counterbalanced loom became the popular loom of Medieval Europe and later of the colonies. The draw loom was used between the thirteenth

and eighteenth centuries to weave the intricately patterned fabric representative of the apex of European weaving. The invention of the **fly shuttle loom,** in 1733 by John Kay, made the insertion of the filling a totally mechanical gesture. However, the handle that activated the **fly shuttle** still had to be pulled by hand; the other motions of the loom were hand- or foot-controlled. The Jacquard loom is the mechanized version of the frame loom. The loom was totally mechanized by 1783, patented by Cartwright. By the nineteenth century, power looms and mills were a reality in England and the United States. This summoned an end to the hand looms.

However, hand weaving did not completely die out; it experienced renewed popularity in the 1920s and 1930s, and once again during the last twenty years. A variety of looms are available for weaving in addition to the counterbalanced loom; the jack-type loom is available as a table or a floor loom; the **countermarch loom** originated in Scandinavia; **folding loom** models for the standard **four-harness loom** and the **multiharness** loom with eight, sixteen, or twenty-four harnesses. Special purpose looms are such as the **tapestry loom** and **rug loom**s; the treadles of these looms activate two sheds and are classified as **upright loom**s.

Novel yet simple looms include the **hoop loom,** which renders a circular woven fabric; the **branch loom,** which becomes incorporated in the woven article; and the **cardboard loom,** which can be rectangular or any shape the weaver desires. The shedding motion in these looms is accomplished by the fingers, or a shed stick and heddle bar.

The size of a loom refers to the maximum width that a fabric can be woven on that loom; **table harness loom**s range from 8 to 32"; foot-powered looms are between 20 and 60" wide and wider ones are built on special order. The primitive looms are available in a variety of widths; some frame looms are built at home to accommodate **wall hanging**s. Looms narrower than 8", such as the **band loom** or the **inkle loom,** are categorized as **belt loom**s. See ill. Also see **dobby loom, Indian weaving, Salish weaving, straw loom.**

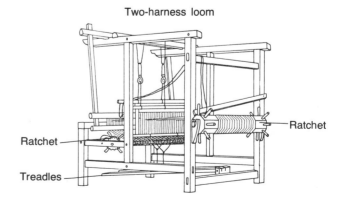

Two-harness loom

Ratchet — Ratchet
Treadles —

loom allowance. Weaving. See **loom waste, yarn calculations.**

loom beading. Beadwork. See **bead weaving.**

loom bench. Weaving. A bench designed to go with a **floor loom.** It is of the proper height and often with a slightly slanting seat so that the weaver does not have to stretch uncomfortably while working on the loom. A store-bought loom bench has either open sides for keeping handy **shuttle**s, **reed hook**s, and other such equipment, or the top is hinged to open up for storage inside the bench.

loom-shaped. Weaving. A term implying that the form of a weaving was achieved mainly through manipulation on the **loom** and with a minimum of cutting and sewing. Although any sort of object can be loom-shaped, the term usually refers to the garment. In this sense, loom-shaped refers to techniques for making buttonholes, slit pockets, the neck opening in a poncho, or the entire front opening of a garment, or also more complex weaving techniques such as tubular **double cloth.** The loom used is frequently a **harness loom,** although loom-shaped refers to weaving made on any type of loom.

loom waste. Weaving. The ends of the **warp** that can neither be incorporated in the weaving nor used as fringe. Loom waste includes the beginning end of the warp, which is the amount of yarn used to tie knots around the front **apron bar** plus the **heading,** and the end of the warp, which extends from the last **pick** of weaving through the **reed** and **heddle**s to the back apron bar. The end of the warp must be long enough for the **shed**s to open. The amount of loom waste varies considerably between weavers, types of **loom**s, yarn elasticity, and the weaving technique employed. In calculating the warp amount needed, it is advisable to allow for an excess rather than just enough or too little. Also see **thrum, yarn calculations.**

loop. Crochet. (Abbr. lp.) The loop of yarn that remains on the **crochet hook** after a **yarn-over** has been drawn through a **stitch** from the **previous row.** This loop is used as a basis for working the next stitch. Also see **Crochet: Basic Procedures, Basic Stitches.**

loop. Lacemaking. Tatting. Created when a thread forms a circle or oval shape, one end of the thread crossing over the other end, or coming together to meet the other end. It may be a decorative embellishment, as in a **picot,** or it may be both decorative as well as functional, as in a joining in tatting. A loop is also a stitch made with a **netting needle** or an embroidery needle and thread. When a series of loops are put together to make a **filling stitch** in **needle lace,** or worked as a main construction stitch, as in **basketry,** it is called **looping.**

In tatting it also refers to the circle made by the **loop thread** going around the outside of the left hand while **making the double stitch.**

loop. Leatherwork. See **belt findings.**

looped edge. Rugmaking. Weaving. Finishing edges where loops are made of the **warp end**s and other ends pass through these loops. These types of edges are variations on knotted edges. One such is the locked loop edge that forms a ridge and in which the ends are so maneu-

vered that they will not come undone. A normal knot is made with two ends, but the right-hand end is pulled through as a loop instead of a straight end. Into this loop goes the left-hand end and then both ends are pulled tightly (**a.**). This left-hand end then joins with the next end in the same manner and the work proceeds from right to left (**b.**).

Looped edges can also refer to the finishing edges done on items woven on a **frame loom** where a **continuous warp** is made from nail to nail, so that there are no cut warp ends. The basic method is **twining** the loops around each other until all the loops are used. Starting at the right edge, the first loop is passed over the loop to the left, twisted and then slipped over the next left loop, twisted again and slipped over. This procedure is followed until the first loop runs out, and then the second loop from the left is picked up and is worked in the same way (**c.**). At the opposite end of the piece, the loops are doubled back on themselves, and then the last two loops can be knotted together or darned down. Variations on this twining of loops would include starting at both edges and working toward the center to form a rounded edge or starting from the center and working out toward both **selvages.** See ill.

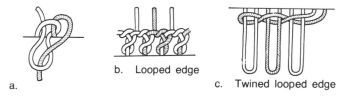

b. Looped edge   c. Twined looped edge

a.

looped knitting. Knitting. Looped knitting creates a highly decorative, loopy, poodlelike knit fabric by wrapping the yarn once or more around some measuring device (usually just one or more fingers). The loops formed are then worked into the fabric by including them into the actual stitch when knit. Several rows of looped knitting can be used on hats, or as fringe on a garment or a blanket. All-over looped knitting is sometimes used to make shag mats and other accessories. See ill.

Looped knitting

looped ribbon. Quilts. See **border.**

looped stem stitch. Crewel. Embroidery. This stitch is worked exactly like the **stem stitch** except rather than pulling tightly, a loop is left on the face of the **background fabric.** A fairly heavy thread in fineweave fabric holds the loop securely. It is an effective raised stitch in **stumpwork.** See ill.

Looped stem stitch

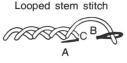

looping. Lacemaking. (Also called knotless netting.) A technique of lacemaking used as a main construction stitch or as a **filling stitch,** especially in **needle lace** and **basketry.**

Use a **netting needle** or an embroidery needle to work the thread for looping stitches. From a **foundation loop,** make the first row of **loops** of thread with a threaded needle. Attach all succeeding rows of loops to the first row.

By wrapping the thread several times around the base of a loop, a twisted loop develops. As a series of twisted loops continue, twisted looping is made. See ill.

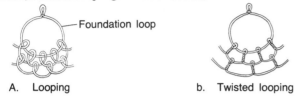

A. Looping   b. Twisted looping

looping. Rugmaking. Weaving. (Also called tufting, wefting looping.) A technique in which the design areas of a rug or fabric are raised in **filling** loops against a flat **plain weave** background. Looping is done in an open **shed** with the use of a round rod or dowel serving as both **pile gauge** and **pick-up stick** for the loops; firmly beaten plain weave in one or more **pick**s follows every row of looping to hold the loops in place because the loops are not secured in any other way and are pulled out very easily.

To do looping, a long, metal rod or a wooden dowel is needed. The rod normally is equal to the width of the piece being woven, and cannot be taken out or slid along the weaving. The loops will fall out if the rod is removed before the first pick of plain weave binds the loops in. Two or three rods can be joined to span a length, should the correct rod size be unavailable. For narrow pieces, extra long knitting needles can be used. The diameter of the rod determines the **pile height.** Fingers can also be used to pick or pull up the loops. However, the loops must then be longer to prevent them from slipping out.

Start at the right with the shed open, preferably with the right-hand outside thread in the upper part of the shed. Insert the filling which can be the same as the main **weft** or an extra thicker one for pattern. A pattern filling is still a long, continuous length, although shorter **laid-in** fillings can also be used. Put this in the shed going from right to left. Do not beat down, but let it lie in the shed relaxed. With the rod held on top of the upper part of the shed, reach down with it between two neighboring threads of the upper shed and draw the filling yarn lying in the shed up onto the rod. Slide the rod to the next two neighboring top **warp** threads and again reach down and pick up the filling yarn and slip it onto the rod. This procedure is followed across the warp width until the entire row has been picked up as determined by the design. This design can be preplanned on **graph paper** or drawn out in **cartoon** form. Looping can be a pattern of dense compact loops, sparsely placed ones, or from **selvage** to selvage. Where the loops are not picked up for the pattern, they will weave plain weave.

When the row is finished, the picked-up yarn remains on the rod until the background filling (plain weave) is put in and firmly beaten down; the rod is removed and the filling

beaten down again. The order of putting in the background plain weave can vary; the background does not have to be plain weave, although it is preferred because it is the firmest weave to hold in the looping. The ground filling can be inserted in the same shed as the pattern filling and a second **shot** in the alternate shed running left to right. Or the shed is changed immediately after the looping and one or more picks of **ground weave** put in. In the popular French Canadian **boutoné,** there are several rows of ground between each pattern row of loops.

There are many variations possible with looping, although in most cases the loops are not cut since they are not attached and cutting them would precipitate their falling out. Only if the warp **sett** is close and the beating is extra heavy can they be cut safely. This was true in the early **candlewick** fabrics where the cut threads were firmly held in and were soft small dots of surface texture. See ill.

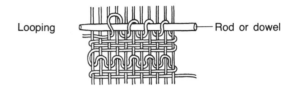

Looping   Rod or dowel

loop pile. Rugmaking. Weaving. See **pile.**

loop stitch. Crochet. (Also called fringe stitch.) The loop stitch produces a loopy crocheted fabric; it is very popular for cardigans and women's hats (best known as the "poodle" hats of some years ago) and in creative crochet.

To form the loop stitch, first work one row of **triple crochet** to the desired length, make 1 ch and turn the work. For the second **row,** insert the **crochet hook** into the first **stitch,** *wrap the **yarn** around a finger to form a loop, yo (**a.**). Draw through the two **loops** on the hook (**b.**). Insert the hook into the next stitch to be worked and repeat from * (**c.**). See ill.

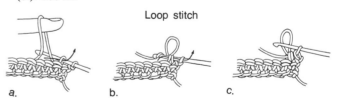

Loop stitch

a.   b.   c.

loop thread. Tatting. (Also called **ball thread.**) The **thread** forming the **loop** around the hand during tatting. The loop thread is passed in a circle around the fingers of the hand with the crossing of the thread forming the loop held between the thumb and index finger of that hand. This is the position of the loop thread in **making the double stitch,** the basic stitch of tatting.

loop yarn. Spinning. Weaving. See **novelty yarn.**

loose warp weaving. Weaving. See **finger weaving.**

Lost Ship. Quilts. See **Rocky Glen.**

lost-wax casting. Jewelry. Metalworking. (Also called

ciré-perdue, investment casting.) A precision casting technique in which a **wax model** is invested in a plaster or clay **mold** and when dry is placed in a hot **kiln** to remove the wax. Molten metal is then forced into the cavity, in any one of a number of casting processes, producing a positive of the piece. Some lost-wax methods are Benin bronze casting, core casting, and **centrifugal casting.** Also see **file wax, investment.**

Lotus Flower. Quilts. See **flower designs.**

loupe. Gemcutting. (Also called magnifier.) A magnifying glass attached to an eyepiece used by gemcutters for examination of gems. Some loupes have multiple lenses for higher magnification and correction of distortion. Single lenses from 2 to 5 power are sufficient for viewing stones during grinding and **sanding. Doublet**s up to 10 power are adequate for examining a gem's internal crystal structure and polished surfaces. Magnification over 15 power requires a system of optical components more complex than the loupe. Also see **Gemcutting: Tools and Materials.**

Love Apple. Quilts. See **Pomegranate.**

Love Knot. Quilts. See **Shoo-fly.**

lover's game. Toys. See **spear-the-fish.**

lover's knot. Quilts. See **border.**

lover's knot stitch. Crochet. (Also called knot stitch.) A highly decorative, open, loopy knot often used as a border or trim on crocheted work. Also see **Crochet: Basic Stitches.**

lover's wheel. Spinning. See **double spinning wheel.**

low-carbon steel. Metalworking. See **steel.**

lower swage. Metalworking. See **blacksmithing tools.**

low firing enamel. Enameling. See **enamel.**

low-relief. Stitchery. Toys. See **bas-relief.**

low-warp. Weaving. (Also called basse-lisse.) A form of **tapestry** weaving where the **warp** runs horizontally from the front to the back of the **horizontal loom.** Low-warp can be done on a regular type of **floor** or **table loom.** Traditionally, however, low-warp is associated with the loom used at Aubusson, France, which is the center for low-warp tapestry weaving. It is a large, horizontal frame with front and back rollers for the warp to be wound around. The **harness**es are below the warp and are equivalent to **heddle rod**s that are attached below the warp instead of above it. Each rod has a cord connecting it to a **treadle.** These foot treadles open up the **plain weave shed**s necessary for tapestry weaving. In France many weavers work on a tapestry simultaneously. This is possible because the harnesses are of small width and each weaver has his own independent harnesses and treadles. Also see **flute, tapestry loom.**

low wheel. Spinning. See **treadle wheel.**

lozenge. Bookbinding. A popular motif used on bindings; it consists of a diamond-shaped figure, or a square standing on one of its corners, usually filled with decorations. Also see **diaper design.**

lubbers process. Glasswork. See **cylinder glass.**

lubricant. Metalworking. Plastics. Woodworking. Any substance which reduces friction and the resulting heat between materials that rub against each other. Lubricants are used on cutting blades, **drill bit**s, and the tips of tools being ground or sharpened on a **grinding wheel.**

In woodworking, occasionally apply a bit of **tallow** to the cutting blade, especially to that of a **table saw** during use of the machine or when cutting heavy stock.

In plastics, the most common cutting and drilling lubricant is mild soapy water, although a paraffin oil may be used. A lubricant may be referred to as a coolant here because it also prevents the plastic from melting during the heat of machining.

In metalworking, the lubricant may also be referred to as a cutting fluid. The following is a sample of some lubricants that may be used on various metals.

Metal	Lubricant
aluminum	kerosene, kerosene and lard oil
brass	brake fluid, kerosene and lard oil
cast iron	air jet (use no liquid)
copper	mineral lard oil, kerosene
mild steel and tool steel	mineral lard oil, sulfurized oil

Lucinda's Star. Quilts. A variation of the **pieced-block LeMoyne Star** pattern. It has a feathered edge of small triangles. See ill.

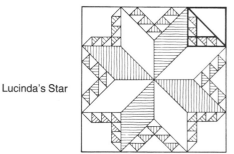

Lucinda's Star

Lucite. Plastics. See **acrylic.**

lucite lap. Gemcutting. See **lap.**

lug. Ceramics. See **Ceramics: Form.**

luke. Basketry. See **short-small.**

lumber. Woodworking. See **wood.**

lumber core. Woodworking. See **plywood.**

lumber size. Woodworking. See **wood.**

luminaria. Papercrafts. A traditional Mexican decoration made with a weighted paper bag and a candle. The bag, with a lighted candle inside it, produces a soft, glowing light. It is traditionally placed outdoors on Christmas Eve.

Place enough sand in the bottom of a brown paper bag to insert a candle and keep it from blowing over. Then fold down the rim of the bag twice, away from the interior, to strengthen the sides. Insert a candle into the sand.

luminosity. See **discord.**

lump pumice. Jewelry. See **pumice.**

Lurex thread. Crewel. Embroidery. Needlepoint. A nontarnishing **metallic thread** in gold or silver; Lurex thread is the only thread flexible enough to stitch through a piece of embroidery or use on needlepoint **canvas.** Care should be taken to use a needle with a sufficiently large eye to prevent tearing the thread when going through the fabric. Also see **metallic thread embroidery** and **Needlepoint: Materials.**

luster. Ceramics. A metallic **overglaze** used as a ceramic decoration. Luster is a mixture of a resin, oil of lavender or **fat oil** as **binder,** bismuth nitrate as **flux,** and a metallic salt. The ware is fired in an oxidizing **kiln** at a low temperature. Also see **oxidation, oxidizing fire, silver luster.**

luster. China and Glass Painting. Liquid **metallic color,** such as **silver, gold,** and iridescent pigments, suspended in a clear solution that, after application and **firing,** form a thin film of lustrous, metallic **glaze** over the surface. Lusters are mixed and used in the same way as liquid gold.

Stir the liquid luster well and apply it thinly with a camel's-hair brush. If thinning is necessary, use **lavender oil** or a commercially prepared essence for thinning gold. Never mix luster with turpentine. The luster is impossible to blend, so apply it by brushing in one direction only. To smooth the coating, pat it all over with a **silk pad.** For a good luster and for iridescent effects, apply three or four coats and fire after each application. Wash the luster brush in alcohol and then moisten it with **lavender oil.**

Lusters for glass are prepared with a different formula than for ceramics. The lusters for ceramics and glass are not interchangeable.

luster. Enameling. See **metallic luster.**

luster. Gemcutting. The quality of light reflected by a gem. The luster of a gem varies with the proportion of light reflected at its surface.

Metallic luster resembles burnished metal and is exhibited by opaque materials such as iron **pyrites.**

Metallic sheen (also called schiller) refers to bright, submetallic **reflections** caused by minute fissures or **inclusions** of small plates such as bronzite.

Vitreous luster is exhibited by transparent gems such as **ruby, emerald,** and **topaz.**

Adamantine luster is characteristic of **diamonds,** appearing as if coated with a metal film.

Silky luster (also called satin luster and sheen) is reflection from many minute points observed in fibrous gems.

Pearly luster is observed on faces parallel to internal **cleavage** cracks.

Greasy luster is shown by gems with low refractive indices.

Waxy luster is exhibited by **turquoise.**

Resinous luster is exhibited by many **garnets.**

Chatoyance refers to a bright reflective band caused by parallel tubular inclusions; when cut as a **cabochon,** chatoyant gems are called cat's eyes.

Asterism is caused by two or more chatoyant bands intersecting; it occurs in **corundum, beryl, quartz,** etc.

Iridescence resembles the **color** quality observed on soap bubbles.

Labradorescence is characteristic of a variety of **feldspar** called labradorite.

Adularescence is reflection from minute mobile points not discernible even under strong magnification.

Tyndall effect (also called opalescence) is a scattering of light by minute particles in transparent gems; in reflected light a pale blue color is imparted, but in transmitted light a yellow-brown color is observed.

Aventurescence is caused by reflections from easily visible plates or separations.

Play of color is a term reserved for the intense colors of precious **opal.**

Iris describes the bright reflections of spectral colors in cracked transparent quartz. Also see **C-axis, refraction** and **Gemcutting: Orientation.**

luting. Ceramics. (Also called sticking-up.) A method of joining pieces of leather hard or dry clay with **slip.** Score the **leather-hard** edges to be joined to insure a secure joint. Luting is used in slab-building, hand-building, and for joining thrown forms. Dry forms are joined using vinegar, a **deflocculent.** Also see **pulling a handle** and **Ceramics: Hand Building.**

lye. Batik and Tie-dye. Any strong alkaline solution. Formerly, lye was made by leaching wood ashes, primarily for use in soapmaking and washing. The solid sodium hydroxide, a brittle white substance, is commercially available. It is sometimes referred to as "concentrated lye." Also see **caustic soda.**

lye. Dyeing. See **caustic soda.**

lying press. Bookbinding. This press is one of the most frequently used pieces of equipment in binding. Into it are inserted the various **boards,** such as **backing boards, grooving boards,** and **cutting boards,** for the different **for-**

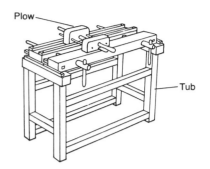

Plow

Tub

Lying press

warding operations, as well as the **plow** for **trimming.** It stands on a **tub** about 30″ high. This press is capable of performing the functions of the **standing press, nipping press,** and **book press** and, with the plow, can be used instead of a paper cutter. See ill.

Lyonnaise style. Bookbinding. A style of binding with broad interlaced strapwork (usually painted) or with large corner ornaments, a prominent center design, and the background filled with dots.

m

maceration. Dyeing. See **lichen dye.**

machine appliqué. Quilts. Stitchery. The attaching or applying of one fabric to another with sewing machine stitches. Any of a variety of **stitch**es may be used, the most common of which are the **machine satin stitch** and the straight machine stitch.

Basting is always important in machine appliqué, especially for satin stitch. An open **zigzag stitch** is first used to **baste** the **appliqué** fabric in place. Then the machine satin stitch is used to finish and completely cover the cut **raw edge** of the fabric. It leaves a solid, wide, smooth line of thread.

A **straight stitch** can also be used for machine appliqué. Edges of the fabric being applied can be **hem**med under or left raw. The straight stitch is used in a single line or in rows.

In cutting the appliqué materials, no **seam allowance** need be added for the machine satin stitch because the edge of the material is not turned under. If a straight machine stitch is employed, the additional ¼″ seam allowance is optional, depending on the method of sewing and the fabric used. If the sewing is done in a forward-and-reverse method, going back and forth over the edge, no allowance is needed. If a hem is to be turned under and sewn with straight stitch, the extra ¼″ is needed.

One of the primary advantages in using machine appliqué is that it requires less time than hand sewing, although it is not necessarily a speedy way to work. The machine stitching is strong and therefore more durable for outdoor or heavy use of any kind, such as for toys, **banner**s, and **soft sculpture.** Machine stitching is especially valuable where the fabric is too stiff or heavy to be sewn through by hand. Sewing machine appliqué is especially adaptable for large-scale work.

Any of a wide range of decorative stitches can also be used for machine appliqué. Most have a very even and somewhat mechanical-looking repeat pattern and for small-scale work are less effective than straight or satin stitch. The various decorative stitches may be used for appliqué according to directions that accompany the sewing machine. Generally they are sewn similarly to the machine satin stitch. Also see **Stitchery: Cutting, Machine Appliqué.**

machine appliqué stitch. Stitchery. See **machine satin stitch.**

machine baste. Stitchery. To temporarily **join fabric**s by means of large, loose machine stitches, using either **straight stitch** or zigzag stitch. The straight machine stitch is used for basting by making the stitches extra long and loose. This makes it possible to check **seam** lines before the final stitching and to remove the straight stitch lines afterward.

To machine **baste** for a satin stitch, the basting should be done with an open zigzag set at about one-half the width that the final satin stitch is to be. The outside edge of the narrow zigzag should be at the cut **raw edge** of the piece to be applied. Then when the wider **machine satin stitch** is used over the top, the basting stitches are completely hidden.

machine bolt. Metalworking. Woodworking. See **bolt.**

machine direction. Bookbinding. See **grain.**

machine lace. Lacemaking. At the end of the eighteenth century the first attempts were made to produce lace on adaptations of the hosiery frame. True lace could not be manufactured by this means. In England in 1808, John Heathcoat and a friend, by a strange coincidence named Lacy, solved the problem of making a strong **net** of a series of entwinements instead of stocking **loop**s. In two years Heathcoat's machines became widely known and their products were in great demand. They were so popular that in 1816 the Luddites, an association of laceworkers, displaced by the net machines, tried to stop this mechanization by breaking into Heathcoat's factory and destroying most of his equipment. In 1823, when Heathcoat's patent expired, many other factories were set up, and soon Great Britain was making quantities of plain netting. In 1813 John Leavers constructed a machine that would combine the making of the motifs and **ground** in one operation. The first such machines were made of wood and hand-operated. From these beginnings improvements have been made, but the highly sophisticated machines that today produce beautiful and delicate laces are still called "Leavers machines."

machine-made glass. Stained Glass. Otherwise known as **cathedral glass,** machine-made glass can be produced in sheets as large as 5′ × 11′ and in many textures, which are referred to as "antique" and "semiantique." These terms are used to designate the type of pattern that has been impressed on the glass with metal rollers. Examples are oceanic, ripple, moss, granite, hammered, figure C, Florentine, and Flemish. Also see **drapery glass, Flemish glass, fused glass technique, granite-backed glass, hammered glass, marine antique glass, Stained Glass: Tools and Materials.**

machine quilting. Quilts. **Quilting stitches** sewn on the sewing machine rather than by hand. The procedure is practical and timesaving, although it lacks the fineness and variation of hand **quilting.** A **quilting foot,** a standard attachment for most machines, is used. For straight lines, an adjustable gauge is also very helpful. For a thick quilt the pressure on the foot may have to be loosened to allow the material to move easily through the machine. Also see **Quilts: Quilting, Machine Quilting.**

machinery. Gemcutting. Machinery for gemcutting is powered by ¼ – ½ horsepower electric motors with a shaft speed of 1725 rpm. This power is transferred from the pulley on the motor shaft to the pulley on the arbor of the tool via a rubber belt (**a.**). The arbor is a spindle securely held in bearings that attaches to the business end of the machine; its purpose is to transfer the rotation smoothly and without vibration to the tool. With a constant motor speed the arbor speed may be varied by moving the belt to different combinations of pulleys. The ratio of the diameter of the pulley on the motor to the pulley on the arbor is equal to the ratio of the motor's speed to the speed of the saw, **grinding wheel,** or **lap.**

Some **tumbling, faceting,** and carving machines operate with direct motor drive, often with variable speed control. Combination machines are units that accept several tools, such as two grinding wheels, two sanding drums, and a polishing buff, on the same arbor. These machines have the tools in vertical positions, and come with drain pans and splash guards. Complete gemcutting machines such as the B & I machine have a vertical arbor in a basin (**b.**).

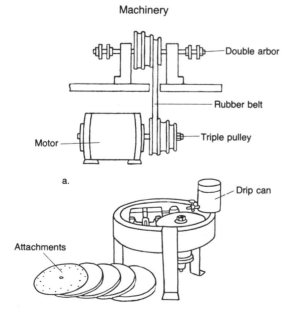

Machinery
Double arbor
Rubber belt
Motor
Triple pulley
a.
Drip can
Attachments
b.   B & I machine

Machine bearings should be sealed to keep out the abrasive grit and should be kept oiled and greased. See ill. Also see **faceting unit, point carver, slabbing saw,** and **Gemcutting: Safety Precautions.**

machine satin stitch. Quilts. Stitchery. (Also called closed zigzag stitch, closed satin stitch, machine appliqué stitch.) A finishing or **appliqué stitch** that can be sewn on most recent model sewing machines. The machine must have a **zigzag stitch** capability. In the satin stitch the needle moves back and forth from one side to the other. The width and the compactness of the stitch can be adjusted. Most sewing machine appliqué uses either the straight or the satin stitch.

Machine satin stitch may be used in either of two ways. In the first the appliqué fabric is cut to the finished size, with no additional ¼″ **seam allowance;** then the mechanism on the machine that controls the stitch size is set for a medium width in an open zigzag stitch. This is used to **baste** the cut shape to the **background.** Several pins may be used to secure the **fabric** in place before the basting begins. Care must be taken to stitch slowly enough so that the appliqué material remains flat. The entire zigzag basting stitch should remain on top of the appliqué fabric—that is, the outside edge of the stitch should be exactly at the cut or **raw edge** of the appliqué material. The stitches should catch and hold any loose threads or **fray**ed ends. When basting is completed any loose threads poking through the basting stitch should be trimmed off. The mechanism that controls stitches is now set for maximum width of the satin stitch. This means a very fine or close setting, so that the zigzags are placed right next to each other. Some experimentation may be required to find the exact setting for each sewing machine. There should be no fabric showing between the stitches, but the stitches should not be so close that they pile up on top of one another. The satin stitches are then sewn over the basted zigzags, making a smooth solid line of thread. If necessary, the stitching may be stopped at a corner, the presser foot lifted, and the material turned so that a sharp corner can be made.

The sewing machine may be set with the tension of the upper thread looser than that of the bottom thread. This assures that none of the crisscross connections between sewing thread and **bobbin** thread will show on the top. Threads are always tied on the back of the material.

A second method of appliquéing with machine satin stitch uses a piece of appliqué fabric on which an outline has been marked or drawn. For example, a circle might be drawn onto a piece of fabric that is about an inch larger than the circle all the way around. The satin stitches are sewn on the drawn line. When stitching of the circle is complete, the threads are tied on the back of the material. Then the excess fabric is trimmed or cut away next to the row of stitching. Care must be taken to cut close enough to avoid loose threads, but not so close as to cut into the satin stitches.

Either of these methods will work easily if the background material has some stiffness, or **body,** to it. Almost any fabric, even a soft lightweight material, can be appliquéd to a background fabric that has ample body. If the background material is very lightweight it may help to put the fabric in an embroidery hoop before stitching. A spray **starch** or an **iron-on interfacing** may be used as a stiffener. Some stitchers baste lightweight materials to sheets of paper the weight of typing or wrapping paper; this offers varying degrees of success.

When the machine satin stitch is used, the thread color becomes very important. Contrasts in value and color make the shapes stand out, or threads can be carefully matched to blend.

The machine satin stitch can also be used by itself—that is, not as appliqué but as embroidery. It makes a strong, colorful line and works especially well on heavy fabrics with good body. It may be used in this way to draw lines for toy animal faces, for linear designs, on **banner**s and **wall hanging**s, or in combination with any appliqué.

The machine satin stitch also has many uses in **quilt**making and provides a sturdy kind of appliqué for fabric toys such as **doll**s and stuffed animals. See ill.

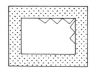

a.   Basted fabric using an open zigzag stitch

b.   Satin stitch or closed zigzag stitch covers basting stitch

c.   Stitches should run at right angles to fabric

machine screw. Metalworking. See **screw.**

machinist's file. Metalworking. See **file.**

machinist's hammer. Jewelry. Tincrafting. See **ball-peen hammer.**

machinist's scriber. Jewelry. A hard-pointed steel tool used for marking metal or as a **soldering point.** See ill. Also see **scriber.**

Machinist's scriber

machinist's vise. Metalworking. See **vise.**

macking. Knitting. An archaic Shetland Island term for the practice of knitting.

macramé. The word "macramé" is thought to be derived from the Arabic word *migramah*, which means "a protective covering." It is also a word for a kerchief, veil, or other head covering. The word "macramé" supposedly came into use during the nineteenth century.

Knotting has been done since the beginning of time. The Chinese and the Japanese were among the first to use it ornamentally. Early Peruvians used it to convey messages, to count, and to record history. Sailors have tied knots for hundreds of years and have played a

major role in the development of fancy knot work, some of which they call "Macramara's lace."

The tying of fringes and braids was an established art in Arabia by the thirteenth century. A century later the French were knotting *filet de carasière.* Much of this knotting was done in convents. There is also documentation of macramé in a sixteenth-century painting found in Valladolid Cathedral in Spain. The Italians were using the term *punto a gròppo,* which means knotted lace, at approximately the same time. Beautiful examples of this outstanding seventeenth-century work are still intact. Samples of macramé worked in silk and metallic threads in the Victoria and Albert Museum in London, England, are dated from 1749. These particular samples are done primarily in the double half hitch. There are also some splendid examples of work done in what is now called Cavandeli work, although this particular name for the knotting did not come into use until the early 1900s. A great deal of early macramé work was done in the double half hitch. In many cases this includes macramé that has been incorrectly placed into lace collections and is not properly identified as knotting. During the Victorian era a great deal of macramé was done in many countries. Elaborate bags, tassels, fringed towels, belts, window coverings, bed canopies, and bell pulls were knotted. Along the Riviera schools and convents began to teach macramé to young children around the beginning of the twentieth century.

Macramé's current popularity began in the mid-1960s as a logical progression of the renewed interest in crafts. Those who wished fast results specialized in articles of adornment, such as belts, bags, jackets, dresses, and bathing suits. Articles for the home were also crafted. The serious, trained craftsperson used it singly or incorporated it with other mediums to produce works of art. The current popularity of macramé is worldwide. Any material that will tie into a knot can be used for this work.

The knotting material is usually referred to as knotting **cord.** Yarns, cords, and twines used in macramé should be durable and smooth-textured, and should have as little elasticity as possible so that the finished macramé won't pull out of shape. A cord that will not fray is best. Cords suitable for macramé include **linen** cord, silk cord, rattail (**satin cord**), **jute,** nylon seine twine, **Marline twine, sisal, leather lacing,** rug wool, and wool roving. Yarns or cords can be used in combination and doubled or tripled to alter the texture, strength, and depth of the macramé work.

Usually **Celotex** or a similar rigid material is used as a knotting surface. The macramé cords are attached to the surface before the knotting begins. As the knotting progresses, a row, or even a knot, is pinned in place on the knotting surface to keep the knotting uniform. Celotex, a board used for insulation, readily lends itself to use as a knotting surface. The Celotex should be wrapped tightly with heavy wrapping paper that has been divided into an all-over grid of 1" squares. **Graph paper** with a large grid can be used. The macramé can be matched to this grid to keep the work even. Cork, sturdy cardboard, and firm foam rubber may also be used as a knotting surface. **Upholsterer's pins, T-pins,** and glass-headed straight pins are essential for **pinning** and **anchoring** the work in place. **C-clamp**s are also helpful for holding the work or holding the cord while measuring and cutting.

You will need **bobbin**s around which to wind the cords to keep them in place, and rubber bands to keep the bobbins secured. Have scissors, a clear glue for securing knots or stiffening a cord end for threading, beads, and graph paper on hand. A tapestry needle is helpful for working loose cords into the piece during **finishing**. An assortment of small hardware, such as plastic or metal rings, buckles, dowels, and small metal nuts, should be kept for use in place of **mounting cords**.

Macramé involves the use of several basic knots and their variations, such as the **half hitch** and **double half hitch** and the **half knot** and **square knot**.

The macramé cord is selected, cut, and attached to a **mounting** with **mounting knots**. The cords are wound on **bobbins,** and the work is pinned to a knotting surface. Various **finishing** techniques can be used to complete the work. Also see **knots, measuring the cord, mounting bar, mounting cord.**

macramé. Lacemaking. A type of knotted lace made with the fingers. It is a revival of the Italian *punto a gròppo,* or "knotted points." This technique was used in Spain and Italy for ecclesiastical linen, church vestments, and other trimmings from the end of the fifteenth to the seventeenth century. The French term for macramé is *filet de carasière.* The original word "macramé" is Arabic, and was used in the East to denote an ornamental fringe added to any material. In Genoa, where macramé lace was chiefly made, the name was at first given to toweling with plain fringed edges, and only gradually became the designation of the lace worked in likeness of the plain knotted fringes.

madder. Batik and Tie-dye. Dyeing. Fabric Printing. Quilts. An ancient, red, **natural dye** obtained from the root of the madder plant (*Rubia tinctoria*) used to obtain a rich color in the dyeing of wool. It grew wild in Europe and Asia, but was also cultivated in northern Europe since the eighth century A.D.

Holland especially became known for the cultivation of madder from the fifteenth century until just before World War II. In Asia, where the dye was first used, the Arabs called the plant alizari, and in a very secret and complicated mixture including such things as ox-blood, cow dung, alum, and rancid olive oil, produced a very fast color for the dyeing of cottons. This fiery color, a favorite in early American quilts, was called Turkey red. The French unlocked the secret mordanting process and carried it to Europe. In 1868, a **synthetic dye,** alizarin, was produced. **Mordant**s used with madder are **alum** for a Chinese lacquer red, **chrome** for garnet red, and **tin** for orange red.

Madame X. Quilts. A modern **pieced block** design made using the **Irish Chain. A border** separates the blocks, interrupting the diagonal effect of the chain.

Madeira border. Basketry. See **border.**

made stitch. Knitting. (As in the term, make 1 stitch. Abbr. m 1 R.) This is the term for the type of increasing done by knitting into the thread that runs between two stitches. Also see **Knitting: Increasing.**

Madison Block. Quilts. A **pieced quilt** design that encloses a six-pointed star within each hexagonal shaped **block**. The design was made in honor of President Madison. See ill. Also see **presidents' quilts.**

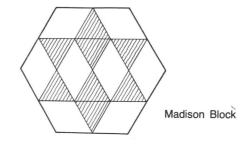
Madison Block

madras tissue paper. Toys. A tissue paper with bands or stripes of color that blend into one another.

magascope. Toys. See **panoptique.**

magic chain stitch. Crewel. Embroidery. The "magic" in this **chain stitch** is created through the use of two contrasting color threads in the needle. One thread at a time is looped to form the chain; the other thread disappears behind the fabric.

Thread the needle with two contrasting threads. Come up at A. Form a loop and put the needle in again at A, holding the loop down with the finger. Come up again at B.

Keeping the light thread under the needle, allow the dark one to go above it. Pull the threads through and the light one will form a single chain stitch and the dark one will disappear behind the material.

Repeat the process, this time holding the dark thread under the needle and allowing the light thread to slip through. Continue to work in this way, alternating dark with light or, if you wish, take two light stitches and two dark. See ill.

Magic chain stitch

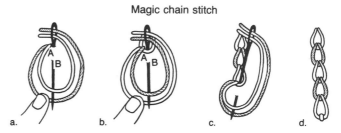
a.   b.   c.   d.

magic disk. Toys. See **phenakistoscope** and **Toys: Optical Toys.**

magic lantern. Toys. An **optical toy** that utilizes a light and lenses to project a slide onto a screen. It was first thought of by Roger Bacon in the thirteenth century, but a newer form was described by an Italian named Kircher in a publication in 1650. It was not produced as a toy until centuries later. Highly decorative and ornamental versions of the magic lantern were available in

England and France by 1840. Hand-painted colored slides were inserted in the lantern one after another and projected to make a magnified image.

The first magic lanterns were for a single viewer who looked through a slot or peephole; later the projection was enlarged to accommodate a number of viewers at one time. These nineteenth-century versions concentrated on educational and moral enlightenment for subject matter. The **polyopticon,** the **panoptique,** and the stereopticon were variations of the magic lantern. Also see **lampscope** and **Toys: Optical Toys.**

magnesium block. Jewelry. A block composed of **asbestos** fiber and carbonate of magnesium, used to support work during **soldering.** Its composition, although firm, is soft enough to allow **steel pins** to be stuck in it to hold work together for soldering. It is longer-lasting than a **charcoal block** but does not hold the heat as well. Also see **asbestos pad.**

magnetic filter. Ceramics. **Slip** is passed over a magnet to attract iron particles; this is done to achieve a pure white glaze. Also see **tramp iron.**

magnetic toy. Toys. Any of a great variety of toys moved or animated by the use of a magnet that attracts parts of the toy containing steel or iron. A popular **bath toy** that employs a magnet consists of a collection of little floating **boats.** One end of each boat has some metal embedded so that the boats can be made to move through the water as they are attracted magnetically.

Other magnetic toys involve the use of iron filings that are moved about in an enclosed glass-topped or plastic-covered container. A magnet is used to slide the filings into various patterns.

magnetite. Gemcutting. See **obsidian.**

magnifier. Gemcutting. See **loupe.**

magnifying toy. Toys. See **water scope.**

mahogany. Woodworking. A generic term for a family of about 75 **close-grain**ed, heavy **hardwood**s that grow in many parts of the world and are prized for **woodcarving, veneer**ing, furniture, and cabinet work. Its **heartwood** varies in color from ocher, yellow, and pink to reddish-brown. Mahogany takes a high polish, has a minimum of **warp**ing, swelling, and shrinking, is resistant to mold and decay, and is available in large sizes. Although some varieties are soft and others brittle, it is generally recommended for carving sculpture.

The hardest type of mahogany is West Indian mahogany (also called Domingan or Spanish mahogany). Honduras mahogany is supposed to be the heaviest and is carved like **walnut.** Tropical American mahogany, grown in Brazil, Guatemala, Nicaragua, Panama, Peru, and northern South America, is white to pink when first cut but changes to a rich golden brown. African mahogany from the Gold and Ivory Coasts is one of the most dramatically **figure**d but

softest varieties, with larger pores than American mahogany. It carves very well.

Lauan or Philippine mahogany is not related at all to true mahogany. It is soft and carves well, but loses its color when exposed to sunlight and is less durable in humid conditions. It is often given a false mahogany finish for commercial use, but is more varied in color and has larger pores than true mahogany.

mahogany obsidian. Gemcutting. See **obsidian.**

maiden. Spinning. (Also called sister.) One of two wooden vertical posts supporting the **spindle** in a **spinning wheel.** The spindle in a **wool wheel** or **spindle shaft** in a **treadle wheel** lies in a horizontal position between the two. In one variety or another they are found on all types of spinning wheels. Also see **spinning head.**

Maidenhair Fern. Quilts. See **Princess Feather.**

main control. Puppets. See **control bar.**

main facet. Gemcutting. See **facet.**

majolica. Ceramics. **Earthenware** covered with a tin lead **glaze,** often with a **luster** decoration. Also see **tin glaze.**

making a platform. Knitting. Creating a buffer for a single **ladder stitch.** A platform is created when the stitch made by the **raised increase** is dropped. To make a platform for a stitch that is to be dropped, make a raised increase. This **made stitch** should be **knit**ted or **purl**ed depending on the pattern until such time as the pattern indicates that the stitch be dropped. When the stitch is dropped, the place will increase in width.

making a throw. Knitting. The movement of passing the yarn around the working needle while making a stitch. "Making a throw" is also used in patterns to describe the elongation of a stitch in the following manner:

Insert the needle into the stitch to be knit, wrap the yarn around that needle twice, and then complete the stitch (**a.**). On the next row, insert the needle through the stitch and drop the second throw when completing the stitch (**b.**). See ill.

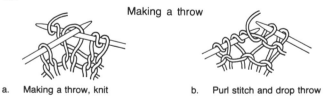

Making a throw

a.   Making a throw, knit   b.   Purl stitch and drop throw

making do. Puppets. Quilts. Stitchery. Toys. The expression describes the philosophic basis of the **patchwork quilt:** using only what is already available. The person who produces a quilt, toy, or wall hanging by "making do" does not buy new fabric but uses what is left over from other sewing projects, from old clothes, and from scraps and patches. In colonial times, this was often a necessity, and the quiltmakers working within these limitations produced works both functional and aesthetic. Examples of the making-do approach are evident in the **crazy quilt,** the **Joseph's Coat** quilt, the **necktie skirt,** and nearly all **folk toys.**

Ecologically, making do is a sound principle. Artistically, it often imposes strict limitations. It should be remembered, however, that the patchwork quilt flowered from a frugal approach to the use of scrap fabrics, suggesting that strict limitations, coupled with ingenuity, may yield surprising results.

making the double stitch. Tatting. The double stitch is composed of two **half hitch** stitches.

After **winding the shuttle,** pull about 15″ of the tatting **thread** from the **shuttle,** holding the shuttle between the thumb and index finger of the right hand (for left-handed persons, reverse directions). Grasp the thread about 2″ from the end with the thumb and index finger of the left hand. Spread the fingers of the left hand and make a loop around them and hold the completed loop in the thumb and index finger. Lift the shuttle thread, the **knot bearer,** with the little finger of the right hand. You are now ready to make the first half of the basic **double stitch.**

Pass the shuttle under the knot bearer and through the loop in the left hand. Bring the shuttle back over the loop and under the shuttle thread; relax the fingers of the left hand and drop the shuttle thread from the little finger. Holding the loop securely between the thumb and index finger of the left hand pull the shuttle thread taut with a quick jerk. Slowly raise the fingers of the left hand, in the loop, and pull the thread up, sliding the left half hitch just completed between the thumb and index finger of the left hand.

Hold the left hand as in the first directions; drop the thread from the shuttle in the right hand, pass the shuttle over the shuttle thread and over the loop in the left hand back through the loop under the **loop thread** and over the

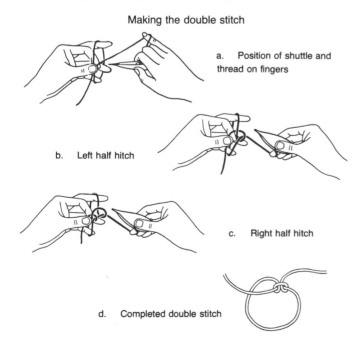

Making the double stitch

a. Position of shuttle and thread on fingers

b. Left half hitch

c. Right half hitch

d. Completed double stitch

shuttle thread. Relax the fingers of the left hand, hold the loop tightly, again pull the shuttle thread taut with a quick jerk. Again, slowly raise the fingers of the left hand and pull the thread up, sliding the right half hitch just completed into position next to the first half hitch. This completes the double stitch of tatting. See ill.

Malacca. Basketry. See **cane.**

malachite. Gemcutting. A carbonate of copper with a **hardness** of 3½, **specific gravity** of 3.5−4, and green **streak.** It **crystal**lizes in the monoclinic system but is more often found in compact masses of nodular or botryoidal (resembling a bunch of grapes) form with prominent bands of light and green **color.** It is cut in **cabochon, flat,** or novelty forms. Malachite is dissolved in hydrochloric acid. It is sanded with 1220-grit silicon carbide **abrasive** on leather and polished with tin or chrome oxide on leather or wood. The dust from malachite is poisonous, so care must be taken to grind and sand it very wet. Also see **polishing** and **Gemcutting: Hand Grinding and Polishing, Rough Shaping.**

male mold. Plastics. See **mold.**

malkat. Beadwork. See **turquoise.**

malleability. Jewelry. Metalworking. The ability of a metal to be easily shaped by hammering or rolling without breaking or cracking. This is not to be confused with **ductility.** A metal such as **lead** is very malleable but it has little ductility and may split if stretched too thin. The following metals are listed in decreasing order of their malleability: **gold, silver,** lead, **copper, aluminum, tin,** platinum, **zinc, iron,** and **nickel.** Also see **annealing, forging, rolling mill.**

malleable iron. Metalworking. See **iron.**

mallet. Block Printing. A small carpenter's mallet with a head about 2½″ long is sometimes used to drive the chisel or gouge when clearing spaces. A mallet with a leather head is easiest to control.

mallet. Fabric Printing. A mallet with a rubber head, such as a tire-changing mallet from an auto supply store, is used for pounding the printing block on the **fabric** to make a clearly printed image.

mallet. Jewelry. A kind of hammer with a barrel-shaped head used for bending and forming metal when scratching or marring of the surface is to be kept at a minimum. Mallets are used with **mandrels** and **stakes.** They come in many shapes and sizes, with flat-faced and rounded surfaces, and are available in fiber, nylon, plastic, horn, and other materials, each of which has a specific use. The most commonly used mallet in jewelry is made of rawhide. Also see **rawhide mallet.**

mallet. Leather. (Also called rawhide mallet.) A hammer made of wood often with a head of tightly rolled rawhide, used in leatherwork with punching and **stamping** tools for flattening areas such as folds and seams and for setting **findings** such as **eyelets** and **snaps**. See ill. Also see **striking stick** and **Leatherwork: Tools and Materials.**

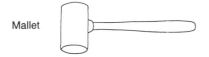

Mallet

mallet. Metalworking. See **hammer.**

mallet. Woodworking. A **hammer**like tool with a broad-faced, barrel-shaped head made of hardwood or weighted rubber. Rubber mallets are used in assembling wood constructions to prevent denting and splitting the wood; wooden mallets are used to hit **gouges** and **chisels** in **woodcarving** and general woodworking when the force of the hand alone is not enough. Mallets come in a variety of sizes classified according to the weight of the head and the diameter of striking area.

Maltese cross. Gemcutting. See **facet.**

Maltese Cross. Quilts. A name given to any of several **pieced block** designs that use the four-armed Maltese cross as the focal pattern.

A basic Maltese cross pattern consists of eight elongated isosceles triangles joined in a radiating pattern with the bases at the outside edge. Usually the triangles alternate from dark to light so that the shape of the Maltese cross shows clearly. Small right triangles are added at the bases of the four Maltese cross triangles to make a square block. This block is identical to the block that makes a **Kaleidoscope** quilt, and resembles **Spider Web.**

In another variation, a plain cross is placed in a square, and sometimes that square is **set** at an angle within another square. Among the variations of this block are **Chimneysweep, Greek Cross,** and **Red Cross.**

Another variation of the Maltese Cross is a **Pineapple** design. It has a four-pointed cross, similar in shape to the Maltese Cross, but with a **sawtooth** edge. See ill.

Maltese Cross

Maltese silk. Embroidery. (Also called horsetail.) A very tightly twisted silk thread with high tensile strength. When waxed it is used for **couching** metallic threads. It is available in various shades of gold and silver. Also see **metallic thread embroidery.**

mandrel. Jewelry. Any metal rod, usually tapered and made of steel, used to hold and form rings, bracelets, wire coils, **bezels,** curves, and metal being prepared for **drawing tubing;** and as a support for working with **wax.** Lightweight aluminum mandrels are available for use in preparation for **casting.** Mandrels can be sized or unsized.

mandrel. Metalworking. A cone of cast metal on which circular objects are forged. A round metal bar or rod of any diameter may be used, but in **blacksmithing** the cone shape is common.

manganese. Metalworking. See **steel.**

manganese oxide. Ceramics. A **pigment oxide** used on **stoneware** and **earthenware** to produce browns. Manganese oxide used in concentrations less than 5% in the body or **glaze** will cause **blisters** during **firing. Frit**ted with **alumnia,** manganese oxide produces a pink **stain.**

manganese oxide. Stained Glass. See **antique glass colorants.**

manger scene. Toys. See **crib set.**

manikin. Toys. See **mannequin.**

Manila rope. Toys. A rope made from Manila hemp or abaca and commonly available in hardware stores and from farm or boat suppliers. It comes in different diameters and is purchased according to the weight it is expected to carry. It is often used to hang **swings** because it is strong. It will wear down and must occasionally be checked for abrasion or rotting. It is also used on **pull toys,** although the surface of Manila rope is sometimes too scratchy to be handled by children; a **nylon rope** or clothesline rope is more smoothly textured for this purpose.

manipulate. Puppets. To move and control the puppet. The animation and articulation are achieved by the way the **puppeteer** manages the **controls.** The skill required in manipulation varies according to the complexity of the puppet—whether it is a simple **finger puppet** or a **string puppet.**

The **hand puppet** is manipulated from below by the hand, which fits inside the **puppet head.** One or two fingers usually fit into the head so that its movements are easily controlled. String puppets are moved by means of **strings** that connect various parts of the figure to the **control bar.** Also see **control point, horizontal control, playing the puppet, vertical control** and **Puppets: Manipulating the Marionette.**

man-made fiber. Batik and Tie-dye. Spinning. Stitchery. Weaving. (Also called chemical fiber). A **fiber** produced by man, not a **natural fiber.** Some man-made fibers have a **cellulose** or vegetable base (such as viscose rayon) or part cellulose base (**acetate**), or they may contain no cellulose at all (nylon, acrylic, modacrylic). The fiber content is of special importance in **dyeing** because it affects the fabric's affinity for dye. Viscose rayon is the only man-made fiber that can be easily dyed. Also see **Batik and Tie-dye: Fabrics for Dyeing, Identifying Fibers.**

mannequin. Toys. (Also called manikin.) A **model** of the human body that has movable and sometimes detachable limbs. The earliest mannequins were made of wood and were **joint**ed. The artist's mannequin can be set in various positions as a guide in drawing the body in various poses. The small French **fashion doll** was a mannequin used to display Parisian styles of dress. Full-sized mannequins are used to model clothes in store window displays. Mannequins are one variety of **simulacrum.**

man-on-a-stick. Toys. See **stick rider.**

manta. Weaving. See **Navajo weaving.**

manufactured gas. Ceramics. See **kiln fuel.**

maple. Woodworking. A tough, strong **hardwood** with a fine, uniform **grain**. It is light reddish-brown to white in color and is used for flooring, furniture, interior work, and **veneer**s for **marquetry**. It takes a high finish well. The common varieties include rock maple, sugar maple, and black maple. The grain is generally straight, with the exception of bird's-eye maple, which is highly **figure**d.

Maple Leaf. Quilts. See **Cactus Flower.**

maquette. Weaving. A French term denoting the small-scale model done beforehand of a large **tapestry** or **wall hanging.**

marble. Mosaics. A hard metamorphic limestone found in a wide range of colors from white through gray, green, ochre, brown, red, and black, and sometimes streaked or mottled. When polished to bring out the natural graining it is used as a **mosaic** material. Before the development of Western glassmaking skills in the fourth century A.D., most mosaics, including the famous **Alexander Mosaic**, were created out of **marble tesserae**. Marble tesserae similar in size to **smalti** (½″ × ¼″ × ¼″) can be found in specialty craft and **tile** shops. Also see **Mosaics: Cutting the Material, Selecting the Material, Tools and Materials.**

marble. Toys. A small **ball** or **bead**like sphere used for the **game** of marbles. The smallest and most common marbles are the **mib**s of unglazed soft-colored **clay**. Larger ceramic marbles, or "shooters," are either unglazed or are decorated with slip painting. Among other marbles popular when the game was played avidly by every schoolboy were glaze-painted chinas, agates, jaspers (polished cloudies) and carnelian agates (blind agates). Marbles today are made principally of glass. The history and collecting of marbles is of special interest to many toy collectors.

marble chips. Stained Glass. Used as a decorative coat on casting, **concrete**, or **epoxy resin**. Also see **dalle-de-verre.**

marbled paper. Bookbinding. Paper of a swirled colored pattern that has been applied by the process of **marbling.**

marble dust. Stained Glass. See **ballast.**

marbleizing. Candlemaking. A decorating process in which the finished candle is coated with a layer of oil paint floated on water. The paint adheres to the candle in a random pattern, producing a marbelized effect.

Mix about 1″ of artist's oil paint squeezed from a tube with paint thinner to the consistency of thick cream. Fill a shallow pan (large enough to accommodate the size of the candle) with water. Carefully spread the paint mixture over the surface of the water in the pan with a spoon so that the paint lies on the surface of the water. Don't try to mix it. Add as many colors as desired, then draw the spoon through the surface of the water and paint to form swirls, but don't stir. Roll the candle in the mixture. Remove and let dry.

marble slab. Leather. See **tooling, stamping.**

marbling. Batik and Tie-dye. The all-over, irregular, or variegated pattern that results from wadding, tying, and **dyeing** a fabric in the **tie-dye** process. The **fabric** is wadded into a ball and bound with string or cord. The end of the cord is fastened, leaving a 6–8″ length by which the ball can be held to dip it in the **dyebath**. The longer the material is left in the dye, the more the dye will penetrate. After dyeing, the ball is rinsed and untied, and the fabric damp-dried and ironed. The process may be repeated for additional colors.

marbling. Bookbinding. The technique of applying a veined colored design to paper, leather, or page edges by floating colors on size in patterns and transferring them to the surface. Also see **marbled paper, marbling comb, marbling vat.**

marbling. Stained Glass. See **oil and water technique.**

marbling comb. Bookbinding. A comblike tool used to form patterns in the colored size used for **marbling** papers and other surfaces. Also see **marbled paper, marbling vat.**

marbling vat. Bookbinding. A container that holds water coated with colored size for transferring marbled patterns to paper and other surfaces. Also see **marbled paper, marbling comb.**

march. Weaving. See **countermarch loom.**

marche. Weaving. See **countermarch loom, lam.**

margin. Bookbinding. The blank spaces surrounding the type on a page. They vary in width from book to book, but generally the top margin is the narrowest, the back (inside) margin the next in size, the front (outside) margin the next to largest space, and the bottom margin is the largest.

A margin is also the hem leather or other cover material that appears on the inside of the cover **boards.**

maria. Glasswork. In flamework, the doughnutlike enlargement that can be formed in rod or tube glass. An area anywhere along the tube or rod is heated in the **glass fire** and the ends of the tube pushed together and turned constantly so that the melted glass is extruded into a ring that is then fused into a solid shape.

marine antique glass. Stained Glass. This glass is technically not **antique glass** because it is rolled out by a machine rather than hand-blown. Although widely used, it lacks the irregularities that add depth to the antique glass. Also see **machine-made glass.**

Mariner's Compass. Quilts. See **Sunburst.**

marine thummel. Stitchery. See **sailor's palm.**

marionette. Puppets. The most complex of all **puppet** figures. Marionettes have **joint**ed bodies connected at various points to **strings** that are attached to a **control.** Also see **card marionette, cloth marionette, control point, horizontal control, leather hinge, perch bar, Pinocchio, playing the puppet, Punch and Judy show, puppeteer, puppet play, rag-doll puppet, rail, screw eye joint, simplified horizontal control, string puppet, transformation puppet, trick puppet, vertical control** and **Puppets: Definition, Making the Marionette Skeleton.**

marionette hand. Puppets. See **hand.**

marionette head. Puppets. The head of the **marionette** is made by the same process as the **puppet head.** The only difference is that the marionette head does not have an opening at the **base** of the neck; the head is solid. A small **screw eye** is later attached under the head to join it to the **skeleton,** or body, of the marionette. Also see **head bar, head string** and **Puppets: Making the Puppet Head.**

marionette stage. Puppets. A specially constructed arena or theater for performances using **string puppet**s or **marionette**s. The marionette stage is similar to a regular performance stage but requires that a **screen** be provided to conceal the **controllers** from the audience view. The operator stands on the operator's bridge, and the marionettes are held over the **bridge bar** to perform on the **stage floor.** Also see **bench, bridge, marionette theater, rear bridge, top drop** and **Puppets: The Marionette Stage.**

marionette theater. Puppets. The entire range of theatrical performance, including the drama, characters, stage, and production. The marionette theater is sometimes referred to as the Punch and Judy theater, although the **Punch and Judy show** is actually a performance of **puppet**s, not **marionette**s. The use of marionettes requires a **marionette stage** to accommodate the **controller** as well as the marionettes.

Mariposa Lily. Quilts. See **Lily.**

Mariposa weave. Basketry. The Navajo version of the **lace coil** weave.

marking gauge. Woodworking. See **marking tools.**

marking out. Jewelry. Producing a full-scale drawing in preparation for **forging.** The drawing then acts as a guide against which the work can be checked as it progresses.

marking pen. Batik and Tie-dye. Puppets. Stitchery. Toys. (Also called felt-tip pen, fabric marker.) Pens with flat or pointed felt tips. Some are nonpermanent and suitable only on paper or for temporary use. Others are permanent markers and may be incorporated into linear patterns and drawings in **wall hanging**s, **stuff**ed **fabric** sculpture, or clothing. The permanent marking pens, available in a wide range of colors, must be allowed to dry thoroughly before they are handled.

For use on clothing, greater stability and permanence of color are required. This can be achieved by ironing with a medium-hot iron to help **set** the colors. Some designers dip the finished fabric into a salt solution, then **press** it with a hot iron.

It requires some experimentation to determine which markers will work on which fabrics. Only laundry markers, or those that specifically state they are permanent, may be assumed to be fast colors. Marking pens are one of the few **dye**s that work well on **permanent press** fabric.

In **batik** or **tie-dye,** marking pens offer an excellent way of adding accents quickly and easily. Also see **alphabet blocks, direct dye painting.**

marking pencil. Batik and Tie-dye. A hard chalk pencil used to mark fabrics. It can usually be brushed or washed off and is commonly available in blue or white. The fabric marking pencil, or dressmaker's chalk, is sometimes used to sketch designs for **batik.**

marking tools. Woodworking. Tools used to mark measurements, points, and lines on a surface, usually in conjunction with **squaring tools** and **measuring tools.**

Any pencil can be used to mark wood. A carpenter's pencil is broad and flat (about ¼" × ½"), has a thick, soft, lead, and can easily be sharpened with a **plane** or **knife.** A pencil line usually can be rubbed away, which may or may not be an advantage. Chalk may be more visible than pencil on dark woods; it also rubs off more easily.

Any sharp, pointed tool may be used as a scribe to score a line that will not rub off; if shallow enough, it can be readily sanded off in the finishing process. **Awls,** knives, and **nails** make good scribes; **combination squares** often have a small scribe in the handle.

A center punch is used for marking points to be drilled. The conical depression formed keeps the **drill bit** from drifting off the mark. An awl or a **bradawl** is often used instead; even a nail will do.

A chalk line (also called a snapline) is a long piece of heavy cord coated with chalk dust. The ends are secured with the cord taut; when the cord is lifted and allowed to snap against the surface, a perfectly straight line is marked in chalk. You can snap a line with any cord rubbed with chalk; there are commercial models with the cord wound on a spool in a case containing chalk dust (**a.**), and some are fitted with weighted **plumb bobs** to serve also as **plumb lines.**

A compass is often used to mark circles on wood. A **divider** can be used instead, to produce a scribed circle. For large circles, a nail for the center, a long piece of string for the radius, and a pencil to mark the circumference is very satisfactory.

A marking gauge is a tool used to scribe lines parallel to the edge of a board (**b.**). A sharp pin at the end of the rule scribes a mark as the other end is moved along the edge. See ill. Also see **centering pin** and **Woodworking: Marking Out and Squaring.**

Marking tools

a.   Chalk line   b.   Marking gauge

mark out. Woodworking. See **Woodworking: Marking Out, Squaring.**

marline twine. Macramé. Marline twine is a cord that has been soaked in creosote to increase its durability. It is primarily a nautical cord and can be obtained at marine supply stores. This type of cord is excellent for knotting hanging planters and other objects intended for outdoor use.

marl yarn. Spinning. Weaving. See **novelty yarn.**

marquetry. Découpage. Woodworking. A decorative woodworking process in which a number of **veneer**s of wood or other material, such as metal or ivory, are glued to a wood ground until the surface is entirely covered. Marquetry is distinct from **inlaying** or **intarsia.**

Marquetry was popular in Holland in the 17th century and later widely used in France. The style has been adapted to découpage by using wood-veneer paper cut and glued to a wood surface, then buried under the découpage **finish.**

Boulle work is a type of marquetry developed by André Charles Boulle (1642–1732). He combined veneers of brass, enameled metal, tortoiseshell, and colored woods on furniture. Boulle was responsible for providing furniture to the French royal household. His craft became the model for all work of that type.

marquise cut. Gemcutting. See **facet.**

marquisette. Stitchery. See **transparent fabric.**

married metals. Jewelry. A technique recently revived by Los Costillo, a family of **silversmith**s working in Taxco, Mexico. Unlike **mokumé,** which is layer upon layer of dif-

ferent metals, married metals are different metals placed side by side, forming **butt joint**s. Metals such as **brass, copper, silver,** and nickel **alloy** are used. Designs made with this technique can be simple or extremely complicated.

The design is made designating the placement of the different metals. The pieces are sawn from a heavy-gauge metal—it is possible to use 18 gauge, but 16 is better—making sure the **sawing** and **filing,** if necessary, are very accurate, providing very close-fitting butt joints. After **pickling,** the pieces are placed in position on a flat sheet of asbestos, such as **transite board,** for **soldering.** The piece is **flux**ed with paste flux, making sure the joints are well-covered. Large solder **pallion**s are then placed over all of the joints, and the work is soldered together. If additional **solder** is required to fill the joints, stick or wire solder can be fed into the areas while soldering. After soldering, the excess solder is removed with heavy **file**s, and the areas smoothed out with finer ones. During soldering, the back of the design is also often flooded with solder, which will need to be removed. If any shaping of the metal needs to be done, such as bending a bracelet or slightly doming a pin, it can be done at this stage, handling the married metals as **sheet metal.** The metal should be shaped with a **rawhide mallet** so as not to mar the design. If a hard solder is used initially, any further soldering necessary can be done with a solder that flows at a lower temperature. The final finishing of married metals is important. As a high polish destroys the color contrasts of the metal, a matte or brushed finish is desirable. The metals can also be lightly heat oxidized to quickly intensify their differences, left exposed to the air for a slower change, or dipped into **liver of sulfur** and rubbed lightly with a fine grade of **steel wool.** Also see **flame, fluxing.**

Martha Washington's Quilt. Quilts. A **quilt** reputedly made by Martha Washington in 1785. It is a **medallion quilt,** featuring copperplate printing on **cotton** in the center depicting "Penn's Treaty with the Indians." Both **appliqué** and **piecing** are used in the surrounding **band**s and **border**s, ending with the **Windmill** design.

Martha Washington's Wreath. Quilts. An **appliqué** design of the early 1800s named for the First Lady. Any of a great variety of **wreath** designs go by this name.

marver. Glasswork. The polished marble or iron plate on which molten glass gathered from a **tank furnace** is rolled and shaped into a cylinder. Size is not critical, but a marver is typically 2' × 4' and at table height. Also see **marvering.**

marvering. Glasswork. The operation whereby a **gather** of glass is centered on the **blowing iron.**

After the gather is drawn from the **tank furnace,** the molten glass at the end of the iron is brought into contact with a polished metal or marble slab called a **marver** and then rolled back and forth by twisting the opposite end of the iron in the hands. By pulling the end of the iron toward you during this operation the glass is forced beyond the end of the iron so that there will be enough material there to encase the first bubble.

Alternatively, the gather can be taken directly to the **glassmaker's chair,** the iron being placed on the arms and rolled with the left hand while a gather is formed with a **paddle** held in the right hand.

Marvering is basic to glassblowing because it is at this point that the necessary **symmetry** is imparted to the gather. If the first gather is not true to the iron, the bubble will form off-center when it is blown, a condition that is not possible to correct with subsequent gathers. Marvering also chills the surface of the glass that comes into contact with the paddle or marver so it will hold its shape during the critical phase of forming the **parison.** Second or third gathers are also subjected to similar forming operations, either with **blocking mold**s or on the marver.

marzipan. Toys. A sweet dough mixture used in **cookie art.** It is an **edible dough** that is a combination of almond paste, powdered sugar, water, flavor, and coloring. Marzipan is a traditional sweet that has been made for several hundred years. Special small **cookie molds** are made for marzipan, or it can be shaped in the hands. It is used in making decorations and **edible toy**s or trifles. Also see **Toys: Ephemeral Toys.**

mascot doll. Toys. See **nursery character.**

mask. Papercrafts. Toys. A disguising covering for the face, part of the face, or for both the face and the upper portion of the body. A mask may be a caricature, a grotesque exaggeration, or an abstraction of human features, but there always remains some likeness of the human face.

Traditional masks of historical significance are seen in such well-known examples as the Greek theater, Japanese theater, religious rites of countries throughout the world, festivals, and parades. In some cultures their use is associated with the supernatural, magical rites, and superstition. In present-day use, masks are usually decorative and may have symbolic or religious significance.

Masks have been devised from materials of all kinds—wood, metal, paper, **papier mâché,** quilted fabrics, and fabrics decorated with embroidery, appliqué, and batik. Various techniques are used in both the construction and the elaboration of masks. The complexity of construction varies from the elaborately hand-carved wood masks with movable parts made by the American Indian of the Northwest to the simple paper-bag masks made by children.

A traditional papercrafts project, a mask can be as simple as a flat, oval piece of **paper** with openings cut for features, or as involved as **papier mâché** strips molded over an **aluminum foil** or **clay** face sculpture.

To add volume to a flat paper mask, slits can be snipped around the outer edges, then overlapped and glued, taking up the paper in small darts for a rounded face. **Curling** may be used for paper-strip hair. For a symmetrical paper mask, the paper can be folded once and the mouth and nose cut into the fold. Eyes are then cut out as desired.

Paper-bag masks are easily made by slipping the bag over the head to mark placement of the eyes and mouth.

The shoulder areas may be cut out for a better fit. Then remove, cut, and decorate.

To make a papier mâché mask over a clay mold, first model the clay face on a board for easy handling. Make the features accentuated so they will have sufficient form after several layers of paper have been applied by the **paper-strip method.** Before applying papier mâché, lightly coat the clay face with petroleum jelly to prevent sticking. Then apply paste-soaked strips in several crisscrossing layers. Allow the mask to dry thoroughly before prying around the edges with a knife to loosen and remove it from the clay form. When completely dry, the mask may be painted. Also see **molding.**

masked print. Papercrafts. See **printing with paper.**

masking. Candlemaking. A technique for **decorating** a finished candle. Make a pattern on the candle with masking tape; dip the candle in wax heated to 200° F. Remove the tape as soon as the layer of wax begins to harden to avoid chipping the edges of the setting wax.

masking. Plastics. Covering a surface with a protective cover, usually adhesive paper or tape, to keep it from being coated with another applied material. Mask areas adjacent to edges that will be cemented with solvent to prevent them from being etched by it. Also see **cellophane, masking paper,** and **Plastics: Cementing.**

masking. Stained Glass. Stenciling. A technique in which areas to remain free of paint are covered with pieces of **masking tape** before paint is applied to the glass. A razor blade or mat knife can be used to trim and shape the masking tape to the desired form. Apply paint boldly as desired without disturbing the areas to remain clear. Remove the tape after the paint dries. Masking is especially important in spray painting. This technique is used in **painting on glass.** Also see **liftground, staining, stenciling ceramics, stenciling with spray paint.**

masking paper. Plastics. A coated adhesive covering plastic sheets to protect the surface from scratches and soiling. Leave this paper on when cutting the sheet and simply peel back the paper from the edges when **filing** or **cementing** them. If you polish the finished edge by **flaming,** not only peel back the paper but also wet it with water. If the masking paper remains intact while working the plastic the surface should not require additional finishing. If plastic sheets are stored in a hot, dry area the adhesive in the paper may dry out, making removal of the paper and adhesive difficult. To soften and remove the adhesive, wipe the sheet with a tissue soaked with clean refined kerosene. Also see **Plastics: Care, Cleaning, and Maintenance.**

masking tape. Plastics. Stained Glass. An adhesive tape used for **masking.**

Masonite. Woodworking. See **hardboard.**

masonry saw. Stained Glass. Also called diamond saw. Used in cutting very fine, precise lines in **dalle-de-verre** slabs. The best type is a water-cooled saw with a 2 hp electric motor. The blade, with a diamond-dust cutting edge, should be about 15−24″ in diameter. It is rather expensive and used sparingly in **dalle-de-verre** because of the expense involved in its replacement.

mason's hammer. Stained Glass. See **dalle-de-verre: Tools and Materials.**

massive. Gemcutting. See **crystal.**

massive amber. Amber Carving. See **amber.**

mast. Kites. The vertical stick on a **diamond kite** or **Eddy kite.** Because of the kinship between sailing and kite flying, many of the terms used for kites are derived from sailing. Also see **Kites: Construction.**

master. A highly skilled practitioner of a trade or craft. Under the medieval **guild** system the master often had one or more **apprentices** in his employ; he was bound by his guild to teach the craft to such apprentices so that they might become **journeymen.**

master lap. Gemcutting. See **lap.**

master mold. Ceramics. A fine mold from which copies are made in plaster or **bisque;** soft soap is used as a release agent to free the castings. The copies are the molds used in mass production.

masterpiece. A production of one's masterly skill in a craft or art; the finest example of one's work.

The medieval **guild** set requirements of expertise for a **journeyman** who sought to become a **master.** In the late Middle Ages, when guilds aimed at limiting the number of masters practicing a trade in a given area, the requirements were often made ridiculously difficult, or sums of money were exacted from journeymen before they would be certified as masters. One of the important tests of a journeyman's skill at this time was his production of a satisfactory sample of his craft. This "masterpiece" was submitted to the board of governors of the guild for their approval.

mastic. Mosaics. Any one of a variety of **adhesive**s or **cement**s made specifically as **bonds** to fix **tiles** to a **backing.** The mastic adhesive is characteristically quick-drying, flammable, and toxic, and therefore should be used with considerable caution in well-ventilated work areas. Also see **Mosaics: Tools and Materials.**

mat. Papercrafts. A framelike border of mat board or cardboard with a cut-out opening the size of the picture to be framed. Beginning at one corner of the cardboard, the desired width of the mat (usually about 3″ or 4″) is measured with ruler and pencil on two sides, then the two remaining sides. Generally, an extra ½″ is allowed on the bottom side of the mat for visual balance. The opening is ruled along the measurements, and all lines are cut with a sharp mat or utility knife pulled gently along a metal rule. A mat is usually cut in preparation for framing a picture under glass. Also see **knife.**

mat. Plastics. See **glass fiber.**

matched mold. Metalworking. Plastics. See **mold.**

Matisse, Henri. Stained Glass. One of the modern painters who designed the Venetian stained-glass windows that are exciting pieces of glass in themselves rather than paintings transferred to glass. **Paul Bony** executed this series of windows.

mat knife. Leather. See **utility knife.**

mat knife. Stained Glass. See **Stained Glass: Tools and Materials.**

matrix. Gemcutting. The dull, surrounding material in which gem material is found naturally. Usually, the gem is removed from its matrix for its perfection. In some cases— for example, spiderweb **turquoise**—the matrix is kept as part of the design of the stone. Gem material in its natural state is called rough.

matta. Rugmaking. Weaving. See **mattor.**

matte. See **gloss.**

matte. Ceramics. A smooth, nonglossy surface due to the break-up of light reflected off its surface. Matte surfaces tend to scratch more easily than glossy ones. Barium carbonate is a common source of matte **glaze.**

matte. Jewelry. A dulled but lustrous finish on metals. Also see **matte dip, Swedish finish.**

matte. Plastics. A dull or flat texture obtained by using paints that yield a flat finish, or by rubbing the surface with very fine steel wool.

matte color. China and Glass Painting. Powdered colors that lack **flux** and do not have a high glaze after **firing;** the resulting dull surface is called "matte." Matte colors are generally used for **grounding.**

matte dip. Jewelry. An **acid** solution used to give the surface of metal a **matte** with a slightly frosted look. First dip the work in a **bright dip** acid solution, rinse and dry, and then dip it into a matte dip solution. The formula for matte dip is 65% concentrated nitric acid, 35% concentrated sulfuric acid, and one pound commercial zinc sulphate ($ZnSO_4$) per gallon of solution. Agitate the work occasionally. The solution will produce the desired surface in a short time. Old acid solutions that have been used a great deal may discolor the metal by redepositing metals dissolved in the solution. Also see **blooming** and **Jewelry: Safety Precautions and First Aid.**

matte finish. Enameling. When a matte, or nonglossy, surface is desired, special **enamels** may be used. The brilliance of the colors may be dulled with a mild nitric acid bath or by swabbing the piece with hydrofluoric acid. Matte salt, which is applied as a paste and rinsed off, is commercially available. Another means of obtaining a matte or eggshell finish is by **stoning** with carborundum, emery, or pumice. Also see **overglaze, underglaze.**

matte gold. China and Glass Painting. See **gold.**

matte salt. Enameling. See **matte finish.**

matte silver. China and Glass Painting. See **silver.**

matte varnish. Découpage. A **varnish** that contains a dulling substance such as talc, wax, or pulverized mica to reduce its luster when dry.

matting. Leather. The technique in **tooling** leather of pressing down background areas of a design with the use of **stamps** and **modelers.**

matting. Stained Glass. Also called badgering. A technique used in **painting on glass** to moderate the light coming through the glass and to create subtle shades and tones. A thin mixture of paint is applied to the glass in broad, even layers with a wide house-painting brush. While the paint is still wet a badger brush is used to push the paint from side to side in a sweeping motion. Using less water in the paint mixture and a slashing movement with the badger on a nearly dry mat produces a beautiful sweep of light. When the mat is completely dry it can be scratched through with quills, wooden sticks, and so on to texture it, or it can be over-painted. Also see **brushes, lettering on glass, staining, sticklighting, shipping.**

matting. Weaving. See **nonloom.**

matting tools. Jewelry. Similar to **grounder punches,** but with a flat working end. When the tool is struck against metal with a **ball-peen hammer,** it imparts its design to the metal. It can be used to create an all-over pattern or texture or a solitary motif. The metal being struck should be placed on an unresisting surface, such as a steel block or piece of hardwood, and struck only once, hard. If two strikes are used, you run the risk of blurring the pattern. It

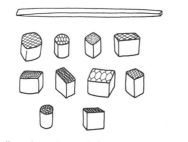

A sampling of matting tool shapes and textures

is therefore important to have the punch well seated on the metal before striking. See ill. Also see **punch.**

mattor. Rugmaking. Weaving. Plural for matta, a Scandinavian **flatweave rug** technique. There are numerous variations on mattor rugs. The simplest version is a **warp-face** rug based on the same principle as the **log cabin pattern,** i.e., the **warp arrangement** is in blocks of color with two colors alternating with each other in each block. If only two colors are used throughout the warp they alternate with each other, and to form the next block the same two colors come together and then begin alternating again. Using colors A and B the order would be A, B, A, B, A, B; B, A, B, A, B, A; A, B, A, B, A, B. Heavy **filling** yarn is used to lift the **warp ends** up over its round form so that the texture of mattor rugs is horizontal ribbing. By the alternation of the colors a pattern of square or oblong blocks can be achieved. Heavy filling yarn can be alternated with fine filling to emphasize colors and to change color blocks horizontally. Because mattor rugs are all warp-reinforced by the heavy filling they are extremely strong.

mattress size. Quilts. See **Quilts: Determining Quilt Size.**

maturity. Ceramics. The point at which a **clay body** hardens and becomes nonporous when fired, or at which the **glaze** ingredients fuse with the clay body, developing a surface texture more resistant to abrasion. Also see **firing.**

maul. Leather. (Also called rawhide maul.) A heavy cylinder-shaped hammer, often wrapped with rawhide, used with **drive punches and stamps.** See ill.

Rawhide maul

maulstick. Stained Glass. A **handrest** for **painting on glass** in an upright position at the easel. It is a wooden stick with a small, soft cloth stop at one end that rests on the glass. It helps provide greater control of the brushwork.

MDC. Plastics. See **acrylic cement.**

Meadow Lily. Quilts. See **Lily.**

measuring. Knitting. Determining how many stitches you have knit in a 1″ row horizontally, and how many **rows** you have knit in a 1″ vertical space. Also see **gauge.**

measuring cord. Macramé. The process of measuring and cutting macramé **cords** to proper length for knotting a piece of macramé. The usual measurement is eight to ten times the intended length of the finished macramé work. Each cord is then doubled and attached to the **mounting cord** with a **double half hitch, reverse double half hitch,** or other **heading.** It is best to always allow extra cord. Also see **C-clamp.**

measuring cord. Weaving. A piece of cord used to measure out the distance on a **warping board** or **reel** that a proposed **warp** is to take during **warping**. The cord is in a contrasting color to the warp and serves also as a guide in showing the pegs the warp will go around on the warping board or the number of turns necessary on a warping reel. It is put on before the warp is started and not tied to it. The warp follows the path set by the measuring cord.

measuring tape. Basketry. Any flexible ruler used to measure rods and the dimensions of a basket. Measure the inside to obtain the length and breadth and the outside to obtain the height. Completed baskets are measured to gauge the quantity of materials used to make them.

measuring tool. Metalworking. Woodworking. Tools used either to measure (in inches or centimeters) or to transfer dimensions in the cutting, **jointing,** and assembly of wood or other materials.

A retractable steel tape is a flexible steel tape measure that retracts into a case (**a.**). It comes in 2–100′ lengths. Long ones are hand wound; those 20′ or shorter are usually spring-loaded.

A folding rule is a ruler formed of hinged narrow wood or steel sections that opens out to a length of 2–8′ (**b.**).

Calipers are compasslike tools used to measure diameters and dimensions where an ordinary rule cannot. Inside calipers have straight legs that turn out at the ends and are used to measure the inside dimensions of bowls, cups, or boxes (**c.**). Outside calipers have bowed legs and are used to measure the outside dimensions of rounded or irregular forms (**d.**).

To use calipers, loosen the tightening screw and open or close the legs on the form being measured. Lock the tightening screw. Remove the calipers from the form and measure the distance between the leg tips with an ordinary rule to obtain the desired dimension.

Wing dividers (also called spring dividers) are com-

passlike tools with straight, pointed legs used to take or transfer measurements and sometimes to scribe circles (**e.**). See ill. Also see **Woodworking: Marking Out and Squaring.**

Meccano. Toys. The patented name for a system of construction used in mechanical toys. Frank **Hornby** developed it after watching a crane at work. He assembled nuts, bolts, and other simple parts to offer a superb **constructional toy** for mechanically inclined children. It was first called Mechanics Made Easy in 1901; in 1907 the name Meccano was adopted. It provides a model for many toys that use the systems and principles of actual construction on a simplified and smaller scale.

mechanical doll. Toys. A **doll** made to walk, talk, or make some other movement through the use of **clockwork** or mechanical devices. The clockwork is usually placed in a box in the body of the doll. It is activated by winding with a key or pulling a string from the box. Also see **automatic toys.**

mechanical fastener. Woodworking. A piece of metal **hardware,** such as a **nail, screw,** or **bolt,** used to fasten pieces of wood together.

mechanical locomotive. Toys. Any of a variety of **toy trains** popular from the early 1800s on. Many were made of cast iron, some of cast tin, and others were a combination of casting and formed sheet metal. They were often elaborately painted in ornate designs of bright colors, as were the **tinplate toys.**

mechanical molding. Ceramics. See **molding.**

mechanical toy. Toys. See automatic toys.

medallion. Batik and Tie-dye. Crochet. Lacemaking. Quilts. Stitchery. A usually circular design, often used as the primary or central **motif** or as one unit of a repeat design.

In lacemaking the medallion is worked from the center on a thread structure. In crochet medallions may be made separately to be appliquéd, used in a series and joined to form a tablecloth or bedspread, or used as a doily or wall hanging.

medallion quilt. Quilts. Any **quilt** in which a **medallion** or large center motif provides a design around which **borders** of **appliqué, piecing,** printed fabrics, or a combination is used. Scenes of historical or mythological interest, printed on **cotton fabrics,** were often featured in this way, as in **Martha Washington's Quilt.** In other medallion quilts, appliqué was used for the central motif.

Medici wool. Crewel. Embroidery. Needlepoint. See **Broder Medici wool.**

medium. See **vehicle.**

medium. China and Glass Painting. An oil or blend of oils used for mixing powdered colors, softening brushes, and

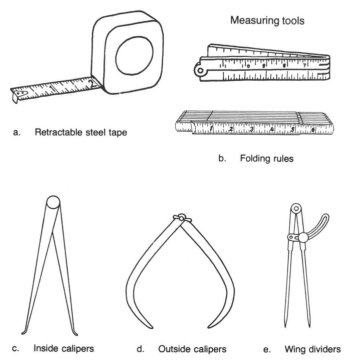

Measuring tools

a. Retractable steel tape

b. Folding rules

c. Inside calipers   d. Outside calipers   e. Wing dividers

keeping the colors on the palette damp. Most of the oils, such as **lavender oil,** oil of cloves, copaiba balsam oil, and oil of tar, are available from the drugstore. **Fat oil of turpentine** can be made in the studio.

medium-carbon steel. Metalworking. See **steel.**

medium fusing enamel. Enameling. See **enamel.**

medullary ray. Woodworking. See **wood.**

MEK. Plastics. See **methyl ethyl ketone.**

MEK-Px. Plastics. See **methyl ethyl ketone peroxide.**

melamine. Plastics. Woodworking. A **thermosetting plastic** made from ammonia compounds called urea-formaldehyde resins. It is used in adhesives for wood, hot gluing (called wood welding), melamine-impregnated cabinet paneling and **Formica,** impregnated **chipboard,** butcher paper, and wallpaper that is grease- and stain-resistant.

melanite. Gemcutting. See **garnet.**

Melon Patch. Quilts. Any of several designs for a simple **block,** that can be either **pieced** or **appliquéd.** It uses an elliptical shape that runs diagonally across a **block.** This is a quilt block in which the **set** is especially important. Set with plain or solid-color blocks, the design is uninteresting. Set as an **all-over pattern** of blocks, the ellipses combine to form large overlapping circles.

melt. Glasswork. The molten glass in a glassworker's **tank furnace.**

melting metal for centrifugal casting. Jewelry. Metals can be melted in a cold **crucible,** but it is better to melt them in a preheated crucible that has already been placed in the **centrifugal casting machine.** When melting nonferrous metals, two important rules should be observed. The flame used to melt the metal should be a hot reducing flame, to minimize the absorption of oxygen in the metal, which would cause a great deal of **porosity** and possibly even small pits in the metal after **casting.** And, the metal should not be overheated, as this too would cause porosity in gold and silver. Overheating produces the same effect in **brass** and **bronze** and also vaporizes the zinc content, altering the characteristics of the metal. Copper, therefore, is not a suitable metal for casting because it becomes brittle and porous. Also see **centrifugal casting, zinc poisoning.**

melting point. Candlemaking. The **temperature** at which solid wax becomes liquid. Most waxes melt at temperatures between 110 to 200° F. The melting point of **paraffin** ranges roughly from 120 to 160° F, depending on how well it has been refined. Also see **Candlemaking: Melting the Wax.**

melting point. Ceramics. The point of change from a solid to a liquid phase as a result of heat. The melting point of a material differs when it is in reaction with other materials from when it is in oxide form or when the material is tested on its own. Also see **chemistry of pottery.**

melting pot. Candlemaking. See **Candlemaking: Melting the Wax, Setting Up a Workshop.**

melting the wax. Batik and Tie-dye. The process of changing **paraffin** or **beeswax** from a solid to a liquid by heating it. The wax should not be placed directly over heat because it can burn if overheated or dripped on the heat source. Keep baking soda conveniently available to smother any fire that may occur. The wax must be hot enough to easily penetrate the fibers and remain **translucent.** If it is **milky,** it is not hot enough; if it smokes, it is too hot. The wax should be placed in a container set into hot water. The water can be held in a heat-controlled utensil such as an **electric frying pan.** It is really an improvised **double boiler** with the advantage of the thermostatic control.

melting the wax. Candlemaking. See **Candlemaking: Melting the Wax.**

memory quilt. Quilts. A **quilt** made from the garments of a deceased friend or relative, usually put together in a **wreath block**—that is, a design that has a plain white center surrounded by a pattern of colored pieces. An inscription in the center of the block gave the name and life-span dates of the deceased, and sometimes included elaborate verses as well. Also see **Kentucky Coffin Quilt.**

Memory Wreath. Quilts. When the **Crown of Thorns block** is sewn using fabrics from clothes of a departed loved one, it is then called by this name. Also see **memory quilt.**

mending. Lacemaking. See **Lacemaking: Cleaning and Care of Lace.**

mending tape. Stitchery. See **iron-on tape.**

mercerize. Batik and Tie-dye. Dyeing. Spinning. Weaving. To treat **cotton** threads chemically with alkali to improve luster and to add strength and elasticity. The mercerized thread also has a greater affinity for **dye.** A **caustic soda** solution is used in mercerizing and the **yarns** or threads are completely immersed in it while being held under tension. In the solution the fiber swells and becomes shorter. The swelling removes some of the **crimp** and opens up the fiber so that it takes dye more easily and permanently than unmercerized cotton. Mercerization can be done only on long staple fibers.

When they are used in **batik** or **tie-dye,** mercerized cottons should not be washed before dyeing because the finish increases the fabric's **affinity for dye.**

mercerized sewing thread. Quilts. Stitchery. Standard **cotton** boilfast **sewing thread** that has been treated by mercerizing. Until recently, this was the commonly available thread. **Synthetic thread**s have virtually replaced these, and **mercerize**d cotton sewing threads are now sometimes difficult to find. Mercerized sewing thread comes in different weights, a regular and a **heavy-duty thread,** and in a wide range of colors.

mercury gilding. Enameling. An alternative process to **electroplating** for producing a thin coating of gold on a **metal** surface.

The area to be gilded must be meticulously cleaned. Dissolve 4 grams of mercury in a teaspoonful of nitric acid and dilute with water to make one quart. Brush this solution on the metal and then rinse it off with water. If the metal was clean, the area should be white. Make an amalgam by combining 1 part fine gold rolled thin with 6 parts mercury in a red-hot firebrick crucible. Cover, heat, and agitate until a white paste is formed; then cool and place in water. The amalgam is stored under water.

When you're ready to use the amalgam, first knead it with a wooden spatula or squeeze out excess moisture in a suede bag. Then spread the amalgam evenly over the treated areas. Because of the poisonous fumes, it's best to do the final step outdoors, upwind from the work. Slowly warm the treated surfaces with a **torch,** and as they shine, spread the mercury with a cotton swab. Continue heating to burn away the mercury. The surface first turns white and then matte gold. Burnish for high luster. Also see **champlevé, cloisonné.**

Merino. Spinning. See **Merino sheep.**

Merino sheep. Spinning. A breed of sheep that yields a wool classified as the finest in the world. The sheep are either purebred or with predominantly Merino blood. It is thought the breed was introduced into Spain between the twelfth and fifteenth centuries or possibly earlier by Moors from North Africa. In the eighteenth century, they were sent to various parts of Europe from Spain as royal gifts. Today, they are found in Europe, North and South America, New Zealand, Australia, and South Africa. The name Merino comes from the Spanish and refers to a sheep that roves from one pasture to another.

merino wool. Spinning. The best wool in the world is obtained from the **Merino sheep.** The **staple** ranges from 1 to 5" and has the best working properties so that it can be spun into very fine **worsted** yarn. The choicest grade of this wool comes from Australia. The merino **fleece in-the-grease** weighs 17 to 22 pounds. After **scouring,** approximately one-third of the original weight remains as wool fiber. **Yolk** and **suint** are heavy, so that the actual wool yield is lower compared to other wools.

merry-go-round. Toys. (Also called roundabout.) A large circular platform on which stationary animals of various kinds are secured. As the platform revolves, the animals move up and down as well as around. Children ride on the animals or on seats adjacent to them. It is the grand spectacular attraction of a carnival or amusement park, accompanied traditionally by calliope music. The hand-carved horses and other animals of the merry-go-round are of great interest to toy fanciers and collectors, and many studies have been made of their carving, manufacture, elaborate decoration, painting, and role in the vernacular arts.

The merry-go-round was formerly called the flying jenny because the carved animals were often jennies (female donkeys), as well as ostriches, camels, tigers, etc. But horses have always been the favorite; painted in every possible way, from dapple grays and sorrels to blacks and bays and pintos.

Modern merry-go-rounds are disappointing to anyone who has enjoyed the elaborate ones of the past. The music of the steam pipes has been replaced by recordings, and cast plastic horses are poor imitations of the wood carver's skills in the originals. The early ones involved the talents of many craftspeople as the merry-go-round was decorated not only by woodcarving, but also by fretwork and painted panels.

Any small toy made with revolving animals is also called a merry-go-round. Also see **carousel.**

Merry Jack. Toys. See **jumping jack.**

mesh. Enameling. See **enamel.**

mesh. Lacemaking. The open spaces created by the loops, as in **needle lace,** and the knotted loops made around a **mesh stick,** as in **knotted lace filet.** In **bobbin lace** it denotes working the threads to form a **net** pattern with a **réseau ground.**

mesh. Needlepoint. See **canvas.**

mesh. Silkscreen. See **Silkscreen.**

mesh canvas. Rugmaking. See **canvas mesh.**

mesh size. Gemcutting. See **abrasive, grinding wheel.**

mesh stick. Lacemaking. (Also called netting gauge.) A tool used in **knotted lace filet** and **circular netting** to regulate the size of the **mesh.** Using the **netting needle,** which has the thread or yarn wound on it, the thread is placed around the mesh stick, and knotted to make a mesh.

meshwork. Weaving. An indefinite term for **sprang,** knotless **netting,** bobbin lace, and other techniques that result in an open, airy fabric that resembles a net rather than lace. A mesh fabric can be constructed by various methods and using various tools or aids. The method and the tools used give it a definite categorical name.

metal. Enameling. Copper is sturdy, inexpensive, and available in a variety of forms—tubes, sheets, rolls, wire, and preformed shapes. To prevent discoloration and pitting of the **enamels** when fired, only pure copper, called "electrolytic," should be used for enameling. Eighteen-gauge is recommended; higher gauges are thinner and lower gauges thicker. Copper is malleable after annealing. It develops **firescale,** a black oxidation, when heated to high temperatures. To avoid contaminating enamels, exposed portions of copper should be coated with Scalex before firing, and the metal should be well-cleaned before the enamels are applied.

Brass, bronze, pewter, and other alloys with high zinc and tin composition have low melting points and may bubble up through the enamel, leaving pits. Before enamel is applied to any of these metals, a firescale layer should be produced on their surfaces for the enamel to adhere to.

Tombac is an alloy of 95% copper and 5% zinc that can be cast and enameled if not overfired. Porcelain enamel on aluminum is used architecturally. Amateur craftspeople use special alloys such as 3003, 1100, or 6061 for enameling. Special enamels that fire at lower temperatures are compounded for use with aluminum. For information write the Ferro Corporation of Cleveland, Ohio.

Iron and steel can be enameled if the material is specifically for enameling. Steel tiles with one or both sides precoated with enamel are also available. Silver-coated steel shapes are available from some suppliers. Avoid the use of abrasives such as steel wool when cleaning them or the thin silver coating will be worn away.

Fine silver does not form firescale. It is soft, not very durable, and cannot be cast. Sterling silver, an alloy, does tarnish but is stiffer and can be cast. It has a lower melting point (1640° F) than fine silver. Silver expands more than copper or gold when fired. Fine silver-coated sterling silver has strength and is almost the ideal surface for enameling. It may be produced by repeated annealing and cleaning or by **casting** sterling silver. Graved or polished silver surfaces are particularly striking under transparent enamels.

Gold is the optimum metal for enameling. Its color is warm and its brilliance high. Fine (100%) gold or 18-karat alloy with 25% fine silver, which is softer than fine gold and has a slight greenish cast, may be used. Gold can withstand high temperatures without deforming or oxidizing. Also see **camels'-hair brush, cleaning metal, cloison, flux, metal foil, metallic luster, plique-à-jour.**

metal. Glasswork. Glass in its molten state. Theoretically, glass is a liquid at all temperatures except when it is held at the **devitrification** temperature and crystals begin to form. Because glass ordinarily has no crystalline structure and there is evidence that glass flows even at room temperatures, physical scientists prefer to think of glass as a supercooled liquid even though it is harder than many metals.

metal. Metalworking. A metal is a mineral element mined from the ground that is opaque, fusible, capable of being polished to a high luster, and conducts electricity. Its mechanical properties include different degrees of hardness, **malleability, ductility, tensile strength,** toughness, elasticity, brittleness, and **corrodibility.** All of these traits are considered to determine the best metal for a particular use.

Metal in its pure state is made up of crystalline patterns called grain held together by a metallic bond. This metal-lic bond is caused by the phenomenon in metal of each atom being closely surrounded by similar atoms, each with free electrons in its outer structure. These electrons are not bound to any one atom tightly and couple with those of any other metal. This allows **alloy**s of many metals to be mixed freely.

The specific atom patterns of grain are formed when the metal is cooled from its melting point. The grain pattern affects the characteristics of the metal; metals with simple grain patterns are highly ductile, and those with small grain are strong. The process of working a metal changes its grain structure. Hot-worked metals have grain patterns that have the same average diameter in all directions, whereas cold-worked metals tend to have elongated grain patterns all pointing in the same direction, causing **work-harden**ing. In alloys and in metals with some impurities, the movement of the grain is restricted and often increases the strength and hardness of the metal.

Pure metals are often difficult to identify by appearance alone, and alloys can be nearly impossible. Steel alloys often look alike. These are graded with numbers developed by the American Iron and Steel Institute (AISI) and the Society of Automotive Engineers (SAE). A series of tests must be made on most metals to determine their basic characteristics. For example, **aluminum** and magnesium look similar and have a similar weight. However, if you apply a torch flame to filings of each, the aluminum filings will melt and the magnesium filings will burn with a brilliant white light. **Ferrous** metals will be attracted to a magnet and nonferrous ones will not. Ferrous metals give off a spark when ground, and nonferrous ones do not. Cast **iron** and cast **steel** have similar color, weight, and appearance, and both are magnetic. But when ground on a grinding wheel, cast iron gives off a red spark and cast steel gives off a white or yellow spark. (The spark test is considered by some to be inaccurate.) The following chart of characteristics is helpful for identifying some common ferrous metals.

Although most steel alloys are not particularly useful for craft work, carbon steel is. It is numbered "1" in the AISI/SAE grading systems. The four digits of the number code indicate the steel's composition. The first tells what kind of steel, the second tells the percentage of alloys, and the third and fourth tell the carbon content in points. One percent of carbon equals 100 points in the code. For example, AISI C190 or SAE 1090 is carbon steel with 90 points (or 90%) of carbon. The letter before the digits tells the kind of furnace in which the steel was made: B means "Acid Bessemer carbon steel," or C "Basic Open-hearth" or "Basic Electric Furnace carbon steel."

Industrially processed metals receive a mill finish. The two most common mill finishes, hot-rolled and cold-rolled, are obtained by rolling metal ingots between huge rollers that squeeze it into sheets, bars, bands, etc.

Hot-rolled metal is rolled while the metal is hot and then sprayed with water to cool it. The water spray forms a bluish film of **oxide** on the surface. Hot-rolled metal is often processed again by cold rolling for further refinement.

Cold-rolled metal is rolled while cold. The sizes of the stock are more accurate and there is a better final surface

Metal	Appearance	Magnetism	Chiseling Quality	Fracture of Surface	Melting
stainless steel	bright, silvery, smooth	depends on the specific alloy	continuous chip, bright color	depends on type	melts fast, becomes bright red before melting
cast iron	dull gray; surface shows evidence of sand mold	strongly magnetic	not easy to chip, brittle small chips of about ⅛"	brittle	melts slowly, becomes dull red before melting
wrought iron	light gray, smooth	strongly magnetic	continuous chip, smooth edges, soft and easily cut and chipped	bright gray, fibrous	melts fast, becomes bright red before melting
low-carbon steel	dark gray	strongly magnetic	continuous chip, smooth edges, chips easily	bright gray	melts fast, becomes bright red before melting
high-carbon steel	dark gray	strongly magnetic	hard to chip	very light gray	melts fast, becomes bright red before melting

finish than on hot-rolled metal. However, the metal sheet is more brittle, and its grain may become distorted in large pieces, causing the metal to crack more easily than hot-rolled stock.

Mill product, or stock, is metal manufactured in standardized shapes and dimensions.

Sheet metal is a flat product **rolled** to less than ¼" thick. Standard metals manufactured in this form are galvanized steel, **tin plate, terne plate, stainless steel, copper, brass,** and **aluminum.** Plate is another flat shape, manufactured in thicknesses of ¼" or more.

A bar of metal is a length of metal ¼" thick or more and 10–24' long. Bars are made in a variety of shapes: square (¼–4½" square), round (³/₁₀–9" in diameter), hexagonal (¼–4" across), octagonal (½–1¾" across), oval, and diamond-shaped. Not all types of steel are available in every length in both hot- and cold-rolled finishes.

A structural shape is a variety of I-beams, channel, H-beams, and angles in various alloys of steel.

A band is a 16' hot-rolled strip, commonly ⅛" thick, with widths of ½", ¾", and 1". It is sold by the pound or by the linear foot.

Wire is a variety of metal sold by the weight of a coil in varying thicknesses. Common **gauge**s are 10, 12, 14, 18, and 20.

Foundry metal, also called casting metal, is pure metal and alloys sold by the pound.

metal foil. Enameling. Extremely thin sheets of pure gold or silver, not as thin as metal leaf, used to simulate the color of precious **metal**s when enameling on copper. It is sold in books of a dozen sheets, each about 4" × 5", interleaved with tissue paper. It is fragile and delicate and should not be touched because it clings to moisture and if contaminated by grease or oil will not adhere to enamels. For handling, sandwich the foil between sheets of tracing paper, paper clip them together, and cut the desired-size pieces with a sharp manicure scissors.

Foils are always placed over a base of prefired **enamel.** Pierce the foil with a needle or a simple tool made of a cork with many needles extending from it. A sewing tool called a pattern marker will also work well. Make about 50–200 holes per square inch to prevent air bubbles underneath from bubbling and buckling the surface. Apply **binder,** pick up the foil with a wet brush, and spread it flat.

When the piece is dry, fire carefully to just melt the undercoat; **overfiring** will burn the foil, making **stoning** and reapplication necessary. Remove the piece from the **kiln** and burnish it with a dull knife or the edge of a **spatula.** Transparent enamels may be applied over metal foil as desired.

Aluminum foil is sometimes used experimentally. Because aluminum melts at 1220° F, low-firing enamels are used with it. The thin aluminum foil used for wrapping food tends to melt into uncontrollable pools; the heavier material from TV dinner plates is easier to handle. Also see **cloison, pallion** and **Enameling: Tools and Materials.**

metal foil. Papercrafts. See **aluminum foil.**

metal frame. Crewel. Embroidery. Needlepoint. See **embroidery frame.**

metal fume fever. Jewelry. See **zinc poisoning.**

metal identification. Metalworking. See **metal.**

metal inert-gas welding. Metalworking. See **welding.**

metaling. Stained Glass. A hard, yellow, metallic deposit that remains on the glass after **firing** when it has been stained with a very strong stain. After washing the glass use acid and a brush to remove the metallic deposit.

metallic color. China and Glass Painting. Colors prepared from metal, available in powdered or liquid form, that, after **firing,** have a shiny luster resembling the metal surface. They range in color from many shades of **gold,** bronze, gold-bronze, green, olive, and brown to platinum and **silver.** Gold and platinum are the most widely used. Directions for mixing are on the package. Generally, the liquid colors are used as they are; the powdered colors are mixed with a **medium.**

metallic fiber. Knitting. A specialty fiber made of metal, plastic-coated metal, metal-coated plastic, or a fiber core that has been completely covered with a metallic thread. This shiny material is often used in the knitting of evening sweaters, etc.

metallic luster. Enameling. Finishing touches are sometimes applied by firing metallic lusters over the **enamel** surface in a manner similar to that used for **overglaze.** Lusters are available in gold, copper, silver, and platinum. They are usually made of finely ground **metal** suspended in an oil medium. They are painted on with a **sable brush** in very thin coats. Lusters must be dried thoroughly for a long period of time. They are fired at a very low temperature, about 1200° F, for a few minutes. This underfiring may cause cracking in the enamel undercoating, which can be remedied by gradually increasing the temperature until the cracks melt away. Also see **raku.**

metallic luster. Gemcutting. See **luster.**

metallic oxides. Stained Glass. See **antique glass colorants.**

metallic paper. Toys. A paper with one glossy, polished, metal-like surface and one plain paper surface. The metallic coating may be gold, silver, or bronze and may be tinted. Foils are then metallic sheets. Also see **gold metal leaf.**

metallic thread. Embroidery. Needlepoint. Stitchery. Sewing threads with a metallic luster, used primarily for embellishing **ecclesiastical needlework** and similar projects. Some threads are metallic with a **synthetic** coating; others have a gold or silver exterior coating. The larger or heavier threads are used for **couching** because they are too heavy to be drawn through **fabric.** Care must be taken in the selection of threads as many are expensive and a nontarnishing surface may be required. Also see **bullion thread, gold purl, Japanese gold and silver, Lurex thread, metallic thread embroidery, passing, pearl purl.**

metallic thread embroidery. Embroidery. In early metallic thread embroidery gold and silver were beaten flat and woven or embroidered to a **background fabric.** The resulting work was both fragile and delicate. Japanese thread is gold or silver leaf wrapped lightly around a silken cone. It produces a stronger stitch when sewn to a background fabric by surface **couching.** Later methods produced **passing,** a finely coiled, fine-wire thread. **Metallic thread**s, passing, and **silk yarn** are combined in **silk embroidery.** In the Middle Ages, the peak of the art, metallic thread embroidery was worked on heraldic banners, knights' trappings, and church vestments. By the sixteenth century, the nobility and wealthy merchants were wearing elaborately embroidered garments. During times of lesser prosperity, the expensive embroideries were laboriously unpicked and the gold melted down. "Drizzling," as it was called, was carried on by ladies taking afternoon tea, and many beautiful pieces of metallic thread embroidery were destroyed.

Today, Lurex thread has replaced metallic thread, which is rare and very costly. True metallic thread embroidery is worked by only a few people in the world. Also see **bullion knot, gold purl, Italian shading, Japanese gold and silver, Opus Anglicanum, pearl purl.**

metallic yarns. Spinning. Weaving. See **fiber.**

metal mesh. Mosaics. Expanded metal mesh designed to be fastened to a surface or mosaic **backing** to provide a better grip for **mortar** or **cement.** It is available wherever building supplies are sold. Also see **Mosaics: Setting the Materials, Tools and Materials.**

metal mold. Candlemaking. See **Candlemaking: Selecting the Mold.**

metal oxide. Enameling. Added to the basic **frit** to produce specifically colored **enamels.** Two to four percent of enamel is coloring. Tin oxide produces white, and is also used to make other colors opaque.

The following oxides are used to produce the following colors: uranium and antimony—yellow; cobalt—blue; gold—red; platinum—gray shades; iridium—black; manganese—purple; and copper—green. Also see **fuming.**

metal reflector. Stitchery. See **reflector.**

metal release. Ceramics. Heavy metals dissolving out of a **glaze** due to the acid corrosiveness of vinegar, fruit juices, or strong acid. The most dangerous chemical commonly used in glazes is lead; it should not be used on tableware.

metal spinning. Metalworking. (Also called cold-metal spinning.) Metal spinning is a process for shaping hollow metal objects over a wood **chuck** on a turning **lathe.** It is a highly skilled craft, practiced little in the United States, but widely practiced in parts of England and Europe. Today, industrially automated spinning, called hydrospinning and shear spinning, produces many rocket and missile parts, especially nose cones. Spinning is also useful for making multiple, identical copies of open symmetrical forms; closed asymmetrical shapes require advanced techniques.

A disk of circular metal is pushed with lathe tools over the spinning chuck with constant pressure. Wrinkling or buckling can only be corrected by removing the metal, **annealing** it, and hand hammering those damaged areas with a rawhide **mallet.** A heavy-duty wood lathe may be used for small home work, but a metal lathe is better suited for enduring the heavy pressure necessary for spinning.

Metals suitable for spinning are gold, silver, **copper, brass, aluminum, zinc, pewter, lead,** and **steel.** Steel is the most difficult metal to spin. Most metals must be annealed frequently (except for gold, pewter, and lead) because spinning **work-hardens** it. Lubricate the spinning work frequently with tallow, soft soap, a soap-and-oil mixture, or a commercially prepared compound for lubricating. See ill.

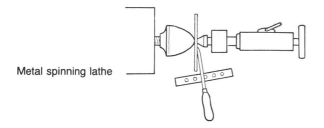

Metal spinning lathe

metalsmithing. Jewelry. Metalworking. See **silversmithing.**

metal tooling. Metalworking. See **tooling.**

metal washer. Toys. A metal disk with a hole in the center used to separate moving parts in **articulated toys** and **wheeled toys.**

metal wire. Enameling. See **cloison,** cloisonné.

metal wire and sheet gauge. Metalworking. See **sheet-metal gauge.**

METALWORKING

Metalworking includes **bench work,** sheet-metal work, art work, **forging, heat treatment,** metal **casting, welding,** and the use of tools and machines for metal construction. The processes and techniques of metalworking and jewelrymaking overlap and are often identical; indeed, the separation of the two crafts is scarcely more than an exercise. Today many metalworkers make what they call "body sculpture," which others might call oversize jewelry, and many jewelrymakers make objects to be displayed, not worn.

Certainly metalworking encompasses the making of larger metal objects than jewelry, the use of more **base metals** than precious ones, and structural and weathering problems peculiar to outdoor constructions. But metalworking also includes many decorative techniques used to create surface reliefs by **tooling, hammering, repoussé, etching,** etc., more commonly associated with the craft of jewelry.

The history of metalworking has been associated with the birth of urban civilization. As soon as metal tools were regarded as a necessity for small agricultural communities, these societies became dependent on imported metal materials. Here the foundation for a new economic system, based on trade, was laid.

Even after metalworking became one of the first specialized industries, the craftsmen still retained their status in the occult sciences. The smith was supposed to be able to forecast future events by examining molten **slags** in his **forge.** The smith's hammer was a symbol of power, and an oath made over his anvil could supposedly never be broken. Metallurgy was believed to influence the regeneration and ripening of stones and ores in the earth. Mines were allowed to rest after periods of intensive digging so the metals could regenerate themselves. Smelting, which was associated with alchemy, was thought to represent a sacred union of male and female ores and to produce products that would give their possessor divine protection. Ancient Chinese metalworking was done with ritual and ceremony by young virgins of both sexes, and by "other persons whose morals were above reproach." One Chinese legend—of the bell-maker's daughter who threw herself into a vat of molten metal so her father could make a perfect bell for the emperor—is based on the idea of a male-female balance of Yin and Yang that had to be achieved in metallurgy. (The rest of the story says that the girl dropped her shoes as she jumped into the metal; and afterward when the bell was rung, it made the sound of "Shoe! Shoe!"—in Chinese, of course.)

By 3000 B.C. the existing urban civilizations in Egypt, Mesopotamia, and the Indus Valley were dependent on metalworking for their economic existence and also preserved a monopoly over **copper** and its **alloys.** Metal equipment for war has been dated from before 2500 B.C. By this time metal had become the standard of exchange (money), thus documenting the growth of a merchant class. By 2000 B.C. a Bronze Age had begun in Europe and Britain. The following Iron Age made cheap iron tools and war implements available to all classes and democratized larger agricultural production, industry, and warfare.

Specific developments, such as **founding** or metal casting, can also be traced, back to about 4000 B.C. Metal was first poured into open cavities in sand, stone, and fired clay. Sandcasting, using the **cope** and **drag flask,** and **core** casting were used in early Egypt. Foundry techniques were refined in the Orient around 2000 B.C., after which the **lost-wax process** was mastered for casting in **bronze.** Iron was cast in China around 600 B.C., and **steel** in India around A.D. 500. This process, used in the West until medieval times, was ultimately lost and never rediscovered. Metalworking techniques were kept secret; they were the property of the clergy, and later of the guilds, until after the Renaissance.

SETTING UP A WORKSHOP By necessity the metalworker will usually have to specialize in only one or two branches of this craft, not only because of the wide variety of tools required to do all of the operations, but also because the working of some metals and processes interferes with the successful crafting of others. For example, particles from hard metals can embed in and ruin the surface of soft ones. **Pewterworking** is rarely done in the same room as **silverwork.** The **lampblacking** of **pewter** is also a messy operation that could contaminate other **buffing** wheels. **Lead** must not be used in a room where you are making any type of food container because lead fumes and particles are toxic.

A great deal of space is necessary for many operations to be done together safely. **Arc** and **gas welding** must be partitioned off with a canvas curtain from onlookers or other workers in the shop without eye protection. Grinding and power-tool work should not be done anywhere near the gas-welding tanks because of possible sparks and deposits of lubricants from the machines. **Forging** and **blacksmithing** also cannot be done safely anywhere near welding tanks, and also require a darkened area for **heat treatment** so that the color of the heated metal can be seen.

General shop requirements include well-lighted, ventilated work areas with dry, nonslip floors and enough space to permit easy manipulation of materials. A cement or metal-covered floor is legally required in any area indoors where welding or forging is done. Adequate electrical wiring for power tools is also necessary. Do not use an open-flame heater, such as a space heater, near welding tanks. Never weld an object against the cement floor; the heat will crack and possibly explode the cement. Protective firebrick is available to cover any metal or cement surfaces for welding.

Position your worktables at a comfortable height. Group related tools together and keep safety equipment near the tool it is used for, e.g., keep goggles hanging near grinding and other power tools, a fire extinguisher near flame- and spark-producing tools, etc. Keep a covered metal can for combustible rags and a metal box or can for hot metal scraps and the remains of hot **electrode**s or **welding rod**s. Provide cabinets or compartments for small tools and accessories in their area of operation.

SAFETY PRECAUTIONS   Provide excellent ventilation in the workshop, and if you are **welding** or working with acids, have an exhaust fan. Both **brass** and **bronze** give off toxic fumes when welded. **Lead** and **zinc** also give off poisonous fumes when heated, so the materials should not be used for any food containers.

Wear protective equipment and clothing when welding, **casting,** or working with acids. Wear **eye protectors** when casting metals, welding, grinding, polishing with a power tool, and whenever there is a chance of flying particles, hot metal, or steam. Clothing for welding should include a long-sleeved, high-necked, flame-resistant shirt or jacket. The cuffless sleeves should overlap leather gloves, the bottom of the shirt should overlap the waistband, and the trousers should overlap leather shoes or boots so there is less chance of a spark becoming lodged in between accessories (e.g., a cinder catching in the top of a shoe or waistband if the torch backfires). **Foundry** workers should wear a leather or asbestos apron or body shield, asbestos gloves, and a full face shield. When using power tools, roll up your sleeves, remove any dangling accessories, tie back the hair or wear a cap, and remove any jewelry such as watchbands and rings. Wear a dust mask when polishing or grinding **copper, brass, lead,** or any other chemically irritating or toxic metals.

Use the proper tool for the job and use it correctly. For example, if a **grinding wheel** that is rated for low rpm is run very fast, it may shatter and fly in the face of the operator of the grinding tool. Keep machine guards in place. Take proper care of the tools by repairing loose handles and by sharpening and shaping dull or battered tools. Dull tools with burrs are more dangerous to cut with than sharp tools because you must exert more pressure on them. Do not carry sharp tools in your pockets.

Make sure your hands are dry before operating an electric power tool, or electric **arc welder.** Do not use electric tools near inflammable gas or let the cords lie on hot or oiled surfaces.

Stop a machine before you lubricate or adjust it. Do not feel the surface of a metal object in motion; first stop the lathe. Do not clean chips off a machine with your hand; use a brush so that you do not get pieces embedded in your hand. Take care of small injuries promptly; blood poisoning and tetanus can result from unattended cuts or slivers.

Cleanliness helps prevent accidents. Scraps of metal on work surfaces or the floor may create hazards. Keep all oil and grease out of welding areas. Clean your tools and machines after use to prevent buildup of any substances that might cause improper functioning, thus creating hazards. For example, clean the **welding torch** tips after use to make sure that no particles have lodged inside that might cause a **backfire** or a **flashback.**

Oil, welding gas, and most solvents are highly flammable, and the utmost care is necessary in keeping them away from the welding and forging flames, spark-producing machinery, and heated metals. Handle gas cylinders or tanks with care, trying not to bump or strike them. Store them away from heat and open-flame heaters. In addition, be sure to store oily rags in a tightly closed metal container in a cool place to prevent spontaneous combustion.

COLD BENDING   Sheet metal may be readily bent with hand tools when large bending machines are not available.

Clamp the sheet on a workbench surface so that the line marked to be bent is even with the edge of the bench (**a.**), or secure it between the edges of hardwood boards in a vise (**b.**). Hammer the metal with a **mallet** with very light blows until the metal lies flat on the wood. For acute or obtuse angles, **plane** one edge of the wood block to the necessary angle and bend the metal over it. For small work, a metal **stake** or **anvil** may be used for bending the metal instead of the wood blocks.

Soft **iron** and **low carbon steel** up to ¼″ thick may be bent cold by clamping the metal in a vise and applying pressure with hammer blows. See ill.

Bending sheet metal

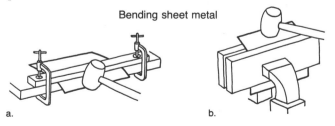

a.   b.

CUTTING   Metal may be cut in a variety of ways. Cold or hot metal can be cut or split with a chisel, as described under **blacksmithing technique**s. Cold metal may be cut with a **cutter, nibbler, shears,** or **snips,** or it may be sawn with a metal-cutting blade in a **bandsaw, hacksaw, hole saw,** or **saber saw.**

Flame cutting with a cutting torch (see **oxyacetylene welding equipment**) is useful for heavier ferrous metals.

To flame cut, support the metal so that there is a space under the cutting line for the **slag** to fall into. Mark the cutting line with chalk or with punch marks along the line with a **center punch.** Check to see that the **torch** valves are closed before setting the **pressure gauges.** The correct working pressure is determined by the size and the type of the tip; consult manufacturer's recommendations.

Open the **acetylene** torch valve and ignite the **flame** with a **friction lighter.** Then open the oxygen torch valve and adjust the flow of gas until you obtain a neutral flame.

Preheat the area at the starting end of the cut to red heat, keeping the inner cone of the flame ⅛–¼″ away from the metal surface. Press the oxygen lever on the torch to cut away the metal. Move the torch steadily forward as the line is cut. If the flame is moved too fast the cut will not go all the way through the metal; if too slow the **kerf** will have a rounded edge and the slag will adhere to the bottom of the cut. In a properly executed cut, the edges are square and the cut lines are vertical.

To pierce a hole for internal cuts, preheat the spot to melting. Raise the torch tip about ½″ above the metal surface. Slowly depress the oxygen lever, moving the torch slightly from side to side. After the metal has been pierced, lower the tip to ¼″ above the surface and continue to cut.

Blowing the sparks against the sides of the cut edges instead of directly downward may cause backfiring as the metal is reflected back from the sides against the torch. Keep the oxygen valve on the hose wide open at all times when cutting; otherwise you may have a backfire.

DRILLING   To drill small holes, up to ⅜″, support the metal on a firm work surface and clamp it as close to the drilling area as possible. Never hold a piece of metal in your hand while drilling it—when the **drill bit** breaks through the metal, it often catches the metal, making it revolve, and it could easily cut your hand.

Frick punch a mark in the center of the hole to make a slight depression, into which you will seat the drill bit. Put a drop of machine oil into the indentation as a lubricant.

Adjust the correct speed on the drilling tool for your material. Proper speed and **feed** of a sharp drill bit into the metal will produce a curled ribbon of metal from the hole during drilling. Use a sharp **twist drill bit.** The following chart gives some recommended speeds for drilling various materials. Carbide-tipped bits are preferred for longer wear; reduce the speed by half for carbon-steel drill bits.

Use just enough pressure when drilling to cut into the metal. Add more lubricating oil frequently for thicker sections. When using a hand drill, position the drill at right angles to the work surface; slowly rotate the handle, applying even pressure to the drill. An electric **drilling tool** is recommended for thick pieces. Reduce the feed pressure as the drill bit begins to emerge on the other side to prevent it from catching the metal.

For countersinking, insert a **countersink** or a drill bit twice the diameter of the already drilled hole into the drill chuck. Adjust the speed to about half that recommended for drilling. Slowly feed the countersink until the proper amount of material is removed to depress the head of the screw beneath the metal surface. The hole to be enlarged by countersinking is always drilled first.

To bore large holes, over ⅜″ in diameter, drill a small center hole first so that a larger twist drill bit will go through the metal or plastic with less friction. Then drill the larger hole. Very large holes may be bored with a **hole saw** or **circle cutter.** Insert either into the chuck of an **electric portable drill** or a **drill press.** Use a slow speed and light feeding pressure until the teeth penetrate the surface, then increase the pressure and speed.

RAISING   Raising is a hand hammering process for making circular or rounded hollow shapes.

Grip the hammer handle near the end for maximum leverage and correct balance. Strike with the whole forearm; hold the wrist stiff but not tensely rigid. Use a heavier hammer for the first **course** and then change to lighter ones.

Keep the same angle between the metal and anvil surface for uniform shaping and overlap the blows (**a.**). Thicken the edge after hammering each course.

Prevent the metal from cracking by **annealing** before starting each new angle on the workpiece and whenever the metal starts to become hard. The sound of hammering becomes high-pitched when it needs annealing. Metal in working condition should sound dull when hammered. **Pewter, lead,** and gold need no annealing.

For angle raising, determine the size of the needed **blank** by adding the depth of the form to its widest diameter in inches. The best thicknesses are 14, 16, and 18 **gauge.** Cut an accurate circle of proper dimensions and **scribe** the exact center with a sharp tool. Mark it with a **center punch** and hammer for future reference in making measurements. File away any excess metal and rough edges with a **double-cut** file, but leave intact a circumference line, also needed for reference.

Position the metal over the common **T-stake.** Start the

Speed in revolutions per minute (rpm)				
Diameter of Drill Bit	Soft Metal (e.g. brass, aluminum, bronze)	Cast Iron, Hard Steel	Mild Steel	Plastics, Hard Rubber
⅛″ or less	9000	2100	4000	5000–6000
¼″	4500–5000	1000	1500–2000	3000–3500
½″	2000–2500	500	500–1000	1000–1500
1″	500–1000	200–500	300–400	400–1000

first course of hammering with a **cross-peen raising hammer,** rotating the blank constantly after each stroke. Strike the metal just above the point of contact of the metal with the stake. Work from the center of the disk to the outer edge (**b.**).

The number of courses required for each angle depends on the hammerer's skill. After completing the angles, **bouge** the object with a heavy rawhide **mallet** over a vertical **mushroom stake.**

Refine the form further by **planishing** it with a **planishing hammer.**

For crimping, hammer the metal with a special **crimping hammer** or a rounded **cross-peen hammer** against a **valley stake.** Hammer the metal into the groove on the valley stake with the narrowing taper pointing toward the bottom of your object. Alternate the hammering grooves on opposite sides of the blank. Start a crimp by hammering either the outer or inner surface of the metal. Anneal the metal after the grooves have been uniformly placed, or as frequently as necessary.

After all the grooves have been made, place the disk at a 45° angle against a **T-stake.** Hammer and rotate the form to remove the grooves and to increase the angle of the raising. Start from the base line and rotate the metal slightly after each blow until you near the outer edge. Anneal; crimp again with the valley stake, and rotate again. Bouge the form, and repeat the process until the desired shape is reached. Planish over a mushroom stake.

For blocking, use an **embossing hammer** for **copper** or harder metal and a fiber mallet for **pewter.** Cut the blank larger than the desired finished object. File off the **burr** edge so as not to damage a wooden mold and to avoid lodging small chips in the metal surface from hammering. Start by placing the disk in a mold larger than the diameter of the blank. For example, for a 10″ disk, use at least a 12″ mold. Hammer around the outside edge with gentle overlapping strokes. Constantly support the blank with the outer edge of the shape against the mold surface. After the edge is uniformly shaped, increase the force of your hammer blows.

After the blank is shaped to the larger mold, force it by hammering into a smaller one, and start hammering at the outside edge again. Tap out all of the dents by holding the mallet closer to the head and using soft blows.

Anneal frequently. Bouging is unnecessary because the form is controlled by the mold shape. Continue hammering until all surfaces are in contact with the mold (**c.**).

For the sandbag method, sprinkle the sandbag with water or oil to reduce dust raised by hammering. Place the annealed disk with the center mark on the bag and start hammering. Use a 1½ lb. embossing hammer in a spiral succession of blows. Rotate the blank slightly after every blow. Hammer methodically in a regular pattern. When the metal becomes misshapen, anneal and work out the wrinkles by bouging it over a vertical stake with a rawhide or wood mallet. Finish by planishing. Start with overlapping hammer blows in the center and work outward.

To repair edge cracks, locate the end of the crack, and drill it by tapping into the metal surface with a **center punch.** Insert a wire or rod of the same metal into the punched hole so that it fits tightly. Cut the wire so that it sticks out of the outside and is flush with the inside of the object. Clean the crack and apply **flux. Hard-solder** (or soft-solder in the case of pewter) the wire into the crack. Clean and file off any excess metal or flux (**d.**).

Incomplete **annealing** and unequal distribution of hammer blows cause uneven shaping. To correct raising faults, first make sure the object is completely annealed. Mark concentric circles on the object with a **compass** and also mark longitudinal lines dividing the surface into equally marked sections between the circles (**e.**). Start hammering from the center in an even series of blows. Count out the blows in each series and rotate the object after each series. See ill.

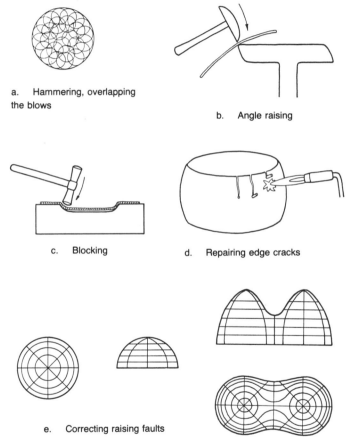

a. Hammering, overlapping the blows

b. Angle raising

c. Blocking

d. Repairing edge cracks

e. Correcting raising faults

HEAT TREATMENT   Heat treatment is the heating of a metal to a specific temperature in order to change its physical properties. This may improve its ability to be shaped, improve cutting edges, remove brittleness and internal strains, and increase the wearability and toughness of a metal. Many metal tools are useless until they are heat-treated. Basic equipment for all heat treatments includes a heat source (e.g. **kiln, foundry** furnace, **forge,** blow torch, or gas-**welding torch**), a quenching liquid (e.g. water, oil, or **brine**), and **tongs** to hold the heated metal. The metals change color within a specific temperature range. Each

Chart of Temperatures for Heat Treatment of Common Metals and
Metal Tools
(in degrees Fahrenheit)

Type of Heat Treatment	Tool or Metal	Color of Metal	Temperature
tempering	steel scribers	light yellow	410
	steel scrapers, lathe tools, twist drill bits, and finishing tools	straw yellow	428
	steel hammer faces, cold chisels, and wood tools	golden yellow	469
	steel plane irons, pocket knives	brown yellow	500
	steel screwdriver tips	light purple	530
	steel hot chisels, dental and surgical tools	dark purple	550
	steel needles, hacksaw blades, small saws, steel springs	pale blue	590
annealing	pure silver		
	aluminum (wrought)	light blue	640
	copper (700-1200°F)		700
	red brass (800-1350°F)	faint red	900
	forging brass (1000-1100°F)	dull red	1050
	bronze (800-1250°F—check the specific alloy temperature)	dark cherry red	1175
	sterling silver		1200
hardening	carbon steel	medium cherry red	1250
	carbon steel (1475-1650°F)	bright red	1550
	alloy steel	salmon	1650
		orange	1725
		lemon yellow	1825
	high-speed tool steel	white	2200
annealing	nickel silver (1100-1500°F)	cherry red	1375
hardening	carbon steel (1475-1650°F)	salmon	1650
annealing	nickel (1500-1700°F)	orange	1727
hardening	alloy steel (1425-1800°F)	lemon	1975
hardening	high speed steel (1800-2425°F)	white	2200

process involves bringing the metal to a critical point or temperature that corresponds to a specific color of the heated metal. However, because each color only approximates a temperature range, a **pyrometer** is necessary for measuring the temperature in accurate or precision heat treatment work. The basic heat treatments are **annealing, hardening,** and tempering.

In annealing, the metal must be heated as uniformly as possible with a torch or in an oven until the metal turns dull red. Keep the metal hot long enough for the heat to permeate the entire piece of metal. Each metal has its own annealing temperature; **aluminum's** (wrought) is 640−670° F, **copper's** is 700−1200° F, **brass's** is 900−1100° F, **nickel silver's** is 1100−1500° F, and pure **silver's** is 572° F.

When possible, anneal the object under a ventilation

hood with an exhaust fan. If you heat the object in a container filled with **pumice** or other refractory material, such as sand, the heat will be retained and distributed evenly.

Do not overheat any metal or you will destroy its working qualities. Judge the temperature by the color of the heated metal, except with aluminum. Aluminum does not change color as it heats, and it melts easily. Mark its surface with blue carpenter's chalk. The chalk will become grayish-white at the correct annealing temperature. Another method is to draw a wood match stick across the hot metal; it will leave a dark charred mark when the proper temperature is reached. **Quench** the metal or let it cool at room temperature.

The hardening process works only with steel that contains 1−3% carbon.

Heat the steel to the specific hardening temperature (see chart). If you underheat it, the metal will not harden properly. If you overheat it the carbon burns out, the grain coarsens, and the metal decreases in strength. Let the heat soak through the metal slowly. Too-rapid heating may cause cracking from unequal expansion.

Quench the metal immediately in water, mineral oil, or **brine.** Test the hardness by running a new file across the corner of the metal. If properly hardened, the file should not cut it or take hold. The piece of metal should now be tempered to prevent cracking.

For tempering, highly polish the end to be tempered with an abrasive so you can see the color changes during heating. Temper the metal by reheating it to the correct tempering temperature and then quenching it (see chart).

Hardening and tempering (also called point hardening) can be done in one set of operations.

Attach abrasive cloth to the end of a rod or stick. Heat the metal tool to the hardening temperature (see chart). Using tongs to hold the tool, quench only the sharpened end. Move the end up and down in the liquid to avoid a sharp dividing line between the hot and cool ends. Remove the tool from the bath after the end becomes black, and rub the end with the abrasive stick. Watch the color of that end as the heat from the hot unquenched part now spreads back to the point. After the right tempering color appears, quench the whole tool.

BLACKSMITHING Blacksmithing is the forging of iron with an anvil and hammer.

Iron heated to dull-red heat is plastic enough to be bent without breaking. Heated further it turns cherry red, bright red, light red, orange, and then white; it melts into liquid at incandescent yellow. Tiny incandescent sparks show that the metal is burning, or at white heat; this is too hot to work steel, but pure iron may be hammered at white heat. Iron and steel may be forged at any stage between bright red and sparking without damage. If it is worked below this temperature, the metal soon becomes brittle and difficult to shape.

Finish hammering each piece with as few heatings or **heat**s as possible, because too much heating affects the metal quality and oxidizes the surface, forming **scale.**

To rest their arm while using a heavy hammer,

blacksmiths often hit the **anvil** face once for every two or three blows on the work. The hard **temper** of the anvil bounces the hammer upward, acting as a start in lifting the hammer for the next blow.

There are several methods for cutting hot or cold iron.

To split heated iron, heat the iron to orange or white heat. Punch a hole in the metal where the split will end to keep the split from traveling further while the iron is worked on. One method is to place the heated section over a **hardie** on the **anvil** and then to hammer the metal directly over it until the cutting edge of the hardie cuts through. Be careful that the last few hammer blows do not cut the iron so quickly that you dull or damage the hardie edge with the sledgehammer. Another method is to use a sledgehammer to strike hot or cold sets or chisels onto metal placed on a **cutting plate** over the anvil face. (When a hot set or cold set cutting head is without a handle it is called a hot or cold chisel.) Use a hot set or hot chisel, which has a thinner blade than a cold set, for cutting thick metal. Use a cold set or chisel for notching, chipping, gouging, or shearing hot or cold metal.

To split cold iron, use the short-bladed cold sets held by a withy or chisels, or else use the hardie as on hot metals. One may also break a sheet of metal by notching a line, placing the line on an anvil edge, and then striking the metal sharply with a hammer. Cutting or splitting cold iron is recommended for thin stock.

Punch a hole in the iron where the split will end to keep the split from traveling further while the iron is worked on. Punch cold metal only when it is very thin sheet iron. Heat iron that is ⅛″ thick or over before punching. Punch the hole over the **pritchel hole** or the **hardie hole** for large holes, over a **swage block** for small holes. Line up the punch on top of the hot iron with the hole underneath the metal. For stock 1″ or thicker drive the punch halfway through. Then turn the metal over and punch the rest of the way through from the opposite side. Take care that the last few hammer blows do not cut the iron so quickly that the hardie edge becomes dulled or damaged.

The hole may be enlarged or reshaped by hammering a **drift** into the already made hole.

To bend the iron, heat the area at the bend line slowly to bright red. Fast heating may cause the metal to oxidize. Place the metal over the anvil face so that the bend line is over the edge of the anvil. Hammer down the protruding part (**a.**).

Another method of bending is to place one end of the metal rod into the **hardie hole** or clamp it into a **vise**, then bend the other end over with tongs (**b.**).

If the metal is thick, bend it to half of the distance. Then reheat it and complete the bend by **upsetting** the end and the side edges to keep the metal from spreading.

To twist the metal, heat it to a bright red. Clamp it in a vise and twist the piece with tongs.

Drawing out (also called forging down, setting down, fullering) is a process of stretching the metal to reduce its thickness or diameter and to increase its length or width. Heat the area to be stretched in the forge to bright red or orange-red.

Draw out small pieces of iron by hammering the heated metal on the face of the anvil. Use a hammer with a flat face without sharp edges for thinner pieces and a **cross-peen hammer** for thicker ones. The first series of blows will raise the surface with ridges, and the second will flatten these ridges as the metal stretches. Drawing out the edge of a flat bar will cause the bar to bend into a curve with the thinner edge outward. Large or heavy bars must be stretched between top and bottom fullers with the help of another person to strike the sledgehammer blows upon the top fuller.

To spread the metal in all directions from the center outward first hammer it with the rounded end of a ball-peen hammer, starting in the center. Then apply the next series of radiating blows with the flattened end of the hammer.

To reduce the diameter of a round bar with a hammer, strike the heated area with slow, well-directed blows, forming it into a square shape. Reheat the bar and then hammer the drawn-out section into an octagonal shape. Don't try to stretch out the previous square diameter without changing it to an octagon or the rod may crack or distort. Continue a gradual reduction in the diameter by next hammering out the edges of the octagon into a round diameter again while continually rotating the bar (**c.**).

In **upsetting**, heat the iron to more than orange-red for maximum plasticity. Hold the bar or rod perpendicular to the anvil face and hit it straight down with a hammer until the end spreads. If it is long and heavy, you may be able to drop the end straight down on a hard surface to spread it. The blows must be straight head-on to keep the metal from bending. Use a few hard blows rather than many light, quick ones.

To upset a section at a distance from the end, heat this part to white heat and then hammer or drop the end against the anvil face. This is difficult to accomplish without bending the metal.

In forge welding, **scarf** the ends of the metal before starting the welding process. Shape the scarfed surfaces to slightly convex rather than concave so that **flux** and **oxides** are forced from the joint when they are hammered.

Position the anvil close to the **forge.** Place the metal to be joined on top of the fire until it is red. Remove it and sprinkle flux over the side to be welded. Place the metal back into the forge. Increase the air from a **bellows** or a **blower** slowly. Turn the metal so that it heats evenly to a white-yellow or incandescent white. Apply more flux if **oxide** is forming on the surface. Rather than staring at the searing fire to check the color, use a small ⅛″ rod with a thin chisel edge as a probe. Touch the thin edge of this probe onto the surface of the metal being heated. When the probe sticks, welding heat has been reached. Pull or twist the probe loose. Take the metal from the forge to the anvil and proceed with the joint.

Hammer the joint sharply in the middle of the two molten convex surfaces to force flux and oxides out of the edges (**d.**). Then use light, quick blows for the edges of the joint, hitting every spot. Finish the weld while the iron is still bright red by smoothing it with a hammer or **flatter.** See ill. See also **blacksmithing tools, blacksmithing techniques.**

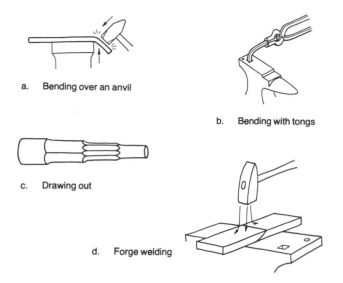

a. Bending over an anvil

b. Bending with tongs

c. Drawing out

d. Forge welding

SANDCASTING   Sandcasting is a process for casting molten metal into a pattern impressed into **molding sand.**

To sandcast a simple one-piece **pattern,** place the pattern on the **molding board** with the smaller, inward-tapering side of the **draft** facing up. Make a mark on one side of the **flask** (for aligning purposes later), and place the **drag** (the lower section) face-down (pins up) on the molding board so it is centered around the pattern. Dust the pattern with a **parting compound.** With some molding sand in the **riddle,** shake it back and forth until the pattern is completely covered by 1″ of sand. Take a shovel and completely fill the rest of the drag with sand until it is overflowing.

Using the wedge-shaped end of the **rammer,** tap the sand down around the outer edges of the mold, then **tamp** the sand firmly around the pattern with the flat end. This is a critical step because if the sand is packed too loosely, it will not hold the impression; if it is packed too hard, the gases from the molten metal cannot escape through the sand.

Strike off the excess sand with a **strike-off bar** by pulling it over the top of the flask. After sprinkling a light layer of sand (for a bed) over the top of the flask, place the **bottom board** on top of the drag. Holding the molding board and the bottom boards together, carefully turn over the drag. Remove the molding board and blow off loose sand from the surface with a **bellows.** Dust this surface with a parting compound and place the **cope** in position over the drag. Insert the **riser pin** into the sand about ¾″ from the casting pattern and the **sprue pin,** about 2–3″ away from the riser.

Repeat by filling in the cope with sand as you did for the drag. Vent the mold by making holes with a ¹⁄₁₆″ diameter rod around the pattern. They should go down into the molding sand to within ⅛″ of the pattern to permit hot gas and steam to escape.

Loosen the sprue pin and riser pin and remove them from the mold. Remove the cope section from the flask and stand it up on edge to check that the sprue and riser holes are clear through. The sand should stay in place if it has been properly prepared to the right consistency. Moisten the sand around the pattern with a **swab** and a little water to keep the sand from crumbling.

Turn a screw into a predrilled hole in the pattern and tap it lightly to loosen and remove the pattern. Carefully cut a small channel or gate between the sprue and riser and from the riser to the pattern. This channel will indirectly feed the pattern. Repair the mold if necessary using the **slick and oval** tool, and blow all loose sand out of the pattern. Close the mold by replacing the cope section over the drag, checking that it is aligned with your mark. Weight or clamp it together and prepare to pour in the molten metal.

Wear protective clothing for pouring: canvas or asbestos gauntlet gloves, leggings, and goggles or a face shield.

Choose a **crucible** that will hold enough metal to fill the cavity in one pour. Heat the metal in the crucible to pouring temperature in a gas furnace or forge. Check the temperature with a **pyrometer,** add a **flux,** and skim off the **slag.** Remove the crucible from the forge or furnace with **tongs** and pick it up for pouring with a pouring or **crucible shank.** Pour the molten metal in a steady stream until the sprue hole is filled.

Let the metal cool. Separate the cope and drag and shake out the sand. Handle the casting with tongs because it is still hot. Do not try to reuse the mold, even though the sand impression may remain, because the sand must be retempered to achieve a good cast and the **gating** system will have to be recut.

Cut off all vents, sprues, gates, and risers with a **hacksaw** or metal-cutting blade in a **bandsaw.** File, grind, and chase off parting lines, rough edges, etc. Chasing hammers and cold or small chisels may be used to further work the surface. Also see **sandcasting, sandcasting molding equipment.**

SOLDERING   For soft soldering, clean the metal with an **abrasive** such as steel wool or sandpaper; **solder** will not stick to a dirty or coated surface. Preheat the **soldering copper** or **iron** to the proper temperature. Check by touching the tip to the solder; if it melts quickly, it is near the correct heat. Do not let the iron become red-hot or the solder will splatter.

Secure the parts to be soldered firmly in place by clamping or weighting them together on a sheet of asbestos or other nonflammable material. Coat the areas to be soldered with **flux. Tack** the joint in several places by touching the point of the hot soldering iron to the metal until the flux sizzles.

Add a small bit of solder just in front of the point—not on the iron. The solder will be drawn toward the heat by capillary action. Keep moving the iron ahead of it, slowly feeding more solder when necessary. Solder the entire seam, moving the iron slowly in one direction. Do not go back and forth. Never set the hot soldering iron on any wood or flammable surface.

Finish by cleaning the surface thoroughly; if you have used acid or corrosive flux, use warm water and baking soda to neutralize the acid. Dry the piece.

If you have used a **galvanized** mild steel, the heat from soldering may have melted and protective **zinc** coating from the joints. They will rust unless again protected. When soldering galvanized steel, use **hydrochloric acid** as a flux.

For sweat soldering, clean and sand the edges to be overlapped, and coat with a flux. Put a smooth layer of solder on each surface of the joint separately. Put these faces together and heat the seam until the heat starts to melt the solder. Press down the metal with a stick or tool end and move the iron along the seam, following it with the hold-down tool. Wipe up any excess solder with a damp cloth.

When soldering **aluminum, copper, tin,** or **lead,** use a solder made with a **zinc** alloy. Clean the oxide off with an abrasive or soldering flux before starting.

Forge brazing is blacksmithing technique for iron and steel.

Put both pieces to be joined in the **forge** and heat them until the edges are orange-red. Place the edges together on the **anvil** with **tongs** and apply **flux** and brass filings (spelter) between them. Tap the two pieces together with a sharp tap when the brass has melted and is evenly distributed. Leave the joined piece in a dying fire until it cools below red heat and the brass solidifies. Remove it from the forge; when it is cool, file and finish smoothing it.

Oxyacetylene fusion welding can be dangerous; always take the necessary safety precautions. Do not use or store grease or oil around the welding area. Do not light the torch with both gas valves open at once. Wear welding goggles, and do not allow anyone else to watch unless they also are wearing welding goggles. Test for gas leaks by brushing soapy water around the fittings and watching for bubbles, which indicate escaping gas; never light a match to test for gas. Turn off your torch when a weld is complete; do not lay it down while lit.

Before lighting the torch, make sure the oxygen and acetylene gauges register the needed working pressure. (See **oxyacetylene welding equipment** for instructions on adjusting the pressure.) Put on the welding goggles and leave them on your forehead, to be pulled down over your eyes as soon as the torch is lit. Open the **acetylene** torch valve about ¾ of a turn. Squeeze the spark lighter about 1″ away from the tip to ignite the torch; never use a match to light it. The flame will be smoky. Open the oxygen torch valve slowly to adjust the **flame** to **neutral.**

WELDING   Welding is the joining or fusing of metals by heat.

Braze welding fumes are toxic; always provide excellent ventilation and an exhaust fan. Worn **steel** may be braze welded only once, but **cast iron** may be brazed repeatedly for repairs. Braze welding is not recommended where parts are subjected to push-pull types of stress.

Clean the metal joint thoroughly by filing off rust or **scale,** then rubbing it with **steel wool. Tin** thick sheet metal by applying a thin layer of brazing metal to the area to be joined. Apply **flux** to the **filler rod** by heating it and dipping it into powdered flux, or use a **brazing rod** that has a flux coating already on it. Adjust the torch to obtain a neutral **flame** for general brazing work or a slightly oxidizing flame for brazing cast iron. Use a tip size on your torch that is one size larger than the one recommended for fusion welding steel of the same thickness.

Preheat the **base metal** until it turns a dull red. Do not melt the base metal into a **puddle** with the torch flame. Do not apply the brazing rod to the metal before the base metal is thoroughly preheated or the filler metal will form beads on the surface and not adhere properly. If the base metal is too hot, the filler metal from the rod will boil away.

Make several **tack welds** along the seam first to secure the position of the pieces to be joined. Then proceed to **run a bead** with the filler metal by stroking the rod slightly ahead of the torch on the preheated base metal. The rod will spread and adhere correctly only when the base metal temperature is just right and the surface is free of grease and dirt.

Hold the inner cone of the flame about ⅛″ from the surface of the base metal, moving it around in a small area until a puddle forms. Hold the **welding rod** so that it is slanted away from the torch and insert the tip of the rod into the puddle. Keep the flame moving on the base metal, not on the welding rod, and move the torch forward. Do not hold the rod above the puddle, thus allowing molten drops to fall into the pool; instead, keep dipping the rod into the center of the puddle. If the rod sticks, play the flame onto the tip of it. **Tack weld** several points on the seam to secure the joint in place while you weld the rest of it.

Now move the puddle forward by advancing the torch flame in a series of overlapping oval motions, moving the torch just fast enough for the heat to melt the base metal thoroughly. If the flame travels forward too rapidly, the heat will not penetrate enough, and the weld will be weak. If you move it too slowly, the flame will burn a hole through the metal. This process is known as running a bead (a.).

To run a bead without a welding rod, adjust your flame to neutral. Tack weld both ends of the seam. Heat the metal with the tip at a 45° angle to the base metal so that the inner cone is between ¹/₃₂″ and ¹/₁₆″ from the surface. After the puddle forms, move the flame slowly forward in a semicircular pattern for a **butt weld,** or in a zigzag for an **edge weld,** where two pieces of metal come together at an angle.

To shut off the torch, turn off the acetylene torch valve first to avoid throwing off soot or creating a slight **backfire;** then turn off the oxygen torch valve. When finished for the day, close the valves on both the acetylene and oxygen tanks. Then bleed the lines by opening the torch valves one at a time to drain the gas out of the hoses. Close the torch valves when no further gas escapes. Finally, loosen the adjusting screws on the pressure regulators.

For arc welding, clean the metal to be welded, both at the joints to be welded and where the **ground clamp** is to be attached. Attach the ground clamp to a part of the metal you will not touch with the **electrode** when welding. If you will be turning the work in order to weld several different areas, attach the ground clamp to the metal worktable.

Adjust the **arc welder** to the correct amperage for your type of electrode. Consult the manufacturer's recommendations for each thickness and type of metal.

Insert the bare end of the electrode into the **electrode holder** and turn the arc welding machine on. Place the helmet in front of your eyes before **striking the arc.** There are two methods of striking the arc. For the scratch method, quickly drag the electrode tip across the **base metal** as if striking a wooden match, but lightly and using only wrist movement (**f.**). For the tap method, tap the electrode perpendicularly up and down on the metal surface (**g.**). While the scratch method is easiest, it leaves pit marks on the surface. Use the tap method when fine surface appearance is important.

After the arc ignites with either method, withdraw the electrode tip to ¼″ from the surface for a second or two, then lower it to ⅛″ from the metal. If the tip is held too far away, a hissing sound will be emitted and the arc will go out. If it is too close, the electrode will stick to the metal. Twist the electrode sharply to release it.

To run a bead, move the electrode steadily along the seam with the tip ⅛″ from the metal. Progress in one direction only, tilting the electrode slightly. As the electrode is burned up, keep lowering the electrode holder to maintain the correct distance from the surface. If you move the electrode too fast you will get a thin bead lacking strength; if you progress too slowly you will get a large bead with a lot of piled-up waste metal. See ill.

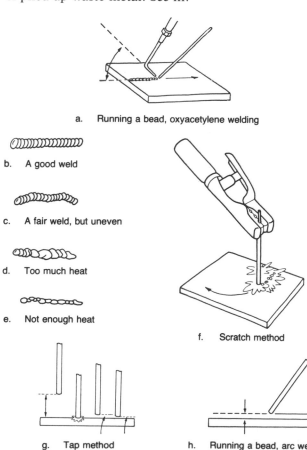

a. Running a bead, oxyacetylene welding

b. A good weld

c. A fair weld, but uneven

d. Too much heat

e. Not enough heat

f. Scratch method

g. Tap method

h. Running a bead, arc welding

FILING Filing is not usually a final finishing operation in jewelry or raising, but it may be in rougher sculptural work. It generally prepares the metal for further surfacing processes. Make the filing strokes as long as possible.

Cross-filing is ordinary filing used to remove metal or to smooth a surface by pushing the file forward across the metal (**a.**).

Secure the work piece in a clamp or **vise.** Protect the surface of the object by covering the vise jaws with wood or sheet metal. Grasp the handle in one hand and the end of the file with the other hand, and push the file forward at a slight angle to the piece of metal, keeping the file face flat on the metal surface through the entire stroke. Release pressure on the return stroke.

Rocking the file will give a rounded surface. On a flat surface, change the filing direction after a place has been filed to check for any uneven areas in the previously cut surface.

Clean the file with a **file card** as it becomes clogged.

Draw-filing is used after cross-filing to give a smooth surface (**b.**).

Secure and protect the work as in cross-filing. Push a single-cut mill file sideways across the work. Release pressure at the end of the stroke. Use a second-cut or bastard-cut file if much metal must be removed. Use a new part of the file for each stroke, employing both sides of the file, so the metal filings do not become packed into the ridges and scratch the surface.

Clean the file frequently with a file card. For a higher polish, wrap abrasive cloth with some oil in it around the file and rub it across the metal surface. See ill.

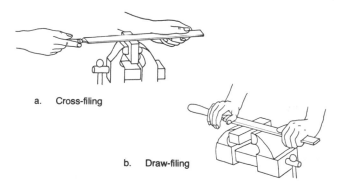

a. Cross-filing

b. Draw-filing

FINISHING The order of processes in finishing is grinding, polishing, cleaning, and coloring. Finishing a **casting** involves extra steps to remove parts of the **gating** system.

Grinding wheels can be mounted on any **grinding tool,** electric **drilling tool,** or lathe.

Wear safety goggles or a face shield and clothing that will not catch in the grinder. Wear a dust mask when grinding or polishing **copper, brass, lead,** or any chemically irritating or toxic metal. Do not grind, polish, or buff sharp objects that may catch on the electrically powered wheel.

A speed of 1740 rpm is recommended. If you have a fixed-speed wheel of 3450 rpm, which is for polishing, use a small-diameter grinding wheel. If you have a motor with a slower speed, you can use a large grinding wheel to increase the surface speed for polishing.

When bringing the metal in contact with the grinding wheel, do not apply excessive pressure or press the metal for any extended amount of time onto the wheel, or the metal will overheat and burn. Also, move the grinder or the object being sharpened to various parts of the grinding face so that one section of the wheel does not become excessively worn down.

Wear the same protective equipment and clothing for polishing as for grinding when working with power equipment.

The wheel should revolve at 3450 rpm toward the operator. Put **polishing compound** on the wheel. Place the object to be polished against the wheel below the center of the wheel so that if the form is caught, it will be pulled away from you rather than driven into your hand. Insufficient pressure may cause deposits of polishing compound on the metal. Do not place the top edge of an opening onto the wheel because the opening may catch in the wheel. Do not hold the object in a cloth, because the cloth may become entangled. Back thin or small objects with a block of wood to support them. Keep turning the object so that it is polished by the wheel in several directions. If the polishing does not seem to be effective, try a different speed, cleaning the wheel, or more or less polishing compound.

A softly scratched appearance called a satin finish may be created by lightly holding the metal against a wire brush fitted onto the grinder or polishing wheel.

To hand-polish, wrap a strip of abrasive cloth around a wood block, if working flat surfaces, or hold it in the hand. Add a few drops of oil to the metal and rub the cloth as if **sanding.**

Follow all polishing with cleaning. Remove dirt from metals by rubbing with a paste of **pumice** and water. Take off grease with a pickle bath or **carbon tetrachloride.** Remove **scale** after degreasing by heating the metal to a dull red and then dipping it in a weak pickle solution. Do not do this for castings, which might crack from rapid cooling in liquid.

The following recipes are a few examples of chemical dips or baths used for cleaning. Always pour acid into water, not the reverse.

For copper: After **annealing,** dip the metal into a bath of 1 part **sulphuric acid** to 8 parts water for about 5 minutes, or swab the solution on. Wash the metal thoroughly.

For brass, gunmetal, and bronze: Dip the metal into a bath of a 5% solution of acetic acid and water. Add table salt to the acid until it stops dissolving before putting it in the water.

For sterling silver: Remove **scale** by rubbing it with a polishing compound or by a quick dip into a cold solution of equal parts of water and **nitric acid.** Because the bath will corrode soldered joints, remove the object within seconds and wash it thoroughly.

For steel and iron: Use a bath of a weak solution of 20 parts water to 1 part **sulphuric acid.** Rinse and brush with a steel brush.

For lead and tin: Clean these metals and their alloys with a caustic soda solution. Do not use acid that has been used on copper or copper alloys on tin, lead, or zinc, because copper deposits, which are difficult to remove, will form on the surface.

Coloring is the last step in finishing, unless you wish to add some protective coating for maintenance. Many metalworkers disapprove of coating metals with any type of extraneous covering whether it be **wax, polyurethane, lacquer,** or paint, and believe the best maintenance consists of constant use or hand polishing to prevent tarnishing. The condition of the surface before coloring does not change after applying a **patina;** dull surfaces remain dull, or matte, and highly polished surfaces keep their gloss. This is because the coloring processes described here are not coatings, but chemicals that combine with the existing surface.

Clean the metal thoroughly or it will not receive an even color. Do not handle the metal with the bare hands or leave it exposed to the air for long periods of time.

For heat coloring, heat the metal in an oven or with a torch flame until the desired colors appear, then **quench** the metal immediately. Heating the surface with a torch and applying chemicals to the surface accelerates chemical action but is regarded as dangerous to the artwork and may not have as long-lasting an effect as cold chemical work. Submerging the object in a hot chemical solution, however, assures uniform coloration.

For chemical coloring you may apply the chemicals to the cold metal surface, immerse the object in the liquid, or expose the metal to chemical fumes. To color with fumes, moisten the clean metal surface with water and place object in a vessel containing the chemical that produces the fumes. Close the container and keep the metal enclosed for several days.

Wear a protective apron, gloves, and eye protection when working with acids or irritating chemicals, and make sure your working area has excellent ventilation.

The following are examples of chemical formulas used for coloring.

To color copper, brass, or silver brown or black: Dissolve a piece of **liver of sulfur** (potassium sulphide) no larger than a walnut in a gallon of hot water.

To color brass or aluminum bronze-red: Dip it in a solution of copper sulfate and water.

To color brass violet, blue, or green: Mix 2 ounces of sodium hyposulphite in 1 pint of water. Dissolve ½ ounce of lead acetate in another pint of water. Mix the 2 mixtures together and heat, but do not boil.

To color iron or steel brown: Mix 4 ounces of iron nitrate and 4 ounces of sodium hyposulphite in 1 quart of water.

To color iron or steel antique green: Mix 3 quarts of water with 1 ounce of ammonium chloride and 2 ounces of salt.

Oil blackening is both a coloring and protective process. Heat the metal in an oven or with a torch, then coat it with a heavy oil. Reheat it for 5 to 8 minutes to burn off the excess oil. This color coating also retards rust.

If a **ferrous** metal must be outdoors and is not **alloy**ed to resist corrosion, it will require a coat of paint or plastic. Clean galvanized steel with special commercial cleaners or vinegar. Apply a primer of red lead, red iron oxide, or zinc chromate (the last also for aluminum exposed to salt water) before painting on a top coat of enamel or lacquer designed especially for use on metal. Transparent plastic coatings like **varnish** have also been developed to resist weathering. Wax coatings are temporary and will wear off with handling.

To finish a cast-bronze object, saw off the **vents, sprues,** risers, and any other remains of the **gating** system with a **hacksaw.** Chisel off **flashing** and other unwanted projections with a **cold chisel** and hammer. Grind off rough details with a **grinding machine.** (This grinding step is not done on **wrought bronzes.**) File the area smooth.

Fill any surface cracks by braze welding or heliarc welding with a **filler metal** of the same alloy.

Clean the surface with a dilute solution of **nitric acid;** scraping with files, chisels, or a stiff wire brush is not recommended while the acid is on the bronze. Then clean the work thoroughly with water to stop the corrosive action of the acid and dry it. Washing with a strong heated solution of brown potash in water is harsh and not recommended.

Remove any **scale** with steel wool. Throwing cold water on the freshly cast metal after its removal from the **mold** while it is still hot will loosen the scale for easier removal later.

Chase off other surface imperfections or add fine details with chisels and punches. Polish the casting if desired. Bronze will tarnish quickly after polishing. To preserve its original shine, apply a coat of floor wax, **beeswax** dissolved in **turpentine,** or **lacquer.** Wax by itself is only a temporary coating.

Patina the metal if desired. Also see **abrasives, grinding wheel.**

CARE AND MAINTENANCE **Ferrous** metals must be protected from rusting (unless the **alloy** has been designed to rust to a protective coat, as in **Corten steel**) by a coating of paint, **lacquer,** plastic, or the like. Brush off any rusted spots with a wire brush and then sand the bare metal before applying another coat.

Nonferrous metals can tarnish rapidly, or acquire heavy **oxide** coatings that not only change their color, but also protects the metal underneath from outdoor weathering. **Aluminum** can acquire water stains as well as a thin coat of oxide. Leave this coating alone for protection of the metal unless you want to maintain the original shine, in which case you will have to apply a transparent lacquer or plastic covering that requires upkeep.

Metal objects for indoor use will retain their shine if used constantly. No coating is necessary, although there are waxes and commercial polishes available to seal the surface for those who dislike polishing their metals frequently. These coatings will wear off with handling. Do not use abrasive household detergents on a highly polished work or you will scratch and dull it.

methyl alcohol. Enameling. See **binder.**

methylene dichloride. Plastics. See **acrylic cement.**

methylene iodide. Gemcutting. See **specific gravity.**

methyl ethyl ketone. Plastics. (Also called MEK.) An organic thinner and **solvent** useful for cleaning **resin**-soaked paint brushes. Also see **Plastics: Care, Cleaning, and Maintenance.**

methyl ethyl ketone peroxide. Plastics. (Also called MEK-Px.) A **catalyst** mixed with 40% **plasticizer** used for **curing polyester resin** at room temperatures. It is a toxic, corrosive liquid that can cause skin burns. Follow the manufacturer's instructions for mixing, and handle it with care.

methyl isobutyl ketone. Plastics. (Also called MIBK.) An organic thinner and **solvent** for **epoxy resin.**

Mexican cotton. Quilts. Stitchery. All plain-weave **cotton fabric** with slightly irregular threads. These fabrics come from Mexico and are brilliant in color, although not all are **colorfast** to washing or sunlight. They are more often available in import shops or fabric stores that specialize in unusual fabrics. Similar cotton fabrics can sometimes be located through interior decorators. Mexican cotton works well for batik or tie-dye. Weights vary from bolt to bolt, although most have good **body,** which makes the fabric suitable for **appliqué,** dolls, and stuffed toys.

Mexican Cross. Quilts. See **Mexican Star.**

Mexican double weave. Weaving. See **Finnweave.**

Mexican lace. Weaving. An **openwork technique** that is actually a more elaborate form of **leno.** The twist here is also between the upper and lower layers of the **shed,** but the twisting order is uneven. This difference adds more curve to the **warp end**s but also more stress, so that care should be exercised in beating down the **filling** or the ends may break.

The common forms of Mexican lace are single Mexican lace and double Mexican lace, so called because of the number of ends twisting together in each. In splitting the groups formed by each twist in the next row of twist it is possible to get elaborate open sheds and patterns.

The exaggerated twist that is characteristic of Mexican lace was developed by early weavers around the world in places as diverse as Peru, Greece, the American colonies, and Mexico. But its prevalence among the Tarascan Indians of central Mexico has earned it the name of Mexican or Tarascan lace. There is little doubt that the early Tarascans and the natives of Peru had trade contact, so perhaps in this way a particular technique found its way from one culture to another.

A **pick-up stick** is the easiest way to do Mexican lace, although some weavers prefer to use a crochet hook to twist and hold the threads and then pull the filling through each set of twisted threads. To do Mexican lace, weave the **plain weave** on the last **pick** going from left to right and open the next shed, having the right edge warp end in the upper part. For the single twist, which is one end twisted over another except at the **selvage,** pick up with the stick the two warp ends in the lower part of the shed. Pull them on the stick toward the right of the first upper end. Go over the next upper end. Continue picking up one end from the lower shed, move to the right and go over one in the upper part. At the close of the area or at the selvage, one lower end goes over two upper ends. Close the shed, turn the pick-up stick on its edge, and put the filling through the new shed going from right to left. Level the pick-up stick and push the filling down. It can be beaten down again with a **beater.** Open the plain-weave shed again and run the filling through, going from left to right, which completes the twist and returns the warp threads to their original positions.

To do double Mexican lace, which involves twisting two lower ends over two upper ones, begin at the right edge by pulling three lower ends to the right and over two upper ends. Go under the next two lower ones, pull to the right and over the next two upper ends. Continue to the end of the area where two lower ends go over three upper ends. Place the filling as for the single Mexican lace. See ill.

Single Mexican lace   Double Mexican lace

Mexican laid-in. Weaving. See **laid-in.**

Mexican onyx. Gemcutting. See **calcite.**

Mexican Rose. Quilts. See **Whig Rose.**

Mexican Star. Quilts. A **pieced block** design of an intersected right-angle cross combined with triangles to make an eight-pointed star shape. In the Mexican Cross, a very similar pattern, the cross is a diagonal form. See ill.

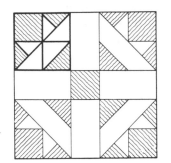

Mexican Star

mezzo-relief. Stitchery. (Also called middle-relief.) A **relief** or sculptured surface in which areas stand out prominently from the background. It is higher than **bas-relief,** but not as three-dimensional as **alto-relief.** In **fabric panel**s, areas that are heavily **stuff**ed stand out in mezzo-relief. **English trapunto** offers a means of forming a mezzo-relief surface and can be used on stuffed forms such as toys or soft sculpture.

mib. Toys. Small, unglazed, fired **clay marble**s, usually soft in color.

MIBK. Plastics. See **methyl isobutyl ketone.**

mica. Jewelry. A mineral that crystallizes into layers of thin transparent or translucent sheets. If transparent, it becomes translucent when heated. Mica is resistant to heat and does not melt or burn at temperatures required for the hottest soldering **flame**s. It is used for delicate work such as **filigree.** The filigree is placed on top of the mica, and the heat of the torch is applied from below for soldering. This produces a heat that simulates soldering on a bed of charcoal, the traditional method of soldering filigree, and that keeps direct flame, which might melt the delicate wire, and the pressure from the flow of gas and oxygen off the delicate work. There are great deposits of mica in the mountains of North Carolina. Thin transparent sheets of mica can be purchased ready for use.

mica mirror. Stitchery. Small shiny-surfaced disks of irregular shape used for **mirror embroidery** in decorating clothing, stuffed animal forms, **banner**s, or other decorative stitchery work. Those that are mica and imported from Pakistan or India may be machine washed. They are available in craft and hobby shops. The mica does not cut the attaching threads as glass mirror does.

micro-balloon. Stained Glass. One of several **ballast**s used in filling out **epoxy resin.** These balloons are tiny plastic bubbles that take up space in the resin but help reduce its weight.

micron. Gemcutting. One-thousandth of a millimeter. It is used as a measure of the size of very fine **abrasive** particles.

middle color. Shell Carving. In **cameo carving,** the portion of the shell that receives the carving and stands in low relief against the **ground color.** It is the layer of shell between the bottom layer of ground color, which provides the background of the **cameo,** and the exterior layer, which is generally removed. Also see **black helmet, bull-mouth helmet, gold ringer cowrie, horned helmet, king helmet, money cowrie, panther cowrie, poached egg, queen cowrie, snakeshead cowrie, tiger cowrie.**

middle-lap joint. Woodworking. See **joint.**

middle-relief. Stitchery. See **mezzo-relief.**

middlesboro. Basketry. A 7–8′ length of **willow** rod.

MIG welding. Metalworking. See **welding.**

Milanese stitch. Needlepoint. This stitch gives the interesting optical illusion of a three-dimensional effect. Four slanting stitches form a triangle, covering one, two, three, and finally four mesh. The triangles are worked in opposite directions. An interesting effect can be achieved by alternating colors with the diagonals. See ill.

Milanese stitch

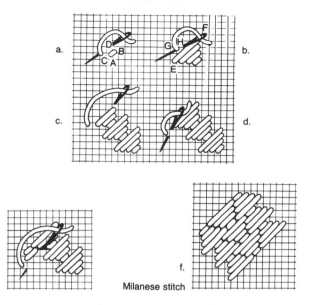

Milanese stitch

mildew-repellent finish. Stitchery. A **finish** given by the addition of various chemicals to **fabric** to retard or prevent its mildewing or rotting. The fabrics most subject to mildew are **cotton, linen, rayon,** and **wool.** Mildewing is easily prevented through proper drying, but if fabric is several layers thick, as it often is in **appliqué,** drying is difficult and mildewing is more likely to occur. Some **ducks** and **canvas**es made especially for outdoor use are mildew-proof. Stuffed toys for children benefit from the use of such treated materials.

mild steel. Metalworking. See **steel.**

military toy. Toys. Those playthings based on any of various aspects of war. The **toy soldier** is among these and is one of the oldest. Mounted soldiers of tin or lead, as well as some of clay, are known to have existed since the thirteenth century. Toy cannons, swords, and shields were popular for hundreds of years, followed by guns and, in this century, tanks, bombers, and other modern weapons of war.

milk-carton container candle. Candlemaking. See **cardboard container candle.**

milky. Batik and Tie-dye. A term used to describe **wax** not thoroughly heated. Instead of penetrating the fabric and remaining clear, the wax partially cools and has a whitish, milky appearance. Also see **melting the wax.**

mill. Ceramics. To grind materials, such as **clay** and **glaze**s. Also, a tool or machine that is used for grinding. Also see **blunge, mortar and pestle, pebble mill, pug mill.**

milled fiber. Plastics. See **glass fiber.**

milled glass decoration. Ceramics. A decorating technique in which cullet, or ground glass, is laid over a **glaze** or **oxide** in a well or cavity on a ceramic surface. When it melts and flows in firing the glass will always craze to form an interesting decoration. Also see **crazing.**

millefiori. Beadwork. A traditional glass **beadmaking** technique, sometimes called mosaic bead, in which rods of colored glass are fused together, sliced into intricately patterned cross-sections, and then processed into millefiori beads.

millefiori. Enameling. Disk-shaped slices of glass with interior geometric designs. These are fired into **enamel** but their thickness may cause them to pop off or crack.

millefiori. Glasswork. A kind of ornamental **glasswork** made by fusing together a number of glass rods of different diameters and colors, **drawing** the bundle into thinner diameters, and cutting the mass into cross-sections. The short cross-sections are then embedded in transparent glass to make paperweights and other objects.

millefiori. Stained Glass. From an Italian word meaning "thousand flowers," these are tiny cylinders of whirls of color also known as Venetian tube beads. They can be melted onto **glass** in a **kiln** for ink-blot effects. They can also be used unheated as eyes in a sculpture, or abstractly in designs and **mobile**s.

millefleurs. Découpage. A style traditionally associated with masses of plants and flowers as used in medieval tapestries. Millefleurs in découpage refers to an all-over pattern using any motifs or figures that seem to go together. Also see **Découpage: Selecting Prints.**

mill ends. Rugmaking. Remnants or short lengths of fabrics obtained from a factory. They make an economical source of material to be cut up into strips for weaving **rag rug**s or making **braided** or **hooked rug**s.

mill file. Metalworking. See **file.**

mill finish. Metalworking. See **metal.**

milliner's needle. Stitchery. See **needle.**

milling. Weaving. See **fulling.**

mill product. Metalworking. See **metal.**

Mill Wheel. Quilts. See **Windmill.**

millwork. Woodworking. Products such as doors, sash frames, **molding,** and cabinets produced in a woodworking plant. Stock millwork includes items of standardized sizes like doors or kitchen cabinets, which are generally mass-produced. Special millwork is custom work done for special architectural situations where stock sizes will not fit.

mineral color. China and Glass Painting. Pigments (powdered color) of inorganic, mineral origin. Metallic oxides are the base of all **onglaze color**s, such as cobalt for blues; lead chromes for yellow, orange and red; metal chromes for greens; iron for reds and browns; antimony for yellow; manganese for blue; **silver** for yellows; and **gold** for rose, ruby, violet, and purple. Gold and silver are the best metals, and the strongest colors. In mixing colors, any gold color will dominate. Some of the iron reds are undependable, needing the addition of **flux** to make them part of the glaze.

mineral fiber. Spinning. Weaving. See **fiber.**

mineral spirits. Batik and Tie-dye. Toys. A combustible fluid, containing distillate used to thin paitns, enamels, and varnishes. It is also used as a **solvent** in cleaning brushes, being substituted for turpentine, a more expensive paint thinner. Caution must be taken to avoid contact with flame or heat. It must be used with adequate ventilation and skin contact should be avoided. Wash hands thoroughly after use.

Mineral spirits are sometimes used by batik artists to remove **wax** from the finished **batik fabric.**

mineral spirits. Metalworking. Woodworking. See **solvent.**

mineral tanning. Leather. The processing of leather with mineral substances such as salts of chromium, aluminum, and zirconium.

Miner's wheel. Spinning. See **spinning head.**

miniature. Toys. A **model** on a very small scale. A miniature is not always of exact ratio, as a **scale model** is. Miniatures are often of interest to collectors, particularly those made for dollhouses. Also see **Toys: Definition.**

minileaf pattern. Knitting. See **Knitting: Construction.**

minimum selvage. Weaving. See **selvage.**

mirror embroidery. Embroidery. Stitchery. The attaching of small irregularly shaped pieces of **mica mirror** to **fabric** by means of embroidery **stitch**es. The work is derived from the shisha embroidery of India and Pakistan; it is believed that the mirrors ward off evil spirits.

The mirrors are first held in place with crossing stitches, then a **Cretan stitch** or a **buttonhole stitch** may be used around them. **French knots** and other decorative stitches are also added. Mirror embroidery may be seen in traditional costumes, umbrellas, **panel**s, and stuffed animals from India and Pakistan. It is currently a very popular kind of embroidery for **body covering**s, **wall hanging**s, and stuffed forms. Also see **shisha work.**

mirror finish. Jewelry. Metal that has been polished to a shine so high you can see your reflection in it. Also see **buffing compound, lapping.**

mirrorwork. Embroidery. See **shisha work.**

mishima. Ceramics. A form of **inlay** in which a design is stamped into **leather-hard** clay and then filled by brushing a **slip** over the depression. Also see **roulette.**

miss. Crochet. See **skip.**

Missouri Puzzle. Quilts. See **Goose-in-the-Pond.**

Missouri Rose. Quilts. See **Prairie Rose.**

Missouri Star. Quilts. (Also called Shining Star.) A **pieced block** design that has a central eight-pointed star outlined in blocks and darts, probably designed in 1821, when Missouri became the 24th state.

miter. Quilts. Stitchery. A method of **fold**ing and sewing **fabric** strips to make a right-angle corner. In mitering a corner, two strips of fabric cut to exactly the same width are joined with a 45° seam. To figure the 45° angle, mark off a square at the end of the strip, using the width of the strip as one dimension of the square. Draw a diagonal line from corner to corner. Place the strips with right sides together and sew on that line. Turn one strip back and, if measurements and sewing were accurate, an exact right-angle corner results. The finished corner has a diagonal line where it is stitched, and is used in **binding** and **edging quilt**s. Mitering gives a neat flat corner with a sharp point, and it evenly distributes the fabric that is turned under.

A similar folding method of mitering is often employed in quiltmaking when there is ample material from the **quilt back**ing to fold it over the front into a **self-binding** edge.

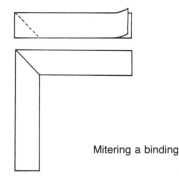

Mitering a binding

miter. Woodworking. An angled cut, other than a right angle, across the **grain** of a board (rather than on the edge, when it is called a **bevel**), usually cut in a **miter box.** Also see **joint** and **Woodworking: Jointing.**

miter box. Woodworking. A U-shaped box or device used to hold a piece of wood while cutting a **miter.** It can have permanent cuts at specific angles or have an adjustable angle guide to hold the saw while cutting.

To use a miter box, mark the angle to be cut on the board with the aid of a **bevel square.** Place the wood into the miter box to align the mark securely where the cut is to be made. Hold the wood firmly and place either a **crosscut saw** or **backsaw** into the miter-box groove. Start the cut by dragging the saw toward you a number of times to establish the cut. Proceed with the regular forward-and-backward cutting until the board is sawed through. See ill.

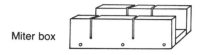

Miter box

mitered corner. Bookbinding. (Also called cut corner.) A separately attached piece of **cloth** or **leather** that serves to protect the corner of a book. It is first glued to the outside of the cover and then turned to the inside where the overlaps butt at a 45° angle. The corners should measure no wider than the width of the back.

Cut four corners the desired finished size plus ⅝" allowance for turning to the inside. Cut away the point of the right angle of each corner at a 45° angle so that the edge is about ⅛" from the board corner when the **corner** paper is in position (**a.**). Mark the position on the face of both **board**s where you intend to place each corner. Paste the corners and align them with the pencil marks. Turn in **head** or **tail** overlaps first, tight to the board edge, and rub down with the **bone folder.** Tuck in the small projection of cloth left at the board corner with your thumbnail or the folder before turning in the **foredge** (**b.**). Turn in the foredge overlap, rub down all four corners with the folder over a clean piece of paper. **Nip** in press (**c.**). See ill. Also see **paring, pasting leather, rubbing down.**

Mitered corner

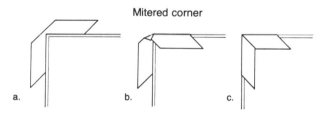

a.   b.   c.

mitered corner. Stitchery. A fitted right-angle corner, made by **miter**ing a **fabric seam.** In **binding,** a mitered corner is sometimes a sharp smooth turn that has a flat appearance and a minimum of bulk.

miter gauge. Woodworking. See **squaring tools.**

mitering lead. Stained Glass. See **Stained Glass: Glazing.**

miter joint. Woodworking. See **joint.**

mitre. Knitting. A knit corner that forms an angle of 45°. Also see **corners.**

mitten-type hand. Puppets. A mitten-shaped **hand** made for the end of an open sleeve of the **hand puppet** or **marionette.** The **controller** of the hand puppet can slip the end of a thumb or finger into a mitten-type hand to control hand movements. Also see **glove-type hand.**

mixed cut. Gemcutting. See **facet.**

mixed-media stitchery. Stitchery. Those **panel**s that employ **fabric**s and **fiber**s in combination with other ma-

terials of a nonfibrous nature, such as clay, paper, plastic, wire, wood, found objects, and natural material. The fabrics or fibers usually provide the cohesive element of the composition.

mixed warp. Weaving. A **warp** made up of many different yarns. The yarns can be different in texture, color, thickness, or **fiber** content; or, within one warp, they can be different from each other in all the above-mentioned qualities. Warps are made of yarn mixtures for aesthetic reasons and they usually result in a cloth that is lovelier and more interesting than one in which just one yarn has been used in the warp. The technical problem that can occur with a mixed warp is uneven tension because each yarn may have different elasticity. A second **warp beam** or extra-heavy **padding** on the warp beam may be the answer. The **sett** with a mixed warp is no longer the standard one, or two per **dent,** but irregular according to the texture and thickness of the yarn. The sett can also be quite varied from inch to inch depending on how the warp is mixed or if there is a repeat to the mixture. Also see **color blending.**

mixing. Ceramics. The process of combining two or more materials to produce a **clay body.** Water is put into a container of the proper size and then the clay is added to ensure that each particle is coated with water. A fluid **slip** the consistency of thick cream is produced. Mixing can be done by hand, using a stick, or by machine, such as a washing machine. Also see **blunger, propeller mixer, pug mill.**

Miyako. Batik and Tie-dye. See **acid dye, direct dye.**

moaning stick. Toys. See **bull-roarer.**

mobile. Papercrafts. Stained Glass. A sculptural form in which multiple shapes are suspended in air by threads or fine wire. The mobile originated in the 1930s with the moving wire and metal sculptures of Alexander Calder. It is a completely American art form.

Papercrafts offer interesting possibilities for mobile-making as the material is lightweight and can be cut or shaped with ease into various forms for hanging. Paper **cutout**s or three-dimensional forms such as **origami** figures may be used. Once the shapes to be suspended are prepared, holes for the thread or wire are punched in the paper shapes at the approximate top center point. The shapes are then individually threaded and hung from pieces of stiff wire, cardboard, balsa wood, or soda straws so that the parts balance and swing independently of each other.

In stained glass, mobiles are made by **copper foiling** pieces of glass or enclosing them in **lead came** or hanging them by themselves by drilling a small hole in each piece and attaching **fishline,** fine wire, or the like to make the hanging arrangement. The wind chime is a form of mobile in which pieces are hung closely together so that wind blows them together, making them chime.

Some experimenting is necessary to achieve a balanced mobile. To begin, balance single hanging shapes on either end of a length of stiff wire. If the two shapes are identical, the designs will be symmetrical, and the supporting wire should balance in a horizontal position from a thread attached to the exact midpoint of the wire. When one shape is heavier than the other, some trial and error adjustment must be made in the positioning of the middle, supporting thread. Move the hanging thread from the center of the supporting wire until the mobile balances. The heavier weight section will be closer to the suspending thread, on the shorter arm.

The number and kinds of shapes and the arrangement of completed suspended sections can be endlessly varied. As a general rule it is best to start with the lowest section, balancing as described above, then build up from the bottom to the major supporting wire. Incidentally, there is no rule to say that the supporting wire or piece must be exactly horizontal—only that it should allow for free movement of the other shapes and wires surrounding it. Obviously, the greater the number of sections suspended from one another, the more complex the piece. In planning a mobile, it should be remembered that because each section must be able to turn freely in response to air motion without bumping into its neighbor, each should be threaded to hang at either a different level or far enough away from the adjacent piece to avoid collision. Also see **fastening, glass drill, millefiore.**

mobile wastebin. Stained Glass. See **Stained Glass: Setting Up a Workshop.**

mock double cloth. Weaving. A fabric with the appearance of **double cloth** in **block pattern**s but not constructed as double cloth. Instead of having two **warp**s and two **filling**s necessary for the two layers of double cloth, mock or false double cloth has two fillings but only one warp. The double cloth appearance is primarily due to the **threading,** which is in blocks; for example, 1,2,1,2,1,2 followed by 3,4,3,4,3,4 and then repeated from the start. The blocks can be any width desired and it is not necessary to have the 1,2 block equal to the 3,4 block. In the **treadling** one of the two fillings works as the **plain-weave ground** with the warp. The other one is a pattern filling woven on a **warp-faced twill weave** that **float**s on the back when not engaged on the front. This makes the fabric not reversible, as opposed to true double cloth. More than one pattern filling can be used.

mock leno weave. Weaving. Weaves designed to cause open spaces in a fabric through the interlacing of groups of **warp** and **filling float**s. It is a **loom-controlled** attempt to simulate a lace effect or true **leno.** It is used chiefly for stoles, scarves, and women's apparel. The open spaces are caused by grouping warp and filling threads in such a manner that the threads in each group slide together easily but are separated from adjacent groups by the interlacing of the first and last threads in each group. This interlacing keeps the groups apart and, at this point, an opening is formed. The openings can be made even wider by skipping **dent**s in the **sleying** so that the groups are spaced apart at the start. Although some **plain weave** is present in order to hold the interlacing, the mock leno can be combined with a plain-weave **ground** or border for a firmer

fabric. Cotton, wool, or any nonslippery yarn is used so that the openings do not shift out of position. Mock leno is also known as imitation gauze. See ill.

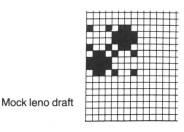

Mock leno draft

model. Toys. A small version or replica of an object, such as the model car and model **airplane.** A **scale model** is produced in exact proportions, whereas a **miniature** is simply a tiny version. Also see **architectural plaything, balsa wood.**

model airplane. Toys. See **airplane.**

modeler. Leather. A tool used for **tooling** and **working** leather. A modeler for all-around tooling work has one pointed, narrow end for line work or tracing, and one flattened end for various types of modeling.

The ball-end modeler is used for **embossing** and **stippling.** The deerfoot modeler is used for beveling, for getting into hard-to-reach areas, and for depressing outlines. The tracer is used for tracing lines on leather. See ill. Also see **matting** and **Leatherwork: Cutting and Edging, Tools and Materials.**

Modelers

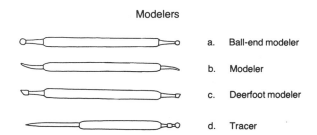

	a.	Ball-end modeler
	b.	Modeler
	c.	Deerfoot modeler
	d.	Tracer

modeling. Ceramics. Modeling can be done by **pinching, throwing,** or slab-building clay. The term also refers to the technique of finishing and decorating clay with **modeling tool**s. Also see **Ceramics: Hand Building.**

modeling clay. Ceramics. A **clay body** used for making sculptures and large pots by hand that contains a large quantity of **grog** to aid in quick drying and to give maximum structure. Also see **casting slip, throwing clay.**

modeling clay. Toys. A mudlike material which is worked while in a plastic state and then dried. The material can be shaped in the hands and modeled to suggest various forms. **Plasticene** is a common one. Some of the doughs used in **baker's art** are referred to as modeling clays, although they are more precisely **modeling dough**s.

modeling compound. Plastics. A plastic paste or putty used for direct modeling or to make **patterns** used in **casting** or **molding. Polymer emulsion** pastes and **gesso** with inert **fillers** such as marble dust may be used directly for modeling. Modeling clays for use with flexible **silicone** molds do not harden and are for patterns only. Claylike modeling compounds, which must be baked in an oven to attain final hardness, are commercially available. Do not use oil-base Plasticene modeling clay with silicone rubber molds. Also see **Plastics: Casting.**

modeling dough. Toys. A mixture of ingredients which form either an **edible dough** or an **inedible dough** and which has enough plasticity to be shaped in the hands. Modeling doughs are used in **baker's art.** Also see **baker's clay, bread clay, salt clay, salt dough.**

modeling material. Puppets. Any material that can be molded. **Papier mâché** and **sawdust mâché** are common modeling materials for **puppet heads.** Often **clay** or **Plasticene** is used as a modeling material over which papier mâché is used in making a molded puppet head. Also see **pulp mâché** and **Puppets: Making the Puppet Head.**

modeling mix. Puppets. Prepackaged material to which water is added to make **pulp mâché.** It is suitable for making molded heads for **puppets** and **marionettes.** Also see **Puppets: Making the Puppet Head.**

modeling tool. Ceramics. There are many types of modeling tools, usually made of wood and sometimes with wire attachments, used for smoothing, trimming, and working clay either on or off the wheel. See ill.

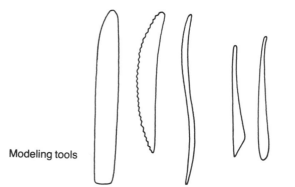

Modeling tools

modeling tool. Jewelry. Tools with flat working ends and slightly rounded corners used in **chasing.** They are used to more fully define an area raised through the **repoussé** process by punching down the areas immediately surrounding the raised areas of the repoussé.

modular quilt. Quilts. A **quilt** design that is based on a **module.** In designing such a quilt, all **blocks** are planned for **finished sizes.** If, for example, a 3″ module was being used, blocks would **finish** at 3″ × 3″, 3″ × 6″, 3″ × 9″, 6″ × 6″, etc. That means each piece must be cut with the additional ¼″ **seam allowance.** If this is not done, the blocks will not **set** properly. Two blocks, each 3″ wide, must be sewn together before they can be joined to an adjacent 6″ block. If the seam allowance has not been added, the 3″ blocks, less the seam, would end up being 5½″ long, which would not fit the 6″ block. When 2 blocks, each cut 3½″, are placed side by side, they make a total length of 7″. When joined they will be 6½″. That will equal the 6″ block, which, with its ½″ seam allowances, will also be 6½″ long.

Modular quilts are joined and sewn in the same manner that blocks are set for any quilt. Straight lines are always sewn, avoiding corners, which are much more difficult to sew.

modular unit. Batik. Quilts. Stitchery. See **module.**

module. Batik. Quilts. Stitchery. The single unit of measurement that is repeated in any modular design. The module may be planned and utilized in any of several ways. In one, the module may be a simple shape with the measurement the same on all sides, such as a square used to produce a **checkerboard** pattern. Other examples of the use of this single unit module are **quilts**, panels, or banners made up of **hexagons** or triangles. In another plan, the module might refer to just one dimension, which is used in multiples. For instance, a 4″ module could be used to make units that are 4″ × 4″, 4″ × 8″, 8″ × 8″, or any such variation as long as each dimension is a multiple of the 4″ module. This assures that all the **blocks** or modules will fit together easily. In a third variation, the module controls only one dimension, which is not used in multiples because the other dimensions may vary. An example of this is the use of a collection of batik or **appliqué** blocks based on the module height of 10″. Blocks of varying widths can be joined to form bands 10″ high. The **strip quilt** utilizes this module. **Pieced** wall hangings are often based on modular units. Batik and tie-dye panels may be planned on modular unit systems, as they allow for the use of easily handled, small fabric pieces.

In each variation listed the modules are **assemble**d to make a larger piece of material. The measurements of a module always refer to **finished sizes,** and **seam allowances** must be added. A modular unit simplifies the planning and arrangement of parts of an **all-over pattern** and makes the assembly of the material an easy task. Also see **modular quilt.**

mohair. Crewel. Embroidery. Knitting. Needlepoint. Spinning. Weaving. The name given to the fiber of the **Angora** goat. Mohair has a **staple** length of 9–12″ and is 2½ times stronger than wool. The fiber has less **crimp** than wool, which gives it a smooth, lustrous surface. It is soft in handling and its extreme elasticity helps to prevent wrinkling in a fabric. The whitish fiber has a good dyeing capacity and its high natural luster shows off brilliant colors especially well. Mohair is also the name given to the fabric made of mohair fiber, with or without the addition of other fibers. Mohair yarn is very popular for knitting sweaters, scarves, and afghans. It is used in crewel to give a fluffy effect to certain stitches, and is especially effective in cut Turkey work for emphasizing softness.

Mohs scale of hardness. Gemcutting. A ranking of the ability of materials to resist scratching. Since its invention in 1820 by Friedrich Mohs, a Viennese mineralogist, this measure of relative **hardness** has been popularly used by gemcutters. The softest material is numbered one, the hardest is numbered ten. This scale does not accurately reflect the vast differences separating the different hardnesses.

The Knoop scale, determined with a **sclerometer,** provides a more realistic view of relative hardness; this scale is given in parentheses following the Mohs arrangement.

1. Talc
2. Gypsum (32)
3. Calcite (135)
4. Fluorite (163)
5. Apatite (430)
6. Feldspar (525)
7. Quartz (750)
8. Topaz (1200)
9. Corundum (2200)
10. Diamond (8200)

A fingernail has a hardness of 2½; a copper coin of 3; window glass of 5; and a knife blade of 5½. Chips of materials of known hardness, mounted in holders, are used to test gems for hardness. Care must be exercised when cut stones are examined; to avoid damaging them, make only a tiny mark on the girdle and use the highest possible magnification. Also see **abrasive** and **Gemcutting: Rough Shaping.**

moisture crazing. Ceramics. **Crazing** due to water absorption after firing in a **ceramic body,** causing slight swelling. Also see **adsorption.**

moki. Weaving. See **Navajo weaving.**

mokumé. Jewelry. A technique derived from an ancient Japanese technique of using varicolored clays in the making of ceramics.

Layer upon layer of **sheet metal** is **solder**ed together. The metals are chosen for change and contrast in color. Many metals can be used, such as bronze, silver, brass, and copper. They should be of the same size but can be of the same or varying gauges. This "sandwich" of metal is a form of banded alloy.

First **pickle** and **flux** the metals and cover each layer with **solder filing**s, or powdered solder. Bind the metals together with iron binding wire and solder them on a flat **charcoal block,** using a large, hot flame. As the solder flows, it is necessary to press down on the metals from above with a **soldering point** for a more complete joining. You should see the solder squeeze out along all of the edges in a bright silver line. If there are areas that do not join after soldering, place the block of metal on a **steel block** and hammer the metals tightly together with a flat-faced hammer such as a **planishing hammer.** Pickle again, rinse, coat all exposed areas with flux, and resolder.

There are several ways of treating this metal sandwich, which is called mokumé. Slices can be cut down through the layers of metal to expose the different colors. These slices should be no thinner than 5 mm, as more work can be done on them. It is nearly impossible to cut through this block of metal with a jeweler's saw. A hacksaw can be used, but an electric jigsaw that can cut metal is ideal.

Put the slices through a **rolling mill,** which spreads them and makes them thinner until they become varicolored sheet metal. They can be used just as they are for the making of jewelry, or can be arranged next to one another to create further patterns and then soldered together with medium solder. This positioning and soldering can be done either before or after rolling. This method produces a rich, fairly regular pattern.

Another method in which this **lamination** can be used is by distorting the pattern by **doming** the metal in areas with a **punch** and filing the domes flat to expose circles on the varicolored metals. The laminets can also be partially filed with a V-shaped file or a square file used on its corner, again exposing the varicolored layers of metals. The metal can then be put through the rolling mill to produce sheet metal or, if a mill is not available, the work can be made flat by planishing with a planishing hammer, hammering the metal alternately from both sides until it becomes flattened.

With any method, if the work becomes hardened, **annealing** will be necessary or the metal will **fracture.**

In building the sandwich, do not use silver as the top metal because it tends to receive the most heat during soldering and may collapse. Brass and silver tend to **alloy** quickly; try to keep them apart when building up the mokumé. Small pits or areas that did not solder can be filled with hard solder after the initial slicing of the metal. Seams that fracture while working the metal can be resoldered. Holes that are too large to be filled with solder sometimes appear. A patch of metal can be soldered over these with a lower-melting-point solder and either rolled down to level it with the rest of the metal or hammered level with a planishing hammer.

If further soldering is required in the **fabrication** of jewelry, you must use solder that has a lower melting point than any solder used in the forming of the mokumé. You may want to consider other methods of joining, such as **riveting** or **tapping** the work or holding it together with screws. There is also the possibility of using the mokumé as an inlay material or setting it in a **bezel.**

Polished mokumé is extremely subtle, even with the contrasting color of the metals. If more contrast is desired, the metals can be heat oxidized, treated with liver of sulfur, and rubbed very lightly with fine **steel wool** to produce a greater contrast and a soft, lustrous finish. Rub lightly, or the entire oxidization will be removed.

mola. Stitchery. A loose blouse of intricate design skillfully made and worn by the Cuna Indian women on the San Blas Islands. The molas are sewn by a process of stacking **fabric** layers and then cutting through in a method called **San Blas appliqué, reverse appliqué,** or **cut-through appliqué.** The blouses are made up of two square or rectangular pieces of **appliqué,** one for the front and one for the back. Any printed material is used to **join** the fabric over the shoulders. The **stitch**ed designs are characterized by intricate linear patterns using **zigzag** shapes, figures, animals, and bird forms in complex overlappings. In more recent years the designs have included adaptations of American advertisements and slogans. Molas are now widely collected and exhibited.

mold. Candlemaking. Any container or receptacle that will not melt or break when subjected to the relatively high **temperature** of melted wax. Molds are available in almost limitless number, either as **found object mold**s or as commercial candle molds. Also see **Candlemaking: Selecting the Mold.**

mold. Ceramics. Any form used to shape clay, usually made of bisque or plaster. See ill. Also see **hollow-dish mold, hump mold, master mold, molding, press mold, slipcasting.**

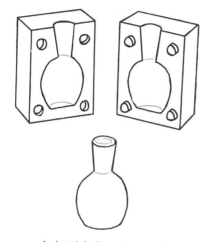

Industrial slipcasting mold

mold. Glasswork. The metal or wooden form used to shape blown **glasswork.** Often the mold has two hinged sections that are closed around the **parison,** the latter being inflated and turned so that the walls of the blown vessel or shape contact the inside of the mold and harden into that shape. Wooden molds acquire a coating of carbon, which serves to polish the glass as it is turned. Commercial iron forms are coated with a carbon-forming material made of resin, linseed oil, and sawdust that serves the same polishing function. Also see **blocking mold.**

mold. Jewelry. The prepared hollow form into which molten metal is poured to produce a **casting.** Also, a hollow form into which metal can be forced with **punch**es. Also see **dapping block, dapping die.**

mold. Leather. See **Leatherwork: Forming Leather.**

mold. Metalworking. Plastics. A form used for **casting** a molten metal or a liquid plastic **resin,** or for **molding** a soft **sheet metal** or heat-softened **thermoplastic** sheet. **Moldmaking material**s for metals must be resistant to greater heat than those used for plastics, but the terminology and methods for the two crafts are essentially similar.

A **pattern** is a full-size model of the finished object made of plastic **foam, clay, hardwood,** etc., used in making the mold. In most cases, it is removed from the mold before casting, but in **foam-vaporization casting** of metals, the foam pattern is left in the mold and vaporized by the molten metal.

The inward slope of the object on the vertical faces of the mold is called the **draft;** it is necessary to facilitate removing the cast object from the mold when it has solidified (**a.**). The draft should be about 3–5%.

A slope in the opposite direction of a draft, which would tend to lock the cast object into the mold and prevent its being removed easily, is called an **undercut** (**b.**). It may be caused by a projection or a depression in either the pattern or the mold; undercuts should be avoided in molds that will be removed intact or reused.

There are several types of molds. The open (or open-face) mold is a one-piece mold, used for a cup or a bowl shape. Plastic or metal may be poured or pressed into or over it, as in **drape forming** with plastics or **slush casting** with metal.

The matched (or male-and-female) mold has a convex "male" half and a concave "female" half; the soft plastic or metal is pressed between the two (**c.**). Multiple editions of soft sheet-metal reliefs may be made by sandwiching the metal between thin male and female halves and rolling the mold and metal through a printing press. Good examples of the quality of work made by this process are the lead reliefs of Louise Nevelson.

The piece (or split) mold is made in two or more sections (**d.**). A carefully planned piece mold permits making castings of complex shapes with undercuts and without draft, as long as each piece of the mold can be removed freely.

The sand mold is a sand container into which molten metal is poured for a single **casting** and that is destroyed as the hardened metal casting is removed. Green sand molds are the least expensive, do not require baking before use, and may be used for practically all **ferrous** and **nonferrous** metals. Their disadvantages are they are not strong, may not be stored for any length of time, and are easily damaged. The moisture in the sand may cause casting defects if not carefully controlled.

The investment mold, also for metals only, is made from a mixture of **casting plaster** and refractory materials, which

Molds

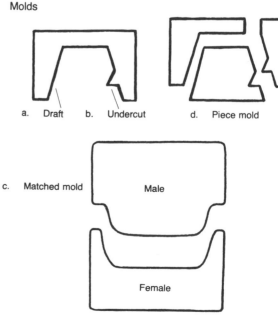

a. Draft   b. Undercut   d. Piece mold

c. Matched mold   Male

Female

is called the investment. It is destroyed as the hardened metal casting is removed. This type of mold is used for **lost-wax process** casting, precision casting, and investment casting.

The flexible mold is used with plastics only; it is a layer of flexible rubber, latex, **silicon rubber,** or **vinyl.** It must be backed with a rigid material such as **plaster** to prevent distortion when casting.

The **pattern** is used as a mold for some types of **thermoforming,** such as vacuum forming, **blow forming,** and **drape forming.**

The waste (or break-away) mold is used only once; it is broken away to remove the cast object. See ill. Also see **investment, molding sand, sandcasting molding equipment,** and **Metalworking: Sandcasting.**

mold. Stained Glass. See **dalle-de-verre mold.**

moldavite. Gemcutting. (Also called bottle stone.) A mineral similar to obsidian but with perfect transparency. It has a **hardness** of 5½, a **specific gravity** of 2.36, a refractive index of 1.5, and is green in color. Also see **refraction.**

molded bead. Beadwork. Beads formed by rolling the bead material between the palms of the hands, then piercing it with a knitting needle to make a hole for hanging; or by shaping the material right on the needle. **Ceramic bead**s, **gesso bead**s and **papier mâché bead**s are examples of molded beads. Also see **perfumed bead**s.

molded candle. Candlemaking. A candle formed by **molding.** Also see **Candlemaking: Molding.**

molded head. Puppets. See **modeling mix** and **Puppets: Making the Puppet Head.**

molder's bulb. Metalworking. See **sandcasting molding equipment.**

molding. Candlemaking. The process of forming candles by casting hot wax in a heat-proof container. Also see **Candlemaking: Molding.**

molding. Ceramics. Any method of forming clay using some sort of **mold** to help determine the final **form.** The techniques vary widely, but fall into three groups: hand molding, mechanical molding, and casting.

Hand-molding methods are similar to (and sometimes combined with) hand-building methods; usually a **slab** of clay is first prepared. The slab may then be shaped over a natural **former** or a **hump mold,** or may be pressed into a **hollow-dish mold. Sandcasting** is a more complex method; a plaster mold is cast in sand and then used to form the clay slab. A **plunge pot** is made by pressing a convex wooden batten into a block of clay.

Mechanical molding uses a heavy **clay body**—sometimes **grogged**—in a **press mold,** or it is used for **extrusion**s.

Casting is largely confined to **slipcasting** and used mainly for mass-producing ceramic objects of all sorts. Often, a **master mold** is made, from which numerous plas-

ter or **bisque** molds can be duplicated. Also see **Ceramics: Hand Building.**

molding. Papercrafts. A **papier mâché** shaping technique consisting of applying **paper mash** or **paper strips** over a form, then removing it when dried to the shape of the form. The shape should be simple enough to permit easy removal of the dried papier mâché. A bowl, a **balloon,** or a **relief** sculpture of **clay,** such as a **mask,** are suitable. More complex forms can be made by using two molds, one for each half, and then joining the halves with additional paste-soaked paper strips.

The mold should be given a light coating of petroleum jelly to prevent sticking. An alternate method to prevent sticking is to dip the first layer of strips in water only; all other layers are soaked in **papier mâché paste.** The paste-soaked strips are applied to the surface, each layer in a different direction (**a.**). The paper must be worked well into all areas, pressing into crevices and indentations firmly because papier mâché tends to flatten when dry. Press with the fingers to remove any air bubbles within the layers. When the papier mâché coating has dried, turn the piece over and remove the form. If using clay, it may have to be scooped out with a spoon. Then trim and repair the edges of the papier mâché piece with additional paper strips (**b.**), and paint if desired. See ill.

molding. Plastics. Pressing or draping soft, heated plastic into or over a **mold.** Also see **Plastics: Thermoforming and Molding.**

molding. Toys. Scraps of molding, sometimes available from cabinetmakers or picture framers, can be used to add detailed trims to **toys.**

molding. Woodworking. A strip of wood designed to add a decorative covering to an edge, or to cover a poorly fit joint or corner. Molding comes in a variety of shapes and sizes. Some common examples are half-round, used to cover joints between various walls or ceiling tiles (**a.**); quarter-round, used to cover inside corner joints between wall and floor paneling (**b.**); the cornice, often used at the top of an interior wall (**c.**); and ogee, an S-shaped molding used as a cornice molding (**d.**). See ill.

molding board. Metalworking. See **sandcasting molding equipment.**

molding sand. Metalworking. (Also called casting sand, founder's sand, green sand.) A mixture of sand (usually quartz or silica sand), binding materials, and other additives used for **sandcasting.** The binders may be clay, cereal grains, plastic resin, pitch, mineral or vegetable oil, cement, or waterglass (sodium silicate). Additives may include wood powder or sea coal, to improve the surface finish and aid in the cleaning of castings, or silica flour, which fills the spaces between the sand particles to reduce metal penetration in the mold. Most sand is used damp (or green), but some processes are done with dry sand.

There are two basic types of molding sand: synthetic and natural. Synthetic or foundry sand is mixed from pure silica sand, clay carbon materials, and water, and is used for casting that requires high temperatures. An advantage of synthetic sand is that it is purchased finely graded for sharply detailed reproduction. Natural sands come mainly from the eastern Great Lakes area, Kentucky, and Missouri.

French sand is a variety of specially prepared reddish-brown molding sand from France. Facing sand is extra-finely ground molding sand with graphite or ground coal added and is used to cover the pattern surface. **Parting compound** is finely ground silica sand or talc that is sprinkled on the outside surfaces of the sand mold to keep the sand in the **cope** from sticking to that in the **drag**.

Temper dry sand by sprinkling it with water and mixing it thoroughly with a shovel. It should retain the impression of your fingers when you squeeze it, and should break off sharply when tapped. If it sticks to your hand, it is too wet.

moldmaking material. Plastics. The choice of a material for a **mold** or a **pattern** depends on the type of plastic being cast or thermoformed, the size of the object to be made, the number of copies desired, and the specific casting or molding process to be used. In both **thermoforming** and **casting** the quality of the surface is determined by the finish of the mold or pattern material facing the plastic.

Casting plaster is popular for casting with **resin**s. It is inexpensive for casting large objects, but it lacks durability and may not withstand multiple castings. The mold pieces may also warp easily when stored, unless the parts are tied in their respective positions with twine or rubber bands. Because it is porous, casting plaster must be sealed with a **sealant,** such as lacquer, shellac, or varnish before a **mold release agent** coating, or plastic sheeting, is applied to its surface.

Silicone plastic gives extremely accurate reproductions and can withstand multiple castings. However, it is expensive and may not cure properly if in contact with any material containing sulfur or some synthetics, like **Mylar**, Teflon, **cellulose acetate**, and **polyethylene**. It must be supported or backed up by a rigid substance, such as plaster or wood, because it is flexible. This flexibility is an asset for removing the mold from work with delicate details without damaging intricate parts.

Single castings of resin may be made by pouring the liquid plastic into sand, aluminum foil, polyethylene and **polypropylene** sheeting, or any material to which a sealant and mold release agent can be applied. **Polystyrene** or **Styrofoam** will be eaten away by **polyester** resin upon contact unless the surface is thickly and thoroughly sealed.

Molds for mass-produced plastic objects are made from hardwood or metal.

mold release. Candlemaking. A **silicon spray** or some form of vegetable oil applied to the inside surface of the **mold** to facilitate the release of the hardened candle. To eliminate an undesired mottling effect, wipe away any excess oil before pouring the candle.

mold release. Stained Glass. See **releasing agent.**

mold release agent. Plastics. (Also called parting agent, compound, separator, internal release agent.) A substance applied to the **mold** surface in contact with the **resin** to prevent the plastic from sticking to the mold. Examples are wax, PVA (polyvinyl alcohol), **alkyd** and **vinyl** paints, PVC (polyvinyl chloride), silicone sprays, lecithin, or **sheeting** such as **cellulose acetate, cellophane,** or **Mylar.** Also see **Plastics: Casting.**

mold release agent. Stained Glass. See **releasing agent.**

molly bolt. Woodworking. See **bolt.**

molybdenum. Metalworking. See **steel.**

momentum toy. Toys. A toy in which the momentum of a moving part keeps it in action. A **yo-yo** is probably the best-known toy of this type. The **moulinet** and **alouette** are based on this principle. Other similarly operated toys are the **apple mill, whizgig,** or **water cutter.** In each, a **string** is pulled or some similar method devised to add impetus to keep the force constant and the toy in motion.

money cowrie. Shell Carving. (*Cypraea moneta.*) A shell of golden-yellow exterior, matte white **middle color,** and a violet **ground color** that can yield one ring-sized, three-color cameo instead of the usual two-colored one. Also see **cameo carving, cowrie, helmet** and **Shell Carving: Shell.**

monkey-on-a-stick. Toys. (Also called performing monkey.) An animated wooden **folk toy** that consists of a jointed figure attached to two sticks. When the sticks are moved it creates a frenzied activity in the articulated figure. It is sometimes called admiral-up-a-stick or acrobat-on-a-stick when a figure is used.

Monkey Wrench. Quilts. A geometric pieced block design, usually a **nine-patch.** One block is nearly identical to Shoo-fly. See ill.

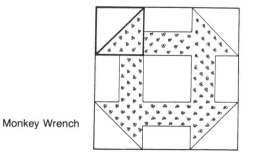

Monkey Wrench

monkey wrench. Woodworking. See **wrench.**

monk's belt. Weaving. A variety of geometric pattern weaves that belong to the **overshot** weave constructions. This is the simplest version of overshot and the patterns are mainly blocklike, without the flowing intricacy of the true overshot. As in overshot, there are three elements in the construction: a pattern **filling** thread that forms the design through **floats**; a background filling thread; and the **warp.** The **drawing-in draft** likewise conforms to overshot in that every pattern **harness** is followed by one threaded to weave **plain weave.** However, in monk's belt the patterns are held to two blocks. One block would always have harnesses 1−2 threaded and the other harnesses 3−4. This is known as threading on **opposites.** The 1−2 and 3−4 combinations may be in even or uneven units and the **treadling** square or elongated. The block effect without the pattern floats may be gotten with other nonovershot types of threadings.

Monk's belt is an ancient pattern and it is suggested that it originated in Scandinavia because it is so popular there. It is also found in old textiles in Italy, Germany, and the United States. It has a variety of uses—border trim on peasant-type aprons or skirts, curtains, coverlets, towels, and table linens (one of its commonest uses). It can also pattern the entire fabric and be used for pillows, bags, or garments. See ill.

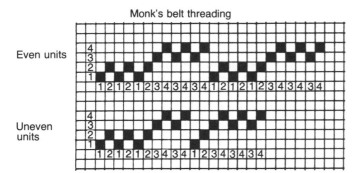

Monk's belt threading

Even units

Uneven units

monk's cloth. Rugmaking. A cloth used as a **rug backing** in hooked or **embroidered rugs.** It is woven of soft durable cotton, usually in a 4−4 **basket weave,** although a smaller, tighter basket weave can also be used, such as a 2−2 basket weave. Monk's cloth is a heavy, pliable fabric in which the yarns tend to slide around, making working on it somewhat difficult. It can be obtained in a maximum width of 184", so that piecing a rug would probably be unnecessary.

monk's cloth. Stitchery. A heavy, loosely woven **cotton fabric,** in **basket weave.** It is sometimes used as **background** material for **banners** and large hangings.

mono canvas. Needlepoint. See **canvas, petit point.**

monochromatic. Compositions or designs executed in only one hue, with variants of **value** and **saturation.** Also see **monochromatic color triangle.**

monochromatic color triangle. An ordered array of colors related to one **hue** and including **tints, shades,** and grayed variants of that hue. A simple, effective way to display these colors was devised by Wilhelm Ostwald around 1920. In his scheme, the pure hue **pa** is at the apex of the triangle. An example of a **pa** color is ultramarine blue straight from a tube of artist's color, or perhaps a phthalocyanine blue fabric dye straight from the bottle.

The vertical row **O** (a,c,e,g,i,l,n,p) represents the **gray scale,** where **a** is white, **p** is black, and **c** through **n** represent increasingly darker shades of gray. (Ostwald used every other letter of the alphabet in setting up the basic matrix, so that intermediate colors could be included if necessary; for simplicity's sake, only the alternate letters are used here.) The oblique row pa,na,la,ia,ga,ea,ca,a, is called the light clear series because it includes the tints of the purest hue with increasing amounts of white until the limit, **a,** is reached. Other rows parallel to this row have increasing amounts of black in the mixture or colors.

The series pa,pc,pe,pg,pi,pl,pn,p is called the dark color series; it is composed of shades ranging from **pa,** the pure hue, to **p,** pure black, in regular steps. All of the other colors in the triangle are grayed colors, the ones having the largest proportion of pure pigment being nc, ne, lc. **Saturation** is reduced as colors approach the gray-scale row, **O.** The array in each vertical row (numbered 0,2,4,6,8,10,12,14) is a group of colors called a **shadow series** that tend to be very harmonious when used together. All colors taken from the color triangle will be fairly harmonious with each other, but the most harmonious combinations will be formed by colors located at regular intervals to each other, and especially drawn from a single shadow series, or from a single row parallel to the light clear series or the dark clear series. See ill.

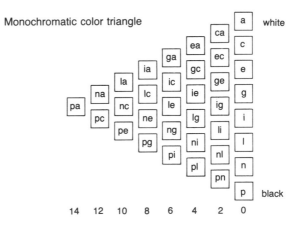

Monochromatic color triangle

monoclinic. Gemcutting. See **crystal.**

monocut. Papercrafts. See **symmetrical cutting.**

monofilament. Spinning. Weaving. See **filament.**

monofilament. Stitchery. A **man-made fiber** or thread formed in one long continuous strand, usually of **nylon.** A **nylon leader** or fishing line is a commonly available monofilament. It is extremely strong, although, as with any other nylon product, it may lose its strength through exposure.

monoprint. Block Printing. (Also called monotype.) A simple printing technique in which **block printing ink** is applied with a brush in the desired design to a sheet of glass and the paper is pressed down on it and then removed to produce a single printed impression. The ink on the glass must be reapplied for each print—hence the name.

Poster or tempera paint may be used, but the work must be done quickly before the paint dries. The ink must not be applied too thinly, or the print will be dull. If the ink is applied too heavily, the print will have thick blotches.

There are many variations to the monoprint technique. Ink can be rolled on the glass sheet with a brayer, then a line drawing done on the inked surface with a stick or a brush handle. After the paper is printed, these lines will appear as white lines, or the color of the paper. For larger areas, torn or cut pieces of paper can be placed on the inked surface before printing, creating identical shapes the color of the paper.

Another monotype method is to ink the glass sheet with block printing ink, then placing paper over it; the ink will make the paper stick. A drawing can then be made with a pencil or a ballpoint pen. The pressure from the pencil or pen picks up ink from the glass on the back side of the paper. This is sometimes called a "print-through" process. Areas of gray can be made by rubbing gently with the finger, which makes the paper take ink and print on the other side, the print side. When the paper is peeled off the glass, the even, harsh lines on the back side (the drawing side) are printed through on the right side with interestingly textured, soft lines.

Individual experimentation can be done for further monoprint variations. Multicolored prints can be made by applying each color to a separate sheet of glass and printing them one on top of another for a final print, taking care that the **registration** is exact.

monotype. Block Printing. See **monoprint.**

monster. Toys. See **bull-roarer.**

montage. A construction or assemblage of materials or elements, borrowed from several sources, such that the visual impression of the whole construction has a balance or order in spite of the disparity of the parts. Also see **collage.**

montage. Découpage. Papercrafts. (Also called photocollage, photomontage.) A term from the French word *monter*, to mount, for an arrangement of photographs pasted to a flat surface. Today the term is used more loosely to describe a composition in which various materials are pasted to the surface.

Montanari. Toys. A family of dollmakers and wax **model**ers in nineteenth-century England. They were famous for the lifelike modeling of **wax doll head**s, among the most highly prized objects of collectors. Also see **dollmaking.**

Montenegrin cross stitch. Needlepoint. (Also called two-sided Montenegrin stitch.) Although this variation of a cross stitch can be worked over two mesh, it is much more effective worked over four. It is good for background and area filling.

Working from left to right, come up at A, count 4 mesh up and 8 mesh over to the right, and go in at B. Come up at C, 4 mesh to the right of A and parallel to it (**a.**).

Go in at D, 4 mesh directly above A and come up at C again in exactly the same hole made by the previous stitch (**b.**).

Go in at E, 4 mesh immediately above C, and come up once again at C in the same hole (**c.**). Repeat to make a row of stitching as shown (**d.**). See ill. Also see **filling stitch, long-arm cross stitch.**

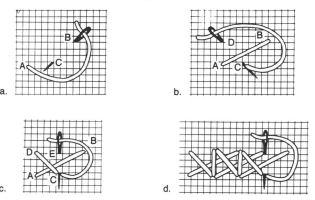

Montenegrin cross stitch

Montessori, Maria. Toys. See **Toys.**

moonknife. Leather. (Also called round-head knife.) A knife with a semicircular blade used for trimming heavy leather and cutting around small corners. To use, lay the leather on a flat surface and push the knife ahead of you, cutting carefully with a rocking, back-and-forth motion of the blade. See ill. Also see **Leather: Cutting and Edging Leather, Tools and Materials.**

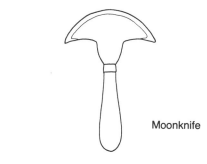

Moonknife

moonstone. Gemcutting. See **feldspar.**

moon winder. Toys. See **buzz button.**

mop. Ceramics. A large, soft, round brush without a point that does not leave brush marks, used for applying **glaze.**

mop. Jewelry. (Also called wig.) **Iron binding wire**s loosely twisted into any form, used to hold small pieces in place during **soldering.** They can be made by twisting the wire over a **heating frame;** they are also available commercially.

mop. Shell Carving. See **nacre.**

mop. Stained Glass. A soft-haired wash brush that can hold large quantities of pigment. It is used for applying washes in **painting on glass.**

mordant. Batik and Tie-dye. Dyeing. Fabric Printing. A substance used in conjunction with **natural dye**s that, through a chemical action, binds the color permanently to the fiber. The color is changed according to the mordant used, so that in many instances several colors or shades of color can be obtained from one **dyestuff.** The word "mordant" comes from the French "to bite," and this is what actually happens to the fiber. The mordant "bites" into it so that when it is dyed the color becomes one with it and it becomes colorfast. Most mordants are metallic salts. These include **alum, chrome, copperas,** or iron and **tin.** Widely used also are **acetic acid** and tannic acid or **tannin.** The metallic salts have an affinity for animal fibers; and wool and silk, in turn, have the property of holding chemicals. With these two fibers, there are seldom problems in having the dyestuff combine with the mordant that already has coated the woolen or silk fibers. Vegetable fibers, however, do not absorb metallic salts readily, and are used with tannic acid, which acts as a mordant or as an agent for fixing another mordant to the fiber. It is not uncommon to use mordants together; for example, cream of tartar (potassium bitartrate), itself a mordant, is frequently used with other mordants to keep colors bright and clear. A few natural dyestuffs may be used directly, but the majority require **mordanting.**

A mordant is not used for batik, but is sometimes used for tie-dye for greater fastness. The tying is completed before the fabric is submerged in the mordant solution. The mordant should not be washed out of the fabric; it should be dyed immediately, while still wet. When the mordant solution dries, it becomes powdery, and may be brushed off. Also see **mordant formula, wetting out.**

mordant. Candlemaking. The chemical solution used in **mordanting,** or pickling, braided bleached cotton to make **wick**ing. (A simple mordant can be made by diluting 2 tablespoons of salt and 4 tablespoons of Borax in 4 cups of water.) The wick should be allowed to soak in this solution for a minimum of 12 hours.

Commercial mordants are much more complex, consisting of ammonium phosphate, ammonium sulfate, ammonium chloride, boric acid, borax, and potassium nitrate. Wicks purchased from hobby shops or candle-supply stores have in almost all cases been treated with a mordant.

mordant. Découpage. See **gold size.**

mordant. Jewelry. An **etching** solution.

mordant chrome dye. Batik and Tie-dye. See **mordant dye.**

mordant dye. Batik and Tie-dye. (Also called mordant chrome dye.) A class of **dye**s, some natural and many synthetic, that have no affinity to fibers but that do have an affinity to metallic salts. The salts may be combined with the dyes or they may be used to treat the **fabric** either before or after **dyeing.**

Mordant dye is sometimes called chrome dye when chromium is used as the **mordant** to **fix** the dye. Chromium and copper are the common mordants for protein and acrylic fibers, respectively.

Other metallic salts, such as iron, aluminum, or tin, may be used in place of chromium. These colors are not **colorfast** to washing on cotton, but are so on nylon. Also see **Batik and Tie-dye: Dyes.**

mordant dye. Dyeing. See **adjective dye.**

mordant dye printing. Fabric Printing. Any printing technique in which a **mordant** is used to set a **dye** in a **fabric.** In **dyed style,** the design or pattern is applied using a thickened mordant before the fabric is dyed. The dye then "takes" only where it can combine with the mordanted design; the rest of the dye washes out. The opposite technique involves dipping the entire fabric in a mordant solution, then applying the design or pattern with the dye. Again, the dye takes permanently only where the dye and mordant combine. Modern techniques combine the dye and mordant in a **dye paste** or **emulsion.** The color is made stable by exposing the fabric to **steaming** at the completion of the printing process. Also see **Fabric Printing: Printing Techniques.**

mordant formula. Batik and Tie-dye. The combination of materials used to make a solution into which fabric is dipped for **mordant**ing in **tie-dyeing.**

For cotton, linen, and viscose rayon use 4 oz. **alum,** ¼ oz. **washing soda** (sal soda), and 4 gal. water (add **Calgon**). Boil one hour and let stand overnight.

For silk use 1 oz. alum, 1 oz. cream of tartar, and 4 gal. soft, warm water. Let the fabric stand in solution overnight (do not boil).

For wool use 4 oz. alum, 1 oz. cream of tartar, and 4 gal. **soft water.** Slowly bring it to high simmer (never boil wool) and continue to simmer for one hour. Allow to cool slowly overnight.

mordant gilding. Découpage. (Also called oil gilding.) See **gilding, gold size.**

mordanting. Candlemaking. (Also called pickling.) The process in which a bleached cotton yarn is treated with a **mordant,** or pickling, solution. Mordanting causes the **wick** to bend as the **candle** burns, thereby creating a cuplike cavity at the base of the wick to hold the liquified wax for burning. Unmordanted wicks do not bend during burning; this causes carbon to form on the wick tip, resulting in incomplete combustion and **smoking.**

mordanting. Dyeing. The soaking of fleece, yarn, or fabric in a **mordant** before, during, or after dyeing. The mordanting controls and enriches the colors of **natural dyes** and makes them permanent. Mordanting was known in the Middle Kingdom of Egypt (2200–1500 B.C.), a fact verified by the finding of mordanted textiles in the tombs. Not only did the Egyptians use it as a means of obtaining **color-fastness,** but also they were well aware that changes in color using one **dyestuff** could be obtained by changing the mordant. The clearest and brightest colors usually come from mordanting the yarn before dyeing, so this has become the most popular method to follow. However, it is best to consult the **dye recipe** as to when to mordant and which mordant to use for a specific color.

General rules for mordanting are as follows. The fiber should be completely clean—wool thoroughly washed of its grease, and silk boiled or washed of its waxy gum. The fiber should be thoroughly wet before going into the mordant bath. Weigh the amount of fiber to be mordanted and weigh the mordant chemical carefully so that the results will be as exact as possible. The mordant should be introduced into the bath, dissolved, and stirred before the yarn is put in. Soft water should be used and replaced as it evaporates during mordanting so that the fiber is constantly submerged. Do not boil the fiber, but rather simmer it. Frequent stirring is important for even mordanting and dyeing as the dye will react according to where and how the mordant has taken. Keep the temperature constant and do not subject the fiber to sudden changes of temperature. At the end of mordanting it is best to allow the bath to cool slowly before rinsing (if necessary) in water of the same temperature.

Mordite. Candlemaking. See **caulking compound.**

morganite. Gemcutting. See **beryl.**

morion. Gemcutting. See **quartz.**

Morning Star. Quilts. A **pieced quilt** design that consists of **hexagon**s surrounded by six-pointed stars.

Moroccan leather. Leather. Goatskin that has been decorated with **tooling** in the same technique as **cordovan.**

morocco. Bookbinding. See **leather.**

morris dancer. Toys. A costumed dancer, popular from medieval times to the nineteenth century, who pranced in a wooden frame shaped like a horse's body. The effect of the costume was to make it appear that the dancer was astride a horse. The costumes were elaborate, giving details of the horse from nose to tail. Ribbons or strips of cloth hanging from the sides concealed the dancer's legs.

Morris, William (1834-1896). Fabric Printing. An English craftsman, designer, poet, and utopian socialist, known for his influence on Victorian taste. In a reaction against the dehumanization brought about by the Industrial Revolution, Morris stressed the importance of complete knowledge by the craftsman of materials and processes. His designs for fabric and wallpaper were based on natural forms.

morse ivory. Ivory and Bone Carving. See **walrus ivory.**

mortar. Ceramics. See **mortar and pestle.**

mortar. Mosaics. A mixture of **cement,** sand, water, and **hydrated lime**—the traditional, and, for many mosaicists, still the very best **bond** for **mosaic** material. Greek and Roman mosaics were all set in a mortar of pounded brick, **lime,** and water, and many of those works are still holding together. The development of a lighter-weight mortar at the start of the Christian era contributed in part to the magnificence of the Byzantine mosaics; the lighter mixture allowed craftsmen to get their works up off the floors and onto the walls at an obviously more spiritual level. For today's craftsperson, mortar has much to offer. It is relatively cheap, extremely tenacious, and, most important, it has the flexibility to accommodate height and angle variations and to allow for the shifting of pieces until the right setting is found. The only drawbacks of mortar are that it is a lot heavier than other bonds and that it takes time and some expertise to prepare and apply to the **backing.**

A cement or **concrete backing** must be thoroughly soaked with water before the mortar is applied, so that the backing will not absorb the water from the mixture. With a wood backing, a **metal mesh** should be attached to provide a better gripping surface for the mortar. Although the proportions of cement to sand to hydrated lime may vary from artist to artist, one typical mixture involves approximately (by volume) 4 parts cement, 4 parts sand, 1 part hydrated lime, and enough water to make the mixture plastic. The mortar should be thick enough to lump up on the trowel but moist enough to remain smooth or porridgelike. Any building supply outlet will be able to advise you on mixing techniques, proportions, and solutions to your problems should they arise. Applying the mortar is a matter of troweling it onto the backing or **buttering** it onto the back of an individual mosaic piece before placing it on the backing. One cautionary note: mortar, to hold, should be allowed to cure slowly. The completed mosaic must be splashed with water several times during the drying process to slow down the drying time and reduce the risk of cracking because of shrinkage. Whatever the problems, anyone interested in the traditions of mosaics must attempt at least one project using mortar as the bond. Also see **Mosaics: Tools and Materials, Setting the Material.**

mortar and pestle. Ceramics. Enameling. Stained Glass. A mortar is a thick-walled semicircular bowl and a pestle is a ball on a handle. Both are made from **bisque**d **porcelain** and used for grinding and crushing stains, paints, or **glaze** in small quantities. See ill. Also see **mill, painting on glass, staining.**

Mortar and pestle

mortise. Woodworking. A rectangular hole cut into a piece of wood. It is usually made to receive another piece of wood called a tenon for a **mortise-and-tenon joint.** Also see **joint** and **Woodworking: Jointing.**

mortise-and-tenon joint. Toys. This kind of mortise joint is sometimes used in **dollmaking** to make movable arms and legs.

mortise-and-tenon joint. Woodworking. See **joint** and **Woodworking: Jointing.**

mortise chisel. Woodworking. See **chisel.**

mosaic. Gemcutting. See **intarsia.**

mosaic. Mosaics. An overall design, pattern, or picture composed of a multitude of **tesserae** or small pieces of material such as **glass** or stone in a variety of shapes and colors permanently held in place with a **bond** such as **mortar** or **adhesive.**

mosaic. Papercrafts. See **paper mosaic.**

mosaic. Stained Glass. A process in which pieces of glass, stone, shells, and so forth are set into an opaque material such as **grout, epoxy resin, plaster of Paris,** or concrete. The distinguishing quality in mosaic is that the material surrounding the glass is opaque, adding an element of design to the finished piece, whereas in **lamination** the surrounding material is clear. The **scrap glass** from other projects can be used.

Using a **portable light box** place the **cartoon** under a piece of **plate glass** and coat the glass with clear epoxy resin. Then coat the bottom of each piece of stained glass or other material with epoxy resin and put it in place on the glass. Let it dry overnight. Then fill in the spaces between the glass pieces with the grout. If epoxy grout is used, remove the excess with epoxy solvent on a rag.

Another method uses transparent contact paper taped to a light box with the adhesive side up and the working drawing underneath the paper. Glass pieces are arranged on the paper and the spaces between are filled in with an epoxy called PC-7. After the epoxy has set up for about 8 hours, the excess epoxy should be removed with a rag dipped in water or denatured **alcohol.** After the epoxy dries, the contact paper can be peeled off. Also see **tesserae; Tiffany, Louis Comfort.**

mosaic amber. Amber Carving. See **pressed amber.**

mosaic bead. Beadwork. See **millefiori.**

mosaic hammer. Mosaics. See **hammer.**

mosaic quilt. Quilts. A **pieced one-patch quilt** in which the **patch**es are unusually small. These are occasionally used to "paint"—that is, to do mosaic pictures using the tiny patches as though they were Venetian tile.

When the **hexagon** is used as the one-patch, the quilt might be called either a mosaic or **hexagon quilt.** A certain arrangement, or **set,** of the hexagons makes it a **Grandmother's Flower Garden.**

If small squares are used as the one-patch, the quilt is called either a mosaic or a **postage-stamp quilt.**

MOSAICS

The history of mosaics glitters with a multitude of breathtaking works and brilliant craftspeople: Rome, Pompeii, the **Alexander Mosaic,** Byzantium, **Ravenna, Galla Placidia,** St. Mark's in Venice, **Gaudi,** La Iglesia de la **Sagrada Familia, Rodia,** and the Watts Towers.

Mosaics were considered an integral part of the art and architecture of the better homes and public buildings of the early Egyptian and Babylonian civilizations. Excavations in Mesopotamia have uncovered highly sophisticated examples that date back as far as the fourth millennium B.C. From the very beginning of Greek civilization through the decline of the Roman Empire, mosaics were the basic decorative floor covering. Greek mosaics, which began as simple patterns created with natural, uncut pebbles, gradually developed into highly refined compositions patterned after paintings of the time. The real beginnings of mosaics as we think of them now—made of pieces with hard, squared edges—date back to the fourth century B.C. and the first importing by the West's craftsmen of cut tesserae from the Middle East. The new, shaped **tessera** of **marble,** stone, and a few colors of manufactured **glass** opened up all kinds of opportunities for further refining the art. By the first century B.C., the new materials had allowed the craft to reach such levels of sophistication that artists were reproducing in stone the most elaborate mythological scenes with subtle nuances. The **Alexander Mosaic,** created in 90 B.C., is composed of approximately one million cut pieces of marble. Although this mosaic, like other creations of the late Roman era, suggests three dimensions and has intricate detail, the artists were slaves to the artwork they were copying and did little to advance the creative nature of the mosaic art form.

If the importing of tesserae can be considered the first great breakthrough for mosaics, the beginning of the manufacture of **smalti** on a broad scale in the fourth century A.D. must be considered the second. Although the number of colors and shades available at first was limited compared to the range available by the time of the late Byzantine Empire, the new material, with its colors and intensified brilliance, very quickly replaced marble and stone as the primary mosaic ingredient. At about this same time, gold tesserae began to be imported from Egypt. What an incredible time it must have been for mosaic workers! All at once the palettes of the mosaicist had expanded wonderfully, and the mosaic artists responded in kind with work of a quality unsurpassed to this day.

Constantine's shift of the capital of the Roman Empire to Byzantium in the fourth century A.D. hastened the decline of Rome and led to the creation of a magnificent civilization centered in the eastern capital, which was renamed Constantinople. When Honorius, with his sister **Galla Placidia,** established **Ravenna** as their capital in the sixth century A.D. they set in motion a creative spirit that resulted in the awesome culmination of Byzantine art under the reign of the Emperor Justinian. The churches of Ravenna, along with the eleventh-century St. Mark's in Venice, are unexcelled examples of Byzantine art—especially in mosaics, its primary art medium.

The mosaics of the Byzantine Empire evolved as an intermingling of early Christian symbolism, Western classicism, and the creative influence of Greek Oriental art, with all its mystical grandeur, richness of color, and decorativeness. The Byzantine mosaicists, primarily of Greek origin, reached their creative zenith in the mosaics of the fifth and sixth centuries. Their method of working involved scratching or painting a design on an existing wall or ceiling that had been freshly coated with a thin layer of plaster. The design was then covered, a small area at a time, with a layer of the relatively new lightweight **mortar** made of local cement, lime, and mortar dust. The tesserae were then pressed into the mortar in an arrangement preplanned to best reflect light. No **grout** was applied to the finished mosaic. The output of those Greek artists working in Ravenna and later in Venice remains the ultimate example of the splendor of the craft.

By the end of the thirteenth century, however, the glory of Byzantium was gone. With it went the artists who had created the great mosaics. The technical knowledge lingered, but the inspiration was gone; production shifted from Greek to Italian hands. Works shifted from a reliance primarily on the strengths of the mosaic materials themselves to a concern for exactitude in copying the paintings of the time. The decline in creativity also saw a change in working techniques. Greek, Roman, and Byzantine mosaics had all been created using a **direct method,** in which the tesserae were set in mortar at the location site. With the commercialization of the craft during the Italian Renaissance, a simpler, **indirect method** was developed. The mosaics were created in reverse in the studio on temporary paper backings and then taken to the final site for installation. It was quicker, it was easier, and it made more money. But the creative surge was over. By and large, no major works of mosaics, in which the technique and material determined the form, were produced between the decline of Byzantium and the rise in the late nineteenth century of **Art Nouveau.** Not until the works of **Antonio Gaudi** and his followers did mosaics regain even a touch of the brilliance it had once known. Today, thanks in part to artists like Gaudi and **Simon Rodia** and his Watts Towers, mosaics is enjoying an exciting, albeit limited, renaissance.

The beginning mosaicist would do well to study the works of the Byzantine artists as well as the more recent works of Gaudi and Rodia. Each example reveals an intense interest on the part of the creator in the strength of the mosaic material and in the technique itself.

TOOLS AND MATERIALS Creating a mosaic involves selecting the type of **tile, tessera,** or material to be used, cutting it if necessary, and setting it with a **bond** on a suitable surface or **backing.** Therefore, the basic tools must include cutting equipment, a **trowel** or **spatula** for applying the **adhesive** or **mortar** to the backing, mosaic material or tesserae (preferably in a broad selection), a variety of agents to bond the material to the backing, and some kind of surface or backing material.

The kinds of material that can be included in a mosaic are almost limitless. The traditional tessera, still the finest material one can use in a mosaic, is **smalti.** However, for reasons of economy or personal design preference, a wide range of other materials, including **ceramic tile, found objects, porcelain tile, pressed glass,** and the very first mosaic materials, **pebbles** and cut **marble,** frequently find their way into contemporary mosaics.

There are several ways to cut mosaic material. Tesserae may be either fractured by placing a tessera upon a hard-edged, chisel-like **hardie** and dealt a sharp blow with a mosaicist's **hammer,** or clipped with tile **clippers.** A pair of square-jawed pliers is useful in holding and breaking off the tessera along the cut-line. Tweezers of some sort should be available to place small bits in place.

The kind of bond used depends on the design of the project and its ultimate location. Small, closely set works that will remain indoors can be adhered to a backing with a **glue, epoxy resin, mastic,** or ceramic-tile adhesive. For larger works, particularly ones that will be left outside, something more durable, such as a waterproof cement mortar, is more appropriate. It should be noted that mortar, unlike glue, offers considerably more flexibility for varying the height and angle of the individual mosaic pieces. In addition to the bond, the mosaicist should have available a supply of **grout** for filling in the crevices between the mortared tesserae.

The backing for a mosaic can be either an existing wall or a base specifically designed and constructed for the project. Backings can be made of a great many materials, including cement or concrete, plywood, masonite, plastic, metal plate, and even plate glass. With other than a **concrete backing** it is advisable to fasten a **metal mesh** to the surface to provide a better grip for the bond, particularly if the bond is mortar.

To this point, the tools and materials recommended could apply to the **direct method** or the **indirect method** of constructing a mosaic; using the latter method adds a couple of materials to the list. Constructing the mosaic in the studio requires some kind of heavy, durable **mounting paper,** and glue for fixing the material to the plan. Plain heavy-weight brown wrapping paper works as well as anything, and, although any water-soluble glue can be used, traditionally **gum arabic glue** is the preferred adhesive.

It should be emphasized that a studio can never have too many, or too wide a selection of, mosaic materials available. The real thrill and the creative pleasure of this craft comes from the manipulation of the materials in their infinite combination.

SETTING UP A WORKSHOP Mosaic work, because of the bulkiness of the materials and the messiness of the technique, requires a lot of space. Light and its reflection plays a large part in the effectiveness of the final mosaic. A diffused north light is ideal; stay away from direct sunlight. A system of overhead fluorescent tubes is the best substitute for natural north light. Two tables are almost mandatory: one large, sturdy one for working on the mosaic, and one neat one for sketching and planning. The **tesserae** and other materials should be stored by individual types and colors in either transparent containers or boxes with a sample of the contents glued to the outside. The **cement, mortar** ingredients, and **grout** should be kept in sturdy, leakproof covered containers. As with any workshop, a convenient space should be available for systematically storing tools not in use. A source of water in the room or very close by is a must. A wall on which to hang sketches and **cartoon**s to give a feeling as to how the piece will look when hung is extremely helpful. Finally, it's nice to have the workshop on the ground floor near an exit, because mosaics, and the materials, are heavy.

CREATING THE DESIGN　Whether the **direct method** or the **indirect method** is used for making the mosaic, all but the most experienced craftsperson should first prepare a rough sketch or **cartoon** of the work. The primary concern at this stage is to create a dynamic design that will make the most of the materials used and the unique characteristics of the mosaic itself, with all its crevices, gaps, and hard edges. Care should be taken in preparing the cartoon to avoid too exact a rendering. The completed sketch is a guide, not something to be slavishly copied. Some mosaicists sketch the cartoon with flat pastel sticks, using short, crisp strokes to simulate individual tessera, but such an approach, if carried to extremes, can inhibit creativity at both the design and the setting stages.

At the earliest sketching stages it must be kept in mind that **tessera** have sharply defined edges; soft, ill-defined pattern shadings should be avoided. Color contrasts should be used to heighten the tension in the design, as should contrast in the direction of the rows and the size of the areas of different materials. Variations in the kinds of materials used within a single mosaic, as well as sizes and heights or depths of the individual settings, must also be given some thought at the design stage. Familiarize yourself with the materials before you begin your plan. Look at your materials from all angles; think how they'd look cut down to smaller sizes or built up to a larger mass, set on edge rather than flat-side out, or shattered into pieces. Look for new materials, like a **found object** or a piece of cut **glass,** to work into your design.

Once the cartoon is completed a rough outline of it can be transferred to the **backing.** In the direct method, the design may be traced or sketched directly onto the backing. To simplify this step, trace the cartoon from the sketch sheet onto tracing paper, then rub soft graphite or crayon on the reverse side of the paper. Trace the design, drawing-side out, onto the backing with a hard pencil or dry ballpoint pen. The transferred design may then be highlighted or touched up with a soft pencil or felt-tip pen. With the indirect method, because the mosaic material is pasted on upside-down, a mirror image of the cartoon must be transferred to the mounting paper unless direction is of no consequence in the final work. Again use tracing paper, but this time the reverse side of the tracing paper should serve as the pattern, and the drawn-on side should be covered with graphite.

SELECTING THE MATERIAL　The variety of materials available to the mosaicist includes practically everything that can be fastened to a **backing** or surface, from alphabet noodles to zircon gems. **Smalti** is still the nonpareil material for the formal type of mosaic, but cost and a greater tendency among modern artists to explore new areas have introduced many exciting materials to the craft. The **found object** itself is now an everyday item in mosaics, shown by the wonderful Watts Towers of **Rodia** in southern California. Along more traditional lines, substitutes for smalti such as **ceramic tile** and **floor tile** are now used skillfully by many artists. The oldest materials of all, the **pebble** and cut stone and **marble** fragments, are enjoying a brilliant renaissance of their own. What is important is that, whatever the material you use, it must be used dynamically. Try to use traditional materials such as smalti, marble, and stone in new ways. You will also have to know the advantages of the various **mortar**s, **epoxy resin**s, and glues, and the reasons for using the **direct method** over the **indirect method** or vice versa.

CUTTING THE MATERIAL　Mosaics would be a much simpler craft if mosaicists could be satisfied with the shapes of materials as they buy them or find them. Cutting glass **tessera** is tough work, and cutting **marble** or stone is even tougher. But if your creative urge demands that you must make smaller pieces out of big ones, consider the possible ways of accomplishing this. Commercial **tile** such as **ceramic tile** or **floor tile** can be rather easily reduced into fragments by giving it a good rap with a hammer. There is very little control with this technique, but one does get a fine mass of smaller chunks or shards with which to work. Random pieces can work very effectively within a mosaic design, and often a pedestrian commercial tile is turned into an exciting selection of material.

But there are situations in which a more formal cut is required; a square tessera must be cut diagonally to form two much-needed triangles, or cut down the center to produce two rectangles, or cut twice to form four smaller squares. The traditional technique calls for placing the tessera on a secured chisel-like **hardie** and then hitting it a sharp but well-placed blow with a mosaic **hammer.** It is a most accurate technique, but difficult to master. A simpler technique involves cutting the tessera with specially designed tile **clippers.** The tile or tessera is held by the fingers and the cutting blades of the clippers are placed over the edge of the tessera on a line with the angle of cut desired. Sure, quick pressure is applied and the tessera or tile should fracture as desired. Considerable waste should be expected at first. For beginners, a 50% success rate is about average, but it gets better. Save the rejects; they can always be worked into another, more spontaneous composition. Marble and stone can be cut with a hammer and hardie or hammer and chisel, but it can be very difficult and slow. If possible, it's really best to use these hard materials in the size and shape in which you find them so as not to become discouraged by the cutting before you even set your tile.

SETTING THE MATERIAL　Mosaic material may be set by either the **direct method** or the **indirect method.** The direct method, as the term implies, involves setting the material directly onto a surface or **backing** coated with a suitable **bond.** The indirect method calls for setting the material reverse-side out on a **mounting paper,** which is then transported to the location and embedded right-side out on a bond-coated surface. The bond for either method can be an adhesive, **epoxy resin**, glue, or **cement**-based **mortar.** With mortar, crevices must be left between the individual pieces to allow the mortar to surround the material, thereby ensuring a better bond. Any **concrete backing** must be thoroughly soaked with water before the mortar is applied, to keep the concrete from drawing off the water in the bond.

The mechanics of the direct method necessitate that the bond be applied to an area of the backing large enough to be a self-contained design unit when completed but small enough to be worked without haste before the bond itself can harden. The proficiency of the mosaicist, coupled with the difficulty of the work and the drying rate of the bond, will dictate just how big an area should be covered. A **trowel, spatula,** or **palette knife** can be used to spread the adhesive or mortar evenly. As a rule of thumb, the layer of mortar should be about half the thickness of the material. Wood stripping tacked around the edge of the backing should keep the bond from overflowing. If a **metal mesh** has been fastened to the backing, the mortar should be carefully worked in and around the wire grid with a tool. The depth of the material to be set will determine how thick the bond should be laid on; particularly thick materials make a mortar bond almost mandatory.

When the bond has been spread on, you should be ready to lay your material. With adhesives or glue the individual pieces can be butted together with no gaps; with mortar, each piece should be firmly embedded, with a small crevice or gap on each side. The material should be set one piece at a time, one row at a time, beginning with the bold contour lines that dominate the design. The remaining areas within the contour lines can be completed after the flow of the design has been established. It is at this stage that the final dynamic flow of the work is determined. Movement is primary in any design. The excitement that you created at the **cartoon** stage must be carried through in the setting. Consult the sketches frequently. If they had flow—and they should have—the work should show it now. If your backing is the permanent site for the piece, play with the light reflections. If you are working horizontally on a backing that is to be moved to a site, continually set the piece in a vertical position as it dries, to be sure the angles of your settings work in the upright position. Work to vary the angle and the elevations of your individual pieces. For work with a great deal of detail, consider **buttering** the individual pieces with the bond one at a time, as you would butter a cracker, rather than coating an entire area of the backing. This method allows you to work at the pace you like without worrying about your bond's drying up on the backing prematurely. Buttering is an excellent technique, but don't become so attached to an area of detail at the cost of losing sight of the overall composition.

The **indirect method** involves some slightly different mechanics. Because the mosaic is first constructed upside-down on mounting paper, the design must be reversed unless the directional flow of the finished work is irrelevant. For the traditionalist, the best temporary adhesive is a **gum arabic glue,** but any strong water-soluble glue (even a simple flour-and-water paste) will suffice to hold the bits in place until the mosaic can be set in its permanent bond. The glue can be brushed on to the paper in a light coat or buttered on the pieces.

With both the direct and the indirect methods, large-scale mosaics can be broken down for easier handling. With the indirect method, where the completed temporary mosaic must be lifted into place and maneuvered until it is set in the permanent bond, the weight factor makes the sectional breakdown almost mandatory. These sections, cut from the mounting paper, can be equal squares or puzzlelike sections cut along the contour lines of the pattern or cartoon. The few individual bits that would fall directly over the sectional dividing lines can be filled in after the segments have been set in the permanent bond.

The only mosaic considerations not necessary in the indirect approach are light reflection and variations in elevation and setting depths. The indirect method naturally produces a relatively flat final surface. One major advantage of the indirect method, besides being able to work out the entire composition within the convenient confines of the studio, is that mistakes are much easier to correct with a temporary adhesive than with a permanent bond. All kinds of adjustments can be made before the glue dries. As one final check before setting the mosaic on the backing, all the sections should be assembled in puzzle fashion to be sure the lines and colors match up. If everything looks good at that point, preparations can be made for bonding the mosaic to the permanent backing. The type of backing and bond to be used will have something to do with the complexity of the steps involved, but basically the procedures are pretty much the same. Once the mortar has been troweled onto the backing, a thin scratch line can be incised along the bottom edge of the planned space to help position the bottom sections. A thin layer of mortar should also be spread on and worked into the crevices of the mosaic on the mounting paper. Each section, one at a time, beginning with the lower left section, can then be carefully placed in position paper-side out. Once placed, it should be firmly but gently tamped into place with a hammer and flat board. Proceed with the placement laterally along the bottom scratch line.

The mounting paper should be removed when the mortar underneath is firm enough to hold, but not completely hardened, so adjustments may be made after the paper has been removed. This partial hardening usually takes a few hours. Because mortar tends to shrink and possibly crack during drying, the mosaic should be splashed frequently with water to allow slow curing. To remove the paper, thoroughly soak it with warm water with a saturated sponge, and then peel it away. Peeling from the top down seems to work best. With the paper removed, pick away any surface bits of mortar, and make any necessary adjustments to the mosaic itself. Some residue from the temporary glue will remain on the surface of the mosaic. This can be cleaned away when the mortar is completely hardened. After all the final corrections have been made, the final surface of the mosaic should again be tamped with a hammer and flat board. Any deep crevices can be hand filled with the mortar mix. The complete mosaic should be allowed to set for at least a full day before cleaning. This decision as to whether or not to grout the piece should be made at this time. If the piece is to be exposed to the elements, grouting material between the crevices will prevent water damage.

The procedure for using the indirect method with an adhesive such as epoxy resin, and with other kinds of backings such as wood, is basically the same as for concrete and mortar, although considerably less complicated. Both the backing and the mosaic should be coated with the adhesive, and the paper removed when the bond reaches a state of semihardness. As with the direct method, if a wood backing is used in combination with a mortar bond, **metal mesh** should be attached to ensure a better gripping surface. For a full understanding of the mosaics craft, both the direct and the indirect methods should be explored, using a variety of backings and bonds. Both techniques have their advantages and disadvantages. There is no one best approach to the art.

CLEANING THE MOSAIC   Mosaics construction with **mortar** is a messy business. The completed surface is almost always encrusted with dried oozings of the **bond**. To clean the debris away, the surface should first be carefully scrubbed with a stiff wire brush. If the final surface is not flat enough to scrub, it should be picked at with something like an ice pick to dislodge the excess surface mortar. Once the big pieces have been brushed or chipped away, the surface can be washed with a full-strength solution of **hydrochloric acid**. An old brush or a rag on a stick is a good tool for this kind of work. Hydrochloric acid is extremely strong and must be handled very carefully. Thick gloves, preferably rubber, and protective clothing must be worn. Allow the acid to sit for a few minutes on the surface; then rinse it away with a mixture of baking soda and water. A final rinse of clear water should bring out the beauty of the completed mosaic. If necessary, the dried surface can be buffed with crumpled newspapers or old rags.

mosaic stitch. Needlepoint. The mosaic stitch worked horizontally consists of three small diagonal stitches, one short, one long, one short, forming a square unit. It has a firm backing and resembles small mosaic tiles when worked up. It is very effective when worked in geometric patterns with various colored yarns. It is worked in the manner of a **flat stitch** except there are only three diagonal stitches instead of five. Also see **mosaic stitch diagonally.**

mosaic stitch diagonally. Needlepoint. (Also called Florentine stitch.) When the **mosaic stitch** is worked

Mosaic stitch diagonally

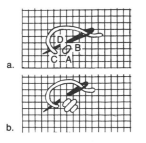

a.

b.

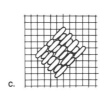

c.

diagonally it is abbreviated by eliminating one short stitch. See ill.

mosaic tile. Plastics. See **fusible thermoplastic.**

mosaic work. Leather. See **appliqué.**

Mossoul stitch. Crewel. Embroidery. See **herringbone stitch.**

moss stitch. Knitting. (Also called seed stitch.) The smallest of checked patterns. It is based on an uneven number of stitches. * K 1, P 1 * across row, end K 1. Repeat every row to desired length. Also see **Knitting: Construction.**

mother-of-all. Spinning. The horizontal wooden bar that supports the **spinning** apparatus in **spinning wheels.** It supports the vertical pieces called **maidens** that in turn support either the **spindle** or **spindle shaft.** Also see **treadle wheel, wool wheel.**

mother-of-pearl. Beadwork. Découpage. A hard, nacreous layer of certain mollusk shells, used as added embellishment in découpage. It is available from craft supply stores in small leaves or 2″ × 5″ sheets, or in tiny flakes.

The hard sheets must be soaked in white vinegar until they are soft enough to cut. Rinse off the vinegar with water. Dry the sheet with tissue and cut out desired shapes with small curved **scissors.** Mother-of-pearl may be **glue**d with **white glue** to any surface that has been prepared for découpage. The coloring of the surface will slightly change the tone of the shell. If desired, the shell pieces can be glued over identically shaped pieces of foil glued to the surface for added luster. When gluing slightly curved pieces, place them curve-down on the surface and press them flat. Continue pressing the piece down until it is firmly glued. Remove excess glue with a damp sponge. After it has dried, the mother-of-pearl will seem dull, but after the découpage design is completed and the **sealer** coat applied it will resume its luster.

mother-of-pearl. Jewelry. The nacreous layer of the inner shell of certain mollusks, obtainable in a range of colors from iridescent blue, green, gray, purple, and yellow. It can be used as an **inlay** material.

mother-of-pearl. Shell Carving. See **nacre.**

moth repellent. Quilts. Stitchery. **Fabric**s treated with colorless chemicals similar to dyestuffs to make them impervious to moth damage. The chemicals are sometimes added to a dyebath and sometimes sprayed on. When part- or all-**wool** fabrics are used in **quilt**s or stitcheries for public installation, a moth repellent product is insurance against damage by the larvae that eat wool **fibers.**

motif. A distinctive feature or figure of design that is repeated or developed in a work of any kind.

motif crochet. Crochet. A complete piece of crochet done in one particular shape and design (a star, a snowflake, a circle, a square, etc.). A series of these motifs can be joined together to form a finished crochet piece, such as an afghan or vest. Also see **joining, medallion** and **Crochet: Patterns.**

motions. Puppets. The seventeenth-century name for **puppet plays,** used by both Cervantes and Ben Jonson. Also see **Puppets.**

motion toy. Toys. See **moving toy.**

mottling. Candlemaking. The technique used in candlemaking to provide a marblelike surface on the molded candle. This surface quality can be achieved by adding **mottling oil** or salad oil to the **wax** prior to the pouring process. One suggested ratio calls for 3 tablespoons of oil to 1 tablespoon of **stearic acid** for every pound of candle wax. Candles should be allowed to cool at room temperature, with no water bath. Mottling can also happen unwittingly when the oil used to coat the mold is used in excess when preparing the mold. Also see **Candlemaking: Preparing the Mold.**

mottling. Dyeing. See **spot dyeing.**

mottling. Weaving. A **tapestry** technique in which several threads of widely differing colors or shades of one color were mixed or wound on the same **bobbin** or **shuttle.** Among many color or texture effects that were possible, mottling enabled a color to be shaded from dark to light by successive combinations on bobbins, always eliminating some of the darks and adding more lights. Today, with the use of heavier yarns in tapestry, mottling is done with single strands of yarn and the mixing or shading is done by alternating the colors in successive sheds rather than the combinations on the bobbins.

mottling oil. Candlemaking. An additive, such as mineral or vegetable oil, mixed with the wax to create a mottled effect on the candle surface. Also see **mottling.**

moulinet. Toys. A **momentum toy** known to have existed since at least the fifteenth century. It consists of a round rod or **dowel** with flat or twisted crosspieces at one end (propellerlike) and a hollow ball at the center. The rod

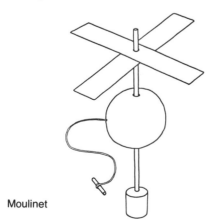

Moulinet

goes through the ball. The toy is operated by winding a **string** around the rod inside the ball, with the string emerging through a hole at one side made for that purpose. The string is pulled to set the rod twirling in a vertical position. The hand operates the toy at the end of the string in much the same way that the **yo-yo** is kept in motion. See ill. Also see **alouette.**

Mound Builders. Quilts. See **Swastika.**

mount. Bookbinding. The material to which maps, plates, or anything is affixed or mounted.

mount. Stitchery. To frame or finish a **panel** by stretching it over a rigid background. Some **fabrics** are mounted over plywood in such a way that the material can be drawn around the edges to the back and **stapled** or tacked in place. Illustration board, **Masonite,** or **Celotex** are sometimes used but they are difficult to frame. The plywood has a thickness to which a strip of wood framing can be nailed. Also see **Stitchery: Finishing.**

mountain bolo. Toys. A skill toy consisting of two small **balls** attached to the ends of a **string.** The string has a loop tied just off-center to serve as a handle. If it is tied exactly in the center the balls will strike one another, so the difference in length must be at least the same as the diameter of the ball. The point of play with this toy is to get the balls to orbit or swing in circles opposite to one another. When an up-and-down movement of the hand is used this can be accomplished, making the balls move vertically or at right angles to the ground. Sometimes buckeye nuts or large wooden beads are used for the balls. The Eskimos used sealskin balls filled with sand in a version of the mountain bolo called the Eskimo yo-yo.

Care must be used in handling this toy because it is possible to injure oneself while manipulating it. Recent mountain bolos have been made from plastic with hard plastic balls. Their use has been outlawed in some areas because of injuries to children playing with them. See ill.

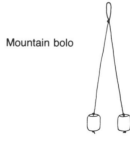

Mountain bolo

Mountain Lily. Quilts. See **Lily.**

mountain oak. Woodworking. See **oak.**

mountain top. Toys. See **spindle top.**

mounted plate. Bookbinding. A plate that is affixed to a sheet of paper or other material.

mounted tweezers. Jewelry. See **third hand.**

mounting. Bookbinding. Affixing the entire surface of one material to another.

mounting. Crewel. Embroidery. Needlepoint. See **Crewel: Finishing, Needlepoint: Finishing.**

mounting. Macramé. The process of attaching macramé cords to a **mounting cord** or bar that is pinned to the work surface to form a **heading** on which the macramé knotting is begun. Also see **Mounting bar, Mounting Knot.**

mounting bar. Macramé. A mounting bar may be made of wood, metal, or plastic and is used in place of a **mounting cord.** It is the starting point of the macramé work. Small pieces of hardware or jewelry findings (i.e., curtain rings), wooden dowels, and curtain rods may also be used for mounting. Also see **mounting knot.**

mounting cord. Macramé. The particular **cord** to which all cords being knotted are attached at the beginning of the macramé work. The mounting cord is the starting point for the knotting. It is essential that this mounting cord be anchored taut to the work surface while the cords to be worked are being attached with **mounting knots.** Also see **mounting bar.**

mounting knot. Macramé. Knots that secure the **cord** to the **mounting bar** or **mounting cord;** they form the first row of knots. Two of the more frequently used mounting knots are the lark's head (the **double half hitch**) and the reverse lark's head (the **reverse double half hitch**). Use the reverse double half hitch as the mounting knot if a loop in

Mounting knot

a.   Lark's head (double half hitch)

b.   Square knots with picots, overhand knot with reversed lark's head (reverse double half hitch)

c.   Circular mounting with lark's head

the front of the work is not desired. Decorative mounting knots are formed by using the double chain knot, the picot knot, and the square knot with the lark's head (double half hitch). See ill.

mounting paper. Mosaics. Paper used as a temporary **backing** for materials mounted by the **indirect method.** Strong brown wrapping paper is frequently used for this purpose. Also see **Mosaics: Setting the Material.**

mountmellick stitch. Embroidery. Mountmellick is a surface stitch traditionally in **white work** only. It gets its name from the town in Ireland where it originated in the 1830s. It is a bold stitch with a raised effect, achieved by working heavy white cotton on a background such as satin or linen. The stitch is worked vertically, and looks best in heavy thread. See ill.

Mountmellick stitch

mouth. Ceramics. See **Ceramics: Form.**

mouth blowtorch. Enameling. See **torch.**

movable joint. Puppets. A connection that allows for movement. Various kinds of movable **joints** are used in the construction of the **marionette skeleton** to allow the figure to be articulated. Cord, leather, or **screw eyes** may be used in making the flexible joints. **Tongue-and-groove** and **hinge joints** allow for movement of limited direction. Also see **leather hinge, swivel point, and Puppets: Making the Marionette Skeleton.**

movable joint. Toys. Any **joint** that allows the connected parts to be placed in various positions. The **stitched joint** is one of the most simple for use on fabric. Others are **ball joints, string joints,** or **mortise-and-tenon joints.**

move number. Weaving. See **satin weave.**

moving toy. Toys. A general description for any **animated toy** or motion toy. It is not necessarily operated by key windup devices or mechanics, as automatic toys are. The **top** and the windmill both move, but the source of energy is supplied outside the toy itself. When **springs** or **rubber bands** are used, the **stored energy** moves the toy. Also see **Toys: Mechanical Toys and Moving Toys.**

Mrs. Cleveland's Choice. Quilts. (Also called Country Fair.) A **pieced-quilt block** design consisting of numerous small triangles of fabric joined to form a complex pattern. Over 60 pieces are used in each block design, and great care and sewing skill are required to sew this design perfectly. It was named for President Cleveland's wife. See ill. Also see **presidents' quilt.**

Mrs. Cleveland's Choice

Mrs. Ewer's Tulip. Quilts. See **Tulip.**

M's and O's. Weaving. A texture weave made up of alternate blocks of plain and **rib weave**s. Texture patterns may be developed with the blocks; equal-size ones would give a check effect, unequal ones a **plaid** effect. In most M's and O's, it is only two **treadle** combinations that alternate to weave the blocks. It is a reversible weave that can give a heavy or sheer fabric. Some uses are for upholstery, drapery, table linens, blankets, and scarves. M's and O's goes back to the pioneers in the Delaware River Valley having probably come from Finland and Sweden, where it has always been common. See ill. Also see **grouped thread, plain weave.**

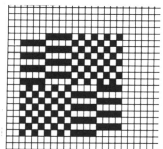

M's and O's weave draft

mucilage. Toys. A gelatinous material from plants used in the manufacture of certain **adhesive**s. These adhesives may be sold and labeled as mucilage and are used on paper and cardboard. It is not easy to remove from the hands and cannot be washed off.

muckle wheel. Spinning. The Scottish name for a **wool wheel.**

mud saw. Gemcutting. See **slabbing saw.**

muffle. Ceramics. An internal lining or box, made of **refractory** material, forming the **kiln** chamber that protects the **ware** from direct flames and hot gases. A sagger is a round-cornered container used in kilns lacking muffles. Glazed ware is placed inside a muffle or sagger to protect the **glaze** during **firing.**

mug. Ceramics. See **Ceramics: Form.**

mulefoot tool. Leather. A kind of **stamp.**

mule spinner. Spinning. See **Spinning.**

mull. Bookbinding. See **crash.**

muller. Stained Glass. A small hand mill made of glass or marble used to grind stains and paint to a very fine powder. It is used on a palette or slab of glass or marble. Also see **mortar and pestle, staining.**

mullion. Stained Glass. A vertical bar used to divide a window opening into smaller sections. Mullions can be made of steel, aluminum, or wood and are used in Gothic architecture to hold up the inner **tracery** of the window. In the studio, wooden bars are used as a simulation of real mullions.

multifaced doll. Toys. A **doll**, usually rag, with from two to four faces. In some the fabric could be folded to reveal a desired face while hiding the remaining faces. Those with two faces were changed by removing a bonnet from front to back. The **topsy-turvy doll** was two-headed; the doll was flipped upside down to reveal the second face. Some manufactured dolls had swivel heads so that the faces could be turned. The different faces usually offered different expressions, such as laughing and crying.

multifilament. Spinning. Weaving. See **filament.**

multiharness. Weaving. (Also called multiple harness.) A term designating **loom**s that have upward of four **harness**es, or weaves done on such looms, including satins, **block pattern**ed **double cloth, damask,** and certain twills. The pattern and weave combinations on a multiharness loom are limitless. It is possible for weavers to buy up to a 16-harness loom without special ordering. Above that number the loom usually does not have **treadle**s because it is very difficult to operate the raising of the **shed**s. There are **shedding device**s to open the sheds on the order of a **dobby loom** head, which is attached to the top of the loom. Also see **satin weave, twill weave.**

multiple band plaiting. Weaving. A type of **chevron plaiting** that involves dividing the **warp** yarns into more groups than two and then interlacing all the groups in the same manner as in chevron plaiting. After the initial interlacing of each yarn in each group to the neighboring group the **plaiting** proceeds across the entire width of the warp.

multiple dovetailing. Weaving. See **dovetailing.**

multiple harness. Weaving. See **multiharness.**

multiple-layer lamination. Stained Glass. See **lamination.**

mummy bead. Beadwork. See **Beadmaking.**

Muntz metal. Jewelry. See **brass.**

Muntz metal. Metalworking. See **welding rod.**

mural. Stitchery. A large **panel,** usually permanently installed, that is planned to relate architecturally to the area in which it is hung. **Stitchery murals** are often stretched over a **plywood** base for hanging. Also see **Stitchery: Stitchery Forms.**

Murano. Glasswork. The island off Venice where glassmaking flourished as early as the eleventh century. The guild system protected the secrets of the industry and maintained the prestige and social position of the glassmakers. Murano produced much of medieval Europe's finest glassware, although, in time, rococo ornamentation almost completely obscured the glass itself. Murano produced fine mirrors before the advent of modern **parallel glass** sheet manufacture, and continued to do so up until the nineteenth century. Through the long history of glassmaking there, many important improvements in technique and glass formulation were evolved. The development of adding manganese oxide to the **melt** to attain a hitherto unavailable clarity in glass was first introduced at Murano.

murex shellfish. Dyeing. See **natural dye.**

muriatic acid. Batik and Tie-dye. See **removing fabric finish.**

muriatic acid. Jewelry. Metalworking. A commercial grade of **hydrochloric acid,** a colorless corrosive used for **coloring, etching,** and **pickling bath**s, and as a **flux.** Also see **Metalworking: Finishing.**

muriatic acid. Mosaics. See **hydrochloric acid.**

Museum of Childhood. Toys. A museum in Edinburgh, Scotland, devoted to the historical objects of childhood. It was created by Patrick Murray and opened in 1955 as a city museum. The collection includes toys from all periods of history from over thirty countries.

mushroom. Stained Glass. A large mushroom-shaped stain of wet cement that develops between two pieces of glass when cementing. It is impossible to clean it out without taking the **glazing** apart. Also see **Stained Glass: Glazing.**

mushroom mold. Ceramics. See **hump mold.**

mushroom stake. Metalworking. See **anvil.**

musical automata. Toys. Automatic toys combined with musical sounds. While it was from Switzerland that mechanically produced musical accompaniment came, it was in Germany that it was developed to such a fantastic level. Musical **automatic toys** reached their peak in the last half of the eighteenth century. Performing toys accomplished incredible feats, using mechanical power and, later, **clockwork** systems. Among the earliest musical au-

tomata were the incredible singing birds and performing animals and orchestras.

musical jack-in-the-box. Toys. A mechanical **windup toy** in which a music box is set in motion by turning a handle on the side of the box. The music may be synchronized with the pop-up action of the **jack-in-the-box.** For example, if the tune being played is "Pop Goes the Weasel," the lid will be set to fly open, releasing the jack, on the final "Pop."

musical top. Toys. A **spring top** in which the spinning creates a series of whistling sounds. The pitch varies with the speed at which the **top** turns.

musical toy. Toys. Any of several kinds of toys in which musical sounds are produced. One group consists of basically **sound toys** such as the singing top or a bell toy. Sound toys are generally very simple.

A second group is made up of toy or real musical instruments. These are meant to be played to produce a musical note or notes. A **drum,** a bottle **whistle,** a toy mandolin, **pipes,** trumpets, cymbals, horns, and **kazoo**s fall into this category.

A third kind of musical toy has mechanically operated sound synchronized with the toy. **Musical automata** offer the best examples. **Musical jack-in-the-box**es are another, in which the winding mechanism operates both music and jack.

Music boxes, with the mechanically operating devices, were sometimes set into the bodies of **dolls** or toys.

muslin. Batik and Tie-dye. Bookbinding. Crewel. Embroidery. Lacemaking. Needlepoint. Quilts. Stitchery. A plain-weave cotton textile of Eastern origin, deriving its name from Mosul, or Moosul, a town in Turkey. India muslins were introduced into England about 1670. Muslin varies from fine and sheer to coarse. It comes in various widths and is usually **size**d and **bleach**ed. Muslin should always be washed before it is used unless it is specifically **preshrunk.**

Fine transparent muslin may be used as a background **fabric** in **white work** embroidery and for **tambour work** in lacemaking. In bookbinding it is used for reinforcing book joints and backs. Coarse muslin is used for making patterns or templates for upholstery in crewel or needlepoint. Because it is available in sheet widths muslin is often used as **backing** for **quilts** or as **filler** in lightweight **coverlets.**

mutascope. Toys. See **kinora.**

Mylar. Plastics. The brand name of a transparent, water-repellent plastic sheeting used in casting. It serves as an **air shield** and **mold release agent** for **polyester resin.** Also see **Plastics: Casting.**

Mylar. Stitchery. A thin plastic material available by the roll or by the sheet. Some semitransparent Mylar is clear and shiny on one side and textured on the other, and is used for doing drawings for reproduction because the textured side offers a good bite, which prevents the running of India ink.

Mylar is also available with a mirrored surface. It is flexible and extremely reflective and is used in **soft sculpture, banner**s, masks, and toys.

myriopticon. Toys. A small device very similar to the **historiscope**, a **panorama toy.** The original showed a pictorial history or panorama of the Civil War. Also see **Toys: Optical Toys.**

mystic paper. Plastics. An **adhesive**-backed paper used for **masking** plastics.

mystic tape. Stitchery. A thin **adhesive tape,** available in many colors, that is very convenient in **stitchery** projects. The adhesive is strong enough to be used permanently on **banner**s or **panel**s where the material will not be washed. It can also be used for decorative details on wood, in wood appliqué, and in toymaking. Although it can be peeled off or easily removed, it is permanent enough for many uses.

n

nacre. Shell Carving. (Also called mop, mother of pearl.) The iridescent interior layer of shell, yielded by many fresh and saltwater mollusks. Nacre is composed of calcite (aragonite) and calcium carbonate (lime), indexed at 3–4 on the Mohs' scale of hardness. On the inside of the shell, occurring only near the valves, is a layer of calcium carbonate. Nacre is covered on the outside by a crusty layer of **conchylin** that is most often removed before working the shell. The iridescence of the nacre is a result of light diffraction by the first few layers of aragonite.

Mop is obtainable in many shades. "White mop" is characteristic of Australia and Borneo, and amber colored mop, referred to as "gold lip," is harvested from beds near the equator (the finest "gold lip" comes from Manila, in the Philippines). Tahiti and the Cook Islands produce multicolored shells. The famous black or smoked pearl variety known as "black lip" originates in the Malay Peninsula.

Much of the nacre that is worked comes from the shell of the meleagrina, fished from tropical waters at depths of 6 to 40 fathoms. Its value is enhanced by the fact that it must be fished by hand and with considerable risk. Also see **abalone, blind, fretwork, grubby, nautilus, scratch carving** and **Shell Carving: Shell.**

nail. Woodworking. A straight, metal **mechanical fastener** used to hold two or more pieces of wood together; it is driven into the wood with a **hammer.** Nails come in a variety of types, sizes, metals (usually **iron** or **steel,** but also **copper** and **bronze**), and coatings (**bright, blue,** and **galvanized**).

Except for brads, the smallest nails, the sizes of which are designated by the **gauge** of wire used to make them, most nails are sized according to a penny system, abbreviated "d." In the fifteenth century, the system represented price—sixpenny (6d) nails cost sixpence per hundred—but now the system indicates length only, as follows:

2d—1″	9d—2¾″
3d—1¼″	10d—3″
4d—1½″	12d—3¼″
5d—1¾″	16d—3½″
6d—2″	20d—4″
7d—2¼″	40d—5″
8d—2½″	60d—6″

The largest nails are called spikes and are sized simply by inches.

There are dozens of shapes and types of nails for more or less specialized uses.

The common nail is the standard nail, with a medium-sized flat head and a relatively thick shank, available in most penny sizes (**a.**). A shingle nail is a short, very pointed common nail used for shingles and siding; it is galvanized to prevent rusting. The roofing nail, another short galvanized nail, with an extra-flat head, is used to hold down roofing paper and shingles; it comes in sizes 1–6d.

The box nail is similar to the common nail but thinner; it is used in building boxes and for other light construction (**b.**). Box nails, sometimes coated with resin for greater holding power, are available in sizes 3–20d. The double-headed nail, also similar to the common nail, has a second head about ¼″ below the first to permit easy removal in temporary work.

The finishing nail, the second most basic type of nail, is used for finishing work (**c.**). The head is only slightly larger than the shank and can easily be **set** below the surface of the wood (**molding**s), with a **nailset** or another nail. It is available in sizes 3d, 4d, 6d, 8d, and 10d. A brad is a small finishing nail, usually 1″ or shorter (**d.**). Thickness is indicated, as in wire, by gauge, with increasing numbers for progressively thinner brads; 8- and 9-gauge brads are common sizes. The scaffolding nail is a double-headed finishing nail for putting up scaffolds.

A casing nail is a large nail similar to the finishing nail but heavier, for heavier work (**e.**). It has a conical head and is available in sizes 4d, 6d, 8d, 10d, and 16d.

A wire nail is a short nail with a thick shank and a flat head. Wire nails are used to fasten heavy strips of wood, such as **lattice** or screen molding. They are graded like brads and are available in lengths up to 1¼″.

A screw nail is a steep-threaded nail with a small head, used for laying floors and for hardwood box construction. It is very strong and rigid and comes in most standard penny sizes.

The ring-shank nail has a large flat head and a horizontally grooved shank to increase its holding power in materials like **gypsum board** and in **softwood**s. Ring-shank nails are available in sizes 3d, 4d, and 6d.

Instead of being formed from a piece of wire as other nails are, the cut nail is cut from a sheet of hard steel, resulting in a rectangular cross-section (**f.**). Cut nails are very strong and are used for laying hardwood floors and securing wood to masonry. They are most commonly used in sizes 4d, 8d, and 10d. See ill. Also see **nailing** and **Woodworking: Nailing.**

a. Common nail   c. Finishing nail   e. Casing nail

b. Box nail   d. Brad   f. Cut nail

nailhead. Leather. (Also called spot.) Decorative metal studs available in many shapes and sizes with prongs which pierce the leather and bend flat in back after inserted. The slits for nailheads must be prepunched. Mark with a scratch **awl,** then pierce with a single-prong **thonging chisel;** after inserting, turn the leather over and press down the prong ends with the end of a screwdriver for a snug fit. If you are setting many nailheads, an adjustable **nailhead punch** is useful. Also see **chisel, ornamental spot, studding.**

nailhead punch. Leather. (Also called split punch, spot setter.) A **drive punch** with two prongs that can be adjusted to the distance between the prongs of the **nailhead**s to be set, to prepunch the holes for the nailhead prongs to be pushed through. See ill.

Nailhead punch

nailing. Jewelry. Carving a wood form and then nailing metal plates to its surface, completely covering the wood core. The nails themselves can have decorative ends. The metal should be drilled first to permit the nails to enter without bending it. This ancient technique is usually reserved for large works such as sculpture or household items and furniture, but can also be used in making jewelry.

nailing. Woodworking. The process of driving **nail**s or similar fasteners into wood or other material with a **hammer.**

Other than straight nailing, the two most common forms of nailing used in woodworking are clinching and toenailing.

Clinching is used to hold thin boards together without screws. Use nails about 1″ longer than the combined depth of the material being nailed. Drive the nails completely through, and hammer the nail points over until they are flush with the surface of the wood and aligned with the **wood** grain.

Toenailing is the process of driving in nails at an angle through the side of one board into the surface of another. This is often done when you can't nail straight in from the flat side of a piece of wood. It is often used when nailing wall **stud**s in place. Also see **Woodworking: Nailing.**

nailset. Woodworking. A small steel tool used to drive **finishing nails** below the surface of the wood—the equivalent of **countersinking** a **screw.** The nailset is a tapered rod about 4″ long with a slightly concave tip at the narrow end to hold the nailhead; the other end is tapped with a **hammer** to set the nail. Also see **Woodworking: Nailing.**

Nanduti. Lacemaking. See **Sol lace.**

nap. Quilts. Stitchery. Short **fiber**s on the surface of a **fabric** that have been **finish**ed by being brushed in one direction. **Velveteen, corduroy,** and similar materials have a nap. Viewed from one direction, looking down on the nap, the color appears lighter. When viewed against the nap, the color appears to be more intense. Care must be taken in using **napped fabric** to be sure that the nap is always used in the same direction if a consistent color is desired. In some **appliqué** projects, the change in nap offers another possibility for color variation.

Nap results from a brushing or **napping** process applied by the manufacturer. A similar soft surface called **pile** results from a process of weaving construction.

nap. Weaving. See **napping.**

naphthol dye. Batik and Tie-dye. (Also called azoic.) A special class of **dye**s not packaged for the craftsperson and not generally recommended for the home dyer. The dyes, called colorfast salts, are mixed into two separate **dyebath**s and involve the use of naphthol and monopol oil (sulfonated castor oil) mixed with **caustic soda** (sodium hydroxide) in varying amounts according to colors. In a second bath, water, **Calgon,** common **salt** and **fast-color salt**s are added. Directions with the dyes must be carefully followed. Also see **Batik and Tie-dye: Dyes.**

napped fabric. Stitchery. Any **fabric** that has a **nap finish.** The soft surface is raised in the napping process by brushing the woven **wool, broadcloth, cotton, flannel,** or knit goods with wire bristle brushes. When **teasel**s are used the fabric is said to be gigged. A napped fabric should be pressed with a **needle board** or over a padded surface to prevent a flattening or matting of the nap.

napping. Weaving. (Also called brushing, teaseling.) A method of **finishing** a fabric by raising the fibers from the surface of the fabric. After weaving and washing, the fiber is raised with a **teasel** or a flat, or cylindrical, steel wire brush. As the fiber is raised, the fabric surface becomes shaggy or fuzzy, which results in a softer and smoother fabric with increased warmth, body, and durability. It becomes more compact as the napping covers up the spaces between the interlacing of **warp** and **filling.** A coarse, loose, and even inferior fabric can often be made more appealing. Napping is done to blankets, throws, and afghans, and sometimes to apparelwear. The soft surface is called a nap. Napping goes back to the Roman era, when dried teasel seed pods were used. Leonardo da Vinci invented a napping machine in 1490, but it was never widely used because workers whose jobs were jeopardized objected. It wasn't until the early nineteenth century that a brass napping machine was operating commercially (in Providence, Rhode Island). In contemporary work, the Canadian weaver-artist Mariette Rousseau-Vermette uses napping to blur the edges of the color changes in her **wall hanging**s. Because the napped fibers reflect light more than a flat surface, the colors become more luminous and intense. Also see **teasing.**

narrowing. Knitting. See **Knitting: Decreasing.**

narrow rope stitch. Crewel. Embroidery. See **rope stitch.**

narwhal ivory. Ivory and Bone Carving. The single horn of the male narwhal, an Arctic whale. It is tapered and grooved spirally from end to end. The rarest and most esteemed ivory, powerful myths were attributed to its medicinal and aphrodisiac properties. During the Middle Ages, it was thought to be the horn of the unicorn—sole proof that the mythical beast existed in some distant land. Specimens have been recorded over 8' long. It has a large internal hollow and is used in the same manner as **elephant ivory.** Also see **Ivory and Bone Carving: Preparation, Carving, Finishing.**

nativity set. Toys. See **crib set.**

natural dye. Batik and Tie-dye. A **dye** that comes from natural sources in contrast to one that is synthetic, or manufactured. Insects, plants, shellfish, and minerals were the source of most color in the Old World and in early American fabric printing. They were, in fact, the only dyes known prior to 1856. In that year the accidental discovery of mauve from coal tar led to the development of the **aniline,** or synthetic, **dyestuff**s known today.

Among the most familiar of the natural dyes are **henna, madder, cochineal, indigo,** and dyes from a variety of nuts, berries, seeds, lichen, and **dyewood**s.

natural dye. Dyeing. Those dyes obtained from a vegetable or animal source. Most of the natural dyes are vegetable in origin with only one animal **dyestuff, cochineal,** still being used. Prior to the discovery of **synthetic dye**s in the latter nineteenth century, only natural dyes were used. The most widely used were **indigo, logwood, woad, weld, madder, fustic,** and cochineal and kermes. Some were difficult to secure and became quite costly. One of the most treasured dyes of the ancient world was Tyrian purple, extracted by the Phoenicians from a murex shellfish similar to a snail. As with many natural dyes, the discovery of this purple supposedly came about by accident in 1000 B.C. when a couple on the coast near Tyre noticed that their dog's throat was spattered purplish-red after killing a shellfish. The dye came from a little vein in a particular shellfish. It was a colorless liquid and oxidized in air to become red-purple. Since such a small amount was in every shellfish, thousands had to be gathered for any sizable amount of dye. It rapidly became a color for the nobility who could afford its high price. Although the Near East was important in the ancient dye world, it was in India and China where natural dyeing became a skillful art and a source of trade. With the discovery of synthetic dyes, natural dyeing became a lost art except for the few people in the mountain and backwoods areas who kept on gathering the leaves, lichens, bark, twigs, buds, nuts, berries, seeds, flowers, and roots that give a natural dye.

Today natural dyeing has become quite popular again and **dye recipe**s are traded and modified as much as cooking recipes. Natural dyeing can be done with common household items such as coffee, tea, onion skins, and cinnamon bark; the substances can be picked in the garden, forest or field, or in cases where certain dyestuffs are not indigenous to a part of the country, the dyestuff can be ordered from a supplier specializing in natural dyes. Natural dyes are divided into two groups: **direct dye**s, those giving fast colors without the use of a **mordant,** and **adjective dye**s, those requiring a mordant. Most natural dyestuffs fall into the adjective dye category.

Natural dyes are much warmer, softer, and more subtle in hue than synthetic dyes. There is also an element of chance in what the color will actually turn out to be, since growing conditions, climate, and geographical location all tend to change a dyestuff. Other factors affecting the color properties are the time of year gathered and in what manner and for how long the dyestuff is stored.

In addition to **mordanting** and dyeing, natural dyestuffs have to go through other procedures before the color is on the fiber. These precede the mordanting and have to do with turning the natural substance into a dyestuff. After the substance is gathered, it must be cleaned of foreign matter, dried, and crushed, unless it is to be used fresh. Since many natural dyestuffs are seasonal, it is best to gather them when you can and dry and store them. If it is to be used fresh, then it must be steeped in a small amount of water from two hours to overnight, and then boiled for half an hour to two hours. The liquid is strained off through cheesecloth and the remaining matter in the cheesecloth is saved for further reboiling in case more dyestuff can be extracted. The liquid can be stored or put in use immediately in a **dyebath.** Also see **colorfast, dye, lichen dyeing.**

natural dye. Egg Decorating. Various colored dyes obtained by simmering natural vegetable matter in water. The vegetable matter is chopped into small sections and covered with water in an enamel pan, then simmered until the desired shade is obtained. Some vegetables produce strong dye without too much experimentation. Ground turmeric, available as a bottled spice at the grocery store, produces a strong, gold dye when simmered in water; mix about 1 tablespoon turmeric to 1 cup water; add 1 teaspoon white vinegar to help set the dye. The dry outer skins from common onions can be simmered in water to produce a brown dye. Again, a teaspoon of vinegar added will help the dye take to the egg. When the desired shade has been reached, pour the hot mixture through a strainer into another pan. This strained liquid is the dye. Simmer eggs in dye until the desired intensity of color is reached. Remove with a slotted spoon and let dry on a wire rack.

natural emery. Metalworking. See **abrasive.**

natural fiber. Batik and Tie-dye. Quilts. Stitchery. The fiber found in a natural form, as opposed to a **man-made fiber.** Used in the manufacture of textiles. The natural fibers are of two kinds: **cellulosic,** or **vegetable fiber**s, and protein, or **animal fiber**s. The vegetable fibers include cotton, **flax, hemp, jute,** and **ramie.** Animal fibers include silk, wool, and hair. Among the most commonly known fabrics made from natural fibers are cotton, linen, silk, and wool. In **batik** and **tie-dye** the natural fibers are always preferred and are sometimes essential because of their receptivity to **dye**s. Also see **alkali test, oil test** and **Batik and Tie-dye: Fabrics for Dyeing, Identifying Fibers.**

natural fiber. Spinning. Weaving. See **fiber.**

nautilus. Shell Carving. Cephalopod mollusks, of the genus Nautilus, native to the South Pacific and Indian oceans with a spiral, chambered shell of **nacre.** The shell is used polished and intact as a shell specimen, often sliced in two to reveal its chambers, and also for carving. Also see **fretwork** and **Shell Carving: Shell.**

Navajo loom. Weaving. A large, vertical, rough **frame loom** used by the Navajo Indians for the weaving of their ruglike blankets. The outer frame of the loom is made of vertical posts or slender trees, and horizontal beams are tied crosswise to form a rectangle. The looms are usually newly built to the specifications of each new blanket. They are easy to disassemble and reassemble when moving is necessary. This type of loom is thought to have developed with the prehistoric Pueblo Indians and is known to have been in use by the Pueblos in the period between A.D. 1050 and 1300. The feature that distinguishes the Navajo loom from other frame looms is the manner in which the **warp** is attached to the loom. In making the warp it is wound as a figure-eight **continuous warp** around sticks that serve as warp bars at the beginning and the end of the warp. They are parallel to each other, and the distance between them determines the length of the weaving, while their length determines the width of the work. The warping is usually done on the ground with the warp bars fixed in position so they will not shift around as the warp is being made. **Twining** is done parallel to each bar so that the warp **end**s will be kept separate and spaced, and so that they will not slide off during transfer to the rectangular frame. A **lease cord** is tied to secure the **cross.** Before the warp bars are attached to the frame, the upper warp bar is tied to another bar serving as a tension bar. The tension bar is then suspended by a rope from the top of the outer frame. During weaving, this rope can be pulled to tighten the **warp tension** or loosened to lower the working area. The lower warp bar is tied to the bottom beam of the frame. The **shedding device** consists of a narrow rodlike **shed stick** in position above the **heddle bar** which has **string heddle**s made by a continuous **heddle cord** of loose loops. The shed sticks serve to indicate one **shed,** but this is kept open and wide by an inserted **batten.** The batten is used also with the heddle bar and can be used to push down the **filling** after it is put through on a **bobbin shuttle.** A wooden comb is used to firmly beat the filling down. The batten is withdrawn and reinserted with each shed. Weaving goes on in this manner with the weaver sitting or squatting in front of the loom until she can no longer comfortably reach the weaving area; then the adjustable warp is lowered to her convenience. The woven cloth is wound around the bottom beam which now serves as a **cloth beam.** Actually the blanket is sewn tightly to itself as it is wound and there are often traces of this sewing left on blankets. Weaving is

completed when the top of the movable upper warp bar is reached. These last few **pick**s, where no shed is possible, are laid in by hand with the aid of a curved sacking **needle.** To beat down the filling in this upper part, the Navajos turn their comb and use the tip of the handle. In former days they used a thick, long wooden pin. See ill. Also see **hand beater, Navajo weaving.**

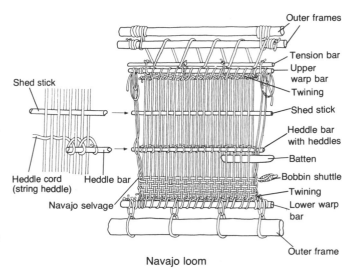

Navajo loom

Navajo selvage. Weaving. A form of **warp twining** used by the Navajo Indians for strength and as a decorative touch at the **selvage**s of their blankets and rugs. Each selvage is made up of two extra threads that are both slightly thicker than the normal rug warp **yarn.** These threads should be the same as those used for twining at the top and bottom of the rug. They are tied on to the top and bottom warp bars of the **Navajo loom** after the warp is on. The **shed stick** goes under one thread of each pair. The other thread is left unattached. After about ¼–½" of the piece has been woven, the two selvage threads change positions. The one on the shed stick is dropped and the other one is picked up. The one on the shed stick is always caught up in the weaving, whereas the other **float**s behind until it is its turn to be picked up by the shed stick as the first thread is dropped from the shed stick. During this switch, the selvage threads are twisted, always in the same direction. The switch happens at every ¼–½", depending on what amount has been established from the beginning. This switch and twist should occur often enough so that the floats of the unattached thread are not too long. The twisting causes a reverse twist in the threads above the shed stick, so at times the selvage ends have to be untied from the top cross bar, untwisted, and retied. At the very end of the piece, the selvage is worked in with a sacking **needle** so that the twist appears identical to the rest of the selvage. As a last step, the two ends of the twining thread and the two ends of the selvage thread are knotted together at the corners. The selvage threads are made about two feet longer than the regular warp to allow for the take up in the twist and the tying at the end. This warp twining can also be composed of three threads making for a more decorative selvage. See ill., next page. Also see **Navajo weaving.**

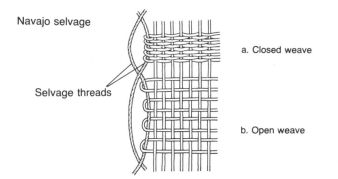

Navajo selvage

Selvage threads

a. Closed weave

b. Open weave

Navajo spinning. Spinning. Weaving. The twisting of the **wool fiber** from the **fleece** of one's own sheep as done by the Navajo Indians. Their spinning differs from other spinning in evidence in the United States today in two ways: the length of their **spindle** and the method of rotating it. The Navajo spindle, called a beedizi, can have a shaft as long as two feet or more. It has a thick, wide **whorl** placed about a quarter of the distance from the bottom tip of the shaft. There is no notch at the opposite tip since the yarn is spun over this tip. Sitting on the ground, a Navajo spins by placing the point of the spindle on the ground at her right side or by sitting it in a little cup placed there. The shaft rests at a slant against her right thigh. She spins either by twirling the upper end of the shaft between the fingers of her right hand, or by rotating the shaft between the palm of the right hand and the upper right thigh. The left hand draws out the fibers from the **rolag** and holds the yarn at the point where **spun yarn** and fiber meet. A length of **spun yarn** is attached to the spindle prior to beginning spinning. This spirals off at the top and is joined there to the fiber. After a length of yarn is spun, it is wound around the spindle. Usually the yarn is spun more than once rather than **plying** it. It is spun twice for filling yarn and three times for a strong, tightly spun **warp** yarn.

Navajo spinning has not changed from its early traditional ways. However, the preparation of the wool has changed considerably. In the old days, due to the scarcity of water in the Southwest, it was never washed. Wool was cleaned by shaking it to remove the sand and then placing it on bushes, where the burrs and sticks were removed by hand. The wool fiber was then pulled over a brushlike implement that took the place of a **carder.** It was made of burrs attached to a wooden frame. The change in wool preparation took place with the influence of the traders on **Navajo weaving.**

Navajo stitch. Basketry. See **figure eight.**

Navajo weaving. Weaving. The weaving, chiefly blankets used as clothing and rugs, produced by the Navajo Indians of northern Arizona and New Mexico. The work is done in a **tapestry weave (plain weave** covering the **warp** entirely) on an **upright loom.** Their colorful and beautiful work is just about the only **Indian weaving** done in any quantity today and has made their name synonymous with Indian weaving. However, they were relative newcomers to this craft, not taking it up until 1680 or shortly after. Up to this point, they were nomad farmers and hunters who raided Pueblos and Spanish towns. The Spanish had introduced domesticated sheep into the American southwest in the early seventeenth century and, through either trading or stealing, the Navajos began to build up large herds of sheep so that they had on hand a ready supply of **wool.** The techniques of spinning and weaving, along with the portable loom, came from the Pueblo Indians, who were the primary residents of the southwest and had been weaving cotton since before A.D. 700. The contact with the Pueblos was made through slaves gotten by raids, or through intermarriage. Still other Pueblos came to join the Navajos for protection against Spanish retaliation after the Pueblo Revolt of 1680. Among the Pueblos the men were the weavers, but when the Navajos assumed the craft, it was the women who learned the processes and techniques. They at first followed Pueblo styles, but soon developed their own patterns. By the 1800s they had become noted even among the Spanish for their taste and sophistication. Weaving declined among the Pueblos to just about nonexistence, but the Navajos in the meantime had surpassed their teachers.

The earliest surviving Navajo blankets date from the late eighteenth and early nineteenth centuries, and mention of their weaving goes back to 1700. These blankets were used as clothing. Both Navajos and Pueblos had similar ideas of apparel. The Navajo rectangular blankets were akin to the Pueblo "manta," the Spanish word for blanket, and used as a shawl or cloak and as a shoulder dress. The shawl became the so-called "chief" blanket, or shoulder blanket, and was worn by both men and women. These were rectangular pieces with the long side running the way of the **filling.** The shoulder dress was made of two pieces of finely woven blanket fastened at both shoulders and sewn together at the sides leaving openings for the arms at the top and for movement at the bottom.

Early Navajo weaving was also like the Pueblos' in that the only patterning was narrow filling stripes. This was woven with only natural colors of **handspun** wool. Wool was used for both warp and filling. Small amounts of vegetables dyed yellow, reddish brown, green and **indigo** blue (the most common) were occasionally used. Red touches came from the bayeta, or baize, and English flannel brought up by the Spanish from Mexico and traded to the Indians. It came in many colors, but a favorite was a scarlet or blue-red obtained from **cochineal.** Before being able to use the fine yarn of the bayeta cloth in their own weaving, the Navajos had to cut the cloth into strips, unravel it, and twist the strands together into a two-, three-, or four-**ply** filling yarn. Sometimes they simply laid it in the shed in multiple strands without twisting. Bayeta has come to mean all **natural dye**d, unraveled yarns. Because the bayeta cloth was **piece dye**d, the dye did not always penetrate the crossing of warp and filling. So Navajo blankets using this yarn often have characteristic undyed white spots. Bayeta cloth was of a higher quality than the American flannel that replaced it after the United States took over the southwest from the Mexicans. This was **aniline dye**d and had a bright orange-red color. Often these unraveled yarns had to be **card**ed and respun.

Knowledge of early Navajo weaving is based on fragments found in Massacre Cave in Canyon del Muerto,

Arizona. The massacre by the Spaniards was in 1805. Other later scant evidence supports these early fragments. Since 1850, however, the quantity of extant blankets and rugs makes a historical and stylistic survey possible. There are four major, yet overlapping, periods that coincide with historical events in the lives of the Navajo people. The first of these, the classical period, covers 1850–75, when the Navajos' weaving attained its pinnacle. It is assumed that, stylistically and technically, they built upon the type of work done prior to 1850, and that the yarn and type of dyes used were the same. However, during this period Saxony yarn was introduced. It was made in Germany and imported into the southwest. This three-ply yarn has a high sheen and was used sparingly by the Navajos in small stripe or design areas. It came in a number of colors, but red seemed to be the preferred one.

Their style also evolved so that more design elements were added to the simple stripes. These elements were in the form of diamond shapes, rectangles, crosses and zigzags. When involved on a diagonal, the elements were stepped or terraced. **Interlocking** or **dovetailing** was involved, so that no slits appeared. Beading or **stippling** was used to relieve the black or brown and indigo, alternately striped, Moki patterns.

The navajo weaving during this time was done for sale and trade in addition to their own needs. In 1863 the American soldiers under Kit Carson rounded up the Navajo people and held them in detention until 1868 at Bosque Redondo, a reservation at Fort Sumner in central New Mexico. This imprisonment brought to an end a great weaving tradition. The style changed as well as the type of materials used. It is thought that the soldiers at Bosque Redondo introduced Saxony yarns to the Indians, who no longer had their own herds of sheep. From 1875 to 1890, the Navajo weavers entered a period of transition. They returned to their home area, but instead of weaving primarily for themselves, their work through contact with the whites was turned toward the tourist trade. The coming of the railroad in 1880 brought more tourists and traders, who introduced the Indians to commercially spun yarns and aniline dyes. The traders bartered yarn goods to the Indians and this helped to turn the Navajos away from their native blanket wear. It was at this time that dimensions changed as the clothing blanket gave way to the weaving of larger and heavier blanket-rugs to answer tourist wants.

The commercial yarns of the transition period were named Germantown, after the place of manufacture in Pennsylvania. They were a four-ply yarn, available in many colors, and used by the Indians for about the next thirty years. Cotton twine also became available and was used instead of wool for the warp of many blankets. The diamond or serrate style appeared at this time. It consisted of smooth, small diamonds along oblique lines and replaced the bold stepped patterns. These small diamonds outlined larger motifs, so that a natural closing was formed, and no interlocking or dovetailing was necessary. In some cases, with slightly larger diamonds, a **slit tapestry** was developed. During the end of this period, the technique of **wedge weave** or pulled warp was introduced.

During the years between 1890 and 1920, the Navajos concentrated almost all their efforts on supplying tourist demands; technique and style deteriorated. However, in this so-called rug period, some interesting styles did develop, notably the "eye-dazzler," an outline style using the brightly colored Germantown yarns. Because the traders had become an important factor in Navajo weaving, they had considerable success when they tried to upgrade it by discouraging the use of aniline dyes, Germantown yarns, and cotton warps. The traders encouraged old techniques such as the **twill weave,** which had come down from the prehistoric Pueblos by way of the Pueblos contemporary to the Navajos. Twill weave fragments were found in Massacre Cave but the Navajos had not produced them to any extent until the 1880s. The traders tended to call this **double cloth** or double weave, but this is due to the thick, sturdy fabric that results rather than to any similarity in construction to true double cloth. The traders also convinced the Navajos to weave new patterns, such as those having a border around the outside edges, and those based on sandpaintings. However, around 1910, contrary to the efforts of the traders, the U.S. government introduced a better meat-producing sheep to the Navajos. Unfortunately, the wool from this sheep was of poor quality and this, along with the lack of good colors and a lack of interest on the part of the Navajos, led to a further decline in Navajo weaving.

Steps were taken beginning in 1920 to reverse this trend and improve the quality of yarn, dyes and color, design, and weaving technique. An interest was shown in reviving classical period patterns, and native **natural dye**s were introduced along with new, softer aniline dyes. These vegetable dyes were mostly new to the Navajos, for in their early blankets there was only a limited use of natural dyes. Most of their early colors depended on the natural color of the sheep and the blending of these colors through carding. This revival period succeeded in various aspects, and today Navajo weavers are creating new designs within an old context or copying patterns from the past. There is much handspinning going on, along with more and more use of vegetable dyes.

A distinctive technical feature of Navajo weaving is a twisted **selvage** composed of two threads at each side that catch and twist around the filling so that there is additional strength at these sides. There is weft **twining** at both top and bottom of the blanket that remains in the piece once it is off the loom. The Navajos also weave narrow sashes on **backstrap belt loom**s. Also see **color blending, eccentric weft, lazy line, Navajo loom, Navajo selvage, Navajo spinning.**

neat's-foot oil. Leather. A commercially available oil used to soften, lubricate, and make leather water resistant. Neat's-foot oil may be applied every six months to leather as a conditioner. Apply several light coats, then polish with a soft cloth. Also see **Leatherwork: Care, Cleaning, and Storage of Leather; Finishing Leather.**

neck. Ceramics. See **Ceramics: Form.**

necking. Ceramics. See **collaring** and **Ceramics: Throwing.**

necking down. Glasswork. Reducing the diameter of the molten glass **gather** beyond the end of the **blowing iron.** A **jack** is used to grasp the glass at the proper point, and then the gather is turned while applying pincer action with the jack. The groove formed by this action facilitates **cracking off** when that becomes necessary. During necking down, the blowing iron is rolled by hand back and forth on the arms of the **glassmaker's chair,** and the jack is squeezed gently and pushed to move the molten material farther off the end of the pipe.

needle. Beadwork. Needles for beadwork are available in packages from hobby shops. **Beading needle**s are longer than sewing needles and usually have a long eye. They are difficult to thread and sometimes are sold with a needle threader in the package. The smaller the size number of the needle, the larger the needle diameter. Ordinary sewing needles are not small enough for **seed bead**s, but may be used for **crow** and **pony bead**s. For stitching beads to leather, #10 or #12 "embroidery" or "sharps" are recommended. For general use, the most common size is #16. For **bead weaving** with a needle and thread, #14 or #16 should be used, preferably the smaller, #16, because the needle must pass through the bead hole twice.

needle. Leather. Many types of needles are available for stitching leather. Large blunt needles are useful for general sewing with waxed thread or fish line through prepunched holes. A saddler's needle or a curved needle may be needed for stitching hard-to-reach areas. Glover's needles have wedge-shaped, three-sided points that pierce the leather as you sew, so they may be used on lightweight leather without prepunching. Sharps, the regular sewing needles, which are available in various sizes, are also widely used for leather. For **lacing,** various **lacing needle**s are available. See ill. Also see **harness needle, running stitch** and **Leatherwork: Sewing Leather.**

Glover's needles

needle. Quilts. See **quilting needle.**

needle. Stitchery. A small, slender piece of steel which is pointed on one end and has a hole at the other through which a thread may be inserted. Most needles for hand sewing come packaged in assorted sizes, offering a range from which to select for various needs. Needle sizes range from 1 (coarse or large) to 10 (fine). The assorted packets usually contain sizes 3 to 9 or 5 to 10.

Among the most common needles are the following: Sharps are the ordinary **round-eye needle**s of medium length, most often used for hand sewing; betweens are extra-short needles with round eyes used for very fine sewing and sewing through extra-heavy fabrics; milliner's needles are long, very fine-shafted needles with round eyes used for basting, hand shirring and other fine stitching; embroidery needles are **long-eye needle**s of medium length which are easily threaded with several strands of **embroidery floss.** Used for many kinds of decorative stitching, crewel needles are similar to embroidery needles but slightly larger. The eye is large enough to accommodate one or more strands of crewel **yarn.** Darning needles or darners are large, extra-long needles with long eyes, which can be threaded with cord or yarn for use on heavy or thick materials; upholstery needles are curved or flattened, extra-long needles made specially for sewing through mattresses or extra-heavy materials; calyx-eyed needles have an opening above the eye to make them easy to thread; leather needles are three-sided needles used for sewing through leather. Blunts are medium-sized round-eye needles which have stouter points than sharps and are shorter than either sharps or betweens. Ball-point needles are made especially for hand- or machine-knitted materials. Also see **beading needle, bodkin** and **Stitchery: Tools.**

needle. Weaving. A long pointed tool with a large eye that is used in **needle weaving** or which is used to finish weaving where it is no longer possible to open a **shed.** Usually the needle is steel and the point is rather blunt; it is helpful if the tip is bent, because this makes picking up the **warp end**s during weaving easier. At one time, it was possible to obtain small **frame loom**s with accompanying bent-tip needles measuring about 6–7″ long. Because of their length, they functioned extremely well in weaving. With the increased use of frame-loom weaving in recent years, wooden needles have appeared in weaving supply stores. They are used to insert the last **pick**s in a weaving when it is impossible to open a shed. They are usually of various thicknesses and lengths, have much larger eyes than steel needles, and are hand-made of exotic woods. A long time ago, the Navajos used a wooden or bone needle for this same purpose. Today, they use a sacking needle, which is a curved **rug needle.** Also see **bodkin.**

needle art. Stitchery. The traditional needlework arts. In commercial use it often refers to a store or department that handles all materials related to needlework and embroidery. It is also sometimes used to refer to needlework or stitchery kits.

needle awl. Ceramics. (Also called pricker.) A pin in a handle that is used for cutting clay (**a.**). It can be made by simply pushing a hat pin through a cork. Used in throwing on a **potter's wheel,** the **pot** is set on the wheel and the needle awl is held horizontally and stationary. As the wheel turns, the pin cuts the **rim** at the desired height (**b.**). See ill.

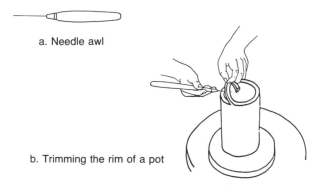

a. Needle awl

b. Trimming the rim of a pot

needle board. Stitchery. A specially surfaced board made expressly for ironing or steaming **fabrics** that have a **nap.** The board has a surface of short, pointed steel pins, and the nap or top surface of the **napped fabric** is placed against the pins. Ironing will then remove wrinkles without flattening the nap.

needle book. Stitchery. A small folder or booklet in which pages of **linen, flannel,** paper, or other soft **fabric** hold a collection of **needles.** It is often in the shape and form of a book, with pages that open to show needles of various sizes. The outside of the book might be carved ivory, carved wood, leather, or worked fabric. Historically, needles have been valuable tools, too precious to lose, so the development of the needle book and the **needle case** were logical. Nowadays, with an abundance of fine needles always available, the elegant containers for needles have disappeared from the scene.

needle case. Knitting. Stitchery. A case or container, often of cylindrical shape and elaborately made, in which **needles** are kept. The needle case has a removable lid or cap. Like the **needle book,** its original purpose was to preserve and protect the precious needles. Needle cases were of bone, horn, wood, ivory, gold, silver, steel, glass, or brass. The care with which these antique needle cases were made suggests the value placed on needles. They are rarely used now, and are found only in antique shops.

needle drill. Coral Carving. Ivory and Bone Carving. Jet Carving. Shell Carving. This easily constructed tool, consisting of a needle in a block or dowel of hardwood, is used for hand drilling slender holes through materials softer than steel. It is especially useful for small, hand-held pieces and for beads.

Drive the point of a needle into a piece of hardwood that will serve well as a handle; file off half of the eye-end of the needle to create a two-pronged end. Draw a triangular file once through the center to sharpen the tool. Slowly rotate the drill by hand against the material. The material may be held stationary in a **lapstick** or **bead-holding jig.** Also see **fretwork.**

needle file. Jewelry. A fine, narrow **file** 4 to 7¾" in length. (The length generally refers to the cutting area.) Needle files come in **cuts** from 0 to 6; #2 is the most commonly used. All needle files have round shanks, except those called **escapement files** which have square shanks. Needle files come in a far greater range of shapes than large files.

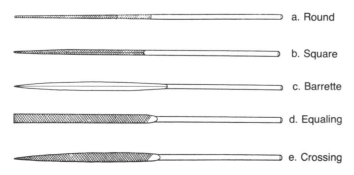

a. Round
b. Square
c. Barrette
d. Equaling
e. Crossing

The six basic shapes are round (**a.**), half-round, square (**b.**), barrette (**c.**), equaling (**d.**), and crossing (**e.**). Needle files can be used for refining areas of metal that have first been worked with heavy files, for **filing** small sculptural forms into metal (each file can make several variations of a specific cut by changing its angle), and for cleaning up areas and edges after **sawing.** See ill.

needle flame. Jewelry. See **flame.**

needle lace. Lacemaking. (Also called needlepoint, point.) **Lace** made with a single **filament** applied with a needle. Needle lace first developed from a type of embroidery called **cutwork,** where threads were drawn from the woven fabric, leaving a structure of threads. It was upon this structure that **buttonhole stitches** were made.

Later in the development of needle lace, the foundation of threads was laid in with a needle, and buttonhole stitches worked upon this foundation. Generally speaking, all needle lace is made in this manner, with buttonhole stitches in the **fillings** as well as over the foundation structure.

The ancient embroideries of the Near East undoubtedly influenced the beginnings of needle lace. From there the art traveled via Italy to all over Europe. By the sixteenth century portraits featured collars of both needle and **bobbin lace.** The laces showed great artistic skill. Two outstanding examples of needle lace are **reticella** and **point de Venise.** Also see **Lacemaking: Needle Lace.**

needle-mark. Quilts. A method of marking a **quilting pattern** on fabric. It avoids any soiling or smearing, as sometimes occurs with pencil or **chalk.** A blunt needle is used to trace around a template. The needle is held almost parallel to the fabric and pressure is exerted against the needle so that it creases the material. Because the material will retain the creases only a short time, as much as is needed for one session of sewing is marked. **Synthetic fabrics** are usually too springy to be needle-marked.

needle-nose pliers. Stained Glass. These are pliers with a narrow, pointed tip, used for such jobs as straightening out the **leaf** of **lead came** or for making hanging loops by twisting copper wire together. Also see **fitting, lathkin** and **Stained Glass: Tools and Materials.**

NEEDLEPOINT

Needlepoint is a type of needlework done on a **background fabric** of open mesh **canvas** or a string fabric with an even weave. The ground is completely covered with stitching in wool, cotton, or any other yarn, to resemble tapestry. **Canvas work** would be the more accurate, though less romantic, name for this type of needlework, which is generally known in Europe simply as **tapestry.** True tapestry is always woven, so the American name "needlework" probably developed to distinguish between the two.

The name "needlepoint" is also given to the various forms of lace done with a needle to distinguish them from laces done on a pillow with bobbins.

Needlepoint can be roughly divided into two basic groups: free designs which are drawn on the canvas, and geometric or repeat patterns which are counted out on the canvas as they are worked.

The most versatile basic stitch, which closely resembles tapestry, is the **tent stitch** or **half cross stitch.** Since the stitches interlock and blend well together, it is very useful for shading. The stitch is worked on a slant across each intersection of the woven background canvas, so its size is controlled by this canvas mesh. Canvas is available in a wide range of sizes, and is measured by the number of threads to the inch. Tent stitch worked on fine canvas (approximately 14–18 threads to the inch) is known as **petit point,** that worked on medium size (10–12) is called **demi point,** and on coarse canvas (5–8) is called **gros point.**

Besides tent stitch, there are literally hundreds of stitches and combinations of stitches which form patterned effects. They may be counted out to form geometric designs, or used to fill areas in free designs.

Needlepoint is well suited to any article which will receive hard wear, so it is ideal for rugs and for upholstery such as chair seats, bench tops, or foot stools, as well as for pictures and wall hangings, slippers, handbags, vests, card-table covers, backgammon and chess boards, tray or table top inserts (under glass), address and telephone book covers, coasters, etc.

Though needlepoint has never been really out of fashion since its beginnings in the sixteenth century, it is today enjoying a renaissance. Artists are discovering needlepoint as a new medium and a wide variety of designs are being produced in a great many different styles.

It is difficult to say exactly when the history of needlepoint began—at least the kind of needlepoint we know today. Its early beginnings were rooted in the all-over patterns and counted stitches which were closely related to the structure of the cloth. These are found in peasant costumes and the hangings and altar frontals worked in Germany during the fourteenth century. In the sixteenth century, more advanced spinning and weaving methods and the ability to produce a strong, even-weave background fabric of hemp or linen enabled the needleworker to make hangings, table carpets, and bed valances with the close all-over stitching we associate with needlepoint today. Later, these fabrics were sized and stiffened to form a clear, open-mesh canvas which was even easier to work on. Stitches were collected on **sampler**s. The earliest, which date from the sixteenth century, were long strips of linen with small areas of patterns and stitches, worked in a haphazard arrangement just for the purpose of keeping a record. The stitches were generally those used in needlepoint: **tent stitch, rococo stitch, cross stitch, turkey work, brick stitch,** etc., and were worked in silk or wool and often with touches of **metallic thread**s as well.

Designs for needlepoint were taken from herbals and bestiaries, the reference books of flora and fauna which were illustrated with beautiful line drawings. These were often written by monks and travelers to the New World and gave detailed accounts of the special properties of each plant and its uses in medicine as well as careful descriptions of the strange and exotic animals found in faraway lands. Where facts were lacking, details were filled in by the author's imagination.

Other designs were taken from engravings and allegorical subjects or Biblical themes. Crests and coats of arms were worked on cushions and table carpets. Because the even mesh of the background made it simple to count out repeat patterns, these were often combined with illustrative scenic designs. For instance, the famous Bradford table carpet in the Victoria and Albert Museum, London, has a border of country scenes drawn with naïve simplicity and without regard for perspective, while the center of the carpet has an all-over design of intertwining grapes. In Great Britain royal ladies such as Mary, Queen of Scots, Queen Elizabeth, and Elizabeth of Hardwicke all did needlepoint. Their designs often had symbolic significance and were sometimes worked on smaller pieces of canvas in the form of medallions which were then applied to velvet or brocade and enriched by outlining with gold thread embroidery.

In colonial America, schools of needlework always included the teaching of needlepoint. Designs were taken from popular engravings and many variations of pastoral landscapes and hunting scenes were worked with charming naïveté. Especially interesting are the Fishing Ladies series, over fifty of which were found in New England. These may have been produced by the same source, a finishing school owned by Mrs. Conde of Boston, who advertised "patterns of all sorts especially pocket books, housewives' screens, pictures, chimney pieces, escritoires, etc., from tent stitch in a plainer manner and cheaper than those that come from London."

During the Victorian era, a certain technique of doing needlepoint was called **Berlin wool work.** A Berlin printer and his wife devised a method of teaching and designing needlepoint by means of a colored chart. The designs were counted out stitch by stitch onto a chart, and from there onto a canvas. Special merino sheep were bred in Saxony to provide the soft wool needed for this needlework. It became so much the rage that eventually all needlework was known only as "Berlin work."

In the 1930s in England, Louisa Pesel designed some beautiful kneeling cushions and choir-stall cushions for Winchester Cathedral. This stimulated a great deal of interest in England and America; in 1956, a similar project was started for the National Cathedral in Washington, D.C.

Since the sixteenth century, interest in needlepoint has been steadily increasing, and today the designs and possibilities available are practically unlimited.

MATERIALS **Canvas** for needlepoint is available in many varieties. The most universally used is called mono canvas; this is a single-thread canvas in sizes from 24 mesh to the inch (very fine) to 10 mesh to the inch (medium to coarse).

Penelope canvas is double mesh canvas available in a very fine mesh size but can be obtained in as bold a weave as 7–5 threads to the inch. The double-threaded mesh makes this canvas firm and stiff, and thus it is quite suitable for rugmaking.

Interlocked canvas has twisted double mesh threads; this gives the appearance of mono canvas and the strength of a double-thread canvas. The mesh always runs straight and square.

Plastic canvas comes in sheets 11″ × 14″ and is firm, yet flexible. It cannot stretch out of shape, so it needs no **blocking** when the article is finished. As it can be cut to the exact size and needs no turnbacks, it is useful for handbags, coasters, belts, boxes, and all kinds of similar articles.

Also available is an imported soft **linen canvas** of deliberately uneven threads which has an antique appearance. In the coarser size mesh it is attractive for rugs, and is often worked with **thrums,** the wool thread remnants sold by most carpet manufacturers. Working on the canvas with its handwoven effect, using this loosely twisted wool in muted colors, can be effective for duplicating the effect of Oriental rugs.

Tapestry needles have blunt, rounded points and are used exclusively in needlepoint as the needle must be able to slide easily between the threads of the canvas mesh without splitting them. For instance, a large rug needle would be #5, the finest needle for petit point would be #26. An average-size needle, good for working on #10 canvas (10 threads to the inch), would be #18. Packages of assorted sizes of tapestry needles are available in most stores. If the needle is hard to push through the mesh, it is too large; if the yarn sticks and jams, the eye is too small for the double yarn. Using the correct size needle can save time.

Whatever **yarn** is used, care must be taken to see that the thread is neither too heavy nor too fine for the background canvas. White spots showing through a partially covered canvas are unattractive, but too heavy a thread makes the stitches irregular and hard to work. A 1″ square practice piece is sufficient to establish the correct texture.

Persian yarn is most popular in the United States. Originally dye by Paternayan Brothers of New York in a wide range of brilliant yet subtle colors, this yarn has now been copied by several manufacturers and is known as "Persian type." Three threads of two-ply wool are lightly twisted together to form a single strand. This can easily be separated to work with as many or as few threads in the needle as the canvas or stitches require. This yarn is versatile and easy to work with.

Tapestry yarn is a rounded thread, four- to six-ply, twisted firmly together. It is difficult to separate, so it is best used as is. Obviously it is not as versatile as Persian, and looks best worked on penelope canvas of the correct size so that the background becomes completely covered.

Various kinds of **metallic thread**s may be used in needlepoint. Those made of **Lurex thread** are the best, as they are the most pliable. All metallic threads (including Lurex) that are twisted with acrylic or silky fibers are superior for needlepoint, because the yarn is strong enough to stand the abrasion of being pulled repeatedly back and forth through the canvas. Only short lengths of thread should be used at a time.

Most **acrylic yarn**s are unsuitable for any needlepoint which is to receive hard wear, such as rugs, chair seats, etc. Like most wool threads it is apt to fluff or "pill" when the finished article is first used. Unlike wool, however, where the fluff is easily removed by brushing, the "pilling" of acrylic adheres firmly to the surface and cannot be removed. The fluff from one color adheres to another, making the whole effect look dirty. Also see **Appleton crewel wool, Broder Medici wool, cotton embroidery floss, D.M.C.**

WORKING ON A FRAME Traditionally all needlepoint was done on a frame, and today a frame is always used by professionals. This is simply because the finished result is smoother, needing little blocking when the canvas has been stretched out firmly as it is being worked, and the stitching has been rhythmically done with even tension, using one hand above and one below the surface. A frame is particularly useful if the needlepoint design is shaded. Several needles can be threaded with various colors, a little of each worked in as you go along, so that you can more accurately judge the amount of each rather than if you stitched in all of one color first, then the next, and so on. For large rugs and hangings, which would be most cumbersome to work in the hand, a frame is almost a necessity. For these large pieces a square frame is best; the work is rolled up on one side, completed, and unrolled on the other so as to expose the unworked design as needed. Also see **embroidery frame.**

PREPARATION AND LAYOUT To apply the pattern to the fabric, outline the design clearly on the acetate, tracing, or layout paper in black ink. Cut the canvas square with a good border all around the design (at least 4″ if possible). You can always trim afterward, but it is much harder to add!

Bind the raw edges with masking tape, bias binding, or by a **whipping stitch,** or turn back the edge and hold it with a **running stitch.** This will prevent the edges from unraveling while the piece is being worked. Rule a straight line vertically and horizontally through the center of the traced design and tape it to a firm surface such as a drawing board. (If acetate or tracing paper is not opaque, place white paper underneath.) Repeat this process on the canvas, folding it in four to find the center lines. Instead of ruling, run a pencil through the center vertically and horizontally. The pencil will easily run between the threads of the canvas and establish a straight line. Center the canvas over the design, lining up the vertical and horizontal lines, and tape it in place.

Trace the design with a black permanent marker: permanent color will not run into the wool when the finished work is blocked and produce a dirty effect (it is advisable to test the marker for washability first).

Once the outline is traced it may be either filled in with color (again, using permanent markers, oil paint, or acrylic which has been tested for permanence) or it may be worked directly on the plain canvas, placing the colors within the outlines by following directly from the original painted design or photograph.

Geometric designs must be counted onto the canvas,

following from a previously worked pattern or graph. Always begin working in the center of the shape to insure balance on all four sides; work the predominant color first, then the others may be filled in more easily around this previously established pattern.

Tramé is a method of applying the design to penelope canvas. Lay horizontal lines in the correct colors across each area of the design on the canvas. The traméed threads are held firmly between the double threads of the canvas. Work the stitching, usually the **half cross stitch,** over the traméed base, matching color to color. The traméed threads indicate the exact areas of the design, and strengthen by forming a padding under each stitch.

COLOR AND DESIGN   Since the background of needlepoint is to be entirely covered, a great variety of color combinations are available for the needleworker. The overall tapestry effect of needlepoint affords more freedom to the needlepointer than can be obtained by the crewel embroiderer, who has to choose a preset, predyed fabric upon which to work.

Great realism can be obtained within the confines of the square canvas mesh, yet perhaps the most pleasing designs are those in which realism bows to the confines of the craft itself. Spare simplicity and stylization often have a more dramatic effect in this medium than a great deal of overbearing fussiness and too-elaborate shading.

FINISHING   Needlepoint should be blocked very carefully. If worked in the hand it may require two or three **blocking**s to get it perfectly straight. If only tent stitch is used, place the needlework face down on a **blocking board;** if other stitches are used, block the piece right side up to prevent flattening the stitches. The corners of the board are a basic means of keeping the piece at right angles and the edges straight, although a plastic right angle—available in most art supply stores—is the best guide. Nail rustproof carpet tacks in each of the four corners, making sure all four sides measure the same. Carpet tacks can next be placed in the center of the four sides, and then in the spaces between, until the nails have been placed at ½" intervals around the edges of the canvas.

In order to stretch it firmly, canvas pliers should be used. After testing for colorfastness, clear, cold water should be used to dab the work all over with a sponge until it is thoroughly soaked. It should be allowed to dry in its own time. If the colors are not fast, use a commercial cleaning fluid such as naphtha or benzine.

Needlepoint can be used for upholstered pieces, rugs, cushions, handbags, belts, wall hangings, etc.—almost any item that can be covered with a sturdy fabric. Most pieces should be mounted professionally. However, pictures, pillows, belts, and small clutch-type bags can be mounted in the home.

Pictures can be mounted on artists' **stretcher strips** and then fitted into a frame. If the canvas is not a standard size, sectional frames are available in all sizes.

Pillows look best with a welting which covers any canvas which might show. Be careful to secure the raw edges so they don't unravel. Since needlepoint is heavyweight, a sturdy fabric such as velvet or corduroy should be used as a backing.

Belts can be easily mounted by folding the raw canvas back and finishing the fold with a whipping stitch or **binding stitch.** A grosgrain ribbon can be used as a backing. No additional backing is needed. Also see **rabbitskin glue.**

CARE AND MAINTENANCE   Needlepoint should never be brushed, as this will fuzz the yarn and spoil the smooth effect of the stitches. After being upholstered, the needlepoint article can be vacuumed lightly. This should not be done too frequently as it will wear the needlework. Dust can be loosened by beating or banging it with a clean, soft duster.

Needlepoint is washable as long as it is tested for colorfastness. It should be soaked in a clean, large tub of cold water and then the back of the work is rubbed with a cake of Ivory or any other pure soap. Rubbing on the back prevents felting the stitches on the right side. Afterward the needlework should be blocked. Pressing is undesirable because the heat tends to shrink the wool used in the needlepoint.

needlepoint. Lacemaking. See **needle lace.**

needlepoint rug. Rugmaking. See **embroidered rug, needleworked rug.**

needle-point scriber. Jewelry. A sharply pointed steel tool used to scratch lines in metal in preparation for **sawing** or cutting, to mark placement, or to cut designs into metal. A **scriber** is very sharp and, except in the case of cutting drawing designs into metal, a very light mark should be made: a deep cut is difficult to remove. There are numerous other types of scribers, such as an engraver's scriber, an engraver's needle-point marker, and a double-end scriber. See ill.

Needle-point scriber

needle stone. Gemcutting. See **quartz.**

needle threader. Stitchery. Any of a number of small devices that aid in threading **needle**s. Usually a fine wire loop is threaded through the needle's eye and a thread is run through the loop. The wire is then drawn back through the eye, pulling the thread with it. There are various antique threaders, and some new plastic "pushbutton" varieties. The needle threader at home, usually the person who is sewing, finds that a sharp diagonal cut on the thread helps in guiding it through the eye. Few seamstresses fail to moisten the thread between their lips to help hold it rigid. Finally, good light is essential.

needleweaving. Crewel. Embroidery. A very old method of decoration dating back over three thousand years; the oldest existing examples have been found in Egyptian tombs.

Needleweaving is a major part of drawn-thread work. After the desired threads are drawn out, a **tapestry needle** is threaded to weave over and under the remaining threads in bundles of one to eight threads. Patterns can be created by varying the size of the bundles of threads. The illustration shows needleweaving alternating with a single thread wrapped tightly.

Hemstitching the edges of the border is optional for needleweaving; it may just be left plain.

Prepare the border as in **drawn thread borders**. Working on the reverse side and using a blunt tapestry needle, weave over a bundle of approximately eight threads, then under a bundle of eight. The needle always goes down in the center of the two groups, first pointing from right to left, as shown, and then from left to right. Push the stitches together with the needle as you go, so that they are even and firmly packed. To end off, run the thread back under the stitching. Needleweaving may be done over three or even four groups of threads, or woven with many variations. See ill. Also see **raised needleweaving.**

a. Single thread wrapped tightly   b. Needleweaving around bundles of threads

needleweaving. Weaving. A technique in which the **filling** is carried by a **needle** over and under the **warp** threads since no **shed** opening is possible. Because needleweaving does not utilize a shed, there is a tendency to classify it as embroidery rather than weaving. However, the worker does start with a series of threads that pass as the warp and then interlaces them with a filling, which need not be at right angles to the warp as in most true weaving. It is conjectured that needleweaving was known to the early Egyptians, who, in some of their white mummy wrappings and household articles, left a strip of warp unwoven and then later filled this in with a pattern in color, presumably with a needle.

In most cases, the loom used for needleweaving is a **cardboard loom,** a circular or **hoop loom,** or any variety of a small **frame loom** in which a shed is not possible or desirable. Other needleweaving looms would include those shaped to the form of the final object, or found object looms, such as **branch loom**s. A household fork, or a **hand beater,** is used to beat the filling either down or up. The needle that carries the filling can be a bent-tip yarn darning needle, a curved needle, a blunt tapestry needle or a **bodkin.** Butterflies can be used in some instances if it is possible to manipulate them over and under the threads. Needleweaving is used to weave a finished and final piece, especially where an unusual shape is desired, and also to weave trial samples before a long warp is put on a bigger loom. Used this way, color combinations, new yarns, techniques, and weaves can be probed and practiced before the final piece is attempted. Needleweaving is used quite often in schools when the students work at home and larger looms are not available. It performs a useful function as a learning tool and also as a quick aid with which to develop design ideas or color problems. In the latter case, it is especially valuable because the weaver is freed from concentration on technique and loom mechanics and can completely devote attention to design and color problems.

Just about anything can be needlewoven; however, in large pieces, needleweaving works best where there are small areas of color, such as there are in most tapestries. Also see **butterfly, tapestry.**

needleworked rug. Rugmaking. Rugs made of yarn applied with a needle to some sort of **rug backing** or foundation fabric. The term is synonymous with **embroidered rug**s except for one or two differences in the usage of the terms. One of the differences refers to the amount of backing covered by the yarn. In needleworked rugs it has come to be assumed that the foundation is fully covered, whereas in embroidered rugs, it can be left exposed if that is the aesthetic intent of the designer. Scandinavian rya rugs are made of a **knotted pile** attached with a needle to a specially woven rug backing, and although the knotted pile is a type of embroidery **stitch,** the rugs are commonly referred to as needleworked rugs. Needleworked rugs are also known as needlepoint rugs and **tapestry rug**s, the latter because some stitches used in embroidered rugs closely resemble those in woven tapestry rugs. Also see **yarn sewn rug.**

negative design. Block Printing. See **negative print.**

negative print. Block Printing. Papercrafts. (Also called negative design.) A **block print** in which the pattern is cut out of the surface, leaving the background raised. When printed, the pattern appears white against a dark background. Also see **Block Printing: Designing and Transferring.**

negative shape. Batik and Tie-dye. Stitchery. The part of a design that is to be subtracted or removed from an area, or that shape "left," as distinguished from a **positive shape,** which is added. Background areas may sometimes be referred to as negative shapes and may be used to suggest a positive form.

negligé. Coral Carving. The name given to a necklace of strung slender tips of the coral branch. The pieces are sanded and pierced for stringing, without further working them. Also see **Coral Carving: Working the Material.**

Nelson's Victory. Quilts. A **pieced block** design of squares and triangles. It is one of the many variations of the pinwheel arrangement used in **Churn Dash, Pinwheel,** and **windmill.** See ill.

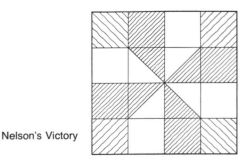

Nelson's Victory

Neolite. Leather. See **Leather: Setting up a Workshop.**

Neozapon. Plastics. See **colorant.**

nepheline syenite. Ceramics. A mineral used in **porcelain** bodies and in **glaze**s. In some ways it is similar to **feldspar;** it contains **potash** and is most commonly used in **stoneware** glazes. Nepheline syenite produces a greater **firing** range and increases thermal expansion, which reduces crazing tendencies in glaze.

nephrite. Beadwork. Gemcutting. See **jade.**

nested doll. Toys. See **nested toy.**

nested egg. Toys. A **nested toy** that consists of a series of **egg**s, one egg fitted exactly inside another.

Some nested eggs are made of painted, **lathe-turned** wood, some of **papier mâché,** and a few rare ones of silver or carved ivory. The egg shape recurs in toys from all over the world.

A traditional Japanese nested egg is made of paper strips. As the paper is unwound, new eggs appear under the preceding ones. Sometimes a small toy or candy is wrapped in the smallest egg.

nested toy. Toys. Any toy in which one shape is designed to fit exactly into its counterpart, one size larger. Usually, anywhere from three to seven parts fit together. Both the Japanese and Russian nested dolls are of this variety, as are the **nested egg**s and similar toys of papier mâché and wood. Some nested toys are now made of plastic.

net. Lacemaking. A very delicate fine mesh fabric. Net, in relation to lace, is a foundation fabric made with **bobbin**s and **needle**s upon which the lace **pattern, motif,** and stitches are worked.

Netting, the art of making net, is so ancient that no date can be fixed for its invention. That it was used for fishing and bird-catching purposes by the earliest inhabitants of the earth is without doubt. From the thirteenth to sixteenth century, net was made with bobbins or needles, and used as a foundation fabric; but in the early nineteenth century, lacemakers were able to get machine-made net, which greatly facilitated the making of certain laces. Also see **appliqué, Carrickmacross, knotted lace filet, tambour lace.**

net. Quilts. Stitchery. A mesh material in which the **fibers** are twisted to form varying **geometric** shapes. Net material ranges from fine to coarse and from sheer to full. It is made from a variety of fibers—**cotton, linen, rayon, silk,** or **nylon.** In **stitchery** it is used on **lace appliqué** to give a shadow or transparent effect. It is a non**ravel**ing material and can be easily **appliqué**d by machine.

net appliqué. Stitchery. The use of **net**s of various weights and meshes in **appliqué** onto another **fabric.** The effect is light, airy, and transparent. The nets may be attached with **machine-appliqué,** or a simple **catch stitch** can be used to secure them in place. Since nets come in a wide range of colors, they offer unusual possibilities in overlays of transparent colors. Net is also used in some **lace appliqué.**

net stitch. Lacemaking. (Also called lattice stitch.) A stitch in **bobbin lace** in which two pairs of **bobbins cross** and then **twist.** In working an area in net stitch, one bobbin moves horizontally; this is called the **worker** bobbin. The net stitch is frequently used in combination with the **cloth stitch** in the **design** areas or in the **ground.**

netsuke. Ivory and Bone Carving. A common form of Japanese **ivory** carving, generally of human and animal figures that are attached to inro, the small portable cases used in place of pockets. The netsuke is attached by a cord into the inro and slipped under the obi, or belt, to keep the inro in place. **Vegetable ivory** was often used.

netting. Weaving. The process of looping and knotting to make an open mesh or net with the openings being secured by knots. The openings are of a fixed size that is determined by a gauge. The construction uses a single element, one thread, that interconnects with itself through looping to form a net. It is also called network or filet work and forms the foundation for filet lace, which is embroidered over it. To do netting, only a **netting shuttle** and a gauge are necessary. The gauge can be a dowel or flat strip of wood slightly wider than the shuttle. This width sets the size of the open spaces. Some craftsmen prefer a freer approach and use just their hands instead of the shuttle, determining the size of the openings by eye. However, there must be a stationary object to attach the first loop or loops to. Fishermen are often seen using their toes as this object. The knot that holds the mesh together has become known as a fishermen's knot or fishnet knot.

The best yarns to use for netting are smooth and not elastic so that the open structure or pattern is clearly visible, and either relaxed or stretched open. The basic mesh or opening is either square or diamond shaped. Other variations can be produced by using different width gauges in one piece and interlacing the loops in a more elaborate manner.

The ancient Peruvians were masters of netting and used other types of knots, as well as techniques, to get a variety of openings and intricate patterning in their nets. The craft, however, goes back much earlier than ancient Peru. Prehistoric man used it to make nets to catch his food. The early Egyptians used it for this as well as for body and head adornment. Today it is used to produce practical

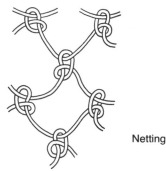

Netting

items like garments, hand bags, or shopping bags, caps or hair nets, curtains, fishing and hunting nets, or for art objects such as filigree **wall hanging**s and **fiber sculpture**. The net can be used for lacemaking, or as the foundation to which yarns or objects are fastened. If in the making process the yarn is merely looped or linked around itself and not knotted, then the process is known as knotless netting or **looping. See ill.**

netting gauge. Lacemaking. See **mesh stick.**

netting needle. Lacemaking. (Also called netting shuttle.) The tool used to hold the thread or yarn in working the **net stitch** for **bobbin lace**. Secure the thread to the needle by making a figure eight around the prongs, then wind the thread around the needle, end to end between the prongs. Also see **knotted lace filet.**

netting needle. Weaving. See **netting shuttle.**

netting shuttle. Lacemaking. See **netting needle.**

netting shuttle. Weaving. An arrow-shaped implement used primarily for making knotted nets. It also goes by the name of netting needle. In weaving it is used by **tapestry** artists, or those weavers engaged in **frame** or **off-loom weaving**. This **shuttle** is of the flat or stick type with a point at one end only. The yarn is wound around from the end opposite the point to a spine or projection in the open center of the shuttle. It is wound first on one side of the shuttle and then on the other side. Netting shuttles are small shuttles averaging about ¾–1″ in width and 6–8″ in length. Today they are usually of plastic, although at one time it was possible to buy bone ones at fishermen's supply houses. See ill. Also see **netting.**

Netting shuttle

network. Weaving. See **netting.**

neutral flame. Jewelry. Metalworking. See **flame.**

New England laid stitch. Crewel. Embroidery. See **Roumanian stitch.**

New Star. Quilts. A **pieced block** for an **all-over pattern**. When four of the blocks are joined, a new star is formed at the intersection. Also see **star patterns.**

new wool. Spinning. Weaving. See **virgin wool.**

New York Beauty. Quilts. See **Rocky Mountain.**

nibbler. Metalworking. A power hand tool used for cutting flat sheets of **mild steel** and other relatively soft metals, most commonly used on sheets 1/16–¼″ thick. It is electrically driven and has a punch and die arrangement that does the cutting. See ill.

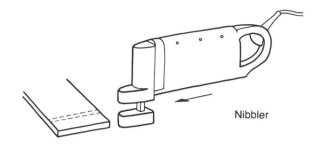

Nibbler

nibbling. Stained Glass. See **grozing.**

nichrome. Enameling. See **firing.**

nicked corner. Bookbinding. The cut corner of a book **board** on the edge that lies near the **head** and **tail** bands.

nickel. Jewelry. Metalworking. A hard, **ductile**, silvery metal that is very resistant to corrosion and wear, used for **alloy**ing, **casting, electroplating**, and **forging** objects. Its most important use is as an alloy in steel, to increase hardness and strength. It becomes work-hardened from hammering and must be **anneal**ed slowly and **quench**ed gradually in a solution of 2% **denatured alcohol** to prevent cracking.

Nickel may be brazed, welded, or soldered. For hard **soldering**, use a phosphorus-free silver solder and a fluoride **flux**. For soft soldering, use the same acid fluxes as you would for **copper**. For **welding** with **oxyacetylene** gas, use a nickel **welding rod** and a reducing **flame**. Lea's Compound is recommended for polishing nickel to a satin finish, but **polishing compounds** that have rouge or lime in them do not cut well enough. Also see **annealing, quenching.**

nickel-chromium steel. Metalworking. See **steel.**

nickel oxide. Ceramics. See **pigment oxide.**

nickel silver. Jewelry. Metalworking. (Also called German silver.) Any of several **nickel** alloys containing 62–65% **copper**, 18–33% nickel, and 5–18% **zinc**. It is commonly used for artwork casting, jewelry, plumbing fixtures, camera parts, architectural ornamentation, and as a base for silver-plated tableware. The larger the amount of nickel, the whiter the color. **Solder** and anneal it as you would **brass**. Stock sheets come in 16 and 20 **gauge** and are sold by the **linear foot**. Also see **annealing, brass.**

nickel steel. Metalworking. See **steel.**

nicolo. Gemcutting. See **intaglio.**

niddy noddy. Spinning. See **reel.**

niello. Jewelry. A man-made metal ranging in color from gray to bluish gray. The term ''niello'' comes from the Latin word meaning black. One **inlay**s niello into decorative depressions created by **etching, engraving, repoussé**, or **chasing** a base metal (commonly **silver**, but gold, **bronze** and steel are also used). It is then filed flush with the level of the surrounding metal. The niello formulas vary, but most require silver, copper, lead, and sulfur. Making niello requires extremely good ventilation. It has an obnoxious odor, and the fumes are very unhealthy to breathe. The technique goes back to ancient Egypt and is still in use in many parts of the world. Raw ingredients are blended together in a **crucible,** then poured into a second crucible, which contains sulfur, and heated until molten. The liquid is poured onto a steel surface and allowed to cool. The niello is then broken up into small chunks and finely ground with a mortar and pestle. It is then washed numerous times to remove impurities. After the washing it is packed into the areas of design that have been previously prepared in the base metal. It is packed high, much in the same manner as enamel while doing cloisonné, and then fired in a **kiln,** preferably only once, as continued firings cause it to become pitted or bubbly. Niello lasts indefinitely; however, unfired niello deteriorates and is especially sensitive to humidity. It should be stored in an airtight container, but even then it will not keep long. Also see **graphite rod, lead block.**

Niger morocco. Bookbinding. See **leather.**

nila. Dyeing. See **indigo.**

Nilghiri. Basketry. See **cane.**

nine-patch. Quilts. A basic, simple-to-make **block, pieced** from nine squares of identical size, usually in alternating colors. It gives a **checkerboard** effect. In some variations of the nine-patch, the central square is larger or smaller than the corner squares. More than half of all quilt patterns are based on the nine-patch and the **four-patch** design. The quilt known by this same name, **The Nine-Patch,** refers to a nine-patch of specific proportions. Some quilters refer to any nine-patch quilt by this name. See ill. Also see **Double Nine-Patch, Ohio Star, Shoo-fly, split nine-patch.**

Nine-patch, The. Quilts. A **block** design for a **pieced quilt** that consists of patches of three different sizes. The center square is large, with smaller squares forming the corners of the block, and with rectangles finishing the **nine-patch** square. The blocks may be **set** so that they alternate with plain blocks.

Nine-patch Chain. Quilts. A **block** design for a **pieced quilt** based on a particular arrangement of the **nine-patch.** Of the nine **patch**es, six are of solid colors and the other three are themselves nine-patches composed of smaller blocks. These nine-patches are placed diagonally into the larger block arrangement, so that when the quilt blocks are **set,** a diagonal chain appears over the entire **quilt.**

nip. Bookbinding. The term "nip in the press" refers to pressing a book in the **nipping press** for a short period, but with substantial pressure, to set the book's shape. If you have no nipping press, the book may be pressed between **board**s in the **lying press.**

nippers. Jewelry. Pliers with side-cutting, diagonal-cutting, and end-cutting blades with tempered and hardened edges. They can be used for cutting thin-**gauge** metal and clipping **solder;** however, their primary function is for cutting wire. Also see **shears, snips.**

nippers. Mosaics. See **clippers.**

nippers. Stained Glass. See **grozing pliers.**

nipping. Bookbinding. A momentary pressing of a book.

nipping press. Bookbinding. The nipping press is used when a material requires a brief pressing to set a shape or to flatten a freshly glued surface. The article is placed between sheets of clean waste paper and then between the **board**s of the press and centered under the screw pillar of the press. Screw the press down tightly and then release immediately. A nip in the press rather than a period of long pressing will not squeeze the glue or paste through the material being pressed. In the absence of a nipping press, a book may be **nip**ped between two press-boards in the **lying press** or **book press.** See ill.

Nipping press

nitric acid. Enameling. See **bright dip, cleaning metal, etching, matte finish, mercury gilding, washing enamel.**

nitric acid. Metalworking. A colorless acid (HNO_3) manufactured by the reaction of sulfuric acid on nitrates, and by the oxidation of ammonia. It is corrosive and should not touch the skin. Use it to clean **scale** from cast bronze objects and to **pickle** metals. It is also used to **oxidize** many metals.

Nitric acid was first made by Raymond Lully, an alchemist, in the thirteenth century, but was not generally used in metallurgy until the late nineteenth century. Also see **Metalworking: Finishing.**

Noah's ark. Toys. A **Sunday toy** probably developed in the late sixteenth century in Oberammergau. It consists of a **boat** or ark, with a ramp at one side with some kind of an opening into the ark. A series of paired animals fit inside. Noah's ark sets are traditionally made of wood.

Noah's ark animal ring. Toys. See **turned-wood animal.**

noble coral. Coral Carving. See **coral.**

noble metals. Jewelry. A small subgroup of the **nonferrous metal**s that have surfaces that are relatively unchanged by air; that is, they oxidize or corrode very slowly. These metals include **fine gold, fine silver,** and platinum and the others of its family group—osmium, palladium, rhodium, iridium, and ruthenium, all generally used for plating as they do not possess workable qualities.

noil. Spinning. The short fibers that remain in the **comb** during the **combing** process. They are used in making felt and low-grade yarns. In order to make them workable, they may also be mixed with longer fibers. **Silk** noil is a by-product of spun silk. It is spun into noil yarns, which are uneven and lumpy in character. Also see **Spinning.**

noisemaker. Toys. Any toy designed for the express purpose of making noise. The **rattletrap, Haman knocker,** and **ticktack** are noisemakers. Some toys produce noise, but it is a by-product, as with the **buzz button. Sound toy**s and **musical toy**s are considered to be noisemakers by many adults.

nominal size. Woodworking. See **wood.**

nonferrous metal. Jewelry. Metalworking. All metals that do not contain iron. Also see **cold forging.**

nonloom. Weaving. Refers to fiber techniques not requiring a **loom** to stretch a **warp** on. This would include single element techniques (those using a continuous single strand of yarn) such as crocheting, knitting, **looping, netting,** and **tatting**; and multiple element techniques such as **bobbin lace, braiding, card weaving, coiling, hooking, knotting, plaiting, twining,** and **wrapping.** There are also nonloom processes, such as **matting** and **felting,** that belong to neither of the above categories. Almost all nonloom techniques and processes can be combined with conventional weaving done on a loom. Also see **off-loom weaving.**

nonmordant dyes. Dyeing. Those **dyestuff**s that do not need **mordant** to produce a fast color. Among **natural dyes** this would include **indigo, woad, kermes** and **lichen dyes.** Also see **colorfast.**

nonobjective. See **abstract.**

nonorganic dye. Batik and Tie-dye. See **aniline dye.**

nonrepresentational. See **abstract.**

nonsewn garment. Stitchery. An article of clothing which has few or no **seams** or none of the usual complexities of **clothing construction.** A poncho is sometimes made with no sewing, and is a nonsewn garment. Other articles can be adapted for clothing so that little sewing is required. Tablecloths or blankets are examples of things which can be altered slightly to make simple **garments,** similar to caftans. They are nonsewn in the sense that the usual procedures for clothing construction are not followed.

nontoxic dye. Toys. See **food coloring.**

nontoxic paint. Toys. See **enamel paint.**

nonwoven material. Stitchery. Any **fabric** or cloth in which threads or **yarns** are joined by some method other than weaving. **Felt** is one of the most commonly known and used nonwoven materials. **Synthetic iron-on interfacing** may be a nonwoven material, as are some shiny plastics or imitation leathers. Other nonwoven fabricmaking methods include knitting, crochet, and macramé.

Noonday. Quilts. See **Sunburst.**

Noonday Lily. Quilts. See **Lily.**

noose. Basketry. A loop attached to the front of a hinge covered basket over which a **hasp** falls to secure the lid.

no-pin filling. Lacemaking. A lace **filling** made without pins. The leadworks are placed checkerboard fashion in alternate rows. This filling is made in the **leaf stitch** with **bobbins.**

Norman slab glass. Stained Glass. A type of stained **glass** whose name and method date back to the revival of the technique of hand glass-blowing, when there was need for rough, irregular pieces of glass to be used with **lead came.** The glass is gathered on the blowpipe and a bubble of glass is blown into a four-sided, rectangular bottle. The bulb of excess glass is removed and the bottle removed from the mold. It is then tapped so that the four sides fall apart. Each piece measures approximately 7″ × 5″ and the bottom measures 5″ × 5″. The pieces are difficult to use because of their irregularity of thickness. The edges are very thin, whereas the middle of the slabs can be ½″ thick. Painting on Norman slab is dangerous because the glass can explode in the **kiln** or develop **firecrack**s. Also see **crossed slab glass, painting on glass, tapper.**

North Carolina Lily. Quilts. See **Lily.**

North Carolina Rose. Quilts. See **flower designs.**

North Carolina Star. Quilts. See **star patterns.**

North Wind. Quilts. See **Kansas Troubles.**

Norway pine. Woodworking. See **pine.**

Norwegian knitting. Knitting. The traditional style of **color knitting** practiced in Norway for hundreds of years; it is characterized by simple, geometric designs—the background color is white, and the designs are navy, dull red, and dark green.

Knitting was practiced in Norway as early as the ninth century, and spread to the Faroe Islands and Shetland Islands through sailors and early settlers. Also see **Faroe Island knitting, Shetland knitting.**

Norwegian rölakan. Rugmaking. Weaving. See **rölakan.**

Nosegay. Quilts. An **appliqué block** design of a nosegay arrangement. It has a central bouquet of bright and delicate flowers, surrounded by buds or leaves, with stems at the base. A nosegay quilt sometimes includes flowers that give a three-dimensional effect through the use of folded **fabric.**

noshi. Papercrafts. The Japanese term (abbreviated from noshi-awabi) for a small folded-paper decoration that is attached to a gift or a purchase as a token of good fortune. This traditional decoration, which developed from an ancient custom, is also called a noshi wrapper.

noshi wrapper. Papercrafts. See **noshi.**

notch. Puppets. A groove or indentation cut into a piece of **wood** to aid in fitting sections together. When a square piece of wood is attached to a **dowel,** the round dowel rod may have to be notched in such a way that a flat surface is created to allow the square and round pieces to be securely joined. A notch is used in making a **tongue-and-groove joint.**

notching. Kites. The cutting of V-shaped grooves in the ends of the wooden **framing** sticks to allow the **guideline** to sit securely in position. Because most framing materials split easily when the ends are cut, it is advisable to wrap them with lightweight thread just below the notch before cutting.

notching. Tincrafting. The cutting of V-shaped patterns into **tinplate.** Notching may be carried out as a design in and of itself, or as a means of cutting out hard-to-cut parts of an overall flat design. In the latter case, the tough area to cut is bypassed during the first broad stroke of the **snips** until more space is available, at which point the snips return and notch out the tight cut. Also see **Tincrafting: Cutting the Tin.**

notion nannies. Toys. See **peddler doll.**

novelty yarn. Spinning. Weaving. A yarn whose structure is such that it has unusual or irregular effects as compared to the ordinary **single** or **ply yarn.** It can be of natural or man-made fibers with effect produced because of a difference in **twist,** tension, **count,** or rate of delivery of one of the yarns while spinning. This makes for loose, curled, knotted, or looped areas in the yarn. Novelty yarn can be single but more often it is ply yarn, consisting of a core yarn, or foundation yarn, around which the decorative or effect yarn is wrapped and held by a binder yarn. Novelty yarns can be made on spinning machines with special attachments, or by the handspinner on her own spindle or wheel. Often yarns have developed with handspinners and then been imitated by machine.

Some common novelty yarns are:

Spiral yarn or corkscrew yarn: made by twisting together two plies that differ in size or twist. Usually it is a soft and heavy yarn combined with a fine one. The heavy yarn is delivered faster than the fine one, and as a result, winds around the fine yarn in a spiral formation. In hand-spinning, this can be achieved by holding the finer yarn more taut than the heavier, so the finer one forms the core for the heavier one to wrap slackly around.

Guimpe yarn or gimp yarn: usually consists of a tightly twisted core yarn wrapped around with a soft twist novelty yarn. Sometimes guimpe has silk fiber, metallic yarn or flat tinsel wound around a soft core, making it one of the more expensive yarns.

Ratiné yarn: a heavy or bulky yarn in a spiral twist around a fine core. A binder of equal fineness holds the heavy yarn in place. The binder is twisted in the opposite direction of the first twist, so that the heavy yarn tends to unwind, but is still caught by the binder. A zigzag or rickrack effect results.

Bouclé yarn: has closed loops at regular intervals in the yarn. It is made of two or more strands, one of which is held taut, while the other forms the soft round nubby loops. A binder yarn twists the two together.

Loop yarn: made like a bouclé, but the loops are larger and more open.

Slub yarn: made by varying the twist so that certain areas are more loosely twisted or left untwisted to produce bulky effects, or slubs.

Flake yarn: soft, thick, elongated tufts of fiber placed at intervals between a core and binder.

Grandrelle yarn: a two-color yarn obtained by twisting two contrasting colors of single yarns or **roving** together. It is also known as marl yarn.

Nub yarn: made by twisting the effect yarn many times in the same place around the core until a small knot appears. Often a binder is added in a second twisting operation. Seed yarns are nub yarns with smaller knots. Other names for a nub yarn are knot yarn, spot yarn or knop yarn.

Chenille yarn: a woven yarn coming from a fabric that has been slit into fine warp-length strips. The yarn looks like a caterpillar with a **pile** protruding at right angles to the center, either on both sides or on just one side. A heavy chenille yarn can be woven on a **handloom** by putting a **warp** on the loom that has open spaces at one-inch intervals. A thick and soft **filling** yarn is used. It floats across the empty spaces. These **floats** are cut down the center when the fabric is off the loom and the strips are chenille yarn. Also see **fiber, leno, textured yarns.**

nub yarn. Spinning. Weaving. See **novelty yarn.**

numbering the design. Stained Glass. See **template.**

numerical order of bobbins. Lacemaking. **Bobbin lace** stitches are always made with four **bobbins** working at a time. Two bobbins constitute a pair of bobbins; a pair is held in each hand. When following instructions, remember that bobbins are always numbered from left to right as they lie on the **pillow.** Within one pair of bobbins, #1 is on the left and #2 on the right; when using two pairs of bobbins, the bobbins number 1, 2, 3, and 4, left to right. Bobbins work in pairs except, when a **gimp** is used, a gimp thread is worked with a single bobbin. See ill.

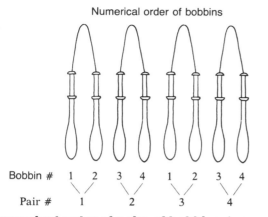

Numerical order of bobbins

Bobbin # 1 2 3 4 1 2 3 4

Pair #   1   2   3   4

numerical order of pairs of bobbins. Lacemaking. Two **bobbin**s constitute a pair of bobbins. When following instructions, remember that pairs of bobbins are numbered from left to right as they lay on the **pillow**. After a movement is completed, the pairs assume their proper numerical order: 1, 2, 3, 4, 5, 6, 7, 8, 9, and so on. See ill.

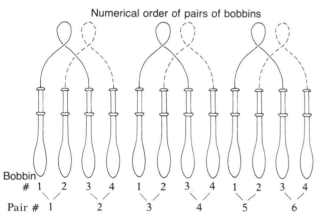

Numerical order of pairs of bobbins

Bobbin # 1 2 3 4 1 2 3 4 1 2 3 4

Pair #   1   2   3   4   5   6

nursery character. Toys. Any popular storybook character, human or animal, with which many children are familiar. Most make the transition from story to **stuffed animal, stuffed figure,** or toy, such as Little Orphan Annie, **Pinocchio, Peter Rabbit,** Humpty Dumpty, **Raggedy Ann,** and Alice in Wonderland. Others move in the opposite direction, starting out as someone's favorite **nursery toy** about whom books are later written, such as Pooh Bear and the **Golliwog.** Many contemporary nursery characters come from television and movies, such as the Sesame Street puppets. These favorite characters are produced from a wide range of materials, often relying on costuming to identify the character. Red Riding Hood and Alice, for example, are identified more by the clothes they wear than by their features.

Nursery characters are often known as mascot dolls or storybook dolls. Similar to these nursery characters are **comic-strip toys.** Also see **celebrity doll, character doll.**

nursery toy. Toys. Either of two general categories of toys. One includes those toys designed for very young babies (sometimes called baby toys) such as **rattle**s, **coral**s, **cradle gym**s, teething rings, and small soft toys.

Nursery toys also refer to any toys found in the children's nursery or play room, usually for preschool age

children. The early-twentieth-century interest in the needs of the preschool child led to rapid development of additional toys for this age group. **Hobbyhorse**s and **blocks** were among some of those that remained popular. Also see **fabric block.**

nut. Metalworking. Woodworking. See **bolt.**

nylon. Macramé. Nylon is a durable man-made fiber available in an extremely wide range of sizes and colors as macramé **cord.** Nylon seine twine is especially well suited to macramé knotting.

nylon. Spinning. Weaving. See **filament.**

nylon. Stitchery. A generic term applied to manufactured filaments or **fiber**s derived from polyamide resin and to **fabric**s made from these fibers. These **man-made fiber**s are obtained from coal, air, and water. Because nylon is lightweight, strong, and elastic, it is a desirable material for many uses. Prolonged exposure to sun and light impair the strength of nylon.

nylon leader. Puppets. Stitchery. A clear nylon monofilament fishing line. It is exceptionally strong and nearly transparent and fills many of the craftsperson's needs for a non**fraying thread** or cord. It can support a large amount of weight, usually specified on the product package by pound. It has the disadvantages of weakening from exposure to sunlight and a tendency to stretch when under tension or with a weight suspended from it. Because of the stretching it is not recommended for **stringing puppet**s. Also see **shadow play, shadow puppet.**

nylon rope. Toys. An extremely strong and slightly elastic rope made from nylon filaments. It is available in various diameters and is described in terms of either diameter or the weight it will hold. Nylon ropes are smooth and pleasant to touch (in contrast to **manila rope**). It is manufactured in a variety of bright colors. If used to hang **swing**s it should be knotted in such a way as to avoid abrasion because nylon will wear away under constant rubbing. The ends of nylon rope can be melted by applying heat or flame to keep them from raveling. Knots may require readjusting on a swing because the nylon tends to stretch when weight is attached. Also see **box swing.**

nylon seine twine. Macramé. See **nylon** and **Macramé: Tools and Materials.**

nylon stocking doll. Toys. (Also called stocking doll.) A doll made from a nylon stocking. If ample stocking length is allowed, the body can be made from the same section of nylon as the head. Arms and legs may be made separately and attached. The dolls are **stuff**ed with **Dacron polyester batting** or **cotton batting.** Also see **alto-relief, blusher, nylon stocking head, sock doll.**

nylon stocking head. Puppets. Toys. A three-dimensional stuffed head made from a nylon stocking filled with **batting.** The features are sculpted by stitching through the nylon and the batting, forcing some areas to protrude and others to recede.

A section of stocking is knotted at one end, then stuffed. The **stuffing** should extend below the area of the head so that when **string** or cord is tied around the stuffed shape to suggest a neckline the string is tied on top of stuffing. That way the head will hold erect. If only a ball of stuffing is tied off, the head will flop from side to side.

After the stuffed head area has been tied off, stitching can begin. Knots are always kept at the back or at the neckline. A double thread should be used, but not too large a needle or it may cause the nylon stocking to run. A ball-point needle will help to avoid runs. An area of the stocking may be pinched to suggest a nose. The stitching to hold the nose in place would go back and forth at the face level, from the left side of the nose to the right, forcing the nose shape to protrude. A stitch at the bottom of the nose will round it out.

Other stitching may go all the way through the head from front to back to create recessed areas, as for the eyes or at the ends of the mouth. **Felt** or fabric may be used to suggest eyes, or features may be added through the use of embroidery. Yarn, batting, braided unspun wool, wiring, felt strips, or old wigs may be used for **hair.**

The stocking head made in this way can be used for a nylon stocking puppet or a **nylon stocking doll.** The faces assume surprisingly realistic expressions, as the soft folds of the nylon are skinlike in appearance.

nylon stocking puppet. Puppets. (Also called stocking puppet, stuffed-stocking puppet.) A **hand puppet** that utilizes a stuffed **nylon** stocking for the head. It is similar to the simple **sock puppet** but allows for a more elaborate kind of facial detail.

A tube is first found or made to fit around one or two fingers. A light cardboard can be rolled and taped or tied, then a **Dacron polyester batting** or **cotton batting** is padded loosely around the tube to make it round and head-shaped. A tubular section of nylon stocking is pulled carefully down over the **stuffing.** Then the nylon is tied around the neck. If more stuffing is needed, it can be inserted from the top before being tied off there. When the head shape is prepared, the features are sewn on the **nylon stocking head.** Hair may be added, and clothes are made to allow for the fingers, as in **hand puppets.** Also see **softhead.**

nylon tricot. Stitchery. (Also called tricot.) A knitted jersey made from **nylon** threads or yarns. It has some "give" or stretch to it and is sometimes used for the top layer of **English trapunto** work, particularly in clothing.

O

oak. Woodworking. A generic name for a group of over 50 varieties of a strong, close-grained **hardwood** that ranges in color from creamy and yellowish white to dark brown.

It is used for furniture, flooring, interior finish work, tool handles, **woodcarving,** and whittling. It tends to check and warp and so must be carefully seasoned and stored, but it takes a high polish and is very durable. American or domestic oak has three classifications: white oak, red (or black) oak, and live oak. Red oak is slightly inferior in quality to white oak. The white oak (also called Eastern or mountain oak) is the most common and, in wood sculpture, is better for broad, simplified designs than for intricate ones. Live oak is relatively scarce. European oak often takes the name of the country it is native to.

Oak Leaf. Quilts. Any of a great variety of **appliqué** designs that use four leaf shapes pointing to the four corners of a **block.** Some resemble a tree shape, others leaves; all have a central square, star, or circular flower form. These blocks are **set** as **all-over pattern**s, alternated with solid blocks, or divided with **band**s. Oak Leaves and Cherries and Charter Oak are two variations of the Oak Leaf pattern. See ill. Also see **Quilts: Quilting.**

Oak Leaf

Oak Leaf and Reel. Quilts. An **appliqué block** that combines **The Reel** with an oak leaf at the four corners.

Oak Leaves and Cherries. Quilts. See **Oak Leaf.**

oak tanning. Leather. See **vegetable tanning.**

oasis morocco. Bookbinding. See **leather.**

oblique Tunisian stitch. Knitting. See **Tunisian stitch, oblique.**

oblong cross stitch with backstitch. Needlepoint. This stitch consists of a tall **cross stitch,** worked four mesh long and two mesh wide. It is tacked down in the center with a small horizontal **backstitch** two mesh.

This stitch works best in one color in an area where an interesting texture is desired. It works up slowly and gives a firm backing. Also see **long arm cross stitch, Montenegrin cross stitch.**

oblong punch. Leather. (Also called bag punch.) A punch for piercing several sizes of oval-shaped slots for attaching bag straps and buckles. See ill. Also see **drive punch.**

Oblong punch

obsidian. Gemcutting. A mineral composed of aluminum silicate with potash, soda, and lime. It is found as volcanic glass. It has a **hardness** of 5½, a **specific gravity** of 2.3–2.6, a refractive index of 1.495, is vitreous to greasy **luster,** has a sharp conchoidal **fracture,** and an amorphous structure. It occurs in black, gray, brown, yellow, red, and blue varieties and is opaque, except in thin sections when it has paler color and translucency. Obsidian, like optical glass, is polished with cerium oxide on a felt buff.

Magnetite is black obsidian, colored by included iron. Mahogany obsidian is a brown-black variety. Perlite (also called silversheen) is obsidian with numerous air-bubble **inclusion**s. Also see **crystal, polishing, refraction** and **Gemcutting: Hand Grinding and Polishing, Rough Shaping.**

obsidian. Glasswork. Stained Glass. Natural glass formed when sandy lava cools. Also see **fulgurite.**

ocean wave. Quilts. See **Quilts: Quilting.**

ochre. Ceramics. A term given to clays containing varying amounts of red iron or **manganese oxide**s. Ochre can be used as a **glaze** or **slip** colorant to render tan, brown, and brick red hues. Also see **burnt sienna, sienna.**

ochre. Enameling. A yellow pigment used by painters that is applied to soldered connections in a piece to prevent the solder from melting when fired. Also see **firing** and **Enameling: Tools and Materials.**

ochre. Metalworking. See **yellow ochre.**

Octagonal Star. Quilts. A **pieced block** pattern of an **eight-pointed star.** It is one of many popular **star pattern**s that may be identified by this name. See ill., page 598.

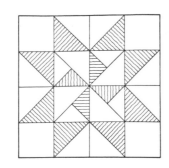

Octagonal Star

Octagons. Quilts. A **pieced quilt** in which the primary shape is an octagon. When the octagonal shapes are joined, a square shape emerges between them. A simple way to make an octagon quilt is to fit and sew a small triangle onto each of the four corners of a square **block,** leaving spaces between the triangles so that eight equal sides remain. Then when the squares of alternating colors are **set,** octagons emerge with **split two-patches** between them.

The Octagons quilt is sometimes called an **Hourglass** because of the shape formed by two of the octagons.

octavo. Bookbinding. A book (abbr. "8vo") made up of groups of eight leaves, or sixteen **page**s. Also see **leaf, section.**

Odd Fellow's Cross. Quilts. See **Odd Fellow's Patch.**

Odd Fellow's Patch. Quilts. (Also called Odd Fellow's Cross.) Any of a variety of **pieced block** designs that are reminiscent of **Birds in Flight.** This block can be used as an **all-over pattern,** or it can be separated with alternating blocks or **band**s. The triangles in this block point inward in bands that cross to form the letter X. Also see **Letter X.**

Odd Fellow's Star. Quilts. See **star patterns.**

odds-and-evens. Weaving. An old term for the **tie-up** to weave **plain weave.** One **treadle** is attached to all odd-numbered **harness**es. The second treadle is attached to all even-numbered harnesses.

Odd Star. Quilts. See **star patterns.**

odontolite. Ivory and Bone Carving. See **fossil ivory.**

off-and-on stitching. Bookbinding. Sewing the **section**s together with the thread running through the sections at every second tape. Also see **sewing on tapes.**

off-center came. Stained Glass. See **lead came.**

off-grain. Stitchery. See **off the grain.**

off hand. Glasswork. Said of glassblowing made by hand with a **blowing iron** and without the aid of **mold**s. Also see **freeblowing.**

off-loom picks. Weaving. See **picks per inch.**

off-loom weaving. Weaving. A catch-all phrase implying different things to different weavers. In the purest sense it means the use of **nonloom** techniques to create a woven structure. This is a very restrictive definition that would limit the practitioner of off-loom weaving to **finger weaving** or **plaiting** alone. In common usage the definition has split into two directions. It means either the use of nonloom techniques to fashion a two- or three-dimensional fiber structure or a woven structure made on anything other than a **harness loom.** This could include anything from a primitive **branch loom** to a **frame loom** with a **continuous warp** and many **heddle bars.** The techniques employed would be both woven and nonloom ones.

offset. Bookbinding. **Offset lithography,** one of the printing processes. Inks transfer to the opposite page, usually occurring when pages are left stacked. The opposite, or offset, page serves in the manner of a blotter. Offset is also called setoff.

Also, a type of printing by indirect image transfer from photomechanical plates. Offset printing is the most common printing method in use today. See **offset lithography.**

offset lithography. A commercial printing process similar to **lithography,** wherein the inked image, carried on a grainy-surfaced (usually aluminum) plate, is transferred or "offset" from the plate onto a rubber-covered roller and then from the rubber surface to the paper. The image area and the nonprinting area on the plate are at the same level and are kept separate by means of a chemical difference in the surfaces. The process is also called photo-offset because the printing image is made ink-receptive by means of a photographic process.

offset printing. Block Printing. An indirect printing technique in which the image is transferred from the **printing block** to a roller or **brayer,** then printed from the brayer onto a sheet of **paper.** First the block is evenly inked with a brayer, then a clean brayer is pressed over the block, picking up the image. The size of the design is limited by the size of the brayer. If a large brayer is available, this technique can be useful for work with fine detail, such as printing leaves or feathers by inking them and then transferring their image to the brayer and then to paper.

off the grain. Stitchery. Not with the **straight** of the **fabric.** Occasionally fabric designs are printed off-grain or off the grain, which means that the lines of the design do not align themselves with the **grain** of the fabric. A **bias** cut is "off the grain" since it cuts diagonally over the threads.

ogee. An S-like curve used as a decorative element of a design. Ogee curves combine concave and convex sections. Such curves are often used as decorative edging or fluting in furniture or architectural details. See ill.

Ogee

ogee. Woodworking. See **molding.**

Ohio Rose. Quilts. Any of several variations of **flower designs** for **appliqué quilt block**s. The best known has a large central flower encircled by leaves and buds. See ill.

Ohio Rose

Ohio Star. Quilts. A **nine-patch pieced block** that depicts an **eight-pointed star**. The nine **patch**es are a combination of **one-patch** and **split two-patch** blocks. It is one of the numerous **star patterns**. See ill.

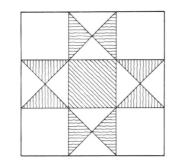

Ohio Star

oil. Ceramics. See **kiln fuel**.

oil and water technique. Stained Glass. This technique for **painting on glass** utilizes the incompatibility of water and oil. To achieve a marbling effect, brush or sponge partially evaporated turpentine onto the glass. Brush watercolor paint over turpentine, forming droplets.

The following procedures do not produce a marbled effect: painting **oil-base paint**s on top of wet water color paint; floating oil paint on a water base. Also see **staining**.

oil-base paint. Stained Glass. (Also called Drakenfield paint.) These are used in **painting on glass** and are as effective and permanent as water-based glass-stainers' paints. They come in all colors and must be used with a nonvegetable oil/turpentine-based medium. Oil-base paints take longer than other paints to dry on glass. The powder is ground first and the medium added (no **gum arabic** is necessary) until the proper consistency is achieved. They fire at lower temperatures than water-base paint—about 1000–1050° F. Also see **oil and water technique, stick lighting**.

oil-base paint. Toys. See **enamel paint**.

oil-base paint. Woodworking. See **paint**.

oiled wool. Knitting. Wool that has been processed with some of its natural lanolin left in to make it waterproof. This wool was originally used in Aran Isle sweaters, and today is often knit into warm, water-repellent fishermen's sweaters.

oil-fired kiln. Ceramics. An oil kiln is used mostly in high fired pottery and it works on the drip-feed principle where oil is transformed into a mist or vapor for use. An oil kiln fires easily and cheaply and the temperature is easily controlled. However, the more unrefined the grade of oil used, the more smoke it makes in firing. Also see **gas kiln, wood firing**.

oil gilding. Découpage. (Also called mordant gilding.) See **gilding, gold size**.

oil of cloves. Enameling. See **binder**.

oil of lavender. China and Glass Painting. See **lavender oil**.

oil of lavender. Enameling. See **binder**.

oil of sassafras. Enameling. See **binder**.

oil of spike. Stained Glass. See **enameling**.

oil of turpentine. Enameling. See **binder**.

oil pencils. Découpage. See **color pencils**.

oil putty. Woodworking. See **wood filler**.

oil resist. Batik and Tie-dye. The use of oil to **resist dye penetration** in **fabric**. Household vegetable shortenings or household cooking oils can be used as resists for **batik** and **cold dyeing**. Thick resists can be applied with spatulas and various tools; liquids can be applied by brush. Oil resists are not as easily controlled as some other resists and do not always resist dye completely, so experimental pieces are essential.

oil stain. Woodworking. See **wood stain**.

oilstone. Jewelry. See **Arkansas oilstone, India oilstone**.

oil stone. Leather. See **Leatherwork: Care and Maintenance of Tools**.

oilstone. Stained Glass. (Also called sharpening stone.) A grinding stone used for sharpening tools such as the **glazing knife**. Also see **Stained Glass: Tools and Materials**.

oilstone. Woodworking. See **sharpening stone**.

oil tanning. Leather. See **Leatherwork: Tanning and Manufacture**.

oil test. Batik and Tie-dye. A simple test used to distinguish between cotton and linen fibers. A drop of oil on linen produces a translucent area. On cotton, the area remains opaque. Also see **Batik and Tie-dye: Identifying Fibers**.

oil varnish. Woodworking. See **varnish.**

Ojibwa loom. Weaving. See **free-hanging warp, Ojibwa weaving.**

Ojibwa weaving. Weaving. The weaving done by the Ojibwa (Chippewa) Indians of the Algonquin tribe that is native to the Great Lakes region. They practiced several types of cloth construction that was categorized as weaving, such as the **plaiting** or **finger weaving** of sashes, bands, pack straps, and garters; the weaving or **twining** of mats made of cattails, bulrushes, birch bark, and basswood bark strips, used as wigwam coverings, floor coverings, table and house partitions; and the twining of intricately patterned flat, rectangular bags used for storage or carrying. It is the last, with its complex and sophisticated design detail, that most weavers allude to when speaking of Ojibwa weaving. The frame on which to construct these bags is known as the Ojibwa loom. However, this is not true weaving, but **weft twining** done on a vertical support which is similar to the **warp-weighted loom,** except that the **warp end**s are not weighted, but are left hanging free and loose, suspended from a cord stretched between and around two stakes.

The early bags were made of false nettle fiber which was spun with moose or buffalo hair into a yarn of roots, rushes, and vegetal fibers with the natural colors of each item forming the pattern. Most bags were tightly constructed, but openwork bags of twisted basswood fibers were used for washing corn. True yarn that was used for these so-called yarn bags was probably spun of buffalo hair. In the seventeenth century when commercial woolen trade fabrics were brought in by the Europeans, the Indians began to fray out and respin the wool from these blankets and cloth. Nettle fiber and basswood bark remained in use as their warp. By 1850, commercial yarn obtained from traders was used to make the bags. When used for storage, the bags were approximately 20″ × 20″ in size. Small bags were used to carry charms or medicines. Early designs were symbolic, stylized birds, butterflies, and animals woven in bands, along with geometric forms. The tightly constructed yarn bags were made in a variety of twined patterns. The most basic was diagonal twining or **twill twining.**

The Ojibwa loom is constructed of two long (about 36″) rods or dowels inserted vertically into a board or the ground. The distance between the upright rods should be the width of the item being twined or slightly wider if the rods are "springy" and tend to pull in during work. Several strands of cord are stretched between and around the outside of the two rods near to the top of them. Pegs or nails can be inserted into the rods to keep the cord from slipping down while working. Warp ends are cut all to the same length (about 2½ times the length needed) and attached to the cord with a **lark's head knot** so that each length becomes two warp ends. This is done around the entire cord so that there are warp ends on both sides as well as on the outside of the vertical rods. There are no side seams, as the twining proceeds downward and around the loom. When the bag is finished it is slipped off the top of the rods and the upper, open ends are sewn together to become the bottom of the bag. The hanging warp ends are braided around the rim or wrapped to form a corded edge. Below the braid or cord an open warp area is left through which another cord is laced in and out and which pulls the bag closed like a drawstring. See ill. Also see **quillwork.**

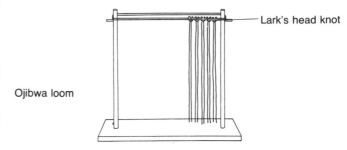

Ojibwa loom — Lark's head knot

Old Colony Star. Quilts. See **star patterns.**

old Florentine stitch. Needlepoint. A technique of alternating pairs of two long and two short stitches, the short stitch always one-third the size of the longer. Work the stitch back and forth horizontally, the long stitches of one row meeting the short stitches of the succeeding row; the short stitches are placed in the middle of the long stitches. The old Florentine stitch is very effective worked in two colors and can be used as a **filling stitch** or a **border stitch.** It is not recommended for an area that will receive a lot of wear, as the long stitches tend to snag. The old Florentine stitch works up quickly and does not use much yarn.

In one variation of the old Florentine the short stitches are placed in the upper third of the long stitch in the first row. In the return row, the short stitches will be placed in the lower third of the long stitch and the entire row interlocks with the preceding one. This variation is an excellent border stitch since two rows form a band. See ill.

Old Florentine stitch

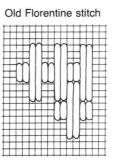

Old Homestead. Quilts. See **Log Cabin.**

old Indian weave. Weaving. See **finger weaving.**

Old Maid's Puzzle. Quilts. See **Letter X.**

Old Maid's Ramble. Quilts. See **Kansas Troubles.**

old shale lace pattern. Knitting. See **Knitting: Stitches and Patterns.**

Old Tippecanoe. Quilts. (Also called Tippecanoe and Tyler, Too.) A **block** design consisting of 32 triangles. They are arranged to suggest overlapping squares and angles so that when the quilt is **set**, new patterns emerge. The block was designed in honor of President William Henry Harrison. See ill. Also see **presidents' quilt**.

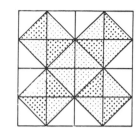

Old Tippecanoe

old woman in the shoe. Toys. A toy based on the nursery rhyme of the woman who "had so many children she didn't know what to do." It consists of a shoe filled with the many figures of the children and their mother. Craftspeople often make the children of fabric or wood.

oleic acid. Stained Glass. See **flux** and **Stained Glass: Glazing.**

oligioclase. Gemcutting. See **feldspar.**

olivine. Gemcutting. (Also called peridot.) A magnesium silicate **crystal**lized in the orthorhombic system with **hardness** of 6¾, **specific gravity** of 3.3–3.4, conchoidal **fracture,** and vitreous to greasy **luster.** Olivine is green, occurring in translucent to opaque varieties. It is soluble in hydrochloric and sulfuric acids.

Chrysolite is a transparent variety of olivine with low refractive indices of 1.66 and 1.7, and strong double **refraction.** It is green, yellow, or brown with weak dichroism. It is **faceted** with main crown facets at 43° and main pavillion facets at 39°, and polished with 14,000 grit **diamond** on a plastic **lap.** Also see **faceting, polishing.**

ombré stripe. Rugmaking. Weaving. See **stripe.**

ombré yarn. Crewel. Embroidery. Needlepoint. The French term meaning "shadowed" and descriptive of a yarn that is shaded with graduated tints from light to dark of one color. This **yarn** works best in a very textured or patterned stitch. It is not recommended for most **shading stitch**es because there is no control over color placement.

once fired ware. Ceramics. (Also called glazed greenware.) Ware that is fired in one long fire that includes both bisque and glaze firing. Glaze is applied to **leather-hard** or dry clay. The glaze must dry completely before **firing.** Also see **bisque fire, glaze fire.**

on-edge lamination. Stained Glass. See **lamination.**

one-fold cutting. Papercrafts. See **symmetrical cutting.**

one-over-one principle. Knitting. This principle is used in **cable knitting** to form the twists in the cable. It is done by holding stitches in reserve on a **cable needle** without

working them, working the stitches immediately beyond them, slipping the held stitches back on the regular needle, then working them. Depending on the particular pattern, these stitches can be held either in front or in back of the knitting. See ill. Also see **stitches in waiting** and **Knitting: Stitches and Patterns.**

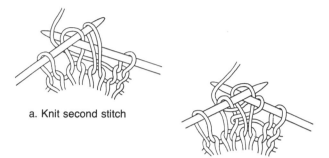

a. Knit second stitch

b. Knit first stitch and remove both stitches

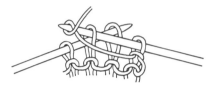

c. Purl second stitch, purl first stitch, and remove both stitches

one-patch. Quilts. A single **patch** or piece that is used to make an entire quilt pattern. All the pieces are identical in size, and in the simplest type there is no attempt at arrangement of colors. Some well-known one-patch quilt patterns are **Brickwork, checkerboard, Honeycomb, Thousand Pyramids, Tumbler.**

one-piece doll. Toys. See **single-shape doll.**

one-piece mold. Metalworking. See **mold.**

one-prong thonging chisel. Leather. See **thonging chisel.**

one-way joint. Puppets. See **hinge joint.**

onglaze color. China and Glass Painting. (Also called china color, overglaze color, or vitrifiable color.) Colors in a powdered form prepared particularly for decorating china that contain **mineral color** and **flux.** The color is mixed with **medium** and painted onto glazed, undecorated china, then fused by **firing** to form a glassy bond with the glaze underneath. Onglaze colors are fired at a much lower temperature than **underglaze color,** so a wider range of color can be used. **Metallic color** is available in hues from greenish bronze to **gold** and **silver.**

onionskin egg. Toys. An **egg** colored by wrapping the hard-boiled egg in the skins of a red onion to impart a linear pattern of deep red and brown. Also see **Easter egg.**

onlay. Bookbinding. See **inlay.**

onlay. Weaving. See **laid-in.**

on-loom picks. Weaving. See **picks-per-inch.**

on the grain. Quilts. Stitchery. Usually, "on the grain" refers to the **lengthwise grain.** Sometimes it means on either lengthwise or **crosswise grain,** running parallel to either **warp** or **weft** threads. When directions specify "on the grain," the warp or weft threads should run straight through the length of a piece being cut. It specifically means the piece should not be cut on the **bias.**

onyx. Gemcutting. See **quartz.**

opacifier. Ceramics. A chemical that is relatively insoluble in the **glaze fire. Tin oxide** and **zirconium oxide** are the major opacifiers. The most effective opacifiers are white. **Titanium oxide** forms minute crystalline structures within the glaze. This type of crystal formation is associated with **matte** glazes.

OPACIFIERS

Color	Oxide	Percentage	Firing temperature	Kiln atmosphere
Pure white Weak blue-white	Tin	5	Any	Either
	Titanium	8−12	Any	Either
	Zirconium	8−12	Any	Either
Weak yellow-white	Antimony	10−12	Low	Oxidizing

opacity. The quality of inks, paints, or other materials that prevents the passage of light. A paint with high opacity is one that has good hiding power—one coat is enough to cover a surface without the surface color below showing through. For example, cadmium yellow **pigment** is more opaque than hansa yellow even though both colors have approximately the same **hue.** One would use a hansa yellow where the opposite quality of transparency was desirable. Similarly, the paper of this book is of medium opacity. It is difficult, but not impossible, to see the image printed on the opposite side of this page.

opacity. Candlemaking. The absence of transparency in candles depends on the amount of **stearic acid** added to the **paraffin.** The higher the proportion of stearic acid, the greater the opacity. For a snow-white effect, the candle should contain as much as 33% stearic acid. Also see **Krystalline.**

opacity. Ceramics. See **opaque glaze.**

opal. Gemcutting. Hydrated silica with amorphous structure, **hardness** of 5½ to 6½, **specific gravity** of 1.9−2.3, and refractive index of 1.45. Opal has conchoidal **fracture** and vitreous, greasy, waxy, or resinous **luster.** Most opal is cloudy or opaque. It is decomposed by hydrofluoric acid and strong alkalis. It occurs in white, brown, yellow,

black, and green with play of color. It fractures easily if overheated, requiring care when **dopping,** grinding, **sanding** and **polishing.** It should be dopped using a heat lamp and shellac **dop** or a cold dop made with acetone cement and cornstarch. Opal is polished with cerium oxide on a rock-hard felt buff or on a muslin buff with tin oxide.

Hyalite is transparent material.

Harlequin opal has a yellow-red body **color.**

Flame opal has a **streak** of color resembling a flame.

Mother of opal consists of specks of material in the dull brown **matrix** called potch.

Fire opal has a red body color with the characteristic play of color.

Petrified wood may become opalized in a manner similar to the **quartz** variety.

Hydrophane is a translucent opal that absorbs water and becomes transparent. It is so porous it sticks to the tongue, and makes a hissing sound when immersed in water.

Cachalong is an opal with alternate light and dark bands.

Black opal is a valuable variety often imitated by cementing opal to a black background in a **cabochon doublet.** Also see **Gemcutting: Hand Grinding and Polishing.**

opalescence. Gemcutting. See **luster.**

opalescent antique glass. Stained Glass. See **German antique glass.**

opalescent glass. Stained Glass. A type of commercially made **cathedral glass** that is semiopaque, usually with a milky appearance and streaked with two or more colors.

opaque enamel. Enameling. See **enamel.**

opaque glass. Stained Glass. This is **glass** too dark to see through. To cut this glass using the cut-lining method: since the **cut-line** cannot be seen through the glass, trace the outline onto the glass with carbon paper; then dust the carbon line with a **pounce bag,** which will leave a white cutting line on the glass.

opaque glaze. Ceramics. A glaze through which light will not pass, but which reflects light back from its surface. Opacity is the result of an uneven or **matte** surface of reflective matter suspended in the glaze. The basic opacifiers are oxides of tin, zinc, zirconium, or titanium. Also see **titanium oxide, zinc oxide, zirconium oxide.**

open binding. Batik and Tie-dye. See **spiral binding.**

open body. Ceramics. Unfired clay mixed with **grog.** The grog content reduces drying and firing **shrinkage** and the danger of thermal shock. It also refers to a **clay body** with large pores.

open canvas. Rugmaking. See **canvas mesh.**

open cutting. Papercrafts. See **open silhouette.**

open-end box wrench. Woodworking. See **wrench.**

open-end thimble. Stitchery. See **Chinese thimble.**

open-end wrench. Woodworking. See **wrench.**

open filling stitch. Crewel. Embroidery. A stitch used for filling in an area and that allows the **background fabric** to show through and become part of the design. The **detached** stitches work well in this manner. **Wave stitch** and **back stitch threaded** are also open filling stitches. Also see **cloud filling stitch, interlaced cable chain stitch, raised honeycomb filling.**

open firing. Ceramics. See **direct firing.**

open grain. Woodworking. See **wood.**

opening. Ceramics. A step in throwing where the mound of clay is opened in preparation for bringing up the walls into a **cylinder.** Also see **Ceramics: Firing.**

opening a new book. Bookbinding. Opening a new book properly the first time prevents damaging the **back lining,** thus extending the life of the book. Stand the book on its **back edge** and allow the covers to drop open. Fold the **endpaper** flyleaf back to its paste line, simultaneously turning down the front and back leaves a few at a time. Run your finger along the groove every few pages. Continue to do this, gradually working your way to the center of the book. Also see **leaf.**

opening the screen. Silkscreen. The process by which the screen material in the **screen frame** is cleared of backing material or other materials that temporarily clog the openings in the screen during preparation of the **stencil.** See **cut paper stencil, photographic stencil, tusche stencil.**

open kiln. Stained Glass. See **kiln.**

open mesh. Crochet. (Abbr. om.) The term for the meshlike sections of **filet crochet** worked with the **double crochet stitch.**

open mold. Plastics. See **mold.**

open out. Basketry. In **woven basketry,** to spread the base **spoke**s radially after the initial **tying-in** of the spokes has been completed and the weaving begun. Also see **Basketry: Woven Basket Construction.**

open satin stitch. Stitchery. (Also called open zigzag.) The **machine satin stitch** that has been adjusted to allow space between the stitches. It makes a **zigzag** pattern. The open satin stitch can be used as either a basting or finishing stitch, depending on the **fabric** and the intended use.

open silhouette. Papercrafts. (Also called open cutting.) A **silhouette** in which internal details are cut, so that it is no longer a true silhouette but a paper **cutout.**

open warp tapestry. Weaving. See **exposed warp tapestry.**

openwork techniques. Weaving. Those **finger-manipulated** techniques or a combination of techniques that give a fabric open areas or openings (eyelets). The openwork is often in combination with **plain weave,** the pattern of the **filling** yarn, and the pattern of **transposed warp** threads. These weaves include **gauze weave, leno, slit tapestry, Brooks Bouquet, wrapping, Spanish lace, Danish Medallion** and **Peruvian lattice.** The openwork can be found in some cases as the total fabric and, in others, in certain areas as a design motif or trim. Openwork weaves are also called **lace weave**s, although the fineness that the word "lace" implies should perhaps reserve it only for **loom-controlled** lacy-looking fabrics.

   Another type of openwork fabric can be achieved by leaving out certain sections of warp ends, i.e., having them spaced apart in the **reed,** and then also spacing the filling so that open areas alternate with the filling beaten in as desired.

open zigzag. Stitchery. See open **satin stitch.**

operator. Puppets. See **puppeteer.**

operator's bridge. Puppets. See **bench.**

opposites. Weaving. A term having dual meanings—one pertaining to the **treadling** and the other to the **threading.** In treadling it is the lifting of two **harness**es in a **pattern weave** that are the direct opposite of those two lifted in the previous **shed.** This applies to the **twill tie-up** used for the pattern in weaves such as **crackle, summer and winter weave** and **overshot.** The pattern **pick** is normally followed by a pick of **plain weave ground.** In weaving "on opposites" each pattern pick is followed by its opposite pattern pick and the plain weave eliminated, i.e., pattern pick 1-2 is followed by pattern pick 3-4, 2-3 by 1-4, 3-4 by 1-2, and 1-4 by 2-3. It is also possible to weave 2-3-4 followed by 1, 3-4-1 by 2, 4-1-2 by 3, and 1-2-3 by 4, although care has to be taken against long **floats.** The **filling** thread is usually the same weight in each pick and, if the ground pick is eliminated and the **sett** is open, a heavy fabric with the **warp** covered results. Since the ground weave is essential in holding the pattern threads together, the reason for these structures not falling apart is that the "opposite" treadling locks or binds the previous pick in place. It is therefore called **boundweave.** Color placement is an important factor since it serves to delineate the design. The weight makes the cloth ideal for rugs, throws, heavy seat cushions, and wall hangings.

   There are also **drawing-in draft**s threaded "on opposites." This involves a two-**block pattern,** where one block would be consistently threaded on harnesses 1 and 2, and the second block on harnesses 3 and 4. This produces a starkly defined pattern without the half-tones produced in such multi-block weaves as overshot. **Monk's belt** is a classic example of threading "on opposites." Also see **boundweave.**

optical paradox. Toys. An **optical toy** consisting of a single glass lens ground into six prismatic segments. The apex of each prism is at the periphery of the circular glass piece. When a picture is viewed through this the image disappears, allowing segmented adjacent designs to appear instead. Its effect is humorous for the incongruous ways in which pictures are apparently cut and reassembled. Also see **Toys: Optical Toys.**

optical pyrometer. Ceramics. (Also called disappearing filament pyrometer.) A tool used to read the temperature of a kiln during **firing.** Also see **pyrometer.**

optical toy. Toys. Any of a great variety of toys invented in the early nineteenth century, most of which demonstrate or illustrate the optical principles and optical illusions from which cinematography was developed. The **thaumatrope** and **phenakistoscope** were among the very popular early ones. Later the **zoetrope** and the **magic lantern** reflected the continuing interest in movement and light. The fascination with animation, as evidenced by the tremendous variety of optical toys, led to early experiments in photography and cinematography. The optical toy is in some ways similar to the **peep show.** Both emphasize visual material of educational value.

Some of the contemporary interest in optics and op art is similar to the Victorian fascination with optical toys. Also see **chromatrope, graphoscope, kaleidoscope, kittiscope, lampscope, optical paradox, panoptique, polyoptique, taleidoscope, Thames tunnel** and **Toys: Optical Toys.**

Opus Anglicanum. Embroidery. (Literally: English work.) A type of ecclesiastical embroidery done in England in the thirteenth century. It was done by covering the entire ground with couched gold metal threads. The strong threads holding the gold were pulled right through to the reverse side of the fabric as each stitch was taken, giving the gold a textured, patterned effect on the right side. This technique was known as **couché rentré,** or reverse side couching. Opus Anglicanum hangings and vestments were of such exquisite workmanship that they were exported all over the then-known world, and had considerable influence on the embroideries of other countries. Also see **couching, metallic thread embroidery,** and **Bargello.**

Orange Peel. Quilts. See **Lafayette Orange Peel, Reel, The.**

Orange Slices. Quilts. See **Reel, The.**

orbital flat lapping machine. Gemcutting. See **flat.**

orbital sander. Plastics. Woodworking. See **sanding tools.**

orchil. Dyeing. See **lichen dye.**

ordnance steel. Metalworking. See **gun metal.**

organdy. Quilts. Stitchery. A crisp, **sheer fabric** of **cotton** which is semitransparent and lightweight. It is similar to **organza,** which is more transparent but less easily handled than the cotton organdy. **Starch** or **sizing** is added to organdy, making it easy to control in sewing.

When batik or tie-dye processes are used on organdy a very delicate pattern can be developed. Some batik artists employ a transparent layer of batik used over a second pattern of batik on a more opaque material. Unusual contemporary quilts have been made using batik on organdy as the top layer.

In **quilting,** organdy may be used as the top layer in a technique called **shadow quilting.** It may also be used as a covering layer over **patchwork** with quilting then going through four layers instead of the usual three.

In stitchery, organdy is used for **transparent appliqué.** Because of the slight stiffness it works well for either **hand-appliqué** or for **machine-appliqué.** Colored organdies are used in a painterly approach of overlapping transparencies.

organza. Quilts. Stitchery. A **fabric** similar to **organdy** but more wiry and more transparent. It is made of **silk, rayon,** or **synthetic fiber**s. Organza is used like organdy, though it is not always washable.

Oriental kite. Kites. See **Kites.**

Oriental Poppy. Quilts. A **block** design from the early 1900s. It is a combination of **piecing** and **appliqué** in which the flower form is **pieced** from small **geometric** shapes and the stem and leaves are appliquéd. The pieced and appliqué parts both form squares, so when the quilt is **set** the two squares alternate.

Oriental rug. Rugmaking. Weaving. Handwoven rugs with a **knotted pile** produced in the Middle East with most of them coming from either Turkey or Persia (Iran). The term can also pertain to rugs from the southeast Balkans, the Caucasus, and as far east as India and China. Oriental rugs are appreciated not just as articles of use, but more as works of art, having a richness of design and symbolism and a highly sophisticated and intricate use of color. They can be divided into those rugs made in workshops in specific regional centers and towns of the Middle East and those made by nomads. The latter also make **soumak** and **flatwoven rug**s. There are hundreds of types of Orientals. Some of the better-known varieties are Kirman, Sarouk, Kashan, Tabriz, Hamadan, and Shiraz.

The craftsmanship of Oriental rugs is usually of the highest quality and is measured by the number of knots per square inch, their fineness and regularity. The average is about 300 knots per square inch. Throughout the centuries they have been treasured pieces and many attempts have been made to copy them in the West in all forms of rugmaking from weaving to painting and printing. Wear gives true Orientals a rich patina; the more they are used the better they look.

Oriental rugs are used as floor coverings, wall hangings, covers for divans and pillows, saddle bags and blankets, and as prayer rugs on which the devoted Moslem prostrates himself at an appointed hour with his forehead resting in a niche pictured on the rug that is pointed toward Mecca. Also see **pile rug, rugweaving.**

Oriental stitch. Crewel. Embroidery. See **Roumanian stitch.**

Oriental soumak. Rugmaking. Weaving. See **soumak.**

orifice. Spinning. The small opening in the **spindle** on a **treadle wheel** through which the spun yarn travels en route to the **guide hook**s of the **flyer.** Also see **flyer assembly.**

origami. Papercrafts. The traditional Japanese art of **paper folding.** Birds, butterflies, etc., are carefully formed by intricately folding small squares of lightweight **origami paper.** The use of symbolic, paper-folded designs for festivals, ceremonies, and entertainment has been a Japanese tradition since the latter part of the twelfth century.

In origami instructions, certain terms are used, such as valley fold for a concave crease, or mountain fold or peak fold for a convex crease. The valley folds are more commonly used, so unless specified, a fold means a valley fold. Directional words are used consistently, such as up for toward the top of the page, down for toward the bottom of the page. Forward means toward you, behind means away from you. Repeat behind means to repeat on the far side only. If the directions seem complicated, pencil marks can be made on the origami paper to correspond with the marks in the diagrams. See ill.

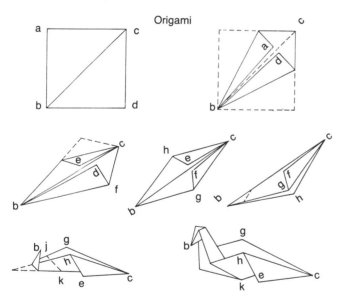

Origami

origami. Toys. The Japanese art of **paper folding.** Animals, objects, and figures of all kinds can be made by folding the papers in prescribed ways. They are often made from special **origami paper**s. Origami is a kind of **paper sculpture.**

origami paper. Papercrafts. Toys. Thin, crisp, tissuelike paper squares (4″ or 6″ square) available in packages of assorted bright colors for use in **origami.** Also see **madras tissue paper.**

Original Rose. Quilts. (Also called Indiana Rose.) An **appliqué block** design that depicts a large central rose surrounded by four leaves. It is one of many **flower designs.** See ill.

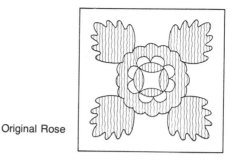

Original Rose

Oriole Window. Quilts. See **Circular Saw.**

ornamental cut. Leather. (Also called dress cut.) Various decorative cuts may be made with the **swivel knife** by varying the pressure applied to the tool. These swift, scrolly, decorative cuts take some practice to master, but they are essential to **tooling** leather, as most freehand embellishment is done in this style. See ill.

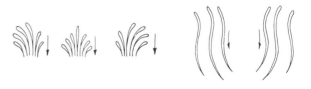

Ornamental cuts

ornamental spot. Leather. A type of **nailhead,** traditional in Western leatherwork, which has a colored faceted stone or glass in the center.

Ornate Star. Quilts. See **Combination Star.**

orrisroot. Beadwork. The fragrant rootstock of the Iris florentina, which is powdered for use in perfumery as a fixative or preservative. See **perfumed beads.**

orthoclase. Gemcutting. See **feldspar.**

orthorhombic system. Gemcutting. See **crystal.**

orton cone. Ceramics. See **cone.**

Osage braid. Weaving. See **chevron plaiting.**

osier. Basketry. See **willow.**

osnaburg. Stitchery. A **cotton** cloth of coarse **plain weave,** usually natural or unbleached, which is often used in **stitchery panel**s and for batik or tie-dye. This fabric was originally made of **linen** in Osnaburg, Germany, and at one time was woven for grain and cement sacks.

osseous amber. Amber Carving. See **amber.**

Ostrich Plume. Quilts. See **Princess Feather.**

ounce. Leather. The thickness of leather is measured in terms of weight. It is determined by the number of ounces in one square foot of leather. If one square foot of leather weighs 1 oz, it is called one-ounce leather and is $^1/_{64}$″ thick. Two-ounce leather weighs 2 oz per square foot and is approximately $^1/_{32}$″ thick. As weight and thickness of a particular hide are seldom uniform throughout, the markings may read 6/7 oz, meaning the skin weighs between 6 and 7 ounces per square foot. This skin therefore ranges between $^6/_{64}$″ and $^7/_{64}$″ in thickness. Also see **Leatherwork: Weight Designations.**

outline stitch. Crewel. Embroidery. See **stem stitch.**

outline stitch. Stitchery. A simple **stitch** used to give a fine, distinct line. It is commonly used with **appliqué** in wall hangings and in defining the features on dolls. It is usually worked from right to left at a slight diagonal, so that each stitch overlaps the last.

outline tooling. Leather. A **tooling** technique in which the design outline only is cut with the **swivel knife** and is pressed down, leaving the rest of the design raised. Also see **embossing.**

outlining. China and Glass Painting. A technique of making very fine lines with fine **brush**es or a **crowquill pen** for delicate accenting and outlining in china painting. Often only the outlines of a design are painted, then the firing is done. Next the areas are filled in with color, then refired. The paint for outlining should be the consistency of thin cream. Mix powdered color with a **medium**, then thin slightly with a drop or two of turpentine until the paint flows evenly. Hold the pen or brush in an upright position and draw the lines with an even, slow pressure, lifting the tip as little as possible.

outlining. Lacemaking. The technique of highlighting the outer edge of a motif or design by using a **cordonnet, gimp,** or an **overcast stitch.**

outlining. Weaving. A **tapestry** technique used to define certain color areas from adjoining ones and used to keep the colors distinct. It can be horizontal, diagonal, or vertical. In horizontal outlining, two **pick**s are inserted in the **plain weave** in a color different from the areas to be outlined. If only one row is put in, the line is very fine and uneven. Three or four picks will result in a thick outline. Diagonal outlining is similar to horizontal outlining with the exception that the picks are not placed at right angles to the **warp,** but placed on a diagonal according to the shape already woven. A very steep diagonal or a rambling shape is outlined differently, since the angle of elevation or the irregular contour does not permit an easy laying in that would not distort the warp ends and that would be beaten in without difficulty. In these cases, the outline is wrapped around the warp ends in a successive progression going forward over two threads and back under one. One or two rows can be put in in this manner, depending on how pronounced the outline is to be. The method is called limning and is a form of **wrapping** said to have originated with the ancient Peruvians (**a.**). Another method that came from the Peruvians is a vertical outline that consists of leaving a warp end vacant between areas and then wrapping it (**b.**). It creates a **slit tapestry** that is not sewn together. An alternate method of vertical outlining that creates a joining of the two color areas is dovetailing or interlocking the adjoining areas to the outline thread. This is almost like lacing the two areas together and it forms an outline that is broken by the colors of the areas with which it is joined. See ill. Also see **dovetailing, interlocking.**

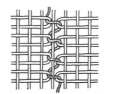

a. Diagonal wrapped outlining or limning   b. Vertical outlining

outlining designs. Needlepoint. When working an intricate design begin by outlining areas of color in **tent stitch** using the same color in which the whole area will be worked. Because of the nature of **canvas** it is extremely difficult to obtain a rounded shape. The needleworker should not be afraid to skip stitches, as the eye will complete the line. The most common mistake of novices is to put too many stitches in one line. A crewel stitch such as **stem stitch** can be worked directly on top of your finished needlepoint, rounding out the shape.

outside caliper. Woodworking. See **measuring tools.**

oval. Basketry. One of the common shapes of a basket. In woven basketry it is obtained by accenting one direction in organizing the loose rods before beginning the weaving. Also see **Basketry: Woven Basket Construction.**

oval. Batik and Tie-dye. An elongated circular shape that may be made in **tritik tie-dye** by **folding** the fabric and then sewing through the double thickness. The running stitch outlines one-half of the oval (or any symmetrical shape) at the fold of the material. It is then drawn up tight, fastened off, and dyed. This gives a **resist** outline of the whole shape.

An oval may be similarly produced by **ruching,** in which the first line of sewing starts at the folded edge, moves in a scallop or dropping arch across the material, and then back up to the fold. Then a second parallel line is needed to make a channel through which the wood can be inserted. A fold is made on the first line of stitching so that the channel follows the shape of half the oval. When tied and dyed, an oval pattern is formed.

oval cut. Gemcutting. See **facet.**

oval drive punch. Leather. See **drive punch.**

oval-head screw. Woodworking. See **screw.**

oval rug. Rugmaking. See **round rug.**

oval rug frame. Crewel. Embroidery. Needlepoint. See **embroidery frame.**

oven. Ceramics. See **kiln.**

oven forming. Plastics. See **thermoforming** and **Plastics: Thermoforming and Molding.**

ovenware. Ceramics. **Pottery** that can be used for cooking in an oven and which can stand extreme changes in heat and cold. If not to be exposed to a direct flame, most **earthenware** and **stoneware** clay can be used to make ovenware bodies.

over. Crochet. (Abbr. "o," "yo." Also called yarn-over.) The process of bringing the **yarn** over the crochet hook from back to front in such a way that the yarn can be caught by the hook and pulled through existing stitches to form new stitches. One of the most essential and basic crochet movements, this procedure is used in virtually all crochet work.

over. Knitting. The "over" is an ornamental increase used to create extra stitches in lace and fancy patterns. It is also used with a decrease to make holes for ribbons or buttons, and to make a **picot edge.** Overs can be used for **fashioning** in a garment. The yarn is taken over the needle before or after a stitch, on either the **knit** or **purl** side of the fabric. Also see **faggot stitch, lace faggot stitch** and **Knitting: Increasing, Decreasing.**

overall. Quilts. A single design that completely covers the **quilt top.** The **Tree of Life** is one example of such a design. Overall design is different from **all-over pattern.**

Overall Bill. Quilts. See **Sunbonnet Girl.**

over-and-under. Basketry. One of the most fundamental weaves, using a simple over-one, under-one stroke. It is also used in **checked plaiting** and **checked wicker weaving** or **randing.** Also see **Basketry: Plaited Basket Construction.**

overarm slab machine. Gemcutting. See **flat.**

overcasting. Rugmaking. Weaving. A stitching device done to prevent the ends of a woven fabric from raveling. It can be done when the fabric is on the **loom** or off the loom. If done off the loom, the fabric should be placed flat on a table with a weight on top of it to make the overcasting easier and faster. Overcasting can be a prelude to **hemming** or it can be a **finishing edge** in itself with the free **warp end**s left dangling unfinished as a **fringe.** The overcasting is done with matching yarn and gives a diagonal line or ridge if the stitches are closely spaced. The stitching goes over the warp end and the last two or three **filling picks** and then under these picks, emerging to the surface at a point just below them and before the next warp end. The same procedure is repeated for each warp end. This is done from **selvage** to selvage with the yarn being caught at each edge with a couple of extra stitches. See ill.

Overcast edge with fringe

overcasting edge. Needlepoint. One method of binding a raw edge before working on the **canvas** is to fold the edge back on itself and securing it with a whipping stitch which simply wraps around the fold. This can be done with any type of thread. Also see **whipped chain stitch, whipping** and **Needlepoint: Preparation and Layout.**

overcast seam. Stitchery. A **plain weave** which is pressed open and then stitched at the **raw edges.** Usually an **overcast stitch** is used to keep the raw edges from **fray**ing. See ill.

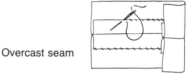
Overcast seam

overcast stitch. Crewel. Embroidery. This stitch is excellent for lines, stems, and especially monogramming. Begin by laying down a **running stitch,** picking up very few threads of the **background fabric** between the stitches. Work **narrow satin stitch**es repeatedly over the running stitches at right angles to them, giving a firm, raised texture. This stitch is much used in **whitework** and fine embroidery.

overcast stitch. Lacemaking. A stitch made with needle and thread to secure together two edges of fabric or a piece of fabric and lace. A continuous row of small stitches is worked parallel and very close together. Place the needle at a diagonal, taking up a small bit of fabric from both layers together. Bring the needle out, and advance it for the next stitch.

In **needle lace,** an overcast stitch is used to outline an area or is worked over a cord to form a **picot,** as in **Carrickmacross.**

overcast stitch. Stitchery. A simple overlapping **stitch** used to attach one piece of **fabric** to another or to **hem** an edge. It is similar to a **whip stitch,** though it is longer and leaves more thread exposed. See ill. Also see **felt appliqué.**

Overcast stitch

overdyeing. Dyeing. See **top-dyeing.**

overfiring. Ceramics. **Firing** a **glaze** beyond the recommended temperature. Overfiring can ruin kiln shelves and cause ware to become distorted. It also causes **matte** glazes to become shiny and run. Also see **flushing.**

overfiring. Enameling. (Also called burn out.) A technique of using higher than usual temperatures in firing enamels to obtain special effects. Opaque whites may discolor into green or gold hues; some soft opaques become transparent or darken. Silver **cloison**s or **pallion**s melt and darken. Since **enamel**s may erupt through layers above, thin coats should be used for overfiring. Experimentation and testing are necessary to control results. Also see **color testing, torch firing, wisteria line** and **Enameling: Basic Operations.**

overfiring. Stained Glass. The **firing** of glass in the **kiln** for too long or at too high a temperature. Overfired glass can be recognized by its excessively glossy appearance; the sides of the glass begin to melt. The complete disappearance of paint is also due to overfiring; the paint should be reapplied. Also see **firing out, firing stain, staining.**

overglaze. Ceramics. Pigments applied over a fired glaze. Overglaze colors are enamels and easily applied. The overglaze enamels are fired at 1085° F. Also see **luster.**

overglaze. Enameling. A finely ground—at least 150 mesh—**enamel** intended for ceramics but applicable over enamels for fine detailing and delicate shading. It is available in both liquid and powder forms. To use the powder, mix it with a small amount of oil to a painting consistency; thin with squeegee oil used as a **binder,** and apply with a **sable brush** or crowquill pen. Allow to dry thoroughly to a **matte finish** before firing at a low (1350° F) temperature. If overfired, the glaze may sink into the enamels beneath and disappear. Testing is necessary for successful results. A final coating with flux is advisable to prevent the overglaze from deteriorating. Also see **color testing, grisaille, metallic luster, underglaze** and **Enameling.**

overglaze color. China and Glass Painting. See **onglaze color.**

overhand knot. Macramé. (Also called cluster.) The overhand knot is a simple knot made by forming a loop with one or more cords and then pulling the loose end through the loop to form a knot. The overhand knot can be worked in a series on one cord to form a **sennit,** or singly, one on each cord, in **finishing** a piece of macramé. See ill.

Overhand knot

overhand knot. Rugmaking. Weaving. A knot formed by a self-loop with the end of the yarn passing through the loop. It is often used as a simple **finishing edge** on rugs, wall hangings and other weavings before they are hemmed, or as the main treatment given to a self-**fringe** or an added fringe. It is done with at least two **warp end**s and often with a group of them. When overhand knots serve to keep the first and last **pick**s of weaving in, they should be

pushed up tight against these picks. As an ornamental fringe they can serve the same function and allow the ends to hang loose to form the fringe. In addition, each group of loose ends can then be divided in half and a second row of overhand knots made of two adjacent half-groups. This gives a second row of knots in a staggered position to the first row. This second row can also be divided in half and the third row made up of these new halves to form a row in the same position as the original row of knots. Since the overhand knot is so simple to make, yet holds so well when pulled tight, it can be placed anywhere in the length of the fringe and combinations of overhand knots can be made to form a lacelike effect. See ill.

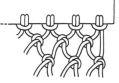
Fringe of overhand knots

overhand stitch. Rugmaking. Weaving. See **lacing stitch.**

overhead beater. Weaving. See **beater.**

overlaid stitch. Beadwork. See **overlay stitch.**

overlaid stitch. Crewel. Embroidery. See **Roumanian stitch.**

overlap. Fabric Printing. See **Fabric Printing: Designing.**

overlapped seam. Leather. A seam-sewing technique in which the seam allowance of one of the layers to be joined is trimmed away. The piece with the seam allowance remaining is then overlapped on the other piece to the depth of the seam allowance. Tape or glue to hold while topstitching along the overlapped edge. For a more decorative look, a second line of stitching may be added near the edge of the overlapped piece. Also see **Leatherwork: Sewing Leather.**

overlay. Crewel. Embroidery. Needlepoint. See **clear plastic grid overlay.**

overlay. Weaving. See **laid-in.**

overlay sheet. Plastics. See **air shield.**

overlay stitch. Beadwork. (Also called appliqué work, couched stitch, overlaid stitch, spot stitch.) A popular method of stitching beads to a background of skin or cloth used in **American Indian beadwork.** The **bead**s are threaded on heavy **thread** and placed in the desired pattern, then held in place by overlay stitches taken between every few beads with a separate needle and thread. When stitching beads to leather, the needle does not go through completely, but passes through the skin halfway, parallel to the surface, with no stitches showing on the wrong side. See ill. on the next page.

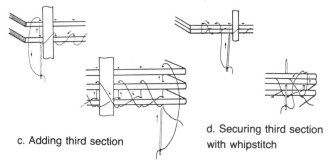

Overlay stitch

over principle. Knitting. The use of **over**s to increase or decrease for a decorative effect, and to create a **picot edge.**

overprinting. Block Printing. Stenciling. A technique of printing one color over another. In block printing, a simple block can be cut with large, plain areas, then printed in a light color. When the paint is dry, a second block, cut with smaller, more intricate shapes, can be printed over the first areas in a darker color. This simple method of multicolor printing can be executed without elaborate **registration.** The total finished design should be planned before the blocks are cut, so that the small applied shapes are compatible with the large ones.

overprinting. Fabric Printing. A printing technique in which **fabric** is printed, allowed to dry, and then printed in another color over the first printed areas.

oversewing. Batik and Tie-dye. A variation of the **tritik** method in **tie-dye.** It uses an overcast or whip stitch on a folded edge of fabric or on a narrow, flat **tuck** of single cloth. The size and the consistency of stitch length and spacing will affect the final design. Stitches must be drawn up tightly as they are sewn. Every five or six stitches the thread should be pulled taut. This causes the fabric to roll beneath the stitches. In variations of oversewing the material can be folded several times before sewing, or a folded edge can be rolled and then overstitched. The oversewing technique is sometimes called "stitched tie-dye."

Oversewing can be used to outline shapes drawn on the surface of the fabric. This method does not draw the material into bunches as the running stitch does. The deeper the stitches are taken, the wider the **resist** pattern will be. The closer together the stitches are taken, the more they will resist the **dye.** After the dye process more stitches can be added, or stitches can be removed and the process started over for the second color.

oversewing edge. Needlepoint. In order to unite two pieces of worked **canvas,** place the two side by side with the fronts facing you. Beginning with your needle at the right, take small whipping stitches. The stitch should be small, regular, and close together. This is especially useful in joining plastic canvas. Also see **joining canvas, whipped cable stitch, whipping.**

oversewing single sheets. Bookbinding. A method useful for manuscripts, books with severely damaged **back section** folds, and magazines. An oversewn book is equal in strength to one that is sewn through the sections. Magazines and books must first have the backs trimmed in the **plow**; trim off as little as possible so the words in the inner margin of the pages will not be lost after binding. Remove the staples from magazines before **trimming.**

Place the material between sheets of heavy white paper or **kraft paper,** clamp in the press, and trim just deep enough to reach the innermost sheets. Brush the cut back with flexible **glue** and allow it to set until tacky. Place the material in the **stabbing clamp** and adjust it until the glued edge is even with the edge of the bar. Drill the back through each of the holes with the **hand brace,** using a $1/16''$ drill bit. The holes should begin about ¾" in from the **head** and **tail.** (An **awl** may be used in the place of a stabbing clamp.) When dry, separate the sheaf into sections of about 8–16 pages, depending on the thickness of the leaves. After stabbing or drilling, crease each section on both sides just inside the line of perforations, parallel to the back, using a **bone folder** and straightedge; this will allow the book to open with ease after binding.

To oversew onto buried **tapes** or **cords,** place the first section in the sewing frame with the tapes positioned between stab holes; whipstitch from head to tail, passing the thread over the tapes, not through them (**a.**). Lay the second section on the first and tie them together at the tail. Whipstitch them together as far as the head (**b.**). Place the third section on the second and insert the needle upward through the sections, down across the outside of the back, and tie it to the trailing tail of thread where you began sewing (**c.**). Insert the needle into the same hole, bring it up through all three sections and then down over the back in a whipstitch and up through the next hole in sections two and three (**d.**). Continue whipstitching section two to section three until you reach the tail. Lay section four in place and pass the needle through all the sections, entering the first stab hole near the tail; whipstitch over the back and up again through sections two, three, and four. Whipstitch section four to section three, working from tail to head. Repeat these stitching procedures until all the sections are joined. See ill.

a. Whipstitch first section   b. Adding second section

c. Adding third section   d. Securing third section with whipstitch

overshot. Weaving. A vast category of pattern weaves whose design are developed through **floats,** or overshots, of **filling** over **warp.** These weaves are perhaps the most popular of all pattern weaves in this country as well as in weaving communities around the world. In America they have a rich history of invention and adaptation; early and simple overshot patterns found their way into complex structures of entwining floral motifs and geometric motifs. Their names are indicative of the pattern's look or history. Some of the more colorful are Wandering Vine, Traditional Roses and Rings, Lee's Surrender, and Blooming Leaf of Mexico.

Although complex in detail, the overshots are logical and direct in construction. They depend on three elements: the warp, the **ground** filling, which is the same thread or weight as the warp and weaving with it, and the pattern filling, a heavier or softer yarn that floats and forms the design. The **drawing-in draft** is composed of blocks which in turn are composed of two-**harness** units. The units are 1–2, 2–3, 3–4, 1–4. It can be seen that the drawing-in draft derives from the **twill treadling**. The units are combined into pattern blocks of any desired size. There is no distinct separation between the blocks, and the last thread of one block may become the first thread of the next block. In weaving, every **shot** of pattern is followed by a shot of ground filling for the **plain weave** interlacing. The **treadling** is either as-drawn-in, which means the pattern is squared with a diagonal of blocks running through the square; in rose fashion, which gives a symmetrical pattern without the diagonal; or a completely original treadling.

Overshot is primarily a four-harness weave, but it can be extended to six or eight harnesses. Its good color effect is made up out of pure pattern color or half-tones of pattern which is sometimes mixed with warp and which make it a favorite for rugs, pillows, drapes, runners, coverlets, linens, and apparel. See ill. Also see **colonial overshot, corduroy, monk's belt, square-off, treadling-as-drawn-in.**

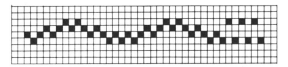

An example of the twill structure of an overshot drawing-in draft

overtwist. Spinning. Weaving. See **twist.**

oxidation. Ceramics. The combination of a substance with oxygen. In **firing,** it refers to the high level of oxygen maintained in the **kiln.** Also see **reduction.**

oxidation. Jewelry. Metalworking. See **corrosion, oxide.**

oxide. Ceramics. See **chemistry of pottery.**

oxide. Jewelry. Metalworking. The coating left on a metal surface as a result of oxidation (the combination of oxygen with the metal). The coating will be blue-green on **copper,** black on **lead,** white or gray on **aluminum** and **zinc,** and reddish-brown on **iron** or **steel** (rust). On certain metals such as aluminum, copper, and copper **alloys,** this covering prevents further corrosion.

oxide. Stained Glass. See **antique glass colorants.**

oxidize. Batik and Tie-dye. To unite with oxygen through exposure to air. In **vat** dyeing, oxidation is the final step that develops the dye color. Oxidation should occur on the fabric after it has been removed from the **dyebath.** Care is always taken so that the vat itself is not oxidized. Unnecessary stirring or the use of a **dye vessel** with a wide top may allow the dyebath itself to oxidize; this must be avoided because it is the reaction between fiber and dye that makes the color permanent. Also see **indigo.**

oxidizing fire. Ceramics. A clear fire with lots of air intake where oxides remain unaltered. **Earthenware** is fired in a fully oxidizing atmosphere. Secondary air must be allowed in the **kiln** in an oxidizing fire, or there will be a **reduction** atmosphere.

oxidizing flame. Jewelry. Metalworking. See **flame.**

oxyacetylene fusion welding. Metalworking. See **welding.**

oxyacetylene welding. Metalworking. See **oxyacetylene welding equipment, welding,** and **Metalworking: Welding.**

oxyacetylene welding equipment. Metalworking. Equipment needed to do oxyacetylene gas **welding.**

Two different tanks, or cylinders, are used—one for oxygen and the other for acetylene. Store them upright in a cool place. Avoid bumping them with objects that might cause sparks or punctures. Return to the supplier any tank that is badly dented or corroded. Keep grease and oil away from the valves and never lubricate them. Never try to repair a leaky cylinder by welding or any other means. Put it outdoors and call your gas distributor. Both oxygen and acetylene tanks are equipped with a cylinder valve that is threaded for connection to pressure regulators. Use a **wrench** to open and close valves. If the threads are damaged, making it difficult to connect the regulator, do not use the tank. Return it to the distributor, reporting the number that is stamped on the side of the cylinder. When returning empty tanks, close the valves tightly and screw on the metal cap if supplied. Mark them "MT" with chalk and store them apart from the full ones to avoid confusion.

To use a tank, clean off and check the threads of the cylinder valve for damage. Stand to one side and **crack the tank** with a rapid quarter turn, opening the cylinder valve to blow out any dirt in the valve. Close again quickly. Leave the cylinder key or wrench on the tank in case you have to shut it off in an emergency.

A regulator (also called a pressure regulator or pressure gauge) is a device screwed on top of the oxygen and acetylene tanks that controls the amount of gas pressure. There are generally two pressure gauges for each tank regulator. One registers the total cylinder gas pressure and the other the working pressure supplied to the torch.

To use a regulator, adjust the working pressure by opening the valve on the torch so the gas is flowing out. Turn the adjusting screw on the regulator until the working pressure gauge shows the desired pressure. If the torch valve is closed when regulating the pressure, the pressure will fall when the torch is in operation.

Do not use acetylene gas beyond 15 lb working pressure because it becomes unstable.

There are two nonporous hoses, a red one for acetylene and a green or black one for oxygen. The acetylene hose connections have left-handed threads (you tighten them by turning to the left) and the oxygen connections have right-handed threads. This guarantees correct attachment of hoses and regulators. Never tighten the connections so tightly with a wrench that you have difficulty removing them, damaging the threads. For safety, do not try to repair a damaged hose with tape. Keep the hoses away from sparks and hot metal. Oil and grease will deteriorate the hoses.

The welding torch mixes the oxygen and acetylene and discharges them through the end of the torch tip (**a.**). The torch has two tubes (one for oxygen and the other for acetylene), a mixing chamber, and valves to control and adjust the flame. Different sized tips, each requiring a specific gas pressure, are available for welding varying thicknesses of metal. (See Table.)

	Tip Number						
	00	1	3	5	8	10	12
Metal thickness (in.)	¹⁄₆₄	¹⁄₁₆	⅛	¼	½	¾	1
Oxygen pressure (psi)	1	1	3	5	7	9	12
Acetylene pressure (psi)	"	"	"	"	"	"	"

To use a welding torch, open each valve and then close it, one at a time, before lighting the torch. This purges the lines, torch, and tip of any impurities or dirt, and prevents premature mixing. Light the torch with a friction lighter, not a match. When changing tips, wipe the threads and connections clean. Dust or dirt can prevent a good fit. Clean or clear the tips with a copper or brass wire of the proper size, or use the specially designed cleaning drills.

A cutting torch is a torch specifically designed for cutting **ferrous** metal (**b.**).

The cutting torch is similar to a welding torch, but it has a large lever control that introduces a stream of pure oxygen through the tip, causing rapid oxidation and cutting of the metal. The torch is designed to produce two types of flames. The preheating flame, which melts the metal, comes from a series of small outer holes in the tip; the cutting flame consists of the preheat flame plus the pure oxygen stream, and comes through a large central hole of the tip.

Cutting tips also come in a variety of sizes and demand appropriate gas pressures. (See Table.)

	Tip Number			
	0	1	2	4
Metal thickness (in.)	¼	½	1	2
Oxygen pressure (psi)	30	40	50	50
Acetylene pressure (psi)	3	4	5	5

A friction lighter (also called flint lighter, igniter, spark lighter) is a device with a piece of flint that produces a spark when the handle is squeezed (**c.**). It is used to ignite both welding and cutting torches safely.

Welding goggles are specially designed for oxyacetylene welding (**d.**). Do not use sunglasses because they will not give protection against the infrared and ultraviolet rays given off by the torch. If after welding you notice white spots before your eyes, the goggle lenses are not dark enough to provide adequate protection. Wear clothing that overlaps areas that might catch sparks. Wear a cap, high shoes or boots, and turn down pants cuffs. The clothing should be free of holes or fringes. Wear leather gloves with gauntlets. See ill.

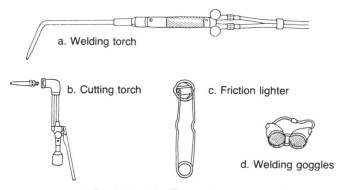

a. Welding torch

b. Cutting torch   c. Friction lighter

d. Welding goggles

oxygen-acetylene torch. Enameling. See **torch.**

oyster knife. Stained Glass. See **stopping knife** and **Stained Glass: Tools and Materials.**

p

packing. Basketry. The technique of building up a particular side of a basket with one or more short turns in a **round** of weaving to compensate for imperfect symmetry.

packing. Metalworking. See **blacksmithing techniques.**

packing chisel. Metalworking. See **blacksmithing tools.**

packing glass. Stained Glass. Packing materials include excelsior (the best all-around material), Styrofoam, and foam-rubber chips for filling up large spaces in a packing crate.

Fill the base of a wooden crate with a thick layer of excelsior. To pack several panels, place the tallest in the center, with a sheet of corrugated cardboard between each panel or sheet of glass. Fill the areas around the sides and top of the crate with either excelsior or foam-rubber chips.

A panel with **Norman slab glass** requires extra packing material around the glass. The crate should be large enough to allow 2–3″ of space for excelsior around the glass.

Do not apply pressure to the glass during packing. The crate should be labeled DO NOT LAY FLAT, so that other crates are not piled on top. See ill. Also see **Stained Glass: Care and Maintenance of Stained Glass Pieces.**

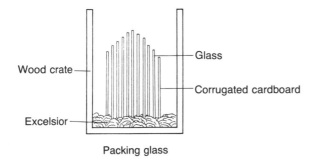

Packing glass

padded appliqué. Stitchery. A small, decorative piece of **fabric** sewn to a larger one and **stuff**ed as it is sewn. The **padding** is usually accomplished piece by piece—that is, by stuffing each individual piece as it is sewn. The padding material may be **Dacron polyester batting** or any other **stuffing** material.

padded stitchery. Stitchery. A decorative approach to **stitchery** which may be accomplished in either of two ways. Individual shapes may be padded, as in **padded appliqué.** In another approach a layer of **batting** or **stuffing** may be placed between the **face** or top material and the **backing** material. Then stitching is done over the whole **panel,** similar to **quilting.** Some quilted **wall hangings** are referred to as padded stitchery to distinguish them from **quilts.**

padding. Rugmaking. Quilts. A thick, soft yarn, or narrow strips of soft fabriclike flannel placed under a stitch as it is being embroidered in order to raise it and bring it into sharper relief. The padding is laid over the backing along the line of stitching. It can be pinned in place if it shifts. It is best to have the padding in a color related to the yarn you are stitching, so that if it shows through the stitches, the effect won't be disturbing.

In quilts it refers to any substance used as **filler** or stuffing for the middle layer in a quilt. In **trapunto,** the padding may be **cotton** cord or **batting.** In **quilting,** the padding is usually a large sheet of batting or a **cotton flannel** sheet blanket, but it can be any other soft and lightweight yardage.

padding. Stitchery. The **filler** used to **stuff** areas of stitched work. Unless **trapunto** is used, the padding is usually inserted from the top. An **appliqué** piece may be sewn about three-fourths of the way around, then the padding is slipped in and the sewing is completed. The padding may be layers of **flannel,** other **fabric,** or **batting.**

padding. Weaving. Placing heavy wrapping paper, lightweight corrugated paper, or a series of smooth, flat sticks between every layer of **warp end**s as they are wound around the **warp beam.** Padding, or layering, is used to insure that every layer of ends goes around the beam as smoothly and evenly as possible, and that there are no sections where the ends pile up on top of each other—a condition which leads to uneven tension while weaving. The padding should be wider than the warp width so that the ends on the edges will not slip off. The paper length should be slightly less than that of the warp. If this is not available, the paper can be overlaid or taped together. The padding is inserted after the warp makes its first revolution around the warp beam. The paper when first inserted must go in straight or it will angle off and the warp yarns will fall off at one end. Tugging at the paper after every revolution keeps the warp tightly wound and brings to the surface any slack threads that may have inadvertently gone around the beam. If sticks are used, they are placed in a continuous alignment around the entire warp beam during the time of the second revolution of the warp. The warp, as it winds around the beam, holds them in place. In successive revolutions, sticks are added one or two per revolution. They are placed at the point where the warp is just ready to go around the beam.

Some weavers also recommend padding the cloth as it is wound around the **cloth beam.** If this is done, heavy wrapping paper works the best and is easiest to use. This paper can be heavy duty grocery bags that are cut open and taped together. See ill.

Padding

paddle. Ceramics. A flat, wooden **beater** with a handle used to flatten clay or for stirring **glaze** and **slip.** Also see **beaten forms.**

paddle. Glasswork. A tool used in glassblowing to flatten parts of the work while it is in a molten state. The paddle is customarily made of wood and has a handle. Because paddles burn or char in use even when used wet, they are considered expendable and are usually made up by the glassblower as needed. Modern paddles are sometimes made of a small slab of graphite with a metal handle. Graphite scarcely burns, and it has the necessary slickness that the charred surface of a wooden paddle provides. See ill.

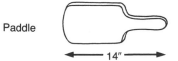

Paddle

← 14″ →

paddle doll. Toys. A small ancient Egyptian paddle-shaped figure made from flat strips of wood. Paddle dolls were brightly painted with strung **bead**s to represent hair. At one time considered to be dolls or toys, they are now regarded as tomb figures, and evidence suggests that they represented concubines or slaves. One theory proposes that they were without legs so that they could not run away.

Also, any doll that resembles a paddle in shape may be referred to as a paddle doll. **Wooden spoon doll**s and **pestle doll**s are similar in form.

paddles. Lacemaking. See **leaf stitch.**

paddle warping. Weaving. A method of **warping** many threads at one time and still maintaining an individual **cross** for each yarn. This method is used when the **warp** is composed of several kinds of yarns or colors which are repeated in the same consecutive order. It saves time in that the weaver does not have to cut and tie on each change of warp yarn. A **warping paddle** is used with the yarns passing from **cone** or **spool** through the holes of the paddle. The number of different yarns that it is possible to use depends on the number of holes in the warping paddle. The yarn is threaded in repeat through the holes, with the first yarn of the repeat going through the top left hole. The odd-numbered yarns are all threaded through the holes at the left side of the paddle and the even-numbered ones are threaded through the holes on the right. After threading, they are tied together and the knot is slipped over the starting peg of the **warping board** or **reel.** The paddle handle is held between the thumb and forefinger of the right hand and the warp is wound from the starting peg to the **lease** or cross **pegs.** Here the paddle is turned slightly so that the first lease peg goes between the even and odd yarns with the even threads on top. At the second peg, the odd yarns are lifted by hand to go over the peg and the even ones stay below. On the return trip, the wrist is turned so that the odd yarns are uppermost on the paddle. These odd yarns will stay on the top part of the peg if the total number of yarns used is an even number. If it is uneven, the even yarns are picked up and become the top part of the cross. At the next peg, the odd yarns will be lifted to the top if the even ones had been lifted at the previous peg; or the even yarns lifted, if it had been the odd ones previously. The warp is continued in this manner until the correct total number of ends have been made.

paddle wheel. Toys. A device used to move or animate certain toys in which a series of paddles is attached to an **axle.** Sometimes sand or water is dropped onto the paddles, turning the wheel so that the axle of the wheel in turn moves other parts of the toy. In some, such as the **paddle wheel boat,** energy is provided by a wound **rubber band** attached to the boat and paddle wheel.

The paddle wheel itself consists of boards or paddles attached radially at the circumference of the wheel. The wheel revolves on a horizontal shaft or axis that is parallel to the object being propelled. Also see **boat.**

paddle wheel boat. Toys. Any small toy **boat** moved by means of a **paddle wheel** attached at the stern. Crossing the **axle** of the paddle wheel, also attaching it to the boat, is a **rubber band,** so that the paddle can be wound to put tension on the rubber band. When released, the paddle turns and the boat moves. The paddle wheel can be made by using two small rectangles of wood, each notched at the center on one side and fitted together as in an egg-crate construction. This boat is essentially a **rubber-band toy,** as torsion on the band stores the energy. The paddles, however, pull the boat over the water.

paddling. Ceramics. See **beaten forms.**

pad sander. Woodworking. See **sanding tools.**

pagination. Bookbinding. The process or method of numbering pages of a book. Also, the process of breaking down galleys, or running proof copies, into pages.

paillette. Beadwork. See **sequins.**

paint. Block printing. See **block printing ink.**

paint. China and Glass painting. See **onglaze color.**

paint. Papercrafts. Almost any type of paint can be used to color papercraft projects. Water-base paints, such as poster color, powdered tempera color, watercolor, or acrylic tempera are most used because they clean up easily and dry quickly. Ink and **dye** may also be used.

For **papier mâché** designs, tempera or acrylic paints are commonly used. Enamels, colored brushing lacquers, or spray paints may also be used.

Paint is generally brushed on, then allowed to dry. For more brilliant color, apply a base coat of white paint before applying the color. **Dry brush texture** may be used for a grained effect.

paint. Stenciling. Any type of paint can be used for stenciling as long as it has a thick consistency and is appropriate for the surface. For example, textile paint must be used on **fabric.** Poster or tempera paint, acrylic tempera, and artist's oil paint are generally used. For designs stenciled over surfaces painted with alkyd enamel paint, use artist's oil paint. For stenciling over surfaces painted with flat latex paint, use acrylic paints. Paints are usually used straight from the tube, without thinning, because stenciling requires thick paint. However, if thinning is necessary, use a few drops of linseed oil for oil paints or of water for acrylics. Also see **Stenciling: Painting.**

paint. Woodworking. Paints, because they are opaque, conceal the natural grain and color of the wood. They are applied to protect cheaper woods where a transparent finish is not desired. Paints may be used for interior or exterior work. The two major types of paint used on wood are oil-base paint and enamel paint.

Oil-base paint may be used indoors or outdoors. It is made from a base of white lead or zinc oxide with pigment added for color. Raw **linseed oil** and turpentine are added to the paint solids to produce a liquid and ease application. Linseed oil is a good preservative and usually is used in greater proportions in outdoor paints than indoor paints.

Enamel paint differs from oil paint in that the linseed oil is replaced by **varnish** to produce a faster-drying, smoother, harder, and glossier surface. Enamels are mostly used for interior work and are easy to clean.

Latex paint is a water-soluble plastic-base paint. It does not penetrate wood as well as oil-base or enamel paints, and therefore is less permanent.

Prepare the wood surface as for any wood finish. In addition, apply a coat of white **shellac** to any knots to prevent the **bleeding** of resin through the paint. Also see **Woodworking: Finishing.**

painted canvas. Needlepoint. A **canvas** on which a design has been painted with oil or acrylic paints which the needleworker covers with stitches, using yarn the color of the paint. Also see **Needlepoint: Transferring a Design.**

painted fabric. Stitchery. Cloth to which color is added by painting it on directly with a brush. Various paints or dyes may be used depending upon the **fiber** content and the function of the article to be painted. The need for a colorfast dye in painted fabric is different in clothing or toys than it is in a **wall hanging.**

Among the possible paints, any **textile paint** may be used according to directions. **Acrylic paint** and silkscreen paint may be thinned and painted directly on the fabric. However, they do not leave the fabric pliable. **Procion** dyes, mixed to the right consistency, will give strong permanent color on **natural fiber**s. India ink or other permanent inks and marking pens will also give good colors. Note that marking pens can be used on synthetic blends such as polyester, Dacron, and other undyeable fabrics.

painted quilt. Quilts. Either of two contemporary **quilting** approaches that combine some of the characteristics of traditional quilting with bright, quickly applied paints. In one, white **cotton** quilted mattress covers provide the base; they come in a variety of prequilted patterns. They are then direct-painted with acrylic polymer emulsion paints.

In another approach, paints are applied to the surface of a bed sheet or any similar fabric. The painted sheet then becomes the **quilt top,** and is placed over **filler** and **backing** to be **basted** together. **Quilting stitch**es are then taken by hand or machine on the edges of the painted areas, giving the effect of a **pieced** pattern.

paint formula. Stained Glass. See **painting on glass.**

painting. Tincrafting. See **Tincrafting: Finishing the Tin.**

painting leather. Leather. See **Leatherwork: Dyeing and Coloring.**

painting on aciding. Stained Glass. Normally the side of glass to be painted is the inside surface, but with acided glass either side can be painted, with differing effects. When the acided side is painted, the dry paint can be rubbed off the high points of the **aciding** to give a glittering appearance. Also see **painting on glass.**

painting on glass. Stained Glass. A technique in which a specially prepared paint mixture is applied to sections of precut glass pieces either set up on an easel or lying flat on a table. After being painted, the pieces are fired in a kiln to bake the paint onto the glass permanently.

In painting stained glass the important quality to achieve is the feeling of light showing through and remaining around the paint. The paint itself is negative. One technique is to put a series of mattes on the glass and work through them back to the light. This is the traditional method used in the fifteenth and sixteenth centuries; it produces rich, somber work. Coventry Cathedral's nave was painted this way.

The other, more spontaneous, way uses a clear piece of glass to which is applied only enough paint to achieve an effect.

Painting on glass is like water-color painting or Chinese calligraphy. How well the paint goes on the glass is determined by the amount of water added to the paint.

It is best to work on the whole window at the same time to keep the paint unified. (An electric hair dryer can be used to dry the paint when working at an easel, to keep it from running.)

MATERIALS Paint **brush**es; **mop**; a piece of ¼–½″-thick **plate glass** about 15″ × 18″, with beveled edges, to be used as a palette; water; **gum arabic**; and containers of water for rinsing brushes.

PAINT FORMULA A mixture of fine **glass dust, iron oxide**—sometimes other metallic oxides—and **flux** such as borax or lead oxide. The flux allows the glass dust to melt and fuse with the glass surface at a lower temperature than the melting point of the piece of glass itself. There are many paint formulas produced by a variety of manufacturers. The paint is like that of ceramic glaze, only it is fired at a lower temperature. The best all-around paint is a black paint that turns a neutral-tinted blue when diluted with water, so that it has a thin consistency on the glass. Dark brown and dark red are other common paint colors.

MIXING THE PAINT The most common mixture is with **gum arabic** and water.

Adding a little **acetic acid** to the gum and water fixes a layer of paint so that subsequent layers can be built up without smearing the original paint.

An **oil-base paint** diluted with **turpentine** or thinner can be used on top of the gum and water, and on top of gum, water, and acetic-acid paint without affecting these water-soluble paints. It is the last paint to go on the glass before it is fired. This elaborate system of painting is not commonly used today.

METHOD FOR MIXING PAINT Make a pile of paint on the palettes, with a well in the middle to receive water.

Pour a little water in the well and make a muddy mixture.

Then add gum arabic to the mixture in a proportion of ¼ to ⅓ of the mixture and mix thoroughly. Add a little more water to blend the paint to a consistency that is easy to paint with. Too much gum will make the paint dry brick-hard or result in **blistered paint** and **frying;** too little gum will prevent the paint from permanently adhering to the glass surface. Also see **aciding, decalcomania, firing out, grissaille, handrest, lettering on glass, lift ground, masking, matting, maulstick, Norman slab glass, oil and water technique, painting on aciding, painting on plating, staining, stick lighting, stippling, tracing, vinegar trace paint.**

painting on plating. Stained Glass. Paint can be applied to both layers of plated glass and given a double-layered blurred effect. Also see **aciding, plating, painting on glass.**

paint remover. Toys. Any of a variety of commercially available **solvent**s, most of which contain methanol, which is poisonous. It will remove paint of all kinds. Directions and cautions must be carefully read and observed for all paint removers.

paint remover. Woodworking. A chemical remover of **paint** or other surface **finishes** such as **shellac** and **varnish.** Caustic paint remover is detergent like lye, beetsol (bisodium phosphate), or washing soda. When dissolved in hot water and applied to a wood finish it chemically dis-

solves and softens the finish. Caution must be exercised in applying this type of paint remover. Use rubber gloves and keep it away from the eyes. There is a danger that the remover may affect the wood—particularly if used on **plywood,** where the **veneers** may separate. Test remover on a scrap piece first to be safe. Solvent paint remover is a ready-mixed chemical solvent that is easier to use and generally safer than caustic remover. It generally contains benzoate, alcohol, and **acetone.**

To use paint remover apply it as you would apply paint, by brushing it on. Cover a small area at a time; a second coat will heighten the penetration. Allow a few minutes for the chemical action to begin; then, with a wide **putty knife,** scrape off the softened finish and discard it. Rub the surface with 1/0 **steel wool,** then clean it with alcohol or benzine to loosen and remove chemicals that might remain in the pores of the wood surface. (Paint rags soaked with these liquids are highly flammable; dispose of them properly.) Let the wood dry thoroughly before refinishing it.

paint thinner. Toys. See **mineral spirits.**

paired warps. Weaving. A technique in weft **twining** where the interlacing or twining of the **filling** yarn goes over and under a pair of **warp end**s each time instead of just once. There are many variations on this; one is to alternate the pairs so what was twined in one row would be split up to form new pairs in the next row. In another variation, a pair of warp ends can also alternate with a single warp end. Also see **twill twining.**

pairing. Basketry. Working two **weave**s, alternately over and under each other, to form a twist. Also see **Basketry: Woven Basket Construction.**

pairing. Weaving. See **twining.**

pairing gouge. Woodworking. See **gouge.**

pair of bobbins. Lacemaking. See **numerical order of bobbins.**

palampores. Crewel. Quilts. Printed or painted cotton hangings imported by the East India Company. These were probably Indian interpretations of English designs sent out by the Company. Palampores greatly influenced embroideries after their introduction into English life in the seventeenth century. English artists were also inspired by the fashion for chinoiserie. The Tree of Life pattern certainly caught the ladies' fancies and exotic fruits, flowers, wild birds and animals, pomegranate trees, strange elephants, and leopards abounded. There are beautiful examples of palampore-inspired designs in the Governor's Palace in Williamsburg, Virginia, which were worked in England and brought to America. These curtains and bed hangings are perfect examples of **Jacobean** embroidery. Pieces of the palampores were often incorporated in **quilts** and **coverlets.** Also see **broderie Perse, chain stitch.**

Palembang. Basketry. See **cane.**

palette. The thin board or plate painters use as a base for mixing colors. Traditional palettes are oval and have a thumbhole at one end, but any hard, nonabsorbant surface, such as a sheet of glass or formica, will suffice. Art supply stores carry pads of plastic-treated paper that can be used for the purpose, the top sheet being discarded after it is used.

The word "palette" can also refer to an artist's or designer's range of colors used in a composition.

palette. Crewel. Embroidery. Needlepoint. A wooden or Plexiglas structure closely resembling an artist's palette used for holding and separating yarns. The cut yarn can be looped through the holes so that one thread at a time can be pulled out. Also see **yarn organizer.**

palette knife. A thin, flexible, usually steel blade fitted with a handle and used for mixing paint or ink on a **palette,** or as a tool for applying paint to a surface. Palette knives may be up to 20″ in length for mixing large batches of stiff paints, but most are 8–10″ long and have an offset handle so that the blade may be brought down flat on the palette or canvas.

palette knife. Mosaics. An artist's tool with long, flexible, flat blade made of thin metal mounted on a wooden handle used in mosaics for **buttering** or spreading **bond** and **grout.** The thin, flat design of the blade makes this an excellent tool for working the bond and grout in between the crevices of the mosaic. Also see **Mosaics: Setting the Material.**

palimpsest. Bookbinding. See **Bookbinding.**

palladium. Bookbinding. An amalgam leaf that resembles silver leaf used in **tooling** bindings.

pallet. Bookbinding. A brass or steel tool used to strike straight lines across the spine of a book. Also, a binder's **type holder.** See ill.

Pallet

pallion. Enameling. A small piece of **metal foil** fused into enamel. Also see **overfiring.**

pallion. Jewelry. (Also called solder snippet.) Small squares of **solder.** Pallions can be cut from sheet solder with **plate shears.** Also, small pieces of **sheet metal** that have been used to embellish a piece of work. Also see **appliqué, married metals.**

pallions. Tincrafting. Small bits of **solder** roughly the size of rice grains that are spread out evenly along the joint to be soldered and then flowed into a liquid bond with a propane torch. Also see **Tincrafting: Joining the Tin.**

Palm, The. Quilts. (Also called Hosanna, Palm Leaf.) A **pieced** pattern of pre-Revolutionary origin, consisting of four jagged sets of leaves. The distinctive element in the design is that the alternating leaves are inverted. When **set** so that the pieced **block**s form an **all-over** design, the leaves combine to produce complex overlapping patterns.

Palm Leaf. Quilts. See **Palm, The.**

pamphlet. Bookbinding. A book of a single section with a paper cover.

panbone. Ivory and Bone Carving. The wide but comparatively thin bone of the lower jaw of the sperm whale, located at the hingepoint between the jaw and the head. The panbone was second only to the tooth of the whale as a medium for the whaler's art of **scrimshaw.** Its broad, flat outer surface provided a larger working area than did the tooth, but unfortunately, as time was to prove, one of short endurance. Many laboriously carved treasures were doomed as the panbone warped and split with age, and soon panbone was used predominantly for chicken feed.

Pandoras. Toys. The name given to the earliest **fashion doll**s.

Pandora's Box. Quilts. See **Box Quilt.**

panel. Bookbinding. A space or area on the **back,** or spine, of a book between the lines made from **tape**s. Also see **sewing on tape.**

panel. Stained Glass. One of the terms used to describe a finished stained-glass leaded or copper foiled flat piece. Also see **cartoon, copper foiling, fishline, full and slack, halation, template.**

panoptique. Toys. A French version of the **magic lantern.** This particular nineteenth-century optical toy utilized homemade pictures or magazine prints to replace the more expensive hand-painted slides. Most had highly moral titles and captions; illustrations from Bunyan's "Pilgrim's Progress" were characteristic and popular. The panoptique was the forerunner of the magascope and opaque projector. Also see **Toys: Optical Toys.**

panorama toy. Toys. An **optical toy** based on a public entertainment in which an audience was seated in the center of an area and a continuous picture, or panorama, was pulled past and around them. The toy panoramas consisted of similar but smaller pictorial strips that were unrolled from a cylindrical box. Some were many feet in length. The first public panorama was presented in 1785. The **historiscope** and **myriopticon** are variations of the panorama toy. Also see **Toys: Optical Toys.**

panther cowrie. Shell Carving. (*Cypraea pantherina*.) A shell with a dark brown and white mottled exterior, a white **middle color,** and a dark brown (sometimes tinged with violet) **ground color,** used for cameo carving. Also see

cowrie, helmet and **Shell Carving: Shell, Tools and Preparations, Cameo Carving.**

pantin. Toys. (Also called pantine.) The original name for the **jumping jack,** imported from France to America as an **adult toy** in the 1700s. The pantin was halfway between a **puppet** and a **paper toy.** The name probably was derived from the town of Pantin, now a suburb of Paris, or from the inhabitants of Pantin, who were famous dancers.

pantine. Toys. See **pantin.**

pantograph. Crewel. Embroidery. Needlepoint. An instrument used for copying designs on any desired scale. Also see **enlarging and reducing designs.**

paper. Block Printing. In general, smooth, fairly soft, thin paper is best for block printing. Fine quality printing paper, such as 100 percent rag content paper with a hot, pressed (smooth) surface, is available from art supply stores. The paper should be unsized. Japanese papers, made from bamboo or mulberry tree bark, are widely used. They are available in various degrees of thickness and opacity, and have a soft, silky surface.

For heavy papers, dampening the paper first is recommended. Dampening the paper improves its ink-retaining properties. Hard, rough papers are impossible to print unless damp. Dampen sheets of blotting paper by alternately stacking sheets of wet and dry paper with two dry to one wet sheet, although the amount of dampness can be controlled by adjusting this ratio. Place a heavy weight on top of the stack until the moisture is evenly distributed throughout. Then stack these damp sheets of blotting paper alternately with dry sheets of printing paper. Keep them under pressure until the moisture is evenly distributed. This process may be done the night before printing.

paper. Bookbinding. (Also called stock.) Cellulose vegetable fibers that have been macerated into individual filaments, intertwined, matted, and dried into thin sheet form. Wood is the most common material used in the United States, but rags, bamboo, esparto grass, and other cellulose fibers are also used. The word "paper" comes from the Latin word "papyrus." Paper was invented in China in the early second century A.D. It was made exclusively by hand until the 1800s, when papermaking machines became common. The process, although mechanized, is basically unchanged from the hand method of lifting a screen up through fibers suspended in water and then pressing the water from the sheets. Handmade papers are available today through art-supply stores, bookbinding supply houses, and specialty paper distributors. Mill paper is available in scores of colors, textures, and weights.

Bond paper is traditionally used for letterheads or other writing paper, and is obtainable in standard sizes of 8½″ × 11″ and 8½″ × 14″, from a very cheap sulfite grade up to 100% cotton fiber, a paper of excellent quality. The most commonly used weight of bond is 20 lb.

Book papers are medium-grade paper, bulkier and softer than a sulfite bond. They are obtainable in various finishes and colors in weights from 50 to 100 lb (60 lb is the most common).

Text papers are much more expensive than book papers. They are available in an extensive range of colors and textures, many with **deckle** edges. The usual weight is 70 or 80 lb.

Cover paper ranges from 65 to 100 lb, but most work uses 80 lb. The colors and textures are as various as those of bond and book papers.

The cost of recycled paper falls between that of bond and book paper. The color is not as rigidly controlled as for other papers, but in other respects it is as easily used.

Paper comes in many standard mill sizes, including papers available from Europe and the Orient. Some common **sheet** sizes used in **offset** printing are 23″ × 29″, 23″ × 35″, 23″ × 38″, and 26″ × 40″. Paper is sold by the ream, a unit of 500 sheets. The paper weight (e.g., 20 lb) is the weight of a ream in full sheet size. Also see **grain.**

paper. Kites. See **Kites: Tools and Materials.**

paper. Papercrafts. Any of various sheets, from heavy and stiff to thin and flexible, manufactured from pulps made from vegetable, mineral, or man-made fibers. Although trees are the major source of pulp, various other vegetable materials, such as straw, grasses, and the inner bark of mitsumata (paper mulberry) have been used. Many fibers are processed from used rags and clothing of cotton, flax, jute, sisal, and manila hemp to produce rag-pulp papers, called "rag-content" papers. Corn stalks, straw, and sugar cane waste are used for pulp. Another important source of pulp material is bags, boxes, and other paper or cardboard waste.

The basic method of making paper has changed little since its invention in China around A.D. 105. The various fibers are processed into pulp, which forms a matted sheet on a screen after the moisture has strained through. To process the fibers into pulp the material is first cleaned and foreign matter removed (bark removed from trees, buttons and heavy seams from rags, etc.). Next the fibers are broken up in water, then washed free of impurities and bleached. The pulp is then ready to be sent to the paper mill. At the mill the pulp is beaten into hairlike fibrils, refined into more uniform lengths, and color, sizing agents, or other chemicals are added. This processed pulp is finally fed to a paper machine. There are various types of paper machines, but the general process is the same. As the moisture is removed from the pulp a web of matted paper is formed. Then the press section of the machine further rolls the matted paper to remove any remaining water and to give surface characteristics to both sides of the paper. The paper then moves into the drier section, where it is exposed to heat and wound into a roll as it leaves the machine.

Many types of paper are used for papercraft projects. Some are easily found, such as newspaper, shelf paper, bond paper, paper bags, **tissue paper,** and wrapping paper. For **cutouts** done on folded paper, thin paper such as bond paper is used. Some projects require a medium-weight paper, such as construction paper, tracing paper, pastel paper, or blotting paper. For projects requiring heavier papers, use Bristol board, chip board, mat board, illustration board, oak tag, or corrugated cardboard. Some designs may require specialty papers such as colored tissue paper, crepe paper, or **origami** paper.

Ribboned or shredded paper, such as paper straw, is available, or paper can be cut into long ribbons by folding a piece many times, then cutting across it in narrow strips.

For **papier mâché**, newspaper is the basic material, although other kinds of paper may be used. Paper toweling, white tissue paper, and facial tissue absorb the **papier-mâché paste** easily, but dry with a wrinkled surface.

For decorative touches on a papier mâché design, a **collage** finish may be used by applying strips or cutouts of wrapping paper, magazine pictures, labels, canceled postage stamps, and so on, as the final layer.

paper airplane. Toys. A triangular-shaped form produced by folding a sheet of paper in any of various ways. It is a **paper-folding** toy of long-lasting appeal to adults and children. The folded paper plane "flies" across a room, utilizing the principles of aerodynamics and often aiding in the understanding of them. Also see **airplane.**

paper-bag mask. Papercrafts. Toys. See **mask.**

paper-bag puppet. Puppets. (Also called brown-bag puppet.) A simple **puppet,** usually made by children or for the amusement of children, from a common paper bag. If a lunch-bag size is used the puppet will fit over the hand. Holes can be cut to allow the child's fingers to be the puppet's arms.

Grocery bags are large enough to allow the child to become the puppet by pulling the bag down over his/her shoulders, animating the puppet from the inside. Holes must be cut for the eyes and mouth, and the child's arms can be stuck through openings at the sides of the bag. In either case, the features may be cut from paper and glued on or they may be painted or drawn with crayons. Bright-colored glazed paper bags are attractive, but they should be the kind that unfold to make a flat surface at the bottom. A **puppet play** may, in this way, be presented with a minimum of material, cost, and time. These puppets are not physically confining and are therefore excellent for young children.

paper batik. Batik and Tie-dye. Paper batik is basic **batik** applied to paper by a **direct-dye painting** method. The **resist** material is put directly onto the paper and the **dye** is painted over the resist. This **roll off** method is easy and inexpensive.

Wax crayons, **wax pencils,** and oil crayons can all be used and have the advantage of adding color. If clear **waxing** is desired, **paraffin** can be used. The paraffin chunks can be used to draw with, or they can be melted and painted onto the fabric. Even leftover candle pieces can be utilized. Colored waxes, along with colored papers, greatly expand the range of possibilities in paper batik. Waxes can be ironed out after dyeing.

The dyes need not be permanent colors, as the papers will not be washed. Watercolors, inks, tempera paint, poster paint, or fabric dyes can also be used.

Soft papers, such as newsprint or tissue, do not work well as they tend to disintegrate under the agitation of brushing and water. Writing bond and watercolor paper are excellent, although many less expensive papers can also be used with richly varied results.

paper beads. Beadwork. Oblong **bead**s are made by gluing and rolling various long shapes of paper. Long, rectangular strips form cylindrical beads, long isosceles-triangular strips form beads with tapered ends, and so on. Paper strips are brushed with white glue, then rolled tightly around a knitting needle. When the glue is tacky, the needle is removed and the bead allowed to dry. Although paper beads are already characteristically patterned from the newspaper or magazine paper used, they may be painted and varnished when dry. See ill.

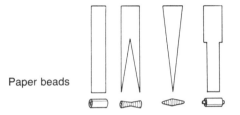

Paper beads

paper beads. Papercrafts. A variety of bead shapes can be made with papercraft techniques. Strips of paper can be glued and rolled around a needle for cylindrical beads. **Paper mash** can be rolled between the hands, then pierced with a needle for rounded, molded beads. When beads are completely dry, they may be painted and given a **protective finish.** Also see **molded beads.**

paper buildings. Toys. See **architectural playthings, cutouts.**

paper construction. Papercrafts. See **paper sculpture.**

PAPERCRAFTS

Any design in which paper is the primary ingredient, such as **collage, cutouts, origami, paper sculpture, papier mâché,** and **silhouettes,** is called a papercraft. Papercrafts range from flat sheets of paper that are cut and folded, to three-dimensional paper sculpture or papier-mâché forms.

In papercraft designs paper retains its own character; in a collage or a paper sculpture, paper is an integral part of the work, adding its own texture and shape to the completed design. Although drawings and paintings are done on paper, the sheet of paper is only a base for the artwork, rather than a part of the work of art itself. This is not to say that papercrafts may not be decorated or painted; they often are, but in papercrafts the form and feeling of the paper is highly evident in the finished work.

Since the invention of paper in China in the early second century A.D., thousands of types of paper have been developed and put to innumerable decorative and utilitarian uses. The Chinese experimented with tearing paper into pieces and mixing it with glue to produce a claylike substance. This early form of papier mâché was used to produce trays, boxes, and other decorative pieces. A rich folk tradition of papercutting also stems from the Orient, where paper effigies were used in burial rites. Paper decorations were also hung in homes as good-luck tokens to ward off evil spirits. Shadow theaters with paper figures were popular in the eleventh century.

One of the best-known paper arts is origami, which developed in Japan; elaborate animals, birds, and other figures were made by intricately folding paper. Even Japanese children mastered these folding techniques.

Paper was introduced to Europe during the Middle Ages; **symmetrical cutting** was used to produce paper stencils for applying decorative patterns. **Paper filigree,** embellished with beads and gold threads, was used in church decorations to simulate gold filigree during the fifteenth century in England. The use of paper filigree combined with seed pearls, small shells, and metallic threads was revived in the seventeenth century. Decorative paper cutouts were made with vegetable-dyed papers in Poland during this same period. In Germany, white cutouts were mounted on black backgrounds (later reversed to black-on-white) of intricately cut scenes, animals, and figures.

During the 1700s in England, **Mary Delany** developed a collage style of delicate paper-flower cutouts mounted on black paper. By this time, paper was used for many decorative arts. In France, papier mâché became extremely popular. Many household accessories such as snuffboxes, trays, door panels, and some furniture were made with **paper mash** or **laminated** sheets of paper. Papier-mâché objects were often decorated with **découpage** techniques to resemble hand-painted or inlaid work, in which intricately cut paper designs were applied to the surface, then coated with a clear, lustrous finish.

In Victorian England, papercrafts again became extremely popular. Lacy paper cuttings were used on greeting cards, especially in **valentines.** Papier mâché and découpage instructions were given in magazines. **Pin pricking** was popular for making lacy paper pictures, and **paper flower**s were widely made for household decorations.

Paper dolls printed on sheets of paper were available in the early 1800s in England and later in Germany and France. Included on the sheet were several changes of costume. The dolls were printed in black ink; sometimes they were pretinted by hand, but most were left for the buyer to color. All pieces had to be cut out with scissors or knives.

In 1854 an American publisher, Crosby Nichols & Co. of Boston, printed a booklet containing a paper doll named Fanny Gray. She had several changes of dress, verses about her, and a wooden base on which to stand her. In 1859 *Godey's Lady's Book* adapted the idea and produced a series of paper dolls: six girls and six boys, with costumes in the latest children's fashions. Magazines and newspapers soon followed the trend, developing their own characters for paper dolls. In no time at all, paper dolls became a beloved tradition.

Papercraft techniques have been used in many countries. Perhaps the best-known products are the brightly colored decorative wares from Mexico, where papier mâché, introduced to Mexico by the Spanish, has traditionally been used for masks. Today all sorts of papier-mâché animals, figurines, and various **piñata** designs are made in Mexico.

From this rich background of papercraft techniques, a wealth of designs and methods have been developed. With a minimum of equipment and materials, and a few basic techniques, a variety of designs from lacy paper cutouts to large papier mâché sculptures can be made.

TOOLS AND MATERIALS Most papercraft projects can be executed with a minimum of tools and materials. For paper sculpture various types and weights of paper should be kept on hand, as well as **cutting tool**s including scissors, a sharp **knife** or single-edge razor blades, and a paper punch for small holes. A pencil and an eraser are adequate for most designing. A ruler with a metal edge is used for measuring and for **scoring.** For very accurate work, a metal square may also be useful. Cutting should be done on a wood backing or cutting board. **Fastening** is done with **glue,** such as white glue, or with tape or staples. Paper clips and masking tape are helpful for holding the paper together while assembling or while the glue is drying. In most cases, the paper sculpture or construction is left as it is, although **dye** or **paint** may be used for coloring. If so, brushes, palette, or mixing cups may be needed.

For **papier mâché,** the basic equipment is newspaper or other absorbent paper and flour, glue, or **papier mâché paste.** The **support** (the form to be covered with papier mâché) can be of **aluminum foil,** paper, or **found objects** joined with masking tape. A bowl will be needed for mixing the paste, and a wire rack, such as a cake rack, will be needed for drying. **Spackle** and fine sandpaper are often used to smooth the dry papier mâché surface. Paint and brushes should be kept on hand for painting and applying **protective finish**es to the completed pieces.

SETTING UP A WORKSHOP Many papercut designs can be done with very casual working arrangements. However, for constructing geometric designs and intricate paper sculptures, or for **scoring,** a well-lighted worktable with a cutting board should be set up so that measuring and cutting will be accurate. For effective designs, the paper should be neatly stored to prevent wrinkling. Since paper is the essential ingredient, it must be clean and crisp.

When working with **papier mâché,** the worktable should be protected with several layers of newspaper or plastic. If the form is to be built from **found objects,** a collection of various containers, paper cups, toweling tubes, etc., should be on hand. Since the completed piece will have to dry for several days, there should be a shelf with a wire rack where it can remain undisturbed.

FOLDING AND CUTTING Folding paper is simple. The surprising aspect of papercrafts is that with very basic, almost intuitive means, beautiful designs can be made. Folding a sheet of paper gives it the strength to stand by itself, as well as the appearance of sculptural dimension. The folds catch the light, and the shadows add to the effects of solidity and depth. Lightweight paper can easily be creased and folded; heavy paper requires scoring in preparation for folding.

Perhaps the best-known way of folding paper is **accord-**

ion pleating, which makes a **fan fold.** This back-and-forth fold is used as a basis for various other folds, such as the **battlement fold** and **diamond fold.**

Paper can be gently rolled, rather than creased, to make forms such as a **cylinder** or a **cone.** These basic shapes, as well as the **circle, square,** and **triangle,** are part of the repertoire of the paper craftsperson. And for those who wish to experiment further, it is possible to construct solid **geometric form**s.

Cutting or tearing paper can produce many other shapes. Tearing paper by hand results in unexpected, irregular edges, often used for **collage.** Cutting designs in paper, usually folded for intricate designs, is a folk tradition in many countries. Whether using scissors or a knife, the tool should feel comfortable and cutting should be done in a relaxed way.

Simply folding a sheet of paper in half is a beginning step. From this a **symmetrical cutting** can be made. Remember that the pieces cut out of the paper, called the **positive design,** as well as the background sheet from which it was cut, called the **negative design,** may be used in designing. Cutout scraps can be saved for additional decoration. Folding the sheet in many repeated folds and then cutting a design into the folded edges will, when unfolded, result in as many repetitions as folds. Variations on folding and cutting may be invented for anything from a lacy paper valentine to a **snowflake.** Simple cuts into the folded edge can be used for geometrical patterning, which, by the additional folding in of the cut section, can add dimensional texture of light and shadow. Such patterning can add interest to an otherwise plain fold in a **paper sculpture.** Other cutting variations, such as cutting into paper at intervals with a knife and then folding these shapes in or out, may suggest feathers, fish scales, or other textures.

By certain methods of folding and cutting, paper can be enlarged, actually **expanding** the size of the sheet to make it fill a larger area. Many folding techniques give the illusion of dimension; expanding paper actually enlarges its size.

Paper can be cut into long ribbons for **paper-strip** designs, or combined with **curling** for hanging ornaments or mobiles.

All these basic methods are used or combined by gluing or fastening for innumerable papercraft projects. See ill.

Geometrical patterning

PAPIER MÂCHÉ TECHNIQUES Papier mâché can be applied using several methods. The **paper-strip method,** in which strips are dipped in **papier mâché paste** and applied one at a time, is suitable for pieces of any size, and can be used over a **support** of **chicken wire** for very large sculptures.

Much of the fun of designing is involved in creating the support. **Found objects,** such as assorted cardboard containers, may be combined to make the form to be coated with papier mâché. Crumpled newspaper or **aluminum foil** may be formed into desired shapes and taped in place. The support, if composed of different materials, must be firmly taped together in the desired position before applying papier mâché. A figure or animal should balance on its legs if it is to be free-standing. A **balloon** may also be used as a support. **Molding** may be done to duplicate a shape, such as a bowl. The strip method is quickly done, and when dry, is hard, strong, and lightweight. It does, however, have a tendency to sag when wet. It is important that the paper strips be applied in layers in alternating directions so that every part of the surface is completely covered and strong.

Another common papier mâché technique is the use of claylike **paper mash,** made by soaking bits of paper in papier mâché paste. The mash can be formed with the fingers to make designs, in the same manner in which clay is modeled, or it can be applied as a coating over a support. While still wet, designs may be incised into the surface with knives, nails, etc., or embedded with buttons, beads, and so on. The mash takes longer to dry than paper strips and has a rather rough surface which can be smoothed with sandpaper.

Another method, **laminating,** involves gluing several layers of paper together and then shaping the thick, damp, layered sheet into the desired shape. Laminated sheets may be molded over a simple base, or torn into small pieces and applied in overlapping pieces until a smooth surface is achieved.

In all papier mâché techniques, the paper should be torn rather than cut, for better adhesion. The paper will tear evenly if torn with the grain. Tearing against the grain is difficult, and produces uneven, jagged strips.

Perhaps the most important step of any papier mâché process is drying. Insufficient drying is generally the cause of any cracking of paint or other finish. Depending on the weather, a piece may dry in two to five days. Drying may be hastened by placing the object in bright sunlight or in a 175° F oven with the door ajar. With the heat method, allow the piece to cool overnight before coating it with any **spackle,** paint, or finish.

The finishing of the completed piece depends largely on the effect desired. The final layer of paper strips could be colored paper for a **collage** finish. In this case, let the piece dry thoroughly, then coat with one of the **protective finish**es. If the piece is to be painted, it is helpful to first smooth the surface with spackle, let it dry, and then sand it with fine sandpaper. A prime coating of white paint or acrylic gesso, allowed to dry before the final painting, produces more brilliant color. When dry, the painted surface may be coated with a protective finish.

CARE AND MAINTENANCE OF TOOLS Bowls and brushes used for spackle, ink, dye, tempera, watercolor, or acrylic paints are cleaned with soap and water and then rinsed and dried. For other paints or protective finishes, use the proper **solvent** (lacquer thinner for lacquer, paint thinner for enamel, denatured alcohol for shellac, etc.) and then wash with soap and water and rinse thoroughly.

papercut. Papercrafts. See **cutout.**

paper cutout puppet. Puppets. A **flat puppet** made by pasting cut-out pictures from books or magazines onto card paper. These are moved by the **puppeteer** from the sides of a stage and are a variation of the old **"penny plain and tuppence colored"** flat puppets.

paper cutouts. Toys. See **cutouts.**

paper cutter. Papercrafts. (Also called guillotine.) A manually operated blade mounted on a board used for cutting or trimming paper with precision. The paper is lined up with the top edge of the board and the blade is brought down in a continuous movement.

paper doily. Papercrafts. An intricate, filigree paper cutout, generally circular. Thin paper is folded many times, then cuts are made into the folds. When unfolded, the cutout areas are repeated in complex patterns. Paper doilies are also commercially available.

paper doll. Papercrafts. See **Papercrafts: Background and History.**

paper doll. Toys. A figure printed on paper to be cut out and to which clothes can be affixed by means of tabs. The **cutouts** came in great variety for a great many years and finally reached a zenith in the 1850s with the advent of colored lithography.

Paper dolls were originally called Protean figures, named after the classical seagod Proteus, who could alter his figure at will. The Protean dolls came with numerous changes of costume, and sometimes with extra heads as well.

Paper dolls, or dressing dolls, have maintained popularity over a period of 250 years. Today the tabs are replaced by self-sticking papers. The job of cutting out the figures has been eliminated by the use of the die-cut by machine, which leaves occasional strands of paper to hold the figures in place on the sheet until they are punched out.

paper fastener. Puppets. Toys. A small brass clip used to **join** sheets of paper together. Each fastener has a head and two flat prongs that can be inserted into a slot or hole and then spread. The prongs are about ¾" long.

paper filigree. Papercrafts. (Also called rolled-paper work or quillwork.) A papercraft technique in which tiny strips of paper are tightly rolled into spirals, scrolls, and cones and then glued on a background in various elaborate arrangements. The technique was popular in Europe during the eighteenth century and again during the Victorian era. These intricate arrangements were often used as borders in combination with shells, beads, wax, metallic thread, or other materials, and framed under glass. Early rolled-paper work, done in a creamy vellum, resembled carved ivory. When gilded paper was used, the work resembled gold so much that it was often called gold filigree.

"Quillwork," a misleading name, was the term used for the rolled-paper work in America. The technique was adapted in freer designs, with mica or ground glass sprinkled over the background for a sparkly effect.

The long, narrow strips of paper should be no more than ¹/₁₆" or ⅛" wide. Various weights and types of paper may be used. The strips are tightly rolled on the end of a toothpick. The toothpick is then carefully removed, leaving a tight coil. The rolled strip is drawn out to the shape desired, the bottom edges are touched in glue, and the shape is placed on the background.

paper flowers. Papercrafts. Various types of flowers can be cut and assembled from various types of **paper,** such as **tissue paper,** or **crepe paper,** and mounted on wire stems. Petals can be cut individually and taped or wired onto the stem, flowers can be made from paper circles made into cones of desired depth with the petals cut or fringed around the edges of the circles. For a simple, fringed, circular flower, concentric circles are cut and the wire stem with a loop at the top is inserted through their centers (**a.**). Many slits are cut deeply around the edges, then the flower is pulled up and secured to the stem with floral tape.

A variation on the fringed flower is made by folding a long strip of paper in half and cutting slits or petal shapes into the fold (**b.**). The end of the strip is taped to the stem and then tightly rolled around it.

For some designs, **curling** may give variety to the petals or fringes. Petals and leaves may be given more depth by **scoring** and then bending the shape as desired. See ill.

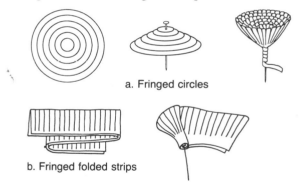

a. Fringed circles

b. Fringed folded strips

paper folding. Toys. The art of creating simple forms by folding sheets of paper. Toys made in this way in Europe were usually all-white, in contrast to Japanese **origami,** which utilized sheets of colored paper. Among the best-known folded paper animals are the traditional chickens (or cocottes) and crows (or krahen). Paper folding is a technique used in **paper sculpture.** Also see **helicopter, paper airplane.**

paper mash. Beadwork. Papercrafts. (Also called paper pulp.) A malleable mixture made of paper pulp used in combination with paste for modeling **papier mâché** forms. The pulp is made by soaking paper or cardboard in water until it deteriorates into a pulp. The mash may be used to cover the entire **support,** or may be used to add sculptural details or textured areas to pieces done by the **paper-strip method.** Small items such as buttons, small stones, or beads may be pressed into the paper-mash surface while still wet for decoration. When dry, the surface is durable and hard, with a moderately rough texture.

To make paper mash, tear a few sheets of newspaper into tiny pieces, then place them in a bucket with enough liquid **papier mâché paste** to completely cover them. Let the mixture soak for about two days, then squeeze out excess moisture. The mixture should be malleable. Cooking the mixture will shorten the soaking period. Facial tissue or cardboard egg cartons may also be used to make paper mash. **Instant papier mâché,** another term for paper pulp, is available at art supply and hobby stores.

paper mold. Candlemaking. The basic paper mold in **candlemaking** is the waxed cardboard container. If the paper mold to be used is not waxed, it should be coated with vegetable oil to facilitate **mold release.**

paper mosaic. Papercrafts. A term for a paper **collage** composed of many small pieces, resembling a mosaic. Bits of paper can be glued to a **support** of heavy paper or cardboard brushed with **white glue.** If the pieces are placed a little apart, small cracks or lines in the background will become part of the design.

paper paste. Toys. An **adhesive** for paper and cardboard that is easy to use and safe for children to handle. Containers usually have a brush attached to the lid. This kind of **paste** is sometimes referred to as "school paste."

paper printing. Papercrafts. See **printing with paper.**

paper pulp. Papercrafts. See **paper mash.**

paper resist. Ceramics. See **resist method.**

paper sculpture. Découpage. (Also called papier tole.) A technique of raising areas of a flat **print** to create a three-dimensional effect, often used in **shadow box** arrangements. An area to be raised can be cut out with a knife, leaving enough connecting paper to keep it attached to the rest of the print. The area can be stuffed behind with a claylike filling, such as **bread-dough mixture** or **papier mâché.** If two identical prints are available, areas to be raised can be cut from one print, then filled and **glue**d to the flat print. This technique of filling raised areas for a bas-relief effect is similar to **repoussé.**

Pinpricking can also be used to make areas pliable enough to press into three-dimensional shapes.

Some details of the paper sculpture can be almost completely cut out, their wrong sides coated with glue to add stiffness, and shaped with the fingers, without adding any filling. The paper itself will retain a sculptural shape. Also see **vue d'optique.**

paper sculpture. Papercrafts. (Also called Paper construction.) Sculpture formed by various papercraft techniques, including, rolling, bending, **scoring,** cutting, and folding. The forms are secured by gluing. The sculpture may be free-standing or attached to a backing or **support.** Also see **Papercrafts: Tools and Materials, Setting Up a Workshop, Folding and Cutting.**

paper sculpture. Toys. The art of making three-dimensional forms in paper or cardweight paper through a process of folding and turning. The traditional Japanese

paper folding is called **origami.** Many other countries have paper folding among their folk arts.

Paper is usually **score**d before being folded so that the line of scoring controls the shape. Some pieces are completed only through folding—others require tabs or **glue** to position them.

Paper sculpture can be large in scale and is used extensively in advertising and commercial art work. Also see **cardboard.**

paper strip. Papercrafts. A long, narrow piece of paper that can be combined with several other strips into many designs. The traditional paper chain with interlocking circles is a basic form of strip designing. The strips may be curved or folded in **accordion pleating,** then glued or stapled in decorative shapes. For a sphere, strips can be laid flat in a starburst shape, stapled at the center, and then all the ends brought up and fastened together to form a ball. Many other three-dimensional shapes can be devised with strips. **Curling** may be done on loose ends. See ill. Also see **weaving.**

a. Paper strip

b. Accordion pleating

c. Three-dimensional sphere

paper-strip method. Papercrafts. A **papier-mâché** technique in which pieces of newspaper or other **paper** are torn with the **grain** into small strips, then soaked or dipped in **papier-mâché paste** and applied to a **support** in smooth layers. The paper is torn rather than cut for better adhesion. The size of the strips depends on the size of the sculpture; an average-sized strip is around 1″ × 3″. However, when covering detail areas such as facial features, these strips may be torn into smaller pieces to fit into difficult areas. See ill. Also see **Papercrafts: Papier-Mâché Techniques.**

Paper-strip method

paper toy. Toys. Any toy devised or fashioned from paper. The range and variety of these toys, produced since the early 1700s, is incredible. Paper toys were both mass-produced and made at home. Paper toys comprise **cutouts, architectural playthings,** the "**penny plain and tuppence**

colored" theater sheets, **origami** figures, **model**s of all kinds, and **paper doll**s. Simple toys that can be made from paper by any child include **pinwheel**s, **paper airplane**s, and **jumping jack**s. **Paper folding** techniques are often used in making paper toys.

paper windmill. Toys. See **pinwheel.**

papier collé. Papercrafts. A French term, first used by Picasso, for **collage.**

papier collé. Stained Glass. A French term for **collage** or arrangements of paper glued down together. This is one way of making a **cartoon** in designing for stained glass.

papier mâché. Découpage. A traditional material of paste-soaked strips of paper or paper mash, used to fill out sculpted or raised areas of a **paper sculpture** or a **repoussé** print for a three-dimensional effect. Papier mâché can also be used to make forms which, when dry, are strong, durable, and suitable for finishing with découpage.

papier mâché. Papercrafts. A French term meaning "chewed-up paper" for the technique of building or covering forms with paste-soaked paper strips or paper mash, and for the medium itself. When dry, the surface is hard and durable. The basic methods of applying papier mâché are **laminating**, **molding**, applying layers in the **paper-strip method**, or forming with **paper mash**. Also see **Papercrafts: Tools and Materials, Setting Up a Workshop, Papier Mâché Techniques.**

papier mâché. Puppets. Toys. A material used to model **puppet head**s. It is made up of torn newspaper, or other absorbent paper, and **wheat paste**. **Pulp mâché** is a papier mâché process which uses soaked paper bits, while **strip papier mâché** uses torn strips, though all fall into the general category of papier mâché.

If wheat paste is not available, a flour and water paste may be substituted. Papier mâché is easily made and is an inexpensive material which adapts to work of small or large scale.

Dried papier mâché objects can be painted with **enamel paint**s, or they can be painted with **tempera** and then given a waterproof finish of **fixative** or **varnish**. Also see **ball cutter, card marionette, liquid soap, modeling material, rag-doll puppet, rod puppet** and **Puppets: Making the Puppet Head.**

papier mâché beads. Beadwork. Paper mash can be rolled with the hands to make **molded beads**. When dry, the surface is rough; it may be smoothed with sandpaper, then painted and varnished.

papier mâché doll. Toys. Any doll or doll head made from **papier mâché**. The doll head can be constructed in the same way as the papier mâché **puppet head**. Some dolls are made in separate parts or pieces which are then **joint**ed; some have a papier mâché head and a **cloth body**; others are formed in one solid piece, with no movable parts. Papier mâché dolls are made inexpensively in various parts of the world and have been commonly available since the 1800s. The recipes for papier mâché vary from one toymaker to another. **Pulp mâché** dolls are sometimes referred to as papier mâché dolls.

papier mâché paste. Papercrafts. Although various pastes may be used as the binder for the paper in papier mâché, **flour paste** is the traditional paste. **White glue** may be substituted, mixing 1 part white glue to a little less than 1 part water. Bottled liquid **starch** also provides an adequate substitute. To add texture and strength, a tablespoon or two of sand or plaster may be added to a quart of liquid starch. A wheat paste can be made from nontoxic **wallpaper paste**, mixing about 1 part paste to 10 parts water. Strain the mixture if it becomes lumpy. Keep the wallpaper paste refrigerated, or add a few drops of oil of wintergreen, available from the drugstore, as a preservative. Wallpaper paste is especially useful for very large pieces. For adding final decorative details, white glue should be used full strength.

papier tole. Découpage. See **paper sculpture.**

parachute. Toys. Any of a variety of toys in which an umbrella-shaped fabric or similar light material is weighted and floated to the ground. It is also a particular toy that consists of a handkerchief-sized square of flexible plastic attached to **string**s in such a way that when folded and tossed into the air it will open, catch the air, and float slowly down. The strings are attached to each of the four corners and joined at the ends with a weight. Some experimentation is required to find the optimum length for the strings and what works best as a weight. The weight should be heavy enough to keep the string end down, enabling the parachute to catch the air. If it is too heavy, the whole thing will simply plummet to the ground. The toy is sometimes referred to as a pocket parachute. See ill.

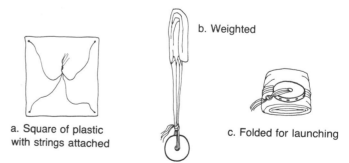

a. Square of plastic with strings attached

b. Weighted

c. Folded for launching

Paradise. Quilts. See **Pine Tree.**

paraffin. Batik and Tie-dye. Candlemaking. A white, translucent, waxy substance refined from petroleum. Paraffin is the primary component of most candles made today. It is available from most hobby shops and all candle supply stores. It comes in three grades, according to how well it is refined: soft, with a **melting point** of 120–135° F; medium, with a melting point of 140–155° F; and hard, with a melting point of around 160° F. The medium-grade paraffin is used for most **molding,** the soft grade for soft cores, and the hard grade for hard outer shells. To improve its overall quality as a candle component, paraffin is frequently mixed with **stearic acid** to produce a harder, better burning candle. Paraffin was first used in the manufacture of candles by James Young, a Scotsman, in the mid eighteenth century.

Paraffin is used as a **resist** agent for **batik.** Melt **wax** in a **double boiler;** do not melt paraffin over direct heat. Most **batiking wax** consists of a combination of paraffin and **beeswax.** Paraffin **fracture**s when painted on fabric and cooled, producing the veining characteristic of batik. Also see **Batik and Tie-dye: Basic Procedures for Batik.**

paraffin. Metalworking. Woodworking. See **wax.**

paraffin. Quilts. See **beeswax.**

paraffin wax. Stained Glass. See **aciding.**

parallel glass. Glasswork. Glass of modern manufacture that has parallel surfaces that minimize distortion when used as window glass. Previous methods of manufacturing window glass, like the Lubbers process for making **cylinder glass,** left wavy surfaces. Highly automated factory methods for making parallel glass draw molten glass from a furnace in a continuous stream.

parallel-jaw pliers. Jewelry. **Pliers** made with a special construction permitting the jaws to close precisely parallel to one another. They can be used in any situation in which bringing two pieces of metal together in a parallel position is necessary: for example, in making a catch or in **bending.**

parang. Batik and Tie-dye. A name given to a particular Javanese **batik** design. This design, from the word meaning "rugged rock," is often composed of diagonal lines or **zigzag pattern**s. Many traditional Javanese designs were specifically identified by name and are still in use today.

Parang Rusak is a pattern once reserved for the use of the Javanese king, but is now reproduced and sold commercially.

parchment. Bookbinding. Sheepskin prepared with lime. Also see **vellum.**

parchment. Leather. A paperlike sheet prepared from animal skins which was used for books and manuscripts in Europe until paper was introduced in the fourteenth century.

parent metal. Metalworking. See **base metal.**

Parian. Toys. Unglazed, pure white **bisque** china used for **doll head**s. It was called "Parian" because the finished material of the unglazed doll heads was hard and marblelike, resembling the marble from the Greek island of Paros. Parian china was developed and patented by the Spode factory in the 1840s. Because of the hardness and fineness of the paste pressed into the molds, great delicacy and detail were possible in the features and hair. The Parian heads are highly valued by doll and toy collectors. Also see **all-bisque** and **Toys: Dolls.**

paring. Bookbinding. (Also called skiving.) Systematically reducing the thickness of leather by shaving it on the flesh side in areas where it folds or overlaps. A **French paring knife** is used for this operation; its blade must be kept exquisitely sharp, so frequent stropping is advised. After marking the areas to be pared, lay the leather face-down on a slab of marble, sheet of plate glass, or lithographer's stone. Be careful not to let shavings get under the leather, as they will create lumps that your blade might catch, producing holes in the skin. Hold the leather with your free hand and hold the knife with your forefinger extended almost to the cutting edge of the blade. Maintain the blade almost parallel to the leather; the higher the handle is held, the greater the danger of making an unwanted cut. With a steady downward pressure and even movement, pare away from you. Do not saw the leather; the cuts must be even, as any ridges will show through to the face of the leather.

paring. Leather. See **skiving.**

paring stone. Bookbinding. A lithographic stone or a marble or plate glass surface used in binding for **leather paring** operations or as a surface on which **adhesive** may be **offset** onto guarding strips.

Parisian embroidery stitch. Needlepoint. An upright stitch formed by alternate long and short stitches over two and four threads respectively. The second row interlocks with the first, the long stitch meeting the short. This stitch is very effective when worked in two colors and is a good background or **filling stitch** with a substantial back. See ill.

Parisian stitch

parison. Glasswork. The first molten mass of glass gathered at the end of the **blowing iron,** which, after having been marvered true and cylindrical, has received its first bubble of air. Introducing a bubble at this point keeps the hole in the working end of the blowing iron clear, and the slight cooling effect tends to stabilize the shape so that subsequent **gather**s can be made around the first one.

To form a parison, twist the blowing iron in the molten glass and pull it so the glass sticks to the end of the iron in a ball (**a.**). The ball of molten glass is called a "gather." After removing the iron from the furnace, twist it in your hands to keep the gather from dripping off the iron (**b.**).

Roll the gather on the **marver** to make it cylindrical and of even thickness around the iron (**c.**). Marvering also chills the surface of the glass slightly so it will hold its shape and provide some resistance to blowing. While still rotating the iron to keep the glass centered, introduce the first bubble of air (**d.**).

You can pick up additional glass on the parison after the bubble is formed (**e.**). **Neck down** the parison off the end of the blowing iron with a **jack** (**f.**).

The **blocking mold** (**g.**) is used to shape and center the parison at the same time that the wet mold chills the surface of the glass and gives the parison stability (**h.**).

You can rest the parison on a metal or marble plate to flatten the bottom (**j.**), and continue to fill the form (**k.**). See ill.

Forming the parison

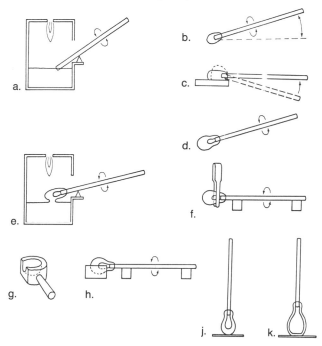

parkerizing. Metalworking. See **bluing.**

parlor wheel. Spinning. See **German wheel.**

parquetry. Gemcutting. See **intarsia.**

partial overprinting. Fabric Printing. A printing technique used for special effects of shadow printing or double printing in which the same block is printed again with the block slightly shifted; the second print covers part, but not all, of the first print.

particle board. Crewel. Embroidery. Needlepoint. See **chipboard.**

particle board. Woodworking. (Also called chipboard.) Wood chips and an adhesive compressed into large, flat panels, sold in 4′ × 8′ sheets of various thicknesses. It has a smooth, hard surface and is very resistant to **warp**ing and moisture. Because it tends to chip easily, it is best surfaced with a **veneer** of wood or **Formica.** It is also used as a core

material for cabinet doors and desk tops, and as a base material for flooring.

particle board core. Woodworking. See **plywood.**

parting. Stained Glass. A term defining the breaking and separating of two pieces of glass. Also see **plate pliers, tapper** and **Stained Glass: Cutting.**

parting. Woodworking. In **woodcarving** or **wood turning,** the process of separating one form from another. In wood turning, a **parting tool** is fed into the spinning wood. In **woodcarving,** a V-shaped **parting gouge** is hit with a **mallet** to make the necessary cut. Also see **Woodworking: Whittling and Woodcarving and Wood Turning.**

parting agent. Plastics. See **mold-release agent.**

parting compound. Metalworking. (Also called parting powder.) A dry powder, often **talc** or a finely ground sand powder, that is sprinkled between the **cope** and drag sections of the **sandcasting** flask to prevent the upper and lower sections of the mold from sticking together. The surface on which this is applied is called the parting line. Parting compound is also used on the **pattern** in sandcasting to ease separating it from the moist sand. Also see **Metalworking: Sandcasting.**

parting compound. Plastics. See **mold-release agent.**

parting gouge. Woodworking. See **gouge, woodcarving tools.**

parting line. Metalworking. See **parting compound, sandcasting molding equipment,** and **Metalworking: Sandcasting.**

parting powder. Metalworking. See **parting compound.**

parting tool. Woodworking. See **wood turning tools.**

passage. Weaving. See **tapestry.**

passementerie. Beadwork. ''Passementerie'' was originally the term for a trim made of gold or silver braid or ribbon, but in eighteenth-century France and later for the Victorians, it was a technique of intertwining braid and beads for decorating dresses.

A wiry cord is shaped in the desired pattern, then stitched onto fabric. Rows of threaded beads are then stitched over the cord pattern, completely covering the cord with slanting rows of beads. Beads must be pushed together in neat rows while working. For added decoration, large beads are sewn over the circles of cord and beaded fringes and tassels are attached.

passing. Embroidery. A wire thread available in various thicknesses of gold or silver, used for **couching** in **metallic thread embroidery.** It is made from a mixture of metals and not pure gold or silver, so it will tarnish. It is very flexible and easy to handle, ideal for a beginner learning the intricacies of metal thread couching. Also see **Lurex thread.**

passive. Lacemaking. (Also see hanger, passive bobbin.) In **bobbin lace,** the **bobbins** that are spread out fan shape and fall down on the **pillow.** The bobbins called **workers** work from side to side through the passives to do the lacework.

passive bobbin. Lacemaking. See **passive.**

passive element. Basketry. The heavier structural element or material used in the formation of a basket. It is called passive because it is woven around and held in place by a more flexible **active element.** It provides the basic shape of the basket, and adds strength. Also see **warp.**

paste. Batik and Tie-dye. In dyeing, to paste a dye is to stir the powdered **dyestuff** into cold water or other medium to make a smooth mixture. The pasted dye can then be mixed with hot water and added to the **dyebath.**

Also, the **flour paste** used in **paste-resist batik.** Also see **household dye.**

paste. Bookbinding. Paste is usually a watered solution of starch or dextrin mixed with gum, resin, or glue to add strength, and antioxidants to retard disintegration. Paste forms a bond after the evaporation of the solvent in the formula. It is widely employed throughout the various binding processes for the adhesion of paper and paper board because it does not readily **cockle,** wrinkle, or warp paper despite the presence of water as the solvent. Paste is also used to soften old adhesive materials so they may be scraped off in preparation for rebinding.

Casing in paste is used to attach **cloth** and **leather** to the boards and for **tipping on endpapers.** Paste for **strip repair** is easily made by mixing 1 tablespoon flour, 2 tablespoons starch, ½ teaspoon alum, and 3 ounces water, stirring until smooth. Simpler and no less effective is cornstarch mixed with cold water, brought gently to a boil, and allowed to cool before using.

paste. Ceramics. A term used to describe any **clay body** mixture, but usually one which is smooth and having low **plasticity.**

paste. Papercrafts. See **flour paste, glue, papier mâché paste.**

paste. Toys. A water-base **adhesive** usually used on paper. **Flour paste** and **paper paste,** or "school paste," are two common examples. These pastes are harmless and can be removed from the hands by washing, and are therefore satisfactory for children's use.

White glue can be washed off the hands with water before it has set and is more permanent than paper paste.

paste filler. Woodworking. See **grain filler, wood filler.**

paste flux. Stained Glass. See **flux.**

pastel colors. Pale colors which result when colors of high intensity are mixed with white. Pastels have low color saturation. Almost any group of pastel colors blend because they share a common element of white, giving them **harmony.**

paste paper. Bookbinding. A decorative paper produced by coating the surface of paper with paste colored with pigments and then making designs in it.

paste resist. Batik and Tie-dye. A **resist** process used in batik. In paste resist, any of a variety of flour-and-water mixtures is used in place of **wax** to block areas of the fabric. A permanent **dye** is then used over the pasted fabric. Sometimes **binders** are added to the **paste,** making it possible to paint water-soluble dye over the paste.

There are many different paste resist recipes; most of the highly skilled artisans of various countries have developed their own. A recipe widely used in Japan consists of rice and bran flour combined with a small quantity of powdered zinc sulfate and **salt.** It is mixed with water and cooked to make a transparent cream.

Paste may be applied in any of a variety of ways. A traditional method is to use a finger to spread the paste over the material. Fine lines can be made by using a **brush** or by squeezing the paste through a tube similar to a decorating tube.

In the traditional paste resist batik, the powdered dye was mixed with gum solution to make a smooth, stiff mixture. Because of the consistency the dye did not run, and any number of colors could be applied cold. Fabrics treated this way were steamed to **set** the dye. A final rinsing in clear, cold water removed the paste, and the material was then ironed.

The paste resist process can be simplified so that it is easily used by children. Children's paste batik utilizes a simple **flour paste.** Its advantage is that it avoids the dangers of melting wax. The fabric is first brushed with a layer of skim milk. If regular skim milk is not available, add ⅓ cup powdered skim milk to a cup of water. When this coating is dry, the flour paste is painted on. When the paste design is dry, the fabric is pulled or stretched to **crackle** the paste. Liquid dye (1 part dye to 3 parts water) is painted over the material. Those areas covered with paste will resist the dye. When the dye is dry, the fabric is folded with paper toweling between the layers to prevent dyed areas from touching one another. The entire fabric is then steamed for 45 minutes to set the dye. Additional colors may be added by repeating the entire process. Only one **steaming** is necessary. The fabric is finally soaked in water for 30 minutes to an hour to remove the paste and skim milk, and is then rinsed clear of excess dye.

The following are a few of the common recipes for paste resist:

Cook 3 tablespoons flour and 1 cup water in the top of a **double boiler** until almost transparent, stirring constantly. When thick and still hot, brush or spread it onto the fabric. Dyes or pigments should be brushed over the dried paste.

Mix 1 teaspoon **alum** with ¼ cup water and add enough flour to make a paste.

Mix 1 tablespoon white flour, 1 tablespoon rice flour, and ½ tablespoon powdered laundry starch. Add a little cold water to make a smooth paste. Then add ¼ cup hot water and cook in the top of a double boiler for about 15 minutes. Use hot.

paste resist painting method. Batik and Tie-dye. A simple method of **batik** that is safe for children. A drawing is made on fabric with charcoal or **chalk** and covered with a **flour paste** mixture. About 1 tablespoon flour is added per ½ cup water for a thin paste that can be brushed on. When the paste is dry the fabric is covered with a somewhat thick **dye**; silkscreen dyes can be used. When a color is dry, another area can be painted with the paste. When all colors are completed, the paste is scraped off and the dye is **set** by **ironing**. This is similar to **paste resist**.

pastiche. A design or work of art with obvious evidence of plagiarism, often done satirically; an assortment or hodge-podge of **motifs** borrowed from other artists.

pasting guard. Bookbinding. A piece of waste paper folded to produce a sharp, straight edge used to protect portions of a surface when pasting a thin margin, as in **tipping** and **pasting up.**

pasting leather. Bookbinding. Cut the leather from a paper pattern; allowing ¾" for turn-in, and paring where it folds or overlaps. Moisten the face of the leather to soften it so that it works easily and to prevent staining from the moisture of the paste. Place the leather on a clean surface and work paste into the pores; fold it in two with the pasted side inside. (With corners, place one pasted corner upon another one.) Let the paste soak in for ten minutes, then paste the leather again. Remove any excess—the paste that has accumulated in the pores will adhere the leather to the **board**s or **back**.

To paste corners, position the leather correctly on the corner of the face of the board, turn the board over, and press it onto the leather. Rub the leather on the edge of the board with the **bone folder**; turn the **head** and **tail** overlaps first, then the **foredge.**

For backs, apply paste to the back strip of leather and the back of the book. Lay the back of the book on the leather and adjust it until the overlaps are equal at head, tail, and all sides of the back. Press the book down onto the leather until the leather adheres to the back when the book is picked up. Wrap the overlap around to the front and back boards, adjusting the leather until it is centered. Lay the book down and **rub down** the back with the bone folder. Lift the leather from the side of one of the boards, being careful not to lift as far as the back, and work it into the **French groove** with the folder. If you do this operation without lifting the leather first, it will stretch too tightly across the joint and pull the sides out of shape. After forming the groove, lay the leather onto the board and rub it down firmly into place. Repeat on the other side of the book, and then rub down all of the back once more to be certain it is well adhered to the **back edge.**

To turn in overlaps to form head bands, place a waste sheet on the pasted leather at the tail and stand the book upright. Place a thick piece of twine the width of the back in place on the leather, level with the head of the book. Rub a little paste on the leather on the outside where it will turn over. Holding the boards, push them back slightly and turn the leather (with your thumbs) over the twine. Keep the twine level with the top of the book and the turn-in flat. Repeat this operation for the tail. Tap the leather along the edges of the boards for squareness. Tie a string around the back so that it lies in the French groove. The knot should fall between the boards at the head or tail to prevent it from making an impression on the leather. Wrap a heavy card or manila sheet around the back of the book at the head band and hold it in place with one hand to prevent the leather from pulling away from the back. With a bone folder, mold the head band to a square or beveled shape; it should not project above the boards. Work out any creases with the folder and make any other adjustments before the leather dries. Place wax paper between the boards and the book to prevent **cockling**; wrap it in clean paper and place it under a light weight to dry. Do not press, as this would force the leather off the spine. If the head band is too tight after the leather dries, lightly dampen the inside of the turn-in near the joint. See ill. Also see **mitered corners, paring.**

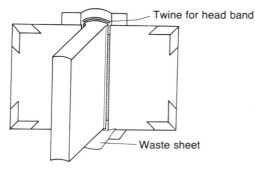

Turning in overlaps to form head bands

pasting up. Bookbinding. A gap will appear between the first or last two **sections** of a **bound book** when opened to these junctures unless they are pasted up. After sewing the sections together and then **knocking down** the **swell**, **jog** the book until it is square at the **back** and **head**. Open out the first section and lay a **pasting guard** across the first page of the second section, leaving a ⅛" margin exposed parallel to and next to the back. Apply paste with your finger to the ⅛" exposed strip. Remove the **pasting** guard and carefully close the first section; make sure that the section is positioned exactly level with the back and head of the book. Repeat for the last section of the book.

pastry tube. Toys. A small kitchen tool made for the purpose of forming pastry into decorative shapes. Some tubes are metal and others are fabric bags with a metal nozzle. Many materials can be put into the pastry tube for decorative work.

In toymaking, either colored or white spackle can be forced through the tube for application on wood or cardboard, or frostings can be squeezed through for use in **baker's art.**

patch. Quilts. The basic unit of a **pieced quilt.** Sometimes the patch and the **block** are identical, as in a quilt that uses only squares, triangles, or hexagons, all of the same size; this simple **geometric** arrangement is usually called a **one-patch.**

Ordinarily a block is made up of a number of patches. For example, a block might be made up of four patches, in which each patch is a square and all four squares are identical in size, but the makeup of the patches may vary. That is, one might be plain or solid while another is made up of four smaller triangles. It is the arrangement of the patches that determines the block pattern.

A small piece or scrap of material sewn on top of another material may also be called a patch. This is sometimes done to mend or repair a garment or blanket. Then patches may be arranged into designs both decorative and functional, and in this sense, to patch means to **appliqué.**

At the risk of adding further complexity or confusion, it should be noted that patch is sometimes used to refer to any finished block design, whether appliquéed or pieced. Here, patch is the smaller unit, and block is the larger repeat unit of the quilt. See ill.

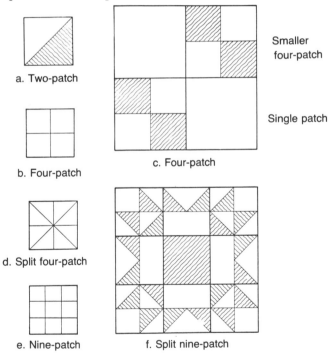

a. Two-patch

b. Four-patch

c. Four-patch

Smaller four-patch

Single patch

d. Split four-patch

e. Nine-patch

f. Split nine-patch

patchouli. Candlemaking. A widely used **scent.** Also see **Candlemaking: Adding the Additives.**

patchwork. Quilts. Stitchery. The **piecing** together of small scraps or **patch**es of fabric to produce a single piece of cloth. The patches are usually cut into basic **geometric** forms to produce simple or complex patterns through the systematic way in which they are joined. The term "patchwork" is often used interchangeably with the term **pieced;** a patchwork quilt is essentially a **pieced quilt.** It is also sometimes used to refer to patching or mending in which one piece of fabric is sewn over the top of another, as in **appliqué.** A garment may, in this sense, be covered with patchwork.

patchwork clothes. Stitchery. A popular approach to clothing design which involves the use of **patchwork** or **pieced fabrics.** Some **recycled clothes** make use of unquilted patchwork **quilt top**s, while others utilize pieced materials made up specifically for a certain **garment.**

Patchwork can also be used in the original sense of "patching." One piece of fabric may be applied overlapping another to produce a random pattern of colors and shapes. Patchwork on jeans or blue denims is currently popular. Many patchwork clothes start out with patches of a functional nature which tend to become more elaborate and decorative.

Yardage can be made up from smaller pieces of fabric which are patched or sewn together. Patterns are then placed over the patchwork and it is used as though it were whole cloth or a single length of material.

patchwork quilt patterns. Quilts. See **pieced patterns.**

patchwork weaving. Weaving. See **scaffold wefts.**

patent leather. Leather. Leather, usually black, with a hard, glossy surface finish; it is mostly used commercially.

patent leather compass. Leather. A compass tool for scribing circles or cutting circle grooves in leather. It usually comes with one point, for marking, and several attachments for cutting grooves of various widths. It is commonly used also much like an **edge creaser,** to mark or groove lines parallel to the edge of leather. See ill. Also see **divider, scratch compass.**

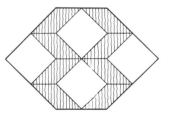

Patent leather compass

Paternayan yarn. Crewel. Embroidery. Needlepoint. See **Persian yarn.**

Path of Thorns. Quilts. See **Tree Everlasting.**

Patience Corner. Quilts. One of the earliest **pieced block** patterns, made up of squares and diamonds. It is an **all-over pattern** of hexagonal blocks, put together in a **hit-**

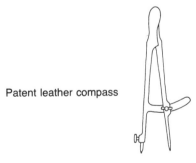

Patience Corner

or-miss arrangement. When the blocks are **set** in certain arrangements of dark and light, a **Box Quilt** pattern results. See ill.

patina. Originally, the layer of chemically caused green corrosion that forms on bronze when exposed to weather. The word is now used to refer to an appealing encrustation, texture, calcification, coloring, or sheen on any material, indicating age or wear.

patina. Jewelry. The surface color and quality that appears on metal—naturally, through the process of aging, or as a result of a chemical treatment such as **antiquing.** Also see **ammonia, coloring, corrosion, heat oxidizing, liver of sulfur.**

patina. Metalworking. The color and finish of a metal surface caused by natural weathering and oxidation, or by chemical or heat treatment; the process of creating this finish. When the process gives the look of aged metal it is sometimes called antiquing. Hundreds of formulas for chemical patinas have been developed over the centuries. Some of these and their methods of application have been kept secret by guilds and craftspeople; others are simple and widely known. For example, **silver** and **copper** may be antiqued or tarnished by applying a solution of liver of sulfur (potassium sulfide). **Bronze** castings take on various surface colors when heated and painted with human urine.

A patina will not disguise surface faults or poor joints, so the form and surface should be completely finished and polished before any patina process is applied to the work. Also see **Metalworking: Finishing.**

patriotic quilt. Quilts. Individually designed one-of-a-kind-quilts incorporating stars, stripes, flags, shields, and eagles in the design. Inspired by patriotism, the women who made these quilts reveled in the bright reds, whites, blues, and golds. One **patchwork** example is further embellished with India-inked inscriptions such as:

"Our country right or wrong, when wrong to be put right, when right to be kept right."

"Abraham Lincoln knows the ropes!"

"While our fingers guide the needle, our thoughts are intense [in tents!"]

Printed souvenir handkerchiefs also found their way into patriotic quilts, as did portraits of presidents or presidential candidates printed on fabric. Also see **bicentennial quilt, centennial quilt, Secession Quilt, Star-Spangled Banner Quilt.**

pattern. Crochet. (Abbr. pat.) The specific combination of **loop**s, **chain stitch**es, and **yarn-over**s to form a design, **motif,** or crocheted objects. Most often, crochet patterns take the form of a row-by-row listing of the working of every stitch. They are usually recorded by using abbreviations for the various crochet terms. Also see **Crochet: Abbreviations, Basic Stitches, Patterns.**

pattern. Knitting. A knitting pattern is the directions for a piece of knitting. It is first composed of **stitch**es, and then stitches and **motif**s. A knitting pattern consists of a row-by-row listing of stitches required to create a specific garment or other knit object; it tells when and how to **increase** for purposes of **shaping,** and—if the knitting is colored or involves many different kinds of stitches—it may include **graph**s that visually mark out complicated sections of the pattern, stitch by stitch. Also see **Knitting: Construction.**

pattern. Lacemaking. **Bobbin lace** is worked over a pattern that has been made with a **pricker** on a piece of strong paper or firm, lightweight cardboard with a smooth finish. It is through these pricked holes that the **pins** are placed and around which the lace is worked.

After drawing a **design** on paper, lay the design over a piece of pricking paper or cardboard, on a firm surface which should be padded to receive the point of the pricker. Securely clamp, pin, or tape the papers so they will not shift during the **pricking.**

Holding the pricker in a vertical position, press the tip of it through the design and the pricking paper to make tiny holes at the points indicated in the design. If the holes are too large, the pins will shift around in the pinholes during the lacemaking, and will likely enlarge and throw the design off.

For a **lace edging** or **insertion,** where many repeats of the pattern are needed, have the pricking of sufficient length to go completely around the cylinder shape of the **pillow.** By placing a few layers of cloth under the pricking, an adjustment can be made so the pattern will be joined perfectly around the circumference of the cylinder.

When the bobbin lace is finished, pull out all the pins and separate the lacework and pattern.

In **needle lace,** designs are usually traced onto a fine fabric. Lay in a foundation of **running stitch**es and work the lace on this. In needle lace **appliqué,** draw the pattern on **blue paper** and arrange the **lace** pieces on the pattern.

pattern. Metalworking. A copy of the finished form used to make an impression in the sand when **sandcasting.** It is made of wood, metal, plaster, or plastic, and has a slight **draft** and no **undercut**s. It is made slightly larger than the desired cast, to compensate for metal shrinkage in casting. Most patterns are withdrawn from the sand after an impression is taken; however, in **foam vaporization casting,** the plastic foam patterns are burned out in the pouring.

Pattern materials are chosen on the basis of how many copies are desired. Foam patterns are used once; wood patterns are used 100–500 times. Metal patterns are used for more detailed work and for 500 copies or more. The table below shows common pattern allowances for shrinkage.

Metal Used	Shrinkage per foot (in inches)
Gray iron and malleable iron	1/8
Steel and white cast iron	1/4
Aluminum and magnesium alloys	5/32
Brass, bronze, and other copper alloys	3/16

A shrink rule is available for calculating shrinkage when a precision fit is required.

When planning the draft, inside surfaces need more draft angle than outside surfaces: 1–3%, or $^1/_{16}$–$^1/_4$″ per foot. Large flat surfaces often warp and should be designed so the pattern has reinforcing ribs on the undersides. Inner corners, which are not seen, are always rounded.

pattern. Plastics. The model used to make a **mold** for **casting.** In **thermoforming,** a pattern is the mold itself. It should not have a rough surface, sharp corners, right angles, or points because the plastic draped over it may stretch thin and tear. For **drape forming,** make a slight **draft** on all vertical edges of the pattern. For vacuum forming, the pattern should have small exhaust holes all over it, so that the plastic is sucked down evenly. The material used should be **hardwood,** or any other sturdy material, and the holes small enough so that they won't mark the soft hot plastic. Also see **Plastics: Thermoforming and Molding.**

pattern. Stained Glass. See **template.**

pattern. Tatting. A pattern is made using a design or motif as a model; the design is accompanied by written instructions for tatting it. Also see **abbreviations.**

pattern draft. Weaving. See **weave draft.**

pattern dyeing. Fabric Printing. See **dye printing.**

patterning. Basketry. Any of a variety of decorative effects obtained by varying the weave or color of a basket material.

pattern knife. Stained Glass. Used in cutting out **template**s, this tool is one of the substitutes for the expensive **pattern shears.** Double blades are set into an angled handle, which must be line up exactly even on the paper and traced around the outline of the shape. See ill.

Pattern knife

pattern shears. Stained Glass. A three-bladed scissors with a single edge on top and a double blade on the bottom used in cutting out **template**s or patterns. It comes in a $^1/_8$″ or a $^1/_{16}$″ size. The thin strip removed represents the **heart** of the **lead came** (a.). A substitute may be made by inserting a $^1/_8$″ or $^1/_{16}$″ cardboard or wood shim between two single-edged razor blades and taping them together (b.). See ill. Also see **pattern knife.**

a. Pattern shears

$^1/_8$″ piece of wood — Tape

b. Handmade substitute single-edged razor blade

pattern weaves. Weaving. Those weave structures that have a definite, recognizable design to them. Every weave has a pattern to it no matter how small the weave, but the term is applied only to larger and more elaborate structures. Pattern weaves usually have their **drawing-in drafts** arranged in groups or blocks to form the basis of the design. The **treadling** then completes the pattern with often a choice of treadling available depending on the pattern desired. In some pattern weaves, color placement brings out the pattern. In others, the pattern stands out as a texture of the fabric. The term is also applied to various **pick-up weaves** that usually have more elaborate and definite patterns than loom-controlled pattern weaves. Also see **block weave, Bronson weave, crackle weave, overshot, spot weave, Summer and Winter weave.**

pattern yarns. Weaving. Usually refers to the **filling pick**s that produce the design in the cloth. They are not part of the **ground weave** and they distinguish the pattern—by being heavier than the ground yarns, by floating over them, or in some other manner. It is also possible, though not common, to place the pattern yarn in the **warp** and have the design travel lengthwise in sections of the cloth.

Pattison, Edward. Tincrafting. A Scottish-born American colonist thought to be the founder of the first tincrafting shop in the colonies. Also see **Tincrafting: History and Background.**

pavé. Jewelry. **Bezel**ed gemstones in lines or groupings so that the metal is paved with stones.

pavillion. Gemcutting. See **facet.**

pawl. Weaving. (Also known as dog.) A wooden or metal piece hinged to the side of the loom near the **ratchet.** It is shaped so that by falling into the teeth of the ratchet wheel, it works as a brake and prevents the **beam** from turning while weaving. **Warp** tension is adjusted by the pawl and ratchet. There can be more than one pawl to a ratchet so that a finer adjustment can be made. See **weaving.**

peacock fan. Quilts. See **Quilts: Quilting.**

pearl ash. Ceramics. Potassium carbonate used to modify color effects. When substituted for lead, sodium, or calcium, in **copper oxide** compounds, the usual green is changed to yellow green or a bright blue. Also see **pigment oxide.**

pearl purl. Embroidery. Pearl purl is a heavy coil which is pulled slightly open before being couched to the **background fabric** with waxed thread sewn between each twist. It has the effect of small beads and is generally used to neatly outline those areas filled with **bullion thread** which have been raised with a felt padding. Since it is such a heavy wire it stays in any position in which it is bent, and is most useful for finishing areas neatly. Also see **couching, metallic thread embroidery.**

pearls. Beadwork. A nacreous growth is formed inside an oyster or other mollusk when a foreign substance such as a speck of sand enters the shell. This growth, the pearl, continues to grow for as long as the oyster lives, sometimes as much as twenty years. Pearls vary in shape, from perfect spheres to disk-shaped button pearls to pear-shaped. The colors, always iridescent, vary from gray, blue, and rose to white.

Because of its curious source, the pearl has been regarded as the tears of the oyster, and because of its beauty, as the embodiment of purity. The Greeks thought that pearl-bearing shells had been struck by lightning. Besides its flawless beauty, the pearl has other fine qualities to make it prized for jewelry and **beadwork**. It is not too difficult to pierce, and it is very durable.

Because pearls are rare, various types of artificial pearls have been made. Seed pearls and chalk have been ground with other ingredients to try to imitate the luster of pearls. The wonderful technique of producing **cultured pearls** was developed in the early twentieth century, making pearls more available to craftspeople. Most of the pearls used for **bead embroidery** come from a small freshwater mollusk, usually called a pearl mussel, found in rivers, lakes, and streams of nearly every continent. Pearl beads are round (seed pearls) or oval (oat pearls).

pearls. Lacemaking. See **picot**.

pearly luster. Gemcutting. See **luster**.

pear shader. Leather. A pear-shaped **stamping** tool used for texturing and shading areas which have been cut with a **swivel knife**. Also see **tooling**.

peasant embroidery. Embroidery. From peasant embroideries and the folk art of all nations has come the inspiration for many of the world's most interesting embroidery techniques. Year after year through long winter days and evenings, mothers would teach their daughters to spin, weave, and embroider, passing on from generation to generation the experience they had gained. Each country had its own special expression, yet all have an overall unity in exquisite craftsmanship and strong design.

The elaborateness of the stitchery, where time was of no importance, is almost unbelievable. A west Bohemian shawl, for instance, is worked to entirely cover the linen with stylized leaves and roses in shades of mulberry colored silk, in the **satin stitch**. Gold-green oak leaves, connected by striped mulberry and green **stem stitches**, are superimposed on this to form a wavy border. The whole shawl is edged with white lace. (The colored embroidery of most peasant costumes is generally set off with frothy frills of white linen, made lacy with cut work.)

A northern Macedonian shepherdess costume has a deep border of geometric patterns in red, green, gold, and white wool at the bottom of the apron, and a repeat of the design stitches at the back of the matching white wool boots. All the Baltic countries have a wide diversity of embroidery, from the brilliant silks of one region to the homespun wools of another. All have striking and dramatic color combinations, often striking in their stark simplicity. The young girl's costume from Romania, for instance, is en-

tirely black and white. It is worn with brilliant flowered silk ribbons tied at the waist, the ends flying out as the wearer walks. Six to eight yards of white linen make the **accordion-pleated** skirt, which is worn over a petticoat of eyelet embroidery. The shirt with its bell sleeves is **smocked** at the neck and the cuffs with fine black stitches. A vest with a delicate design of lacy flowers is worked in black **buttonhole stitch** on white linen.

peashooter. Toys. (Also called beanshooter.) A simple **folk toy** that consists of a hollow tube or **blowpipe** through which peas, beans, or **spitballs** are blown. In some more complex peashooters, a plunger or piston is used to force the air through. If the end of the shooting toy or toy gun is plugged with a spitball, the piston can force it out at great speed.

pebble. Mosaics. A natural stone made round and smooth by the natural action of water over a long period of time. Many of the earliest **mosaics,** before the development of **tesserae,** were constructed out of pebbles. The making of a mosaic with pebbles can be made much easier if they are graded by size before the project is begun. The shift away from the more formalized approach to mosaics by many contemporary artists has greatly revitalized the interest in the pebble as a **found object** mosaic material. Also see **Mosaics: Selecting the Material.**

pebble jet. Jet Carving. Jet obtained from the beach, as opposed to jet that is mined. The outer skin of blue or yellow lias rock has been removed by the tumbling of the sea, leaving a dull, gray, abraded surface. The fractures will be black, or a few scrapes with an emery board will produce brown lines, thus revealing its identity. Also see **hard jet, jet, soft jet** and **Jet Carving: Tools and Materials.**

pebble mill. Ceramics. A tool that is used to grind and mix materials in pottery. Usually, **glaze** or **slip** and water are placed in a jar with flint pebbles. Also see **ball mill.**

peccary. Leather. The leather, similar in appearance to **pigskin,** from skins of a wild boar from Central and South America.

peck. Woodworking. See **wood: defects.**

pecking bird. Toys. Any of a variety of mechanically operated birds from the early twentieth century. The windup mechanism tightens a spring that, when released, causes the tin birds to bob up and down, suggesting a pecking movement. The name is sometimes used to refer to the **pecking chickens toy.**

pecking chickens. Toys. A **swinging-weight toy** in which cut or **carved wood**en chickens or other birds are set in a circle on a base to which a short handle is added. Each head is hinged and attached to a string that runs down through a hole drilled in the base; all the strings are attached to a single weight. When the base is moved in a circular horizontal motion by means of the handle, the weight swings under the base and activates the pecking motion.

Some pecking chickens are made with a weighted pendulum that swings back and forth, setting two chickens in motion in an alternating action. The weight is pulled to one side and then dropped, so it is unnecessary to rotate the paddle or platform. The toy must be hung or held over the edge of a table to allow the pendulum to swing.

The pecking chicken is a **folk toy** of Russia and Eastern Europe. The chicken or bird form itself makes it something of a **universal toy**, being found so frequently in toys the world over.

This toy is sometimes called a **pecking bird** or pecking sparrow.

pecking sparrow. Toys. See **pecking chickens**.

pedal. Weaving. See **treadle**.

peddler doll. Toys. (Also called notions, nannies.) A replica doll of the itinerant salespeople who were licensed to sell **knickknack**s, toys, and housewares in various parts of England. They were carefully costumed to represent a specific locale. Some peddler dolls that were kept as parlor ornaments eventually became the toys of children. The peddler dolls were always outfitted with **miniature**s of the actual items sold.

peen hammer. Metalworking. See **hammer**.

peep egg. Toys. Any **hollow egg** that contains a **miniature peep show**. One such **egg**, popular in the middle 1800s, was of alabaster and contained two small scenes. Each scene was viewed through a lens set into a small opening at one end of the egg in a variation of the peep show.

Sometimes real eggs are used for peep eggs. Small openings are made at the ends of the egg so that the contents can be forced out by blowing. Much careful work is required to arrange the scene in place because it must be done through a tiny opening, using tweezers and similar tools. **Sugar egg**s are also sometimes used. Also see **Toys: Ephemeral Toys**.

peep show. Toys. A popular entertainment toy of the nineteenth century in which the viewer peers through a small opening, and often through a magnifying lens, to view a scenic arrangement or an object. The scenes were usually partially animated, changeable, or movable, although in the **peep egg** they were stationary. The peep show and the **optical toy** are similar and it is sometimes difficult to identify where one leaves off and the other begins.

Some peep shows were coin-operated and were placed for amusement in penny arcades. A coin dropped in a slot set the peep show in motion or released the handle so that, by hand cranking, a series of pictures could be viewed. Some shows promised in lurid advertisements to offer a sensational glimpse into the wicked, impure, or unvirtuous side of life in the 1800s. Also see **kinora** and **Toys: Optical Toys**.

peg. Basketry. A short length of dowel or **stuff** often used to secure the lid **hasp** to a **noose** on the body of a basket, or put through the **bow** of a **cross handle** to prevent the handle from slipping out of the weaving. See ill.

Peg

peg. Toys. A wood pin or a short length of **dowel** used in various ways in toymaking. The peg-jointed doll has **peg-joint**s for each movable limb.

peg awl haft. Leather. See **awl** and **haft**.

pegboard. Needlepoint. A board with evenly spaced holes which can be used for large-scale contemporary needlework designs where an evenweave **background fabric** is desirable.

peg clamp. Jewelry. A hand-held tool for holding small pieces while working them. It consists of a wooden handle attached to the bottom of a ¾″ circular face plate which is partially pierced through with many holes. Different-shaped pegs are available which may be fitted into the holes around a symmetrical or irregularly shaped piece to secure it. In addition, the circular face plate is divided in half and can be expanded to hold somewhat larger work. It is primarily used to hold work for **engraving**. Also see **clamp, electric engraving tool**.

peg doll. Toys. See **penny wooden doll**.

pegged rug. Rugmaking. Also called "brodded" rugs. Predecessors of **hooked rug**s, made in the Yorkshire region of England and Scotland. **Thrums** of wool yarn or cloth scraps were poked through **canvas** or **burlap rug backing** creating a rough **pile**. Another method was to poke the thrum up and down through the backing so that loops were formed on the surface. These loops were later sheared to make a more uniform **pile height**. Also see **thrummed rug**.

peg joint. Toys. A **joint** often used in **dollmaking** in which **peg**s or **dowel**s are used as the connecting device in completing joints. A **tongue-and-groove** joint with a peg run through the center was sometimes used to allow the movement of knees, hips, and elbows, usually with another peg joint to connect the arms to the shoulders. The **peg-joint doll** had this specific type of joint instead of **ball joint**s, **cord joint**s, etc.

peg-joint doll. Toys. A **doll** whose arms and legs are made movable by **peg-joint**s. The Dutch doll or **penny wooden doll** is made in this way and is sometimes referred to simply as "peg-jointed," or peg-wooden.

A **pin-joint** doll can be made with a **peg** used to replace the pin. Such a doll is also called a peg-joint doll.

peg knitting. Knitting. A primitive type of knitting, traditionally done by American Indians, similar in technique to **frame knitting**. Peg knitting was done by interweaving yarn from finger to finger or peg to peg, then slipping the loops off in a locked manner to form rows of "knitting." See ill.

Peg knitting

pegmatite. Ceramics. A natural igneous rock formation. It is a variety of granite that is generally characterized by an extremely coarse texture.

peg plan. Weaving. See **chain draft, dobby loom.**

peg top. Toys. (Also called casting top.) A spinning toy similar to the **spin top.** It is a pear-shaped **top** with a metal tip or point.

peg-top doll. Toys. See **pestle doll.**

peg wooden. Toys. See **peg-joint doll.**

Pekinese stitch. Crewel. Embroidery. A very effective decorative stitch when used in a straight line or as a **border stitch.** The **backstitch**es initially laid down should be small and not too tight. The loops are worked around the back stitches with a **tapestry needle** and should not be too long. It is especially effective when the loops are worked in a contrasting color to the backstitch. See ill.

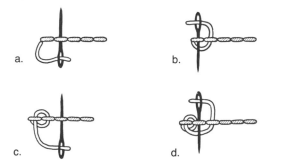

a.   b.

c.   d.

pelle d'angelo. Coral Carving. See **coral.**

pelt. Leather. An untanned skin or hide which still has the hair on it.

pen blade. Woodworking. See **whittling tools.**

pencil. Bookbinding. A small camel's-hair brush used to apply **glaire.**

pencil line. Quilts. See **Quilts: Marking and Cutting.**

pencil puppet. Puppets. Any **puppet** that is attached in some way to a pencil. **Stick puppet**s may be made quickly

by attaching picture cutouts to pencils. Or small fabric or **felt puppets** can be slipped over the end of a pencil and used in a **puppet stage.** The pencil merely substitutes for the finger.

pendeloque. Gemcutting. See **facet.**

pendulum toy. Toys. A toy in which parts are made to move by the swinging motion of the pendulum. Often the weight at the end of the pendulum is sufficient to alternately animate more than one figure, as in the **pecking chickens.** It is sometimes referred to as a **swinging-weight toy.**

penelope canvas. Needlepoint. See **canvas, petit point.**

penetrating oil stain. Woodworking. See **wood stain.**

pen knife. Woodworking. See **whittling tools.**

pennant. Stitchery. A long narrow **flag,** usually triangular in shape. Pennants are made in either solid colors or may be **appliqué**ed and embroidered.

Pennsylvania Dutch quilt. Quilts. Those quilts, frequently identified by color and style, that were originally made by the Pennsylvania Dutch. Nowadays their use of color and form is duplicated, or at least imitated. The quilts made by these women, usually **appliqué**d, are vigorous and strong in design and full of exuberant color. There is a charmingly naïve aspect to the free play of their designs. Flowers (especially tulips) and hearts and birds are some of the most prominent motifs. Among the most copied of all their designs are the so-called hex signs, design motifs painted on the sides of barns. Nearly all the Pennsylvania Dutch motifs have been utilized in appliquéed quilt designs, to the advantage and benefit of the quilts.

penny. Woodworking. See **nail.**

"penny plain and tuppence colored." Puppets. The original English **flat puppets.** They were moved by the **puppeteer,** who stood at the side of the stage and slid the figures on and off stage by means of a stick or wire. As the name suggests, they were sold "plain" to be decorated and colored at home, or "colored" and ready for use. Also see **cut-out figure, Juvenile Drama, paper cutout puppet, toy sheets, toy theater.**

pennywood doll. Toys. See **penny wooden doll.**

penny wooden doll. Toys. (Also called Dutch doll, Flanders baby.) A **peg-joint** doll of **carved wood** that was made from the late 1700s to the early twentieth century. The face and head were **finish**ed and painted, usually with black hair. The legs, hands, and shoes were painted on. The dolls were made in a wide range of sizes, from ½" to 2' tall, and were sometimes called "Nurnberg Fille." Large pennywood dolls or peg dolls were made with **ball joints** instead of peg joints. Also see **Bartholomew baby.**

Peony. Quilts. A **pieced** and **appliquéd block** design that usually features a large single flower, or sometimes three flowers. There are many variations of this design. The name is also used to refer to a number of the **Tulip** patterns. Many of the pieced peony flowers are based on the **LeMoyne Star,** as is a variation of the Peony called Cactus Rose. See ill.

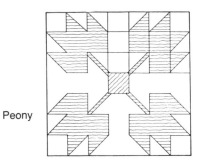

Peony

percale. Stitchery. A **cotton fabric** of close, **plain weave.** It is similar to **muslin,** but finer, and is used in **appliqué** and in quiltmaking.

percel-gilt. Jewelry. The partial or complete goldplating of metal. Also see **fire gilding.**

perch bar. Puppets. (Also called **rail.**) A bar with a row of hooks attached, affixed to the **rear bridge. Marionette**s not in use are suspended from it to keep their **string**s from tangling.

perch control. Puppets. See **vertical control.**

perforated cardboard. Needlepoint. A **background fabric** used in **counted-thread embroidery.** The large holes make it helpful as a background fabric for teaching needlework to a child.

perforated pattern. Quilts. See **pounce** and **Quilts: Quilting.**

performing monkey. Toys. See **monkey-on-a-stick.**

performing toy. Toys. An **animated toy** of an animal or figure made so that it mimics human behavior. Highly skilled toymakers of the eighteenth century made remarkable **musical automata** and **clockwork** animals and figures. The earliest record of clockwork toys is in Nuremberg in 1672. Among the popular early **automatic toy**s were performing monkeys who played **drum**s, cymbals, and **bell**s; dancing bears; and sometimes entire orchestras, complete with a synchronized sound track in an early phonograph cylinder. **Autoperipatetikos** were so highly developed that some stuffed toy animals could actually write on a paper as the paper moved mechanically under the pen.

perfumed beads. Beadwork. Various traditional techniques have been used to make scented beads. The fragrance was obtained from ground cloves, myrrh, oil of cloves or geranium, or rose petals ground into a malleable pulp. This was added to powdered **whiting,** finely shred-

ded cotton, or other fiber thickening mixed with a gum solution and powdered **orrisroot** for a preservative. The mixture was made into **molded beads.**

peridot. Gemcutting. See **olivine.**

perishable toy. Toys. See **ephemeral toy, edible toy.**

perla. Shell Carving. See **Shell Carving: Cameo Carving.**

perlite. Gemcutting. See **obsidian.**

perloir. Jewelry. A **punch** on which the working end is concave, in the form of a small half bead, used for modeling balls on metal. Also see **beading tool.**

permanent finish. Batik and Tie-dye. Stitchery. A **fabric finish** that cannot be removed by washing, abrasion, light, or heat. This offers assurance that a particular finish will survive repeated use and laundering.

In **batik** or **tie-dye,** it means that the finish cannot be removed to make the fabric receptive to the **dye** process, so the fabrics are unsuitable for use.

permanent marker. Batik and Tie-dye. Stitchery. Toys. See **marking pens.**

permanent press. Batik and Tie-dye. Stitchery. A **fabric finish** used on materials to keep them from wrinkling. This particular finish prevents the **fiber**s from absorbing or accepting **dye.** Also see **wash-and-wear.**

permeability. Ceramics. The degree to which a solid will permit a gas or liquid to pass through. In ceramics, it refers to the rate at which water will pass through fired clay, giving an idea of the size of pores in the **pottery.** The degree of **vitrification** determines the permeability; glazes are often necessary to make pottery impervious.

Persian embroidery. Quilts. See **broderie Perse.**

Persian knot. Rugmaking. Weaving. See **knotted pile.**

Persian rug yarn. Rugmaking. A long-**staple** wool of superior quality that gives excellent wear. It is spun and dyed in the United States, not in the Middle East, and was originally produced to facilitate the needs of repairers of **Oriental rugs.** The yarn became known to rugweavers because of its lovely luster and very wide range of colors. Today it is more popular in embroidery than in rugweaving due to several factors, including the rise in price of the yarn, and the emergence of other yarns made specifically for rug use.

Persian stitch. Crewel. Embroidery. See **Cretan stitch.**

Persian yarn. Crewel. Embroidery. Needlepoint. (Also called Paternayan yarn.) A three-stranded yarn that can be easily separated to use as many strands as are required to cover the **background fabric.** It is generally sold by the ounce (approximately 40 strands), but can be purchased by the skein in a wide range of weights and colors. Generally this yarn has a high sheen and is mothproof. Paternayan is one of the major suppliers, and because of its fine quality, Persian wool is often referred to as paternayan yarn. Also see **coarse weave linen** and **Needlepoint: Yarns.**

perspective. A technique in drawing for representing three dimensional objects and depth relationships on a flat **picture plane.** The development of techniques for "foreshortening"—showing near objects as large and more distant objects as small—occurred mostly in medieval times. Some medieval paintings show a kind of reverse perspective in which nearer things are drawn shorter than more distant things, so that space seems to open up behind the picture plane.

Two commonly used schemes for showing more distant things smaller than near ones in a consistent way are one-point perspective and two-point perspective. For one-point perspective, some point is chosen on the picture plane, more or less arbitrarily, and then lines of real objects that run away from the picture plane are drawn so that they would meet at that point, called the vanishing point. Two-point perspective is similar, except that it makes use of two vanishing points at the same level in the picture. See ill.

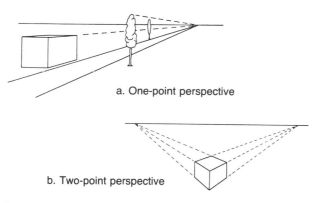

a. One-point perspective

b. Two-point perspective

Perspex. Plastics. See **acrylic.**

Peruvian double weave. Weaving. See **finnweave.**

Peruvian ingrain weave. Weaving. A **double cloth** construction that gives a compact, patterned **warp-face** fabric. The weaving is done with a **pick-up stick** so that the pattern is reversible; i.e., what is color A on one side, is color B on the other, and vice versa. The two **warps** are intermeshed so that, actually, a single fabric results. The weave is used in Peruvian and Bolivian Indian belt weaving, where bright colors are often used for the two warps. The **filling,** a heavy yarn, appears only at the edges of the belt. **Card weaving** is ingrain weaving, also, as is the weaving of **ingrain rugs** with two or three warps.

Peruvian knotting. Weaving. See **Brooks Bouquet.**

Peruvian lace. Weaving. See **gauze weave.**

Peruvian lattice. Weaving. An **openwork** technique that diverts the **warp** in sections from proceeding in parallel,

vertical lines, and in so doing, achieves a fabric composed of slanted solid areas interspersed with diamond-shaped openings. The warp sections are pulled together by the **filling** and woven tightly so that they remain close in a group. After a few **picks,** each group is divided into two equal numbers of warp **ends** and these new groups are woven as individual units. Eventually the new groups join through the filling with similar woven tabs to the right and to the left. As a group is pulled to its neighboring group, the latticelike openings are formed. The dividing and rejoining goes on for the length of the design. The Peruvians employed this technique in many fabrics, using it either as a whole area of the fabric, in bands across the fabric, as corners, or as border trim. See ill. Also see **diverted warp.**

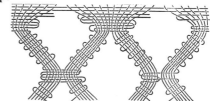

Schematic diagram showing two possible ways of joining sections in Peruvian lattice work

Peruvian weaving. Dyeing. Spinning. Weaving. The textiles of the pre-Columbian Peruvian Indians. This would include a period from 2500 B.C., when weaving was already well established (preceding the development of pottery and metallurgy by more than 1000 years), to the time of the Spanish conquest in 1532. Weaving is still an important craft in Peru, but the intricacy and artistry of the textiles have dwindled. Owing to the burial customs of the early Peruvians, which included wrapping the body up in yards of fabric, and the extreme dryness of the burial grounds on the Peruvian coast, many of these early textiles have been preserved for 3,000 years, so that contemporary weavers can today study their elaborate techniques and the artistry that these early weavers showed in putting together designs, images, colors, and techniques.

They are of interest to weavers because on simple equipment such as the **backstrap loom,** these preconquest weavers wove fabrics that were technical feats done with absolute mastery. Not only were they familiar with the usual weaving concepts and techniques, but they had in their repertoire techniques unknown to their contemporaries in other parts of the world; their work was very often superior to what was being done in the Old World. In addition, Peruvian textiles encompass not just weaving but **netting,** needle-made and needle-ornamented (embroidered) fabrics, and **braiding** and **plaiting.** A great number of today's American weaver-artists have been inspired by the invention and daring of the Peruvian weaver-artists.

The Peruvian weavers were also excellent spinners, using a **spindle** twisted by hand. They obtained a very fine, tightly twisted yarn, and sometimes **plied** it into a 2-**ply** yarn. **Cotton** and wool obtained from the **llama, alpaca** and **vicuña** were the fibers they used. In dyeing they had an extensive range of colors based on **natural dyes** of the area and an extensive knowledge of the workings of **mordants.** Among other natural **dyestuffs** they used **indigo** and cochineal. Also see **Brooks Bouquet, cross weave, dovetailing, eccentric weft, exposed warp, feather fastening, gauze weave, interlocking, Mexican lace, openwork techniques, outlining, Peruvian lattice, pile, scaffold wefts, slit tapestry, Spanish lace, sprang, tassels, triple cloth, twining, wrapping.**

pestle. Ceramics. See **mortar and pestle.**

pestle doll. Toys. A simple doll made from an English pestle or champing tree used for mashing fodder. One of the oldest examples is from 1800. The shape became well known for dolls. The peg-top doll was made in the same wood form. Pestle dolls are among those toys considered to be **emergent toys.**

Petal Quilt. Quilts. See **Hearts and Gizzards.**

Peter Rabbit. Toys. A popular **stuffed toy** and **nursery character** from the late 1800s on. The character was taken from Beatrix Potter's "The Tale of Peter Rabbit." Squirrel Nutkin is another well-known toy drawn from her writing. Because the author herself had tried to produce the soft toys in England, she was indignant that pirated versions were imported from Germany. The situation led to her activity in the campaign for tariff reform in 1910.

petite beads. Beadwork. Round **glass bead**s smaller than $^1/_{16}''$ in diameter. Also see **seed beads.**

petit point. Needlepoint. (Literally: "tiny stitch.") A French term referring to the scale of the **tent stitch** done on a penelope or mono **canvas** of size 18 or smaller. As the size decreases, the **background fabric** is more likely to be a fine gauze or a silk fabric with an **even weave.** Also see **silk canvas.**

petit point. Rugmaking. See **tent stitch.**

petrified wood. Gemcutting. See **flat, opal, quartz.**

pewee. Toys. See **caddy.**

pewter. Metalworking. An **alloy,** now made of approximately 91% **tin,** 7% **antimony,** and 2% **copper,** that is shiny white, soft, ductile, resists corrosion, and expands when cooled (giving sharp casting impressions). It is used for **raising, casting, metal spinning,** and stamping. It does not **work-harden** when hammered so does not need to be **annealed,** and it is easily **soft soldered** with a **flux** made for use with pewter. The melting point of pewter ranges between 425° F and 471° F, depending on the specific proportions of the metals used. It is a **eutectic** alloy; that is, it melts at lower temperatures than any of its components. Stock forms of pewter come in sheets up to 24″ × 36″, in **gauges** from 10 to 30 (14- and 16-gauge are most often used), circular blanks, strips, ingots for casting, and round,

half-round, and square wires $^1/_{16}''$ to $1\frac{1}{2}''$ in diameter. Pewter is sold by the pound.

Pewter was known by many other names throughout the centuries—poor man's silver; prince's metal; white metal; trifle or common pewter (83% tin and 17% antimony); lay or ley metal (20% or more lead), which was used for organ pipes; tin and temper; Pemberton's alloy (90% tin and 10% antimony); and black metal (60% tin and 40% lead). It was named Britannia metal in the 1760s when lead was replaced by antimony. Early in the twentieth century, legislation was created to limit the percentage of lead allowed in pewter; the lead limit was set at 10%. Now, no lead is allowed in pewter.

pewterware. Metalworking. Objects made of **pewter.** The history of this craft dates back to the Greeks and Romans, who often used as much as 3 parts **tin** to 1 part **lead** in their ware. After the Dark Ages, the manufacture of pewterware spread throughout Europe; England became the pewter center during this time. Most pieces were cast in **brass** or **bronze** molds, except for large ones, which were hammered. Metal spinning was restricted, because spun ware was considered inferior in quality. The Worshipful Company of Pewterers or The Pewterers Company, the officially recognized guild, beginning in 1348 graded pewter according to its lead content. Trademarks were registered, like the hallmarks in silversmithing.

Popular Britannia metal pewterware, such as the Sheffield plate made in England in 1770, had induced American craftsmen to manufacture pewterware by 1814. Art pewterware was later revived at the beginning of the twentieth century by the Art Nouveau movement, examples of which are Tudric ware from England and Kayserzimm from Germany. France also produced excellent pewterware, with organic, figurative, and floral designs.

pewterworking. Metalworking. The process of making objects out of **pewter.**

Working pewter generally requires different techniques and tools than working other metals does. Use wooden **stake**s and **anvil**s as a base for **raising** and **hammering,** because those of hard metal will mark the soft pewter. Files must be cleaned with a **file card** more frequently than when used with other metals because the softer metal tends to clog them. Also, files used on pewter should not be used on other metals, especially silver and gold, because pewter particles can cause the other metals to pit. This is especially noticeable when the metals are **solder**ed or **anneal**ed.

Pewter may only be **soft solder**ed with a solder that has a melting point below that of pewter (e.g., bismuth solder, which is very weak and brittle and melts at 240° F; a mixture of 60% tin and 40% lead, which melts at 370° F; 63% tin and 37% lead, which melts at 358° F; and 50% tin and 50% lead, which melts at 420° F). When soldering a series of joints near each other, such as a handle on a seam, start the first seam using the solder with the highest melting point and progress to lower-melting solders on the following seams. This will prevent the first seams from melting as you solder the succeeding ones. Never use a soldering iron whose heat is not easily controlled, or you may melt the pewter. Use a commercial pewter flux or mix your own by adding 7 drops of **hydrochloric** (muriatic) **acid** to 1 ounce of **glycerin.**

Pewter requires no annealing when hammered. It may also be cast into thin hollow forms by **slush casting** the metal into chilled bronze molds. Allow the metal to harden and etch the surface with a solution of 20% **nitric acid** and water.

Finishing pewter involves three steps: cutting or abrading the metal, blending the scratches, and polishing with **lampblack.**

When abrading the metal, do not use an **abrasive** cloth like emery or the particles may rub off and become embedded in the surface because of the heat of the **buffing wheel.** Instead, apply a polishing compound such as semidry tripoli, which has a nongreasy base, to the wheel. Do not use compounds with animal fat or **tallow,** because they tend to leave a clouded surface that is difficult to remove. A muslin buffing wheel is preferred to fell, which may cut grooves in the pewter.

To blend scratches, use a loosely stitched muslin buff with tripoli, exerting light pressure against the wheel. Move the work so the metal is buffed entirely in one direction and then turn the object so the buffing strokes overlap. Continue until the scratches are all blended to an even finish.

Apply a lampblack and kerosene mixture to the pewter (not to the muslin buff or it will fly back at you). Do not apply much pressure or you will create brown stains. After the mixture is spread all over the surface, put a clean soft buff wheel on the polishing wheel and take the lampblack off the object. Do not overwork it or you will stain the metal.

Wear cotton gloves during the various finishing procedures to avoid getting fingerprints on the metal. Keep different pairs for each stage and have two pairs for lampblacking—one for putting it on and one for removing it. Also, keep all polishing wheels separate.

peyote beadwork. Beadwork. See **Beadwork.**

phanascope. Toys. See **phenakistoscope** and **Toys: Optical Toys.**

phantamascope. Toys. See **phenakistoscope.**

phenacite. Gemcutting. See **phenakite.**

phenakistoscope. Toys. (Also called phenakistrope.) An early **optical toy** invented in 1833. It was identical to the strotoscope, which was invented at the same time. It worked on the principle of rotating cogs and wheels that showed visual images in rapid succession and demonstrated the persistence of vision. Numerous toys are made based on the phenakistoscope. Among them are the kaleidorama, or koleidorama, magic disk, phantamascope, phanascope, and tantascope. See ill. Also see **Toys: Optical Toys.**

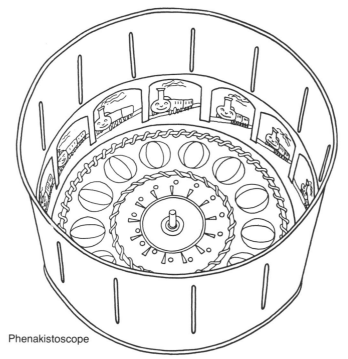
Phenakistoscope

phenakistrope. Toys. See **phenakistoscope.**

phenakite. Gemcutting. (Also called phenacite.) Beryllium sulfate **crystals** of the orthorhombic system with **hardness** of 7¾, **specific gravity** of 2.95–3, refractive indices of 2.95 and 2.97, conchoidal **fracture,** and vitreous **luster.** Phenakite is transparent to translucent, occurring in colorless, brown, rose, or yellow varieties. It is **facet**ed in brilliant form. Main crown facets are cut at 43° and main pavillion facets at 39°. Phenakite is polished on a tin **lap** with tin oxide. Also see **faceting, luster, polishing, refraction.**

phenolic. Woodworking. A **thermosetting plastic** commonly used in **adhesives** and synthetic **resin** varnishes for interior and exterior surfaces and floors. It is also one of the components of **Formica.** Resorcinol glue is a waterproof adhesive made for wood from phenolic; it may be sanded and machined, and is suitable for outdoor use. Phenolic is derived from phenol, also called "carbolic acid," which is derived from coal and benzene.

Philippine edge. Rugmaking. Weaving. A band of continuous knots that are worked **selvage** to selvage as the **finishing edge** on a rug or weaving. The edge looks a little like **plaiting** and is called a weft protector because it holds the first and last **filling picks** in place. Ridges are formed on the side of the work facing the worker as he knots going from the left side to the right side. The edge is wrapped over, two **ends** at a time, and the "up" thread doing the wrapping is then brought down beside the other two. Starting from the left side, wrap end #3 around and under #1 and #2 and over itself. Take end #4 and work this in the same motion over #2 and #3. This is repeated across the width of the item, always picking up a new **warp** end on the right and dropping the end that has been held on the left. A fringe is formed by the discarded ends. The ends that have the working end going under are always held firmly in the left hand and are pulled down to tighten, while the working end is pulled up.

If working on a rug, care should be taken that there are not too few warp ends or the knots will not be tied securely enough and the rug edges may be pulled in. More than one row of this knotting can be done, although one row will suffice to secure the filling. If more rows are done, the knots should always be started on alternate sides of the work so that ridges will appear on both sides and a sideways shift of the finishing edge will be avoided. The fringe can be made thicker by increasing the number of warp ends worked together. For example, instead of using one warp end, 2 or 6 in a bundle could be used and a bulkier knot with a thicker fringe will result. See ill.

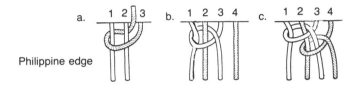

Philippine edge

Philippine mahogany. Woodworking. See **mahogany.**

Phillips-head screwdriver. Woodworking. See **screwdriver.**

Phillips Screw. Woodworking. See **screw.**

Phoebe Warner Coverlet. Quilts. An extraordinary **coverlet** of **appliqué** and embroidery from the early 1800s. A huge appliquéed urn occupying the center of the coverlet contains an extravagant arrangement of flowers, vines, and birds. Beneath the urn a flock of sheep stand quietly near a shepherd while deer rush past. A man and woman stand admiring a bird cage held between them, and children play, complete with dog and bow and arrow. Large birds hover over the tiny figures beneath the urn. It is a beautiful coverlet of intricate pattern and detail. It is in the Metropolitan Museum of Art, New York City. Also see **Sarah Furman Warner Coverlet.**

photocollage. Découpage. See **montage.**

photoelectric pyrometer. Ceramics. A heat-measuring device for high temperatures. It measures and transforms the light given off by a hot body in a **kiln** into an electric current that is registered on a dial.

photogram. An image made on light-sensitive photographic film or paper without the use of a camera. Man Ray, an American painter working in Paris, and Laszlo Moholy-Nagy, a Hungarian painter working in Berlin, worked with the art form independently around 1921, Ray calling his work Rayographs and Moholy calling his photograms.

The techniques and the results are rather similar. Two- or three-dimensional objects are placed on or next to light-sensitive paper and light is then permitted to fall upon the paper in such a way that the objects cast shadows, or a movable light source like a penlight can be played over the assembly. Shadows cast by solid objects, textures of transparent materials, even the path of a concentrated light beam can be recorded on the light-sensitive paper, which is subsequently developed in the usual way.

The kinds of images produced in this way are often surprisingly cohesive. Most of the best work done in the medium has been done by artists who were more or less committed to the principles of **abstract** art. The methods and materials necessary for the making of photograms are few and fairly simple, which makes the process well suited to developing visual ideas on an experimental basis before application to another medium. All necessary supplies can be purchased in photo-supply stores.

photograph. Découpage. Photographs can be used in découpage, but the results are not permanent. In time they will fade, and they may buckle underneath **varnish** coatings. Black-and-white photographs can be soaked and peeled to remove thick backing paper. Color photos cannot be soaked or thinned, but must be pasted to the surface dry. Otherwise, traditional découpage techniques can be used if care is taken during sanding not to mar the photo surface. Also see **thinning prints.**

photographic cartooning. Stained Glass. A method in which an original drawing for stained glass is photographically blown up to size required for the **cartoon.** The limitations of the method are its expense and the fact that it produces distortions around the edges.

photographic stencil. Silkscreen. Any of a number of kinds of **stencil** for silkscreen printing made by the use of light-sensitive materials.

The direct method involves coating the silkscreen smoothly with a mixture of water, gelatin, and a bichromate (potassium bichromate, ammonium bichromate, sodium bichromate) and allowing the coating to dry, at which time the coating becomes light-sensitive (**a.**). Exact formulas for the mixing of the coating material are available with the products from screen-process suppliers. After the screen is coated, further operations must be carried out in a room lighted only by photographic safe lights.

Designs to be copied must exist in the form of a film positive. A film positive can be created by drawing on transparent plastic film with crayon or paint or through photomechanical methods, using a darkroom, enlarger, and litho film. Many commercial silkscreen printers rely on photoengraving shops to supply the necessary film positives. An area for exploration is the making of a positive image by drawing or working on a sheet of glass. In any case, the image to be reproduced must exist as opaque material or photographic emulsion on a transparent sheet.

The film is placed against the light-sensitive coating on the screen so that the side of the plastic film with the design or lettering on it contacts the coating intimately. Commercial equipment uses a vacuum to ensure this close contact between film and screen. The studio craftsperson can improvise, using weights, sheets of foam material, and glass.

To expose the screen, strong light is allowed to fall through the transparent film onto the sensitized screen (**b.**). Industry uses arc lamps as a light source. The studio worker could use 1000 watts of flood lamps at a distance of about 3 feet for 15 minutes or so, but the exact time, which is important, will have to be determined by experimentation. When the exposure is sufficient, the areas of the screen that have become light-hardened will turn a darker color than the protected areas. The areas that were protected from light and are not light-hardened remain soluble in water. To open the screen, the whole screen is soaked for a few minutes; the softened image areas are flushed out of the screen with a stream or spray of warm water (**c.**). When the screen is dry, it is ready to be mounted on the printing base, and printing can begin. Reclaiming gelatin/bichromate stencil screens is very difficult; many workers merely stretch a new piece of mesh on the frame.

In the transfer method, the light-sensitive medium is a piece of film from which the image is transferred to the screen by adhering, much in the manner of the **cut-film stencil.** The most-used and best systems require proprietary materials like Ulano Wet-Shot photo film, McGraw presensitized film, and Kodak Ektagraph film; instructions for their use are included with the film and developing materials.

Photographic stencil methods are still in limited use by studio workers, but they are increasingly easy to use and offer intriguing possibilities for the craftsperson and artist. George Pollack of Denver is one of the very few screen artists making studio prints using four-color process separations. See ill.

Photo silkscreen preparation

a. Coating the screen   b. Exposing the screen   c. Opening the screen

photomontage. Découpage. See **montage.**

photo-offset. See **offset lithography.**

pick. Stitchery. See **filling.**

pick. Tatting. The extended tip of the **shuttle** used to "pick up" the **thread** to **attach** one **motif** to another.

pick. Weaving. A single passage of the **filling** yarn through the opening or **shed** of the **warp** yarns. Also, "pick" may be used when referring to the horizontal threads in a fabric as a unit or collectively, i.e., as a synonym for filling.

pickage. Weaving. See **picks-per-inch.**

pick-and-pick. Rugmaking. Weaving. (Also known as alternating weft.) These are single **pick**s of alternating colors in alternating **shed**s. For example, in a **plain weave** fabric using two colors in the **filling,** one color would go in the shed formed by raising **harness**es 1-3, the second color would go in the shed formed by raising harnesses 2-4, and they would alternate in this manner throughout the entire fabric. When plain weave is woven in a tapestry or a **flat-weave rug** technique, so that the **warp** is entirely covered, pick-and-pick colors will produce vertical or warp **stripe**s. See ill. Also see **stippling.**

Pick-and-pick weaving with rows of alternating color

pick count. Weaving. See **picks-per-inch.**

pick glass. Weaving. A magnifying glass used in analyzing and dissecting **cloth.** The glass is attached to a stand that has a ¼", ½", 1", or 2" square opening in the base. This opening rests on the cloth as the weaver looks through the glass to determine the number of **ends** and **picks**-per-inch and the weave structure. Both base and glass are hinged to the stand, so that the whole may be readily folded up. A pick glass is widely used in fabric and **weave analysis.** It is also known as a **linen tester.**

picker. Weaving. See **fly-shuttle loom.**

pickets. Weaving. See **cross weave.**

picking. Basketry. See **pick off.**

picking. Spinning. See **teasing.**

picking. Weaving. The action of throwing the **shuttle** containing the **filling** through the open **shed.** It comes after the **shedding motion** and before the **beating,** but unlike the other two terms, it is seldom used in handweaving today.

picking knife. Basketry. See **knife.**

picking stick. Weaving. See **fly-shuttle loom.**

picking up stitches. Knitting. See **knitting up.**

pickle. Enameling. See **cleaning metal.**

pickle. Jewelry. Metalworking. (Also called pickle bath.) An acid and water mixture used to remove **oxide** and **scale** from a metal surface, especially after heating. Pickling is the process of immersing or painting the metal object in a bath of **sulfuric acid** or **nitric acid.** Also see **Metalworking: Cleaning.**

pickle bath. Metalworking. See **pickle.**

pickle formula. Jewelry. See **pickling.**

pickling. Candlemaking. See **mordanting.**

pickling. Jewelry. Immersing metal in an acid **pickle** solution. It is used to remove any dirt or grease from the metal, as these will prevent **flux** from adhering properly and **solder** from flowing. Work should be placed into and removed from the pickle with copper **pickling tongs.** Pickle is kept in a pyrex container with a lid. If **Sparex #2** is used, it is heated to speed its cleaning action. If the pickle formulas below are used, the work can be dropped into the cold pickle solution while it is still hot from **soldering** or **annealing,** although these too can be heated. They produce, however, much more powerful fumes than Sparex #2. When dropping heated work into the pickle, it should be released from the copper pickling tongs and dropped all the way into the pickle, because putting it partially into the solution and then dropping it can create stresses or even cause the metal to fracture.

Pickling is done prior to **fluxing** the metal; after soldering, to remove any of the hardened flux and **firescale;** after annealing, to remove any of the hardened flux and firescale; and prior to coloring metal or creating a **patina,** to make sure the metal is absolutely free from any grease.

After pickling in Sparex #2, or the following formulas, the work must be rinsed in water. With Sparex #2 a bowl of fresh water will do, but with the formulas, the work should be flushed under running water.

With Sparex #2 and the pickle formulas, iron or steel should never come in contact with the pickle or it will contaminate the solution. Copper is instantly pulled out of the steel and deposited on any work in the pickle. Hence, work that has been bound with **iron binding wire** during soldering must have the iron wire removed before pickling. Steel tweezers should not be used to drop work into the pickle as the solution can splash, hit the steel tweezers, and roll off back into the solution and contaminate it. Use only copper or bamboo pickling tongs.

When dropping work into the pickle, always hold the lid of the pickle container between you and the pickle, close to the end of the container, to prevent the pickle from splashing skin, eyes, or clothing.

If there are small hollows where the pickle can collect, the work must be neutralized. This can be done by boiling the work in a solution of 1 tablespoon baking soda to 1 cup of water, and then rinsing the work under running water.

Pickle formulas for gold, silver, and copper are: 10 parts water to 1 part sulfuric acid; 8 parts water to 1 part nitric acid; and 6 to 12 parts water to 1 part sulfuric acid.

Always pour acid slowly into water—never the reverse, as it can cause splattering, heavy fumes, and even an explosion. Also see **cleanliness, electric pickler, married metals, waterbreak** and **Jewelry: Safety Precautions and First Aid.**

pickling. Metalworking. See **pickle.**

pick off. Basketry. (Also called picking.) To cut off or trim the loose ends of a completed basket.

pick-out. Weaving. See **weave analysis.**

pick soldering. Jewelry. (Also called point soldering.) A method of **soldering** in which the **solder** is picked up on the tip of a **soldering point.** It is used to quickly solder small **joints,** such as the seam between two pieces of round wire or on a **jump ring.** The solder is clipped and **flux**ed, then the tip of the soldering point is heated and placed on top of the solder, which is on an **asbestos pad** or a **charcoal block.** The heat from the **torch** is played on the soldering point and the solder. The solder will melt and form a small ball that will attach to the tip of the soldering point. This piece of solder is immediately moved to the area where the work, which has been previously fluxed, is heated. When it nearly reaches the point at which the solder will flow, the soldering point with the solder attached is touched to the joint of the work, and the solder flows off the soldering point into the joint. This is an extremely efficient and fast way to do multiple soldering of small links. Also see **chain soldering.**

picks-per-inch. Weaving. (Abbr. PPI, p/in. Also known as pickage, pick beat, pick count.) The number of individual passages of the **filling** yarn back and forth through the **warp** in one inch of fabric. The picks-per-inch help to establish the character of a cloth. If the picks-per-inch are equal to the **ends-per-inch,** the result is a balanced cloth. If the picks-per-inch are scanty in relationship to the warps, the cloth will be either **warp-faced** or a gauzy one. If the picks-per-inch are much more than the ends-per-inch, the filling will predominate. If they are so packed in that the warp is entirely covered, then a stiff fabric like **tapestry** is achieved.

On-loom picks are measured as the weaving progresses to see exactly how the fabric is being woven. This is important for keeping records for future orders or changes in the cloth. Off-loom picks are slightly more to the inch than on-loom picks. This count is taken after the fabric is cut off the **loom** and no longer stretched taut. The last count, finished picks, is after washing, **fulling** or whatever **finishing** method is employed to treat the yarn and fabric so it is in a state ready for use or display. Finished picks-per-inch usually have the highest count of the three. If there has been much compression or shrinkage during finishing, then the count can be much more than was originally counted on-loom. In some cases the yarn is not affected by the finishing method and there is no change in the picks-

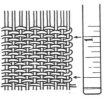

Picks-per-inch

per-inch from the off-loom count to the finished count. See ill.

pick-up design. Weaving. See **Finnweave.**

pick-up stick. Weaving. A thin, flat, and very smooth stick with beveled edges and a pointed end. It is used as an aid in making extra **shed** openings for certain **openwork techniques** or in some types of **free weaving.** To make the shed for openwork weaves, the stick is inserted in a flat position as it picks up and twists the **warp end**s; it is then turned on its edge and an opening results. The height of this opening is determined by the width of the stick, which is usually between 1″ and 2″. Its length can be just long enough to do a section of the warp or it can be slightly wider than the warp width if the pick-up or new shed is to extend across the entire warp. Also see **gauze weave, leno, pick-up weaves.**

pick-up-sticks. Toys. A modern version of the old **game** of **jackstraws.** It consists of a collection of small, smooth, sticks about 10″ long and the diameter of a matchstick. The ends are painted in various colors to denote differing score values. The sticks are dropped in a pile and picked up one at a time, the purpose being to pick each stick up without moving any of the remaining sticks.

pick-up weaves. Weaving. Those **weaves** that require a **shed** or part of a shed to be picked up and opened by the fingers, a needle, a flat **shuttle,** a **batten,** or a **pick-up stick** rather than by a **harness** or a **shed stick** and **heddle bar.** Pick-up weaves result when the design to be woven calls for more shed openings than are possible with the available **shedding devices.** These patterns are usually so complex that either a **draw loom** or a **Jacquard** mechanism would be required to weave them if they were to be done without pick-up. Fine examples of these weaves are to be found in Mexico, Guatemala and Peru, countries where **backstrap loom**s are prevalent. Often the pick-up is assisted and speeded up through the use of a whole series of pick-up sticks. This method necessitates the removal of the stick after the **pick** is woven and its reinsertion when that pick is called for again. However, since the next row of the pattern is picked up while the previous pick-up stick is still in place, it is quicker and easier to find the correct threads to pick-up. Many extra heddle bars with **string heddle**s can be used in which the shed is pulled open with the bar and a batten inserted to keep the shed open while the **filling** is put through. The pattern pick-up weaves are done in combination with a background weave, which is usually plain weave.

The term "pick-up weave" is also given to those techniques where the filling does not pass through the shed from one **selvage** to the other, but weaves a pattern in a given area. This would apply to **free weaving** such as the **laid-in weaves.** Pick-up is also used to describe the method employed in obtaining the pattern in **Finnweave** or **looping** and the structure in a **gauze weave** or **leno.** In the latter techniques, the **warp end**s are not only picked up but

twisted before the shed is opened. Also see **dukagang, double cloth, quiltweave.**

picot. Lacemaking. A small ornamental **loop** on the edge of the lace or on either or both sides of a **braid.** In **bobbin lace,** they are also called pearls, purls, purl pins, or turn pins. The common way to make a picot is to make a small **loop** and cover it with **buttonhole stitches.**

The picots in **needle lace** are worked with needle and thread, and are sometimes referred to as bobs. One way to work a picot is to put the tip of the needle into the work, taking up a very small bit of the foundation thread, wind the thread several times around the needle, put the left thumb on the wound thread, and pull the needle through. The wound loops from the needle will then transfer to the end of the thread, completing the picot. See ill.

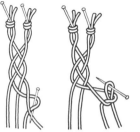 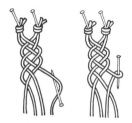

a., b. Bobbin lace double picot   c., d. Bobbin lace single picot

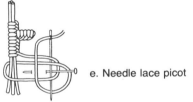

e. Needle lace picot

picot. Macramé. Tatting. (Abbr. p.) A tiny loop on the perimeter of a **ring** or **chain** in tatting. It is decorative as well as useful, adding a different look to the tatting because of the **double stitch**es. To **attach** one **motif** or area to another, nothing is more useful than a picot.

To make a picot, make a few double stitches on the **knot bearer.** With the next double stitch do a **left half hitch** a little distance from the last stitch on the knot-bearing cord; it is this **space** that will give the length of the picot (**a.**). Do a **right half hitch** and push that double stitch, completed, back to the previous double stitch. The distance between the last two stitches will form a loop, i.e., the picot. It is the **loop thread** that forms the picots.

Do a prescribed number of double stitches and repeat the spacing for another picot, complete the double stitch, and push back to form the second picot (**b.**). When the ring or chain has the required number of stitches, draw the knot bearer tightly to close (**c.**). See ill., next page.

To use a picot for a joining through a picot previously made on another motif, pick up the loop thread of the ring you are working and make a loop; pass the shuttle carrying the knot bearer through this loop and pull up on the loop thread. Check to see that the knot bearer pulls easily back and forth through the joining. Continue tatting. This procedure may be used in joining chains also.

The **pick** or hook of the tip of the shuttle, the **pin and ring,** a **crochet hook,** or a straight pin are useful for picking up the loop for making joinings.

In macramé, picot refers to a small loop that protrudes from a completed macramé knot. Picot knots are highly decorative and are often worked in the formation of **mounting knot**s. Also see **Josephine picot, square knot with picot** and **Macramé: Basic Procedures.**

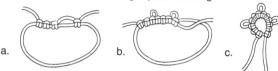

Making a picot in a ring

picot border. Knitting. See **border.**

picot casting on. Knitting. See **Knitting: Casting On.**

picot edge. Knitting. See **hem.**

picot eyelet. Knitting. A picot eyelet is a heart-shaped eyelet hole in the knitting fabric; it is often used in a series to create geometric eyelet patterns in a solid knit fabric. This design motif is made with double paired increases and a double yarn over in between.

Row 1: K 2 tog, yo 2, s1 1, K 1, psso.
Row 2: P 1, K 1, P 1 into yo 2 from previous row, P 1.

picot knot. Knitting. A knot of stitches made and completed within one stitch.

To work a picot knot, cast on by knitting four or more stitches, using one stitch as the base. The stitches will all be on the left needle (**a.**). Knit the cast on stitches, including the stitch used as a base for casting on (**b.**). There will now be four or more stitches on the right needle. Lift the cast-on stitches on the needle over the first cast-on stitch (**c.**). See ill. Also see **motif.**

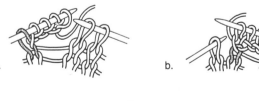

c. Picot knot

picot-point chain. Knitting. A small lacelike point protruding from a knit **edge.** Picots are usually used this way as a simple, decorative trim.
To knit the picot:
Row 1: Cast on 3 stitches by knitting, and knit into the backs of these 3 stitches.
Row 2: Cast off 2 stitches, leaving 1 stitch.
Repeat the two-row pattern.

picture plane. In drawing and painting, the imaginary flat surface on which objects are portrayed, equivalent to the plane on which film rests in a camera.

pieced. Quilts. Stitchery. **Join**ed, put together, or **seam**ed; made up of smaller parts or pieces. Usually **geometric** shapes of fabric are joined to form the squares or **block**s of **pieced quilt**s. When a block has been pieced, all **stitch**es and seams are on the back. Almost all blocks are either pieced or **appliqué**d. Also see **Quilts: Definition, Marking and Cutting, Sewing and Assembling.**

pieced-border designs. Quilts. Quilts are often finished with **borders** of **pieced** pattern designs. These are identified by name, and some of the best known of these pieced borders are: **Birds in Flight,** cat track, chained square, **checkerboard, diamond, Irish chain,** rickrack, **sawtooth.**

pieced quilt. Quilts. A quilt of traditional design made of **patchwork** or **pieced fabric**s. Pieced quilts resulted originally from an ingenious combination of the need for bedcovers and a scarcity of available fabrics, along with a bold use of color and pattern. The variety of designs produced by the simple method of **piecing,** or joining, is evidence of lively artistic invention. The pieced quilt has remained the most popular and versatile of all quiltmaking forms and is currently very popular. Almost all quilts that use **geometric** repeat patterns are pieced quilts.

pieced quilt patterns. Quilts. See **pieced patterns.**

Pieced Star. Quilts. A **star pattern**—pieced—that was designed to use small scraps. The center of the **block** shows a pinwheel design surrounded by the eight points of the star, which form the corners of the octagonal block. It is **set** with small squares between the octagons. See ill.

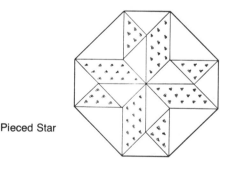

Pieced Star

pieced work. Quilts. Stitchery. **Patchwork,** or the joining of many small pieces of material in such a way as to produce patterns in the larger piece of material thus made. Usually **geometric** shapes are used. Also see **Quilts: Marking and Cutting, Sewing and Assembling.**

piece-dyed. Batik and Tie-dye. Stitchery. A term that indicates that **yarn**s were **dye**d after they were woven into cloth, in contrast to **yarn-dyed.** Color penetration is not always as thorough in piece-dyed **fabric**s.

piece dyeing. Dyeing. Dyeing of a fabric after it has been woven or knitted. Piece dyeing for the home dyer can be a relatively simple matter as long as the **dye bath** container is large enough so that the fabric is not crowded in it. Piece dyeing is done commercially in a variety of ways which either pull, rotate, or roll the fabric through the dye bath. A variation on piece dyeing is cross dyeing. In this case the fabric is composed of different fibers. When placed into a single dye bath using a particular dye, some fibers will absorb the dye, others in different degrees, and some not at all. This will produce a variegated shade of the color or, in some cases, a tweed or mottled effect.

piece in. Basketry. See **joining in.**

piece mold. Metalworking. Plastics. See **mold.**

piecing. Quilts. Stitchery. The joining, or sewing together, of small pieces of fabric to produce patterns and at the same time to form a larger piece of material. The pieces, or **patch**es, are sewn on the wrong side with a **running stitch** (if by hand) or a **straight stitch** (if by machine). In piecing, shapes are always cut with a ¼" **seam allowance** at each edge. The success of piecing depends upon sewing skills as well as the use of colors. By placing dark and light **value**s to repeat arrangements, the entire effect of a pieced design can be changed. Quilts using identical patterns of piecing may appear to be completely different in design, depending upon the arrangement of the colors. Piecing is often used in the design of banners and clothing and on wall hangings. It is a **making do** process.

When piecing fabrics, one may press the seams to one side, or press them open; quilters have different preferences. The advantage to **press**ing seams all in one direction, which means that both of the seam allowances go the same way, is that if there is any stress on the seam, there is fabric underneath the stitches. When seams are pressed apart or open, pull on the pieces might open up a slight gap between the stitches. When lightweight fabrics are used, such as **percale,** there is no problem of bulkiness from having both seams go the same way. The advantage to pressing seams open is that heavy materials (**Mexican cotton, kettle cloth,** sports cottons) may get very **bulky** if both seam allowances are pressed flat in the same direction. This is especially true where squares intersect. When **quilting stitch**es outline blocks, falling ¼–½" from the seams, the open seams give equal fullness to the quilted areas. Also see **Quilts: Marking and Cutting, Sewing and Assembling, Pressing.**

piecing. Rugmaking. Weaving. A process of joining two ends of yarn or fabric strips together for use as **filling** in weaving or for use in making **braided rugs.** In weaving, the simplest method of joining filling yarn in the middle of the **warp** is by overlapping the ends of the new and old yarn in the same **shed,** and then beating them into position. If the yarn is very heavy, these ends may be tapered so that no bulking appears. Fine yarns may be twisted together into one strand. Knots are never made in the filling unless they serve a decorative purpose. Overlapping is also used at the **selvage** when using fine yarns. With heavy yarns, the splicing is accomplished by cutting out half of the strand of yarn and placing the now thinner strand in the next shed.

The new yarn is placed over this tapered strand and both are beaten into place. Selvage splicing is used to avoid a rapid build-up of extra filling. **Thrums** can be spliced in any of the above methods and, in so doing, are put to good use as filling.

Fabric strips used in **rag rug**s or braided rugs can be spliced with or without sewing. In weaving, if the rag strip is about four yards long, there is no need to join pieces. The ends can be overlapped with tapering or, perhaps, twisting if very fine fabrics are used. However, with smaller pieces and in braiding, they should be overlapped at right angles and sewn by hand or machine in a diagonal line. This is known as a bias joining. For weaving there are also other methods of sewing rags. A very strong splice is made when the ends are overlapped and folded lengthwise and then stitched.

To splice with no sewing, slits about 1" long and at least ½" from the end of the strip are cut into the ends of the rag strips. The end of one rag strip is slipped through the slit of the other. The free end of the second strip is then pulled through the slit of the first. Both are pulled tightly together. There are variations on this method when a tighter and more secure joining is needed. With stocking or circular fabrics, the rag strips should be cut in circles and then the circles looped together to form a longer strip. See ill. Also see **joining.**

Splicing rags without sewing

pierced carving. Woodworking. See **woodcarving.**

piercing. Jewelry. Perforating holes in metal for functional or decorative purposes, using either hand or power tools. Complete pieces can be made entirely by piercing. Also see **automatic center punch, beeswax, center punch, chisel cutting, drillpress, flexible shaft machine, hand drill, reamer, sawing.**

Pierotti. Toys. A family of dollmakers who came to England from Italy in the 1780s and made **doll**s through the 1800s and into the 1900s. They were famous for their wax-head dolls in which real hairs were set individually into the wax. The wax heads were stitched to bodies of white calico. Also see **dollmaking.**

Pierrot's Pompom. Quilts. See **Hearts and Gizzards.**

pietra dura. Gemcutting. See **intarsia.**

pig. Glasswork. A notched bar set at the lip of the **tank furnace** mouth and used to support the **blowing iron**s or **punty**s while these are heated to the temperature sufficient to enable the irons to pick up and hold the **metal.** The opposite ends of the irons are supported on a horizontal metal bar.

pig iron. Metalworking. See **iron.**

pigment. A coloring material, usually a solid, that has been ground fine and mixed with a medium or **vehicle** in which the pigment is insoluble. Most paints and inks are such suspensions of pigments in vehicles. As the vehicle dries, the pigment is left on the painted surface (cloth, wood, ceramic, etc.). An example of a historically important pigment still in use is ultramarine blue, formerly made by crushing lapis lazuli, a natural, deep blue stone. Also see **dye.**

pigment. Fabric Printing. A substance that colors fabric by coating the fiber, as a paint. Also see **textile color.**

pigment. Plastics. See **colorant.**

pigment finish. Leather. The coloring of the leather surface with colored pigments dispersed in chemicals, called binders.

pigment oil stain. Woodworking. See **wood stain.**

pigment oxide. Ceramics. Metallic oxides that provide **color** and opacity in **glazes** and **slips.** Pigment oxides added to **silica,** a **flux,** and **alumina** produce a colored, complete glaze. The basic pigment oxides are **cobalt, copper, chromium, iron, manganese, nickel, antimony,** and **rutile. Zinc, tin, zirconium,** and **titanium oxides** are the basic **opacifiers. Fri**tted glazes and **stains** are commercially available. The following table indicates the color produced by specific oxides, the amount used in solution (based on the whole unit equaling ten), and the firing temperature and conditions. Also see **barium, burnt sienna, crocus martis, Egyptian paste, flambé, kiln log, ochre, oxidization, pearl ash, reduction, sienna, umber, underglaze pigment, uranium oxide, vanadium.**

COLORS PRODUCED BY SPECIFIC OXIDES

Color	Oxide	Percentage	Firing temperature	Kiln atmosphere
Black	Cobalt	1–2	Any	Either
	Manganese	2–4	Any	Either
	Cobalt	1	Any	Either
	Iron	8	Any	Either
	Manganese	3	Any	Either
Blue	Cobalt oxide	½–1	Any	Either
	Turquoise–copper oxide (alkaline flux)	3–5	Low	Oxidation
	Slate blue–nickel (with blue)	1–3	Low	Oxidation
Brown	Rutile	5	Any	Reduction
	Chrome (with magnesium oxide, zinc oxide)	2–5	Low	Either
	Iron	3–7	Any	Oxidation
	Manganese	5	Any	Either
	Nickel (with zinc)	2–4	Any	Either
Green	Copper oxide	1–5	Any	Oxidation
	Gray-green iron	1–4	Any	Reduction
	Nickel-magnesia	3–5	Low	Oxidation
Red	Pink chrome-tin (1 to 18)	5	Any	Oxidation
	Coral chromium (with high lead oxide)	5	Low	Oxidation
	Purple manganese (with KNaO)	4–6	Any	Oxidation
	Copper	1	Any	Reduction
	Iron (with flint-KNaO no CaO)	2–5	Low	Oxidation
Tan	Iron	2	Any	Either
	Manganese	2	Any	Either
	Rutile	2	Any	Either
Yellow	Uranium (yellow and orange)	5–8	Low	Oxidation
	Tin-vanadium stain	4–6	Any	Either
	Antimony yellow stain (high lead oxide)	3–5	Low	Either
	Praseodymium yellow stain	4–6	Any	Either
	Zirconium vanadium stain	5–10	Any	Either

pigskin. Bookbinding. See **leather.**

pigskin. Leather. The leather from the skins of pigs, usually from Argentina or Brazil. Pigskin is durable and has a distinctive **grain.** It is generally used for gloves, billfolds, and linings. Also see **peccary.**

pile. Rugmaking. Weaving. The upright loops or cut ends that project from a foundation to form the wearing surface of a rug or fabric. The word "pile" comes from the Latin *pilus,* meaning "hair." In fabrics, it refers to the downy nap of a cut surface such as velvet or **corduroy** pile. In rugs, it is denser and longer and can be composed of small loops as well as being cut. It can be formed in woven, **hooked, latch-hooked,** and **needleworked rug**s, or added onto **crochet, knitted,** and **braided rug**s. Short or low pile is ½" to 1" high and is closely spaced so that it stands upright. The loops (uncut pile) can be left totally intact or intermingled with the cut pile that, as a contrast, forms a softer surface. In weaving rugs, a cut, short pile is often referred to by its Scandinavian name, **flossa.** Long or high pile is between 1" and 4" in height, but the most commonly used heights are 2" to 3". Long pile is widely spaced so that the yarn falls every which way and subtly mutes definite designs and color outlines. This effect has been called "shag," but it is better known by its Scandinavian name, **rya.** Both short and long pile can be cut pile, but in rugs, only short pile is left uncut, or in loops, since long loops would constitute an accident hazard should a heel or toe get caught in them. In **wall hanging**s or other weaving where long loops are used for a decorative purpose, there is no need for such a precaution. Besides having a mixture of cut and loop pile and various **pile height**s, it is also possible to have pile areas against a background of another flat technique. No matter how the pile is formed or how it is used, its density is a factor with which the craftsperson must reckon. If the pile is too sparse, then the **rug backing** or foundation will show through and the pile itself will look "thin." If the pile is too thick, then the rug will tend to buckle. The density of the pile is planned according to its height and the thickness of each yarn strand or knot. A general rule of thumb is that the shorter the pile, the closer the tufts or knots are to each other; the longer the pile, the further apart is the spacing. For example, **Oriental rug**s are very dense but their pile is extremely short and the yarn is of medium weight.

The height of **knotted pile** is determined by a **gauge** over which it is constructed. This is particularly true for short pile, for a gauge facilitates the making of short pile and also keeps it uniform. With long pile, where uniformity is not a main concern and may be quite undesirable if a shaggy look is intended, the pile can be constructed over a gauge or one's fingers, or be precut into lengths, a method which allows for more color and texture freedom.

In weaving, knotted pile is a third element added to the **warp** and **filling.** This element is knotted to the wrap in a Ghiordes, Sehna, or Spanish knot, with Ghiordes being the most commonly used. Cut pile can also be formed by a **laid-in** technique. Loop pile can be formed by **tufting** or looping and cut pile by the corduroy or imitation pile

technique, or the use of chenille yarn to make a **chenille fabric.** In these cases the filling becomes the pile. Warp can also become pile with the use of two beams to give long enough floats to loop or cut into pile.

Pile can be found in pillows, purses, bags, hats, garments, and drapery as well as rugs and wall hangings. It can also be double-sided (found on each side of the fabric) as was the case in many of the early Finnish rya weavings which were used as sleigh covers and blankets as well as rugs. Also see **novelty yarn, pile weave, Peruvian weaving, rugweaving, warp pile.**

pile. Stitchery. The soft clipped or unclipped loops of yarn which are added to the surface of a pile fabric during the weaving. Various pile-weave methods may be used, each requiring either extra **warp** or filling threads to produce the pile. After weaving is completed the loops may be cut as in **velvet** or they may be uncut as in **turkish towel** fabric or **terry cloth.** Among the best-known pile fabrics are **brocade, corduroy,** plush, terrycloth, **velour,** and velvet. Upholstery fabrics made with pile weave give a soft, luxurious surface, often suitable for **stuffed fabric** forms, **wall hanging**s and toys.

pile gauge. Rugmaking. Weaving. See **gauge.**

pile guide. Rugmaking. Weaving. See **gauge.**

pile height. Rugmaking. Weaving. The height of **pile** measured from the surface of the backing to the top of the pile, and not including the thickness of the backing. Also see **rug backing.**

pile rug. Rugmaking. See **hooked rug, knotted pile, latch-hooked rug, needleworked rug, pile, rugweaving.**

pile weave. Rugmaking. Weaving. Constructions which require two or more **warps** and one **filling,** or two or more fillings and one warp. The extra warp or filling forms the **pile** in loops, usually just on the face of the fabric. The loops can be cut or left uncut. **Corduroy** and tufting are examples of a pile weave with extra filling, while terry cloth is a **warp pile** with loops on both sides of the fabric.

pillar doll. Toys. See **Frozen Charlotte.**

Pillement, Jean Baptiste (1719–1808). Découpage. A French artist and designer whose **chinoiserie** scenes of Chinese figures, bridges, and trees are still widely used in decoupage. Many of these **prints** were reproduced in "Ladies' Amusement," published in England in 1760. He also designed scenes for **toile de Jouy** fabrics and for the silklooms of Lyon.

pilling. Weaving. The tendency for the hairy **fibers** of **wool** and **synthetic** yarns to roll up into small balls. It is a common occurrence in **warp**s as they are being wound onto the **warp beam,** and more so when the warps are overcombed or overhandled. Pilling also occurs in woven and knitted garments where the surface is exposed to rubbing. Sometimes known as "fuzz," pilling results from short fibers escaping from the yarn and collecting on the surface to eventually join together and form the little balls.

pillow. Lacemaking. A pillow is the article upon which the lace is worked. It is used for both bobbin and needle lacemaking. There are several shapes of pillows, whose use depends on the type of lace being made.

The mushroom or flat pillow, used for both **bobbin lace** and **needle lace,** is made of a thin, circular piece of wood, approximately 12″ to 24″ in diameter. It is padded to be about 2″ deep at the center and slope down to a thin edge. The padding is very firm, usually of pounded straw, and covered with a stretched tightly cloth that is secured at the edge, either by tacking or turning and sewing on the underside. This mushroom pillow is used when small **motifs** are made, placed within a **design,** and then joined together in a larger piece with a **ground** (a.).

The cylindrical pillow is rolled as the work progresses. This type of pillow is suitable for bobbin lace, which is worked in one piece. It is well padded so that when the pins are inserted, they are quite secure (b.).

A small cylindrical pillow is often set in a well of a larger mushroom pillow. This pillow is suitable for bobbin laces. As the lacework develops, take out some pins from the back, leaving enough in the front to secure the work. Roll the lace up in back as it is freed from the pillow. Then roll the cylinder back to expose more **pattern.** The pillow extending beyond the cylinder is useful for laying the bobbins in their respective positions. This pillow is excellent for **lace edging**s and **lace insertion**s made with bobbins where considerable lengths of lace are required (c.).

The long pillow is a half round cylinder; it rests in the lap while the top is propped against the table or wall (d.).

A **celotex** board, thinly padded and covered with cloth, works very well for sample work and large contemporary pieces. See ill.

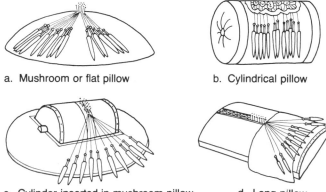

a. Mushroom or flat pillow

b. Cylindrical pillow

c. Cylinder inserted in mushroom pillow

d. Long pillow

pillow. Stitchery. A **stuff**ed cushion, usually made of **muslin, ticking,** or similar **cotton fabric.** The muslin pillow form may be slipped inside a pillow cover which has been treated decoratively by **hand appliqué** or **machine appliqué.** Among the most popular treatments for pillow designs are **cut-through appliqué, felt appliqué, lace appliqué, quilting** and **trapunto.** The materials selected and the use for which the pillow is intended are significant in determining the most appropriate way to decorate.

The decorative work is always done on the top or face of the pillow cover before it is sewn to the **pillow back**ing. This way, the sewing is done on a flat piece of fabric which is easily handled.

Pillow covers may be sewn with a knife edge or they may be boxed. The knife-edge pillow has a single straight line of stitching inside each of the four edges. The boxed pillow has a strip of **bias** or **straight** cut fabric set into the sides to give it a boxed appearance. Either may have a **piped seam** or a **corded seam** at the edges.

A knife-edge pillow may be any shape, though a circular form is sometimes difficult to keep smooth at the **seam** lines. Square or rectangular shapes work better. Almost any complex shape can be sewn with the knife-edge method, including figures and plant forms. The result is similar to **single-shape doll**s or to some **soft sculpture** forms. In these, the outline seam is sometimes sewn through the two layers of the pillow cover and it is stuffed directly. No separate pillow form is used, because of the complicated shapes involved.

When sewing a knife-edge pillow, place right sides of the decorative **pillow top** and pillow back together. Machine stitch, being sure to sew all four corners and to leave a slot so that the pillow form can be inserted. A common stuffing for the knife-edge pillow is **kapok** or **Dacron polyester batting.**

The boxed pillow can be stuffed with either kapok or Dacron polyester batting, though **foam rubber** or other polyfoam forms are available in sheets of various thicknesses. Boxed pillows are commonly made in simple squares, rectangles, or circular forms. The pillow tops and the pillow back are cut identically, then a strip of material is cut to form the sides. If a boxed pillow is to be 2″ thick, a 3″ wide **band** is cut, which allows a half-inch seam at each edge. The foam filler is cut from a 2″ thick block. Some boxed pillow covers are made for pillow forms which have a knife-edge seam. For best fit, however, the pillow form should also be boxed.

A way of suggesting a boxed effect which is more easily sewn is the Oriental floor cushion. The outside seam lines are first sewn on the two layers of fabric placed right sides together (a.). All four corners are sewn, though an opening is left on one edge so that the pillow form can be inserted. Each corner is opened and refolded so that two side seams are face to face. Then a stitch line is sewn across the corners at right angles to the side seams (b.). Turned right side out, this makes a tailored or partially boxed corner. See ill.

Pillow forms may be purchased already stuffed or they may be made at home. The advantage in having a pillow form and cover made separately is that the cover can be removed for cleaning or washing. If the pillow cover itself is stuffed, without a separate pillow form, all the stuffing must be taken out for cleaning.

Two average-sized pillows can be made from one bed pillow. Two parallel lines of stitching should be sewn crosswise through the center of the pillow before it is cut into two parts. This will prevent the stuffing or feathers from scattering. The **raw edge**s can then be tucked in or turned back and stitched.

Pillows are often further decorated with **tassels** or

fringes. These can be inserted in the edge seam or they can be added by hand after the pillow cover is completed. Openings left from stuffing are closed with the **whip stitch** or the **slip stitch** (**c.**). The pillow covers may also be hand sewn to finish the opening, or one side may have a zipper sewn in to ease removal of the pillow form. When a zipper is used it is inserted before the side seams are completed. See ill.

Almost every method of fabric treatment can be adapted for pillows. The use of latching, hooking, **batik**, quilting, and **appliqué** are all appropriate.

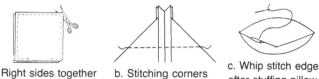

a. Right sides together   b. Stitching corners   c. Whip stitch edge after stuffing pillow

pillow doll. Stitchery. Toys. A doll with a pillow for the main part of the body. In some cases a rectangular pillow is used as the body, with head, arms, and legs attached. In others, made in the manner of a **single-shape doll**, the head and body are in one pillow shape with only the arms and legs added. Simple **baby doll**s may be made as small oval pillows with the faces **appliqué**d and the rest wrapped in a blanket.

Some pillow dolls are essentially pillows and the doll aspect is incidental. Quilted, embroidered, or **trapunto** figures sewn to a pillow top may be referred to as pillow dolls, although they are used more as pillows than as toys.

pillow lace. Lacemaking. See **bobbin lace.**

pillow quilt. Quilts. Any quilt made by stitching together a series of prestuffed pillow forms. Technically these are not quilts at all because no stitching goes through to hold three layers together. They do, however, have a top, a **backing**, and a **filler** between.

The small pillows may be identical in size, such as a series of rectangles, triangles, or squares, or they may vary, being based on a **module**.

To make a pillow quilt, a number of fabric squares identical in size are cut. Each square is folded diagonally and stitched on the seam allowance, and stuffing is inserted into the opening. If the pillows are larger than 6″ square, the stuffing may shift. When working with other shapes, always keep one dimension less than about 6″. For example, pillows cut 4″ × 10″ will not be a problem. Pillows as large as 8″ square will need to be secured in the center, as in the **puff quilt.**

After the pillows are stuffed, the open end is closed with a **slip stitch** or **whip stitch.** Then the pillows are joined to one another by stitching with a strong thread. Heavy-duty thread, buttonhole twist, or sewing cord is suitable. A slip stitch may be used but should be sewn twice, once from the front and once from the back. **Faggoting** is an excellent joining stitch. The pillows should be joined in rows or sections to make the handling easier. The sections can be joined last so that the entire weight of the quilt is not handled continuously. The **biscuit quilt**, puff quilt, and

raised patchwork are all variations of the pillow-quilt approach.

pilot bit. Woodworking. See **drill bit.**

pilot hole. Woodworking. A hole drilled to ease driving a screw and prevent the wood from splitting. In **hardwood** the hole should be slightly smaller than the diameter of the screw; in **softwood** the hole can be about ⅔ the diameter of the screw core. For larger screws, a series of graduated holes may have to be drilled to compensate for the taper of the screw; drill the largest hole first. An alternative is to use a pilot bit. In hardwoods and at the ends of all woods, it is a good idea to drill pilot holes for nails, using a bit ⅔ the nail's diameter. Also see **Woodworking: Screwing.**

pilus. Rugmaking. Weaving. See **pile.**

pima cotton. Quilts. Stitchery. A high-quality **cotton fabric** from the extra-long **fiber**s of the pima cotton plant. It is next in quality to **sea island cotton,** which is considered to be the best. It is sometimes referred to as **Egyptian cotton.**

pimpilowe. Stitchery. See **pincushion.**

pin. Jewelry. See **steel pin.**

pin. Lacemaking. A good quality pin is a very important piece of equipment in **bobbin lace.** The function of the pin is to hold a thread or threads in position until the **lace** is worked far enough to hold its own shape. Insert the pins into the pillow at a slight angle away from the lacer, as the threads pull a little against the pins. On the inside areas of the lace, work the stitches around the pins.

A lacemaking pin is of fine-quality steel, about 1⅜″ long, and has a very small head, much smaller than the common pin, or straight pin, used by dressmakers. A glass headed pin, about 1¼″ long, is also useful for coarser lacemaking. The insect specimen pin, used by entomologists, makes a very good lace pin.

pin. Stitchery. See **dressmaker's pin.**

pin. Toys. See **skittle.**

pin. Weaving. See **tapestry tools.**

pin and ring. Tatting. An accessory used in the eighteenth and nineteenth centuries to pick up the **loop thread** through a **picot** to attach one **motif** to another motif. It was a ring large enough to go on the little finger of the left hand; a cord was attached and a hook was secured to the end of the cord. The ring was put on the little finger during tatting: when a joining was necessary, the little hook was put to use.

piñata. Papercrafts. A festive Mexican decoration, usually shaped like some kind of animal and traditionally made of a low-fired clay. The ceramic shell is filled with toys and candy, and the filled piñata is hung low from the ceiling during festivities, to be broken by the children with a stick, showering down the gifts. Piñatas are also made from bright, ruffled paper.

A piñata can be made of **found objects,** such as toweling tubes for legs, a round container for the body, and so on, securely taped in position. The form is then covered with **tissue-paper** ruffles, made by snipping into the folded side of a long, folded strip of paper, as described for cutting **paper flowers.** The paper fringes are glued, curl outward, to the form in rows with **white glue,** overlapped so that the surface is filled with the fluffy ruffles. Because a cardboard piñata cannot be broken easily, an opening should be left for inserting and removing gifts.

pinchbeck. Jewelry. A **brass alloy,** very close to gold in color, made of 88 parts **copper** and 5 parts **zinc.** It was used primarily during the Victorian period; its modern counterpart would be red brass.

pinching. Candlemaking. A technique for **decorating** a finished candle. The candle must first be warmed to soften the surface wax, then pinched or crimped immediately with assorted sizes of pliers or other pinching tools to produce rows of decorative indentations. When the crimping is completed, the candle is dipped in a cold **water bath** to set the design. The traditional pinched candle made by Spanish candlemakers has the same pinch marks in each row around the circumference, with variations between the rows rather than within.

pinching. Ceramics. See **Ceramics: Hand Building.**

pinch pot. Ceramics. An object made by pinching, a simple method of making pottery by hand. A hollow is formed in a ball of clay and pressure is applied to the walls until the desired shape is made. A **rim** can be added when the pot is leather hard. Also see **coiled pot, pressing, slab pot** and **Ceramics: Hand Building.**

pin closed. Lacemaking. (Also called enclosing the pin.) A procedure in making **bobbin lace.** When **pattern** instructions say, "close **pin,**" or "close the pin," it means to do the same stitch after placing the pin into the **pillow** as was done immediately before placing the pin. In other words, a stitch is made, a pin is placed, and the same stitch is repeated.

Pincushion. Quilts. See **Cathedral Window.**

pincushion. Stitchery. (Also called pimpilowe, pinpillow.) A device of incredible variety and invention used since the sixteenth century to hold pins and needles. One early eighteenth-century pincushion was made to resemble a carrot; pale yellow **velvet** with tissuelike glazed **ribbons.** Another was a carved ivory basket, containing a cushion. From then on, pincushions assumed divers forms—some on clamps, or weighted, others made to resemble fruits, vegetables, or animals. The red **flannel** tomato with a small strawberry attached is a well-known favorite. Pincushions may be filled with **wool,** sawdust, hair, or scrap fabrics.

pine. Woodworking. The generic name given to a group of forty light-colored (straw-white to reddish-brown), even-grained **softwood**s. Pine is generally light weight and easily worked, with a fine, **close grain.** Although classified as a softwood (i.e., a conifer), some pine is quite hard. Knotty pine (also called Idaho white pine) is often used for paneling. White, clear, and sugar pines are especially good for fine carving and interior work. Yellow pine is strong, heavy, and resinous, and is used in building construction. Norway pine is the hardest variety of white pine.

Pineapple. Quilts. A **pieced block** design made up of long, narrow trapezoids surrounding a central square. It makes a **sawtooth** edge within the square. It is sometimes called a **Maltese Cross.**

This name also identifies another similar block, which is a variation of **Birds in Flight.** See ill. Also see **pineapple quilt.**

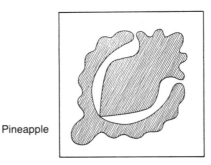

Pineapple

Pineapple Log Cabin. Quilts. A particular **set** of the **Log Cabin block.** In this combination the dark areas of the blocks join to form a pineapple shape with **sawtooth** edges. Also see **pineapple quilt.**

pineapple quilt. Quilts. Any **quilt,** either **pieced** or **appliqué**d, in which shapes suggest a pineapple. In the pieced patterns, there is usually a **sawtooth** edge. Some quilts use the pineapple **block** repeated in a diagonal pattern. In others the pineapples point toward each of the four corners of a block **set** to make an **all-over pattern.** Also see **Pineapple, Pineapple Log Cabin.**

pine-cone bird. Toys. A **folk toy** in the form of a bird, made from a pine cone with wings of cotton balls or seed pods. Seeds, found materials, or **papier mâché** may be used for the head. The bobwhite and cardinal are two familiar birds made of pine cones from the Appalachian region.

pine-cone flower. Toys. Slices of pine cone, cut crosswise, that are flowerlike in shape and pattern. They are used in many **folk toy**s to suggest parts of birds or animals and also in wreaths and table decorations.

pine-cone toy. Toys. Any of a variety of **folk toy** birds or animals in which a pine cone is used for the body. Sometimes several cones are joined, or they may be cut into sections or slices. Owl, woodpecker, and turkey are among the most common pine-cone toys.

Pine Tree. Quilts. (Also called Christmas Tree, Forbidden Fruit, Live Oak, Paradise, Temperance.) A **pieced** pattern using many small triangles combined to suggest a tree shape. It originated in Massachusetts and was a quilt known in all of the original thirteen colonies. It is an old and popular pattern with many variations.

The pieced **block**s are sometimes used in an **all-over pattern,** and sometimes separated by **band**s or **border**s. The trees may be **set** diagonally or straight up and down, and it is most often a two-color **quilt top.** In some quilts, the tree trunk is **appliqué**d, the leaves pieced. See ill. Also see **Tree of Life.**

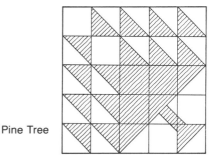

Pine Tree

pin filling. Lacemaking. A lace **filling** in **bobbin lace.** Each square leadwork has a small hole in the center, made by the twisting of the threads. It is done in the **leaf stitch.**

pinhole. Ceramics. A pinhole results from blisters or bubbling in a **glaze** that has not quite settled down. This can be avoided by applying the glaze thinner, using more **flux,** or by a heat soaking at the melting temperature. Also see **blistering, bloating, bristol glaze.**

pinhole. Enameling. See **Enameling: Repair and Care.**

pinholes. Stained Glass. See **bubbles, frying.**

pin joint. Toys. A **joint** used in **dollmaking,** often found on ancient **doll**s. In the pin joint the ends of two parts are fitted together and a single pin is run through the parts to connect them. The parts move by turning on the pin. Sometimes a wooden **peg** was used in place of the pin; some of the joints on the **penny wooden doll** are made this way. A similar joint, but one that uses a string in place of the pin, is called a **string joint.**

pink compound. Jewelry. See **buffing compound.**

pinked seam. Stitchery. A **seam finish** used on a **plain seam** in which the **seam** is **press**ed open. The **raw edges** are then cut with a **pinking shears.** Sometimes a line of machine **straight stitch**es is sewn at the raw edge before it is pinked. See ill.

Pinked seam

pinking shears. Stitchery. **Shears** which have **zigzag** or sawtooth edges on the blades. The decorative-cut pattern is used to finish **raw edges,** thus making a **seam finish** called a **pinked seam.**

In some **felt appliqué**s, the **felt** pieces are cut with pinking shears to make a decorative edge which is hand sewn in place. This pinked edge is effectively used in **banners** and toys. The **scalloping shears** are similar, but of a different edge pattern.

pin lace. Lacemaking. See **bobbin lace.**

pin nail. Puppets. Toys. A thin-shafted small nail, just larger than a pin.

pinning. Macramé. Pinning is the process of securing macramé cords and knots to the knotting surface. Be sure to pin into the knots, not in between them, slanting the pins away from the working area. As the work progresses, the pinning should be moved evenly down the length of the work to ensure that each row of knotting will be worked evenly. Also see **anchoring.**

Pinocchio. Puppets. Toys. A wooden **marionette** from the children's story of the same name. According to the story, the woodcarver Gepetto carved a figure that became a live boy who experienced a series of adventures. Marionettes and dolls are often made with a long, pointed, wooden nose to resemble Pinocchio. Also see **nursery character.**

pin open. Lacemaking. A procedure in making **bobbin lace.** "To leave the pin open" means you make a stitch, place the pin into the **pillow** at the place indicated in the **pattern,** and do not follow with another stitch. In other words, do not enclose the pin with another stitch.

pinpillow. Stitchery. See **pincushion.**

pin-pivot method. Batik and Tie-dye. A method used in **tie-dye** to create patterns. A rectangle of fabric is placed on a surface into which a pin can be firmly stuck, such as wood, Celotex, or carpeting. The pin is placed at top center. The fabric is pulled lightly against the pin into rolls or **pleats** and held firmly. It is then unpinned so that it can next be either covered with line **binding** or hand tied. By placing the pin off-center, variations in the **dye** pattern can be achieved.

pin poppet. Stitchery. A small metal or wooden case to hold pins, which was carried in the pocket.

pin pricking. Découpage. Papercrafts. (Also called pin-prick work.) A papercraft technique, used since the seventeenth century, of piercing pictures on paper with pins or needles in hundreds of tiny holes, the results resembling lace so much that they have often been called lace pictures. Details in drawings of cuffs, lace edgings, or patterned dresses were especially embellished. Pins and needles of varying thicknesses were used for effects of light and shadow, giving the picture an embossed appearance. Pin pricking was usually combined with painting. The pictures, usually mounted over a foil background, were often used for valentines. The paper used for pin pricking should be strong and porous, such as rag or linen, so that it has some give to it. The needles may be inserted in corks for easy handling.

pin-prick work. Découpage. Papercrafts. See **pin pricking.**

pins. Macramé. Essential equipment for macramé. T-pins, **upholsterer's pins,** and long, glass-headed straight pins are used in **anchoring** to hold macramé work securely and evenly in place on the knotting surface. Also see **Macramé: Tools and Materials.**

pinstem. Jewelry. See **findings, riveting, tapering wire.**

pin stripe. Rugmaking. Weaving. See **stripe.**

pin vise. Bookbinding. A small hand tool with a drill chuck head that holds a needle. It is used to pierce thick papers.

pin vise. Jewelry. A small **hand vise** used to hold tools such as **fine drills** and **reamers.** It is usually fitted with a **collet** and a **chuck** that can be hand tightened to hold the tools. It is available in a number of different shapes and sizes. Also see **riveting, vise.**

pinwheel. Crochet. See **Crochet: Patterns.**

pinwheel. Papercrafts. A traditional papercraft design formed by cutting slits into a square and rolling and fastening the corners to the center. It is generally tacked to a stick. The rolled spokes catch the wind and move the pinwheel. See ill.

Pinwheel

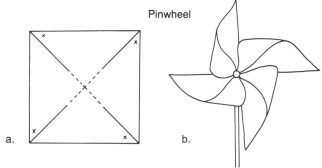

a.   b.

Pinwheel. Quilts. A **pieced block** design of squares and triangles in which the triangles are **set** to suggest a whirling movement. The block design is a common one, used often but varied greatly through different combinations of color and placement of the triangles. Two of the pattern variations are **Churn Dash** and **Nelson's Victory.** See ill. Also see **Windmill.**

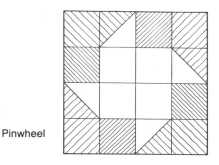

Pinwheel

pinwheel. Toys. (Also called paper windmill, spinning star wheel, windmill.) A **wind toy,** popular at least since the fourteenth century, in which blades or propellers are attached to a stick. When moved rapidly through the air the blades turn. During medieval times, they were made from wood in a variety of shapes. The propeller mechanism was usually attached at the end of the stick; in later versions, it was attached to one side, near the end. They are now sometimes made of plastic and are designed also to be **optical toys;** that is, when the propellers spin, the visual images painted on them merge to form designs.

Pinwheels are easily made by small children. A 5″ to 8″ square of paper is cut from each corner toward the center, leaving the very center of the square uncut. Of the 8 points thus formed, every other point is brought to the center. A pin is run through the points and then through the center of the paper so that it extends out the back. It is then pinned to a stick or a **dowel.**

In the early 1800s, the pinwheel was sometimes called a turnabout-Johnny.

pipe. Toys. A **musical toy** or **sound toy** consisting of a tube through which air is blown to produce a tone. Pipes may be made of reed, straw, bamboo, clay, wood, or metal. In some the air strikes a sharp edge to produce the sound; in others it may flow over a reed, causing it to vibrate and create a tone. Sometimes holes are made in the pipe so that tones can be varied, as with the flute.

pipe clamp. Woodworking. See **clamping tools.**

piped seam. Stitchery. A **plain seam** which has a band of **piping** inserted for decorative effect. If the piping is of a contrasting color, the importance of the **seam** is exaggerated.

piping. Stitchery. A strip of **bias fabric** which has been **fold**ed over lengthwise through the center and **basted.** This piping can then be inserted in a **seam** so that the **raw edges** are concealed and the folded edge extends beyond the seam. The piping adds a decorative effect to the seam. A **piped seam** is sometimes used on **pillow covers,** in **costumes** and clothes, or on any fabric article using **plain seams.**

piqué. Shell Carving. *Piqué* means ''pricked'' in French. Piqué is the technique of inlaying or hammering small round gold or silver wire into tortoiseshell, most usually in geometric patterns. Piqué work was common in Victorian England as a form of decoration for small boxes, cigarette and watch cases, jewelry combs, and other tortoiseshell items. Also see **Shell Carving: Tortoiseshell.**

piqué. Stitchery. A **cotton fabric** which is firmly woven and which has raised patterns in the weave. Fine ribs or cords pattern most piqué, though a **waffle-weave** is also popular.

piqué. Weaving. A fabric with **cords** running parallel to the **filling.** In its original form, it was **double cloth** with **stuffer picks** in between the front and back layers to achieve the cords or ribs where desired. Today piqué has come to mean a **warp**-wise **rib** called **Bedford Cord.** However, there is no similarity of structure between the two; Bedford Cord is a single-layer fabric without stuffer picks.

piqué work. Jewelry. A type of **inlay** in which metal dots or shapes are put into a nonmetallic base such as bone, ivory, tortoise shell, horn, or **plastic.** Drill holes into the base material. They should be of an even depth but should not pierce it. The diameter of the **drill** being used must be the precise diameter of the wire to be inlaid. Clip off short pieces of wire of **fine gold** or **fine silver,** somewhat longer than the length of the drilled hole. Fine gold and fine silver are used because they possess great **malleability.** These metals are especially excellent for use in thin materials such as tortoiseshell or thin plates of bone or ivory. Drive the metal into the holes with a lightweight hammer such as a **rivet hammer.** The work, particularly if the base metal is thin, should be supported on a solid base, such as a **steel block** or surface plate. After the inlay of the piqué work is completed, the base material and the metals can be filed flat and the work polished either by **hand polishing** or on a **buffing machine.** The metal can also be left raised like **rivet** heads.

Small pieces of flat **sheet metal** in **karat** golds, sterling silver, **brass, copper,** or **bronze** can also be inlaid into tortoiseshell, horn, and plastic, by means of heat. With your first attempts the pieces of metal should be fairly small, about ¼", so you can get the feel of just how it works. It is a good idea to make tests. Horn, tortoiseshell, and plastic all react somewhat differently, but the basic concept is the same. The small pieces of metal must be heated upon the base material until they sink into it. This must be done carefully, because a direct **flame** cannot be applied to the material or it will be destroyed.

When working with acrylic sheet, place the pieces of metal one at a time on top of the plastic. A small **soldering iron** with changeable tips, of the type used for lead soldering, is used for heating the metal. A tip that comes to a point is nearly useless, unless you are setting in tiny dots of metal. The changeable tips, which screw off and on, are made of either brass, copper, or aluminum. They can be filed and reshaped so that they have broad, flatter tips. When the tip is hot, place it on top of the metal. As the metal heats it will begin to sink into the plastic, but you must apply a rather heavy, steady pressure straight down, otherwise the hot metal will stop and leave a mark or pit in the plastic. As the metal sinks in, the plastic it is displacing comes out around—but not over—the metal. This makes it somewhat difficult to see how deep the metal has gone, but with some practice it is possible to tell rather accurately. The idea is to have it sunk into the plastic as near to the level of the surface of the plastic as possible, but not below. Eighteen-**gauge** metal works quite well; because later on in the technique some metal will be removed, a thinner gauge is not practical.

As you are pressing the heated metal into the plastic, an amazing amount of pressure is built up. If you remove the soldering iron the metal will pop out and even fly across the room; you must therefore hold the metal in position both while you are sinking it in place and when you remove the iron. The metal can tip from uneven heating or uneven melting of the plastic as the heat is being transmitted through the metal. You must hold the metal in position until the plastic becomes hard enough itself to hold the metal, which takes at least 10 seconds, although the cooling time depends on the size of the heated metal and the plastic. You must support the metal at more than one point, otherwise the one supported point acts as a fulcrum, and the metal will tip or slide and go in crookedly. Balance the metal by placing **tweezers** so that one point is on either side of the soldering iron, pressing down, and slowly removing the heating unit so you can accurately gauge the pressure you are applying through each point. Uneven pressure makes the metal slip. With larger inlays you may need an assist from someone to apply pressure to the metal from several positions. Be careful when attempting to place pieces next to one another. If they are too close, the previously set-in piece of metal can pop out as the plastic surrounding it becomes too warm. When all the pieces have been inset, file down the entire surface. It can be polished either by hand or on the buffing machine.

If polished on the buffing machine, it must be done very carefully, as the plastic gets hot very quickly and melts. Another way of finishing the surface of the work is to use **carborundum paper** to give both the metal and the plastic a scratched finish. It will change the tone of color in the plastic, however, so tests should once again be made.

Your soldering iron should be lightweight. You must be careful not to overheat the metal, which happens easily with a large soldering iron, or it will cause the plastic to bubble and begin to deteriorate. You must not touch the plastic itself with the heated tip, as it can instantly make a deep mark. An excellent inexpensive soldering iron for small-to-medium-sized pieces of metal is made by Black & Decker—No. 7990 Solder and Craft Kit-Type 1—and can be purchased in a hardware store. Large, intricate pieces of pierced and sawn out sheet metal can be used with the heat method, but this may require the use of several larger soldering irons, and require more than one person for both the heating and holding the metal in position as it cools.

A face mask with charcoal filters should be worn while working in this technique with acrylics because the fumes are harmful to breathe. Work in a well-ventilated area. Also see **horn hammer.**

pirn. Weaving. See **fly shuttle.**

pit amber. Amber Carving. See **amber.**

pitch. Jewelry. A form of tar that may have other components added to it, such as brick dust, rosin, tallow, or linseed oil, to provide elasticity. The pitch is used to hold work in place and for an elastic supportive material in the processes of **chasing, repoussé,** and, sometimes, **engraving.** Although pitch may be purchased ready to use, below is a formula for making pitch. Pitch is used in a **pitch bowl** or in a larger pan, or spread on a close-grained wood such as sycamore. The wood may be chiseled out to form a shallow dish, or a wooden rim may be nailed around it to contain the pitch if it is particularly runny when heated. Slightly heat the surface of the pitch with a **torch.** Take care not to ignite the pitch, as it can be a fire hazard, and charred pitch is useless. Place the metal to be worked on the pitch and push it into the warmed surface. The pitch should not be too warm and the metal should not be pushed too hard or it will simply sink below the surface of the pitch. Allow the pitch to cool, but while it is still slightly warm, begin work. For curved work that cannot be placed on the flat surface of the pitch, the pitch can be heated and pushed with a piece of wood to form a mound of the desired height and width to support the work. To remove the work from hard pitch, drive a repoussé tool between the metal and the pitch, using some leverage. If this does not work, and more leverage would cause damage to the piece, heat the metal: the pitch in direct contact with it will soften. The piece can then be lifted from the pitch bowl with **pliers.** Pitch can be removed from the work with a rag. If the pitch is too cool, the work can be heated until the pitch flows for easy removal. Do not burn the pitch, as it will then be more difficult to remove. Some pitch may be soaked overnight in turpentine to remove it. With the formulas below, paraffin can be used to dissolve the partially melted pitch. It can also be removed by **annealing** the work and **quenching** it in water. Generally, this must be done more than once. Pitch is sticky and somewhat of a mess to handle, but it will help if it is removed when it is not too hot. If your hands are kept wet, it will not stick to them.

Different companies make pitch of differing qualities. If possible, experiment with a small quantity on a board to feel its qualities. Most commercially prepared pitch is black in color. The following formula is made from a pitch known as Stockholm or Swedish, and is a dark brown: 6 parts pitch, 8 parts brick dust, 1 part resin, and 1 part linseed oil. Melt the pitch and resin in an iron pan. When they are liquid, add the brick dust, stirring well. Then add the linseed oil.

pitch bowl. Jewelry. A cast-iron bowl for holding **pitch.** The bowl rests on a **ring pad,** which makes it easy to maneuver. See ill. Also see **chasing, embossing, repoussé.**

Pitch bowl on ring pad

pitch cement. A semirigid waterproof sealing cement prepared by melting 70 parts pine pitch and 2 parts **rosin,** and dusting in 28 parts plaster of Paris.

pitcher. Ceramics. See **Ceramics: Form.**

pit firing. Ceramics. See **clamp kiln.**

pith. Basketry. The center or core of the **rattan** palm. It is easy to work and sometimes called **reed, center cane, pulp cane,** or **pith cane.**

pith. Woodworking. See **wood.**

pith ball. Toys. A **marble**-sized **ball,** very lightweight, made from the soft center of a dry cornstalk or similar material. The pith is dug out, trimmed to a roughly spherical shape, and then sanded or rolled in the palms of the hands for final shaping. Pith balls are used in **flipperdingers** and other toys requiring lightweight balls.

pith cane. Basketry. See **cane.**

pit loom. Weaving. See **ground loom, warp-weighted loom.**

pitman. Spinning. See **footman.**

pitmarks. Candlemaking. Small pinpoint blemishes on the surface of the molded candle usually caused by air bubbles trapped within the **mold.** Also see **Candlemaking: Possible Problems with Candles.**

placing sand. Ceramics. Fine silver or white sand used in **firing** under large **earthenware** pots and forms. The sand acts like tiny rollers, over which a piece can move as it **shrink**s, thus preventing the ware from sticking to the shelves and cracking from the resistance. Also see **kiln furniture.**

plaid. Weaving. A fabric consisting of various color blocks in the **warp** and then crossed by the same colors in the same sequence in the **filling.** This is known as a true plaid. Various rectangles are formed by the crossing, but in a true plaid there will also be squares running in a diagonal across the fabric. They are formed by each color crossing itself in the warp. "To plaid off" is an expression often used when the intention is to weave a true plaid. False plaids are fabrics where warp and filling are not in the same colors, or, if they are, the sequence and amount of the filling colors are not that of the warp. Balanced plaids have the same sequence of color blocks arranged around a center point so that each side of the center is symmetrical with the other. Scotch plaids are good examples of balanced plaids. Unbalanced plaids have a random **warp arrangement** without a center point. Also see **stripe.**

plain crochet. Crochet. (Also called slip stitch.) Plain crochet is worked either through a **chain** of stitches or into stitches in a **previous row.**

Insert the **crochet hook** into the uppermost stitch of the chain or the previous row, bring the yarn over the hook, and pull it back through both loops at once. This is a plain crochet. Repeat this the length of the **row** or as specified by the particular pattern. Also see **Crochet: Basic Stitches.**

plain knitting. Knitting. (Also called garter stitch.) One of two basic stitches in knitting (the other is **purl**). Also see **Knitting: Basic Movements.**

plain laid-in. Weaving. See **laid-in.**

plain quilting. Quilts. Any **quilting** that makes use of simple patterns of **all-over** designs. Only straight lines of stitching are used, sometimes combined with **fancy quilting** stitches. Also see **Quilts: Quilting.**

plain quilting patterns. Quilts. The best known of the "plain," or simple quilting patterns are: crossbar, diagonal, diamond, double crossbar, double diamond. Also see **fancy quilting patterns.**

plainsawed. Woodworking. See **wood.**

plain seam. Stitchery. A simple and much used line of stitching which **joins** two pieces of material together. Since a **seam** is usually intended to be inconspicuous as well as strong, the right sides of the **fabric** are placed together and stitching is done on the wrong side on the seam line. The seam line is sewn at the edge of the **seam allowance** which is usually ½" to ⅝" from the **raw edge.** The seam is **press**ed open and flat. This is the most common seam for all construction and joining of fabric. See ill. Also see **bound seam.**

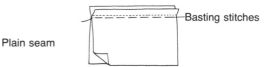

Plain seam — Basting stitches

plain weave. Quilts. Stitchery. A simple weaving pattern in which a **crosswise** thread crosses over one **lengthwise** thread, under the next, and so on. Also see **basket weave.**

plain weave. Weaving. The most basic and simplest weave structure, formed by an over and under interlacing that repeats every two **warp ends** and every two **filling picks.** The symbol for plain weave is $\frac{1}{1}$ and is read as "one up, one down." This means that every other warp end is raised and the warp ends in between are lowered, so that the filling pick that is shot through the warp ends goes under one, over one. In the following pick, the order is reversed and what was raised is lowered and what was lowered is raised. The filling pick now goes over one, under one. The third pick repeats the first pick. Plain weave can be woven on any even number of **harness**es, but since it repeats on only two ends, it is a favorite for two-**harness loom** weaving and **frame loom** weaving.

   Plain weave gives the tightest interlacing possible between the warp and filling. It is used in about 80% of all commercially woven fabrics and is found as gingham, taffeta, seersucker, and crepe, to mention a few fabrics woven in this construction. In handwoven cloth it is also widely used. It can be used as a **balanced cloth** with as much **warp** as **filling** showing. The warp can be completely covered, as in a **tapestry weave** or some **flatweave rugs.** If the warp is all that shows, and the filling is completely covered, then a horizontal **cord**ed or **rib** effect is achieved. Other variations on plain weave can be gotten by color variations in the warp and/or filling, irregular **threading,** irregular **sleying,** and the use of **textured yarn**s. Plain weave is used as the **ground weave** in patterned fabrics and as a **binder** in many weave constructions. **Finger-manipulated** structures, such as some of the **lace weave**s, have plain weave in some areas. Two repeats of the warp and filling are shown in the **weave draft** with one repeat outlined. See ill.

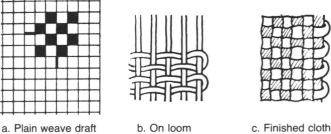

a. Plain weave draft   b. On loom   c. Finished cloth

plait. Lacemaking. See **braid, leaf stitch.**

plaited bar. Lacemaking. See **bar, braid.**

plaited basketry. Basketry. One of the three major basket structures. It utilizes only flexible, **active element**s in the **weave.** These are usually flat strips or **splint**s of uniform widths and thicknesses. They are woven together to produce **checked, twilled,** or **lattice plaiting.** Also see **Basketry: Plaited Basket Construction.**

plaited basket stitch. Knitting. The plaited basket stitch is used to create a handsome knit fabric that resembles the diagonal basket weave fabric. This pattern is based on the **one-over-one principle,** using an uneven number of stitches and applied to both the knit and purl rows. Also see **Knitting: Construction.**

plaited border. Basketry. See **border** and **Basketry: Woven Basket Construction.**

plaited edge stitch. Rugmaking. See **braid stitch.**

plaited Gobelin stitch. Needlepoint. A stitch worked over four mesh vertically and two mesh diagonally. Each row changes direction and results in an open zigzag look. This stitch is recommended for background and filling. See ill. Also see **filling stitch, Gobelin stitch.**

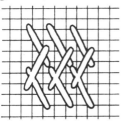

Plaited Gobelin stitch

plaited palm basket. Basketry. A **plaited** basket woven from palm leaves that utilizes both the leaflets and the ribs of the leaves in the structure. Most commonly, the ribs are used to form a natural boundary (corner or edge) of the basket and remain passive while the leaflets are actively woven together in a **checked, twilled,** or other plaited pattern. See ill. Also see **plaiting.**

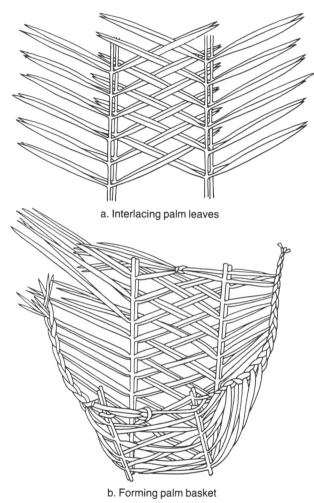

a. Interlacing palm leaves

b. Forming palm basket

plaited Slav stitch. Needlepoint. See **long-armed cross stitch.**

plaited stitch. Crewel. Embroidery. Needlepoint. See **close herringbone stitch.**

plaited wick. Candlemaking. See **braided wick.**

plaiting. Basketry. The **weaves** used in **plaited basketry.** Also see **Basketry: Plaited Basket Construction, Basic Weaves.**

plaiting. Weaving. A fabric technique employing a single set of elements (yarns) which are interlaced over and under each other in the manner of **plain weave.** This single set of elements is the lengthwise **warp** threads that serve as both warp and **filling** by **interlacing** with one another. The warp hangs loose and the work progresses downward. Each warp thread in turn becomes a **weft** thread and is drawn by the fingers, without a **shuttle,** through a **shed** formed by separating the alternating warp threads with the fingers. The shed is kept open by the fingers until the warp **end**s serving as weft have completely passed through. The shed is then closed and the fingers are used to push or beat up the filling compactly into the warp. After the passage through the shed, the weft thread is dropped and left to hang once more as a warp thread. A new shed is again opened by the fingers for the next warp thread acting as weft. Each warp end may serve many times as a weft thread.

Because the fingers are the main tool used, plaiting is often called **finger weaving.** There is also a tendency to use the words "plaiting" and **braiding** interchangeably, which is partially correct, since both techniques work over and under warp being used as weft. However, in a braid, all the threads or rag strips start from a common point and interlace downward in one direction. The result can be a three-dimensional finished strip. In plaiting, the threads or strips are spread out like a warp, can interlace in two directions (back and forth across the warp) and form a flat, narrow fabric. Several of these narrow fabrics can be sewn together or otherwise manipulated into wider fabrics or even three-dimensional structures.

Plaiting is believed to have been in use earlier than weaving by primitive peoples who employed it to construct shelters, baskets, and mats, and also for belts, straps, and bands. The early Peruvians, who were known to have used it as early as A.D. 300, developed complex forms and techniques in plaiting. Plaiting was also used extensively by the Indian tribes of North America. The Utes, Hopis, and some California tribes plaited strips of rabbit fur into winter robes. The Indians of the Great Lakes and Northeast plaited vegetable and animal fibers into bags and sashes, and reeds and bark into mats. An important item in the East was ornamental or ceremonial sashes which were worn around the head, turban style, across the chest in bandolier fashion, or around the waist with the long fringe trailing on the ground.

Patterns in a plaited fabric come from the arrangement of colors in the warp and the direction of the plaiting. Often both elements run on the diagonal. Plaiting is done over a support rod or dowel used as a holding device for the warp elements. The support rod, which can be removed later on, is attached to, or hung from, some stationary object. The yarn to be plaited should be cut into lengths about four times the length of the desired band or fabric. Each strand of the yarn is doubled over the support rod by means of a double-hitch knot or it can be merely looped over. The rod is in the center of the warp strands so that half of the fabric is constructed first and then the work is turned around and the other half is plaited. While the first half is being plaited the strands of the second half can be pinned or taped out of the way.

Plaiting is begun by picking up the yarn strand at either the extreme left or right and interweaving it as filling under and over the other yarn as if it were plain weave. Once it reaches the opposite side, it once more becomes a warp strand. The next yarn on the dowel is interlaced in the same manner with the other yarns and also with the first yarn, which is now in the warp position. A diagonal band develops as the process is repeated with each strand. The dowel is removed before starting the second half and the warp is straightened out. The second half is made in exactly the same way the first was. When the fabric is completed, the ends can be finished off by knotting, making small braids, or with some other type of **fringe**. Variations on the diagonal plaiting include **chevron** (Osage braid) **plaiting**, and **multiple-band plaiting**. Another variation is that the yarns lock or link around each other, instead of going over and under. This idea, but with the yarns in a stretched position on a frame, is known as Egyptian plaiting or **sprang**. A contemporary weaver-artist who is noted for her brilliant use of plaiting in constructing woven walls is Olga de Amaral from Colombia. As her warp and weft, she uses prewoven strips of fabric or wrapped multicolored rope strands, which she then plaits into large structures. See ill. Also see **Assumption sash, ceinture flechée, double plaiting, Hopi Indian wedding sash.**

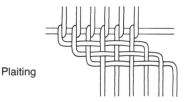

Plaiting

plane. Ceramics. A tool similar to a woodworking plane that is used for smoothing. A useful and valuable item of equipment for making ceramics by hand.

plane. Woodworking. A tool used to level and smooth wood surfaces by shaving down the high points or rough areas. There are two basic categories of planes: long bench planes, used for planing larger stock, and shorter block planes, used for **end grain** and smaller pieces. Both cut with a plane iron or blade that can be adjusted to vary the depth of the cut; in bench planes it is set at an angle of 45° and in block planes at 12−20°. Bench lanes usually have a cap iron that breaks the resistance of the shavings on difficult woods.

There are several types of bench planes. The jack plane is a two-handed plane 12−15″ long with a plane iron 2″ wide (**a.**). It is the standard bench plane used for leveling long edges and surfaces; a smoothing plane is similar to a jack plane but shorter—8″ to 10″ long. A fore plane (or jointer) is also like a jack plane but much larger: 18−30″ long and up to 2½″ wide. It is used to plane large boards. The power plane is a portable electric tool with a rotating plane iron used for **dressing** rough lumber.

Most block planes are for one-handed use. The block plane is the standard small shop plane, used to plane small pieces or end grain. It is 6−8″ long and has a plane iron 1⅝″ wide (**b.**). The trimming plane is the smallest plane, 3″ long and with a 1″ iron, used for small planing and smoothing. The rabbet plane, used for **rabbeting** the edges of boards, has a 1″ plane iron with a large handle. The bullnose rabbet plane used for rabbeting has a removable face or nose plate to permit planing to the very end of an obstructed interior edge (**c.**). The router plane is a double-handled plane with a heavy, narrow **plane iron**. It is com-

monly used to remove the waste wood in between the outer **kerfs** in cutting **grooves** and **dados** (**d.**). See ill.

Some planing tools do not fall into the categories of bench and block planes. A spokeshave is a double-handled tool somewhat like a drawknife, but with a blade more like that of a cabinet **scraper**. It is used for fine planing of curved surfaces where a regular plane would be unsuitable. It is available with two basic types of blades: flat, for shaving rounded surfaces, and convex, for hollow surfaces. A jointer is an electrical shop tool with a long, flat, two-part table with a series of flat revolving cutters recessed in the center. It is primarily used for planing the edges of a board but can also be used for surface planing. **bevel**ing, **chamfer**ing and some types of **rabbet**ing. A planer is an electric shop tool used in **dressing** boards. It is most commonly used to correct boards that are cupped or twisted, or to plane to a uniform thickness boards that have been edge-glued together. Also see **Woodworking: Planing and Squaring.**

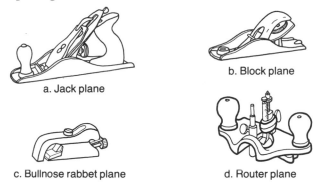

a. Jack plane

b. Block plane

c. Bullnose rabbet plane

d. Router plane

plane iron. Woodworking. The adjustable steel blade of a **plane** that shaves the wood.

planer. Woodworking. See **plane.**

plangi. Batik and Tie-dye. A Malay word by which **tie-dye** is known in many countries.

planing. Glasswork. See **fining.**

planing. Woodworking. Smoothing or **dressing** a rough, irregular edge or surface of a piece of wood. Any of a variety of **plane**s may be used depending on the size, shape, and location of the lumber being planed. Electric **jointer**s are power shop planes used for product planing. Also see **Woodworking: Planing and Squaring.**

planisher. Jewelry. A **punch** used for **planishing** (smoothing) forms; it is used when the form is too small to be planished with a **planishing hammer.**

planishing. Jewelry. A forming process used to smooth the surface of metal after **forging**. The work is supported against a **stake** or an **anvil** and the surface is systematically hammered in light, overlapping blows with a **planishing hammer.**

planishing hammer. Jewelry. A hammer with two faces, one slightly domed and the other flat, used for **planishing.** Available in a number of sizes, shapes, and weights, it is used to take out or smooth down irregularities in metal after **forging, forming,** or **doming** it over a **stake.**

planishing hammer. Metalworking. See **hammer.**

plank. Basketry. See **lapboard.**

plank. Woodworking. See **wood.**

plaquée. Stained Glass. See **flashed glass.**

plasma. Gemcutting. See **quartz.**

plasterboard. Woodworking. See **gypsum board.**

plaster mold. Candlemaking. Plaster molds, like **ceramic mold**s, must be treated or coated before filling with hot wax, to keep them from absorbing the liquid. Several layers of a **spar varnish** should adequately seal the mold. Also see **Candlemaking: Preparing the Mold.**

plaster of Paris. Ceramics. **Calcine**d gypsum that when mixed with water hardens into a soft, porous stone. It is used to make **bat**s and **mold**s. Most commercial pottery is made in or on plaster molds. To mix plaster, add powdered plaster to water, without stirring, until an island forms in the container. Then stir, and it is ready to use. Retardants such as milk and vinegar can be used to slow down drying time; salt and warm water can be used to hasten it. Don't try to dry plaster in a hot kiln because it can be dead-burned, or decomposed to a white powder.

plaster of Paris. Plastics. See **casting plaster.**

plaster of Paris. Stained Glass. Powdered dehydrated gypsum, which when mixed with water becomes a soft, porous stone. Drying time can be hastened by the addition of salt and warm water or retarded by milk or vinegar. Also see **Stained Glass: Tools and Materials.**

plastic. Jewelry. A relatively new medium for the jeweler that is blooming into an expressive jewelry form both on its own and in combination with metal and other materials. As the prices of metals soar, especially gold, more and more craftspeople will be turning to other materials, and plastic will surely be one of them. See ''Plastics for Jewelry'' by Harry Hollander. Also see **piqué work.**

plastic. Kites. See **Kites: Tools and Materials.**

plastic. Plastics. A synthetic material made of large molecules called **polymers,** which are derived from substances containing carbon. Also see **Plastics.**

plastic bubbles. Stained Glass. See **micro-balloons.**

plastic canvas. Needlepoint. See **canvas** and **Needlepoint: Materials.**

plastic clay. Puppets. Toys. See **Plasticene.**

plastic clip peg. Batik and Tie-dye. A simple plastic clamp designed for hanging fabrics or clothes. It is a one-piece clip and is often used in the **gadget tie-dye** process to secure fabrics. It works well in cold or warm water, but hot water may warp the plastic, causing it to loosen.

plastic-coated fabric. Stitchery. A woven or knitted material which has a plastic film over it. It has some special advantage in **banner**s, **soft sculpture,** and **stuff**ed toys, since the plastic serves to protect the material from soiling. Some plastic-coated **fabric**s are available with very shiny surfaces and can therefore be used to suggest certain unusual textural or metallic effects.

plastic emery stick. Jewelry. See **emery stick.**

plasticene. Beadwork. A clay that can be used instead of a vise to hold wood or other hard materials securely in place on the workbench while drilling holes in beads for stringing.

Plasticene. Puppets. Toys. (Also called plastic clay.) Modeling clay made with oil. It is unlike natural **clay,** which contains water. **Puppet head**s formed of Plasticene can be used as they are. Plasticene is never fired and is not permanent. The surface hardens to some extent, however, and if the features are dented or misshapen, they can be remodeled. Also see **ball cutter, liquid soap, modeling material.**

plasticene. Stained Glass. An oil-based, nonhardening sedimentary clay used for temporarily attaching pieces of glass to forms during **soldering.** Also see **dalle-de-verre, lampshade construction, lampshade molds.**

plasticity. Ceramics. The quality of malleability that is unique to clay.

plasticizer. Plastics. (Also called flexibilizer.) An **additive** mixed into **rosin** to make the plastic softer and more flexible after **curing.**

plastic memory. Plastics. (Also called elastic memory.) The ability of many **thermoplastics** to return to their original shape when heated. They may be repeatedly heated, but if heated beyond their melting point they will decompose.

plastic mold. Candlemaking. Highly sophisticated plastic resin molds, in a wide variety of shapes, are becoming readily available through hobby shops and candlemaking supply stores. They come with complete instructions for **molding.** Unless the heat resistance of the mold is indicated, care should be taken in pouring hot wax into plastic molds because certain types are not able to withstand high **temperature**s. When in doubt, allow the melted wax to cool to approximately 165° F before pouring. Also see **Candlemaking: Selecting the Mold.**

plastic resin glue. Woodworking. See **adhesives.**

PLASTICS

The craft of plastics explores the properties of **plastic** for aesthetic and practical ends and develops and exploits, rather than disguises, the material itself. The field opens a whole new direction for crafts exploration, because plastics have some unique qualities. For example, plastic can be more transparent than glass, its impregnated colors can be more saturated and intense than painted coverings, and its capability for large-scale molding and casting makes possible free-form, flowing shapes that would be too expensive to produce in other mediums.

Plastic compounds were first made in the nineteenth century. Between 1828 and 1846 explosives, chloroform, aniline dyes, lubricants, perfumes, medicines, and other products were developed from **polymer** compounds. In 1863 an American, John Wesley Hyatt, compounded **celluloid** in an attempt to win a prize offered for a substitute for ivory in billiard balls. Celluloid was too brittle for that purpose, but the plastic, despite its flammability, came to be used for collars, combs, table-tennis balls, and photographic film. In France in 1889, Hilaire de Chardonnet made an "artificial silk" from an acetate compound, but it was too flammable to succeed commercially. **Cellophane** was made in 1912, **polystyrene** in 1929, nylon in the 1930s, and synthetic rubbers in the 1930s and 1940s. The term "plastic" was given to this family of products in technical journals in the 1920s, because at that time it was felt that plasticity in some stage of manufacture was their only common characteristic.

The craft of plastics began shortly after industrial manufacture. American vocational high schools taught machining and forming of plastics in the 1940s much as they taught woodworking and metalworking. These skills spread as more and more plastics—many of them originally classified as secret materials for defense efforts—became available to the general public.

Many basic plastics operations can be accomplished at home, such as **casting, thermoforming, lamination, lathe turning,** coloring, **carving, cementing, embedment,** and finishing. Because plastics is a relatively new craft, there are many brands of plastic that disappear as they are replaced by improved varieties. Always read instructions carefully when using plastics and related chemicals; ask your plastics distributor not only for advice about the best plastic for a specific use, but also how best to use a given plastic.

SETTING UP A WORKSHOP The first requirement for a workshop is excellent ventilation and a good exhaust fan, because many of the materials used in crafting plastics are toxic or flammable or both. If you are going to work with **casting** or lamination **resin**s, there must be no open flames in the workroom (such as from space heaters), because the fumes produced are highly explosive.

Tools and materials needed will depend on the particular processes you intend to use. Probably you will specialize in just one or two basic areas, so purchasing equipment for all plastics operations would be expensive and wasteful.

Store sheets of plastic flat on a level surface if possible, or on edge at only a slight angle, to prevent warping. Store rods and tubes similarly. Do not store plastic in hot or excessively dry or humid areas, or near heating pipes; the **masking paper** will deteriorate, or the plastic may craze, warp, or become cloudy. Do not spray paint near sheet or solid plastics; the paint fumes attack the plastic. Tools and blades designed for soft metals are the type used on plastics. Carbide cutting tips retain their sharpness longer than ordinary steel tips. Power tools are preferable to hand tools for machining. Also see **cloudiness, crazing, distortion.**

SAFETY PRECAUTIONS AND FIRST AID A clean work area is a must in plastics. Cover working surfaces with vinyl or other plastic sheeting or with waxed paper when using resins. For accuracy in weighing, cover your **balance scale** and all other weighing equipment with plastic or paper when not in use; dust can distort the weights. Clean away chips and machining dust as you work. Chips may become embedded in your plastic surfaces and mar them, and inhaling dust is potentially harmful.

Minimize the danger of fire. Do not pour **catalyzed resins** into trash bins with other combustible materials; the heat of the curing resin can start a fire. Do not use an open-flame heater in the immediate area of casting, and do not smoke in the area where plastic fumes or dust may be present. Most vapors of **solvents** are flammable or explosive at certain concentrations and temperatures. A ventilation system that changes the studio air six times an hour is considered necessary to prevent dangerous vapor concentrations.

Some plastics will corrode metal cans. Store potentially reactive chemicals in separate locations in case there is leakage. Use safety containers for liquid solvents.

Read labels carefully before mixing chemicals. Weigh your chemicals and use them in the correct proportions to minimize combustion hazards. Inquire about the flammability of all your plastics before you store them. Carefully consider the flammability of plastics to be used for objects of interior furnishing and apparel.

For your personal safety: use vinyl, rubber, or disposable gloves and aprons (or smocks) when **casting** with resin. When machining solid plastics, wear a **dust mask,** and when working with resins, plastic-based spray paints, or solvents, wear a **chemical mask.** When spraying plastic chemicals, use a spray booth and a mask designed to filter organic chemicals.

Do not eat in the area where plastics fumes or dust may be present. Inhaling or eating plastics sprays is dangerous because of the toxic solvents, even when the plastics themselves are nontoxic. All **plasticizers, catalysts,** and solvents are potentially dangerous. While many plastics are classified as nontoxic by their manufacturers, some people develop allergies to them. Poisoning from the inhalation of vapors from resins and solvents can be cumulative!

Burning plastic is also potentially dangerous because many plastics release carbon monoxide, hydrogen cyanide, hydrogen chloride, and **hydrocarbons.** Carbon dioxide, the main waste product from burning plastics, is not toxic but can be suffocating.

Foaming-agent chemicals for making **foam** are also dangerous and require the use of a chemical mask. Freon, one foaming agent, can "freeze" your lungs.

Excellent ventilation cannot be overemphasized!

If you spill resin or catalyst on your skin, dry the area with a cloth, then wash it with soap and water. Wash again with **denatured alcohol** if any resin is still left on the skin. Do not (!) use **acetone** because it will spread the chemicals and make them penetrate deeper into the pores.

If chemicals get into your eyes, flush them immediately with water for at least 15 minutes and see a doctor.

Cold cream or adhesive tape will aid removal of **glass fiber**s from the skin.

TOOL CARE AND MAINTENANCE   Sharpen cutting blades and router bits when dull. Keep saw teeth even. Lubricate cutting blades and drill bits with water when working thick or heavy pieces of plastic.

Clean off any fused or heat-melted plastic immediately. It is easier to remove when soft or uncured. Clogged cutting blades and **drill bit**s will damage the quality of the cut. Clean **resin**-filled brushes before the resin **cures**. If this is not possible while working, immerse the brushes in a container of **solvent** and clean them thoroughly as soon as possible.

Keep tools for use with **mold**s and **casting resin** dry and free of dust to prevent **cloudiness** in the **curing** plastic.

CUTTING   Cut or saw plastic with power saws, using metal-cutting blades. Circular saws, table saws, band saws, jig saws, and sabre saws may all be used. Use blade with fine teeth for fine cuts. Keep the blade sharp and the teeth of even height; **carbide**-tipped blades give a better cut and stay sharp longer than ordinary **steel** ones.

Leave the **masking paper** on the plastic when sawing. Keep the adhesive on this paper from gumming up the saw by applying white soap or **tallow** to the cutting blade. Do not allow deposits of adhesive or plastic to accumulate on the saw.

Feed the plastic into the blade (or blade into the plastic) slowly and evenly. Hold the plastic firmly so that the piece does not rattle or move. You may have to clamp thin plastic to scrap lumber to saw it. Put soapy water on the blade as a coolant when cutting heavy stock.

Use a table saw or circular saw for long straight cutting. Adjust the height of the blade so that it is just a little greater than the thickness of the plastic to be cut. Use hollow-ground high-speed blades with teeth of uniform height, shape, and rake. Do not use a combination blade. Feed material a bit faster when using a carbide-tipped blade because it does not tend to bind when cutting thick sheets. Use the normal woodworking speed of 3,400–4,000 rpm with a 1-horsepower motor for sheets under ¼" thick, or a 1½- or 2-hp motor for plastic over ½". Keep the table saw surface clean of chips and particles of dirt that can scratch plastic.

Use a band saw for cutting curves and irregular shapes and for straight cuts in thick material. Use a guide bar for straight cutting operations and a speed 2,500–4,000 surface feet per minute. The thinner the plastic sheet, the greater the number of blade teeth per inch necessary—for example, for ⅛" thick use 18 teeth per inch, for ¼" use 14 per inch, for ½" use 10 per inch, and for 1" use 8 per inch.

Use jigsaws and saber saws to cut closed holes. Cut only one sheet at a time, because the saws heat the plastic quickly and it tends to gum up the blade with fused material. Use a fine-toothed blade with about 14 teeth per inch. Support and clamp the work while cutting. If the saw has a switch for fast and slow speeds, use a fast tool speed but a slow feed.

Cut a thin sheet of plastic by hand by scoring it with a sharp metal hand tool, such as an **X-Acto** knife or **burin**, several times, using a straight edge as a guide. Then place the deeply scored line over the edge of the worktable or any raised straight-edged surface, with the line facing up, and press down on both sides of the line with both hands. It will break cleanly on the line.

For drilling, use an electric drill or drill press with a high-speed twist drill bit at speeds of 1,000–2,000 rpm. Cut large holes at a slower speed with a hole saw or **circle cutter**.

Leave the **masking paper** on the plastic to help protect the surface and prevent chipping. Clamp the plastic securely and protect the surface by shielding the clamp or vise jaws with pieces of a softwood. Back the plastic with wood when drilling thin sheets to reinforce the sides of the hole and to prevent it from spreading with increased heat.

To prevent a hole from tearing, file the point of the drill flat so that the point does not go all the way through the plastic before the full diameter of the drill has entered the material. Decrease the rate of **feed** as you increase the depth of the hole.

File rough edges of sheet and solid plastics to remove machining marks, and to prepare the edge for **cementing** and finishing. File the surfaces of cast plastic objects to remove imperfections created during the **casting** process before finishing the surface.

Acrylic tends to clog standard mill files, so you will have to clean the **file** frequently with a **file card.** File only on the forward stroke; do not drag the file on the surface on the return stroke.

CEMENTING   **Cementing** is one of the easiest and most common methods of joining plastics, but practice is needed to avoid **crazing** and weak joints. If a part is to be subject to heavy pressure or wear, reinforce the joint by inserting a pin or screw.

If you spill **solvent** on a plastic surface, blot it up immediately or not at all because the spilled solvent will smear the surface as you wipe it. If the solvent is allowed to evaporate undisturbed, the surface may be unharmed.

When bonding cast parts, use the **resin** they are made of; it makes a better bond than glue. Use about 10 drops of catalyst in ½ oz of resin. Work very quickly; do not use the catalyzed resin after it starts to **gel.** For bonding dissimilar plastics, ask your plastics distributor to recommend an **adhesive** for your particular materials.

Do not machine or polish the cemented joint until it fully **cures.** This takes 8–24 hours, depending on the temperature of the room. Speed the curing process by exposing the plastic to 125° F either from a heat lamp or a warm oven with the door open. Humidity may cause **cloudiness** or a joint; **annealing** strengthens the cemented joint.

Always use the manufacturer's recommended solvent for a particular plastic. Mask the areas around the joint with **masking** or **cellophane tape** to prevent etching by the **solvent.** Fit the pieces to be joined together accurately without forcing them. Sand or scrape the surface for fitting, but do not polish the area.

For capillary cementing, apply the solvent to the joint with an eyedropper, syringe, paint brush, or pipe cleaner. Do both sides when possible. The solvent will spread over the jointed surface by capillary action. Apply light pressure until the solvent sets. The setting time varies according to the type of solvent, the size of the plastic joint, and the room temperature. Do not try to cement when the temperature is below 60° F. Under ideal conditions it will dry in 3–10 minutes and may be machined in 4 hours. Scrape off the excess solvent, clean and polish.

For soak cementing, hold one of the edges to be joined in solvent until soft, usually at least seven minutes. Remove it from the soaking container carefully, avoiding splashing. Briefly tilt it at a slight angle to drain off excess solvent. Join the surfaces and keep them together under light pressure to let the soaked edge moisten and soften the other surface. Then add more pressure by weighting the joint for at least one hour. Discard solvent left in the soak pan. Do not pour it back into the original bottle, because one of its ingredients evaporates upon exposure to air.

CASTING   Casting is used to reproduce three-dimensional objects, especially models made in clay or other impermanent materials. The number of copies that may be made depends on the type and quality of **mold** and **mold-making materials.**

Assemble all tools and materials. These include:
polyester or **epoxy casting**-grade **resin** and **catalyst accelerator,** if desired
additives such as **colorant**s, if desired
lacquer thinner or **acetone** to clean equipment
denatured alcohol to clean any chemicals off your skin
rubber gloves
a **chemical mask**
measuring tools: a **balance scale,** and a graduated eyedropper or syringe (without needle)
disposable waxed-paper cups (not plastic or Styrofoam, which would be dissolved by chemicals)
stir sticks
masking tape
newspaper, waxed paper, or plastic sheeting to cover all work surfaces
cellophane or **Mylar** if the resin lacks **air-shield**ing additives
modeling compound or Silicon Seal for caulking cracks and joints in molds
pastry cutter or sharp knife to cut **gel**led resin
mold release agent, unless resin has such an additive
sealant, if mold is porous

If the completed mold is porous, prepare it with a sealant to keep it from absorbing the resin. If the resin does not have a mold release additive, coat the surfaces of the mold that will face the resin with two or more coats of mold release agent. A sheet of cellophane or Mylar may be used instead if the shape is simple enough.

Measure the chemicals carefully and pour the catalyst into the resin. If you will be pouring a thick layer of resin, reduce the amount of catalyst slightly, or the curing resin will get too hot. For a thin layer, you may add accelerator to the resin after the catalyst has been mixed in, but do not add accelerator directly to the catalyst—an explosion may result. Mix the chemicals thoroughly, but stir slowly and avoid excess agitation to prevent air bubbles in the mixture.

Pour the catalyzed resin into the mold and, if there is no air-shield additive, cover the surface with an air shield of cellophane or Mylar. Keep the casting out of drafts and allow it to cure.

Ideal casting conditions call for relatively dry atmosphere and temperatures above 67° F. If this is not possible, put the curing resin in a box with a heat lamp over it. Warmth is necessary for adequate curing. Lack of warmth will result in imperfect curing and a sticky surface. Weight the surface if the casting shows signs of warping.

Remove the cast from the mold when cured. If a harder, more scratch-resistant surface is needed, coat the cured surface with **surface resin.**

EMBEDMENT   An **embedment** is a simply shaped casting with **inclusion**s put in during the pouring. Paperweights with embedded coins are familiar examples of the technique.

Assemble the tools and materials, and prepare the **mold** and **resin** as for casting.

Pour the **base pour** of resin into the mold slowly to avoid trapping air bubbles. Tap the mold to free any trapped bubbles to rise to the surface. Let the base pour **gel**; it will heat up and then cool.

Before embedding the inclusions, dip them into resin to coat them thoroughly. It may be necessary to dip them several times to avoid trapping air bubbles in the crevices. Objects that are lighter than the resin should be dipped in resin and then secured to the base pour with an **anchor pour.** Make sure the object is positioned properly, and let the anchor pour gel.

Catalyze more resin and pour it. This may complete the castings, or you may make deep castings containing many levels of embedments.

Cover the resin surface after the last pour with an **air shield.** Allow the casting to cure. If the surface remains tacky, place the mold in an oven at 120–180° F or under a **heat lamp.** Remove the casting from the mold when fully cured.

LAMINATING   Use laminating procedures when you wish to build a strong, thin shell or wall. Laminate a casting into an open mold or a piece mold and then put the pieces together after they cure, or laminate over an armature (support) that is left inside the completed object. Assemble the basic tools and equipment used for casting plus paintbrushes for applying **resin; laminating resin** (either **epoxy** or **polyester**) and a **catalyst;** a **thixotropic** agent; **reinforcing material**s and a fiberglass surfacing mat; a roller to press out air bubbles from between the layers; and **colorant** and an accelerator (if desired).

Prepare the surface upon which you will lay the reinforced resin by coating the mold as for casting (if you wish to remove the plastic from it later) or by roughening the surface with any abrasive (if you want the plastic to cover and adhere to the armature).

Cut all necessary pieces of reinforcing material to the desired sizes before **catalyzing** the **resin.** Determine how much you need by positioning the cut pieces in the mold or on the armature as you cut them. Remove them from the mold and lay them out within reach.

Calculate the amount of catalyst based on the weight of the laminating resin; do not include the thixotropic filler, colorants, or reinforcing materials in the calculations. Use the percentage of catalyst given in the product instructions.

Mix in thoroughly any internal colorant before catalyzing. Next add the catalyst and stir thoroughly. Add accelerator if desired, but do not add more catalyst, or excessive shrink and warping may result.

Brush on the **gel coat** with a paint-brush and let it **gel.** Make sure you brush out any air bubbles. Impregnate your reinforcing material by soaking it in resin or by brushing the resin on it. Lay it over your gel coat, again brushing out or pressing out air bubbles. A roller may also be used here instead of your gloved hands. Alternate layers of impregnated reinforcement and layers of resin without waiting for the lower layers to **cure.** Also alternate the direction of the reinforcing material on subsequent layers. Keep working out the air bubbles to help prevent **delamination.** The number of layers depends upon the size, shape, and function of the completed form. The layer nearest the final exposed and visible surface on the completed objects should contain the **glass fiber** surfacing mat.

Finish by applying a final coat of resin.

COLORING Most colored plastics are internally colored in the manufacturing process by mixing pigments, dyes, or metal flakes into their resins; thus the colors will not wear off. Various paint and dye coatings may also be applied to the surface of plastics, but they are not as durable and must be touched up if scratched. Add internal **colorant**s to the resin according to product directions before **catalyzing** the resin, and mix thoroughly. Colorants may slow the **gel time.**

Do not spray **lacquer** or any other spray paint on **polystyrene** foam. Test all paints on a trial area of the surface first. Solvents in many paints attack the **foam** surface. Certain smooth plastics, such as **vinyl,** may need to be slightly roughened by fine sanding or require a primer paint to help the color coat adhere securely.

Sheet **acrylic** may be painted with acrylic and other **polymer-emulsion**-base paints. Silk-screen stencils can also be used to print on acrylic. Aerosol spray paints cause stress; do not use them in an area subject to wear and pressure. Allow aerosol paint to dry 4 hours before using the plastic.

When using external dyes to color the surface, mask out areas not to be dyed with cellophane tape. Clean the plastic thoroughly and do not get fingerprints on it. Dip the plastic in a dye bath made from a commercial plastic dye—consult your plastic distributor for reliable brand names. Dye may also be painted on the surface with a paintbrush.

CARVING Most rigid plastics, whether solid or **foam,** can be carved.

Solid plastics like **acrylics** can best be carved with various **burr tip**s and **tapered drill bit**s on a flexible-shaft machine (**a.**). The design is often carved into the back so the front surface remains smooth. Blocks of plastic can have shapes carved into the interior from the bottom with the same tools. The surface may be engraved by the **intaglio process** with **burin**s or other sharp hand tools.

Plastic foam can be shaped with hand tools such as knives, files, sandpaper, and **Surform tools.** High-density foam may be worked with a flexible-shaft machine, but care must be exercised to avoid overheating the material.

Foams can also be cut by pulling a hot wire through them. However, the denser the foam, the hotter the wire must be; if the wire is too hot, small knobs of melted foam develop along the cut line and become scorched.

Do not try to carve **polystyrene** foam with a flame; a flame will not only melt and bead the foam, but also will burn it, producing noxious fumes. See ill.

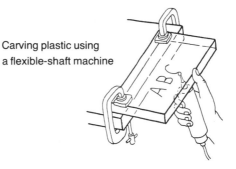

Carving plastic using a flexible-shaft machine

THERMOFORMING AND MOLDING **Thermoforming** and **molding** with **mold**s and **pattern**s is particularly useful for making multiple copies of objects. Oven forming and **strip heating** are suited to free-form one-of-a-kind objects, although multiple identical copies can be made if the soft plastic is cooled in a **jig.** Plastic sheets used for vacuum forming are **polyvinyl chloride, acrylic, polyethylene,** cellulose acetate butyrate, and ABS plastic.

Assemble all materials and equipment. You will need a heater—an oven, **strip heater,** or heating element for use in vacuum forming or **blow-molding;** sheet **thermoplastic** (e.g., **vinyl,** acrylic, **styrene**); cotton gloves; flannel or other soft material to drape over holding surfaces; holding tools (**jig,** clamps); and a power **saw** to cut sheets to size.

For oven forming, remove residual **adhesive** with facial tissue moistened in refined kerosene. Dab the plastic to remove softened adhesive; do not wipe. Wash off any caked dirt with a nonabrasive soap or mild detergent; remove grease or oil with naphtha, kerosene, or isopropyl alcohol. Never use window sprays to clean plastic.

Heat small trial pieces of the plastic in an oven to determine exact heating time for the desired degree of plasticity. Keep the oven temperature at 320–340° F for **acrylic.** Overheating will cause the surface to blister, decompose, or ignite. Do not leave the plastic in an oven (or any heater) unattended. Prop a home oven door open a bit to prevent any fumes from building up inside. Ventilate the room well.

Handle heat-softened sheets and rods on the edges or ends. Wear clean, lintfree cotton gloves to prevent finger impressions. Do not force-bend the plastic or it will craze. Return the material to the heater if it offers any resistance. If dissatisfied with the cooled shape, reheat it until it returns to its original form, to prevent distortion from shrinking, and then remold it.

For strip heating, first clean the plastic as described above. Support the plastic sheet at least $1/16''$ from the **strip heater,** or even further away for a bend with a large radius, so that a larger section of plastic will be treated. It is ideal to have two heaters, one on each side of the sheet, for thick pieces. Bend the plastic while soft, following the same procedures as for oven forming.

For vacuum forming, design your pattern so that it has at least a 3–5% **draft** on the vertical sides and no **undercut**s. Sharp corners, points, and edges may tear the soft plastic. Drill small exhaust holes in the horizontal surfaces.

Secure your pattern on the **vacuum former**s platform with tape. Turn on the vacuum compressor to build up the vacuum pressure while you prepare the plastic sheet.

Cut the plastic sheet larger than the pattern size. Add extra inches to the dimensions, equal to the depth or height of the pattern plus 2% to allow for shrinking of the sheet as it cools.

Clean the plastic sheet, and position and clamp it into the vacuum former in a holding frame. Turn on the heating element, which is suspended over the holding frame, and pull it down close to the plastic. Heat until the plastic sags. When the sagging accelerates, pull the holding frame away from the heat and down over the pattern. Quickly turn on the vacuum release, which sucks the plastic to the pattern. Leave the plastic in the holding frame on the pattern until cool. Remove and cut or file off waste edges. See ill.

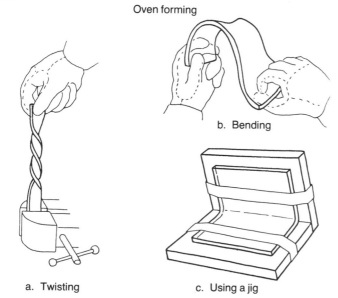

Oven forming

a. Twisting   b. Bending   c. Using a jig

FINISHING **Casting** and laminating **resin**s must be completely **cured** before using any finishing process. Purchased shapes may need little or no finishing if protective **masking tape** or paper has been left on the surface. Do not scrape, sand, or ash a surface unless the imperfections are too deep to be filled with polishing **wax** or **tallow** or to be made invisible by **buffing.**

Scraping is done on the edges with a sharp scraper or the sharpened back edge (without teeth) of a hacksaw blade to remove marks left by machining. Rough edges will cause improper bonding of cemented joints. Do not further sand, ash, polish, or buff edges that are to be cemented; edges not to be **cemented** may be further finished.

To hand sand, wrap the sandpaper around a wood block when sanding flat areas to avoid making finger indentations in the surface. Use progressively finer grades of wet-or-dry sandpaper or garnet paper, ranging from 150 to 400, depending on the depth of the surface marks. Wet-sanding with wet-or-dry sandpaper is preferable because it reduces frictional heat and keeps plastic dust from filling the air. Wear a **dust mask** when dry-sanding to avoid inhaling the dust.

For machine or power sanding wear **eye protectors** and a dust mask. Clamp or hold the object in a vise or, when using a portable electric drill with a sanding attachment, secure the drill and move the plastic shape against the sanding or grinding wheel or disk. Use disk or belt sander mainly on edges rather than flat surfaces. Avoid overheating and gouging: use only light pressure, keep the sander in constant motion, and when using waterproof sandpaper, sprinkle water on the surface as a coolant.

For **ashing,** apply a thick paste of 00 pumice and water to a **buffing wheel** and operate the wheel at a speed of about 2,000 rpm for **thermosetting plastics,** or about 1,500 rpm for **thermoplastic**s. Wash off the pumice and dry the plastic when finished. Bring the surface to a high polish with a little more final buffing.

Polish **polyester** surfaces without **polishing compound**s by painting highly **catalyzed** resin over scratches and machined edges to fill them. For other plastics, apply a polishing compound such as tripoli or jeweler's rouge to the buffing wheel. Again, when working with portable electric hand tools, clamp either the plastic or the tool securely for control. Speeds of about 2,000 rpm are recommended. Use separate buffing wheels for different plastics. For example, wheels used with polyester may become gummed and transfer polyester to **acrylic.** Use only light pressure and avoid overheating the plastic.

Flaming is a form of final edge-polishing using a **propane torch.** Prepare the edge by scraping and sanding to remove any machining marks. Remove the protective paper from the edge, and wet any other paper on the sheet. Do not flame edges to be cemented or bonded together. Move the lit torch with a constant motion at a distance of at least 6″ from the edge surface. Use extreme caution to avoid overheating and bubbling of the surface. This process is not recommended for novices.

When buffing, first use a dry, clean cotton buffing wheel with tallow or other recommended wax. Then buff with another clean wheel of unstitched flannel for a higher polish. Apply antistatic wax by hand with a soft, clean cloth.

CARE, CLEANING, AND MAINTENANCE Remove protective masking paper. If any **adhesive** remains on the sheet, moisten facial tissue with clean refined kerosene and dab it on the plastic until the adhesive softens. Remove the softened adhesive by again dabbing, not wiping, with the tissue. Wash off any caked dirt with a nonabrasive soap or mild detergent and water, using a soft, lint-free cloth, sponge, or chamois.

Remove grease or oil with naphtha, hexane, kerosene, or isopropyl alcohol. Never use window sprays, kitchen scouring compounds, or **solvent**s that may attack the surface, such as **acetone, benzene,** carbon tetrachloride, dry-cleaning fluid, fire-extinguisher fluid, or **lacquer thinner.**

Cleaning processes do not prevent the return of an **electrostatic charge** and its accompanying dust and dirt. Apply an **antistatic** coating or wax in a very thin, even coat with a soft, clean cloth. Remove excess coating if beads appear during application. Let the coating dry, and polish the surface with a soft cloth.

Repeated dusting of a plastic surface unprotected by an antistatic coating will cause the build-up of tiny, almost invisible scratch lines that in time will dull the surface. Any of the protective coatings applied after the initial cleaning will reduce maintenance to a very light dusting with a soft, clean cloth or feather duster. Cheesecloth, muslin, or shop cloths may scratch the surface. Scratch removals are accomplished by filling minor scratches with a paste wax or hard automobile wax. Remove deeper scratches by hand-polishing with jeweler's rouge or other compounds. Do not try to erase heavy scratches or large areas of blemishes without power buffing equipment. Also see **antistatic treatment.**

plastics. Mosaics. A synthetic compound commercially molded into any one of a variety of shapes or glasslike sheets. Sheet plastic, cut by the artist into bits and pieces, can be bonded with a **plastic adhesive** to a transparent surface such as plate glass to produce stained-glass-window types of mosaics. Plastic sheets are also used as translucent mosaic **backing**s.

plastic toy. Toys. Plastic was first introduced in toymaking at the end of the first quarter of the twentieth century. By 1934 it had been developed enough to make it competitive with wood, metal, cloth, and rubber. It had the advantages of speed in production, reasonable production cost, great variety, low cost, and the ability to provide realistic and fine detail. **Hardwood** is still preferred over plastic for building **blocks** and **constructional toy**s, especially for preschoolers. Wheels are still best made of metal. Dolls, however, are almost exclusively made of plastic.

The tremendous renewed interest in toymaking by designer-craftspeople since the 1960s is in part a reaction to the use of plastics in toys. The current interest is in a return to simple **folk toy**s of wood, cloth, and natural materials. The emphasis in handcrafted toys is on the personalized toy.

plastic wood. Puppets. Toys. (Also called wood putty.) A soft, plastic or puttylike material used to fill holes or cracks in wood to give it a smooth surface. It is a hard-setting substance about the consistency of cream cheese. It is used in filling, smoothing, or repairing wood and is excellent to use in filling in the gaps between layers of **plywood.** It is available in cans and is applied with any flexible knife blade or with a piece of cloth. It will adhere to other materials but is most commonly used on wood.

In applying the wood dough, it is usually spread onto the area slightly thicker than needed. It can later be sanded.

Most plastic woods have an acetone base and are cleaned with **acetone** or a thinner or **solvent** designated on the container. It is extremely flammable and precautions should be taken to avoid breathing the vapors.

In **puppet head**s of **sawdust maché** or in **carved wood,** plastic wood may be used for minor modeling as well as for mending. It comes in natural wood color and **stain**s can be added to it so that it will more closely resemble or match any wood. When dry and hard it can be sanded smooth and level and painted or treated like the rest of the wood. Also see **Puppets: Making the Puppet Head.**

Plastic Wood. Woodworking. See **wood filler.**

plated glass. Stained Glass. See **plating.**

plate finish. Leather. A term for the smooth finish given to leather by plating. Also see **Leatherwork: Finishing Leather.**

plate glass. Stained Glass. Used in lamination and in situations in which a reinforced, polished, thick, clear **glass** is needed—for example, mirrors, shop windows, and so on—and where window glass, easily shattered, would not be strong enough. Use a **diamond glass cutter** to cut plate glass. Also see **fused glass technique, gemmaux, glass stress.**

plate metal. Metalworking. See **metal.**

plate pliers. Stained Glass. (Also called glass pliers.) A very useful instrument in cutting glass. They are a heavier-weight pliers than the **grozer** and have smooth inner jaws that get a firm grip on the glass and help in **parting** it. See ill. Also see **Stained Glass: Cutting Glass, Tools and Materials.**

Plate pliers

plate shears. Jewelry. Scissorlike tools used to cut plate metal, available with curved and straight blades of various lengths. Small plate shears, more accurately termed

Plate shears

"snips" because of their size, are useful for cutting thin-**gauge sheet metal,** bezel wire, wire, and solder **pallion**s. See ill.

plating. Leather. See **Leatherwork: Tanning and Manufacture.**

plating. Stained Glass. (Also called plated glass.) The term for using two pieces of glass together as one piece. They are cut separately, using the same **template.** The lighter piece of glass goes on top.

In **painting on plating,** paint the heavier piece of glass. In **glazing** the painted plating, reverse the pieces of glass so that the surface with paint is on the inside of the window and is not placed in between the pieces. Double wide-channeled lead is used to glaze plating. The process is called **double glazing** or **doubling.** Also see **aciding, painting on aciding.**

playboard. Puppets. The board over which **hand puppet**s appear. Since there is no **stage floor** in the hand-**puppet stage,** the area on which the performance occurs is called the playboard. Also see **"boxed in"** and **Puppets: The Puppet Stage.**

Play-doh. Toys. The trade name of a modeling compound available in bright colors. It is malleable, flexible, and can be air-dried. It is a nontoxic and nonpermanent material.

"playing the puppet." Puppets. Operating or animating the figure. With **hand puppet**s this means moving the hands in such a way as to suggest action. With **marionette**s, it means to **manipulate** the **control**s to suggest action.

play of color. Gemcutting. See **luster.**

play pretties. Toys. A name used in the southern United States to refer to any toy or **game** of amusement, usually a **folk toy.** It could include **whittle**d animals or toys such as the **whimmydiddle.**

pleat. Batik and Tie-dye. To **fold** a fabric into narrow strips before **binding** to produce a pattern in **tie-dye.** Also, the **flat double fold** produced in this way. The fold is of an even width for its entire length. When used in a series, this fold or pleat is called an **accordion pleat.** The pleats may be formed in any direction, although they are usually parallel. A series of pleats may be used within another shape. For example, there could be a pleat pattern within an **oval,** or fabric might be pleated as it is wrapped over a rope.

pleating. Papercrafts. See **accordion pleating.**

pleochroism. Gemcutting. See **color.**

Plexiglas. Plastics. See **acrylic.**

Plexiglas. Puppets. Stitchery. Toys. See **acrylic plastic sheet.**

Plexiglas. Stained Glass. A synthetic resin cast into sheets, either in a clear state or colored through the addition of colorants. Also see **lampshade construction.**

plied fringe. Rugmaking. Weaving. A fringe that is made of a number of **warp end**s separated, twisted into two thick cords, and twisted together. The warp ends are first divided into two equal groups. The initial twisting or **plying** is done in one direction (Z-twist) and the second plying is achieved by allowing the two cords to twist together in the reverse direction (S-twist). They will do this naturally as the first twists oppose each other. This will also hold the final twist, but not completely, and either an **overhand knot, wrapping,** or some sort of tight holding device must be at the end of the plied cord to hold it completely. See ill.

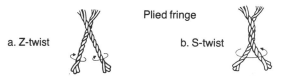

Plied fringe

a. Z-twist   b. S-twist

plied yarn. Spinning. Weaving. A yarn in which 2 or more **single** yarns are twisted together to form a heavier yarn. Any number or types of yarn may be plied together. The counts of the individual yarns need not be the same. A plied yarn of the same count for all individual yarns is written as two numbers with a slash line between them—for example, 2/10s. The smaller number is the ply number. Plied yarn is stronger and more expensive than a single yarn of the same weight. Also see **yarn count.**

pliers. Beadwork. A long-nosed pair of jeweler's pliers or sharp needle-nose pliers with serrated cutting edges is used in **bead flowermaking.**

pliers. Enameling. See **Enameling: Tools and Materials.**

pliers. Jewelry. There are two groups of pliers—pliers whose jaws remain parallel when open, and pliers whose jaws pivot around a rivet. Sometimes the jaws are serrated to facilitate gripping, and sometimes they are smooth, leaving the metal, for the most part, unmarked. There are many types of pliers manufactured and each has specialized uses, although many of them are multipurpose. Some uses are **bending** wire around the pliers which act as a gripping device and a **mandrel,** especially when shaping thin **gauge sheet metal;** setting small **rivet**s; and forming **bezel**s. Some types of pliers and a few of their uses are given below.

Chain-nose pliers are for forming chain links. Both jaws are flat inside, round outside.

Flat-nose pliers are for bending metal at or toward right angles (a.).

Forming pliers have one jaw round, the other flat.

Half-round pliers have one jaw half-round, the other flat.

Parallel-jaw, flat-nose pliers are the same as flat-nose pliers, except the jaws open and close parallel to each other.

Parallel-jaw, round-nose pliers are the same as round-nose pliers, except jaws open and close parallel to each other.

Chain-nose pliers with cutter are the same as chain-nose pliers, except with a cutting jaw along the side for snipping wire.

Three-prong pliers are for bending very fine flat wire.

Rivet-setting pliers are for forming rivets in **finding**s.

Prong-setting pliers are for pushing **prong**s against a stone or pearl.

End-cutting pliers are for **clipping** wire.

Diagonal-cutting pliers are for clipping wire (**b.**).

Four basic pliers would be: flat-nose pliers, round-nose pliers (**c., d.**), half-round pliers, and end-cutting pliers (**e.**).

Pliers that are used for bending metal can be wrapped with masking tape to protect the metal from scratches. This will work particularly well on round-nose pliers. To bend metal with pliers: Cut a strip of masking tape about 1½" long with scissors to make a clean edge; round-nose pliers are tapered, small at the end, larger toward the handle. Place the tape at a diagonal to compensate for the taper in the nose of the pliers and wrap tightly no more than twice. Trim the excess tape off with scissors. The tightness and neatness of the tape is important as the pliers are acting partially as a mandrel. If the tape is loose, you will have a mushy-looking bend. The tape will last for only a short period of time and must be replaced as it wears through. If a period of time passes while the wrapped pliers are not in use, when the masking tape is removed the jaws will be sticky from the adhesive on the masking tape. This can be removed with benzine or lighter fluid. See ill.

a. End-cutting pliers

b. Diagonal-cutting pliers

c. Round-nose pliers (long)

d. Round-nose pliers (short)

e. Flat-nose pliers

pliers. Jewelry. Metalworking. Woodworking. Standard slip-joint pliers are used to hold or grip a **nut** while tightening or loosening it.

pliers. Tincrafting. A pincerlike gripping tool used in tincrafting to help shape the metal plate. Pliers come in a wide variety of shapes, including pairs with both completely rounded and half-rounded (or half-flattened) gripping ends. The rounded type allow for shaping, **rolling**, and curling or decurling tin with no hard edges or bends; the flattened or needle-nose type permit angled bending and flat shaping. Also see **Tincrafting: Tools and Materials.**

plique-à-jour. Enameling. An enameling technique in which transparent **enamel**s are fired in openings in the **metal** to achieve an effect like a miniature stained-glass window. The technique may involve piercing holes in a sheet of silver and filling the holes·with transparent enamels, or finishing a piece in the standard **cloisonné** manner to a copper base which is then etched away leaving a fragile membrane of enamel and wire. Also see **etching, trivet.**

plow. Bookbinding. The plow is attached to a **lying press** to trim the edges of the leaves and **board**s of a book. The blade of the plow is advanced on each forward stroke by turning a handle. Only a few leaves are cut with each stroke and only on the forward stroke, unless cutting with the **grain**, in which case it is possible to cut on the backward stroke without tearing the material. An adjustable blade is recommended as it is necessary to keep the blade sharp. The blade must be kept square with the lying press. See ill. Also see **trimming.**

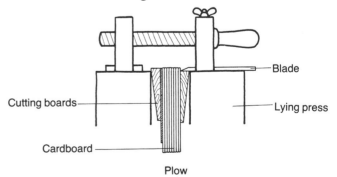

Plow

plucked ware. Ceramics. Pots that are scarred as a result of touching and sticking to the kiln wall or furniture during firing and must be plucked off. A common occurrence of **salt-glazed ware.**

plug. Woodworking. A small, round piece of wood used to cover the head of a screw after **countersinking** it. A **plug cutter** is used if it is desirable to match the grain of the wood, or a piece of **dowel** may be used; the plug is glued in place and sanded flush with the wood surface. Some furniture styles use mushroom-shaped plugs, the heads of which are left protruding.

plug cutter. Woodworking. A **drill bit** with a hollow center used to cut standard-size **plug**s. It is best used in a **drill press** for accuracy.

plug tap. Metalworking. See **tap.**

plumbago. Jewelry. A combination of powdered graphite and clay from which some **crucible**s are made. Also see **centrifugal casting.**

plumb bob. Woodworking. See **plumb line.**

plumber's solder. Metalworking. See **solder.**

plumb line. Woodworking. A string with a weighted plumb bob on the end used to mark a vertical line or to locate one point directly below another.

To use a plumb line to mark a vertical line on a wall, coat the line with chalk and tie the unweighted free end to the point you designate, letting the plumb bob swing free. When it stops moving, secure the bob to the wall with one hand, then pluck the string away from the wall and let it snap back to mark the surface with the **chalked line.** See ill.

Plumb bob with line

plunge pot. Ceramics. A pot built around a wooden batten which is forced into a block of clay; the clay is thinned by stroking it upward around the batten, and the excess is trimmed away with a wire. Also see **press mold.**

plush. Quilts. Stitchery. See **velour.**

plush stitch. Crewel. Embroidery. Needlepoint. See **turkey work.**

ply. Knitting. The single strand of yarn made from spinning. Woolen knitting yarns are of various weights and are created by twisting together a number of plys (2-ply, 3-ply, etc.). In cotton yarns, it is the size of the ply rather than the number of plys that creates the thickness of the yarn.

plying. Spinning. Weaving. The twisting together of two or more **single ply** yarns. Plying is done either by machine or by hand using a **doubling stand** or **spinning wheel.** Done on a doubling stand the **twist** is very slight. On a spinning wheel, it is a tighter twist. For **novelty yarns,** plying must be done on a spinning wheel so that the yarn delivery and tension can be controlled and adjusted to obtain whatever novelty effect is desired. Also see **novelty yarn, spinning.**

plywood. Woodworking. A **laminate** of an odd number of thin layers of wood **veneers** glued together with the grain of each layer at right angles to the one beneath. All plywoods are graded for interior or exterior use. Exterior grade uses a moisture-resistant glue bond. The two basic types of plywood are softwood plywood and hardwood plywood.

Softwood plywood is essentially a utility material, used as a substructure in building construction and cabinet work. It is made of Douglas **fir,** southern **pine,** or **cedar,** and comes in 4′ × 8′ panels and in thicknesses of ¼–1¼″. It is graded according to the quality of both the face and back veneers used; some grades are as follows:

A—has few repairs, is of good quality, and is smooth
B—may have circular plugs or knots
C—has limited splits and knotholes
C—plugged like C grade, but holes are filled
D—poor quality and used for backs and interior use where it is not visible
N—a special defect-free grade made of select **heartwood** or **sapwood**

When labeled, the face veneer is noted first and the back second: A–C indicates a good face with a medium-poor back.

Hardwood plywood has a fine face veneer of a quality hardwood such as **birch, walnut, cherry, maple,** or **oak.** It is used for interior paneling and fine cabinet work. It is available in panels 24–48″ wide and 4–8′ long. Thicknesses range from ⅛″ to 1″. It is graded by number, such as:

1—flawless, best grade with well-matched grains
2—less precisely matched, with some small knots
3—good if painted

There are three types of inner plies: Lumber core is three-ply board with a very thick central ply made of **poplar** or **bass** and used for doors and tabletops. Particleboard core has a **particle board** center faced with veneers; this type of plywood is used mostly in cabinet work. In veneer core the inner plies are the same thickness as the face veneers. This plywood is used where strength is needed.

poached egg. Shell Carving. (*Ovulo ovum.*) A shell used for cameo carving that has a shiny, bright white exterior layer, a matte white **middle color,** and an extremely thin port wine **ground color.** The greatest strength of color is shown near the mouth. Also see **cowrie, helmet** and **Shell Carving: Shell, Tools and Preparation.**

pocket chisel. Woodworking. See **chisel.**

pocket hone. Gemcutting. See **lap.**

pocket parachute. Toys. See **parachute.**

point. Lacemaking. A term used to indicate **needle lace**s. The term is sometimes loosely applied, and will also refer to a lace of very fine quality—whether it is needle or **bobbin** made.

point. Weaving. See **herringbone.**

point carver. Gemcutting. Gemcutting **machinery** used for carving, engraving, and sculpturing **cameo**s and **intaglio**s. It consists of an arbor which supports a **carving point** at speeds up to 6,000 rpm, although normally operated at speeds from 2,000–4,000 rpm. Higher speeds are more efficient for the smaller carving points.

The point carver is tilted downward toward the operator at an angle from 30° to 45°; some models can be adjusted to any angle. Often the speed may be regulated by means of a foot treadle, as on a sewing machine. A hand rest is provided for holding the work against the carving tool. Some models have multiple arbors for using several different points in series. Also see **tube drill** and **Gemcutting: Tools and Materials.**

point de Venise. Lacemaking. (Also called Venetian point.) One of the finest examples of **needle lace.** Reticella and point de Venise share the same working technique (**buttonhole stitch**es and needle-worked **picot**s), but they differ greatly in design. Reticella is geometric, and point de Venise is quite curving and graceful, worked in a floral design. The units of design are always outlined with a **cordonnet.** When the cordonnet is especially heavy, the lace is called Venise à gros relief. Other variations of this lace are Venise à relief, Venise à la Rose or point de Rose, and Venise au lacet.

Lay a pattern drawn on paper over a double layer of cloth. With needle and thread make a structure of foundation threads over the pattern, 3 to 5 together, using a thread of fine, smooth quality, indicating the design motifs. Secure these with a stitch over them at widely spaced intervals, making these holding stitches through the paper pattern and the two layers of cloth. Upon this structure of foundation threads, work the buttonhole stitches, picots, and the cordonnet.

When the lace is finished, cut the securing stitches by sliding the scissors between the two layers of cloth, thus releasing the lace from the pattern.

point draw. Weaving. A **drawing-in draft** that takes a **straight draw** and runs it first in one direction and then in another, with a point occurring at the **harness** on which it reverses directions. In its simplest form, the draft begins at the first harness, proceeds to the last harness, and then comes back again to the first. This is often called an even point draw since both directions are the same length. However, the variations are many, some of which depend on the number of harnesses available. There should be at least 4 harnesses. The harness at the point of reversal has only one thread, whereas the other harnesses always have 2 threads to account for both directions. The thread at the point of reversal is called the point thread. To see the point

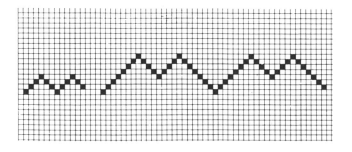

Point draws

drawing-in draft as a weave pattern, a **twill weave** treadling should be used. See ill. Also see **bird's eye pattern, diamond twill, goose-eye pattern, rose path.**

pointed threading draft. Weaving. See **point draw.**

pointed twill. Weaving. See **twill weave.**

pointillé. Bookbinding. A term used in book cover design that denotes a dotted background. It also refers to a seventeenth-century style of cover decoration characterized by tooled forms with dotted outlines. Also see **Lyonnaise style.**

pointillism. Rugmaking. Weaving. See **color blending.**

pointing. Stained Glass. The final procedure in fitting a stained-glass **panel** into place. A mastic gun (purchased in building-supply or hardware stores) is used to fill up any holes or grooves that remain.

point lace. Lacemaking. See **bobbin lace.**

points. Woodworking. Saws are graded by points, based on the number of teeth per inch. There is always one more point than the number of teeth per inch: if a saw has 10 teeth per inch, it is an 11-point saw.

point soldering. Jewelry. See **pick soldering.**

point tempering. A heating process that hardens the working edge or end of a steel tool.

point thread. Weaving. See **point draw.**

poker. Metalworking. See **blacksmithing tools.**

poke shuttle. Weaving. See **stick shuttle.**

polarization. Enameling. See **electroplating.**

pole horse. Toys. A **push horse** that has a single pole, or support, for the front half of the horse and a single pole at the back; the animal rests on two legs instead of four. Also see **cock horse.**

polish. Leather. See **Leatherwork: Finishing Leather.**

polisher. Bookbinding. A polisher is used to smooth irregularities from leather covers before **tooling.** See ill. Also see **bone folder.**

a. Polisher for the sides of a book

b. Polisher for the back and inside margins

polishing. Amber Carving. See **Amber Carving: Finishing.**

polishing. Ceramics. See **burnishing.**

polishing. Enameling. (Also called buffing.) A process of producing a smooth, lustrous, continuous surface by rubbing with buffs, ultrafine abrasives of medium hardness on soft but firm materials such as linen, canvas, felt, or leather. Polishing machines consist of an electric motor driving an arbor, either directly on the shaft of the motor or by a belt and pulleys, which has one or two tapered spindles which hold the disk-shaped buffs for rotation. The buff should turn its edge from the top toward you as you face it.

Enamel surfaces can be sanded and smoothed with fine emery paper used wet or dry, and buffed with tripoli or cerium oxide. **Metal** is polished with rouges consisting of **metal oxide**s in an oil or grease base. Also see **champlevé, cleaning metal, cloisonné.**

polishing. Gemcutting. The process of smoothing and refining gem material by rubbing to produce a perfect **luster.** Polishing is an abrasive operation using **abrasive** particles of various grits; sometimes the polishing compound is of lesser **hardness** than the gem material being polished.

Faceted gems are polished on polishing laps.

Polish unfaceted stones on a felt buffing wheel, or on leather, canvas, or muslin buffs, with polishing compounds mixed with water. The compounds are mixed to a creamy consistency and applied to the buff by hand or with a mop or brush reserved for this particular purpose. Use each polishing compound on its own buff uncontaminated by dust, grit, and other compounds.

The polishing **machinery** is operated horizontally or vertically, similar to **sanding** machines and **grinding wheels**. In vertical operation, the running edge of the buff is used; in horizontal operation, the flat surface of a wooden disk padded with leather is used.

Operation of buffs is done at speeds of 1,200 feet per minute on the perimeter, equivalent to 570 rpm for a leather buff 8″ in diameter. Faster speeds, up to 1,400 surface feet per minute, are used with felt buffs (equivalent to 670 rpm for an 8″ rock-hard felt buff).

For rapid polishing of many small similar articles, polishing is sometimes done by **tumbling.** Also see **cabochon, faceting, flat** and **Gemcutting: Hand Grinding and Polishing, Tools and Materials.**

polishing. Jet Carving. See **bead-polishing board, bow-drill** and **Jet Carving: Polishing.**

polishing. Jewelry. The process of rubbing a metal surface to refine its coarseness and produce a lustrous finish. An **abrasive polishing compound** differs from an abrasive **cutting compound** in that it removes less metal and does it more slowly.

If an abrasive is loosely applied to a buffing wheel, as opposed to being bonded to a paper or cloth or bonded to itself in the form of abrasive wheels and heads, the operation is known as **buffing.**

Technically, buffing follows polishing as a finishing procedure. Instead of abrading the metal, it rearranges the surface molecules to produce a **luster;** this is known as the Beilby effect.

Burnishing is another final surface treatment that increases luster without abrading.

Various articles lend themselves better to **hand polishing** because of their delicate construction. Others may be polished on **buffing machine**s or with **flexible shaft machine**s with special buffing or polishing heads. Also see **bright dip, buffing compound, heat oxidation, polishing cloth, thrumming.**

polishing. Plastics. See **Plastics: Finishing.**

polishing. Shell Carving. See **Shell Carving: Polishing.**

polishing. Tincrafting. Tin, a relatively soft metal, is subject to easy scratching and marring. In shining the material, it is advisable to proceed with caution. A gentle rubbing with fine steel wool will produce a soft burnished effect on the metal. With **tincan**s that have been lacquered by the manufacturer, use only soft soapy rags to avoid removing the colored surface.

polishing. Woodworking. See **Woodworking: Finishing.**

polishing buff. Gemcutting. See **polishing.**

polishing cloth. Jewelry. A cloth electrolytically impregnated with abrasive flour, powder tarnish retardant, or chemical polisher. Polishing cloths are used for **polishing** chains, beads, and other fragile pieces by hand when machine buffing would be unwise. Some abrasive agents used on the lintfree (often flannel) cloths are crocus powder, **aluminum oxide** (corundum), **emery,** rouges, and **tripoli.** Chamois skin can be used for both cleaning and polishing. Many fine chemically impregnated polishing cloths are commercially available. Also see **hand polishing, red rouge cloth.**

polishing compound. Gemcutting. See **abrasive.**

polishing compound. Jewelry. Metalworking. There are two basic classifications of polishing compounds: **abrasive**s (cutting compounds) that wear away the metal to remove surface imperfections, and coloring compounds that intensify color and sheen. Powdered natural abrasives such as **whiting, pumice,** and lime and cutting compositions such as tripoli, bobbing, crocus composition, white diamond polish, and greaseless compound are abrasives. Application of coloring compounds follows cutting. Some examples of coloring compounds are standard red, green, white, and porcelain rouge, and **lampblack.** These must be scrubbed off with soap and water after buffing because of their greasy or oily binding agents.

In pewterworking, a semidry tripoli with a nongreasy base is used for the beginning polishing, called cutting, and then lampblack mixed with kerosene is used for the final nonabrasive polishing and buffing.

Other polishes are called cut and color compounds (e.g., white, pink, green, and gray compounds), perform both functions at the same time, and are designed for use on particular metals. For example, green compound is used on stainless steel, chrome, and platinum. Also see **buffing, buffing compounds, pewterworking** and **Metalworking: Finishing.**

polishing compound. Plastics. A paste, **wax,** or powder used for polishing surfaces. When the polishing compound cuts or wears away the plastic, it is an **abrasive.**

For polishing plastic, use any of the commercially available brands—jeweler's rouge or tripoli—followed by a wax. Also see **Plastics: Finishing.**

polishing hood. Jewelry. A hood that fits around the **buffing** wheel to catch the dust thrown off by **buff**s and **brush**es. The more expensive units not only have polishing hoods, but also fans and filters to pull and catch the flying compounds. Less expensive units may merely fit around the buff; there is usually a pan in the bottom that should be filled with water that has a little detergent in it to help catch the dust. It is a good idea to purchase one with lights for good visibility when buffing. The polishing hood will also catch the work if it slips from your hands while buffing. See ill.

Light switch

Polishing hood

Politec. Plastics. See **acrylic paint.**

polka spider web lace. Lacemaking. See **sol lace.**

Pollack's Toy Museum. Puppets. Toys. A **toy theater** and museum in London that continues the tradition of juvenile drama. It is based on the original Pollack's that sold **toy sheets** from the 1870s into the 1930s. After a series of changes and closings, the museum is again open and producing colorful and original plays.

pollucite. Gemcutting. A white mineral used for **facet**ed gems. Pollucite has **hardness** of 6½, **specific gravity** of 2.86, and refractive index of 1.52. It is polished with Linde A on a tin **lap** or cerium oxide on a plastic lap. Also see **faceting, polishing, refraction.**

polyester. Plastics. A **thermosetting** plastic used primarily in liquid **resin** form for **casting** and **laminating.** It is also sold as premixed **molding compounds,** pastes, films, cast sheets, rods, and tubes. Its properties vary according to the ingredients with which it is mixed. Polyester **casting resins** are designed specifically for **casting;** they have comparatively low **exotherm** and may be a clear watery-white. Polyester **laminating resin** (artist's resin) must be reinforced with **fillers** or **reinforcing material** to control shrinking, warping, and **brittleness,** and to improve impact strength. Polyester resin has a limited **shelf life** and should be stored in a cool place. It may be dissolved by chlorinated **solvents** and strong alkalis and deteriorates in

sunlight unless **light-stabilized.** Polyester was developed between 1938 and 1942 and was then a classified defense material. The **catalyst** most widely used with polyester resin is methyl ethyl ketone peroxide (MEK-Px). Also see **Plastics: Casting.**

polyester. Stitchery. A generic term applied to manufactured **fiber**s which are made from a chemical composition of ethylene and terephtholic acid. Most polyesters do not take dye readily and have limited use for the batik or tie-dye artist. Even **fabric**s which are **blend**s of polyester with **natural fiber**s are not suitable for dyeing. Stitchers find polyesters difficult to handle in **hand appliqué,** but their advantages of wrinkle-resistance, strength, and quick-drying properties make them desirable for other uses.

polyester batting. Quilts. Stitchery. Toys. See **Dacron polyester** batting.

polyester resin technique. Stained Glass. (Also called casting polyester resin.) A technique similar to **lamination,** used with fused or single layers of stained glass. The technique encapsulates the glass layers in polyester resin. Before being cast in the resin, the glass may be stained, fired, acided, and painted, as for leaded glass. Scrap pieces can also be utilized in this technique.

The best mold is made of clear acrylic, its advantage being that it can be placed over a light box and all work done there. A curved mold can be made of shellacked **plaster of Paris.** Wood or metal covered with a rubber sheet can be used.

To prepare the glass for use, clean all the pieces with **acetone** or **alcohol** and dry them. When the resin has been mixed and hardener and any colorants have been added, pour a ¼″ layer of resin into the mold and place the first layer of glass onto it. Pour a second layer of resin so that it just covers the glass and add a second layer of glass. Then add more resin, and so on. The glass must be completely surrounded by the resin. The final layer is polyester resin floated over the whole composition. When it has set up, it can be planed and polished to a high gloss.

There is also a technique using layers of fiber glass with polyester resin to bond pieces of **antique glass** together into a window. In this technique layers of fiber glass and polyester resin are packed around the glass, leaving the glass free of the resin. Also see **aciding, firing, fused glass technique, painting on glass, staining** and **Stained Glass: Safety Precautions.**

polyester thread. Stitchery. Any of several kinds of sewing thread, similar in weight to **mercerized sewing thread,** but made of **polyester.** Some are springy or wiry and tend to twist when used for hand-sewing. **Synthetic thread**s are usually part or all polyester.

polyethylene. Plastics. A translucent, milky-white **thermoplastic** that feels warm and waxy to the touch. It is rigid or flexible depending on the thickness and is used for squeeze bottles, packaging, and sheathing for electric cables. It makes a good container for **resins** and **catalysts** because it is not affected by **solvents** at ordinary temperatures. It will, however, be dissolved by a number of solvents above 140° F. Polyethylene sheets may be used as a **mold** if supported by another rigid form. It may be used only for short-term or temporary needs, because it scratches easily. It needs no **mold release agent** for use with **polyester** and **epoxy.** Chill it in a refrigerator if the form does not release easily.

polyethylene binding. Batik and Tie-dye. A **tie-dye binding** method that uses polyethylene strips under the **binding materials.** It makes the material more resistant to the dye. The plastic can be used in narrow or wide strips over which rubber bands, thread, cord, or other binding can be used.

polymer. Plastics. An organic compound made up of repeated linked units of small molecules. It is synthesized in the making of **plastic.**

polymer emulsion. Candlemaking. (Also called polymer medium.) A transparent acrylic polymer latex varnish (water-soluble until dry) available in most art-supply stores. Polymer emulsion can be used as a binder to add to the durability of the sand mold in the creation of a **sand candle.**

polymer emulsion. Plastics. A synthetic emulsion (suspension) of minute particles of synthetic **resin** in water. It is used as a vehicle for binding color pigments in paints or as a protective **sealant.** There are three common types: an **acrylic** resin base (called acrylic polymer medium or acrylic emulsion); a polyvinyl base, which was an early invention; and a copolymer base, which combines two or more kinds of plastics to give flexibility and durability. Acrylic emulsion paints will mix and thin with water, are fast-drying, nontoxic, and nonflammable. Do not mix polymer emulsion paints with oil paints. Popular brand names include Liquitex, Acquatec, Shiva Acrylic, and Cryla (England).

Polymer emulsion also comes in gels (called gel medium), pastes for modeling, and **gesso.** The gel medium is polymer emulsion thickened to a consistency of heavy cream. It is white when wet but dries transparent and colorless unless mixed with pigment. Polymer emulsion paints may be mixed into it to create a viscosity and texture similar to that of artist's oil paints. It may also be used as a sealant on **foam.** Also see **acrylic paint, molding compound.**

polymerization. Plastics. The process of linking monomers (small simple molecules) with each other to form a **polymer** that has different characteristics from the original components. This process occurs in **curing.**

polymer medium. Candlemaking. See **polymer emulsion.**

polymer medium. Découpage. Papercrafts. (Also called acrylic emulsion.) A transparent acrylic polymer latex **varnish** that is water-soluble until it dries. It is available from art-supply stores as a liquid with a glossy or matte finish.

Although not a traditional découpage material, it can be used in shortcut projects as both a glue and a varnish.

polymer medium. Plastics. See **polymer emulsion.**

polymethyl methacrylate. Plastics. See **acrylic.**

polyolefin. Plastics. See **polypropylene.**

polyopticon. Toys. A less elaborate and cheaper version of the **magic lantern.** It was developed in America and, as did other **optical toy**s, represented the nineteenth-century fascination with early projection and photographic techniques. Another version was called the wonder camera. Also see **Toys: Optical Toys.**

polyoptic pictures. Toys. See **les métamorphoses** and **Toys: Optical Toys.**

polypropylene. Plastics. (Also called polyolefin.) A **thermoplastic** in film, fiber, sheeting, and molding compounds, that may be used for **mold**s. It is more durable than **polyethylene** but must be backed up by another material for rigidity and strength.

polypropylene cord. Macramé. A shiny cord used in macramé. Also see **Macramé: Tools and Materials.**

polyscope. Toys. See **debusscope.**

polystyrene. Metalworking. Plastics. Woodworking. (Also called styrene.) A plastic derived from coal (benzene and ethylene). It is produced in liquid, **foam,** and solid forms. Although it has been known since 1839, it was not put into commercial use until World War II. Styrofoam and Dylite are popular polystyrenes often used for making decorative objects. They are lightweight, easily carved, and can be covered with other materials such as **epoxy,** which adds durability. Styrene liquid is used as a dilutant for **polyester resin.** Also see **Plastics: Carving.**

polyurethane. Macramé. A man-made fiber available as macramé cord. Also see **Macramé: Tools and Materials.**

polyurethane. Metalworking. Plastics. (Also called urethane.) A plastic used for **adhesive**s, rigid and flexible **foam,** and protective coatings. The solid, film, sheet, and liquid forms are **thermoplastic;** the foam form is thermosetting. Urethane deforms at between 200° and 300° F and burns slowly, although flame-resistant types are available. It resists water and common **solvent**s. Ultraviolet rays from sunlight discolor white foam. Chemicals can be purchased to fix foam urethane in place, but the fumes given off are toxic. Wear an organic vapor mask, have excellent ventilation, and keep the chemicals off your skin. The foam can be cut with a hand **hacksaw** blade, a **band saw,** or a hot wire.

In metalworking, liquid urethane is painted or sprayed on finished metal as a protective sealant to help prevent discoloration from weathering.

In plastics, urethane in foam form is used for direct

carving of sculpture and model making. Also see **Metalworking: Finishing.**

polyurethane. Woodworking. (Also called urethane.) A synthetic **varnish** that produces a very tough and flexible surface for both exterior and interior wood surfaces. It is highly resistant to acids, alkalis, grease, hot and cold water, and alcohol. Polyurethane is relatively fast drying, and is applied like varnish. Also see **Woodworking: Finishing.**

polyvinyl alcohol. Plastics. (Also called PVA.) A product of **acetylene** and **acetic acid.** It is used in sheet, film, and liquid forms as a **mold release agent** for **polyester resin,** in white glues, such as Elmer's Glue All and Sobo, and in patching paste compounds filled with wood flour. It is also a main ingredient in **polymer emulsion** paints.

polyvinyl chloride. Plastics. (Also called PVC and vinyl chloride.) A plastic formed in a reaction between **acetylene** and chlorine. It was discovered in France 130 years ago but was not made commercially available until World War II when military researchers found a **plasticizer** for it. It may be used in sheets for vacuum forming or in film form (e.g., Saran Wrap) as an **air shield** or protective covering for work equipment. One derivative called Vinylite VMCH, a vinyl chloride acetate, is used for outdoor mural painting. This plastic is commonly used in plumbing pipes and as an ingredient in some hair sprays. Current cancer research indicates that constant exposure to the atomized spray form and to the uncured product is hazardous to one's health.

polyweb. Stitchery. Toys. A trade name for a **nonwoven material** that has **adhesive** on both sides. It is **set** by heat and is made for use on hems, trims, and facings. It is both washable and dry cleanable, and is therefore excellent for adding details to **fabric** for **stuffed toy**s and various cloth **doll**s.

Pomegranate. Quilts. (Also called Love Apple.) An **appliqué quilt block** design using a single pomegranate, sometimes with leaves, as the central design.

Pomeranian. Basketry. See **willow.**

pommawonga. Toys. See **spear-the-fish.**

pompom. Weaving. A small ball of yarn attached to a finished woven article as trim. Pompoms are made of a soft yarn around two cardboard disks with holes in the center. The yarn is threaded through a needle in order to cover the disks with close stitches that pass through the hole in the center and over the outer edge. When the whole surface of the disks is abundantly covered, scissors are inserted between the two disks and the outer edge threads are all cut. A piece of yarn is very tightly wound several times around the yarn that is seen between the two disks. It is secured with a firm knot and left with ends long enough to attach the pompom. The disks are then cut and removed from the finished pompom. The outer yarn tips can be fluffed up if desired. See ill. Also see **tassel.**

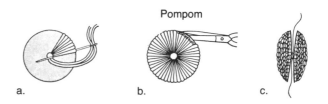

Pompom

a.   b.   c.

pompon. Quilts. Stitchery. A ball or **tuft** which results from the tying together of a number of short threads or **yarn**s. The fluffy balls or puffs are used decoratively on **pillow**s and **banner**s. They look similar to the commercially available **ball fringe,** though in making your own you can determine color and size.

In a **tufted quilt** or **popcorn quilt** the pompon results when the cotton cord or **candlewicking** is sewn into place and then clipped. The ends of the yarns spread to form the tufts or pompons.

To make a pompon, two circles are cut from cardboard the size the finished pompon is to be. A quarter-inch hole is punched or cut in the center of each circle. With the cardboard circles placed together, two strands of yarn are sewn through both. Stitches are merely wrapped around the cardboard and through the center, wrapping around and around the cardboard rings. When the cardboard disks are well covered, yarns are snipped between the two disks, cutting all strands at the outside edge. A strand of yarn is drawn down between the disks to tie all the yarns tightly together. The end of this yarn is knotted and trimmed to the same length as the others. When the disks are removed, the yarn ends are fluffed out to make a ball. Any uneven yarns are trimmed.

poncho. Stitchery. A blanketlike **garment** which has a hole in the middle for the head and hangs over the shoulders like a cape. The poncho came originally from Spanish America and has become a popular design for handwoven and hand-decorated use because of its simple lines. It is a preferred design for batik and tie-dye **fabric**s since it is a single piece, or nonsewn garment, requiring no cutting and no **seam**s in the treated fabric.

pontil. Glasswork. See **punty.**

pontil mark. Stained Glass. See **rondel.**

pony bead. Beadwork. The first **trade bead** to be widely distributed to the North American Indians. Pony beads, so named because they were carried in by the traders' ponies, were used on the plains from about 1800 to 1860. These round beads varied in size, usually around $\frac{1}{8}''$ in diameter with large holes, making them adaptable for stitching with sinew onto leather. Pony beads were limited to blue, black, white, and occasionally yellow and red.

Pooh Bear. Toys. See **Winnie-the-Pooh.**

pool retting. Spinning. See **flax.**

"Poonah" work. Stenciling. See **theorem work.**

poor child's doll. Toys. An imaginatively made doll made using almost any object for a body. The **shoe doll** is one example. The **Museum of Childhood** in Edinburgh contains other **slum toy**s made from **knucklebones** and rolled fabrics. Almost any child will devise such a doll when no other is available. A **spool**, a handkerchief, a **skittle**, a rolled blanket, a wooden spoon—all become dolls to the imaginative child. In India today, children even fashion dolls from rolled newspapers. The doll devised from any available material is also a **universal toy**. Because these dolls are usually played with and then discarded, they are seldom saved or collected. Also see **Toys: Dolls.**

poor man's lacquer. Découpage. See **arte pover.**

"pop." A shortened version of "popular" which refers to the utilization of trite and ordinary everyday "popular" subject matter in various art forms. In **wall hanging**s or **banner**s, subjects from comic strips, such as "Wonder Woman," and advertisements become the focal points of the design. Pop art usually involves the replica of a popular or familiar object in another medium, often taking commercial advantage of the familiarity of the subject. Also see **funk.**

popcorn quilt. Quilts. (Also called snowball quilt.) **Pompom**s or puffs of **tufting** and **candlewicking** produce a pattern of soft white balls. These are sometimes referred to as "popcorn," and quilts using this method may be referred to as "popcorn quilts." They are usually **white-on-white.**

popcorn stitch. Crochet. A stitch that creates a **raised pattern** similar to the **cluster**, but worked more tightly to form a ball or "popcorn" shape. Also see **Crochet: Basic Stitches.**

popgun. Toys. (Also called cork gun.) A **folk toy** that, because of the loud noise it makes, is also a **sound toy**. It consists of a tube and piston attached to a handle. A cork is attached by string to the end of the piston and drawn back through the tube to fit tight in the end of the tube. When the piston is pressed forward the cork is forced out with a loud pop. Although it is a shooting toy, it is safe and enjoyed primarily as a **noisemaker**. See ill.

Popguns

a.   b.

poplar. Woodworking. (Also called aspen.) A lightweight softwood that varies in color from light yellow to dark yellow-green with brown heartwood. Although it is not strong and bruises easily, it has excellent working qualities and is good for beginning woodcarvers. It is also used for boxes, **plywood** core, painted furniture, and whittling.

poppet. Toys. An old name for a **doll**, and one sometimes used to refer to the **Flanders baby**, or **penny wooden doll.**

popping. Metalworking. See **backfire.**

popsicle stick. Toys. See **craft stick.**

popular arts. Those arts which, along with the **folk art**s, comprise the **vernacular arts** of any area or place. The popular arts tend to follow a general pattern of acceptance. They are enjoyed, used, and appreciated by the common man. As styles and customs change, they are discarded and ignored. Sometime later they appear again, popular to intellectuals or artists who enjoy them in a different way. Soon after this they appear in antique shops, and finally as collector's items much prized by collectors and museums.

The popular arts may be garish, crude, bright, and vulgar. There is often an air of complexity, vitality, and elaborate detail. Impermanent materials are often used, and much of horror and the macabre may be found. All told, the popular arts are full of energy.

These arts are almost always ignored or disregarded while they are in popular use. Later, they will be collected. Those areas which comprise the popular arts include parade floats, mannikins, fireworks, funeral accessories, campaign buttons, posters, and signs. The popular arts of a century ago would have included carousels, taxidermy, the wagons, carts or boats of itinerant workmen or repairmen, stages and tents of performers of all kinds, horsehair wreathes, and greeting cards.

popular theater. Puppets. Historically, a theater "of the people" in which **marionette** and **puppet** performances were presented on portable stages. The shows used **stock character**s and were common, public, and immensely popular. Now, a few remaining **Punch and Judy show**s, mostly in England, are all that have survived of the once spectacular plays. The theaters were usually transportable, and performances, while professional, were improvised and unliterary, and filled with stock characters. Also see **street theater, "zanni."**

porcelain. Ceramics. A type of **clay body** comprised of **kaolin** and combined with **feldspar** and **flint.** It fires white at high temperatures and matures into a hard, scratch-proof, dense, **vitreous** body resembling glass. Porcelain objects are generally made from **mold**s because of the low level of **plasticity** in the clay body. When a porcelain clay body is fired in **oxidation**, the color is a warm off-white; when it is fired in **reduction**, the color is a bluish white although it appears as pure white.

porcelain doll. Toys. See **china doll.**

porcelain glaze. Ceramics. A hard **glaze** used on **porcelain ware**, with a high **silica** content. **Feldspar** is the principal material in porcelain glazes, which are fired to **cone**s 8–13. Also see **celadon, feldspar glaze.**

porcelain rouge. Jewelry. See **buffing compound.**

porcelain tile. Mosaics. Commercial **tile** made of a porcelain-type ceramic material and sold with both glazed and unglazed surfaces. This tile is produced in a variety of shapes and sizes, including hexagons and rectangles, but the most common version is the 1″ square. The unglazed variety has a soft, smooth surface; the glazed type comes in a range of colored-glass glazes over a white ceramic base. Porcelain tile is both cheap and readily available, but has a rather uninspiring uniformity of shape and color. Also see **Mosaics: Tools and Materials.**

porcupine. Stained Glass. See **striations.**

porcupine quill embroidery. Embroidery. This type of work was carried out by North American Indians. Quillwork was done on moccasins, knife cases, leggings, and costume accessories of all kinds. It was done in four different ways: by sewing, weaving, wrapping, or, in the case of birchbark, by inserting the quills into holes made by an awl. The most usual varieties were done on leather.

Quills were dyed in a beautiful range of shades, laid down one by one on the surface, and sewn in place with a fine leather thong. In order to conceal the sewing thread, each quill was lapped back and forth over the stitches as they were taken.

The Iroquois tribes of New York State decorated their costumes for war dances with quill embroidery, the Sioux Indians of South Dakota made gloves decorated with it, and the Plains Indians worked their jackets with quills in crosshatched designs. Sometimes quill embroidery was combined with **beadwork.**

pore spacing. Gemcutting. See **grinding wheel.**

porosity. Ceramics. The degree of **absorption** in a **ware.** **Bisque** is porous, whereas fired ware is nonabsorbent, or **vitreous.**

porosity. Jewelry. The density of holes that can be seen at or just below the surface of a **casting** after filing. They can appear singly or in numerous groupings throughout a casting. Small holes are caused by the incomplete escape of gases during the casting, due to improper venting; during cooling, due to the slight shrinkage of the metal; or from overheating the metal immediately prior to casting. To a certain extent porosity can be driven deeper into the casting by **annealing** the metal after casting. Also see **centrifugal casting, vent.**

porosity. Shell Carving. Shell is a fairly porous material and accepts dye well. Shell is most easily worked when soaked in water 3–21 days previous to carving. Unfinished pieces should be stored in water between carving sessions. Keep tools lubricated with water while working to avoid clogging and undue wear.

porrey cross. Weaving. The crossed **warp ends** coming at the end of the warp. This would be the end to come last as the warp is being wound in the **beaming.** Porrey crosses are usually necessary only with certain types of beaming where the **cross** is transferred from one spot to another. Some weavers, especially those using **warping reels** in making the warp, automatically put the porrey cross in whether or not it is needed. Also see **cross, warping.**

portable belt sander. Woodworking. See **sanding tools.**

portable electric drill. Woodworking. See **drilling tools.**

portable grinder. Metalworking. See **grinding tools.**

portable light box. Stained Glass. (Also called light box.) A square or rectangular frame of wood on short legs used as an aid to transfer a drawing or **cartoon** to paper or glass; also used to facilitate assembling and cutting glass pieces. The frame is constructed with a groove all around the box near the top edge so that ¼″ **glass** or **Plexiglas** can slide into the top. Several fluorescent lights should be attached to the bottom of the box about 2–3″ away from the top so that the glass does not crack from the heat.

If an alternative to fluorescence is preferred, an ordinary light bulb can be attached to one end. A tin reflector lining covering the bottom of the box will cause light to be reflected through the top. Also see **backlighting, cutting bench.**

portee cross. Weaving. The crossed **warp** threads coming at the beginning of a warp. This is the **cross** or lease used by most weavers to maintain the order of the warp. The beginning of the warp is the end left out of the **chain** that is wound around the **warp beam** first. Also see **warping.**

Porter, Rufus. Stenciling. A nineteenth-century American artist, craftsman, and jack-of-all-trades who developed and popularized a rapid method of combining stenciling and freehand painting for mural decoration. Using the method he could cover an entire room with scenes in a few hours. Generalized scenes of country panoramas were depicted rather than particular local scenes. Porter traveled throughout Maine, New Hampshire, and Massachusetts as an itinerant painter, producing murals of the New England countryside with the short-cut aid of stencils, which were applied to a hand-painted background for all the detail work. Porter later founded and edited the "New York Mechanic and Scientific American" journal. Also see **Stenciling: Background and History.**

portfolio. Quilts. A collection of **quilt blocks** in **pieced** or **appliquéd** designs. In planning a new quilt, a quilter may select a pattern from his or her portfolio. Also see **sampler quilt.**

portrait doll. Toys. Any doll made to resemble a real person. Such dolls have been manufactured at various times to depict current celebrities. Now they are usually individually made dolls and are sometimes produced in jest or satire as soft sculpture. Photosilkscreening may be used in a realistic portrait doll, although any **dollmaking** method lends itself to portraits.

Portuguese border stitch. Crewel. Embroidery. A technique in which a series of parallel stitches (bars) are laid down as the foundation for the raised slanting stitches. Start at the base of the laidwork, and use a blunt tapestry needle. Work four straight stitches around the first two bars. Do not go through the material. At the fourth stitch, pass only under top bar (**a.**). Work two slanting stitches around the next two bars. Work the second stitch only under the second bar (**b.**). Work the other side beginning at the base and slanting the needle in the opposite direction (**c.**). See ill.

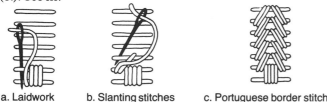

a. Laidwork   b. Slanting stitches   c. Portuguese border stitch

Portuguese knot. Crewel. Embroidery. A single **stem stitch** over which two tight loops are wrapped. This is recommended for a thin line effect.

Using a blunt tapestry needle, begin with a stem stitch. Come up at A, go down at B and holding the thread to the right of the needle, come up at C, midway between A and B. Pull thread tight so the stitch lies flat.

Slide the needle under the first stitch at D, and bring it out on the other side just below C. Do not go through the material. Pull thread tight, then slide the needle under the stem stitch again, so that it lies in place just below the first coil (**a.**).

Pull thread tight and make another stem stitch, going down at E and coming up in the same hole formed by the stitch at B. Hold the thread to the right of the needle (**b.**). Pull thread tight. Now slide the needle through both the first and second stem stitch where they overlap, just below B (**c.**).

To continue, slide the needle under the second stem stitch and again wrap it twice around (**d.**). See ill.

Portuguese knot

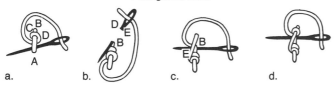

a.   b.   c.   d.

positive design. Block Printing. Papercrafts. See **Papercrafts.**

positive print. Block Printing. Papercrafts. A **block print** in which the pattern is cut in **relief,** with the background cut away. When printed, the pattern appears dark on the white paper. Also see **Block Printing: Designing and Transferring.**

positive shape. Batik and Tie-dye. Stitchery. The prominent part of a design that is added to a **background.** It suggests a specific form, in contrast to a **negative shape** whose form is dependent on the positive form. The use of positive and negative forms in design offers a play between foreground and background in which the parts can be transposed and reversed.

post. Woodworking. See **wood.**

postage-stamp quilt. Quilts. A **pieced quilt** made up from tiny squares, sometimes measuring less than an inch across. The number of stitches per inch of **quilting,** or the minuteness of pieced **block**s, sometimes became an obsession of quiltmakers'.

poster paint. Puppets. Toys. Somewhat **opaque water-base paint**s of a creamy consistency, similar to **tempera,** available in a variety of bright colors. When dry, they are not waterproof and will smear easily. A coating of **lacquer** or **fixative** will make the painted surface more permanent.

post stitch. Crewel. Embroidery. See **bullion knot.**

post vise. Metalworking. See **vise.**

pot. Ceramics. See **Ceramics: Form.**

potash. Enameling. See **frit.**

potassium permanganate. Batik and Tie-dye. **Dye** crystals that produce a brown color. The crystals are water soluble and can be used to dye cotton, linen, or rayon, although they work best on wool and silk. While inexpensive and commonly available, the color **fade**s badly. To use the dye, dissolve ½ teaspoon potassium permanganate crystals in 1 cup hot water. (Increase proportions for dyeing anything larger than a small sample: approximately 2 tablespoons potassium permanganate crystals to 3 quarts water.) Immerse fabric that has been **wetted out** and keep it in the liquid for from a few seconds up to 5 minutes. Remove from **dyebath** and let the material sit until it changes in color from purple to brown. Repeated dippings will deepen the color. Rinse, wash, and iron.

Fabric dyed in this way can readily take **discharge dyeing.** A **lemon-juice discharge** works well.

potassium sulfide. Enameling. See **liver of sulfur.**

potassium sulfide. Jewelry. See **liver of sulfur.**

potato block. Fabric Printing. A common potato, or other hard vegetable such as a turnip or carrot, that has been cut in half and a design cut into the cut side to produce a **printing block.** This cut side is then coated with **textile color** and printed as desired. Also see **potato block printing.**

potato block printing. Block Printing. A simple block printing technique in which the flat side of a halved raw potato is used as a **printing block.** Other hard vegetables, such as carrots, turnips, or beets, may be used. Because of the nature of the vegetable surface, it is best suited for relatively simple patterns.

Select a crisp potato or hard vegetable. Cut it in half across or lengthwise. The moisture in the potato should be wiped off with paper toweling, or the potato may be drained, cut side down, on toweling for about half an hour. Both halves of the potato may be used as blocks (**a.**).

The potato half can be printed just as it is, or with lines or patterns cut into the surface. The pattern may be incised to produce a negative print, or the background cut away to produce a **positive print (b.)**.

Potato printing is done with traditional block printing methods. **Block printing ink** or tempera paint may be applied by brushing the ink onto the raised part of the design. Inking can also be done by pressing the potato block onto ink that has been rolled out with a **brayer** onto a piece of glass. For a clear print, a stack of six or so layers of paper toweling, or napkins, should be placed underneath the paper to be printed. The potato block is stamped down on the paper and care is taken not to smudge it as it is removed.

Designs for potato printing should be simple, not requiring elaborate joining or **registration. Stamping** a repeated design with spaces between each motif is the most successful approach. See ill. Also see **Block Printing: Designing and Transferring, Printing Techniques.**

a. Potato block   b. Positive print

potato block printing. Fabric Printing. The procedures for printing **fabric** with designs cut into potato blocks are basically the same as those for block printing on paper, except that **textile color** must be used. Also see **Fabric Printing: Designing.**

potch. Gemcutting. See **opal.**

pot gauge. Ceramics. (Also called throwing gauge.) A measuring tool for production or **repetition throwing** of a series of pieces the same size, such as cups and bowls. It can be a stationary **caliper** or a stick stuck in a wad of clay to gauge the height of pots to be thrown. Also see **Ceramics: Throwing.**

pot glass. Stained Glass. See **pot-metal glass.**

potichomania. Découpage. See **découpage on ceramics.**

pot life. Plastics. (Also called working life.) The length of time that a **catalyzed resin** will remain liquid and workable before **setting up.** It can range from a few minutes to several days, depending on the temperature, humidity, and other variables. Not to be confused with **shelf life.**

pot-metal glass. Stained Glass. (Also called pot glass.) The term for **antique glass** made of a single color spread uniformly throughout the **glass.** The pot is the steel-lined vat in which the molten glass is kept in flux while the antique glass is being blown. All hand-blown glass is theoretically pot glass because it is colored in the pot in a molten state.

Potomac Pride. Quilts. See **Coronation.**

pot-scrubbers. Stained Glass. See **brushes.**

potter's knife. Ceramics. See **fettling knife.**

potter's wheel. Ceramics. A flat disk that revolves on a vertical stick and holds the clay used in throwing. A power wheel is a motor-driven potter's wheel. The speed is controlled by a foot or hand lever which engages or disengages the motor. See ill.

Potter's wheel

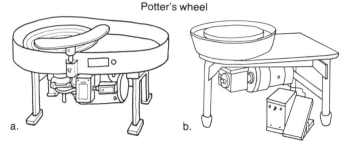

a.   b.

pottery. Ceramics. Generally, any fired **earthenware** clay object; more specifically, containers such as pots, dishes, and similar forms. Also, the factory or studio where pottery is made.

potting. Plastics. See **embedment.**

pounce. China and Glass Painting. See **silk pad.**

pounce. Crewel. Embroidery. See **Crewel: Transferring a Design.**

pounce. Quilts. To print a design, usually on fabric, by forcing a powder of charcoal, **chalk,** or clay through small perforations in a paper pattern. The pattern produced is called a perforated pattern. This method is rarely used today. Also see **Quilts: Quilting.**

pounce. Stenciling. A small velvet pad used to apply bronze powder through a stencil to a tacky varnish surface. Also see **Stenciling.**

pounce bag. Stained Glass. A small cloth bag filled with **whitening,** used to trace **template** shapes onto **opaque glass.**

pouncer. Quilts. A tool used for pouncing. Powdered **chalk** or charcoal tied tightly in fabric and attached to the end of a stick may be used as a pouncer. It is used in a light beating motion, like playing a drum. The powder is forced out of the pouncer through a perforated paper pattern, transferring the design onto the fabric beneath. Also see **Quilts: Quilting.**

pounce wheel. Crewel. Embroidery. See **sawtooth wheel.**

pounce wheel. Leather. See **space marker.**

poupard doll. Toys. A legless doll, usually a **baby doll** wrapped in gowns or blankets. Early ones were made of **papier mâché** or wood. In some cases, the wooden heads were attached to a dowel that ran the length of the body and emerged at the bottom as a handle. This made it possible to move the doll's head from side to side.

poured candle. Candlemaking. A **taper** formed by pouring. The term also applies to **molded candle**s. Also see **Candlemaking: Pouring.**

pouring. Candlemaking. See **Candlemaking: Pouring.**

pouring basin. Metalworking. (Also called cup.) The cup-shaped depression cut into the top surface of a **mold** for **casting**, into which the molten metal is poured. This cup connects to a system of tubes within the mold to the mold cavity, enabling the metal to fill all parts of the casting. This cup shape is necessary to minimize the turbulence caused by casting metal directly into the **sprue**. It also lets the caster reach a good pouring speed before any metal enters the mold cavity.

pouring glaze. Ceramics. See **Ceramics: Glazing.**

pouring shank. Metalworking. See **tongs.**

pouring tongs. Metalworking. See **tongs.**

Poussah. Toys. See **balance toy.**

powdered asbestos. Jewelry. **Asbestos** in a powdered form. Water is added and kneaded into it, producing a doughlike consistency. Areas to be protected from heat during **soldering** can be covered with the mixture, or it can be used to form a wall that will keep the flame from hitting specific areas that you do not want brought to a high heat. Powdered asbestos can also be used to support pieces during soldering. After soldering it becomes hardened, but it can be broken away by tapping or pulling with **tweezers** after it has cooled. Remove asbestos before **pickling**, or it will contaminate the **pickle**. Powdered asbestos is not good for use in protecting a gemstone, unless the stone is far from the area that is being soldered, as the heat conducted through the metal can crack the stone. Also see **bismuth block.**

powdered pumice. Jewelry. See **buffing compound, pumice.**

power plane. Woodworking. See **plane.**

power sanding. Plastics. See **Plastics: Finishing.**

power saw. Metalworking. Plastics. Woodworking. Any of a variety of motorized saws used to cut and shape wood. Large versions of many of these saws replaced **hand saw**s early in the Industrial Revolution, powered first by watermills and then by steam and internal-combustion engines. Modern stationary shop tools are now usually run by electric motors, and the chain saw is the only portable saw sometimes powered by a gasoline motor instead of by electricity. Skilled supervision and instruction are necessary before attempting to operate any power shop equipment.

Power saws may be classed according to type of cutting **blade** and action (circular, continuous, and reciprocating); because of the overlapping functions and the rapid prolif-

eration of portable power tools recently, there is considerable confusion in the names given by manufacturers to some of the reciprocating-blade saws.

In all circular-blade saws the blade is circular and rotates in the direction of the cut; blades for **crosscutting**, **ripping**, cutting **veneer**, **dado**ing, and other special functions are readily interchangeable, although a combination blade will do most simple cutting adequately.

A circular saw is a portable power saw with a circular blade 6–10″ in diameter (**a.**). The blade angle and depth of cut are usually adjustable, making it possible to **bevel**, dado, and cut **groove**s.

A table (or bench or arbor) saw is a shop saw with an 8–15″ blade mounted beneath the cutting table and adjustable for both cutting height and angle; it is used primarily for production cutting and precision cabinet work (**b.**). The wood is fed over the turning blade; the saw has an adjustable **fence** and a slotted table surface to accept a **miter gauge** for cutting **miter**s and squaring ends.

A radial arm saw is a circular saw suspended in an adjustable track above the cutting table; the wood is placed on the table and the saw and motor move across to do the cutting, although for ripping, the wood may be fed through the stationary saw. Although versatile, this is potentially one of the most dangerous shop tools.

There are 2 main continuous-blade saws. A band saw is a power shop machine that uses a continuous band of flexible steel with teeth cut on one edge (**c.**). Easily interchangeable blades may be used for wood, metal, plastic, or other materials; they come in varying widths for heavy or light material. The saw may be used for cutting irregular scrollwork and curves as well as for regular straight cuts. The size of the band saw is measured by the diameter of the pulleys on which the blade runs (14–30″) or by the length of the blade.

A chain saw is a gasoline- or electric-powered portable saw with an exposed blade and a continuous toothed chain. It is used to fell and cut up trees and for rough construction work; its **kerf** is too wide for any fine work. Extreme care is necessary in its operation; the exposed blade can lop off an arm or leg with no trouble.

Reciprocating-blade saws most closely imitate the back-and-forth motion of a hand saw, and are powered developments of the compass saw, keyhole saw, and coping saw. Blades are of two types: the slender blade, which must be held taut on both ends (as in the hand coping saw and the power scroll saw), and the rigid, pointed saberlike blade (similar to that of the keyhole and compass saws, but smaller), used in the reciprocating and saber saws.

A scroll (or jig) saw is a stationary saw with a coping-saw blade held vertically between an arm over the small table and the reciprocating motor beneath, used for cutting fine irregular shapes in thin wood or plastic. Many scroll saws may also be used with the rigid saberlike blades. The saw size is measured from the blade to the rear support for the upper arm, and is commonly 18–24″.

A saber (or portable jig or bayonet) saw is a popular and versatile small saw useful for cutting curves in relatively thin material; the saber blade runs perpendicular to the body of the saw (**d.**). Some models have variable-speed motors. Special blades for plastic, metal, and wood are available.

A reciprocating (or large saber) saw is larger than, but similar to, the saber saw; it uses similar blades but they are larger and run parallel to the elongated body (**e.**). It is used for fast roughing in construction, where a compass saw might be used. See ill.

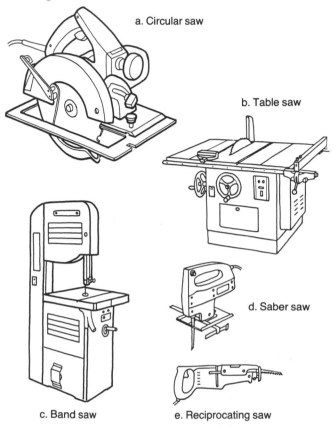

a. Circular saw

b. Table saw

c. Band saw

d. Saber saw

e. Reciprocating saw

power wheel. Ceramics. See **potter's wheel.**

pozzuolana. Mosaics. A volcanic rock used in the powdered state as a natural **cement** by early mosaicists.

Prairie Flower. Quilts. See **Prairie Rose.**

Prairie Lily. Quilts. See **Lily.**

Prairie Rose. Quilts. (Also called Missouri Rose, Prairie Flower, Rose Tree.) An **appliqué quilt block** design bold in pattern and color. It shows a central stem flanked by two

Prairie Rose

smaller stems that join at the base to make the letter U. Leaves, flowers, and buds adorn the stems. The block is reminiscent of the Pennsylvania Dutch style, combining strength, vigor, and a charmingly naïve use of natural forms. See ill.

Prairie Star. Quilts. See **Harvest Sun.**

prase. Gemcutting. See **quartz.**

praxinoscope. Toys. An **optical toy** similar to the **phenakistoscope.** It uses two drums on which a series of figures is shown. The background, or scenery, remains stationary. Through the use of mirrors the images of moving figures appear on the screen of the background. As do many other optical toys, it illustrates the persistence of impressions on the retina. Also see **Toys: Optical Toys.**

praxinoscope theater. Toys. A box containing a **praxinoscope** and the screen on which animation is shown. The box housed the equipment and then opened to become the theater.

precious coral. Coral Carving. See **coral.**

precious metal. Jewelry. Primarily gold, silver, and platinum. Although there are other precious metals, these are most often used by craftspeople. Some of the others have undesirable qualities, such as extreme **brittleness.** Also see **base metal, noble metal.**

precipitated chalk. Ivory and Bone Carving. See **chalk.**

precision casting. Metalworking. See **lost-wax casting.**

precut yarn. Rugmaking. Weaving. Yarn that has been cut into short lengths in order to knot into **pile.** This can be done over a homemade **gauge** or the yarn can be bought precut and packaged in small bundles. It is used in making **woven, needleworked** or **latch-hooked** pile **rug**s. Also see **rya.**

preform. Gemcutting. A stone that has been ground to an approximation of its final shape prior to **faceting.** Sometimes material for **tumbling** is performed on a **grinding wheel** to approximate geometrical shapes. A shape sawn from a slab for **cabochon** cutting is called a blank.

A preform for a brilliant cut should be rounded, not conical. The crown, the widest portion, should be ⅓ the overall height and the pavillion, the truncated portion, should be ⅔ the height (**a.**). For a double-mirror brilliant cut the proportions should be ¼ to ¾ for the extra row of facets in the pavillion. The girdle should not meet in a sharp line, but in a thin (¹/₆₄–¹/₃₂″) band to prevent chipping.

A preform for the step or emerald cut is square with the lower portion curving to a ridge. The crown can be ¼ the total height, the pavillion being ¾ (**b.**). A deeply colored gem material can be preformed ⅓ crown, ⅔ pavillion. The corners are just barely touched, as they must be ground to exact size on the **faceting unit.** See ill.

a. Preform for brilliant cut   b. Preform for step or emerald cut

preforming. Gemcutting. Preforming is the process of rough-shaping a gemstone for **faceting.** Examine the stone carefully for color and clarity and decide where the table (the flat top of the finished gem) should be. If the stone has **cleavage,** the table should be cut at least 15° off the cleavage plane. Holding the stone by the fingers, first grind a flat area where the table will be on a 220 grit wheel. Use water abundantly to prevent overheating and to flush away the cuttings. Still holding the stone by hand, continue the grinding of the table, first on the coarse side of a **lap,** and then on the fine side. The table is now ready to be polished. Moisten the polishing compound with water in a little jar until it reaches a thick, creamy consistency. Apply the polishing compound to the polishing lap and polish the table until all scratches are removed and examination with a 10 power **loupe** shows a smooth surface. Go back to the 220 grit wheel and proceed to grind the girdle, keeping the edges at exact right angles to the table. Check the roundness of the stone in a **template.** Try to produce the largest **preform** possible, but remember that the finished height should be three-quarters of the finished diameter of the stone. Use a sharp set of dividers or a vernier caliper for making measurements. Having ground the girdle edge at right angles with the table, turn the bottom of the piece of rough to the wheel and carefully grind away any excess material till you achieve a form looking like half an onion set on top of a slice of tomato—the slice of tomato representing the girdle edge. The preform for a brilliant is completed.

For grinding a preform for a step cut, use a rectangular blank. At least two-thirds of the preform should be below the girdle. Also see **dopping, facet.**

preheat. Metalworking. To heat a metal to red-hot in preparation for **flame cutting, brazing,** or **fusion welding.** This is done by moving the welding torch around the area, usually in a circular pattern. When flame cutting, hold the cutting torch in one spot after heating the general area until a **puddle** develops, then depress the oxygen lever for a **kerf** cut. When welding, the puddle is started in the same way and a bead is run along the seam to be welded. Thorough preheating is especially necessary for metals that disperse heat rapidly, such as cast **iron** and **aluminum.**

prehnite. Gemcutting. Calcium and aluminum silicates **crystal**lized in the orthorhombic system or in compact crypto-crystalline masses. It has **hardness** of 6, **specific gravity** of 2.8 to 3, refractive indices of 1.615 and 1.645, vitreous **luster,** and granular **fracture.** It is translucent and occurs in colorless and yellow-green varieties. Prehnite is polished with tin oxide on a leather buff for **cabochon**s and on a tin **lap** with Linde A for **facet**ed gems. Also see **faceting, polishing, refraction.**

Premium Star. Quilts. See **Bear's Paw.**

preparing fabric. Batik and Tie-dye. See **removing size, removing fabric finish** and **Batik and Tie-dye: Fabrics for Dyeing, Preparing the Fabric.**

presentation quilt. Quilts. A quilt made by a group, with each individual contributing a **block.** The presentation was sometimes at a public gathering, where each block was presented separately. The blocks were then **assemble**d and quilted. Ministers, doctors, or notable community leaders were the most likely recipients of these quilts. Because of their sentimental value, these quilts were often wrapped and stored, not used. Therefore, many good examples are available for viewing in private and museum collections. The presentation quilt is often called a **Friendship Medley** or a **friendship quilt.** Also see **album quilt, autograph quilt.**

preserving quilts. Quilts. See **Quilts: Care of Quilts.**

preshrink. Stitchery. To wash a **fabric** for the purpose of **shrink**ing before it is used. If fabrics of uncertain origin are to be used or combined, it is always safest to preshrink them by running them through a laundry cycle. Even a fabric marked or labeled "preshrunk" may need to be laundered for this purpose.

President and the World. Quilts. See **presidents' quilts.**

President's Quilt. Quilts. See **Coronation.**

presidents' quilts. Quilts. Patterns of **appliqué** and **patchwork** were often made to honor a president or first lady. If an election campaign was particularly exciting, it was likely that a **block** would be designed to commemorate it. There are several appliqué designs named for George Washington, including **Potomac Pride, Washington Sidewalk,** and **Washington's Puzzle.** President James Madison and his wife Dolley were honored in the **Madison Block** and **Dolley Madison Star,** respectively.

The Indian fighter William Henry Harrison aroused enough response with his spirited campaign of 1840 to inspire several blocks, including **Old Tippecanoe** (sometimes called Tippecanoe and Tyler, Too), **Whig Rose,** and **Harrison Rose.**

Lincoln's Platform is the best known of the **Lincoln quilts** named for Abraham Lincoln, although **Log Cabin** may also have been in his honor.

President Garfield was honored in a block that depicts the **Garfield Monument.** President and Mrs. Grover Cleveland inspired the blocks **Cleveland Lilies** and **Mrs. Cleveland's Choice.** President Roosevelt inspired a design called Rose of the Field. It was made with a row of buds denoting the president's five children.

The custom of designing quilts for current presidents has nearly disappeared, although the Eternal Flame was designed in honor of President Kennedy. A design honoring President Johnson was named the President and the World; the most recent was Forward Together for President Nixon.

press. Bookbinding. See **book press, lying press, standing press.**

press. Stitchery. To smooth a **fabric** and remove wrinkles from it by ironing or steaming. When straight seams are sewn it is usually important to press them open. In pressing fabrics with a **nap** or **pile**, a **needle board** helps prevent any flattening of the surface threads. A **pressing cloth** is usually placed over **wool** before applying the iron. This prevents the wool from flattening and developing a shine. A lightweight cloth may be used over **silk** and **synthetics**. Care must always be taken in pressing to adjust iron temperatures to the proper range for the **fiber** content of the fabric. Steam is very helpful in pressing **cotton, linen,** and other fabrics, but must be used with great care on any woolens to avoid **shrink**ing. Also see **Stitchery: Finishing.**

pressboard. Woodworking. See **hardboard.**

press cheeks. Bookbinding. The tops of the two wooden blocks of a press.

pressed amber. Amber Carving. (Also called ambroid, antique amber, mosaic amber.) Small pieces of amber may be welded together to form thin sheets when subjected to heat and great pressure. Amber plate is used in mosaics, inlay, and the fabrication of various articles. This process does not alter the workability of the material. Also see **Amber Carving: Carving.**

pressed dish. Ceramics. A dish made by pressing clay into **press mold**s to form dishes, after which excess clay is trimmed away.

pressed glass. Mosaics. (Also called Venetian glass or vitreous tessera.) Flat, uniform, ¾″ cast or pressed **glass** tile, originally manufactured only in Venice, hence one of its alternate names. Now it is also produced in Mexico. Pressed glass lacks the elegance and the brilliance of **smalti** or Byzantine glass, but its relatively lower cost adds considerably to its appeal as a mosaic material. As compared with smalti, pressed glass is much less consistent in color quality and surface characteristics and far more difficult to cut accurately. Because of the difficulty in cutting, it is advisable to score the cut-line on the **tessera** with a **glass cutter** before applying pressure with the **clippers**. Probably the most effective way to use pressed glass is in combination with the more striking smalti. Also see **Mosaics: Tools and Materials.**

pressed glass. Stained Glass. See **slab glass.**

Press Gently (Koomi Malie). Quilts. See **Hawaiian quilt.**

pressing. Batik and Tie-dye. The process of smoothing a **fabric** or making it free of wrinkles by applying heat and weight. Pressing is referred to as **calendering** in the textile industry, and as ironing in the home. Pressing temperatures vary according to fiber.

pressing. Ceramics. A method of making **pottery** forms by using pressure and two plaster **molds**. Also see **coiled pot, pinch pot, press mold, slab pot, slipcasting** and **Ceramics: Throwing.**

pressing. Metalworking. See **raising technique.**

pressing boards. Bookbinding. Plywood boards placed on each side of a book before inserting it in a **lying press** or **standing press,** to prevent marring of the cover by any irregularities in the plates of the press.

pressing cloth. Stitchery. A heavy cloth placed between **wool fabric** and the surface of an iron when the wool is **press**ed. It prevents the wool from developing a shine. A lightweight pressing cloth is used over **silks** and **synthetics** when they are ironed. Special pressing cloths are available in fabric shops, though they may be made from any lint-free **cotton** material.

press mold. Ceramics. A two-part **mold** in which clay, rather than **slip,** is formed. The slab of clay is placed in one part of the mold and the other part is hydraulically pressed against it; any excess is squeezed out and trimmed away. A sheet of clay can also be pressed manually. The advantage of pressing over slipcasting is that **grog**ged and mixed clay bodies can be used to form thicker walls.

press-on tape. Stitchery. See **iron-on tape.**

press pin. Bookbinding. An iron bar used for turning the screws of presses.

pressure gauge. Metalworking. See **oxyacetylene welding equipment.**

pressure regulator. Metalworking. See **oxyacetylene welding equipment.**

pressure-sensitive tape. Puppets. Strips of paper, cloth, or plastic with an adhesive coating on one side. Pressure is needed to fix the tapes to the surface. Among the most commonly used:

Cellophane tape is good for short-term use. It is yellowish in color and on paper turns brown and sticky with time.

Cloth tape comes in assorted colors and widths and is fabric-backed.

Drafting tape is a smooth-textured tape that is excellent when a temporary adhesive is needed. It can be peeled off without tearing or damaging the paper.

Masking tape is a crinkly-textured brown paper with adhesive on one side that comes in a variety of widths. It will adhere to any hard, dry, nonfibrous material.

Plastic tape is made in bright opaque colors and can be used for quick, though nonpermanent, decorative effects.

Transparent mending tape has a matte surface and appears colorless. It is more permanent than cellophane tape and does not change color.

Two-faced tape is similar to masking tape but has adhesive on both sides. It is convenient for quick mounting.

All pressure-sensitive tapes should be considered to be temporary.

previous row. Crochet. (Abbr. prr.) The previous row of crochet is the **row** that has just been completed. It is into the loops of these stitches that the succeeding row of stitches is worked.

prick. Basketry. See **pricking.**

pricker. Ceramics. See **needle awl.**

pricker. Lacemaking. A tool used in **bobbin lace,** consisting of a needle driven into a handle, used to make **prickings** and, sometimes in fine lacework, to take up the **loop** in **sewings.**

pricking. Basketry. A process used to prevent cracking when bending a **willow rod** sharply up or down, as in **upsetting,** or when weaving a border.

Insert the pointed end of your **knife** well into, but not through, the rod to be bent (**a.**). Twist the blade in the cut and at the same time bend the rod down or up to the desired angle (**b.**). See ill.

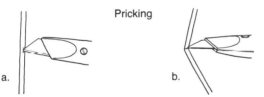

Pricking

pricking. Lacemaking. A **pattern** in **bobbin lace.** It is usually made of strong paper or firm cardboard with a smooth finish; because the pattern is likely to be used many times, a high quality paper is important. The **design** is "pricked" through the cardboard with a **pricker** from a drawing indicating the pinpoints where the pins will be placed during lacemaking.

An early term for prickings was "cards." When some lacers were asked where they got their patterns, the response was, "Why, from the cards," indicating that the patterns, or cards, were handed down from generation to generation.

pricking powder. Crewel. Embroidery. See **Crewel: Transferring a Design.**

Prickly Path. Quilts. See **Tree Everlasting.**

Prickly Pear. Quilts. See **Kansas Troubles.**

prick punch. Metalworking. See **punch.**

prick rand. Basketry. A method of **joining in** new **weavers** while **randing.** It utilizes the **pricking** technique to bend the **rod** ends down into the weaving so as not to leave any projecting ends while joining in. See ill.

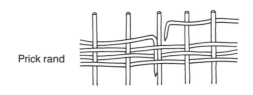

Prick rand

Pride of the Forest. Quilts. A complex **appliqué block** design that incorporates fern leaves into a modified **wreath** surrounding a pine tree. Cones point to the four corners of the block. See ill.

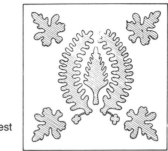

Pride of the Forest

primary clay. Ceramics. See **Ceramics: Clay.**

primary color. Any one of three or four colors that theoretically can be combined with other primary colors in various proportions to produce all other colors in the **spectrum.** Yellow, red, and blue are commonly considered to be the primary colors of **pigments,** but no matter which shades of these colors are selected, the resultant **palette** of colors available by mixtures is inadequate for some purposes. The three primary colors used in photographic color film and so-called full-color printing are yellow, cyan, and magenta. Cyan is a light greenish blue similar to turquoise blue and magenta is a purplish red. Available pigments in artist's colors close to these theoretical primary colors are cadmium yellow, phthalocyanine blue, and acra violet. Of any three primary colors that might be chosen to mix paints of any color, these will produce the most nearly satisfactory range of colors.

The primary colors proposed by some systems include four primary colors—yellow, red, blue, and green, the blue and red being altered in hue from the norm. The range of colors available by blending these four primaries is somewhat more satisfactory, although saturated purples like dioxizine purple are not approachable.

Colors made by mixing roughly equal amounts of primary colors are called secondary colors. **Hues** made by mixing roughly equal amounts of primary colors with secondary colors are called tertiary colors. An example of a secondary color is orange. Orange-red is a tertiary color.

Pigment primaries like those described above must be differentiated from the primary colors of light, which everyone agrees are red, blue, and green. These are the primary colors that are used in points to construct the image on a color television screen. Also see **hue circle.**

primitive loom. Weaving. A simple **loom** that does not contain **harnesses** with **heddles** or a **beater** with a **reed.**

The weaving is accomplished by passing the **filling** over and under the **warp** as in darning. A refinement on this is the use of **shed sticks** and **heddle bars** to act as a **shedding device.** Primitive looms need not signify primitive weaving. On the contrary, some of the finest fabrics, most complex weaves, and most intricate patterns have been woven on the simplest looms, as attested to by the fabrics made by the weavers of Peru, Guatemala, and Mexico. Very rough, primitive looms and subsequent refinements evolved through the centuries with man's quest for better and easier ways to interlace fibers. Although the coming of the **harness loom** is an outgrowth of this evolution and has replaced the primitive loom in many parts of the world, primitive looms are still found among many cultures, tribes, or sections of the world. Primitive looms can be either **horizontal** or **vertical loom**s, and include **warp-weighted loom**s, **ground loom**s, **Navajo loom**s, **backstrap loom**s, **bow loom**s and **frame loom**s. Not all primitive looms were intended for weaving. The **Chilkat blanket** loom, which is warp-weighted, and the Ojibwa loom, with a free-hanging warp, are for **twining.** Also see **Ojibwa weaving, Peruvian weaving.**

princely toy. Toys. A toy made without consideration of expense—thus, one that could be afforded only by the aristocracy. Sometimes it was the use of precious materials that made the toy costly, as with cast silver or gold **toy soldier**s and motor cars of ivory. In others, the complex **clockwork**s made the toys prohibitively expensive. Also see **coral.**

Prince of Wales toy. Toys. See **yo-yo.**

Prince Rupert's Drop. Glasswork. An interesting illustration of the forces developed in cooling glass. A piece of molten glass is dropped into water, which cools the drop so quickly that high internal stresses develop between the surface and the interior of the drop. If the drop does not fracture immediately, there is a good chance that the stresses will be so balanced that even a hammer blow will not be sufficient to break the drop. However, if the rather fragile "tail" of the globule is snapped off, the piece will shatter into countless fragments.

Tempered glass makes use of this effect of stressed glass.

Prince's Feather. Quilts. See **Princess Feather.**

Princess Feather. Quilts. (Also called Fern, Maidenhair Fern, Star and Plumes.) Any of a great variety of **appliqué** patterns showing a squared-off feather that curves to form an arc. These curved feathers are combined, using four, six, or eight of them in a radiating pattern. The feather design sometimes surrounds a star or flower at its center. The single or double feather motif is often used as an appliqué **border** pattern. The design originally came from the crest of the Prince of Wales. It came to America in crewelwork and was then used in appliqué. It was known as Prince's Feather, and later became Princess Feather.

Medallion quilts also use the Princess Feather appliqué as the large center block design. The Pennsylvania Dutch quilters made a very bold, strong use of this pattern as the primary **overall** appliqué.

Ostrich Plume, or Ben Hur's Chariot Wheel, is a variation of Princess Feather. When this pattern is used so that individual feathers surround other designs, it may assume new names that are really combinations, such as Princess Feather and Tulip, or Rising Sun and Princess Feather. Also see **Quilts: Quilting.**

Princess Feather and Tulip. Quilts. See **Princess Feather.**

printed batik. Batik and Tie-dye. A term used to denote either of two kinds of batik fabrics. The first is the authentic **batik** in which **dye** is applied by means of a stamp or **tjap.** This process is known as **tjap printing,** and the finished fabrics are called stamp batik or printed batik. The second fabric is a printed one that imitates and debases the art of batik. The printed materials may even mimic the traditional Indonesian styles and the characteristic **crackle** pattern.

printing base. Silkscreen. The flat surface to which the **screen frame** is hinged and on which stock or material rests while the image is screened onto it. In cases where the screen frame has been hinged directly to the top of a table, the table itself is the printing base. Often it is more convenient to use a piece of plywood or masonite as a printing base, both of these materials being flat and free of dents or bumps.

Commercial silkscreen machinery includes provision for holding stock in position by applying a vacuum through pin holes in the printing base. The studio craftsperson can approximate this effect by spraying the flat base with a pressure-sensitive adhesive commonly available in aerosol cans. The stickiness of the surface will prevent smudging the print should it stick to the bottom of the screen and stencil after the print is made. After the first application of spray adhesive the surface may be too sticky for prints to be removed easily, but after a few prints, fibers from the stock will adhere to the base and reduce its tackiness.

In designing the printing base/screen frame combination, it is a good idea to plan the hinge arrangement to leave ⅛" to ¼" between the screen and the print, with the screen frame in printing position. Prints made so that the screen contacts the print only at the line of travel of the **squeegee** give maximum sharpness. This out-of-contact method is especially valuable when printing fine detail

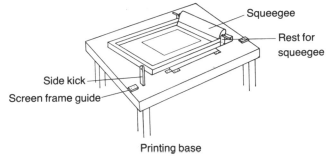

Squeegee

Rest for squeegee

Side kick

Screen frame guide

Printing base

like half-tone illustrations or textures arrived at through the **tusche stencil** method. See ill.

printing block. Block Printing. Fabric Printing. Blocks of various materials are cut so that the design to be printed is in **relief.** The portion to be printed remains uncut; areas not to be printed are cut away. Any part that is not cleared away will make a printed impression. The cut block is inked or painted, and printed on fabric or paper. Different printing-block materials have different printing characteristics: a **linoleum block** prints smooth, solid colors, and a **wood block** tends to print a grained texture.

printing ink. Block Printing. See **block printing ink.**

printing ink. Fabric Printing. See **textile color.**

printing paste. Fabric Printing. See **dye paste.**

printing table. Fabric Printing. See **Fabric Printing: Setting Up a Workshop.**

printing with paper. Papercrafts. (Also called masked print.) A printing technique in which the glass or cardboard surface is rolled with ink, then cut or torn paper shapes are placed over the ink. When paper is placed over them and pressed down, a print is made that has a solid-color background, with paper showing through wherever the cutout was placed. For a technique that resembles **block printing** or **relief** printing, heavy, smooth paper can be cut into shapes and adhered to a cardboard backing. The protruding shapes are rolled with ink, then printed on paper.

prints. Découpage. An endless variety of pictures printed on lightweight paper can be used for découpage. Prints are available in crafts shops, découpage studios, and antique shops. Museum reproductions and pictures from books and catalogues are commonly used. Colored or black-and-white pictures can be used. Avoid glossy magazine papers and newspaper because the ink tends to bleed and the print shows through from the back side. Also see **Découpage: Selecting Prints.**

Prip's flux. Jewelry. An excellent **flux** invented by John Prip, a fine **goldsmith** and **silversmith** from Rhode Island. It is superior to any commercial flux for gold and silver. The formula is: 64 grams borax, 64 grams sodium phosphate, and 96 grams boric-acid powder. Using a small amount of water, make a paste. Gradually add one quart of water and bring to a boil. This produces a clear flux that is excellent in preventing **firescale.**

Priscilla. Quilts. See **World Without End.**

prisoner's lock. Toys. (Also called ring puzzle.) A **puzzle** containing a series of seven rings pinned to a base; a double wire bar is threaded through them. The puzzle is sim-

ple to make but complex to solve, requiring both patience and skill. A puzzle of this type is on exhibit in the National Museum of Finland as a Finnish **folk toy.** It was supposedly devised by a Prussian baron imprisoned for ten years by King Frederick the Great. A later name for the puzzle was Trenck's lock. Another tale suggests that the puzzle was invented by a secret agent in the English army around 1810, giving it the name Sinclair's lock after the supposed inventor. The name Chinese rings suggests another origin. In Italy, the puzzle was attributed to a sixteenth-century mathematician and named Cardan's rings after the inventor. The puzzle is so complex that it has been used to lock boxes and doors, excluding all but the most ingenious intruders! See ill.

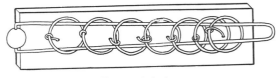

Prisoner's lock

pritchel hole. Metalworking. See **anvil.**

Procion dye. Batik and Tie-dye. Dyeing. A **cold water dye** that chemically adheres to the fiber (**fiber-reactive dye**). Procion dyes are **colorfast** and are used to dye silk, cotton, linen, leather, and viscose rayon. Heat the dyebath when dyeing wool. The Procion M series is the preferred dye for batiking; but due to colorfastness it cannot be used for **discharge dyeing.** Usually fiber-reactive dyes are packaged and available for home dyeing. The fixing solution is in a separate envelope. Follow manufacturer's directions carefully. Brand names of fiber-reactive dyes are: Fabec, Hi-Dye, Dylon, Color Fast, and **Putnam.** Also see **direct dye painting, dye, dyestuff, synthetic dye** and **Batik and Tie-dye: Dyes, Dyeing.**

Procion M. Batik and Tie-dye. See **Procion** and **Batik and Tie-dye: Dyes.**

profile draft. Weaving. A condensed version of a large and complicated **weave draft.** It is a graphic, short **draft** done in order to save time and paper, yet it gives a true picture of how the pattern will look. There are several ways to do profile drafts, depending on the original weave draft. In patterns like **overshot,** the **ground** weave can be eliminated and only the pattern blocks indicated. In weaves which have their structure based on blocks, like **Summer and Winter,** one filled-in square of the **graph paper** can represent a group of threads which normally would have each occupied a square to themselves. This forms one block of the pattern structure and the other blocks are handled in the same manner. For very large designs, a block plan is drawn on graph paper that proportionally reduces each block, so that the design as a whole is still seen and the correct relationship of one block to another is kept. One square could represent an inch or more. Instead of condensing an established pattern, the profile draft can be used to design new block patterns and then convert them to conventional weave drafts. See ill. on next page.

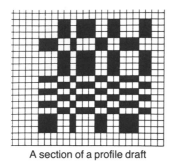

A section of a profile draft

pro-gauge. Leather. An adjustable guide tool which can be attached to the **swivel knife** to incise lines equidistant from the edge of the leather.

promotor. Plastics. See **accelerator.**

prong setting. Jewelry. A setting in which small flattened wires, or prongs, are pushed into position against a gemstone to hold it in position. This type of setting can be done on the face of the work, or from behind, showing the stone through the front of the piece but hiding the prongs. Also see **bezel, bezel pusher, crown setting, gypsy setting, reverse bezel.**

prop. Ceramics. See **kiln furniture.**

prop. Puppets. An article used on stage in a **puppet theater** that helps to describe or provide a setting for the characters. In the shadow theater, both props and **set** are suggested in **silhouette.** In stage productions, three-dimensional objects are used. Props are usually kept at a minimum in puppet performances, though a few will always be essential, depending upon the specific tale being told. Also see **prop shelf** and **Puppets: The Puppet Stage.**

propane. Ceramics. See **kiln fuel.**

propane torch. Enameling. See **torch.**

propane torch. Tincrafting. A gas-fuel torch used during the **soldering** process to heat the **tinplate** to be joined, the **soldering iron** tool, and the **solder** itself. Soldering can be accomplished by using a soldering iron to apply the solder or by melting small bits or **pallions** of solder directly onto the tinplate, using the torch without any soldering iron. Also see **Tincrafting: Joining the Tin.**

propeller mixer. Ceramics. A machine used to mix clay and water to produce **slip.** It has a propeller that spins very quickly and is used for mixing clay with no lumps in it. It is valued for its efficiency. Also see **blunger.**

propeller stick. Toys. See **whimmydiddle.**

propeller toy. Toys. Any toy that consists of propellerlike parts or that uses a propeller or moving blades to animate or activate it. Some propeller toys are the **flying machine,** the **alouette,** and the **whimmydiddle.**

proportion. Relationship, mostly of size, between a part of something and the whole, or between or among several things. We tend to say that a room is of good proportions when its length and breadth are related to its height in such a way that no one dimension seems to predominate. Balance and symmetry imply equal proportion. **Asymmetry** implies a proportion not equal, but related by a mathematical or other ratio. Consistency of proportion among several things is perceived as ordered by the eye and tends to make objects, spaces, and shapes harmonious or in agreement. The **golden section** is a proportion most eyes see as agreeable.

prop shelf. Puppets. A shelf inside the hand-**puppet stage** where puppets can be laid temporarily while not in use and where **props** needed in the play are stored. **Hand puppets** are transferred to hooks if they are not needed for a long time, since the prop shelf is reserved for those things that must be kept readily available.

proscenium. Puppets. The front of the stage, the part that is visible to the audience when the **curtain** is closed. The proscenium may extend several feet below the stage level to conceal the **puppeteers,** and sometimes there are side extensions of the proscenium for this same purpose. Also see **bridge, canopy, front bridge, proscenium arch** and **Puppets: The Puppet Stage.**

proscenium arch. Puppets. The arch-shaped opening in the **proscenium** that reveals the stage. It is sometimes referred to as the **proscenium opening.** Also see **Puppets: The Marionette Stage, The Puppet Stage.**

proscenium opening. Puppets. A rectangular or arch-shaped opening in the **proscenium,** or stage front, which allows a view of the stage. There is usually a way to cover this opening by means of a **draw curtain.** Sometimes an additional curtain on the stage front allows for an adjustment in the size of the proscenium opening. Also see **proscenium arch** and **Puppets: The Marionette Stage, The Puppet Stage.**

proscenium toy. Toys. A toy made to be viewed through an opening or a window. Many of these are also **optical toys,** as are **peep shows** and **dioramas.** The **Thames tunnel,** which relies on perspective changes, is a good example of the proscenium toy. Also see **Toys: Optical Toys.**

Protean figure. Toys. See **paper doll.**

protean view. Toys. An **optical toy** that made use of double images, sometimes involving two pictures that were attached together. They were viewed in a **diorama** and either of two images could be shown, depending upon the source and amount of light. In other protean views a scene would be shown, then other images were placed in front of it between the scene and the light source, giving another kind of double image. These were later used with the **zogroscope.** Also see **Toys: Optical Toys.**

protective finishes. Papercrafts. Various materials are used as a transparent glaze over completed, dried papier mâché designs to preserve and strengthen them. Clear plastic spray is easy to use if there is adequate ventilation. The spray can should be held about 10″ from the piece, spraying in a circular motion to cover the piece with several light coats. Liquid-plastic coatings are also available. Clear polyurethane varnish, available at the hardware store, can be brushed on the surface. When dry, it provides an excellent, durable, rather glossy, water-resistant surface. **Polymer medium,** available in glossy or matte finish from art supply stores, is used in the same way. Clear liquid epoxy is available in a kit of hardener and epoxy which are mixed just before applying. Epoxy is extremely durable, but care must be taken to avoid contact with the skin while applying. Wear rubber gloves and work in a well-ventilated room. If some should spill on the skin, wash immediately with alcohol and then wash with soap and water. **Varnish** also provides a durable, water-repellent surface. Clear lacquer, also from the hardware store, is often used, usually brushed on in several applications, allowed to dry in between for a lustrous, durable finish. **Shellac** may be used as a final coating, although it is not water-resistant, and moisture may cause spotting. Directions are given on the containers for mixing, as well as for the proper **solvent** to use for thinning and for cleaning brushes.

protein fiber. Batik and Tie-dye. Stitchery. See **animal fiber.**

prunt. Glasswork. An embossed or debossed print left in molten glass by application of incised metal molds or stamps. Commonly, prunts are applications to a vessel of additional glass, which is subsequently impressed with designs or motifs. The tool used to impress the molten glass is also called a prunt. Also see **knop.**

pucella. Glasswork. See **jack.**

puddle. Metalworking. The small liquid pool of molten metal made by the torch flame or electrode when **welding.** It is made in preparation for **running a bead** when **oxyacetylene welding** and maintained throughout the welding, adding **filler rod** to it if necessary for a thicker weld. The penetration of the weld will depend on the depth of the molten pool or puddle. When **arc welding,** the electrode is used to make and control the puddle.

Puerto Rico rose. Crewel. Embroidery. See **bullion knot.**

puff. Quilts. A soft, lightweight, resilient, fully **stuffed comforter.**

puff quilt. Quilts. A puffy bedcover that is easily made from a series of pre**stuff**ed shapes. Technically it is not a quilt at all because it requires no **quilting** to join the layers. It is a variation of the **pillow quilt** and uses squares of fabric identical in size, of about 4″ or 5″. Two squares of fabric, placed with their right sides together, are joined on the **seam allowance** at three edges. The material is then turned right side out.

Nylon stockings are used for the stuffing. The stocking is gathered at the center, as though it was to be put on, then the flattened stocking is slipped into the pillow form and pinned in place. The open edge is **whip-stitch**ed shut. The blocks or puffs are then tied in the centers as in the **tied quilt.** Finally, the puffs are joined with overcast stitches or **slip stitch**es.

pug mill. Ceramics. A machine used for **mixing** and **kneading** clay for large-scale production purposes. The clay is forced through a chamber with a turning screw. A de-airing pug mill is a machine that combines mixing clay and removing air pockets. It constitutes a refinement of the pug mill in that it holds clay in a vacuum while it is being forced through a chamber. It produces a dense, smooth clay unobtainable by hand methods. See ill. Also see **ball mill, wet-pan mixer.**

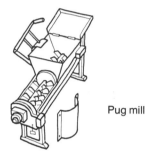

Pug mill

Pulcinella. Puppets. (Also called Pulchinelle.) A **stock character** who emerged from the **commedia dell'arte** around the 1600s. He was one of the "**zanni,**" dressed like a sixteenth-century peasant, and was the forerunner of **Pierrot** and **Punch.** His face, a mask, became standardized, as did his character. Pulcinella was a seemingly slow-witted peasant with a spirited character, but full of cunning and guile; however, he fled at the sight of danger. He was not the wife-beater and fighter into which Punch later evolved.

pulled. Bookbinding. A book that has been cut away from its cover and from which all **section**s have been freed from each other.

pulled warp. Weaving. See **wedge weave.**

pulled work. Embroidery. See **whitework.**

pulley. Spinning. See **bobbin pulley, spindle pulley, whorl.**

pulley. Weaving. A small mechanical device attached to a **roller** above the **harnesses** in a **counterbalanced loom.** Two pulleys are suspended from a roller and from them in turn two harnesses are suspended. The pulley and roller working together raise and lower the harnesses. Also see **counterbalanced loom.**

pull-in. Weaving. See **draw-in.**

pulling. Bookbinding. The operation that detaches the thread and removes the glue that holds the **sections** together in preparation for rebinding. It is done by opening each section at its center, cutting through each loop of thread without damaging the paper, and gently pulling the sections apart.

pulli punta. Ivory and Bone Carving. See **vegetable ivory.**

pull string. Toys. A cord, thong, yarn, string, or light rope by which a toy may be pulled, especially a **wheeled toy.** It may also refer to the string by which some toys, such as a **jumping jack,** are animated. A pull string often has a **bead** added at the end to weight it, making it easy to locate and hold on to.

pull toy. Toys. Any toy attached to wheels or a wheeled base that can be pulled along by a **string,** cord, or long handle. Many pull toys are designed so that the action of the turning wheels animates other parts of the toy. These toys are especially popular with small children and toddlers.

Some pull toys are animals, such as the well-known sheep on a platform and the model of the Trojan Horse. Among others are vehicles of all kinds—**wagon**s, trains, **boat**s, ships, and carts. Also see **Toys: Wheeled Toys.**

pulp cane. Basketry. See **cane.**

pulp mâché. Puppets. Toys. A **papier-mâché** process for the **puppet head** that uses soaked bits of newspaper mixed with **wheat paste.** This makes an excellent **modeling material,** which dries slowly but becomes hard. Prepackaged pulp-mâché mix, called **modeling mix,** is available at hobby shops. Also see **Puppets: Making the Puppet Head.**

pulp mâché doll. Toys. Any doll or **doll head** made from **pulp mâché.** Usually pressed in a mold, the mixtures were similar to those used for **papier mâché dolls.** They were ground or kneaded to a fine pulp, however, rather than used in layers.

pumice. Amber Carving. Ivory and Bone Carving. A porous volcanic material, essentially obsidian, that consists of aluminous and siliceous glass with fibrous to scaley structures. A brittle substance, it breaks down readily into numerous minute sharp-edged shards. As an abrasive powder, it is used on materials with a hardness of less than 6. It can be sawed into **pumice pencil**s to use for carving soft substances.

pumice. Découpage. A sharp, abrasive powder made from pulverized volcanic rock, used to smooth a **varnish** surface. Apply the pumice with lemon or linseed oil and rub with a pad made from felt until a smooth finish is achieved.

pumice. Jewelry. A form of porous volcanic glass. It is extremely lightweight and is available in two forms, lump pumice and powdered pumice. The powdered pumice is available in two grades, coarse and fine. In lump form, it can be used in an annealing pan to set and support work for **annealing,** as it does not burn. In powder form, it is used for cleaning and **polishing.** A paste of pumice and water can be packed down against a metal surface and wire-brushed to produce a **matte** finish. To produce a subtle matte finish without the use of a motor-driven device, take a cloth or your thumb, dip it in water and then in pumice powder, and rub the work. Such finishes are produced after the final **pickle.** Also see **abrasive, buffing compound.**

pumice. Metalworking. Plastics. Woodworking. See **abrasives.**

pumice pencil. Amber Carving. Ivory and Bone Carving. Jet Carving. Shell Carving. A hand-shaped piece of pumice used for digging crevices and outlines in carving soft materials; it was one of the tools used by the ancient amber carvers of Greece and Rome.

Saw 2–3″ lengths of pumice from a block (about ½″ wide) and file them into various chisel profiles. Form and size them to meet the individual requirements of the particular piece you are carving. The pumice can be sandwiched and glued between two strips of wood to provide a handle.

pumice powder. Amber Carving. Ivory and Bone Carving. Shell Carving. A light, porous volcanic rock with a spongy look ground to different degrees of fineness for use in polishing wood, ivory, and other organic substances, as well as marble and metal. It is used with water or linseed, olive, or lemon oil to make a paste. Also see **pumice** and **Amber Carving: Finishing.**

punch. Bookbinding. The indentation of type into a page.

punch. Jewelry. The movable part of a punch-and-die combination that, when hammered, forces the metal into the die. This term is also used in reference to **chasing** and **repoussé** tools. Also see **automatic center punch, beading tool, center punch, circle cutter, dapping punch, embosser, grounder, matting tools, perloir, planisher, tracer.**

punch. Leather. Any of various punches which are used to make holes in leather for hand sewing, slits for straps and **lacing,** and for attaching buckles and fasteners. Prong and **drive punch**es are placed on the spot then struck firmly with a **mallet** to pierce the hole. A **revolving punch** is used for punching various sized holes in lightweight leather. For hard-to-reach areas use a single drive punch. Also see **combination punch, drive punch, split punch, stitching punch.**

punch. Metalworking. A tool for piercing, marking, or stamping a surface; it is tapped with a hammer or pressed by hand into the object.

A prick punch is a narrow steel rod tapering to a fine point for making light indentations, and especially to mark measurements on metal (**a.**). Use it with a small, lightweight hammer.

A center punch is a heavier rod than the prick punch,

used for enlarging prick-punch holes as a preparation for **drilling** (b.). Mark the spot to be punched and lightly tap the prick punch with a hammer. Next, hammer the center punch in the same position to enlarge the indentation.

To sharpen a punch, rotate the punch slowly against a **grinding** wheel to keep it round without flat spots. Grind the tip to an angle of 90° for a center punch, and to 30° for a prick punch. Be careful not to burn the point. Grind it only at the cutting tip, not at the sides. See ill. Also see **blacksmithing tools.**

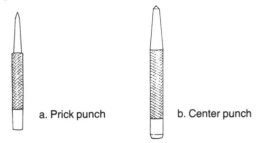

a. Prick punch   b. Center punch

Punch. Puppets. The immensely popular puppet hero of the **Punch and Judy show**s. Punch was known in his present character from about the eighteenth century, though he has undergone some changes. There is a magic charm in his personality, some delicious perversity that has a very widespread appeal, not the least of which is the gay abandon of his approach to life. While he is often represented as a wife beater, he was originally the henpecked husband. He may commit mayhem and murder, though usually his bragging and bravado are cover-ups for the beatings he himself receives. Punch, in the last century at least, usually wins out in his climactic battle with the devil, though formerly Punch fell victim to the gallows or the guillotine.

Punch was derived from the seventeenth-century **commedia dell'arte**'s braggart Pulchinelle, or **Pulcinella**. In Russia he became Petroushka, and in France, Polichinelle. He has remained popular because the **stock character** of Punch represents man.

punch. Woodworking. (Also called center punch.) To make a starting or centering hole in a piece of wood with the aid of an **awl, bradawl,** or a center punch. This hole is usually made to center a drill bit to keep it from **drift**ing, particularly in hardwoods.

Punch and Judy cast. Puppets. The **stock characters** that make up all **Punch and Judy shows**. These include **Punch** and **Judy**, the main figures, and a variety of others, usually numbering between 8 and 12. There are 16 identifiable characters in all, as well as 3 animals, but never do all the known characters appear in any one performance. Some of the regular characters are the Baby (whom Punch throws out the window), the Hangman (who sometimes gets hanged himself while demonstrating to the uncomprehending Punch how to slip his head in the noose), the Officer, the Devil, the Clown, Toby (a dog), Hector (a horse), and a Crocodile or Dragon.

Punch and Judy show. Puppets. (Also called Punch and Judy theater.) The one remaining example of the tradi-tional **popular theater,** which still exists in English-speaking countries today. In it, all the characters are **stock character**s: they remain the same from play to play. **Punch** and **Judy** have been known in their present form since the late 1700s, but they carry with them the vestigial remnants of some more antiquated theater. The staging itself was known to medieval minstrels, and the face of Punch seems to come directly from the Italian masks of the **commedia dell'arte.** Even the bawdy humor and primitive buffoonery are elements of more ancient theater.

The Punch and Judy show includes any of many variations of the popular puppet performances. In their heyday in eighteenth-century Europe, the main characters, Punch and his wife, Judy, became so celebrated that the performances became known generally as Punch and Judy shows. Even today, "Punch theater" refers to a stage for puppets. The characters of a Punch and Judy theater were made in several ways. The **hand puppet**s were most common, though many elaborate **string puppet**s, or **marionette**s, were also made to represent these figures.

The Punch and Judy theater was well loved by both peasants and royalty. Itinerant **puppeteer**s performed on the streets, as well as by royal request in the palaces. There are many versions of the plays performed.

In some interpretations, the Punch and Judy performances becomes a morality play: Punch (the fearless!) conquers his bodily appetites (Judy), the tyranny of civil power (the uniformed officer), the mockery and shallowness of existence (the clown), superstition (the ghost), and physical pain (the crocodile), makes a mockery of death (the hangman), and finally slays sin itself (Satan). Most of these characters are a part of the **Punch and Judy cast.** Also see **Bartholomew Fair, marionette theater, Punch stage, puppet theater.**

Punch and Judy theater. Puppets. See **marionette theater, Punch and Judy show.**

punch blade. Woodworking. See **whittling tools.**

punch box. Toys. See **jack-in-the-box.**

punch hook. Rugmaking. See **punch needle.**

punching. Metalworking. See **blacksmithing techniques.**

punching. Tincrafting. The technique for making small holes in **tinplate** as part of an overall decorative pattern or as an opening to receive a cotter pin, rivet, or binding wire to join two pieces of metal. Punching is best accomplished by striking an **awl** that has been carefully positioned on the tin with the flat end of a **ball-peen hammer.** It helps to strike the tin from both sides. A **hammering board** can be used to absorb the end of the awl. If neatness is required it also helps to hammer the hole between awl punchings to flatten the metal burrs. Also see **Tincrafting: Cutting the Tin.**

punch needle. Rugmaking. A heavy metal needle with a wooden handle used to make **hooked rug**s by pushing or punching the yarn from the back to the front on the **rug**

backing. The needle became popular in the 1930s; it is meant for yarn but fine fabric strips can be used also. There is a gauge on the needle to regulate the pile height, which ranges from about ¼″ to 1″. The metal part of the needle is usually interchangeable to accommodate different thicknesses of yarn. There are several models on the market; most have a hollow center down through which the yarn goes to be threaded through the needle. When the needle is being used, the slotted or threaded side of the needle faces the direction in which the work is proceeding. It is pushed through the rug backing as far as the gauge will allow. The needle works best for novices if the loop that forms on the underside (the front of the rug) is caught between thumb and index finger and held in place as the needle is pulled out and then pushed in again for the next loop. If not held, the loop might pull back with the needle until experience is gained on how to compensate for this. The punch needle is also called a punch hook or a hollow handle hook. See ill.

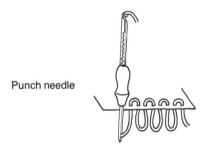

Punch needle

Punch stage. Puppets. (Also called Punch-type stage.) A small stage built for **puppet show**s. It takes its name from the original **Punch and Judy show**s which used such a stage. Also see **Puppets: The Puppet Stage.**

Punch-type stage. Puppets. See **Punch stage.**

punchwork. Rugmaking. Making **hooked rug**s with a **punch needle.**

punctured quilt pattern. Quilts. See **pounce** and **Quilts: Quilting.**

punty. Glasswork. A solid-steel or stainless-steel rod ⅜″ to ¾″ in diameter and 4−5′ in length, used as a support for molten glass after the glass is removed from the **blowing iron.** Attaching the punty to a blown form is a little tricky for a lone worker and is usually managed with the aid of a helper.

While the blown form on the blowing iron is allowed to cool slightly, a small **gather** is taken from the **tank furnace** on the end of the punty and formed on the **marver** into a conical shape (**a.**). Sometimes the tip of the conical gather is indented with a file or dipped into coarse sand before attaching so that the joint made is imperfect and therefore more easily cracked off.

While an assistant keeps the piece on the blowing iron centered by rolling it back and forth on the arms of the glassworker's chair, the point of the conical gather on the punty is pushed into contact with the center of the piece (**b.**). The relative temperatures of the two pieces are some-

what critical. The gather on the punty should be glowing and quite flexible or it will not be sticky enough to form a bond, and the bottom of the piece has to be cool enough not to deform substantially while the joint is made. Also the piece on the blowing iron cannot be allowed to cool so much that the heat of the gather on the punty will crack the bottom.

After the joint between the punty gather and the blown form is accomplished, the piece is removed from the blowing iron by **cracking off.** A few drops of water are applied to the necked-down area of the vessel, or a wet **file** is used to score the glass at that point (**c.**).

A gentle rap with the handle of a jack is usually enough to crack off the vessel from the blowing iron at the desired point (**d.**).

The opened mouth of the vessel can be smoothed by **fire polishing** in the furnace mouth or in a **glory hole** (**e.**). The mouth can also be smoothed by grinding.

The glass can also be reheated and other forming operations performed. For instance, the glass can be reheated and formed with **jacks** and **paddles,** or it can be spun by twisting the punty in the hands at high speed until the glass forms a plate or for a longer time still to form **crown glass.**

To attach a handle to a blown-glass form supported on a punty, take a small gather of glass from the tank furnace on a second punty. The new gather is allowed to drip and flow from the punty and to attach to the vessel; **shears** are used to cut the handle from the punty. The cut end is brought into contact with the vessel using a jack (**f.**). See ill.

Attaching the punty to a blown vessel

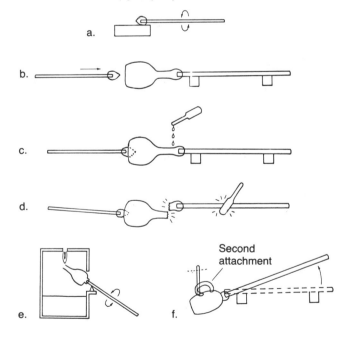

a.

b.

c.

d.

e.

Second attachment

f.

puppet. Puppets. Any of a great variety of figures made for use in performances in the **puppet theater** or the **marionette theater.** The puppets range in complexity from very simple **finger puppet**s and **hand puppet**s through the most complicated **string puppet**s, or **marionette**s. Also see

apple-head puppet, articulated puppet, cut-out figure, paper-bag puppet, puppet master and **Puppets: Definitions.**

puppeteer. Puppets. (Also called manipulator, puppet player.) The person controlling any of the various puppets or the **string puppets,** or **marionettes.** The term "operator" is sometimes used, though less commonly. **Controller** is more specific, usually referring to the puppeteer who **manipulates** marionettes, since a **control bar** is used. "Puppeteer" is sometimes used to refer to anyone who designs and constructs the puppets, costumes them, or produces the **puppet show.** Also see **control, proscenium, puppet master, UNIMA.**

puppet hair. Puppets. Hair for the **puppet** or **marionette** may be made of any material that gives the desired appearance. Fur, fabric, wool or cotton yarn, ball fringe, fluffy cotton or dacron batting, ribbon, or cut strips of **felt** can be sewn or glued to the head, depending on how the **puppet head** is made. Also see **Puppets: Making the Puppet Head.**

puppet hand. Puppets. See **hand.**

puppet head. Puppets. The head of a **hand puppet,** which fits over the fingers so that the hand can **manipulate** the puppet. There must be either a **flange** or holes at the **base** of the neck so that clothing or costumes can be added, covering the hand and giving the suggestion of a body to the puppet. Puppet heads may be made of **felt, stuffed fabric** or stocking, **papier mâché, found materials, pulp mâché,** or **carved wood.**

Marionette heads are made from the same materials and by the same methods, though the finger hole is eliminated in favor of the solid base to which a **screw eye** can be attached. Also see **balsa wood, caricature, finger hole, modeling material, plastic wood, redwood, sawdust, soft head, two-faced puppet** and **Puppets: Making the Puppet Head.**

puppet master. Puppets. The head **puppeteer,** or one who manages or is in charge of the **puppet show**—sometimes, any puppeteer who is performing and is, therefore, master of a **puppet.**

puppet opera. Puppets. An opera composed especially for use on the **puppet stage,** particularly fashionable in court circles during the eighteenth century. Bach, Haydn, and Mozart all composed for the puppet operas. These operas were performed as miniatures of real operas, and often as parodies.

puppet play. Puppets. A play adapted or written especially for use in a **puppet show** and one that takes into consideration the kinds of movements that the puppets can perform. The parts are usually spoken by the person who is controlling the puppet, and a **puppeteer** may sometimes operate two **hand puppets** at one time, one on each hand. Since two hands are required for the manipulation of each **marionette,** there must be a **controller** for each character

on the stage. The cast must necessarily be limited to the number of people who can be accommodated **backstage.** Also see **articulated, control, topdrop.**

puppet player. Puppets. See **puppeteer.**

puppetry. Puppets. The art of producing **puppets** and **puppet shows.** Also see **swazzle, UNIMA** and **Puppets.**

PUPPETS

Puppetry includes any theatrical use of small figures that are **manipulated** by the **puppeteer** on a stage or **screen.** These figures include **finger puppets, hand puppets, shadow puppets, rod puppets, marionettes,** and many variations of each of these. The **puppet** can be manipulated by hand from below, as in the case of hand puppets, shadow puppets, and rod puppets. Marionettes are **controlled** by **strings** from above, and the figures are commonly articulated by **movable joints.** In either case, the **controller,** or manipulator, is usually concealed.

Puppetry is probably less well developed in the United States than in most other countries. Here we do not have familiar characters that can be identified for their attitudes or characteristics of good or evil. The Sesame Street puppet characters are probably the first to be recognized and enjoyed by a large following, although through television rather than through the immediacy of the **puppet theater.**

Puppet shows have been performed for centuries, although there are few documented records of their existence. One of the earliest illustrations of puppets is found in the "Romance of Alexander," by Jehan de Grise of Flanders; it is dated 1338 and depicts a **puppet stage** with puppets in action watched by a group of girls.

The shadow puppets of the Wayang culture of Java are probably the earliest use of puppets; although the Chinese were also early to develop the art of **puppetry.** Today, there are few cultures where puppetry does not exist in some form.

The traditional shadow puppet of Java is identified as the Wayang Purua and is used to perform ancient stories of ancient kings. The shadows are cast from leather **silhouettes,** painted in great detail, onto a white screen. In this way tales are passed from generation to generation. The Balinese used similar puppets, also for relating tales of historical and religious significance rather than entertainment. The Javanese plays were cast with royalty and animals; the Chinese were to use peasants, demons, and clowns.

Shadow puppets moved from China, probably via Persia, to Turkey; the chief character in the Turkish plays is Karogoz, a slapstick comedian similar to **Punch,** whose counterpart is found in almost every country.

The **glove puppet,** precursor to the **hand puppet,** was extremely popular in Victorian England, as were the characters of the **Punch and Judy cast.** In Germany, the **marionette theater** was accepted as legitimate theater; professional authors wrote for it and replaced the previous repertoires. Hand puppets also flourished in Germany, their repertoire including much of the grotesque. Some of the nineteenth-century performances included such thrilling titles as "The Death Bell at Midnight,""The London Body Snatchers," and "The Murder in the Wine Cellar."

In Italy, the marionette theater was professional and important; grand opera was performed and referred to as the **puppet opera.** The Spanish **puppet theater** had a characteristic half-romantic, half-religious series of performances. An 1808 performance of the "Death of Seneca" used narrow red ribbons to simulate blood flow and ended with the philosopher making a profession of faith on his arrival in heaven.

Today, puppetry is known everywhere. Commercially made hand puppets and marionettes are readily available, although they rarely meet the specific needs of a puppeteer as well as does the handmade puppet. In fashioning the head, the puppetmaker gives focus to the puppet's character, which is conveyed by a combination of several elements: the appearance (including the features and costume), the movements, and the voice. These must be correlated so that each is part of a unified whole.

Puppets are now being used more extensively in education, since even a simple production involves students in a wide range of activities from playwriting and direction to painting and speaking.

Many museums have collections of puppets and marionettes, especially folk museums and those devoted to toys or children. Many nineteenth-century puppets remain in collections all over Europe. Among some of the better-known collections are those in the City Museum at Munich, the City Museum at Lyon, and the Paul McPharlin Collection in Detroit. The Victoria and Albert Museum in London possesses an eighteenth-century Italian marionette theater as well as stage models, and the British Museum contains the Raffles collection of Javanese puppets. Two other centers that have shown an interest in historical puppets are the Puppet Museum at the Central Puppet Theater in Moscow and the Folk Arts Museum in Basel, Switzerland. **Toy theater**s may be seen in the Victoria and Albert Museum and in Pollock's Toy Museum in London.

DEFINITIONS **Puppet**s are basically of two kinds: those held upright by the hand and those that are controlled by strings from above. The term "puppet" may be used to refer to the entire range, but the ones **controll**ed by **strings** are usually designated **marionette**s or **string puppet**s.

Puppetry sometimes falls on a borderline between actual toys and theater. Marionettes that require a high degree of skill to **manipulate** are designated within the theatrical area, even though simple ones are devised for children. Much of the real art of puppetry lies in **"playing the puppet,"** not in making it; in animating a figure, a performance occurs. It is in this sense that puppetry is used here. All puppets are performance figures, and even the simplest are in the theatrical arena.

The simplest, smallest puppet is the **finger puppet.** The **hand puppet,** or **glove puppet,** ranges in complexity from a paper bag to a modeled head. The head may be moved on the end of a wood **dowel** or rod, like a **stick puppet,** or op-erated behind a **screen,** with the shadow of the animation being observed, as with the **shadow puppet.**

The string puppet, or marionette, is the most complex of all. The marionette is a puppet form manipulated from above, in contrast to the hand puppet, which is manipulated from below. The head of the marionette is attached to a wood frame or **skeleton** and made flexible with **swivel joint**s and **hinge joints.** Strings are attached to a **control bar.** The **puppeteer** holds the control bar and manages the movements of the marionette.

The skeleton is built of square sticks, usually pine. Sometimes doweling is used, depending upon the size and weight of the figure. Hinge **joint**s may be made with strips of leather; these **leather hinge**s, or leather joints, allow for a swinging movement in one direction only—the leg can move back below the knee, but not forward. Swivel joints are used at the neck, shoulders, and hips, and may consist of a pair of **screw eye**s, linked together. Use a strong thread for **stringing,** such as **linen thread, carpet thread,** or **nylon leader.** Nylon leader is nearly transparent but has the disadvantage of stretching slightly with time. Tie the strings lightly until the positions are checked; untie them to **dress the figure.**

A marionette may, of course, be a very simple form, using only a few strings. But the marionette used by a professional puppeteer may have strings for every joint—hand, wrist, elbow, shoulder, etc.

MAKING THE PUPPET HEAD   The **puppet head** can be made by a great variety of processes, any of which can be used whenever the head is formed separately, whether for a **hand puppet** or for a **marionette.** When the head and body are to be made as one single unit, as in the **finger puppet, paper-bag puppet,** or **stocking puppet,** those directions are given under their specific names. The following processes are for heads that are formed separately, then painted and added to bodies, whether of cloth or of wood.

Heads for marionettes are made with a flat solid base, so that a **screw eye** or similar device can be used to join the head to the **skeleton.** The clothes are then hung from the skeleton or framework.

By contrast, all heads for hand puppets must have an opening into which the fingers can be inserted, and some provision must be made on the neck for attaching clothes.

Heads for hand puppets are usually 3–5" high, which means they are proportionately a little large for the bodies. There is greater variation in the sizes of heads for marionettes, although most fall into this same general size range. The puppet head must be lightweight if it is to be supported easily by string or two fingers.

SOFT HEADS   **Fabric** is the least expensive and most readily available flexible material from which to form a puppet head. For the hand puppet, the head can be **fabricate**d over a cardboard tube that slides over one or two fingers. For the marionette, use a wood spool or wood cylinder as a core.

Quilt **batting** or **stuffing** can be added to make the head round, or in lieu of these, strips of cloth will do. This padding or batting can be tied on or attached with masking tape; then flat fabric head shapes, cut so that one piece forms the face and the other piece forms the back of the head, are sewn together and slipped on. A tie or ribbon at the neck will secure it. Features, hair, etc., are easily added to the fabric by sewing.

Other similar methods that use fabrics are **felt puppet, nylon-stocking puppet,** and the **sock puppet.**

STRIP PAPIER MÂCHÉ HEAD   To form a puppet head of **strip papier mâché,** there must first be a shape over which to work. The basic shape can be cardboard and paper, or it may be **Plasticene** or clay. The cardboard tube, padded with paper, will do nicely for the hand puppet. If a marionette head is made by this method, the bottom of the tube does not have to remain open.

Fit a cardboard tube over the fingers: snug fit will allow the movements of the head to be easily controlled. A cardboard tube from paper towels will work well; a tube can be made from any lightweight cardboard and secured with tape at the end. The tube is cut to a 4″ length, or shorter, for the marionette head; form a ball with wadded newspaper secured with masking tape to the tube base. Apply **papier mâché** to the rough head shape. Details such as the nose are added with the papier mâché strips.

Tear newspapers into strips about ½″ wide, dip into a **wheat-paste** solution, wrap around and adhere to the wadded newspaper head. A minimum of six layers of pasted papers is required to get a smooth surface. Place the layers at right angles to each other (**a.**).

A thinned household **white glue** may be substituted for wheat paste. It is more expensive, but dries hard and leaves a smooth surface.

It is best, if time permits, to let each layer of the paper strips dry before the next is added. If all layers are added simultaneously, several days are required for drying.

Add small pieces of paper for facial details; cover with additional strips to blend with the head. When the head is finished, it must be left to dry thoroughly for at least a day before it is painted. If the head feels cool to the touch it is still damp. The more layers of paper strips used, the longer the time required for drying, and the stronger the head will be (**b.**).

For extra strength, alternate layers of gauze cut in 1″ strips with the paper strips. Dip gauze in paste and place over several layers of papier mâché; work extra paste into the gauze layer and shape as needed. The head for a hand puppet has a **flange** at the base of the neck; close the bottom of the tube for the marionette head so that a screw eye can be inserted.

Paint the face using poster paint or tempera. Seal the dry surface with a spray-on fixative or lacquer. If acrylic paint is used, no sealer coat is needed; enamel paint requires a longer drying time. Do not use sealer or enamel paint on the top of the head if the hair is glued.

Using wadded paper as a base for strip papier mâché is easy and simple and suitable for beginners. Plasticene or clay allow for more control of facial details. The Plasticene serves as a bone structure; the neck, head shape, chin line, and forehead are all suggested in the form. Cover the Plasticene with a thin layer of liquid soap, petroleum jelly, or wet paper strips to facilitate removing the Plasticene model. Cover the model with paper strips dipped in wheat paste as described above.

When almost dry, slit the head all the way through to remove the Plasticene or clay. Do not allow the clay to dry completely within the head because it will be too hard to cut through. Make the incision behind the ears and over the top of the skull. Separate the two parts and remove the Plasticene or clay; glue the two hollow halves together; cover the seam with more paper strips and add facial details (**c.**). Some puppetmakers prefer not to cut the head, but to dig the clay or Plasticene out through the opening in the neck using a ball cutter. This method is most successful with clay rather than Plasticene. In either case, the modeling material is removed before the papier mâché is dry enough to hold its shape. See ill.

Making a strip papier mâché head

a.   b. Plasticene base   c.

MODELED HEAD   A puppet head can be shaped or molded from any malleable material that will harden. Keep in mind that a hand puppet requires finger space in the head and a marionette requires a head with a solid base.

Sawdust mâché is a modeling material made from a mixture of sawdust and wheat paste. The finer the sawdust, the smoother the finished surface of the modeled piece. Sawdust can be run through a sieve to assure an even finer material.

To mix sawdust mâché, stir the sawdust into the ready-mixed wheat paste, which has the consistency of heavy cream. Use half as much wheat paste as sawdust; more of either can be added as necessary to work it into a malleable batter. If the mixture crumbles or falls apart, more paste is needed. Do not add water to thin the mixture because the sawdust will absorb it and expand. If the mixture sags and will not hold its shape, it is too thin, and more sawdust is needed. When a workable consistency is found, shape or mold the head. Set the finished head upright or lay it flat and let it dry. As it dries, check to make sure it is retaining its shape. It is not necessary to be overly concerned if the back of the head flattens slightly, since it will probably be covered by hair.

Sawdust mâché is a slow-drying material. If it feels cool to the touch it is still damp. Cracks may occur in the surface, and they can be patched later with **plastic wood** or wood putty. Mix in a little sawdust with the putty to give it the same texture. The sawdust mâché works best for small forms, because it does not have great strength in large chunks.

When the sawdust mâché is used to model the entire head for a hand puppet, a hole must be dug out for the fingers. For the marionette, the dried sawdust mâché is strong enough to hold the screw eye that attaches it to the marionette skeleton. Sand the dried head for a smoother finish.

Pulp mâché is paper pulp mixed with wheat paste; it is used like sawdust mâché. Tear newspaper into tiny bits and soak in water for 1–3 days. Squeeze out excess water and add paper to prepared wheat paste to make a workable clay consistency. Shape the pulp mâché into a head. Pulp mâché can be modeled over a cardboard tube, or padded and shaped over a wadded newspaper form, Plasticene, or clay base.

The Plasticene or clay base is a solid, simplistic head shape; facial details are added with the pulp mâché. The clay or Plasticene is removed when the head is dry, therefore no finger hole is necessary in the model. Cover the clay head shape with a few strips of wet paper, or a thick layer of petroleum jelly or liquid soap, before adding the pulp mâché. This will ease the separation of clay from the pulp mâché. The pulp mâché must be at least ¼″ thick; thinner layers will break while drying.

Remove the clay before it dries, using a small scoop, apple-corer, ball cutter, or a table knife. Although Plasticene does not harden, it does have a stiff consistency and should be removed before the pulp mâché dries.

Pulp mâché modeled over a cardboard tube padded with paper will dry faster than the same material over clay. It is advisable to keep the head damp until all modeling is completed because the mâché shrinks as it dries. Cover the head with a plastic bag to retain the moisture. If patching is necessary on a finished head, do the patching from the inside.

Pulp mâché is available commercially; the paste is pre-mixed with paper pulp; just add water and shape. Add hair and features to the pulp mâché heads in the same manner as described for sawdust mâché.

CARVED WOOD HEAD   The most elaborate of all puppets or marionettes are those with **carved-wood** heads. The carving requires a woodworker's skill, and the head for the hand puppet must be hollowed before carving begins.

The hollowing may be done in either of two ways. In the first, the block from which the head is to be carved is cut in half. Then the inside can be gouged out with hand tools. The two halves are then glued back together and it is ready for carving. In the second, the block is drilled out from the bottom using a large drill bit. In either case the **finger hole** must be large enough to accommodate one or two fingers, whichever is used.

For the marionette, the head should not be hollow. The solid base is needed to join the head to the **skeleton**. In either, a **flange** should be left at the base so that clothing may easily be attached.

The carved-wood head usually has exaggerated features, since the figure is to some extent a **caricature**. The head will be slightly large for the size of the body.

Softwoods, such as basswood or **balsa wood,** are most commonly used for the carved heads, especially by beginners. The experienced woodworker may prefer birch, beech, pine, or redwood. The wood grain must always run lengthwise through the head (from crown down through the neck) for greatest strength.

A block of wood approximately 3″ × 3″ × 5″ will do to begin with. The size varies depending upon the size planned for the finished figure. Hand puppets vary in total length from a 7–8″ simple form to some that are 12–15″ long. Marionettes, not limited by the size of the **puppeteer's** hand, may range from a few inches up to 3 feet. Most marionettes, however, are from 10–20″ tall.

It is helpful to do a drawing of the **marionette head** first. Then the front view (which is the same as the back view) is marked onto two opposing sides of the block and sawed. A coping saw or jigsaw is needed for cutting these full-face and back views. In using the coping saw, a bench vise is essential. The first cutting will round the head at the top above the ears, and will indicate the ears and shape of the neck. The wood block is then turned so that the side views, or profiles, can be marked and cut. This leaves a rough suggestion of the head in the block of wood, with cutting completed on all four sides. A wood rasp is then used to bevel and round the rough cuts to suggest the brow line and chin line.

Chisels are used to clear areas at the sides of the nose, back of ears, eyes, etc. A cut is made at the base of the nose as well as above and below each lip. The chisels are always used on wood that is held securely in a vise. All chisel cuts are made away from the grain. Final rounding is done with sandpaper. Two coats of ground paint or **undercoat** are needed if **enamel paint**s are used. If **acrylic paint** is used, give one solid skin-color coating before attempting to color specific areas. **Puppet hair** may be carved on the **puppet head** or it may be added with fur, wool, yarn, or any other material that offers the desired effect.

Another simpler way of making a wooden head is to start with a wood ball or a round wood **finial,** available at hardware stores. A hole must be drilled at the base for the fingers if a hand puppet is being made. For some marionettes just the ball is adequate—hair may be added, features painted, and a **screw eye** added at the base. To suggest simple features, like a nose or chin, pound in a few small nails or **pin nail**s to suggest the shape, then use wood putty or **plastic wood** to cover them, modeling the face. The plastic wood will not stick to the smooth wood surface without some support.

Some round wood finials can be found that already have a neck or base attached. For these, add a screw eye at the base to aid in fastening the marionette head to the body. If the "neck" is large enough it can be drilled out to make the **finger hole** for the hand puppet.

FOUND MATERIALS   A little ingenuity will turn up a surprising variety of ready-made objects or **found material**s suitable for puppet heads. Pulp mâché flower pots are lightweight and work especially well on their sides as animal heads. A pig or donkey can be easily represented in this way. A small coconut, with holes **drill**ed to the correct size for fingers, makes an excellent head for an animal. If it is sawed in half to remove the coconut meat it can be re-joined by gluing. Heads from old dolls will sometimes work, and thrift shops often carry inexpensive ones in need of repair. These usually have a ready-made **finger hole** in the bottom. With imagination, cardboard tubes wrapped with fabric, rubber balls, **Styrofoam** balls, or even a ball of yarn can be used.

DRESSING THE HAND PUPPET The **hand puppet** can be dressed in any simple smocklike garment that allows ample freedom for the **puppeteer**'s hand and arm. The puppet's garment will drop to about mid-forearm on the puppeteer, which means that the wrist is near the puppet's waistline. Bowing and bending of the figure are therefore possible.

The size of the hand or **glove puppet** body must be relative to the size of the operator's hand, and ample room should be left in the garment for the puppet's arms to move forward. Since the hands are **control**led by the puppeteer's fingers, hand puppets can pick things up and move them. First determine whether 1 or 2 fingers are needed to support the puppet head. If the head is held by the index finger, the puppet arms should equal the distance between the outstretched thumb and middle fingers. As a general guide, the hand puppet smock is 5–6" across and 7–8" long. The garment is securely tied or fastened at the **flange** on the **base** of the puppet head. Sleeves, with hands attached, must be wide enough for the fingers of the puppeteer. Length depends, of course, on the size of the person animating the puppet as well as the scale of the puppet. Experiment using plain **muslin** to determine the correct proportions. Make a trial garment using a large handkerchief; cut a hole in it and tie or attach it to the puppet neck; take a few stitches in the sides to make sleeves.

The hands of a puppet are added along with the clothes. An easily made **hand** is one sewn from two pieces of **felt**. They are cut so that there is a thumb and a flat palm area. Stitches are sewn through both layers to outline the hand, and then additional lines suggest spaces between the fingers. A **mitten-type hand** can also be made of felt. If **fabric** is used, it can be sewn, turned, and **stuff**ed. The operator's finger can slip right into the hand. If the fingers are stitched or stuffed, as in the **glove-type hand**, the operator's finger must remain behind the hand. If the puppet must be able to pick things up and move them, the mitten-type hand is better.

Hands can also be made from lightweight wire, such as **florist's wire**. If individual fingers are needed, they can be formed this way and then wrapped with tiny bits of cloth. The ends of the fabric pieces are glued.

Hands for both puppets and marionettes can also be made of **papier mâché** if they are kept simple. Fingers can be cut by making slashes of equal length into a heavy paper, such as construction paper. This piece can be dipped in the **wheat paste** until it absorbs some of the adhesive and then curved slightly to suggest bent fingers and left to dry.

The bottom of the puppet's skirt or smock requires a narrow hem. Lightweight wire is run through the hem, and a loop of the wire is extended through the hem on the back side. The wire helps hold the garment out and away from the arm and at the same time provides a hanging device, since hand puppets are stored hung upside down.

MAKING THE MARIONETTE SKELETON It is a challenge in engineering to construct the figure and **controls** for a **marionette**. The design and construction often become an end in themselves. Ideally, however, the voice, character, music, performance, and physical form of the marionette are all controlled by one person. This gives a sense of cohesive unity to the character in performance, making it more believable.

The simplest of all the marionettes, or **string puppet**s, are those that use a ready-made stuffed doll or animal. A basic doll shape may also be specifically made for that purpose. The **cloth marionette** is one type. Another, made from paper, is the **card marionette**. Beyond these, the making of a marionette is a complicated, though not necessarily difficult, task.

The finished **marionette head** will help determine the size and type of body needed, as will the character being represented. As a general guide, the head is about 1/6 of the total body height in a marionette, which gives the head greater size in relation to the body than it has on its human counterpart. A cloth head probably needs a cloth body. The **carved-wood** head may need the more complex many-**joint**ed figure. There are several possible ways of forming either of these marionette **skeleton**s.

Papier mâché, because it is versatile, inexpensive, and readily available, is an excellent material for the marionette skeleton or framework. If the head is of papier mâché, the use of the same material for the skeleton is also appropriate, although papier-mâché bodies can be used with any kind of marionette head.

First, the body is divided into two parts—shoulders and chest in one part, and the pelvis-hip area in another. These parts are formed in **Plasticene** and then covered with strips of papier mâché, as described in **Puppets: Making the Puppet Head.** After the body is split to remove the Plasticene, additional strips are layered over the glued seams.

These body parts will be firm and durable but can still be punched with an **awl** to sew or **string** them. The arms and the legs are made in two parts. Cut a length of dowel for each section. If the lower arm is to be 3" long, the dowel cut for it should be approximately 2" long. Wrap the dowel with either papier mâché or a rolled card-weight paper, so that the entire surface of the dowel is covered. The rolled paper or strips of mâché extend a half inch beyond the dowel at each end; press the end flat. A hole is poked through the flat extension for **stringing.** The dowel adds needed weight to the joints. **Hand**s and feet are made similarly, either with papier mâché or card-weight paper. If the latter is used, the paper should be cut to the proper size and then glued and stacked until adequate thickness and weight are achieved. The parts of the marionette are then joined as described in **Puppets: Stringing the Marionette.**

Another simple method of making the skeleton uses **dowel**s for the shoulder line and hip line, and a rectangular piece of wood in between. Lengths of dowel are then cut for arms and legs, with joints at elbows and knees. **Screw eye**s are used to connect at upper arms, elbows, and wrists as well as at hips, knees, and feet. **Leather hinge**s at the joints prevent them from bending in the wrong direction. See ill. on next page.

A variation of the dowel method substitutes small

square strips of **wood** similar to those used in model building but stronger than **balsa wood.** The parts of the body are cut the same as for dowel construction, except wood blocks are used for the shoulders, hips, and limbs. Joints at elbows and knees are **hinge joint**s, made with leather strips. Two blocks of wood—for example, the lower and upper parts of one leg—are placed end to end. Then, on the back side of the leg, both pieces of wood are tapered in toward the knee to make a shallow V. The leather strip is glued over the angled ends of the wood. This arrangement allows the knee to move forward but prevents it from bending backward.

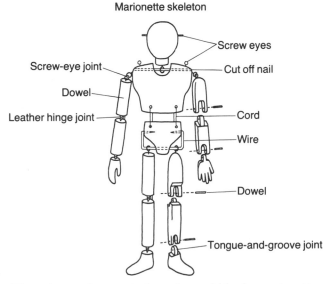

Marionette skeleton

Labels: Screw eyes; Screw-eye joint; Cut off nail; Dowel; Cord; Leather hinge joint; Wire; Dowel; Tongue-and-groove joint

There is another variation of wood-block construction that has the advantage of being very simple, although movements are somewhat limited. The body is cut from a thick piece of wood, 2″ thick or more, depending on total size. When one looks directly at the front of the marionette, it appears to be a solid block. When the figure is turned sideways, the profile shape shows. This shape is sawed from the block of wood, and no carving is done to round the edges. Arms are also cut flat and are set next to the body, held in place by a **screw** with a flat **felt** washer between the two parts. This allows the arm to move in one direction only—up or down. Legs are similarly attached. This marionette requires fewer strings, since there is only one motion for the arms. Instead of a string for elbow, wrist, and hand, only one string is needed. The movements are somewhat rigid, but it is a simplified form and more easily **manipulate**d than other more complex ones. A final advantage is that costumes can be suggested with the sawing, and then painted directly on the wood.

The carved-wood body of a marionette is usually made in two parts from wood chunks about 2″ thick and 3″ wide. The top is about 3½″ long, the bottom 3″. The upper part, shoulders and rib cage, has a half circle cut out so that the neck can fit into it. The neck and shoulders may be connected by means of screw eyes—one on the **base** of the neck and the other in the depression of the shoulders. Or, a long nail or wire can be used to run crosswise through the shoulders, going through the screw eye of the neck to join these parts. The shoulders should slope slightly, and there

is a tapering from the arm joint to the waistline, although the lower body (hips and pelvis) is sawed or carved so that it tapers at the base. Two holes are **drill**ed from front to back on the lower body at the waistline edge. Two corresponding holes are drilled into the upper body. Cord is then used to join these parts, giving a **movable joint** so that the figure can be bent forward or backward at the waist. Again, screw eyes can be substituted, but they make a very **free joint** between those parts. Arms and legs are carved from 1″ square wood strips. The lengths will vary, but the lower arms might be 3″, upper arms 2¼″, thighs 3½″, and lower legs 3″. The wood is shaped by carving or with the use of a **wood rasp** and **file**s. The upper and lower arms are joined, ideally, with a tongue-and-groove joint. The groove is cut into the upper arm, the tongue in the lower. They are carefully measured so that the parts slide together. Then each is drilled, and a thin nail or pin is fitted in and bent at the pointed end to make a round loop. The leg parts are joined in the same way. Screw eyes can be substituted for tongue-and-groove joints, though some of the control of the marionette's movements is sacrificed.

To fasten arms to the body, a hole is drilled in the upper arm, about ¼″ from the top edge. Then a sturdy cord is double-knotted in the center. The knot is left on the outside of the arm, and the two ends are strung through the hole. They are tied securely to the screw eye, which emerges from just below the shoulder line on the body. To attach the legs to the lower body, first drill a hole from side to side through the pelvis about ¼″ from the lower edge. The upper legs should have screw eyes attached. Then using a stiff **galvanized wire,** run the wire through the screw eye of one leg, through the pelvis, and through the screw eye of the other leg. Leave an even amount of wire at each side. Then bend the wires up, at right angles to the cross wire. Now drill a hole into each side of the pelvis, straight above the first holes, make second right-angle bends in the wire, and hammer the ends of the wire into these drilled holes.

Hands, somewhat exaggerated in size, are carved from wood that is about 2″ wide, an inch thick, and 3″ long. A tongue-and-groove joint connects the hand to the lower arm with the tongue cut into the wrist and the groove cut into the arm. Or screw eyes can be used on both arm and hand. Feet are cut and attached in the same way, with the tongue extending from the foot to form an ankle. If the hands and feet are made of lightweight wood, **lead** may have to be added to the bottoms of the feet or in the palms. The added weight aids in the control of the figure. Chamois also works well for hands, offering flexibility and a natural color.

The hands and feet of the marionette have often, in traditional puppetry, been made of **sheet lead.** It is easily worked and attached to the body parts. Hands with fingers may be cut by using scissors, and an awl can be used to force a hole through the lead. The hands should be cut with an extra long wrist so that the joint will be concealed by the sleeve. For the feet, lead is bent so that a vertical extension can be attached at the ankle.

DRESSING THE MARIONETTE Before the clothes are made, all **screw eye**s for **stringing** must be installed in place on the **marionette** body. The actual stringing, however, cannot be done until the marionette is dressed. Placement of the screw eyes is given in **Puppets: Stringing the Marionette.**

Clothes for marionettes are sometimes fitted and attached to parts of the body, the clothes being assembled, in effect, on the figure. It is never easy to change the clothes on a marionette, even when they are made as separate costumes, since all the **strings** must be removed first.

If a change of costumes is needed in a performance, it is sometimes better to have two identical marionettes, each wearing one of the necessary costumes. That avoids the necessity of untying, dressing, and retying the marionette under the time pressure of a performance.

Soft fabrics are used for costumes when the movements of the **joints** are to show. A stiff fabric would lose the effect of manipulating the elbows or knees. A fabric of soft texture that does not wrinkle or crease easily is best. Chiffons work beautifully to show movement, and many of the soft permanent-press cottons work well. Knitted materials are excellent, though those which are foam-backed are too heavy. Velveteen has an elegant texture and is soft enough to move or give with the body changes. Avoid any stiff or hard fabrics, such as organdy, duck, hopsacking, or kettle cloth.

An allowance will sometimes have to be made in the costume for the screw eyes. If a seam in the clothing crosses a screw eye, it may then simply be a matter of leaving an opening in the seam. Otherwise, a tiny hole can be cut into the fabric and a **buttonhole stitch** sewn around the hole to prevent fraying. Another possibility is to place a piece of iron-on tape on the inside of the garment over the area where the hole is needed. Then the cut hole will not ravel.

The dressing of the marionettes is an individual operation. Each garment is **fabricate**d in terms of the character, the historical setting, the materials available, and the extent of elaborate detail needed. Sometimes the simplest clothing is the most effective. At other times, refined and extensively detailed apparel is appropriate.

STRINGING THE MARIONETTE The number of **strings** attached to a **marionette** is determined by the kinds of movements it will have to perform. This will vary from one marionette to the next, but generally the strings should be attached as follows: to the top of each shoulder, to each temple (just in front of the ear), at the top center of the pelvis on the back side (for bowing), on each thigh, just above the knee, and at each palm. The professional **puppeteer** may have additional strings for more sensitive control—for instance, a shoulder bar and strings, or two hip strings to replace the back string—but these are all that are ordinarily needed or used.

A good, strong thread is needed for **stringing,** and **linen thread,** or **carpet thread** is best. A #18 is a good weight, though any smooth, hard cord will do. If the string is black it will be less visible than if it is white.

The strings are usually about 3 feet long (and longer for those that go to the feet rather than the head). The height of the stage and the position of the operator will determine the final length needed in a theatrical production.

To attach the strings to the marionette's body, small

screw eyes must be inserted at those points indicated on the head, shoulders, and back. The thighs and palms should be drilled so that a string can be tied through the openings. To string the thighs, drill a hole just above the knee, and then run the thread through the hole and tie it securely, so that just one thread comes up from the knee. Only one small opening is made in the garment for each **knee string.**

When strings have been attached to each of these **control** points, the marionette is ready to be attached to the controls.

The strings attached to the marionette must now be attached to the controls. The stringing arrangement assists the puppeteer in animating the figures and helps him manage the numerous strings.

The control is a fairly simple arrangement of a **control bar** or **rod** and **cross bar**s. The arrangement may be vertical or horizontal.

Sometimes the **vertical control** is the arrangement of the **vertical rod,** to which cross bars and wires are added. The entire arrangement is called the upright control or perch control. In this reference it will always be referred to as the vertical control. The central rod of this vertical control will be referred to as the vertical rod.

The vertical rod is made from a square piece of wood or **dowel** about 9″ long and ¾″ in diameter. A large hook is added at the top so that the marionette, when not in use, can be hung. A coat hanger may be clipped off to supply such a hook, or one with a screw end is available at stores. A second, smaller hook is needed about 1″ below the top. A screw eye is inserted in the bottom end of the control bar. That completes the vertical rod, except for the cross bars, which are now added to complete the vertical control.

A cross bar, about 4″ long, must be added about 3″ from the bottom of the vertical rod. This will be the **head bar.** If a dowel was used for the 9″ piece, it will have to be **notch**ed to let the cross bar rest flat. If a square length of wood was used, the cross bar can be glued and screwed to the vertical rod. It must be held securely. A hole or screw eye is needed at each end of this 4″ bar.

About 3″ from the top of the **rod** a hole must be drilled through the middle of the rod, parallel to the cross bar that was added. A 10″ length of **galvanized wire** is run through the hole, centered, and then bent at right angles to extend out over the cross bar. The ends of the wires are bent, using **pliers,** to make small loops or rings. These wires function as the **arm bar** and will eventually connect to the **hand**s or wrists by the **hand strings.** The final attachment to the rod is a bar about 3″ long, which projects outward in the opposite direction from the wires just described. A screw eye must be fitted into the end of this projecting bar. It is the **shoulder bar.**

The last cross bar is not attached to the rod at all but hangs from the small hook at the top of the rod. It is the leg control, or **leg bar,** which is 12″ long with a hole drilled at each end and one in the middle. Screw eyes can be used to replace all three drilled holes.

To tie the marionette strings to the vertical control, start with the **head string**s. They are attached to the ends of the head bar. The strings must be exactly equal in length. When those are evened and tied, pick up the **shoul-**

der strings. It will be helpful now to hang the vertical control from the large hook extending out of the top of the vertical rod.

The shoulder strings must also be exactly equal in length if the marionette is to stand straight. They are attached to the **shoulder bar,** with both strings being tied to the same screw eye in the end of the projecting 3″ bar.

The remaining strings should now be tied and kept firm, but not taut, when the limbs are in a relaxed position. The hand strings run free through the rings at the ends of the galvanized wire. When the wire is dropped, the hands are down.

The **back string** is attached to the screw eye that was inserted at the base of the vertical rod. The leg bar is hung from the small hook near the top of the vertical rod, and the knee strings are attached to the holes or screw eyes in the ends of the leg bar. The vertical control is now finished, and the stringing of the marionette to the control is complete (**a.**).

The **horizontal control** is less common than the vertical control, although it is more suitable for four-legged creatures. The arrangement of bars is similar to that in the vertical control. The **horizontal rod** is a square stick of wood ¾″ in diameter and about 9″ long. (A dowel can be used, but the notching to fit the parts is more difficult.) The entire arrangement is called the horizontal control. The **central rod** or bar of the horizontal control will be referred to as the **horizontal rod.**

The leg bar will again be a separate cross bar, which can be removed or hung back on the horizontal rod.

Starting at the left hand end of the horizontal rod, a hook is inserted into the end of the rod. Next a cross bar of about 6″ in length is added, notched into the horizontal rod, firmly attached by gluing, and strengthened with a screw or nail. Screw eyes are attached on the side pointing to the left—that is, in the direction of the leg bar. This will be the arm bar, to which **arm strings** will eventually be attached.

About ⅔ of the way down the horizontal rod another cross bar, about 4″ wide, is attached in the same way as the arm bar. The screw eyes, however, are inserted into the ends of this cross bar. The shoulder strings will later be attached to these screw eyes.

At the right-hand end of the horizontal rod, two screw eyes are inserted, one at each side of the horizontal rod, to which the **hip strings** will be attached. Note that here is one change from the vertical control. In that control a single string came from the back. Here, two strings come from the sides of the hips. Either method of stringing can be used with either control, though generally the double hip strings are better for the horizontal control.

Finally, a screw eye is attached under the horizontal bar, near the shoulder bar. This will later hold the head bar. A large hook is now added to the very top, so that the marionette may be hung when it is not in use.

To string the marionette to the horizontal control, follow the general order given for the vertical control. Head strings are tied on first, and the two must be of identical length. These are attached to two screw eyes, which have been inserted into the ends of a 2″ length of dowel. This length of dowel is attached to the small screw eye that was placed under the horizontal rod. A string goes from one end of the short dowel, up through the screw eye, and back down to the other end of the dowel. Once this head bar has been joined to both puppet and horizontal rod, the rest of the stringing can proceed.

Shoulder strings are next attached to the screw eyes at the ends of the 4″ cross bar. The marionette should now be checked to see if it hangs evenly. The control may be propped up on something or held from above to check position.

Now the strings from the hips are tied to the screw eyes at the end of the horizontal bar. Arm strings are tied to the arm bar. Finally the leg strings or knee strings are attached to the leg bar. The horizontal control is now finished, the stringing is completed, and the marionette is ready for action (**b.**).

A simplified version of the horizontal control is one commonly seen on marionettes made for children. Most toy stores carry this kind. It consists of two flat sticks that look like sections of a yardstick cut about 8″ long. These are securely attached at right angles to make a cross. The

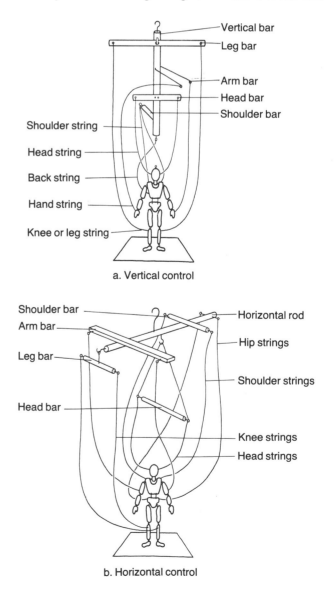

a. Vertical control

b. Horizontal control

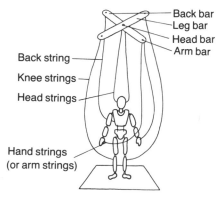

Back bar
Leg bar
Head bar
Arm bar
Back string
Knee strings
Head strings
Hand strings
(or arm strings)

c. Simplified horizontal control

strings are generally attached following the directions for the more complex horizontal control (**c.**). See ill. Also see **simplified horizontal control.**

MANIPULATING THE MARIONETTE   Nothing is of greater value in developing facility in manipulation than practice. It helps to work in front of a mirror.

To begin, grasp the **control** firmly in one hand; the **leg bar,** which lifts off the **rod,** is held in the other hand. Changing the hands on controls is helpful in developing ambidexterity, which is valuable when more refined movements are needed.

Most of the **strings** are attached in pairs so that a **rocking** movement of the **cross bars** makes an alternating movement of the parts of the figure. Walking, which is difficult for the beginning **puppeteer,** is accomplished by rocking the leg bar, which will cause alternate legs to rise. By a lifting of the control as each foot comes up, the **puppet** can be made to perform this difficult task. This coordination of leg and body movements will require time, patience, and practice.

The **marionette**'s **hands** may be controlled by either the right or left hand of the puppeteer. If the puppet's legs are at rest, the leg bar can be hung on the **control bar,** and that free hand can do the manipulating. The marionette's hands may be moved individually (by the **hand string**) or together (by the control or **arm bar**). To make the head nod, the control is tilted forward, to make the body bend forward at the waist, the **back string** is lifted.

As skill in operation is developed, each puppeteer makes his own alterations in arrangement, adjusting strings and controls to suit his particular needs.

THE PUPPET STAGE   Different kinds of **puppets** require different stages for their performances. The general requirements remain the same: the **puppeteer** should be hidden from view, the puppet must be clearly visible, and the voices must carry to the audience. There are many simple makeshift solutions for **puppet stages,** and sometimes the spontaneity of the construction is appropriate to the quickly devised puppet. If the more elaborately detailed **string puppets** or **marionettes** are used, then a more elaborate stage may be required. The requirements of the various types of stages are listed separately as follows:

SHADOW PUPPET STAGE   All that is needed for the **shadow-puppet performance** is a **screen,** since the puppets' shadows must be projected on a flat surface. The screen can be made of **fabric** stretched over a rigid frame. Many ready-made frames are available, such as picture frames, canvas stretcher bars, window screens (with screen removed), or window frames (glass need not be removed). Or for a stage of specific size, the frame can be built. The size depends in part upon the size of the puppets themselves. The frame must be rigid, since a fabric must be stretched over it tightly enough to be completely smooth and wrinkle-free.

The frame is covered with some semiopaque colorless material. White window shade will do, and has the advantage of being slightly stiff. Cotton **sheeting, muslin,** or **broadcloth** will work. Nylon or other white **synthetic fabric**s work well, although they are sometimes difficult to stretch smooth. Avoid a material that is too soft; instead, use one with a little stiffness or body. The advantage in using a woven fabric is that scenery can be pinned to it, though **pressure-sensitive tape**s that have adhesive on both surfaces also work on almost any material.

The completed screen must be set or hung vertically and held firmly in place. It may be clamped to a table edge so that the puppeteer stands behind the table. Another simple and very effective method is to hang the screen in a doorway. However the screen is set, the surrounding area should be blacked out so that no light comes from behind the screen. The doorway system works well, since much of the background is already blacked out. Curtains should be hung below and above, as necessary.

A strong light is needed and is directed from behind the puppets, facing the screen. If too transparent a fabric has been used on the screen, the light will glare through. There must be a single source of light, usually of 150 watts or more, depending on the size of the screen. The larger the screen, the further back the light must be in order to illuminate the entire surface. Care must be taken to be sure that the puppeteers' shadows are not cast on the screen. A desk or floor lamp with a cone-shaped metal shade and a flexible neck is ideal for lighting.

Stage **set**s or properties are best kept simple, since the screen must be kept open and free for the movement of the puppets. If the screen is tilted forward slightly at the top, **prop**s can be set on the frame and rested against the screen.

A permanent stage for shadow puppets can be made, giving consideration to the above requirements. Space must always be allowed for the puppeters. If only one or two people will be operating the puppets, a small screen is adequate. If a larger group, as in a school situation, is to work together, more space must be given to avoid overcrowding **backstage.**

FINGER-PUPPET STAGE   **Finger puppet**s, the tiny figures that fit over just one finger, require a stage similar to, but smaller than, that for **hand puppets.** The directions for the hand-puppet stage may be followed, with all areas reduced in size.

Because finger puppets are so quickly and easily made,

it seems appropriate to have a stage that can be made in an equally simple way. The simplest stage is an empty box that allows the characters to emerge from behind it. Taking this a step further, a stage opening can be cut into the front of a cardboard box, with a slot cut in the bottom of the box for the **puppeteer**'s hands. This leaves the back for scenery or stage **set**s.

Many kinds of simple stages can easily be devised for finger puppets. If a slot is cut in either a vertical or horizontal stage, a finger puppet can move at ease. The finger-puppet stage requires ingenuity, and each play performed may demand a different arrangement.

FLAT-PUPPET STAGE   **Flat puppets**, contemporary versions of the **"penny plain and tuppence colored,"** require a simple stage that is open at both sides. The puppeteer stands at the sides, and the figures are moved in and out of the open areas at the sides of the stage by means of wires or sticks attached at their bases.

A **stage floor** is needed, since the puppets must rest on a flat surface to be **manipulate**d. A low, flat box will do. An easy stage can be made from a flat box that has a telescoping lid, where the top of the box fits down over the bottom. A box about 20″ long, 12″ wide, and 4″ deep would be ideal. Anything close to those proportions will work.

The bottom of the box, turned upside down, makes a raised stage floor. The top or lid of the box, set on one side and slipped under the back of the stage floor, makes the back of the stage. The 4″ sides make a narrow roof, and the ends form the side panels. When the lid is slipped under the back edge of the stage floor, it is held upright and a support is provided for the **proscenium.**

The proscenium is a flat cardboard cut so that its width fits within the edges of the inverted box of the stage floor and its height goes from the stage floor to the inside top of the stage back. The exact measurements will vary depending upon the thickness of the cardboard or the wood, if it is used instead. The approximate measurements of the proscenium are 18″ wide and 8″ high. A section is cut out to allow a stage opening. What is left is the **proscenium arch**—a flat area, facing the audience, on the two sides of and above the stage opening. The approximate size of the stage opening is 10″ × 6″, leaving a proscenium 4″ wide at the sides and 2″ wide at the top. Bracing is needed from the proscenium to the stage back, and **wings** are also attached to these. If the stage is made of wood, slots for the proscenium arch and wings to fit into are very helpful (**a.**). See ill.

The only other essential requirement of the flat-figure stage is the curtained area at the sides. This is essential to conceal the **controller**s, or puppeteers. Folding screens may be used, although a **curtain** on a separate stand would also provide a means of curtaining the stage before a performance or during changes of scenery.

This simple type of production is usually done with daylight or ordinary room light. Some kind of flood lighting can be added if desired, coming from in front of the stage and preferably from above.

HAND-PUPPET STAGE   Any puppet manipulated from below may be used in the **hand-puppet** stage. This includes hand or **glove puppet**s, **stick puppet**s, **finger puppet**s, and **rod puppet**s. Shadow puppets are the one exception.

Basic considerations must be given to the freedom of the puppet on stage and to visibility to the audience. The puppeteers (if there are several) may get crowded or cramped if the stage is not made to accommodate the number of performers.

Makeshift puppet stages are available to anyone. A rectangular or square table turned on its side provides a simple but good solution for a quickly devised stage. The puppeteer sits behind and is screened by the overturned table, and the puppets appear over the top edge, which becomes the **playboard.** With a large table of the kind found in schools, five or six puppeteers may perform at once.

A curtain stretched across a doorway makes another simple stage. Or cardboard cartons can be stacked two on each side of a stage area with a curtain hung across the open space between them. Such a stage can be expanded by moving the boxes farther apart and using a wider curtain. This arrangement helps hide the puppeteers. Many other possibilities will occur to anyone with the puppet on his hand.

A "real" puppet theater is the kind used in the original **Punch and Judy show.** In fact, these stages are sometimes referred to as Punch-type stages or the **Punch stage.** This stage is like a huge empty carton, vertical in shape, with the top and back removed. It allows the puppeteer to be inside, and the puppets appear over the top edge of the box, which becomes the **playboard.** The **backdrop,** or **backstage set,** is rigid and attached by vertical supports to the sides of the main box. The bottom of the backdrop should line up with the top front edge of the box, or stage. This type of stage allows for maximum visibility. A curtain can be added to conceal the puppeteer (**b., c.**). If it is to be used repeatedly it is best made from wood, but a cardboard carton is a good place to begin. In fact, if cardboard cartons are used for the initial attempts, only one or two performances are required to determine if changes should be made in the more permanent structure. The number of performers and the types of plays to be produced help determine the specific needs. See ill.

A similar stage can be devised from one huge carton. (A refrigerator carton makes an easy beginning.) A doorway is cut in the back of the vertical box for the entry and exit of puppeteers. A stage hole is cut about ⅓ of the distance from the top. A curtain is hung from the inside top of the

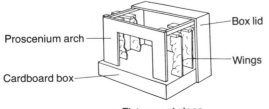

Proscenium arch
Box lid
Wings
Cardboard box

a. Flat-puppet stage

box, and another devised to drop or pull over the stage opening. This completely conceals the puppeteers.

Either of these stages should also include a **prop shelf** and hooks for hanging the puppets during a performance.

Hand puppet stage

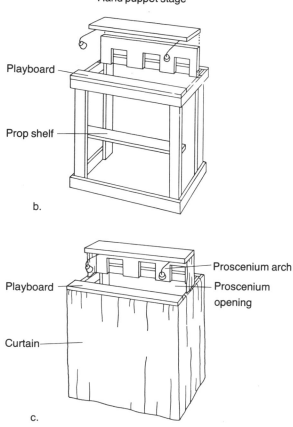

Playboard

Prop shelf

b.

Playboard

Proscenium arch

Proscenium opening

Curtain

c.

If the puppeteer is **"boxed in"** beneath the stage, his voice may not carry. It would be helpful to cut vents into the proscenium under the stage area to facilitate in carrying the sound to the audience.

MARIONETTE STAGE **Marionette stage**s can range from simple makeshift devices to elaborately constructed and intricately painted theaters. The type constructed depends on many factors, including the ultimate use of the stage, the plays to be performed, and the costs in terms of materials and time. However simple or complicated, there are some considerations that remain constant. All marionette stages must include the following essential features: the **stage floor,** over which the **marionette** moves; a background, against which the action occurs; a place where the operator may stand and be concealed from the audience's view.

The **puppeteer** or operator should always have a convenient and secure position from which to **manipulate** the marionette. The structure that offers this support is called the **bridge.** The operator leans over the **bridge bar** to hold the **control bar** over the stage floor. A **curtain** is hung from the bridge bar to conceal the operator from view.

Marionette theaters may have a bridge built in as part of the stage, or the bridge can be separate, or any convenient table or bench may be used for that purpose. The simplest of all marionette stages is one in which two heavy boards are placed flat and parallel, and as far apart as the entire stage is to be wide. At one end of each board a vertical post is firmly attached, and a third post is used to join the vertical ones at the top. This makes a large doorway or bridge. A second shorter and smaller bridge is built parallel to the first and behind it. This structure fills all the basic needs of a marionette stage. The larger bridge, or **front bridge,** is hung with curtains to form the **proscenium,** of which the center curtains are cut short to make a stage opening. The bridge bar is hung with a curtain to provide a **backdrop** and to conceal the operators. The **rear bridge** has the **perch bar** and is the back edge of the stage.

This stage may be placed on a table so that the bridge bar is at a convenient height for the operators' arms. If the height is not comfortable, an adjustment can be made by using a **bench** for the operators to stand on, by raising the table or (in a permanent arrangement) by cutting off the necessary amount from the table legs.

This stage should be built with regard to the height of the operators. The front bridge must be enough higher than the bridge bar to conceal the operators' heads. Depth and width of the stage are determined by the size of the marionettes and the action involved in the play. Generally, a marionette stage is not less than 4' wide or there will not be enough space for two operators to work at one time. A larger and more complex marionette stage is not usually portable but is the ultimate goal of a **puppet master,** who wishes to acquire great skill and control. It is a somewhat more professional stage.

For a free-standing marionette stage the proscenium can be cut from **plywood.** A 5' × 10' sheet is used in the center, and another sheet of the same size is cut in half lengthwise, so that a 2½' × 10' piece is added at each side. Reinforcements of 2 × 2s are used on all edges and at the joints. The stage parts will also be attached to the 2 × 2s, so they serve a double purpose. A bridge 6' high and 5' wide is built 30" behind the proscenium wall, or front bridge, and the stage floor goes in between them. The stage floor is 30" above the ground. A bench is built for the operators to stand on (**d.**).

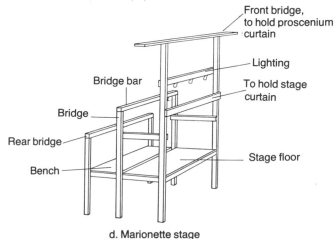

Front bridge, to hold proscenium curtain

Lighting

To hold stage curtain

Bridge bar

Bridge

Rear bridge

Bench

Stage floor

d. Marionette stage

A **canopy** over the **proscenium opening** can hold the curtains from underneath and will support lights above. Lighting may become a complex arrangement using colored bulbs or stage gelatins for various colors to give dramatic effects, and dimmers to bring lights up or down in intensity. The entire stage must be well constructed and reinforced so that it will not wobble or move when in use. Each marionette stage, of whatever design, should include a **rail** on which to store the marionettes when they are not in use, to prevent tangling of the strings.

puppet show. Puppets. A performance of **hand puppets** or **marionettes** presented on a **puppet stage. A puppet play** is usually written, giving consideration to the special needs of **puppetry.**

The number of **controllers** may be limited by the size of the **puppet theater** or **marionette theater,** so the action may have a limit to the number of puppets that appear at any one time. The puppet show must coordinate all the various aspects and limitations of puppetry. For example, if marionettes move across stage, the **controls** may pass from one person to another, but the part is always spoken by the same person. Also see **Bartholomew Fair, Punch stage, puppet master.**

puppet stage. Puppets. A specially constructed performance area for the presentation of **puppet show**s. The puppet stage consists of an arrangement that conceals the **puppeteer** from audience view and provides a **playboard** on which the puppets move. When the **string puppet,** or **marionette,** is used, rather than the **hand puppet,** the requirements change, so the marionette stage is of different design. Also see **articulated, "boxed in,"** draw .**curtain, pencil puppet, prop shelf, puppet opera, topdrop** and **Puppets: The Puppet Stage.**

puppet theater. Puppets. The full range of the **puppet show,** including the drama, characters, stage, and production. The phrase **Punch and Judy show** is used in this sense to refer to the entire performance. Also see **Judy, playboard, prop, puppet, sheeting, stage floor.**

purl. Embroidery. See **bullion thread, pearl purl.**

purl. Knitting. One of two basic knitting stitches (the other is simply called knit, or **plain knitting**). It is the reverse of the plain knitting stitch. Also see **Knitting: Basic Movements.**

purl pins. Lacemaking. See **picot.**

purls. Lacemaking. See **picot.**

purl together. Knitting. (Abbr. P 2 tog.) Purling together is a method of **decreasing** done by purling two stitches together to create one new stitch instead of two. Also see **Knitting: Decreasing.**

purse knitting. Knitting. See **bead knitting.**

purse stitch. Knitting. See **Knitting: Construction.**

push and punch. Quilts. A **quilting stitch** taken individually, or one stitch at a time, to produce a very fine pattern of stitches on both the front and back of the quilt. The needle is punched straight down from the top and is drawn through the quilt so that it emerges under the quilt. Then, with the left hand used as a guide in placement, it is reinserted and pushed back to the top. This **fine stitch** is much more time-consuming than the **running stitch,** which is more often employed in **quilting.**

push drill. Woodworking. See **drilling tools.**

push horse. Toys. A wooden horse built onto a wheeled platform so that it can be rolled or pushed along. Push horses were usually small, although some were made to be large and sturdy enough to support a young rider. The **cock horse** and **pole horse** are variations of this toy. It is sometimes called a billet horse because it is made with polelike legs.

push toy. Toys. A **wheeled toy** that moves easily when it is pushed. It is a child-activated toy rather than one run by mechanical or windup devices or batteries. Also see **Toys: Wheeled Toys.**

Puss-in-the-Corner. Quilts. A name given to several different **block** designs for **pieced quilts.** One uses a **nine-patch set** in such a way that it becomes one patch of another, larger nine-patch. This version is also called **Double Nine-patch** and Burgoyne's Surrender. Another common version is identical to **Shoo-fly.** A third variation sets nine-patch blocks alternating with solid blocks, each of which has a triangle set in the corner. This effect is similar to **Irish Chain.**

put in. Quilts. To put the quilt into the **quilting frame.** This involves attaching the **backing** fabric to the **rails,** layering the batting or **filler,** and placing the **pieced** or **appliquéd** top over all. These layers are carefully **basted** together. When the quilt is ready to be quilted, it has been "put in." Also see **Quilts: Quilting.**

Putnam. Batik and Tie-dye. Trade name of a commonly available **fiber-reactive dye** that can be used in a **dyebath** temperature of 90−100° F, which will not melt **wax.** Also see **color remover, Procion dye** and **Batik and Tie-dye: Dyes.**

Putnam All-Purpose. Batik and Tie-dye. See **household dye.**

putty. Woodworking. See **wood filler.**

puttying. Stained Glass. See **Stained Glass: Glazing.**

putty knife. Woodworking. A tool used to apply **wood filler** to wood. It consists of a wide, thin, flexible blade with a squared end and a handle attached at the other end.

To use a putty knife, hold the tool handle and load the flat end with filler or putty. Place the material over the hole or crack to be filled and draw the tool down and across the surface, letting the natural spring of the blade press the filler into the crevice.

putty powder. Amber Carving. Ivory and Bone Carving. White to yellowish impalpable powder obtained through calcining tin and lead to oxides. High-grade material is 85–90% **tin oxide.** The lower grades, which contained barely 50% tin oxide, were once used for polishing glass, but as it caused lead poisoning its use was discontinued in favor of the higher grade. It is an excellent polishing powder for soft materials, but because rare earth oxides are cheaper, more reliable, and faster, the use of putty powder has become less common.

putty powder. Gemcutting. See **abrasive.**

puzzle. Toys. A toy or device designed to test ingenuity, so called because it is puzzling, perplexing, and sometimes confounding. The simplest and oldest of puzzles are knots. The Chinese **tangram** is another early one. Most of the string and wooden puzzles to be disentangled and reassembled are Oriental in origin. Also see **jigsaw puzzle.**

puzzle bag. Toys. A container, usually cloth, in which the many pieces of a **puzzle** may be kept. Puzzle bags are usually made to accompany homemade **jigsaw puzzle**s; commercially produced ones are usually packaged in boxes.

PVA. Bookbinding. Polyvinyl acetate, a thick white emulsion adhesive that may be thinned with water but is waterproof after it sets. After setting, it will remain soft and flexible, but tough.

PVA. Plastics. See **polyvinyl alcohol.**

PVC. Plastics. See **polyvinyl chloride.**

pycnometer. Gemcutting. See **specific gravity.**

Pylam. Batik and Tie-dye. See **fiber-reactive dye** and **Batik and Tie-dye: Dyes.**

pynpillow. Stitchery. The sixteenth-century version of a **pincushion.** Up until then, the treasured pins were kept in boxes.

pyramid blocks. Toys. See **telescoping box.**

pyramid box. Toys. See **telescoping box.**

pyramid figure. Toys. See **acrobat.**

pyramid stitch. Needlepoint. (Also called raised stitch.) A textural stitch done in a square with the stitches laid counterclockwise, creating a raised area in the middle of each square.

pyrite. Gemcutting. (Also called iron pyrite.) Iron sulfide cyrstallized in the isometric system with **hardness** of 6½, **specific gravity** of 5, and yellow brassy color and metallic **luster.** It is decomposed by nitric acid but not by hydrochloric acid. It sparks when struck with steel and, when heated, gives off a rotten-egg smell. Pyrite is polished with Linde A or diamond powder on leather or with rouge on muslin.

pyrometer. Ceramics. Jewelry. A temperature measuring device used in **kilns.** A pyrometer measures actual heat only. Pyrometric **cones** are more reliable for judging how ceramic ware is firing. Also see **optical pyrometer, thermocouple.**

pyrometer. China and Glass Painting. Stained Glass. The instrument that gauges the heat inside a **kiln** and registers it on a dial outside. The heat is registered on the thermocouple, the part of the pyrometer that is exposed to the heat and either built into the kiln or inserted into a hole in the peephole plug.

pyrometer. Enameling. An instrument which measures **kiln** temperature. Kiln color is an additional guide to kiln temperature for experienced crafts workers. Also see **firing** and **Enameling: Tools and Materials.**

pyrometer. Metalworking. A device used for measuring the temperature of molten metals for **casting,** or to determine the correct temperature of a metal object to be **annealed, tempered,** or **harden**ed in a furnace.

pyrometric cone. Ceramics. See **cone.**

pyrometric cone. China and Glass Painting. Cones composed of various materials set inside the **kiln** for use as a heat gauge. The cones are available in different numbers to deform, or bend, at different given temperatures. Two cones, close in number, are placed in the kiln so that they can be seen through the peephole. When the cone of lower number bends, the degree of heat required is nearly reached. When the remaining cone bends, the kiln has reached the required amount of heat and should be turned off.

pyrope. Gemcutting. See **garnet.**

pyroplastic deformation. Ceramics. The **warping** or bending of ceramics as they soften at high temperature; usually refers to **kiln** shelves bending under a load in firing. Also see **distortion.**

pyroxene. Gemcutting. A class of minerals closely related to the amphiboles which includes **diopside, hypersthene,** jadeite, nephrite **jade, rhodonite, spodumene,** and **actinolite.**

Pysanky. Batik and Tie-dye. Egg Decorating. The traditional Ukrainian art of decorating and dyeing **eggs** with a wax **resist** technique similar to **batik.** The egg is usually divided into geometric areas, then completely filled with intricate, symmetrical, linear designs that require great skill and control to produce. The batik is applied to uncooked eggs that are washed in a solution of warm water and vinegar. **Wax** designs are then added with a **kistka, brush,** or **tjanting.** The waxed egg is dipped in Easter egg dye or **household dye** for color, then may be rewaxed and redyed for additional colors.

The first coat of dye should be the lightest, such as yellow, and each additional dye progressively darker. Traditionally, the final dye coating is black. The completed design must be cleaned of wax by placing the egg on paper toweling in a pan in a warm oven for a few minutes. The wax will melt to a glossy sheen on the egg. Remove the egg and wipe the wax off with toweling. This process may be repeated until the wax is completely removed.